Writing Dancing in the Age of Postmodernism

Sally Banes

Wesleyan University Press
Published by University Press of New England
Hanover and London

Wesleyan University Press
Published by University Press of New England, Hanover, NH 03755

Printed in the United States of America 5 4 3 2
CIP data appear at the end of the book

Acknowledgments

I would like to thank the following individuals and institutions for granting me permission to reprint articles and chapters, and for supplying illustrations: Janet Adshead-Lansdale and the National Resource Centre for Dance; K.C. Bailey; Boston Review; Tom Brazil; Martha Cooper; Paula Court; Sophie Fiennes; Ain Gordon and the Urban Bush Women; Lois Greenfield; Lauren Shaw and The House Foundation for the Arts; Pooh Kaye; James Klosty; Paul Kolnik; Sarah Lazin; MIT Press (for the article from *The Drama Review*); Dona Ann McAdams; Jonas Mekas; Parachute; Wendy Perron; Patricia Reynolds; Robert Robertson and Harwood Academic Publishers (for the articles from *Choreography and Dance*); Jim Self; Patricia Tarr and Dance Ink; Carmelita Tropicana; University of Pittsburgh Press; Wisconsin State Historical Society Film Archives.

I am also grateful to Val Bourne, Maria Reardon Capp, Noël Carroll, Terry Cochran, Selma Jeanne Cohen, Mike Shea, Janice Ross, and Elizabeth Souritz for their assistance and advice.

Writing Dancing in the Age of Postmodernism

To my editors

Contents

Introduction xi

I. Writing Criticism/History 1

1. Jill Johnston: Signaling Through the Flames 3
2. Working and Dancing: A Response to Monroe Beardsley's "What Is Going on in a Dance?" (with Noël Carroll) 10
3. Criticism as Ethnography 16
4. On Your Fingertips: Writing Dance Criticism 24
5. Power and the Dancing Body 43

II. The Euro-American Avant-Garde 51

6. Balanchine and Black Dance 53
7. An Introduction to the Ballets Suédois 70
8. Soirée de Paris 82
9. Kasyan Goleizovsky's Ballet Manifestos 92
10. Merce Cunningham's *Story* 103
11. Cunningham and Duchamp (with Noël Carroll) 109

III. The African-American Connection 119

12. To the Beat, Y'All: Breaking Is Hard to Do 121

13. Breakdancing:
A Reporter's Story 126
14. Lock Steady 133
15. Critic's Choice:
Breakdancing 137
16. Breaking 143
17. A House Is Not
a Home 153
18. Breaking Changing 156
19. The Pleasin'
in Teasin' 159
20. The Moscow Charleston:
Black Jazz Dancers in the Soviet Union 161

IV. Other Subversions: Politics and Popular Dance 169

21. Stepping High:
Fred Astaire's Drunk Dances 171
22. The Men at
John Allen's Dance House 184
23. Red Shoes:
The Workers' Dance League of the 1930s 199

V. Postmodern Dance: From the Sixties to the Nineties 205

24. Judson Rides Again! 207
25. Choreographic Methods of the
Judson Dance Theater 211
26. Vital Signs:
Steve Paxton's *Flat* in Perspective 227
27. Meredith Monk and the Making of *Chacon*:
Notes from a Journal 240
28. Dancing on the
Edge 252
29. "Drive," She Said:
The Dance of Molissa Fenley 259

30. Self-Rising
Choreography 268
31. Transparent
Living 273
32. No More Ordinary
Bodies 277
33. Happily Ever After?
The Postmodern Fairytale and the New Dance 280
34. Pointe of
Departure 290
35. Classical Brinksmanship:
Karole Armitage and Michael Clark 297
36. Terpsichore in Sneakers, High Heels, Jazz Shoes, and On Pointe:
Postmodern Dance Revisited 301
37. Dancing [with/to/before/on/in/over/after/against/away from/without] the Music:
Vicissitudes of Collaboration in American Postmodern
Choreography 310
38. La Onda Próxima:
Nueva Latina Dance 327
39. Dance and Spectacle in the United States in the
Eighties and Nineties (with Noël Carroll) 333
40. Dancing in
Leaner Times 341
41. Going Solo 348

Notes 353
Index 387

Introduction

This book is a collection of my published and unpublished essays and talks on dance since the 1970s. I began writing about dance twenty years ago, in 1973. Suddenly, I found myself in possession of a contract with Chicago Review Press to write a book on contemporary dance. (That book became *Terpsichore in Sneakers*, a history and critical study of postmodern dance that was eventually published by Houghton Mifflin.) Although I had both danced and written since childhood, and although I worked for the Chicago *Reader* as a professional, free-lance journalist, I hadn't yet written about dancing. I mainly wrote restaurant reviews, sometimes theater reviews, and occasionally articles that pertained to feminism and culture. But a friend had a friend who was starting a press and wanted a book on contemporary dance. My friend couldn't bring himself to write it, since he had a number of phobias that prevented him from traveling to New York or watching dance concerts in enclosed spaces. Besides, he had a novel to write. I inherited the dance book assignment.

I realized that I had to become an instant expert on dance to write the book. I therefore wrote myself into existence as a dance historian and critic, training myself in public to look at and think about dance, in the dance column my *Reader* editor, Bob Roth, readily provided on my request. I asked him to name me the paper's dance editor so I would have some credentials when I, a recent college graduate, visited New York to interview the dancers and choreographers I planned to write about. He said OK. Things were that easy and informal then. A few years later, I had moved to New York and found three more permissive editors, Robb Baker (at the *Soho Weekly News*), Burt Supree (at the *Village Voice*), and Tobi Tobias (at *Dance Magazine*), who were equally willing to let me regularly trot out my research on postmodern dance in public. And over the years, there were more supportive editors: Joan Acocella, Mindy Aloff, Jack Anderson and George Dorris, Tom Borek, Thulani Davis, Lise Friedman, Michael Kirby, Alan Jabbour, Francis Mason, Erika Munk, M Mark, Wendy Perron, Robert Pierce, David Vaughan, Ross Wetzsteon.

When I look back on those beginnings, it seems to me I entered the field of dance scholarship by the back door. It was the alternative papers and presses (and one unusual editor at *Dance*) that first gave me space in which to write about dance. Perhaps that is why mainstream dance has never been my bailiwick. Then, too, I grew up in the sixties and was formed by the oppositional culture that swept youth, art, performance, and politics all up into a compelling, vital, interdisciplinary brew. When I first turned to writing dancing, it was Jill Johnston, the *Village Voice* dance critic in the sixties, whose outrageous style and heterodox subject matter most influenced and inspired me. The postmodern dance, art, and performance I discovered in 1973 when I read her book *Marmalade Me* have preoccupied me ever since.

However much I admired Johnston, I soon opted for a more sedate style, and I have discovered additional historical obsessions — most notably, the European and Soviet avant-garde of the 1920s, and various facets of the African-American dance tradition. These research areas are not as unconnected as they might at first seem, as I hope this collection shows. All three repertoires mix forms, treating dance as inseparable from music, visual art, and theater. But more importantly, all three occupy an uneasy space in our own society, circulating between "high" and "low" art and between the acceptable (even desirable) and the margins. These, of course, are some of the terms in which we have come to define postmodernism and its roots in modernism.

If in 1973, when I began writing dancing, postmodernism was a relatively new term that meant something different for each art form (according to its own history and its own definitions of modernism), in 1993 the term postmodernism has come to define an era. Since I explore the meaning of the term in both dance and culture in Chapter 36, "Terpsichore in Sneakers, High Heels, Jazz Shoes, and on Pointe: Postmodern Dance Revisited," I won't rehearse it at length here. But it is worth noting here that writing dancing in the age of postmodernism not only encompasses what has come to be known as "postmodern dance" — the post-Cunningham, post-Balanchine, post-Halprin, post-Waring American avant-garde of the sixties through the nineties. It also includes the other emblematic dance genres of our era and contemporary ways of looking at and thinking about dancing. That is, postmodernism refers simultaneously to a historical movement in dance, the present moment in dance, and a method of analyzing dance. What is officially labeled as postmodern dance itself has changed since I began writing about it in the early seventies; it has become less formalist, more concerned with content — in particular with the politics of identity — and, demographically speaking, its practitioners have become more multicultural.

And those of us who write about dancing have changed since then, too. Influenced not only by Johnston's experiments in critical writing but also by Susan Sontag's essay "Against Interpretation" — a sacred text for my generation — as a critic and historian I initially staked out an aggressively descriptive, anti-interpretive stance. I was also an enthusiast, a missionary for the kind of dancing I found moving, both intellectually and kinesthetically. When I began graduate school at New York University in 1977 to study with Michael Kirby, he reinforced the documentary approach. But by the early 1980s, like many of my generation, I found myself gravitating toward other, more analytical, interpretive, and contextual approaches to writing culture.

Perhaps this was in part an Oedipal gesture that let me differentiate myself from my teacher. But certainly the dancing I was writing about in some measure catalyzed this shift. A new generation of choreographers was injecting postmodern dance with manifest content of all sorts that seemed to demand interpretation. Around the same time, I began looking at breakdancing. It was an easy, even attractive critical and historical move to make, since I had long been interested in African-American dance and had studied aspects of it in graduate school; now the postmodern dance I followed was, simultaneously, breaking barriers between cultural strata by alluding to vernacular and popular dancing. Searching for a way to make sense of breakdancing forced me to take cultural context into account and led me into conversations with folklorists and anthropologists who turned my thinking in new directions. Further, a feedback loop between the two worlds of dance was soon established, not simply by critics and historians, but more importantly by choreographers and curators. A potent transfer of the imagery of popular culture and issues of political identity from one genre to another seemed to symbolize the emergence of a multiplex but shared postmodern aesthetic across class, gender, ethnic, and cultural lines.

The discourses of semiotics, poststructuralism, and cultural studies molded me to some degree even when I was engaged in criticizing them. Three key theorists of the body, Mary Douglas, Michel Foucault, and Mikhail Bakhtin, have continually provided insights for finding ways to think about bodies, their social meanings, and their political forces. The analytic precision of semiotics exerts a continuing attraction, although my own approach is neither orthodox nor explicit. (Chapter 26, on Steve Paxton's *Flat*, is an exception in that it was a conscious exercise in performing a semiotic analysis of a dance, and it was first written for a course in theatrical semiotics taught by Paul Bouissac.)

The first section of this book, "Writing Criticism/History," is concerned with metacriticism and metahistory. It maps out certain options for methodologies of dance writing, and it attempts to raise questions about the political and social position of the critic and historian. At the same time, it is obliquely autobiographical, in that the arrangement of the articles tracks my own development as a dance writer, beginning with my tribute to Jill Johnston's criticism and ending with my most recent thoughts about how to write dance history in terms of the political negotiation of moving bodies.

The second and third sections cover components of the backdrop to postmodern dancing. In "The Euro-American Avant-garde," I trace two types of modernist dancing: the first is experimental ballet of several kinds, from an anticanonical aspect of Balanchine's choreography, to alternative companies to the Diaghilev Ballets Russes in Paris in the 1920s, to the work of Kasyan Goleizovsky, a leading Soviet innovator; the second is the formalism of Merce Cunningham's modern dancing. Although we often think of Balanchine as a mainstream American ballet choreographer, in this section I examine the ways in which his interest in African-American dancing led him to expand and alter the ballet canon. This topic is related to the third section, "The African-American Connection," which traces African retentions as well as transformations in African-American dancing, primarily but not exclusively in the arena of breakdancing. Breakdancing is perhaps the quintessential form of popular dancing in the age of postmodernism, incorporating mixed allusions to the mass media and to high culture, and creating ironic narratives of personal and political identity. Thus the third section includes information on both the background and the expression of the postmodern in dance.

The fourth section investigates politics and popular dancing. Again, although the popular Hollywood film dancing by Fred Astaire and social dancing of the kind done at John Allen's dance house in one sense may be considered mainstream, the consideration of the underbelly of these forms prompted these essays. Astaire's drunk dances are subversive antidances, undermining the very canons of grace and agility he establishes in his main repertory. Allen's place specialized in the kind of dancing rejected by high society, catering to the seamiest sectors of society and introducing, through its sailor clientele, an international mixture of bodily moves. Finally, the Workers' Dance League of the 1930s was an overtly subversive movement. A left-wing cultural formation, it sponsored the making of dances with progressive political content—antiracist, antifascist, antiwar, and anticapitalist.

All these aspects of dancing contribute to the material discussed in the fifth section, "Postmodern Dance: From the Sixties to the Nineties." Postmodern dance has changed in many ways over the last thirty years, and these essays are arranged in an order that charts those changes. Once a predominantly Euro-American avant-garde movement, by the nineties postmodern dance has become multicultural in every sense. It is multiethnic; it advocates diversity of gender, sexual choice, age, and physical ability; and it includes within its vocabulary every available genre of dance, gleaned from the entire hierarchy of cultural levels. Further, it restores the speaking voice to the dancer's body. And it is a historically conscious movement that reproduces, recycles, and renews dances from different eras.

Perhaps to some readers this collection simply will appear to be a mélange. But I am convinced that it is emblematic of postmodernism, in a number of ways. It is, first of all, concerned with crossovers between "high" and "low" dance cultures — the avant-garde, the popular, the commercial, and the vernacular. Moreover, it analyzes relationships between mainstream dance and its counterstreams, which contest, challenge, subvert, and undermine the mainstream traditions. In terms of methodology, my approach is postmodernist in that it has a tendency toward the contextual, historical, and ethnographic. It is also concerned with bringing the margins to the center.

This book not only reflects but also participates in the production of the postmodern moment. It is for this reason that in the title I speak of writing dancing, because it is partly through writing and talking about dancing that we, as a culture, collaborate in producing it.

I

Writing Criticism / History

1

Jill Johnston: Signaling Through the Flames

Jill Johnston is important to modern dance history not only because her writings afford us a vivid glimpse of avant-garde New York dance in the 1960s (much of which disappeared with little documentation elsewhere), but also because of the kind of writer she was. A champion of the avant-garde — not only in dance but in all the arts — from her first essay published in *Dance Observer* in 1955, Johnston chose subject matter, language, and structure that have profoundly influenced a subsequent generation of critics and choreographers who have learned much about dance through her writings.

Johnston's passions as an art critic (she worked for *Art News* as a reviewer from 1960–66) and dance critic often led her to see parallels between fine art and dance, or to use metaphors from the visual arts to describe choreography. She also wrote at a time when boundaries between various art forms were beginning to blur; and it seems only logical that her two volatile interests should have combined explosively to produce a cultural "cryptic."[1] Writing about theater, dance, music, happenings, environments, and art panels in the pages of the *Village Voice*, she both noted the intermedia connections (the sculptor Robert Morris's dances; the writings and influence of composer John Cage, Merce Cunningham's music director; Yoko Ono's performances; Fluxus and poetry performances, et al.), and made her own. In her critical writing she began, in the midsixties, to use forms and strategies analogous to those she wrote about: the found phrase paralleled the found objects of pop art and neodada, or the found movements of postmodern dance; stream-of-consciousness correlated to assemblage and improvisatory dance composition.

Johnston is often remembered as the dance critic who created a precedent for personalized, descriptive criticism.[2] That aspect of her writing, as I have suggested, suited the temper of her times. Yet I think a careful reading of Johnston's early reviews and essays (1957–65 — after the 1955

New Performance 2/1 (1980)

essay she did not write regularly on dance until 1957) show another valuable contribution: a rigorous, analytical, yet generous approach to the avant-garde that still found room to acknowledge the contributions of the old guard.

Johnston's first dance essay, "Thoughts on the Present and Future Directions of Modern Dance" (1955), sets forth themes that will recur throughout her career as a dance critic. While vague (it mentions no names), often pedantic, and embracing an oceanic, organic-idealist notion of art — proposing that art has life cycles, like living creatures, and that those cycles are an evolving progression — the essay hints that a "rebel group" will revitalize choreography, and calls for a constructive criticism to meet the challenge recent dance experiments have raised. "Here and there in this boiling pot of arm waving, choreography by chance, egos in vacuums, and styles of all descriptions may be detected snatches of original inspiration, and an occasional work of breadth," it notes optimistically.[3]

Two years later, in "The Modern Dance — Directions and Criticism," Johnston's language has relaxed and her thesis is more specific. She names José Limón and Merce Cunningham as the leading exponents of two opposing tendencies in modern dance. In Limón's camp she puts Anna Sokolow, Pearl Lang, Ruth Currier, Sophie Maslow, and Natanya Neuman. These are the choreographers who will consolidate and extend the traditions of the modern dance pioneers of the 1930s. The other group consists of rebels — besides Cunningham, Alwin Nikolais, Sybil Shearer, and Katherine Litz. Though Johnston generalizes that this group is engaged in depersonalizing movement, excluding emotional subject matter, and breaking with the past, she finds that they have little in common apart from their strong individualism, and concludes by calling again for a new criticism, an objective criticism that will no longer judge artists by predetermined standards, but rather will "[penetrate] the style, method and content of its subject, *in the interests of the public it serves*" (italics Johnston's).[4]

It was the rebel choreographers, including also James Waring, Paul Taylor, Merle Marsicano, Aileen Passloff, and after 1962 Yvonne Rainer and other members of the Judson Dance Theater, to whom Johnston chiefly directed her own attention and criticism, both at *Dance Observer* and the *Village Voice*. However, until around 1963, even while delivering polemics against the old modern dance, she continued, in print, to appreciate the accomplishments of a Limón or a Sokolow in extending an honorable tradition.

A third essay, "Abstraction in Dance," written in 1957, further clarifies Johnston's sympathies by invoking abstract expressionism in painting and arguing that any discussion of the abstraction process in dance must account for the fact that it is not movement that is abstracted — "Movement is what it is" — but choreography. Through the organization of movement, the gestures become divorced from dramatic content. This notion of abstraction has historical precedents, from Petipa's ballet divertissements to Limón's "stylized decoration." Johnston hopes that her essay has made the term less mysterious and threatening.[5]

Besides these three essays, Johnston wrote seven reviews for *Dance Observer* between March 1957 and October 1959. Her first review for the *Village Voice*, published February 3, 1960, was of Alwin Nikolais's *Totem*. Her tone is still somewhat pompous. But here she has the space for discursive argument, rather than a paragraph or so for each dance, as she had at *Dance Observer*. The leisurely, logical, and analytical style she would use for the next five years is already evident in the *Totem* review. It opens with a paragraph setting forth its premise that Nikolais creates a science fiction of the dance. It then talks about the choreographer's style in general, giving only short descriptions to support a point in its argument. These descriptions summarize the action, rather than dissect the movements in detail; for example, "In *Reliquary* Murray Louis looks like a harlequin-skeleton-monkey in the role of a relic. He cavorts amiably on a bar (which must be his reliquary) supported by two impassive bearers." The last third of the review analyzes the impact of the dance; in this case, Johnston concludes that Nikolais sacrifices choreography for special effects. In this, her first review of Nikolais, Johnston is forebearing. Yet her patience with his work soon runs short. The following year she complains about his "shenanigans" and the "indignity suffered by the dancer in the role of prop for the props," the deadening effect of his predictably symmetrical shapes. By 1964, she has dismissed Nikolais's work summarily, conceding, however, the talent of some of his dancers. "*Sanctum* is a bombastic bag of noise and color. . . . The manipulation of props and costumes is as predictably naive as ever."[6]

After an initial enthusiasm for Paul Taylor, especially for his use of stillness, Johnston soon finds his style gimmicky and habit-bound. By the end of 1962, she pronounces the passing of Taylor's experimentalism, judging his distinctive style a trap. "Now it seems proper to stop thinking about Taylor as the man with the golden heel. He did what he did; . . . he continues to be an interesting dancer with interesting ideas; there is no longer a need to anticipate what is not a probability," i.e., that Taylor's future works will be as astonishing or important as, for example, his *Epic* (1957) or *Three Epitaphs* (1960). Johnston does not write about Taylor again until 1967, in a review that declares, "Paul Taylor is like one of those great-looking animals with a low I.Q. . . . Since [1958] it's been all downhill for Taylor. . . . [He] remains a terrific dancer . . . but he needs a choreographer."[7] Johnston's passion for Merce Cunningham's works never flags, from her first review, of the premieres of *Rune*, *Summerspace*, and *Antic Meet* (1960), to her comments on the first performance of *Winterbranch* (1964). (That advocacy continues in her writings, of course, beyond 1965.) Her commitment to Cunningham stems in part from his commitment to pure dancing, a step both revolutionary and radical, in the literal sense. "He has *brought us back* to the reality that dancing concerns dancing" (italics mine). Yet she does not deny that his movements are expressive; rather, she celebrates the expressive intensity of abstraction, which "implies much more than a simple defined emotion. Which, in the end, is more powerful, more human and exacting, than the sledgehammer technique of a doubled-over grief or a chest-expanded joy."[8]

Because of the nature of Cunningham's choreography, in which the structures seem to disappear to set forth the dancing, Johnston is content to describe the works, rather than to analyze their workings, although generally she introduces the reviews with ruminations on how to look at the dances. At first she has difficulty evoking the movements; discussing *Rune* (1959) and *Summerspace* (1958) she can only analogize them to paintings seen as one passes through a room, to which one would like to return for a closer look: "*Rune* . . . contains some typically swift and dazzling passages, but the dominant tone is a rich, slow brown. By contrast, *Summerspace* is light and resilient . . . it has the quality of the speckled backdrop and costumes — something like the dappled play of light and shadow caused by the sun when it glints through leaves."[9] (Johnston's later renderings of the qualities of Cunningham's movement are among her finest, most concise images: "I have a vivid recollection of an 'incident' originating as a vibration in [his] thighs, transferred to the stomach, travelling upward to the arms and shoulders and exploding like a geyser at the top," she would say of Cunningham's dancing in *Aeon*. And of *Winterbranch* she would write, "The dancers move through the sound like hunters going calmly about their business in the animal kingdom of a jungle night. The sound is wild. The action is spare and remote. It takes a long time for a dancer to push himself the length of the stage on his back, the beam of a flashlight raking from under his shirt. Mostly I recall a beautiful tumble as they all clasp arms and make a slow, massive rise and fall of liquid branches following after a long stretch of flotsam burlap drifting across the bleak stage."[10])

By 1962 Johnston's writing style is informal, personal, still authoritative but in an appealing, if brash manner. With a review of works by Fred Herko and Yvonne Rainer in March of that year, Johnston prophetically announces that "fresh winds" are blowing from the direction of Robert Dunn's composition course, taught from 1960 to 1962 at Merce Cunningham's studio. (Herko and Rainer, along with Ruth Emerson and Trisha Brown, whom Johnston here singles out as interesting dancers in the concert, had been among the active members of the Judson Dance Theater from its beginnings in July 1962.) She identifies Herko's *Edge*, a piece for dancers and actors, as a "combine-dance," correlating his style to Robert Rauschenberg's in painting, and writes, "The movement of the dancers was large, lyric, unassumingly original. The actors thrashed, snarled, wrestled, and in general made themselves bigger than life in a barroom brawl. When the dancers and actors were on together, the tension . . . made a charming uproar. . . . Mr. Herko kept switching tactics and if you think about it, which I am doing, it really was a mismash of styles, events, media, and it all made excellent sense." Rainer's static method of repeating movement fragments without climax or development—in *The Bells* (1961), *Satie for Two* (1962), and *Three Seascapes* (1962)—moves Johnston to quote Gertrude Stein on repetition: "From this time on familiarity began and I like familiarity. It does not in me breed contempt it just breeds familiarity. And the more familiar a thing is the more there is to be familiar with. And so my familiarity began and kept on being." This comparison was quite a compliment to Rainer, in view of the fact that Johnston herself was emulating Stein's writing style with increasing frequency around this time.[11]

With her review of the first Concert of Dance (1962) given by Judson Dance Theater, which presented works by fourteen choreographers in one evening, Johnston announces the arrival on the scene of a group of choreographers "who could make the present of modern dance more exciting than it's been for twenty years." It is this group, including Rainer, Herko, Emerson, Brown, David Gordon, Judith Dunn, Steve Paxton, Lucinda Childs, Elaine Summers, Carolee Schneemann, Robert Morris, Deborah Hay, and Alex Hay, as well as the older choreographers showing work at the Judson (Waring, Litz, Marsicano, Passloff), to whom Johnston is to devote the majority of her writing for the next several years.[12]

Johnston's stylistic innovations are present in embryonic form almost from her first articles for the *Voice*. There is a casualness and abruptness in her diction that easily segues into the later experiments with cliché, sentence fragments, and fractured paragraphs. She introduces the pronoun "I" into the first *Voice* review, and within a few months would be using it often, in a direct and conversational tone. By June 1960, she has already introduced a review with a long anecdote about her dealings with press agents—a reworking of Kafka—that prefigures the picaresque columns of the later sixties, in which her adventures before, after, and in between dance concerts are as important as the dancing itself. "Fluxus Fuxus," her inspired treatise on events by the neo-dadaist music group Fluxus, published July 2, 1964, is an early and nearly complete model of Johnston's later modus operandi. A single paragraph nearly a thousand words long, it begins:

> Fluxus flapdoodle. Fluxus concert, 1964. Donald Duck meets the Flying Tigers. Why should anyone notice the shape of a watch at the moment of looking at the time? Should we formulate the law of the fall of a body toward a center, or the law of the ascension of a vacuum towards a periphery? The exposition became a double bloody mary. Some Fluxus experts went to the Carnegie Tavern also. Fluxus moved into the street and onto my typewriter. Polyethylene and people everywhere and some of them have all these voices. Soren Agonoux said (that). The voice of being kind to your fine feathered friends. Put your favorite sounds in a

> tube and see how they come out at the other end. Be kind to Your Fine Feathered Friends was never so palatable. Take a loaf of tip top bread and try constructing a staircase. What did George Macunias mean by saying that "all other pieces have been performed whether you notice them or not?"[13]

Johnston's participation in the aesthetic revolution of the sixties was so direct that her style and method of writing changed drastically; she passed from writing about events passively observed to writing about her own activities at dance concerts as well as on art panels, in lecture events, at artworld parties, and on her journeys to and from these incidents. Ironically, her attempts to be true to the material she wrote about led her directly back to her self. A fragmented, visionary, yet matter-of-fact style, studded with clichés and puns, became Johnston's hallmark after 1965. It was that year, after her first breakdown, that she decided "[to explain] myself to the universe . . . [to] exonerate and redeem myself and hopefully plead the case for a visionary life . . . to shatter and reorganize the language for myself."[14] For this enormous goal, the field of dance alone was clearly too narrow; for someone whose writings about dance had helped to widen dance to include more of life, the only territory left was all of life. Her structures became fluid, open-ended, dense, full of compound words, montage sentences without paragraph breaks, and autobiographical revelations. Dance was sometimes still the content, but usually only secondarily so. Through 1968, "Dance Journal," as Johnston's column in the *Voice* was titled after mid-1965, was primarily about the daily adventures and mental processes of the critic-as-artist. "The artists were never pleased that I began to find their lives more interesting than their work," she wrote later.[15]

In January 1969 her third schizophrenic break began. Perhaps significantly, for the first time she was not hospitalized, pursuing instead a self-prescribed Laingian therapy, and continuing for the first time to write her column throughout the episode.[16] The "dance of life" absorbed her then and thereafter. She never again wrote arts criticism.[17] Finally, in 1971, acknowledging what had in fact become the subject of her column, she changed its title to "Jill Johnston." After she came out in print as a radical lesbian July 2, 1970, the columns became a soapbox for her evolving political ideology.

What Johnston respected in the choreography of Rainer and other postmodern dancemakers was a theme that in the sixties had preoccupied the work of avant-garde artists in a range of media: the matter-of-fact, the everyday, the objective. Just as pop art and, later, minimalism can be understood as rebellions against the subjective excesses of abstract expressionism, the revolution fomented by the Judson choreographers, which Johnston applauded and explicated in her columns, can be understood as a rejection of the theatricalization by modern dance of emotion, character, and finally, human movement. It is interesting to note how Johnston's interests and loyalties gravitate toward the Judson group, paralleling her activities as an art critic. Like Rainer, Paxton, and others, Johnston celebrated "the heroism of the ordinary," as she wrote of Rainer's *We Shall Run*. "No plots or pretensions. People running. Hurray for people." It is this directness, this immediacy in vividly presenting the kinesthetic facts of life that informs Johnston's writing as well as the dances and other events she wrote about.[18]

Yet her criteria for modernity and progress in both art and dance emerge, throughout these early writings, as a curious blend of factualism and romanticism. Her advocacy of coolness, of paring down emotional affect, her attacks on the pretentiousness of "meaningful" modern dances and social passion, and her attention to the ordinary seem to signal a conception of art that values detachment and abstraction. Yet Johnston is not a formalist critic. She glories in, even mythologizes, the direct experience of "reality"—chaotic, messy, raw vitality of movement and materials unmediated by deadening forms. The trouble she finds with the ballet *The Sleeping Beauty*, for instance, is that it is too far removed from its roots in mythic fertility rites.[19] The *Weltansicht* Johnston sets forth in her columns implies a set of values for art and society of which form for its own sake is not a member: freedom, democracy, pluralism, modernity, attacks on logic and legitimacy, participation, moral engagement, honesty, the presentation of self as center of perception. From this perspective, she rejects ballet and old modern dance as tokens of a set that unites royalty, hierarchy, masterpieces, European aesthetics, museums, and even stylized symbol systems. "The aristocracy is dead and cornflakes are profound for breakfast," she writes in a review of Limón and Cunningham.[20] In hindsight, we have come to see that cornflakes and soup cans are expressive symbols too. Yet Johnston goes farther, calling for an art that "signals through the flames"—as she frequently quoted from Artaud, evoking the image of the artist as an ecstatic martyr[21] and projecting a romantic vision of nature and reality, and of the innocent grace of artists who can make life yield its secrets. That is a view as freighted with political and social meaning—albeit an alternative meaning—as the art of the academy.

Writing about Surplus Dance Theater in 1964, Johnston concludes, "This review is about process and reality, which reminds me of Whitehead, who said someplace that philosophy—and I'll substitute criticism—is the analysis of the obvious."[22] In order to effect that analysis, Johnston staked out for herself a new criticism both in terms of the breadth of her subject matter and the openness of her writing style. "As I see it now," she wrote in "Critics' Critics" in 1965,

> The land looks level enough to be a wide open field and I'm ready to run or walk on it without encountering a boogie man. . . . I'll take a plot of

level territory and stake out a claim to lie down on it and criticize the constellations if that's what I happen to be looking at. I also stake out a claim to be an artist, a writer, if that's what I'm doing when I get to the typewriter and decide that I liked something well enough to say what I think it's all about. . . . The future is upon us and the Art of Criticism has already come into its own in those public places where the critic is lying down on a soft piece of ground to enjoy a bit of blue and yellow scenery. . . .[23]

2

Working and Dancing: A Response to Monroe Beardsley's "What Is Going on in a Dance?"

With Noël Carroll

Professor Beardsley's paper is distinguished by his customary clarity. Many of the distinctions he draws will undoubtedly be useful, not only for dance theoreticians, but for dance critics as well. Nevertheless, the way that these distinctions are placed in the service of a putative characterization of what constitutes a dance "moving" seems to us problematic. This brief note will be devoted to exploring the adequacy of Professor Beardsley's proposal.

Beardsley appears to conclude his paper by stating a condition requisite for a motion to be counted as a dance "moving." He writes, "If, in other words, there is more zest, vigor, fluency, expansiveness, or stateliness than appears necessary for its practical purposes, there is an overflow or superfluity of expressiveness to mark it as belonging to its own domain of dance."[1]

We interpret Beardsley's basic point here as the claim that a superfluity of expressiveness (above the requirements of practical exigencies) is a defining feature of a dance "moving." However, in our opinion, this attribute represents neither a necessary nor a sufficient condition of dance.

First of all, "superfluity of expressiveness" is not exclusive enough to define a dance moving. We often hear of the fervor of socialist volunteers, urbanites, who travel to rural areas to help with a harvest and boost produc-

Dance Research Journal 15/1 (Fall 1982).

tivity. Imagine a truckload of such patriotic workers arriving at a cane field somewhere in Cuba. Some of them may even be professional dancers. They raise their machetes much higher than necessary, use more force than is required by their task, and perhaps their swinging becomes rhythmic. Their activity is expressive of patriotic zest and revolutionary zeal, but it is not dance. Here we have an overflow of expressiveness, and it is not related to the practical purpose of the event, which is aimed at increasing productivity, not at displaying class solidarity. Of course, a journalist might describe the harvest as a dance, but we would have to understand this as poetic shorthand, meaning "dancelike." To take the term "dance" literally in referring to such an event would commit us to such unlikely ballets as some sweeping infantry maneuvers and the dramatic tantrums of an adolescent. If a dance critic were to review these events, we would be very surprised.

Undoubtedly, a choreographer could take our truckload of harvesters, place them on a proscenium stage, and transform their enthusiasm into a dance. But in such a case, it seems to us that it is the choreographer's act of framing, or recontextualizing, rather than an intrinsic quality of the movement, that is decisive. In general, whether one is speaking about art dance or social dance, the context of the event in which the movement is situated is more salient than the nature of the movement itself in determining whether the action is dance.

Professor Beardsley's definition not only fails to be exclusive enough, but also falters in inclusiveness. There are, we believe, incontestable examples of dance in which there is no superfluity of expressiveness in the movement. One example is *Room Service* by Yvonne Rainer, which was first performed at the Judson Church in 1963 and again the next year at the Institute of Contemporary Art in Philadelphia. Rainer describes it as "a big sprawling piece with three teams of people playing follow-the-leader thru an assortment of paraphernalia which is arranged and rearranged by a guy and his two assistants."[2] Part of the dance includes climbing up a ladder to a platform and jumping off. A central segment of the Philadelphia performance (and of particular interest for this paper) was the activity of two dancers carrying a mattress up an aisle in the theater, out one exit, and back in through another.

Although *Room Service* may appear similar to a dance Beardsley discusses—Anna Sokolow's *Rooms*—it differs from it in important ways. The ordinary movement in *Room Service* is not marked by "the intensified way"[3] in which it is carried out. The point of the dance is to make ordinary movement qua ordinary movement perceptible. The audience observes the performers navigating a cumbersome object, noting how the working bodies adjust their muscles, weights, and angles. If the dance is performed correctly, there can be no question of superfluity of expression over the requirements of practical purposes, because the raison d'être of the piece is to display the practical intelligence of the body in pursuit of a mundane, goal-oriented type of action — moving a mattress. That is, the subject of the dance is the functional economy of a movement in the performance of bodies involved in what Beardsley calls a working. *Room Service* is not a representation of a working: it *is* a working. But it is also a dance — partially because through its aesthetic context it transforms an ordinary working (the sort of thing whose kinetic intricacies usually go unnoticed or ignored) into an object for close scrutiny. Rainer immediately went on to make another dance, *Parts of Some Sextets*, comprising a variety of activities involving ten dancers, twelve mattresses, and gears, string, rope, and buffers. Again, the emphasis in the dance is on the working human body.

Room Service is not an atypical dance. It is an example of a genre of avant-garde performance that might loosely be referred to as task dances, which have been made continuously since the sixties. The roster of task dances includes other works by Rainer, Trisha Brown's Equipment Pieces and her *Rulegame* 5 (1964), and Simone Forti's "dance construction" *Slant Board* (1961), in which three or four people move constantly across a wooden ramp slanted against a wall at a forty-five-degree-angle to the floor, by means of knotted ropes.[4] The existence of this genre is an important motive in writing this reply to Professor Beardsley, because we fear that his definition is unwittingly conservative, operating to exclude prescriptively some of the most exciting work of contemporary choreographers.

Of course, Beardsley may wish to defend his definition by arguing that *Room Service*, and works like it, are not dances. This seems ill-advised for several reasons. First, the dance shares a set of recognized aesthetic preoccupations with contemporary fine art. For example, it is what has been called "anti-illusionist." That is, it attempts to close the conceptual gap between artworks and real things — a major theme of modernist sculpture and painting. In this vein, Jasper Johns reportedly has said that "people should be able to look at a painting 'the same way you look at a radiator.' "[5] Johns's flag paintings, especially *Flag* (1955, Museum of Modern Art), ingeniously implement this "demystifying" attitude toward artworks, since in certain pertinent respects the painting is a flag (or one side of one), rather than a representation (or "illusion") of one; schoolchildren could pledge to it with no loss of allegiance. Johns's bronzed beer cans or his Savarin can with paint brushes are sculptures that likewise attempt to narrow the categorical distinction between mundane objects and works of art.

The choice of ordinary working movement as the subject of *Room Service* is on a par with the "demythologizing" tendency toward fine art that one finds in many of Jasper Johns's pieces. Stated formulaically, we might say that "ordinary object" in art is equivalent to "ordinary movement" in dance. Now, Johns's work is (rightfully, we believe) considered among the major accomplishments of the art of the fifties, sixties, and early seventies. There can be little doubt that it is art or that his patterned canvases are paintings. Why? One answer is that his works are the intelligible products of a century of animated interplay between art making and art theorizing. Since the rise of photography, anti-illusionist arguments for the role and destiny of painting abound. Part of the rhetoric of this theorizing is that a painting is essentially an object (a "real" object), like any other (for example, a radiator or beer can), rather than a cypher (a virtual object) standing for real objects. The Johns examples, as well as Warhol's Brillo boxes, attempt to literalize this type of theory by proposing masterpieces that in terms of certain relevant features are indistinguishable from everyday objects. *Room Service* bears a *strict genetic resemblance* to the above cases of modernist painting and sculpture. If they are full-blooded examples of painting and sculpture, as we believe their position in the history of twentieth-century art establishes, then *Room Service* is a dance.

Specifically, it is an art dance, since the tradition it directly emerges from is that of the artworld rather than custom, ritual, or popular culture. Indeed, it is an art dance in a triple sense. First, it is presented to the spectator as an object of aesthetic contemplation and not as a social or ritual activity. Second, and more importantly, it mimes (or, less metaphorically, transposes) the theoretical *données* of fine art in the medium of dance. And third, in doing this it is also in the domain of art dancing proper, since both the balletic and modern traditions of dance have always made a practice of exploring other arts for inspiration and invention.

In making this argument, we hasten to add that we do not believe that it is necessary for the anti-illusionist theories that form the conceptual background of Johns, of Warhol, or of Rainer to be true or even compelling philosophically in order that the putative paintings, sculptures, and dances be classified as paintings, sculptures, and dances. It is enough that the theories have currency in their appropriate communities of discourse and that the works in question can be seen as their consequences. We are assuming this on the grounds that a genetic link between an evolving artistic tradition (including theory, practice, and the cross-fertilization between the two) and a candidate for inclusion in that tradition is a prima facie reason for classifying the candidate as part of the tradition. *Room Service* is both art and art dance because of such genetic links. Indeed, insofar as it is even less ambiguously an ordinary working than painting the design of the Stars and Stripes is a flag, it is perhaps a more effective implementation of modernist concerns than the Johns example. In terms of our use of *Room Service*, and dances like it, as counterexamples to Beardsley's characterization of dance, it is important to iterate that these dances are able to articulate the modernist theme of anti-illusionism precisely because their movements are completely practical—a literal performance of a task—with no superfluity of expressiveness.

A related, though less persuasive, reason to believe that *Room Service* is a dance (specifically, an art dance) is that it performs a major (though not essential) function of art in general and art dancing in particular. Namely, it symbolically reflects major values and preoccupations of the culture from which it emerged. In other words, it behaves the way we expect dances to behave. Its anti-illusionist stance and its disavowal of representation, formal decorativeness, and the kinds of expressiveness found in most modern dance (for example, Graham, Humphrey, and Limón) evince a reductive bias, a quest to get down to basics, to eschew the layers of convention, coded symbolism, and elaborate structure that "obstruct" the spectator's perception of movement. This search for fundamentals is in many respects utopian. Nevertheless, it does reflect a particular postwar mood — a positivist search for the hard facts of dance, bereft of illusionist "nonsense." Again, whether there are such hard facts is beside the point; it is the quest implied by this dance that reflects the temper of the times. And, to return to Beardsley's definition, *Room Service* reflects the values and prejudices of its cultural context because of the sheer practicality of its movement. (Interestingly, a Labananalysis of Rainer's nontask dances of this period shows a striking similarity between the efficient motions used in work and those used in the dances: a somewhat narrow and medium-level stance, an even flow of energy, and sagittal gestures — in two planes, forward and backward plus up and down — rather than the three-dimensional shaping, gathering, and scattering movements of much modern dance.)[6]

Admittedly, *Room Service* is an extremely complex dance, with several levels of symbolic import. It is not our intention to argue that it is not expressive. For example, it communicates a conception of dance, albeit a reductive one, and, as the previous paragraph argues, it espouses identifiable values. However, this sense of expression is different from Beardsley's. It is not a matter of the movement having intensified, nonpractical qualities, but of the movement implying certain polemical commitments, easily statable in propositions, resulting from the art-historical and cultural contexts in which the dance was produced. Here the propositional import of the dance hinges on the practicality of the movement; this level of expression, in other words, cannot be mapped in terms of an overflow of intensified qualities, above and beyond the functional. Though *Room Service* has propositional meaning, it is not what Beardsley calls a saying, nor is it a representation of a saying. Professor Beardsley's sayings are highly conventionalized signals; for example, a wave of the hand is regularly associated with "hello." However, we do not "read" the significance of the movement in *Room Service*, but infer it as the best explanation of Rainer's choreographic choices within a specific historical context.

Room Service might also be called expressive in the sense that the choreography metaphorically possesses certain anthropomorphic qualities; we have already called it "positivist." It might also be called factual or objective. But each of these labels fits the dance specifically because of the theoretically "hard-minded," anti-illusionist position it promotes. That the subject is work in the context of a culture that often identifies art and dance with play also has expressive repercussions: the choreography is "serious" rather than "sentimental" or "frivolous" (in the idiom of the Protestant ethic). Again, it is the choice of unadorned workings as its subject that is the basis of its expressive effect as well as the basis, as previously argued, of its being recognizable as an art dance. Given this, Professor Beardsley's stipulation, identifying dance with a superfluity of expressiveness above practical purposes, does not seem to fit the facts of a major work of postmodern dance and, by extension, a genre of which it is a primary example.

Professor Beardsley's paper also raises issues relevant to postmodern choreography in the section where he argues that the basic constituents of dance are not bodily motions as such. Instead, Beardsley holds that dances are composed of actions that he calls "movings" and "posings." It is interesting to note that in certain postmodern dances and dance theorizing it is presupposed that dance is fundamentally bodily motion and that the function of a dance is to make the spectator see bodily motions as such. The motive behind this enterprise derives from the modernist bias outlined earlier. In brief, in contemporary theoretical discussions of fine art, the conception of a painting as an *ordinary* object easily becomes associated with the idea that it is an object as such. It is a surface. Thus, the role of an artist like Jules Olitski is seen as acknowledging the flat surface of the painting. Painters are cast in a role akin to nuclear physicists, exploring the basic physical constituents of their medium, as if plumbing the mysteries of the atom. The result is paintings "about" paint or, to change media, films "about" celluloid. This anti-illusionist move is also in evidence in postmodern dance. Dances like Trisha Brown's *Accumulation* identify dance as a concatenation of physical motions without any ostensible formal, conventional, expressive, or representational unity. *Accumulation* is a list of abstract gestures—simple rotations, bends, and swings of the joints and limbs—that are accumulated by repeating the first gesture several times, adding the second gesture and repeating gestures one and two several times, and so on. There are no transitions between gestures. *Accumulation* suggests a position about the nature of the basic elements of dance, a position which holds that dance consists of bodily motions.

The philosophical problems raised by dances like *Accumulation* can be quite vexing.[7] But in our opinion, such dances are not counterexamples to Beardsley's claim that dances are made up of actions and never mere bodily motions. Our reasons for believing this are, for the most part, contained in our gloss of *Room Service*. We have admitted that the search for the fundamentals of dance by postmodern choreographers is utopian. Making dances like *Accumulation*, which are designed to *imply* that dance essentially consists of bodily motions, requires that the basic movements chosen for the dance be purposively made so that (a) they are not straightforwardly classifiable in terms of traditional categories of dance actions (for example, Beardsley's "suggestings") and (b) they are intelligible, owing to their historical context, as rejections of the traditional categories. In meeting the first requirement, each movement is a type of action—namely, a *refraining*. Specifically, each movement is a *studied omission* of the movement qualities found in ballet and modern dance.[8] In the context of the sixties, this sort of refraining implied a commitment to the idea that dance consists primarily of bodily motions. However, the movements used to articulate that position were actually anything but mere bodily motions. They were actions, refrainings whose implicit disavowal of the traditional qualities of dance movements enabled them to be understood as polemical. Thus, though we feel that certain developments in postmodern dance, specifically task dances, threaten Professor Beardsley's concept of dance, we do not believe that the existence of dances like *Accumulation* challenge Beardsley's point that dances consist of actions rather than mere bodily motions.

3

Criticism as Ethnography

About a month ago, I told a philosopher friend the topic of my talk for today. "I can immediately think of two important differences between dance critics and ethnographers," he said. Now this friend, the son of an African statesman and an upper-class British woman, grew up in Ghana, was educated at Oxford, and teaches at Cornell. Not only does he literally embody cross-cultural experience; he is also one of the leading contemporary philosophers of mind. "This is great," I thought. "I'm about to get a brilliantly insightful theoretical groundwork for a complicated topic. The talk is as good as written." "So . . . ?" I asked, taking out a mental notebook, and gearing up for some subtle philosophical discourse. "It's this," he replied: "Ethnographers get a lot more grants to go to *much* more interesting places." Well, here we are in San Francisco, as we know, the site of the first DCA annual conference outside of New York. That's already a more

Keynote address, Dance Critics Association Conference, San Francisco, 1989.

interesting place for many of us, but I doubt that any of us is here on a hefty National Science Foundation grant.

Ironic and lighthearted as my friend's comment was, one thing about it seemed to me a valuable starting point. And that is the hidden antitopic in the title of my talk. That is, if we are going to think about critics as ethnographers, I want to begin by looking at the differences between the two, differences that, as I will address, have become complicated in the last decade or so, when both ethnography and dance criticism have undergone changes in method and substance. I would next like to ask why this has become a topic—that is, why we are now interested in thinking about ourselves as a particular type of social scientist. And finally, I want to suggest where this comparison might (or might not) prove useful in conceptualizing in our own field.

In order to mark some of the differences between ethnography and criticism historically but briefly, I'd like to divide both practices into two stages: the modern and the postmodern, or, if those labels seem too problematic, the "traditional" (in quotes because for ethnographers this is, of course, a loaded term; I mean it here in its common usage) and the current; or, roughly speaking, presixties and postsixties twentieth-century practice. Of course, within those two large stages one could trace much more detailed processes of change, and I will talk about some of those changes, although in broad strokes. But it is still important to divide those two stages, for in the first the distinctions between criticism and ethnography are much more salient, while the second stage is perhaps closer to raising the kinds of questions we are here today to address.[1]

Both ethnographers and dance critics share a certain intellectual task: our role is that of a translator of sorts, one who translates, not between two languages, but between experience and language, between experience and (by and large) the page. In looking at the work of each discipline, then, we might divide it into two steps: the experience that is to be cast into writing, and the writing itself, or the event and its representation. For the ethnographer, the experience or event is fieldwork; for the critic, going to the theater. (Here it should be understood that I am referring to "traditional" ethnography and dance criticism.) This aspect of the work involves a number of components. What exactly is the nature of the experience? Who undergoes it? When and where does the experience take place?

For ethnographers like Bronislaw Malinowski, A. R. Radcliffe-Brown, and Margaret Mead—those who, among others, defined and shaped the discipline in the 1920s and 1930s—*who* did the traveling, witnessing, and writing was as key to professionalizing the discipline as what they did: that is, data-gathering through intensive fieldwork, which became the distinctive method of social and cultural anthropology. Establishing the method of participant observation and naming the players (university-trained social scientists) marked ethnography off from nineteenth-century armchair anthropological speculation by scholars like Sir E. B. Tylor and Sir James Frazer, on the one hand, and reports by travelers, missionaries, colonial administrators, and other such "men on the spot," on the other hand.

In dance criticism, there is an early parallel between some of the nineteenth-century amateur anthropologists—writers, artists, and adventurers—who wrote about their encounters with exotic cultures, and the balletomane critic. In fact, Théophile Gautier and his ilk not only reported on an alien world of bare legs and human flight for their readers, but were also close to anthropologists in writing about a genre of ballet that prized exotic, often Orientalist locales. But while we, too, have a generation of the twenties and thirties—John Martin, Louis Horst, Edwin Denby—who, in a sense, tried to impart more analytic rigor to our field, not until the present generation has dance criticism begun to professionalize itself as an academic discipline. Many of us work completely outside academia as journalists. But, over the past decade and a half, many of us have joined the academy, teaching both history and criticism, even establishing graduate training programs, and this trend has had the double effect of historicizing present criticism (more on that later) and institutionalizing dance criticism as an academic discipline. As well, the past twenty years have seen the rise of smaller-scale critics' institutes—sponsored by the American Dance Festival, the DCA itself, and local critics' groups—which, while not exactly turning working critics into graduate students, do have the effect of institutionalizing training and creating "family trees" of influence; one might even go so far as to speak of "schools." Perhaps our own field's long-standing nonprofessionalism—attracting poets, novelists, sports writers, philosophers, art critics, musicians, and even dancers themselves—has been salutary, as Edwin Denby once suggested.

Of course, one major difference between ethnography and dance criticism has been the locale in which the research is carried out. Ethnographers have been distinguished by their study of the Other—usually in what used to be called primitive cultures, in what we now call colonial or postcolonial, third-world cultures. Part of the point, as George Marcus and Michael Fischer argue in *Anthropology as Cultural Critique*, was the intrinsically comparative process that allowed the ethnographer to make sense of the strange by contrasting it to Western culture, and at the same time to suggest critiques of our culture by locating it in a field of relative values. This liberal project was explicit, for example, in Mead's studies of childhood and child-rearing in Samoa and other cultures.[2]

There is another, perhaps more conceptual, locale that has traditionally preoccupied the ethnographer, and that is the space of everyday life. To be sure, many ethnographers have described rituals and other extraordinary, even theatrical events, and some have specialized in one or another layer of cultural life—dance or music or economic processes. And yet, even those specialists would probably agree that ethnography is above all a holistic science, that sense can only be made of those special activities or aspects of culture by rooting them firmly in the context of daily life.

Both of these spaces are quite far from those of the dance critic, who for the most part is an observer staunchly grounded inside her own culture, except that her own daily life is completely taken up with what for most people is an extraordinary activity—going to the theater. Even when she writes about exotic dance, traditionally it has been the dance imported to the theaters of her own city. When we read Carl Van Vechten on African dance, we are still reading about the New York dance world.

And, of course, this difference in conceptual spaces leads to another important distinction—that of one's research method. As I noted earlier, intensive fieldwork, characterized by participant observation, is the distinctive method of ethnography. What this means in practical terms is that the ethnographer learns a foreign language, travels to a different and distant culture, and spends one or two years living in difficult circumstances learning about that alien culture from the ground up. Going through this initial rite of passage is part of how the ethnographer establishes her scientific authority. She finds native informants who help interpret the strange practices of the Other. She lives the other culture, so to speak, like a child being educated in its conventions—eating its food, speaking its language, dancing its dances, and perennially asking, "Why?" And while she might not participate in every single event she studies, her observations from the outside are confirmed and validated by her intensive (but always limited) experiences of participation from the inside.

How different is the experience of the dance critic, who might interview the choreographer or attend rehearsals, even take a dance class, but whose skill and authority finally depend on observing the finished product across the footlights. A distant observer of her own culture, she is the exact opposite of the ethnographer who works hard to become intimate with a culture not her own. An ethnographer spends years with her subjects, and usually returns, in subsequent years, for follow-up studies; we may spend a season with a company—or we may even return season after season, studying its conventions closely—but many of our encounters are one-night stands and most of us cover a broad range of different artists and ensembles.

Once the fieldwork or performance is over, the next step for both ethnographer and critic is writing. Here, too, the differences loom large. For the ethnographer's genre conventions demand, above all, descriptive detail as a basis for interpretation. In the traditional genre of ethnographic realism, the analysis includes not only the interpretation of a culture's practices, beliefs, and values, but also a representation of the conditions of fieldwork, a novelistic sense of the conditions of everyday life, a holistic functionalist account, and a feeling of translation across both conceptual and linguistic borders. For the dance critic, a key element is missing here.

Like the ethnographer, we are also interested in contextualization, description, and interpretation. But for us those elements are but a first step toward criticism's raison d'être—evaluation. And while we might contextualize our artworks in terms of other artworks or more broadly in a social milieu, for the most part we turn our attention to Culture with a capital C; even more specifically, to fragments of Culture—single works or groups of works.

Since the sixties, both ethnography and dance criticism have changed. The realist ethnography of the functionalist anthropologists who dominated the first half of the twentieth century was challenged, in the sixties, by a shift to structuralist and linguistic models. Claude Lévi-Strauss, for example, looked for an underlying universal grammar shaping all cultural systems, and posited culture as a system of differences in which the meaning of any particular unit emerged in contrast to other units. Clifford Geertz's symbolic analysis concentrated on deciphering a complex network of meanings made of actions, words, and other symbolic forms. In the work of these and other anthropologists, the study of mental and cultural systems—of meaning—replaced the study of behavior and social systems. Linguistic models were attractive, not only because language is the central medium of culture, but also because linguistics seemed to offer more scientifically rigorous ways of studying cultural patterns.

The seventies and eighties, however, have seen new shifts in anthropology that are both outgrowths of and responses to sixties structuralism. Influenced by phenomenology and deconstruction, hermeneutics, Marxism, semiotics, and the various other forms of poststructuralism, what is now known as interpretive anthropology conceives of ethnography as a dialogue across cultural codes. A renewed and revised relativism stresses multicultural awareness tempered by a more modest view of the diminished global status of the Western perspective. Interpretive, or postmodern, anthropology not only moves the emphasis in ethnography from description to interpretation, but also, given the current "crisis of representation," engages in a critique of ethnography, from fieldwork (including what kinds of sites are appropriate or possible to study) to writing (including the use of political and historical perspectives).

Given a shrinking world, the complex influence of the West on non-Western nations, and the shifting global power relations since the sixties, the whole issue of the ethnographic Other is in question, leading some American anthropologists to study cultural diversity right here at home. For instance, in "Ethnicity and the Post-Modern Arts of Memory," Michael Fischer analyzes autobiographies by members of North American minorities.[3] As well, those shifting political dynamics and an acute awareness of the ahistorical nature of much previous anthropology have raised the related question of how to represent cultural difference, leading some anthropologists to conceptualize—even to write—ethnography as a polyphonic, reciprocal dialogue between scholar and informants, a dialogue that ranges over cross-cultural aesthetics, psychology, and epistemology. Such works range from Kevin Dwyer's *Moroccan Dialogues*, which represents barely edited field interviews, to *Piman Shamanism and Staying Sickness*, collectively produced by Donald Bahr, anthropologist, Juan Gregorio, shaman, David Lopez, interpreter, and Albert Alvarez, editor—three of whom are Papago Indians.[4]

A related question that also affects ethnographic writing is the question of how to represent experience itself, in the past more the domain of artists than of social scientists. To this end, postmodern ethnologists have experimented with stretching the boundaries of their genre, not only studying poetry, fiction, autobiography, and film, but also producing it. John O. Stewart, for instance, presents life in his native Trinidad in short story and poetic form as well as in standard ethnographic essays in *Drinkers, Drummers, and Decent Folk*, and Ákos Östör has made a trilogy of films on Hindu ritual.[5]

Both of these issues—how to represent experience and cultural difference—tie into ways that dance criticism has also changed since the sixties. Guided at first by the New Journalism and by *Village Voice* critics like Jill Johnston and John Perrault, a whole generation of dance critics in the late sixties and early seventies plunged into description and prose experiments of all kinds. In retrospect, it seems to me that Susan Sontag's call for a descriptive criticism in "Against Interpretation," which influenced so many of us, might have been an urge fueled by her interest in French anthropology; one of the essays in the collection titled *Against Interpretation*—"The Anthropologist as Hero"—celebrates Lévi-Strauss.[6]

Description was a technique that fit well with the formalist dance of the period, especially in the avant-garde. Now, partly in response to a decade of description, and partly in response to new dance in which content has triumphed over form, dance critics in the eighties, like their contemporaries in other fields, have turned back to interpretation. We, too, have been influenced by poststructuralist and feminist inquiries, although probably at a slower rate than critics in other humanities disciplines, such as film and literature. We have also been influenced by inquiries in our own field, such as Labananalysis.

As well, partly as a result of the temper of the times (with its refined sense of historical consciousness), but also partly because (as I noted earlier) we have sometimes made our living teaching dance history—while writing criticism "on the side"—our writing has willy-nilly become more historically inclined. Deborah Jowitt's *Time and the Dancing Image*, an iconographic history, and Marcia Siegel's critical biography of Doris Humphrey, *Days on Earth*, are two exemplary instances of this trend.[7]

Since the sixties, our genre of critical writing has been stretched by paratheatrical events, deriving both from avant-garde challenges to the borders of theater and from a multicultural awareness. That is, our beat includes the ballet, postmodern dance, recent hybrids of the two, modern dance, tap dance, jazz dance, and musicals; it also includes breakdancing, capoeira, flamenco, wayang, kathak, ballroom dancing, parades, ice skating, possessions. And when we cover an event like this week's Ethnic Dance Festival, we're expected to write about a panoply of traditions at a glance. There's no hope of our becoming instant experts, the way we might if only one esoteric tradition turned up, a sore thumb in a familiar landscape. We turn to ethnographers, whose work it is to study the products of alien cultures, for some answers.

No wonder we are attracted to ethnography. As the boundaries between genres of criticism as well as art blur, and as a diversity of cultures presents its dances to us, we are tempted to view ourselves as ethnographers of sorts. For one thing, in an era of slippery meanings, anthropology is attractive because social science seems more rigorous than humanistic inquiry. (This, of course, overlooks the fact that social scientists consider anthropology the softest of the social sciences, and that anthropology itself, in quest of more rigor, turned to linguistics in the sixties.) Anthropology (at least, in its popularly known, modern version) seems to offer techniques more solid, more objective, more credible than our own highly personalized, rarely articulated systems.

Secondly, in the wake of sixties political consciousness, anthropology seems more capable of conceptualizing and embracing social context, especially the present challenge of American multiculturalism. Ethnography, like history, provides a bigger context for discussing a single event, even the kind of Euro-American event with which we are familiar. But, at the same time, it goes beyond history by seeming to promise tools for the more practical problem of having to write about dance from a culture not our own — a task that has challenged us since the turn of the century but that, in a postcolonial world, we feel a diminishing authority to undertake. So many dance and music critics find themselves opting simply to describe a performance from another culture — or at best to provide a kind of program note's worth of background along with the description — that the anthropological paradigm seems to offer a shot of confidence, if not real methods, to get beyond pure description. (And this, of course, overlooks the fact that anthropologists are also suffering a crisis of confidence and are trying to free themselves from authoritative paradigms.)

I can think of a third appeal anthropology holds for us, as well. In a cultural moment when the avant-garde seems to be dying, if not already dead, when the tradition of the new has been replaced by a postmodern pastiche of the old, ethnography (again, as popularly conceived) seems an answer from another direction for our quest for novelty. And I think this actually gets us back, in a more serious way, to my friend's joke. How can we get to more exotic places? If the avant-garde can no longer provide us with originality and novel aesthetic experiences, where will we find aesthetic adventure? Perhaps in the dance of other cultures, even those that are subcultures at home. Perhaps even through the defamiliarization of Euro-American dance, as Joann Kealiinohomoku suggested in her article, "An Anthropologist Looks at Ballet as a Form of Ethnic Dance," in which, as the title implies, she took the stance of an anthropologist from another culture, looking at our dance as a mysterious phenomenon.[8] Ethnography, as the science that uncovers and explains other cultures, seems to offer an inroad to unfamiliar or defamiliarized terrains, even though its method, participant observation, may be rejected. If this route seems to have an historic precedent in the ethnographic experiments of the cubists, the dadaists, and the German expressionists, perhaps we, too, are on the brink of an artistic and critical experiment, one that will, however, undoubtedly use ethnographic materials in different ways.

There is an enormous temptation, then, to view criticism as ethnography. But we should keep in mind that, as we veer toward social science, ethnographers are equally tempted to view themselves as critics. Ironically enough, we want to be traditional anthropologists, while they want to be traditional critics. But neither discipline is standing still. The rigor, the confidence, the authority, the paradigms, the access to and deciphering of the exotic Other that we would like to borrow from ethnographers are no longer there. But just because there are increasing correspondences and parallels between the two activities, just because it is sometimes useful to unite them metaphorically (as Victor Turner linked theater and anthropology), they should not be mistaken as equivalent. Sometimes dance critics depart from the usual role to write about the daily lives of dance companies, as Joseph Mazo did when he covered the New York City Ballet in *Dance Is a Contact Sport*.[9] Sometimes anthropologists study institutions of Euro-American dance, as Cynthia Novack did in her dissertation on contact improvisation.[10] But that doesn't make Mazo an anthropologist, nor Novack a critic.

I would be the first to admit ethnography's attractiveness, and I was trained in a graduate program that has been moving closer and closer to anthropology. In fact, when I first began to write about breakdancing in 1980, before the form had been theatricalized, there seemed no other way to even get to see it than to hang out in the Bronx, and an ethnographic approach seemed to offer certain advantages to interpreting an art form so inextricably rooted in its subculture. I may not have asked all the questions a trained anthropologist would have, nor was I even interested in recording all the microprocesses of these kids' lives. But I did feel that a cultural context had to be limned in order to capture the sense of the dancing.

But I would also be the first to admit that that situation was unusual, that as critics we mostly see dance made for the theater or uprooted from its context and theatricalized. And that is an important distinction. The differences between the two kinds of inquiries are simply greater than the similarities. Interpretive anthropologists are engaged in making critiques of their own interpretations; dance criticism is not nearly so reflexive. Ethnographers are moving toward a dialogic construction of cultural texts, but as critics we remain—and, I would argue, *should* remain—distant observers. Who wants to coauthor their review with the choreographer? But we are distant observers at home. Anthropologists work outside their culture, or as outsiders to subcultures within their culture; we work, for the most part, right inside the mainstream of our culture, and we write about events for other people inside our culture who share our expectations and values. Shouldn't there be room in the world for both kinds of discourse?

Above all, as I suggested earlier—and this, I believe, is connected to our writing as insiders, for insiders—we bring to bear on our object of study an evaluative purpose that ethnographers have historically shied away from. If ethnographers, operating from cultural relativism, refuse to make judgments—whether aesthetic or moral—but, rather, look for evaluative criteria outside their own experience, inside the other culture, our job as critics is constantly to internalize, refine, create, and apply our culture's criteria to our culture's products. We are less like the ethnographer and more like the ethnographer's native informants, who do the evaluation for her, using emic judgments, who lead the anthropologist to the best artwork or the master artisan, who act as messengers from deep inside the culture.

4

On Your Fingertips: Writing Dance Criticism

Paraphrasing Goethe on theater criticism, Edwin Denby once wrote that "a writer is interesting if he can tell what the dancers did, what they communicated, and how remarkable that was."[1] This statement sounds almost banal, if not obvious. But in fact it sums up several different, often

This material is taken from the forthcoming book *Anthology on Dance Criticism*, Lynne Blom and Susan Lee, eds. Used by permission of the University of Pittsburgh Press.

complex operations that a critic can perform. These are: description (what the dancers did—what does the work look and feel like?); interpretation (what they communicated—what does the dance mean?); and evaluation (how remarkable it was—is the work good?). To Denby's list I would add another critical operation: contextual explanation (where does the work come from aesthetically and/or historically?). For the critic's job is to complete the work in the reader's understanding, to unfold the work in an extended time and space after the performance, and to enrich the experience of the work. This may be done, of course, even for those who have not seen the work.

Not all critics perform all these operations, for reasons ranging from ideological commitments to the practical constraints of their jobs. It goes without saying that these are not *the* explicit rules of our profession; many critics perform some or all of these operations intuitively. The purpose of this essay is to bring these critical activities to light and to begin an analysis of their role in dance criticism.

Evaluation pure and simple is the function often forced on the daily critic. This is criticism at its crudest—the critic as consumer guide. Here, for instance, is Théophile Gautier's review of *Le Lutin de la Vallée*. Gautier explains that what is key to this ballet is the dancing. "The work," Gautier writes, "does not exist by itself and could be described in four lines; but it furnishes the dance with an auspicious frame and that is all that is necessary." He does give a plot summary (more than four lines long), but adds that he considers this information quite perfunctory: "Now that we've done away with the plot, and we must give it this credit that it is neither long nor complicated, let us immediately get to what is important—to the dance." And then he goes on to treat the dance, in terms that are primarily evaluative:

> Mme Guy-Stéphan exhibits as natural talent an extraordinary lightness; she bounds up like a rubber ball and comes down like a feather or a snowflake. Her foot strikes the floor noiselessly, like the foot of a shadow or a sylphide, and each jump is not echoed by a dull sound of the dancer landing which recalls the marble heels of the statue of the Commander [in Molière's *Don Juan*]. Study has given her a cleanness, a precision, a finish that are rare nowadays when real dancing is neglected for voluptuous attitudes and precarious poses for which the partner is the pivot or the springboard. Her *jettés-battus* are extremely clean; her *pointes*, which are rigid and clear, never waver; and she has remarkable elevation.
>
> The *pas* that she dances in the moonlight with the elf of the valley, who skips on the silvery spray of the waterfall, is delightfully poetic. No one could imagine anything lighter, fresher, nor more nocturnally vaporous, nor more endearingly chaste.

Absolute terms like "extraordinary," "remarkable," and "delightfully" signal Gautier's approval of Mme Guy-Stéphan's dancing. So, too, for those who know the style of the Romantic ballet, do words like "lightness," "feather," "snowflake," "noiselessly," and "vaporous." But also Gautier uses comparison and contrast to make clear his judgment that this was an excellent performance. The dancer's foot is compared to that of a shadow or a sylphide (the template for the Romantic ballet ideal); her cleanness and precision are praised as qualities "rare nowadays when real dancing is neglected for voluptuous attitudes and precarious poses."

About the choreography, Gautier gives us only this much description, then quickly returns to his evaluative mode:

> While the girl balances in a pose of innocence and love, the elf bounds about, hovers, and traces around her circles of benevolent magic. It is charming. To be able to compose such a dance and to execute it, one has to be Saint-Léon, an exquisite intelligence served by hamstrings of steel; one has to have both mind and legs, rare attributes, even when separated.[2]

To be sure, Gautier couches his evaluation of Guy-Stéphan's dancing in metaphors that supply some description—at least of the feeling qualities, energy, and texture of the dancing. It is light, resilient, and delicate. But of the choreography—the movements, phrasing, floor patterns, and overall structure of the ballet—we learn very little.

It may be that ballet—because it is founded on a conservative, academic tradition that foregrounds the dancer over movement invention—prompts an evaluation of the performance and the performer herself. After all, the choreography of classical ballet no longer needs to be described, interpreted, or evaluated in our day, since both the ballets in the repertory and the general vocabulary of steps are so familiar. It is presumed that the choreography is a known (and perhaps already evaluated) quantity—even if it isn't. So what seems to remain to be evaluated is the performance—which usually comes down to the dancers' dancing. Even in Gautier's day, as he notes, the plot of the ballet—and, he implies, even the choreography itself—was just an excuse for pure dancing. That was what the interested spectator came to see and the critic to judge. But, in fact, dance history, criticism, and theory have suffered from this propensity—carried to an extreme by balletomane critics—to render verdicts simply on the dancer's performance.

Clearly, evaluation may be applied to choreography as well as to performance. Historically, the emergence of modern dance and modern ballet raised new issues to be approached in evaluating choreography, bringing dance criticism into the twentieth century. Yet even choreographic evaluation may become too exclusive a preoccupation. Here, for instance, is an even more radical example of pure evaluation in Clive Barnes's rave review of Paul Taylor's *Arden Court*:

> Someone once described a critic as [a] person who stood in front of a work of genius and made noises. Last night at the City Center I myself

> had the privilege of standing — in fairness they gave me a seat — in front of a work of genius. . . .
>
> My one problem is how I'm going to take dance all that seriously after Paul Taylor's *Arden Court*. I am convinced that this is one of the seminal works of our time.
>
> Dancers leap — and my God how they leap — twirl, and oddly enough coquette, before your very eyes. Taylor has created many good, even great ballets, but *Arden Court* represents something new, not simply in Taylor's career, but something extraordinary in the history of dance.[3]

The superlatives are piled on: "a work of genius," "one of the seminal works of our time," surpassing Taylor's previous "great ballets," "something extraordinary in the history of dance." In fact, the critic himself is moved to remark on his inability to express himself adequately, giving the reader the impression that even these superlatives are not lavish enough. (By contrast, but in the same vein, Louis Horst's notorious "blank" review of Paul Taylor's 1957 minimalist concert seemed to carry a purely negative evaluative message.) In terms of the four critical operations, both Gautier and Barnes exemplify an extreme position. Both these reviews are primarily evaluative. They are so meager in the way of description, interpretation, and contextualization that I believe they may be counted as purely evaluative reviews.

Now evaluation — making judgments — is a crucial responsibility of any critic. But if that is all there is, a review is bound to fail. What's wrong with pure evaluation? It doesn't contribute to an understanding of the work because it supplies no grounds to support the evaluative argument. Unless the reader has already seen the dance, she must rely on the critic's pronouncement. She never *sees* the work in the review, and therefore has no way of knowing whether or not she agrees with the critic's judgment. While this method is often employed by the daily critic, it in fact conflicts with one of the basic functions of a daily paper. For most of the paper's readers will not have seen the dance performance in question and will find pure evaluation simply incomprehensible. Moreover, dance — unlike theater with its long runs — usually has a short box-office life. A particular work has either a one-night or a one- or two-weekend run, or it is shown only a few times during a season. Since dance disappears relatively quickly in the culture business, on the most practical level the aspiration to serve as a consumer guide is thus rarely the most fruitful one for dance criticism.

Let us turn now to a "pure" example of another critical operation: *interpretation*. By this process the critic tells what she thinks the dance means, performing a hermeneutic procedure that plumbs the connotations and denotations of the movements and their designs. In the following review of several new ballets, Jack Anderson seems above all concerned to allot the short space he has for each piece to a reading of the dance's significance:

> Jennifer Banks, of the New Jersey Ballet, and Albert Evans, of the New York City Ballet, seldom touched during much of their pas de deux. When they did, they soon broke apart, as if happy to be free. Even when complex lifts and balances required them to cooperate closely, they still appeared ready to assert their independence. . . .
>
> Patrick Corbin, of the Paul Taylor Dance Company, surely had serious ideas in mind when he created "Psychedelic Six Pack," to recordings by the Beatles, Jefferson Airplane, Donovan, Pink Floyd and Jimi Hendrix. A scrapbook of images of the 1960's, the choreography included intentionally disconnected movements that presumably symbolized the effects of drugs. A scene in which a chained figure was freed may have referred to civil rights struggles and an all-male sequence was a reminder that the 60's saw the beginning of the gay liberation movement. But these vignettes remained snapshots in an old scrapbook, for Mr. Corbin never revealed what personal significance they had for him today.[4]

Interpretation is often difficult in dance, since movements, unlike words, have few combinatory rules that guarantee a clear, unambiguous communication of ideas. Dance is unlike verbal language, for it usually creates meaning only vaguely. When it becomes more specific, it tends to move into the realm of pantomime or sign language, or even to introduce verbal language. Therefore the hermeneutic task the critic fulfills is an important one. One can see, as well, why in a concert by young choreographers a sympathetic critic might be more concerned with understanding the dances than with passing judgment on them. However, interpretation alone is as baffling as evaluation alone. In Anderson's review, description only comes as part of a decoding operation. We know, for instance, that the dancers in the pas de deux broke apart, lifted and were lifted, and balanced. But we don't know exactly what movements they did or what movement qualities they used—in other words, how they did these general things differently than in any other pas de deux. Context here, too, is kept to a minimum, primarily surfacing in the identification of dancers and choreographers according to the dance companies they work for. As well, Anderson avoids evaluation. Except for the opening paragraph, in which he notes that "whereas the evening's ballets always had polished surfaces, they sometimes lacked choreographic depth," and the very last sentence quoted above, we know very little about his opinion of these dances and dancers.

An opposite approach to both pure evaluation and pure interpretation in criticism is pure *description*. In arts criticism generally, description was often used in the 1960s as an antidote to what was seen as an overemphasis by previous generations on evaluation and literary interpretation. In dance, this approach to criticism fit well with certain dominant and emerging choreographic practices. For instance, although they were unlike in other respects, both Cunningham and the generation of early postmodern dancers that followed and rebelled against Cunningham refused to pinpoint meaning in their dances. Yvonne Rainer, for instance, aimed at making dance that was factual, "objective," nonstylized, and nonillusionistic.[5] The postmodern dancers deliberately undercut evaluation—of dancers, for instance, by using untrained performers. And, faced with new aesthetic ground that broke previous standards of taste, critics were willing to suspend judgment. This approach in criticism was akin to the artistic practice in film of *cinema verité*—the notion of a noninterpretive, nonevaluative, objective camera that simply records reality without imposing a point of view. And this domestic approach to culture, so to speak, also fit with a post-World War II, relativistic, anthropological approach to comparative cultures that eschewed judgment regarding alien cultural practices. For the most part, artists were not literally likened to the makers of cultural artifacts in distant cultures, but the same values of nonintervention and nonjudgmental appreciation of the world's variety of art held forth in the avant-garde and its critical discourse.[6]

Susan Sontag dispatched her famous rallying cry for descriptive criticism in her 1964 essay "Against Interpretation."

> Like the fumes of the automobile and of heavy industry which befoul the urban atmosphere, the effusion of interpretations of art today poisons our sensibilities.
>
> . . . Interpretation is the revenge of the intellect upon art [at the expense of energy and sensual capability].
>
> Even more. It is the revenge of the intellect upon the world.[7]

Sontag calls for descriptive criticism in order to "reveal the sensuous surface of art without mucking about in it." Critics must stop searching for content in art, she argues, in order to be able to see the work at all. Indeed, she complains, the critic's search for content perpetuates the myth that artworks have content. Both interpretation and evaluation, it was felt during this period, were hierarchical and authoritarian, closing off alternative meanings and values, but above all, as Sontag suggests, denying the physical, sensory pleasures of art. Description was meant to recreate the work by representing it in all its physical detail.

In the 1970s, *The Drama Review* under the editorship of Michael Kirby was particularly active in promoting this "objective" type of descriptive criticism. It also vigorously documented the analytic, gallery-connected phase of postmodern dance.[8] Burt Barr's 1979 review of David Gordon's dance *What Happened* is an exemplary piece of the type of descriptive dance criticism *TDR* offered. I quote this review at length to give the reader a sense of how full and fine-grained Barr's description is:

> David Gordon's dance piece, *What Happened*, opened at the American Theatre Lab, in September, 1978.
>
> The stage is well-lighted when seven women enter. Some of the women are wearing white walking shorts with kneesocks, others are in

white pants, and all are wearing white tops. Across the width and depth of the stage dancers take random positions, paces away from one another. They face the audience, looking straight ahead, arms at their sides—a group of women simply being themselves.

A car being started is heard; the car moves away, then there is a crash, followed by police and ambulance sirens. When the sound of sirens dies in the distance, the women begin speaking and moving, the stage is awash in words and gestures.

Over the sweeping view of the stage the dancers turn and pivot, some take steps, all of them talk, gesture, but none leave the given spheres in which they began. Each dancer is performing full-out, the movements crisp and short, the words loud and distinct. Singling out one performer, then others, certain words are heard: an old man . . . a baby . . . an old friend . . . not an old man but a grandfather.

What Happened is composed of seven different but similar stories. In each story there are words and passages common to all of them, thus certain words are heard many times and the same movements, dependent on the words, are seen repeatedly. When a dancer utters the words "the old man," she bends forward, places her hands on the small of her back, then points to herself. For the word "baby," another common word, a dancer links her arms together as if cradling a baby and rocks them back and forth. The word "friend" is shown by a performer who extends her arm as if to drape it around someone's shoulder, then her hand droops and swoops downward into the gesture for a handshake. Also there are movements related to the sound of a word and not its meaning. "Avail" is depicted by a dancer drawing her hands downward over her face. The word "way" is shown by two cupped hands, palms up, going up and down as if weighing something. The word "would" is shown by a dancer touching the wood floor.[9]

Again, this review is helpful as far as it goes, but it doesn't go far enough. What's wrong with pure description? It doesn't provide a structure for thinking about the work or for understanding it. Certainly it is useful to future dance historians or reconstructors to pile on the descriptive detail. But, in terms of helping the contemporary reader understand the work, it leaves one in suspense. What do we do with the work after we are able, thanks to a detailed description, to see it clearly? In fact, contra Sontag, it seems to me that often, the more description, the harder it becomes actually to see the work. That is, the more trees, the more elusive the shape of the forest becomes.[10] It's useful—indeed, I would argue necessary—to have *some* description. But a description needs to be shaped by conceptual categories in order to have meaning. It needs to be hooked at least to interpretive machinery, if not to evaluative and contextual frameworks as well.

As with evaluation, there are different aspects of a performance that may be described. And again, these aspects seem to be distributed logically according to genre. In modern and postmodern dance, the critic must often describe not only the design of the choreography, but the movements themselves, since the vocabulary may not be a given. Ballet critics use description, too. But often they focus on the dancers, and even on the dancers' bodies, since ballet is built on a bodily canon that demands homogeneous standards of perfection. This review by Arlene Croce of the Bolshoi Ballet certainly includes the other critical operations. In this excerpt her description is interwoven with interpretation and evaluation. But her characterization of Nadezhda Pavlova's dancing is particularly interesting here because of the close attention she pays to the dancer's body—and to how the ballerina's body itself creates meaning. Her description is extremely rich, and, like Barr, she has the space to go into full detail:

> Physically, Pavlova is a well-shaped, small girl with abnormal leg extensions and feet. Maybe it's the abnormality that gives her stage personality its "dark" intonation; even when the steps are light and zestful, she almost terrifies you. Like many phenomenal dancers when they first appear, she exaggerates elements of the classical style, so that they appear to carry new meanings, but nothing in the exaggeration violates the implicit sense of the style. Her leg in full extension is precisely that series of subtle S curves which is drawn in dotted lines in the dancing manuals. Although the leg is held perfectly straight, the eye can follow one large S (from the back of the knee along the high arch of the foot to its point). This is how all ballet legs look in theory, but it is strange to see the principle enunciated so fully on the stage, and it is doubly strange to see these paradigmatic legs sweeping the air in their high-voltage arcs. The energy of the gesture seems to pulsate from hip to point as steadily as a beam from a lighthouse. The hip joint operates so freely that in the leg's release no part of the force that belongs to the leg is kept back. In the *Nutcracker* pas de deux, she completes each of a series of supported pirouettes by opening smoothly to the highest of high développés—a hundred and eighty degrees—and without tipping from the vertical axis to do it. That leg just seems to go home by itself.[11]

Croce assumes the reader knows ballet movements like pirouette and développé, and the choreography for a standard pas de deux like *The Nutcracker*. Similarly, Gus Solomons assumes that readers know basic ballroom steps like the waltz when he reviews the American Ballroom Theater. So in his description he concentrates, not on the choreography, nor on the bodies themselves (for the ballroom dancing genre doesn't enforce canons of body shape and structure as rigorously as ballet), but on the distinctive performance style:

> To open *Two Hearts in ¾ Time*, the finale tribute to that grandest of ballroom dances, the waltz, noted authority on nineteenth-century social dances Elizabeth Aldrich has staged *Salon Waltzes*. The dancers' mincing, stiff-backed tiptoeing to the staccato strains of a brass ensemble adds a

> refreshing bit of historical authenticity to ABRT's otherwise frothy entertainment. . . .
>
> Then, who could resist the ultimate waltzing extravaganza: six lovely ladies in miles of swirling white chiffon in the arms of handsome swains in white tie and tails, gliding around the floor to the three-quarter lilt of "The Blue Danube"? Champagne![12]

The fourth critical category is *contextualization*. It is possible to find reviews that focus almost entirely on explaining the dance or the choreographer's work, either in biographical, historical, political, or artistic terms. Take this example, a review by Allen Robertson of Lucinda Childs's *Dance*, presented at the New Dance Festival in Minneapolis in 1981:

> Boos and shouts of disapproval boomed in Northrop Auditorium Saturday as many people in the audience viewing the Lucinda Childs Dance Company's performance of the highly repetitive "Dance" stamped out of the hall in disgust.
>
> Choreographed by Childs in 1979, enhanced with visual design and film by Sol LeWitt and performed to a commissioned score by Philip Glass, "Dance" is a milestone in minimalist art. . . .
>
> Granted, "Dance" may not be everyone's cup of tea, but it is not a hoax.
>
> No one is compelled to like minimalist art, but to deny there is either deep thought or the most stringent craft involved in its creation is unfair. . . .
>
> The dance boom of the last decade has weighed down dance with an overriding burden of glamour. It has become, like rock, one of the 20th century's instant-gratification art forms. Most audiences want their dance hot, and this performance doesn't allow that kind of response. Childs' work is cool, controlled, yes, even contrived art—but it *is* art.
>
> In fact, it is art older than Western civilization, it is art whose roots can be clearly seen and heard in Bali, Java, Korea, Africa—almost in any culture where time is allowed to exist on more than our own moment-to-moment level.
>
> Childs and Glass compress their art, like angels, onto the head of a pin. The concentrated result is either something so tiny it can't be seen or it is a microcosm capable of expanding to the edges of the universe. Take your pick.[13]

As with interpretation, this focus on contextualization can serve to explain the dance to the reader. In Robertson's case, it seems that the audience's negative reaction prompted him to defend the dance by setting it in an aesthetic context that is centered on the minimalist art movement of the 1970s but that has a relationship to world dance and music. Admittedly, Robertson makes clear his positive evaluation of the piece in the vigor of his defense. But nearly all the work of the review is devoted to explicating the dance, not in terms of its meaning but in regard to the situation of its making. Neither description nor interpretation plays a role here.

I have been citing critical writing that focuses on only one critical activity, in order to isolate the four operations. But most critics mix several of these key critical operations. I would like now to analyze a few different approaches that use these activities in combination. Here, for example, is an excerpt from a long essay by John Mueller on Doris Humphrey's *Passacaglia*:

> The lead man moves to the top of the risers for the tenth entrance. As with the ninth, all other movement suddenly stops, and he is given the entire burden of expressing the powerful fugal entrance with a development of the teetering pose of Figure 6 [a "five-point star" balancing on one leg with the other leg and arms outstretched]. He moves again among the seated dancers and, in a most beautiful sequence, seems to rouse them, group by group, into canonic waves of rises and falls.[14]

This very useful and detailed formal description of the tenth entrance in the Fugue section of the dance includes evaluative terms like "beautiful." The description-cum-evaluation follows a section of the essay in which the dance is contextualized, partly in terms of Humphrey's own shifting interpretations of the work. Yet Mueller himself never essays his own interpretation, nor does he choose to favor one of Humphrey's. Thus his essay combines contextualization, description, and evaluation, but shies away from interpretation.

Here, in contrast, are some excerpts from a review, by Jean Nuchtern, of an Antony Tudor ballet. The review is long on interpretation. Yet it also includes strong evaluations and quite a bit of contextualization:

> While Antony Tudor's *The Tiller in the Fields* (New York City premiere) will never be my favorite Tudor ballet, it's a sweet and simple fantasy in which a gawky, ugly duckling (Gelsey Kirkland—if you can believe she's awkward) wins the object of her affections, Patrick Bissell. . . .
>
> Cinderella/Kirkland never takes her eyes off Bissell. From the intensity of her looks, it's obvious that this waif has been hankering after her hero for a long time. When Kirkland approaches him, it's apparent that he doesn't know her and isn't interested in such a pathetic girl. Out of shyness, Kirkland rushes off like the sylph in *La Sylphide*. The three couples resume their dance, which reminds me of the grape harvest peasant dances from *Giselle*. . . .
>
> I like the way Tudor delineates characters' emotions as well as the stages of their love relationship through movement. I know Kirkland's shy because she steps with pigeon-toed feet. I also know that she's transformed and becomes direct in Bissell's presence: To communicate her adoration she kneels at his feet. . . .
>
> The ballet lacks density and depends not upon interesting choreographic ideas—as well as a good story—but only upon identifying with the shy girl's predicament through the ballerina's performance. . . .
>
> Bissell is exceptionally appealing as the farmer/lover. His dancing and

> his personality gain dimension as he begins to fall in love. Kirkland's role is not a new one for her. In several ballets she excels as the shy adolescent experiencing love for the first time. In *Tiller*, she's not only a technical whiz-kid but is soft and vulnerable. I'd compare her dancing with a Chopin composition. The content and feelings are romantic, but the composition and performing techniques are classical.[15]

In terms of context, we are told how this role compares with Kirkland's other roles, and in a section not quoted we learn something about how this ballet fits into Tudor's oeuvre. There is a great deal of interpretation, for every movement is assigned its codified meaning. And terms like "exceptionally appealing," "a technical whiz-kid," and "lacks density . . . and . . . interesting choreographic ideas" supply artistic evaluation, both for the dancing and for the choreography. The one operation that is missing here is description. Of course, in order to decode some of the poses and gestures, a minimal amount of description is introduced. But often comparisons or similes—"Kirkland rushes off like the sylph in *La Sylphide*"—substitute for movement description. Perhaps Nuchtern's refusal to describe the choreography stems from her judgment that it is inadequate. That is, her lack of description may itself be a form of evaluation.

A different combination of critical functions appears in Noël Carroll's review of a dance by Kenneth King. Carroll's review stresses interpretation as well, but it also includes contextualization and description:

> In much post-Cunningham dance, for example Yvonne Rainer's classic *Trio A*, the idea that dance is essentially movement is taken quite literally, producing strings of ceaseless changing bursts of movement without reference to a pre-existing system of gestures or to an easily discernible choreographic design. But in Kenneth King's latest piece, a work-in-progress called *Wor(l)d (T)raid*, the emphasis is less on movement as such and more on gesture and choreography. He handles these equally basic aspects of dance in a very painterly way, stressing gesture in terms of line and shape, and choreography as composition in space. . . .
>
> The conclusion includes the trio walking as a group at a hearty pace. They are virtually marching. They set out in one direction and then suddenly make sharp, forty-five-degree turns along another vector of movement. With each turn, two of the dancers will exchange positions in the group. The spectacle is engrossing; its emphasis is less on the movements of the individuals and more on the qualities of the movement of the whole group. At times it appears as a machine; with some turns, it reminds you of a snake. But above all, its stress is on directionality. The space around the trio seems to disappear and an exhilarating feeling of propulsion evolves. Whereas the previous dancing underscored space as such, this phrasing promotes an intensified experience of a trajectory through space. Corresponding with the earlier sections, King's preoccupation is still with the formal qualities of choreography. He enables the spectator to papably feel the dancing as a veritable *line* of movement.

Whereas many contemporary performers strive to make the audience aware of the concrete dimensions of dance, King wants us to *feel* its abstract qualities.[16]

Carroll's review sets King's work into the context of the work of other postmodern dancers of his generation. Although he doesn't try to describe every movement in the dance, he balances enough selected movement descriptions, together with structural and stylistic descriptions, to give the reader a strong sense of the look and feel of the dance. And even though this is an abstract dance that has no story line to tease out of the movement, Carroll is always concerned with interpretation. He seems to see as his primary task the explication of what King is doing in the dance and what this means, in dance terms. The one critical operation that Carroll refuses to perform here, however, is evaluation. There are two words in the above excerpt that seem at first to be evaluative: "engrossing" and "exhilarating." However, in this context, both these words are used as descriptive indicators, not as matters of opinion or aesthetic judgment.

There are various combinations and permutations of these critical operations—fifteen, to be exact! For instance, Mueller's essay is contextual, descriptive, noninterpretive, and evaluative. Nuchtern's review is contextual, nondescriptive, interpretive, and evaluative. Carroll's review is contextual, descriptive, interpretive, and nonevaluative.

The grid showing the fifteen possibilities of combining these four operations is as follows:

1. contextual, descriptive, interpretive, evaluative
2. contextual, nondescriptive, interpretive, evaluative
3. contextual, descriptive, noninterpretive, evaluative
4. contextual, descriptive, interpretive, nonevaluative
5. contextual, nondescriptive, noninterpretive, evaluative
6. contextual, descriptive, noninterpretive, nonevaluative
7. contextual, nondescriptive, interpretive, nonevaluative
8. contextual, nondescriptive, noninterpretive, nonevaluative
9. noncontextual, descriptive, interpretive, evaluative
10. noncontextual, descriptive, noninterpretive, evaluative
11. noncontextual, descriptive, interpretive, nonevaluative
12. noncontextual, descriptive, noninterpretive, nonevaluative
13. noncontextual, nondescriptive, interpretive, evaluative
14. noncontextual, nondescriptive, interpretive, nonevaluative
15. noncontextual, nondescriptive, noninterpretive, evaluative

It would undoubtedly be too tiresome to demonstrate the entire gamut of possibilities. Rather, having demonstrated seven already (2, 3, 4, 8, 12, 14, and 15), I will now give several examples of what seems to me to be the fullest kind of dance criticism—number 1, the rich balance of all four operations—and then return to the subject of critical evaluation.

Here is the conclusion of Marcia B. Siegel's essay on Kurt Jooss's ballet *The Green Table*:

> The opening and closing scenes, with the Gentlemen in Black around the Green Table, have a tremendous pictorial and pantomimic effect, but even here the movement qualities contribute to the overall atmosphere. The diplomats, in their rusty black tailcoats, spats, white gloves, and senile masks, palaver back and forth in a continual discord that ranges from amiable to tense. They are devious, with weaving heads and wagging fingers, or aggressive, as they lean forward across the table. Their groupings are constantly shifting; one side of the table will work in a unit against the other, they scatter off into huddles, relax and shake hands with their opposite numbers, return to the table to argue as individuals in stiff, angular postures. The only time the ten men do anything in unison is when they line up facing the audience, draw their pistols, and fire into the air, thus by common consent precipitating the next war.
>
> *The Green Table* works as a profound human statement because Kurt Jooss consistently selected the particular dynamic and spatial qualities that would best strengthen his narrative. I think most ballet and modern dance has become bottled up in its own movement conventions; it has nowhere to go but to repeat itself. Choreographers who use movement more fluently, for what it is, may have found one way out, and *The Green Table*, as a pioneer work in this genre, not only survives but surpasses a lot of later choreography in its vitality.[17]

Siegel gives a visual sense of what is seen on the stage, in her description of the politicians' costumes, as well as a kinetic sense, in her movement descriptions that incorporate postures, gestures, groupings, specific movements and movement sequences, and the deployment of varied energies. Other descriptions (not quoted here) also treat the ordering of time and space in the dance, and at one point she gives a summary of the dance's overall choreographic structure. Earlier in the essay Siegel has contextualized the dance in several ways: the situation leading to its revival by the Joffrey Ballet (the occasion for the present essay); the genre—antiwar dance—of which she sees it as an outstanding example; the larger genre—expressive dance-theater, specifically of the Central European variety—within which Jooss made the dance. She returns to the contextual mode in the last two sentences of her review, when she contrasts *The Green Table* with current ballet and modern dance. Since the explicit point of her essay is to show *how* Jooss's movements create narrative and symbolic meaning, Siegel interweaves interpretation throughout. One example in the extract above is the sentence describing the motions she interprets on two levels: not only may they be read pantomimically as a pistol shot, but also the group pistol shot itself has symbolic long-range implications, signaling the beginning of the next war. Finally, that Siegel finds this work excellent is clear, starting with the essay's title—"*The Green Table*: Movement

Masterpiece"—continuing with such words (before the section quoted here) as "stunning," "radiant," and "immortal." The ending reffirms Siegel's view of the dance's excellence: "a profound human statement . . . surpasses a lot of later choreography in its vitality."

Another good example of dance-critical writing that interweaves all four operations is Deborah Jowitt's review of Merce Cunningham's *Sounddance* (two paragraphs in a long review of the choreographer's season):

> *Sounddance*, too, acknowledges the fact—without paying special attention to it—that Cunningham is no longer working with a company of near peers, that he is a man in his late fifties surrounded by the splendid young dancers he has trained. (Meg Harper has been with him since 1967, but the rest from between five years and a matter of months.) *Sounddance*, like *Rebus*, begins with a solo for Cunningham. I can't remember it clearly, except that I found no peace in it either. The other dancers enter with great vigor—not all at once—from behind a fold in the heavy, poured-looking white curtain that Mark Lancaster has draped over a partially lowered light pipe. Lancaster's costumes are pale cream and beige; his lighting dazzlingly white. David Tudor's brilliant score, *Toneburst*, shakes and quivers from speaker to speaker—over our heads, behind us, back to the stage speakers. The highest vibrations sound like a gaggle of raucous birds. Sometimes, in the distance, you hear the quiet echo or afterimage of a pattern; but most of the time the volume and the energy made me feel like a cat in an electric storm—frightened and exhilarated.
>
> Maybe the music causes the dance to seem wilder than it is. And the lights. I see the dancers as playing with fierce energy on an empty shore at high noon. Here's the moment I remember seeing in Cunningham Events when Morgan Ensminger parallels his body to the ceiling, holding his weight on hands and feet (a backward crab-walk, would you say?), and two of the other men swing Ellen Cornfield into the air over him and let her down on her knees on his groin, while he folds up under her weight. Something reckless-looking about a game like that no matter how much the dancers smile. *Sounddance* has a lot of couple work—men and women fastening onto each other, falling under each others' weight. Cunningham with Meg Harper sometimes makes me think of a sentinel. Does he see things they don't? They dash off the way they came, and after a moment in which we have time to wonder, Merce spins after them and disappears through the flap in the curtain.[18]

Appropriately for a review of a major choreographer's season, the contextualization of this particular dance is brief and is mainly concerned with relating this dance to other works in the choreographer's oeuvre. Jowitt uses occasional, specific movement description together with atmospheric metaphors to flesh out a concise, vivid picture of the work. Her descriptions are very complete, not in the sense of a moment-by-moment reckoning, but in that they include the various theatrical elements that surround the dancing as well: music, lighting, costumes, decor. Jowitt's interpretations, too, often take the form of metaphors and, again, appropriately enough for a choreographer who shrinks from overinterpretation, are offered most unaggressively, couched as personal opinions with which the reader might or might not concur. "I see the dancers as playing with fierce energy on an empty shore at high noon." Or "Cunningham . . . sometimes makes me think of a sentinel." Similarly, Jowitt's evaluation is understated but explicit. A word here and there—"splendid . . . brilliant . . . exhilarated . . . wonder"—together with the pronouncement of Cunningham's "persistent genius" in the final sentence of the entire review make clear her commitment.

Excerpts from Joan Acocella's long essay on Mark Morris's 1990 season in New York show a different style that still combines all four elements. First she supplies a contextual introduction, which begins:

> When Mark Morris, won over by a generous offer from Belgium's national opera house, moved his modern-dance company from New York to Brussels in 1988, he left behind him a reputation as a dark-souled character full of "edge" and irony. . . . The other main aspect of his reputation—that he was the world's most musical choreographer . . . in no way offset his angry-young-man image.

Even within her long contextual introduction, Acocella supplies descriptions and interpretations of Morris's early work to point up the basis for the American controversy over his work. She fills the reader in on the circumstances of Morris's return to tour the U.S. and the transformation of his image—"the artist who was formerly a bad boy is now being taken very seriously"—then moves on to analyze—through description and interpretation—and to evaluate the work she credits with changing the choreographer's reputation.

> *L'Allegro*[, *il Penseroso ed il Moderato*] (1988) was the first piece Morris created in Brussels, and he made it to match the scale of his new opera-house home and the hopes that had brought him there. Everything about it is expansive—big, burgeoning, bursting. . . . Not only did Morris embrace [Handel's and Milton's] Renaissance-like program, he fulfilled it with amazing, unstrained inventiveness. For two hours his stage bloomed with nymphs and goddesses, birds and bees, shepherds and plowmen, variously moving in line dances, circle dances, arcs and Xs and wedges and rosettes, solos and duets and full-cast, 24-person ensembles. . . .
>
> In [Morris's] conjunction of classicism and grief there is no paradox. . . . To the classical mind, nothing is singular, and everything is knowable; it is just that not everything is bearable.
>
> Mark Morris has such a mind. That, in fact, is probably what allowed him to imagine the golden world of *L'Allegro* and at the same time the dark terror of his other recent work. To envision each takes nerves of steel, for each carries the other buried in its heart.[19]

I want to return now to the question of evaluation. In performing the evaluative function, the critic asks whether the work is good according to certain standards. However, there are several different dimensions along which these standards might be applied.[20] One is the moral dimension. Surely, for instance, part (but not all) of Siegel's positive assessment of *The Green Table* comes from her appreciation of the antiwar sentiment of the dance. The moral dimension includes political judgment. In the following review of a work presented in New York by the Ballet Nacional de Cuba, written by Rob Baker, the political aspects of the dance include class, race, and gender, and are, the critic argues, crucial elements in the work:

> [Alberto Mendez's] *Dolls* . . . takes the rather hackneyed ballet staple of dancing dolls and puts it into a sociopolitical context that is rather astounding for such a short, simple work. The male doll is a typical prerevolutionary aristocrat and soldier. He takes a decidedly sexist and elitist attitude toward his homespun partner, and this is apparent from every stiff-jointed move he makes, as well as from his stuffy, old-fashioned uniform. Besides that, in the New York casting . . . the partnering is notably (and I think intentionally) interracial. Her rag doll was black to his white, tatterdemalion to his fastidious, naughty to his proper, sexy to his stuffy, civilian to his military, womanly to his macho, populist to his elitist. And nowhere is this more apparent than in the way she moves, her flexibility contrasting perfectly with his jerky stiffness.

Indeed, Baker insists, even the apparently "apolitical" works in the Cuban company's repertory—like *Giselle*—may be read as political. Baker takes issue with the "liberal" New York critics who "were all too quick (as usual) to praise the company for what they considered the apolitical nature of its repertory."

> Putting art above politics is a typical ploy of well-meaning liberals, but in this case somebody's missing the boat. . . . Cuban dance exists at least partly (if not primarily) as an arm for spreading the prorevolutionary message—the party line, if you will. This doesn't make it bad dance . . . and it doesn't necessarily make it all that different from the kind of probourgeois, procapitalist dance . . . that we've been reared on and, in our own way, brainwashed with here in the United States.
>
> Curiously enough, [Alicia] Alonso's *Giselle* in a way remains the consummate statement of the company, both in terms of its brilliantly precise dancing style and its revolutionary message. . . . Surely no classic ballet contains a clearer statement about the temptations of bourgeois corruption than does *Giselle*. Albrecht's deception of Giselle; the way the peasants bow and curtsy to the aristocracy, putting on a little show for them; Bathilde's condescending liberal gesture to Giselle in offering the cute little peasant dancer a doodad.
>
> And, after Giselle's death, Albrecht, for all his money and social prestige, cannot right the wrongs that he and his class have committed

> while Giselle, ironically, is able to dance until dawn to keep him alive—a true, forgiving populist heroine.
>
> The fact that Alonso has made *Giselle* relevant to Cuba today is proof positive that art has "survived" the revolution. . . .[21]

Baker not only finds a political interpretation in the dance, but also judges the dance good on the basis of its political message.

In her essay "The Balanchine Woman: Of Hummingbirds and Channel Swimmers," Ann Daly takes a feminist stance, criticizing what she sees as the sexism underpinning Balanchine's choreography—as well as the silence with which dance history has treated this bias. She writes:

> When people say that "Balanchine glorified Woman," it is generally considered a laudable accomplishment. But in an age of backlash against feminism, when women's efforts toward progressive social change are losing ground to blithe conservatism, "glorification" smacks of regressive sexual politics. . . .
>
> If the ballerina has been only a passing subject of critical feminist thinking, the Balanchine ballerina has been strictly off-limits. During his life, Balanchine was enveloped by a mythology that ascribed to him near-mystical inspiration, and now, four years after his death, Balanchine's legacy is generally considered sacrosanct. Yet Balanchine's statements about his idealized "Woman" openly declared their patriarchal foundations. . . .

Daly supports her assertions with specific examples from *The Four Temperaments*, analyzing the movement in terms of gender-specific qualities in our culture. For instance:

> The erotic undercurrent in the [third] theme surfaces when the ballerina's arabesques shoot between her partner's legs. In another sequence, the ballerina ends up in an elegant sitting position, with bent knees properly together and on her toes. Before repeating the phrase, she briefly looks at him, then coyly lowers her gaze and cocks her head as she frames the sinuous curve of her face with an open palm. Like the Romantic image of the female and the image of a geisha girl in Japanese prints, she is revealing her feminine charms in a demure yet provocative way.[22]

Thus Daly evaluates Balanchine's choreography negatively on the moral/political dimension, for dichotomizing genders and subordinating women.

I predict that, for two reasons, political evaluation will come increasingly to the fore (as it has already begun to do, most noticeably, in American and British academic dance criticism). One reason for this is that, as Daly suggests about her own feminist project, a generation of younger critics is responding to a world ever more sharply polarized along dimensions of political identity: "race," ethnicity, class, gender, sexual preference, religion, age, disability, and others. The other reason is that younger choreographers themselves tend to opt now for political or cultural-political themes.

Thus even those critics who may not bring politics to their criticism find themselves willy-nilly confronting more political issues in the theater.

A second dimension that may serve as an evaluative standard is the cognitive. The philosopher Susanne Langer supplies an underpinning for this approach when she writes that dance can display the ethos of a culture and gives objective shape to the subjective "inner life."[23] More recently, writers on dance who have been influenced by or trained in ethnographic methods have turned to analyzing and judging dance in these terms. The folklorist Elizabeth C. Fine, for instance, writes about African-American stepdancing in terms of the form's cultural meaning. Step dancing, or stepping, is a form of competitive exhibition dancing, derived from African-American folk traditions, performed by black college fraternities and sororities. Fine writes about this form as a "social drama" and is concerned with its links to the African-American tradition; the "vitality" of the dance form as a signifier of identity is the evaluative term that she stresses in her essay:

> Fundamentally, stepping is a ritual performance of group identity. It expresses an organization's spirit, style, icons, and unity.
>
> One can't hope to comprehend the complexity and richness of the stepping tradition by surveying only a few groups or routines. . . . All . . . draw on such African-American folk traditions and communication patterns as call-response, rapping, the dozens, signifying, marking, spirituals, handclap games, and military jodies. . . .
>
> Stepping performances have become a key venue for displaying and asserting group identity, as well as for negotiating the status of each group within the social order. . . .
>
> [The] agonistic nature of step shows makes them a performance tradition charged with high energy and life.[24]

In her analysis, Fine emphasizes the cognitive dimension of stepdancing. She finds the stepdancing performances to be good because they teach us about African-American culture. They have cognitive value as a key to African-American identity, and therein lies their vitality. The cognitive contribution is linked to a positive evaluation.

Similarly, Sondra Fraleigh, writing from a phenomenological perspective, often evaluates dances and choreographers in terms of what we learn from them:

> Martha Graham's dramatic works, for instance, speak their psychic truth through sharp angular movement. . . . Her works take on a fuller meaning when we understand that they reveal familiar inner landscapes through archetypal figures. Likewise, Merce Cunningham's works reveal truths beyond their cleanly etched motion, as they engage us in mystical world views and meditation on the accidental moment. Twyla Tharp's dance . . . sheds light on our tensional body-of-action, allowing us to see and experience the dancing body in new terms.[25]

Thus Fraleigh judges as "good" dances with cognitive value—dances that provide knowledge, not only about the "outside" material world and the inner life of the psychic landscape, but also about the dancing body itself.

The third dimension along which a work may be evaluated is the aesthetic. This is the arena that Jill Johnston works in when she writes about Yvonne Rainer's *Trio A*:

> I've seen *Trio A* a number of times and still think I haven't really seen it. . . . The trio is actually one solo. The three dancers perform the solo simultaneously but are almost never in unison since each performer moves at his own speed. The solo seems to consist of innumerable discrete parts or phrases. The intricacy lies in the sheer quantity of diverse material presented in a short space of time. Yet all this detail is assimilated by a smooth unaccented continuity rendering some illusion of sameness to the whole thing. . . . Here's the crux of a departure from conventional phrasing . . . [undermining] the whole hierarchical structure of traditional dance.[26]

Johnston argues that Rainer's dance, though it may to some seem boring by virtue of its overall consistency, nevertheless pleases because of its intricacy and condensed quality. Here Johnston seems to agree with the philosopher Monroe Beardsley, who claims that there are objective standards—general canons, as he calls them—by which we can judge the aesthetic value of an artwork. They are unity, complexity, and intensity. Thus Rainer's *Trio A*, while refusing one of the canons—unity—supplies plenty of complexity and intensity.

The aesthetic dimension seems to be both the most important and the most difficult to judge. After all, the feminist or Afrocentric critic, for example, will have a ready-made set of standards by which to judge any work, and in the case of writing about explicitly political art even those critics who have no particular political program will usually be able to decode the political commitments of the artist. But even if we agree—or disagree—with the artist's political message, we will still want to say whether the work is good or not. We may be pleased with the antiracist message or the celebration of gay life or the prochoice commitment of a dance and still find it boring or lacking organization. Or we may find ourselves disagreeing strongly with the hierarchical, imperial politics of a dance—say *The Sleeping Beauty*—and nevertheless find it brilliant. Leni Riefenstahl's *Triumph of the Will* is a case in point.

Yet this is not to say that the moral or cognitive dimensions of the work are outside of the critic's domain of judgment. Nor is it to insist that these three realms are entirely separable. Both artists and critics bring to their work aesthetic values that are culturally specific. To ignore or avoid what some might see as the extra-aesthetic dimensions of the work—especially where those elements are evident in the work—is to be ahistorical and amoral. It fragments and diminishes the experience of the work, for artworks are made and judged in a world that is moral, social, and cognitive.

We are witnessing a shift in critical values during the present period. An "anxiety of evaluation" has manifested itself in American criticism in many ways over the past thirty years or so—from an insistence on pure description to debates about cultural relativism. Even the growing emphasis on the political dimension of evaluation noted above is linked to an anxiety of aesthetic evaluation when artists and critics themselves challenge the "right" of the critic to judge a work created by someone outside of her "race"/ethnicity/class/gender/etc. This anxiety now deserves to be put to rest. Although evaluation should not be the only function the critic performs, it is a valuable and crucial aspect of the critic's work. If evaluation causes anxiety, it is, nevertheless, unavoidable.

5

Power and the Dancing Body

Dancing Bodies Change the World

Dance historians often start from the premise that dance *reflects* society. For instance, in *Time and the Dancing Image*, Deborah Jowitt writes:

> Western theatrical dancing . . . has always been *responsive* to current trends. At its most profound, like the other arts, it *reflects* aspects of the current world picture; at its most superficial, it acknowledges the current fashions. . . . The dancer's image has been subject to many alterations since the beginning of the nineteenth century *in response to* the immense social, political, scientific, and technological upheavals that have characterized the period. . . . Trying to view the dancers of the past as *products* of their age . . . is a challenge [italics added].[1]

For Jowitt, dancing and dancers do not produce culture, but are products of it. Dancing and dancers reflect intellectual and material trends in other spheres of human activity; they do not catalyze trends.

Choreographing History Conference, Riverside, California, 1992.

Similarly, on a panel on American bodies and American culture in the mid-1980s, I insisted that the physical body reflects the social/political body. I used a binary model—influenced by the anthropologist Mary Douglas—that contrasted smooth versus shaggy body styles as symptoms of tightly versus loosely controlled cultural styles. And I argued that the smooth, controlled, virtuosic bodily images purveyed through various strata of both black and white dance cultures in the eighties (from the heroine and the breakdancers in *Flashdance* to Michael Jackson to the avant-garde choreographer Molissa Fenley) were metaphors for a "greed and glitter" era that stood in direct contrast to the hot effervescence and improvisation of sixties and early seventies dance styles (from James Brown to the twist to the postmodern group the Grand Union).[2]

The presupposition assumed by reflection-theory dance historians is that, whether on stage or in social life, dance is a mirror or a microcosm where the workings of culture, everyday life, and even government are actively registered from above on passive bodies below. In a variation of this notion of cultural modeling, Sally Peters writes that "the roots of [exhibition] ballroom dance are popular and mirror views of male/female relations specific to period or culture," even though she sees this as "ironic since performance requires artistic collaboration, not mere submission as may occur in social dance."[3] Thus, for Peters, a double reflection takes place in the theatricalized arena of exhibition ballroom dancing, for the gendered roles that society has inscribed on bodies on the mass level "trickle up" to the level of artistic choreography.

However, I want now to advance another view of the role of dance in society. I do not want to deny that dancing bodies may at times reflect the way things are, but I want to emphasize that they *also* have the potential to effect change.[4] While we might easily acknowledge that ritual dancing in traditional societies alters reality (or at least is believed to by the faithful), we tend to diminish the efficaciousness of both theatrical and social dancing in modern Western culture. Yet even the standard dance history books supply proof that Western theatrical dancing has the capacity to change the world.

For instance, Catherine de Medici's court spectacles were not merely the expression or reflection, but the very medium of political negotiations. Queen Catherine's ballets were part of political life, and they were usually conciliatory, uniting opposing political and/or religious factions. But Lincoln Kirstein suggests that the Massacre of St. Bartholomew and the civil war in France that ensued from it were, in part, the results of some bad casting choices in *The Defense of Paradise*. In other words, a political error in arranging the ballet led to massive bloodshed. The reconciliation backfired. The event in question was an allegorical combat ballet staged for the Navarre-Valois wedding magnificences, in which Catherine's son Charles IX, the Catholic king of France and brother to the bride, defended Heaven, aided by his royal brothers, while the Protestant bridegroom, Henry of Navarre, guarded Hell and led his forces in an attack—doomed to fail, of course—on Heaven. Kirstein asserts that the tenuous peace between Catholics and Protestants was shattered by their symbolic combat in this ballet when violence erupted a few days later in the form of an assassination attempt on Admiral Coligny, the leader of the Huguenots, by a retainer of the Duc de Guise. The St. Bartholomew's massacre was the royal response to the panic.[5]

Jowitt herself points out that both *Swan Lake* and *The Sleeping Beauty* were cautionary tales for the nineteenth-century Russian imperial court. Like the literary genre of eighteenth-century French fairy tales that included *The Sleeping Beauty*, these ballets didn't merely reflect, but actually formed—through ethical instruction—a class of courtiers in proper behavior. "The story," Jowitt writes of Petipa's masterpiece, "has a moral: a breach in royal courtesy, even to such nasty adversaries as wicked fairies, can allow chaos to upset the orderly flow of events."[6]

Numerous dance historians have pointed out the deleterious effect of nineteenth-century minstrelsy on the moral fiber of American life. Vicious racist stereotypes of African-Americans took the form of both verbal and physical "humor" on both the white and the black minstrel stage, in ways that still pervade popular culture, not only in the United States but in Europe and Japan as well. In this case, too, it seems that dancing not only reflected racist attitudes already present in the culture, but actually helped to form prejudice, with images of shuffling, lazy clowns and overdressed, shifty dandies.[7]

In an example from our own century, Natalia Roslavleva writes that the dance practices of Isadora Duncan as taught in the Soviet Union in the 1920s eventually entered the public school curriculum in the form of "artistic gymnastics" sports events. The system as it was developed in the Soviet Union after 1947 was based on Duncan "plastique," and Roslavleva attributes the expressive style of Soviet champion gymnasts, like Olga Korbut, to the influence of Duncan's technique.[8] In other words, Duncan's way of dancing formed the everyday practices—indeed, the bodies—of recent generations of Soviet youth.

"Your Body Is a Battleground"

The contemporary body has become a battleground not only in the struggle in the public sphere over abortion rights but also in scholarly debates on cultural theory.[9] Cultural historians working from a feminist Foucauldian perspective arrive at a similar position to that of the reflection-theory dance historians when they argue that culture wreaks utter tyranny on individual bodies. Bodies, they claim, are disciplined, molded, and rearranged by dominant powers, which simultaneously promote the illusion that people are "free" to construct their own bodies — in the matter of shape, say — as they wish. For instance, Susan Bordo writes that:

> Popular culture does not apply any brakes to these fantasies of rearrangement and self-transformation. . . . Of course, the rhetoric of choice and self-determination and the breezy analogies comparing cosmetic surgery to fashion accessorizing are deeply mystifying. . . . The general tyranny of fashion — perpetual, elusive, and instructing the female body in a pedagogy of personal inadequacy and lack — is a powerful discipline for the normalization of *all* women in this culture.[10]

Now, Bordo insists on the power of culture over the body not because she subscribes to a view of the arts as imitative. Rather, she has entered into a dialectical relationship with two other current theories of the body in contemporary culture. The first is that of postmodern theorists, like Susan Rubin Suleiman, who celebrate the body as protean, capable of slipping out of any fixed role or "voice," entering instead into a flux of "endless complication and creative movement."[11] The second is that of cultural studies theorists, like John Fiske, who celebrate the body as a "site of resistance" where ordinary people — those who have no political power — become empowered, creating their own social identities by manipulating and reworking the oppressive body images produced by the dominant ideology. Writing about Madonna, for instance, Fiske states that the star is not "an agent of patriarchal hegemony," as her stereotyped gender role-playing (especially in terms of her subordination to male sexual fantasy) might suggest. Rather, she empowers her primary audience, young girls, supplying "gaps or spaces in her image [of physical and sexual pleasure] that escape ideological control and allow her audiences to make meanings that connect with *their* social experience."[12] Bordo challenges Fiske's claim, pointing out that Madonna once seemed to embrace the unruliness of her own rounded physique, but now, thinner and more muscular as the result of an exacting exercise regimen, has simply traded a fifties ideal of voluptuousness for an eighties/nineties ideal of taut control.[13]

Are we, as material persons, thoroughly victimized by or thoroughly resistant to our culture? It seems to me that both positions are too extreme. To deny agency altogether doesn't square with the range of choices people *do* seem to exercise (even within certain strictures of "race," class, gender, age, and so on).[14] After all, to take only one example, transvestites, the exemplary corporeal chameleons, come in all colors, ages, and income brackets (not to mention genders). But at the same time there *are*, undeniably, limits to agency regarding our bodies. These are stringently, if not forcibly, imposed on our bodies by a range of rules: laws, medical regimes, moral codes, etiquette, fashion, and local community or family ethos. In the United States, for instance, our national policy is that smoking is unhealthy. In certain places it is illegal, and in other places it is as morally repugnant as spitting in public was to our grandparents. To take another example, unless one is Michael Jackson, with no ceiling on one's cosmetic surgery and bleach budget, it is very unlikely that one can easily change from looking black to looking white. In fact, for some, like Jackson's brother Jermaine, to make that change might be physically possible, but morally reprehensible. It seems that the relationship between bodies and culture, like that between bodies and nature, occupies a middle ground between discipline and creative expression. That is, we *can* make our own bodies, but only to a limited extent.[15]

Bodies Are Ensembles of Social Meaning

To study dance history in a way that breaks out of our field's often myopic condition means to study not only the bundle of arts that enter into an artistic dance production — music, scene and costume design, lighting, and so on — but also an interdisciplinary ensemble of social practices. And here the debates in cultural studies on the body should be instructive. We should be asking questions about bodies and power. And that requires taking into account the various powers that restrict or release physicality.

Can we do research on either social dancing or ballet without taking into account the kinds of bodily codes Norbert Elias traces in his *History of Manners: The Civilizing Process*?[16] For dancing is part and parcel of everyday social life and, if not usually highly regulated by society in our own day, has in past times figured prominently in the basic training of manners, especially at court (and the court's equivalent in democratic societies, like Washington society). Ballet emerged in the courts of Europe in the sixteenth through the eighteenth centuries, not only as a symbolic theatrical enactment of royal power, but as part of a package of physical discipline in daily life for the noble classes. To this day it remains the upper-middle-class method for training daughters in proper carriage and deportment. To study the history of manners, then, is to learn what has been both acceptable and possible in dancing events — in regard to, for instance, proximity of partners' bodies, individual posture, positions of the limbs, eating, drinking, clothing, odors, sexual expression, and so on. As well, dancing has begun to be studied as one of the *channels* for, not just the repository of, the pedagogy of etiquette.[17] Did the waltz, for instance, reflect or actually *alter* the acceptable distance between male and female bodies in public? Did Elvis Presley's hip swivels (derived from black dance) change the way white youth in the fifties and early sixties stood and carried themselves? Even more than in the macropolitics of states and governments, dance plays an active role in the micropolitics of how persons interact as bodies.

Medical studies shed light on dance events. Elizabeth Aldrich's compilation of texts on nineteenth-century ballroom dancing includes advice on avoiding wearing poisonous lead-based makeup to social events.[18] What is considered safe or unsafe in terms of contemporary ballet dancers' body weight has already entered the discourse of the dance field, although dance historians have not rushed to find such information for earlier periods.[19] In studies of the effect of breakdancing spins on the head and spinal cord or of aerobic dancing on heart rates, the dancing body is the subject, not just the reflection, of medical discourse that reaches beyond dance itself. In lore about the physical dangers of dancing, the cultural struggle over the way bodies erupt out of control becomes clear.

We need to study legal codes when issues of licensing affect dance performances, whether in legitimate theaters, burlesque houses, or in shopping malls. How much of the dancing body must be covered in public, whether in the theater or at a social dance gathering is sometimes simply an issue of fashion but at times becomes a legal issue—as in the case of the New York law that until the late 1960s forbade total nudity for moving, but not still, bodies onstage. Where and when are certain kinds of dancing criminalized? Religious codes, like those of the Puritans, shape and are shaped by the dancing body. For the dancing body's energy is dangerously sexual and uncontrollable.

Practices of everyday life, like fashion, furniture, and even architecture affect and are affected by dancers' bodies and dance designs. We know that Marie Taglioni's hairstyle was imitated all over Europe in the 1830s and that the fashion designer Paul Poiret dressed Paris society in colors and patterns borrowed from Bakst's costumes for Diaghilev's Ballets Russes. Loïe Fuller's wavelike draperies gave organic shape to all sorts of art nouveau craft items, as well as to the building in which she performed at the Paris Exhibition of 1900. In the 1980s, the torn off-the-shoulder sweatshirt Jennifer Beals wore as an aspiring ballerina in *Flashdance* became de rigueur attire for American girls and young women.

Social Bodies Are Dancing Bodies

This paper, then, is a call for dance historians to note and analyze how dance not only reproduces, but actually produces cultural practices outside of the dance world itself. It is also a call for cultural historians to acknowledge dance as a vital, active element of society when they write their histories of bodies. Perhaps the Choreographing History conference is a step in that direction.

A recent article by Tim Armstrong in the journal *Textual Practice* serves as an example of how dance's role in forming the culture is often overlooked. Armstrong's fascinating article is entitled "The electrification of the body at the turn of the century." In it, he considers the complex cultural attitudes toward the uses, at the end of the nineteenth century, of this new resource in relation to the body: its repressive role in state executions as well as its productive energy for technology that promoted scientific research and increased the production and consumption of goods. Electricity began to serve as a rich store of metaphoric language for representing the body, in particular the nervous system and sexual desire. In his analysis of images of electricity and the body in Theodore Dreiser's novels, Armstrong even shows how in *Sister Carrie* the new language of electrification was used metaphorically in the theater (Carrie "electrifies" her audience, and her name goes up "in lights").[20]

Armstrong is interested primarily in what literature has to say about these aspects of electricity and the body, but to a dance historian there is a notable gap in his cultural survey. For dance participated conspicuously in that cultural obsession with electrification, from Loïe Fuller's patented lighting designs (some created in collaboration with the Curies) to Isadora Duncan's and Genevieve Stebbins's theories of human movement as analogous to electrical currents.[21]

I would like to close with a final, more extended example of the role dance plays in producing culture by considering the wedding dance. Of course, the wedding dance plays an important role in European theatrical dancing; it is a theme that deserves an analysis too lengthy to take on here.[22] Also, the differences between wedding dances in different ethnic cultures would be useful to analyze but impossible to do here. Rather, I want to talk about the implicit and explicit normative rules of dancing in mainstream Euro-American culture.

According to Emily Post, the set order in which the dancing partners at the reception pair off is as follows: first the bride and groom dance together. Next the bride dances with her father-in-law and the groom with his mother-in-law, while the remaining parents (the groom's mother and the bride's father) dance together. Finally each dances with his or her own parent (of the opposite sex, of course), while the other two parents—the groom's father and the bride's mother—pair up.

The structure of this choreography is as finely tuned in terms of hierarchy and social relations as a court or military ball. The bride and groom are king and queen, leading out the assembly. And although they are more likely to dance a version of the foxtrot or two-step than a cotillion step, in fact the choreographed switching of partners in the foursome closely resembles a cotillion or quadrille. There is a narrative here of political unification, the incorporation of two opposing groups—two families—into a harmonious social body. Generations are joined, split up, and re-allied in the literal performance of kinship structures. The dance doesn't stand for or reflect these relations, but enacts, encodes, and ratifies them in a legal and often religious context.

At many American weddings, not just Jewish ones, after a period of couple dancing by the majority of those assembled, the pairs dissolve into a large group hora. Thus the narrative has a second chapter: the nesting of the individual in the nuclear family is itself nested in the larger community.

The ecstatic line of dancers pulls in stragglers, swallows up those who can't dance—not because it is particularly tolerant, but because it brooks no bystanders. These dances may be symbolic, but they are also meant to do real work—to join families and to enfold the new family into the community.

For dance history to take its place on the stage as a branch of cultural history, dance historians need to show that dancing bodies have not simply created divertissements. Perhaps then cultural historians will be convinced to take seriously the centrality of dance in our culture.

II

The Euro-American Avant-Garde

6

Balanchine and Black Dance

In 1967, at the peak of his career and at the very beginning of the dance boom, George Balanchine choreographed *Jewels*, an enormously popular evening-length ballet. Its three sections constituted a sampler of ballet styles: *Emeralds*, to music by Gabriel Fauré, danced by women in long tutus, evoked the perfumed elegance of late nineteenth-century Paris; *Diamonds*, to Tchaikovsky, was a glittering celebration of Petipa's Imperial Russian ballet. However, the middle section, *Rubies*, set to music by Stravinsky, Balanchine's closest collaborator, was a primer of a distinctive Balanchinian style. Critics saw it as the American section of the triptych, and it encapsulated a style Balanchine had invented. *Rubies* set forth his canon of modern neoclassical ballet, with its speed, broken lines, off-center weight placement, intertwining bodies, and syncopated accents. Both the critics and the dancers also saw this section as a near relative of black jazz dancing. Deborah Jowitt has described Balanchine's typical " 'Stravinsky' steps" in *Rubies* in terms that invoke black style: "the jutting hips, the legs that swing down and up like scythes, the paw-hands, the prances, the big, quick lunges, the flexed feet, the heel-walks."[1] Robert Garis wrote that "[Marnee] Morris's provocative poses in the opening section are like sexy show-dancing of the twenties and thirties" and noted "the powerful thrust down toward the floor."[2] Dancer Suki Schorer reported that *Rubies* was "tricky . . . half jazz, half elegant."[3] Another dancer, Edward Villella, also noted the jazz connection.[4] A French critic, observing Balanchine's way of "stopping movements abruptly and letting his dancers freeze," unwittingly described a typical African-American dance movement.[5] And Clive Barnes noticed a number of black dance features, such as flat-footed stepping and the Charleston, when he wrote, "The dancing is sharply accented, with a quirky yet quite unforced kind of invention. Legs fly out at high and unexpected angles, feet that you expected pointed are made flat, and flirtation is given an edge of delicate and even urbane malice. . . . At one moment a girl with India-rubber legs is diverting the attention of four suitors. . . ."[6] More recently, Joseph Mazo has written that *Rubies* "suggests

Choreography and Dance 3/3 (1993).

jazz dancing with its brisk attack and sharp changes; its changing accents; its turned-in legs and thrust-out hips; its joyously outrageous show-dancer sexiness; and—very importantly—its humor."[7]

So little attention has been paid to the influence of African-American dance on Balanchine's work that, taking these remarks together, one has no context in which to interpret them. One might ask first whether these dancers and commentators noticed the black dance connection because the late sixties was also a time when the dramatic struggle for civil rights and black power took center stage in American culture. Or one might ask whether Balanchine included these elements of African-American popular dancing because it was timely to do so and because he came, at the height of his choreographic powers, to appreciate a different genre of dance enough to quote it in his own work. One might even wonder whether he embraced black culture then as a political gesture.[8]

But obviously, if this ballet set forth a Balanchinian canon, these elements were not new, nor does anything in Balanchine's biography lead us to think that they were suddenly produced as agit-prop for civil rights. Indeed, these borrowings from black dance were long-standing cor-

Helene Alexopoulos and Kipling Houston in George Balanchine's *Four Temperaments*. (Photo: Paul Kolnik.)

nerstones of the modernist strand of his choreography and had been noticed by critics previously.[9] This strand had a very important impact on the technique in which his dancers were trained. And yet while this aspect of his work has been noted frequently in passing, it has never been closely examined. The purpose of this essay is to initiate such an examination.

It is well known that Balanchine loved things American, from Western movies to jazz music. Even before he moved to the United States he was inspired by black dance styles, to which he was probably exposed even in his youth in Russia, and which he must have seen in Paris during the jazz-era twenties. In the first few years after he arrived in New York, he worked closely with several dancers and choreographers whose work in the black idiom inspired him. Moreover, several modernist composers whose music he choreographed were deeply influenced by black jazz. Balanchine's interest in black dance and black music—whether performed by whites or African Americans—is evident not only in his various works for the popular musical stage; aspects of the black dance tradition also thread through Balanchine's concert choreography, like *Rubies* and other ballets.

I want to argue here not that Balanchine appropriated African or African-American dance wholesale or singled out black dance as his sole inspiration. For Balanchine's initiation into choreography took place during the height of the modernist era, characterized by its mixture of forms. Rather, his interest and participation in American popular entertainment fed back into his ballet choreography. His connoisseurship of dance in popular culture inevitably led him to experiment with one of the crucial forms and styles that have shaped American twentieth-century social and popular dancing—viz., the venerable tradition of African-American dance.[10] (I am defining "black dance" here as the group of social and popular [theatrical] dance genres that originated and were passed down in the African-American community, evincing survivals and transformations of West African practices. It should be understood that black dance has had a complex history, involving a syncretic fusion of European and African elements, and that it has sometimes passed back and forth between African-American and Euro-American performers.[11])

As I have noted, the black dance influence is an aspect of Balanchine's work that has long been sporadically commented on by critics. For instance, Edwin Denby wrote in 1953 that "as folk and ballroom steps have been classicized in the past in many ways, so Balanchine has been classicizing movements from our Negro and show steps."[12] It may even be, as Elizabeth Kendall has suggested, that Balanchine's love for tapdancing shaped his choreographic style in the most fundamental way, generating a consistent emphasis on multiple, complex steps and intricate, syncopated rhythms, with a relatively understated port de bras that at the same time allowed for a flexible torso.[13]

To be sure, African-American dance was not the only source of the rich technical and choreographic style Balanchine developed. He was fascinated with African-American dancing; he was also fascinated with popular images of the "Wild West," with white square dancing, with baroque European rhythms and postures, with romantic style, with the waltz, with both the classical ballet idiom and the stylized representation of folkdancing in Russian nineteenth-century ballet, with Shakespeare, with parades and military drills, and with much else besides. He worked in cabarets, opera houses, the circus, on the variety stage, in Hollywood, on Broadway, and of course in his own theater at Lincoln Center. From the beginning Balanchine's work smudged the boundaries between high and low culture. Moreover, the ballet tradition in which he was reared had deep roots in social dancing and popular entertainments and continually borrowed back new forms. So it should not surprise us that, in creating a distinctively American ballet, he threaded it through and through with African-American popular dancing—not only the exhibition and "show-business" genres, but also the social dances of his time. Although this essay focuses on Balanchine's use of black dance and argues that it had a fundamental influence on his work, it should in no way be construed as asserting that this was the only or even the primary focus of an oeuvre that ranged over many styles and developed in many different directions.

Although genuine African-American jazz dancing arrived with a splash in the Soviet Union only in 1926, two years after Balanchine emigrated to Europe, ragtime (an earlier form of African-American music) and its associated social dances—the cakewalk, the one-step, the Boston, and the foxtrot—had already spread throughout Russia between 1910 and 1917. According to Bronislava Nijinska, as early as the 1890s the black tapdancers Jackson and Johnson toured Russia.[14] However, popular black ballroom and exhibition forms had largely been mediated through white Euro-American culture. A Russo-French brand of jazz arrived in 1922, when the poet, dancer, and jazz enthusiast Valentin Parnakh returned home from Paris to organize, in Moscow, the first Soviet jazz band. He gave a concert, demonstrated his version of the latest Parisian jazz dances, and published articles in the Russian émigré Berlin journal *Veshch* on "The New Dances" and "The Jazz Band."[15]

Parnakh's efforts were part of an influx of Western culture into Russia during the years of the New Economic Policy, when limited capitalism was in place, Western culture was imported, and the borders of the Soviet Union were relatively permeable. The influence of American films, a free-flowing cultural exchange between Russian cosmopolites and European capitals (in particular Paris and Berlin), a market economy, and the lifting of liquor prohibition laws made cabarets and jazz clubs a familiar item in Moscow and Petrograd. In 1924, Parnakh's jazz band appeared in Vsevolod Meyerhold's production of *D.E.* (Give Us Europe), in a scene ostensibly showing the decadence of American culture. (The Soviet audience loved it.) Thus even before the first visit of American jazz musicians and dancers in 1926, the jazz age had already penetrated Russia.[16]

Several of Balanchine's early pieces from the Russian years testify to his au courant interest in jazz and black dance. In 1921, he choreographed a foxtrot for the guests at a party celebrating the Anglo-Soviet trade agreement signed on March 16.[17] In 1922 he choreographed a ballet to Stravinsky's *Ragtime* (1918). And in 1924, the same year *D.E.* toured to Petrograd, the Young Ballet presented another Balanchine foxtrot, presumably a solo for Nicholas Efimov. Working in the Maly Opera Theater in 1923, Balanchine staged the dances for a modernized version of Shaw's *Caesar and Cleopatra*, which included a prologue in a bar. The humorist Alexander Flit described the production thus:

> To show the queen in a bar
> They struggled with all their might
> Egyptian vignettes and foxtrots
> Academically to unite.

During that season, the same theater presented Ernst Toller's *Eugen the Unfortunate*, again with choreography by Balanchine; the literary critic Boris Eikhenbaum commented that the audience saw "shadowy dances in the latest fashion." Also in the year before he left the Soviet Union, Balanchine worked as a pianist and dancer in cabarets and cinemas. He was, as well, connected to the Factory of the Experimental Actor (FEKS), an avant-garde theater group that tried to "Americanize" their work by quoting jazz, sports, and films.

Finally, Balanchine rehearsed, but never finally staged, Darius Milhaud and Jean Cocteau's 1920 music-hall ballet, *Le Boeuf sur le toit*, which featured two black characters in a Prohibition-era American bar. Thus even before leaving Russia Balanchine had already demonstrated his interest in American black dance forms, worked in popular venues, and choreographed dances to music by two composers—Stravinsky and Milhaud—whose modernism (or at least, certain aspects of it) was directly inspired by the polyrhythms and syncopated accents of American jazz.[18]

By the time Balanchine left Petrograd in 1924, later that year joining Serge Diaghilev's Ballets Russes, two important avant-garde ballets on African and African-American themes had recently been given in Paris. Les Ballets Suédois had presented in 1923 both *La Création du monde* and *Within the Quota*. The first was a "ballet nègre" based on Blaise Cendrars's renderings of African creation myths, choreographed by Jean Börlin to jazz-inspired music composed by Darius Milhaud for a Harlem-style jazz orchestra. Milhaud recounts in his autobiography how he had long been interested in experimenting with the forms of jazz he had heard in Harlem nightclubs, and also how the collaborators on the ballet (Börlin, Milhaud, and Fernand Léger, who designed the sets and costumes) planned it during visits to popular dance halls in Paris.[19] The second was a "ballet américain" about immigrants, the American dream, and Hollywood myths. Although it did not focus on African-American characters, it was set to a jazz score by the as-yet-unknown Cole Porter, it featured black-based social dance forms like the shimmy and the foxtrot, and it included in its cast of characters "A Coloured Gentleman" (danced by Kaj Smith in blackface).[20] Balanchine missed these ballets, but surely he had access to the same popular dance halls Börlin had visited with Milhaud and Léger. And he would easily have had the opportunity to see performances by black jazz dancers and musicians, including (after 1925) the legendary Josephine Baker. According to Phyllis Rose, Baker's biographer, in the 1920s "all the nightclubs in the area of Pigalle had at least a few blacks in their orchestras. At the Casino de Paris, a leading music hall, the orchestra was entirely black."[21] According to Patrick O'Connor, Balanchine gave Baker private ballet lessons in Paris in the early 1930s, and Lincoln Kirstein remembers that "he was a great friend and admirer of Josephine Baker, and . . . may have staged some small numbers for her in Paris."[22]

It may be that Balanchine's ballets for Diaghilev's troupe were flavored with jazz dancing. There are suggestions of this direction in photographs of *Le Chant du rossignol* and *La Chatte*, at least. He never went so far as to make a "ballet nègre" for Diaghilev, and, even if he had wanted to, it is not clear that Diaghilev would have allowed it. But two characters he created in 1926 brought black dancing onto the Ballets Russes stage. One was The Black Dancer, played by Alexandra Danilova, in *Jack in the Box*. The other was Snowball, "a Blackman," danced in blackface by Balanchine himself in *The Triumph of Neptune*. This ballet, with a book by Sacheverell Sitwell and music by Lord Berners, was based on nineteenth-century English pantomimes. Snowball was modeled after a lame black man who sold flowers on the Scarborough streets during Sitwell's childhood. Of course, black men in nineteenth-century England—whether in real life or as represented by whites on the pantomime stage—did not dance twenties-style jazz steps. But Cyril Beaumont's description of Balanchine's depiction of this character suggests that historical authenticity was not what he had in mind. It was, Beaumont wrote, "a dance full of subtly contrasted rhythms, strutting walks, mincing steps and surging backwards bendings of the body, borrowed from the cake-walk, the whole invested with a delicious humour derived from the mood of the dance, a paradoxical blend of pretended nervous apprehension and blustering confidence."[23]

Soon after he joined Diaghilev's company, Balanchine became friendly with the composer Vladimir Dukelsky. Under the name Vernon Duke, Dukelsky later composed jazz-based film and musical comedy scores. And, after Balanchine moved to the U.S., he renewed his acquaintance with Duke and worked with him on several projects, including the Ziegfeld Follies, the film *The Goldwyn Follies*, and the Broadway musical *Cabin in the Sky*.

Between 1929 and Balanchine's arrival in the United States in 1933, several of the choreographer's activities indicate the presence of the jazz thread in his artistic production as well as his professional associations. One was his work on the variety stage. This included his uncredited choreography for *Wake Up and Dream!* (the 1929 Charles B. Cochran London revue, with music and lyrics by Cole Porter); a jazz number for four women (to recorded music by Jack Hylton and his Orchestra) in Sir Oswald Stoll's variety shows at the London Coliseum in 1931; and collaboration with Buddy Bradley on *Charles B. Cochran's 1931 Revue* (to music by Noel Coward and others).[24]

The collaboration with Buddy Bradley is a crucial one, for Bradley, an African-American tapdancer, teacher, choreographer, and coach, put his stamp on numerous Broadway musicals in the late twenties and early thirties, before moving to London where he opened a school. Not only did he devise group numbers, but he also coached and designed dance routines for various white solo and duo performers, including Mae West, Ann Pennington, Adele and Fred Astaire, Ruby Keeler, Eleanor Powell, Paul Draper, and especially Jessie Matthews, whose stage shows and films he choreographed. What Bradley gave Broadway was a fresh combination of tap-dance steps combined with body movements taken from African-American vernacular dances, set to the rhythms of jazz improvisations in music. His ideas permeated Harlem clubs as well as black and white Broadway and helped shape popular theatrical dance as we know it today.[25]

Another jazz thread during this period was Balanchine's work with Bertolt Brecht and Kurt Weill on *Les Sept Pechés capitaux* (The Seven Deadly Sins) for Les Ballets 1933. This was a refraction of American bourgeois materialist culture through German 1920s cabaret performance style, set in the form of a morality play. Anna-Anna's tour of America's cities and vices thematically motivated a jazz ballet style that anticipated Balanchine's *Slaughter on Tenth Avenue*.

It was in 1933 that Kirstein, visiting Europe, invited Balanchine to come to America. Balanchine was already thinking of the U.S. as a blessedly racially mixed country, and he looked forward, according to Kirstein at the time, to establishing a ballet school and company that would feature an equal number of black and white dancers. "For the first he would take 4 white girls and 4 white boys, about sixteen yrs. old and 8 of the same, *negros* [sic]. . . . As time went on he would get younger children from 8 yrs. on. He thinks the negro part of it would be amazingly supple, the combination of suppleness and sense of time superb," Kirstein wrote to the director of the Wadsworth Atheneum in Hartford. He went on to describe some of the ballets he himself planned for the company's repertory, including *Uncle*

Tom's Cabin, a "ballet au grand serieux avec apothéose: by E. E. *Cummings*. . . . Music by Stephen Foster."[26] The totally racially integrated ballet company described here — whether indeed it was Balanchine's own idea or Kirstein's — never, of course, materialized. Yet some plans for including black dancers may have been discussed from time to time, for Denby wrote, in 1952, that the New York City Ballet "is as likely to be as Negro as white in another decade or so."[27] Again, whether this was Denby's interest or a plan of Balanchine's is unclear. In any case, it was not until 1955, when Arthur Mitchell joined New York City Ballet, that the company had even one African-American member.[28]

However, Balanchine began to work with a number of African-American dancers on the popular musical stage shortly after he arrived in the U.S. Beginning in the fall of 1935, he devised the dances for the 1936 edition of the Ziegfeld Follies (with music by Vernon Duke), where part of his job was to choreograph numbers for Josephine Baker, who was making her triumphant return to New York after ten years in Paris. Although he did not compose their dances, he met the acrobatic tapdancers Fayard and Harold Nicholas (the Nicholas Brothers), who were also part of the revue.[29] In 1936, Balanchine choreographed his well-known jazz-tap ballet "Slaughter on Tenth Avenue" for the Rodgers and Hart musical *On Your Toes*. Although the leading dancers — Ray Bolger and Tamara Geva — were white, the black tapdancer Herbert Harper, who also served as the assistant to the choreographer, must have taught Balanchine a great deal. Probably it was Harper who choreographed the tap sections. According to Fred Danieli, "In *On Your Toes* he was tremendously taken with the black tap dancer Herby Harper, who was also his assistant on the show. Balanchine was fascinated with American rhythms. Absolutely loved tap. Tried to learn it."[30] Balanchine worked with the Nicholas Brothers again in the Rodgers and Hart musical *Babes in Arms* (1937), for which he choreographed a surrealistic dream ballet — "Peter's Journey," in which one of the lead characters takes a fantasy trip to Hollywood, Europe, and Africa. The piece presaged the vogue for dream ballets in Broadway shows whose origins are usually attributed to Agnes de Mille. Fayard Nicholas describes how in *Babes* Balanchine combined the Nicholas Brothers' acrobatic stunts with the actions of the chorus girls: "There were eight chorus girls bending over, and I started out running, doing cartwheels and flips and leaping over one, then two, and finally all eight girls and landing in a split. Then the girls lined up with their legs apart, and Harold slid into a split beneath all of them from the rear and snapped back up as he came out in front."[31]

Balanchine's first Hollywood musical, *Goldwyn Follies*, was released in 1938. Although no African-American dancers appear in it, tapdance plays a crucial role, for in the Romeo and Juliet Ballet, the conflict between the ballet-dancing Montagues and the tapdancing Capulets is symbolized in the clash of opposing dance styles.[32] In retrospect, this ballet prefigures not only *West Side Story*—in that Jerome Robbins made a jazz version of the Romeo and Juliet legend—but also the various breakdancing films of the 1980s, beginning with *Flashdance*, in which breakdancing itself does battle with other dance forms, from ballet to whitewashed contemporary Broadway jazz. Indeed, the precedent had been set as early as *On Your Toes*, in which there had also been a "competition ballet" between ballet dancers and jazz dancers, and in which the entire plot revolves around the "feud" between classical and popular music.[33]

In 1940 Balanchine directed the Vernon Duke-Lynn Root musical *Cabin in the Sky*, collaborating with Katherine Dunham on the choreography for the all-black cast, which featured Dunham's company in the dance numbers. The choreographic style was a mix of classical ballet and the technique Dunham had synthesized from ballet, modern dance, and Afro-Caribbean ritual and folkdance. Dunham recalls that Balanchine had intended to choreograph the production himself, "but watching us in our own classes and training and the company's use of their bodies, he finally felt that we should work together. . . . He felt the rhythms, you know. . . . We worked together with no problem. . . . He really seemed to love our style. . . . the rhythm and the percussion of our dances." Dunham muses that "He had no prejudices that I know of. . . . He picked us out, remember. It was an ideal collaboration."[34] He worked with Dunham again when they both choreographed numbers (along with Donald Dare) for the all-star wartime film musical *Star-Spangled Rhythm* (1942).

In 1954, Balanchine choreographed Peter Brook's production of *House of Flowers*, a musical by Truman Capote and Harold Arlen. The all-black cast included Pearl Bailey, Diahann Carroll, Geoffrey Holder (who choreographed his own Banda dance), Walter Nicks, and Arthur Mitchell, and, later, Alvin Ailey.[35]

In all these musicals, as well as in those such as *I Married an Angel* (1938), *The Boys from Syracuse* (1938), *Keep Off the Grass* (1940), *Louisiana Purchase* (1940), and *The Lady Comes Across* (1942), Balanchine borrowed heavily from black tap and jazz dancing, the reigning dance styles of both white and black Broadway musicals since the smash all-black musicals of the early 1920s. Like many white dancers and choreographers of the period, he learned the nuances of these dance styles directly from African Americans, whether from collaborators who were credited in programs (like Buddy Bradley and Herbert Harper), dancers whose choreographic contributions remained relatively anonymous (as dancers' contributions often do), or nonprofessional dancers he observed on social occasions at dance halls and nightclubs. He also learned something from the white tapdancers he admired, in particular Fred Astaire and Ginger Rogers. Edward Villella remembers that Balanchine hoped to give Astaire a role in the 1961 jazz ballet *Modern Jazz: Variants*.[36]

That Balanchine respected and was respected by the black community becomes clear in perusing his list of works. For instance, for a 1953 Negro Debutante Ball in Harlem sponsored by the *Amsterdam News* he arranged a Cotillion Promenade for five hundred couples, led by two New York City Ballet stars — Tanaquil Le Clercq and Jacques d'Amboise. On the occasion of Martin Luther King, Jr.'s, death in 1968, the company officially mourned with the performance of *Requiem Canticles*, to Stravinsky's 1966 composition of the same name. More a memorial procession than a ballet, it featured Arthur Mitchell as the figure of King. Soon after, Mitchell founded the Dance Theater of Harlem. Balanchine became a board member and a vice president of the company. The year of the new company's debut, Mitchell and Balanchine, with dancers from both companies, collaborated on *Concerto for Jazz Band and Orchestra* (1971) for a New York City Ballet gala benefit evening at the New York State Theater. The ballet, to music by Rolf Liebermann (performed by the Tonight Show orchestra, conducted by "Doc" Severinsen), included sections called "Blues" and "Boogie-Woogie," and concluded with a "Mambo" danced by the entire integrated cast. All the sections were collaboratively choreographed, and dancers from the different companies partnered one another.[37] It was the only time Balanchine's vision of a totally integrated ballet company was ever realized.[38]

Jazz and other African-American dance themes (sometimes in the form of Latin American dances) appear overtly and consistently in the titles, subjects, and musical choices of Balanchine's American ballets, from *Alma Mater* (1935; music by Kay Swift), a ballet on college life in which the heroine is a flapper and the final number a "Salvation Rhumba," to *Tango* (1982; music by Stravinsky). These obvious references include: *Pas de Deux — Blues* (1940), to music by Vernon Duke (performed at the Winter Garden in an *All Star Dance Gala* for British War Relief), and *Fantasia Brasiliera* (1941), to music by Francisco Mignone, with choreography based on Brazilian folkdances, especially the samba. The list also contains the Blackamoors' Dance in *Night Shadow* (1946), which was originally performed (by Ruthanna Boris and Leon Danielian) in blackface, and *Bayou* (1952), with music by Virgil Thomson, a ballet that Denby describes as "a sort of Dunham number." And the list includes: *Ragtime (I)* (1960), to Stravinsky's 1918 composition (with scenery from Lew Christensen's 1947 ballet *Blackface*), which had cabaret-style, jazz-based choreography (*Ragtime [II]*, a different pas de deux to the Stravinsky piece, for Suzanne Farrell and Arthur Mitchell, was done in 1966); and the above-mentioned *Modern Jazz: Variants* (1961; music by Gunther Schuller), which featured the Modern Jazz Quartet playing onstage, an orchestra in the pit, and choreography that mixed ballet and jazz. (Denby, reporting in detail the choreographic process of this ballet, describes a "stylized Lindy-kick figure" in 5/8 time, and notes that the entire ballet, with its "very rapid, unexpectedly complex, quite confined . . . figures, sharply contrasted, [that] kept changing direction," had the feel of "a Lindy-type couple dance." He also notes that Balanchine "wanted half the cast—two solo boys and eight ensemble girls—to be Negroes, but the girls weren't found." Arthur Mitchell was one of the men, and John Jones, appearing as a guest with the company, was the other.) This category of work also includes *Clarinade* (1964), to music by Morton Gould, featuring Benny Goodman playing solo jazz clarinet with the City Ballet orchestra—the first ballet Balanchine choreographed for the New York State Theater stage. And it includes *Who Cares?* (1970), the well-known suite of solo and group numbers to George Gershwin's songs from Broadway musicals.[39]

But there are African-American influences that subtly pervade even the modernist pieces in Balanchine's oeuvre. Indeed, given the African and African-American influence on modernism in the other arts, from Picasso's cubism to Stravinsky's polyrhythmy to dada's fascination with "the big drum," it should not surprise us that Balanchine's modernism is also tinged with the black dance heritage. In cubism, what was seen as pure abstraction in fact came from a different aesthetic tradition, one that among other things used stylized forms, rather than the "illusionistic" representation of the West. In the same way, some of Balanchine's "anticlassical" innovations were created simply by injecting African-American elements into the classical vocabulary. These elements include characteristic positions of the arms and hands, for instance the arms held akimbo and "jazz hands"—palms presented, with the wrists flexed.[40] They also appear in frequent pelvic thrusts, crouches, bent legs, flexed ankles, and flat feet, and in rhythmic features like syncopation (suspended beats or freezes). (Obviously such elements as bent legs or suspended beats, per se, do not constitute Africanisms. However, the more these elements appear in clusters, the more they resemble African-American dancing.) Denby refers to the "Negro dynamics of the jazz style (such as an overslow follow-through, a razor-sharp finesse in the rhythmic attack, an exaggerated variety of weight in playing with the beat)," and he even notes that the dancers in the 1952 company "all have shagged from way back."[41] African-American elements in Balanchine's work also include recognizable steps, like the soft shoe in the second theme of *The Four Temperaments* (1946), the shag in *Symphony in Three Movements* (1972), or the Charleston in *Stravinsky Violin Concerto* (1972).

According to Arthur Mitchell, "Jazz elements show up in all his ballets. And that's why his style is called *neo*-classical." Mitchell explains,

> One of the bases of his technique is what we call jazz, because everything is off the hip rather than being on the leg. And that's why when you see his ballets danced by a regular classical ballet company, something is missing. Because he says, "Dancing is movement through time and space." He does not want you to stand on one leg and balance. He wants a sense of movement. So the hip thrust, which we consider jazz, is very important. And that is the premise of the neo-classical technique.

> This is why when Dance Theater of Harlem dances his ballets, because of [the dancers'] awareness [of African-American vernacular style] it looks like it's been created on them. It's the same thing as when you listen to Stravinsky's music. Whenever I work with an orchestra conductor or a pianist, I tell them, "To get the syncopation, think of jazz." Then all of a sudden it makes sense.
>
> And to take it a step further, this is what Dance Theater of Harlem is doing by bringing a feline quality [to the dance]—which is also one of the things he talked about, landing like a cat. But we use the base of the spine and the fluidity of the back that comes from what we call ethnic dance [or African-American vernacular dance]. That's what Dance Theater of Harlem is bringing to the neo-classical dance. There's no word for it yet. And that's why when you see Dance Theater of Harlem dance Balanchine it's so vibrant, so alive. Because it comes from a core or a center that's not being placed or being rigid.[42]

Arlene Croce seems to concur with Mitchell when she notes how his company stresses the African-American dance features in the "abstract" Balanchine ballets they perform. "*Agon* contains an element of New York Afro-Latin rhythm to which the [Dance Theater of Harlem] dancers respond excitingly, just as they respond to the syncopation and jazzlike counterpoint of *Concerto Barocco*," she writes.[43]

African-American elements may be seen in Balanchine's avant-garde ballets as early as *Apollo* (1928). Although this dance has often been flagged (even by Balanchine himself) as the choreographer's reaffirmation of classicism, it was, as Nancy Reynolds has pointed out, "classicism with a difference." The difference resulted from such "distorting" African-American elements as a multi-unit torso, thrusting hips, flexed feet, crouches, shuffles, and jazz hands. Some of these elements, and of course the complex rhythms of the dancing, including suspended beats, were inspired by the structure of Stravinsky's music. Croce has written that certainly Stravinsky, in writing the music, had in mind not only ancient Greece and the French seventeenth-century neoclassical ideal, but also "contemporary Paris of *le jazz hot*." Villella has commented that Terpsichore's entrance in the coda, especially her hip gestures, are "pure show-biz—pure jazz." And Patricia McBride has stated, "The Terpsichore role is very jazzy, the variation especially. The rhythm is interesting—it's delay, then you change the rhythm in it." The role of Apollo, too, incorporated jazz style (see, for instance, the photo of Jacques d'Amboise on page 47 of *Repertory in Review*). According to André Eglevsky, "In the Coda, you come out with a big jump, then twist in the air, then there's a slide and stop; slide and stop. You don't know where you are. Mr. B. said, 'You have no bones in your back. Slide like rubber.' "[44]

Balanchine was deeply immersed in his Broadway work when he choreographed *Concerto Barocco*. Indeed, *Cabin in the Sky* opened only seven months before the ballet was first given in New York at an open dress rehearsal in May 1941 (its premiere took place in Rio de Janeiro the following month during American Ballet Caravan's South American tour). Given his interests and influences at the time, Balanchine's lacing of classical ballet with black jazz dance seems an appropriate, if anachronistic, response to the intricate rhythms of Bach's Double Violin Concerto in D minor. One reviewer wrote that the ballet "captures the soul of polyphony." Denby invoked tapdancing when he wrote, "Here the sound of the dancers' toe steps is part of the effect." And he noted that "the syncopations of the first and third movements are wonderfully apt and American."[45]

Even more revealing are Suki Schorer's remarks about Balanchine's instructions to her in the soloist's role: "More difficult than precision in technique is exactitude in timing—the syncopation. . . . For all its refinement, he likes it 'jazzy.' There's one place where the corps almost does the Charleston on pointe. In some of my most brisk and classical movements, he kept saying, 'Make it jazzy. Lead with the hip.' " Danieli also specifies an African-American influence: "He always took from American dancing. In *Concerto Barocco*, the corps does a walking step in the adagio, snapping their fingers. That gesture was from a popular social dance in 1941. He danced everything and he made us dance it too." The dancers recognize the African-American influence in Balanchine's work because Balanchine spoke to them about it, as when, rehearsing *Symphony in Three Movements* (1972), he gave Villella this correction: "You know, dear, it's the shag—the *Boston* shag."[46]

Like *Apollo*, *The Four Temperaments* (1946) is often seen as a turning point in Balanchine's choreography, one that expanded his technical vocabulary in avant-garde directions. Both the musical score and the dance were conceived on a medieval theme—the four bodily humors—yet at the time it was created the overall look of the ballet was deemed modernist in its distortions. At the time, critics spoke of what Balanchine might have borrowed from modern dance. However, here Balanchine's modernism seems to be created partly by juxtaposing to the familiar classical vocabulary jazz and vernacular movements and energies, taken from the black dance material he had so recently worked with. The evidence shows that the angular, oblique, distorted lines and syncopated rhythms owe as much to Balanchine's stint on Broadway and in Hollywood—and to Hindemith's own jazz inspiration—as to the idea of "angular archaisms" generated by the medieval theme. Denby refers to "dragged steps . . . and easy syncopated stepping." And Arthur Mitchell, who found his part difficult to learn, recalls, "It was the rhythm, not the steps [that presented difficulties to the dancers]. Several things were going on at once. The actual steps were just kind of like a tricky tap dance."[47]

From the very beginning of the dance, African-American elements appear. In the first theme, early on the foot flexes quite deliberately; the dancers crouch facing away from one another in a "get-down" posture; the woman crouches even while doing attitudes and arabesques. Both lean back in the cakewalk pose that Beaumont had seen in Snowball's dance in *The Triumph of Neptune*. (This, like the other movements in the theme, is a characteristic posture that recurs throughout the ballet). Croce writes: "The image created by the third girl as she is spun is blithe, even comical; could Balanchine have been thinking of the bass fiddle the forties jazz player spins after a chorus of hot licks?" The same turn in fact appears even earlier, in the second theme, along with a sprightly soft-shoe dance, hip thrusts, and a boxlike position of the arms with palms facing forward, very similar to the ecstatic arm gestures associated with religious possession in African-American culture. In the third theme, the action of jazz hands "pushing through" as the torso twists against lunging legs is introduced, while the cakewalk pose appears even more strongly as the woman does slow kicks while her supporting leg bends and she leans back against the man's chest.[48]

Perhaps there were intimations of a flash act[49] or the virtuosic breaks of the lindy in William Dollar's especially acrobatic version, no longer performed, of the Melancholic Variation. In any case, in its most recent incarnation, Melancholic is striking for its use — by both the man and the women — of the typical above-mentioned jazz movement that places the legs in a wide fourth position lunge and twists the torso, setting the shoulders against the plane of the hips, while the hands push their way into an overextended straight-arm fourth position with jazz hands, reaching out in opposition to the legs. It is notable, too, for the way the four women advance leaning back, thrusting their hips, and stretching out their arms to the sides, palms forward. Sanguinic, too, emphasizes the off-hip use of weight, the hip counterposed to the shoulders in profile, jazz hands "pushing through" and the cakewalk posture of the couple.

According to Mitchell, "throughout Phlegmatic, you had to keep the rhythmic thing going with your feet, while the body is supposed to be loose, boneless. . . . To get the accents with the feet and retain fluidity in the body — that was the challenge." Indeed, as Phlegmatic leans over, one hand on hip, one is reminded of the conventional rhyme in black songs: "Put your hand on your hip; let your backbone slip." Croce refers to tap in describing this variation: "[Phlegmatic's] little dance with the corps includes cabalistic gestures toward 'his' floor, and he hovers close to the ground, repeating his mumbo-jumbo (a syncopated time-step) as if he expected the ground to answer him." Phlegmatic postures, left hand on his hip and the other held out, in an iconic black gesture that Robert Thompson has traced through African-American and Haitian usage to Kongo origins and that John Szwed sees in the African-derived baton-twirling pose of majorettes. The women, too, take up this gesture. As the music takes a jazzy turn, the man lines up with the corps to form a chorus line, complete with kicks, and the whole group "steps it down." Finally, the way Phlegmatic's torso hunkers over his footwork at the end of his variation is reminiscent of a typical tapdancer's posture in performing the step Over the Top.[50]

Choleric stresses the asymmetrical placement of the weight over one hip in several stances, including one (threading through the entire ballet) in which one leg is placed, turned-in, in front of the other. It's the stance of a fashion model or a showgirl, and it is one of Balanchine's favorite poses for presenting women, but it can eventually be traced back to the African-American dance practice of treating the body as an assemblage of shifting planes that move in multiple, at times perpendicular, relationships to one another.[51] Moreover, the movement in and out of that stance—the rotation of one or both legs by twisting the foot—is a characteristic jazz move.[52] The quick épaulements, enlarged for a moment into a full-scale shimmy, add to this impression of shifting planes. Choleric, too, strikes the majorette posture. When the corps enters for the Finale, the ballet is crowned with all the African-derived movements that had been set out in the theme and developed in the variations, and more: the slow cakewalk, crouching steps and lunges, outstretched arms with jazz hands, a prancing step with hands flopping forward, ecstatic arms, and a plunging reach by one hand to the opposite foot.

As in *The Four Temperaments*, in *Agon* (1957) Balanchine's modernism seems based in the unpredictable rhythmic complexities and cool performance demeanor of African-American style, even though the ostensible model is a palimpsest of Greek athletic contests overlaid with seventeenth-century French social dances. Again, Denby in particular was attuned to the borrowings from black jazz dancing in Balanchine's work. For instance, he describes Melissa Hayden's solo, *Bransle gay*, during the second pas de trois, in jazz terms: "As she dances, she keeps calmly 'on top of' two conflicting rhythms (or beats) that coincide once or twice and join on the last note." (In a different article, written the same year, he notes that " 'on top of the beat' is a jazz expression.") Moreover, he writes that "The dancers [in *Agon*] have been 'cool' in the jazz sense—no buildup, inventions that did not try to get anywhere, right after a climax an inconsequence like the archness of high comedy. . . . At the end, the imaginary contestant froze, toughly confident. The company seems to have figured jointly as the offbeat hero." Four years after the ballet was made, Denby contrasted the subtle infusion of jazz steps and dynamics in *Agon* with Balanchine's unsuccessful attempt to make a "real" jazz ballet in *Modern Jazz: Variants*. Denby concluded that "*Agon* . . . in some unliteral way came closer to the image of jazz than any jazz ballet yet has." Indeed, by the early sixties, although Balanchine was still interested in jazz music, apparently he was no longer in touch with "authentic" jazz dancing, which had so influenced him twenty years before. Denby reported that "the dance fans" objected, in

Variants, "to the thirties-type jive steps, to the show biz-type gesture, to the sour night-club look of the staging." Moreover, he complained, "the partners couldn't let each other alone for a moment, the dances couldn't leave out a beat, nobody could dance except on top of the beat." And he pointed out that "current jazz dancing separates partners, omits beats, lets the beat pull away, anticipates it, and that elasticity of attack characterizes the gesture, and varies it."[53]

In his abstract works, Balanchine was by no means trying to create jazz ballets, as he had, for instance, in *Slaughter on Tenth Avenue* or *Modern Jazz: Variants*. Rather, he was transforming and adapting material that undoubtedly attracted him for many reasons. Perhaps most important to him as a transplanted European was the iconic "American-ness" of black vernacular dancing; it was, after all, the basis for most American social dancing by the 1930s, when he arrived in the U.S. But surely he was attracted to black dance for other reasons as well. In terms of structure, its virtuosic rhythmic play was deeply compelling to this most musical of choreographers, just as jazz music had been a "revelation" to the European composers of his generation.[54] And it offered an equally attractive bodily aesthetic that created contrast and variety when juxtaposed to the classical ballet lexicon.

Balanchine was not looking for an alternative genre of choreography, the way Dunham was, for instance, when she began to incorporate Haitian folkdances into her spectacles; rather, he imagined an academic ballet genre expanded, enlivened, and enriched by references to the popular dancing of the culture he and his dancers inhabited. According to Mitchell, "He would say, 'I am using the kinetic energy and the rhythms and the bodies of Americans. If I were in another country, I would probably choreograph totally differently.' " Villella describes Balanchine's use of black vernacular dance as typical of his approach to the balletic incorporation of other folkdance motifs, as in *Tarantella*, for example. "The form would be intact but it would be perfectly classical. He had a unique ability to adhere to the original rhythm and step of the folk dance, while still making constant reference to the classical tradition as well. Also, he could see something once and completely understand it—he was a phenomenal jazz dancer. And when you see social dancing in his works it's so networked that it's stuff you've seen before but you don't know you've seen it before; you're comfortable with it and yet it's new and fresh."[55]

Of course, Balanchine was not the only Euro-American ballet choreographer to use black dance or African-American dancers. Both Jerome Robbins and Agnes de Mille worked on Broadway; de Mille choreographed *Black Ritual* for American Ballet Theater in 1940, using Dunham's dancers, to Milhaud's *Creation of the World*, and Robbins's ballets in the fifties, like *New York Export: Op. Jazz*, as well as his *West Side Story*, were heavily informed by jazz style. In Chicago, Ruth Page choreographed the jazz-based *Frankie and Johnny* (1938) for the Federal Theater Project and worked with Dunham, Talley Beatty, and several other African-American dancers on *La Guiablesse*. Yet Balanchine is the one choreographer who seems to have taken this interest further than a passing fancy for Americana; he incorporated his deep and abiding love for African-American dancing into the very heart of his technique and choreography. And his modernist incorporation of black dance into his ballets, like his blurring of the boundaries between corps and soloist in *Serenade*, seems to be an expression of his liberal view of modern American society.[56]

At the same time, this liberal aspect of Balanchine's work has its problematic facets, confined and limited as it was by the nature of American race relations. His initial dream of a racially integrated American ballet company never materialized, for reasons that remain unknown. Strikingly, although he used jazz music, it was almost never by an African-American composer.[57] Often the black dancers in his company, like Mitchell and Mel Tomlinson, although cast in many different types of roles, also played stereotyped roles, either exotic or nonhuman, like the African Oni of Ife in *The Figure in the Carpet*, Puck in *A Midsummer Night's Dream*, Pluto in *Persephone*, and Hot Chocolate in *The Nutcracker*.[58]

Yet this aspect of Balanchine's choreography was also exemplary in many ways. To cast a black man in a leading role and as an intimate partner for a white woman in the fifties and sixties, as Balanchine did many times with Mitchell, was a radical political statement on the ballet stage. Moreover, as Mitchell pointed out, since Balanchine's was a technique that used jazz principles, it fit well on a company of African-American classical ballet dancers. In an era when people still debated whether blacks had the "wrong bodies" for ballet, Balanchine's choreography saluted black dance and the black body on the New York City Ballet stage and also provided a vital core for the Dance Theater of Harlem's initial repertory.[59] It may be that if Mitchell had not formed an all-black ballet company, more African-American dancers would have gravitated to the New York City Ballet. But since the critical mass of black dancers Denby predicted would belong to the company by 1962 never appeared, one has to conclude that the company's priorities did not include minority recruitment.[60] It took an African-American leader to form a ballet company composed entirely of African-Americans. But Balanchine had already altered the face of American ballet by incorporating within it the African-American dance tradition.[61]

7

An Introduction to the Ballets Suédois

The year 1920, in which the Ballets Suédois made its début in Paris, was not a good year for Sergei Diaghilev and his Ballets Russes. His tours were not successful, and his financial situation was complicated by theft and lawsuits. The following year, Diaghilev's choreographer and lead dancer, Léonide Massine, quit the company precipitously because he wanted more independence. *Chout (Le Bouffon)*, the impresario's newest modernist ballet, with choreography hastily conceived by the painter Mikhail Larionov, was badly received in Paris. It seemed as though Diaghilev's influence was losing ground. He began a strategy of retrenchment, for example producing (in 1921 in London) a lavish revival of *The Sleeping Princess*, the Russian Imperial Theater's greatest classic ballet. That production was a commercial failure that nearly brought about Diaghilev's bankruptcy. It was several years before the company would recover from the problems it faced in the first two years of the decade.[1]

Another impresario and another avant-garde ballet company had arrived in Paris in 1920. This company had been instituted directly as a result of the prodigious impact the Ballets Russes had made on the European stage. Rolf de Maré and his Ballets Suédois would, for the next five years, produce modern theater works incorporating dance, mime, painting, and music that would rival anything Diaghilev had created in terms of their avant-garde aspirations. It was perhaps partly due to Diaghilev's reaction to the success of the Ballets Suédois that the Ballets Russes began to turn away from Russian painters and composers and instead employ the newest French artists as collaborators.

Both de Maré and his choreographer and lead dancer, Jean Börlin, were influenced profoundly by the Ballets Russes. De Maré, a wealthy Swedish landowner who had studied agriculture and managed his own estates, was also an amateur ethnographer who collected folk art and lore not only in Sweden but also in other parts of Europe and in Africa, Asia, and the Americas. When Mikhail and Vera Fokine left Diaghilev and came to northern Europe to perform and teach, they became friendly with de Maré

Ballet Review 7/2 & 3 (1978–79).

and often stayed at his estate at Hildesborg in southern Sweden. It was there that they spoke of forming a new ballet company, which would present the folk art of Sweden as translated into theater by modern artists, just as Diaghilev had brought Russian culture onto the stages of Europe with his ballets beginning in 1909.[2]

Fokine and de Maré agreed that Jean Börlin, a young Swedish dancer who had left the company of the Stockholm Royal Opera to study with Fokine in Copenhagen, should be engaged as the "animator" of the new troupe. Börlin was born in 1893, the son of a sea captain, in Haernoesand in northern Sweden. Raised by an aunt and uncle, he was encouraged to follow his rhythmic inclinations and given piano lessons at an early age. At nine he was sent to Stockholm to study ballet with Gunhild Rosén at the ballet school attached to the Royal Theater. There he learned both the Danish Bournonville technique and the virtuosic Italian academic method. In 1905 Börlin joined the corps de ballet at the Opera, and five years later he was promoted to deuxième sujet. In 1913, the year Börlin was further promoted one rank to second dancer, Mikhail Fokine arrived with his wife to stage several ballets at the Royal Theater.[3] Fokine had recently left Diaghilev's company, angry that Vaslav Nijinsky had been appointed second choreographer. From the Russian choreographer, Börlin learned parts in several of Fokine's ballets, including *Cléopâtre*, *Schéhérazade*, and *Le Dieu Bleu*. Börlin danced the role of a faun in *Cléopâtre*, and years later Fokine remembered his impressions of the young man:

> He skimmed the stage with immense jumps, dropped with all his weight, and glided over the floor, among the groups of bacchantes. What a nature! What ecstasy! The fanatical sacrifice of a bruised body in order to create the maximum choreographic expression. It was a revelation for me. . . . These Scandinavians. . . . A northern people, cold and stony. Where did this fervor come from? From where did this ardent flame burst forth?[4]

The mixed strains of dance traditions in the Opera school—the Bournonville technique, which preserved the mid-nineteenth-century French romantic ballet idiom, and the Italian school, which stressed technical virtuosity above all—had produced in Sweden an academic, gymnastic style. It was a similar academic rigidity, along with the gradual degeneration of the artistic possibilities for ballet within this style, that had led Fokine, while still working in the Imperial Theater in Russia, to call for reform. Börlin was losing interest in the ballet, preferring to study singing and, when his voice broke, practicing piano and harmony. To him the daily "monotonous gymnastic" was overly fastidious and could not possibly lead to dancing.[5] But with Fokine's arrival his interest was rekindled and his talents were inspired. Perhaps Börlin had also seen in Stockholm Isadora Duncan's recital in 1906 and Anna Pavlova's first dance performance outside of Russia in 1908.[6]

In 1918 Börlin was proposed as first dancer at the Royal Theater. But he chose instead to leave the Opera ballet in order to study with Fokine, who was teaching in Copenhagen. According to Pierre Tugal,

> the technique of Jean Börlin was already very assured; he was flexible, elegant, and gracious. Nevertheless, the vivacity and nervous elasticity of the dancers born under the midday sun and the completely oriental frenzy of the Russians were still foreign to us. At this time Börlin, to [use] the image of Nietzsche, was solely under the influence of Apollo. But in the studio of Fokine, the impetuous god [Dionysus] was awakened in him. The art of Börlin—sober, intellectual, pure-bred—came from audacious pursuit and at times attained sublime stylizations which delighted Fokine.[7]

Fokine had radically reformed the Russian academic style in accordance with five principles, which he summarized in a letter to the London *Times* in 1914. He believed that in each ballet the movement should correspond to the subject matter, period, and musical style, instead of being simply another combination of preordained steps; that dance and gesture should advance dramatic action; that the entire body, not just the hands and feet, should be used in gesture; that the rôle of the corps de ballet should be expressive rather than merely ornamental; and, finally, that dance must be allied with the best in the other arts but still maintain its own independence.[8] These principles were formulated directly in opposition to the rigid codes and formulas of the Imperial Russian ballet as it developed under Marius Petipa during the second half of the nineteenth century, reaching its apogee in the symphonic *Sleeping Beauty* of 1890. Fokine's reforms, carried out primarily in Western Europe under the aegis of Diaghilev, revitalized ballet through radical transformation, creating a modern ballet in much the same way, and with many of the same goals, as Isadora Duncan had done with modern dance. Fokine's ballets were one act instead of three. They were concise, too, in terms of their expressive action, for, instead of alternating passages of pure dance with pantomime gesture, he made the dancing itself dramatic. The dramatic requirements led to an expansion of the ballet vocabulary.

De Maré and Börlin, who was in total agreement with his teacher's theoretical goals, put together a troupe of dancers culled, for the most part, from the ballet company of the Stockholm Royal Opera. Jenny Hasselquist, Carina Ari, and Ebon Strandin were their leading danseuses. But because the Opera was short of good male dancers, they went to Denmark to find men. "I did not have a single scruple about demolishing the corps de ballet at the Stockholm Opera," de Maré wrote, "considering that I had decided to present it as a magnificent troupe dedicated to performing abroad."[9]

In March 1920 Börlin gave a solo concert in Paris at the Théâtre des Champs-Elysées. He performed two harlequin studies, to music by Chopin;

Derviche, a reenactment of a dervish dance, to music by Alexander Glazounov (this piece was in the Ballets Suédois repertory during the first season); a series of Swedish airs; and *Negro Sculpture*, to a Scriabin nocturne.[10]

De Maré had taken over the lease of the Théâtre des Champs-Elysées, and it was there that the Ballets Suédois gave its first performance on October 25, 1920. The first program consisted of *Jeux*, *Iberia*, and *La Nuit de Saint-Jean*. Later in the season, several more ballets were added: *Maison de fous*, *Le Tombeau de Couperin*, *El Greco*, *Derviche*, *Les Vierges Folles*, and *La Boîte à Joujoux*. All of the works were choreographed by Börlin.

The twenty-four ballets produced by the Ballets Suédois during its five-year life span fall into three basic categories: ballets derivative of the Diaghilev style and themes; dances based on Swedish folklore; and original, avant-garde productions. Some of the works, of course, fall into more than one category. To present Swedish folklore in a modernist theater setting was an act that had a precedent in the Ballets Russes productions that artfully recast Russian images and legends. *Within the Quota* (1923), a Swedish fantasy about an immigrant who encounters typical American stereotypes, danced to a score by Cole Porter and with décor by the American artist Gerald Murphy, must certainly have been partially inspired by the success of the Massine-Cocteau-Satie-Picasso *Parade* (1917), created for Diaghilev. And yet *Within the Quota* also claimed certain avant-garde distinctions. It was the first authentic jazz ballet, and the first ballet score written for a European company by an American composer.

Not surprisingly, the first season's ballets are the most suggestive of Diaghilev's predecessors. De Maré admitted that "despite [his] desire for innovations, [he] called on musicians and painters who were advanced, but also well-known," to create a series of "sensible ballets" for the first season.[11] *Jeux*, to music by Debussy and with décor by Pierre Bonnard, had already been choreographed by Vaslav Nijinsky. According to Bengt Häger, Börlin rechoreographed the piece as a "polite gesture to Nijinsky."[12] Apparently (judging from photographs) the new version had none of the curled-in, fetal awkwardness and abruptness of gesture that characterized the Ballets Russes ballet of a modern love triangle. Börlin's version was "an amiable sportive ballet," in contrast to Nijinsky's, which had been "a little brusque."[13] The later Ballets Suédois *Skating Rink* (1922) was also based on the use of sports as a microcosm of more generic social relations. Its cubist décor and costumes by Fernand Léger, its "dance poem" by Riciotto Canudo (the publisher of the prewar journal *Montjoie*), and its modernist score by Arthur Honegger gave the later ballet an original, machine-inspired vision of the monotony of the modern world. Apparently, during that first season dances from Fokine's *Chopiniana* (*Les Sylphides*), performed by the Ballets Russes during its first season, were reconstructed by

Börlin. *Iberia*—with music by Isaac Albeniz, orchestrated by D. E. Ingelbrecht (a pupil of Debussy's and the conductor of the orchestra that accompanied the Ballets Suédois, and later the husband of Carina Ari), and with décor and costumes by T. A. Steinlen—even though it was based on Börlin's observations of Spanish and North African dances while touring those areas, must have reminded Paris audiences of the Spanish atmosphere of *Le Tricorne*, the Massine-Picasso ballet given the previous year. And *La Boîte à Joujoux*, to another Debussy score (orchestrated by André Caplet), with décor and costumes by André Hellé, had nearly the same plot as Massine's *La Boutique Fantasque* of 1919—the activities of toys in a toy shop.

When de Maré and Börlin decided to set a ballet to Maurice Ravel's 1919 piano suite "Le Tombeau de Couperin," Ravel orchestrated it (1920). This suite has since become a popular concert piece, and from it three sections—Forlane, Menuet, and Rigaudon—were choreographed and danced in the setting of an eighteenth-century fête galante. Highly successful, Börlin's *Tombeau*, a delicately tinted recreation of period dances, was performed 167 times by the Ballets Suédois; at the Théâtre des Champs-Elysées, Ravel conducted the one-hundredth performance in 1923.[14]

Yet already during the first season the ballets *Maison de fous* and *El Greco* created controversies. *Maison de fous* (music by Viking Dahl, décor and costumes by Nils von Dardel) had a sinister feeling, very different from the divertissements offered by ballets like *Jeux* and *La Boîte à Joujoux*. The scenery depicted a gigantic man in anguish, and the story—of a young woman who wanders into a madhouse and is strangled by one of the inmates after having gone mad herself—was told through odd rhythms and gestures. Börlin created different dance motifs for each inmate, symbolizing human follies. Each dancer repeated and varied the motif monomaniacally. Börlin was accused of using gestures that were overly pictorial, of making a ballet that was not really a ballet.[15] *El Greco* (music by D. E. Ingelbrecht, scenery by Georges Mouveau after paintings by El Greco, and costumes by Börlin) was a dramatic recreation of tableaux from works by the painter, again attesting to Börlin's expressive use of gesture rather than combinations of dance steps. Especially important to the style of the dance-drama was the use of the crowd. In a storm, as the crowd in the market square become fearful of violent nature, a young man watches the funeral procession of his brother, who has been struck by lightning. A Christian girl comforts him and restores his faith. The skies clear and light returns to the square.[16]

These works contrasted strongly with the ballets deriving from Swedish folk art and traditional dances, whose bright, naïve décor and homely peasant mood had a direct, unsophisticated appeal for the spectator. *La Nuit de Saint-Jean* (1920)—with décor and costumes by Nils von Dardel and music by Hugo Alfven—and *Dansgille* (1921)—with music arranged by Eugene Bigot from Swedish folk songs, scenery taken from folk paintings, and traditional costumes—both used the theatrical framework of a scanty plot involving a folk festival to support scenes of pure folkdance. It was these works, and *Les Vierges Folles* (1920)—with music by Kurt Atterberg, scenery and costumes by Einar Nerman, based on a Swedish folksong that tells the parable of the wise and foolish virgins—that most pleased the American critics during the company's tour of the United States in 1923–24. The avant-garde offerings were confusing and often puzzling, but the hearty folk spirit of *Les Vierges Folles,* for instance, was "full of delightful forthright humor of a homely sort. . . . It is not 'sicklied o'er with the pale cast of thought,' nor the more vivid streaks of morbidity."[17] The contrast, apparently, is with the other three works on that evening's program: *Skating Rink, Les Mariés de la Tour Eiffel,* and *L'Homme et son Désir.* The critic compared *Les Vierges Folles* favorably with the White Russian revue *Chauve-Souris.*

A Boston critic, reporting from Europe, described *Les Vierges Folles*:

> The set consists merely of a gray drop, in the centre of which is painted a quaint church-façade broken by a doorway hung with black curtains. The virgins are all dressed in bobbing, bouncing, hoop skirted dresses, with little tight basques, and high, black, stovepipe hats; the wise ones in green and the foolish ones in orange; each carrying her lamp in hand. The bride's dream of her groom, while the virgins sleep with drooping heads like wilted flowers; the difficult waking of the virgins; the discovery that the frivolous ones are out of oil, and their pleas for the loan of a few drops from their righteous and unyielding sisters; the inimitable bridal parade led by the proud fiddler; and the exclusion of the poor foolish virgins by two yellow angels with swords of yellow flame that look like sticks of candy—the whole action of the piece is presented with deliciously and delicately nonsensical steps to the most charming and danceable of tunes.[18]

Les Vierges Folles was the most popular ballet in the repertory of the Ballets Suédois, and it was performed a total of 375 times.[19]

The least popular work, however, was also based on a Swedish folk theme. *Offerlunden* (1923) was billed as a ballet-pantomime, with music by Algot Haquinius and décor and costumes by Gunnar Hallström. The plot was reminiscent of the Stravinsky-Nijinsky *Rite of Spring* produced by the Ballets Russes: "In a prehistoric forest, the holy fires have died out. In spite of incantations, rites, and magic dances, the flames will not rise up again, unless the king voluntarily gives himself up as an offering."[20] *Offerlunden* (the Swedish title translates as *The Sacrificial Grove*) was performed only five times and then dropped from the repertory.[21]

Le Porcher (1924), based on a tale by Hans Christian Andersen, also used music from old Swedish folk tunes to tell of a prince who disguises himself as the swineherd at the emperor's palace to win the love of the emperor's daughter.

The most important works given by the company, in terms of their historical and avant-garde importance, were the collaborations with French modern composers and painters. The first of these was *L 'Homme et son Désir*, the result of a three-way collaboration between Paul Claudel, who conceived the scenario, Darius Milhaud, who wrote the music, and Andrée Parr, who designed the scenery and costumes. The ballet had been planned in 1917 in Rio de Janeiro, where the three friends had seen Nijinsky perform. Claudel wrote of that inspiration:

> He is the greatest human creation, lyricism incarnate, standing like a god among the jerking puppets that we are. He paints our passions on the canvas of Eternity, he takes our most misused gestures, as Virgil took our words and images, and transports them into the blissful realm of all that is intelligent, powerful, and ethereal. . . . He walked as tigers walk; it was not the shifting of a dead weight from one foot to the other, but all the complex of muscles and nerves moving buoyantly, as a wing moves in the air, in a body which was not a mere trunk or a statue, but the perfect organ of power and movement. Every tiny gesture, as for example when he turned his face toward us and his small head swung round suddenly on his long neck, was accomplished gloriously, with a vivacity both fierce and sweet, and at the same time an overwhelming authority.[22]

From these impressions, Claudel conceived the theatrical image of a man caught in the Brazilian forest both by the overpowering night and by his own obsession. The man was to be played by Nijinsky. However, at this time Nijinsky's sanity began to disintegrate. And when Milhaud played the music for Diaghilev, he rejected it. Milhaud—who felt that Diaghilev did not like his music because, unlike that of his colleagues Auric and Poulenc, it was not pleasant and direct—thought that *L 'Homme et son Désir* was too symbolic and dramatic for Diaghilev's present needs. Milhaud went then to de Maré, whose "dancers did not have the virtuosity of the Russians, but their sincerity and their love of the art made them very attractive."[23]

Claudel's notions of gesture as it related rhythmically to speech, the plastic expression of the poetic image, correlated to Börlin's ideas of translating forms in painting into dynamism. Claudel had already worked on these ideas with Milhaud; for instance, he had asked the musician to write a score for his play *L 'Annonce faite à Marie* that would be "muffled, like countryside breathing," and serve as a commentary on the action of the play.[24]

L 'Homme et son Désir was first performed June 6, 1921, at the Théâtre des Champs-Élysées. Claudel wrote an introduction to the ballet in the magazine *La Danse*:

This little drama in movement had its birth in the atmosphere of the Brazilian forest which, in its vast uniformity, seemed like an element in which we were immersed. It is most strange at night, when it begins to be filled with movement, cries, and gleams of light; and it is one such night that we are trying to show in our poem. We have not tried to reproduce its inextricable tangle with photographic accuracy. We have simply spread it like a carpet—violet, green, and blue—around the central blackness on the four tiers of our stage. This stage appears vertical to the eye, like a picture, or a book being read. It is, if you like, a page of music in which each action is written on a different stave. The Hours of Night, all in black with gilded headdresses, move one by one along the topmost ridge. Below, the Moon, led across the sky by a cloud, like a servant walking before a great lady. At the very bottom, in the waters of the vast primeval swamp, the Reflection of the Moon and her Servant follows the measured walk of the celestial pair. The drama proper takes place on the platform halfway between heaven and earth. And the principal character is the Man in the grip of primeval powers, robbed by Night and Sleep of both face and name. He enters led by two women, identical in their veils, who confuse him by turning him round and round like a child blindfolded for a game. One is Image and the other Desire, one is Memory and the other Illusion. Both mock him for a while, then disappear.

He remains there, standing with outstretched arms, sleeping in the brilliance of the tropical moon, like a man drowned in deep waters. And all the animals, all the noises of the eternal forest come out of the orchestra to watch him and din in his ears: the Bells and the Panpipes, the Strings and the Cymbals.

The man begins to move in his dream, and to dance. And his dance is the age old dance of nostalgia, Desire and Exile, the dance of captives and deserted lovers, of those insomniacs who pace in a fever from one end to the other of their verandah, of caged beasts that fling themselves and fling themselves again—and again, and again—upon the impassable bars. Sometimes a hand from behind pulls him back, sometimes a fragrance which saps all vitality. The theme of obsession becomes more and more violent and frenzied, and then, at the darkest of the dark hours before the dawn, one of the women returns, and circles round the man as though fascinated. Is this a dead woman? or a live one? The sleeper grasps the corner of her veil; she whirls round him and her veil unwinds until he is wrapped around like a chrysalis, and she is almost naked—and then, joined by the last wisp of stuff, very like that of our dreams, the woman puts her hand on his face and both move away to the side of the stage.

Of the Moon and her attendant all we see is the reflection, down below.

The black Hours have ceased to file past, and the first white Hours appear.[25]

Less than two weeks later, on June 18, the company performed in Cocteau's play *Les Mariés de la Tour Eiffel*. Jean Hugo, the grandson of the writer Victor Hugo, designed the masks and costumes that gave the performance a cartoon appearance. Irène Lagut designed the scenery, a bird's-eye view from the Eiffel Tower. Music by the group known as Les Six (minus Louis Durey) used popular French tunes as source material. The action takes place on July 14. A bourgeois wedding party arrives on the first platform of the Eiffel Tower for a nuptial lunch. The photographer's "birdie" — which, it seems, is an ostrich — has escaped from his camera, and in the course of the play other unlikely characters emerge from it: a bathing beauty from Trouville, who poses as if for postcards; a lion which eats the general who gave the wedding toast; and the couple's future child, who massacres the wedding party. Finally, after a cyclist passes through, five telegrams do a dance, the birdie returns to the camera, and the whole wedding party is sold to an art collector. The general comes back to life by emerging from the camera, into which the entire party shortly disappears. The narrative was spoken by two announcers inside booths representing phonograph loudspeakers.

Cocteau himself was quite pleased with the Ballets Suédois production of *Les Mariés de la Tour Eiffel* — his first work, he believed, that was not at all derivative of other works.[26] In a 1922 preface to the text, he enthusiastically extended his appreciations to his collaborators:

> Thanks to Jean Hugo, my characters, instead of being, as so often happens in the theatre, too tiny, too true to life to justify the extent of the lighting and décor, were constructed, corrected, built up, enlarged by every device of artifice to a resemblance of epic proportions. I rediscovered in Jean Hugo a certain atavism of monstrous reality. Thanks to Irène Lagut, our Eiffel Tower suggests forget-me-nots and flowering compliments.
>
> George Auric's Overture, "The Fourteenth of July," marching bands whose music blares out at a street corner and moves on, also evokes the potent enchantments of the sidewalk, of popular fairs, of red-festooned grandstands like guillotines, around which drums and trumpets start stenographers dancing with sailors and clerks. And his *ritournelles* accompany the pantomime just as a circus band repeats a certain motif during an acrobatic act.
>
> The same atmosphere pervades in Milhaud's "Wedding March," in Germaine Tailleferre's "Quadrille" and "Waltz of the Telegrams," in Poulenc's "The General's Speech" and "The Trouville Bathing Beauty." Arthur Honegger amused himself, in the "Funeral March," by making fun of what our musicologists gravely call Music. Needless to say that they all fell into our trap. Hardly had the first notes of the "March" sounded when all those long ears were lifted. No one noticed that this march was as beautiful as a sarcasm, written with great taste, with an extraordinary appositeness. Not one of the critics, all of whom praised this piece, recognized the waltz from *Faust* which served as its basis.
>
> How can I express my gratitude to MM. Rolf de Maré and Börlin? The former by his clairvoyance and generosity, the latter by his modesty, made

it possible for me to crystallize a formula I had been experimenting with in *Parade* and *Le Boeuf sur le toit*.[27]

Apparently, however, the production hampered the efforts of the choreographer. Because the dancers could hear neither the music nor the voices of the announcers through the masks, they had enormous cuing problems, and all the movements had to be planned with great care and utter precision.[28]

On October 25, 1923, de Maré presented *La Création du monde*, a "Negro-jazz ballet" inspired by the current vogue for black art from Africa and America. Blaise Cendrars, who had recently compiled an anthology of black folklore that included a section on cosmogonic legends, wrote the scenario. Darius Milhaud, who had long been interested in the forms of jazz he had heard in Harlem clubs, composed the music for a jazz orchestra, and Fernand Léger designed the curtain, scenery, and costumes. At first, Milhaud recalled, Léger had imagined using skins to represent flowers, trees, and various animals. At the moment of their creation, they would be inflated with gas and fly away like balloons. But since the complicated installations for blowing up the skins would clutter the stage and interfere with the music, Léger had to abandon his plan, settling for animal disguises like those worn by African dancers during ritual ceremonies. Milhaud also remembered that the three collaborators planned the ballet during visits to popular dance halls.[29]

At Léger's suggestion that an "American" ballet be the curtain raiser for the much anticipated *Création*, Gerald Murphy and Cole Porter (not yet a popular success) devised *Within the Quota*. Murphy's libretto, like his décor, satirized American life and the instant-success myth. A Swedish immigrant meets American types (part myth, part real) whom he knows from the movies, but his joy is horned-in on by a puritan type who poses successively as social reformer, revenue agent, uplifter, and sheriff. Eventually, the immigrant meets "Mary Pickford," who makes him a film star—as movie cameras click away. Börlin used popular dance forms such as the shimmy and the foxtrot in choreographing Porter's satiric, eighteen-minute, ragtime- and jazz-influenced piano score, which was orchestrated by Charles Koechlin. Before the première Léger—sensitive that the lively "curtain raiser" might overpower the principal work—had de Maré reverse the order of performance. (Both ballets triumphed in Paris; on the American tour immediately following, New York gave *Within the Quota* mixed notices while it found favor in Chicago.)[30]

In *La Création du monde*, at first the stage is dark; one perceives a tangled mass of bodies. Three enormous creation gods, Nzame, Medere, and N'kva, move around it slowly, reciting incantations. The mass begins to move, a tree grows, drops a seed, and another tree grows. As leaves of the trees touch the ground, they tremble and swell and turn into animals. The stage grows lighter with each birth. During a round dance of the creatures, a man and a woman are born, execute a dance of desire, and couple. All the creatures, including the shamans and sorcerers, join the dance, which reaches a frenzy. Finally it dies down, and the couple remains isolated in their kiss.[31]

After giving a ballet on Persian themes (*Le Roseau*, with music by Daniel Lazarus and scenery and costumes from Persian miniatures); a modern erotic debate-as-ballet, *Le Tournoi singulier* (music by Roland Manuel, scenery and costumes by Foujita, based on a poem by Louise Labé); and a realist tale of an impoverished Italian village, *La Giarra*, based on a story by Luigi Pirandello (music by Alfredo Casella, scenery and costumes by Giorgio de Chirico), all in 1924, the Ballets Suédois created its final work, *Relâche*. Called "An Instantaneous Ballet in Two Acts and a Cinematographic Entr'acte, and a Dog's Tail," it was conceived by Francis Picabia, the film made by René Clair, the music composed by Erik Satie, and the choreography by Börlin. *Relâche* means "no performance," and the title already suggested a dadaist inspiration. The opening scene of the film shows Satie and Picabia firing a cannon from a Paris rooftop (this was perhaps among the projected scenes that preceded the ballet). As Noël Carroll suggests, the image is hostile and destructive toward bourgeois culture. "They fire a volley, literally a moral salvo, that is echoed throughout the film [and the ballet], articulated through pejorative metaphors of Parisian society and aggressive renunciations of bourgeois aesthetic, ethical and social values."[32] The advertisement for the performance describes the work as "a ballet which is not a ballet, nor an anti-ballet," and warns, "above all, don't forget your dark glasses and some cotton to stop up your ears."[33]

Ironically, Jean Börlin had fallen ill, and on the proposed opening night, November 20, the theater actually was closed, much to the confusion and dismay of the audience. The ballet finally opened on November 27, 1924 (according to some accounts, December 4, 1924).[34] One critic recalled that "many believed it all another prank of Satie's, and when, a week later, the orchestra sounded the prelude to *Relâche* based on the student song 'The Turnip Vendor,' the audience howled. They roared out the scandalous chorus, heckling and laughter interrupted the performance."[35] The curtain rose on an inner curtain decorated with graffiti, including the names of the collaborating artists, the legend "Vive Relâche," and "Erik Satie is the greatest musician in the world." The designs were transparent on a black background; and, lit from behind by a flickering light, they gave the impression of neon signs. The curtain was soon replaced by a screen, on which several logically connected cinematic images were projected. Finally, the stage decoration—several enormous arches covered with reflective discs—was revealed. A fireman entered, smoking. A woman in evening dress walked onto the stage from the auditorium and smoked a cigarette. She danced, without music, and when her dance ended the music resumed. Several men from the audience went up on the stage and danced with the woman, and one of them carried her off the stage.

The curtain fell; and the cinematic entr'acte, accompanied by repetitive music structured as a montage, was projected. There were shots of a dancer from below (through a transparent floor); of Man Ray and Marcel Duchamp playing a game of chess; of an egg resting on a jet of water, which, shot by a hunter, released a bird. A funeral rushed headlong toward the ridiculous, speeding through Paris and metaphorically suggesting the moral disintegration of the city. Finally, the coffin toppled from the hearse; and the dead man, now a smiling magician, emerged and made everyone disappear.

In the second scene of the ballet, the décor showed broken lines and posters on which one could see sentences like "Those who are dissatisfied can go to the devil!" The dancers returned, took off their evening clothes, and — in flesh-colored tights decorated with colored spots — resumed dancing. The woman entered with a wheelbarrow, the fireman poured water from one container to another. For the curtain call, Satie drove onstage in a small Citroën and "ironically greeted the worthy audience whom he had just ridiculed magnificently."[36]

Relâche, Picabia wrote, is "as much alcohol and opium as sports, strength, and health; it is baccarat or mathematics. . . . You will see a beautiful woman, a handsome man, many handsome men, blazing lights, everything turning in a movement as rapid and agreeable as that which we can get at 300 HP on the best route bordered by trees tilted for a speed-producing illusion."[37]

After *Relâche*, de Maré and Börlin decided that they could go no further. Neither was it possible to retreat from the vanguard position they had staked out for the Ballets Suédois. De Maré dissolved the troupe, Carina Ari remained in Paris, later becoming the head of the ballet company at the Opéra Comique in Paris and première danseuse étoile at the Opéra, where in the 1930s she choreographed three ballets.[38] Börlin toured South America, contracted jaundice in Brazil, gave two more dance concerts in Paris in 1929, and, with a concert planned for Carnegie Hall in December 1930, went to New York. He died there on December 6. De Maré continued to produce theatrical performances at the Théâtre des Champs-Elysées — most notably the first appearance of Josephine Baker in musical revues — and in 1931 established in Paris the Archives Internationales de la Danse, with material not only from the Ballets Suédois performances but from his dance researches around the world. In 1932 the Archives held a choreographic competition in Börlin's memory, at which Kurt Jooss won first prize with his ballet *The Green Table*. In 1950 the Archives was dissolved, and many of its contents moved to the Dansmuseet in Stockholm.

8

Soirée de Paris

Soirée de Paris was a month-long season of ballet and theater organized by Count Étienne de Beaumont at the Théâtre de la Cigale in May and June 1924.[1] According to the souvenir program and the poster, the season was a charity benefit for the Society for Relief for the War Widows and the Committee to Help Russian Refugees, under the patronage of the President of the Republic and Mme Millerand; the President of the Council and Mme Poincaré; Marshal and Mme Foch; and the Princess Sixte de Bourbon; its committee of honor and roster of patrons include diplomats, political and military officials, and minor royalty.[2] In his biography of Cocteau, Francis Steegmuller suggests that the season was organized to "refloat" Léonide Massine, who had been dismissed by Diaghilev in 1921, had organized his own, unsuccessful companies, and had asked to be readmitted to the Ballets Russes in 1922, but was refused.[3] Massine reports modestly that "I was very surprised and flattered when [Beaumont] asked me to collaborate in a new venture he was planning, . . . a charitable venture for the assistance of French war widows and Russian refugees. . . . He asked me to choreograph five productions for him."[4] In his preface to the souvenir program, Beaumont states as his goal to combine all the arts—dance, painting, music, and poetry—which in their own ways reveal the new spirit and the youngest countenance of France.[5]

Perhaps Beaumont, who was an avid ballet fan and friendly with Misia Sert, Valentine and Jean Hugo, Jean Cocteau, and others in Diaghilev's circle, aspired to become as active an impresario as the producer of the beloved Ballets Russes. He directed his social life with all the care of a metteur-en-scène, and the borderline between private life and theater in his social set was not always clear. In their biography of Misia Sert, Fizdale and Gold call Beaumont "the Diaghilev of costume balls."[6] They describe one party in which "Max Jacob appeared as a monk, Jean Hugo as an Imperial Guard, and Lucien Daudet . . . as the Spectre de la Rose."[7] Reginald Bridgeman, a secretary to the British ambassador in Paris, reported that each Beaumont ball had a theme—the French colonies, the court of Louis XIV—and that at the first of these parties, in 1919, the guests were requested to arrive "leaving exposed that part of one's body that one consid-

Unpublished.

ered the most interesting."[8] At Beaumont's Bal des Jeux in 1922, Raymond Radiguet came disguised as a shooting gallery, carrying clay pipes and wearing a cardboard target over his evening dress; Valentine Hugo appeared as a merry-go-round, Jean Hugo represented a game of billiards, and Misia Sert's nephew Jean Godebski was a house of cards.[9] At the Bal de Mer, Jean Hugo was one of four men disguised as waiters from Prunier's who carried the Maharanee of Kapurthala, as caviar, on a tray.[10] And in 1923 at the Bal Louis XIV, the Countess de Castries, as "La Malade Imaginaire," was carried in on a chair; Raymond Radiguet was in attendance as "a patient, made up with spots, meaning measles."[11] The Duchess de Gramont, in mourning, appeared as an executioner bearing the head of John the Baptist on a platter, attended by Jean Hugo as Herodias and the Prince de Chimay as Salomé.[12]

Despite its caché — besides its list of dignitaries, the program announces that the lighting was designed by Mme Loïe Fuller — the Soirée season was somewhat haphazardly organized. Programs were changed or substituted at the last minute, and announcements in the newspapers often conflict, even in the same publication. The souvenir program and poster give 17 May 1924–30 June 1924 as the dates of the season, as does Massine in his autobiography, but the listings in *Le Figaro* indicate that performances were given every night between 18 May and 18 June, but not before or after. Because *Le Figaro* gives last-minute details on *répétitions generales* and changes of program, and upcoming events, I have used its listings in compiling the following classification of the Soirée de Paris season.[13]

The opening program, listed as playing 18 May–23 May, was listed under "Spectacles and Concerts" daily in *Le Figaro* as follows:

> À La Cigale (Nord 07–60), à 9 heures, "Soirées de Paris," organisées par le Comte E. de Beaumont. *Vogue, Mouchoir de Nuages, le Beau Danube, Salade.* Projections lumineuses de miss Loë Fueller.[14]

Vogue, according to the souvenir program, was "three danced pages," conceived and designed by Valentine Hugo, and produced in collaboration with *Vogue* magazine. Costumes were made by Jeanne Lanvin, with additional men's costumes by Hermes and Lus and Befve, and boots by Perugia. In the first "page," "Les Filles Mal Gardées," two girls escape from a boring picnic, find a four-leaf clover while walking in the garden, and fight over it. In "Le Favori," two young women talk to a jockey in the paddock just before a race, making him forget the time, until a bell rings to remind him to mount the favorite. "Le Bain de Minuit," to a poem by Paul Morand, tells of a couple who go bathing in a river after a ball. The man falls asleep, a young man dances with the woman, and after the sleeper awakes, angry, he joins them in their dance. The first scene was danced by Mlle Zaria and Jane Hawitt; the second by Mlle Allan, Joyce Meyrs (sic), and Harry Wills. In "Le Bain de Minuit," Mlle Pietruckewitz played the woman, Mme Miklaschewskaja the young man, and Rupert Doone the sleeping escort.[15] In its review of the second season, *Le Monde Musical* calls *Vogue* "an agreeable ad for the magazine of the same name."[16]

Mouchoir de Nuages was a "tragedy in fifteen acts" by Tristan Tzara, directed by Marcel Herrand, with costumes by Lanvin and projections by Fuller, and Andrée Pascal's shoes by Perugia.[17] The "tragedy" is a comic romance, based on a triangle involving a banker, his wife, and a poet, and a number of chorus members who comment on their actions. Each tiny act takes place in a different locale and involves a different theatrical style, ranging from classic Greek theater, to Shakespeare, to French symbolism, to detective films. The staging was anti-illusionist:

> The action takes place in a closed space, like a box, from which the actors cannot leave. All five sets are the same color. In the back, at a certain height, there is a screen that indicates where the action occurs, by means of reproductions blown up from illustrated post cards. These are rolled up on two rollers by a stagehand, who is visible at all times to the audience.
>
> In the middle of the playing area there is a platform. To the right and the left are chairs, makeup tables, properties and the actors' costumes. The actors are on the set for the duration of the play. When they are not performing, they turn their backs to the audience, change costumes, or talk among themselves. . . .
>
> All the actors in the play keep their own names. . . . The Poet, the Wife of the Banker and the Banker are the principal characters. A, B, C, D and E are the Commentators, who also play all the secondary roles.[18]

One scene, a flashback, is played behind a scrim. Three scenes from *Hamlet* are combined into one scene, which functions as a play within the play and leads to the banker's murder. Throughout, the commentary, which is structured as the final part of every act, offers a discourse on conflicting levels of reality:

> C: . . . Even though we are the Commentators, that is to say, the subconscious of the drama, the playwright never even let us know why the Poet does not love Andrea.
>
> E: Yet she is pretty and intelligent; you are aware that I know her very well myself.
>
> B: The fact that you act the role of Andrea's friend on stage does not give you the right to believe that you are her friend in real life.
>
> A: But she could easily be his friend outside this dramatic action, this play, in real life, in her own life—how would you know?
>
> C: Oh! There is nothing so tedious as these endless discussions on the difference between theatre and reality![19]

The poet was played by Marcel Herrand, the wife of the banker by Andrée Pascal, and the banker by Dapoigny.[20]

G. Allix, reviewing *Mouchoir de Nuages* in *Le Monde Musical*, remarked that the play was "not at all my cup of tea," but that, nevertheless, a person "would not be bored by it for an instant," with its uproarious style and its successful parodies of Maeterlinck, Victor Hugo, and Shakespeare. He thought the use of the chorus ingenious, and complimented the young cast, especially Pascal and Herrand, but wondered why the title of the play was so nonsensical.[21]

Le Beau Danube, "a character ballet in two acts," was choreographed by Léonide Massine to music by Johann Strauss, orchestrated by Roger Desormière, who conducted the music for Soirée de Paris. The décor by Vladimir and Elizabeth Polunin was based on a painting by Constantin Guys, as suggested by Étienne de Beaumont.[22] In the first act, a painter (Ladré) works on a painting in a square, surrounded by rubbernecks, milliners, and salesmen. It is a holiday. The king of the dandies (Stanislas Idzikowski) and the other dandies dance a waltz with the "cocodettes." A hussar enters, flirts with two girls, and dances a mazurka with the prettiest. A troupe of comedians arrives: an athlete, a dancer, and a comic actor. The dancer (Lydia Lopokova) recognizes the hussar (Massine) as her former lover and faints. The girl (Eleanor Marra) also faints. The dancer revives and dances the "Blue Danube" with the hussar, and the girl also revives, vanquishing the dancer and dancing a mazurka with the hussar. The girl's parents give the young couple their blessing. In the second act, the wedding of the girl and the hussar is celebrated. Young people dance quadrilles, and the dancer arrives with a new friend to hide her chagrin.[23]

Gilson MacCormack, reviewing the first performance, wrote in *The Dancing Times*:

> Either this is the most banal and puerile ballet ever composed, or else Massine is pulling the leg of the Parisian public and foisting on them as a work of the modern school a ballet of the mid-Victorian epoch of the feeblest and most sentimental kind. Even if meant as a burlesque, it fails because it lacks sufficient humorous exaggeration to warrant the assumption that such is the case.
>
> Not even the excellent dancing of Massine, Idzikowski, and that irrepressible "gamine," Lopokova, could redeem such an effort. It was a pity to see Idzikowski's superb technique wasted on so poor a show. His dazzling cabrioles and entrechats caused gasps of delight from those who love grace and perfect finish in an artist.
>
> The corps de ballet was, without exception, the worst I have ever seen.[24]

The first program concluded with *Salade*, choreography by Massine to music by Darius Milhaud, with a scenario by Albert Flament, décor and costumes by Georges Braque. The "choreographic counterpoint" was danced by Massine (Polichinelle), Marra (Isabelle), Allan, Witzansky, Baikow, Streletsky, Ignatow, Sergieff, Domansky, Ochimonsky, Plier, Ladré, and Zmarlik. It was a typical commedia dell'arte plot. Milhaud writes that he incorporated music given to him by Massine, as well as certain themes from serenades he himself had heard in Sardinia.[25] Four voices sang a rhythmic accompaniment to the orchestral music and the dancing.[26] The rhythmic libretto, which Massine describes as a mixture of singing and recitation,

> exactly caught the flavour of Naples, as did Braque's setting, with its sober greys and maroons suggesting the raw, hard-working side of Neapolitan life with its street vendors and artisan families living in one room and ceaselessly struggling for survival. The melodies I had chosen for it were orchestrated by Darius Milhaud, . . . who completely transformed them, producing harsh, aggressive, broken rhythms which exactly suited my conception of the ballet. To bring the audience into direct contact with the action, I made the dancers carry lanterns, which they placed along the front of the stage before each scene. These threw a wavering light over the sculptural choreographic tableaux. My inspiration for this came from my desire to emulate the sculptural effect of the works of Donatello and other Renaissance masters, and also from the cubists' use of layer-upon-layer of colour surfaces, particularly apparent in Picasso's larger still-lifes.[27]

Paul Collaer describes Massine's choreography as "very interesting and at times thrilling," a gestural counterpoint in which no group was ever completely at rest, "creating a simultaneism to which our eyes were barely accustomed," and remembers that as Polichinelle Massine danced subtly and perfectly.[28] MacCormack thought *Salade* similar in epoch and spirit to *The Good Humoured Ladies*, and called the score one of the best Milhaud had written, though wholly modern and far removed from "the quaint archaic beauty of Pergolesi."

> The choreography is virile, as is everything undertaken by Massine. The gestures and poses are stark and angular, relieved by none of the grace and beauty that Fokine gave us, but this choreography is an integral whole with the music. . . . Massine's dancing is full of individuality and vigour, but the quick, stiff, nervous movements of the arms to which he is addicted becomes [sic] rather wearisome when repeated continuously. One French critic went so far as to say that he "gave the finest display of physical agony that had been seen for many a day."[29]

And Allix wrote that the "hectic choreography exhausted the eyes and the spirit," and that the dancers seemed like marionettes hung from imaginary strings.[30]

The second program in the Soirée de Paris season opened on Saturday, May 24, with *Gigue* and several divertissements. On the same night an exhibition of art by late nineteenth-century impressionist masters opened in the foyer and ground floor of the theater. These works on themes from the music hall, theater, and circus included drawings, paintings, and lithographs by Cézanne, Daumier, Dégàs, Delacroix, Constantin-Guys, Manet, Seurat, and Toulouse-Lautrec.[31] On the following night *Le Beau Danube* was added to the program, which ran through Monday, June 2.[32]

Massine describes *Gigue* as:

> an elegant trifle set in a corner of the garden at Versailles, designed by Derain. As the Prince I wore a shimmering gold costume. Idzikowski made an elegant courtier and Nina Nemchinova a lovely princess in a deep blue robe embroidered with flowers. For the overture we used music by Scarlatti, and for the ballet itself music by Bach and Handel played by the pianist Marcel Meyer.[33]

The *Figaro* theater columnist Maxime Girard wrote in a preview of *Gigue* that Massine was an erudite as well as virtuoso dancer, since he had scrupulously reconstructed all the variations prescribed by Beauchamps.[34] The divertissements on the program are not named in any reviews or previews, but perhaps they comprised an unnamed dance by Massine, set to a waltz by Lanner and with décor and costumes by Étienne de Beaumont, which he describes as light and romantic,[35] and two other dances listed in the souvenir program: *Ballet Espagnol*, by José-Maria Sert, danced by Ida Rubenstein, and *Danses Actuelles*, by Harry Wills.[36]

The next program to be given at the Cigale was Jean Cocteau's *Romeo et Juliette*, which had its *répétition générale* either on June 2 or June 4.[37] Cocteau had been friendly with the Beaumonts since before World War I. He served in Beaumont's volunteer ambulance unit, corresponded with him about his work on *Parade*, went with him and others of their circle to the circus, the ballet, masquerade balls. Steegmuller suggests that Beaumont served as a model not only for Raymond Radiguet, Cocteau's lover, in his novel *Le Bal du Comte d'Orgel*, but also for Cocteau in life. According to Steegmuller, Beaumont invited Cocteau to contribute something to the Soirée de Paris season that did not include Massine at all, in order to cover up the real purpose of the program.[38] During the war Cocteau had wanted to produce a version of *A Midsummer Night's Dream* with the Fratellini clowns and with music by Satie. After Beaumont asked for a contribution, Cocteau planned to produce a five-act verse play at first named *Bajazet*, later *L'Impromptu de Montmartre*. It had characters, including a dog, named after those in Racine's tragedy *Bajazet*, as well as a sea horse and a glazier who carried his equipment on his back. Sketches for the glazier were realized in the character Heurtebise in Cocteau's *Orphée*, written in 1925 and first performed in 1927.[39] Cocteau abandoned his plan for *L'Impromptu* and decided to use instead an adaptation he had made of *Romeo and Juliet*, drastically paring down Shakespeare's poetry in order to substitute a poetry of mise-en-scène. As Neal Oxenhandler points out, Cocteau reduced Romeo's lines on seeing Juliet in Act I scene 5—

> O, she doth teach the torches to burn bright!
> It seems she hangs upon the cheek of night
> Like a rich jewel in an Ethiop's ear;
> Beauty too rich for use, for earth too dear!
> So shines a snow-white swan trooping with crows,
> As this fair lady o'er her fellows shows.
> The measure done, I'll watch her place of stand,
> And, touching hers, make blessed my rude hand.
> Did my heart love till now? forswear it, sight!
> I never saw true beauty till this night.

—to the following three sentences: "Je n'avais jamais aimé. Un seul diamant orne l'oreille de la nuit, c'est elle. A quoi servent ces lustres ridicules?"[40]

Inspired by Miss Aerogyne, the Flying Woman whom he had seen in a sideshow in 1920 with the Hugos and Paul Morand, Cocteau planned a prologue in which the speaker "flew" in an acrobatic posture. Miss Aerogyne's setting had been all black, against which she stood out in white tights and rhinestone accessories. For *Romeo et Juliette*, "With Jean and Valentine Hugo I had invented an entirely black set, in which only the colors of certain arabesques, costumes and props were visible. Red lights framing the stage kept the audience from seeing anything else."[41] The costumes were black dresses, doublets, and hose, and black tights, painted to look embroidered and framed by white cuffs and collars. All the men of Verona had a stylized way of walking, aggressively and with a hand on the hilts of their swords, which contrasted with Romeo's sleepwalker's pace. The actors rehearsed to music that was suppressed during the performance, in which a medley of Elizabethan airs, orchestrated by Roger Desormière, accompanied the action. Cocteau directed the production and acted the role of Mercutio; depressed by Radiguet's death the previous December, from typhoid, Cocteau wrote to Jacques Maritain that he always hoped during the duel scene "that my pantomime would deceive Death and induce it to take me."[42] Marcel Herrand played Romeo, Andrée Pascal Juliet, and Yvonne George the Nurse.[43] There was also, according to Jean Hugo, a miniature ballet danced by two English women.[44]

The reviewer for *Le Théâtre* approved of the simplicity of the setting, likening it to the scenery of Shakespeare's time. The costumes, he thought, were exactly the opposite of the décor—sumptuous yet original, combining Renaissance style with an extreme modernism. "Finally, the characters, instead of walking naturally, perform a sort of rhythmic dance, at first disconcerting, which makes them resemble marionettes, but which allows for certain peculiar attitudes, in the manner of the Ballets Russes." Contrasting with the pruning of the poetry in the text, the reviewer noted a contrasting conservation of the comic passages, newly rendered in familiar argot. "In this astonishing *Romeo et Juliette*, the dominant character is neither Romeo nor Juliet, but the Nurse."[45]

Romeo et Juliette was performed at the Cigale through June 8, interrupted on June 9 and 10 by a program comprising *Salade*, *Gigue*, and divertissements, then performed again from June 11 through 13. On Saturday, June 14, *Mercure* and *Les Roses* were danced at a gala subscription performance; on June 15 their *répétition générale* was held. These two ballets were given, with *Premier Amour*, a duet by Idzikowski and Lopokova to Satie's *Morceaux en forme de Poire*, and *Vogue*.[46]

Premier Amour is not listed in the souvenir program, but is mentioned by two reviewers. Gilson MacCormack simply calls it a "mimed playlet" and states that "in both *Premier Amour* and *Les Roses* M. Idzikowski danced with his usual extraordinary skill."[47] Maurice Boucher, writing for *Le Monde Musical*, calls it "a ballet scene in which Mme Lopokova and M. Idzikowski are comic and charming."[48]

Les Roses is listed as a divertissement conceived and choreographed by Massine, to music by Henri Sauguet, with décor and costumes by N.[49] N is immediately recognizable as Marie Laurencin, from the designs reproduced in the program.[50] Boucher calls this ballet "a pretty play of colors," but wonders wryly whether the music has been substituted, since it "resembles exactly the celebrated waltz which has nothing to do with 'the youngest countenance of our France.' "[51] Perhaps this was the divertissement Massine mentions having made to a waltz by Lanner, but with décor and costumes by Beaumont. MacCormack reports that, "In *Les Roses* an amazing series of grands jetés en tournant caused tumultuous applause, whilst the technical precision of Mlle. Lopokova's grands jetés portés en diagonale was also appreciated by the enthusiastic ballet lovers present. The *corps de ballet* had greatly improved since the beginning of the season."[52] Later that year Idzikowski performed *Les Roses* at the London Coliseum, with Vera Savina. Described as a "classical poem," the dance was, according to "The Sitter Out," inconsistent but "vastly better than any of the arrangements shown by Pavlova at Covent Garden." Only Idzikowski's perfect technique "saves the piece from being merely a mediocrity," however.[53]

Perhaps the most eagerly awaited event of the season was *Mercure*, "poses plastiques," a collaboration among Massine, Erik Satie, and Pablo Picasso. For three days before its premiere *Le Figaro* reminded its readers of the event, promising that the ballet would "disconcert, amaze, surprise," and that "inanimate objects would play preponderant roles,"[54] and remarking that only in Paris could such a fantastic event happen.[55] In an interview in *Paris-Journal* before the ballet opened, Satie explained:

> Though the ballet has a subject, it has no plot, It is a purely decorative spectacle and you can imagine the marvellous contribution of Picasso which I have attempted to interpret musically. My aim has been to make my music an integral part, so to speak, with the actions and gestures of the people who move in this simple exercise. You can see poses exactly like them on any fairground. The spectacle is related quite simply to the music-hall. There's no stylization, and no attempt to relate it in any sense to things artistic.[56]

The action in the ballet, in three tableaux, was meant to illustrate the aspects of Mercury's mythological personae as a god of fertility, a thief, a magician, a messenger, and the henchman of the underworld.[57] Ornella Volta suggests that the dance was also replete with alchemical symbols, an interpretation in light of Satie's Rosicrucian ideas.[58] In the first tableau Mercury finds Apollo and Venus in an embrace, surrounded by the Signs of the Zodiac. Mercury kills Apollo and then revives him. In the second tableau, the three Graces bathe, Mercury steals their pearls, and is chased by Cerberus. In the third tableau Mercury, at a feast given by Bacchus, invents the alphabet and dances, and Proserpine is carried off by Pluto and Chaos.[59] Massine danced Mercury; Vera Pietro, Venus; Cywinsky, Apollo; Plier, Ladré, and Baikow (men in wigs and red-painted false breasts) played the three Graces; Ignatow, the Philosopher; Vuorisola, Polichinel; and Wysnansky, Domansky, Zmarzlik, Ochimovski, and Streletzki danced Chaos.[60]

According to Douglas Cooper even Massine has noted that the ballet was largely Picasso's. The sketches indicate that Picasso planned groupings as well as the décor, costumes, and *praticables*. The basic setting for each tableau was a set of white and grey canvas flats with either a white or black backdrop. In the first scene, Night was an outline figure of a reclining woman, made of black-painted rattan, with a moveable head and neck that rocked during the dance, surrounded by stars, also moveable. When in the bath, the Graces were played by men but, when out of the bath, they were cut-outs with heads that could move up and down, manipulated by dancers. Cerberus was a black praticable with three heads painted in white outline on a circle, and a rape of Proserpine was drawn on two white cut-outs.[61]

On the opening night there was a demonstration by some members of the Surrealist group, criticizing Picasso for working for the aristocracy. André Breton, Louis Aragon, Max Ernst, and others wrote a letter of apology, praising Picasso, to *Paris-Journal*.[62] Boucher, describing the ballet, remarks that, despite the little demonstration, there was not much to get angry about; the décor was so simple and its degree of invention so impoverished that it resembled the sort of thing everyone has made at some time in their lives, perhaps when a little drunk. The music he found exactly like "the ordinary pom-pom of the Music Hall," and only the dancers—Lopokova, Pietro, and Idzikowski and their partners—were "truly astonishing."[63] According to MacCormack, "The ballet fully came up to our expectations. It is humorous in content; and the fantastic humour of Picasso's décor and costumes is quite equalled by the music . . . and the choreography. . . . The choreography of Massine was full of whimsicality. The fantasy was admirably danced by all concerned."[64] Cyril Beaumont, who saw *Mercure* when Diaghilev produced it in 1927, was less enthusiastic: "All I can remember of this production is that it contained some male dancers, crudely attired to represent women, who wore crude wigs with thick plaits dangling over their shoulders, and were provided with enormous imitation breasts. There were also strange contraptions in iron wire—designed by Picasso—which were carried on the stage. The whole thing appeared incredibly stupid, vulgar, and pointless."[65]

Serge Lifar saw Diaghilev either on the opening night of *Mercure* or at the closing performance on June 18 and noticed that Diaghilev was "pale, agitated, nervous," because he felt threatened by the success of his former collaborators.[66] Diaghilev had already tried unsuccessfully to dissuade Milhaud from creating *Salade*, and Braque had written to promise that his designs in *Salade* would not be seen before those in *Les Facheux*, though this turned out to be untrue. And Cocteau felt moved to defend his collaboration with Beaumont by writing to Diaghilev that "I am doing nothing that is in any way like your productions, and am confining myself to the theatre."[67]

Milhaud remembers the 1924 Paris ballet season, with the rival performances organized by Diaghilev and Beaumont, as "particularly brilliant,"[68] and Collaer remembers Soirée de Paris, too, as brilliant: "What talent, what beauty, and what charming ease! One drank, one smoked, one chatted. This light, music-hall ambiance, this air of spontaneity around works of art was very pleasant. . . . Were we at the Cigale, or at Count de Beaumont's home? The most aristocratic thought was joined to a powerful popular instinct, and out of this meeting a series of essentially French spectacles was born."[69]

The season was successful for Massine, not only in terms of the reviews, but for his career with Diaghilev. In London at the end of 1924, Massine met Diaghilev and heard his reactions to the Soirée de Paris. "Don't let's talk about *Le Beau Danube*—that's pure trash," he said, but he "had been intrigued by *Mercure* and thought the choreography and lighting of *Salade* had marked a definite step forward."[70] Diaghilev then commissioned two ballets from Massine, who rejoined the Ballets Russes in January 1925.[71]

9

Kasyan Goleizovsky's Ballet Manifestos

Kasyan Yaroslavich Goleizovsky was born in Moscow in 1892. As a child he studied dance in Moscow, where his father was a soloist with the opera and his mother was a dancer. Beginning in 1906, he attended the Maryinsky Theater school in St. Petersburg. His teachers there included Mikhail Obukhov, the great mime Pavel Gerdt, and the young reformer Michel Fokine. In 1908, Goleizovsky danced in the graduation concert of Bronislava Nijinska and Lyubov Tchernicheva. In 1909, the year Serge Diaghilev produced the first season of Russian ballet in Paris, Goleizovsky graduated from the Imperial Ballet Academy; and, after a short term in the corps de ballet at the Maryinsky Theater, he transferred to the Bolshoi Theater in Moscow in 1910. There he studied production with the choreographer Alexander Gorsky, who installed a new dramatic realism in the ballet, and with Gorsky's assistant Mikhail Mordkin, an exponent of dramatic expressivity who later left Russia to tour with Anna Pavlova. (Mordkin eventually settled in the United States, where his Mordkin Ballet Company became the precursor of American Ballet Theatre.) Goleizovsky danced with the Bolshoi Ballet until 1918.[1]

During World War I, Goleizovsky choreographed ballet miniatures and grotesque dances, as well as directing plays and operettas, for Nikita Balieff's cabaret La Chauve-Souris. After the October Revolution, while still dancing at the Bolshoi, Goleizovsky opened his own experimental studio, where he choreographed ballets using students from the Bolshoi Ballet School. At the same time, he organized children's performances, using his youngest students in such works as *The Sandman, Max and Moritz,* and *Snow White,* until the group disbanded in 1920.[2]

Goleizovsky began work in 1919 on *The Masque of the Red Death,* inspired by Edgar Allen Poe, to music by Nikolai Tcherepnin. In this allegorical ballet, a feasting king was visited by death, symbolizing the destruction of the Russian monarchy by the revolution. According to the Soviet dance historian Elizabeth Souritz, both Gorsky and Vladimir Nemirovich-Danchenko (who was collaborating with Gorsky in an attempt

---

Ballet Review 11/3 (Fall 1983).

Scene drawing from Goleizovsky's *Faun.*

to bring the Stanislavsky approach to ballet) supported Goleizovsky in this project, which was planned for the Bolshoi Theater; but the company received it coldly, and it was never produced.[3]

The years 1921–25 saw intensive experimentation in Goleizovsky's choreography. He organized his Chamber (Kamerny) Ballet, which in 1921 performed three evenings of his work, including dances to music by Medtner and Scriabin. In 1922 he produced *White Mass* to Scriabin's Tenth Sonata, *Faun* to Debussy's "L'Après-midi d'un faune," and *Salome* to music from the opera by Strauss. *Faun* was performed on a set constructed of platforms and stairs. As proclaimed in the two manifestos by Goleizovsky that are reprinted following this introduction, he was interested in finding new movements generated by the exigencies of the stage surface, which changed by means of constructivist décor. In *Faun*, the Faun, stationed on the upper platform, flirted with the half-naked nymph Walenta, stationed on a lower platform. Other nymphs were arranged in ornate, angular poses along various levels of the stairs; two satyrs commented on the action with ironic postures. Like Nijinsky's startling *L'Après-midi d'un faune* of 1912, Goleizovsky's *Faun* made no attempt to reconstruct Greek mythology, but, rather, created an atmosphere through abstract movement. The critic Truvit (A. I. Abramov) wrote that in *Faun* there was no subject, no aesthetic complication, no mythological cliché, "just a magnificent play of movements. Just a wonderful mastery of composition. Just an effective combination of poses." The verticality of the action, the powerful rhythms of the design, and the bare bodies of the dancers all contributed to the originality of the new forms that Truvit praised in Goleizovsky's choreography.[4]

In the fall of 1922, Goleizovsky showed *Faun*, *Salome*, and his Medtner and Scriabin pieces in Petrograd. Yuri Slonimsky, the critic who during the early twenties was a member of George Balanchine's circle, later wrote in *Ballet Review* that Balanchine and his friends went to every one of the Kamerny Ballet's performances in Petrograd, and that they found the dances so astonishing and Goleizovsky himself "so talented that we at first thought he had answered the question 'How shall we proceed?' The resources of the human body, the wider range of colors and movements, could not leave an audience unmoved." Slonimsky notes that Balanchine's early works definitely show the influence of Goleizovsky's erotic, gymnastic style.[5]

In 1923, Goleizovsky choreographed a cycle of *Eccentric Dances*, with costumes commissioned from the Ukrainian constructivist designer Anatol Petrizky. In the same year he made a series of more classically based dances to Chopin études, a group of Spanish dances, and a cycle of Danube Slavic folkdances. This interest in folkdance redeemed Goleizovsky in the thirties, when his early productions were criticized as too erotic, individualistic, and New Economic Policy-Style (i.e., bourgeois). In 1924, he choreographed the Western dances (foxtrot and shimmy) in Meyerhold's *D. E.* (*Give Us Europe!*), which were performed by women in black mesh stockings to the accompaniment of a jazz band.[6]

Goleizovsky's best-known work of this period was *Joseph the Beautiful*, set to music by Sergei Vassilenko and designed by Boris Erdman. Erdman had acted with Tairov's Kamerny Theater in 1917–18, before he was twenty years old. Interested in constructivism, he soon turned to theatrical design; and by around 1920, close to the imagist writers, he began to illustrate and design their literary works. While working in the State Institute of Theatrical Art he collaborated with Meyerhold, Baratov, and others, and he designed costumes for dancers in the Moscow State Circus. Erdman believed that the dancer's body should be revealed in order to show the workings of the muscles and to unencumber the body's action.[7] Zakhary McLove described *Joseph the Beautiful* in the New York *Times Magazine*:

> The stage, contrary to ballet laws that demand clear floor space for dancing, was filled with stairs and platforms, on which the entire ballet was performed. There was not much dancing, in the traditional sense, but there was plenty of beautiful posing, magnificent grouping, and choice "plastics." To this the gorgeous, if scant, costumes of Erdman lent color. The performers' bodies, too, were colored from head to foot. There were orange Jews, red Egyptians, brown Ethiopians. Joseph was a lemon-yellow youth with feminine features; Taich, Potiphar's wife, was white as

> milk. Taich was danced by Miss [Lyubov] Bank. . . . She appeared upon the stage with only narrow silver strips over bust and hips. Her bobbed black hair was parted in the middle by a string of diamonds. The face was immovable, sardonic.[8]

In Act I, Joseph's entrance variation depicted his sensitive, poetic nature. His brothers entered and tried to kill him, and Joseph danced a second variation of dramatic confusion. Act II opened with a huge pyramid, with Potiphar at its center, surrounded by warriors holding round shields and other figures turned in flat, profile poses. Joseph's role was a passive, steadfast one as he struggled against the violence in Potiphar's court. Souritz points out that in Fokine's *Legend of Joseph* (choreographed to Strauss's music in 1914), an angel saved Joseph from execution and Potiphar's wife was killed by thunder, whereas Goleizovsky did not believe in magic endings and kept his Joseph imprisoned in a dungeon:

> The immovability of despotic power came into question. The pyramid crumbled. Joseph, squeezed between the columns, which moved toward the center of the stage, threw himself down. Taich and Potiphar gazed from the height of their power onto the earth, which had devoured the disobedient. There, where he recently stood, the servants danced. One had to grovel, to show one's devotion to the ruler, to delight in the destruction of the man who was not like all the rest. But he existed and did not submit. And these swarming, mingled figures, these groups broken into small particles, never again gathered into their former majestic bas-relief.[9]

In 1925, Goleizovsky showed his appreciation for the romantic ballet style evinced in his manifestos in his production of *Teolinda*, to music by Schubert, which was presented on the same program with *Joseph the Beautiful* at the Experimental (Bolshoi Filial) Theater.[10]

In his agitprop ballet *The Whirlwind* (1927), Goleizovsky made use of the same contrast between the "decadent" dances of the bourgeoisie and the healthy, upright dances of the proletariat that he had used in *D.E.* Lunacharsky suggested the graphic style for this work, choreographed to music by Boris Beer for the tenth anniversary of the October Revolution, commissioned for the same program as *Heroic Action*, an allegorical opera: "I ask you to make a poster and only a poster," he told the choreographer. The ballet showed the class struggle between foxtrotting capitalists, royalty, clerics, and the stirring masses (led by a man in the first act and a woman in the second). Recalling both the stylistic contrasts of the exemplary ballet *The Red Poppy* (Lev Lashchilin and Vassily Tikhomirov, 1927) and *D.E.* and the themes of Goleizovsky's own aborted *The Masque of the Red Death*, the ballet *The Whirlwind* began with a king carousing in his castle and ended with the entrance of a death-bearing Spirit of the Revolution and an orgy. "The servants of tsarism, which is dying out and devoured by the indignant people, hide in palaces that have been preserved here and there. Dreaded, red Death — the Red Whirlwind chases them and overtakes them everywhere," Goleizovsky wrote.[11]

Vladika, the fat king in *The Whirlwind*, was a caricature straight out of ROSTA* posters of "Capital," surrounded by noblemen in white gloves and shirtfronts, senators in ribbons, and diplomat buffoons. A soloist emerged from the funnel-shaped mass filling the stage, where the scene showed the silhouette of a ghostly city with a sky on which, lit up by raging fires, appeared the black crosses of gallows. The crowd led the Spirit of the Revolution to the castle, where the king rolled down the steps to his throne, losing his clothing along the way. "The abominable pile of flesh will wallow with a final spasm. All the courtiers, seeing him in such a state, will understand that there is no redemption. Without adornments, their god turned into dust," Goleizovsky wrote.

According to Souritz, the orgy was a fantasy of horror. A decadent violinist accompanied erotic dances; a bacchanalian frenzy that combined wild folkdances with foxtrots followed. "Monks of all creeds threw themselves into the dance, together with the half-dressed bacchantes. The black cowls of Orthodox monks and the tonsures of Catholics flashed by; shamans and Tibetan lamas raged. The monks turned into satyrs during the dance: their soutanes fell off, and antlers and tails appeared." The final apotheosis was the "pyramid of victory" over the fallen court. "Below, the motley harlequins and personages of the court lie, their writhing finished; above, the workers build a new life. The entire scene is covered with slogans," Goleizovsky wrote.[12]

Like Meyerhold in *D.E.*, Goleizovsky was accused in *The Whirlwind* of making the aristocracy attractive and exciting, while the proletarian heroes were boring and stilted. The critic V. Iving complained in *Pravda* that the ballet was an unhappy fusion of attenuated eroticism with bold propaganda, and that the agitprop itself seemed only an excuse for the eroticism. After its dress rehearsal at the Experimental Theater on 6 November 1927, when spectators walked out in the middle of the performance, *The Whirlwind* was withdrawn from the repertory.[13]

After the failure of *The Whirlwind* and the increasing repression of avant-garde art in the Soviet Union, especially after 1932, Goleizovsky worked independently in Moscow and in various other Soviet cities, staging ballets and sports festivals as well as ballets for the theater. He studied the folklore of various nationalities and based his 1941 ballet *Two Roses* on Tadjik folklore. In 1964 he wrote the book *Images of Russian Folk Choreography*. In the late 1950s, Goleizovsky again began to work at the Bolshoi Theater, on themes that recalled his earlier work. He choreographed a new

* ROSTA, the Russian Telegraph Agency, commissioned artists, including Vladimir Mayakovsky, to make propaganda posters that were put in store windows all over the USSR.

Scriabiniana, an abstract suite of dances, in 1962 (it has since been recorded on film) and *Leili and Mejnun* in 1964. At the time of his death in 1970; Goleizovsky was working on plans to restage *Faun* for television.[14]

As the following manifestos show, Goleizovsky joined with his mentors Fokine and Gorsky in bitterly criticizing the sterility of academic ballet conventions, still prevalent in the early twentieth century, that were inherited from Marius Petipa. "The Old and the New: Letters about Ballet" in many ways echoes Fokine's letter to the London *Times* of 1914. And perhaps Goleizovsky also refers to the eighteenth-century ballet reformer Noverre in the title as well as the concerns of these manifestos. Goleizovsky complains that, even after the revolution, the right wing in ballet still holds power.

As a "leftist" choreographer, always interested in innovations for the sake of greater expressivity, he invented two new positions of the feet: sixth position, in which the feet are close together with the legs held parallel; and seventh position, in which one foot is in front of the other, also in parallel (rather than turned-out) position. Goleizovsky makes reference to these new positions (and to criticisms of them) in "The Old and the New." He expanded the ballet vocabulary further with acrobatic movements, gymnastics, and arabesques either tilted forward, performed par terre, or in the air with the support of a partner's arm or knee. The legs of the ballerina were then free to gesture expressively. Goleizovsky's dances proceeded in a flow of intricate, changing poses and circular or spiral shapes. The parallel positions of the body, the unusual partnering arrangements, and the flowing chains of dancers are all elements of Goleizovsky's choreography that seem to have influenced not only George Balanchine but also later generations of Bolshoi choreographers.

These manifestos originally appeared in *Ekran* (*Screen*), a biweekly magazine published in Moscow that carried articles about and reviews of all the arts, as well as listings of film screenings and theatrical performances. The publication of "The Old and the New: Letters about Ballet" coincided with a season of performances by the Kamerny Ballet at the GOSET Yiddish Theater in April and May 1922.[15]

The Old and the New: Letters About Ballet

I.

"The works of the leftist ballet masters are too technical. They do not correspond to the music, they are erotic, and so on. Classical dance may evolve, but it is impossible to call the works of the present-day leftist ballet masters dance." Nowadays we hear such voices rather often.

But isn't dance really the expression of an idea by means of movements? Sometimes even the instinctive expression of a subconscious part of our imagination?

And a votary of the art of ballet who neglects any kind of movement is a bad one.

Every position of the body is beautiful and necessary. A new movement for a ballet master is the same thing as a new paint for a painter. The more there are of them, the more possibilities there are.

Can one and need one take into consideration the opinions of the pundits, who have become hardened on entrechats, bourrées, and so on, and who employ these few pas—where they are needed and where they are not needed? Pundits who have become exhausted in a useless struggle against their own imaginations? Those who force unhappy, moaning performers—who have bound their heads up with the traditional little ribbon and put on all the glittering goods, without considering whether the artistic point of view demands it or not—to perform these pas day in and day out, not only in a tunic and a tutu, but also in an ordinary skirt? Or must one consider the opinion of nonballet people, who at the time of their discourse on this art remind one of birds with clipped wings? I would say it is impossible to take their opinions into consideration, but also necessary. We are compelled to consider them, because all of the major stages on which a choreographer can now create anything are occupied by them.

The masses get used to the new more quickly than their leaders do. The masses unconsciously believe that everything created by nature is admissible. The masses are not a rival for the artist. The masses are more of an artist than the pundit, because they judge by first impressions.

It is possible to find ugliness in anything beautiful. In fact, aesthetics says that the essence of beauty does not lend itself to precise definition.

The pundits, the old ballet masters, even made the crowd come to believe that the second position of the so-called classical ballet was beautiful. Or it would be clear to people who look for "indecency" that the attitude position may remind one of a dog during its natural animal functions, and so on.

Even the nonrecognition of the leftist masters of ballet is no more than a misunderstanding, which is a result of the lack of imagination of the ballet pundits and their stagnation, their fanatic, blind faith in the precepts of old men.

We observe interesting phenomena—a new ballet master, M. M. Fokine, is born—in Russia he suffers ruin; Western Europe crowns him with laurels. In Paris the dancer V. Nijinsky conquers the audience in the ballet *Les Sylphides*—in Petersburg after this ballet (which grand dukes and so on attended), he receives an order to leave Russia immediately.[16]

Can there be two opinions about whether the dance of Taglioni, Elssler, Grisi, and so on was beautiful? The distinctive, naïve beauty of the dance of the [18]30s and 40s is so perfect, original, and logical that not only a specialist, but even a layman barely interested in the art of movement, will feel it unconsciously. And an absence of that technical quality that presently prevails in every choreographic work is the most salient feature of this dance of the 30s, 40s, 50s. This type of dance elucidated an idea in original and uncomplicated movements. This dance has been preserved in only a few classical ballets.

The variation in the first act of *Coppélia* is still the closest of all to the old dance. There we see what the dancer wants to say with her movements. There the meaningful set of pas is a harmony of movements, which as a whole express a definite idea. And in the dance of Taglioni's time, as in ancient dance, an idea appears as movement.

In the old ballets of Marius Petipa, especially in his last works, we already see less meaning in the movements.

At the present time the art of that classical dance is experiencing its decadence. The stunt on which this dance is built, unpoeticized, is not illuminated by an idea, but, on the contrary, is bared, and the spectator goes into raptures chiefly over such combinations as thirty-two and more fouettés, six or eight turns à terre, etc.

And we observe a transition to technique, but a cautious transition, in which, besides the big, special, technical accomplishments and taste, a knowledge of the history and evolution of one's art is felt.

Really, isn't any significant ballet in Moscow a machine? Isn't it really naked, puzzling, tedious technique and nothing more? How inexpressive and monotonous the choreographic variations are! And, in the majority of cases, what terrible music accompanies the creation of the ballet master, at a time when serious, "genuine" composers lie in the library and bide their unknown time!

The stage on which a ballet performer arranges his movement is the keyboard of his art. It is not made use of at all by the fanatics of the old. But the creative work of a performer who has finished his technical training cannot be constrained by any kind of decorative or musical fracture. For him, every unexpected turn, bend, rise, step, and so on, should serve as an object of reflection, as a chance to amplify (intensify) his movement, as a possibility for some kind of new achievement.

The ballet dancer, like the ballet master himself, should rejoice at every unexpected obstacle on his keyboard, because such an obstacle is, in truth, not an obstacle but the possibility for some kind of new achievements. The interest of creative work lies in these possibilities.

The leftist ballet masters are accused of making combinations and poses to which the eye is unaccustomed. It is said that these are not dances but circus tricks.

But in the Bolshoi Theater, in the second act of *Vain Precautions*,[17] we ourselves see a real circus "splits" en l'air, which the ballerina performs supported by the premier danseur. I find that this circus trick does not in the least disturb the impression of high artistic value. It is as much a circus trick as all the other movements in that dance — which those who err term "old" classical — are inherent in the circus.

I maintain that there is no position of the body in the art of ballet that could not be found in the movement not only of the circus but also of the dramatic or operatic performer. In all three cases, the movements have their own nuances and are complex in their own ways.

All movements are inherent in life. The art of ballet is an extract of all the arts in general.

The Bolshoi State Academic Theater, as the single museum of this art, should collect all movements inherent in life, without ignoring a single one.

And whether a given movement is pleasing or displeasing is really not so important. It pleases some people; displeases others.

One can superciliously not acknowledge the leftist trend, but it is impossible to forget that all progress in art is made by leftist artists.

If an artist-innovator is educated and technically accomplished, don't persecute him; lend an ear to what he says.

Really, it is only thanks to the innovators that we have now surpassed "abroad." Thanks to them we teach our former teachers. We have traveled to draw knowledge from Gordon Craig, Isadora Duncan, and so on.

And now both could learn a great deal from us, which, it seems, is in part being realized.[18]

II.

How can one explain that the revolution, which allowed leftist artists of all types of art to express themselves, did not give this opportunity to the leftist masters of ballet?

Funds for ballet were allocated only to the academic theaters, where they were sown and are sown to this day. The *Little Humpbacked Horses* and the *Bayaderkas* are the communal graves of Russian ballet dancers; for the breeding grounds of the future beggars — of smatterers — there are the ballet studios. True, there are ballet studios in which attempts to express something new are made, but these attempts remain attempts.

Thanks to this sort of circumstance, a new ballet art is born in the very writhings in which the old perishes.

We still have a school for those who devote themselves to ballet. There they train their bodies over the course of seven or eight years. In the last years of training, a student must master the technique of the ballet to perfection. Training mechanically and disciplining their bodies, they prepare themselves for their future creative work, where all the five famous positions should become only a means of achievement, for the creation of some kind of image.

But our ballet is situated in the hands of people who are chiefly occupied with the continual repetition of what was done before them, without creating anything new, and they have reduced this art to such a state that, after looking in on a ballet class, you couldn't say what is going on. Is this a class or the rehearsal of some "old" ballet? But where is the creative work of the performer?

What is performed in class is now done exactly onstage. In every ballet you find the very same pas, the very same combinations. And these pas and combinations, as I have already said, are attached to any costume. Arabesque en l'air looks very pretty in tutus, for instance, in the ballet *Vain Precautions*, and was absolutely out of the blue in the ballet *Eunice*,[19] where this arabesque was set into a tunic. But, of course, a school should be just a means of achievement and nothing more.

One of the pundits of the Bolshoi State Academic Theater pointed out to me that in one of my works the dancer does a circus culbute (he somersaults over his head). "Is this really dance?"

But in the Bolshoi Theater, in the first act of the ballet *Swan Lake*, doesn't the dancer V. Efimov actually turn a somersault over his head several times, according to the instructions of the extreme right-wing artist A. A. Gorsky?[20] It is difficult and unnecessary to argue about which movement can be called dance and which cannot.

Princess Brambilla and *Phèdre* at the Kamerny Theater[21] are genuine, beautiful ballets; to reach them, *The Little Humpbacked Horse* and so on would need to grow for a long time.

And the monologue of Tseretelli in the play *King Harlequin*,[22] thoroughly saturated with dynamic movements . . . well, this is a beautiful, meaningful variation, which I am sure would never be accepted as dance by the fanatics of "the old classical dance."

The sixth position—when both a person's feet are on the floor, touching one another closely at the heels and the big toes—is absolutely not acknowledged by these very fanatics. Nor is the seventh position—that is, an amplified fifth.

I was accused of the indecency of several poses and pas, and the indecencies are attributed to "leftism" in general. But where is the indecency? Surely not in sixth position, which I propagate. In a position of modesty. In a position indigenous to the East and the ancients, where the naked dancing woman, who has no veil, covers up with her knees. But really, is the second position of the old classical dance—when a person stands with legs wide apart while the toes and knees are turned out—is this really more decent than my sixth position? And is the costume of our ballerina really decent, when the woman is undressed to the point where her nudity may be felt more strongly?

Maybe these guardians of chastity would also find Longus's *Daphnis and Chloe* indecent? It is the nature of the pathological person to find "indecency" in everything that excites his sensuality.

The judges say further that the dance of a leftist ballet master is in most cases vapid. It makes no difference to me whether or not these judges let me abolish the traditional tutus and the glittering ribbon worn on the head. But I think that it scarcely ever happens that a spectator sees a dancer in my work turning for some unknown reason like an open pair of compasses, for a duration of two or three minutes to the music, which is written by either Medtner, Scriabin, Debussy, or Prokofiev, and so on. But in the interpretation of classical dance, which is aged, faded, and has now lost any meaning, such pirouettes are inalienable appurtenances and accompany any musical composition. The chaînés of the above-mentioned dance are yet more such hackneyed appurtenances. Almost every variation performed by a woman ends with them.

I have already said that the movements of the old classical dance are attached by the right-wing choreographers to any costume, thus depriving the movement of its style and expressiveness. A dance of pure fantasy, a dance outside of time, depends entirely on the imagination of the artist, and hence may not be constrained by any cliché. I want to speak here not only about costume but also about movement. For if a person is given four or five positions, tutus, a headband of sham diamonds, and is ordered to create — the fantasy flies away. This is no longer creative work but merely a job.

I heard from a certain right-wing ballet master that "every movement is international." I can agree with him when it is a case of a discussion of ethnographic dance. Even then he is not quite right, since the structure of the body of the person of the country in question has great significance. For example, among the Spanish the pelvis is pushed forward; among the Jews the curve of the waist is weakly outlined; among Negroes the feet are turned in; and so on. And all of this plays a very large role in the construction of a dance. Lately, the ethnographic dance of the right-wing masters has been reduced to such a state that it has become completely indistinguishable from a parody of ethnographic dances, performed by variety dancers, where all the movements are vulgar, hackneyed, calculated for thunder, crash, glitter, and sensation and, chiefly, to catch the ear of the spectator, to the detriment of the character and pithiness of the dance.

The so-called classical dance belongs to everyone and to no one; it is a dance of pure imagination and mood. It always evolves and it cannot die. The classical dance of the 1840s and 1850s is beautiful, aromatic, like an old, expensive perfume. Now, it's true, it has lost both beauty and form; now, for all intents and purposes, it temporarily does not exist.

We who love our art, "the left wing," are restoring it in due course and will show it, like an old, precious engraving. But the new — onward! Don't pay attention to the disdainful grimaces of the ballet academics. What can these decadents say? They have reduced our ballet to the point where it is barely noticed and is not considered an art.

If a spectator even attends ballet performances, it is only because there is nowhere else to go. If we also could only periodically show our works, as these old masters do, then the public, which loves ballet, would have something to live by. Let us hope that someday our ballet will be given more consideration in Russia than it has been spared up to now. But for the time being—onward, innovators! For innovators are always the renascence.

10

Merce Cunningham's *Story*

Story, a dance Merce Cunningham choreographed in 1963, signaled a new phase of experimentation for the man who had moved in the radical vanguard of modern dance at least since 1951, when he first used chance methods in his choreography. Through the use of chance—employing charts, coin-tossing, dice-throwing, and clues from the *I Ching* to select elements in a predetermined gamut of movements, body parts, or stage spaces—Cunningham had developed a technical style characterized by unexpected juxtapositions of actions.

For Cunningham, chance had the salutary effect of loosening the choreographer's conscious control over the dance, a goal augmented by the well-known autonomy of his collaborative method with composers and designers. To a great extent, choreography by chance produced unexpected and unpremeditated results. However, the initial gamut of movement choices from which the chance combinations were made still came from Cunningham's personal inventions. Also, once the chance procedures were followed, the resulting movement combinations, phrasing, spacing, and other components would then be set in an unchanging choreographic pattern.

With *Story*, Cunningham introduced two elements that would further minimize his own control in the dance, by transferring choice from the choreographer to the dancers: spontaneous determination and improvisation. The choreographic structure allowed the dancers at points to make certain decisions regarding the given movements and in other sections to

Society of Dance History Scholars, Tempe, Arizona, 1989.

invent their own movements. But, for several reasons, *Story* was not a success. Hence it is useful to examine it precisely as a departure from Cunningham's usual methodology.

Story is also notable for other reasons. It established the basic ad hoc structure for the flexible Events, which Cunningham began to present during the world tour of 1964. In *Story* for the first time, Cunningham decided just before each performance which sections of the dance would be performed, in what order, and for what durations, posting the instructions backstage. The ironic title, further, serves as a paradigm for Cunningham's attitude toward the interpretation of his dances, since *Story* (obviously) implies that the dance will have a narrative structure, and yet, as with so many of his dances, Cunningham left any final exegesis up to the spectator.

Story marked a transition in Cunningham's working relationship with Robert Rauschenberg, the painter who since 1954 had designed sets and costumes for the company. In 1961, that role had intensified, when Rauschenberg became the lighting director and stage manager of the Merce Cunningham Dance Company, traveling with the group on tour. Eventually, during versions of *Story* given on the company's world tour of 1964, Rauschenberg began to create "live décor." Inscribing his own and his assistant Alex Hay's performances in the décor of the dance was a decision that had deep repercussions, since ultimately it led to his leaving the company, in 1965.[1]

Story was first performed at Royce Hall at the University of California, Los Angeles, in July 1963. The company had recently undergone a change of personnel: Judith Dunn and Marilyn Wood had left, and Barbara Lloyd had recently joined. This necessitated a change in the repertory.[2] The group spent June and July in residency at UCLA, and Cunningham choreographed *Story* during that time. Seven dancers were in the first performance of the work: Merce Cunningham, Carolyn Brown, Viola Farber, Shareen Blair, William Davis, Barbara (Dilley) Lloyd, and Steve Paxton. The dance was open-ended in terms of the number of performers; Cunningham writes that it was "a dance for x-number of people."[3] In the nineteen performances of the dance in the United States, the number of dancers ranged from five to eight. For the performances in Europe and Asia during the world tour of 1964, the dancers for *Story* usually included the entire company: Cunningham, Brown, Farber, Blair (until she left the company during the tour), Davis, Deborah Hay, Lloyd, Sandra Neels, Paxton, and Albert Reid. Because the structure was so flexible, the duration of *Story* also ranged widely—from fifteen to forty minutes.[4]

Cunningham has written of *Story*:

> The title does not refer to any implicit or explicit narrative but to the fact that every spectator may see and hear the events in his own way. Within a

> section the movements given to a particular dancer could change in space and time and the order the dancer chose to do them in could come from the instant of doing them. Also the length of each section varied each time. The sections were given names for reasons of identification.
>
> The dance was made up of a series of sections, solos, duets, trios, and larger units, that could freely go from one to the other, so their order was changeable. . . .
>
> We played it a great many times as it could involve one or all of the dancers, and be given under any kind of extreme circumstance. Rehearsals consisted of each dancer doing all the parts of a given section.[5]

Thus *Story* was composed anew for each performance, from a series of eighteen sections. Their (identificatory) titles were: "Solo #1," "Solo #2," "Solo #3," "Floor," "Object," "Tag," "Space," "Exit," "Entrance," "Fall Trio," "Duet & Solo," "5-Part Trio," "Triangle," "Hopping," "CB & MC," "Arm-Trio," "SB & MC," and "VF & MC." In "Object," for instance, the dancers manipulated, moved, and carried an object that Rauschenberg made or found—a different one for every performance. In the film of *Story* that documents a performance in Helsinki, this is the most dramatic section of the dance—or at least the part most freighted with possible narrative import, for each dancer looks at, handles, carries, drops, or otherwise interrelates with the object in a way that imbues it with an almost totemic power. (This resulted from Cunningham's rules that the dancers could touch the object a specified number of times—though the manner of contact was unspecified.) In "Floor," Brown and Farber started at any point (either on- or off-stage) and then, according to Cunningham, "move[d] in a pronounced, slow tempo across the area, possibly separated, but more often together." In "5-Part Trio," three dancers executed five quick phrases.[6]

The dancers consulted lists posted in both wings to remind themselves which section came next, as well as how long it should last. Also in the wings were clocks provided for the dancers to synchronize their timing; while onstage, they tried to estimate the duration of a section.[7]

In terms of performance style and contact, Carolyn Brown remembers that overall the dancers "were free to relate to others on the stage or to ignore them." One option the dancers could also exercise was to stay offstage during a particular section. And further, she notes that where there was room for the dancers' invention of movement, the rules were tightly constructed, involving choices regarding direction, level, and duration. "This section was improvised, or should have been. Cunningham expected the dancers to choreograph spontaneously and not pre-set and rehearse and repeat. This proved to be more difficult for some than others."[8]

Albert Reid, for instance, found *Story* "a big nuisance. I hated it. There were so many insertions in your supposed improvisation that you were in knots. You couldn't do it as well as something that was set. And I have a terrible time remembering things, so I made something up and set it.

I pretty much did the same thing after the first attempts to do it extemporaneously."[9]

Much of the dancing—at least in the film documenting the Helsinki performance—remains recognizably Cunninghamesque. There are slow lunges, brisk leg extensions, quickly changing facings, repetitive jumps with arms moving or held in asymmetrical positions, a singular movement that flings the body open and closed, and—at the very end—a stunning trio partnering sequence in which Cunningham supports Brown, who leans off-balance in arabesque, with his left hand, while Farber repeatedly turns and flops over his outstretched right arm. All these postures and movements, as well as the extreme contrasts in dynamics, clearly bear the imprint of Cunningham's choreographic style.

Not only the dancing, but also all the other elements of the dance were indeterminate. In instructing Rauschenberg regarding the costumes and set, Cunningham notes that he told him only that "the piece would change its order from night to night." Cunningham had indicated that he wanted the costumes "to simply be picked up in the area where we were," and Rauschenberg translated this idea into an arrangement that left the costume design partly up to the dancers. They wore a basic outfit of yellow leotard and tights, and to this each dancer added items chosen from bags stationed—along with the scores and the clocks—in the wings. These items included dresses, shirts, pants, and sweaters from second-hand stores and Army-Navy surplus stores; a football player's shoulder padding; an old pair of longjohns; and a gas mask. Thus each dancer's costume varied, not only from evening to evening, but also during the course of a single performance. Often the garments were worn in unconventional ways: a dancer might extend one arm through the sleeve of a dress and the other through the neckline; a sweater might be tied around a dancer's neck. One evening, Brown remembers, "Barbara Lloyd [put] on all the costumes she could manage, leaving the rest of us with next to nothing, and making herself so large and encumbered she could barely move. What effect this had on the choreography was interesting indeed."[10] Lloyd experimented in the opposite direction with costumes in Tokyo, where she undressed completely, including her leotard and tights, and then matter-of-factly got dressed again in a new costume.[11]

The lighting, too, was indeterminate, ranging from quite light to dark. Rauschenberg used the lights at hand in a given theater, often using work lights or arranging the lighting instruments in the audience's field of vision as part of the set. On the world tour, especially, this extemporaneous system of lighting caused some technical problems with the theater crews. The technicians for the most part did not want Rauschenberg and his assistant, Alex Hay, to handle the instruments, and, Rauschenberg recalls, "They couldn't understand the concept that we didn't know where the dancers were going to be, which was part of the dance. . . . And [the crews] couldn't understand that. They just kept saying, 'Bring me the light chart, your cue sheet, and we'll do it.' "[12]

The set was composed of objects and equipment found in and around each theater. Often Rauschenberg began by stripping the stage bare of wings and drops so that the back wall was visible—at the time, a radical treatment of the stage space. According to Rauschenberg, "I never repeated the set. A new one was made for each performance from materials gathered from different places. . . . I never knew where anyone was going to be; the space was not defined. The set had to be made out of what you could find, given the amount of time that you had in a particular locale, out of stuff that was there . . . out in the alley or any place you could get it."[13] At La Fenice, the theater in Venice where the company performed during the Biennale in 1964, the stage had platforms, which Rauschenberg raised and lowered; in Helsinki, part of the stage began to revolve near the end of the dance. In Augusta, Georgia, in a hall with two theaters back to back, the audience saw the empty theater behind the stage as the backdrop. At UCLA, the vista included the open doors, hallway, and scene shop behind the stage.[14]

Rauschenberg claims that the "live décor" began at Dartington, a British arts school in Totnes, Devon, where the theater was so tidy that nothing else could be found to decorate the stage. "I didn't know what to do. I couldn't find anything. And so finally, like five minutes before we had to be back at the theater, I asked Alex [Hay] if he had any white shirts that needed ironing. And he had one and I think I had one, and I told Merce that I had something to open the show, that Alex and I were going to be on stage." The company performed next in London, where Rauschenberg created a new performance that occurred simultaneously with the dancing. He began a painting, continued making it during the four-night run, and finished it on the final evening; meanwhile Alex Hay performed tasks such as reading a newspaper or drinking a cup of tea.[15]

The music for *Story* was Toshi Ichiyanagi's *Sapporo*, a composition with a number of variable elements. In terms of personnel, the score calls for a conductor and performers numbering up to fifteen. Ichiyanagi made sixteen different scores, notated with a limited set of symbols. These indicated sustained sounds, sliding sounds, and attacked sounds; in some cases, the players were to produce more than one sound simultaneously or to choose, out of a group of possibilities, only one or two symbols to interpret. Any instrument capable of producing sounds required by the score could be used. The players were meant to be as far apart as possible in the space.[16]

Obviously, like the set and the costumes, as well as the movement itself, the rules governing the music in *Story* generated different sounds at each performance. A critic described the music in Warsaw as "harsh, shrill squeaks, rattles, and clacks." Among other musical events in that performance, John Cage played a mirror by rubbing it with a cut bottle. According to the critic, this produced "a genuine sensation," and "seven persons sensitive to squeaks left the hall."[17]

Story was performed in various United States cities (although never in New York) and throughout the company's world tour in 1964. On the company's return to the United States, the dance was taken out of the repertory. According to Rauschenberg, his steadily increasing participation in *Story* raised Cunningham's ire.[18] Certainly the dance could not be performed without Rauschenberg's participation. And in many ways, given what has remained in the memories of both critics and dancers, *Story* seems more indelibly stamped with Rauschenberg's signature than with Cunningham's.

Company member Albert Reid remembers that the dancers disliked the dance and that eventually Carolyn Brown wrote Cunningham a letter asking that the dance be removed from the repertory; as Reid recalls it, the dance was quietly dropped soon thereafter. According to Carolyn Brown, the dance was dropped because Cage "didn't trust us to do indeterminate dancing" and, furthermore, she asserts flatly, Cunningham "hated [*Story*], because he couldn't control it."[19]

Although it remained in the repertory only a short time and was a favorite neither with the choreographer nor with the dancers, as we have seen, *Story* is important for reasons both dance-political and dance-historical (as well as art-historical). It catalyzed Rauschenberg's departure from the collaborative relationship with Cunningham and from the company, enabling him to pursue his own more idiosyncratic performance path, but leaving the company without a resident designer. Its creation signaled Cunningham's interest in maintaining his own threatened position in the vanguard of modern dance, in the face of a rising generation of younger experimental choreographers. As I have noted, its structure prefigured that of the Event, a staple of Cunningham's activity since 1964. That *Story* was discontinued seems to indicate Cunningham's unwillingness to go beyond certain boundaries in choreography and in dance performance — setting him apart from the postmodernists, who reveled in improvisation and ordinary movement.

In looking at how *Story* contrasts both with the rest of Cunningham's oeuvre and with the more radical departures of the Judson group (and other postmodern choreographers), the differences between chance choreography and improvisation are clarified. And further, in understanding those differences, one can see clearly why Cunningham does not fit in the category of postmodernism.

In giving up control (via chance techniques) over such elements as timing, spacing, and sequencing, Cunningham needed to assert even more careful control in a different direction over his dancers. For one thing, if the dancers were not carefully coordinated, the varying speeds and complicated movement patterns might lead to accidents. For another, strict direction was necessary since the dancers could not rely on musical phrasing or other conventional methods to synchronize their movements. In other words, the creator's vast freedom in handling his compositional materials led to a richness of content but, simultaneously, to a tightening of the reins over his performers.

By contrast, improvisation allows for the spontaneity that was prized by the younger generation, but only through totally conscious control, residing anarchically in each individual performer—the exact opposite of the surrender to fate implied by using chance techniques. It also allows for movement content and performance style beyond any gamut of the choreographer's imagination. Improvisation democratizes the choreographic procedure by relocating it in the performers. But it also creates the risk of a "failed" performance.

Hence the conflict in *Story* goes much deeper than a power play in a dance company; it is the friction between two irreconcilable ways of making artistic choices.[20]

11

Cunningham and Duchamp

With Noël Carroll

Marcel Duchamp has suffered the fate of certain great artists: he has become an adjective, a handy category for puzzling, verbally playful, inaccessible, and "intellectual" painters, sculptors, composers, and performers. But applying the concept "Duchampian" on the basis of characteristics like puzzlement, inaccessibility, and word wit often seems too broad to be informative. One must exercise great care in examining the

Ballet Review 11/2 (Summer 1983).

relation of Duchamp to current artists. Thus our first task is to consider not only the analogies that can be drawn between Merce Cunningham and Duchamp, but the disanalogies as well.

One very general area of congruence between the two is signaled by our willingness to attribute certain of the same qualities—for example, "intelligence"—to the oeuvres of both. In Duchamp, this "intelligence" derives from his spinning paradoxes, explorations of "the limit" of the concept of art, and hermeticism. In Cunningham, on the other hand, "intelligence" is a quality of the movements and bodies that his choreography comprises. We don't paraphrase his dances into propositions about the nature of art, as we do Duchamp's ready-mades, nor do we take them to be alchemical allegories, as many do regarding *The Large Glass*. Rather, "intelligence" pertains to the movement's most significant expressive quality in Cunningham's dance.

In opposition to the technique of the Graham style (from which he emerged), Cunningham's movement is light. It is directionally flexible and often rapier fast, covering space both quickly and hyperarticulately. At the same time, it is characterized by what followers of Laban call bound flow; the energy is liquid and resilient inside the dancer, but it stops at the boundary of the body. It is strictly defined and controlled. It does not rush vectorially or spill into the surrounding space. It has an air of exactitude and precision. In turn, these formal bodily properties—lightness, elasticity, speed, and precision—suggest a particular description of the mind as an agile, cool, lucid, analytic intelligence of the sort once referred to as Gallic or Cartesian, but also appropriate as an ideal of post-World War II America. Whereas the image of human thought in Graham was heavy, organic, brooding, and altogether nineteenth century, in Cunningham it is permutational, correlational, strategic, exact, rarefied, and airy. This is not to say that Cunningham presents a pantomime of the mind, but that he presents the body as intelligent in a specifically contemporary way. Indeed, the idea of bodily intelligence itself is contemporary, while the mode of that intelligence in Cunningham's work is clearly analogous to Duchamp's preferred style of thought.

Another increment of "intelligence" in Cunningham's work is a quality of clarity. Most often, this amounts to a principle of separability—that is, each element in a dance has its own autonomy and must be apprehended in isolation from the other elements of the spectacle. This is most evident in Cunningham's relation to his composers, most notably John Cage. Music and dance are presented as disjunct, unsynchronized events, each comprehended in its own right. They are not fused in a single Gesamtkunstwerk. This division of music and movement distinguishes Cunningham from George Balanchine, a choreographer who in many other respects shares some of Cunningham's ideals of bodily intelligence. Cunningham's sets also have an existence discrete from the dancing. For example, Robert Morris's column of light moved inexorably across the proscenium stage in *Canfield*, and some of Robert Rauschenberg's actions that composed a live décor in *Story* (such as painting a painting onstage, or ironing shirts) at times upstaged the dancers. Moreover, this tendency toward separability extends into the choreography itself. In Cunningham's Events, phrases from different dances are lifted and spliced together to produce new works. This presupposes that the separate phrases in a dance are not unbreakably connected to their original context, but that they have a pristine individuality of their own. Of course, a similar point might be made about Cunningham's use of chance in certain dances, like *Untitled Solo* or *Torse*. To appreciate the individuality or integrity of a phrase, presented as such, demands a very focused, literally discriminating, variety of attention from a spectator, who must attend to each movement bundle separately and see each for what it alone is—that is, see clearly and distinctly. Again, Cunningham offers what can be thought of as an artistic interpretation of the Cartesian mentality.

Causality, or, rather, the absence of certain feelings of causality, provides another point of comparison between Duchamp and Cunningham. Duchamp, influenced by Raymond Roussel's *Impressions d'Afrique*, specialized in a kind of fantastic causation that could only exist in words, but that because it was physically imponderable, seemed curiously insubstantial, ghostly, and perhaps nonexistent. *The Bride Stripped Bare by Her Bachelors, Even* (*The Large Glass*) represents a machine, but we have no palpable intuition of its possible causal system apart from what we are told, and that not only is unbelievable but also evades the possibility of our constructing an inner, sensuously felt representation of it. How can an antique chocolate grinder, given its physical structure, be a functional part of the elaborate, sci-fi, chemical, electrical apparatus Duchamp outlines in *The Green Box* and *The White Box*? The problem here is not that of magical causation. We can imagine enchanted swords flying of their own power, and we can vicariously feel their impact as they plunge into imaginary dragons. But we cannot develop a bodily sense of the causal interactions and forces in *The Large Glass*. They exist only as words, imparting a sense of hollowness, bereft in feeling of what Hume called the cement of the universe.

Similarly, in Cunningham one feels the absence of causation in several respects. This is not to say that his dancers do not obey the same physics as balls on an inclined plane, but, instead, that his pieces lack many of the most typical and conventional representations of causation found in dance. The most conspicuous of these absences involves agency (which is, of course, at root a causal concept). Since Cunningham's dances are not dramatic, his dancers do not appear impelled by motivations. But, if they are not personal agents, neither are they social agents. They often seem unaware of each other as they dance different phrases juxtaposed at opposite ends of the stage. Undoubtedly a large measure of this effect derives from their performance masks, which are generally free of every emotion save concentration. But there is also a sense of detachment that is related to Zen and Hindu philosophies; Cage has written of the tranquility that pervades each dance despite kaleidoscopic appearances of emotions, as in the Indian tradition. Thus, when the dancers perform a cooperative task — a lift, a pull, or a support — it does not seem expressive of conventional communality. The dancers are businesslike, alone even when joined in a coordinated feat. They are not so much persons driven by a common purpose as atoms that happen to lock into each other. Their mien, their detachment, supplies another qualitative link with Duchamp, as well as another factor in the principle of separability, denuding the choreography of an aura of continuous causal process.

The discontinuities of Cunningham's choreography divest it of a deep-seated, pervasive illusion of process that is typical of most dance and that led Susanne Langer to define dance as a realm of virtual powers. Cunningham's phrasings appear as discrete operations, intricate, planned, and self-contained; they do not engender the illusion of power — magnetic or propulsive — coursing through them and binding them to adjacent movements. It is the illusion of such power in pre-Cunningham dance styles that imbues much traditional choreography with a sense of coherence and interconnectedness — a sense of overarching intelligibility grounded in the illusion of causal linkage. Without such a framework, we have not merely a strong impression of the separateness of the phrases, but concomitant feelings of the presentness and presence of each movement unit. This quality of inexplicable *thereness*, achieved through radical juxtaposition and disorientation, is also something that confronts us in Duchamp's later work, attested to by the very title of his final masterpiece, *Given*.

Duchamp said, "The creative act is not performed by the artist alone; the spectator brings the work in contact with the external world by deciphering and interpreting its inner qualifications and thus adds his contribution to the creative act." Read as a brief for the participatory spectator, this statement not only correlates with some of Cunningham's most significant innovations as a choreographer, but has been echoed by both Cage and Cunningham. By placing several different actions onstage simultaneously (for instance, the L'Amour and the Bounce Dance section in *Gallopade*) in such a way that they make equal bids for the viewer's attention, Cunningham decenters the dance composition, democratizing the space so that any place on the set can be important. He pioneered an all-over, antiarchitectonic style of choreography. At the same time, this has invested the audience with the role of determining where to look and when. (Interestingly, Cunningham first arrived at this combination of audience freedom and responsibility roughly a decade after André Bazin and film realists enunciated a similar aesthetic in regard to the cinematic image. In both film and dance, the viewer was now required to consciously interact with the imagery.) Yet for Cunningham, it is important to emphasize that what the spectator is free to choose is *which movement* to look at. In the preceding quotation, Duchamp is saying that the spectator brings his own meaning to the work of art. But meanings are precisely the sort of things that Cunningham's work is designed to deter and deflect.

With the distinction between movement and meaning, we reach the point of sharpest contrast between Duchamp and Cunningham. Duchamp strove for an art of ideas, an art that was discursive, an art that was allegorical. Duchamp opposed his ideal to art that was merely painting, merely "retinal." In this regard, his readymades can be glossed as the reductio ad absurdum of the proposition that art should seek objecthood. Cunningham, on the other hand, is a modernist in the reductive vein, creating an art based on what he conceives to be the essential material of his medium, viz., movement. And this movement is supposed to *be*, not mean—it is the functional equivalent of the paint in something like Jules Olitski's *Shake Out*. If Cunningham's movement is said to be emblematic of the philosophical system of Zen, we must remember that this is John Cage's position and not, primarily, Cunningham's. For Cunningham is concerned only with movement as such, what might be thought of as the animate counterpart of painterly objecthood. He uses chance methods to dispel the intrusion of his personality into certain dances, just as Duchamp experimented with various means of eliminating the painter's touch from his creations. But in the long run, in contradistinction to Cunningham, Duchamp mixes references to cosmology, philosophy, literature, psychosexual symbolism, puns, spoonerisms, and the like, which, though hermetic, nevertheless invite, rather than frustrate, interpretation.

Psychologically, Duchamp's disdain for retinal art led him to curtail his output. He had a reputation as a painter who did not paint. He said he loathed paint. But Cunningham has no such reservations about his materials, as his endless stream of production confirms. In this Cunningham resembles Picasso—the artist of whom it is said Duchamp's silence reflects upon him as a bad conscience. Cunningham's abundance shows his utter confidence in his medium. He manipulates a stylistic vocabulary, readily recognizable as dance, with the ease, untroubled facility, and fecundity of a Bournonville. Indeed, it is Cunningham's very reliance on dance technique that led the succeeding generation of Judson Dance Theater choreographers to question his practice. Perhaps in this respect they were more Duchampian than their mentor.

Duchamp's distrust of the "retinal" art object increasingly prompted him to create works that went against the grain of certain classical modes of aesthetic attention. He created works (like the readymades, *The Large Glass*, and *Given*) that were first and foremost discursive—that is, that were pretexts for theoretical or hermeneutic discussion. They were not objects that could be gazed at for hours in the rapt contemplation of the classic aesthetic attitude. In fact, Duchamp ridiculed this mode of aesthetic appreciation in his *To Be Looked at (from the Other Side of the Glass) with One Eye, Close to, for Almost an Hour*. Duchamp's later works are intentionally not much to look at. Rather, they are occasions for puzzles and codes that the spectator could glean from a brief visit to the gallery and ruminate about at home. Cunningham's dances, however, are made for immediate, sensuous, total consumption. Aesthetic engagement at the moment of performance is paramount; residual meditation on the meanings of the work is secondary, if important at all. *Nowness*—that is, the committed aesthetic perception of the physical and formal properties of the dance as it unfolds—is the point of Cunningham's work.

At present, Duchamp's major contribution to twentieth-century art is dialectical (in the Platonic rather than the Hegelian sense). As befits the son of a notary, Duchamp was concerned with the question of what authorizes or authenticates something as a work of art. His readymades Socratically posed this embarrassing question, and suggested the unsettling answer that contextual factors surrounding the putative artwork, such as the reputation of the artist, were (rather than the work itself) the decisive factors in determining whether something was an artwork. Thus Duchamp's ready-

Merce Cunningham and Dance Company in *Walkaround Time*, 1968. (Photo: James Klosty.)

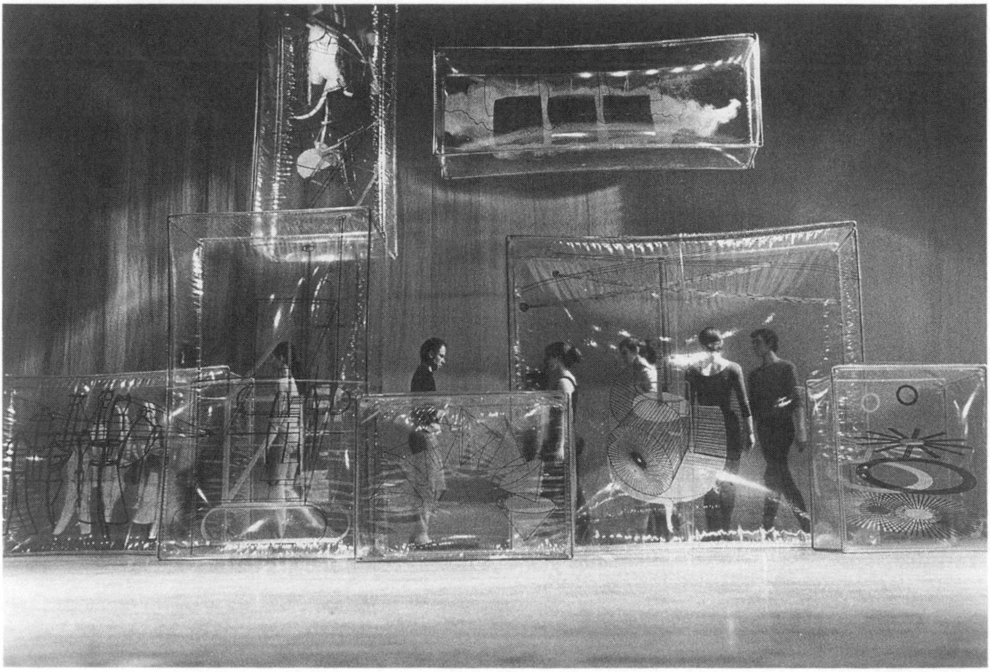

mades were not only reflexive (for example, about art) but revelatory (disclosing both something unexpected in itself and something with wildly unexpected ramifications about the concept of art). Cunningham, however, is not involved in revelatory reflexivity. His dances can be said to manifest (rather than reveal) a certain modernist conception of dance—that it is pure movement. And one can say that his dances are about dance if this means that they present the period-specific ideal of pure movement—that is, they are dances composed of what we regard as dancing and nothing else. But one cannot say that Cunningham's work explores and discloses the conditions of dance. Rather, it inhabits, manifests, and exercises them. One does not leave a Cunningham concert with the sense that one has garnered a new theoretical insight or question about the nature of dance; one leaves feeling one has just seen what is incontrovertibly dance.

For all the speculations about analogies and disanalogies between Duchamp and Cunningham, there is a concrete historical connection between the two artists. The dance *Walkaround Time* was choreographed by Cunningham in 1968, with décor by Jasper Johns based on *The Bride Stripped Bare by Her Bachelors, Even* and with music by David Behrman titled . . . *for nearly an hour*. . . . The piece was Johns's idea; Duchamp approved it; and it was Duchamp's suggestion that during the dance the pieces of décor be moved into a relationship that emulated the painting. As with many of Cunningham's collaborations, Cunningham saw the set and Johns saw the dance for the first time the day before the premiere.

Walkaround Time is a dance in two parts, with an onstage intermission for the dancers, for a company of nine.* It lasts for nearly an hour, and much of the dancing takes place behind or among transparent plastic boxes of various heights on which were silkscreened designs from *The Large Glass*, including the Chocolate Grinder, the Oculist Witnesses, the Sieves or Parasols, the Nine Malic Molds, the Top Inscription or Milky Way, and the Bride. The dance opens with the entire company arrayed on the stage, surrounded by the décor, saluting the work in an open-armed knee bend. Several movement themes and qualities thread throughout the work. Cunningham twice runs in place, at first behind the Chocolate Grinder and then behind the Malic Molds. Various partnering structures for two or three dancers imitate the rolling, turning, and interlocking of machine parts and gears (echoed by the grinding, whirring, crunching sounds, interspersed with long silences, of the music). Valda Setterfield and Carolyn Brown each perform slow solos that involve intricate shiftings of body parts on a minute scale (a shoulder, a hip) and then a large scale, while standing in place. Setterfield, Brown, and Sandra Neels each traverse the stage in slow-motion runs at various points during the dance, sometimes to the counterpoint

* An excellent film of *Walkaround Time*, made by Charles Atlas, is available. For purposes of cross-reference, in describing the performance of the dance we refer to the dancers and actions recorded on the film.

motion of other dancers walking or swiftly running across the stage in separate zones. There are many entrances and exits, but this does not make the dance seem busy. On the contrary, the entire group is rarely onstage together, and the sparse look is accented by the stillnesses that often capture even those few dancers who populate the stage. Dancers turn in place, lift their limbs evenly and desultorily, take large steps, but then suddenly swoop circularly into new spaces or run off. During the intermission the dancers don robes, sit and converse, or saunter onto the stage, to the tune of cocktail music. In the second half of the dance, Cunningham changes from one set of clothes to another while running in place, Brown repeats and expands her solo, women are carried and lifted aloft and caught in leaps, a chorus of overlapping women's voices talks about *The Large Glass*, and finally the dancers pick up the plastic boxes to move them into their final arrangement center stage.

According to Cunningham and to several other company members, Duchamp was very much on the minds of all those who worked on creating this dance — both its designers and its performers. Cunningham has spoken of several direct references to Duchamp deliberately choreographed into the dance — the readymades, the entr'acte (recalling *Relâche*), and the awareness of time. In fact, there seem to be two different categories of references to Duchamp's works or ideas in *Walkaround Time* (aside from the décor and the music). First, there are direct allusions to Duchampian subjects. The most obvious of these is the solo in which Cunningham changes clothing while running in place — a direct reference to *Nude Descending a Staircase* that escapes few viewers. The solos for the women in the dance, especially Brown's solo, cast them squarely as aspects of the Bride. This is not a matter of obvious but vague correspondence; the three instances in which women move in "filmic" slow motion across the stage seem like analogies for the three cinematic blossomings the Bride is said to undergo in *The Large Glass*. Cunningham has said that the repetitions in the second half of sequences from the first half are his way of referring to the readymades. This interpretation seems to ignore the most obvious feature of readymades — their ordinariness. Yet there is a correspondence to readymades in the offstage behavior of the dancers made visible in the intermission.

Still other correspondences take the form not of allusions to Duchamp but, rather, of translations of Duchamp's ideas in *The Large Glass* and other works to the medium of dance. *The Large Glass* is, first and foremost, a complicated, fantastic machine. The overarching choreographic theme of *Walkaround Time* is mechanic, in terms of the style as well as the steps. It is not that the dancers mime robots or form themselves into machine parts à la Nikolai Foregger. The verticality of the spine in Cunningham's style here stiffens into a kind of rigidity. There is also a pronounced sense of mechanical action occurring in the dancers' bodies and in their interactions. Legs and arms lift and lower sequentially like so many levers. Slow turns that revolve around a still axis give the impression of so many bolts being riveted into the floor. And, as in the moment when Cunningham does a sidestep that moves him while creating the illusion that he is walking in place, often the dancers seem to be moved by outside forces rather than by their own bodies. And, of course, underscoring this mechanical aura are the motor, creaking, and grinding sounds of the musical score.

But further, this dance makes machine references of a very specific sort. *The Bride Stripped Bare by Her Bachelors, Even* is a special kind of machine—a mechanism for effecting sex through a series of convoluted, alchemical operations. That meaning is conveyed in *Walkaround Time* through the use of partnering, a traditional symbol in dance for sexual union. In this respect Cunningham's choreographic style is an appropriate medium for a translation of *The Large Glass*, for, not only does the machinelike grace of anatomical coordination and rhythmic repetition appear in many of his other works, but also his use of classical partnering techniques and subversions of such techniques is one of the hallmarks of his style. Cunningham's partnering is little remarked upon, perhaps because critics feel there is nothing unusual in partnering, while there *is* something unusual about the separation of dance from music or the decentralization of stage space. In Cunningham's dances instances of partnering become saturated with polyvalent meaning precisely because they are *not* lodged in a narrative, as in *The Sleeping Beauty*, or in some other poetic causal chain of events, as in many of Paul Taylor's ballets. In Cunningham's works the sexual meaning of the partnering act hovers in the dance, evoked by centuries of social iconography, but then dissolves, leaving a mysterious, vague feeling that resists categorization.

There are many moments of such fleeting but explicit contact in *Walkaround Time*. Cunningham carries Brown offstage. Brown leaps across the stage, led by a partner who holds her hand. Susana Hayman-Chaffey takes a flying leap, arms and legs outstretched to the sides, landing in a man's open arms in a moment that simultaneously signals coitus and the end of the dance's first half. The dancers coolly execute their maneuvers with machinelike detachment and precision; themes of passivity and of the quickening and slowing-down of action seem to act as both sexual and mechanical metaphors at the same time.

Yet another aspect of Cunningham's choreography is apparent here: his use of slowness and stillness. This quality makes him an appropriate choreographer for translating a painting or a sculpture, and it is especially apt here. Carolyn Brown seems to wax ecstatic in her steadily flowing turns; as she poises on demi-pointe for long moments, she seems to become the Bride exuding commands. In general, the frequent long stillnesses (and silences) in *Walkaround Time* seem to render it fixed, static, highly legible, and transparent—qualities especially suited to a painting/sculpture on glass. Where there is motion in this dance, there are often drastically contrasting rates of speed, as when one dancer runs in slow motion while another passes her, running in (actual) rapid time.

Thus, in the most salient features of *Walkaround Time* one finds references to Duchamp that are not actual uses of the latter's methods or materials but, rather, translations of certain themes in *The Bride Stripped Bare by Her Bachelors, Even* into the dance terms of the vocabulary Cunningham has already evolved. These elements of Cunningham's style are unique and make *Walkaround Time* a work that, stripped of its décor, we would still recognize as a Cunningham work, although we might be hard pressed to identify it as a work devoted to Duchamp.

III

The African-American Connection

12

To the Beat Y'All: Breaking Is Hard to Do

Chico and Tee and their friends from 175th Street in the High Times crew were breaking in the subway and the cops busted them for fighting.

"We're not fighting. We're dancing!" they claimed. At the precinct station, one kid demonstrated certain moves: a head spin, ass spin, swipe, chin freeze, "the Helicopter," "the Baby."

An officer called in the other members of the crew, one by one. "Do a head spin," he would command as he consulted a clipboard full of notes. "Do 'the Baby.'" As each kid complied, performing on cue as unhesitatingly as a ballet dancer might toss off an enchainement, the cops scratched their heads in bewildered defeat.

Or so the story goes. But then, like ballet and like great battles (it shares elements of both), breaking is wreathed in legends. "This guy in Queens does a whole bunch of head spins in a row, more than ten, he spins, stops real quick, spins. . . ."

"Yeah, but he stops. Left just goes right into seven spins, he never stops."

"There's a ten-year-old kid on my block learned to break in three days."

"The best is Spy, Ronnie Ron, Drago, me [Crazy Legs], Freeze, Mongo, Mr. Freeze, Lace, Track Two, Weevil. . . ."

"Spy, he's called the man with the thousand moves, he had a girl and he taught her how to break. She did it good. She looked like a guy."

"Spy, man, in '78—he was breaking at Mom and Pop's on Crotona Avenue in the Bronx; he did his footwork so fast you could hardly see his feet."

"I saw Spy doing something wild in a garage where all the old-timers used to break. They had a priest judging a contest, and Spy was doing some kind of Indian dance. All of a sudden, he threw himself in the air, his hat

---

Village Voice, April 10, 1981.

flew up, he spun on his back, and the hat landed right on his chest. And everyone said, 'That was luck.' So he did it once more for the priest, and the hat landed right on his chest. If I didn't see it, I would never have believed it."

The heroes of these legends are the Break Kids, the B-Boys, the Latino and black teenagers who invent and endlessly elaborate this exquisite, heady blend of dancing, acrobatics, and martial spectacle. Like other forms of ghetto street culture — graffiti, verbal dueling, rapping — breaking is a public arena for the flamboyant triumph of virility, wit, and skill. In short, of style. Breaking is a way of using your body to inscribe your identity on streets and trains, in parks and high school gyms. It is a physical version of two favorite modes of street rhetoric, the taunt and the boast. It is a celebration of the flexibility and budding sexuality of the gangly male adolescent body. It is a subjunctive expression of bodily states, testing things that might be or are not, contrasting masculine vitality with its range of opposites: women, babies, animals; illness and death. It is a way of claiming territory and status, for yourself and for your group, your crew. But most of all, breaking is a competitive display of physical and imaginative virtuosity, a codified dance form cum warfare that cracks open to flaunt personal inventiveness.

For the current generation of B-Boys, it doesn't really matter that the Breakdown is an old name in Afro-American dance for both rapid, complex footwork and a competitive format. Or that a break in jazz means a soloist's improvised bridge between melodies. For the B-Boys, the history of breaking started six or seven years ago, maybe in the Bronx, maybe in Harlem. It started with the Zulus. Or with Charlie Rock. Or with Joe, from the Casanovas, from the Bronx, who taught it to Charlie Rock. "Breaking means going crazy on the floor. It means making a style for yourself." In Manhattan, kids call it rocking. A dancer in the center of a ring of onlookers drops to the floor, circles around his own axis with a flurry of slashing steps, then spins, flips, gesticulates, and poses in a flood of rhythmic motion and fleeting imagery that prompts the next guy to top him. To burn him, as the B-Boys put it.

Fab Five Freddy Love, a graffiti-based artist and rapper from Bedford Stuyvesant, remembers that breaking began around the same time as rapping, as a physical analogue for a musical impulse. "Everybody would be at a party in the park in the summer, jamming. Guys would get together and dance with each other, sort of a macho thing where they would show each other who could do the best moves. They started going wild when the music got real funky" — music by groups like Super Sperm and Apache. As the beat of the drummer came to the fore, the music let you know it was time to break down, to free style. The cadenced, rhyming, fast-talking epic mode of rapping, with its smooth surface of sexual braggadocio, provides a perfect base for a dance style that is cool, swift, and intricate.

But breaking isn't just an urgent response to pulsating music. It is also a ritual combat that transmutes aggression into art. "In the summer of '78," Tee remembers, "when you got mad at someone, instead of saying, 'Hey man, you want to fight?' you'd say, 'Hey man, you want to rock?' " Inside the ritual frame, burgeoning adolescent anxieties, hostilities, and powers are symbolically manipulated and controlled.

Each segment in breaking is short—from ten to thirty seconds—but packed with action and meaning. The dancing always follows a specific format: the *entry*, a stylized walk into the ring for four or five beats to the

Frosty Freeze of Rock Steady Crew with Fab Five Freddy and Friends. (Photo: Martha Cooper.)

music; the *footwork,* a rapid, circular scan of the floor by sneakered feet while the hands support the body's weight and the head and torso revolve slowly—a kind of syncopated pirouette; the *freeze,* or stylized signature pose, usually preceded by a spin; the *exit,* a return to verticality and to the outside of the circle. The length of the "combination" can be extended by adding on more footwork-spin-freeze sequences. The entry, the footwork, and the exit are pretty much the same from dancer to dancer—although some do variations, like Freeze from the Breakmasters crew, who stuffs a Charleston into his entry, and then exits on pointe. But it is largely in the freeze that each dancer's originality shines forth, in configurations that are as intricate, witty, obscene, or insulting as possible. A dancer will twist himself into a pretzel. Or he will quote the poses of a pinup girl. He might graphically hump the floor, or arch up grabbing his crotch. Someone else might mime rowing a boat or swimming, or emphasize acrobatic stunts like back flips and fish dives. Sometimes two breakers team up for a stunt: imitating a dog on a leash, or a dead person brought back to life by a healthy thump on the chest. According to Rammellzee, a DJ who's gotten too tall to break, the set of sequences adds up to a continuing pantomimic narrative. It is each dancer's responsibility to create a new chapter in the story. "Like if you see a guy acting like he's dead, the brother who went before him probably shot him."

When you choose your moves, you not only try to look good; you try to make your successor look bad by upping the ante. That's one way to win points from the crowd, which collectively judges. Going first is a way to score a point, but so is coming up with a cool response, chilling out. Through the freeze, you insult, challenge, and humiliate the next person. You stick your ass in his direction. You hold your nose to tell him he stinks. You put a hand to your spine, signaling a move so good it hurts. But the elegant abstract dancing that couches these messages counts, too. B-Boys from the Bronx and Manhattan look down on the "uprock" prevalent in Brooklyn, a mere string of scatological and sexual affronts without the aesthetic glue of spinning and getting down on the floor.

Naming and performing the freezes you invent are ways of laying claim to them, though some poses are in the public domain. A lot of breakers are also graffiti artists, and one way to announce a new freeze is to write it as graffiti. Speed and smoothness are essential to the entire dance, but in the freeze humor and difficulty are prized above all. "You try to put your head on your arm and your toenails on your ears," says Ken of the Breakmasters. "Hard stuff, like when I made up my elbow walk," says Kip Dee of Rock Steady. "When you spin on your head." "When you do 'the Baby' and you balance on one hand and move your legs in the air." "When you take your legs and put them in back of your head out of the spin."

During the summers the B-Boys gravitate to the parks, where DJs and rappers hang out. Younger kids learn to break by imitating the older kids, who tend to outgrow it when they're about sixteen. Concrete provides the best surface for the feet and hands to grip, but the jamming is thickest in the parks, where the DJs can bring their mikes and amplifiers. During the winters, breakers devise new moves. Crazy Legs, of Rock Steady, claims the "W," in which he sits on doubled-back legs, was an accident. "Once I was laying on the floor and I kicked my leg and I started spinning," says Mr. Freeze, of Breakmasters. But inventing freezes also demands the hard daily work of conscious experiment. "You got to sweat it out." You don't stop, even when you sleep. "I have breaking dreams," several B-Boys have told me. "I wake up and try to do it like I saw it." Kip Dee dreamed he spun on his chin, "but I woke up and tried it and almost broke my face."

Part of the macho quality of breaking comes from the physical risk involved. It's not only the bruises, scratches, cuts, and scrapes. As the rivalry between the crews heats up, ritual combat sometimes erupts into fighting for real. And part of it is impressing the girls. "They go crazy over it," says Ken. "When you're in front of a girl, you like to show off. You want to burn the public eye, because then she might like you."

Some people claim that breaking is played out. Freddy Love disagrees. "The younger kids keep developing it, doing more wild things and more new stuff. We never used to spin or do acrobatics. The people who started it just laid down the foundations. Just like in graffiti—you make a new style. That's what life in the street is all about, just being you, being who you are around your friends. What's at stake is a guy's honor and his position in the street. Which is all you have. That's what makes it so important, that's what makes it feel so good—that pressure on you to be the best. Or to try to be the best. To develop a new style nobody can deal with. If it's true that this stuff reflects life, it's a fast life."

13

Breakdancing: A Reporter's Story

Breakdancing is a craze that has easily surpassed the twist for media attention and wildfire popular diffusion — its energy and ambition seem to symbolize the 1980s. It is also a richly complex phenomenon to examine. First, breakdancing is not an isolated form of expression but is integrally linked to rapping (a form of chanted poetry descended from black oratory), scratching (the music made from record-mixing techniques), subway graffiti, slang, and clothing fashion. To study breakdancing is to study an entire energetic urban adolescent subculture called hiphop, that has spread from New York City black and Latin ghettos across the United States and beyond the Americas to Europe, Asia, Africa, and Australia. And to analyze breakdancing and hiphop is also to consider the ways in which the spread of that subculture has inevitably fragmented and distorted it and to note how the popular global media serve as both imagery for and agent of hiphop culture. Second, because breakdancing builds its unique style on the solid foundations of the Afro-American dance repertory, it opens a window not only on the present youth culture but also on the history of black dance on both sides of the Atlantic. Its study sheds light as well on the continuous process by which folkdance is transmuted into theatrical dance and vice versa. And further, in terms of its own short history, breakdancing is particularly compelling because new generations of dancers arise so quickly on the heels of the old. The telescopic story of its permutations and transformations, as well as its tenacity and flexibility in the face of various changes, lets us observe the vicissitudes of an oral tradition in an incredibly short time span. And finally, partly because of its close relationship with the media, the observers and recorders of the form — myself included — are willy-nilly participants, since they have had such an enormous effect on its meteoric history.

In the fall of 1980, I received a call from Martha Cooper — a photographer, a visual anthropologist who specializes in children's play, and a working journalist. For several years she had been documenting subway graffiti (her book, *Subway Art*, with Henry Chalfant, was published in 1984). She told me that as a staff photographer for the New York *Post* she had been sent to a police station in Washington Heights the previous winter

Folklife Annual (1986)

"to cover a riot." When she got there she found only a few dejected-looking kids who had been arrested for allegedly fighting in the subway when they claimed they were dancing. Marty's interest in them was fueled by seeing the confiscated cans of spray paint and martial arts paraphernalia that marked them as part of the graffiti subculture. According to the kids, the cops had to admit defeat, drop charges, and release them because the kids proved conclusively that they had, in fact, been doing a shared dance. Marty asked them to take her back to the subway station and show her their dancing moves. She photographed them and took down their phone numbers. When she called me, she was just getting around to looking them up and asked if I would be interested in writing an article about this kind of dancing for the *Village Voice* (where I frequently wrote about dance and performance). It was something she'd never seen before — solo performance with wild acrobatics and poses — and she found it hard to describe.

But having a second look turned out to be harder than we bargained for. For one thing, these kids were shy about demonstrating their dancing for adults, even for two encouraging and sympathetic reporters. Their mothers disapproved of their breakdancing indoors, since they invariably knocked into the furniture, and they also disapproved of their breakdancing outdoors, since (although the dancing itself wasn't, after all, fighting) the activity seemed connected to all kinds of illicit behavior and institutions — like graffiti and street gangs. (The word *crew* replaced *gang* when the talk was of graffiti or dancing rather than fighting.) And the competitive nature of the dancing at times did lead, in fact, to actual combat.

A further difficulty for our investigation was that these kids — members of the High Times crew — assured us that this kind of dancing no longer interested them or their friends. It was out of fashion, they insisted. Roller disco was now the going thing. They ran a little karate school in the basement of a neighborhood apartment building, where they finally hesitantly showed us bits and pieces of the form. Even the name hadn't crystallized; when we tried to tell them (and afterwards tell new informants) what it was we wanted to see, they referred to it as "B-Boy," "rocking," "breaking," or even "that kind of dancing you do to rapping." We recorded some improvised a capella raps and they invited us to several occasions where they thought a jam would materialize, but by Christmas, when we went to the karate school's recital for friends and families, we had yet to reach our elusive goal — to see "the real thing." It occurred to us that perhaps the form was hibernating and would reemerge the next summer in the parks. It also occurred to us that perhaps this was, indeed, a fad that had appeared and already disappeared without attracting mainstream attention and that we'd missed our chance.

But we were determined to satisfy our curiosity before a possible summer revival, and though we continued to search for the form at rap concerts, school dances, and other events, we tried another method: we began to track down more breakdancers by sending out feelers among graffiti-writers. Henry Chalfant, Marty's colleague, was planning a slide show of his photographs of subway graffiti at Common Ground, a loft in Soho, to be accompanied by live rap music. When Marty asked him whether the graffiti-writers he knew did breakdancing and Henry discovered that they did, he decided to include that too as part of the show. A crew — Rock Steady — was found, and it promptly split itself into two for the sake of competition. The "fake" crew called itself Breakmasters. We supplied both sides with T-shirts ornamented with crew insignia — "colors" in hiphop slang, which serve as prizes in real jams, with the winner taking the loser's. At the time the T-shirts and the wide colorful sneaker laces were the most elaborate parts of the breakdancers' outfits. Later, crews developed entire uniforms as well as a style of layering and slashing clothing that formed a visual analog to the mixing and scratching of records by the DJs. Fab Five Freddy (Braithwaite), the graffiti-writer-turned-easel-artist who wrote Blondie's hit song "Rapture" and later would be the musical director of Charlie Ahearn's film *Wild Style*, served as both DJ for the event and knowledgeable informant for us. Rammellzee was the MC — an acronym reworked, in the hiphop manner, to mean "mike control" or rapper. As they all rehearsed for the upcoming "Graffiti Rock" show, we photographed, asked questions, and took notes (and even dance instruction); gradually other people dropped by to film and videotape the goings-on.

The form as a whole looked like nothing I'd ever seen before, though it did include very familiar moves. Its spatial level called to mind capoeira, the spectacular Brazilian dance cum martial art form that incorporates cartwheels, kicks, and feints low to the ground, but the two were dissimilar enough in shape and timing that capoeira seemed at most only a distant relative, and certainly one the breakdancers weren't acquainted with — at least on a conscious level. There was a Caribbean beat to the rapping and music that most often accompanied the early breakdancing — and rocksteady is a form of music related to reggae — but the dancing, though it shared with Jamaican ska and other Afro-American forms the use of pantomime and narrative capacity, wasn't a close relative of reggae dancing either. Though in certain ways breakdancing as a pastiche of pop culture in the 1970s and 1980s — with its references to TV, *Playboy*, comic books, kung-fu films, and even the spinning turntable — seemed utterly new, in other ways it was clearly a direct descendant of African and Afro-American dance traditions, from its format (a solo performer inside a ring) to its rhythmic structure (syncopated), to its movement vocabulary (the leg wobbles of the Charleston, the acrobatic spins of black dance from Africa to the flash acts of New York nightclubs, the mimed freezes), to its rhetorical modes (the boast and the insult), to its function (male exhibition and competition). It was a distinctive new dance, but one with a solid pedigree.

The term *breakdancing* continued (and continues) to provide food for research. In music, the term refers to brief improvised solos in jazz, often making use of a suspended beat and inventive flourishes. It was exactly the break in swing music that made it "hot." The parallel with breakdancing seems clear. When I first asked kids what *breakdancing* meant, they told me, "It's when you go crazy on the floor," and that it was the change in the musical phrasing that compelled one to break out into the most outrageous possible movements. As Fab Five Freddy put it, "They started going wild when the music got real funky," when the drummer's beat took over. The term *breakdown* refers to both the dance and the music of a nineteenth-century black vernacular dance, a kind of reel that entered the white repertory as well—and by extension entered American slang to mean a raucous gathering. But also, the *break* in vodun is a technical term that refers to the point of possession in the dancer, controlled by the playing of the drummer. And further, in French Guiana a traditional dance is called, in Creole, *cassé-ko* (breaking the body). Clearly this linking of ecstatic dancing, suspending the beat, and the term *break* itself is a continuing idea in Afro-American dance culture. And further, the various violent, destructive meanings of the word see their parallels in the scratching of records by DJs and the ripping of clothes in hiphop fashion.

In April 1981 I wrote the article for the *Village Voice* that would serve as the preview for Henry's concert, scheduled for two performances in early May. The response to the article was overwhelming. By the following weekend, three extra shows had to be scheduled and the Rock Steady crew had performance dates lined up at several summer festivals and filming dates for various television news specials. In retrospect, it seems it was that article that introduced breakdancing aboveground.

But Rock Steady's sudden fame had other repercussions. Before they could reap their rewards, they had first to pay for their hubris. After the first of the "Graffiti Rock" concerts, a rival crew, from Brooklyn, appeared at the performance space and threatened violence. Rock Steady was an uptown crew and had overstepped its turf, though it was never clear whether the Ballbusters, as this group was called, were rival dancers or simply fighters. Henry and the crew members decided to cancel the remaining shows. And our faith in what one breakdancer had told us—that breakdancing had replaced fighting among street kids—was shaken.

But the rise of breakdancing, and of the Rock Steady crew, was already unstoppable. What began as a folk form, a dance-game among adolescent boys that symbolically asserted various aspects of personal identity and group solidarity, became theatrical and then, in turn, was taken by its younger acolytes back out into the parks and streets. Every new performance situation initiated changes in the form. For instance, a few weeks after the "Graffiti Rock" show, Marty and I presented a paper on breakdancing with slides at a conference on the folklore of the Bronx. Members of the Rock Steady crew, entirely at home behind microphones and in front of a mesmerized audience, served as commentators, and the next day they were given a local roller skating rink to perform in. The space and the equipment inspired them to new heights of invention: breakdancing on roller skates, group choreography, open-field performance. In another few weeks they had already outgrown the status of folk performers as Henry Chalfant and Tony Silver, who had met as a result of the *Voice* article, filmed them competing with a Queens crew, the Dynamic Rockers, in another roller rink, for the documentary film *Style Wars*, which appeared on PBS in 1983. The logistical needs of the film crew created yet more stylistic changes in the dance form. For example, the man who ran the roller rink kept telling the kids to open up the circle to give the cameraman room. The next time we saw breakdancing in the park—by now people were jamming in parks again—we happened to run into Rock Steady. Crazy Legs, by now president of the crew, was walking along the edge of the circle telling everyone to open up the circle.

The widespread media dissemination not only changed but also for a time homogenized the form. What at first had been moves of idiosyncratic personal style, with imaginative invention at a premium, though firmly rooted in the basic conventions as passed on from older cousin or brother to

Headstand in Subway Station.
(Photo: Martha Cooper.)

younger apprentice, were copied ad infinitum and became fashion. At a party the following fall I saw a group of neighborhood kids my host had hired for the evening's entertainment and noted their stylistic similarity to the Rock Steady crew; I asked them where they'd learned to breakdance. From seeing it on television, they told me.

Rock Steady began performing regularly at the Negril, a reggae club in the East Village, and refining their choreography with the instant feedback of video as well as audience response; at first Chalfant set up some jobs and then they took on as their manager Kool Lady Blue, who organized hiphop nights at the Negril, then at the new wave club Danceteria, then at the notorious Roxy. The professionalization of breakdancing had begun: downtown choreographer Julie Fraad organized the Magnificent Force and gave their performances a narrative structure; Michael Holman managed the New York City Breakers; the Kitchen, a Soho center for avant-garde music, video, and performance, presented an evening of Rock Steady as part of their dance series. The independent filmmaker Charles Ahearn shot *Wild Style*, a musical with a fictional narrative that featured real graffiti-writers, rappers, scratchers, and breakdancers. Patty Astor (who in the film plays a white reporter who discovers hiphop culture as she researches graffiti in the Bronx) opened The Fun House disco. The Hollywood film *Flashdance*, with the Rock Steady crew, came out in the same year, 1983, and, though its breakdancing sequences lasted less than two minutes, it made the dance a national phenomenon. *Breakin'* and *Beat Street* followed fast, as did an entire stream of movies that hasn't ended yet. These films documented another phase in the development of breakdancing: its merger with the West Coast form, electric boogie, an upright style (as opposed to the floor-oriented breaking) inspired by robotics (as opposed to the martial arts imagery of breaking).

At the same time, breakdancing as an amateur activity proliferated. By 1984, you could buy several how-to-do-it books as well as even more numerous how-to-do-it videotapes. All over the suburbs, middle-class housewives and professionals could take classes at their local Y's and dance centers. (Much of this instruction, however, centered around electric boogie rather than the more physically demanding breakdancing spins and freezes.) And the road from amateur to professional could often prove a very short one, as kids took to street corners to perform for donations from the crowds of spectators they attracted. The very term *street dancing* had changed its meaning in regard to breakdancing, from private to public performance, from folk to theatrical status, from performing for one's peers to performing for money.

The meaning and nature of the competitive element of breakdancing have also taken on new dimensions. In its original, folk form, breakdancing was a dance-game, a cooperative (though not always friendly) competition in which kids tried to top one another in order to win honor and fame (sometimes symbolically expressed in tangible form by the above-mentioned "colors") not only for themselves as individuals but also for their crews. It was in the crucible of the contest that the form's moves were forged. Its vocabulary alluded to fighting in its use of martial arts maneuvers. That combative heat and pressure generated a style that was intricate, witty, raw, and flamboyant—inventive by necessity. The film *Breakin'* portrays (albeit in Hollywood fashion) just such a competition, where one senses that the dancing does metaphorically stand for fighting in proving power and virility. (Contrary to the norms of street life, in this movie women also enter into the fray.) As breakdancing became more theatrical, with public performances as interactions, the element of contest reemerged in a new form. At clubs like the Ritz and the Roxy, crews began to vie for cash prizes and movie roles in contests organized not by the kids themselves but by the club managements or movie producers; they were judged not by their peers but by panels of "expert" judges.

But with the rise of breakdancing on the Hollywood screen, yet another level of competition has appeared—the battle of the dance genres. From *Flashdance* to *Breakin'* to *Beat Street* to *Body Rock*, the plot of the hiphop movie inevitably takes a crucial turn when the youthful vitality and (literally) down-to-earth quality of the breakdancing is pitted against an entrenched form—ballet or jazz dancing—that is shown as effete, decadent, and creatively exhausted, if not downright offensive. The battle lines are clearly depicted as class lines. And, of course, breakdancing always wins.

Breakdancing was invented by a generation of kids raised on television, movies, radio, and video games. The relationship between the dance form and the mass media is densely layered, beginning with the use of pop culture imagery and with brevity of format, and evolving with the succession of responses to media coverage and dissemination. The very success of the form and of some of the dancers, in fact, seems an American dream-come-true that could only have been concocted in Hollywood. These kids' sensitivity to—and sophistication in the use of—the popular media is essential to the nature and development of this urban folk dance.

14

Lock Steady

I'm walking down Lafayette Street and I see some graffiti: DONDI ROCK ON BROADWAY WITH TWYLA THARP — TALKING HEADS. I'm trying to learn the basic breaking steps from the B-Boys, and Frosty Freeze tells me, "You gotta keep your head facing front while your whole body turns, then snap your head around at the last minute, just like in ballet." Toni Basil mixes white ballet dancers with black street rockers from Los Angeles in a remake of the four cygnets section of *Swan Lake*. Roll over, Tchaikovsky. Who says there's a separation between high art and popular art in America?

Of course, Western high art has always borrowed from folk and popular forms, both Western and non-Western, scoring a quick hit of vitality just when things threaten to get overrefined. You could look at the history of theatrical dancing, for instance, as a cyclical process that continually transforms vibrant social dances into legible forms for spectators. Twyla Tharp's appropriation of vernacular music and dance steps is nothing new; part of what went on in the original *Swan Lake* was Petipa's lively setting of czardas and mazurkas and polkas — nineteenth-century European equivalents of rock and roll — into an imperial jewel of ballet, encrusted with academic steps. But we sometimes forget that this kind of borrowing is a two-way street, and that in America traffic moves fast. Street artists borrow mainstream and avant-garde art. In dancing, steps and styles move from theater, film, and television to the street and back again. Our folk dancing updates its tradition daily, amalgamating Afro-American moves that reach back to ancient cultures with modern images of high-tech urban living, shifting from black to Latino to white culture, from kids to adults, with amazing fluency. And where do you draw the line between pop culture and high art? It may depend only on where you see it. Rock bands use film, video, theatrics, and choreography as sophisticated and far-out as anything postmodern artists are using. Graffiti artists paint murals on subways that quote Andy Warhol quoting commercials. Art school graduates form rock bands. And in New York the downtown museums and performing spaces show punk art that revels in "bad art" and trash imagery, and present street art and performance untransformed by the "trained" artist's hand.

This weekend at the Kitchen, the Soho center where all sorts of such

Village Voice, October 21, 1981.

exchanges have been going on for years, Toni Basil is bringing to New York a review of ten years of Los Angeles street dancing. Basil is a kind of one-woman exemplar of two-tiered art, standing with one foot in the entertainment world and one foot in the avant-garde. She has appeared in the films *Easy Rider, Five Easy Pieces, The Last Movie,* and *Greasers' Palace*. She has choreographed for Bette Midler on film and on tour, and for David Bowie's "Diamond Dogs" tour. Basil's choreography and video effects for the Talking Heads' *Cross-Eyed and Painless* are strangely surrealistic. Recently, Basil made a video album of her own, called *Word of Mouth*. Basil has become a choreographer in the entertainment world, but the real stars of her show at the Kitchen are the kids and the dancing she has been inspired by and borrows freely from. For ten years, Basil, who is white, has been documenting on film and videotape the dancing black kids are doing in Watts, and for eight years or so she has been organizing and producing theatrical and TV revues that feature street dancers. The Kitchen show will not only include Basil's documentaries but also dancers from the various groups with which she's worked: the Lockers, the Electric Bugaloos, and performers of a dance called the "Vogues."

In the early 1970s, Basil met Donald Campbell, also known as Campbellock, also known as Camelot, who claimed he invented a new dance form called "Locking." Combining elements of the "Football" and the "Funky Chicken"—most notably, the conspicuous flapping of elbows that is descended from the early Afro-American animal imitation dances—Campbellock improvised a new twist, a framing device that, in the competitive spirit of street dancing, called attention to his performance. Rolling his wrists in time to the music, he froze and pointed to spectators in a gesture that demanded all eyes turn his way. Toni Basil was amazed by "Locking," started bringing all her friends to clubs in Watts to watch people dance it—"It was like stumbling into a Busby Berkeley film," she remembers—and eventually organized a group of dancers, most in their early twenties, to perform the dance in a theatrical format. Although the Lockers had known each other, or known of one another, before Basil got them together, they had preferred solo forms and a freewheeling, competitive relationship, and had never been interested in organizing as a group. Under Basil's direction, they began putting their moves into set patterns, and soon were appearing on TV specials for Carol Burnett, Roberta Flack, and Doris Day. Each Locker brought his own specialty to the group. Fluky Luke, already famed as a cheerleader at Crenshaw High in Watts, specialized in acrobatics, Russian splits, and dancing on his toes. Penguin stressed a slow-motion walk and a heavy, waddling step. Slim the Robot introduced a mechanized somnambulist's mannerisms. Greg Campbellock, Jr., and Shabba-doo had a concept of unison movement that cemented the group.

Wearing outrageous uniforms of knickers, striped socks, thick-soled elaborate shoes, and fancy hats, the Lockers flapped, leapt, jumped, danced on their hands, and scoo-be-dooed to music by the O'Jays, Sly and the Family Stone, James Brown, and Joe Tex. They did foot stomps and chants, mimed killing roaches with well-aimed slaps of the hands on the floor. They perfected their elbow movements by practicing on refrigerator handles. In their choreographed acts, they danced with female partners—besides Basil, there were Pat Davis, Damita Jo Freeman, and Janet Lock. The women had their own specialties too, but essentially their dancing was background material for the more assertive, flashy, macho "Locking."

Inevitably, the move from street to stage diluted the form. The music became a problem, especially on television appearances—"Did you ever hear a TV orchestra try to play 'Jungle Boogie'?" Basil comments—and all sorts of compromises had to be made for the sake of programming and the camera. And Basil's own role as choreographer/producer was problematic. She often used a story format to tie the dancers together with narrative and characters, devising rock versions of *Little Red Riding Hat, Casey at Bat*, and rechoreographing the prologue to *West Side Story*. But "Locking" was essentially an improvisatory, solo, competitive form, and the demands of unison dancing and rehearsing sapped its strength. The Lockers preferred to go out dancing at clubs over pressing the stuff into molds at rehearsals and in public performances, and their dancing went from what Basil remembers as a fine, vital madness—"everyone jumping around and freely improvising while I frantically called the cues"—to a watered-down, refined, predictable act. Basil's own ambitions expanded after she worked with Midler and Bowie. She wanted to be more of a choreographer, and to bring her childhood ballet training—with Edna McRae in Chicago—into the act. "It seemed to me that ballet and ghetto dancing matched up when you saw them together. I thought there was an audience of rock people who could love ballet but weren't interested in the music, and I also thought the ghetto dancing held up as an art form to the ballet. Besides, as a choreographer I thought it was a heavy idea."

At the same time, a new dance form emerged among gay black dancers in Los Angeles: the "Vogues," also known as "Posing," or "Punk." But this was a black version of punk that had nothing to do with the frenetic style of white punk dancing. Andrew Frank, Star, Tinker, and other male dancers Basil soon brought into her own shows knew about "Locking" but were interested in creating a feminine style. They took elements of "Locking," embroidering on the freeze-frame pointing of the finger and transforming the wrist-rolling into a gesture that moved decoratively around the head, and they added deliberately campy poses, quoting from *Vogue* magazine and from photos of movie stars like Greta Garbo and Marilyn Monroe. Shabba-doo of the Lockers worked out his own take on the "Vogues," turning transvestite imagery back into macho imagery by posing as a gangster or a muscle-man.

Basil's next hookup was with the Electric Bugaloos, members of the Solomon family and their friends, who had already organized themselves into a group. The disco craze of the midseventies had instilled new values of unison and precision in social dancing, and the Bugaloos have embellished all the smoothness and mechanization of dances like the "Hustle" and the "Bus Stop" with idiosyncratic gestures, pantomime, and special steps that have sources as diverse as cartoon characters, dada performance, African dancing, and silent film comedy. Their names are indicative of their specialties: Bugaloo Sam, Poppin' Pete, Puppet Boozer, Robot Dave, Ticking William, Creepin' Sid.

Wearing costumes that are part pure elegance, part funk—ultra-baggy pants, vests, ties, shirts, and canvas round-toed shoes, all in shades of gray, black, and white—the Bugaloos have developed a style that, for all its diverse motions, is essentially about physical dissociation. The "Tidal Wave," a virtuosic belly roll, harks back to Voudoun possession dances belonging to Damballa, the serpent god. The baggy pants emphasize the corkscrewing and jackknifing leg motions, but also create the illusion, as the torso twists, that the legs are walking away from the upper body. Arms spatter the air with sudden paroxysms, or else the hands flop loosely from upheld wrists. Feet slip backwards secretly beneath a body turned in profile, making the dancer appear the pawn of external forces. The body shudders with microscopic convulsions that make flesh seem to turn to jello. The dancers form lines and patterns, moving out two-by-two or four-by-four, bending over, standing up, and regrouping with a clockwork, deadpan slipperiness that conjures up superhuman robots.

To look at ten years of social dancing telescoped into an evening is to see a microcosm of American change. At the end of the sixties and into the seventies, the dance floor was an arena for letting go, for wildness, for individualistic creativity at its height. Ten years later, from Lincoln Center to Soho to Harlem and Watts, our dancing mirrors the fact that we no longer want to let go. We want to hang on, to survive, and the watchword is control.

15

Critic's Choice: Breakdancing

Breakdancing may have made it from the black and Latin ghettos of New York City to suburban shopping malls and the cover of *Newsweek*, but the surest sign that it's gained a foothold in mainstream American culture is its appearance in the dance studio and, fast on those heels, on how-to and feature movie home-video programs.

Social dance is a skill we usually think of as passing from teacher to student through live contact—whether the teacher is a professional or an older sister or brother—but in Western culture written notation has aided in the process, at least since the Renaissance. In the twentieth century, every shift in technology has afforded dance instruction new and more ingenious ways of shaping itself. Radio and records made it possible to spread local dance music around the world. In the sixties, a rash of "instruction" lyrics ("Put your hand on your hip and let your backbone slip . . .") taught whites to do black dances, while TV revolutionized dance fashions by providing mass training to teenagers via studio sock-hops such as *American Bandstand*.

With home video, dance instruction has been doubly enhanced: Not only do we get the appropriate music and the visual model, but we can also rewind to repeat and practice those elusive, difficult moves. Now, with breakdancing, the dance craze that has captured today's American, European, and Japanese imaginations, we have video instruction for the one dance form that seems most apt for TV tutelage, born as it was in a generation obsessed by the medium—its imagery, its rapid-fire pacing, its drama, and the instant stardom it promises.

Breakdancing was an invisible underground current for years. (It had already been pronounced out of fashion by kids in the Bronx, Harlem, and Brooklyn who created it, by the time it got its second wind and rocketed into flamboyant visibility in '81.) But it took to TV instantly, not surprisingly, since at times it seems like a live version of a videogame. Breakdancing and all the culture of hiphop (the umbrella term for graffiti, breaking, rapping, scratching, and their immediate social context) incorpo-

Video Review (December 1984).

rate and use media style and imagery in a homemade, funky form. As usual, though, the media have polished hiphop and homogenized it.

At this point, therefore, any reference to breakdancing has to distinguish between prefame and postfame versions of the dance. Prefame breaking was (and, for some, remains) a folk form that emphasizes playful competition just this side of gang warfare. The urge to top a rival gave rise to the virtuosic acrobatic maneuvers, done close to the floor, that originally embellished the real climax of the dance—the pose or freeze, a personal signature that also served to insult one's opponent and win status for one's crew. Postfame is, of course, the version of breakdancing familiar to most of us through the media. Theatricalized and sanitized, it emphasizes gymnastics over meaning, and it has broadened to include various forms of "electric boogie"—an upright, pantomimic, elegant articulation of body parts.

Nowadays, breakdancing is utterly common as a TV image, from ads for Burger King and the U.S. Army to events such as the closing ceremonies of the Olympics. Those who want to learn or simply to savor the spectacle now have a wealth of footage at their fingertips, from the ads they can tape to the four major movies so far released commercially that feature breakdancing, to the mushrooming quantity of how-to videotapes. The reviews that follow offer first a history of the image of breakdancing in movies—its increasing role and appeal—and then a survey of the instructional tapes. With the movies, the ratings reflect the quality of the breakdance numbers they include, not their overall quality as pictures.

Flashdance (1983) ★ ★ ★

Flashdance was the movie that first catapulted breakdancing to fame, although the breakdancing sequences last for less than two minutes of the picture. The plot here is that of an up-dated Depression musical in which the heroine wins her audition at a prestigious ballet school with her nerve, a throbbing disco song, and a jazz routine that features a well-placed backspin, inspired by seeing the Rock Steady crew breakdancing on the streets. The heroine's ripped clothing and T-shirts slung low on one shoulder set a new style that also fits with hiphop fashion.

The scandal about the movie that later emerged was that Jennifer Beals, the lead actress, didn't do the dancing. (The uncredited stand-in was Marine Jahan.) It's hard to tell who does the winning backspin in the audition routine. The rumor is that it's Crazy Legs, from Rock Steady crew. Earlier in the movie, Crazy Legs and other members of the crew appear for barely a minute to show off quite an eyeful of the standard breakdance moves: backspins, freezes, a mimed puppet duo, and what later would become renowned as the moonwalk—the illusion of being pulled backward while walking in place.

Also with Mr. Freeze, Frosty Freeze, Prince Ken Swift, others. Directed by Adrian Lyne.

Wild Style (1983) ★ ★ ★ ★

This witty, vibrant, fictional account of the travels of hiphop from the Bronx to Manhattan, from the subways to the art galleries, and from anonymity to fame lovingly and accurately portrays hiphop culture as a multifaceted whole and preserves some captivating early performances by the cream of the scene. Although the narrative is fictional, the actors are the graffiti writers, rappers, scratchers, and breakdancers who created hiphop, playing characters very much like themselves, including Fred Braithwaite (musical director and collaborator on the movie, who's formerly of the Fab Five graffiti crew and the author of Blondie's rap hit "Rapture") as an impresario.

The plot is thin — one graffiti-writer tries to hold out as a purist and still paint subway cars while his friends make murals in the Bronx and canvases in Soho — and the tone is romantic, but the performances and the spirit of the movie are exhilarating. That there are only four brief breakdancing sequences — two in a club setting in the Bronx, one in a playground rhythmically intercut with footage of a DJ scratching records and graffiti artists painting a bandshell, and one in the bandshell that is the picture's finale — is a comment on the lower status of breakdancing compared to other forms of hiphop when the movie was being researched.

But, in a larger sense, the picture is full of choreography, showing us that the music, poetry, and movement here are all intertwined, on the basketball court as well as on the dance floor, in the hands of a DJ spinning discs as well as in the pretzeled limbs of a breakdancer.

Also with Chief Rocker Busy Bee, Grandmaster Flash, others. Directed by Charlie Ahearn.

Breakin' (1984) ★ ★ ★

Released in the summer of '84, *Breakin'* was the first movie to focus on breakdance. The acting is terrible, the heroine is unappealing, and the scene in which the jaded jury is astounded by the vitality of breakdancing is lifted straight from *Flashdance*. But there are sixteen breakdancing scenes, ranging from a few seconds (the Spider walk that flashes on after the final credits) to a full ten minutes (a showdown between two crews at the Radiotron). And the dancing is good — or, in hiphop lingo, *bad*. What's more, you really get the sense of breakdance as something urgent, even vicious, and of its importance in the lives of the breakdancers in a number of ways: for the older kids, as a way to win honor as well as to be creative; for the younger kids, as a way to be initiated into social life.

The competitive aspect of breaking emerges in another sense here when as a dance form it competes against Broadway-style jazz dancing . . . and of course it wins. The scene is Los Angeles, where the electric-boogie side of the breakdance family originated, and the cast features some of the pros who were in the vanguard of its creation.

With Lucinda Dickey, Adolfo "Shabba-doo" Quinones, others. Directed by Joel Silberg. Choreographed by Jaime Rogers.

Beat Street (1984) ★ ★ ★

Beat Street is a kind of *Wild Style* writ large, Hollywood fashion, with a more complex (but just as romantic) plot and professional actors—with the notable exception of Robert Taylor, who plays the younger, breakdancing brother of the DJ whose career and love interests are one of the central narrative threads. He falls in love with a composer who lives in a ritzy neighborhood in Manhattan, which provides contrasts with life in the Bronx.

A second thread tells the story of a graffiti-writer who decides to "become a man," leave the streets, and make a home for his young wife and baby in an abandoned building, but who's killed when he falls on the electrified rail during a fight in the subway. The final scene is a tribute to his life, to his art, and to hiphop.

Beat Street, like *Wild Style* before it, shows the underlying moral and aesthetic code that links the various elements of hiphop and gives them a shared style and meaning. Plot development takes precedence over scenes of pure breakdancing, but there is a wonderful battle between two dance crews in a futuristic subway station, scenes in a Bronx club, and a fast-paced audition scene that presents a wealth of dancers, rappers, and DJs. This movie uncompromisingly locates hiphop within its social context—not shirking the violence and ugliness of street life—as well as showing its joyful, tender, and beautiful side.

Also with Rock Steady and Magnificent Force. Directed by Stan Lathan.

Breaking with the Mighty Poppalots (1984) ★ ★ ★

The best of the four how-to-breakdance tapes available (although the perfect one has yet to be made), perhaps because much of the control over the program seems to have rested with the dancers themselves, this tape offers instruction by the four members of a Washington, D.C., crew: Breakin' Bett (Steve Durham), Crazzy Leggs (Jerry Cooper), Sly C (Donny Walker), and Red Rooster (Dale Hurd). The dancers take turns, each one teaching his forte, demonstrating the basics and variants of popping, the moonwalk, various mime specialties (from facial expressions to the rope pull), and both elementary and advanced features of breaking per se.

After showing the moves, with the narrator talking the viewer through them and offering both encouragement and stylistic commentary, this how-to tape provides something none of the others do—a broader context to give all these separate moves coherence. We learn a routine, find out about crew-dancing through interviews and shots of the Poppalots performing, and even glimpse the roots of the form in inner-city fighting, with shots of "uprock" (which most resembles Oriental martial arts).

The instruction is very clear: The movements are broken down, put back together slowly, and then sped up while the narrator talks rhythmically and the dancers themselves chime in. The camera shows close-ups of crucial body parts, but also pulls back to show the configuration of the entire body for each move. Each sequence is well ordered and well timed, and the progression of the whole is nicely done. The Poppalots themselves are appealing performers with impressive physical technique and an infectious joy for dancing.

Produced by Harmony Vanover.

Let's Break (1984) ★ ★

This tape is notable for the fact that one of the instructors is a woman, a rare creature in the world of breakdancing. Like all four how-to tapes, pure breakdancing accounts for less than half of the lesson; it begins with electric boogie and moves on to the moonwalk (called gliding here), before getting down to the floor.

The approach is a little cutesy, with a studio rendition of a ghetto street as a set, endless graffiti titles, and a computerized voice constantly booming "Practice! Again! One more time!" But the camerawork is often ingenious, beginning with close-ups to focus on whichever body part is in motion and then pulling back as the movement is put together with the music, giving a good sense of the whole. The occasional use of slow motion distorts the style in the section on popping, but the overhead shots that are used help explain visually what a thousand words never could.

The emphasis throughout is on showing what the moves are, rather than explaining them verbally, though there are some helpful stylistic comments. Finally, this is the only tape that takes an appropriately laissez-faire attitude toward the form, reminding us again and again that, ultimately, the moves are just a raw vocabulary that each dancer will combine and elaborate on in his or her own way.

With Susie, Tony Rodriguez, and Frank Vega. Directed by U. Roberto Romano.

Breakin' in the USA (1984) ★

This tape is a lesson in the theory that dance consists of more than the sum of its movements. Here we learn all the moves, but without being shown how they fit together, what they mean, and in what manner they should be performed, we still have a long way to go before we're breaking.

The time spent on various components is out of proportion to their importance in the dance, and with long sections on how to warm up and endless previews, repetitions, and wrap-ups, you get the sense that the makers of this tape had a lot of extra time to fill. The solarization and other special effects are more distracting than helpful, the dancers look self-conscious, and the movements are so overanalyzed ("Now move your weight to the inside of the right knee. Now move it to the outside of your knee.") that most of the time you feel like the centipede who fell over when someone asked him which leg he starts walking with.

With David "Mr. Fantastik" Breaux, David "Fresh Jome" Robinson, and Mark Vincent. Directed by James L. Percelay.

Breakdance/You Can Do It! (1984) ★

The only good things about this tape are the scenes from *Breakin'*. (Some of the sequences are outtakes from *Breakin'*.) The setting is a breakdancing class taught by Odis Medley, and after he demonstrates one move quickly—often telling you to make twists and turns that leave your back to the TV set—you get to see his students practicing it. Gee, thanks, Odis.

Instead of using the music as a way to propel you into the dance, Medley drones out a relentless eight-count phrase, like a parody of a jaded Broadway musical director; only at the end of each section does he reward you with a song to dance to. Missing information is a problem, too. In teaching the moonwalk, he leaves out the crucial element of which foot takes the weight, and his suggestions for improvisation are downright embarrassing. ("You can use an everyday situation—like eating! Ooh, that spaghetti is good!") The camerawork only makes things worse.

But this tape has one virtue: When the students strut their stuff in the final jam, we see that—while one's become a virtuoso—anyone *can* do it.

16

Breaking

Breakdancing is a style of competitive, acrobatic, and pantomimic dancing. It began as a kind of game, a friendly contest in which black and Hispanic teenagers outdid one another with outrageous physical contortions, spins, and back flips, wedded to a fluid, syncopated, circling body rock done close to the ground. Breaking once meant only dancing on the floor, but now its definition has widened to include electric boogie, uprock, aerial gymnastics, and all sorts of other fancy variations.

Although breaking is the newest part of hiphop culture, it's the part that has made hiphop a media obsession. Five years ago the only people who had ever heard of breaking were the kids in New York's ghettos who did it. They didn't even have a definite name for the form—they sometimes called it "breaking," but they also referred to it as "rocking down," "B-Boy," or just "that kind of dancing you do to rap music." By 1980—when the form had already been around for a few years—they weren't even very interested in it anymore. This kind of dancing was a passing fad, they felt, that would soon be replaced by roller disco. But history was to prove them wrong. Not since the twist, in the early sixties, has a dance craze so captured the attention of the media.

By 1984 only a hermit could *not* have known about breaking. It had arrived, not only in the United States but also in Canada, Europe, and Japan. Breaking had been featured in the 1983 Hollywood film *Flashdance*, the independent hiphop musical film *Wild Style*, and the documentary *Style Wars* (which aired on PBS), served as the inspiration for the 1984 films *Breakin'* and *Beat Street*, and was rumored to be the subject of fifteen forthcoming Hollywood movies. Countless how-to books and videos had hit the market. Breaking had been spotlighted on national news shows, talk shows, and ads for Burger King, Levi's, Pepsi-Cola, Coca-Cola, and Panasonic. One hundred breakdancers heated up the closing ceremonies of the 1984 summer Olympics in Los Angeles. And Michael Jackson had given the form national currency.

Breaking made the cover of *Newsweek* in 1984. Newspapers all over the country regularly carried stories on its latest ups and downs. The paradox emerged, as you flipped the pages of the *Washington Post* or the

Fresh: Hip Hop Don't Stop. Co-authored with Nelson George, Susan Flinker, and Patty Romanowski. New York: Random House/Sarah Lazin, 1985. © Sarah Lazin Books.

Los Angeles Times, that breakdancers who'd come up in the ghetto were banned from city streets and shopping malls for causing disturbances and attracting undesirable crowds, while at the same time middle-class housewives and executives could learn to breakdance in their spare time at classes proliferating throughout the suburbs. Doctors added to the form's acceptability by giving medical advice on how to survive it unbruised. And the *New York Times* began using breaking as a metaphor even in articles that had nothing to do with hiphop.

By now, breakdancing was happening at bar mitzvahs, children's dance recitals, high school proms, college dances, in prison talent shows, at ballet galas, and on Broadway, as well as in clubs and discos—and, in a second-generation revival, in city parks and on the streets once again. Even President Reagan was delighted by breaking when he saw the New York City Breakers perform in Washington, D.C., at a Kennedy Center gala.

The media hype about breakdancing has changed both its form and its meaning. So to talk about breakdancing you have to divide it into two stages: before and after media. Before the media turned breaking into a dazzling entertainment, it was a kind of serious game, a form of urban vernacular dance, a fusion of sports, dancing, and fighting whose performance had urgent social significance for the dancers. After media, participation in breakdancing was stratified into two levels: professional and amateur. For the pros, breakdancing had become a theatrical art form with a technique and a vocabulary that, like ballet's, could be refined and expanded. On this level, competition took on new meaning. It was no longer a battle for control of the streets, for neighborhood fame, or to win your opponent's "colors" (T-shirt with crew insignia). Now cash prizes, roles in Hollywood movies, and European tours were at stake. For the amateurs, the element of competition had diminished. The appeal was a mixture of getting physically fit, tackling the challenge of breaking's intricate skills, and even becoming more like street kids, who've suddenly become stylish thanks to the meteoric vogue of hiphop.

Breaking first entered media consciousness when Martha Cooper, a photographer who had for years been documenting graffiti, was sent by the *New York Post* to cover "a riot" and found some kids—members of the High Times crew, friends and relatives from West 175th Street—who claimed they'd been dancing, not fighting, in a subway station. One kid demonstrated some moves to a policeman, who then called in the others one by one. "Do a head spin," he commanded as he consulted a clipboard full of notes. "Do the baby." As each crew member complied, performing on cue as unhesitatingly as a ballet dancer might pirouette across a stage, the police had to admit defeat.

Or so the story goes. But, like ballet and like great battles (it shares elements of both), breaking is wreathed in legends. Since its early history wasn't documented — the *Post* never ran Cooper's photos — it lives on only in memories and has taken on mythological form.

The heroes of these legends are the B-Boys, the original breakdancers, black and Latino teenagers who invented and endlessly elaborate the heady blend of dancing, acrobatics, and warfare that is breaking. Like other forms of ghetto street culture and like the other elements of hiphop, breaking began as a public showcase for the flamboyant triumph of virility, wit, and skill. In short, of style.

The intensity of the dancer's physicality gives breaking a power and energy even beyond the vitality of graffiti and rapping. If graffiti is a way of "publishing," of winning fame by spreading your tag all over the city, breaking is a way of claiming the streets with physical presence, using your body to publicly inscribe your identity on the surfaces of the city, to flaunt a unique personal style within a conventional format. The body symbolism makes breaking an extremely powerful version of two favorite forms of street rhetoric — the taunt and the boast. The razzing takes the form of insulting gestures aimed at your opponent, while the bragging is expressed through acrobatic virtuosity. Breaking is a competitive display of physical and imaginative prowess, a highly codified dance form that in its early stages served as an arena for both battles and artistic invention and that allowed for cracking open the code to flaunt personal inventiveness.

The High Times crew told the cops they were dancing, not fighting, and as breaking captured mainstream attention it was touted in the media as a transfiguration of gang warfare. Breaking may be a stylized, rhythmic, aesthetically framed form of combat — but it still escalates, at times, into actual violence. Peace is volatile when honor is at stake, and the physical heat of the form itself makes for situations that are highly combustible, as scenes from both *Breakin'* and *Beat Street* show.

Until breaking became frozen and legitimated by media hype, it was, like much of kids' culture in our cities, self-generated and nearly invisible to outsiders, especially adults — who just didn't want to even think about it or know about it, much less watch it. It was both literally and figuratively an underground form, happening in the subways as well as in parks and city playgrounds, but only among those in the know. Its invisibility and elusiveness had to do with the extemporaneous nature of the original form and also with its social context. Breaking jams weren't scheduled; they happened when the situation arose. You didn't get advance notice of a breaking "performance"; you had to be in the right place at the right time. In other words, you had to be part of the crew system that provided social order among the kids of the Bronx, Manhattan, and Brooklyn ghettos.

Since May 1981, when Henry Chalfant presented the Rock Steady crew at Common Ground in Soho as part of a graffiti rock show, breaking has taken to theatrical presentation like a duck to water. The first article on the form, by Sally Banes with photos by Martha Cooper, appeared in the

Village Voice just before the concert, giving breaking instant visibility. By the end of that summer, breakdancers had appeared outdoors at Lincoln Center and at other festivals, and endless filming had begun. The Rock Steady crew signed up for an appearance in *Flashdance*, and kids were already learning to break, not from older brothers and cousins on the street, but from watching Rock Steady on TV. Breaking had entered the public eye and left the underground for the mainstream, and this new theatrical context, with a style largely disseminated by the Rock Steady crew, quickly crystallized the form for spectators.

Through breaking, in its original form, all the pleasures, frustrations, hopes, and fears of adolescence were symbolically played out in public spaces. Breaking was inextricably tied to rapping, both in terms of its style and content and because the rap provides the insistent percussion that drives the dance.

The format of the dance was at first quite fixed. The dancers and onlookers formed an impromptu circle. Each person's turn in the ring was very brief—ten to thirty seconds—but packed with action and meaning. It began with an entry, a hesitating walk that allowed him time to get in step with the music for several beats and take his place "onstage." Next the dancer "got down" to the floor to do the footwork, a rapid, slashing, circular scan of the floor by sneakered feet, in which the hands support the body's weight while the head and torso revolve at a slower speed, a kind of syncopated, sunken pirouette, also known as the helicopter. Acrobatic transitions such as head spins, hand spins, shoulder spins, flips, and the swipe—a flip of the weight from hands to feet that also involves a twist in the body's direction—served as bridges between the footwork and the freeze. The final element was the exit, a spring back to verticality or a special movement that returned the dancer to the outside of the circle.

The entry, the footwork, and the exit were all pretty formulaic, with very little room for showing off personal style, although some dancers created special versions of these elements—Frosty Freeze, for instance, often exited "on point," walking on the tips of his sneakers. The entry, the footwork, and the exit were like the stock expressions and nonsense syllables that sandwich narrative content in a rap. They provided a rhythmic frame for the freeze, an improvised pose or movement, which broke the beat. They also provided a nicely textured, comfortably predictable backdrop against which the freeze stood out in bold relief. And, besides their aesthetic function, these segments were a way for the dancer to "tread water" between strokes, to free the mind for strategizing while the body went through familiar uninventive paces.

The simplest combination of a breaking sequence was entry-footwork-spin-freeze-exit. But turns in the center could be extended by inserting more footwork-spin-freeze segments. In other words, you might get entry-footwork-spin-freeze-footwork-spin-freeze-exit. And so on.

The entry, the footwork, and the exit framed the freeze, a flash of pure personal style, which was the most important part of the dance. The main thing about the freeze was that it should be as intricate, witty, insulting, or obscene as possible. "You try to put your head on your arm and your toenails on your ears," explains Ken of the Breakmasters crew. "When you spin on your head," says another B-Boy. "When you take your legs and put them in back of your head out of the spin." A dancer might twist himself into a pretzel, or strike a cocky salute. He would quote the sexy poses of a pinup girl, or perhaps present his ass to his opponent in a gesture of contempt. Through pantomime, he might extend the scatological insult even more graphically, pretending to befoul his opponent. Or he might hold his nose, telling the other guy he stinks. He might put his hand to his spine, signaling a move so good it hurts. Sometimes the dancers in the opposing crew joined in, razzing the performer from the sidelines.

Some of the freeze motifs prophetically rehearsed possible futures for the B-Boys. Several images quoted sports actions—swimming, rowing a boat—and even more suggested the military. The freeze celebrated the flexibility and budding sexuality of the gangly male adolescent body, and looked forward to sexual adventures or commemorated past ones. The gun imagery of the military pantomimes doubled as phallic imagery. A dancer would often grab his crotch or hump the floor for a memorable finale.

Another important set of motifs in the freeze section was the exploration of body states in a subjunctive mode—things not as they are, but as they might be—comparing and contrasting youthful male vitality with its range of opposites: women, animals (dogs, horses, mules), babies, old age, injury and illness (e.g., a heart attack à la Richard Pryor's routines), and death.

Various dancers had their specialties, especially in the freeze, but also sometimes in the other sections of the dance. Crazy Legs got his name from his rubber-legged way of walking into the ring, a move descended from the Charleston, and he also takes credit for the W, both face-up and face-down. Kip Dee claims he invented the elbow walk. As breaking moved from the streets to the stage, dancers teamed up to make group freezes, a development that has been elaborately extended over the past two or three years.

In the broadest sense, freezes were improvised. Few were devised on the spot; they were imagined and worked out in advance. But they allowed for the greatest range of individual invention, and the choice of which freeze to use at a given time was often an extemporaneous decision. The B-Boys used a variety of methods to create new freezes, including techniques, such as accidents and dreams, preferred by shamans and by the dadaist and surrealist painters and poets. Not all freezes have names, but to name your specialty—and to write it as graffiti—was a way of laying claim to it, a kind of common-law copyright.

In breaking as street competition, the freeze was the challenge that incited, a virtuosic performance as well as a symbol of identity. As each dancer repeatedly took his turn and, through a series of strategic choices, built excitement with a crescendo of complicated, meaning-packed freezes, he won status and honor for himself and for his group.

The B-Boys organized themselves according to neighborhood or family ties into crews, which were networks for socializing, writing graffiti, and rapping, as well as dancing, held together by a strict code of ethics and loyalty. Crews performed in a spirit of friendly competition at jams where the crew leader directed the group's moves. One kid would set up a challenge, and a B-Boy from the opposing crew would try to top him, or "burn" him. The crew leader was in charge of sending in new players to spell someone who had run out of moves. Onlookers—more friends, relatives, and neighbors—would judge the contest by consensus. B-Boys learned to dance in a system of master-apprentice, referring to each other as father and son—even though the "father" was usually only a few years older than his "son"!—and even chose names that reflected their relationship, like Ty Fly and Kid Ty Fly.

In those days, although there were some girls who joined in, most of the breakdancers were boys from the ages of about eight to sixteen. One reason that girls were the exception was that breaking was a specific expression of machismo. Part of its macho quality comes from the physical risk involved—not only the bruises, cuts, scratches, and scrapes, but also the risk of real fighting that might erupt. And part of it is the deliberate attempt to impress the girls.

Breaking was one kind of "rocking," which also included uprock, a more pantomimic, narrative style of dancing done jumping down and up to standing level, kicking, jabbing, and punching right in a rival's face, without actually touching. In uprock every move is intended to insult the opponent, and besides actual fighting gestures, a dancer might mime grabbing his rival's private parts, smelling his hand, making a face, and then throwing the offending odor back. Uprock is funny, but like a rapper's boast it has a mean edge.

The breakdancer's "costume" was born of necessity as well as style. T-shirts and net overshirts provide traction on the spins, and sneakers are important to the footwork. Their critical role in the dance is emphasized by making the feet look gigantic and by nearly fetishizing the shoes with embellishments like wide, bright laces loosely tied so that the tongues stick out. The insignia of the crew, as well as colors and outfits that coordinate with those of fellow crew members, play a part in intensifying group solidarity. And the overall look of militarized athleticism creates an image of power and authority. The other accessory for breakdancing is a mat, made of cardboard or linoleum, that originally protected the dancers from scraping against concrete.

For the current generation of B-Boys, it doesn't really matter that the breakdown is an old name in Afro-American dance for both rapid, complex footwork and a competitive format. Or that a break in jazz means a soloist's improvised bridge between melodies. Or that *break* is a technical term in Haitian vodun, referring to both drumming and dancing, that marks the point of possession. Katherine Dunham defines the term as "convulsive movements and sharp temporary changes in a ceremonial . . . rhythm." Or that in a different Afro-American culture, in French Guiana, there is an old dance called, in Creole, *cassé ko* (translation: breaking the body). All these connections have obvious links with breakdancing as we now know it. For the B-Boys, memory is short and history is brief; breaking started in the midseventies, maybe in the Bronx, maybe in Harlem. It started with Afrika Bambaataa's Zulus. Or with Charlie Rock. Or with Joe, from the Casanovas, from the Bronx, who taught it to Charlie Rock. "Breaking means going crazy on the floor," one B-Boy explained back in 1980. "It means making a style for yourself."

As Fab Five Freddy (Fred Braithwaite), the musical director for *Wild Style*, remembers it, breaking began when rapping did, as an intuitive physical response to the music. "Everybody would be at a party in the park in the summer, jamming. Guys would get together and dance with each other, sort of a macho thing where they would show each other who could do the best moves. They started going wild when the music got real funky"—music by groups like Super Sperm and Apache. As the beat of the drummer came to the fore, the music let you know it was time to break down, to freestyle. The cadenced, rhyming, fast-talking epic mode of rapping, with its smooth surface of sexual braggadocio, provided a perfect base for a dance style that was cool, swift, and intricate. The structure of the rap, with its play of quick, varying rhythms going on and off the beat within a steady four-square pulse, is like the off-balance, densely packed, lightning-speed pace of the breaking routine. The sense of inclusiveness, of all being in on a fun time together ("Everybody say ho!" "This is the way we rock the house!" "I *am*! We *are*!"), of turn-taking, is there both in the rap and in the dance. At times the lyrics of the rap even dictate the breakdancing moves, as the MC calls out the names of the dancers and the steps.

For the current generation of B-Boys the history of breaking may reach back only to recent memory—and even those stories conflict—but of course in a broader sense the history of breaking goes back to the slave trade, when Afro-American dancing was born. Breaking *is* something new and original, born of American ghetto culture in the seventies and (in its latest manifestation) in the eighties, but its basic building blocks are moves from the Afro-American repertory, which includes the lindy and the Charleston and also includes dances from the Caribbean and South America. Capoeira a Brazilian form of martial art that, since slaves were forbidden to practice it, evolved as a dance to disguise itself, bears a striking resemblance to breaking, with its crouching, circling, cartwheeling moves.

And, as the Africanist Robert F. Thompson has pointed out, capoeira is a pretty direct descendant from Angolan dance. But while breaking is not capoeira, but something unique, and while breakers may never have seen capoeira until others pointed out to them the similarities of the two forms, the two dance/sport/fight forms have the same roots, just as rapping and the collage of music that comes with it are new and at the same time firmly rooted in a tradition of black and Latino music and verbal style.

The main source of the movement in breaking is black dance, but, like the rest of hiphop, breaking is an exuberant synthesis of popular culture that draws on everything in its path. Some moves can be traced to the Caribbean, some to the black church, some to the Harlem ballrooms of the twenties and thirties, some to such dances as the lindy and the Charleston, and others to such diverse sources as kung-fu movies—which were immensely popular in the seventies—*Playboy* magazine, French pantomime, cartoons, comics, and TV.

Like any form of dance, breaking is more than the sum of its movements; it is also the way movements are combined, as well as the costumes, music, setting, audience, and the interaction between dancers and spectators. And its context. As an integral part of hiphop, breaking shares many stylistic features with graffiti, rapping, and scratching. Like wild-style graffiti, it emphasizes flamboyance, and the embellishment of the tag finds its parallel in the freeze. The act of writing graffiti is, despite its acceptance on canvas at the Fifty-seventh Street galleries, an act of defacement, and breaking, in its days before media hype, was an act of obscene gestures, a threat. In both graffiti and breaking, each piece or freeze is a challenge, a call to rivals to try to top this, and at the same time a boast that it is unbeatable. Graffiti, rapping, and breaking alike celebrate the masculine heroes of the mass media—Superman and other comic-book heroes, the Saint of detective book and TV fame, athletes, kung-fu masters, and great lovers. The obscure gestural ciphers of breaking find their parallels in the (deliberately) nearly unreadable alphabets of wild-style graffiti, the (deliberately) nearly unintelligible thicket of rap lyrics, and the (deliberately) barely recognizable music that is cut up and recombined in scratching.

Graffiti-writers make up new names for themselves, choosing tags partly on the aesthetic grounds that certain letters look good together; breakdancers, too, rename themselves, either after their dancing specialty or style—Frosty Freeze, Kid Glide, Spinner, Little Flip—or, like rappers and DJs, with an alliterative name that sounds good—Eddie Ed, Nelly Nell, Kip Dee. And they name their crews in a similar fashion: Breakmasters, Rock Steady, Dynamic Breakers, Magnificent Force, Rockwell, Floormasters, Rockers' Revenge, Supreme Rockers, Furious Rockers. Just as graffiti-writers mark off city territory and lay title to it with their tags, breakers claim space by tracing symbols on the streets with their dancing and penetrating public space with their ghetto blasters. To write on subway trains, to strike obscene poses, to wear torn clothing, to scratch records, to talk in secret codes, and to sing one's sexual exploits and other praises are transgressive acts. But it is a mark of our times that even such acts, vivid, proud, and aggressive, transmuting destruction into imaginative creation, can be defused as mainstream culture adopts them. Instead of dreaming of becoming revolutionaries, as they might have in the sixties, in the eighties the B-Boys aspire to be stars. And, at least for some of them, the dream has already come true.

After media exposure, the form of breakdancing immediately began to change as theatrical and other experiences—such as a panel at a conference on the folklore of the Bronx—were brought back to "home base." The folklore conference arranged a jam at a roller disco in the Bronx, and, soon after, Henry Chalfant and Tony Silver, the directors of *Style Wars*, shot a battle between the Rock Steady crew and the Dynamic Rockers (later Dynamic Breakers) at a roller disco in Queens. The stage was set for the scene at the Roxy, a roller disco in Chelsea, in Manhattan, that soon replaced the Negril as the venue for Wheels of Steel hiphop nights. When *Style Wars* was being filmed, the owner of the Queens disco kept clearing out the circle so the cameramen could get in. The next time Rock Steady was breakdancing in the park, the crew's president, Crazy Legs, was walking back and forth saying, "Open up the circle."

By now, the circular format has opened up so far it's become linear, for greater theatrical legibility. Less improvisation takes place as well-worn popular moves become standard. As is often the case in the development of a dance form, acrobatic transitions are elaborated, while the freeze, which once concentrated personal expression, competitive gestural dialogue, and group style into a single significant image, has dwindled away to almost nothing and sometimes even merges with the exit. What once was a dance for adolescents is now the terrain of young adults, professionals whose bodies are less gangly and whose higher level of skill is commensurate with their years of practice. Group choreography and aerial spins, reminiscent of the spectacular balancing acts of circus gymnasts, have added to breaking's theatrical brilliance, as has the influx of electric boogie, popping, locking, ticking, King Tut, the float, and other moves that are not break dancing per se, into the genre.

Locking is a comic dance that creates the illusion that a person's joints are stuck in one place while his extremities are swinging in wild, rapid circles. It was originally popularized in the early seventies by dancers on the popular black dance television program *Soul Train*, which spawned a dance group called the Lockers, whose flamboyance made locking and the related popping—where one segment of the body moves while others stay still—nationally known. Fred Berry, star of the seventies television comedy series *What's Happening!!*, Jeffrey Daniels, ex-member of the pop-funk vocal group Shalamar, and choreographer Toni Basil were key members of the dance troupe. Berry's bouncy body and beefy face were symbolic of locking's comic appeal. Daniels, a willowy stick figure with an enormous Afro, not only locked and popped, but did a mean robot (the moves look like they sound)—and, along with Michael Jackson, helped spread the moonwalk, a pantomimed illusion of walking backwards, via Shalamar tours and videos. Basil, a choreographer since the sixties, when she worked on the television series *Shindig!* and the legendary film *The T.A.M.I. Show*, worked throughout the seventies and eighties integrating the Lockers' moves into progressive film and video projects, such as her contribution to the Talking Heads' trailblazing "Once in a Lifetime" video. Another noteworthy ex-Locker is the Latin dancer Shabba-doo, who went on to star in the breakdance film *Breakin'*.

The electric boogie is a mimelike movement of the entire body, full of wiggles and robotic head turns, that refined the Lockers' movements into a more fluid, less jerky style. It was inspired by moves seen on a summer replacement television show hosted by mimes Shields and Yarnell. Kids picked up on it from TV, as they had locking, and embellished it, though the mime artists' white gloves are often worn by street dancers. Also via television came the King Tut and its kissing cousin the Egyptian after comedian Steve Martin appeared on *Saturday Night Live* in mock Egyptian garb to perform his hit single "King Tut." With his arms aimed out at sharp right angles, Martin resembled a talking stonecarving, and this move was quickly assimilated by youngsters.

All these moves—locking, popping, the electric boogie, the King Tut, and the Egyptian—were similar in that each emphasized arm and upper-body motions, and, unlike breakdancing, kept the dancers in basically upright positions.

As kids began to learn breakdancing moves by watching the pros on TV or at dance classes, instead of from breakers on the street, the performance style became homogenized. There's now more of a tendency to copy personal style directly instead of making one's own signature. Amateur breaking still happens—in fact, more than ever, as children as well as adults of all classes and ethnic backgrounds get down at school dances, country clubs, shopping malls, in living rooms, and even on street corners, not in the original competitive mode, but as a money-earning public performance.

The flexibility and resilience of breaking is evident in the way it incorporated electric boogie and other new moves, rather than letting itself be replaced by them. B-Boys vow that it will never die out but, like ballet, become an honored tradition. Interviewed by the *New York Times*, Kid Smooth, sixteen years old, imagined having a son and that son having a conversation someday with his friends: "One kid says, 'My father is a doctor.' The other kid says, 'My father is a lawyer.' And my kid, he says, 'My father spins on his head.' "

At a time when youth culture is again taking center stage in America, the rest of the country is fascinated by black and Latin kids' street life precisely because of its vivid, flamboyant, energetic style. It symbolizes hope for the future—born of a resourceful ability to make something special, unique, original, and utterly compelling out of a life that seems to offer very little. As Fab Five Freddy puts it, "You make a new style. That's what life on the street is all about, just being you, being who you are around your friends. What's at stake is a guy's honor and his position in the street. Which is all you have. That's what makes it so important, that's what makes it feel so good—that pressure on you to be the best. Or to try to be the best. To develop a new style nobody can deal with. If it's true that this stuff reflects life, it's a fast life."

17

A House Is Not a Home

Kool Lady Blue moved her theater of operations from the Negril to Danceteria while Negril is closed for repairs. The Negril is a reggae club where for the past few months, on Thursday nights, KLB Productions/Wheels of Steel has been presenting the best deejays, emcees, and performers in evenings of rapping, dancing, and entertainment. It's a fluid scene like a party in someone's basement where white, black, Latino kids mix to dance with one another, and to perform in every sense. To be out there. To get down.

At Danceteria, the immense space cast this heretofore friendly occasion in a new light. Take last week's event. Somehow the buildup was much bigger than the reality. The ads promised "girl rappers" and "electric boogie." Blue let everyone know that she had found the best dancers in the Bronx and tracked them down and they'd be performing on Tuesday at Danceteria. I got there early—around 10:30—and saw Take One and Crazy Legs from the Rock Steady breaking crew, there to watch the show too, maybe learn some new electronic moves. Not too many other people

Village Voice, April 13, 1982.

were there, but the deejays were spinning discs and a few people were dancing. Take introduced me to the guys who would be performing—Loose Bruce and Paulie Gee. They were over in a corner practicing unobtrusively and I could see that Blue was really right. These guys could segment their bodies with a drawn-out shudder that looked like a cold electric shock was passing slowly through their veins. Their feet always seemed bolted to the ground while their bodies swiveled robotlike along a vertical axis. Or else they'd do a slippery step, miming walking backward, as though they were stuck on a conveyor belt. And all the time their bodies were going through these contortions, they smiled with a spacy grin on their faces.

I didn't see any girl rappers around.

Take introduced me and Marty to Phase Two and we all went upstairs to talk because you couldn't hear anything over the music. The upstairs at Danceteria is decorated like someone's awful rec room from the fifties and numerous TV sets were broadcasting what looked like chance-edited imagery. It all seemed very homey.

At midnight we went back downstairs to see if the show had started. Well, some kind of show had started, even if it wasn't *the* show. The way the white kids were dressed up in punk regalia and dancing as outrageously as possible, not partnering, just presenting themselves as dancing beings, turned social dancing from an act of personal pleasure, or a way to dance *with* someone, to a mode of dancing *for* someone, anyone. At the same time, closer to the stage, the black and Latin kids, friends or competitors of the evening's acts, were performing in a much more conscious style, lining up in formations to mark the time of a reggae tune, in a kind of undulating marching step, or stepping out into a circle of space to underscore a funk tune with a spasm of footwork.

The space made everything strange. You kept waiting for the show to start but you weren't sure where it would happen. Loose Bruce and Paulie Gee would start up over in a corner and the crowd (by now it was crowded) would rush over to take a look. Then it turned out they were sort of only practicing. They sat back down and people started drifting back onto the dance floor. Around one o'clock Crazy Legs got down on the floor to start breaking and a wide circle cleared out on one side of the room. But when he went back into the circle to let someone else take a turn, the space stayed empty. Nothing happened. Finally a blissed-out white hippie bounced across the circle and people kept waiting, stubbornly but passively, for *some* kind of show to begin. You'd hear an emcee's voice start an announcer's rap and you'd go over to the stage—maybe now it would start—but then it would turn out to be a false alarm, just a recorded rap simulating intimate spontaneity.

But then around two, a live emcee introduced Silver Star, and two black women in silver outfits ran onto the stage formed by the wide steps leading up to the turntables. They rapped and sang a funky version of "Old MacDonald Had a Farm"—a string of nursery rhymes spiced up with sexual content with the refrain, "Ee-I-Ee-I-O." And then they ran off. Was that it for the girl rappers? After another half hour or so of just dancing, the emcee introduced the electric boogie dancers. Loose Bruce and Paulie Gee moved to the center of the dance floor. They smiled and popped, played a clapping game, passed the action back and forth—Paulie Gee mimed shaking hands and Loose Bruce mimed playing a guitar. And then they bowed and disappeared. Was that it for the electric boogie dancers? It was almost 3 A.M. and the place cleared out fast.

The evening was more satisfying in terms of watching the impromptu performances that coalesced from time to time out of the general dancing and music playing than in the planned acts. At the Negril the Wheels of Steel evenings depend on the intimate atmosphere where nobody notices what race, age, or style distinguishes you from anyone else, where different groups truly feel at home, where the entertainment parts of the evening dovetail comfortably with recorded and live rapping, dancing, drinking, sitting, visiting, partying. Negril's homey ambience is an appropriate setting for the meeting of punk style and street style; it makes public the private party, a youth culture occasion that densely layers all domesticizing symbolism of a special world. It is a world bound by special rules, conventions, and secrets, often inaccessible or invisible to outsiders, deliberately obfuscated—as in the complex gestural codes of breaking, the incomprehensible patter of rapping, and "wild style" graffiti, art forms through which street kids evolve their own social organization and education. They learn from one another in a spirit of competitive cooperation, exploring and articulating issues of identity, creativity, and autonomy; negotiating the complex spaces and meanings of the city; claiming territory an status for themselves and their groups. They inscribe their environment with their style, not only by literally writing their names and messages on subway cars and public walls, but also by tracing symbols on the ground through dancing and by penetrating public space with blasts of music or, the other side of the same coin, making space private with Sony Walkmans. Street style domesticates public space, turning the omnifarious city into a familiar, manageable place, making it human scale. Punk style also mobilizes themes of domesticity with its fifties nostalgia, and both streams of American youth culture share a sense of disenfranchisement that finds its expression not in political organization but in extreme physical sensation—drugs and dancing.

White America has perennially turned to black America, especially to black and Latin dance and dancing music, for revitalization in times of cultural exhaustion, and white punk culture is currently fascinated by black and Latin street culture precisely because of its vivid, flamboyant, energetic *style*. At the Negril this fascination seems to point to some kind of real fusion, some hope for the future, some alternate route to social harmony. But Danceteria, try as it might to be like home, can't seem to stop being a factory run by white entrepreneurs to market pleasure. And here the social relations were more reminiscent of the nineteenth-century minstrel show, or the Cotton Club of the twenties, where blacks performed for all-white audiences, than signposts for an uncharted future.

18

Breaking Changing

It's been almost five years since some cops arrested kids for breakdancing in the New York subway, thinking they were fighting, and Martha Cooper, then a *Post* photographer, began to track down this elusive form of adolescent street dancing. Now, with breakdancers in poster ads for WPLJ and the movie *Beat Street* plastered all over the subway stations, if a bust happened all a B-Boy would have to do to explain his activities is point. But what cop these days, whether in New York, Philadelphia, Oakland, Tokyo, or even Moscow, has escaped the media obsession with breaking? Hiphop culture—the world of breaking, rapping, scratching, and wild-style graffiti, with its special slang and clothing—was once an underground current (both literally and figuratively) but has now burst into the mainstream of art, fashion, and entertainment full flood.

The front cover of *Vogue* this month sports a beautiful (white) model in a graffiti-decked hat. Perhaps the same inner-city elementary school teachers who four years ago told me breaking and graffiti were equally criminal will be moved to buy just such a hat, or designer Terry McCoy's graffiti shoes or chairs, or Willi Wear graffiti clothes. They must have seen *Flashdance*. And I hope they'll see *Breakin'*, which, for all its technical shoddiness, has a real feel for the vivacity of the style and its social roots. Certainly they should see the two movie musicals that, on different scales, wonderfully capture New York hiphop's exuberance—*Wild Style* and *Beat Street*. At least fifteen more breakdance movies are said to be in production or preproduction in Hollywood.

Burger King ads on TV show breaking, McDonald's ads feature

Village Voice, June 12, 1984.

rapping, and General Electric plans ads that include graffiti. Thom McAn shoe stores have ordered 17,000 pairs of *Wild Style*-brand sneakers — with their rubber shell-head toes, they're the preferred style for breaking. A flooring business near Philadelphia advertises linoleum mats for breakdancing for only $25. Meanwhile, graffiti-based art sells in 57th Street and Soho galleries, and even President Reagan was delighted when he watched the New York City Breakers crew perform at the Kennedy Center. The Roxy has become legendary. The first of a rash of books on breakdancing, a how-to-do-it-yourself guide, has appeared. Hiphop has moved so far from its folk origins that when Steven Zeitlin tried to hire the Dynamic Breakers, originally a Queens neighborhood crew, for the City Play festival this weekend in Flushing Meadows, he learned their fee was out of his range — $10,000.

The media hype of breakdancing has changed both its form and its meaning. The form itself (like much of hiphop) has always drawn flexibly from TV, radio, magazines, comic books, and movies, so it's not surprising that media appearances create instant feedback. The original format for breakdance jams in neighborhood parks was a circle with the soloist in the center. I remember that when Tony Silver and Henry Chalfant, who made the documentary *Style Wars*, were filming Rock Steady and Dynamic Rockers at a roller disco in Queens in 1981, the owner of the place kept clearing out the circle so the cameramen could get in. The next time I saw Rock Steady breaking in a park, Crazy Legs, president of the crew, kept walking back and forth saying, "Open up the circle."

By now the circular format has opened up so far it's become linear, for theatrical legibility. Less improvisation takes place as popular moves become standard. Acrobatic transitions are elaborated, while the "freeze," which once concentrated personal expression, competitive gestural dialogue, and group style into a single, significant image, has dwindled away to almost nothing and sometimes even merges with the exit. What once was a dance for adolescents is now the terrain of young adults, professionals whose bodies are less gangly and whose higher level of skill is commensurate with their years of practice. Group choreography has added to breaking's theatrical brilliance, as has the influx of electric boogie, popping, locking, ticking King Tut, the Float, and other moves that are not break dancing per se.

Another way the media has changed breaking is that the performance style has become homogenized as kids begin to learn the moves by watching the pros on TV or at dance classes instead of from older brothers and cousins on the street. There's more of a tendency to copy personal style directly instead of making one's own signature. Amateur breaking still happens — in fact, more than ever, as children of all classes and ethnic backgrounds get down at school dances, bar mitzvahs, shopping malls, in living rooms — and even on street corners — not in the original competitive mode, but as a money-earning public performance. *Breakin'*, *Beat Street*, and *Street Dreams*, Peter Gennaro's musical at St. Clements, occasionally amalgamate Broadway-style jazz dance with breaking, to its detriment.

No doubt the book *Breakdancing*, by Mr. Fresh and the Supreme Rockers, will contribute to the whitewashing process. To begin with, it's hard to imagine that anyone could learn to do this kind of dancing by reading instructions, especially these instructions. But, then, the pictures are muddy, the prose repetitive and dull, informative descriptions lacking, and the data shallow when not downright wrong. Of the twenty-one lessons, only five are devoted to actual breaking moves, the rest to electric boogie. And readers are constantly warned that breaking is dangerous unless you study with a pro. Come on, folks! Breaking has only *had* pros for a couple of years.

The history of breaking, in this book, begins in New York in the seventies, instead of with the slave trade, when Afro-American dancing was born. Breaking *is* an original form, born in a particular context in the last decade, but its basic building blocks are moves from the Afro-American repertory, including the lindy and the Charleston, as well as moves from kung-fu films, *Playboy* magazine, French pantomime, cartoons, comics, and TV. But, like any form of dance, breaking is more than the sum of its movements; it is the way movements are combined, and also the costumes, music, setting, audience, and interaction between dancers and spectators. This book deals with the music, costumes, and dance imagery in an utterly cursory way. There is no analysis, for instance, of *why* certain poses are chosen, or *why* athletic clothes are worn (other than the obvious, ease and cost). Nor does anyone bother to mention the taste for military uniforms, special hats, wide shoelaces left untied, studded belts and chains, layered and slashed T-shirts, or to meditate on the significance of this deliberate, exaggerated iconography of the sinister and the outcast. And the book claims that as a result of breaking, gang warfare has stopped in the Bronx(!). Here's hoping Steve Hager's illustrated history of hiphop will offer more insight.

Hager also wrote the script for *Beat Street*, which opens this week and serves up some beautiful, sustained scenes of breaking at its hottest. Lots of different performers—including dancers, rappers, and deejays—are lovingly presented, and even the media influence on hiphop is wittily shown. The film uncompromisingly locates hiphop in its social context (not shirking from the violence and ugliness of street life), as well as in its joyful, tender, and beautiful side. Unlike *Breakdancing* and *Breakin'*, in *Beat Street* we can see that an underlying moral and aesthetic code links the various aspects of hiphop and gives them analogous stylistic features as well as a shared meaning. To write on subway trains, to strike obscene poses, to wear torn clothing, to scratch records, to talk in secret codes, and to sing one's sexual exploits are transgressive acts. The vivid, proud, and aggressive tones of hiphop transmute destruction into imaginative creation.

19

The Pleasin' in Teasin'

The last in a series organized by Tina Pratt to celebrate black dancers in America, this program had a special resonance because all the dancers in it were women. The black woman as dancer and the images she has managed to create within the stereotypical roles assigned to her could fill volumes. Pratt's program dealt with one of those roles. Shake and exotic dancers, in plain parlance, are striptease artists, and therefore, this tribute was in part an exploration of the artistry of striptease.

The performance took place on a Sunday afternoon at a crowded jazz club with a small stage. The context was entirely different for this kind of dancing, and the de-contextualization provided a new perspective on what really happens in the striptease performance. During the course of the afternoon each of the women presented her specialty, like a gift, to the audience, and this relaxation of the sexual tension usual in such performance created a spirit of generosity. That most of the spectators were singers, musicians, dancers, and other friends and associates of the performers also lent an air of friendly enjoyment. And there were as many women (if not more) in the audience as men; as viewers called out words of encouragement or appreciation, it seemed to me that, on this day at least, the women were dancing for other women.

Louise (Li'l Bits) Brown, a tiny, gray-haired, compact woman, started out the program with a mixture of comedy and eroticism. Dressed in a devil's outfit complete with horns, she not only vibrated movable parts of her anatomy with the expertise of long experience, but made everyone crack up as she toyed with the thick pink glittery devil's tail that swung between her legs. Betty Brisbane did a more conventional act, removing layer after layer of a seemingly endless supply of underwear of every description. Tina Pratt danced elegantly in a long gown, creating a friction between the seamlessness of the movement of the covered body and the articulation of individual body parts, once revealed.

Gerri Wayne did a remarkable drunk dance, wobbling on high heels and taking all sorts of objects out of a sacklike dress, until what at first

---

Village Voice, March 22, 1983.

seemed like an unattractive, misshapen, out-of-control, sexless person became extremely sexual and shapely partly through sudden immaculate control. Comanche let her hair down and swung it over the faces of unsuspecting targets in the audience and, as her body emerged from her American Indian-style costume, she twirled her breasts in opposite directions. Chinki Grimes cast angry glares at the viewers as she dropped articles of clothing with cold determination.

Beyond individual characters, special skills, and atmospheric costumes, the dancers were united in their incredible sense of performance style, a verve and flair that has less to do with the dancing per se than with the power of the gaze, the subtle handling of fabric to partially hide or emphasize planes of the body. They used expert timing to build suspense, and an equally knowledgeable sense of space—breaking the audience barrier, for instance, or turning suddenly to face away. All of these things are aspects of dance style, but when Pratt called up various women in the audience to sing or play music, they all showed the same masterful presence, from the ancient, wizened Cousin Ida to the Playboy bunny, perhaps still in her teens, who belted out a hot blues song. That presence takes shape in the dancing as a luxurious, confident enjoyment of one's own moving body, a pleasure in both sensing and revealing the dance as one makes it that exactly parallels the structure of the sexual act and seems, more than the particular movements of the dance, to supply the erotic edge.

In certain ways exotic dancing is like jazz music, which began as raunchy whorehouse entertainment. Historically, jazz music was an avenue open to black (male) musicians who were barred from "high art" musical performance when neither training nor jobs were available to them. Until late in the twentieth century it has been almost impossible for black women dancers to find jobs that did not involve sexually entertaining men. In fact, most of the lucrative jobs for black and white women dancers have always been provocative dancing. And the vocabulary of provocation draws on the body-oriented arts of Africa, on the hip-swinging, torso-undulating, physically proud dances of the various ancestral tribes of American blacks.

Black dancing has traditionally embarrassed mainstream white culture in the way that any dance of an unfamiliar culture shocks, intrigues, and revolts, because it is in our dancing that we most powerfully and directly manifest our views about the body. In Euro-American culture, one of the most deeply entrenched rules of dancing style is that the sexual power of the body is masked and controlled, rather than flaunted. The very exoticism of Oriental and African dance styles made them provocative in the nineteenth century, when striptease became an industry. I've seen West African tribal dances on film in which a woman turns her back to the dancing group, crouches forward, and vibrates her buttocks in exactly the same sequence favored by American shake dancers. But the meaning of the movement changes drastically when the context shifts.

Roland Barthes has written that French striptease is a kind of harmless family entertainment that takes the evil out of sex by innoculating a nation with a dose of clinically sterilized voyeurism. The climax of the striptease—the ultimate revelation of the body—does nothing more, he writes, than turn the woman into an undesirable object. American striptease, especially as seen in this program, can be something else. As they taunted the men whose attention they held, these women became wielders, not victims, of power. The importance of their act lay in the process of unveiling, in the dance of undressing, rather than in the static nude image produced by that dance, almost as an afterthought. In the limitations of the economic and social structures of striptease—of marketing sexual appeal—they have managed to let the brilliance and ease of performance shine through.

20

The Moscow Charleston: Black Jazz Dancers in the Soviet Union

In 1926, authentic jazz dance arrived for the first time in the Soviet Union when an American black musical revue toured to Moscow and Leningrad.[1] *The Chocolate Kiddies* reached Moscow in February 1926. Billed as a "Negro operetta," the show played at the Second State Circus in Moscow and then moved on to the Leningrad Music Hall, remaining in Russia for three months. The advance publicity tantalized Soviet audiences with its lure of American exotica and at the same time assured them they could be as sophisticated as audiences in Paris, London, and Berlin.

It was the middle of the jazz age in Western Europe. Although Russia was a backwater—uncharted territory for black dancers and musicians—

Society of Dance History Scholars Conference, Riverside, California, 1992.

this was the middle of the NEP period. From 1921 to 1928, the New Economic Policy allowed limited capitalism and foreign trade, opening windows between the Soviet Union, Europe, and America, and creating a Soviet consumer culture as well as a nouveau riche bourgeoisie. During this relatively lax time of economic openness and exchange, a great many cultural commodities were imported from the West. And jazz was one of them. But at the same time, a political struggle over the value and meaning of this cultural exchange ensued. On the one hand, jazz was seen as *the* symbol of Western decadence. However, official Marxist ideology simultaneously celebrated African-American culture as the expression of an oppressed proletarian class. Thus American jazz had a special, more complex and contradictory significance for Soviet culture than for the other foreign cultures to which it was regularly exported in the 1920s.[2]

The Chocolate Kiddies was a group put together in the United States by an émigré Russian impresario for a European tour, beginning in Berlin, in May 1925. Consisting of thirty-five dancers, singers, and musicians, the troupe was a merger of part of the cast of the recent Broadway musical revue *The Chocolate Dandies* and Sam Wooding's jazz band, which had recently moved from Atlantic City to Harlem to Club Alabam in Times Square. This troupe had already toured Europe and North Africa for nearly a year when they accepted the attractive offer made by Rosfil, the Russian Philharmonic Society, to visit the Soviet Union.

In fact, the program was not an operetta, as billed (perhaps in order to capture—however inadequately—its multimedia nature).[3] It was, as later ads made clear, a two-part show: the first act was actually *The Chocolate Kiddies* (a song, dance, and comedy revue) and the second act was a jazz music concert by Sam Wooding's band, which had served up the accompaniment in the first act.[4]

Wooding, the grandson of a slave and the son of a Philadelphia butler, had conservatory training in piano and music theory. During World War I he was in the army in France, playing tenor horn with the 807th Pioneers military band. When he returned to the U.S., he played jazz at nightclubs in Atlantic City. Although trained as a classical pianist, he remade himself into a jazz musician, he writes, to "[earn] my bread and butter."[5] The conflict between Wooding's symphonic aspirations and his commercial success in the jazz world led to a conservative big band approach that garnered an uneven critical reception in Europe. He was often considered "too symphonic," and even in Russia some complained that his band was not at all "hot."

The Chocolate Dandies had opened on Broadway in September 1924. Originally titled *In Bamville* in its pre-Broadway tryouts, it was the second black Broadway show composed by Noble Sissle and Eubie Blake, though this time without their earlier collaborators, the comics Miller and Lyles. Like this quartet's 1921 surprise Broadway hit *Shuffle Along*, which set the pattern for the 1920s black musical, *Chocolate Dandies* was a series of song, dance, and comedy routines straight out of vaudeville (and not far removed from minstrelsy), hung together by a flimsy plot. In this case it was a love story in a racetrack setting that allowed for scenes of Ziegfeld-like splendor. (The book was by Sissle and Lew Payton.) Although not a commercial success (it closed after ninety-six performances), this show got some favorable reviews. However, it suffered financially because it was much more expensive to run than *Shuffle Along* had been and it charged relatively low admission for Broadway. As well, its cast was raided by the road tour of another black musical, *Runnin' Wild*. But as Allen Woll suggests, "perhaps the major problem that *The Chocolate Dandies* faced was that it was condemned by the white critics for 'ambition.' "[6] *Variety*'s Chicago critic wrote: "The absence of spirited stepping . . . looks as though it were deliberate in a plan to make the whole piece 'high toned.' It is that, but the results are achieved at the expense of a genuine negro spirit."[7] Ashton Stevens wrote in the *Chicago Herald and Examiner* that "the show seems to suffer from too much white man."[8]

Despite its short run, *The Chocolate Dandies* was notable for several reasons (besides its simulated race with three live horses on a treadmill, à la Belasco's *Ben Hur*). One was that in it Josephine Baker became a star. Although still a member of the chorus line, in it she had a special role as a clown. As well, she had several solo turns, both comic and elegant, and she was given equal billing with the four female stars. Baker, however, did not join *The Chocolate Kiddies* tour because by then she had been recruited for the starring role in *La Revue Nègre* in Paris. Another reason the show was memorable was one of its musical numbers, "That Charleston Dance," in which Baker did an amusing parody of the dance that had recently swept the country. *The Chocolate Dandies* may not have introduced the dance to the mass public — the Charleston had arrived on Broadway a year earlier, in the show *Runnin' Wild* — but the unforgettable image of Baker parodying the dance in *The Chocolate Dandies* engraved it on posterity's imagination. And the precision chorus line of *The Chocolate Dandies* danced the Charleston to perfection. As Baker herself described it:

> The first impression made by the Charleston was extraordinary. . . . As if excited by the dance to the point where they did not care whether they were graceful or not, the chorus assumed the most awkward positions — knock knees, legs "akimbo", toes turned in until they met, squatting, comic little leaps sidewise. And then the visual high point of the dance, these seemingly grotesque elements were actually woven into a pattern which was full of grace and significance, which was gay and orgiastic and wild.[9]

Although Baker doesn't mention it, what was seen as awkward or grotesque by white eyes is, of course, an African-based bodily canon of bent limbs, angular lines, and acrobatic moves.

It was *The Chocolate Dandies*, reconstituted as *The Chocolate Kiddies*, that brought the Charleston to Moscow.[10]

Moscow audiences may only have seen their first authentic black jazz dance performance in February 1926, but they had earlier been exposed to African-American music and dance performers. As early as 1873, the Fisk University choir sang spirituals in St. Petersburg, and in 1910 a Russian couple, the Nazarovs, introduced the cakewalk to Russian high society. They had learned it from an African-American couple at a Petersburg dancing school. In prerevolutionary days, Russian music publishers couldn't turn out dance tunes fast enough. They not only produced versions of the cakewalk, but also the tango, the maxixe, the one-step, the Boston, and the foxtrot.[11]

However, after World War I, when jazz was spreading rapidly throughout Western Europe, Russia was slow to absorb it, for several reasons: revolution and civil war isolated the country; debates raged about the relationship of native proletarian music to high culture; the popular music industry was strictly licensed; and certain requisite instruments like the banjo and saxophone simply were not available.

Finally, in 1922 (a year after the new freedom of the New Economic Policy was introduced), the first Russian jazz concert was given in Moscow, but not by African-Americans. The Russian-Jewish poet, dancer, and avant-gardist Valentin Parnakh, having already sent reports home from Paris about the latest black music and dance, came home to spread the gospel of jazz: it represented, he wrote, not only modernity, but also freedom. Parnakh organized "The First Eccentric Orchestra of the Russian Soviet Federated Socialist Republic" and put on a jazz concert in October 1922. At his second concert, in December, he demonstrated the shimmy, the foxtrot, and the two-step. Though Parnakh's band was anything but authentic, it appealed to the public's imagination—and that of the government and the intelligentsia. The film director Sergei Eisenstein requested foxtrot lessons. Parnakh's band appeared in Vsevolod Meyerhold's production *The Magnanimous Cuckold* (1922) and then was featured in a key cabaret scene in Meyerhold's *D. E.* (1924) as a potent (and popular) symbol of the decadent West. Ironically, however, the band also entertained at government and Communist party functions.[12]

Jazz, its meanings, and its forms, quickly became a hotly debated topic and thus had already become an object of connoisseurship in the Soviet Union by the time first Benny Peyton's Jazz Kings and then, a few days later, *The Chocolate Kiddies* arrived in 1926. But authentic African-American jazz musicians and dancers had not yet been seen. Previews in the press included enthusiastic statements by artists and cultural leaders—

including Meyerhold, the theatrical directors Konstantin Stanislavsky and Alexander Tairov, and Petr Kogan, the president of the Academy of Artistic Sciences. The filmmaker Dziga Vertov augmented the publicity by including the group in scenes in his poetic agit-documentary *One-Sixth of the World*.[13] Depicting graphically how capitalism destroys human relationships, through parallel editing Vertov compares African-American entertainers both to slaves and to toys of the bourgeoisie. Thus several scenes from *The Chocolate Kiddies* are recorded on film. These include: a high-stepping chorus line behind a singer, with men in suits, spats, and straw hats and women in dresses; a tapdance done in the manner of a military drill; a pair of acrobatic dancers in overalls performing a choreographed fight; a plantation scene with some women in mammy outfits and some in short dresses doing the Charleston; and an "exotic" number with women in grass skirts and wigs shaking their shoulders, swiveling their hips, and pressing their thighs. For Vertov, the Chocolate Kiddies—and all African-Americans—are indubitably exploited innocents, systematically devoured by the capitalist machine.

I want now to analyze two items. The first is the most detailed review available of the dance aspects of the show, written by the dance critic Vladimir Blum for *Zhizn Iskusstva*. The second is a poster for the show by the well-known Soviet artists the Stenberg Brothers.

Blum complains that, although the publicity "kindled the public's interest in this exotic sensation," and "Meyerhold himself, having returned from his travels in enlightened Europe, declared that the Negro operetta was amazing, a work of genius, stupendous"; in fact: "What we were shown, it turned out: 1) was not in the least an operetta, and 2) was not even very 'Negro,' so to speak, since nearly the entire troupe are obviously mulattoes, and two ladies are quite white-looking. . . ." Blum writes (and I quote him at length):

> There is neither plot nor theatrical acting in the revue. It simply consists of an unconnected montage of specifically circus attractions. And why the scenery changed twice is completely incomprehensible. Maybe for an American proprietor of a remote ranch out of O. Henry these silly rags are in some measure convincing and even necessary. . . .
>
> The attractions actually work splendidly. But they are monotonous. In the end, they are all either tapdancing—squared, cubed, raised to the nth power—or partnered acrobatics. You can watch this genre for a half-hour—maybe forty minutes—but the performance stretches on for two hours. . . . By way of contrast, the furious hullabaloo of tap and acrobatic numbers breaks off from time to time into a "serious"—that is, a clearly non-Negro—solo or duet song. This pitiful singing is beneath any criticism, but is probably very pleasing to a sensitive and unexacting habitue of a New York . . . cheap dive.

> Because that is precisely the origin—the vulgar Euro-American "cafe chantant" (as not long ago such haunts of vice were called)—of this so-called performance, which came to us in the USSR "directly via steamship."
>
> Thus fifty percent of this spectacle is covered with a thick layer of filth. The women—a good half of the troupe—accompany and alternate the attractions with indecent, cynical body movements and dances. They are frankly untalented and "act" exclusively by means of their natural resources. There is nothing "exotic" in their dances and "plastique"; no ethnography ever spent the night here. . . .
>
> But one has to do justice to the men. They are masters of their craft. They accomplish the most puzzling rhythmic tasks with ease, with spirit, carefree as a child. In general these people have rhythm—and contemporary European music could learn something from them. . . .
>
> The premiere of the "Negroes" was quite a public success. The great majority, of course, was happy that it finally got to a "European" entertainment. But there were naive souls who didn't even suspect that they had ended up in the ambiance of a cheap Euro-American dive, where not only was a decadent bourgeoisie celebrating its orgies, but where it even reconstructed these unfortunate Negroes according to the image of its own likeness, forcing them to spice up their unaffected, simple-hearted gaiety with the most vulgar, most international obscenities.[14]

Blum's review, itself deeply ambivalent (and the briefer review he wrote under the nom de plume Sadko in *Izvestiia*), exemplifies perfectly the warring sentiments with which the Soviet tour of *The Chocolate Kiddies* was received. To begin with, the show isn't black-looking enough. Moreover, when the group presents "white" material, its performance is contemptuously dismissed as "beneath criticism." The women are vilified as lascivious and are accused of having no skills, but only "natural resources." The men, stereotypically branded as having "natural rhythm," are "masters of their craft," but at the same time they are also childlike. While it is true that, as we have seen, American critics also condemned *The Chocolate Dandies* for its "white ambitions," Blum's reaction is slightly different. For running through the entire review, and exploding at the conclusion, is a thread of anti-European and anti-American suspicion, rooted in Soviet xenophobia, that identifies all that is bad about this performance with the machinations of the white bourgeoisie and all that is good with primitivist fantasies.

Blum doesn't mention the Charleston, and he focuses on the tap-dancing. Yet the Stenberg Brothers' poster—which must have been made from a publicity photograph—clearly shows the woman, at least, doing the Charleston, and we know from the Vertov film that it was part of the show. The Stenbergs' poster, like Paul Colin's for *La Revue Nègre*, emphasizes the "blackness" of the show. The features are those of minstrel-show blackface. And, while the Stenbergs probably could not have known this, the man's pose is one of the most recognizable, iconic African-American gestures in the repertory. His left hand on his hip, his knees slightly bent, he holds out his right hand, fingers apart. An ancient Kongo pose, it shows up in generations of African-American and Caribbean dances.[15] Yet, in gender terms, the poster upholds the division Blum so bluntly draws up in his review. The woman's dress is short and revealing; the man's body is completely covered. Moreover, the man, wearing glasses, has an intellectual cast—suiting him to understanding the mysteries of "puzzling rhythmic tasks," while the woman is all body.

Both theatrical dancing and social dancing were profoundly influenced by *The Chocolate Kiddies*' ebullient performances of the Charleston, tapdancing, and other black dances. Shortly after their visit, the Blue Blouse movement—a network of actors and other artists that created "living newspapers" to promulgate Communist policy, mixing avant-garde techniques with popular variety-show formats—began performing their highly physicalized theater to jazz music, and even doing movements that look like jazz dance.[16] On the lyric stage, the avant-garde ballet choreographers Kasyan Goleizovsky and Feodor Lopukhov were influenced by the group.[17] And, on the popular stage, exhibition dance acts like that of Lydia Iver and Arkady Nelson demonstrated the new social dances.[18] Finally, after 1926, Soviet youth caught up with the rest of the Western world by Charlestoning the night away at clubs and private parties. They provoked the same old debates about the sexual element in these dances, but this time in a new context, for Soviet youth were supposed to be "high-minded and austere."[19]

The visit of *The Chocolate Kiddies* was both a catalyst and a symptom of Russia's Jazz Age. The troupe never would have even been invited to Moscow and Leningrad without the ground already having been prepared—politically, legally, socially, and artistically. However, their performances further inspired professional and social dancers. They became a point of reference as a symbol of truly excellent ethnic dancing in the Soviet dance world, and of freedom and individual expression in the larger world of Soviet society.[20] The new steps they introduced into the stage repertory were short-lived; those of the social-dance repertory persisted much longer. In certain ways the show reproduced and marketed racial stereotypes, which many Europeans, even the Soviets, were eager to receive. But some, like Vertov, criticized those stereotypical roles, and many saw beyond them to appreciate the artistry of these bravura performers.

IV

Other Subversions: Politics and Popular Dance

21

Stepping High: Fred Astaire's Drunk Dances

Fred Astaire made three "drunk" dances in three films, all in the 1940s. Although they are quite different from each other, all three dances are striking both in terms of their functions in the film narratives and in terms of their formal expressions of drunken sensations and drinking images. I will analyze here the New Year's Eve duet in *Holiday Inn* (1942); the solo number "One for My Baby (and One More for the Road)," in *The Sky's the Limit* (1943); and the "Heat Wave" production number in *Blue Skies* (1946), looking at the ways in which Astaire uses choreography to project social views and feelings of drunkenness, and sets up tensions between those qualities of inebriation and the notions of precision and agility his dancing embodies.

During the 1940s, the dominant public attitudes toward drinking and alcoholism were undergoing change. Before Prohibition, the prevalent position on alcoholism had been a morally judgmental one. Drunkenness was considered an immoral activity, the result of a moral flaw or spiritual degeneration, and alcoholism was simply the constant practice of drunkenness. Alcohol was thought to be intrinsically evil, but also special groups in society exacerbated the problem by tempting the morally weak. It was this kind of attitude that saw the legislation of temperance as a useful solution. By the mid-1930s, the repeal of Prohibition and the rise of Alcoholics Anonymous began to spread another conceptual model, that of alcoholism as a disease. Alcoholics were thought to be genetically determined, and therefore not morally responsible for their problem. But if they did not choose treatment for their "illness," they were doomed to continue, indeed increase consumption. However, in the 1940s, coinciding with the expanding practice of psychoanalysis in the United States, for the first time a more internal yet morally neutral model for conceptualizing alcoholism became prevalent. Rather than falling prey to social evils, moral flaws, or a predes-

CORD, American Dance Guild, Dance History Scholars Joint Conference, Los Angeles, California, 1981.

tined disease, the alcoholic was considered a product of unresolved childhood traumas which, if understood and resolved, through the will of the patient and the process of psychoanalysis, would provide the key to curing the alcoholism. Thus, with the rise of the biological and then the psychological model in the decade after the end of Prohibition, the social stigma of drinking and alcoholism decreased considerably.[1]

Still, the Hays Office Production Code of 1934 states that "the use of liquor in American life, when not required by the plot or for proper characterization, will not be shown,"[2] a precaution that harks back to the belief that external factors speed the moral degeneracy of the potential alcoholic. Prohibition attitudes and their lingering aftereffects added a darker note to the portrayal of drinking in film than had previously been known. Film had inherited certain modes of using drunken behavior, especially for comic effect, from theater—both popular entertainments and high art. John Durang, the American dancer, actor, and clown, wrote that in 1797 his clown act in John Bill Ricketts's circus included "[riding] the foxhunter, leaping over the bar with the mounting and dismounting while in full speed, taking a flying leap on horseback through a paper sun, in character of a drunken man on horseback, tied in a sack standing on two horses while I changed to women's clothes. . . ." He also "performed the drunken soldier on horseback, still vaulted, I danced on the stage, I was the Harlequin in the pantomimes, occasionally I sung a comic song."[3] John Towsen describes a burlesque equestrian act popular in the nineteenth century in which a clown disguised as a drunken audience member attempts a bareback horse ride. The clown Joe Pentland transformed the role, in the midnineteenth century, to that of a drunken sailor, and Dan Rice (1823–1901) made the inebriate a backwoodsman, a beloved, mythic comic figure of his day.[4] Towsen also tells of the British acrobatic team, the Hanlon-Lees, whose most famous production in the 1880s, *A Trip to Switzerland*, included among its antics "a brilliant drunk scene in which [the villain's] servants experience great difficulty in trying to light a candle while drinking, with one of them even sticking the lit candle, rather than the bottle, down the throat of the other."[5]

The American Broadway musicals and revues presented drunken behavior as pretexts for physical gags, as did the British music hall, and it is interesting to note in this context that Vernon Castle's early Broadway parts often demanded that he play the inebriated socialite, for example the role of Souseberry Lushmore in *The Midnight Sons* (1909). Similar comic dancing roles were the specialties of Jack Donahue and Nick Long, Jr. in the 1920s.[6]

Even on the ballet stage the role of the inebriate was mined for comic effect. George Balanchine's *The Triumph of Neptune*, itself inspired by the conventions of the old English pantomime, and choreographed for Diaghilev in London, 1926, had a scene in which "A drunken negro [danced by Balanchine himself] upsets the magic telescope and so all connection with the fairy world is severed."[7] Catherine Littlefield's *Café Society* (Chicago, 1938) not only named among its cast of characters an Intoxicated Gentleman, but even anthropomorphized drinks: Champagne, Rock and Rye, Gin, and Scotch and Soda.[8] There is a tipsy guest, Josephine, in Frederick Ashton's *A Wedding Bouquet* (London, 1937), the ballet accompanied by a reading of Gertrude Stein's text *They Must. Be Wedded. To Their Wife.*, and there is A Drunkard, as well as a tipsy Timid Man (originally played by Massine), in Leonide Massine's *The New Yorker* (New York, 1940), an impression of nightlife based on drawings from *The New Yorker* magazine.[9]

Charlie Chaplin's earliest roles in the English music hall troupe of Fred Karno included that of the inebriated "swell," as in *Mumming Birds*, a Karno routine that ran for more than thirty-five years, in which Chaplin first appeared in 1908 (at the Folies Bergères in Paris) and which a Karno company brought, again with Chaplin in the leading role, on tour to Chicago, New York, and San Francisco in 1911, under the title *A Night in an English Music Hall.* Chaplin went on to memorialize that music-hall character in many of his own films, including *The Rounders* (1914), *A Night Out*, (1915), and the quintessential drunk film *One A.M.* (1916), in which Chaplin's intoxication transforms his entire house into one huge obstacle course.[10]

Another performer who capitalized on the incongruity of drunken numbness mixed with unexpected agility was the magician Cardini. He relied less on comic business than on a surprising display of coordination, juxtaposed to the image of intoxication. The same age as Astaire, by 1927 Cardini, *né* Richard Valentine Pitchford in Wales, had developed his persona as an upper-class, inebriated London clubman, whose "hallucinations" of recalcitrant objects continually befuddled him.

> "Paging Mr. Cardini! Paging Mr. Cardini!" A spotlight picked up the slightly tipsy, monocled Britisher as he walked unsteadily from the wings reading a newspaper. The page took the paper and used it to catch the fans of cards that began appearing at Cardini's gloved fingertips. Obviously annoyed, he threw aside one perfectly formed fan after another. The page took his cape, cane, top hat, and gloves. Cardini steadied his hand, and after considerable effort fitted a cigarette into the holder he gripped between his teeth. The cigarette disappeared and reappeared several times to his distress. He finally lighted the cigarette with a match from nowhere. Then a sudden blast of fire above his head startled him. The red flower in his buttonhole whirled dizzily. The white silk handkerchief he tried to knot untied itself. Billiard balls appeared between his fingers; they changed colors and multiplied.
>
> Lighted cigarettes plagued him. Sometimes he was so astonished when one appeared that the monocle dropped from his widened eye. Then a

> lighted cigar materialized from thin air. He puffed on it contentedly as the page brought him his cape, cane, hat, and gloves. As he strolled toward the wings, he tossed away the cigar—and two more cigarettes. Before he walked off, a large, lighted meerschaum pipe startled him by its sudden appearance. Smoking this, he left the stage.[11]

Cardini's act ran at the Palace Theater on Broadway in 1927, and during the 1920s and 1930s he played extended runs in London at the Palladium Theater.[12]

Despite this theatrical heritage of an image of the inebriate as comically inept or uncannily dexterous, it is the darker, more tragic psychological image of the drunk and drinking—in fact, of life in general—that pervades the films of the 1940s. Robert Sklar notes in *Movie-Made America* that with the onset of World War II most American films—not only the classic *film noir* but even the "escape" comedies—had a gloomy, claustrophobic look.[13] The films of the 1940s temper the often comic (though also sometimes moralizing) message drinking conveyed in earlier films with a bleaker note. Compare *The Thin Man* (1931), for instance, with its continual, endearing references to and portrayals of liquor and drunkenness, with *The Lost Weekend* (1945), the exemplary film tragedy on alcoholism. The bars and clubs in *Holiday Inn*, *The Sky's the Limit*, and *Blue Skies* are as ubiquitous as those in the Astaire-Rogers films of the 1930s. But in Astaire's earlier films the drinking is never foregrounded—through dance—nor shown as problematic, as it is in the later movies.

All three of the Astaire films with drunk dances are set in environments where drinking is taken for granted. Yet, within these arenas, there are differences in the role alcohol plays. In the essay "On Alcohol and the Mystique of Media Effects," Andrew Tudor draws distinctions between four modes of portraying drink in movies and on television: *routinized background*, in which drinking is a normal feature of the social world of the narrative, taken as a matter of course and not in any way emphasized, a format in which norms of acceptable drinking behavior are presented, learned, and legitimized by the audience; *routinized foreground (nonproblematic)*, in which drinking is emphasized but without appearing to cause problems for the characters, at times even seeming positive (for example, advertisements for liquor on TV, *The Thin Man*); *routinized foreground (semiproblematic)*, in which drinking and alcoholism may be treated as problems, but the specific plight of alcoholism is not the central theme, in which different patterns of drunkenness are presented; finally, *exceptional foreground*, in which alcoholism is treated as a serious dilemma, and typification of ideas about alcoholism and alcoholics is created.[14] Using Tudor's classification, we can differentiate between the ways in which Astaire's drunk dances function to support varying social messages in the three films.

In *Holiday Inn*, Fred Astaire plays a nightclub performer, Ted Hanover, whose milieu always includes the social drinking of the sophisticated club set. One of his partners, Jim Hardy (Bing Crosby), decides to give up the performing rat race and take up farming. Their third partner, Lila Dixon (Virginia Dale), Hardy's fiancée, reneges on the retirement plan and remains with Hanover, both professionally and romantically. Crosby discovers that farming is even more taxing than crooning, has a nervous

Fred Astaire in Irving Berlin's *Holiday Inn*, Paramount Pictures, Inc.
(Photo Courtesy of Wisconsin State Historical Society Film Archives.)

breakdown, and then decides to open his Connecticut farm as a club open only on holidays, a rural but still sophisticated retreat for urbanites. Linda Mason (Marjorie Reynolds, sung by Martha Mears), a shop clerk, seems to be the only person who auditions for Hardy and, once they sing "White Christmas" together, not only does she get the job, but they fall in love. Meanwhile, Lila leaves Ted for a rich Texan. Ted arrives at Holiday Inn on New Year's Eve roaring drunk, dances a two-minute, totally disoriented jitterbug with Linda—which the guests at the Inn take to be a choreographed, comic dance number—and then promptly passes out. The rest of the film concerns his efforts to relocate his mysterious dancing partner, whom he was too drunk to remember; Jim Hardy's dissembling strategies to keep Linda for himself; and Ted's own tricks, once he finds Linda, calculated to win her away from Jim.

In *The Sky's the Limit*, the setting is also the nightclub world, in which drinking is part of the general background, erupting into dance only when the hero has been rejected by the heroine (although in *Holiday Inn*, Jim Hardy is arguably the hero). *The Sky's the Limit* differs from *Holiday Inn* in that, though the latter film makes reference to World War II with its patriotic celebration of the holidays and its political montage in the Fourth of July number, the movie is basically a comic revue with a sentimental plot threading through it, whereas the former, though it has its comic moments, has dark undertones throughout. In *Running Away from Myself: A Dream Portrait of America Drawn from the Films of the 40's*, Barbara Deming sets up several categories of the films that seem to project on screen the predicaments of the collective American psyche in the war and postwar years. *The Sky's the Limit* falls into two of Deming's categories: the war hero, tough, lonely, and cynical, whose ambiguous motives and uncertain actions, stemming from a crisis of faith, form the narrative suspense of the film; and the Hollywood Ariadne, the plot in which the good woman must rescue the embittered hero from his bleak fate, viz., confronting himself in the hell of living. In the latter plot, the hero is the rolling stone, the wolf, but the heroine is the aggressor, the one who proposes marriage though she originally rebuffed his advances, the one who guides him safely home.[15]

In *The Sky's the Limit*, Joan Leslie plays a photographer, Joan Manion, whom Fred Astaire, as Fred Atwell, alias Fred Burton, sees in a bar and tries to woo. He's a Flying Tiger who's slipped away from a hero's tour for some fun in New York; she's a society magazine photographer who tries to convince her publisher to let her do serious work as a war correspondent. At first Fred chases Joan, to her annoyance, but gradually they fall in love. He hides his real identity from her and she, thinking him a ne'er-do-well, proposes marriage and then tries to push him into getting a decent job. After he ruins an important job interview, she rejects him, he makes a tour of several bars and, in drunken desperation, he finally breaks into a dance of destruction, tapping violently atop the bar and smashing the glasses and mirrors. A tour de force of nihilism, ultimately the dance cathartically reveals Fred's assertion of self-control—confirmed when Joan shows up just as he leaves for his tour of duty. Yet the film ends ambiguously, leaving one to wonder whether Fred will return from that tour.

In *Blue Skies*, the drinking takes the form of a much more problematic routinized background, and, through metaphor, emerges as an exceptional foreground. Astaire plays a revue performer, Jed Potter, who tries to seduce a woman in the chorus line, Mary O'Dare (Joan Caulfield). But she falls in love with Jed's old vaudeville partner, Johnny Adams (Bing Crosby), who now has a habit of buying and selling bars, at which he sings. As Mary and Johnny's marriage teeters through compulsive business transactions, symbolizing Crosby's instability—an unmistakable transformation of the pattern of alcoholism—Jed still tries to win her love. Eventually Mary leaves Johnny, returns to show business as Jed's partner, and even makes plans to marry Jed. But they run into Johnny on tour and Mary realizes she still loves him. Jed begins to drink heavily. The drunk dance in this film, however, suppresses drunken behavior while simultaneously communicating internal sensations of intoxication. Here Jed must perform in a production number as though perfectly sober, though the previous scene shows he cannot walk a straight line. As he dances on a high bridge, Jed becomes dizzy and falls, never to dance again. He becomes a radio announcer, Johnny redeems himself with war work, and, in the end, Jed's nostalgic retelling of the story as a retrospective of Irving Berlin songs broadcast over the radio brings Mary back to be reunited with Johnny.

In all three films Astaire's character becomes drunk when rejected by a woman. But both the meaning of the drunken act and its consequences vary from film to film. In *Holiday Inn* two views are given of Ted's intoxication, adding up to an ambivalent view projected by the film itself. The guests at the Inn, and Linda as well, see the stumbling drunk as comic, putting on an act, whereas Jim, and Danny Reed, Ted's manager, know this behavior is not only real, but self-destructive. Yet beyond a hangover the next morning, and the undertone of tragic romantic loss, the drunkenness has no lasting repercussions in a negative sense. It even has positive connotations, for during it Ted has found the perfect dancing partner to replace the woman whose loss brought on the drinking jag. Drunkenness is almost a state of grace, of transformation, like Cinderella's when she meets the prince at the ball. Perhaps without experiencing this liminal state[16] Ted would not have made the transition between rejection by Lila and the resumption of work. And in his state of sublime semiconsciousness he improvises a prodigious dance. He loses Linda in the end, but not because of his drinking.

In *The Sky's the Limit*, the drunk dance again begins as angry, frustrated, even suicidal behavior. Astaire's helplessness is dramatized when the glass he is holding seems to jump from his hand and smash itself, inaugurating a ripple of violence that permeates the dancing and ends in an apotheosis of destruction. Yet this episode gets the anger out of Fred's system in an ultimately nondestructive way. After this purging the hero can flip his hat on his head and walk out the door with perfect coordination. In the end he "gets his girl." Yet, as I have noted, this new strength and romantic triumph is equivocal, subverted by a melancholy suspicion that the hero may never return, and that the control he regained was a grim setting of his jaw to meet his fate.

In *Blue Skies*, as in *Holiday Inn*, Jed is doomed to be rejected by the woman he loves. But here the drunken dance number is even more sinister than in the two earlier films. It is almost a reversal of the drunk dance in *Holiday Inn*, for again there are spectators, but here they must not know that the character is drunk. Only the heroine knows the dangerous truth, and knows her role in Jed's condition. And Jed is able to fake perfect coordination until the very end of the "Heat Wave" number, when his drunken state causes a disaster. It injures Jed, preventing him from working as a dancer again, but at the same time it provides the means—his radio broadcasting job—for finally reuniting his friends.

The three drunk dances are striking in that each one is a palpable expression of certain images and qualities of intoxication, yet all three are different from each other. The differences come, not only from the various narrative functions the dances play, but, primarily, from the choreography. In each case Astaire makes an entire dance out of one or two salient qualities.

The duet in *Holiday Inn* is only two minutes long, but it is a wonderfully detailed, complex study in disorientation and balance. It is necessary, for the plot's sake, that this dance be a duet, for Ted Hanover can only dance with a partner, and also the dance begins as a social dance rather than as a performance. But this narrative requirement adds a useful formal element, since we already have seen a duet, between Ted and Lila, with which to compare and contrast the New Year's Eve dance. "You're Easy to Dance With," which Linda had seen Ted dance with Lila in the New York City nightclub on Christmas Eve, is the song to whose reprise the drunk dance is performed. But the later version with Ted and Linda is a total inversion of the earlier number. The first duet is a straightforward, simple dance that emphasizes verticality of the body and unison movement between partners. On New Year's Eve, from the moment Ted and Linda bump into each other and fall into each other's arms, the dance is structured like a series of accidents, embellished with fortuitous meetings. The music is a fast $4/4$ rhythm, repeating two melodic phrases in a dogged ABAB pattern. The dance, however, changes constantly, in typical Astaire fashion. It begins in a standard closed partnering position. Astaire does a little scramble and slide with his feet, repeats it, and he and Reynolds step around in a small circle. They step-hop backward and forward, do a buck and wing, then open up to walk in a circle, but Astaire trips and switches directions. Regaining his balance momentarily, he ends up on tiptoe and circumnavigates, bewildered, as Reynolds orbits him, always just behind him. Astaire staggers about on the outside edges of his curled feet. The two locate each other and, resuming the jitterbug format, slide out from each other's arms to lean at arm's length—but Astaire keeps on leaning and falls down onto an onlooker, who tilts him back upright. After a quick pivot back and forth, Astaire gives Reynolds a fast turn, but her arms become tangled and he neglects to let go of them. As he walks away he unwittingly drags her, arms still tangled, on his back. Finally, the two unsnarl themselves, resume the standard partnering position, and, after turning in large circles, Astaire collapses forward and falls to the floor, exactly in time with the music.

The dance is everything a dance should not be; no one could be less "easy to dance with" than the drunken Ted Hanover/Fred Astaire. And yet, in its utter recalcitrance, the dance becomes a kind of gem of impossibility. The same actions that keep threatening to disintegrate into total chaos actually keep time perfectly with the music, changing movement motifs with every musical vamp. It is as if the character were willfully rejecting that side of him that is "easy to dance with," finding it useless emotionally and boring choreographically; being drunk frees Ted to improvise wildly, cracking open the jitterbug form and adding ornate embellishments flowing from his lack of balance. *Holiday Inn*'s drunk dance presents alcoholism as an only partly bitter anodyne, and Ted's disequilibrium as a blissful state of being—out of synch yet full of grace.

In *The Sky's the Limit* the drunk dance is a solo, as befits the lonely, "tough guy" character Astaire plays. Fred's frustration at realizing he's fallen in love with his conquest, Joan, and his anger at being rejected by her, spur him into an acrimonious, violent intoxication. The violence seems almost unconscious, externally motivated. The dance number begins when Astaire sets down a glass so hard that it breaks. Startled by the mutiny of the object, Astaire breaks into song, in the form of the archetypical confession to the bartender, "I've got a little story you ought to know. . . ." About four minutes long, the number plays itself out melodically in an ABAB pattern.

The dance begins with a ballet of hand gestures, a motif that continues throughout, almost as if Astaire's hands, like the whiskey glass, were separate objects with wills of their own. At first the hands play out a legible pantomime accompaniment to the lyrics. Astaire beckons the bartender, motions him to "set 'em up, Joe," points and rests his head on his fist in a gesture connoting frustration. In another bar, on the second stanza of the song, he motions to "put another nickel in the machine," flips out a coin, wags his finger to show that telling the details of his problematic romance is "not in a gentleman's code," and, this time, rests his head on his open hand, indicating resignation. On the B stanza, in a third bar—which is, in fact, the same bar where the character Fred had met Joan—Astaire stands with one hand in his pocket and the other holding a drink. He rocks back and forth—dramatizing the "tipsiness" of inebriation—and points and gesticulates volubly with the hand that holds the glass. Suddenly he throws down the glass, backs up startled—more mutiny!—and, shaking off the liquor and smoothing his hair, breaks into a total-body dance.

He beats out a violent tattoo with his feet, throws down his hat, and walks over to a pillar. Now the music switches into a reprise of "My Shining Hour," the song Joan had sung at the bar, and Astaire smoothly moves arms and body into a partnering position, reliving the dance with Leslie. But then the music changes again, and here the dance moves down the body, from hands and arms into feet and legs. Astaire jumps up on the bar, taps and slides first to the right end, then all the way to the left end. He comes back down the length of the bar whirling. It is an episode of pleased discovery, as if the storm had subsided in the turning and as if his body were surprising him now not with mutiny but with agility. He jumps down from the bar and violence erupts again: He kicks at the glasses on a table, smashing them, but, unsatiated, glances around for another target.

The music (still on a long B section) speeds up as Astaire jumps neatly on a stool, then the bar, drums out a barrage of taps in place and turns quickly with legs held close together in a parallel pirouette. His legs cling together, and their separation after each turn is like an explosive afterthought. He looks around him more and more urgently as he turns and, spying the three-section glass display in front of the mirrors, he aims three well-placed kicks in precise rhythm, jumps down to the floor, and throws the barstool at the mirror.

As the music returns to the conclusive A theme, Astaire smooths his hair (as he had at the beginning of the dance), collapses onto a barstool, and, as the bartender enters, sings a last, conciliatory stanza, resuming the gestural pantomime, pulling out his money, pointing, and making appeasing gestures. With his foot he flips his hat on his head and leaves the room jauntily, his left hand in his pocket as he opens the door, just as it had been when he broke that first glass. After a frenzy of activity and destruction, the number has left him cool, in control.

Besides the hand gestures, a number of distinct movement motifs thread through "One for My Baby," unifying the dance even while it progresses linearly toward mayhem. Even the motif of attack itself is stylized and streamlined, accelerating with well-timed bursts and accenting the storminess with frozen poses. At the same time that Astaire displays control and finesse—stopping his slide down the bar on a proverbial dime; stepping in complex rhythms; jumping up on the bar and back down to the floor with accuracy—this projection of control is constantly undermined with formulaic signals of drunkenness. These begin with the unsteady, rocking position at the beginning of the song, continue with leaning postures and the wavering path that lead Astaire to the pillar (where he leans again), and end with his shock of unrecognition when he peers into the mirror and sees himself, like a surprising hallucination. All these themes, added to the explosive energy and movements, and the outbursts of destructive violence, correlate inebriation, not only with loss of balance, but also with belligerence, drastic shifts of mood, and unpredictable fits of destruction.

As I noted above, in *Blue Skies* there is another ambiguous message conveyed about drunkenness. The choreography in "Heat Wave" makes legible two distinct images of intoxication. One is shown by negation, a suppressed image of appearances: Jed must appear sober, and so Astaire's stance in most of the number is alert, tense, cheerful, and agile. The audience of the film—though not of the revue in the film—knows this stance is a false one and makes the necessary logical transformations. The qualities of drunkenness conveyed by their suppression here, then, are carelessness, inattention, relaxation (or lethargy), unhappiness, and clumsiness. In fact, the previous scene has shown some of these qualities to be true of Jed. But far more striking in "Heat Wave" is the second, internal sensation that the choreography evokes. In its very structure—its windings and circlings, and its use of spatial levels—the dancing of Astaire, Olga San Juan, and a large corps creates a dizzying feeling that makes Astaire's ultimate plunge seem inexorable.

The "Heat Wave" number is staged as a tropical revue. The women are dressed in halter tops and full skirts, while Astaire wears a sailor's suit, and the rest of the men are dressed in islander's costumes. The song is a mambo, with a 4/4 beat in an ABA pattern. The narrative plot of the dance is quite simple: Astaire sees San Juan, flirts with her, and follows her up to the top of the bridge, where the fall takes place. But this progression from one side of the set to the other, then up the stairs, happens in the most roundabout, stylized way, full of hesitations, reversals, turns, and backings-up, as if the whole number were a giant breakaway mambo step. At first Astaire is seated on a platform. His glance is caught by San Juan, who is singing and swaying her hips, atop a bar. He starts up into a lunge. The intense articulation of levels in space, leading logically to the proscenium-high bridge, has started.

Astaire does a few tight turns, smoking a cigarette and advancing toward San Juan. The rising sexual tension mirrors the boiling heat described in the song. Astaire lifts San Juan down from the bar, the music changes to a suspenseful B motif, and the two move out into a clearing, where the group awaits them in the background. This moving into the clearing is a formalized stepping back and forth. San Juan moves first; Astaire follows, his back to her, his arms crossed. She moves forward, then back, a beckoning with her entire body; he stamps out his cigarette and shadows her, catlike. They finally face each other and continue the back-and-forth stepping, accentuating the held note at the end of each measure with a pause and a quick, distinct gesture—a different gesture for every measure. The lyrics stop, suggesting the dwindling away of conversation when serious lovemaking begins, and the music changes to an instrumental version of the A motif, and speeds up systematically over the next twenty bars. Astaire puts his arm around San Juan's waist, drops her and catches her (the same movement will be repeated twice on the top of the bridge), and both plunge into a full-scale mambo, stepping, swinging their hips, striking a side-by-side position, and even decorating their arm gestures with some Continental obliques. When the B motif returns to heighten the intensity, they break away from each other, hesitating, then whirling and each kicking a leg up behind them.

San Juan whirls to her knees, then leaves, while Astaire begins a fast, virtuosic tap solo to a jazzed-up variation on the A theme. His legs turn in and out, his hands flutter, held low; he executes a number of turns, tracing a semicircle away from the staircase, and then comes forward. He stamps, salutes, "trucks" for half a measure, wings, and ends the flashy two-minute catalog of stunts with a triumphant grin, his hands clenched, his body forming a proud stride.

Now a musical bridge starts the corps of dancers whirling. It is as if the solo had momentarily deflected the relentless vortex heading Astaire up on the bridge, to destruction. Astaire and San Juan resume their flirtatious back-and-forth pattern to the A music motif, but this time their pace is more urgent, and the whirling, jumping dancers around them have become a kind of obstacle course for their staccato chase. Reaching the staircase, both walk up it in a patterned, almost ceremonious design. Both revolve once to the right, step, toss their heads back and extend an arm, then run up a few stairs; next each revolves to the outside, then takes a step, tosses the head back, extends the arm, runs up more stairs. When they reach the top, they face one another and turn once again.

Once on the bridge—still to the A theme—Astaire turns his partner, drops her into one arm, obviously awkwardly (the first hint he gives of drunkenness or lost control), both whirl and then reverse direction. He drops her to one arm again, this time more slowly and carefully. Now San Juan stands still while Astaire spins around her on a circular path. But as we see his orbit widening we can predict his fall a split second before he dramatically puts his hand to his head, topples . . . and the orchestra concludes the final bar of music.

So many other parts of the film presage and buttress both the formal and substantive qualities of the "Heat Wave" number that one is tempted to read the whole movie as an antialcohol morality story. The nostalgic format makes a sentimental frame for a plot in which the alcoholic loses the girl, while the man who sublimates his alcoholism by buying and selling bars wins her. And true love triumphs over all obstacles, in the form of a solid, homey marriage. In formal terms the whirling that undoes Jed is the answer to the whirling staircase dance that begins the film, in the number "A Pretty

Girl Is Like a Melody," when Jed begins to court Mary. In terms of the social message, alcohol pervades each scene. Besides Johnny's string of clubs, there are endless mentions of drink, portrayals of Prohibition days, a song about the pleasures (chiefly alcoholic) of "C-U-B-A," Astaire miming a young man who enters a saloon and exits drunk in "Song and Dance Man," and Billy DeWolfe's Mrs. Murgatroyd act, in which he plays a matron who gets inebriated on her anniversary and complains about her marriage to her friend. (This small act would be interesting to analyze as a comic inversion of the sentimental plot of the film itself.) But, after the "Heat Wave" number, the glamor and comedy of the references to alcohol and inebriation are tinged with tragic consequence.

In these three drunk dances, as in most of his choreography, Fred Astaire manifests not only his choreographic inventiveness in moving a dance forward by constructing seemingly endless variations, rather than simply repeating movement motifs; he also plays with the formal incongruities of making a dance about physical difficulties that would ordinarily preclude virtuosic dancing.[17] The satisfaction in watching these dances stems directly from that incongruity, from watching Astaire the dancer triumph ingeniously over every hurdle Astaire the choreographer has contrived. The illusion of the loss of agility in fact, as we have seen, requires a great deal of skill. Yet it is a sly, never overt virtuosity we see in the drunk dances, a coup de théâtre of near misses and surprising resolutions.

22

The Men at John Allen's Dance House

In order to understand how the experiences of the men at Allen's dance house contributed to the dancing, it is relevant to look at the role of the dance house in the lives of those men. Therefore in this chapter we will consider the men other than Allen who attended the event—the customers, employees, and observers of various kinds.

The Customers: Seamen

John Allen's was known as a "sailor dance-house,"[1] a "sailor dive."[2] He must have opened the dance house especially to cater to seamen, for in the 1840s and 1850s New York port was at its height, crowded with clipper ships unloading their crews and cargoes; with markets, hotels, and businesses catering to the needs of the shipowner—chandlers, sailmakers, clerks, and so on; and with those who catered to, or rather exploited, the needs of the sailor ashore.

John H. Warren, Jr., was a detective who surveyed various types of houses of prostitution in *Thirty Years' Battle with Crime*. He describes the Water Street dance houses as "the lowest, if not the very lowest, link of the Upas of lewdness." Warren explains succinctly why the dance house thrived:

> It seems to have been invented originally by some fiend to catch the sailor on his return from a voyage. The first thing "Jack" wants when he gets on shore is a glass of grog, a female companion, and then a dance; and when all these are in his possession there is no happier creature alive, until the last cent goes into the till of the "lubber" who robs him, and then kicks him into the street. Armed with these, he will spend in a single week, the earnings of a year, and do it with a lavish generosity known to no other spendthrift.[3]

This essay was part of a collective research project written when I was a graduate student at New York University's Graduate Drama Department, for a course on nineteenth-century popular dancing taught by Gretchen Schneider. The other sections of the project were written by Ginnine Cocuzza and Sally R. Sommer; they concerned other aspects of the dance house run by John Allen, dubbed by journalists "the wickedest man in New York."

The changes industrialization had brought to shipping made it a growing business that by midnineteenth century paralleled the factory system. Instead of small vessels owned singly or in small fleets by families, ships were larger, parts of fleets that were owned by corporations, and carried heavier cargoes and bigger, unskilled crews. The hierarchy of authority on board, always observed when crises demanded discipline, crystalized into impersonal, stratified social systems. Though ships traveled faster, they went to places that were further away, and therefore voyages were longer. This created a new development in the lives of sailors that had a double effect: they were torn from sustained participation in communities on shore; and they became participants in new, cramped, transient communities—all male, without privacy but without conditions for close personal relationships, highly regimented in terms of time and space, and inescapable for the duration of the voyage. But these communities dissolved when the voyage ended, leaving the sailor once again without home, family, or community ties.

The nineteenth-century sailor was an outsider to normal American society. Richard Henry Dana, Jr., describes in *Two Years Before the Mast* the harsh authoritarian organization of a ship in the 1830s, likening the status of a sailor to that of a prisoner or a slave. Dana argues that the sailor's special code of dress sets him outside the pale of the community, though he reports from the vantage point of a landsman who perceives himself as the outsider:

> A sailor has a peculiar cut to his clothes, and a way of wearing them which a green hand can never get. The trousers, tight round the hips, and thence hanging long and loose round the feet, a superabundance of checked shirt, a low-crowned, well-varnished black hat, worn on the back of the head, with half a fathom of black ribbon hanging over the left eye, and a slip-tie to the black silk neckerchief, with sundry other minutiae, are signs, the want of which betrays the beginner at once. Besides the points in my dress which were out of the way, doubtless my complexion and hands were quite enough to distinguish me from the regular *salt*, who, with a sunburnt cheek, wide step, and rolling gait, swings his bronzed and toughened hands athwartships, half opened, as though just ready to grasp a rope.[4]

Sailors who jumped ship in one port, or who were unemployed, would soon find work—either voluntarily or through the ruses of a crimp*—on another vessel, perhaps one belonging to another country. There were more jobs than men. In the United States, the frontier could easily absorb the more industrious and ingenious of adventurers. The conditions on board ship would not have attracted any but those who were forced, by economic or social circumstances, to live there. And those who spent their lives on the dirty, crowded ships would be further demoralized,

* A crimp was a procurer of seamen, either by swindle or by force.

if not literally sickened, by the quarters. Dr. Heber Smith, writing on "Sailors as Propagators of Disease," complains that "our statute books define the limits of space which shall be allowed immigrants, but I am not aware that any such provision has ever been made for our sailors."[5] Smith quotes from a report describing living quarters in the forecastles of several American ships.

> "Steamship *Helvetia*, 3,327 tons. Lower forecastle twenty-seven feet from stem to bulkhead; twenty-four feet in width at bulkhead; seven and a half feet between decks. Light and air admitted by a hatch six by four feet, and two air ports, each nine inches in diameter, and which are closed at sea, occupied by twenty-eight men in two watches. Very dark; wet from leaky decks; air close and offensive. . . ."
>
> "Steamship *City of Antwerp*, 1,625 tons. Upper forecastle. Sailors' quarters on the port side, approached by a narrow and circuitous passage by stooping under a portion of the anchor machinery. Light and air admitted by passage of entrance; a four-inch stove-pipe hole, and five air-ports, open only in smooth weather; occupied by twenty-two men in two watches. Dark and damp; air close and offensive; berths, bulkheads, and deck, in a dirty condition. The firemen's quarters, on the starboard side, are similar to those of the seamen on the port side, but exposed to the further annoyance and offense of proximity to the passengers' water-closets."
>
> "Ship *Constantine*, 1,280 tons. Lower forecastles for starboard and port watches; twenty-three feet from stem to bulkhead; ten feet wide at bulkhead; seven feet between decks. Companion way steep and difficult. Light and air admitted by companion hatch, thirty inches square, and two air-ports closed at sea. Ten berths in two tiers. Dark and damp; air close, and charged with ammoniacal odors. Bulkheads and berths black for want of scrubbing. Deck slippery with filth. . . ."
>
> ". . . In the hundreds of total wrecks and disappearances occurring annually, if the actual truth in each case were ascertained and acknowledged, it is reasonable to suppose that an alarming proportion is due to the reduction of the working power of the crew by unhealthy quarters, unreasonable overwork, and, in some cases, by maltreatment."[6]

Smith concludes that the designers of these ships and the designers of some American prisons must have been governed by a similar desire: "To see in how small a space human life could be maintained."[7]

The lack of manpower, the crews hastily recruited in each foreign port, the amazing growth and industrialization, especially with steam, of the American shipping trade, was the subject for alarm in "An Appeal to Merchants and Ship Owners on the Subject of Seaman" by Robert Bennett Forbes in Boston, in 1854. Forbes warned that

> The American flag, the boasted stars and stripes, droops in sorrow and mortification at the position in which our commerce finds itself for want of American seamen! We are on the eve of a European war, and we may,

> by the chances of commerce, be involved in it; if we should be, whence are to come the "brave Yankee Tars" to man our ships—where are they? And if we preserve our neutrality, and go on increasing our tonnage, now amounting to about four millions of tons, where are we to get the bone and muscle to manage our ships?[8]

He compared sailors to children, blaming their inability to protect themselves from abuses at work and ashore on natural deficiency, rather than on the structure of their jobs.

> I speak as an *expert* in this matter, and I maintain that good order and discipline can no more be kept up in the navy and in the merchant service, without the *power* to inflict summary punishment, than it can be in a family without submitting the children to wholesome restraint. . . .
>
> I love sailors, (when they behave themselves,) and I would, therefore, treat them with parental kindness. I would feed them well, clothe them well from the ship's chest, when, by their improvidence, they have no clothes of their own; give them good quarters at sea, and, on shore, furnish them with seamen's homes, and, in their old age, give them an asylum in snug harbors; treat them tenderly when sick at sea, and on shore give them good hospitals: and, in return for these *duties*, I would exact the strictest obedience, even if obliged to restore the *power* to use the lash in certain cases.[9]

But he did acknowledge sympathetically the low status of the seaman on shore.

> We have been too much accustomed to consider the seaman, the foremast "Jack," as a mere machine—a mass of bone and muscle, to bear all the "slings and arrows of outrageous fortune" without a murmur, and for the smallest pittance. The seaman may be said to have no political existence; he cannot vote because of his absence, or for the reason that when present near the polls, he may not have been there long enough to warrant the exercise of this right. His wages are smaller, considering the amount of labor and the responsibility devolving on him, than are the wages of any other class of our working population. He must be up day and night incessantly, when duty calls; and, when the Sabbath, that great boon of the landsman comes, his rest depends on the faithless winds of Heaven. He has no day, no night which he can call his own, and when he begins to feel the effect of age, (and there are not many of this class,) he often has *no home*.[10]

Forbes told how foreign sailors managed to get past the law that a certain percentage of American ships' crews must be U.S. citizens; they simply Americanized their names and, often bribing Customs house personnel, were allowed to pass. "It is fortunate that American landsmen are not made as easily!" he remarked.[11]

The easy mixture of nationalities as ships replenished their crews at various ports around the world was troublesome to Americans who perceived the growing waves of immigrants as a threat to the country's stability and morality. With the advent of the Civil War and the abolition of slavery, blacks were seen as a similar threat: to working-class people they constituted a competing labor force; to middle-class and wealthy people they were an unpredictable social force, symbolizing chaos and loss of control.

Sailor's shanties (worksongs) tell graphically about the practices of various kinds of landsharks who capitalized on the shortage of labor.

De boardin' house masters wuz off in a trice,
  A-shoutin' an' promisin' all that wuz nice;
An' one fat ol' crimp he got cotton'd to me,
  Sez he, "Yer a fool lad, ter follow the sea."

Sez he, "There's a job as is waitin' fer you,
  Wid lashin's o' liquor an' beggar-all to do;"
Sez he, "What d'yer say, lad, will ye jump 'er, too?"
  Sez I, "Ye ol' bastard, I'm damned if I do."

But de best ov intentions dey niver gits far,
  After forty-two days at the door of a bar,
I tossed off me liquor an' what d'yer think?
  Why the lousy ol' bastard 'ad drugs in me drink.

Now, the next I remembers I woke in de morn,
  On a three-skys'l yarder bound south round Cape Horn;
Wid an' ol' suit of oilskins an' three pairs o' sox,
  An' a bloomin' big head an' a dose of the pox.

Now all ye young sailors take a warnin' by me,
  Keep a watch on yer drinks when the liquor is free,
An' pay no attintion to runner or whore,
  Or yer head'll be thick an' yer fid'll be sore.[12]

So warns "The Liverpool Judies," a capstan shanty that probably originated in the 1840s, describing a shanghaiing out of New York. "Whiskey Johnny," a halyard shanty* that sings the praises and rues the dangers of drink, carries a similar warning.

If yiz ever go to Frisco town,
Mind ye steer clear o' Shanghai Brown.

He'll dope yer whiskey night an' morn,
An' he'll then shanghai yiz round Cape Horn.[13]

* Shanties, or worksongs, had different rhythms according to the jobs they accompanied. At the capstan, where the crew hove up anchor, a long, constant haul was needed. Halyard shanties, used for setting upper topsails, upper top gallant sails, for bending sails, and other intermittent work, required shorter hauls with hitches.

James Holley Garrison, the brother of William Lloyd Garrison, was an alcoholic who became a sailor in the 1820s. It was the only occupation that could regularly provide him with employment, shelter, and clothing, while rationing out the liquor sparingly. (In the first half of the nineteenth century, the abuse of liquor, even by women, children, and clergymen, had reached alarming proportions.) Garrison served on many ships in his nearly twenty years at sea, including one in the British navy; on most of his voyages he suffered brutal treatment, including a multiple flogging after jumping ship in Cuba. Often, after getting paid, Garrison would find himself in port intoxicated and broke. His ship would have sailed with all his belongings, but without him. Or he would have been robbed of all his money while asleep. Or he would have spent it all, "laid it out in rum, treating all that came past, untill I became once more intoxicated. So hardened had I became that nothing could make an impression on my mind."[14] Constantly disoriented by drink and by the loss of his belongings and the instability of his employment, he would ship out again. Once, while in London,

> I took board with a man by the name of Wm. Chapman, a notorious crimp, who kept a dance hall for prostitutes on the corner of Ratcliff Cross. I had about 10 dollers comeing to me when paid off, which amounted in all to 60 dollers. My clothes I valued at one hundred if not more. I was pretty cunning and they could not get me to drink. One evening his daughter with the servent girl invited me into the ball room. I drunk some beer, and wether it was drugged or not I can not say. But I became insensible and awoke in the morning on the stair case, with my pockets picked and money gorn. I accused the girls of the robbery, and they abused me shamefuly. The landlord denied me my breakfast, said I owed him five shillings, and kicked me into the street. In vain I asked for my clothes, that I might sell some of them to pay him, and get something to eat for my self. But he turned a deaf ear to all my entreaties, and I was left to perish with hunger in the streets.[15]

Of the Water Street area in New York, the *Police Gazette* declared:

> Many of the houses here and the population, as well, subsist for one purpose alone, and that is to prey upon unwary Jack ashore. . . .
>
> Most of these places are nothing less than crimps where sailors are drugged and not only robbed, but shanghaied while still insensible. For years these desperadoes from Water Street have fastened on seamen as quickly as they left their ships and then through a system of advanced wages and exorbitant charges and "drinks for the house" have placed their dupes in debt. Once this fleecing was accomplished they were hustled on board some outbound ship while still intoxicated. Captains often had no other resource when it came time to make up their crews but to deal with these landsharks. Over one thousand girls between twelve and eighteen years of age were found in these places.[16]

In *New York by Gaslight,* George Foster reported that

> . . . the dance-house is a favorite resort with sailors ashore, who almost invariably, with that improvidence which marks their character, come with all the money they possess in the world in their pockets, and of course are generally robbed by their partners, whose profession combines theft with something a great deal more infamous. Not unfrequently worse tricks than mere robbery are practised upon these good-natured and unsophisticated creatures. Being well plied with poisoned liquor, the old hag who happens to be his partner commences making the most outrageous demonstrations of love and tenderness, which end in a proposal of immediate marriage! This startling proposition jumps with the adventurous and excited temper of Jack, exactly. He takes a fresh quid, splices the main-brace, and a magistrate (sometimes a *real* one!) appears, who performs the ceremony and poor Jack is by the enlightened laws of New York the legal husband, protector and defender of a miserable, rum and disease-eaten harridan. The next morning, with the fumes of the liquor dissipated but its sickening poison remaining, he slowly recalls the history of the night and finds that he has, as usual, made a "—fool of himself." But he hasn't yet begun to be aware of the extent of his folly: for when his vessel is ready to go to sea, and the poor husband, half dead with the wifely hardships he has endured on land, looks forward with joy to the moment when he shall find himself at the belaying-pin or yard with no drunken wife at his elbow—lo! comes a warrant summoning him to satisfy the law that he will either stay on shore or give security for the maintenance of his wife and family, under penalty of a prosecution for abandonment! Of course, he knows nothing how to act; and it depends entirely upon the lawyer or the magistrate into whose hands he may fall whether he is let off by giving an order on his owners for the whole or only half of his next three years' wages. Used up, probably diseased, and completely chapfallen, Jack resumes his station before the mast, and sees his native land sink under the blue wave with a fervent hope that the next solid place he exchanges for the deck of his vessel, will be the bottom of the sea.[17]

The sailor in port was a highly recognizable outsider, a potential source of danger to middle-class society. He had no home or family to stay with; his home was at sea and his community was highly heterogeneous. His clothing, stance, and language—part slang, part technical, part traditional—marked him off as distinctive from landspeople. In the course of his voyage, he would have experienced adventures and danger, as well as tedium and cruelty that would be incredible to others. But he would have few resources—though the dance floor might serve as one possible means—to express his experiences. He would have made contact with foreign cultures radically different than his own—with disparate political, economic, and social codes. Nevertheless, for two to four years he had lived in a confined, isolated group with its own special codes of behavior; he had worked and lived closely with men of other national, racial, and religious backgrounds.

On shore, the sailor was either unemployed or on holiday, in either case a person who had suddenly been released from the constraints of an organized, authoritarian life. He was in a liminal state;[18] his sense of time, of balance, of space was altered. Marginal to polite society, he had amassed an enormous repertoire of behavior and now had the freedom and company with which to test it. He had his collected pay to spend, and probably was as unfamiliar with the value of a dollar as he was with the currency of the European, South American, African, or Asian ports he had visited or lived in. No wonder an economic system developed in the ports specifically to welcome the seaman, provide social space for him at the edge of the city, take his money, and sell his labor power when his money had run out.

> Oh, ships may come and ships may go, as long as the seas do roll,
> Each sailor lad, likewise his dad, he loves that flowing bowl.
> A lass ashore, he does adore, one that is plump and round.
> But when his money's all gone it's the same old song, "Get up
> Jack! John, sit down!"
>
> When Jack gets in, it's then he'll steer for some old boarding house.
> They'll welcome him with rum and gin and feed him a pork souse.
> He'll lend and spend and not offend till he lies drunk on the ground.
> When your money's gone, it's the same old song, "Get up Jack!
> John, sit down!"[19]

Sexual energy was another currency the sailor had to spend. But the sexual life of the transient sailor was inextricably bound up with the entire exploitative economic system that could cater to his needs for food, drink, shelter, companionship, and sex, and rob him at the same time.

> Shipmates, if you'll listen to me,
> I'll sing you a song
> Of things that lately happened
> When I come home from Hong Kong.
> To me way, you Santy, my dear Anny.
> Oh, you New York Gals, can't you dance the Polka?
>
> As I walked down from off the docks,
> A fair maid I did meet.
> She asked me for to see her home;
> She lived on Bleecker Street.
>
> "If you will take me to my house,
> If you will be so sweet,
> I'll give you something good to drink,
> And something nice to eat."

When we got down to Bleecker Street,
We stopped at 44.
Her 'mother' and her 'sisters'
Were a-standing in the door.

They gave me wine,
It tasted fine and went right to my head,
And then they peeled my clothes off me
And put me right to bed.

When I awoke next morning,
It was early in the dawn.
My clothes and all my money
And my lady friends were gone.

Now, I don't mind the money,
As some other sailors might.
But I wish someone would tell me
If I had some fun last night.[20]

The sailor's "sea legs," unsteady on land, symbolized his tenuous balance in American society. "After a Long Cruise (Salts Ashore)," an 1857 painting by John Carlin, shows three sailors creating havoc as they try to walk down a waterfront street; they hang onto each other, but still manage to knock down a vendor's tray of fruit, and one grabs a well-dressed woman. A bystander laughs at them; another eyes them apprehensively. The sailor literally brought to the dance floor this instability as well as a need for release—release from physical confinement and from the political and social hierarchy of the ship. Drinking between dances would intensify his condition, lowering inhibitions and physical competence at the same time.

To a WASP ruling class, concerned with taming chaos, organizing and managing space and time to fit the needs of growing industrial America, the sailor ashore was unpredictable, rough, untamed. He might be black, or Irish, Chinese, East Indian, South American, or Polynesian. He might be Catholic or without religion altogether. (Certainly, as the predominance of black spirituals and Irish tunes among shanties and forecastle songs shows, there was an internationalist experience of exchanging culture.) And he was a potential propagator of disease—smallpox, scurvy, venereal disease, foreign fevers—and strange, heathen customs.

Frederick Pease Harlow, a white sailor from New England in the early 1870s, describes his disorientation on debarking in Melbourne, Australia. "While walking up the dock everything looked bright overhead, because there were no heavy yards and hemp rigging above. . . . I began to stumble."[21] Harlow brings this sense of dizzying displacement, this discomfort with land life, with him to Mother Shilling's dance hall.

Mother Shilling was very anxious to have Kitty teach me to dance and on learning that I was a novice, she took both my hands and in her winning way urged me to permit her to show me.

Her touch was magnetic and holding her small, plump hands in my horny, calloused flippers, I never held a main brace with a firmer grip; in fact, I wanted to bowse away and take a turn and belay. She smiled as I squeezed her hands and with a nod of her head towards the floor (for she couldn't point with her hands), her gentle pleadings found me a willing lad.

"Really, you'll find the flawh not hawful bad," said she, tugging away till at last she succeeded, and bidding me put my arm around her she proceeded to show me the waltz step.

Counting one-two-three, first forward, then backward, with a bend of the knee, etc., I was surprised to find how easy I was getting along. Then, at the turn, this little dame threw herself into my arms—"head on." Another squeeze and my feet got mixed up with hers and we started all over again. Under her guidance with a whirl first to starboard and then to port—never complaining when I occasionally hit her foot as I misstayed, coming into the wind, she complimented me at almost every whirl.

It is surprising how hard one works when trying to learn and although I was loath to release my hold around her waist, a sense of politeness told me it was time to give her a rest for we both were perspiring freely. Taking her hand, which she permitted me to hold, I led her back to the table where Dave and Julia both complimented me at my showing.

Whether it was the beer or my confidence in Kitty's teaching, I was so elated, as I stood wiping the perspiration from my forehead, that I felt obliged to order another round of sheoak. In fact, I was willing to buy anything and drawing my chair close to Kitty, I noticed that Julia was sitting on Dave's lap. I saw no reason why Kitty shouldn't do the same with me and putting my arm around her she offered no resistance and so we sat sipping beer, while every remark seemed awfully humorous.

. . . By this time my head was whirling faster than my feet and consequently I held her tighter than I had previously done.

"Are you afryed of losing me?" she asked, laughingly looking into my eyes and I couldn't resist the desire to make a clove hitch around her waist, with my two arms, right there, when she gave a little scream and we bumped into a couple.

"I s'y! Square th' main yard, me 'earty, an' give 'er a good full!" the sailor laughingly said.

"Quite in order! A good full you have it!" I replied, wearing ship only to run foul of another couple.[22]

But, while the landsharks attended to the sailor's body, the Church competed for both body and soul. Runners from seamen's churches tried to reach the docks before the pimps and boardinghouse masters got there. At the Sailor's Mission at Melbourne, Harlow related,

> The entertainment consisted of songs, instrumental pieces, recitations and temperance speeches, winding up by passing around a Total Abstinence Pledge which our crew all signed. Alas! The next night, I am sorry to say, all hands were drunk except Falmouth and myself. The runner from the Mission evidently knew of it for he was always watching for us at the head of the dock, night after night, beseeching us not to get lu'arded into Mother Shilling's saloon as we went ashore.[23]

Banks, homes, bethels, employment exchanges, and floating churches for seamen were built on the waterfront in New York beginning in the 1820s. The vision of the American Seamen's Friend Society, for instance, was vast:

> *Resolved*, That in the opinion of the committee the shortness of the time that sailors remain at home, and their unrestrained exposure to temptation while in our ports, forbid the hope of a very general reformation among them by means of domestic operations alone.[24]

The society obviously disapproved of the mingling of races.

> Early in its history The American Seamen's Friend Society set out resolutely to the task of providing decent, safe places for seamen to stay while ashore. In 1830 plans were made for erecting a Sailors' Home in New York. . . . By 1840, the Society was operating three sailors' boarding houses, one of them exclusively for negroes.[25]

If segregation was one of the criteria for decency, then the integration of blacks, whites, and various shades of brown at John Allen's may have been one reason it was considered indecent.

The churches warned equally against drinking, dancing, the theater, and houses of ill fame. *Seamen's Narratives*, a book of several morally didactic tales published in pocketbook format by the American Tract Society in 1860, includes several injunctions against dancing. In "Tom Starboard and Jack Halyard," Tom persuades Jack to become temperate and to stay at the Sailors' Home that night, after praying at the Bethel. Jack recalls some of his past misdeeds.

> Well, when the Alert's cruise was up, and we were paid off, about a dozen of us went to lodge with old Peter Hardheart, at the sign of the Foul Anchor; and as we had plenty of money, we thought we would have a regular blow-out. So Peter got a fiddler and some other unmentionable requisites for a jig, and we had a set-to in first-rate style. Why, our great frolic at Santa Martha, when Paddy Chips the Irish carpenter danced away his watch and jacket and tarpaulin, and nearly all his toggery, you know, and next morning came scudding along the beach towards the Alert, as she lay moored near the shore, and crept on board on all-fours, like a half-drowned monkey, along the best bower, wouldn't have made a nose to it. Well, next morning I had a pretty smart touch of the horrors,

> and felt rather muddy about the head; but old Peter soon set us agoing again, and we kept it up for three days and three nights, carriage-riding and dancing and drinking and theatre-going, etc.; and we thought the world was too little for us: when all at once old Hardheart took a round turn on us with, "I'll tell you what it is, you drunken swabs, I'll not have such goings-on in my house; my house is a decent house: you must all ship; yes, ship's the word. I must have the advance; you're more than a month's wages apiece in my debt." Tom, I was sober in an instant. My conscience smote me. In three days I had squandered the wages of a three years' cruise, and had not a dollar left to take to my poor old mother in the country, whom I had intended to go to see after the frolic was over, and give all my money to.[26]

In "Conversation in a Boat," a similar exchange takes place between religious Harry and impressionable Tom.

> . . . you don't know what religion is, or how it can make a man happier than fiddles and dancing, and noise and racket; but the thing is true, although you do not understand it. You know, Tom, that I was once as mad-brained and thoughtless a fellow as ever sailed out of Shields harbor. I have tried what grog and noise and songs and fiddles can do; and now, Tom, whether you will believe me or not, I can say from experience, that these things do not go half so far towards making a man happy as religion does.[27]

"Letter to Seamen on First Coming Ashore" tells of the consequences of "THE GROGSHIP. I think THE ROAD TO RUIN would be a better title . . . THE THEATER, or, as it should be called, THE GATEWAY TO HELL . . . THE HOUSE OF ILL FAME, or, AVENUE TO THE GRAVE."

> Many go there "to kill time," as they say, when every moment is a precious talent, for which we must render a strict account to God. So very precious is time, that it is measured out to us by seconds. . . .
>
> Jack, have you ever been the victim of the smooth-tongued wanton? Have you lent a willing ear to her honeyed accents and professions of love, but found that all was false and hollow by the emptied purse, the gnawing conscience, the aching bones, the decaying constitution, and all the other painful and disgraceful consequences of your folly? And will you now venture to sail within even hailing distance of this perilous reef? Up helm and scud; with such an enemy in front, flight not only insures safety, but honor. But though you may not yet have been her victim, Jack, you well know that scores upon scores of our shipmates have, and what shocking penalties they paid. Therefore take warning from their sad experience.[28]

In the fall of 1868, the missionaries heightened their approach by taking over Allen's dance house for religious meetings. But, according to the newspaper reports, "most of those present were of the respectable classes, very few laborers or workingmen being present."[29]

The Customers: Gangsters and Workers

George Foster describes Saturday night at Pete Williams's, a dance house in Five Points which Charles Dickens visited on his trip to the United States: "The company begins assembling early, for Saturday night is a grand time for thieves, loafers, prostitutes and rowdies, as well as for honest, hard-working people."[30] Foster also mentions "the b'hoys, members of rowdy clubs, and those who 'run' with the engines."[31] Junius Browne calls the clientele of Five Points dance houses, just a few blocks from Water Street, "thieves and burglars, sailors and bar-tenders, cracksmen and murderers."[32]

Gangsters and criminals certainly frequented Allen's, for "by 1845 the whole area [the Fourth Ward] had become a hotbed of crime," writes Herbert Asbury. The dives in the neighborhood "sheltered the members of such celebrated river gangs as the Daybreak Boys, Buckoos, Hookers, Swamp Angels, Slaughter Housers, Short Tails, Patsy Conroys, and the Border Gang." Allen's place, in particular, "soon became one of the principal recreational centers for the gangsters of the Fourth Ward . . . one of the worst the city has ever seen."[33]

Up the street from Allen's, at 273 Water Street (an address that has also been given for Allen's), was Sportsmen's Hall, a rat pit run by Kit Burns, where in an interior amphitheater huge rats fought with dogs. George Leese, also known as Snatchem, an habitue of Sportsmen's Hall, was a member of the Slaughter Housers and

> . . . an official bloodsucker at the bare-knuckle prize fights which were frequently held in the Fourth Ward and Five Points dives. With two revolvers in his belt and a knife in his boot-top, Snatchem was an important figure at these entertainments, and when one of the pugilists began to bleed from scratches and cuts inflicted by his opponent's knuckles, it was Snatchem's office to suck the blood from the wound.

Asbury says that a contemporary journalist described Snatchem as "a beastly, obscene ruffian, with bulging, bulbous, watery-blue eyes, bloated face and coarse swaggering gait."[34]

Jerry McAuley, who later ran the McAuley Water Street Mission at 316 Water Street, was probably, in his youth and before his conversion, a typical customer at Allen's.

> His father had been a counterfeiter. He had been of the Catholic faith, if any. In his youth, Jerry McAuley had been a prize fighter in the Water Street dens and he had thieved on the river by night. He had committed enough crime, in his own words, to deserve prison a half-hundred times. Before his twentieth birthday he was sentenced to prison for a fifteen-year stretch. And in 1872, the same year The Seaman's Exchange came into existence, Jerry McAuley founded his Water Street Mission.[35]

Perhaps, during the Civil War years, some soldiers found their way to Allen's, using the dancing and the sex to spend nervous energy as they got ready to fight. In April 1861, when New York City served as a staging area for Union troops, temporary barracks in the Battery and City Hall Park housed 8,500 soldiers.

Perhaps, too, some of the thousands of homeless, orphaned newsboys shunned the Newsboys' Lodging Home, built in 1854 above the *Sun* offices on Fulton Street, preferring to scrape together enough money for an occasional dance, drink, and some sex at Allen's.

And probably a few working men in the neighborhood—fishermen, country merchants, military suppliers, warehouse or store clerks, block-makers, ship chandlers, cotton brokers, sailmakers, "forwarders," pickle dealers, grocers, flour merchants, bakers, fishermen, fish dealers, printers, masons, or stove dealers—would have stopped in occasionally, especially if they lived in one of the hotels in the neighborhood.

Allen's Employees

About Allen's employees we know very little, except that if he was like other dance house owners, he employed, besides the women, a bartender, runners to meet the ships, and procurers to find women. He also would have employed between three and six musicians. And if the orchestra at Allen's resembled that at Pete Williams's, we can visualize their style clearly:

> In the middle of one side of the room a shammy platform is erected, with a trembling railing, and this is the "orchestra" of the establishment. Sometimes a single black fiddler answers the purpose: but on Saturday nights the music turns out strong, and the house entertains, in addition, a trumpet and a bass drum. With these instruments you may imagine that the music at Dickens's Place is of no ordinary kind. You cannot, however, begin to imagine *what* it is. You cannot *see* the red-hot knitting needles spirted out by that red-faced trumpeter, who looks precisely as if he were blowing glass, which needles aforesaid penetrating the tympanum, pierce through and through your brain without remorse. Nor can you perceive the frightful mechanical contortions of the bass-drummer as he sweats and deals his blows on every side, in all violation of the laws of rhythm, like a man beating a balky mule and showering his blows upon the unfortunate animal, now on this side, now on that. If you could, it would be unnecessary for us to write.[36]

The Observers

Even those who considered themselves decent men came to Allen's. Policemen came to keep order. Warren, a detective, came to conduct studies of civilization, ostensibly so that others might not have to suffer the sight themselves.

> The maxim that vice to be abhorred must be seen, has no application to such a scene as we have described from actual observation. No man or youth still unsullied, should ever lay eyes upon a dance house. It is enough to know that it is a sad reality. Human nature, under its most favorable aspects is bad enough, but this phase of it, once thoroughly photographed upon the memory, reveals possibilities of depravity and baseness in man that can never be effaced, or forgotten,—he has experienced a shock from which he will never recover.[37]

Similarly, "The Missionaries are constant visitors to these dens. They go with hope that they may succeed in rescuing some poor creature from her terrible life. As a rule, they meet with the vilest abuse, and are driven away with curses, but sometimes they are successful."[38]

Not only missionaries, but writers, like Dyer, Foster, McCabe, and others, went to the dance houses to observe, purportedly to alert the city to its darker side, but perhaps, judging from their persistence, to get some kind of secret pleasure out of watching the free, rough, giddy activity at Allen's. Oliver Dyer had been going to Allen's for at least two years before writing the article in *Packard's Monthly* that made Allen famous. And Dyer brought missionaries with him.

> In the year 1865, the Sabbath after President Lincoln was assassinated, we began an exploration and sub-soiling of New York city, as to its crime, poverty, want, wo, wretchedness and degradation, which we have pursued ever since, as other engagements would permit. Of course, it was not long before we found out John Allen. We at once recognized his genius for wickedness and made him an especial study. . . .
>
> Since that occasion we have repeatedly visited the abode of the Wickedest Man in New York, for the purpose of "studying him up," and of trying to hit upon some means of inducing him to abandon his course of life, and of saving his boy. For in truth, we not only feel an interest in, but also rather like him, wicked as he is. And so does nearly everybody whom we have taken to see him; and we have taken scores—most of them clergymen.[39]

For those people who were not forced to frequent Allen's, who had other social channels for the release of sexual and emotional energy than the Water Street dives, who had comfortable beds to sleep in, stable jobs, and secure family lives, Allen's could function as a tourist attraction, a freak show like Barnum's. "Strangers and New Yorkers often visit dance-houses for curiosity; but they take the precaution to go armed, and under the direction and guidance of a policeman."[40]

The observers who visited dance houses out of curiosity, rather than necessity, or desire, are those who had the resources to write about them, and they are the ones who call the participants "thieves, harlots and desperadoes," and the event "orgies revolting to the last degree . . . shameless sin . . . unrelieved grossness."[41]

One wonders what they thought was sinful and gross about Allen's. The mixture of races, nationalities, and religions? The frank acknowledgement of sexual needs, symbolizing submission to irrational forces the middle-class tried to repress? Dancing that looked free or chaotic? The anonymity of the partnering? The mood of immediacy, of urgency, of the squandering of money and strength in play? The clash of cultures and languages erupting into physical violence? Self-defined, improvised uses of time and space in a culture that with increasing industrialization valued hierarchical management and ordering of time and space?

Perhaps the participants in the event found other aspects sinful—drugging and robbing disoriented sailors, profit-making by a man from women's sexual relationships, the loneliness of urban life and the dissolution of family ties that would have brought them there. Perhaps, had the participants themselves the means to describe and preserve their perceptions, we would have a different view of John Allen's dance house today.

23

Red Shoes: The Workers' Dance League of the 1930s

The past few years have seen an upsurge of political activity among downtown dancers, from organizing for nuclear disarmament to making dances against U.S. intervention in Central America to making statements about black identity and history. This alliance between the avant-garde and progressive politics might seem surprising (in the U.S., though not in Europe). Yet there are precedents, not only in the 1960s, but from the beginnings of American modern dance. Operating in a less fragmented political scene and a smaller, tighter dance world, the Workers' Dance League of the 1930s was a highly organized, polemical body for producing political dance and organizing dancers.

Although the history of American dance has whitewashed it from

Village Voice, April 24, 1984.

memory, avant-garde dance and the rise of left-wing culture in the United States in the 1930s collided at a critical moment. During the late 1920s, Martha Graham, Doris Humphrey, and Charles Weidman broke away from Denishawn to form their own groups. In 1931, Hanya Holm founded the American branch of the Mary Wigman dance school. At the same time, a number of workers' theater troupes sprang up in New York City, offering a radical, serious alternative to what they saw as the frivolous Broadway stage.

After the economic crash in 1929, the left-wing theater brigades found larger audiences than ever among the millions of unemployed. In the context of widespread depression and the organizing efforts of masses of workers, aided by a growing Communist party, the workers' theater movement burgeoned, fueled by the CP's Third Period policies, which emphasized the imminence of worldwide revolution and called for suitable artistic theory and practice as part of political strategy and action. Unlike the activity of so much avant-garde theater and dance today, these groups found large working-class audiences, given the political context and the tight CP organization as well as its goals.

Today we have no models. But then, the obvious model for left-wing American artists and intellectuals was the young Soviet Union, which had managed to create modernist, avant-garde, politically charged artworks in every genre. In the United States, CP officials urged the building of radical working-class culture through its literary magazine, *New Masses*; through literary John Reed Clubs; and through various theater, music, film, dance, and sports groups. Through these arts and pastimes, class consciousness would be sharpened into a "weapon," to be wielded in the coming revolution.

Some of the young dancers who studied and worked with Holm, Graham, Humphrey, Weidman, Tamiris, Fe Alf, and other "bourgeois" modern dancers were working-class women, often the daughters of immigrants, who marched in May Day parades and stood with their parents on picket lines. They brought to the artistic "revolution" of modern dance a political commitment that led them to repudiate the work of their teachers as too abstract, mystical, or nostalgic. They looked to the model of the workers' theater movement for themes and social forms, a new content for the new dance forms they were discovering. And naive as it may seem to us, they really meant it when they wrote things like "Dance must be used to teach workers' children that they belong to the working class. . . . Use themes of nature to teach children to dance together in harmony, just as workers on a Soviet collective work together." Thus, Kay Rankin explained, children could be won over through dance to join the revolutionary movement and, in particular, the Young Pioneers of America. These dancers believed that, ultimately, they had the power and the obligation to change the world. We feel the obligation, but the sense of power is gone.

By the spring of 1932, the workers' theater movement was so active that a national festival and competition was organized. A League of Workers' Theaters formed, and took over the publication of a radical journal, *Workers' Theater.* The workers' dance groups, although not as numerous, soon followed suit; they formed the Workers' Dance Council, which by March 1933 had become the Workers' Dance League (WDL). The organization boasted seventeen theater groups in New York City.

The Red Dancers, organized in 1929 by Edith Segal, performed at CP functions, at union meetings, and in at least one benefit for striking workers; they held summer classes for adults and kids. Esther Porter praised one of their 1932 performances: "Here were workers throwing all their energies into expressing in a strong and thrilling way the power of their class." Segal also organized the Nature Friends Dance Group in 1931; its first dances were *Red Army March* and *Red Marine.* The group was an outgrowth of a workers' hiking club, the Nature Friends, which campaigned against the 1932 Olympics and also sponsored an agitprop theater troupe.

New Dance Group (NDG), an amalgam of modern dancers led by students from the "bourgeois" studios and by performers in the "bourgeois" companies—most notably, Jane Dudley, Sophie Maslow, Miriam Blecher, and Bill Matons—was the most professional and prolific of the workers' dance groups. Within a year of its founding, NDG grew to a membership of 300, and it helped to set up similar groups in other cities. NDG reported that it had organized "large sections of workers who meet to dance and talk every evening."

Not only did NDG offer dance classes to workers in order to salutarily combine recreation with art, but also members collectively built a repertory of what they hoped were revolutionary dances. At its first anniversary concert, in March 1933, the program included satiric dances (*Parasite, Charity,* and *Peace Conference*), folk dances, and works on serious themes intended to rouse audiences to sympathy, if not action, for the working class (*Strike, Uprisings, Hunger,* and *On the Barricades*).

NDG experimented with improvisations on themes taken from workers' daily lives and—although they criticized themselves for problems arising from their own differences in dance technique, their self-admitted lack of understanding of the working class, and their perennial lack of headquarters—they continued to grow and to redefine their organization (which still exists today, offering evening classes at reasonable rates in a variety of techniques, but without any political emphasis). In the thirties, their pedagogy was organized along the lines of political cells, rather than ordinary dance classes; in 1933, NDG's stated policies included assigning specific themes (e.g., unemployment) to all classes for two weeks of exploration each; dividing students into squadrons of thirty according to ability; and discussing the work after each class session. Students in intermediate or advanced classes were eligible to join the performing company, and thus to help choose the repertory. Classes cost a fraction of their price at the "bourgeois" studios. By 1934, NDG offered courses in teacher training (including Marxist theory), theory of dance, and practical dance technique in various methods: Dalcroze, Graham, Duncan, Humphrey, Wigman.

In the early thirties other dance groups sprang into being from classes at NDG, unions, and community centers. The principle of comradely competition put into practice by the workers' theater groups inspired the Workers' Dance League to organize its First Annual Spartakiade in June 1933. Seventeen groups entered the competition, including NDG, and the Jack London Rebel Dancers of Newark, and, although the organizers admitted that some dances were technically immature, they were proud that the content was strikingly new.

At a forum held in October 1933 called "What Direction Shall the Negro Dance Take?" Hemsley Winfield, a black choreographer, performed with his group, and the Red Dancers performed Segal's *Black and White*. At the 1934 competition, the NDG won first place for *Van der Lubbe's Head*, a collectively choreographed dance based on a poem by Alfred Hayes that castigated Nazi repression. Second prize went to the Theater Union Dance Group, led by Anna Sokolow, for *Anti-War Cycle*. And in third place was the Nature Friends Dance Group's *Kinder, Küche, und Kirche*, a sharp criticism of Hitler's program for women; the dance ended by urging German women to ally themselves with the revolutionary youth movement against Nazism. Other dance groups included the New Duncan Dancers, the Junior Red Dancers, and the Revolutionary Dancers. Reporting on the festival, Grace Wylie, an officer of WDL, wrote that many of the dances treated depression and revolt too generally, and that more specific dances were called for. "We hope that by next year all our groups will have gotten a *Revolt* (sometimes called *Uprising, Upsurge, Red Tide*) off their chests and find means of bringing forward themes which are of direct import to our audience."

Emanuel Eisenberg satirized in *New Theater* a typical revolutionary dance on the program: "Six or ten young women, clothed in long and wholly unrepresentative black dresses, would be discovered lying around the stage in various states of collapse. Soon, to the rhythm of dreary and monotonous music, they would begin to sway in attitudes of misery, despair and defeat. . . . This must be the proletariat in the grip of oppression. . . . The swaying would continue for a couple of minutes . . . and then, a vision. Sometimes it came in the form of a light flooding suddenly from the wings of the balcony; sometimes in the form of music intensity; sometimes as a dynamic figure in red, running passionately at the startled tragedians. . . . And always the group would respond with victory: hope had arisen, strength had come, freedom was here, the revolution had arrived."

There were benefits for *New Theater*, for the *Daily Worker*, and for the Committee to Support Southern Textile Organization, among other efforts. Although it was the modern dancers who felt most strongly linked to the aims of the Workers' Dance League, the movement was not monolithic. It welcomed tapdancers, ballet dancers, chorus girls, and untrained hopefuls. It urged men to join in. Articles in *Workers' Theater* and *New Theater* noted the victories and (more often) the working problems in the dance industry.

Reviews and announcements of performances and classes appeared in the journal. But also, debates raged on topics basic to any new vision of culture. There were questions of technique, criticisms of "bourgeois" approaches to dance, articles on the problems of how to operate collectively within the groups, and, of course, the question of what subjects were appropriate to dance about. Eisenberg criticized a program called Revolutionary Solo Dances, holding that a truly revolutionary dancer would find a different idiom than that of the bourgeois studios. Nathaniel Buchwald retorted that socialist and communist dances could only emerge by growing dialectically out of the best of the bourgeois techniques. Just as the problem of what constituted proletarian literature vexed the writers of the time, the question of what, exactly, proletarian dance should be was fundamental. Did proletarian dances mean those made by workers, for workers, or about workers?

With the end of the CP's Third Period and the inauguration of the Popular Front in 1935, some of these questions were put aside. In the alliance of leftists and liberals against fascism, the brashness of the previous period abated, the vocabulary of class struggle vanished, and the expression of enthusiasm for the Soviet Union gave way to sentiments that spoke more clearly of American patriotism. The word *communist* was used less often. The left sought a new image that would court, rather than threaten, progressive liberals. Also, it shared in the hopeful mood of the nation as economic and social conditions seemed to swing upward.

In 1935, the League of Workers' Theaters changed its name to New Theater League, and changed its style as well, using previously disdained Broadway techniques to attract wide, diverse audiences. Yet it still managed to present themes of racial injustice, war, antifacism, and labor's right to organize. The same year the Workers' Dance League was transformed into the New Dance League; it expanded its thematic range as well as its membership, inviting choreographers it had so recently repudiated, such as Tamiris, Humphrey, Weidman, and Graham, to appear in its programs, and urging "dancers, choreographers, teachers, leaders of groups, dance students, regardless of other political or artistic differences . . . to join the New Dance League at once." Out of this expanded group Tamiris led the groundswell to form a dance wing of the Federal Theater Project. Lincoln Kirstein wrote several articles in *New Theater* that proposed ballet as the most revolutionary form for dance.

Seen in one light, the alliance with the modern dance liberals diluted the message of the radical dancers; in another light, the bourgeois choreographers were moved through that alliance to politicize their performances. (For instance, a number of liberal choreographers, including Graham, contributed dances to a Spanish Civil War benefit program.) Ironically, when the dancers of the early sixties rebelled against older modern dance in the name of democracy and freedom, they protested against the genre's bombastic social messages. The McCarthy era had laundered modern dance, along with the rest of American culture, of its redder tints. Its revolutionary content was lost for the next generation, which had, in any case, to find a new way to make its own revolution.

V

Postmodern Dance: From The Sixties to the Nineties

24

Judson Rides Again!

Judson Dance Theater has become the kind of legend whose reality is lost in a mist of nostalgia and imperfect remembrances. The people who were involved in the group nearly twenty years ago remember only fragments and each one, of course, has a particular perspective on that past. The people who weren't involved, either as participants or spectators, feel compelled to justify their absence. Dance historians and critics invoke Judson for all sorts of reasons, many of them inaccurate. And meanwhile, no one can agree on what, exactly, Judson Dance Theater *was*. With two programs of Judson reconstructions taking place this weekend at Danspace at St. Mark's Church, a great deal of light will be shed on just what happened at Judson Church in the sixties and its pervasive effect on new dance over the past two decades.

The strictest definition of Judson Dance Theater is that it was the loosely organized collective of choreographers who met in a weekly workshop at the Judson Memorial Church on Washington Square from 1962 to 1964, producing over two hundred dances in twenty concerts, mostly one-night stands. The first concert, on July 6, 1962, was a marathon that lasted over three hours, attracted hundreds of spectators (mostly Village writers and artists), and pointed a way for the future of avant-garde, downtown dance. That first concert, organized by students in a choreography class taught at the Merce Cunningham studio by Robert Dunn, set up a model for producing dance cooperatively and cheaply that corresponded to similar activities at the time in the poetry, film, and theater worlds. The brash, iconoclastic energy and ambition of the event foreshadowed the impulse toward physical and political liberation that captured the American imagination in the sixties. Jill Johnston wrote about this concert in the *Village Voice* and called it "Democracy." She also rang Judson Dance Theater's death knell in the *Voice* in 1965, after zealously covering nearly every concert in her column.

A broader definition of the Judson Dance Theater begins with that same concert but moves back in time to encompass the social and artistic networks that impinged on the workshop group. It also includes choreographers who gave concerts at the Judson Church but were never part of the

---

Village Voice, April 20, 1982.

weekly workshop. So James Waring, who began to give concerts at the church after the group, but in whose company some of the group danced, and who shared a studio with Aileen Passloff and Yvonne Rainer where he taught many of the Judson dancers, is part of the bigger sense of Judson Dance Theater, as are Passloff and Katherine Litz, and Remy Charlip. It also includes people like Simone Forti, who was in the Dunn class but never appeared at the church, and people like Meredith Monk, Phoebe Neville, and Kenneth King, who began performing at the church after the initial workshop had disbanded.

In any case, the Judson Church, with its Dance Theater, Poets' Theater, Gallery and numerous political events, was a lively place in the sixties and the Judson Dance Theater was a particularly vital gathering place for artists in all fields. In the early years, anyone who abided by the democratic rules of the workshop could make a dance, whether trained as a dancer (like Yvonne Rainer, Steve Paxton, Ruth Emerson, Fred Herko, Elizabeth Keen, David Gordon, Lucinda Childs, Judith Dunn, Sally Gross, Trisha Brown, Elaine Summers) or as a musician (like John Herbert McDowell, Philip Corner, Malcolm Goldstein, James Tenney) or as a visual artist (like Carolee Schneemann, Robert Rauschenberg, Alex Hay, Robert Morris). The notion of choreography was an open field waiting to be explored.

Although we think now of Judson as the seedbed for the reductive, at times austere, style that characterized postmodern dance in the seventies, diversity of style and method was key to the group's operations. It was an attempt to plumb that diversity that led to the current Judson reconstructions. Wendy Perron, a dancer, choreographer, and writer, led her students on a search for their shared "roots" and began excavating Judson Dance Theater two years ago. Perron and Tony Carruthers set up the Bennington College Judson Project, which commissioned performances by Trisha Brown, Steve Paxton, and Yvonne Rainer at Bennington, videotaped interviews with over twenty Judson Dance Theater "members," and mounted an exhibition of photographs, scores, programs, and videotapes (seen at Bennington and at New York University's Grey Gallery earlier this year).

One problem with the excavation was that very few documentations of the dances on film or videotape existed. Portable video technology was practically nonexistent in the sixties, and few of the dancers could afford to film their work. Even the best photographs could only suggest what the dances looked like in motion. Perron finally embarked on the reconstruction project, and found a place for the performances not at the original church site—at this point, Judson Church has cut back on performance production—but at St. Mark's Church in-the-Bowery, where since 1974 the Danspace project has been sponsoring concerts and avant-garde dance. The Judson reconstructions will take place in the sanctuary of the church, celebrating its reopening after it was gutted by a fire in 1978 and then gradually rebuilt.

Perron and Cynthia Hedstrom, the director of Danspace, invited a number of choreographers to contribute to the program of reconstructions. In a sense, the final program is, as the Judson programs were, a mixture of choice and chance. Not all of the Judson choreographers will be represented because some have died, some are out of town, some chose not to contribute work. But the dances that will be performed still show a remarkable range of content and form.

Elaine Summers, who has been making films since the time of Judson Dance Theater, will show (on Program B) *Judson Nights*, a film collage that includes the projections from her multimedia piece *Fantastic Gardens* (1964) and also some documentations of other dances on the Judson programs. Aside from an Andy Warhol film now unavailable for viewing, *Judson Nights* may be the only surviving record of performances by Fred Herko, who committed suicide in 1964. Thc othcr film is *Woton's Wake* (1963), a very early film by Brian De Palma that has music by John Herbert McDowell and perhaps for that reason was shown on A Concert of Dance #11 at the Cramercy Arts Thcatcr. A thirty-minute black-and-white trance film satire about an alchemist named Woton Wretchichevsky, who looks like a Hasidic version of Tiny Tim, it anticipates De Palma's later works, in that it is full of parodic but loving quotations—not only from Ingmar Bergman and Maya Deren, but also *The Bride of Frankenstein* and *King Kong*.

Edward Bhartonn's *Pop #2*, which originally followed *Woton's Wake* on Concert #11, will also be seen in Program A at St. Mark's. *Pop #2* and its predecessor, *Pop #1* (from Concert #10 and also on Program A) were miniatures in which Bhartonn unrolled a mat, blew up a balloon, and then did a back three-quarter (in #1) or a back three-quarter and a flip (in #2) onto the balloon, bursting it. Program A also includes Elaine Summers's *Dance for Lots of People* (1963), a mass dance reminiscent of German expressionist dances or films like Fritz Lang's *Metropolis*, and Remy Charlip's *Meditation*, an expressive solo of slowly building drama based on moving along the body's chakras. Judith Dunn's *Dewhorse* (1963), a solo done in collaboration with musician Bill Dixon, will be recreated by Cheryl Lilienstein. Simone Forti will reconstruct her *Slant Board* (1961), a climbing game first performed pre-Judson on an evening of Five Dance Constructions and Some Other Things, at Yoko Ono's loft on Chambers Street. Philip Corner will rework his *Keyboard Dances* (1964), in which he used his entire body to play thc piano, and *Flares* (1962), a dance that involved slide projections, darkness, and the simultaneous translation of a written score into musical and movement terms. Program A also includes Yvonne Rainer dancing her seminal *The Mind is a Muscle, Part 1, or Trio* A (1966), a "populist" dance that redefined the notion of phrasing and set the style for the uninflected dances of the seventies. For fifteen years, Rainer did it nearly every day to keep in shape. Thursday she'll do it cold: she hasn't even rehearsed it since August 1981.

Program B includes two pre-Judson pieces—Aileen Passloff's *Structures* (1960), a chance dance, and James Waring's *Octandre* (1957–58), reconstructed by Passloff from Waring's notes. It also includes a post-Judson dance, Deborah Hay's *Ten* (1968), for ten dancers and nondancers dressed in white, lining up in various formations, and a rock band. Steve Paxton will perform his *Jag ville görna telefonera* (1964), a dance that was originally performed in Sweden and involved three chickens, a full-sized overstuffed chair made of cake and yellow frosting, and clothes with zippers in the seams that could be taken apart and put back together in new ways. Paxton's recently rediscovered score for this dance, a collage of sports photos, was on display at Grey Gallery. Lucinda Childs will perform her *Carnation* (1964), a dance with curlers, a colander, socks, and a blue plastic bag that related to pop art paintings and undercut the drama of human presence in the dance, substituting the cool presence of objects, an abiding theme in postmodern dance that later allied it with minimalism in the visual arts. Threading through Program B, as it originally threaded through Concert #13 (the collaboration by the Dance Theater with sculptor Charles Ross) will be Carolee Schneemann's *Lateral Splay* (1963), a group dance of running at top speed and energy.

This weekend's programs bring up basic questions about reconstruction, if not the identity of a dance itself. Does the performance of *Dewhorse* depend on its being danced by Judith Dunn herself? Was there some tangible interaction between dancer and musician that eludes notation and coaching and can never be recaptured? Does an Edward Bhartonn in his forties doing a back flip perform the same dance as the *Pop #2* he did in his twenties? Will even the choreographers themselves remember the dances precisely enough to reconstruct them "exactly"—given the constraints of different spaces, bodies, and, of course, a totally different time? When we see these works made in a different era, can they possibly have the same meaning for us that they had for us or others in the sixties? Or are these discrepancies unimportant in the long run? Twenty years later, the Judson Dance Theater still provides food for thought about dance.

25

Choreographic Methods of the Judson Dance Theater

The Judson Dance Theater, the legendary amalgamation of avant-garde choreographers in Greenwich Village in the early 1960s, represents a turning point in dance history for many reasons. Its cooperative nature as an alternative-producing institution was a conscious assault on the hierarchical nature not only of academic ballet but also, more directly, of the American modern dance community as it had evolved by the late 1950s. The youthfulness of Judson's original members signified a changing of the guard in terms of generations and, emblematic of the Kennedy era, a cultural shift in authority from the wisdom and experience of age to the energy and creativity — the modernity — of youth. Aesthetic questions about the nature and meaning of dance and of movement were raised in the workshop and in the concerts, among them — fundamentally — the identity of a dance work, the definition of dance, and the nature of technique. The cooperative workshop was a training ground for most of the key choreographers of the next two decades.[1]

But perhaps the most important legacy the Judson Dance Theater bequeathed to the history of dance was its intensive exploration and expansion of possibilities for choreographic method. In their relentless search for the new, coupled with an intelligently analytic approach to the process of dancemaking, in repudiating their elders' cherished compositional formulae, the members of the Judson Dance Theater experimented with so many different kinds of choreographic structures and devices that for the generations that have followed their message was clear: not only any movement or any body, but also any method is permitted.

Choreography: Principles and Practice, Janet Adshead, ed. (University of Surrey: National Resource Centre for Dance, Guildford, Surrey, 1987). Reprinted with permission.

Robert Dunn's Choreography Class

The open spirit that animated the group had its roots in the sensibilities of the composition class taught by Robert Dunn out of which the Judson Dance Theater blossomed. Dunn's aspirations as a dance composition teacher were informed by several sources (he himself was, of course, trained as a composer, not as a dancer or choreographer). Most crucially, he translated ideas from John Cage's experimental music class, especially chance techniques, into the dance milieu; Cage's class, in which Dunn had been a student, already originated in an expanded view of music that encompassed theater and performance in a more general sense. Not only Cage's methods, but also his attitude that "anything goes," was an inspiration that carried over into Dunn's class. Certainly this permissive atmosphere was reinforced by the inclinations of the students, who were all engaged in various ways and to various degrees in the groundbreaking artistic scene in the Village, from the Living Theater to pop art to happenings to Fluxus, and some of whom studied as well with Ann Halprin, the West Coast experimentalist. But beyond this generative urge toward license, Dunn and his students consciously disavowed the compositional approaches taught in the modern dance "academy." Dunn remembers that he had watched Louis Horst and Doris Humphrey teach their choreography classes and was determined to find another pedagogical method; he found them too rigid and the dances by their students too theatrical.

The original class had started out with only five members—Paulus Berenson, Marni Mahaffay, Simone (Forti) Morris, Steve Paxton, and Yvonne Rainer. By the end of the second year, the participants included Judith Dunn (whose status as student sometimes seemed to blend with that of teacher), Trisha Brown, Ruth Emerson, Alex Hay, Deborah Hay, Fred Herko, Al Kurchin, Dick Levine, Gretchen MacLane, John Herbert McDowell, Joseph Schlichter, Carol Scothorn, and Elaine Summers. Valda Setterfield and David Gordon attended occasionally; Robert Rauschenberg, Jill Johnston, and Gene Friedman were "regular visitors," and Remy Charlip, David Vaughan, Robert Morris, Ray Johnson, and Peter Schumann, among others, came from time to time to observe. The composition of this population alone—it included visual artists, musicians, writers, a theater director, and filmmakers as well as dancers—made for an interdisciplinary brew.

The basis of Dunn's approach at first was to find time structures, taken from musical compositions by contemporary composers (Cage, Stockhausen, Boulez, and others), that dance could share. The principle technique was chance scores, but others included more wide-ranging methods of indeterminacy and various kinds of rules. Students were assigned to use a graphic chance score along the lines of that which Cage had made for his *Fontana Mix*. Another assignment involved using number sequences derived from Satie's *Trois Gymnopédies*. Several students remember dances involving time constraints, for instance, "Make a five-minute dance in half an hour." Trisha Brown recalls distinctly the instruction to make a three-minute dance:

> This assignment was totally nonspecific except for duration, and the ambiguity provoked days of sorting through possibilities trying to figure out what time meant, was sixty seconds the only difference between three minutes and four minutes, how do you stop something, why, what relation does time have to movement, and on and on. Dick Levine taught himself to cry and did so for the full time period while I held a stopwatch instructed by him to shout just before the time elapsed, "Stop it! Stop it! Cut it out!" both of us ending at exactly three minutes. (21)

Other assignments involved collaborations in which autonomous personal control had to be relinquished within a "semi-independent" working situation. Others had to do with subject matter, for instance, "Make a dance about nothing special." Still others required the use of written scores or instructions. This had partly to do with Dunn's convictions about "inscrib[ing] dances on the bodies of the dancers, . . . on the body of the theater," and the notion of choreography as a kind of physicalized writing. "By planning the dance in a written or drawn manner, you have a very clear view of the dance and its possibilities," Dunn says. "Laban's idea was very secondarily to make a *Tanzschrift*, . . . a way to record. Laban's idea was to make a *Schrifttanz*, to use graphic — written — inscriptions and then to generate activities. Graphic notation is a way of inventing the dance" (7).

An interest in Labanotation and the theoretical issues of recording dance was on the rise in the dance community. Dunn's use of scores was certainly also related to the influence of Cage and other contemporary composers who were inventing new methods of scoring music in order to fit their new methods of composition and performance. But the dancers' use of written scores had a practical basis as well. According to Ruth Emerson: "There was no rehearsal space, and Bob understood that. It was well understood by everybody that most people didn't have a studio of their own. But in another week, you were expected to come in with something. [Scores were] the only practical way of conveying information. . . . [They were] expedient" (25–26).

Dunn recalls that his approach developed generally into supplying a "clearinghouse for structures derived from various sources of contemporary action: dance, music, painting, sculpture, Happenings, literature" (3). (However, because the previous generation of modern choreographers had so tied the meaning of their dances to literary ideas, the verbal arts were the least plumbed.) Beyond the freedom of method and the inspiration by other art forms, a crucial element in Dunn's pedagogy was the discussion of choice patterns as part of the presentation. Through this "postmortem" verbal analysis, the importance of the dancemaking process was underscored. Choreographic method came to be seen as an arena for creativity prior to, sometimes even instead of, movement invention.

Before moving on to the Judson Dance Theater itself, let us examine some of the methods for student works presented either in Dunn's class or at the first end-of-the-year showing for the class, since the students' input, as well as Dunn's, served as a catalyst in that situation, and not all of the students went on to participate in the concerts at Judson Church.

As I have noted, chance was a favored technique, not surprisingly in light of Merce Cunningham's influence on the group (several danced in his company and several more studied with him, and the class itself was given in his studio). And John Cage's influence was even greater. For Marni Mahaffay, the marvel of chance was that it seemed to create limitless possibilities: "I used the rotation of the moon to make one structure, but it could have been anything—for instance, the routine of getting up in the morning and cooking an egg. The path of the moon indicated where things could happen in space, in the dance" (8).

Chance was compelling, not only for its generative capabilities, but because it performed an important psychological function in forcing the choreographer to give up certain features of control. Mahaffay recalls, "To give up your own clichés, to give up your own movement that you were so attached to, was very exciting. You might only be given enough time to do the beginning of your favorite movement, or to do it much less than you would have preferred to. You ended up putting movements together in ways that weren't at all obvious or expected" (8). According to Ruth Emerson, chance also seemed an escape route from the domination of hierarchical authority: "For me it was a total change from controlling the process of how you made movement, which was first of all that you were supposed to suffer and . . . struggle with your interior, which I couldn't bear. I hated it. . . . It was such a relief to take a piece of paper and work on it without someone telling me I was making things the wrong way" (25).

Once one accepted all kinds of previously unacceptable formal choices that chance engendered (for example, stillness and repetition), all sorts of other choreographic devices became possible—repetition or stillness or arbitrariness by choice, rather than simply by chance. Despite the calculated formality and fragmentation of these methods, the movements they organized were not always abstract. Rainer wrote, about her movement choices of that period:

> I dance about things that affect me in a very immediate way. These things can be as diverse as the mannerisms of a friend, the facial expression of a woman hallucinating on the subway, the pleasure of an aging ballerina as she demonstrates a classical movement, a pose from an Etruscan mural, a hunchbacked man with cancer, images suggested by fairy tales, children's play, and of course my own body impulses generated in different

> situations—a classroom, my own studio, being drunk at a party. I am also deliberately involved in a search for the incongruous and in using a wide range of individual human and animal actions—speak, shriek, grunt, slump, bark, look, jump, dance. One or many of these things may appear in a single dance—depending on what I read, see, and hear during the period I am working on that dance. It follows, therefore, that no single dance is about any one idea or story, but rather about a variety of things that in performance fuse together and decide the nature of the whole experience. (14)

Here Rainer is laying a groundwork for what would replace chance as the key choreographic structure for postmodern dance: radical juxtaposition. Collage—with roots in dada and Duchamp, but also reflecting the crazy-quilt of the American urban landscape—was a preferred method for many visual artists of the period; the *Village Voice* dance critic, Jill Johnston, likened a 1962 piece by Fred Herko to a Rauschenberg combine. In Rainer's *The Bells* and *Satie for Two* (also of 1962), Johnston finds a precedent for the repetitive choreographic strategy in Gertrude Stein's circular, repetitive writing.

Another choreographic method used in Dunn's class, the stripping down of movement to "one thing," which later would resurface as a stringent asceticism paralleling that of minimalist sculpture, characterized dances by Simone Forti and Steve Paxton. Forti's "dance constructions" from that period dealt in ongoing activity, a continuum of motion rather than phrases or complex movement designs. Even her response to one of Dunn's Satie assignments is telling: rather than ordering her movements to the counts given by the number structures, she used the numbers to cue certain singular actions: "If it was a five she put her head down. If it was a three, she just put her two feet down. It was an exquisite dance," Remy Charlip remembers. Paxton made a dance in which he carried furniture out of the school office a piece at a time, and another in which he sat on a bench and ate a sandwich.

And at least three other devices that would be used in future Judson dances or works by Judson members arose in the Dunn class: rule games, interlocking instructions for a group, and using or "reading" a space (or some other structure not originally made as a score, such as a child's drawing or the activity of other people) as a score.

A Concert of Dance (1)

The second year of Dunn's class culminated in a public showing of work in the sanctuary of the Judson Memorial Church on Washington Square in Greenwich Village. It was this marathon, hours-long evening, with twenty-three dances by fourteen choreographers, that snowballed into what soon became known as the Judson Dance Theater. As with Dunn's class, the choreographic devices represented on this roster of works were many; since most of the dances had been composed as assignments for the course, the methods reiterate those discussed above, with some additions.

The connection between aleatory techniques and the automatism of surrealism emerged in the first event of the evening, which was not, strictly speaking, a dance, but a chance-edited film by Gene Friedman, John Herbert McDowell, and Elaine Summers. (It was not the last film to be billed as a dance event at a Judson concert.) Ruth Emerson's *Narrative*, the first live event on the program, used a score of interlocking directions involving walking patterns, focus, and tempo, as well as cues for actions based on the other dancers' actions. The "drama" in this "narrative" was physically, rather than psychologically motivated; a change in spatial or temporal relationships between people, no matter how abstractly based, seemed to carry psychological, interpersonal meaning. Emerson's *Timepiece*, based on chance (its very title was a tribute to the stopwatch, the renowned insignia of both John Cage and Robert Dunn), was structured by making a chart that had columns for movement quality (percussive or sustained), timing (on a scale of one to six, ranging from very slow to very fast), time limits (fifteen second periods, multiplied by factors ranging from one to six), movement material (five possibilities: "red bag, untying; turn, jump, jump; hands, head, plie; walking forward side back side side; heron leg to floor"), space time (10, 20, 30, 40, 50, or stillness), space (five areas of the stage plus offstage), front (direction for the facing of the body, with four square directions, four diagonals, and one wild choice), and levels in space (high, low or medium). The qualities having to do with movement and timing were put together, along the graph of absolute time, separately from the qualities dealing with space. Thus changes in area, facing, and level in space might occur during a single movement phrase. Given the fact that there were usually six elements in a gamut of choices for a given feature, the choices were probably selected by the roll of a die.

Emerson was a trained mathematician as well as a dancer; chance choreography appealed to her, and her *Timepiece* serves as a paradigm for chance choreography in its categorical exhaustiveness (for this reason, I have described it in detail). Elaine Summers's semiparodic approach to aleatory techniques in her *Instant Chance* signaled a growing impatience with a method that, for many, was becoming unfortunately fetishized. David Gordon complained that in Dunn's class, "Judy and Bob were really very rigid about this chance procedure stuff they were teaching. And I had already been through a lot of this chance stuff with Jimmy [Waring]. I wasn't very religious about it." Rainer wrote, "The emphasis on aleatory composition reached ridiculous proportions sometimes. The element of chance didn't ensure that a work was good or interesting, yet I felt that the tenor of the discussions [in the Dunn course] often supported this notion."[2] In Summers's *Instant Chance*, the "hidden operations" of the chance procedure were made part of the piece when the dancers threw large numbered styrofoam blocks in the air and performed whatever movement sequences were dictated by shape, color, and number of the block.

The use of "one thing" as structure surfaced in two dances that, despite their formal simplicity, were extremely theatrical: David Gordon's *Mannequin Dance*, in which, wearing a blood-stained biology lab coat, he slowly turned and lay down on the floor while singing and wiggling his fingers; and Fred Herko's *One or Twice a Week I Put on Sneakers to Go Uptown*, which Jill Johnston described as "a barefoot Suzie-Q in a tassel-veil head-dress, moving around the big performing area . . . only the barefoot Suzie-Q with sometimes a lazy arm snaking up and collapsing down. [And] with no alteration of pace or accent" (43). Implicit in these works was the austere, formalist approach that would become rampant in the period I have elsewhere called "analytic postmodern dance" in the seventies;[3] although it had been introduced by Forti at least a year before, it was not yet a favored method in the "breakaway" years of the early sixties.

Two dances that had been made for a class assignment about "cut-ups" were Carol Scothorn's *Isolations* and Ruth Emerson's *shoulder r.* Scothorn's involved cutting up Labanotation scores and Emerson's included Laban material, among other elements. The cut-up is a subcategory of chance procedures that was favored by the dadaists. Tristan Tzara gives instructions for how to make a dadaist poem based on cutting words out of an article, shaking them up in a bag, and reassembling them. Through Cage, the young New York avant-gardists were familiar with Robert Motherwell's book on *The Dada Painters and Poets*, published in 1951, in which these instructions appear. Perhaps the Tzara manifesto was even the source of this choreography assignment. But, in any case, many of the methods used by the dadaists and surrealists to undercut meaning or to release new meanings—from chance to collage—were consciously explored in the dance arena. That is, through their knowledge of the historical avant-garde, the Judson dancers could find a methodological treasure trove for their own, similar purposes.

The use of instructions is related to chance in that it foregrounds issues of control. Chance undermines the choreographer's control by subverting personal choices. (That, at least, is the theory; ultimately, however, the choreographer's choices are revealed in the original gamuts out of which the chance-decisions are made.) Instruction scores given to the dancer(s) by the choreographer exaggerate control, making palpable and objective the normally implicit, hegemonic position of choreographer over dancer—at least, making it explicit in the choreographic process (since neither chance nor instruction as a generating device is necessarily evident to the spectator). However, depending on how strictly the score codes instructions, such a method can also permit a great deal of freedom of interpretation by the dancer, recasting hegemony into partnership. Steve

Paxton's use of a score for *Proxy* grew directly out of thoughts about such issues. He was attempting through the score to make the learning and rehearsal process more objective and impersonal, to get away from the cult of imitation that he felt surrounded modern dance, a cult that began with the direct transmission of movements from teacher to pupil and ended with a hierarchically structured dance company. At the same time, he attempted through the score to go beyond what Cunningham and Cage had done in using chance techniques, for, as he puts it, "My feeling . . . was that one further step was needed, which was to arrive at movement by chance. That final choice, of making movement, always bothered my logic. . . . Why couldn't it be chance all the way?" Paxton's score was made by randomly dropping images and then gluing them in place on a large piece of brown paper: cut-out photographs of people walking and engaged in sports, plus cartoon images (Mutt and Jeff, and one from a travel advertisement). A moveable red dot marked the beginning the dancer had chosen. The score, then, served to mediate between choreographer and dancer, to distance the movements themselves from the choreographer's body and hence his personal style. According to Paxton:

> That was a selection process but one removed from actually deciding what to do with the pictures, because I made the score and then handed it over to the performers, and they could take a linear or circular path through the score. You could start any place you wanted to, but then you went all the way through it. You did as many repeats as were indicated, and you went back and forth as indicated. But how long it took and what you did between postures was not set at all. It was one big area of choice not at all influenced by the choreographer. The only thing I did in rehearsing the work was to go over it with them and talk about the details of the postures. (58)

Summers used a newspaper as a score in *The Daily Wake* for similar reasons. She describes her procedure:

> I took the front page and laid it out on the floor and used the words in it to structure the dance, and used the photographs in it so that they progressed on the surface of the page as if it were a map. If you start analyzing that way, you get deeper and deeper. You get more clues for structure, like how many paragraphs are there? Beginning with *The Daily Wake*, I became very interested in using photos as resource material, and other structures as maps. (53–54)

Another way to distance movement from personal style or personal expression, anathema to this generation precisely because it had become so overblown in the works of "historical" modern dance, was the completion of tasks or the handling of objects. Summers had this in mind in her *Instant Chance*. Robert Morris programmatically developed this method in *Arizona* (to be discussed below).

Yet another term in the debates about choreographic control and the boundaries of chance was the use of indeterminacy, that is, intervention by the performers through limited use of improvisation. This exceeded even Cunningham's relinquishing of control through chance (he was later, in *Story* [1963], perhaps inspired by some of the Judson experiments, to try his hand at indeterminacy, but he was not pleased by the results). Rainer's *Dance for 3 People and 6 Arms*, also performed at Concert 1, was a trio in which the dancers could choose when to perform one of a series of predetermined movement options, most of which, as the title suggests, were concerned with gestures and positions of the arms. Rainer dubbed this method, which combined chance and improvisation, "spontaneous determination." William Davis, one of the dancers, remembers of the first performance (at the Maidman Playhouse in March 1962):

> I think it was the first time dancers were waiting for a curtain to go up without having any idea whatsoever of the shape the dance was going to take.
>
> That kind of thing was being done musically [in the work of Cage and his colleagues]. What it really resembled was jazz musicianship, more than chance operations, because we were all working for a time when we might, for example, do this, or seeing what someone else is doing, think "Oh yes, I can connect this to that," or "They're doing fine, I'll just let them go at it." It's a sense of shape taking place in three people's minds as the dance is going on. (52)

Without going into detail about the rest of the dances on this historic program, I would like to note several other choreographic devices appearing in this first Judson concert (some of which have already been discussed in the section on Dunn's class or will be discussed further below) that would remain rich lodes for the Judson choreographers to mine: children's and adult's games (Gretchen MacLane's *Quibic*); quoting other artworks, either dance or in other media (Rainer's *Divertissement*, Deborah Hay's *Rain Fur*); the use of popular music and social dancing (Herko's *Once or Twice a Week . . .*, Davis's *Crayon*); collaboration (*Like Most People* by Fred Herko and Cecil Taylor; *Rafladan* by Alex Hay, Deborah Hay, and Charles Rotmil); and the collage, assemblage, or list format (Paxton's *Transit*, Gordon's *Helen's Dance*, Deborah Hay's *Five Things*, Rainer's *Ordinary Dance*, among others).

The Judson Workshop

Shortly after the momentous Concert of Dance in July 1962, Elaine Summers had organized A Concert of Dance 2 in Woodstock, New York, an artists' summer colony (before it became famous for the rock festival held there in 1969). Several dances from the Judson Church concert were shown and some new works by additional choreographers were added.

When in the fall of 1962 Robert Dunn did not continue his choreography class, Rainer and Paxton organized meetings of the group, at first in the studio Rainer shared with James Waring and Aileen Passloff on St. Mark's Place in the East Village, and then, after about a month, at the Judson Church, where they met weekly in the basement gymnasium. The purpose of this workshop was understood to be analytic and critical; new dances were not rehearsed there, but performed for peer scrutiny and feedback. Thus the emphasis in workshop discussions was on compositional method as well as such related issues as performance style.

By January 1963, the Judson weekly workshop had accumulated enough material to organize two concerts. The press release for Concerts 3 and 4 specifically underscored the workshop's emphasis on choreographic method. And, importantly, it pointed out that even though the search was on for new devices, new structures, and new theories, even traditional methods were permitted as but one more possibility in a wide, unrestricted range. "These concerts," it read,

> are in the series initiated at the church . . . with the aim of periodically presenting the work of dancers, composers, and various non-dancers working with ideas related to dance. The methods of composition of the works in this series range from the traditional ones which predetermine all elements of a piece to those which establish a situation, environment, or basic set of instructions governing one or more aspects of a work — thus allowing details and continuity to become manifest in a spontaneous or indeterminate manner.
>
> It is hoped that the contents of this series will not so much reflect a single point of view as convey a spirit of inquiry into the nature of new possibilities. (82)

Some of the dances in these two concerts were partly structured by the physical space of the venue: the church gym (for instance a collaboration by Robert Huot and Robert Morris, *War*, which put La Monte Young playing the musical accompaniment in the cage). The constraints of the physical performance space would affect or directly shape the dances in several future Judson concerts, in fact becoming a hallmark of the innovative spirit of the group. One long thread leading from such works was the spate of "environmental" dances in the late sixties and early seventies. But even where such considerations were not explicit in the dances, the space still governed such elements of performance as the intimacy or distance between spectator and performer and the shape and visibility of the "stage." In Concert 5, held in a rollerskating rink in Washington, D.C., Robert Rauschenberg built his entire dance (*Pelican*) on place; in it, Carolyn Brown danced in pointe shoes partnered by two men on roller skates. As well, the enormity of the space led the group to perform in various parts of the rink, making the audience mobile, and sometimes to fill the space (and challenge audience attention) by performing two dances simultaneously in different places. Concerts 9–12, held in the Gramercy Arts Theater—which had a proscenium stage so small one could barely move without moving off it—gave rise to a number of works in which motion was either minimal, very slow, or spilled into the house. These three radical approaches to movement, emerging here out of necessity, would also become approaches of choice, badges of the Judson heritage. Steve Paxton's *Afternoon*, sponsored by the workshop, took place in a forest in New Jersey; for this dance, Paxton was directly concerned with how the natural ground surface and "scenery" would change the movement, which had been constructed in a studio.

Many of the dances for Concert 13 were united both by spatial considerations and by the use of a physical structure (they all happened in, on, or around a sculpture commissioned from Charles Ross) as well as by performance style (the sculpture, evoking a jungle gym, sparked a common spirit of playfulness). Once again, a Judson emblem—dance and art as play—was strikingly condensed in a single event. Finally, a single concert, 14 (one of the last given jointly by the workshop before it disbanded in 1964), was organized around a single choreographic method: improvisation. Although improvisation was not, statistically speaking, a common device for the Judson choreographers, this concert, too, seemed symbolically to lay claim to a new alternative method for making and performing dances.

Some Exemplary Pieces

Nearly two hundred dances were produced by the Judson Dance Theater between July 1962 and October 1964, the time of the last concert officially sponsored by the workshop. After the workshop disbanded, dance performances continued to be produced at the church on an individual basis—the "bus-stop situation," as Judith Dunn later called it. A "second generation" of Judson dancers, including Meredith Monk, Kenneth King, and Phoebe Neville showed work at the church, as did members of James Waring's company (such as Toby Armour, Carol Marcy, and Deborah Lee), Waring himself, Aileen Passloff, and various original members of the Judson Dance Theater workshop. There was even a revival of Judson "hits," presented at the church, as early as 1966.

As I have noted above, many of the seeds of the methodology for the workshop were already planted in the Robert Dunn class; the first concert and those selected concerts discussed in the preceding section represent a sizeable cross-section of the techniques that would continue to provide food for dancing over the next several years, and by the next several cohorts of choreographers. I am concentrating here on the pioneering choreography by the members of the original workshop, but obviously space does not even permit a discussion of every dance performed over the year and a half of the Judson Dance Theater workshop's lifetime (and, of course, since not every dance was the result of an entirely new method, such a review would be tedious). Therefore I would like to devote the next section of the paper to discussing selected dances that not only exemplify the choreographic concerns of the group and of individuals in the group, but that also point in directions that have proved fruitful for the succeeding generations of choreographers in the postmodern mode.

The first full-length evening dance by a single choreographer sponsored by the Judson Dance Theater was Yvonne Rainer's *Terrain*. This dance, in four sections, in retrospect seems a treasure trove of choreographic devices, structures, performance attitudes, and other aspects of style; in it one sees the preoccupations that wend their way in one form or another through the rest of Rainer's oeuvre, reaching their fullest expression in her *The Mind is a Muscle* and *Continuous Project—Altered Daily*. The title is prophetic, for this dance represents the "terrain" of dance Rainer continued to map out in her choreographic career and even in her film work. The dance used methods culled from child's play and rule games (the sections "Diagonal" and "Play"). It had an entire section based on parody through pastiche ("Duet," in which Rainer performed a ballet adagio and Trisha Brown performed a balletic sequence in the upper body with burlesque bumps and grinds in the lower torso, ending with both assuming "cheesecake" poses, all to a collage of music that included African drumming, American jazz, and fragments of Massenet's opera *Thaïs*). The technique of "spontaneous determination" that had provided the armature for *Dance for 3 People and 6 Arms* also surfaced here, as did elements of repetition and chance, the list as organizational tool, and the generating of movement by turning to another art form—in this case, erotic Hindu temple sculpture. Talking while dancing, a technique by which Rainer had electrified spectators in *Ordinary Dance*, surfaced here in the two sequences from the "Solo" section that used texts by Spencer Holst.

Rainer also used several objects for some of the solos in the "Solo" section of *Terrain*. For the Judson choreographers, as for their contemporaries the pop artists, the ordinary object was particularly resonant. Robert Morris wrote in *The Drama Review* that objects and task behavior were two preferred methods for rinsing the dance of excess expressiveness and to find new ways of moving the body:

> From the beginning I wanted to avoid the pulled-up, turned-out, antigravitational qualities that not only gave a body definition and role as "dancer" but qualify and delimit the movement available to it. The challenge was to find alternative movement. . . . A fair degree of complexity of . . . rules and cues effectively blocked the dancer's performing "set" and reduced him to frantically attempting to respond to cues—reduced him from performance to action. (143)

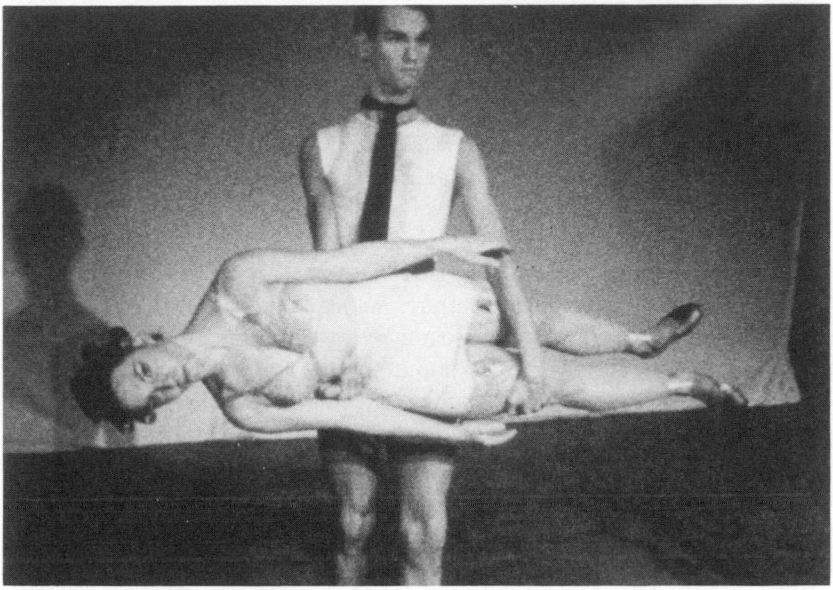

Phoebe Neville and Kenneth King in King's *cup/saucor/two dancors/radio.* (Photo: Jonas Mekas.)

For Morris, objects were superior to tasks as a means to solve problems and thus create a structure for the dance. The manipulation of an object generated movement without becoming more important than the performer or the performance. In *Arizona*, Morris threw a javelin, swung a small light while the stage lights dimmed, and adjusted a T-form; all these objects, he wrote, "held no inherent interest for me but were means for dealing with specific problems," such as setting up relationships among movement, space, and duration, or shifting focus between the "egocentric and the exocentric" in the small light contrasting to the dimming stage lights.

Lucinda Childs in *Carnation* (and in several other works) also built a dance around the cool manipulation of everyday things. Yet here the deadpan attitude itself and the *kinds* of objects used (things associated with women's beauty care or domestic activities such as cleaning and cooking) add up to a seething "hot" significance. (Kenneth King's *cup/saucer/two dancers/radio*, a slightly later dance by a member of the "second generation" of Judson choreographers, radically extends the sense of alienation Childs hints at humorously, partly by equating all the elements listed in the title.) Undoubtedly the fascination with the object—the mute, ordinary, everyday object—reflects a growing consumer society, the burgeoning cornucopia of available goods of the United States during this period.

Yvonne Rainer's *Some Thoughts on Improvisation* (part of Concert 14) is another paradigmatic piece for several reasons: its use of improvisation as a structuring device, its baring of the devices, its analytic reflexivity. This dance, too, like so many others by Rainer during this period, includes a spoken text, but in this case the words are taped, serving as the "musical accompaniment" to the dance—or a sound track, to liken the event to Rainer's later terrain, the cinema. As Rainer improvised the dance, dressed in a black dress and high-heeled shoes (a costume that not only stands for a certain image of femininity, but that also severely limits movement possibilities), her voice described the improvisatory process, both in general and in this specific case. Her monologue moves from an almost phenomenological description of thoughts and experiences ("So I keep on sizing up the situation, see. And I keep on walking. And I make decisions. He has left the room, I will run; she is standing stockstill, I will bring my head close to hers; that man is moving his arms around, I will do as he does; the wall looms close, I will walk until I bump into it . . . [196]") to a dissection of the choicemaking patterns in improvisation. She lists three aspects of choice: impulses, anti-impulses, ideas. The action, she notes, can come from any of these, including the decision not to follow an impulse. It is, finally, the instinct of the performer, including the assertion of physical and mental control and the mastery of anxiety, that fuels the performance, she concludes. "When it goes forward it moves with an inexorable thrust and exerts a very particular kind of tension: spare, unadorned, highly dramatic, loaded with expectancy—a field for action. What more could one ask for" (197).

Although improvisation is often remembered as one of the most important legacies of the Judson Dance Theater, this particular concert (14), with its eight dances all conjoined by the shared method of improvisation, was not considered successful. Jill Johnston wrote:

> Ironically, one of the concerts on this last series . . . was a great improvisation, with minimal restrictions on freedom, and the most impressive collection of vanguard dancers and artists . . . couldn't get this tacitly accepted Open Sesame (free play) off the ground. Everybody was very polite except for Yvonne Rainer . . . and the response to her nerve should have been pandemonium if anybody had faced the assertion squarely. (198)

Yet it was this improvisatory side of the Judson Dance Theater, signaling freedom, that would later give rise to, for example, the Grand Union—one of the most brilliant projects of the postmodern dance.

Another key outgrowth of the Judson Dance Theater was the use of multiple media, or intermedia, especially film, in the dance. This seems only fair, since, although many of the dance ideas of the group came from searching for the essence of dance per se, still others came from the inspiration or influence of other media and other art forms, in particular the visual arts, new music, and film. Of course, in the spirit of breaking down the boundaries between the art forms, artists in different fields were making events that so traded in mixing media that it was often difficult to categorize them, except by the author's label. An early mixed-media event at the Judson Dance Theater was Beverly Schmidt's *The Seasons*. It was a vignette from a larger "film-stage" performance, called *Blossoms*, conceived by the choreographer's husband, Roberts Blossom. For *The Seasons*, Schmidt memorized the dance she had improvised for the film shown in the earlier performance, then choreographed a new live solo, which was performed simultaneously with the film projection, sometimes in counterpoint or opposition and sometimes in unison. The dance was in four sections, with live music by Philip Corner and Malcolm Goldstein, and recorded music by Purcell. Each section had a distinctive movement quality, costume, and color — a distinctive mood, which Schmidt made correspond to the four seasons.

The Seasons served as a model for future events in both dance and film. The following year, two evening-length concerts by individual members of the workshop incorporating film into the dancing were sponsored by the Judson Dance Theater — Elaine Summers's *Fantastic Gardens* and Judith Dunn's *Last Point*. Meredith Monk, who arrived on the Judson scene after the end of the workshop, made the fusion of dance and film central to her work from the beginning, in such pieces as *Sixteen Millimeter Earrings* (1966). Reading Johnston's review of Schmidt's dance, one is even reminded of Lucinda Childs's recent collaboration with Sol LeWitt, using film as décor, in *Dance*:

> The interplay of images — the soft, majestic volume of the figure on the screen with the diminutive flesh and blood on stage — made a shifting mirror of the kind of dimension that reached far beyond, in the past and future, the moments of reckoning on that small stage. Near the end I had the uncanny feeling of an ancient presence when her head loomed large in an instant of immobilized totemistic grandeur. (159)

The list goes on and on: dances built on parodies of other dances or of performance styles (such as David Gordon's *Random Breakfast*); dances structured like sports events or based on sports movements (for example, Judith Dunn's *Speedlimit*), dances generated out of pure flashes of energy (Carolee Schneemann's *Newspaper Event*, et al.), repetition, tasks, free association, "ritual," unfinished work. As well, choreographers continued to use all the methods and devices I have mentioned above: time structures taken from music, chance, indeterminacy, "spontaneous determination," rules, limits, collaboration, written scores, interlocking instructions for a group, and using or "reading" a space (or some other structure not originally made as a score, such as a child's drawing or the activity of other people) as a score, children's and adult's games, quoting other artworks (both dance and other media), the use of popular music and social dancing, the collage, assemblage, or list format, "a situation, environment, or basic set of instructions governing one or more aspects of a work," automatism, satire, cut-ups, handling objects, responding to physical space, improvisation, verbal content, mixing media — and even traditional methods of composition, such as classical musical structures, image construction, and aspiring to values of unity, complexity, and coherence.

I might say a word here about *my* methods. I have tried to get at choreographic structures or devices in a number of ways, not all of which were available for each dance. The dance historian is like an archaeologist, digging up fragments and — depending on the quantity and quality of the shards, their capacity for transmitting various types of information — she puts them together, with a glue partly consisting of informed speculation, to form a picture of the thing as it was. But this picture will almost always still be incomplete.

Using the scores and the oral and written memoirs of the choreographers, on the one hand (which tells us something about sources, intentions, and process), and the descriptions, interpretations, and evaluations of witnesses — colleagues, critics, and spectators — on the other hand (which tells us something about reception and product), I have pieced together the preceding accounts — accounts that, as you have seen, vary in terms of fullness and even in terms of accuracy.

The structures and methods of some Judson Dance Theater works are simply lost and will never be retrieved. (Deborah Hay, for example, destroyed her written records afterwards and does not remember most of her dances of that period.) For other works, we may know about the methods in a general way without gaining any sense of the way the dance looked and felt — its movement details, its performance style. Yet other works are well-documented and well-remembered enough to live on — some even in live reconstructions (though it is important to realize that reconstructed dances may not necessarily replicate the original exactly).[4]

A ground was cleared at the Judson that created new challenges for the following generation; in the 1970s, an entire wing of analytic, formalist postmodern dancers extended and consolidated that passion for revealing choreographic process, which sprang from the freedom of method (and the concomitant articulation of method) of the 1960s. But, by the 1980s, choreographic process seemed less important than choreographic product — for obvious cultural reasons, but also perhaps because methodological innovation was a frontier so thoroughly explored, to many it seemed no new devices could be discovered. But the 1980s are another story.

26

Vital Signs: Steve Paxton's *Flat* in Perspective

The dance *Flat*, by Steve Paxton, was first performed in Concert for New Paltz (an event organized by members of the Judson Dance Theater at the State University of New York at New Paltz) on January 30, 1964. I saw Paxton perform a reconstruction of *Flat* at Bennington College on April 18, 1980. The description of *Flat* given here is based on that viewing and on viewings of a videotape made at that performance.

The purpose of this study is to perform an in-depth analysis of a dance and to gain an understanding of its meaning through an assessment of its formal components, its cultural icons, and its style. To some, this analysis may seem overly detailed, especially in the section on description. However, I have deliberately approached this dance in an obsessive manner for several reasons. First, too many dances (in particular, too many postmodern dances) are poorly documented, if they are documented at all, and so disappear instantaneously. Therefore this essay is in part, like the recent reconstruction of the dance it glosses, an attempt to make a contribution to dance history. But, second and more importantly, this discussion is an illustration of a general theoretical point meant to apply not only to *Flat* but to other postmodern works as well, which is that postmodern dances not only *are* but also *mean*. Therefore I have tried here to present a model for an analysis that seeks to find the meaning given by form and style, an analysis that could be performed on any dance, postmodern or otherwise, and I have made this model as full and as detailed as possible, preferring too much information to too little in the process of unfolding the performance in a larger time and space. Often in taking apart an artwork for the purpose of analysis, one takes steps that might seem mundane or obvious or (as in the case of pure description) even tedious, for the purpose of amplifying and enriching the final interpretation. In trying to examine the cultural categories Paxton manipulates in *Flat*, then, I have tried to dissect the dance exhaustively.

A *Spectrum of World Dance: Tradition, Transition, and Innovation,* Lynn Ager Wallen and Joan Acocella, eds., CORD Dance Research Annual XVI (New York, 1987).

One problem in this study is that I have had to base my observations on one performance only. Although with the help of video I have been able to examine this performance closely, I still cannot know how the dance changes from one performance to the next; I cannot know the constants and variables in the structure of the work. Judging from the choreographer's description of *Flat*, there are features that change, such as the order of the incidents.

Description

In a chronology of his works, Paxton describes *Flat* as follows:

> Photographic score-catalogue performed in unset order. Score mixed with activities: lean against wall, circle walks, removal of shoes, jacket, shirt, and pants; clothes hung on 3 hooks taped to body. Performer redressed and exits.[1]

In the performance of *Flat* under discussion, the performer (Paxton) did not lean against the wall. Perhaps this was because the back of the stage area was marked by a curtain rather than a wall. In addition to the activities Paxton describes, the dance also included poses, standing still, and movements frozen in mid-action; these probably are parts of the "photographic score-catalogue." All these actions and stillnesses were repeated and rearranged in a way that was both aesthetically symmetrical and meaningful.

A light comes up on the stage, revealing a wooden chair without arms—a plain, old-fashioned library chair (in fact, a chair from the Bennington dining hall)—standing stage right. A man enters from the upstage right corner and walks across the space to stand just slightly left of center, upstage. He wears a beige suit (jacket and pants), a white shirt, no tie, dark socks, and black canvas Chinese shoes. He stands, showing the audience his left profile. He faces away from the chair, which is downstage relative to him. He then walks in a large circle, stopping for a few seconds, then repeating the circular path. After tracing nearly two and a half rounds, he suddenly crouches, facing the chair, his left leg higher than his right, both elbows bent and hands curled into fists, the left arm held higher than the right. He holds this pose for a few seconds, then gets up and walks, making one and a half circles that widen to bring his path to the chair.

He starts to sit down, freezes momentarily just before making contact with the seat, then completes the action, sitting still in the chair in a relaxed manner, his knees open a bit, his hands resting on his thighs, and his feet flat on the floor.

The man gets up, walks in a circle again, then sits down in the chair, crosses his right leg over his left so that his right ankle rests on the left thigh, and removes his right shoe, then his right sock. As he pulls the sock off, he freezes. He completes the action, then puts the shoe, with the sock inside it, on the floor underneath the chair. He repeats the operation on the other side, but this time he does not stop until he bends over to put the shoe on the floor. He returns to his neutral sitting position.

After taking off his shoes, the man gets up, walks to his original place on the perimeter of the circle, and stands. He takes a few steps, tracing only a small arc along his round path, and stands again. Then he circumambulates once more, strikes the crouching pose for just a few seconds, then briefly a second pose that looks like a baseball player up to bat, then the crouching pose, this time for fifteen seconds (that is, what feels like a rather long time). He then strikes a new pose: sitting on the floor with both legs folded toward his left, his torso tilted toward his legs, his left arm bent outward with the hand forming a fist, his head turned left, and his right arm bent up so that his right hand is behind his head, as in bathing beauty "cheesecake" poses or, perhaps, as in the Hungarian folkdance *czardas*. He holds this pose, too, for fifteen seconds, then returns to the crouching pose.

After this series of poses, the man gradually undresses. First he makes another circuit, then takes off his jacket, unbuttons a few buttons on his shirt while holding the jacket in his left hand, and hangs the jacket on a hook taped to his chest. With the jacket hanging down the front of his body, he again walks a full round, then strikes a new pose: standing with his back to the audience, his legs apart and straight, both arms bent but reaching up toward the ceiling. He walks a short arc, one quarter of the circle, strikes the batter's pose, then immediately strikes a second crouching configuration, recognizable as a baseball catcher's position.

Standing up in the same spot, the man takes off his pants. He holds them in his right hand while he unbuttons the rest of the buttons on his shirt and removes it. He transfers the pants to his left hand, then hangs the shirt up on a hook taped to his back, using his right hand. He takes his pants with his right hand and hangs them up on a second hook taped to his back. He stands still. Then he assumes the first crouching pose (fifteen seconds), the sitting pose (fifteen seconds, this time with the left hand open), then the batter's pose (ten seconds). He walks around the circle again until he reaches his original station, and there he gets dressed.

He takes the pants off the hook with his right hand, begins to put them on—freezing after inserting his left leg in the trousers—and then completes the operation. He takes another circular walk, takes his shirt off its hook with his right hand, puts it on and stands still, then unhooks the jacket with his right hand, and puts it on.

He walks another round, widening the circle so that he reaches the chair. This time he pauses before beginning to sit down. Then he puts on his left sock, his left shoe, his right sock, picks up his right shoe and freezes for ten seconds, and then puts on his right shoe. He sits in the neutral sitting position for fifteen seconds, then gets up and exits out the upstage right corner.

Figure 1 illustrates the fourteen segments I have isolated in this dance. The dance is not organized into rhythmic phrases. Rather, the recurring circle forms a natural marker for the segments. This repudiation of rhythmic organization is important to the meaning of the dance in several ways, as we will see in the final sections of this study. I have used each circle or portion of a circle as the starting point for a new segment of activity, no matter how much activity follows the circle. Figure 2 illustrates the gamut of numbered poses used in the dance and gives the exact timing for each. In addition to the numbered poses, I refer to the neutral standing and sitting poses as the zero standing and sitting positions.

Toward an Analysis

Figures 1 and 2 show that the main categories manipulated in this dance are space, time, movement and poses (absence of movement), and objects. This may seem trivial or obvious, but it is important to notice that dances often also emphasize other features, including the use of musical accompaniment, and that many dances do not employ objects. Verbal language, absent here, is not considered a usual element in most traditional theatrical dances (that is, in ballet or modern dance), yet in the early 1960s avant-garde it was often used. Facial expression is another feature that usually comes into play in dance and theater. The fact that here the facial expression, lacking in affect, never changes, is in itself meaningful.

Space is used in two ways in *Flat*. First, one can clearly see a floorplan, with a circular path carved out by virtue of repetition and with three stations on the circumference of the circle where various activities take place (see fig. 1). There is also one station outside of the circle—the chair—where more actions occur (although at one point Paxton widens the circle to envelop the chair in his path). The orbit the performer follows only deviates when he crosses the space toward or away from the chair and when he enters and exits. The fact that nearly all of the activities take place along the rim of the circle and that the tracing of the circle (or part of it) sandwiches every segment of the dance is important to the poetics of the work. It (literally) provides a shape. The circular walk acts as a kind of rinse for the spectator's visual "screen," clearing the way for each new set of actions. The circle also acts as an all-encompassing leveler, reducing all of the segments to a state of equal importance. Similarly, the coexistence in space of the circle and the chair serves to equalize the man and the object, which always stand in visual opposition to each other.

The second use of space is in terms of levels (see fig. 2). Activities take place at a high level (pose 4), at a medium level (zero standing and pose 2), at a medium-low level (zero sitting), at a low level (poses 1 and 5), and at an extremely low level (pose 3). Thus, although the dance seems very simple and even monotonous, in fact it densely articulates the various levels of

Figure 1. Fourteen segments in *Flat.*

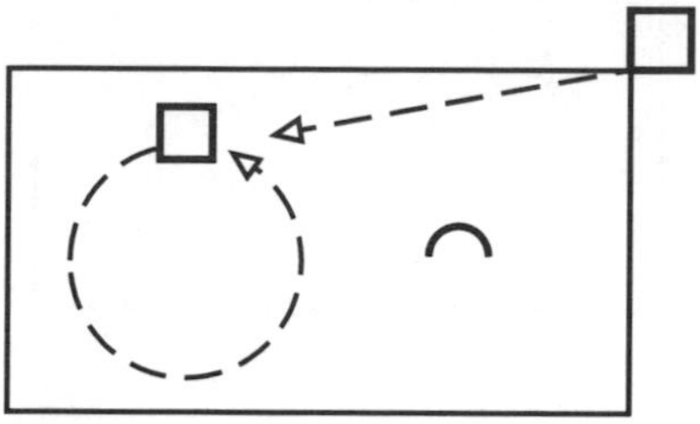

1. Enter.
   Pause: 10 seconds
   Circle: 1
   Action: stand
   Pause: 20 seconds

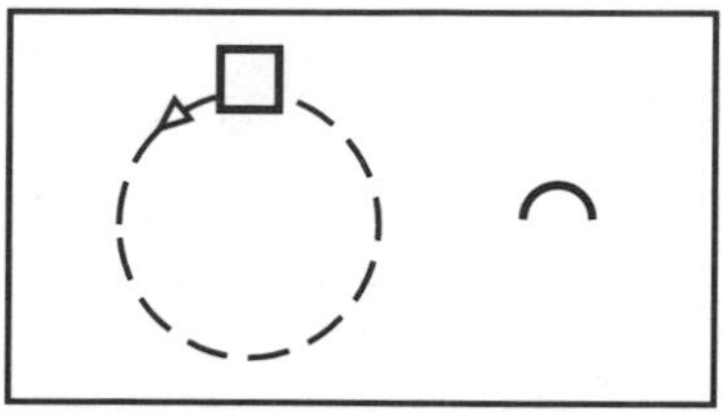

2. Circle: 1+
   Action: stand
   Pause: 15 seconds

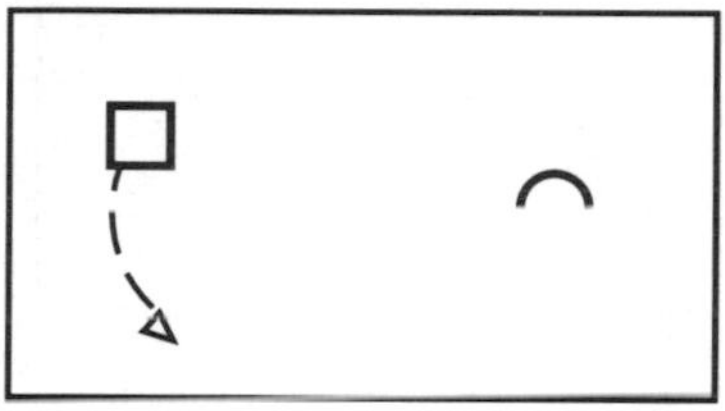

3. Circle: ⅓
   Action: Pose #1
   Pause: 15 seconds

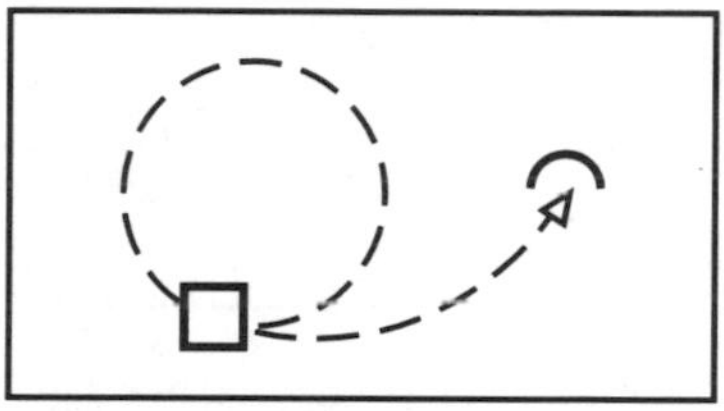

4. Circle: 1½ (widens)
   Action: start to sit down
   Pause: 10 seconds
   Action: complete sitting down, i.e., assume zero sitting
   Pause: 10 seconds
   Action: stand up, walk

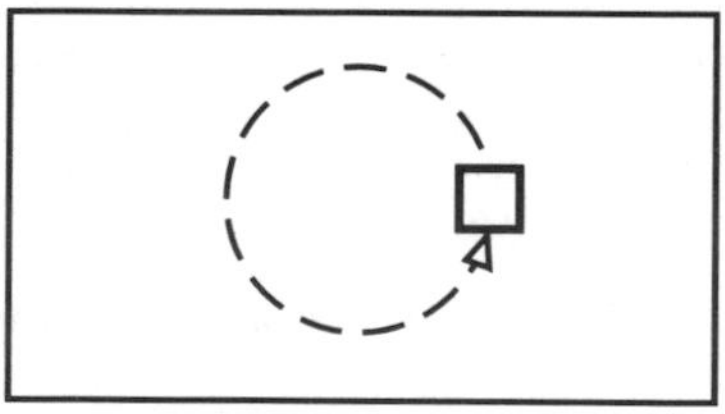

5. Circle: 1
   Action: sitting pose
   Pause: 15 seconds
   Action: cross right leg over left, take off shoe and begin to remove sock
   Pause: 5 seconds
   Action: complete sock removal, put down, sit
   Pause: 5 seconds
   Action: take off left shoe and sock, put down on floor under chair
   Pause: 10 seconds (bent over)
   Action: sit
   Pause: 2 seconds
   Action: stand up and walk

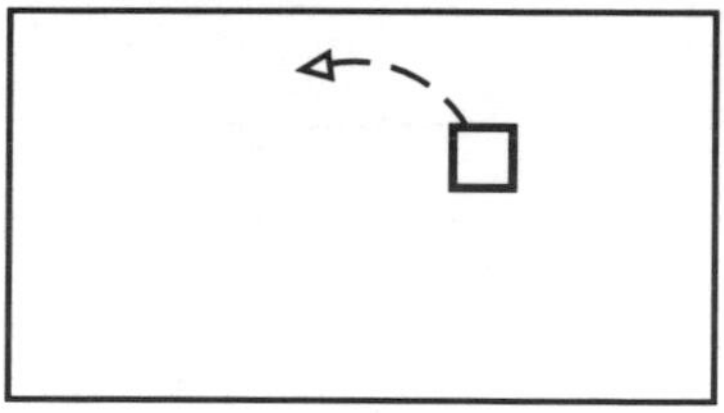

6. Circle: ¼
   Action: stand
   Pause: 10 seconds

KEY

Path – – – –
Starting point of path □
End point of path ▷
Chair ⌒

Figure 1. Fourteen segments in *Flat.* (continued)

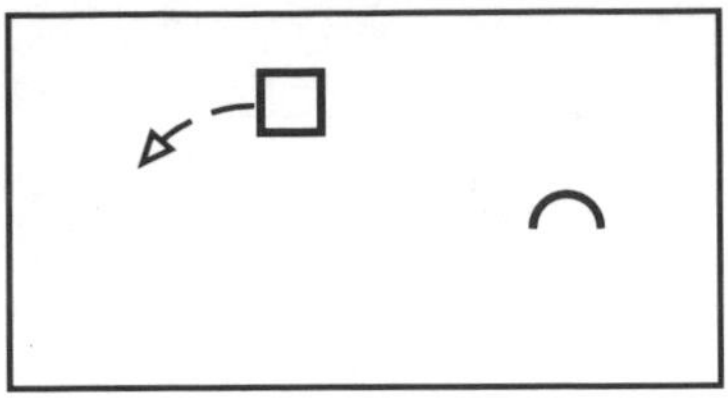

7. Circle: ⅛
   Action: stand
   Pause: 15 seconds

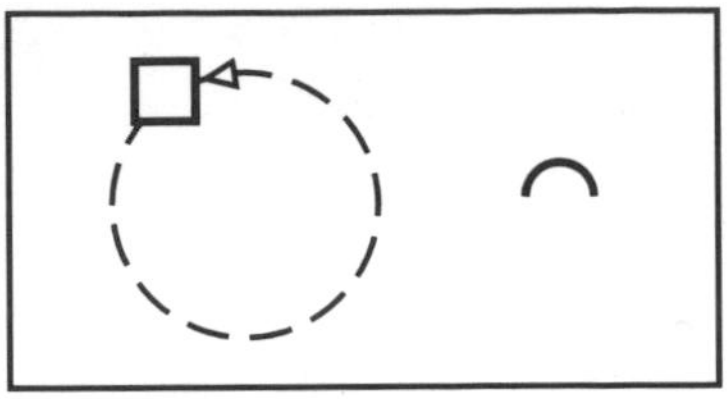

8. Circle:
   Action: Pose 1 Pause: 5 seconds
   Action: Pose 2 Pause: 5 seconds
   Action: Pose 1 Pause: 15 seconds
   Action: Pose 3 Pause: 15 seconds
   Action: Pose 1 Pause: 15 seconds

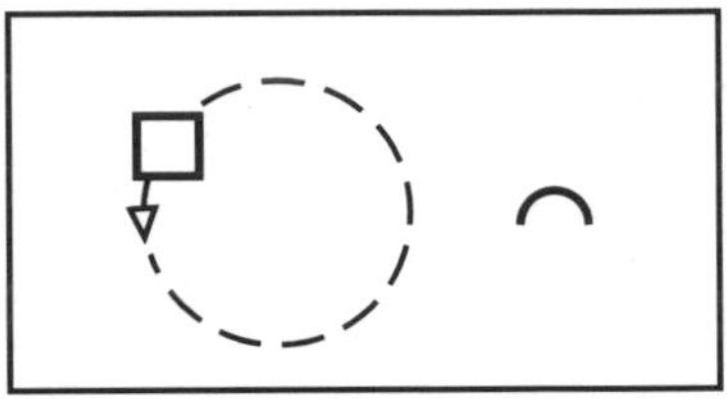

9. Circle: 1+
   Action: take off jacket,unbutton shirt, hang jacket on chest, stand
   Pause: 15 seconds

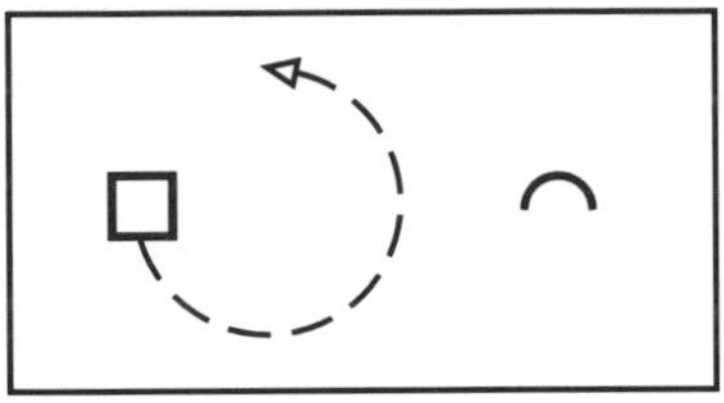

10. Circle: ¾
    Action: Pose 4
    Pause: 7 seconds

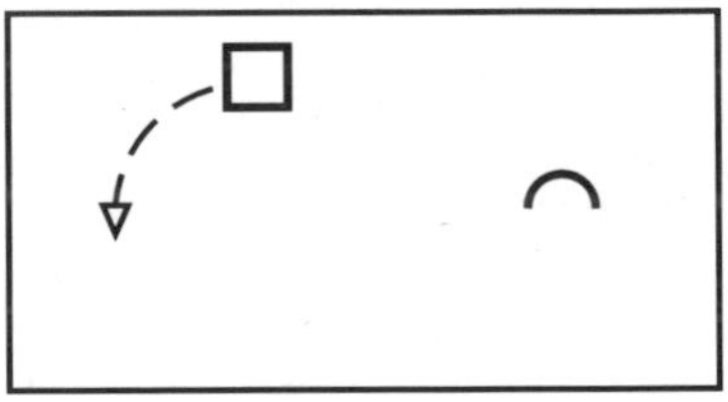

11. Circle: ¼
    Action: Pose 2 Pause: 2 seconds
    Action: Pose 5 Pause: 2 seconds
    Action: remove pants, remove shirt, hang shirt on back, hang pants on back
    Pause: 10 seconds
    Action: Pose 1 Pause: 15 seconds
    Action: Pose 3 Pause: 15 seconds
    Action: Pose 2 Pause: 10 seconds

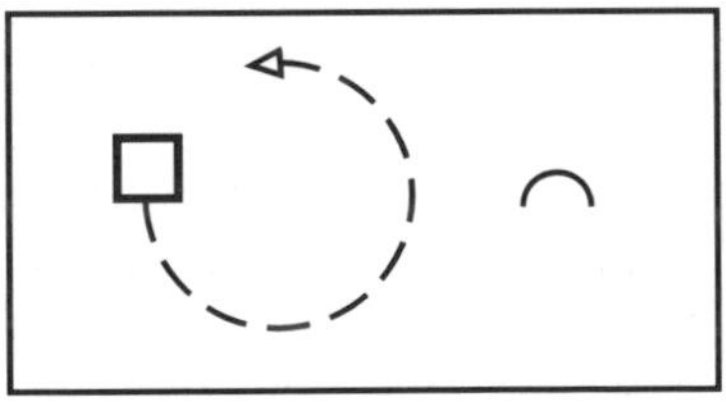

12. Circle: ¾
    Action: stand
    Pause: 20 seconds
    Action: take pants off hook, put on left leg
    Pause: 5 seconds
    Action: finish putting on pants

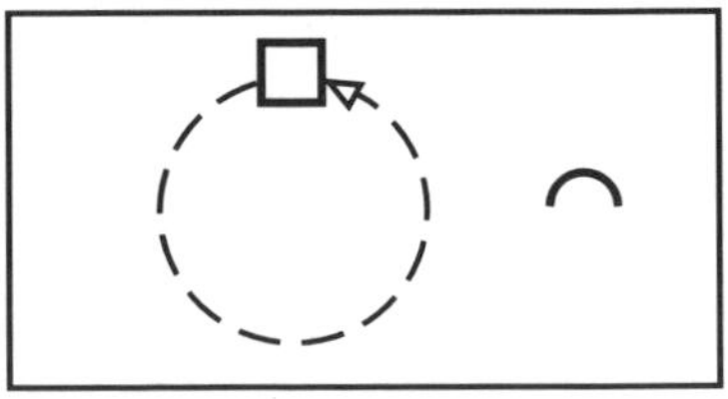

13. Circle: 1
    Action: take shirt off hook, put on, stand
    Pause: 2–3 seconds
    Action: take jacket off hook, put on

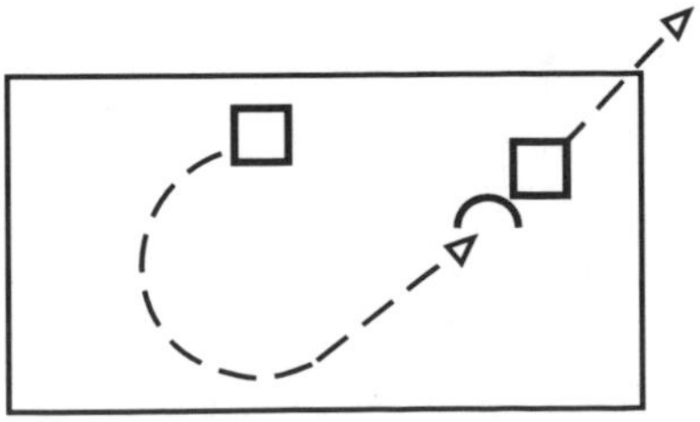

14. Circle: ¾ (widens)
    Action: sit down
    Pause: 2 seconds
    Action: put on left sock and shoe, right sock
    Pause: 10 seconds
    Action: put on right shoe, sit
    Pause: 15 seconds
    Action: stand up
    Exit.

Figure 2. Five emblematic poses in *Flat*.

space in which people operate. Although his path is unvarying and constricted, through the range of levels of space the "hero" of the dance assumes a complex, variegated human dimension.

Like the path in space, the way time is used also serves to flatten and equalize events. Timing is not used for the kind of phatic function one finds in many dances, where a marked climax draws the audience's attention and where the alternation of slow and fast movements maintains contact as well as operating poetically. Here the timing is both steady and arbitrary. The poses are sustained for different lengths of time, but one notices their differences only in that the timing fluctuates unpredictably and does not operate with a rhythmic pulse. In other words, one feels that this pose is brief and that one long, not that the dance is changing from a four-count to a twelve-count phrase.

Most of the variation in the dance comes, as one might expect, in the realm of movement and poses. However, none of the movements here are technical dance movements. They are, rather, ordinary, everyday movements, movements that are "natural" in the sense that, although they function as cultural signs in that they identify the mover in terms of culture, class, and so on, they are not especially stylized, abstracted, or ornamented. These movements are: walking, sitting down and getting up, and manipulating clothing (that is, dressing and undressing). In fact, where these movements are stylized by freezing in the act of performing them, that simply serves to underscore their ordinariness as actions and the casual, untheatrical way in which the actions are performed. The poses include neutral standing and sitting, both of which, like the movements, fall into the category of the everyday. In addition, there are five special poses, which can be considered emblems; that is, they are postures that have a set, specific meaning in our culture. The total gamut of poses, then, comprising both the neutral and the special poses, includes three standing poses (zero, pose 2, and pose 4), two sitting postures (zero and pose 3), and two crouching positions (poses 1 and 5). The total range of activity in the dance consists of combinations of these movements and poses, together with stillnesses, frozen movement, and one variation in gesture in pose 3, from a hand held in a fist to an open hand.

As Marcel Mauss and Gordon Hewes have shown, no movement or posture is natural and universal.[2] "Techniques of the body," as Mauss refers to the repertory of body movements, are learned cultural traits, and these techniques include such basic functions as walking, sitting, sleeping, excreting, sexual intercourse, giving birth, and nursing, as well as more specialized techniques such as dancing and sports. For any given position, Hewes shows a number of alternative styles. Thus the very way one sits or crouches, and not merely the fact that one is sitting or crouching, is rich with meaning. The walk that Paxton uses in *Flat* is a relaxed, efficient walk, with no excess movements of the arms and legs. The arms swing slightly in opposition to the leg movements; the legs bend just enough to permit a medium-sized step. The back and neck are erect, and the head faces in the direction of the walk. It is a relaxed, comfortable, yet correct, and not at all sloppy, American white middle-class male walk. The movements of dressing and undressing, sitting down and getting up are all done in the same nonchalant, unhurried, unexceptional, efficient way.

The zero standing and sitting postures are, again, typical white middle-class male postures. The standing position shows a man standing up straight, in a relaxed yet alert position. The sitting position has the same connotation; the man's back is straight, his knees are slightly apart, and his hands rest on his thighs just above his knees.

In terms of the special poses, the first crouching pose, pose 1, corresponds to the crouching posture Hewes labels number 127. The arms are held forward of the body with the elbows bent, the left arm higher than the right, and the hands forming fists, as if grasping an instrument. This pose is emblematic of the warrior grasping a spear or the sportsman handling an oar. The second crouching pose, pose 5, corresponds to Hewes's posture number 131, but with the right hand placed on the right hip. This is the emblematic pose of the baseball catcher. Standing pose 2 is the stance of the baseball batter. Standing pose 4 corresponds to the action of a weight lifter.

The sitting position that falls into this category of emblems, pose 3, is more problematic. It has different connotations when it is performed in different states of dress. According to Hewes, in almost every culture to sit with the legs folded to one side is a "strongly feminine custom" (1955:240). Certainly that is true in the United States. The gesture of holding the hand behind the head is also considered feminine in mainstream American culture. When a man wearing a suit strikes this pose with this gesture, he presents a token of effeminacy. However, when Paxton strikes this same pose a second time, he is clothed in draperies (formed by the clothes he has taken off and hung on his body) that create a classical look, and his left hand is now open. Now the image is redolent of the masculine beauty and strength expressed in Greek sculpture and in Michelangelo's painting *The Creation of Adam* on the ceiling of the Sistine Chapel. The change in clothing and the alteration of a single gesture transform the image from one despised in mainstream American culture to a treasured icon of masculinity in the Western world.

Thus in *Flat* Paxton presents a set of actions with several meanings. One ensemble of actions calls to mind an ordinary, conventional, even humdrum white American upper-middle-class man, perhaps a lawyer, an accountant, or an advertising man. Another ensemble of activities connotes other, highly symbolic images of masculinity from sports and from fine art. And still another pose represents femininity.

The activities in the dance (that is, the entire range of doings, from motions and poses to transitions and stillnesses) function in a number of ways. First, they operate poetically. There is a symmetry in the order of the movements. Both the circling and the symmetrical structure of undressing, striking poses in various stages of undress, and then dressing provide artistic unity in the dance. The array of poses in different levels of space, from standing to crouching to sitting, is formally quite pleasing.

Second, the doings are referential in the ways noted above, in that they refer to specific meanings in the culture. But also, they comment on the code of dance elements. They are an illustration of a theory of movement for dance that challenges the notion that a dance is an arrangement of special technical movements or even an arrangement of ordinary motions that have been imbued with extra expressiveness or energy.[3] Instead, *Flat* illustrates the proposition that a dance can consist of artfully arranged movements no matter how ordinary those movements or the style in which they are performed. This fits with the practice not only of Paxton in his earlier dances—which included such basic nonspecialized body motions as walking, moving furniture, and eating—but also of several other choreographers in the Judson Dance Theater, of which Paxton was an active member.[4] In *Flat* a full complement of the categories of movement and pose is arrayed: moving and not moving, posing and not posing, walking and not walking, and so on. The stillnesses often function analytically. Like stop-action photography, they freeze a movement one might think of as a single flow of action, rendering the movement less familiar and also dissecting it as a series of actions, revealing its multiplicity. Thus the action of sitting down or of taking off a sock proves to be an ensemble of motions and is enriched and imbued with aesthetic value.

In terms of their referents, the movements and poses in *Flat* fall into two distinct categories: those that refer to natural functions and those that refer to cultural functions. On the natural side fall the actions of walking, standing, sitting down, and getting up. As I have noted above, these are not natural in the sense that they are universal in terms of style. Rather, they are natural in the sense that all people do them and animals can, too. On the cultural side fall the activities having to do with getting dressed and undressed and also the designated poses, which are emblematic of social meaning.

I have discussed the use of space, time, and movements and poses in the dance; the use of objects remains. There are three categories of inanimate objects in *Flat*. One is the chair, which is a particular kind of chair. It is a Windsor chair, an armless wooden chair with a back made of an oval frame surrounding numerous narrow vertical rods. It is the type of chair one sees in intellectual institutions like libraries and universities, or in tasteful upper-middle-class homes, or in restaurants and men's clubs. It has a specific Anglo-American identity; it connotes stability, rural modesty, taste, and intelligence. Paxton has used such chairs in other dances, and he is well aware of their implications.

> [They represent] stolidity. In *Section of a New Unfinished Work* a bentwood chair was assembled, but the other chairs were very sturdy oaken old-fashioned office chairs. And I just quite like them. I think they're an amazing form, the engineering is rather complicated, and they were good solid comfortable chairs as opposed to a lot of the stuff that gets made, mostly a kind of quasi-modern design office furniture, which I think is weird shit. (Paxton with Béar 1975:28)

The second group of objects is the ensemble of clothing Paxton wears. This consists of a beige jacket and matching beige pants, a white long-sleeved shirt, dark socks, "kung-fu" shoes, and jockey-type underpants. Paxton has a closely trimmed mustache and beard, but I think this is irrelevant to his costume, for two reasons. First, he did not have facial hair when he first performed the dance in 1964; that means that a beard and mustache are not integral to the costume. Second, in the United States in the 1970s and 1980s, facial hair no longer categorizes men in regard to age, occupation, class, conformity to social conventions, and wealth, as it did in the 1960s, when it marked a man as a member of a specific social set. Now men of all classes, incomes, ages, and social aspirations may wear beards. Except for his shoes, the rest of Paxton's costume in the dance identifies his "character" as a man to whom the chair might easily belong. He is a man who is somewhat conventional and formal. (He does not, for instance, wear jeans and a T-shirt, nor does he wear a pastel or brightly patterned shirt.) However, he is not so authoritative or formal that he wears a three-piece suit or even a tie.

The shoes are an interesting deviation from the rest of the costume. They are black canvas shoes that slip on. They are more casual than shoes that tie; they are even more casual than leather loafers. But they are not, for instance, sneakers. They simultaneously carry associations both of the "macho" heroes of martial arts films and of a countercultural choice of exotic dress. When Paxton takes off his jacket, the costume is rendered even more casual. The effect is that he is about to "roll up his sleeves and get to work." But this expectation is subverted when he hangs the jacket on his own body, and then when he hangs the rest of his garments on his body the subversion deepens. In fact, this action creates a third category of "object": the human body, which I will discuss further below.

Besides the different articles of clothing, the clothes appear in different combinations. First the man appears fully dressed. Next he is barefoot but otherwise fully dressed. Third he is barefoot, dressed in shirt and pants, and has a jacket hanging from his chest. And fourth he is naked except for his underpants, and the other three articles of clothing, which all hang from his body, form a kind of free-floating set of draperies. In fact, the draperies make him no longer naked but a nude—a work of art. When the same movements and poses occur in the different states of dress and undress, as I have noted above, they seem to mean different things.

Thus the costume functions in a number of ways. As Petr Bogatyrev has observed, clothing acts simultaneously as object and as sign. As a pure object it protects the wearer from nakedness and from climate; as a sign, it indicates such attributes as social status, sex, nationality, age, and occupation.[5] In *Flat*, it also functions as equipment. It transforms the body of the dancer from an animate to an inanimate object in terms of the cultural message of the dance. The human body is rendered a thing whose function is to hang clothes on, like a coat rack; it becomes equivalent to the chair. And this leveling is another aspect of the title of the dance. Also, the clothing literally functions as a frame for the postures and gestures, surrounding the bodily configurations in disparate contexts in a physical sense.

Given the social context of the modern dance concert, the costume also comments on the code of dance "language"[6] by deviating from the standard costume for the dancer: the leotard. By substituting a specific kind of ordinary clothing for the dancer's costume choice, Paxton sends his audience a clear message not only about the character he plays in the dance but also about dance costume and, more generally, about theatrical costume. He illustrates the proposition that the costume need not be a "sign of a sign," in the sense in which Bogatyrev uses that expression (that is, something that is not a suit of clothing but signifies it),[7] but the sign itself (that is, the suit of clothing itself). There is a certain irony here, however, since the dancer's leotard is meant to reveal the muscles and sinews of the body without reaching a state of total nudity, and strongly resembles underwear, while Paxton, overdressed at first for a dancer, violates the taboos both of undressing on stage and of appearing in one's underwear in public. The rules of the dancer's appearance have preoccupied Paxton in several other dances. *Word Words*, a duet with Yvonne Rainer in which the two danced nude (or as close to it as New York State law allowed at that time—pasties for Rainer and g-strings for both), was inspired in part in response to a disparaging remark by a member of the modern dance establishment that the members of Judson Dance Theater all looked alike. In *English* he tried to make his eleven dancers all look alike by putting pale pancake makeup over their faces, lips, and eyebrows. In *Afternoon*, an outdoor performance, some of the trees were dressed like the dancers. Paxton has worn as a costume an entire plastic room, deflated (*Music for Word Words*), a telescoping set of cardboard boxes (*Rialto*), and a set of clothes that had zippers in the seams so that they could be taken apart and put back together in new ways (*Jag ville görna telefonera*). His 1970 plan to do a performance of his *Satisfyin Lover* with forty-two naked red-haired performers was vetoed at the last minute by the sponsor.[8] More recently, in *Bound*, he wore costumes that were either altered or hidden by slide projections, as well as a bathing cap with holes placed such that a string traversing the room seemed to pass through Paxton's head.

Some Conclusions

Paxton's *Flat* is meaningful on at least two levels. On the one hand, it is a dance about a kind of character. On the other hand, it is a dance about the art of dance.

I said earlier that the facial expression in *Flat* is fixed. The fact that it is unchanging makes it recede from the list of prominent features of the dance. However, the very stoniness of expression, like the prosaism suggested by the title and the reduction of the body to objecthood, supports the meaning given in the symbols of constancy, evenness, and monotony discussed above. The affect in this dance is flat. This apparent lack of expressiveness in the face, clothing, style of walking and standing, and in the other activities is expressive in its own way: it intimates a cool stance.[9] But the cool stance is also a sign of repression. On the narrative level, this dance is a small tragedy about a man who is bound and inhibited by his social role. He is "the man in the gray flannel suit," who is nothing more than an object, a coat rack, an automaton who unfeelingly stands, sits, undresses and dresses himself in a routinized, mechanical way, in stops and starts, over and over. His cultural identity, expressed in his clothing and his actions, is stripped away when he takes off his clothing, and it is contrasted with alternative images. The man "tries on" the role of a sportsman, a woman, an idealized classical male figure. But finally he returns flatly to his culturally assigned definition of self.

The other level of meaning given by the dance, the one I have outlined above, also has to do with identity. The dance is a reflexive artwork. By substituting ordinary clothes for costume, everyday movements for technical ones, repetition and monotone for the rhythms and climaxes of traditional dance, Paxton in *Flat* comments on the codes of dance and calls into question the identity of a dance. If dance consists of neither special movements nor metered movements, what is it? *Flat*, along with other dances of its genre, illustrates the proposition that a dance can consist of movement organized poetically, familiar movements made strange by virtue of a new context.

27

Meredith Monk and the Making of *Chacon*: Notes from a Journal

In 1973 a small Chicago publisher sent me to New York City to write a book about contemporary dance. I had been performing, designing and constructing costumes, and writing in Chicago; that summer I had met Jill Johnston, read her writing for the first time, and discovered Judson Dance Theater and the "postmodern" dance aesthetic. In New York, hungrily devouring all the dance I could see, reconstructing history, trying to define the focus of my book, and wondering how my own conflicting desires to write and to perform would be resolved, I was increasingly attracted to the work of Meredith Monk. She, Ping Chong, and Monk's company, The House, planned to make a new piece during a three-week residency at Oberlin College in January 1974; I decided to go along and watch.

At Oberlin, I threw myself into the routine of both the students and the company, taking dance classes and workshops taught by members of The House during the day and, to my delight, was invited to take part in the creation of *Chacon* as a member of The House in the evenings. Because I had decided that the book, *Terpsichore in Sneakers*, would be an investigation into how people make dances, the following "Notes from My Journal" are an attempt to record how Meredith Monk, Ping Chong, and The House collaborated on the realization of *Chacon*.

Notes from My Journal

1/10/74

Arrived in Oberlin yesterday. It's quietly snowily cold here, beautiful peace, quite a change from NY. It's wonderful to dance so early in the morning (practically in the dark, because of the switch to daylight saving time) in the barnlike gym. I'm taking technique classes in the mornings and workshops in the afternoons along with the Oberlin students. MM [Meredith Monk] gives nice stretchy classes, teases herself in disbelief ("What?! Me, teaching

Dance Chronicle, 1/1 (1977).

technique classes?"). But they're not muscular classes, not fast classes, we just work hard at waking up, warming ourselves, opening our joints, becoming flexible. After class I asked her if I could watch the company rehearse tonight. They're making a new piece here — actually she and Ping Chong are making the piece together: *Chacon*, not the French dance form but the name of a town in New Mexico where MM & PC spent the summer visiting MM's sister, who lives there. *Chacon* will be the second part of *Paris*, a duet by MM & PC which I haven't seen, although I did see a videotape of it a few months ago.

So I asked if I could come to the rehearsal. And she said, I don't like the idea of your sitting there watching us all the time. Why don't you just do it with us?

The rehearsal: We warmed up to one side of a record (Bulgarian folk music, which reminds me of Arabic music — nasal, repetitive), everyone doing his/her own warmup. I checked out what everyone else was doing and copied them. Then MM led us in vocal warmups: scales and chords. Then the work began.

Nothing about the piece has been planned or made except the title (even that is up in the air, MM keeps reverting to *Bernallio*) and the ambiance (deserty) and that there would/might be a villain and a birth. Tonight, then, we worked on villain's entrances. One at a time we came in the door of the studio. Monica [Moseley] — who ordinarily looks elegant and genteel, steel-blue eyes and bony balletic carriage — icy, a ramrod. Tall, beautiful Sybille [Hayn] slouches sleazily, tossing blonde hair behind one ear. Danny [Daniel Ira Sverdlik] is all bent-up, hobbling, a frizzy-haired mad-scientist sort of villain. Skinny, spectacled Ping stands in the doorway, smiling so calmly and blandly he looks evil. MM plays on her smallness, gutsy and defensive: her arms crossed, she sticks up her chin: "Hey!" Huge gray-haired Lee [Nagrin] does a slow dramatic stab. Haan [Endred] is subdued nastiness, twisting his ring slowly and deliberately around his finger, glancing sideways. And I am last, channeling my nervousness into a paranoid, nail-biting villain.

We enter again, just to crystallize things, and then come in two at a time, this time trying to turn the entrance into something longer, developing a "bit" to frame the character. We walk around the studio in groups of three, walking and walking in our own particular villain-character-walk. Then all of us walk around, letting interactions — glances, gestures, attractions, distances — happen between our characters, trying to push the movements we find in the characters *beyond* the characters and into more abstract arrangements, repetitions, suggestions. MM is the only one using her voice as well. "Hey! Hey hey hey! . . . . heyHey!"

When that reaches an impasse, we sit down and talk. About stereotypes and archetypes, how they differ, when to use them, how to transcend them, how to avoid them. I wonder how it all works — rehearsal dynamics, that is. Everyone giggles, acts corny, fools around and then also knows when to straighten up and take care of business. There seems to be some unspoken agreement about letting impulses arise and take their course, about surrendering to the rhythm of the group's activity. Nothing, no matter how off the wall, is tossed away without first examining it, mining it for material. The balance between playing and working seems natural and fruitful.

We sit in a circle to sing. MM wants to use again a small round she composed for *Education of the Girlchild*. She sees nothing wrong with reusing material; this song, she points out, didn't get used nearly as much as she'd have liked. So we sing the song. No words to it, only vocalized syllables. Heh heh/heh heh/heh heh heh/heh heh heh/hoi. MM tries punctuating the singing with a simple repetitive motion, a fist pressed against the floor. She looks at PC: Won't a repetitive song with a repetitive gesture be too boring? PC: Well, repetition is a crazy thing. The first few times you do something it's interesting. Then after a while it gets boring. But if you do it for an hour it turns into something else entirely.

We sing all the rounds anyone can think of: madrigals, French songs, "Row, Row, Row Your Boat," spirituals, beautiful baroque intricate songs. And then to the Student Union to drink beer.

1/11

Rehearsal: warmup. Then: walking around the space as if it's a wide open plain, all of us at once.

Then (MM is giving the instructions) one at a time we run across the studio as if it's a wide open etc. And it's amazing how this light, bare, manmade room transforms into plains. Because of the slowness of Danny's sliding, the way Sybille holds her cheek to the wind, the breadth of PC's arms, the way Lee seems to look deep deep into the distance?

We stand in a circle. Think about birth, MM says. And for a few minutes we all stand there thinking or visualizing. Then we take turns showing our birth-thoughts. (It doesn't have to be the act of giving birth, MM tells us. Just whatever comes into your head or your body when you think about birth.) Lee squats. Her face goes through incredible contortions. Labor pains? Orgasms? She mumbles a lot of unintelligible stuff that finally gets shaped into a single spat-out word, and her whole body releases. Sybille lies on the floor on her back with her head toward us. Her whole body tenses and she lifts off the floor, pelvis thrust skyward, all her weight on one shoulder. Ripples of tension pass through her. A thin high scream.

Monica squats, her head between her knees. Quiet private tensing. Danny, clowning, holds the baby in one arm and points to it. I squat, thinking unconvincingly about contractions. All I feel is the discomfort of not knowing what I'm doing while people are watching me. Haan gets down on the floor in a sort of air-raid defense position, his hands covering the back of his head. His whole body contracts and releases beautifully, gently. Is he a baby being born? I wonder.

MM stands in a lunge, holding one arm out straight, bracing it with the other arm. She is pulled, hangs on to her own weight, waiting. She is released. Pull, release. Pull, release, pull. PC watching lilliputian activity very far below him sends the child off with an omnipotent godfather pat.

MM & PC look at each other. MM: Yep, Sybille is going to be the birthgiver, all right. Nevertheless, we teach each other our different births, explain what it was we were feeling, thinking, and doing. Then Sybille does four of our different births in a row, walking off and on stage in between each. No, MM & PC look at each other and frown. Maybe. . . . Monica tries it, without exits and entrances. Then Lee does only Sybille's birth, in a series that develops: walking around, starting to lie down, walking around some more, almost lying down, walking again, etc. MM & PC exchange glances. Well, not exactly . . . but it is the right track. . . . Haan refines Lee's (Sybille's) thing. And then Sybille tries it. But this time the walking in the circle has too much momentum. As Sybille keeps pacing, PC suddenly caws. She stops, listens. Yes. She paces slowly, stopping and listening irregularly. Suddenly lies down. MM tells the rest of us to close in the space just slightly and stand there watching her. Danny as doctor must now zigzag, skating, behind and then come in front.

Whew. A whole section has just been created.

It's amazing how naturally all this flows. MM directs the currents of our material, rather than telling us precisely what to do. It's unclear how much MM and PC discuss privately; mostly she does the talking, he modifies or adds to what she says. One of them will give a problem, then all of us (including the two of them) work on it. We take turns showing our solutions, then we all talk about it. Maybe fool around a bit. Maybe some sparks from fooling around. MM lets it all happen, the looseness, the bullshitting, the playing—I have this image of her as our kindergarten teacher, going off somewhere mentally to sort out the material she's just seen, leaving us to play while she busily tries to figure what to do next. But she's also leaving half an ear open to our playing to maybe pick up on more good material, then she comes back to us and we move on.

1/12

In the costume shop.

We all play, trying things on, kids in a candy shop. Villains, farmers, housefraus. We look for things that feel right for us, keeping in mind MM's dicta: stick to brown; blue for the farmers. I can't help being drawn to yellow and white, though (I've just found out that I'm a farmer)—I feel summery and fieldish in worn white overalls, a faded yellow plaid shirt, ivory scarf on my head. Monica, meanwhile, has come up with the same things only in beiges and browns.

Sybille fluctuates between a homespun brown skinny dress that bags down to her calves, and a flimsy tennessee williams lavender print, lace-edged. We all mess around, trying on this and that, sudden inspirations, gravitations back to certain pieces. And then occasionally MM lines us up and looks at us as a cluster, as a composition.

How to put the "edge" on things? The crucial question of the day. The costumes can't be too period, nor too modern; not too matching (we look like a high-school musical, MM wails) but not too makeshift either.

What about the villains. Is wearing black too clichéd? All the villains try on hats. (MM, PC, Haan are the villains, Sybille is the mother, Lee the painter/poet, Danny the doctor, and Monica and I are the farmers, along with Blondell [Cummings], who hasn't arrived from NY yet.) MM wants to wear an eyepatch, an evil touch that has personal significance as well (she had to wear one as a kid). Now the problem is—where does one find a black eyepatch in Oberlin? Or should the patch simply be a folded-over bandana?

Everyone is getting hungry and, back at the dorm where the company eats, lunch is almost over. So we stop, taking our costumes with us, with alternate choices, to be seen/felt at rehearsal.

Rehearsal. At which I feel uncomfortable because I wanted to go to Columbus, three hours away, to see Twyla Tharp's company perform. But I had felt too guilty to even ask MM if I could be excused from rehearsal, especially to go see someone else's work. Now, is my first responsibility to MM, because I am performing in her piece, or to my own work, the book, which means having to see other people's work as well as hers? Everyone in The House loves to see movies and so rehearsals are always scheduled around whatever movie is showing on campus. But my role is not too clear here, I can't expect special treatment. At the rehearsal my discomfort is increased when I sense that MM is beginning to mistrust me-as-reporter. She doesn't let anyone watch her rehearsals and I think she is beginning to regret letting me do this.

The rehearsal is short. Damn, I think, I should have gone to Columbus after all, but by now am too tired from struggling with the whole dilemma to even care. We do the farmer plowing/singing in rounds, singing the hoi song as two lines of farmers, starting at the walls, move to the center of the floor. We make plowing or farming motions on the first and last beats of the round. MM & PC keep trying out other formations with the same song, but keep coming back to these two lines.

We do villains' entrances, which keep dribbling off and not working, and I feel it's my down energy, my discomfort that's interrupting. We decide to end the rehearsal and let the villains work separately tomorrow.

1/14

A very exhausting day. To begin with, it's Monday. Yesterday MM and I talked about our feeling cagey with each other, our mutual feelings of vulnerability. It must be double nervousness for her this time, the normal state of wondering whether this piece will work and then on top of that having this stranger around all the time. I, however, always have to prove my sympathy and valor to dancemaker after dancemaker; they have every right to be defensive but it taxes me, and don't I wonder enough on my own about my legitimacy as a writer. I gave her some of my writing to read, and that and the talk made us both feel better.

So today: a very demanding and mind-blowing workshop by PC, a lesson in concentration. And then, immediately, a heavy rehearsal. Will I recover in time for tomorrow's work?

Ping's workshop: First in the upstairs gym (where the workshops are usually held), he gave us instructions. Go to the downstairs gym. Walk slowly and regularly, single file, around the room, your bodies flush against the inner wall that goes all the way around the gym. You will be walking at right angles to the wall, your head turned to the right, so that you will be looking to your right at all times even though you are constantly moving forward. Look carefully but only at those things that are directly in your line of vision. Let your eyes be like a camera with only dead-ahead focus.

He had augmented the already marvelous environment. The gym—wooden lockers with rows of open doors, golden wood, cinder blocks, mirrors, the shower rooms with their shiny tiles and their translucent, peony-patterned shower curtains; the partitions, the slats, the panels, the spaces. And then inside this space: Sybille sitting in the showers, sometimes facing one direction, sometimes sitting somewhere else, reading symbolic logic, muttering in German, reading a magazine. A shower dripping. Ping and Haan arriving at postures. Whispering, a hand raised, a hand placed on the piano. Bulgarian music starting and stopping.

We were free to sit down in the middle of the room if we got tired, and that variable too became part of the landscape that began to get macroscopic. Dilations occur because of total concentration. Like LSD. Three times around the gym took me an hour.

Recognizing a piece of dust on the wall. Seeing my own eyeball abrupt and large in a mirror after turning a corner. Coming to a crack after a long stretch of the inner golden wall and suddenly seeing a whole magnified world inside: the piano, Ping and Haan, mats, mirrors, and, through a space in the opposite inner wall, a whole line of people shuffling slowly by, staring, their heads expressionless turned perpendicular to their bodies.

The rehearsal: We go over the birth again. We go over the farmers again, teaching it to Becky [Gilford] and Jan [Jones], Oberlin students augmenting the cast. Teaching it gives it a kind of permanence.

Now Lee as painter/poet/narrator figure walks in, sits down, pulls out a pipe and lights it. Look around, MM directs, make a horizon out there, very distant. Lee will paint a mural on the back wall during the whole piece. Lee, a painter in real life, making her own personal metaphor become a performance metaphor; the mural will be a landscape and we will simultaneously make the same landscape with our bodies and voices.

And what the villains resolved yesterday was that there will be only one villain now, Haan. Haan enters as villain. Then we run through the whole thing, in order. The beginning. Birth. Farmers. Lee. Villain.

1/15

Rehearsals are becoming more linear now, the material is getting pieced together in an order. . . .

Tonight we rehearsed in the big gym where we do our technique classes and workshops, instead of in our small familiar beautiful studio. Our energy diffused in this new, overlarge, unfamiliar space, but this is where we will perform in two weeks. For some reason we kept losing our orientation, forgetting the sequence of things, forgetting which sides to enter from. Danny writes down the correct order of events so this won't happen again, and I do too:

1. Piano music, written by MM, which she sits and plays, since she's no longer a villain.
2. Sybille paces in a circle. She lies down and screams. We farmers move in from the sides and watch.
3. Danny zigzags across the floor, doctor's bag in hand, as if ice skating to the scene. Then he crosses front, where he gives a speech on bonding (chemical). Another personal metaphor: In real life, back in NY, Danny is a chemistry professor. And from time to time he looks or points in front, although Sybille is behind him, and says, "How's the baby?"
4. Monica comes on and gently walks him off as he continues to explain bonding, antibonding, and nonbonding.
5. Lee comes on and sits. Pipe. Horizon.
6. Dawn (light cue). We back out, having been standing there since watching the birth.
7. Sybille gets up, goes to the side and gets a pitcher of water, washes or drinks while Lee behind her sits and smokes.
8. Monica comes on and does a preview of the farmer-plowing thing with a faint hoi song, stops and looks for rain. Backs out.
9. Lee empties her pipe and starts painting.
10. Farmer thing with round singing. Lines of farmers cross once and get to the other side (my line picking up Sybille along the way).
11. Haan enters as villain, drinks the water Sybille has left there.

1/16

No rehearsal today, MM's voice concert and party after.

1/17

Today MM gave the workshop: Lie down on the floor on your back, she said. Listen to your body. . . . Find three sounds. . . . Listen to them. . . . Make the first sound, but with your voice (i.e., don't cough but do with your voice what a cough *is*). Now make the sound very low and slowly. Very high and quickly.

Still lying on your back on the floor with your eyes closed, be in a desert. Have the whole gym become a desert. This desert might have other beings in it. Use the sound to become part of the desert.

Now leaving the desert and body-sound behind, use sound and movement to make that world consist only of the floor and flatness. . . . Now go find a place on the wall; eyes closed, let the surface of the wall be your only world.

Divide up into groups of seven. Make a sound landscape. Let an event happen that changes the landscape. (Our group made a mountain top, very still and delicate; our event: the sunrise.)

Assignment for next time: staying with the same group, make a full landscape, with movement, sounds, characters, animals, anything. Have in it one cosmic event—a wedding, birth, or death—and one food ritual. Design it to be viewed from a specific place in the gym (ours to be seen from the balcony/track).

The rehearsal. Now we have even more Oberlin students as farmers. So we begin by teaching the farmer thing and working on it; the farmer thing is becoming the touchstone for the piece. But today MM is impatient with it, it plods and drags too much, it looks and sounds too much like the "Song of the Volga Boatman," there's not enough variety, dancing, or magic in it, no "edge."

We make our singing more nasal—and yes, that helps, it puts an edge on the weighty regularity of the singing, also seems to free our movements. The movements now begin to turn into something more abstract than farming movements; more like symbols or ritual gestures. Throwing in delicate variations and shifting the focus of our eyes lightens matters.

We work on *Paris*, choosing which of us will be the puppet announcer, laughing at each other, at ourselves, clowning; disembodied heads mouth disembodied words, made by PC across the room. It's a relief to be able to let go, to act as hilarious and bizarre as possible; after all, *Paris* was made long ago, performed, videotaped, known, familiar territory now.

Paris is a duet for MM & PC, a duet they made together, which will be the first part of the performance here; *Chacon* is the second part. Now they rehearse parts of it with Jan at the piano. It's stunning: the sitting still for durations, the skittering, falling, greeting gravely. The strolling and humming. Transforming into monkeys and back again, swatting invisible flies. Moustaches, coats, glasses appear and disappear and reappear. MM taps the pianist's shoulder and he stops playing.

After *Paris* we start to leave, realizing that the performance is in a week and a day, and that *Chacon* is just beginning to grow. MM starts talking about deadline pressures, about how much work there is left to do and it was we, not she, who insisted that we return to rehearse more after dinner.

I got a letter from Ellen today, a xeroxed quotation from Isadora Duncan:

> The dancer of the future will be one whose body and soul have grown so harmoniously together that the natural language of that soul will have become the movement of the body. The dancer will not belong to a nation but to all humanity. She will dance not in the form of nymph, nor fairy, nor coquette, but in the form of woman in her greatest and purest expression. She will realize the mission of woman's body and the holiness of all its parts. She will dance the changing life of nature, showing how each part is transformed into the other. From all parts of her body shall shine radiant intelligence, bringing to the world the message of the thoughts and aspirations of thousands of women. She shall dance the freedom of woman. . . . Oh, she is coming, the dancer of the future: the free spirit, who will inhabit the body of new woman; more glorious than any woman that has yet been; more beautiful than the Egyptian, than the Greek, the early Italian, than all women of past centuries—the highest intelligence in the freest body!

After dinner: We sit around and talk about costumes. How do we find that infamous "edge"—overalls for the farmers have to go. Too corny. What should we wear instead? Suits? Fur coats? We make another appointment for the costume room.

We talk the play through. And then we start accumulating material like crazy! Enough of this business of repeating the beginning over and over! Time to invent the middle and the end.

No slot for this yet, but at some point the farmers enter diagonally from the upstage corners doing the *Education* walk (looks like genuflecting). Then once we reach the center we form a tableau. MM & PC look at each other and say: "It's perfect for the rain scene, now comes the rain scene."

"What's the rain scene?" we ask.

"We don't know yet," MM says. "We haven't made it yet. But anyway, now we have a transition *into* the rain scene. And we should also have a preview of the rain scene, a fake rain scene, like Monica's preview of the farming scene; visual rhymes."

Now, what does the villain do? What makes him a villain? And how does he die? He has to die, but not too melodramatically. We try a funeral dance for the villain.

We try things for the end: Lee comes forward with her family portrait and starts giving life histories of her ancestors. What if Sybille were to give a simultaneous translation in German? We try it and it is bizarre. Time to quit then, all of us tired from so much progress.

Tonight I have been thinking about what an extraordinary woman MM is. Obsessed marvelously with her visions, thoroughly and lucidly and diligently working toward them. Her fascination with St. Joan (*Vessel*, and her momentary appearance as Joan in PC's *I Flew to Fiji; You Went South*).

At times she's unapproachable and formidable. Intent, worried about things not working, having hysterical fits; people reassure her and take care of her. She is a wonderful knot of charm, megalomania, energy, needs, strength, innocence, demands, gentleness, obstinacy, capriciousness, fanaticism, nervousness, sensitivity, spontaneity, spirituality. She's quite beautiful from some angles, not from others. When I stand next to her I am always surprised at how small she is; her presence is huge and commanding. Her hair is sometimes braided into a thousand tiny gypsy braids, sometimes into one thick braid down her back, sometimes hanging straight and loose. Her usual clothing here: overalls, purple brocade Chinese jacket, and workboots.

Today she got a letter from a friend advising her to stop doing group work and only work on solo stuff if that's what she feels drawn to. She talks to me about my writer/performer conflict, tells me how she works on her music and her dancing, bringing them together when she can, devoting herself to them separately when she can. It's a struggle. Then don't these things ever end?

1/23

How long since I last wrote. A week? I've been totally devoted to and exhausted by dancing every morning, working on the student workshop presentation, rehearsing afternoons and evenings.

Tomorrow night is dress rehearsal. So much more has been added and changed and edged.

Now the farmers wear suits, funky countryish Sunday-best suits, with white shirts tinted slightly with tea, to cut the glare. At various points various of us remove our jackets, and bandanas appear and disappear and reappear in pockets, around heads, around arms (reflection of *Paris*).

Haan as villain walks into the space, into Sybille's circle, and sneakily, stingily drinks out of her cup. Blondell (who is both a farmer and a secret folkwitch villain, who has power over Haan) walks straight across the stage not even looking at Haan, who crouches there holding the cup. She walks to the little portable phonograph and puts on the rain record. Some farmers do the *Education* walk diagonally into the space from stage right (since this is happening in the gym, we are completely visible even when offstage; we stand there watching quietly when not on). We form the tableau. Blondell takes the record off, Sybille starts to sway and recite a fairy tale in German. The rest of us in the tableau glance loadedly at each other and at points in space. Then we get up and start walking off, falling and getting up again repeatedly.

Then Blondell does strange gestures and sounds, she approaches the cup and backs off from it. Then she wraps the cup in a bandana and leaves. Sybille walks around in the circle again, and Haan follows her. He teaches her a gesture. They stand there side by side, a strange wondering childlike look on the face of this tall gaunt woman in workboots. Haan walks away and taps the pianist on the shoulder; the music stops (reflection of *Paris*). The woman finally does the gesture on her own; learning it is her death and she crumbles. Then the farmers cross the stage again, farming, this time in silence.

Danny comes on again as doctor. This time he does a transmutation of the bonding speech—tracing maps or acupuncture charts with his fingers. Monica again gently leads him off. Then the farmers cross a third time, this time singing and embroidering the gestures with jumps and flyswattings. We again pick up Sybille along the way (her resurrection).

Haan is onstage. Monica, Danny, and Jan walk diagonally upstage as

Chacon, by Meredith Monk and Ping Chong, at St. Peter's Church in New York City. (Photo: Phillip Hipwell, Courtesy of Meredith Monk, The House Foundation for the Arts.)

town criers, skewing the hoi round into something even more repetitive, more nasal, and much louder. Monica is carrying a camera (in real life she is a photographer and has been taking photos at rehearsals); she takes a picture of the villain as she passes him. He cringes.

Blondell walks onto the stage backwards. Puts on the rain record—the real rain. She stands there with her arms crossed. Haan walks on behind her and walks over to her, wiggles his fingers as if about to strangle her. He touches her, and immediately falls to the ground. Blondell turns and walks to the phonograph, takes the record off, walks quickly in a zagzag path to the real door in the back wall of the gym, opens the door and goes outside.

Then there is a false ending. Lee genuflects forward with her family portrait. Everyone else walks on, some of us genuflecting, to form a line, everyone with their right hand on the shoulder of the person in front. Blondell (who has come back from outside) puts banjo music on the record player. Then we do a figurine dance, making little characters for twenty-four counts, holding hands on shoulder in front with head tilted for twenty-four counts, always snaking the line forward. When the song ends, we freeze. Lee slowly walks forward with the family portrait, slowly says some sentences which Sybille translates simultaneously: The shoe is made of brown leather. The stitches on it are handcrafted and the leather is well-worn. Today is January 25, 1974.

MM and PC in their *Paris* costumes, who have been sitting in front watching (MM playing piano) during the whole thing, come on stage walking and looking around—as they do in *Paris*—swatting flies.

Ellen will be here Friday to see it. I am anxious; will she like it? What is it that she'll see? I have no idea of what it looks like.

7/4/77

My performance journals always seem to end just before the climax. Maybe the climaxes aren't the same in the writing as they are in life. Two different reasons for the abruptness of the narrative's end occur to me: First, the demands (time and energy shortages) of those last two crucial days of the performance process. A very practical reason. And second and more mysterious, the quality of those final stages. One can only record and observe up to a point; in the performance itself, one is swept into another state of consciousness that narrows the vision drastically, destroys any pretense of objectivity. Perceptions are heightened and distorted, the air is saturated with all the familiar material and with something else too: the exchange of energy between performers and audience, the new relationships between the performers, the life of its own that the piece assumes.

And then, it's over, and there's no vocabulary to capture all that complexity and changing with. And somehow, it no longer seems important to capture it. The piece exists as a separate object, in the videotapes, the photographs, the reviews, the muscles of the performers, the retinae of the audience—and the future editions performed on other stages.

Chacon was performed at Oberlin only once, on January 25, 1974. It has since been performed in a revised form, first as part of *Paris/Chacon* (Spring 1974), and then in *Paris/Chacon/Venice/Milan* (1977).

28

Dancing on the Edge

In the West, where the history of the arts since the Renaissance has been the story of specialization, theater and dance are not twins (as they are in many other cultures), but merely siblings—and at times rival ones. The interpretation of the various arts in the 1960s, however, has made an impact on recent dance, bringing the literary and physical aspects of theatrical spectacle close together in ways that are reminiscent of the Renaissance or Greek drama. Although this has happened on every level of dance, it is especially clear in the area of postmodern dance, where choreographers stake out their theories and practice at the edge of what we still consider to be dance.

In the sixties and seventies, avant-garde choreographers tried to find out what is specifically dancelike about dance—how it is different from other arts and other theater forms. By rejecting theater, they were setting themselves apart from classical modern dance and from traditional ballet. But, in recent years, postmodern dance has moved from denying theatricality to embracing it.

The first two generations of modern dance choreographers began by repudiating the academic ballet vocabulary and grammar, which seemed to them sterile and too formal, as well as the fairy tale plots of the nineteenth-century ballets. The forerunners of modern dance (Loïe Fuller, Isadora Duncan, Ruth St. Denis, Ted Shawn, and others), many of whom had training in popular theater troupes at the turn of the twentieth century, and then the pioneers of modern dance (Martha Graham, Doris Humphrey, Charles Weidman, Helen Tamiris, Hanya Holm, and others) of the 1920s and 1930s, all found individualized vocabularies for expres-

TheatreCommunications (May 1983).

sing feeling tones and social messages in stylized movements and energy levels.

By the 1950s, Merce Cunningham in modern dance and George Balanchine in ballet had become the leading proponents of dance for its own sake, rebelling against the age-old situation of dance as the stepchild of theater. They embraced a new formalism that posed questions about the essential qualities of dance as an independent, kinetic art, not one that substituted movement for words.

By the 1960s, a new branch of modern dance was emerging and experimenting with the very limits of what could be defined as dance. Judson Dance Theater, a choreographer's collective that operated out of Judson Memorial Church in Greenwich Village, was the center for young artists in various fields, and was instrumental in redefining dance in every way, from training and technique, to choreographic content and style, to the relationship of audience to performer, to the venue itself.

Out of this laboratory came an interest in the nonillusionistic presentation of pure dance, of movement per se, especially in the work of such choreographers as Yvonne Rainer, Steve Paxton, Trisha Brown and Lucinda Childs. During the later 1960s and 1970s, these choreographers made dances that were antitheatrical in that they deliberately dispensed, not only with character and plot, but also with other theatrically expressive elements such as music, special costumes, and suggestive stage lighting.

Ironically, while the avant-garde choreographers of the 1960s were involved in stripping their dances of every vestige of theatricality, the nontheatrical arts borrowed from the theater, and the theater, stressing physicality, became more dancelike. In "happenings," visual artists called attention to the processes rather than to the products of their activity; poets chanted and sang their poems in public; experimental theater groups such as the Living Theater, the Open Theater, and Jerzy Grotowski's Theater Laboratory incorporated various aspects of physical work into their "dramas."

In the plays of these groups and the many groups influenced or inspired by them, including the Performance Group (later The Wooster Group) and Mabou Mines, physical actions spoke as loudly—sometimes more loudly—than words. The emphasis on the verbal text was diminished. Perhaps the only difference between these performances and dance performances was that these groups still marketed themselves as theater.

Since the late 1970s, postmodern dance has entered a new phase. It hasn't exactly returned to the drama or literary connections of the older modern dance; it has become more theatrical with a new twist. Sometimes this new theatricality is the result of a new emphasis on the mise-en-scène of the dance. In the 1960s and 1970s, avant-garde choreographers operated in a spirit of pragmatism, embracing the ordinariness of everyday actions, enjoying the discovery of the "natural" body and attempting to present dance as a unique art by refusing to let it share the limelight with any other art. Today the upcoming generation of postmodern choreographers as well as the earlier generation are once again willing to share the focus with the visual and aural aspects of staging. The technology and artifice of the theater is no longer seen as false, but as enhancing.

Of the earlier generation, Trisha Brown has begun to collaborate with other artists to create multimedia spectacles, à la Diaghilev or Cunningham, in which the choreography nonetheless remains the prime ingredient. Her *Glacial Decoy* (1979) featured magnificent décor—slide projections the height of the proscenium that slipped in sequence across the stage—as well as costumes by visual artist Robert Rauschenberg. She used music (Robert Ashley's *Atalanta*) for the first time in years for *Son of Gone Fishin'* (1981), which also featured moving drops in watery colors, by artist Donald Judd. Currently Brown is working on a project with Rauschenberg and performance artist Laurie Anderson, to be given its premiere this fall at Brooklyn Academy of Music.

Similarly, Lucinda Childs, whose work of the early seventies was a model of the austere, analytic school of postmodern dance, has made two large-scale collaborations: *Dance* (1979), with visual artist Sol LeWitt (who contributed films and a lighting design) and composer Philip Glass; and *Relative Calm* (1981), with Robert Wilson and composer Jon Gibson. In both of these dances, the sets and the music added layers of mood and atmosphere, adding a grand sense of scale to the clarity and rhythmic brilliance of the dancing. Another collaboration, David Gordon's *T.V. Reel* (1982), created with visual artist Power Boothe and video artist Dennis Diamond, translates Gordon's penchant for infinitely interlocking patterns into several complementary media.

The younger postmodern choreographers draw their inspiration from popular entertainments and social dancing, from the fashion industry and the art world, and from the garish colors, shapes, and sounds of punk rock, new wave, and street style. Molissa Fenley, an American who grew up in Nigeria, mixes memories of West African ritual dance, gestures from American social dancing, cosmic iconography and driving percussion in endless streams of movement. Fenley's recent *Eureka* (1982) was a complex, long solo for the choreographer that changed mood and character with shifts in the music. Karole Armitage, formerly a member of the Merce Cunningham Dance Company, draws on punk rock iconography and has frequently collaborated with composer Rhys Chatham and his new wave band. Armitage's *Drastic-Classicism* (1981) used six dancers and five musicians on stage. The dancers wore bright costumes in strange shapes (designed by Charles Atlas, the artist and filmmaker who often collaborates with Cunningham), the music's high volume assaulted the ear, and the dancers' movements were rapid, abrupt, almost violent. The presence of

Pooh Kaye in her *Home Life of a Wild Girl.*
(Photo: Wim Riemens.)

the musicians onstage at times made the piece look more like a rock concert than a dance performance.

Yoshiko Chuma and Pooh Kaye work sometimes together and sometimes independently. Their work often invites narrative interpretation, but, at the same time, it eludes being pinned down precisely. Both women revel in animal and infantile movements and sensation—crawling, jumping, falling, and snuggling, throwing dirt and leaves with joyous abandon, building houses out of bricks and concrete blocks.

However, another strand of postmodern choreographers has worked since the mid-1960s in a more metaphorical vein. Unlike the analytic dancemakers, whose dances became objective as they presented pure, often simple movement in ways that called attention to the workings of the body, choreographers such as Meredith Monk and Kenneth King have, since 1964, used dance as one element in their *gesamtkunstwerk*, which incorporate gesture, movement, music, the spoken word, light, and sometimes taste and smell. Monk's performances have a homey, folktale quality; they seem to symbolize the processes of seeing, hearing, remembering, and even art-making. For instance, her recent *Specimen Days* at the New York Shakespeare Festival evoked both the context (Civil War America) and the content (a celebration of the physical) of Walt Whitman's poetry, with references to composers Louis Moreau Gottschalk and Matthew Brady as well. The humdrum rituals of daily life deepen in Monk's work into rich, multilayered metaphors for teaching, learning, making art, loving, and building communities—as well as seeing them destroyed. King's dances, with their verbal puns, films, and dances-within-dances, are like complex riddles that pose questions about life's mysteries on many levels; very often, they seem to be metaphors for technology, information, and power systems. Robert Wilson's spectacles, such as the twelve-hour *The Life and Times of Joseph Stalin* or *Einstein on the Beach* (an opera with music by Philip Glass) fall into this category as well—a dense collage of elements located somewhere between dance, theater, and opera, or a "theater of images," as critic Bonnie Marranca has called it.

Bill Irwin (a former member of Herbert Blau's group Kraken), whose technique most closely resembles that of a silent film comedian, is another performer who seems hard to categorize. In the nineteenth century, he might have been simply thought of as a vaudevillian whose specialty was clowning; on a variety theater bill, no one would have worried about precise labels. but in these days of specialization, newspapers have to know in advance which critic to send to an event, and grants agencies need to know which panel to send an application to. A theater-trained performer like Irwin, whose humor is more physical than verbal, may still be claimed by the dance critics even if he doesn't call himself a dancer. Tim Miller, who began working in New York five years ago under the vague rubric of performance artist, blends autobiography and history, words and movement, as he cooks hamburgers, pushes a lawnmower, steps on a string of lightbulbs, and paints his name on his chest. He, too, has been claimed by the dance world, and in his newest work, *Cost of Living*, he is working with a group of trained dancers.

Traditionally, the main—and vast—difference between dance and theater has been the script or text. Once ballet separated itself from opera in the nineteenth century, dance spectacles could be thought of as wordless plays, and even before the nineteenth century dance theorists had advanced just such an idea. Although mime in ballet served as a kind of sign-language substitute for verbal text, and although modern dance choreographers have experimented with poems and other documents since the early part of this century, it is in the postmodern genre of dance that language has definitively emerged as an inalienable right of the choreographer. And it is in the "talkie" dance concert—as in the "new talkies" of the avant-garde cinema—that new dance presently finds itself closest to theater in the literal sense. The work of the Grand Union (1970–76) was an apotheosis of various postmodern concerns, including questions of improvisation and permanence, the various relationships among choreographer, performer, and spectator, and the overlap of movement and language. These dancer-choreographers (Becky Arnold, Trisha Brown, Barbara Dilley [Lloyd], Douglas Dunn, David Gordon, Nancy Lewis, Steve Paxton, Yvonne Rainer, and Lincoln Scott) were as articulate with words as they

Bill T. Jones and Arnie Zane in *Rotary Action.*
(Photo: Lois Greenfield.)

were with movement, and, using every channel of expression available, they not only created work in the moment of performance, but also commented on their activities, planned their strategies, and engaged in all sorts of word wit. Watching a Grand Union performance, one began to wonder why so many dancers robbed themselves by assuming that language was not their terrain.

Bill T. Jones and Arnie Zane are like a duet version of the Grand Union, as comfortable talking as dancing, and equally comfortable doing both at once. The moment-to-moment responses of the two performers to their materials (objects, environment, music, movement themes, two contrasting bodies, and a long friendship and collaboration) are the subject of the dance, and a stream-of-consciousness narration makes the dancing richly resonant.

Gordon's recent *Trying Times* (1982) not only incorporated text in the form of incessant storytelling (in a confessional mode) as the dancers performed exacting physical tasks; it also included a paradigmatic courtroom scene (recalling not only Perry Mason and the Marx Brothers, but also *The Merchant of Venice*) and went on to poke fun at the dance critics, as Gordon's troupe accused him of various choreographic crimes. Trisha Brown's dances have also, from time to time, involved verbal instructions and commentary.

So many younger choreographers use language and plot structures now that P.S. 1, a performance/art center in Queens, has sponsored two "Paranarrative" festivals in the past two years, and the critic Ann Barzel noted recently in *Dance Magazine* that one disgruntled Chicago viewer implored the dancers to stop talking and get on with the dancing. Charlie Vernon, from Chicago, often uses taped stories as the "music" for his dancing. The dancers' partly abstract, partly referential gestures slip in and out of specific meaning as they coincide with, then separate from the words. Johanna Boyce, of the younger generation of choreographers most interested in pedestrian movement and activities, set her dancers singing and playing childlike word games (as well as running relay races, flipping coins, dressing and undressing, and performing other tasks). Jim Self has also been talking and dancing since the early seventies, and in his recent choreography he has collaborated several times with writer Richard Elovich, juxtaposing abstract movement sequences with very specific stories, so that at times the two match up, but at times (for instance, in the long solo *Lookout*, 1982) there are separate stories going on in the quirky dancing and in the spoken text.

Because postmodern choreography has radically redefined dance, our traditional theories for categorizing what we see on stage have crumbled. We can now go to an event advertised as a dance concert and see movement that is neither rhythmic nor wordless. Similarly, the experimental theater movement has redefined what constitutes a play, and we can see dramas that have very little written text. Part of how we decide whether it's dance or theater that we're seeing depends on what the thing is called. Part also depends on "genetics": in which art form were the artists in question born and bred? But perhaps one of the most salutary features of the breakdown of boundaries characterizing postmodernism in the arts is a certain freedom. Whether what we are watching is a dance or a theater piece is not the issue; that settled, we are free to see the work, in all its aspects, simply for what it is.

29

"Drive," She Said: The Dance of Molissa Fenley

Molissa Fenley's choreography bewilders the eye, entices the ear, and challenges both the memory and the intellect. Incessant, everchanging motion, saturated with polymorphous arm gestures, performed to a driving, repetitive, percussive beat, the dances are complex series of tensions between constancy and mutability, structure and disorder, abstraction and imagery, exoticism and familiarity, social and theatrical forms.

American dance audiences are accustomed to watching ballets composed of legible phrases, often matched to equally distinct musical patterns. The traditional modern dance creates a succession of expressive postures and gestures that prompt the spectator to arrange them in a narrative flow or a metaphoric gestalt. The achievement of postmodern dance was to isolate an even smaller unit of perception in dance—to frame the posture, gesture, or movement itself as the central subject of the dance—either by repetition or by complexification. To a choreographer of Fenley's generation (she was born in 1954), the dilemma of how to make dance new is increasingly problematic; her situation is unusual in that she is an American who grew up in another culture. In some sense an outsider to two dance cultures—a white American growing up in Nigeria, Fenley returned to the United States as a young woman who had lived through neither the theatrical nor the social dance traditions of the 1950s and 1960s in the U.S.—she has a certain objectivity about movement styles that seems to free her from conventions. She blends an African sensitivity to ritual dance, in which music, song, movement, and the symbolism of cultural expression are inextricably interwoven, with an acute awareness of her heritage as a modernist, American choreographer. For Fenley, what is singularly American about dance—and what she stresses in her own choreography—is speed, motion, and change, in both an immediate and a historical sense.

Fenley was born in Las Vegas but at six moved to Ibadan, Nigeria, where her father worked for the USAID mission of the United States State

The Drama Review 24/4 (T-88; December 1980). Reprinted with permission of the MIT Press.

Department. She went to intermediate school in Spain, and in 1971 she returned to the United States to study dance at Mills College. Although she never studied Nigerian dance, she remembers the power of the experience of watching festivals.

> You'd see fifty people in a line just moving their heads back and forth for two hours! The colors, the costumes, the makeup were just incredible, and the beat was constant. I think that had a strong effect, not on my choreography, but on my person. I don't think I'm doing a ritual dance. African dance is highly ritualized, and it is narrative. There's a reason for all those people to be out there bopping; someone is going through puberty or whatever. There's a definite psychological or calendrical reason for the dancing.

She suspects that her own choreography has been more inspired, stylistically and formally, by the popular Nigerian modern social dance, the Highlife.

> It's a hip-swinging, finger-snapping thing, extremely sexual, with lots of gyrations. It's all about the hips and genitals, constantly rhythmic, and wonderful to watch. People enjoy themselves when they dance Highlife. Social dancing here has more to do with attitudes than actually getting into the dancing, actually getting inside your body and being involved with your partner and having the sense that there are all these other people gyrating around you.

In school in Spain, Fenley took a few lessons in Flamenco dancing, which contributed some arm gestures to her current vocabulary. But, for the most part, her physically active childhood and adolescence were spent without dance instruction. She jogged, played basketball, cut down trees on safaris. She chose dance as her college major, she says, because she had become fascinated by motion. "Even cars passing would interest me. It didn't coalesce as an interest in speed until I started working that way. But I had an interest in the perception of motion in space. I wanted to be involved in it somehow."

At Mills, Fenley recalls, "I spent the first two years in a state of culture shock." She studied Graham and Humphrey technique and learned Louis Horst's methods of composition, including his analyses of preclassic and modern forms. She found Horst's use of strict rules in relation to musical structures useful, and she began to set up her own arbitrary rules as a device to rhythmically order her own dances.

Fenley graduated from Mills in 1975 and the following year moved to New York, where she danced with other choreographers, including Carol Conway and Andrew deGroat. She steadily worked toward gathering a company to perform her own choreography. Her initial strategy in sparking movement innovation was the use of stylized arm configurations. The first dance Fenley presented in New York, *Planets* (1978), was informed by the iconic arm gestures of sculptures and paintings of Greek and Egyptian gods and goddesses. The spatial patterns in the dance were inspired by the orbits of the planets, abstracted and elaborated in a set of colored drawings Fenley used as visual scores for each section of the dance. Small running, stamping, and jumping steps set up a baseline of rhythm at times overlaid by the contrasting percussion of ankle bells, sandblocks, woodblocks, wrist castanets, afuches, and a percussion hammer. The propulsive rhythms, the repetitive stepping patterns, the circling and weaving of the dancers, the impassiveness of their faces, and the purposeful—even hieratic—sequences of arm gestures, all lent a mysterious, ritual quality to the dance. This borrowing of ritual forms—significantly, the circle—has been current in postmodern dance throughout the 1970s: in Deborah Hay's communal Circle Dances, Simone Forti's primal circular crawls, the ecstatic spinning of Meredith Monk, Kenneth King, Laura Dean, Andrew deGroat. But perhaps nowhere was the cosmic symbolism of this ritual dance form as explicit as in *Planets*.

A forty-five-minute work in six parts, *Planets* was originally choreographed for performance in the Hayden Planetarium. At first, the plan included not only eight planets, but also a chorus of comets, asteroids, and meteoroids. According to Fenley, the planetarium staff was apprehensive about putting on a dance performance, and ultimately *Planets* was performed, with only the eight main dancers, at the Cunningham Studio. The first section, "Solar Nebula," began with the dancers gathered in a tight circle, facing inward, their arms clasped behind one another's backs. Swelling and contracting the size of the circle, breaking away to move as individuals, only to return to the rotating circle, the dancers represented the beginnings of the solar system in an expanding mass. In the second section, "Iconic Gesturing," each planet repeatedly executed two identifying, metaphoric arm signals within a rhythmic framework. The dance continued through "Orbiting," "Planets' Dance," solos for Mercury, Mars, Venus, and Pluto, and, in a final coda, a burst of motion. The general movement of the dance was a rhythmic progression from slow, nearly static positions to a flurry of action. But the central position that questions of rhythm would later occupy in Fenley's choreography was not yet established; the emphasis in this dance was on positions in space, and especially the diagrammatic arrangements of the arms and hands.

The use of the arms evolved. Fenley remembers, "Once I'd seen them in *Planets* and worked with them very statically, then I started to move them, to make them a matter of dancing." She wanted to find a way to deploy the dancer's arms that was neither decorative, as in the fixed arm placements of classical ballet, nor communicative, as in pantomime and other signaling systems. "I allowed the gestures to become more motional, rather than stopped in space, gestural. I wanted to use the back as fully as I could, and to use the arms as more than simply extensions of the spine, as they are used in most techniques. After *Planets*, I did not want to use gestures to conjure up metaphoric meaning in the spectator." Although now she culls hand and arm motions from a variety of sources, the changefulness of those gestures and the fact that they are embedded securely in an overall rhythmic context, without any narrative continuity, discourages interpretation. But, on the other hand, the centrality of the arm movements to the motion of the rest of the body prevents one from seeing them as simply embellishments.

Fenley's second dance was a twelve-minute duet for herself and Rick Guimond: *The Willies* (1978). Although the title suggests a misspelling of the ghostly maidens in the Romantic ballet *Giselle*, Fenley's reference was not to ballet history. In Yoruba, "willy" means cat. In this dance, Fenley's choreographic project was twofold: she wanted to speed up the tempo and to create a social relationship between the dancers that grew concretely out of the situation of dancing together. This was in contrast to both the statuesque and the metaphoric qualities of *Planets*. Although she used cat movements as sources for the choreography, the imagery was not explicit in the dance. The two faced the audience, stepping several steps forward, then back, in a steady four-count beat accentuated with ankle bells. Their hands and arms sculpted the space around their bodies, rising and circling overhead, or stretching stiffly along oblique lines radiating from the body. The wrists flexed, palms changed facings, fingers hyperextended backwards or curled in scooping motions. At other times, the arms counterposed two disparate shapes—straight and angled—or swung metrically across the body. After dancing side by side in unison, the dancers changed orientation, dancing to each other rather than to the audience, and the texture of the dance thickened. The paths began to interweave and to cross the entire space, making use of the diagonals; the steps became at times lighter and bouncier, at times heavier, with an almost military tread. The dancers set up a steady pulse with clapping, allowing the stepping patterns to stop and start in complex rhythms. They alternated erect postures with quick forward swoops, the arms carrying the torso over with force. Finally, as their movement tempo sped up, Guimond and Fenley picked up maracas, adding one more layer of sound to the relentless, roving movements. The dancing reached a peak of fullness, not only because of the countervailing visual and aural rhythms, but also because the creation of music and movement were so inextricably fused, as if the dancing were the flesh that gave body to the skeleton of sound. Then it ended abruptly.

For Fenley, *The Willies* was a new stage in terms of the evolution of her choreographic style. The next three dances, *The Cats* (1978), *Red Art Screen* (1979) and *Video Clones* (1979), were arenas for the consolidation and elaboration of several elements: speeding up the dancing; plumbing the depth of the stage space; making pathways that interweave asymmetrically; meshing the aural and kinetic elements in an ongoing flow; and creating an authentic, intimate interaction between the dancers through touch and glance. In these dances, Fenley kept the movement and the rhythm going at a steady pace.

Mix, comissioned by The Kitchen Center in 1979, was a more ambitious attempt to keep the pulse of the dance fast and steady while varying the dynamics of the movement itself. Fifty minutes long, *Mix* mobilized four dancers in a variegated structure of floor patterns, hand and body gestures, and the manipulation of percussion instruments. The tempo remained at a brisk 4/4 beat, but it was expressed in various ways. In the first section of the dance, the performers' clapping and stamping sounds were amplified by a miked floor, and they reverberated through the use of an Echoplex. In this section, the visual patterns began symmetrically. The dancers moved counterclockwise in a circle, stamping and shuffling, crossing in couples, taking turns moving in and out of the center of the round. Clapping out diverse patterns, scooting out to the edge of the circle with head down, arms stretched up, hips wiggling, the dancers looked as spontaneous as square dancers, except that Fenley had inserted a red thread of irregularity into the dance's design, whenever it threatened to become regular. They left the circle at times to gallop, whirl, hop. They reentered the round, dancing with a hand on each neighbor's shoulder. In the second part of *Mix*, the dancers played sandblocks and then maracas, and, as in *The Willies*, the movements flowed visibly from the physical action of making music.

Mix was striking in a number of ways. The complexity of the combinations of deceptively simple steps, hand positions, and other "kinemes" gave the dance a rigor that was only slightly relieved by the demeanor of the dancers—a lively, engaging interplay of glances, touches, and smiles that added to the folkdance impression. But in fact the intricacy and heterogeneity of the movement combinations were not only quite the opposite of the redundant figures of folkdance; these qualities also made *Mix* distinctive in terms of the pattern genre of postmodern dance. Unlike Lucinda Childs, one of the leading pattern choreographers, Fenley used duration as a salient element and put the arms, hands, and head into play in elaborate ways. Childs's group dances, usually about ten minutes long, are austere and precise, building a concise set of variations on the internal tensions of a single geometric shape and a single, albeit complex, rhythmic structure. One might compare the brilliance and clarity of Childs's method to Bach's music. There is an impersonal, cool sense of formal invention in the dance that distances it from the spectator. The dancers function like fine instruments tracing out an elegant design. Compared to Childs's work, Fenley's choreography, with its deliberate asymmetries, erratic moments, warm sociability, bright costumes, and exhilarating sensuality, is expansive and inviting. The rigor of Fenley's work is not as readily apprehensible as that of

Childs's, because the minute scale of Childs's variations provokes the spectator to sort and assemble visual data until, by the end of the dance, a complete paradigm has become legible. With Fenley, the variations play themselves out on such a broad scale and in such an unfathomable order that even if one attempts to systematize them, they are perpetually elusive. In the face of such a protean stream of dancing, one is tempted simply to plunge into the kinesthetic experience of it, rather than catalog. And, in fact, to catalog the motions presents a problem, because of both the swiftness of their execution and the richness of the vocabulary. One action erases the preceding action, so that the memory replaces, rather than accumulates, images.

In this way, Fenley's choreography also differs from that of Laura Dean, even though some of their hand gestures are similar: the hands that revolve around each other as if winding a ball of yarn; the flat hand, flexed up from the wrist, that wipes the air with a side-to-side motion; the oriental flourishes and arabesque formations made with the hands overhead; the stiff extensions of arms and hands at times contrasting with the play of hips and feet. But Dean's strategy is to repeat such movements over and over in unchanging, easily recognizable configurations over long periods of time. Like the Sufi whirling dervishes, Dean weaves a serene, uninterrupted fabric of motion whose simplicity, over time, draws attention to the individual expressiveness of each dancer, inducing in the spectator a hypnotic flow of peaceful sensations. Fenley's dances are about excitement, rather than order. Although *Mix* was difficult both for the performers — they did not rest for nearly an hour — and for the spectators — its length and complexity overloaded the perceptions at a certain point — it was an important dance in terms of focusing on these contradictory elements.

The next work Fenley choreographed was *Boca Raton* (1980), commissioned by Elisa Monte and David Brown of the Martha Graham Company. Fenley performed the duet several times in New York with Elizabeth Streb. The piece began with a long musical prelude, a calypso beat electronically produced by repeating the first four bars of a Talking Heads song on a tape loop and distorting it with electronic effects. Fenley and Streb, wearing striped t-shirts, pants, and jazz shoes, ran onto the stage and, as in *Mix*, mingled wiggling hips, undulating arms, quick steps and stamps, and a vivacious presence with an exacting, if mercurial, structure. Playing off the Latin-sounding beat, the two built an elaborate couple-dance, swirling arms close around head and shoulders — both their own and one another's — and breaking away to run and leap, all the while moving through a rapid fire of gestural shapes. Also as in *Mix*, any threat of redundancy or dry tidiness was always subverted by spatial asymmetries and changing movements. After a few minutes, the two disappeared; the music continued for several minutes, leaving the impression that the dance had been a sudden, fleeting vision, an accidental embodiment of the ongoing music.

Fenley's latest work, *Energizer* (1980), shows a choreographic intelligence that has synthesized previous concerns in a sophisticated theatrical presentation. More concise than *Mix*, but just as ambitious, *Energizer* is an evening-length work in three parts: a fifteen-minute quartet, a ten-minute duet, and a second fifteen-minute quartet. Each section is structured by its electronic score, which Fenley composed with a rhythm box and synthesizer in collaboration with Mark Freedman. In contrast to most of her earlier dances, in which the music issued from the dancers' bodies either directly (as claps, steps, or stamps) or in a mediated way (by wearing ankle bells or shaking maracas while moving), in *Energizer* Fenley worked in the opposite direction, fitting the dancing to the sound. "My interest is in speed," she said. "In the past, I worked by always making myself go faster. In that way, an underlying rhythmic sensation would evolve, and I would either stay with it or change it. Then it would start to become very clear. The movement would make the rhythm occur." In choreographing *Energizer*'s three sections, Fenley would begin with the piece of music—multilayered percussive fabrics threaded with the open tones of an acoustic organ, and twangs and shrieks that evoke jungle images—and improvise

Molissa Fenley, Susana Weiss, Lynne Allard, and Patricia Graf in Fenley's *Energizer*.
(Photo: © 1980 Paula Court.)

alone to find dance themes she then expanded. She thought of the score as "the initial generator and overall energizer" for each of the three dances. The warm-hued lights and the bright, stylish costumes, along with the exotic-sounding music, added to the juiciness of the dance. The visual attractiveness, the loudness of the music, and the pure speed of the dancing created an extremely exciting bombardment of the senses.

In the first section, all four dancers (Fenley, Lynne Allard, Pat Graf, and Susanna Weiss) enter from the four corners of the stage several minutes after the music has begun. An organ note has faded, and a clicking beat has begun, moving closer and closer and seemingly bringing on the four women. They move in and out of a central circle, their arms circling, tilting in long oblique lines, thrusting forward and back, swinging around the body. Quick side tilts of the head mark rhythmic accents; sudden forward curves of the spine stress new climaxes. The dancers extend their paths into crossings of the stage, occasionally punctuating a stream of forward motion with a spin. They dance in pairs, arms twined; they separate to dance out individual figures. They leave the stage for a moment, clearing the visual screen, and, when they return, the tempo seems to speed up. The imagery courses unpredictably through this flood of motion: at one moment these women look like warriors, their arms snapping crisply in salutes and feints; the next moment, they line up facing the audience and back up, rhythmically shaking shoulders and hips like a cancan line; then they gallop friskily across the floor like small wild animals. Their broad-shouldered, nappy jumpsuits in black, blue, violet, and pink make them look at times like models and at times like infants refusing to lie down to sleep.

In the second part, Fenley and Allard appear, more sirenish in one dark blue and one taupe silk outfit. Their gestures are both closer to their bodies and more powerful than in the previous section, and the music seems thicker with squeaks, shrills, bird calls. They stalk up and back, tossing their heads back languorously as they turn. The motions of their arms whip their bodies into spins they articulate with their feet. They spring and prance. Their movements are so indirect, one part of the body constantly facing away from another, arms scooping and spiraling, cheek pressed against shoulder, that they seem to prowl.

The third section combines motifs from the first two parts. For the first time the dancers enter and exit separately and repeatedly during the dance. This section is different, too, in that it constantly seems to move toward a crisis or climax. In fact there are three. Short solos for each dancer stress the individuality of their combinations of gestures, adding, too, a sense of competition and virtuosity. The legs trace wider arcs as they run, skip, leap; the arms slant and arch with more vigor. The patterning of organ crescendoes, dancers' variations, and entrances and exits, as well as the quicker tempo in this section, all contribute to the sense that the dance is moving toward a state of frenzied intoxication, broken only as they exit and the lights dim. Yet within this frenzy the dancing itself never moves toward chaos, but remains highly articulate.

From the conscious use of floor patterns and static arm signals in *Planets*, Fenley has arrived, in *Energizer*, at a "wall of dance" whose dynamics are so dense and so rapid they are almost impossible to index. In devising movements for the dance, she says, she was interested in neither floor patterns nor body shapes, but simply in motion. "The endurance of performing fast motion seems to hold the key to new experimentation," she has stated. She varied her movement themes, once she had devised them, in somewhat traditional ways. But the spatial interactions, what Fenley calls "space consciousness," came about only after she had taught her dancers the movement patterns and very concretely moved them through space. In the course of setting up weavings, crossings, and plumbings of up and downstage space, she sees the dance as altering space in a way that a stage set would. She is interested in perceptual afterimages, and sets up paths through which dancers move successively, each one following the traces of the previous dancer.

Energizer creates a curious dialectic of discipline and ease. The demands it puts on the performer are visibly enormous, not only in terms of pure stamina, but also in terms of memory and concentration. Fenley rehearses wearing weights, like a long-distance runner. "I want to get rehearsals to the point where we just absolutely *kill* ourselves, so that in performance, when we have everything else to deal with — nervous energy, lights, costumes, the objective of reaching the audience — we're not tired out by the endurance level we really need to have." The dancers are constantly counting and listening for music cues in order to keep track of the often arbitrary movement changes. Fenley thinks of herself primarily as a choreographer rather than a dancer; although, watching her perform, one has the sense that the movements she invents come easily to her and suit her small, full-hipped body well, she constructs those movements through a series of intellectual choices, and not because they "feel good." Yet finally, in performance, the dancing has all the exuberance and lightness of a spontaneous outburst. "I think dancing is an optimistic, joyful art form, and that the social interaction of people dancing together is really quite beautiful. Ideally, the audience is sharing this pleasurable experience."

For avant-garde choreographers in the 1960s, everyday movements, untrained bodies, and simple tasks were the stuff of dance, infinitely compelling, not only because they represented a break with academic conventions, but also because through them one could present the human body and its actions in a down-to-earth manner. A wave of democratic romanticism in the arts, valorizing the natural, the spontaneous, the commonplace, reflected the optimism of a country in motion. Twenty years later, the American temper has changed. In an age of economic distress and political cynicism, we seek glamour, style, and artifice in life and art. Molissa Fenley is one of a second generation of postmodern choreographers, who has reinstalled a new virtuosity in dance performance. Yet it is a nonillusionistic virtuosity that builds on the achievements of a previous generation, presenting dancers in a ritual of technical brilliance that seems to coax the spectator to join in. In the 1980s, art no longer frames real life; it turns toward something better. But the gulf between artist and spectator has been irrevocably bridged. Fenley's dances turn matters of community, drive, and vivacity into energy.

30

Self-Rising Choreography

The first time I saw Jim Self dance, he was eighteen and I was twenty-one. He had just graduated from high school and was already dancing professionally in one of Chicago's few modern dance troupes. I had just graduated from college and had no idea that I would become a dance critic. But I remember that there was already something clear and authoritative about his dancing. There was a strength in his stage presence that contrasted with his physical appearance: willowy, double-jointed (with arms that bent backwards when he held them taut), he had an angelic, snub-nosed face, long straight hair, and looked rather androgynous.

A year or so later, I was looking at dance more seriously, and I saw him in his first dance, *Miami Beach* (1973). He danced and ran in white overalls, a hat, a jacket, and red tennis shoes. He tested the floor, checked out his body, at one point turning his back to the audience to peep inside his jacket. He took off all his clothes except for bathing trunks, shoes, and socks. He kept looking at the audience, turning us all into voyeurs. He took off one shoe and sock and listened to his foot while standing perfectly still. He was clearly the kind of person who comes alive on stage and makes every action, no matter how unrelated to the previous action, look like the right thing to do next.

Over the next few years, I found Self the most consistently interesting

Village Voice, October 15, 1980.

and inventive choreographer working in Chicago. It wasn't just that our lives became more intertwined, which they did. The world of avant-garde art, theater, performance, music, and dance in Chicago was small enough that if you did any of them you were involved with everyone else. But also, I think we became friendlier because we discovered our interests and tastes often coincided. I was writing about dance, but I was also making performances. I took dance classes from Self at MoMing, a center for dance and performance in Chicago that was run by a collective we both helped to found. It was a lively time for dance in Chicago. We brought people like Sally Bowden, Trisha Brown, Douglas Dunn, Barbara Dilley, Kenneth King, and, later, Grand Union to MoMing. Meredith Monk came to the Dance Center a couple of times; so did Viola Farber. Merce Cunningham and Company performed and taught at University of Chicago. Yvonne Rainer showed an early version of *Film About a Woman Who. . . .* Dance companies in Chicago were splitting and proliferating, and younger choreographers were finding it easier to show their work.

As Self reminded me recently,

> It was an active time artistically and politically. I felt the freedom to try out anything I had ever seen or heard about, and it was all happening in a community where everyone knew one another very well. You were writing a book about postmodern dance and bringing back a lot of ideas from New York I'd never known about. With our friend Ellen, I was writing about sex, work, and romance, and how people's personal lives affected their art. We were trying to figure out how to work collectively, but at the same time I was doing solo work. Everything about everybody's life became more information that could be put in the work. We were doing things inside and outside, with and without music, improvised and structured, formally and informally. It was one great experiment, and there were so many things to do, I didn't stay with any one thing too long. Before I finished one project, I was well into another.

Self was incredibly prolific, choreographing solos and group pieces for dancers with varying degrees of training, presenting a twelve-week series of Monday evening *Self Studies*, teaching classes, leading a performance group called Huperbody that made events for parks and at the airport. He seemed to learn from everyone he came in contact with, syncretizing various discoveries into a personal brand of powerful theater.

Born in Greenville, Alabama, in 1954, Self moved with his parents to Phoenix City, then Tuscaloosa, and then, at fifteen, to Evanston, a suburb of Chicago. In high school, he studied art, started to paint and make collages, and took dance classes as a gym elective. Soon he started taking classes at night with Shirley Mordine, and then started ballet training with Ed Parish. In 1972, Self asked Mordine if he could join her company, and he danced with her until 1974. In the postmodern tradition, many of his choreographic ideas were linked to visual art concerns.

> My painting teacher, John Neimanas, was always encouraging. One thing I learned from him was a sense of collage, of taking different things and putting them together. Another was a compositional sense—for instance, using color in one place and picking it up again in another place. You do the same thing in a dance when you emphasize relationships between different things. But in a dance you do it in terms of time and memory.

Self says that at eighteen he felt he had to choose between painting and dancing. "I decided that since I was young I would take advantage of that. I decided that I would begin by putting together dances, but that I would only do it for five years."

In 1976, Self came to New York to study with Merce Cunningham, and by the end of that year joined Cunningham's company. Dancing with the group from 1976 to 1979, he found little time to make his own work. And when he reached his five-year limit, he was so busy touring and performing that he forgot his vow. "When I turned twenty-five, I felt the need for another decision, and I quit dancing." He left the Cunningham company and thought about what to do next. But after two months he realized that dancing and choreographing are "how I make meaning of the world."

Self's concert at American Theatre Laboratory (Tuesdays through October 28) show a new side of both the choreographer and the dancer. Works ranging from 1976 to the present show the Chicago and the New York side of Self. In Chicago, he had already shown certain consistent stylistic features: a strong sense of formal structure; the use of theatrical elements, especially props, characterization through gesture, and talking, all of which added another suggestive layer of meaning to the otherwise stringent formalism of the dance; a vocabulary that combined quick, quirky articulations of the body with a fluid sense of phrasing; an iconic use of popular music; a childlike absorption in the movement; a pictorial use of the performing space.

I still have strong images of *Tuscaloosa* (1974), performed to various Aretha Franklin songs, in which Self at one point danced up the steps and against a door jamb leading to a tiny proscenium stage behind the general dance floor, then slunk along the back wall of the stage doing a series of stripteaser's high kicks. He did some technical dancing, told stories, and later put on a cowboy hat and tailored jacket, said "You don't kiss very good," lit a cigarette, and smoked it languorously while looking at the audience, then exited slowly on an upstage diagonal, came back, left again, while Aretha sang "Life can be so lonely/Without the one you love."

His dancing in those days had a look of naturalness that came from that fluidity, from his use of everyday gestures, the social dancing moves he sometimes borrowed (swiveling pelvis, swaying to the music, shaking shoulders), and the simplicity and directness of presentation. His *White on White*

(1976) was an evening-long work for two men and two women that drew formal contrasts between movements and between bodies, mixed technical and idiosyncratic gestures and movements, and involved strewing objects like beer cans and cigarette packs on the floor. In most of his dances he liked to drop things, throw things away, change appearance, and go off balance — in the literal and figurative senses.

In Self's recent work, the same ingenious theatricality prevails, the same methodical construction, the same evidence of an intelligent structure underlying the flyaway gestures. But Self's way of moving, and even the way he looks, have changed. He has a polish and physical strength that come from the daily discipline of Cunningham's technical demands. His body has become fuller and more muscular. And his choreography calls for much more complicated and precise technique. He's learned how to partner and to jump. Cunningham's greatest influence on him, he thinks, was in giving him a new, more objective and precise way of measuring time. "My movement is still not as precise as Merce's. But before I worked with him I had a totally personal sense of time. If I had an idea, I would do the idea, and if I did the same piece three nights in a row, it might take three different lengths of time.

"I also learned about a dancerly physicality from Merce. Before, dancing was the tool for making a theatrical experience. I learned about dancing as something that requires an intensity, maintenance, and consistency, an understanding of how to work the body, to keep it going and do movements over and over again, and to make them clear. I didn't always even know how a particular movement fit into the overall picture of his pieces. In Chicago, I was involved in developing as a performer — experimenting with dealing with the audience, coming up with different ideas about making dances. I feel that with Merce I learned how to be a dancer."

Self's work in New York has another dimension; collaborating with writer Richard Elovich and visual artist Frank Moore, he has expanded the textual and decorative aspects of his choreography. Where in the past he often danced in blue jeans, the recent and the older works in the Tuesday concerts at ATL are spectacularly designed. Last June at the Cunningham studio, Self performed a duet with a stool while Elovich read a story about a teenage boy who dances alone in his parents' attic. On that concert and at ATL, Self showed *Marking Time* (1980) a trio that operates on both a formal and a dramatic level. In its current version, danced by Self, Ellen van Schuylenburch, and Joel Luecht, the dance exploits the wings, entrances, and exits. The dancers leap in and out of sight. They are three vaguely defined characters — Luecht dressed in a blue leotard festooned with white skeleton's bones, van Schuylenburch in a cartoonlike red dress decorated with outlines of shells, and Self in a bright yellow fishnet outfit with black and white piano keys running up the sides. The tempo is steady while the actions change, giving the illusion that time is being "marked" differently. But the three dancers also play the roles of three people who have different ways of marking time in the sense of waiting. Luecht is steady, functioning almost like a timepiece; van Schuylenburch is more tentative; Self is wild, constantly in motion, careening through space. The result is an abstract but witty comedy of manners.

In *Scraping Bottoms* (1976), a new version of the last piece Self made in Chicago, he walks onstage dressed in a black suit that has been wired to hold a bulky, angular shape, and a little hat. At times he looks like dadaist Hugo Ball in his famous paper column costume, at times like a Kabuki warrior, at times like Buster Keaton as he slouches, stonyfaced, tripping gracefully, waltzing at a tilt, throwing things around. He whistles a few bars of "As Time Goes By." Suddenly he puts his hands in pockets that one would not believe exist in such a bizarre getup, and pulls them inside out, flinging coins everywhere. He touches and talks about different body parts as if they had suddenly appeared to surprise him. He turns on a tape of distorted disco music, tosses three big cushions on the floor, moves in jerky slow motion, and finally sinks to the floor.

The newest dance on the program is a duet for Self and van Scuylenburch. Called *A Domestic Interlude* (1980), this dance suggests two playful characters while sticking to a strict conceptual formula. Dressed in pastel sleeveless jumpsuits that look like pajamas, and accompanied by the almost inaudible sounds of a digital clockradio that sits on stage, blue numbers glowing, the two repeatedly circle one another, do a sort of strutting gallop, hold hands, travel quickly, tumble to the floor, and later lie down for long stretches of time. Self does spinning, off-center turns. He looks at his partner with an exaggerated expression of disbelief mingled with pleasure. He lifts her to sit astride his shoulders. It's an appealing, totally unsentimental romantic duet, mixing humor, action, and affection to convey fleeting emotional shapes.

Self says that in making the dance he began with the idea of making movement for van Schuylenburch that would be different than the balletic movement she is often given to perform. "I wanted to use her strength but without accentuating that perfect, stretched line. I wanted to get her moving fast, using her back, dancing in a relaxed, weighted way." He then set up the structure: Choosing an arbitrary time limit of ten minutes, he subdivided it into ten sections of six counts each. The first half of the dance is deliberately stuffed with as much activity and movement as possible; the second five minutes contain half as much activity and movement as possible; the second five minutes contain half as much action. Later, Self says, partly through Moore's suggestions as he watched the dance to get ideas for the costumes, the dramatic meaning began to emerge. "At first he thought Ellen was a honeycomb and I was a bee, or that she was a web and I was a bug. He thought of it as playful, and that changed the way I thought about it. It's not so much about a couple, but about some kind of generalized, physical relationship between two animals, or two humans regardless of sex."

Self is one of a number of younger choreographers whose work—partly in reaction to a generation of antitheatrical choreography—deals in drama, characterization, artful costumes, and vivid decor. It's strange to realize that after choreographing for nearly a decade, Self stands in another vanguard in dance.

31

Transparent Living

Wendy Perron's dances open onto the world like a window. They are frames that intelligently but plainly reveal particles of daily life. You see, in a group of fresh-faced, sturdy, thoughtful women, moving together, a steady flow of fleeting images: the awkward grace of children playing, the cool sensuousness of slowly twisting bodies, spastic energy, a femininity that evokes both tenderness and strength. Nothing you could put into words, exactly, or that remains as a distinct statement. The pleasure of watching Perron's dances comes from the ongoingness, changeability, and ambiguity of those crowding impressions. You are absorbed into careful viewing, especially because the dancing is often done in silence. The pleasure comes, too, from the curious mixture of wit and sobriety that unfolds through a frank, generous physicality.

A member of a generation that turned to formalist movement invention as an antidote to the excessive symbolism and literary underpinnings of "old" modern dance, Perron has recently become interested in reinstalling narrative. But—like some of her contemporaries, not only in postmodern dance, but also in film, literature, and visual art—Perron approaches plot in a very unconventional way. Her newest work, *The Paris Sciences* (at The Kitchen, March 5–8), is structured not so much by narrative as by a fascination with the notion of narrative—its power to hold one's attention and to unify the artwork. Yet Perron's sensibility is too porous to let her material fall under such neat control. *The Paris Sciences* emerges from a welter of story fragments; its title is a result of free-associating with words like parasites and parasciences. If this performance is a story, it is one that

Village Voice, March 4, 1981.

refuses to end: Perron has asked artist Sophie Healy to write a story based on watching the dance. Then she plans to use Healy's story, along with any unsolicited submissions, as a score for a new dance.

Perron is one of those rare grown-ups who still have a child's insatiable curiosity about new ideas, new images, new mental associations. Her inspirations can come from anywhere: songs, books, films, social situations, even other dancers. One inspiration for the deliberate narrative confusion of *The Paris Sciences* was the film *Men Who Are Men*, in which the filmmakers directed men on the island of St. Lucia to perform tasks while speaking in a combination of their native patois and pure nonsense words. Then the directors wrote a series of English subtitles that gave fictitious explanations for the action.

Wendy Perron in *A Three-Piece Suite.*
(Photo: Lois Greenfield.)

Building on this notion, Perron gave her dancers fragmented images whose meanings are contradictory. "One image is of lifesaving, the way you have to knock someone out," she says. "You're saving their life, but you also have to get them into a weird, dead position to do it. Another came from seeing *Raging Bull* and being struck again by the way, in boxing, you sometimes can't tell if they're hugging or fighting."

The open look of Perron's work comes partly from the postural style of the dancers, with their straight, vertical torsos, relaxed arms, open palms, springy legs. But it also comes from the openness of her choreographic method. "A lot of things I bring into rehearsal are half-baked. I don't want to finish them, because they can be finished by the dancers, or by my working on them in the studio. Sometimes someone makes a mistake, and that brings you somewhere else. You *have* to keep that option open. And I want the piece to be open enough that that can happen in performance, too. So there are parts we don't rehearse very much." She was impressed, when she recently read *POPism*, by Andy Warhol's habit of asking people around him what to do. "I used to feel that I should come into rehearsals with everything fully planned. But other people's ideas are as good as mine, so why not use them?"

Perron studied ballet with Irine Fokine as a child, and later at the Joffrey school. At fifteen, she began modern dance classes at the Martha Graham studio. She went to college at Bennington, where, she says, she first started to connect dancing with the mind. In 1969, after graduation, she came to New York to choreograph her own dances, perform in the works of other choreographers, and write about dance and performance art. She now characterizes her early pieces as "cautious, lovely dancing." In *Shorts* (1972), to the music of B. B. King, and *Oath* (1973), to traditional African drumming, that loveliness became sharper, more specific, the product of an analysis of movement flow. In 1976 she made *The Daily Mirror*, a solo that was a process of accumulating material, a kind of journal in which she explored her own movement preferences. "I thought of it as my playground. It was a field day for my own eccentricities."

Perron managed to keep working independently as a choreographer while performing other people's work. An important influence was Twyla Tharp, in particular *The Hundreds*, which Perron saw in 1971. "The way the dancers would start at the back and move forward doing the phrase, then walk to the back to start the next phrase still sticks in my mind. It was so pure. They just did the movement. It held my attention every second. That influences every piece I do." Working with Tharp the following year, Perron was impressed by her emphasis on the movement impulse. "It didn't really matter where the movement took you, or where it ended. I always liked that way of thinking—'What does the movement do to you?' rather than 'Be sure you finish at this point.' " Perron also danced with Rudy Perez, Frances Alenikoff, William Dunas, Kenneth King, Sara Rudner, Risa Jaroslow,

Stephanie Woodard, Susan Rethorst, and, from 1975 to 1978, with Trisha Brown.

Perron also wrote criticism, first for *Dance Magazine* and then for *Soho Weekly News* (where she edited Concepts in Performance), and the *Village Voice*. "Ingrid Bengis once said that what makes a person a writer is energy. I'm sure that for me writing criticism came from an overflow of energy in my reactions to seeing dance. I remember rehearsing with Sara Rudner. She and Risa Jaroslow and I would come into rehearsal and talk about what we'd seen. Then Sara and Risa would finish talking, but I couldn't stop!"

In 1978, Perron began teaching dance at Bennington College, where she is now chairperson of the Dance Department. She divides her time between teaching and choreographing, between Vermont and New York. She made the move partly because she felt inundated by the volume of dance and performance in New York. "I started feeling 'Why do I need to do anything? There's already so much going on.' "

Teaching has opened up a new set of issues: How do people communicate ideas about dancing, physically and verbally? "It all has to do with *seeing*. Sometimes you have to be very patient with beginners. Often someone will ask me, 'Should I repeat that phrase later in the piece, maybe with a little variation?' and I say, 'You don't have to repeat it for me—I saw it the first time.' But maybe there are people who need that repetition, or who like it. For me, one movement has an impact that remains for a long time."

One hallmark of Perron's recent style is a sweet awkwardness that signals innocence, directness, but also requires a certain abandon from the dancers. "I try to let everything in, like a vessel. But the awkwardness is also a reaction to studio training, which leads you in the direction of finding the most control, the most speed, the most articulation of all parts of your body. That can close everything off. I try to give the dancers license to feel awkward. First, I have to find people who can and will do that. But also, I give them as much information as I know about the movement. I say things like 'Feel like your bladder is full,' instead of just demonstrating the movement. Or I ask them to do something that is physically impossible. I use analogs of situations with irregular rhythms, like stuttering, or a bird flapping its wings to take flight. It's important to verbalize what's going on, so they know what I have in mind. It's like writing criticism."

The frankness in Perron's dances also lies in the sense of unity among the dancers that seems more than physical—a glimmering of emotional bonds, of attentiveness. Perron's ideas about unison in dance are more social than kinesthetic. "I like to keep an eye on everyone when I'm performing, instead of feeling that it's just me out there performing, hoping I'm in synch with everyone else. I use counting less and less; it tends to deaden things. Instead, we try to breathe together, to feel where everyone else is in the phrase. I like feeling connected to the other dancers when I'm performing. And, as a spectator, I like watching people who are watching people. It's so much more interesting than watching people who are just dancing for an audience."

32

No More Ordinary Bodies

The line between play, games, and sports, on the one hand, and dance, on the other, is not always a clear-cut one. For one thing, key to many children's games is a dance element, movement sequences savored for all sorts of qualities, from vertiginous pleasure, to the development of muscular or hand-eye coordination, to social glue. But even in theatrical dancing there is a sense of a tenuous border between the two realms. In times when ballet has become overly virtuosic, critics have complained of performances that have "degenerated" into gymnastics, while to see the dancerly qualities in a gymnast's routine is to praise it. And yet it would be hard to say what, beyond context, distinguishes the one from the other. When a baseball team plays the game sans ball, has the performance become a dance? When we decide to pay attention to the movement of the players even as they use the ball, have we turned the game into a piece of choreography?

These kinds of questions vexed the first generation of postmodern dancers in the 1960s, as did questions about the blurry boundaries between dance and other arenas: not only specialized nondance movement forms like sports, but also ordinary, pedestrian actions, and of course the other art forms. The problems of defining dance in distinction from other events provided these choreographers with important structures and materials in regard to play, games, and sports. I think of Simone Forti's *Huddle*, *Rollers*, and other pieces using children's play as source; Yvonne Rainer's follow-the-leader format for the pivotal *Room Service*, one of several dances in a

Village Voice, April 23, 1985.

Judson Dance Theater collaboration with the sculptor Charles Ross that used a jungle-gym-like structure, springs, platforms, and other equipment. I think of Trisha Brown's rule games, Steve Paxton's use of iconic baseball postures, Judith Dunn's references to wrestling, and the more general playful attitude in such strategies (used, not only by the dancers at the time, but also by musicians, filmmakers, poets, happenings-makers, visual artists, and theater people) as improvisation and spontaneous determination.

Play, games, and sports were fascinating to this generation for other reasons than those of definition. These activities, though specialized in their own ways, were easily accessible and had a more democratic feeling than the modern dance or ballet of the time. You may have to know the rules governing the game in order to play it, but you don't have to go through years of rigorous training or become an acolyte in a cult of personality. It was the democratic commitment of the early postmodern choreographers that led them to use children's games and quintessentially American sports like baseball; you didn't see dances based on Olympic events.

But also, the view of the body and of behavior in the sixties had something to do with it. In dance, the ordinary body executing its mundane tasks and functions suddenly emerged as something surprisingly extraordinary, something amazingly graced. To perform a task, in the theory of such choreographers as Forti, Rainer, and Robert Morris, was a way of presenting the intelligently engaged body modestly stripped of the alluring gaze so typical of theatrical performance. Game structures, like the chance techniques of Merce Cunningham and John Cage, served as more strategies for depersonalizing performance; play activity served as a kind of task that simultaneously generated movement invention.

So notions of spontaneity, democracy, the naturalness of children, and the pleasures of the liberated adult body were united in these artists' fascination with play, games, and sports. Beyond that, in dance, as in Fluxus events, happenings, and other art of the early sixties, to present play as art was to deflate the grandiose seriousness of the previous generation's "high art" and to stake out a claim for a new generation of artists who partly celebrated their own youth.

Games and sports have again seized the imagination of choreographers in the eighties. But the differences between the way these themes emerged then and now show us two eras that are worlds apart. Compare, for instance, Forti's *Slant Board* with Elizabeth Streb's various uses of equipment, including a slant-board. In the former, the spectator feels a sense of kinesthetic empathy as s/he watches people like herself scrambling along a difficult surface by navigating along knotted ropes. In the latter, we marvel at two sleek athletes performing difficult feats of skill and endurance. In Charles Moulton's precision ball-passing pieces, in Molissa Fenley's driving "walls of dance," which require the dancers to rehearse wearing weights, in

Colleen Mulvihill's and M. J. Becker's gymnastic excursions (and in Batya Zamir's aerial dances foreshadowing these, not to mention Twyla Tharp's choreography for John Curry), as well as in the verbal games of Wendy Perron and Johanna Boyce, the dancer's mind/body resumes specialist status—with a vengeance. But this is not exactly a return to older values, especially in light of the current generation of avant-gardists' dialectic with the past.

Perhaps the new virtuosity is a response to the changing American body. The choreographers of the sixties were preoccupied with the ordinary body, but in the eighties the "ordinary" body is no longer simply that with which nature has endowed us. With the rise of jogging, health spas, and body-building machines, the ante has been upped; even the average person now is some kind of athlete.

If in the sixties we wanted to free the body—to let go—today we are no less obsessed by our anatomy, but we express it in opposite ways. In a difficult economy, no one is embarrassed by ambition and control. And one of the cheapest, most convenient things to master is one's body. So it's not surprising that, contra the "natural" beauty of the sixties, our present culture demands an appearance that is fully constructed, a body that is reimagined, padded, dyed, trimmed, molded, decorated, and pumped up. You can literally shape your own destiny, the rhetoric of physical culture promises. In an age seemingly bereft of resources, and certainly short on hope, the Horatio Alger myth reappears in its most concrete, physical form.

33

Happily Ever After? The Postmodern Fairytale and the New Dance

Now I am going to tell you the story of the postmodern fairytale in the new dance, which is really four separate stories. All four of these stories — the history of recent postmodern dance; the history of theatrical dance since the nineteenth century; the history of the folktale and of recent folktale scholarship; and the intellectual history of modernism and postmodernism — converge in this new genre. Space will not, of course, allow me to unfold these stories in full. However, as I weave together strands from each story, the reader should keep in mind that the postmodern fairytale in the new dance can only be understood as located, not in a single context, but in several separate though overlapping contexts, and that this particular new genre of postmodernism in dance expresses a dense web of dance-historical and cultural issues.

The 1980s have seen a broad trend toward the narrative in avant-garde dance. One of several strategies to rebut the modernist, essentialist, antinarrative preoccupations of the previous generation of choreographers in the sixties and seventies (that is, the group that we now call postmodern), the new narrative in dance, like the "new talkies" in avant-garde film and the "new textuality" in avant-garde theater, raises old issues for the art form, but in new ways.[1] In the age of poststructuralism, narrative in general has captured the intellectual and artistic imagination, where it has been analyzed, dismantled, demystified, and deconstructed. The fascination with narrative — its conventions, its meanings, and its reception — seems a logical sequel to the repudiation of narrative that earlier characterized the modernist project overall. And the field of avant-garde dance, where in fact the notion of the seamless narrative had already perished before the current generation of dancers was born, shares this fascination.

Merce Cunningham in the fifties and then the postmoderns of the sixties and seventies wanted to get rid of narrative partly for essentialist

La Danse au Défi (Montreal: Parachute, 1987). Reprinted with permission.

reasons — if they wanted to tell stories, to paraphrase John Cage, they would have been writing, not dancing. But these same artists opened up choreography to so broad a field of action that, even while attempting to pare dance down to its essence, they planted the seeds for a postmodern proliferation of techniques, styles, and functions.[2] By 1980, anything could be in a dance — but that meant not only walking, playing games, talking, silence, and untrained bodies, but also character, plot, music, and virtuosity.

Certainly the new narrative is a response in the dance dialectic to the obdurate "inexpressivity" of the seventies.[3] Some of the early postmodern choreographers themselves began to turn to narrative forms by the late 1970s. The pursuit of the story led Rainer from dance per se into performance art and then film. Gordon for a time specialized in a kind of semiotic of the gesture, playing with the various meanings of bodily movements as they shifted function and context, especially in relation to words; a notable example is his *What Happened*. Brown moved her signature pure-dance piece *Accumulation* into a new era first by telling the story of its making as she performed it, and then by telling several stories simultaneously while interpolating another dance into the sequence. Yet the generation of choreographers that emerged in the eighties has outstripped the earlier postmoderns in its insatiable appetite for narratives of all kinds: autobiography, biography, fiction, political document, interview, the use of sign language and other emblematic gesture systems. And, this in a development that at first glance seems improbable — the fairytale.

The fairytale was, of course, the exemplary narrative form of the nineteenth-century ballet, reaching its apotheosis in Petipa's works for the Russian Imperial Ballet; the paragon of this genre was *The Sleeping Beauty* (1890). For a number of different reasons (its rigidity of form, technical "magic," extravagant mise-en-scène, hierarchical politics, and seemingly trivial themes) the fairytale ballet, with its sparkling divertissements punctuated by literary pantomime to advance the plot, became a despised old chestnut for most of the twentieth century, especially for artists who aspired toward the modern. If the fairytale speaks of otherworldly marvels, Duncan, for one, wished to show the here and now of the human body; if the fairytale is a myth writ small, Graham, for one, aimed at monumentality; if a fairytale stylizes and condenses experience into glittering symbols of consciousness, Rainer wanted to explore reality in all its mundane, unmanipulated glory. One might think that, other than the academic reworkings of nineteenth-century classics, this genre had disappeared. Yet the fairytale ballet has not perished. On the contrary, it is presently emerging in the new dance in a richly provocative manner.[4] When one examines what I call the postmodern fairytale — the fairytale reread — both in terms of its use in the dance and in terms of its broader cultural context, one sees that, far from improbable, this "return" (or more accurately, revision) is perfectly apt.

If for no other reason than to flaunt narrativity in the face of the previous avant-garde, the new choreographer of the 1980s might have turned to the fairytale as a special kind of story, as a paradigm of narrativity per se. In fact, for a generation of folklorists, literary critics, and art historians — Western structuralists inspired by Propp's *Morphology of the Folktale* (English translation, 1958) and also by the writings of Lévi-Strauss — the folktale, in particular that enigmatic type of folktale known as the *Märchen*, or fairytale, or wondertale, seemed, not just a type, but a prototype of narratives in general. Indeed, the structuralists of the 1960s and 1970s were not the first to advance this theory that the fairytale is a paradigm for narrativity. Robert Petsch wrote in 1942 that the *Märchen* is the "archetype (*Ürform*) of human narrative art."[5] Joan Jonas's dance/performance *The Juniper Tree* (1976) and later *Upside Down and Backwards* (1979), based on the Grimm brothers' tale "The Boy Who Set Out to Learn Fear," were early gestures in the direction of the postmodern fairytale, and for their time these pieces were anomalous both by their references to wonder and by the fact that they had a story at all. Meredith Monk's works in the seventies had a folktale quality — especially *Education of the Girlchild* (1973) — but hers were idiosyncratic visionary tales that seemed to offer an alternative, not a return, to tradition. In general, structuralism's heyday in the sixties and seventies may have been, in other disciplines, related through Propp to the fairytale, but in dance it was not even distantly related. Structuralism corresponded, in dance, to the formalist, antiexpressive proclivities of the earlier generation of postmodern choreographers mentioned above.

And, in turn, the new generation of folklorists and literary critics who search for meaning in the tale beyond either its morphology (Propp) or its style (Lüthi) or even psychoanalytic interpretation (Bettelheim)[6] corresponds in dance to the later generation of postmodern choreographers who insist that dance has content — in particular, historical and social content. Twenty-odd years after the powerful impact of Propp and Lévi-Strauss, folklore analysis has turned away from form, toward an analysis of content, codes, performance, and reception.[7] In dance theory and dance practice, the impulse is analogous. So avant-garde dance turns to fairytales — a subject that, despite an historical intimacy, its own formalist and essentialist constraints could not allow it to explore during the age of structuralism. The present interdisciplinary spirit in both intellectual and artistic life allows for a heady (some might say even dizzying) alloy of methods, fields, genres, mediums, and styles. That dance finds itself once again attracted to the fairytale, then, stems from a network of newer concerns that may be characterized as postmodernist and poststructuralist — concerns that begin, to be sure, with a mediumistic desire to examine *how* dance can narrate (a question with roots in the analytic dance of the seventies), but concerns that at the same time fan out beyond the medium itself to embrace questions about dance history, the "genre" division within dance (for example, ballet, modern, and folk dance), the relation of dance to literature and other art forms, the relation of "high" art to folk and mass culture, and, as well, larger social questions about gender roles, ethnic identity, and moral/political education.

In the examples that follow, we can see that there is a family resemblance between the postmodern fairytale and the ballet fairytale, and yet we can also see how the former diverges from the latter, in formal terms primarily by its use of verbal narration. The use of words adds an extra communicative channel, but it also geometrically increases the possibilities for new meanings in the dance overall. That is, the Petipa fairytale was univocal: the music, the costumes, the scenery, the pantomime, as well as the dance steps, all told the same story. In the postmodern fairytale, the relationships among the different elements become unstable, generating new meanings. The choreographers sometimes irreverently adopt the fairytale precisely because it is a despised genre; sometimes in all seriousness present it as wondrous; sometimes debate the social values the tale upholds; sometimes anarchically parody the moral message of the tale; sometimes frame it specifically *as* a moral, and hence politically laden, tale; sometimes acknowledge its unmistakable power, beauty, and allure.

In *Folktales* (1985) by Ralph Lemon, folktales and fairytales are mixed.[8] Here the narrative method is also varied, for some of the tales are told in words only, some via dance and spoken text, some more theatrically with gestures, scenery, costumes, and objects as well as words, and some with pure dance. Altogether there are eight "stories," including a dance-game that has two additional, verbal tales inserted in it. The origins of the tales range from Africa to Europe (Germany and Russia) and America. The juxtaposition of the tales, with the ensuing friction of cultures, of classes, of eras, of individuals, gives each separate tale new meaning. Anthologized, each tale becomes a coded fragment of a culture, a piece of a puzzle that may never be resolved, since its various parts shift meaning, or even lose meaning, out of context.

Not only is *Folktales* a synthesis of tales of various national origins and a sampler of narrative methods; its choreographer is Afro-American and the cast includes blacks and whites, adults and children. Both the (heterogeneous) form and the (multicultural) content of *Folktales* bespeak an ambiguous vision of the creolized traditions that have formed America. For, taken individually, the tales are small gems, seamless and spellbinding, and apparently innocent of political meaning. But when we start to put them together, as the pivotal tale of the Tar Baby—with its explicit commentary on tales as socializing agents—instructs us to do, we also begin to ask questions about these traditional, seemingly timeless, seemingly universal repositories of wisdom.

"The Wonderful Tar Baby Story or Bayin' at the Dixie Moon," from

America, is the one tale that is both presented and commented on. It deserves some description here. First, in the deep blue light of a bright blue moon, a man in the shadows tells a Brer Rabbit story in contemporary jive talk, while another man rows a cardboard boat. The lights brighten, and the speaker of Black English turns out to be white. He stands on a box to tell his own "story" about Brer Rabbit—about hearing the tales first on the Disney screen (in *Song of the South*), then hearing them from a teacher in an all-white school, about discovering racism among friends, parents, and in himself, about wondering what the image of the "Tar Baby" could have possibly meant to black kids.

After we hear "Tar Baby" we begin to associate verbal images from the earlier tales in the piece, to compare and contrast them. It is as if the commentary embedded in the performance suddenly triggered the spectator's analytic reasoning. Why does the lazy, greedy daughter in "Mother Holle," who comes home from the "other" world covered with pitch, resemble the Tar Baby? Why is it that what is bad is signified by black? Why, in the German tale, is the good daughter the one who is unquestioningly obedient to any authority? But many other issues than that of race and ethnicity are raised by these tales. We ask, as well, about other divisions between people, particularly between generations. We are led, then, to ask, What are all these binary differences between people that fairytales so sharply and unmercifully delineate? And why do we long for an image of Eden, as in "Tale with Men, Boys, and Oranges," that is undifferentiated? At the same time, this motley collection makes us realize that our own American culture, whether we are black or white, young or old, male or female, *is* formed of fragments—that pastiche is our cultural style.

The pastiche of styles and methods, then, results partly in a political understanding of the tales, and partly in a peculiarly postmodern understanding of choreography itself. If the postmodern choreographers of the sixties and seventies used collage to circumvent literary meaning and narrative structure, the pastiche of the eighties situates narrative in a new framework. Here narrative can be enjoyed, even as it is subverted; it can be perceived as discontinuous, even while we watch it working.

Peter and the Wolf (1985) by Arnie Zane was originally commissioned by the Dance Division of SUNY-Purchase as a performance for schoolchildren. Zane ended up choreographing a punk version of the Prokofiev piece that probably mystified the young audiences but delighted the adults who saw it. Zane used a woman on pointe in the role of the wolf, a man in drag in a campy version of the bird, and various splintered characters; he told the story in several languages, at one point had the animals cavorting at a disco party with boomboxes, and suggested kinky sex as the red-cheeked farmboy Peter captured and tied up the vampish wolf.

Peter and the Wolf is not entirely a traditional folktale, but a modern version of one. Sergei Prokofiev wrote the libretto (based on old stories) and the music in 1936 as a "symphonic fairytale," a didactic piece for orchestra and voice that was intended to teach children to recognize the individual instruments in the ensemble, for each character is represented by a different musical "voice" that the narrator identifies before the tale proper begins: the bird is the flute, the duck the oboe, the cat the clarinet, the grandfather the bassoon, the wolf the French horns, Peter the strings, and the hunters the drums. (It was also a political-moral tale, for Peter's full name is Peter the Pioneer, and he could serve for Soviet youth as a model of self-reliance, attuned to nature, and a cooperative worker as well.) In 1940, Adolph Bolm did a ballet version of *Peter and the Wolf* for Ballet Theater in New York; critics praised the music by comparing Prokofiev to Walt Disney![9] Since then the ballet has been reworked ad infinitum by choreographers in Europe, America, and the Soviet Union.

In a sense, *Peter and the Wolf*, probably a familiar work from the childhood of many young choreographers of the 1980s, provides a crucial template for the mode of storytelling preferred in the postmodern narrative. Unlike the classical ballet, which advances the plot through mute pantomime, here the narration takes place on two simultaneous levels—verbal commentary and dancing. While this form of storytelling seemed far too repetitive to many in the early versions of the ballet in the 1940s (Cyril Beaumont said, about Frank Staff's 1940 version of *Peter and the Wolf* for the Ballet Rambert, that the musical expression was so clear and the verbal description so vivid, the dancing often seemed superfluous[10]), in the eighties that redundancy along multiple channels not only heightens the postmodernist irony but also, paradoxically, creates the possibility of multivocal meanings. The Cunningham-Cage model of discrete channels whose (nonnarrative) meanings do not necessarily harmonize connects to a new narrative sensibility and is transformed. The new model is, on the one hand, deliberately "dumb" and literal-minded; on the other hand, it provides a multilayered "text" punctured by allusions, subtexts, plural voices.

For Zane's *Peter and the Wolf* is an impish inversion of the piece as a received cultural artifact. It is both the *Peter and the Wolf* we already know and something else. It can be seen simultaneously in two ways. Suddenly it is a tale, not only for children, but at the same time for adults; it not only teaches us, but also upsets what we already know; it upends our notions of gender, of sexuality, of good and bad, even of unified character. Its humor, of course, is parodic. Zane relies on our already knowing the "right" version of the story, to which he can refer without having to make sense—a point that is underscored by the conglomeration of voices speaking in foreign tongues. Yet the very naughtiness of this dance, its spirit of *épater le bourgeois et l'avant-garde aussi* (because it is both avant-garde and retrogressive), makes even its adult sophistication yet another playful pose.

* * *

The Snow Queen (1986) by Kinematic (Tamar Kotoske, Maria Lakis, Mary Richter) is based on the fairytale written by Hans Christian Andersen. It tells of the boy Kay—whose heart is frozen by a splinter of ice and who, increasingly impervious to humanity, is abducted by the Snow Queen—and of his warmly loving friend Gerda, who ventures out to save him and returns him to this world. In Kinematic's version, a group of children (Kinematic plus Thom Fogarty and Carlos Arevalo) watch TV and seem to become possessed—or enchanted. First one child acts out a cartoon and then, when the television narrator's voice suddenly starts telling a fragmented version of "The Snow Queen," they all begin to take on aspects of the characters in the story, to dance to the sundry music, and to gesture as if in some half-forgotten, vestigial code. By the end of the tale, it seems they have been dancing out their own story, for isn't television our own modern version of Andersen's distorting mirror that shrinks human souls—the very mirror whose splinters are the bits of ice lodged in Kay's eye and heart? But who is the Gerda who will rescue these children?

The Snow Queen is the most ambitious and the most complex of the

Kinematic, *The Snow Queen.*
(Photo: Tom Brazil.)

fairytale ballets explored here. With its interludes of abstract dance and pseudo-folkdance and its main text of gesture language, it seems to quote the Petipa format—even though it is a wild version of that format, fills its structure with distinctly unPetipaesque dancing, and also adds the framing device of the TV (verbal) narrator. Dressing its adult dancers as children, the dance not only poses a question in regard to the tale about what has happened to Kay and Gerda (their travails and triumphs seem to be equated with the process of growing up, and, at the end of the story, they have acquired "grown-up children hearts"), but also it is has a very up-to-date punk look. And that punk aesthetic is further double-edged, for it is both utterly contemporary and at the same time nostalgic for the 1950s—that is, for the early childhood of the present generation of artists. Dressing both men and women in unisex pinafores, the dance suggests a cartoonish androgyny that is equally suited to the infantile (pre-splinter, pre-Snow Queen, pre-Fall) world of Kay and Gerda and to the cultural style of the eighties. The image of the dancers as automata (at first out of control, but increasingly regulated by the invisible television voice) is paired with their image as children (passive and malleable, and in the process of acquiring language), and further is yoked to the slipperiness of the characterizations (not only do the dancers-as-children seem to play at being the various fairytale characters, and sporadically at that, but, when the voice begins to interact with them, they even have difficulty identifying themselves), to impart a chilling view of our puny helplessness as our docile minds and bodies are molded by the instruments of socialization—from fairytales to dancing to advertisements and TV shows. The view is particularly chilling because the TV is the source both of the disembodied authority that controls and of the story that tells the "truth" about control.

Space does not permit me to discuss a number of other interesting examples of this genre, such as Pina Bausch's *Bluebeard*; Hope Gillerman's *The Princess Story*, in which the sexual and class codes of the traditional fairytale are overturned; Susan Foster's *Lac des Signes*, a deconstruction of the Russian classic *Swan Lake*; Diane Martel's dances, which rework folkdance and folk music motifs in transgressive contexts; and the work of Jawole Zollar of the Urban Bush Women, who takes her inspiration from African and Afro-American folktales.

As I suggested earlier, one reason the modern and postmodern choreographers preceding this generation found the fairytale anathema was simply that it was associated with the ballet, and, more specifically, with the peak of the academic style in the late nineteenth-century Russian Imperial Ballet. In fact, the European literary fairytale, whose history begins with the French writers Charles Perrault and the Countess d'Aulnoy in the seventeenth century, was the perfect form to inspire the Russian court ballet, for their tales, often new versions of traditional oral tales, were a kind of guide to the young aspirant to Versailles, codifying in graphic form the language, values, and manners of the exceedingly ritualized society of Louis XIV's court—an era the Romanov court itself tried to emulate.[11] By the late nineteenth century, fairytales were no longer written as exemplars for ambitious courtiers, but, repopularized through chapbooks and other cheap editions, played a new socializing role. They had come full circle from their original, feudal, folk origins, through the aristocratic and bourgeois forms developed by Perrault, the Brothers Grimm, and Andersen, to the popular literature and mass media of the modern industrial age.

In the 1970s, Marxist and feminist analyses of the social values coded by the literary fairytale, particularly in regard to status and gender, led to attempts to rewrite the classic tales from antiauthoritarian, nonsexist perspectives. And, by the 1980s, a postmodern consciousness focused on the fairytale not only as a literary genre that straddles both "high" and "low" culture, but also as an ambiguous thing, both pleasurable and dangerous. Hence the British writer Angela Carter lovingly reworks the classic fairytales in a feminized, neosadeian erotic manner, while the recent exhibition at Artists Space in New York entitled *The Fairy Tale: Politics, Desire, and Everyday Life* took as its organizing principle "a critical analysis of the fairy tale as a form of representation that embodies cultural notions of authority, power, morality, and sexuality" and noted that "The fairy tale inserts the child into a discourse that reduces social complexity to simple, unproblematic oppositions such as good vs. evil, male vs. female, power vs. weakness. . . . The use of the fairy tale in the mass media perpetuates a split between fantasy and reality, at the same time that it confuses one for the other."[12] Ericka Beckman's films, most recently and explicitly her *Cinderella* (1986), poetically explore the complex relations among fairytale forms and imagery, dreams, children's play, games, sex roles, and consumer culture. The juncture of various poststructuralist concerns—psychoanalysis, feminist reevaluations of gender roles and the early socialization of children, and Marxist critiques of consumer society with its mass media—excites a new interest in the form of literature most of us knew first.

One major difference between the "old-fashioned" fairytale ballet and the new, postmodern one, is a political and historical consciousness that criticizes and questions "fairytale discourse," as Zipes terms it. How is this difference expressed in concrete terms—through the form of the dance? The presence of the spoken word in the new fairytale ballet is a key departure, and one that serves as a wedge to pry open the meanings of the dance. I noted above that the presence of multiple channels allows for disparate meanings—the undermining or ironic contradiction of a single fixed meaning—in the work. The nineteenth-century ballet fairytale used pantomime to advance the plot, but verbal narration is much more specific than gesture language can be—at least, than the pantomime vocabulary of the ballet allowed. But—unlike what happens in modernist works, where a cryptic verbal text might rub against the kinetic element to create ambiguous poetic sparks — here when the verbal channel presents a narrative as clear-cut, direct, and familiar as a fairytale, a contrasting movement component doesn't rub, it abrades. And out of that abrasion postmodern irony is born.

While the ballet, with its illusions of flight and its brilliant stagecraft, has been, historically, a form of dance-theater particularly suited to magical transformations, the fairytale is appropriate to postmodernists for other reasons. For one, the flatness of the fairytale characters and the formulaic plot allow for a narrative without character development or suspense — that is, a narrative that is still antirealist. This stylized, abstract quality of the fairytale satisfies the part of postmodernism that is heir to modernism.[13] For another, the mixing of styles, techniques, and genres that characterizes postmodernism's "tradition of the old"[14] — which satisfies the part of postmodernism that attacks modernism — characterizes the fairytale as well. And the seemingly primal emotion that saturates the fairytale fits well with the return of feeling to eighties' new dance.

The fairytale is, perhaps, one of the most mysterious narrative forms because it appears to be so old and so marked, like a palimpsest, by the traces of successive cultural transformations. Linda Dégh writes of both the oral and literary forms of the *Märchen*:

> We now know that the magic tale is a precious document of human history. Like the zone-rings in a very old tree trunk, important events in the cultural evolution of man can be traced through a Märchen. A relative chronology might be set up by scrutinizing the Märchen motifs in one and the same narrative. The oldest layer and also the most impressive for modern man is the reflection of a strange [totemistic] world. . . . All animals, natural forces, and objects in the universe are humanized.[15]

But there is a further reason for the fairytale's new appeal in dance. The postmodern dance of the eighties has, for a variety of reasons — including, but not limited to, its historicist imagination and the emergent "tradition of the old" — become interested in working in the ballet arena, in a way that, despite occasional forays, its predecessors never were.[16] And to work in this arena means, not only trying on the technique and appropriating the scale of the opera house, but also experimenting with ballet's most cherished themes.

The intriguing, paradoxical fairytale, so old and yet so oddly emblematic of postmodern culture, has, as I have noted above, captured the imagination, not only of choreographers, but also of artists in film, literature, and the visual arts. While fairytales have not necessarily always been told or written for children — in *The Blue Fairy Book* Andrew Lang quotes an eighteenth-century lady of the French court who explained, "J'aime les jeux innocents avec ceux qui ne le sont pas," and Ralph Manheim translated the title of the Brothers Grimm as *Grimms' Tales for Young and Old*, explaining that not until the tales reached England did they become rationalized, sanitized, and "gift-wrapped" for children[17] — in our day they have come to be almost entirely relegated to children's culture. Thus the fascination they hold for the current avant-garde can be seen as part of a larger fascination with childhood associations of all kinds (as in the "toy-puppet" performances of Stuart Sherman and Paul Zaloom, the relay races and early reminiscences of Johanna Boyce's dances, Jim Self and Frank Moore's cartoonlike cine-dance *Beehive*, and even the fifties "rec-room" atmosphere of Lower East Side performance clubs). This tendency seems to be a dialectical response to a mainstream cultural obsession with childhood, not surprising in an era of the most recent American baby boom. The postmodern fairytale ballet places itself in a position of resistance, as I have suggested, to that uncritical mainstream celebration of children and childhood.

In 1984, Noël Carroll remarked that the new dance images of play and childlike "fun" seemed to assert themselves as antidotes to the austere minimalism of the seventies, contributing to a more general return of expression in postmodern dance that signaled a yearning for rejuvenation.[18] The genre of the postmodern dance fairytale that has emerged in the mid-eighties conjoins that infantile, polymorphous pleasure, focused on the body, with the very adult pleasure of analysis, focused on the text.[19]

34

Pointe of Departure

If the 1960s prized speaking directly, the eighties is an age of irony. Quotation marks surround everything; originality becomes a matter of quoting differently, of wearing tuxedoes *and* tennis shoes. Call it pastiche. It is the aesthetic of postmodernism. An about-face from modernism's "tradition of the new," it at the same time represents an extension of the collage techniques beloved of the modernist avant-garde. No less than in the other arts, this nostalgic eclecticism has swept through the contemporary dance

Boston Review (October 1986).

scene. And nowhere has it more strangely—or more revealingly—expressed itself than in the current invasion of avant-garde choreographers into that bastion of choreographic conservatism, the ballet stage.

At the Metropolitan Opera House last spring, American Ballet Theater audiences viewed Mikhail Baryshnikov as quick-change artist portraying a series of character types from Dr. Jekyll/Mr. Hyde, to a Pavlova-as-Camille ballerina dying of a cough, to Mata Hari's accomplice, to Smith the butler in a murder case where everyone's surname is Smith. This was David Gordon's *Murder* (with music by Berlioz and sets by Edward Gorey), a work that combined a balletic vocabulary and opera-house scale with the typical Gordonian choreographic devices his loft audiences have come to know: spoken texts; a narrative structure that shifts meaning and coils around itself to end, with a surprise, at the beginning; a patterned, almost obsessively repetitive way of manipulating objects and dancers with the same comfortable casualness; transitions effected not by logical causation but by "moving furniture" to literally create a new space (here taken to ceremonial extremes in a recurring funeral procession); quotations of Gordon's own choreography as well as loving allusions to film and ballet classics.

A heretofore fiercely independent experimental choreographer, Gordon designed the movement for the Philip Glass opera *The Photographer* at the Next Wave Festival of the Brooklyn Academy of Music (BAM) in 1983. This is Gordon's second ballet for the American Ballet Theater (ABT), which in 1985 premiered his *Field, Chair and Mountain*, and his third ballet on the Metropolitan Opera stage, where Dance Theatre of Harlem in 1985 performed his *Piano Movers*.

Those same ABT spectators last spring saw quite a different avant-garde ballet in Karole Armitage's *The Mollino Room*, with décor by David Salle, music by Paul Hindemith, and dialogue by Mike Nichols and Elaine May. The tone of the ballet is an oblique tribute to the twentieth-century Italian architect and designer Carlo Mollino, who championed kitsch and prefigured (the press release informs us) "the current thesis of banal design." Yet despite the dancers' awful fifties clothing and the monstrous everyday objects painted on Salle's drop curtains, *The Mollino Room* is anything but banal. Armitage's first important work, choreographed for modern dancers and set to punk/new wave music by Rhys Chatham, was *Drastic Classicism* (1981). As Arlene Croce wrote in the *New Yorker*, "Classical values that were flayed alive stayed alive." Armitage, who danced with Merce Cunningham but had earlier danced Balanchine as a member of the Geneva Ballet, seems a true choreographic heir of both men, wedding a spiky, elongated, off-center neoclassic line, elegantly erotic partnering, and startling costumes and sets, with open-field choreography and a self-conscious commitment to "deconstructing" dance conventions.

The Mollino Room is both an attack on and celebration of the ballet event. Its scale absolutely dictates the need for an opera-house performance, yet the dancers are dwarfed by gigantic objects on the backdrops, which rise and fall according to their own choreography during the piece. One curtain, depicting enormous shoes several times human size, seems actually to squash the tiny, insignificant dancers as it ominously descends. Baryshnikov's role as a soloist is diabolically undercut; his dark costume makes him blend into the corps de ballet as the corps itself seems to fuse into so much décor, and he performs his virtuosic aerial embroideries hiding among a moving forest of bodies. When the voices of Nichols and May boom out their outrageous *My Son, the Nurse*—in a recording that includes the comedians' guffaws, false starts, and reworkings of the theme—one loses sight of the dancers altogether. But the jokes about gender codes are poignantly iterated, redirected home to ballet, as the dancers enter dressed as cartoon boys in shirts and ties and cartoon girls with bright toy falsies studding their leotards.

These are but two examples of the burgeoning ballet repertory by avant-garde choreographers. It all began in 1973 when Robert Joffrey commissioned Twyla Tharp to make *Deuce Coupe*, a bold mix of ballet dancers and Tharp's own company dancing to music by the Beach Boys, with graffiti writers spray-painting fresh décor during each performance. Utterly anomalous as it seemed at the time, this project did have certain historical precedents in some of Diaghilev's collaborations. A later precedent was the 1959 New York City Ballet production of *Episodes*, with separate sections choreographed by Balanchine and Martha Graham, and a guest appearance, in one of Balanchine's sections, by modern dancer Paul Taylor. But Tharp's irreverent pastiche of "high" and "low" art demonstrated a new postmodernist sensibility that flew in the face of the austere, formalist, high modernism that dominated the dance avant-garde of the seventies. That sensibility has infected the dancing of the eighties, and its central arena has become the ballet stage.

Since *Deuce Coupe*, Tharp herself has been working regularly for Joffrey, ABT, and even the New York City Ballet (in a 1984 collaboration with Jerome Robbins). Joffrey invited Laura Dean to make her first ballet for the company in 1980 and that association has continued. More recently Lucinda Childs, known for her "minimalist" dances in the seventies, has choreographed for the Pacific Northwest Ballet and the Paris Opera Ballet; the Ohio Ballet's latest season included works by Molissa Fenley and Laura Dean; the Boston Ballet has a new dance by Mark Morris and a work-in-progress by Jim Self; Armitage has choreographed for the Paris Opera Ballet.

The impetus comes partly from the company directors. By comparison with modern dance, which since the turn of the century has bred generation upon generation of choreographers, American ballet was until

Karole Armitage's *GV-10*, choreographed for the Paris Opera Ballet, 1984. *L* to *R*: Sylvie Guillem, Karole Armitage, Isabelle Guerin.
(Photo: Randolphe Torette.)

recently dominated by a single generation. And for over fifty years the presiding figure was George Balanchine, whose roots were in nineteenth-century Imperial Russian ballet. Even the younger choreographers—like Jerome Robbins—belonged artistically to the world of Balanchine, Antony Tudor, and Agnes de Mille. When Balanchine died in 1983, the end of an era tolled; and the lack of great, up-and-coming ballet choreographers became painfully apparent. A frantic search for new talent began.

Baryshnikov's desires to refresh the ballet repertory and to challenge himself as a dancer are well known. Ballet West (whose director, Bruce Marks, has recently moved to the Boston Ballet) sponsored an open-ended laboratory in 1985 for young experimental choreographers to work with ballet dancers. Liz Thompson, at Jacob's Pillow Dance Festival, has for several years commissioned young postmodern choreographers to make new works for the dancers in the Festival's annual Ballet Project. In London, the Ballet Rambert is now headed by Richard Alston, one of the founders of the British New Dance movement. In addition to showing Alston's own choreography, the troupe is committed to work by young choreographers like Michael Clark. Clark, who has worked with Armitage, recently made a film for British Channel 4 with the American cinedance director Charles Atlas, and will appear on BAM's Next Wave this fall.

And this cross-fertilization between the avant-garde and institutional dance is itself becoming institutionalized. The National Choreography Project, for instance, was established three years ago with money from the Rockefeller Foundation, Exxon, and the National Endowment for the Arts to fund just such (but not only such) connections, and to spread new work to repertory companies around the country. It has sponsored work by Meredith Monk for the José Limón Company, Merce Cunningham for the Pennsylvania Ballet, Mark Morris for the Boston Ballet and the Joffrey, Susan Marshall for the Dallas Ballet, and Charles Moulton and Nina Wiener for the North Carolina Dance Theater, among others.

While not every avant-garde choreographer is drawn toward working with ballet dancers — Trisha Brown, for instance, will not choreograph for any company but her own, and Steve Paxton remains committed to alternative body techniques — a parallel impulse toward spectacle is taking place in the avant-garde arena itself. I have dwelt on the ballet invasion at length here because it seems emblematic of the current avant-garde's great shifts of attention and aspiration. The recent collaborations sponsored by the Next Wave Festival — like Childs's *Dance* (1979), with music by Philip Glass and décor by Sol LeWitt, or Brown's *Set and Reset* (1984), with décor by Robert Rauschenberg and music by Laurie Anderson — are very much in the same ambitious vein. And work by the younger generation of avant-garde choreographers — Johanna Boyce, Pooh Kaye, Tim Miller, Ishmael Houston-Jones, and Fred Holland — is also impelled by a multimedia imagination, contra the pure dance tendency of the seventies.

The shift has practical as well as aesthetic origins. For one, the older members of the current cohort have, after twenty-five years, become established. Dipping into the mainstream, they are discovering that a certain amount of theatricality is desirable, if not necessary. Brown, for instance, says she began using music partly because she felt it made spectators more comfortable with her work. Childs was inspired to infuse her work with theatrical magic after working with Robert Wilson and Philip Glass (on the avant-garde opera *Einstein on the Beach*), but also notes that she had to change her choreography to accommodate the scale and frontality of the opera-house stages where her company now appears. The Next Wave Festival has increased its houses by selling tickets to collaborative efforts whose spectators are drawn equally from the art, music, dance, and theater worlds. And such projects are looked upon more kindly than media specialization by funding agencies.

But the major impetus for the move into ballet, into the contemporary opera house, and, in general, into spectacle and out of the intimate venues and bare-bones dancing of the seventies, comes from the choreographers themselves. In the eighties we are witnessing a new stage of avant-garde dance—one that may ultimately result in full cooptation by the mainstream. Earlier I called the ballet experiments of the eighties strange. What makes them so unlikely? While ballet choreographers have repeatedly looked outside the academy for new inspirations, ballet's adversaries—and that is the stance modern and avant-garde dancers have historically struck—have, until recently, generally disdained entering ballet's ivory tower.

Modern dance began when Isadora Duncan and others challenged the academic vocabulary of classical ballet, borrowed from popular entertainments and various systems of physical culture, and made a new, distinctively American art dance that embodied an individualistic, pioneering spirit and created emblems of freedom through movement. The generation that followed—Martha Graham, Doris Humphrey, and their contemporaries—crystallized individually coded movement vocabularies to communicate personal feelings and social themes. Their models were musical forms; the underpinnings of their dances were literary.

By the mid-1940s, Merce Cunningham was experimenting with abstraction. Working with the composer John Cage, Cunningham sought to free dancing from the constraints of music by letting the two simply coexist in time and space. By the late fifties and early sixties, when in all the other arts a new postwar generation exploded on the scene (and when the hallmarks of those arts were performance, vitality, and motion), dance too produced its own young vanguard.

Working at first in the Judson Church in Greenwich Village (which also housed an off-off Broadway theater and a gallery that showed pop art and happenings), the new dancers made their task a total reconsideration of the medium; and, to discover the essence of dance, they broke every rule. They walked, carried out written instructions, played games, enacted rituals, used chance techniques, improvised, and presented films, lectures, visual art, music, and everyday action as dances. The identity, nature, history, and function of dance were the objects of their animated inquiry.

By the 1970s, a wide range of questions about dance had been asked and a new phase of consolidation and analysis had begun. Choreographic structure was emphasized, and pure movement (movements without expressive or illusionistic references) predominated in the lofts, galleries, churches, and other alternative spaces that had become the venues for postmodern dance (as it was called by the midseventies). For such analytic postmoderns as Yvonne Rainer (now an independent filmmaker), Paxton, Brown, Gordon, and Childs—as well as for their contemporaries, the minimalist sculptors (like Donald Judd and Robert Morris) and the new music composers (like Philip Glass and Steve Reich)—the basic axiom was "less is more."

This postmodern dance in fact had much in common with "modernism" in the other arts: it was reductive, reflexive, and abstract. What, then, to call the new dance of the eighties? Post-postmodern? Certainly it looks and means very differently from analytic postmodern dance. "More," dancers have now decided, "is more." Taken up with popular culture, parodic historicism, and entertainment values, the new dance has everything to do with what in all the other arts we call postmodernism. Perhaps the very impossibility of finding another label — the feeling that we've run out of labels — is one of the marks of the postmodern age.

In dance, the mistress of the age is Twyla Tharp, whose work exemplifies Charles Jencks's definition of postmodern architecture as doubly coded: entertainment for the general public and esoteric historical reference for the cognoscenti. Her rigorously structured choreography uses vernacular dance, blends genres, takes hedonistic pleasure in dancing to the music, and stands with one foot in the avant-garde and one foot on Broadway. In the seventies she seemed utterly sui generis, but she heralded a new generation of "new dance" choreographers who mix the casualness and eclecticism of postmodern dance with the expressiveness of modern dance, the gusto of social dance, and the virtuosity of ballet.

And not only its virtuosity. In the sixties and seventies, many postmodern dancers studied ballet technique as an antidote to the personal style of teaching in modern dance; others had first studied ballet as children and found in its vocabulary yet more material for their pluralistic view of dance. In the spirit of both pluralism and pastiche, if anything can be used in a dance, why not the Western high art tradition as well as social dance, non-Western dance, and nondance movements? But also, the same technical perfectionism, narrative capacity, and expressive power that made ballet anathema in the sixties make it attractive to both dancers and spectators in the eighties.

Our dancing is always shaped by our attitudes toward the body. In the sixties we wanted to let go, to relax, to improvise; in the eighties the mode is one of control — of the organism as well as of the images it produces. From body-building to fashion to sexual mores, our body culture attests to this desire to rein in, mold, and remake our physical selves. It is encoded in our clothing, our hairstyles, our eating habits (and disorders) — and in our dances. From aerobics to ballet to the avant-garde, the quest for technical perfection and the urge toward capturing meaning mark our present mania for control.

The avant-garde choreographers of the sixties were fascinated by the "natural" body of the untrained dancer. In the eighties, when everyone is jogging, swimming, or lifting weights, what it means to have an ordinary body has changed, the very notion of the natural body has come under fire, and even social dancing is highly choreographed. On the concert stage, the level of dance-technical training has skyrocketed. Choreographers of all aesthetic persuasions are making works for superbly trained dancers with multiple performance skills—in different dance genres, but also in sports, gymnastics, acrobatics, even circus arts. Like the omnicompetent dancer, the dance itself has become a multimedia event, a polymorphous meeting of all the arts in the lived moment, in the singularly postmodern presence of performance.

35

Classical Brinksmanship: Karole Armitage and Michael Clark

There are times, it seems, when the classical tradition in dance needs massive shocks to the system to renew itself. Karole Armitage and Michael Clark, working on opposite sides of the Atlantic, in their separate ways, keep dreaming up those shocks. Like Diaghilev in an earlier era of crisis, Armitage and Clark both understand the need to infuse the dance performance with the tonic verve of the other contemporary arts. But also, as exemplary postmodernists of the 1980s, they traffic in a different kind of astonishment, one that wryly mixes classicism and kitsch, the high modern and the vulgar, abstraction with eroticism, the beautiful with the satanic—and the sardonic.

Both Armitage and Clark have been commissioned to bring their wrenching, revitalizing spirits to major ballet companies—Armitage has worked with the Paris Opera Ballet and last year made a dance for Mikhail Baryshnikov and the American Ballet Theatre; Clark has choreographed for the Scottish Ballet, Paris Opera Ballet, London Festival Ballet and Ballet Rambert. But as they dance here in Los Angeles with their own, smaller companies, one can see how they bring a classical spirit—especially discernible in their own dancing—to invigorate modern dance as well.

Armitage was born in Kansas in 1955 and studied ballet as a child with a transplanted former New York City Ballet dancer. Abroad with her family at sixteen, she joined the Geneva Ballet, dancing in a Balanchine-

Program note, *Performing Arts: Los Angeles Festival*, September 3–27, 1987.

dominated repertory. But, feeling rebellious toward even that brand of abstract ballet, she came to New York, where from 1976 to 1981 she was the marvel of the Merce Cunningham Dance Company, with her poise, speed, and pliable, seemingly infinite extension. Certainly in Cunningham's company she had already become part of a world where innovations in dance, art, and music intermarried.

By the time she left Cunningham, Armitage had already been experimenting with her own choreography for several years. The titles of some of the early works, such as *Ne* (1978), hint at both her humor and her spirit. *Vertige* (1980), a duet for herself and new wave musician Rhys Chatham, first performed in a downtown Manhattan club, asserted a bracing frenzy. *Drastic Classicism* (1981), in which her company performed movements from the ballet canon with raw energy, literally in concert with a live punk rock band, articulated a logical direction—given her ballet background, her years with Cunningham, and her proclivity for new wave music. Writing in the *New Yorker* of the way Armitage "flayed [ballet] alive," Arlene Croce concluded that *Drastic Classicism* "transcended its own wildness to become a vindication of formal values in dancing." Though her tastes in music have shifted and the visual element has grown in importance, that direction, a radical classicism, remains constant.

In *The Watteau Duets* (1984), Armitage again deconstructed ballet as she and Joseph Lennon, another ex-Cunningham dancer, explored partnering techniques clad in a variety of costumes, including spike heels for her (that functioned much like the pointe shoes she wore later), a leather skirt for him, and, for both, huge block-stilts. Not only the erotic and sadistic elements of the classical pas de deux, but also its cumbersome spectacle was apparent in this piece, which was performed to a blast of sound from David Linton's band that, like the dance, was both exquisite and tortuous.

Critics dubbed Armitage the "punk ballerina." But while she has used its music and shares with punk a gift for assaulting the senses and a nostalgia for fifties style, Armitage's scheme is more consciously interwoven with artworld and danceworld achievements. "What I want to do is make ballets for this time," she has stated. "The work does not have a pioneering spirit. It is tied to the four hundred years of steps and technique and style that have evolved in ballet, and it is trying to take that somewhere else."

Armitage's compositional style resembles that of her collaborator, the painter David Salle, with whom she lives. Salle has designed the décors and costumes for a number of her works, including *The Elizabethan Phrasing of the Late Albert Ayler*. Both artists specialize in a kind of aesthetic version of cognitive dissonance, juxtaposing part against part in clashing styles, quoting both high and pop culture, art and everyday life. The resulting ironic distance is very much in tune with the fifties style they often appropriate, but is tempered with a singularly eighties tough elegance.

With the Salle collaborations, Armitage's musical requirements have become correspondingly more complex and eclectic; her sense of rock as an energizing, liberating force has simultaneously waned. So the sound for *Phrasing* moves from the Shakespearean declamations of Lord Buckley (a fifties hipster comedian), to Webern, to Yo-Yo Ma performing traditional Japanese music, to Stravinsky, to the jazz musicians Albert and Don Ayler. Yet, though rock has disappeared, the importance of syncopation as a dislocating force remains.

Sex and gender are at the heart of much of Armitage's work, sometimes revealed as the unacknowledged subject of traditional ballet, and

Michael Clark.
(Photo: Richard Haughton.)

sometimes (as in *The Mollino Room*, the piece for ABT), commented on, goofily tongue-in-cheek. Michael Clark, who has danced with Armitage on several of her European tours, sees his outrageous sexual content as a direct frontal attack on the antiquated, rigid codes of classical ballet, with which he, like Armitage, grew up. "The whole sexual side of dance is something that is quite often ignored or even rejected," he has pointed out. And yet ballet's ideas in general "are so straightforward, so rigidly defined. . . . So male and female."

The glorious stew of polymorphous sexual identities and sexual action in Clark's work goes far beyond unmasking the amenities of ballet, however. The English see it as a protest against Thatcherism and an emblem of post-punk London in the 80s — not just a symbol, but an embodiment of the club scene, for the company includes designers (Leigh Bowery and David Holah of Bodymap) and musicians (The Fall and the Yugoslav band Laibach) as both collaborators and performers. "The idea of having your own company is to have people you care about around you, even if it means changing the way you work to incorporate those people," Clark says. It also means making dances that partake of the sights and sounds of life outside the dance studio.

Clark, who was born in Aberdeen, Scotland, in 1962 and began doing highland dancing at age four, trained at the Royal Ballet School and at seventeen joined the Ballet Rambert. The Rambert has always been a company that experiments, and there Richard Alston, the young artistic director who had been a pioneer of British New Dance and had also spent time in New York studying with Merce Cunningham, made Clark a showpiece in dances both classical and contemporary. It was clear that as a dancer Clark was extraordinarily gifted, with fluid grace and élan that have prompted comparisons to Nijinsky.

When Clark left Rambert in 1981, it became clear that he was also a gifted choreographer, one who was able to glean from his ballet training technique and phrasing that could be reused in new contexts. For, despite his criticisms of the ballet as a social institution, and, unlike an earlier generation of avant-garde choreographers, Clark acknowledges that "ballet is a very rich technique, and it can be used in all sorts of ways." Those ways include parody — as when in his dances men wear tutus while women wear combat boots, or when in *Pure Pre-Scenes* he reinterprets the Bluebird Variation and sets women dancing to Chopin piano music — but they also include the seriously dazzling virtuoso dancing that is the essence of classicism.

Ballet is not, however, the only tradition of dance that shows up, reworked, in Clark's choreography. There is a whacky, quintessentially British pantomime-inspired aspect to the cross-dressing, phallic byplay and fantastic costumes. That popular, bumptious strand of dance history rears its head in rebellion in Clark's work.

Is Clark just a chronicler of the wild world he puts on stage, with its narcissistic glitter and its fascistic overtones, or is he a political critic? One British critic saw in *Now Gods*, one section of a longer ballet called *No Fire Escape in Hell*, "a powerful hypnotic vision of the sort of violent society which seems just an election away."

In the 1970s, avant-gardists saw the body as material for art and the performance as a moment both for rinsing movement of all the excess trappings of theatricality that distracted from the dance itself and for technical innovation. In the eighties—the age of the postmodern spectacle—Armitage and Clark lead the way for a new generation of dancers to reinvest the body with sexual and emotional meanings, to reinstall the other arts in the theatre and to rediscover the wealth of dance history.

36

Terpsichore in Sneakers, High Heels, Jazz Shoes, and on Pointe: Postmodern Dance Revisited

In dance, the term "postmodern" came into use in the early 1960s, when Yvonne Rainer and other emerging choreographers used it to differentiate their work from that of the preceding generation—modern dance. By the midseventies, it had become a critical term to label a movement. Now, in the late 1980s, when the term has been theorized not only in the arts, but in cultural criticism generally, "postmodern" has come to mean something quite different for dance—though clearly our current usage is an evolution from those original ruptures with the dance academy in the sixties.

For we in the late twentieth century are everywhere enmeshed in "the postmodern condition."[1] In one sense, everything about our current first-world, post-industrial, mass-media culture is postmodern. But postmodernism, it should be remembered, has had specific, though disparate,

Dance 89 (Munich, 1989).

meanings in the various spheres of culture, meanings that are tied to the particular history and practice of each discipline.

Charles Jencks, the architect and critic, popularized the term (which was first advanced in the 1930s, and then entered literary-critical discourse in the early 1960s) for his own field, beginning in 1975. In his recent book *What is Post-Modernism?*, Jencks reiterates his definition: that postmodern architecture involves "double coding," in two senses. Deliberately hybrid, it appeals to two separate audiences; it both continues and transcends modernism by mixing it with classicism—combining old and new styles, materials, and techniques—in order to engage both the general public and the experts. For Jencks, this eclecticism has a moral and political, as well as aesthetic mission. It is entertaining, decorative, and symbolic, reanchoring architecture in the public service; at the same time, its playfulness is professionally informed, reinstalling the art in the depth and breadth of its historical tradition. But Jencks is adamant about protecting his category from what he considers easy elisions with postindustrial culture generally.[2]

Jencks disputes the definitions given by such critics as Hassan and Krauss, which ally postmodernism with experimentation, radical discontinuity, and deconstruction. For these critics, Jencks argues, any break with high modernism is labeled postmodern. But in his view, because such artists as John Cage, William Burroughs, and Robert Morris still work in a singly coded, hermetic avant-garde tradition—without the symbolism, ornament, and pluralism that characterize postmodern architecture—they should be categorized as late-modernist, not postmodernist.

In literature, John Barth and Umberto Eco, among others, have used the term postmodern to refer to the ironic use of traditional forms, again doubly coded, in that postmodern literature will be enjoyable to broader audiences (say, than Beckett's), yet will still intrigue the literary expert. Fredric Jameson has theorized postmodernism as pastiche, signaling cultural schizophrenia. Charles Newman sees it as an expression of inflationary culture. In the practice and criticism of the visual arts, the term refers to appropriation from mass culture, the "death of the subject," a Lyotardian "loss of master narratives." In theater, postmodern has been used to mean the death of character.[3]

But this jumble of meanings should not paralyze us in looking at dance history. Jencks disagrees with the way the term is used in literature and the visual arts because his definers for architecture are not necessarily applicable across the arts. Since modernism dictated that each art specialize in its own unique essence, it is not surprising that postmodernism has taken different directions in each art. And yet a fundamental part of postmodernism—or postmodernity—is the antimodernist, interdisciplinary mingling of these previously separate spheres. By the eighties, it seems clear that there is a shared project across the arts, but also that the disparate paths to it may not all look the same.

In dance the term "postmodern" also has had a specific meaning—as in the other arts, a meaning particular to the discipline, though that meaning has changed over the last three decades. And it is certainly not accidental that its use in critical discourse began to spread first in the midseventies in order to track developments, dating from the early sixties, parallel to those in the other arts.

The meaning of the term "postmodern" in dance is partly historical and descriptive, as I have suggested. It began as a choreographer's term to call attention to an emergent generation of new dance artists. Those choreographers—many, but not all, of whom were connected with the Judson Dance Theater—were not necessarily united stylistically. Their methods ranged from chance procedures to improvisation to picture-scores to rule-games and tasks, and from a minimalist interest in sustaining "one thing" to a welter of multimedia. Their vocabulary, too, partook of a uniquely early sixties spirit of democratic pluralism, embracing unstylized ordinary activities—child's play, social dancing, daily tasks—as well as the more specialized actions of athletics, ballet, and modern dance techniques. In their work lay the seeds of both the analytic, reductive work of the seventies and a baroque, theatrical style that has reemerged in the eighties. Although these choreographers in no way represented stylistic homogeneity, they were, however, united in their antimodern project—that is, their desire to make dances that departed from the values and practices of the modern dance of Wigman, Graham, Humphrey, Limón, and followers.

By the late sixties and early seventies, however, as members of this generation increasingly allied themselves with the gallery artworld, a more unified style emerged—what I have called "analytic postmodern dance."[4] This is the style that in 1975 Michael Kirby pinpointed as postmodern dance.[5] Its practitioners included Yvonne Rainer (until, by 1973, she was working exclusively as a film director), Steve Paxton, Trisha Brown, David Gordon, Lucinda Childs, and the group Grand Union. Conceptually (rather than musically or literarily) based, analytic postmodern dance was reflexive—not only abstract and shorn of excess theatrical trappings, but also framing these features as revealing the essential characteristics of the medium of dance. It was, that is, *modernist* according to the criteria set down by the art critic Clement Greenberg,[6] and it shared methods and goals with the high modernist project of minimalism, which dominated visual art in the seventies. In postmodern dance, too, the analytic style prevailed, and yet simultaneously another strand of choreographers (such as Meredith Monk, Kenneth King, and Laura Dean), working in a more overtly theatrical vein, pursued in the seventies what I have called "metaphoric postmodern dance."[7]

But, by the eighties, a second generation of what could by then only be called postmodern choreographers—many of them students and followers of the first generation—as well as various formations of postmodern movements abroad (such as butoh in Japan, poor dance in Germany, new dance in England, danse actuelle in Montreal and Paris) had joined the first generation. And, as well, a range of institutions, networks, and festivals had been developed for producing and distributing postmodern dance. Once again, stylistic diversity prevailed, though certain traits recurred—notably, an alliance with the avant/pop music world (and its logical outcome: increased popularity) and an interest in both narrative and the traditions of dance history.

This is true, to varying degrees, not only of the upcoming generation of younger choreographers, but of those who had come of age in the sixties, at the beginning of the postmodern dance movement, as well. And in this respect, recent work by the avant-gardists of the sixties and seventies and their progeny joins forces with the historically dissimilar projects of choreographers like Twyla Tharp and Mark Morris. Its references to classicism and to other dance cultures, its plenitude of theatrical means, and its increased accessibility make this latest chapter of postmodern dance more like what Jencks narrowly admits to the canon of postmodernism than the analytic postmodern dance of the seventies had been.

Yet all three (or more) of these chapters are part of the story of postmodern dance. This is partly because at various points its practices have meshed with aspects of postmodernism in the other arts. But, more importantly, it is because practices that are (compared to the visual arts, for instance) both *modernist* and *postmodernist* have already both been subsumed under the rubric "postmodern dance." Historically—no matter what its twists, turns, digressions, and alliances along the way—the movement has called itself postmodern, and many of its practitioners still use that title. There is no turning back the clock, in this particular case, even if to do so would provide the relief of categorical neatness. In a sense, postmodern dance began as a *postmodernist* movement, underwent a *modernist* interlude, and has now embarked on a second *postmodernist* project. Let us now look in slightly more detail at those three chapters, which fall more or less into three decades.

The Sixties

In the experiments of the early sixties, the groundwork was laid for both the (*modernist*) analytic postmodern dance of the seventies—characterized by minimalism—and the (*postmodernist*) postmodern dance of the eighties—characterized by abundance, appropriation, and theatricality.

The early departures from the modern dance had to do with both form and content; they paralleled the concurrent breaks in visual art from modernism—even though modern dance was never *modernist* in Greenberg's sense. And, although this feature is often forgotten nowadays, one way early postmodern dance broke from historical modern dance and seized artworld status was to ally itself with the visual art world. Simone Forti's earliest New York concert took place at the Reuben Gallery, home of happenings and junk art, in 1960; her second concert installed "dance constructions" meant to be viewed in the round, like sculpture, in a downtown loft. Avant-garde dance in the early sixties shared with pop art (as well as happenings, underground film, and the Off-Off Broadway theater movement) a playful exuberance, a democratic impulse, and a visionary faith in the concrete truth of the human body that challenged modernist academicism in American culture at large. Dance, in particular, foregrounding the artist's body, became a central vanguard arena not only for trained dancers, but also for visual artists, musicians, poets, and filmmakers. Further, it was not seen simply as a vanguard arena, for it both borrowed from popular, folk, and mass arts and also sought wider audiences. And, simultaneously, choreography was rendered less esoteric exactly because it had opened itself to nonprofessionals. Often akin to dada in its blurring of boundaries between life and art, between artist and spectator, and between art forms, early postmodern dance in this regard seemed the opposite of Greenberg's modernism, where every art form reveals its special essence.

But (again peculiar to dance), because the earlier generation's concerns were symbolic and expressive (rather than abstract) one way to break with the tradition of modern dance was to embrace modernist—reflexive—concerns, to bare the devices. Merce Cunningham and others had opened the door to abstraction and the short-circuiting of personal expressivity through chance methods. But modernist reflexivity requires something more—namely, that the formal elements of abstract work be seen as revealing essential characteristics of the medium. Historically, this required an added semantic dimension—that the work not merely be itself but that it be about being the kind of thing it is. Something from the internal structure of the work or from its context was necessary to establish that this sort of reflexivity was operative. The postmodern dancers of the sixties transmuted Cunningham's (and others') abstraction into reflexivity through a variety of means—including manifestos, the insertion of verbal material in the dance itself, nudity, and ordinary movements.

Hence the ways dancers sought to challenge the artistic status quo in their own field in the sixties had elements in common with *both* modernism and postmodernism in the other arts. Their work was often abstract and reflexive, but just as often ironic, dealing in everyday materials and inspecting historical and vernacular conventions. Perhaps because the body is so drenched with social and political symbolism, it was possible to create such symbolic meanings even in ostensibly nonrepresentational dance.

For instance, in Yvonne Rainer's *We Shall Run* (1963), the dance consisted, on one level, of people running at a steady pace in different floor patterns, grouping and regrouping. But a number of factors—the grandiose music by Berlioz, the serious calm of the dancers' demeanor, the variety of their body types, the very steadiness of their pace, and the way the paths allowed neither any one person nor any one gender to take a leader's role (while they did allow for individual forays from the group)—made this dance seem to be as much about a vision of a utopian, democratic community as it was a dance "about" a particular kind of movement or choreographic structure.[8]

Other cultural themes of the early sixties pervaded these dances, not only reflecting many of the issues of post-World War II American society, but at times contesting, and even, at times, creating them. In this time of a "troubled feast"—where despite a teeming cornucopia of goods and an economy more and more geared toward pure consumption, there were pockets of poverty and overarching racist inequities—these dances spoke of freedom and democracy, embracing improvisational and collective methods. The superabundance of objects was satirized in such dances as Lucinda Childs's *Carnation* (1964)—where, under attack from household items like sponges, a colander, and a plastic garbage bag, a young woman remakes her body into a surrealist object; or Kenneth King's *cup/saucer/two dancers/radio*, in which all the items in the title are leveled into a frighteningly dehumanized homogeneity. But also, in this prefeminist moment, dance performance was a venue where the woman artist was fully empowered, carving out a zone for women's work and a status for the woman artist that foreshadowed feminist demands of the seventies.

These dances redefined the body, releasing it from the heroic, symbolically overinflated images of modern dance (for instance, Martha Graham's Greek mythological heroines or the distillation of Shakespearean passion in José Limón's *Moor's Pavane*). Instead, the body became what the Russian literary critic Mikhail Bakhtin had earlier called "the grotesque body": festive, exorbitant, confusing inside and outside, focusing on the "lower" processes of sex, ingestion, and digestion, and all the orifices that lead into and out of the body.[9] Appropriate to the expansive sixties, the grotesque body is itself a figure of abundance. From Simone Forti's playful *Huddle* (1961); to Carolee Schneemann's orgiastic *Meat Joy* (1964); to Steve Paxton's *Physical Things* (1966) (in which the audience passed through a 100-foot plastic tunnel decorated with trees and fake grass); to the "love" section of Yvonne Rainer's *Terrain* (1963) (where she and William Davis assumed a sequence of erotic poses based on Indian temple sculpture); to Robert Morris's appropriation of Manet's *Olympia* in his own *Site* (1964), the facts of the body were aggressively asserted, expressing a cultural moment of confidence, economic expansion, and teeming creativity.

The Seventies

By the early seventies, a new phase of consolidation and analysis began, as many choreographers pursued specific projects unearthed by the wide-ranging experiments of the sixties. This research aspect of the avant-garde laboratory superseded the playfulness of the earlier decade, as a serious work ethic emerged in both the rhetoric and the methods of the post-modern choreographers. The "work" was factual, down-to-earth, objective, a style often arrived at through task activities that, as Robert Morris noted as early as 1965, served as a useful strategy for producing concentrated, unself-conscious, "real" movement.[10] Scores, verbal commentary, and ordinary movements and postures also contributed to the search for movement detached from personal expression. The absence of music and special lighting, scenery, or costumes increased the movement's importance—since the movement became all there was to concentrate on. The antiillusionist approach demanded close viewing and clarified the smallest unit of dance, shifting the emphasis from the phrase to the step or gesture, inviting the spectator to concentrate, in an almost scientific way, on the choreographic structure and the movement per se.

Rainer's *Trio A* (1966), also known as *The Mind is a Muscle, Part 1*, was a harbinger of this trend. A single phrase, four-and-one half minutes long, it dispenses with phrasing, development, climax, the virtuosic feat, and the fully extended body of modern dance, substituting energy equality, equality of parts, found movement, and human scale, as Rainer herself explained.[11] The movements are all abstract, yet they are performed with a tasklike energy and concentration. The various strategies for shortcircuiting the performer's gaze add to the neutral, objective performance demeanor. The choreographic structure is that of a list; one movement follows another without any particular dancerly logic, underscoring Rainer's observation that "Dance is hard to see. It must either be made less fancy, or the fact of that intrinsic difficulty must be emphasized to the point where it becomes almost impossible to see."[12]

Similarly, Brown's Accumulation Pieces and Structured Pieces and various dances by Lucinda Childs, most notably *Calico Mingling* (1973), used structural devices such as repetition and reversal, mathematical systems, geometrical forms, and comparison and contrast to encourage the perusal of pure, often simple movement.

Analytic postmodern dance was consistent with—and consciously aligned itself with—the practice of minimalist sculpture. It was also a fitting art for a post-Watergate, post-oil-crisis America—sober, factual, conservationist in terms of energy and theatrical means.

The work of Twyla Tharp, which had its roots in the modernist project of the analytic phase of postmodern dance, seemed by the mid-seventies to diverge from these structuralist, minimalist—and, admittedly, specialized—concerns. As she began to explore popular music and dancing, at times going so far as to insert the vernacular into the ballet tradition—in works like *Eight Jelly Rolls* (1971) and *Deuce Coupe* (for the Joffrey Ballet, 1973)—she became a practitioner of *postmodernist* dance in Jencks's sense. The rigor of her choreographic structures persisted, while her musicality and catholic musical taste gained her wider, more popular audiences.

The Eighties

Tharp's moves prefigured and meshed with several key directions of the eighties. For a number of reasons—ranging from the aesthetic to the economic—the interests of the first generation of postmodern choreographers shifted to large-scale, spectacular, multimedia collaborations (often under the auspices either of the Brooklyn Academy of Music's Next Wave Festival or of progressive ballet companies). Childs's *Dance* (1979), a collaboration with the visual artist Sol LeWitt and the composer Philip Glass, is paradigmatic of this shift, as is Trisha Brown's *Set and Reset* (1983), a collaboration with visual artist Robert Rauschenberg and composer Laurie Anderson. At the same time, a younger generation emerged in the 1979–80 season—including Bill T. Jones and Arnie Zane, Jim Self, Johanna Boyce, Molissa Fenley, Karole Armitage—who, themselves impatient with the seemingly puritanical seriousness and dry asceticism of the analytic approach, independently found various means to reinstate theatricality while remaining committed to the avant-garde venue. Further, a post-Tharp generation—whether directly descended from her company, like Sara Rudner and Nina Wiener, or inspired by her example (one with wider circulation and impact than that of her analytic colleagues)—began to appear as well. And further, by the mideighties, a wing of choreographers who identified themselves as both black and postmodern—among them Blondell Cummings, Bill T. Jones, Bebe Miller, Ishmael Houston-Jones, and Fred Holland—integrated what had hitherto been a predominantly white arena, often introducing explicitly political themes of black identity in their dances. Other political concerns—notably feminist and gay—surfaced at this time too.

Besides the desire for political representation, there was an aesthetic cultural pluralism at work in the eighties that broadened both the pool of participants and the audience appeal. A number of Japanese dancers, including Kei Takei, Eiko and Koma, and Yoshiko Chuma, introduced techniques from butoh and Japanese avant-garde theater; the alternative techniques plundered by various choreographers and producers—from capoeira, salsa, and breakdancing to tapdancing and juggling—showed the postmodern proclivity, not only for traditions from other cultures, but also for those despised or overlooked from American subcultures and popular culture.

Mikhail Baryshnikov's appointment as director of American Ballet Theatre in 1980 and the death of George Balanchine in 1983, the Joffrey Ballet's success with Tharp's ballets, commissions by such producers as the Jacob's Pillow Dance Festival, and the growing regional ballet movement with its demand for new choreography, as well as a postmodernist interest in history and tradition, all contributed to the move into the ballet arena of a number of postmodern choreographers, including David Gordon, Lucinda Childs, Laura Dean, Karole Armitage, Mark Morris, Molissa Fenley, Jim Self, and Ralph Lemon. In another variation on the same theme, a number of postmodern choreographers, working in alternative venues, have exploited the narrative appeal of the story "ballet"—notably the group Kinematic, with their trilogy of fairytale works. The collaborative turn, the move toward ballet, and the interest in cultural pluralism are all factors that have aligned eighties postmodern dance with developments in the music world—which has itself undergone similar changes.

As the term postmodernism has taken on a broader cultural, interdisciplinary meaning, postmodern choreographers are consciously bringing their work in line with the term as it has been theorized across the disciplines over the last decade or so. Thus Mark Morris makes a series of dances based on Roland Barthes's *Mythologies*; Susan Foster deconstructs *Swan Lake* and makes references to Barthes and Foucault; Stephen Petronio describes his *Simulacrum Reels* as history flashing past the eyes of the spectator.[13] In the eighties, "postmodern" is no longer a descriptive term, categorizing directions already in motion, but a prescriptive one—a commitment to a project that takes postmodernist, poststructuralist theory as a set of directive guidelines.

In the sixties, many of the aspects of postmodernist dance we note today were already present. In fact, those features of post-World War II avant-garde culture with which early postmodern dance was connected originally gave rise to the term postmodern, in literature and the other arts, as well as in dance. But, owing to the historical circumstances of avant-garde dance, as theory informed practice, dancers moved away from multimedia, interdisciplinary experiments and quotations from both popular culture and dance history, in order to explore their chosen medium. That analytical, often austere research program, in a modernist key—which dominated the seventies—gave way in the eighties to new interests in pluralism, in politics, in narrative, in ballet, and in collaborations between the disciplines. And, at the same time, contemporary developments in the other arts have aligned this phase of postmodern dance—which eschews the essentialist bias of modernism—with *postmodernist* practice in current cultural theory and in the other arts. This third phase of postmodern dance shares with the sixties the desire to bring dance into contemporary artistic discourse. But the making of the postmodern dance of the eighties—partly because it is descended from developments in the avant-garde dance of the sixties and seventies, which defined "postmodern" through practice, and partly because art-cultural discourse has redefined postmodernism—is guided now by the theoretical prescriptions the term has come to imply.

37

Dancing [with/to/before/on/in/over/after/against/away from/without] the Music: Vicissitudes of Collaboration in American Postmodern Choreography

In thinking about collaborations in American postmodern dance and music, several distinctions in the relations between the two arts that have emerged in the broader history of theatrical dance are useful. As well, it is helpful to review briefly the history of postmodern dance in terms of its connections to (and disconnections from) music in general. For it may be that the ways postmodern dance has treated music and the composer-choreographer partnership make collaboration itself a problematic term. How much consultation does it take to make a commission a collaboration, and how much must the separate components fit together in the finished work? Or is a commission itself the minimal act of "laboring together," as the etymology of the word collaboration suggests? What happens when the choreographer is the composer, or the dancers the musicians? What if a composer chooses to choreograph? These, indeed, are some of the kinds of

Choreography and Dance 1/4 (1992).

questions that have animated the postmodern choreographic inquiry from the start.

One distinction in the broader history of theatrical dancing is that between first-rate and second-rate music — the debate, as ballet began to detach itself from opera in the early nineteenth century to become a separate art form, as to whether the music should refrain from calling attention to itself (and away from the dance) by its excellence. The idea was advanced that the music should support the dancing in specific ways: by providing, first of all, a clear rhythmic basis for the dancers' timing, and, second, a "dancerly" (*dansante*) melody for modulating the flow of energy and expression. Yet these "program-music" aims were not necessarily consistent with the goals of serious composers — as they had been, for instance, during the baroque era — once dance-music and symphonic music diverged, and once social dance and theater dance were no longer congruent. Serious composers could play around with dancing music and ballet music, but it was not their most serious work; and the composers — mostly hacks — who specialized in such music were not expected to aim for excellence in musical composition. It was even reasoned that the music should avoid innovation, for familiar tunes, by context, could augment the mise-en-scène with the narrative and emotional development that pure dance could not supply on its own.

Closely intertwined with this idea that the music should not upstage the dance — and hence should stay in the hands of dance-composer specialists without aspirations toward serious music — was the slightly different nineteenth-century notion that, in the collaborative process, the dance came first. That is, the music played second fiddle to the dance, not only in terms of quality, but also in calling the tune, so to speak. Ballet, it should be remembered, had grown out of social dancing; in that model, of course, the dance form structures the music. But this hierarchy continued to apply even when the dance vocabulary had become more specialized and even when choreographers used first-rate music — not only in the parts of the ballet based on social dances (mazurkas, waltzes, and so on) but also in the more abstract sections of pure classical ballet as well.

Thus Tchaikovsky was surprised, in working on the 1877 version of *Swan Lake*, to see Julius Reisinger reverse the usual work process by choreographing to the music — rather than ordering the music by the measure to fit the dances. Despite Tchaikovsky's growing reputation as a symphonic composer, Marius Petipa did not hesitate to dictate complete requirements for the music for *The Sleeping Beauty* (1890), and we know that Tchaikovsky was happy to comply. This was the standard method of their collaboration. Nor, as we also know, did Petipa and Lev Ivanov hesitate to rearrange the composer's music for their own 1895 version of *Swan Lake*.[1]

The working methods may not have changed since the earlier part of the century, but the artistic potential released in these late nineteenth-century ballets—when as a result of theater reforms I. A. Vsevolozhsky did away with the position of staff musician and commissioned first-rate music—was an important inspiration to members of the younger generation of Russian artists and intellectuals. Out of their group would issue the Diaghilev paradigm that combined both these concepts—a full collaboration between music and dance (and visual art), in which, ideally, composer and choreographer were both serious, first-rate artists in their own right, and in which they worked together to make a unified artwork where neither art form was subjugated to the other.

In modern dance, too, the early twentieth century was characterized by a new attitude toward music. Duncan's interpretations of the great composers and St. Denis's music visualizations each in their own ways parallel the aspirations of modern ballet choreographers to foster a more symbiotic relationship with the work of serious composers, albeit to already existing works. Yet, as the century wore on, there were instances when modern dance struggled to free itself from conventional musical support. In tune with the primitivism of the dadaists and the German expressionists, Mary Wigman substituted pure percussion—on non-Western instruments—for the melody previously considered essential to European music and dance performance. In the late 1920s and early 1930s, several choreographers choreographed in silence, either adding the music when the dance was completed or presenting the finished dances entirely without music, as in Doris Humphrey's *Water Study* and Tamiris's *The Queen Walks in the Garden* (both 1927). From the midthirties, Martha Graham and others consistently commissioned new music by American composers.

Merce Cunningham's dance theater, with John Cage as musical director, represents a watershed moment in which dance wrenched itself free of music—although not from musical collaboration—for the first time.[2] In the Cunningham-Cage model, the work of both artists stresses the rhythmic complexities at the core of dancing, but the choreography and musical composition present autonomous rhythms that rarely connect, and, when they do, connect by chance. As Roger Copeland has pointed out, one might protest that this separation of elements barely seems to constitute collaboration; but perhaps this "collaboration at a distance," as he calls it, is but one extreme on a spectrum of possibilities for artistic partnership.[3]

I have argued in the previous chapter that the movement we call modern dance was never "modernist" in the Greenbergian sense. That is, unlike the reflexive work of modernist painters and sculptors, historical modern dance never revealed its own essence as an art form. Though the way was paved by Merce Cunningham's abstraction and his separation of the dancing from the music, it fell to the analytic postmodern choreographers of the 1970s to take on this modernist task. This, of course, is why the nomenclature of artistic generations in dance differs from that in the other arts; our "postmoderns" include both what I have termed the "analytic" (modernist) choreographers of the seventies and the postmodernists (in the more general cultural sense) of both the early sixties and now again in the eighties. This also helps explain why, in the analytic stage of postmodern dance, music was often avoided altogether. Let us look, then, at how the different stages of postmodern dance—in its "modernist" as well as "postmodernist" phases—have treated music and the notion of musical collaboration.[4]

The Sixties: Anything Goes

If postmodern dance as it conceived itself in the early sixties was a criticism as well as an extension of modern dance, one form that criticism took was to transcend the various models of the choreographer-composer collaboration—even the Cunningham-Cage model—and to ventilate even more possibilities for the sound component in dance, both during the choreographic process and in performance.

The reigning theory of dance composition at this time was taught by Graham's musical director, Louis Horst, who had already formed several generations of modern-dance choreographers in his well known classes. For Horst, emotion inhered in the very forms of music; whether one chose sacred medieval music or American folksongs as one's source, the meaning and shape of the dance, as well as its vocabulary, were already dictated by expressive qualities Horst found in the musical genre. The goal was to imitate an entire zeitgeist of an era by using the music—as well as painting and architecture—as a program for style. For example, in the medieval sacred dance (not, he warns, to be confused with either medieval secular dances or Renaissance religious dances), Horst recommends using the parallelism that, he finds, pervades this period, from painting style to the musical structure of the organum, and that symbolizes "the meek acceptance of earthy trials" typical of the Christian figure dominated by the Church. Though unique to its own era, Horst reasons, the distortions and irregularities of the medieval period style resonate with our own; therefore modern dances imitating such highly coded notions of a generalized medieval style will be easily accessible now (in the early sixties).

> [This] style is based on religious ecstasy. It is weak with a weakness born of meekness and a paleness born of self-denial. Dance movement based on the parallel designs of medieval religious art is attenuated or twisted out of natural postures to a point of torture. It is apt to be performed in a very limited area; for the most part moving from one parallel design to another without covering much floor space. . . . The dance will repeat the elongated, reaching, contorted art of those times. The conception of medieval man suffering under an inner, self-inflicted pain is plainly

> analogous to many of our familiar modern psychological ideas of emotional conflicts and complexes. . . .
>
> Dances about self-inflicted penance, fasting, flagellation, denial of the world suggest themselves; or in psychological terminology: guilt complexes, withdrawals, etc. Lives of medieval saints and martyrs can be examined for subject matter . . . — the hair shirt, the straw pallet. . . . Mixed and uneven rhythm give the needed uneven, asymmetrical, oblique character to the dance design.[5]

Despite their specific, historically rooted styles, these dance forms, he claims, are all easily assimilable into the modern temperament. And amazingly, the appropriate dance structure for each one of these musical styles, though they are unique products of their culture and time, Horst concludes, "is usually a relative of the basic ABA form" (even though the musical structure may not be).[6]

Not surprisingly, many young dancers in the sixties looked for alternative approaches to dance composition. They found a stimulus in the choreographic workshop that was to spawn the first Judson Dance Theater concert in 1962 — a course also taught by a musician, Robert Dunn, rather than a choreographer. Dunn, a former student in John Cage's experimental music class, took a different path than Horst. He asked his students to transpose more formal music composition problems and concepts (including the use of scores) to movement — rather than making a dance that would mimic a given musical style as part of an expressive package. In Dunn's class, the music that generated a piece of choreography might not even end up accompanying the dance.

The first Judson concert included an improvised collaboration between a choreographer and jazz composer (Fred Herko's and Cecil Taylor's *Like Most People — for Soren*), a dance choreographed by a composer (John Herbert McDowell's *February Fun at Bucharest*, set to music by the baroque composer Charpentier), and an appropriation of rock and roll (William Davis's *Crayon*, to records by the Volumes, Dee Clark, and the Shells). As well, there were pieces in which the dancers sang (David Gordon's *Mannequin Dance*), squeaked (Yvonne Rainer's *Dance for 3 People and 6 Arms*), and talked (Rainer's *Ordinary Dance*), and one in which the audience was instructed to blow up balloons and let the air out slowly (James Waring's musical score for part of *Mannequin Dance*). There were also dances to music by Erik Satie (Fred Herko's *Once or Twice a Week I Put on Sneakers to Go Uptown*) and by John Cage (Carol Scothorn's *Isolations* and Ruth Emerson's *Shoulder r*, both to Cage's *Cartridge Music*). And there were several dances performed in silence.

After the first Judson concert, a number of other young contemporary musicians besides McDowell joined the group — Philip Corner, James Tenney, and Malcolm Goldstein. The composers in the group collaborated on dances by supplying musical accompaniment (Corner and Goldstein, for instance, wrote music for Lucinda Childs's *Pastime* and *Three Piece* [both 1963], respectively; Tenney often worked with Carolee Schneeman; Goldstein and McDowell wrote the music for Elaine Summer's *Fantastic Gardens* [1964]; and even Robert Dunn contributed a musical piece, *Doubles for 4* [1959], as an accompaniment to Judith Dunn's *Index I* and *Index II* [1964]). They also made their own dances. Sometimes, as in Corner's *Certain Distilling Processes* (1963), the dancers' movements became a living score for the musicians to interpret (in Corner's piece, four dancers choreographed individual solos to a calligraphic score by the composer, and their gestures, in turn, were translated into sounds during the performance by seventeen musicians and a singer, each assigned to watch a particular dancer). Sometimes pure musical compositions, with no dancing whatsoever, were presented as part of a dance concert, encouraging the audience to think of music itself as dancing. The physical act of making music was sometimes framed as a dance (Corner's *From Keyboard Dances* [1964]). And dancers, in turn, made music (e.g., Steve Paxton's *Music for Word Words* [1963], which was a sound-producing action—the inflation and deflation, using a vacuum cleaner, of a twelve-foot-square plastic cube with arms and legs, which eventually became a costume. This took the separation of "music" and dance to an extreme, since it was performed the day after his and Rainer's silent duet *Word Words*).[7]

Although a great many younger dancemakers presented work at the Judson Dance Theater, it was not the only site of early sixties experimentation. Simone Forti, on arriving in New York after dancing with Ann Halprin, worked with Rainer, Robert Morris, Trisha Brown, and others who would later form the Judson group. Forti incorporated singing, talking, shrieking, reading aloud, laughing, and other sounds made by the dancers themselves. The ongoing nature of her early dance structures was partly influenced by La Monte Young's use of sustained sounds; and one of Forti's dances—*Accompaniment for La Monte's "2 sounds" and La Monte's "2 sounds"* (1961)—deliberately reversed the usual relationship between dance and music by announcing itself as an accompaniment to Young's *2 sounds*.[8]

James Waring, never part of the Judson workshop itself, was a contemporary of Cunningham's and Halprin's who presented his own work at various venues, first in San Francisco and, beginning in 1948, in New York—including the Living Theater, the Master Institute, and the Judson Church (after 1963). Waring was teacher to several of the Judson group and many younger choreographers danced in his company. In retrospect, Waring's musical practice alone (not to mention his movement inventions) qualifies him as an early model for postmodernism. He was a master of pastiche, juxtaposing Bach and George Brecht; Couperin, McRae Cook, and Maria Alba; Glière, John Herbert McDowell, Rossini, Louis Alter, and traditional Spanish music. In the early sixties he collaborated with a number of contemporary composers, commissioning music—often assemblages—by McDowell and Richard Maxfield especially, but at the same time he choreographed entire dances to Bach or Mozart. In the later sixties he was inclined more toward romantic and modern composers, from Liszt and Chopin to Stravinsky, but often mixed them in collages with popular song. In the fifties Waring had turned to the use of musical forms to structure his dances, specifically as a way of rinsing his choreography of overbearing narrative or drama. (Perhaps he was not aware that even literary choreographers like Graham also, following Horst, worked from musical structures). But his later use of musical collage not only created new musical forms by which to structure dances, but also served, as well, as atmospheric—often nostalgic and theatrical—coloring. Don McDonagh (1971) describes Waring's phrasing as "embroidery around rather than on the music." Much of the music he used—the sound assemblages, for instance, of contemporary composers—might not provide any handles at all for dancerly phrasing, while, in using more traditional music, Waring's choreography often deliberately strayed from following the rhythmic and melodic structure precisely. Partner to the whimsical eccentricity of gesture and costume was an unconventional, slightly off-kilter use of the musical basis.

So the early sixties were marked by a wide-ranging use of music in different styles, as well as a wide-ranging practice in terms of how the music was (or was not) incorporated into the choreographic process. In these breakaway years of early postmodern dance, every tenet of the reigning choreographic methods was called into question. (And even some of the early experiments of the modern dance masters, unknown to this generation, were repeated.) The grandeur of certain musical choices now seemed pretentious and was treated ironically (e.g., Rainer's *We Shall Run* [1963], to Berlioz). Partly as a result of John Cage's teachings, which advocated the acceptance of all sounds as part of music, material formerly considered inadmissible was incorporated in the sound track of a dance—words, popular music, vocalizations and breathing by the dancers themselves. Yet while "lowbrow" music was suddenly permitted, much "highbrow" music, especially that of the twentieth-century pre-Cage composers favored by the modern dancers, began to seem like the old-fashioned, second-rate program music. The relationship, not only between dance and music, but also between choreographer and composer, was explored with a vengeance—and new relationships were imagined.

The Late Sixties and Seventies: Museums, Laboratories, and Silence

In the late sixties and the seventies, an expansive, wide-ranging sense of interdisciplinary experimentation gave way to a situation in which artists returned to their "home" disciplines. In a modernist vein, minimalist painters and sculptors concentrated on exploring the limits and possibilities of their given media. For both aesthetic and social reasons, the choreographers who emerged from the Judson group were gallery-oriented. That is, they participated in the visual artworld discourse;[9] their venues were often museums, galleries, and international art festivals; their audiences were artworld audiences. There were parallels, as Rainer charted in her essay "A Quasi Survey of Some 'Minimalist' Tendencies in the Quantitatively Minimal Dance Activity Midst the Plethora, or an Analysis of *Trio A*," between the work of the visual artists and choreographers of this period.[10] But, although minimalist art shared values and goals with both analytic postmodern dance and minimalist new music during this period, the arts did not usually meet in performance — for one of the values of that minimalism dictated that each art devote itself to refining and reflecting on its own essence. Thus the late sixties and seventies were largely a time of separatism, in the arts as well as the political arena. When the choreographers did use music, often it was "found" sound — popular music in particular. One exception was Simone Forti, whose collaborations with Charlemagne Palestine and Peter Van Riper explored improvisatory interactions between dancer and musician in performance. Another was Deborah Hay, whose *Ten* (1968) was accompanied by a rock band, the Third Eye.[11]

In dance as in visual art, a serious work ethic emerged in both the rhetoric and the methods of postmodern choreographers. The style of the "work" was factual, down-to-earth, objective. Tasks and scores were among the strategies employed to strip movement of personal expression. And movement per se was foregrounded further — scrutinized, as if under a laboratory microscope — by revealing choreographic structure, on the one hand, and by abolishing such theatrical trappings as special lighting, scenery, and costumes — and, often, music as accompaniment — on the other. Moreover, by now the choreographers deliberately shied away from borrowing as dance structures even the kinds of musical structures that had been avant-garde in the fifties and early sixties (e.g., Erik Satie's repetitions). Instead, they used scientific models — geometrical forms (for example, Lucinda Childs's *Calico Mingling* [1973]) or mathematical systems (Trisha Brown's Accumulation Pieces [from 1971]).

Yvonne Rainer used various kinds of sound — including rock and roll, a recording of Lenny Bruce's monologue *On Snot*, a composition by Gordon Mumma, and movie music — for her various "composite" pieces of 1968–70. One section of accompaniment in *Performance Demonstration* (1968) was a tape of Rainer's voice delivering a jeremiad against the use of music at all, a diatribe that was ironic (since music was used in the piece) but at the same time offered a thoughtful critique, forcing the viewer to consider the various theories and possibilities of music-dance correspondence:

> . . . I would like to say that I am a music-hater. The only remaining meaningful role for muzeek in relation to dance is to be totally absent or

> to mock itself. To use "serious" muzache simultaneously with dance is to give a glamorous "high art" aura to what is seen. To use "program" moosick or pop or rock is to generate excitement or coloration which the dance itself would not otherwise evoke.
>
> Why am I opposed to this kind of enhancement? One reason is that I love dancing and am jealous of encroachment upon it by any other element. I want my dancing to be the superstar and refuse to share the limelight with any form of collaboration or co-existence. Muzak does not accompany paintings in a gallery. . . .
>
> . . . I simply don't want someone else's high art anywhere near mine. . . . I *don't collaborate*. . . . Furthermore, I am all for one medium at a time.[12] (emphasis mine)

In *Rose Fractions* (1969), Rainer stated her attitude toward musical accompaniment even more forcefully when she included in the program's list of elements to be found in the first section the term "Mucis"—assimilating music to the social impropriety, later in the list, of "Body and Snot (Lenny Bruce)."

While this period was dominated by the analytic, modernist concerns I have outlined here, the seventies also witnessed a different strand of postmodern dance, one I have called "metaphoric" or "metaphysical." While it shared many stylistic aspects with the first and second phases of postmodern dance, the metaphoric postmodern dance by such choreographers as Meredith Monk, Kenneth King, and Laura Dean took a holistic approach to dance-theater.

In the late sixties and early seventies, King was for the most part using verbal texts as sound elements in his dance pieces—including readings from philosophers, political fantasies, and lectures on dance theory. In the late sixties, Monk collaborated briefly with Don Preston (of the Mothers of Invention) and other musicians on the scores for her dance pieces. But by 1970 she alone composed the music for her often site-specific, epic-scale performances. From 1970 on, she simultaneously choreographed, directed, and carried on a career as a new music composer in a minimalist mode, publishing recordings—the first was *Key* (1971)—and giving concerts for voice, piano, and less conventional instruments like wineglass and jew's harp. These concerts, including *Raw Recital* (1970) and *Our Lady of Late* (1973), were primarily musical in focus, but always theatrical in presentation. The exploration of the voice—its range and expressive qualities, in solo, chamber, and choral form—has been fundamental to both her music and dance-theater works. During the same period, Dean collaborated with the minimalist composer Steve Reich, and by the late seventies began writing her own music in a similar vein. In Dean's work, repetitive modules of movement keyed precisely to music accumulate, serving, like a mantra or the incessant whirling of Sufi dervishes, to reach an intense, meditative, almost mystical pitch.[13]

In a separate arena from either the analytic or the metaphoric postmoderns, Twyla Tharp explored musicality in choreography to existing music, using both classical and popular scores. If the analytic improvisatory group The Grand Union—in its at times surrealistic, at times antiillusionist demystifications of theatricality—put on an omnium gatherum of favorite records to dance to, those interludes were marked as ironic, often incongruous acts. But Tharp, choreographing dances to Jelly Roll Morton, Haydn, the Beach Boys, or Chuck Berry, while sophisticated and ironic in her own way, clearly began with an appreciation for the phrasing, rhythms, and dynamics of the music. In this regard, she is more like Balanchine or Paul Taylor than like the early postmodernists whose pop sensibility she shared. When, as in *The Bix Pieces* (1972) and so many of her other works, the dance is choreographed to one piece of music (or in silence) and then set to another, contrasting composition in performance, the ensuing stylistic and rhythmic tensions create a complex, multilayered structure—though the sources of those tensions (the echo, as it were, of the original music, set in conflict with the later accompaniment) are not always clear to the audience.[14] And the eclecticism of Tharp's musical choices from piece to piece, as well as her catholic taste in dance vocabularies—from the baton-twirling and tapdancing of her childhood to classical ballet moves to quotations of black jazz to the intricate movements generated by structural permutations—put Tharp more squarely in the purview of the term "postmodernist" as it is used now in culture generally. That is, to use Charles Jencks's definition from architecture, her dances are doubly coded, mixing elements from classical and vernacular traditions, but also appealing, on different grounds, both to a general public and to specialists.[15]

Thus in the late 1960s and throughout the 1970s, collaboration was not a dominant practice in the avant-garde, even for a musicalist choreographer such as Tharp, who used preexisting musical works from both "high" and "low" culture. For the analytic choreographers, to dance in silence, to verbal texts, or even to sound collages that included music—that is, to refuse, one way or another, to "dance to the music"—was a way to clarify and focus on movement for its own sake. For the metaphoric choreographers, an opposite aspiration—a coveted union of music and dance—often led, in its own way, to a move away from collaboration and toward an omnitalented single creator, a metteur-en-scène who produced a total artwork combining sight, sound, and kinetics.

The Eighties: Culture Clubs

Simultaneous with the arrival in the eighties of a new generation of postmodern choreographers, the disparate interests of two streams of seventies postmodernism—the gallery-oriented analytics and the more theatrical metaphoric choreographers—began to merge, though not always for the same reasons, and to join as well with the interests of Tharpian musicalists. The result was a striking congruence of themes and preoccupations among both older and younger generations, now joined as well by previously peripheral groups.

As the early postmoderns came to the end of the analytic phase, their own interests began to shift toward new collaborations, similar but not identical to the more casual partnerships of the early sixties. When three minimalist arts met in Lucinda Childs's *Dance* (1979; music: Philip Glass; décor: Sol LeWitt) the quantitatively increased result was a qualitative turn toward a new aesthetic of maximalism. Laura Dean's own forays into composition began that same year, with *Music*. And, while Trisha Brown did not admit music into her work until 1981 (when Robert Ashley's *Atalanta* accompanied *Son of Gone Fishin'*), her collaborative turn also came in 1979, when Robert Rauschenberg designed the sets and costumes for *Glacial Decoy*. Brown's 1982 *Set and Reset* also featured sets and costumes by Rauschenberg, but the music by Laurie Anderson opened an alliance with a younger generation of new musicians. David Gordon initiated a different kind of "sound track"—the dance equivalent of avant-garde film's "new talkies" (of which Yvonne Rainer, who had moved from choreography into film during the seventies, was a leading exemplar)—with his *What Happened* (1978). But, also notably, in his *The Matter* (*plus and minus*) (1979) he made his first in a series of postmodernist allusions to classical ballet: he presented a minimalist version of The Entrance of the Shades from Petipa's *La Bayadère* (1877), to the well-known music by the nineteenth-century ballet composer Léon Minkus.

It seems that, after a period of rinsing dance clean of visual and aural accoutrements, analytic postmodern choreographers were becoming interested in the increasing possibilities music and visual art could provide. But the specific reason for the renewed interest in music varied with each choreographer. Childs, for one, had worked with Glass when Robert Wilson invited her to perform her solo choreography as part of *Einstein on the Beach* (1976) and, sensing that their styles were compatible, she wanted to work with Glass in a production of her own. Brown has frankly stated that she was tired of seeing the larger audiences for which she was booked by the eighties walk out during her performances and wondered—in a reversal of the seventies principle in which it was claimed that the music obscured the dance—whether the absence of music created too much discomfort for them even to see the dancing. In general, the style of the visual art world, performance art, and new music was also changing from austerity to spectacle, and in the culture generally, perhaps as a result of Reaganomics, the partnership of music and dance (from breakdancing and rap music to MTV to tango) commanded a new fascination, reminiscent of 1930s dance films and dance crazes.

If Twyla Tharp, some of whose early pieces had been performed in silence at the Judson Church in 1966, had diverged from the analytic postmodern line of inquiry exactly because her choreography was so musically inclined, by the 1980s, when the analytic choreographers "rediscovered" music and its various uses, that interest realigned her—and her followers, such as Sara Rudner, Kenneth Rinker, and Nina Wiener—with the postmoderns. Like Tharp, the analytic choreographers explored the tensions between music and dance: Gordon delighted in repeating the same dance to different music in a single performance, showing how changing contexts shift meaning; Childs made her spare but complexly arranged vocabulary of steps, hops, skips, small leaps, and turns at times fit and at times disengage from the precise rhythms of Glass's music (and then music by Jon Gibson, Michael Riesman, John Adams, Michael Nyman, and others); Brown choreographed *Set and Reset* to an earlier song of Anderson's and then Anderson composed "Long Time, No See" (to which the dance was ultimately performed) after watching a videotape of the silent dance.[16]

Meanwhile a new group of younger choreographers had stirred up such musical interests on their own—in part to differentiate themselves from their minimalist, analytic, antimusic forebears in a way that fit with the general cultural trend; in part to engage with their own artistic contemporaries in other fields. For by the late seventies and early eighties, the younger generation of new music composers were often hybrid creations, art students turned punk or new wave musicians, that is, avant-gardists with pop ambitions—or with pop experience. Peter Gordon, for instance, claims he founded his Love of Life Orchestra in 1977 to reconcile his classical and avant-garde musical training with his job experiences as a rock saxophonist. "I wanted . . . to make an intelligent, and intellectual, music that can still feel good and still be fun to play. I wanted to use the vernacular in serious music."[17] Whether for theoretical or personal reasons, the lines between popular culture and high art, between visual art and music, between Western and non-Western musics were on their way to a postmodernist disintegration.

Such endeavors took various forms. Karole Armitage, trained in Balanchine ballet (first by Tomi Wortham in Lawrence, Kansas, and then in the corps of the Grand Théâtre de Genève) and a member of the Merce Cunningham Dance Company, collaborated at first with Rhys Chatham, a raucous new wave composer. Armitage's *Drastic Classicism* (1981) presented, among other things, members of Chatham's band sharing the stage space equally with the dancers and sometimes even interacting with them. In her 1985 critique of ballet partnering, *−P=dh/dq* (later retitled *The Watteau Duets*), Armitage commissioned an original score by David Linton (formerly a drummer with Rhys Chatham and one of the musicians who had performed in *Drastic Classicism*) titled "The Simpleton's Guide to the

World's Greatest Music." A mix of live percussion, guitar, and taped musical selections (including Wagner, Stravinsky, and Handel), it was played at such loud volume that at the piece's premiere at Dance Theater Workshop in New York, audience members were given cotton to protect their ears. Yet those who braved the loudness often found its atmospheric pandemonium an exhilarating foil for the precision and delicacy of the dancing. As Robert Greskovic (1985) put it, "I found the hurly-burly atmosphere compelling and quite an ideal landscape for her and her dancing . . . the idea of a long, supple, willowy Karole Armitage stretching simple tendus or raising silky battements amid a tornado of sound is . . . riveting and magical." In these collaborations, the music provided no easily discernible rhythms or melodies for the dancers to follow. Instead, on the Cunningham-Cage model (though not in their style), music and dance created separate dense channels, provoking the spectator's senses in multiple directions. But in subsequent works (especially after her collaboration with painter David Salle began), such as *The Mollino Room* (1986) for American Ballet Theater or *The Elizabethan Phrasing of the Late Albert Ayler* (1986) for her own company, Armitage forsook the thicket of sound of contemporary art-rock composers for taped sound collages that mixed jazz, comedy routines, and classical music.

Molissa Fenley began her choreographic career without any particular interest in collaboration with composers. For instance, in her early *Mix* (1979) dancers made their own percussion with maracas, bells, and sandblocks. But by 1980 Fenley had collaborated with Mark Freedman on the high-energy, repetitive sound score for *Energizer* by manipulating a beatbox, the omnipresent instrument of late disco music. She assimilated her own image of choreography at the time to the Phil Spector ideal, in sixties rock music, of a diffuse, unbounded "wall of sound." She was also influenced by a childhood in Nigeria witnessing West African ritual and social dances, as well as schooling in Spain that exposed her to flamenco dancing. A shared interest in both popular and non-Western musics eventually led Fenley to commission scores from important new composers of her generation, including Peter Gordon (*Eureka*, 1982) and Anthony Davis (*Hemispheres*, 1983).[18]

Bill T. Jones and Arnie Zane for several years had collaborated with Helen Thorington, who contributed avant-garde atonal electronic music for their trilogy *Monkey Run Road* (1979), *Blauvelt Mountain* (1979), and *Valley Cottage* (1980). But beginning in 1982 they also moved into the art-rock effect when they worked with Peter Gordon, on their jointly choreographed *Rotary Action* (1982) and *Secret Pastures* (1984), and on Jones's own choreography for *Fever Swamp* (1983). A different kind of collaboration took place in Wendy Perron's and David Van Tieghem's *Divertissement* (1986), in which both choreographer and composer danced and spoke; Van Tieghem (who has worked as a percussionist with Laurie Anderson and the

Talking Heads, among others) added both sound and drama as he rattled objects littering the stage.

Other examples of young choreographers collaborating with their contemporaries in music include Yoshiko Chuma and Christian Marclay; Wendy Perron and Craig Bromberg (who played in Glenn Branca's band), Bosho, Andy Blinx, and Don Hunerberg; Jawole Willa Jo Zollar and Edwina Lee Tyler. Or, to look at it another way: composer Scott Johnson has collaborated with Charles Moulton and Jim Self; Lenny Pickett with Chuma, Bebe Miller, Stephen Petronio, and Marta Renzi; David Linton with Armitage, Kinematic, Fred Holland; Van Tieghem with Tharp, Perron, Elisa Monte, Jennifer Muller, and new vaudevillean Michael Moschen. The list could go on and on. And the types of correspondence range from amorphous sounds that surround or underline the dancing in a general way, at one extreme, to exact parallels in rhythmic and melodic patterns.

In the early eighties, Charles Moulton's dancers did precision ball passing to A. Leroy's pleasingly melodious version of electronic new wave cocktail music. It was the meticulousness of the twin phrasing of both music and arm motions that made this "routine" a delightful dance (in fact, whenever a dancer dropped a ball, Leroy dropped the phrase and went back to the beginning). Marta Renzi made *You Little Wild Heart* (1981), a proto-MTV videodance, for the public television station WBGH. In it, teenage couples partied, fought, and made love, to the successive cuts in a Bruce Springsteen album, choreographed and edited exactly in the style of MTV's rhythmic montage. Lisa Kraus's *Going Solo* (1983) was a collaboration with a woman rapper. Wendy Perron was the choreographic consultant for Laurie Anderson's film *Home of the Brave* (1985). As these particular examples suggest, when contemporary music began to slouch toward rock, the synthesis of art and rock music provided new models for choreographers—the social dancing act itself, as well as the dancing acts of rock performers. And this was true whether the music was found or commissioned.

Or perhaps it is more correct to say that the new postminimalist interest of art composers in popular and non-Western music forms coincided—or collided—with the interest of eighties postmodernist choreographers in social and ritual dancing (and, hence, the most persistent forms of dance-music relations). As popular and subcultural dance—from salsa to hip-hop to *Black and Blue* on Broadway—captured the world's imagination, the avant-garde took its lead from popular culture. Popular culture itself, a creation of the McLuhanesque electronic global village, had already taken on a "one-world," internationalist beat. Postmodern music and postmodern dance found themselves newly wedded in venues from dance clubs (Danceteria, Pyramid, The World) to television (Alive from Off-Center); but also, avant-garde venues (The Kitchen, P.S. 122,

DTW, Brooklyn Academy of Music) presented popular music/dance—from breakdancing to African highlife to samba to polka—sometimes even arranging their audience in cabaret style. And even rock clubs like the Ritz or the Roxy, where no avant-garde choreography was to be seen, shared audiences with the rest of the venues on this spectrum. Susan Marshall's company played with ballroom dance forms in a witty, poor man's version of the more upscale American Ballroom Theater. Even the renewed interest in baroque dance (a period in which not only were the music and dance still firmly rooted in social dance forms, but also the discovery of the anthropologically exotic Other was an important theme) seems part of this postmodern, interdisciplinary, multicultural project—as does the 1987 reconstruction by Millicent Hodson, Kenneth Archer, and the Joffrey Ballet of that milestone of modernism, the original Nijinsky-Stravinsky-Roerich *Sacre du Printemps*.[19] That multidisciplinary, cosmopolitan, internationalist culture is inspired by—and appropriates in jarring juxtapositions from—the fusion of the arts we have come to think of as disparate, in cultures distant from our own high-art notions of separation and specialization either geographically (e.g., West Africa or Japan), temporally (eighteenth-century Europe or pre-Christian Russia as interpreted in Diaghilev's Paris), or in terms of class stratification (the Bronx or Chicago's Milwaukee Avenue).

In other words, as postmodern dance in its later phases turned away from the *modernist* essentialism of earlier postmodern dance to a *postmodernist* (in the more general sense) interdisciplinarity, there was a binding of the splits between social and theatrical dancing, on the one hand, and between art music (previously altogether separate from the theater) and popular music (whether for social dancing, or for program music in ballet, film, etc.) on the other. And although the notion of collaboration was at first celebrated (for example, in the marketing strategies of the Brooklyn Academy of Music, which devoted the catalog of its first Next Wave Festival, in 1983, to the topic of collaboration), the very desire to bind the splits eventually made the marking off of collaboration as a special method superfluous.

As in the sixties, the many ways dance and music may be parceled out among performers is under exploration, further rendering the very term collaboration problematic. The dancer may function as musician (Fenley's *Mix*; Zollar's many works for her singing, acting, and dancing Urban Bush Women; the sounds of pouring water that counterpoint Richard Munson's piano music in Johanna Boyce's *Women, Water, and a Waltz* [1987]); the musician may function as dancer/performer (Bebe Miller's and Linda Gibb's *Vespers* [1982], Robert Kovich's and John King's *The Dialogues* [1988]; Perron's and Van Tieghem's *Divertissement* [1986]). The figure of the choreographer as composer (Monk, Dean, Tim Miller, Diane Martel, Kumiko Kimoto) or of the composer as choreographer (Van Tieghem in his recent *Caution to the Wind* [1988]) once again serves, as it did in the sixties, as an agent of interdisciplinary admixtures.

Given the cultural context of the eighties, such hybrid activity now tends to signal double specialization, rather than antispecialization, as it did in the sixties. Still, the desire for a unified culture—in terms of blasting open categories such as high and low art, as well as separate art disciplines—is a motive power. Thus the kinds of nineteenth-century distinctions I raised in the introduction to this essay—the progressive splintering of high and low art music, theater and social dance music, and the creation of hierarchies between the spheres of music and dance—all come under postmodernist attack as the twentieth century comes to a close.

One important trend in the eighties has been the mutual attraction between postmodern dance and ballet (discussed earlier in "Pointe of Departure"). This trend is worth looking at briefly here, not because it has spawned new composer-choreographer collaborations, but because in a way it has pointed many choreographers in the opposite musical direction.

Not only does Armitage now run an "alternative" ballet company; she amalgamates a Balanchinian vocabulary—the bent wrists of a fashion model, quick high extensions, brilliant allegro work, a taut line that breaks into sudden, surprising angles—with the shrugs, shimmies, and overtly sexual partnering of contemporary (African) American rock dance, as well as with more lurid gestures that border on porn fantasies. She has, as well as his vocabulary, a Balanchinian approach to the music—making movements ride the melody as well as the (often quite complex) rhythmic design. Armitage takes the musical approach further; she has noted that in *Slaughter on MacDougal Street* (1982; music: Rhys Chatham), as in many of her ballets:

> [A] tightly metered rhythm gave the dancers a base upon which to swing the quarter note—to dance on the beat, behind the beat, or in front of the beat. My interest in using music with a steady beat was precisely to give the dancing that kind of flair and drama and hipness. . . . We would use [a combination of classical and popular styles, with a steady beat] to demonstrate an attitude of liberation, a sophistication, and an irreverence toward the rule of the beat or toward other unbending rules of dance behaviour.[20]

Yet, despite Balanchine's own stylized forays into jazz and Armitage's own quite conscious homages to her guru (her ballets include the abovementioned *Slaughter* and *Kammerdisco* [1988; music: Jeffrey Lohn]), no one would mistake Armitage's brazen, thoroughly postmodern pastiche for Balanchine's modernism. The title of her recent piece, *Go Go Ballerina* (1988; to songs by Jimi Hendrix and the rap groups Schoolly D. and the Hard-Ons), is apt. Mark Morris, too, has the musicality of a Balanchine or Taylor, making him the darling of the ballet world starved for new choreographic blood. Like Armitage, Morris delights in kitsch and sometimes uses both movements and messages that would set the previous generation of ballet choreographers whirling in their graves. Yet his recent commissions—including *Drink to Me Only with Thine Eyes* (1988; music: Virgil Thomson) for American Ballet Theater, the success of the season—and the installation of his company (replacing the Béjart Ballet) in residence in Brussels have thrust him squarely into the mainstream.[21] The roster of other "downtown" choreographers who have moved onto the ballet stage—from Tharp's pioneering forays in the seventies to those, in the eighties, ranging from David Gordon and Lucinda Childs to Jim Self and Ralph Lemon—grows by the season.

Although working on the ballet stage would certainly not in itself preclude musical collaboration, many of these choreographers have chosen to concentrate on collaborating with ballet dancers, rather than with composers (perhaps due to time constraints). They have often used preexisting music or musical collages as accompaniment, rather than commissioning new scores. Childs, for instance, working with the Paris Opéra Ballet on *Première Orage* (1984), used music by Shostakovich; David Gordon's *Murder* (for American Ballet Theater, 1986) was set to music by Berlioz.

Perhaps this trend is responsible for another recent proclivity, in the late eighties, toward musical masterpieces from different eras—whether classical (Stephanie Skura used Beethoven's Fifth in *Cranky Destroyers* [1987]); romantic (Arnie Zane's *The Gift/No God Logic* [1987; music: Verdi], or Wendy Perron's *Schumman Op. 102* [1986]); or modern (Fenley's *State of Darkness* [1988; music: Stravinsky's *Rite of Spring*] or Ralph Lemon's *Les Noces* [1987; music: Ravel and Debussy]). Or perhaps, since that staunchly antiballet choreographer Steve Paxton recently improvised to two Glenn Gould renditions of Bach's *Goldberg Variations* (1987), one can see in the use of classical music yet again a current point of convergence by different routes. If in postmodernism anything can be used, why not old music, beautiful music, highbrow music—as well as the lowbrow, hackneyed, and despised? Why not canned music as well as commissioned? In other words, all the contradictory sides of the dance-music debates seem to coexist comfortably in late eighties postmodern dance.

It has often been noted that the eighties is a period marked by spectacle, on the one hand, and the desire to have it all—to deny denial—on the other. As Jim Self put it in the film *Retracing Steps*, "Yvonne Rainer said no to all those things. . . . And I felt like saying yes."[22] These two postmodernist tendencies are embodied in the latest developments of postmodern dance—in its maximalist, expansive mode, where other artists are brought into the work, and where a pronounced virtuosity, ambitious set design, stylish costuming, and a savage beauty exploit music for all it's got.

38

La Onda Próxima: Nueva Latina Dance

Recent scholarship in multiculturalism and issues about alternative canons and cultural authority have raised questions not only about how national, racial, ethnic, gender, and sexual identities are produced, but also about how the histories of peoples and cultural systems are written. Dance is usually overlooked as a site where cultural experience and knowledge are produced. Nevertheless, there are many instances, especially during the present period, of dances that are distinctly meant to critique the discourse as well as the ideological assumptions of the culture in general, and of choreographic practice in particular, with respect to these issues of political identity. Among the most vital of the current challenges to the dance canon are works by postmodern choreographers that focus on the politically conscious articulation of difference in regard to "race," class, gender, ethnicity, and sexuality.

To be sure, some issues of political identity have been and continue to be explored and celebrated in dance, by such groups as the Alvin Ailey Dance Theater, Dance Theater of Harlem, and Ballet Hispanico. But in the 1980s for the first time various groups of young choreographers have identified themselves as bicultural in a specifically avant-garde mode: black *and* postmodern; gay *and* postmodern; Latino *and* postmodern. Their work is equally informed by their postmodern dance heritage and their political identities. That is, they see their affiliation with political groups as a radical engagement that impinges on and disrupts their artform's discursive practices.

This essay on the work of several Latina choreographers in New York is part of a larger project of documenting and analyzing the articulation of gender identity, the recognition of sexual preference, and the affirmation of ethnic identity on the part of contemporary American choreographers. As we will see, in Latino postmodern dance at times these themes are interwoven.

The group of Latina choreographers I am concerned with here emerged on the New York scene in the eighties and nineties. Their dances

Choreography and Dance (1994)

have been presented in "downtown" venues in New York like Dance Theater Workshop, P.S. 122, Movement Research, and P.S. 1. Their work has also been produced in festivals celebrating new dance, film, and performance art by Latinos—such as La Misma Onda, Tour de Fuerza, and ¡Muévete!.

A number of issues arise in analyzing this work: the stance of the choreographer in terms of group identity and history; how notions of ethnicity are constructed in the representational practices of the dance; how ethnicity is seen to be constructed in the culture at large; what devices are used as signifiers of "race," class, gender, and sexuality in the dances; where and how language is used as part of the discourse of the dance; what other postmodern interventions take place; what kinds of images of Latinos these signs produce, reproduce, or critique; what audiences the choreographer addresses in the work. Space does will not permit me to discuss here all of these items for each dance. However, I hope to suggest the trajectory of my larger research project, in which I plan to analyze the strategies of pursuing identity in dance, in this case Latina/Latino identity. I view these strategies as fundamental to a twin project that challenges the master narratives and myths of homogeneity in our culture as well as the specific discursive practices of mainstream dance.

The Latino postmodern dance I am discussing originated in New York City. So, before turning my attention to specific dances, I would like to sketch a brief demography of Latinos in New York. Also, I would like to point out that I am using the term Latina/Latino, which is preferred by many scholars in the field of Latin American studies, rather than the term Hispanic. As Xavier Totti explains, "*Hispanic* excludes racial and cultural differences, evoking only Spaniards and their descendants. *Latino* (from Latin American) is a more inclusive term accounting for those who come or descend from a specific geographical area where the Spanish and Portuguese legacy is dominant but not exclusive. It recognizes the presence and importance of nonwhite populations (Amerindian and African) in the group."[1]

There were already Puerto Rican and Cuban communities in New York City in the nineteenth century. But a much larger Latino population arrived in New York after World War II. The demography shifted even more radically after changes in the immigration laws in 1965 and 1978, and with the rise of illegal immigration. Because the largest wave of immigration began during the rise of suburbia and the decline of urban centers, and peaked in the seventies, during the last recession, the Latino working-class population in New York has suffered from increasing unemployment, mounting housing costs, and deteriorating social services.

Although Puerto Ricans still constitute the largest group of the city's Spanish-speaking population, the Latino community is at this point quite varied. It comprises Puerto Ricans, Cubans, Dominicans, Colombians,

Ecuadoreans, Salvadoreans, Chileans, Argentinians, Uruguayans, and people whose origins are in other Latin American countries.

Despite differences in national, political, and class backgrounds, Latinos in New York share a sense of unity, partly because of their exclusion from mainstream American culture, and partly because of their shared language—and their common communication systems (including two Spanish-language daily papers and several local and national television and radio stations). Many (though not all groups) also share economic and social discrimination.[2]

So various aspects of the current move to assert a unified, though not homogeneous, Latino identity in the arts, and in particular in dance, should not surprise us. For one, Puerto Ricans predominate, but are by no means the only nationality represented—for example, of the artists represented in Tour de Fuerza and ¡Muévete!, Viveca Vázquez, Merián Soto and Pepón Osorio, Arthur Aviles, Karen Langevin, and Evelyn Vélez are Puerto Rican; Carmelita Tropicana and Ana Vega are Cuban; David Zambrano and Livia Daza Paris are Venezuelan; Eva Gasteazoro is Nicaraguan; and Patricia Hoffbauer is Brazilian. For another, issues of class emerge in various ways in these dances. And third, common themes and common markers of identity, from language to music to clothing, thread through many of the works.

Works in the Latino postmodern mode are at this point too numerous and too varied in style to analyze in a short essay; therefore, now I would like to focus on three exemplary works.

Viveca Vázquez is a Puerto Rican choreographer, trained at New York University, who has deliberately chosen to embody the geographical schizophrenia of many Puerto Rican New Yorkers by dividing her time between the island and the mainland. Her choreography explores this state of being. *Mascando Inglés* (Chewing English) (1984), for instance, is, according to the choreographer, about the cultural displacement and linguistic frustration suffered by Puerto Rican migrants to New York. But there is almost nothing literal about Vázquez's treatment of this theme, except, perhaps, for the few moments when the collage sound track mixes a lecture on language with a list of English words and their correct pronunciations. Rather, as Joan Acocella has noted, Vázquez uses dance metaphors for this enstrangement. "Forced to speak a new language, Vázquez forces the body to do the same."[3]

In *Mascando Inglés*, five dancers perform erratic phrases of movement, at times in unison, and at times completely out of synch with one another. To the danceable sounds of a cante jondo, they stand stock still, then make somewhat mad, repetitive gestures in front of their faces. In silence, they move. Their arms flail up and out, sending their bodies into jumps and turns. Suddenly, they fall into a Spanish stepping dance, tapping out a smart rhythm with their sneakers and raising their arms in full flamenco curves. Their movement phrases are fragmented. They fall on the floor, push themselves backwards; they crouch, hop, and fall like children at play. The constant interruption of the movement impetus and the mismatch of movement and music join to create a feeling of dislocation that is structural, rather than expressive. Only at one point—when a man and a woman seem to enact a parting of lovers, to the strains of salsa music—is there a suggestion of character or story. But then the dance shifts gears, concluding with what is perhaps a memory of a time when life was not fragmented, as the dancers remove their shoes and African-rooted movements take over their dance. These movements *do* constitute a new language, but one that acknowledges its dance heritage as a mosaic of legacies: African, Spanish, and downtown New York postmodern.

In *No Regrets* (1988), Merián Soto and Pepón Osorio mix live performance with specifically Latino popular genres—soap operas on Spanish TV and the fotonovela, a cross between a comic book and a romance novel, told with photographs. Maria, a clerk in a fabric store, meets Roberto, a cabdriver. Fantasies about him make her feel guilty about her sick mother, her macho husband Miguel, and her kids. One Sunday she leaves the kids, the husband, and the laundry at home to go with Roberto to P.S. 122, where they see his cousin in a dance show about Puerto Rican political consciousness. Anxious about her dilemma—should she remain a faithful wife or run away to Puerto Rico with Roberto?—Maria searches her soul. The upshot is that she leaves both men, gets a college degree, and becomes a social worker—with no regrets.

Aspects of the story are romantic, satirical, serious, silly, politically pointed, melodramatic, and reflexive. Though the love affair is the pretext for the story, the predictable conventions of the soap opera and fotonovela are subverted when the heroine takes control of her own future and makes the surprising choice to settle for no man. And this particular love affair is firmly rooted in its social context: working-class people who live in the Bronx, Maria's determination to find upward mobility through education, Miguel's machismo, Roberto's homesickness for the island.

The shifts in tone are partly accomplished through the shifts in media. For instance, as the soap opera of Maria and Miguel unrolls on the giant video screen in the theater, we see Maria watching herself kissing Roberto on her own TV. The fotonovela format stylizes the drama even more drastically than the video. But when the mass-mediated action gives way to live dance, a very different kind of representation takes over: the characters' inner lives are given body, but in ways that are more abstract. The movement vocabulary makes no reference to Latino styles. Rather, it is the juxtaposition to culturally specific forms like the fotonovela and Latin music, and also the presence of Latino characters, that creates the strong sense of ethnic identity in this piece. And just as Maria found it hard to see just how Roberto's cousin's dance show—in which people dressed in black jumped around, shimmied, and fell on the floor—represented political consciousness, so we are challenged to see multiple layers of meaning in the seemingly abstract movements of the dancers.

Carmelita Tropicana is a Cuban-born performance artist. *Candela*, her mixed-media collaboration with Ela Troyano and Uzi Parnes, is not strictly dance. However, it is included here for several reasons: it was part of Tour de Fuerza, it overlaps with postmodern dance in embracing multimedia, and also dance is the topic of the performance piece. Like *No Regrets*, *Candela* invokes various forms of popular culture, here both Latin and Anglo: the zarzuela (a Spanish form of operetta) and the American film Western, the Cuban nightclub floorshow in pre-Castro Havana and the glitz of Las Vegas. But the staging—with its deliberately bad song and dance routines, its ironic representation of nostalgia, its film quotations, its transvestites, and its endless, feverishly colored scarves, shawls, and shmates—also owes something to the camp performances of the underground filmmaker Jack Smith.

To condense the wandering, surrealistic plot enormously: Just when Carmclita Tropicana is about to find fame dancing in the floorshow at the

Candela, by Uzi Parnes/Ela Troyano/ Carmelita Tropicana. *L* to *R*: Parnes, Tropicana, Maureen Angelos. In movie, Ishmael Houston-Jones. (Photo: Dona Ann McAdams.)

Tropicana nightclub in Havana, the choreographer, Mr. Rodney, is shot by gangsters from Las Vegas, and Carmelita's brother, Machito, is framed for the murder. Possessed by Rodney's spirit, Carmelita becomes a successful choreographer, and she and Machito flee to Las Vegas (via the New York City subway) to avenge Rodney's death.

It's a backstage musical of sorts, in which the plot keeps being interrupted by dance routines, including an enchanted conga line that owes something to *The Red Shoes*. *Candela* is also, like the zarzuela and the Western, concerned with honor and moral responsibility. But, unlike these conventional forms, here ethnic identity is both satirized and asserted as the ultimate strength. Carmelita, with her fake heavy Cuban accent, is an endless source of malapropisms, and the great Cuban dance Mr. Rodney died to protect is utter kitsch by any standards. But there are other Cuban dances, done outside of the nightclub show, that are shown as vital. And it is memories of Havana that give the Tropicanas their hope and determination (and the idea for their show-stopping number). And finally, as Carmelita says of Mr. Rodney's dream, "Is no piece of cake, is a flan. Rodney gonna turn a deaf ear every time he hears/ . . . "You're black, you're poor, you're queer. No you can't."/ . . . Rodney just grits his teeth and tell his feet/"Come on, feet, dance, dance, dance!"

One striking aspect of these and other Latino postmodern dances is that certain formal elements of postmodern dance are valued as compositional choices: these include the use of ordinary movements; collage structure (even in the use of narrative); and dancing in silence. As well, the postmodern embrace of language in dance is quite apt in these works, where verbal material serves, not only to comment on the situation or forward the plot, but also to underscore linguistic and ethnic difference. Just an accent can signal ethnicity. But also, featured in several of these dances is a kind of linguistic fancy footwork, a virtuosic display of verbal speed and dexterity that has to do with the rhythms and tempo of the Spanish language itself.

One characteristic of postmodernism that these choreographers relish is the appropriation of popular culture. This they share with Anglo postmodern choreographers, such as Jim Self, who borrows from cartoons, domestic comedies on TV, and pop songs in his works; Barbara Allen, who has made dances inspired by Harlequin romances; and Marta Renzi, who uses an MTV music-cum-story structure. However, in Latino postmodern dance, the soap opera, fotonovela, zarzuela, and Western provide structures and images, while also supplying grounds for expressing cultural differences and pointing to the worldwide domination of the U.S. mass media. As well, the use of popular Latino music asserts ethnicity, while the contrast between various popular music forms stresses the heterogeneous class and national affiliations within that ethnicity.

Finally, the ambiguous, ironic tone many of the choreographers adopt is postmodern, as well. Popular culture is appreciated, but it is also parodied. And there is a certain evident delight here in creating stereotypes, even when the point is to undercut them.

Thus postmodern techniques have been adapted to create a political identity. This tendency connects with the eighties trend toward content in postmodern dance. But in nueva Latina dance, the content is in the interest of a specific community.

39

Dance and Spectacle in the United States in the Eighties and Nineties

With Noël Carroll

American avant-garde dance of the seventies captured the international imagination. Building on the formal inventions of Merce Cunningham as well as the tendencies of minimalism in the visual arts and music, the makers of what began by 1973 to be called postmodern dance were steadfastly antitheatrical. Paring away such trappings of spectacle as costume design, special lighting, even musical accompaniment — not to mention character, plot, and emotional content — these choreographers turned their attention to pure movement and dance structure. Yvonne Rainer's famous "NO" manifesto — in which she rejected virtuosity, glamour, role-playing, and even the gaze of the audience — is emblematic of that repudiation of theatricalism.

However, after a decade of formalist abstraction, postmodern dance radically changed its course at the turn of the decade. In the eighties, postmodern dance met postmodernist culture, and the result was the emergence of a pastiche that reintroduced — albeit in new ways — many of the values of the generations preceding the sixties and seventies. An aesthetic of

Il Corpo Parlante Conference, Rome, 1990.

abundance and pleasure emerged from the ashes of minimalism. As the choreographer Jim Self put it, "Yvonne Rainer's thing was saying no to . . . all those things. . . . And I felt like saying yes to all those things. So I did. I said yes to theatricality, yes to costumes, yes to virtuosity, yes to staging works on a big scale, yes to creating ballets, yes to everything I could think of to say yes to." Moreover, the new, interarts eclecticism characterized the work both of an upcoming generation of young artists and of the older Judson Dance Theater generation that had begun working in the sixties.

For a number of reasons, from aesthetic restlessness to the economic and political anxieties of the seventies that culminated in the drastic contradictions of the Reagan years, a generalized quest in the culture for meaning was sparked in the eighties and continues into the nineties — and dance is no exception. This search for meaning in dance was matched by a shift to large-scale, multimedia formats, often under the auspices of the Brooklyn Academy of Music's Next Wave Festival or progressive ballet companies. First-generation postmodern choreographers such as Trisha Brown, Lucinda Childs, David Gordon, and Laura Dean were becoming more marketable and were beginning to be presented in large proscenium theaters (instead of the galleries and lofts of the seventies). The addition of music, costumes, and décor by well-known composers and artists — like Philip Glass, Laurie Anderson, Robert Ashley, Robert Rauschenberg, Donald Judd, and Sol LeWitt — was appealing to both choreographers and producers in these situations, for not only would they command the attention of a wider, less esoteric audience, but also these other art forms would bring their own respective followers to fill larger houses with audiences of varied interests.

At the same time, a younger generation emerged in the 1979–80 season — including Bill T. Jones and Arnie Zane, Jim Self, Johanna Boyce, Molissa Fenley, and Karole Armitage — who, themselves impatient with the seemingly puritanical seriousness and dry asceticism of the analytic, antitheatrical approach, independently found various means to reinstate theatricality while remaining committed to the avant-garde venue. Further, a line of descent from Twyla Tharp — including Sara Rudner, Nina Wiener, Timothy Buckley, and Bebe Miller — appeared simultaneously. This group reveled in a Tharpian appreciation for musicality and virtuosic movement. Also, by the mideighties a wing of choreographers who identified themselves as both black and postmodern — among them Blondell Cummings, Bill T. Jones, Bebe Miller, Ishmael Houston-Jones, and Fred Holland — integrated what had hitherto been a predominantly white arena, often introducing explicitly political themes of black identity in their dances. Other ethnic groups — such as the Latina choreographers Viveca Vásquez and Merián Soto and the Japanese choreographers Eiko and Koma and Yoshiko Chuma — have helped push postmodern dance toward multiculturalism; while other political concerns — notably feminist and gay — surfaced in the eighties as well. Finally, by the end of the eighties, yet another group of young choreographers was coming to the fore, including Diane Martel, Kumiko Kimoto, Jawole Willa Jo Zollar, and Susan Marshall, for whom spectacle was already the mother's milk they were raised on.

In terms of the desire for meaning, we would like to suggest a number of modes that emerged in the United States in the eighties as ways to install content in the dance, besides the above-mentioned political themes. One important method is the interest in narrative, which corresponds to the coterminous rise of the "new talkies" in film (e.g., the work of Yvonne Rainer) and storytelling in performance art (e.g., Spalding Gray). This fascination with narrative form is not, however, simply a return to old methods. Often the new narrative in dance makes use of verbal language to advance the story, either in spoken narration or in the lyric of a song (à la MTV). A whole subset of this category of dances makes use of the fairytale as an exemplary narrative structure. The group Kinematic, for instance, has made an entire trilogy of fractured fairytale ballets, beginning with *The Snow Queen* (1986).

Another subset is the autobiography, as practiced by choreographers such as Johanna Boyce, Tim Miller, and Ishmael Houston-Jones, which often—stressing the seventies maxim that the personal is political—deliberately takes on political overtones. In Tim Miller's solo *Me and Mayakovsky* (1980), for instance, he cooked, told stories about his childhood, set things on fire, and worried about war.

It was feminism that began to frame the personal as political, but not only the dance autobiography has served as a vehicle for feminist concerns in dance. Means for invoking feminist analyses also appear in explorations of the conventions of partnering, new images of women onstage—as in the Urban Bush Women's images of strong African-American women—and overt investigations into the cultural signs of gender—as in Susan Foster's *Corpus Delecti* (1988), in which she transforms herself from a cartoon muscle-man into a delicate figure of a lady. These means also contribute to gay issues in dance, as in the Mangrove contact improvisation group in California and the many participants in the Men Together festival in New York in the early eighties, and more recently in the work of Tere O'Connor, Creach and Koester, and Mark Morris.

In a more general way, beyond narrative and political content there has been a "return of the repressed" in terms of character, mood, emotion, and situation—in the "new primitivism" of Pooh Kaye (who explores infantile and animal movements), Ellen Fisher, Jo Andres, and others; in the passionate relationships explored by Marta Renzi (who makes duets to rock and roll love songs), Victoria Marks, or Susan Marshall; in the genre-based, sometimes parodic works by Stephen Petronio (in the film noir style), Barbara Allen, Carol Clements.

Another method to make the dance meaningful has been to reinstate technical virtuosity in a number of ways. This may in part be a reaction-formation to "the less is more" ethos of the seventies, but it is also connected to an eighties attitude of professionalization and control, as well as to the related changes in body culture in that decade of aerobics and health clubs. The turn to virtuosity is manifested in ways ranging from the use of highly trained, multicompetent dancers, often with professional degrees in dance; to the presence onstage of dancing bodies that look athletic and built; to the building of permanent companies and repertory; to the rediscovery and proliferation of techniques, from ballet to baroque, tap, and ballroom dancing; to the use of complicated steps and partnering devices; to a fascination with stamina, precision, and balance; to a refined sense of musicality. Molissa Fenley, for example, uses muscular women and music with a disco beat in ongoing "walls of dance" that display skill and endurance. The entry of postmodern choreographers after Twyla Tharp onto the ballet stage—from Laura Dean, David Gordon, and Lucinda Childs to Jim Self, Mark Morris, and Susan Marshall—and the creation of "downtown" ballet companies—like that of Karole Armitage—are paradigmatic instances of the avant-garde urge toward virtuosity.

We have already mentioned a return to musicality. Of course the often-mysterious workings of emotional states in music have been key to much of the new-found expression in recent postmodern dance. Choreographers have gone far indeed from the seventies position of eschewing music. They work with contemporary composers (ranging from Philip Glass to punk bands), recorded music of all kinds (from rock and roll and folk music to Bach to standard ballet music) and even, following Meredith Monk, to composing their own music (like Laura Dean and Diane Martel). Mark Morris's sensitivity to an entire gamut of musical styles has made it possible for him to work consistently in mainstream opera-house theaters, despite the often outrageous content of his dances—the cross-dressing, for instance, of *Dido and Aeneas*.

Given this alliance with the music world, it is not surprising that both postminimalist composers and postanalytic choreographers share an interest in popular music and dance forms. Social dancing provides an historically rich context for the wedding of music and dance. And as social dancing—from MTV to hiphop to theatricalized tango and ballroom dancing on Broadway—began to rivet the world's attention in the eighties, the avant-garde took its lead from popular culture. Postmodern dance and postmodern music found themselves newly joined in New York dance clubs like Danceteria and The World, and on television. And in avant-garde venues popular music and dance—breakdancing, tango, polka—entered the limelight. The splintering of culture into high and low, the splintering of music and dance into theater versus pleasure, and the traditional hierarchies among the spheres of music and dance all come under postmodernist subversion.

The music connection and the popular dance imagery enhance the accessibility of postmodern dance for larger audiences. In this and many other ways, the return to theatricality itself—in the context of American dance—is a move to make dance more approachable, in contrast to the formal austerity and dance-specific hermeticism of the seventies. The introduction of character and narrative is key to framing the movement, and spectacle overall has served as a means of motivating the significance of the dance movement as it has come to be embedded in an informationally rich image. In a more extended sense, these contribute to content, which, of course, attempts to connect the dance to a wider world of concern.

In order to illustrate some aspects of the new theatricality in American dance of the eighties, we would like to discuss Jim Self's recent piece entitled *Dream Maker/Heart Breaker.*

Self is a choreographer with a tremendously diversified background. Born in Alabama, he was raised both in the American South—a legacy he acknowledges in his work in many ways, including the use of country and western music—and then moved to Chicago, where he began choreographing at the age of eighteen. Self originally was drawn to the fine arts, and the aesthetic principles he learned from his painting teacher, John Neimanas, continue to inform his modus operandi as a choreographer. Of Neimanas, Self says: "One thing I learned from him was a sense of collage, of taking different things and putting them together. Another was a compositional sense—for instance, using color in one place and picking it up again in another place. You do the same thing in dance when you emphasize relationships between things. But in dance you do it in terms of memory."

The Chicago of the early seventies, where Self began his career, was an exciting place. An important venue for touring avant-garde artists from New York, Chicago afforded Self the opportunity to see not only a great deal of contemporary dance but also important examples of the emerging theatrical style called performance art, of which there was also an indigenous branch stemming from the Chicago Art Institute School. And the fluid idiom of performance art—mixing the concerns of theater, dance and painting—has remained a continuing influence on Self's development.

In 1976, Self moved to New York and joined the Merce Cunningham Dance Company. From this experience, Self learned a highly disciplined technique as well as a sense of how to pace an evening of work. The demanding schedule of a performer left Self with little opportunity to pursue his own choreography. So he left the company in 1979 in order to resume the development of his own style.

Self's work of the early eighties at first bore the formal and abstract stamp that was virtually inevitable, given his intensive immersion in the

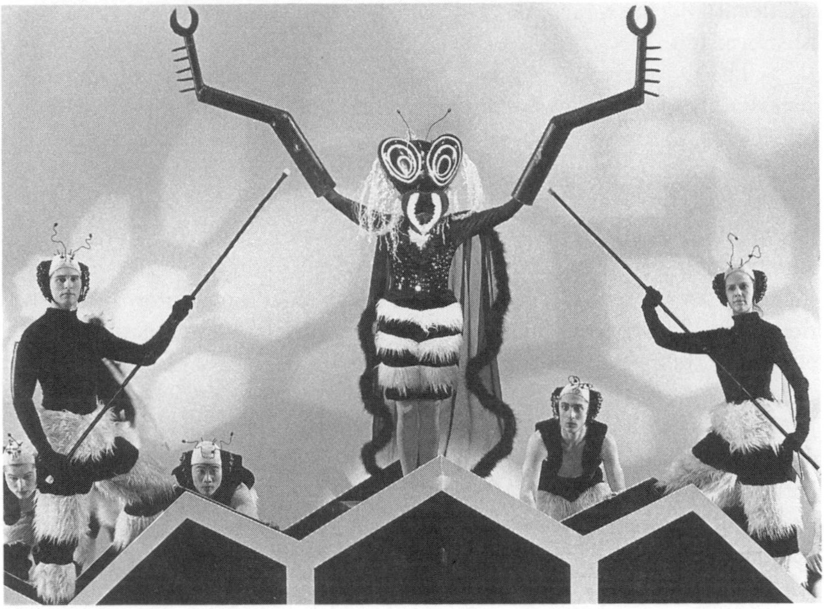

Jim Self and Frank Moore, *Beehive*.
(Photo: © 1991 Patricia Reynolds.)

Cunningham vocabulary. But, while explaining one of his abstract dances to the visual artist Frank Moore, Self realized the degree to which his own method of composing even abstract dances relied on his concocting story lines in his head—story lines that generated the movement, but that the audience could never know. Self decided to break with the abstract constraints of Cunningham-style dance, asking himself what would happen if he showed the audience the fragmented stories that gave rise to the heretofore abstract imagery.

One result was the ballet and the dance-film, both called *Beehive*, two interrelated collaborations with Frank Moore, involving the anthropomorphic representation of the life of bees on a spectacular set. As the outlandishness of the conceit indicates, these works are comic in their delirious, so to speak, "immaturity," but the irony afforded by their very outrageousness provides Self with the opportunity to reflect on the human condition rather in the manner of chatty updates of Aesop's fables. We commented earlier on the importance of content for contemporary choreographers in making their work accessible, and Self's deliberately campy, though witty, imagery—at once infantile and kitschy—supplies the audience with the wherewithal to recognize his gentle satire. At present, Self asserts that he is opposed to an approach to choreography in which the audience is confronted by something that is "mysterious and impenetrable"; instead he prefers to work with images, often alluding to media icons and stories — or story fragments — that the spectator can identify.

Self has worked extensively with Robert Wilson, the metteur-en-scène perhaps most renowned for his oneiric dramas, and the theme of dream suffuses *Dream Maker/Heart Breaker* — as its title indicates. The piece begins as a solitary male figure in a nightshirt enters the softly darkened proscenium stage; the moon appears, as strains of the once popular song "Moon River" start up. When the song refers to "my Huckleberry friend," three oarsman, outfitted like Huckleberry Finn on his raft, glide across the background, raising the question of whether they are the dream of the solitary figure, or vice versa.

Another male dancer joins the first figure. They behave like madmen, intermittently straightjacketed, but then flailing out like asylum inmates when they intrude into each other's territory. As the word "lunatic" indicates, they seem to be under the thrall of the moon. There is a narrative here, but it's dreamlike, the presence of the lunatics alerting us that it will be imagistic and irrational.

As in a dream, sense in *Dream Maker/Heart Breaker* is juxtapositional. But, consistent with Self's earlier remarks about collage, certain motifs thread through the piece as a whole, giving it a casual structural unity. For example, the moon functions as the central image of the first movement of the piece. Subsequently, it reappears by means of playful associations — a crawling dancer, for instance, "mooning" the audience. The last section then tops off this motif as the cast howls at the moon, reasserting the theme of the lunatic, now ululating wildly at a serenely magnetic, lunar image.

Dream Maker/Heart Breaker, like much of Self's recent work, is very dependent on the use of music, particularly popular songs. These songs provide references, often stories, that the movement and action incompletely illustrate in various ways. For instance, "Moon River," with its allusion to Huckleberry Finn, as already noted, provides the motivation for a transitory image of Huck-figures gliding down the Mississippi.

Self plays with the imagery supplied by the songs in different registers. A rendition of "Harlem Shuffle," for instance, is accompanied by a trio of women performing exaggerated versions of the "monkey" and the "shimmy" — popular dance phrases that naturally go with the music — in a way that is satiric, but also life-affirmative; while in a similar gesture of comic defamiliarization, Self also turns a Russian folkdance into a zany image of clockwork gone crazy. The song "I won't say I will" enables Self to create a coquettish character who seduces and then rejects male suitors with the authority of a larger-than-life movie actress as if interpreted by a female impersonator. And when the piece concludes with the country-western favorite "The Wayward Wind" — perhaps a nod in the direction of Self's southern heritage, albeit one leavened by a parody of the pop icon of the singing cowboy—not only do the dancers move as if windswept, but the "Christ-figure" appears at just the point when the song portentously announces "I met him there. . . ."

The "passion" in the song is limned by a mock passion play. A "Christ-figure," outfitted in black bikini briefs, effectively comments on the thin boundary between religion and sexual desire; he is hoisted on a set of overhead cables, calling to mind a crucifixion, but also the ambiguous ecstasy of martyrs like St. Sebastian, who provide serviceable erotic icons for the gay subculture. However, as soon as this observation takes hold, Self leavens it with goofy antics—the crucified figure is bombarded with multicolored water balloons, which may be read either as dousing the eroticism in a cold shower or as culminating a wet dream.

A certain overt gay sensibility runs through *Dream Maker/Heart Breaker*; it is not only detectable in the ironic and camp perspective, but also it appears in the male partnering, among other images, such as the crucifixion, as well. Indeed, the piece that Self created for the August 1990 Lincoln Center's summer program, "Serious Fun," was entitled "Jim Self and Julio Torres in Getting Married—A Wedding for the 90s." This was a literal enactment of a marriage ceremony between Self and his real-life male lover Julio Torres, accompanied by comic metamorphoses such as the newlyweds jumping into a basket that becomes a car, while the song "I'm putting all my eggs in one basket" fills the auditorium. The geniality and humor here is vintage Self, while the affirmation of gay rights represents Self's effort to give voice to social content that until recently has been suppressed.

40

Dancing in Leaner Times

Improvisation *was* the sixties. From social dancing to politics, on fronts of culture as varied as free jazz, Off-Off Broadway theater, and Judson Dance Theater—whose members at times questioned the convention of the "choreographer-as-boss-lady," as Yvonne Rainer put it—liberation and spontaneity were the twin watchwords.

Now, in the nineties, improvisation is back, at least in theatrical dancing. Once again, a generation of dancers is finding value in spontaneous choreography. But this is not a nostalgic return to old times. Improvisation means something different in the post-Reagan era.

Of course, in a sense, improvisation has always been the very stuff of dance. When people make dances, they usually begin by experimenting with movement material and choreographic structures, even when the genre of dance is highly conventionalized, like ballet. We know that the choreography in nineteenth-century ballets was loose enough for star ballerinas regularly to embroider their own solo variations upon set choreography, even though partnering required much more predictability, and corps de ballet work an exacting unison. In the twentieth century, however, just as the theater director became a powerful manager, controlling the actors' contributions and the entire mise-en-scène, in dance, the figure of the choreographer took on more authority, not only in ballet, but also in the new art form of modern dance. It was the choreographer, not the dancers, who invented the movement in the studio, to be presented onstage intact.

Cynthia Novack suggests in her recent book, *Sharing the Dance: Contact Improvisation and American Culture*, that perhaps modern dance's model of authoritative choreography and its repression of improvisation grew out of a desire to differentiate the professionalization of modern dance in the twenties and thirties from what was seen as the taint of amateurism in educational "creative dance." If self-expression was the goal in the university studio, where students freely improvised to discover their own individual ways of moving, in the world of professional modern dance a fully formed creative genius rigorously molded her movements into art. In fact,

Dance Ink 2/3 (Winter 1991–92).

Anna Halprin, who made improvisational performances on the West Coast in the late fifties and early sixties and taught several of the Judson dancers, had studied the form under Margaret H'Doubler in the dance program at the University of Wisconsin.

One way for the sixties dancers to break with the generation that came before them, then, was to put the despised "amateur" form of dancing right there onstage, often in venues that weren't really theaters (to the horror of teachers and critics, who looked for a finished product on a proper stage). Moreover, the values of amateur activity—dailiness, equality, and dancing for pleasure—were attuned to the ethos of the period. The improvisatory impulse that began in American dance in the sixties peaked in the seventies in two arenas: the dance-theater group Grand Union, and the contact improvisation network that spread across the United States and Europe.

Jawole Willa Jo Zollar in her *LifeDance I . . . The Magician* (*the Return of She*). (Photo: Hakim Mutlaq.)

Although some of the sixties values appeal to the current generation of improvisers, their motives—as well as their styles—often diverge sharply from the earlier generation. In a period of economic expansion, improvisation symbolized an abundance of choices; during the present recession, improvisation offers a welcome shoestring approach to production. In the sixties, white improvisers may have picked up black influences from the culture at large; in the eighties and nineties a number of African-American postmodern dancers bring distinctive improvisatory traditions from their culture into the downtown dance world. As well, in a society daily increasing its threshold of violence, improvisation today has a tougher edge.

For instance, Jawole Willa Jo Zollar, the artistic director of the Urban Bush Women, attributes her interest in improvisation to the influence of jazz music and her admiration of the group dynamics of the jazz ensemble. Studying traditional jazz dance and Dunham technique, she learned movement invention from the start. And she feels a historical link to the form, for improvisation is fundamental to most African and African-derived music and dance. Her own ways of approaching improvisation vary from musical ideas to dramatic ideas (derived, in part, from her work with Joseph Chaikin, the experimental theater director).

"Improvisation gives the individual a voice," Zollar asserts. "It allows for—to put it in political terms—what I call collective individualism." Zollar's dances have political messages: they speak of women's experience, of black women's experience in particular, as founded in and supported by community. So it seems appropriate to choose a collective political method to create that content.

Zollar looks for dancers who are open to experimenting with improvisation. But she has recently been frustrated at auditions for new dancers. She concludes that the educational system squelches spontaneous self-expression in blacks, especially poor blacks. And this frustration has led her to propose improvisation as a far-reaching tool beyond the stage, for educational reform and social change. Giving workshops in different communities, and reaching both adults and children through grass roots organizations, she uses the radical pedagogical principles of Paulo Freire to do community organizing through culture. Zollar believes that improvisation can be empowering to those who have been disenfranchised, for it can teach people how to be independent and "to move through situations, to structure a path."

"Improvisation is a spiritual philosophy as well as a movement tool," she insists. "It includes the Marxist concept of collectivity, the African notion of cooperative tribal action, the Native American council."

Like various other dancers who emerged in the eighties and nineties, Zollar uses improvisation both in the studio, to create pieces that will eventually be set, and onstage, in dances that will happen only once, then disappear. Some, like Stephen Petronio or Donna Uchizono, ask their dancers to contribute to the choreography by assigning them choreographic tasks or by "throwing" them material that may look quite different when what's "caught" is shown. Others, like Stephanie Skura and Sally Silvers, may make videotaped improvisatory material permanent by setting it on the dancers.

Silvers is committed to keeping space open for spontaneous invention in her solos — "it keeps the performance fresher for me," she notes — but rigorously avoids asking for individual contributions in group pieces, because so many of the dancers she uses also work with other downtown choreographers and contribute to their choreography. "It tends to make everybody's pieces look alike and creates a potential for the generic in postmodern dance. And it's confusing for the dancers."

Petronio, who started dancing as a contact improviser, then learned various methods of incorporating the dancers' contributions when he worked with Trisha Brown, finds himself now moving, as he puts it ironically, "from democracy to dictatorship." Where formerly he gave his dancers a great deal of freedom, he now asks them to learn more material "by rote." A few years ago, he says, "I wanted an anarchic, chaotic look and letting the dancers improvise was the best way to get it. Now I know how to get it better by making it myself." Though the dances are about "the body as

Urban Bush Women in Jawole Willa Jo Zollar's *Bitter Tongue*.
(Photo: Cylla Von Tiedemann.)

a political battleground" where notions of freedom, control, gender, and sexuality are played out, those ideas are not necessarily expressed through the method of creating the dance. "I'm not so interested in rules or structures," Petronio explains, "as in physical and emotional ideas."

However, there are other dancers, such as Jennifer Monson, Yvonne Meier, John Jasperse, and Clarinda Mac Low, who are committed to improvisational performance itself, who see improvisation not just as a means to a finished product but as a statement about what dance is and what bodies mean in our culture. Mac Low, a biologist who earns her living doing AIDS research, has an almost scientific curiosity about dancing. She also asks questions about the social and political implications of dancing in these trying times. "I ask myself why I continue to dance. But in our society it seems more important than ever, because the body is being de-emphasized, as if it isn't part of you. If you dance, your body is your instrument and you intuit connections between mind and body. Improvising communicates that most eloquently, because everything about you is reacting immediately to the situation at hand. And you can push the limits of your physical body. That's important for people to do or see." Moreover, Mac Low values improvisation, or what she refers to as "creating situations where things can happen," over choreography, since "a dance feels like a solid thing to me; I'm interested in fluid things." And she is interested in the humor, wit, and sometimes clumsiness that improvisation opens up as well.

The daughter of poet Jackson Mac Low, she arrived at improvisation partly through an Oedipal struggle against the chance methods favored by his generation, while still remaining attracted to the egalitarian aspects of an experimental project ("Anyone can do it," she reasons). Her thesis at Wesleyan University was on chance methods as an artistic pursuit of freedom: "The next logical step is informed improvisation, because then you're free even of the rules that govern chance."

"It's hard to shake your first experiences," admits Mac Low, who appeared at age three or so in a mixed-media performance by her father and remembers her first conscious experience of performing, in Meredith Monk's *Vessel* when she was five. "But I have subtle arguments with my father and his generation." Even contact improvisation comes under fire. "By the time I got to it," she says, "it had a certain preciousness that bugged the hell out of me—and a lot of people in my generation."

As its name suggests, contact improvisation stresses systems of support, usually in duet form, through diverse modes of touching, from lifting to ducking, with various body parts. Though it requires strength and quick reflexes, its appearance is calmly organic. But the new generation of improvisers, like Mac Low, Monson, and Meier, is looking for a focus different than the gentle cooperative partnering of contact. Meier believes that improvisation is political because the audience is made privy to the dancer's creative process: hierarchies that remove the performer from the spectator

Donna Uchizono's *San Andreas.*
(Photo: Tom Brazil.)

are undercut. Also, in a group improvisation, "you have to be able to dance with anybody." But beyond that, intimations of violence often lurk in her improvisations. "Violence is something that's happening these days. And dance is political in showing that."

There is a search for simultaneous pleasure and virtuosity in some improvisation that also stamps it as a product of more recent times. "I need to throw myself around in an articulate way," Meier puts it simply. But also, "Improvisation is much more fun for the performer—it frees people up, and everything is new each time. You tap into a different system when you improvise than when you choreograph."

Monson notes that in her duet work with Meier, there is a movement-oriented investigation that is "more complex and virtuosic" than in her group work—where unison movements inspired by folkdancing express community, often among people from different backgrounds. Improvisation now, Monson feels, is different from that of the sixties and seventies in its fierceness and urgency. "The times are so different. The world we're living in is harsher. We're responding to tragedy and hopelessness. And performances are getting shorter and shorter. People then were willing to take more time with their explorations. I want to cut back to the leanest amount and just go out on the streets and perform."

Like Zollar, Meier, and Monson, Donna Uchizono takes inspiration from musical improvisation. Two years ago Uchizono and Marga Guergué began curating the series Bread to the Bone at the Knitting Factory (a music club on East Houston Street) to give dancers a chance to work with new musicians. They also wanted to invite dancers who don't usually improvise in public (like David Thomson, Lisa Schmidt, and Lance Gries, from Trisha Brown's company, and independent choreographers Bebe Miller, Sarah Skaggs, and Vicky Schick) to let down their hair and try it, with some dancers who usually do (like Monson, Jennifer Lacey, David Zambrano, John Jasperse, and Donald Fleming). Bread to the Bone was a chance for dancers to "jam" without the pressure of fund-raising, high-tech production, and reviews (there weren't any, until the series was presented at St. Mark's Church last February). "After her evening, Bebe Miller told me, 'I forgot how much fun you have when you dance.' " Uchizono remarks, "Marga and I wanted to give dancers and choreographers a break from what they normally have to deal with, and at the same time to do something different than Hothouse at P.S. 122, because it's in a music venue. Everyone is there to have a good time. We called it Bread to the Bone because we wanted to keep it minimal — no costumes, no press releases, just music and dancing. Something basic, like bread — without butter, jelly, or jam — that we could feed each other with."

Meier notices that improvisation seems to be coming back into fashion in the nineties. Perhaps, Uchizono muses, improvisation is the appropriate dance form for the recession. Grant money is evaporating and companies are shrinking. There's no longer much money to pay dancers or to rent rehearsal space. If the eighties were a producer-driven period in dance, with high production values, perhaps with improvisation we are moving into a new period of minimalism that keeps control at the lowest level of the dance production pyramid — that of the dancer herself.

41

Going Solo

It seems clear that there are more choreographers working solo these days.

Is it a sign of the times? Of the recession economy? A producers' gimmick? Or is it a standard feature of modern and postmodern dance? Wendy Perron, who organized the week-long Solo Flights program at Jacob's Pillow last summer, speculates that the solo is appropriate for a recession economy because "it has always been cheaper to book solos." Solo Flights came about because "the idea had been brewing for a long time," Perron says, having collected in her mind's eye several memorable pieces. "And it occurred to me that it could be a very economical week."

Even before planning the program, Perron was thinking of putting together a solo evening for herself, featuring works by other choreographers, from Isadora Duncan to Meredith Monk and Trisha Brown. "I thought, Oh, this would be so affordable. I would get booked so easily." But, she admits, the project will probably never materialize—she likes having the dancers in her company around, in the studio and on tour. Still, solo choreography attracts her because, she notes, "You know yourself without asking yourself questions. You don't have to conceptualize when you choreograph for yourself. Somehow it's all preverbal." Beyond her immediate satisfaction with the process of solo choreography, she finds the form particularly striking to view. "Once you've seen a terrific solo, you'll never forget that dancer."

Molissa Fenley, who disbanded her company in 1988 to work almost exclusively as a soloist, says going solo was an artistic choice, not a fiscal necessity. "I felt that my relationship to my work needed to change. All along I've been very interested in the idea of the individual transforming herself through the work. And there seemed to be something missing in the ensemble form. I wanted to work the way a painter or a writer does—there's no translation between thought and action." Fenley acknowledges that "there might be a trend toward going into solo work because people don't want to deal with the finances of a dance company. The point is, a choreographer should keep working no matter what, in whatever form she can manage. It's wrong to think about solos as a purely economic solution.

Dance Ink 3/4 (Winter 1992–93).

But of course, ultimately, everything is an economic response. You don't live in a huge house, because you can't afford it. You don't play the Met, because you can't rent it."

Unlike Perron, Fenley chose to forgo the collegiality we usually associate with dancing. "Dance is notorious as a social art form. It's you and the company. I felt that I would find something very interesting in the solitude of being not only alone on the stage, but also alone every day in the studio. I felt that there was some kind of intense research that could take place in that kind of isolation. I think I've found it; it's a very deep, profound experience. There's never any sense of loneliness. The daily doings of going to the studio — I give myself class every day and then work on whatever I'm working on — have really changed how I feel about my art and dance in general."

Blondell Cummings thinks the solo option is sometimes more a matter of saving time than saving money. "I started out as a soloist because it was practical. I could work around my own schedule. And it gave me more control." And Lisa Nelson feels that the economic side of solos is simply beside the point. "Choreographers make solos for many reasons: to look at work in a different dimension, to be able to work by oneself."

The solo, of course, was a distinctive marker for early modern dance. That Isadora Duncan and Ruth St. Denis dared to hold a stage alone was a programmatic offensive against ballet, which usually embedded its solo variations in an onstage social world, an interlocking pattern of solos, duets, and groups of various sizes. Perron speculates that modern and postmodern choreographers continue to be drawn to solo work "because it's so familiar — it's where we all started." And this is true both historically and pedagogically; college composition classes usually treat the solo as the basic building block from which the more "advanced" forms — duets and groups — develop in an organic progression. But Fenley, for one, argues that "that notion simply has to be revised."

For Dennis O'Connor, the solo form was initially a way of wiping the slate clean after leaving Merce Cunningham's company in 1989. "I needed to start over. I knew so many things about dance that I had to forget. I had to deal with myself first." But, by now, other motives impel his solo work, and it is not exclusively for his own body. *Sacra Conversazione*, the piece O'Connor is currently making, includes four solos for friends — "all dancers whom I love." If Fenley thinks of her solos as an absorption into "a persona, a psyche," and the audience's experience as "the opportunity for people to involve themselves with what's going on with that person, the transformations, the changes, the different experiences," O'Connor holds almost the opposite view, part of the Cunningham principle that he still values. "I don't want to involve the audience in a clear psychological journey in a mid-twentieth-century vein. I require from the audience the willingness to engage in a conceptual field."

Steve Paxton's stance as a soloist is not so much a fiscal one as a radically democratic political choice that has remained constant since his earliest work, in which he felt "the need to see if a democratic situation could exist in a world where it was professed." For many in the fifties and sixties, Cunningham's choreography seemed to topple hierarchies and symbolize democracy. But for Paxton, who danced in the company in the early sixties, "even the Cunningham company was in fact a dictatorship." Paxton turned to the use of scores and rule-games "to acknowledge the performer's creativity." And now, thirty years later, he muses, "I still refuse to manipulate other people. I'm a soloist by default. It has nothing to do with art or choreography. I haven't thought of a way to work with others the way I work myself. I can't ask them to do my movement. I can't have a company." Even contact improvisation, the duet form Paxton initiated in the early seventies, has proved insufficiently democratic for his taste. "I thought it would create so many movement possibilities and enrich choreography. And in a way it has — in terms of sexual equality and the positioning of partners. But its form was set right at the beginning and hasn't been questioned enough." Through his solos — most recently, *The Goldberg Variations* and *Unknown Solo*, set to Bach's *English Suites* — Paxton is involved in "using improvisation as a force" to discover architectural and emotional forms simultaneously, exploring "movement as a reason, not just as an expression of someone's momentary need."

If Paxton's ideal of democracy means refusing to manipulate a group, Deborah Hay, who was nurtured by the same communal ethos of the early sixties, finds the group workshops she leads each year essential to her own solo choreography. "I need the group to make the solo," she states simply. "The process is a whole system. I choreograph for a group, and then I distill the material that I see reflected back to me day after day, three hours a day, for four months. When that group leaves my life, I spend the next six months refiguring that material into a solo for myself." Rather than giving the members of the large group specific movements, Hay "creates parameters" — images and verbal directions — that result in twenty individual views, which, in turn, enrich the vocabulary for her own solos. Hay compares the difference between her large-group and her solo work to something like the difference between grade-C and grade-A maple syrup — and, she hastens to add, she loves both kinds. "In the large group, your eye can jump around all over the place. You can take in the group; you can take in different people. It's like a feast. But a solo is one long trip that you go on. It's like one drink of water."

Timothy Buckley made the solo *The Grave Digger* (1992), to music by Béla Bartók, partly out of the frustration of having to communicate his ideas to other dancers. In this case, after making a group work to the first movement of Bartók's *Sonata for Two Pianos and Percussion*, he felt the other dancers couldn't learn the complexities of the music well enough.

"They weren't having the same responses and impulses as I was. I always had to remind them when something was coming up. Their performance drama came out of exhaustion, not the music." So Buckley decided to tackle the whole Bartók work, head-on, himself. Buckley had stopped dancing and choreographing in 1987. When he began again in 1991, having moved from New York to Chicago, he was also involved in theater. And he created another solo, *Middleman,* that included dramatic monologue and the physicalization of images. His interest in acting has contributed to his view of solo choreography as providing room for improvisation. "There are places where you can create just an outline, so the performance can have some in-the-moment truthfulness, so you only discover what's going to happen when you're actually there. I find that dancers aren't

Blondell Cummings.
(Photo: © 1993 K. C. Bailey.)

trained to do that the way actors are, partly because they've been subjected to the discipline of absorbing and executing steps."

If dances are partly about relationships, where are the relationships in a solo? For Buckley, it is the relationship with the audience that becomes central, but there is, as well, one between "the inner self and the outer self." Perron created *Ten Thoughts Slipping* while thinking about the situation of constantly having to leave her young son in order to work. She thinks of that solo "as a duet with an absent partner." Paxton notes that in *The Goldberg Variations* he has a relationship with Bach and Glenn Gould, the pianist, as well as with the performance space. "Can you take your capacity for dialogue into nonhuman and nonliving realms?" Paxton asks. "The answer seems to be yes. I find myself entering into little conversations with a tree, with gravity, with momentum, but not very much with the audience; the work has its own life." For Nelson, there are also many partners: the audience, the light environment, even the sound person, who in her solo *Terminal Defense* responded in performance to her live instructions. "In a way," she muses, "the whole idea of a solo is spurious. In the theater, one isn't alone."

Cummings finds solo work a welcome respite from creating from the outside in, on a group. "There's something about the solo choreography process that's centering. When I'm doing group work, after a while—because I'm working outside of myself—I start feeling the need to reaffirm my work processes, how I go about making choices and creating movement." And yet she sees the solo as the very opposite of private. "Every person has a solo voice. There are times when you're with other people, and you bring them into your realm. But you're born alone and you die alone. So whenever I'm creating a solo, I feel like I'm speaking for that part of each of us that is always alone. Even though I'm representing a solo voice onstage, I'm definitely going through a lot of different voices to feed that solo, to try to make it universal so it connects to a lot of diverse people. The act of doing it might be a solo, but the sharing of the information is definitely not. To me, choreography is always the act of sharing."

The solo seems to be a hallmark of modern dance, but postmodern dance has left its own imprint on the form. Perron points out that "after Yvonne Rainer's *Trio A*, the solo has never been the same. Now solo choreographers always have to confront the issue of narcissism. It's like the way composers had to think differently about sound after John Cage. The ante has been upped."

Notes

1. Jill Johnston (pp. 3–10)

All references are to articles or books written by Jill Johnston.

1. "Dance Journal," *Village Voice*, February 20, 1969, p. 25.
2. See *Marmalade Me* (New York: Dutton, 1971) for a selection of Johnston's later reviews.
3. "Thoughts on the Present and Future Directions of Modern Dance," *Dance Observer* 22 (August–September 1955): 101–102.
4. "The Modern Dance—Directions and Criticisms," *Dance Observer* 24 (April 1957): 55–56.
5. "Abstraction in Dance," *Dance Observer* 24 (December 1957): 151–52.
6. "Totem," *Village Voice*, February 3, 1960, 10; "Nikolais at Henry St.," *Village Voice*, February 16, 1961, p. 7; "The Gentle Tilt," *Village Voice*, March 26, 1964, p. 5.
7. "Paul Taylor," *Village Voice*, November 22, 1962, p. 7; "Dance Journal: Paul Taylor on Broadway," *Village Voice*, January 12, 1967, p. 20.
8. "Old Hat and New in Connecticut," *Village Voice*, September 8, 1960, p. 10.
9. "Merce Cunningham & Co.," *Village Voice*, February 24, 1960, p. 6.
10. "Cunningham in Connecticut," *Village Voice*, September 7, 1961, p. 4; "Cunningham in Hartford," *Village Voice*, April 9, 1964, p. 19.
11. "Fresh Winds," *Village Voice*, March 15, 1962, p. 13.
12. "Democracy," *Village Voice*, August 23, 1962, p. 9. Out of 57 reviews between this review of the first Judson concert and the end of 1965, Johnston devotes 30 (in whole or in part) to Judson Dance Theater and related choreographers like Waring and Passloff, and concerts by Judson Dance Theater members given elsewhere. Eight of these 57 reviews are of related nondance events, happenings, music, Fluxus, etc. She reviews Cunningham twice during this period.
13. "Fluxus Fuxus," *Village Voice*, July 2, 1964, p. 7.
14. "Preface," *Marmalade Me*, p. 14.
15. "Lois Lane Is a Lesbian," *Village Voice*, March 4, 1971, p. 9. Reprinted in Jill Johnston, *Lesbian Nation* (New York: Simon and Schuster, 1973), p. 143.
16. Personal communication from Diane Fisher, Johnston's former editor at the *Voice*, January 21, 1980.

17. Johnston began writing on dance and art again after this article was published.
18. "Judson concerts #3, #4," *Village Voice*, February 28, 1963, p. 9.
19. "Kings and Queens," *Village Voice*, June 27, 1963, p. 9.
20. "Cunningham, Limón," *Village Voice*, September 5, 1963, p. 10.
21. In "Boiler Room," *Village Voice*, March 29, 1962, p. 14, Johnston quotes Antonin Artaud: "There is still one hellish, truly accursed thing in our time, it is our artistic dallying with forms, instead of being like victims burnt at the stake, signaling through the flames."
22. "Pain, Pleasure, Process," *Village Voice*, February 27, 1964, p. 15.
23. "Critics' Critics," *Village Voice*, September 16, 1965, p. 18.

2. Working and Dancing (pp. 10–16)

This paper was originally an invited response to Monroe Beardsley's paper for the expanded proceedings of the "Illuminating Dance" conference. The authors wish to express their gratitude to Monroe Beardsley, Maxine Sheets-Johnstone, Selma Jeanne Cohen, Adina Armelagos, and Anne Hatfield for their careful readings of this paper.

1. Monroe C. Beardsley, "What Is Going On in a Dance?" *Dance Research Journal* 15/1 (Fall 1982): 31–36. All mentions of Beardsley refer to this paper, given at a conference entitled "Illuminating Dance: Philosophical Inquiry and Aesthetic Criticism," cosponsored by CORD and the Dance Department of Temple University, held at Temple University May 5, 1979.
2. Yvonne Rainer, "Some retrospective notes on a dance for 10 people and 12 mattresses called *Parts of Some Sextets*, performed at the Wadsworth Atheneum, Hartford, Connecticut, and Judson Memorial Church, New York, in March, 1965," *Tulane Drama Review* 10 (T-30; Winter 1965): 168. Reprinted in Yvonne Rainer, *Work 1961–73* (Halifax, Nova Scotia: The Press of the Nova Scotia College of Art and Design; New York: New York University Press, 1974), p. 45. In her discussions of *Room Service in Work 1961–73*, on pp. 45 and 294, Rainer may give the impression that the first performance of the work was the one in Philadelphia in April 1964. However, it was first performed as a choreographic collaboration between Rainer and sculptor Charles Ross at Concert of Dance 13, on November 10–12, 1963, at the Judson Memorial Church in New York City.
3. Quoted from Marcia B. Siegel by Professor Beardsley, p. 33, in order to show why the movement in *Rooms* is dance.
4. Trisha Brown's Equipment Pieces are well documented in Sally R. Sommer, "Equipment Dances: Trisha Brown," *The Drama Review* 16 (T-55; September 1972): 135–41. Simone Forti writes about her dance constructions and other works in her *Handbook in Motion* (Halifax, Nova Scotia: The Press of the Nova Scotia College of Art and Design; New York: New York University Press, 1974). See also the chapters on Trisha Brown and Simone Forti in Sally Banes, *Terpsichore in Sneakers: Post-Modern Dance* (Boston: Houghton Mifflin, 1980).
5. Michael Crichton, *Jasper Johns* (New York: Harry N. Abrams, 1977), p. 31.
6. For an analysis of the workly movements of Rainer's *Trio A*, see "Yvonne

Rainer: The Aesthetics of Denial," in Banes, *Terpsichore in Sneakers*, pp. 41–55.

7. Some of these problems are examined in Noël Carroll's "Post-Modern Dance and Expression," a paper delivered at the American Dance Festival at Duke University in July 1979, published in Gordon Fancher and Gerald Myers, eds., *Philosophical Essays in Dance* (Brooklyn: Dance Horizons, 1981), pp. 95–104.
8. We are indebted to Paul Ziff for the suggestion that concepts like omission, forbearance, and refraining, as used in both legal theory and action theory, would be useful in the description of avant-garde dance.

3. Criticism as Ethnography (pp. 16–24)

1. In my account of the changes in recent ethnography, I have relied on several sources: James Clifford, *The Predicament of Culture: Twentieth-Century Ethnography, Literature, and Art* (Cambridge: Harvard University Press, 1988); James Clifford and George E. Marcus, eds., *Writing Culture: The Poetics and Politics of Ethnography* (Berkeley: University of California Press, 1986); and George E. Marcus and Michael M.J. Fischer, *Anthropology as Cultural Critique: An Experimental Moment in the Human Sciences* (Chicago: University of Chicago Press, 1986).
2. Marcus and Fischer, *Anthropology as Cultural Critique*.
3. Michael M. J. Fischer, "Ethnicity and the Post-Modern Arts of Memory," in Clifford and Marcus, pp. 194–233.
4. Kevin Dwyer, *Moroccan Dialogues: Anthropology in Question* (Baltimore: Johns Hopkins University Press, 1982); Donald Bahr, Juan Gregorio, David Lopez, and Albert Alvarez, *Pinman Shamanism and Staying Sickness* (Tucson: University of Arizona Press, 1974).
5. John O. Steward, *Drinkers, Drummers, and Decent Folk: Ethnographic Narratives of Village Trinidad* (Albany: State University of New York Press, 1974).
6. Susan Sontag, "The Anthropologist as Hero," *Against Interpretation* (New York: Farrar, Straus, and Giroux, 1966).
7. Deborah Jowitt, *Time and the Dancing Image* (New York: William Morrow, 1988); Marcia B. Siegel, *Days on Earth: The Dance of Doris Humphrey* (New Haven: Yale University Press, 1987).
8. Joann Kealiinohomoku, "An Anthropologist Looks at Ballet as Form of Ethnic Dance," *Impulse* (1969–70): 24–33.
9. Joseph H. Mazo, *Dance Is a Contact Sport* (New York: Saturday Review Press/E. P. Dutton, 1974).
10. The dissertation has since been published as *Sharing the Dance: Contact Improvisation and American Culture* (Madison: University of Wisconsin Press, 1990).

4. On Your Fingertips (pp. 24–43)

1. Edwin Denby, "Criticism, Dance," in Anatole Chujoy and P. W. Manchester, eds., *The Dance Encyclopedia* (New York: Simon and Schuster, 1967; revised edition), p. 237.

2. Théophile Gautier, Review of Marie Guy-Stephan, in Arthur Saint-Leon's *Lutin de la Vallée, La Presse*, February 1, 1853; excerpts translated by Edwin Binney III in Selma Jeanne Cohen, ed., *Dance as a Theatre Art* (New York: Dodd, Mead, 1974), pp. 88–90.
3. Clive Barnes, "Taylor's 'Court' Judged Genius," *New York Post*, April 16, 1981.
4. Jack Anderson, "A Potpourri of Works By a Passel of Performers," *New York Times*, September 23, 1991.
5. See, for instance, Yvonne Rainer, "Some retrospective notes on a dance for 10 people and 12 mattresses called *Parts of Some Sextets*, performed at the Wadsworth Atheneum, Hartford, Connecticut, and Judson Memorial Church, New York, in March, 1965," *Tulane Drama Review* 10 (T-30; Winter 1965); reprinted in Yvonne Rainer, *Work 1961–73* (Halifax, Nova Scotia: The Press of the Nova Scotia College of Art and Design; New York: New York University Press, 1974), pp. 45–51.
6. However, for an early essay that did use anthropological methods "at home," see Joann Kealiinohomoku, "An Anthropologist Looks at Ballet as Form of Ethnic Dance," *Impulse* (1969—70); reprinted in Roger Copeland and Marshall Cohen, eds., *What Is Dance?* (Oxford and New York: Oxford University Press, 1983), pp. 533–49.
7. Susan Sontag, "Against Interpretation," *Against Interpretation* (New York: Farrar, Straus, and Giroux, 1966), p. 7.
8. Indeed, the special postmodern dance issue of *The Drama Review* 19 (T-65; March 1975) spread the critical label "postmodern" in regard to dance and set forth a definition.
9. Burt Barr, "David Gordon's *What Happened*," *The Drama Review* 23 (T-83; September 1979): 33–34.
10. Noël Carroll makes the same point in "Options for Contemporary Dance Criticism," in Lynn Blom and Susan Lee, eds., *Anthology on Dance Criticism* (Pittsburgh: University of Pittsburgh Press, 1995).
11. Arlene Croce, "Prizewinners," *The New Yorker*, August 27, 1973; reprinted in Arlene Croce, *Afterimages* (New York: Knopf, 1977), p. 4.
12. Gus Solomons, Review of American Ballroom Theater, *Dance Magazine* 62/3 (March 1988): 50.
13. Allen Robertson, "Dance audience boos performance," *Minneapolis Star*, October 12, 1981.
14. John Mueller, "Notes for the Film, *USA: Dance—Four Pioneers*, including Doris Humphrey's 'Passacaglia,'" *Films on Ballet and Modern Dance: Notes and a Directory* (New York: American Dance Guild, 1974), p. 37.
15. Jean Nuchtern, "Cinderella Makes Good," *Soho Weekly News*, May 10, 1979.
16. Noël Carroll, "Choreographic Canvases," *Soho Weekly News*, December 1978.
17. Marcia B. Siegel, "*The Green Table*: Movement Masterpiece," *At the Vanishing Point: A Critic Looks at Dance* (New York: Saturday Review Press, 1973), p. 65.

18. Deborah Jowitt, "Merce: Enough Electricity to Light Up Broadway," *Village Voice*, February 7, 1977.
19. Joan Acocella, "Mark Morris and the Classical Vision," *Art in America* (January 1991): 51–55.
20. See Monroe C. Beardsley, "Critical Evaluation," *Aesthetics: Problems in the Philosophy of Criticism* (Indianapolis: Hackett, 1988; second edition), pp. 454–99, for a fuller discussion of these three evaluative dimensions and the three general canons, to which I refer below, under which aesthetic judgments may be subsumed.
21. Rob Baker, Review of Ballet Nacional de Cuba, *Dance Magazine* (October 1978): 112, 119.
22. Ann Daly, "The Balanchine Woman: Of Hummingbirds and Channel Swimmers," *The Drama Review* 31 (T-113; Spring 1987): 8, 14.
23. See Susanne Langer, *Problems of Art* (New York: Scribner's, 1957), p. 12.
24. Elizabeth C. Fine, "Stepping, Saluting, Cracking, and Freaking: The Cultural Politics of African-American Step Shows," *The Drama Review* 35/2 (T-130; Summer 1991): 40, 56–57.
25. Sondra Horton Fraleigh, *Dance and the Lived Body: A Descriptive Aesthetics* (Pittsburgh: University of Pittsburgh Press, 1987), pp. 86–87, 89.
26. Jill Johnston, "Rainer's *Muscle*," *Village Voice*, April 18, 1968.

5. Power and the Dancing Body (43–50)

1. Deborah Jowitt, *Time and the Dancing Image* (New York: William Morrow, 1988), pp. 8–10.
2. Panel on "American Dances, American Bodies, American Culture," organized by Cynthia Novack, Dance in American Culture series, The Center for American Culture Studies, Columbia University, 1986. Susan Manning's question to me at that panel regarding my use of the term "reflect" to characterize the relationship between dance and society has in part prompted the present essay.
3. Sally Peters, "From Eroticism to Transcendence: Ballroom Dance and the Female Body," in Laurence Goldstein, ed., *The Female Body: Figures, Styles, Speculations* (Ann Arbor: University of Michigan Press, 1991), p. 147.
4. Anthropologist Cynthia Novack, for instance, writes (in *Sharing the Dance: Contact Improvisation and American Culture* [Madison: University of Wisconsin Press, 1990], p. 8) that "culture is embodied. . . . We perform movement, invent it, interpret it, and reinterpret it, on conscious and unconscious levels. In these actions, we participate in and reinforce culture, and we also create it,"
5. Lincoln Kirstein, *Dance: A Short History of Classic Theatrical Dancing* (New York: G. P. Putnam's Sons, 1935; reprint Dance Horizons, 1969), pp. 146–47. Roy Strong has the same interpretation in *Splendor at Court: Renaissance Spectacle and the Theater of Power* (Boston: Houghton Mifflin, 1973), pp. 149–51.
6. Jowitt, p. 243.

7. See Lynne Fauley Emery, *Black Dance in the United States from 1619 to 1970* (New York: Dance Horizons, 1980), and Robert Toll, *Blacking Up: The Minstrel Show in Nineteenth Century America* (New York: Oxford University Press, 1974).
8. Natalia Roslavleva, "Prechistenka 20: The Isadora Duncan School in Moscow," *Dance Perspectives* 64 (Winter 1975): 43–44.
9. The reference in the section heading is to an agit-photo by Barbara Kruger. The text reads: "Your body is a battleground. Support legal abortion/birth control/and women's rights." Susan Bordo uses Kruger's artwork to illustrate her position on the cultural struggle over the body in " 'Material Girl': The Effacements of Postmodern Culture," in Goldstein, pp. 114, 120.
10. Bordo, pp. 109, 113. I should make it clear that, although I disagree with Bordo specifically about the extent of "the grip of culture on the body" (p. 117), there is much in her article, particularly in regard to representations of racial difference in mass consumer culture, that I find illuminating and accurate. For other feminist appropriations of Fourcault, see Irene Diamond and Lee Quinby, eds. *Feminism and Foucault: Reflections on Resistance* (Boston: Northeastern University Press, 1988), and Jana Sawicki, *Disciplining Foucault: Feminism, Power, and the Body* (New York and London: Routledge, 1991).
11. Susan Rubin Suleiman, "(Re)Writing the Body: The Politics and Poetics of Female Eroticism," in Susan Rubin Suleiman, ed., *The Female Body in Western Culture: Perspectives* (Cambridge: Harvard University Press, 1986), p. 24.
12. John Fiske, "Madonna," *Reading the Popular* (Boston: Unwin Hyman, 1989), p. 97.
13. Bordo, pp. 122–29.
14. I put "race" in quotation marks because, following Henry Louis Gates, Jr., and others (see Henry Louis Gates, Jr., ed., *"Race," Writing, and Difference* [Chicago: University of Chicago Press, 1986]), I want to avoid suggesting "natural" or biological difference where cultural difference is meant.
15. Useful here is Robert C. Allen's point (in *Horrible Prettiness: Burlesque and American Culture* [Chapel Hill: University of North Carolina Press, 1991]), that a dichotomy between "domination" and "resistance" oversimplifies these matters. Allen prefers the terms "ordination" and "insubordination" to describe the dynamic of cultural struggle, since in our contemporary society direct force rarely comes into play in the sphere of ordinary life, at least in matters of fashion, health, theater, and so on. This is not to deny the repressive use of force in our society but, rather, to say that it is not employed to enforce on a mass level the representations purveyed by popular culture. Indeed, it seems to me that one would want to maintain the distinction between, say, police brutality or tape and the "disciplining of bodies" in aerobics classes. In *Making Sex: Body and Gender from the Greeks to Freud* (Cambridge: Harvard University Press, 1990), the historian Thomas Laqueur makes a similar point regarding the balance between cultural and biological construction of the body. He upholds "a distinction between the body and the body as discursively constituted, between seeing

and seeing-as," and notes that although he believes that biology is not given, but is shaped by culture, at the same time he believes that a material body is "*really* there," underlying representations. He cites his revelation, on spending a year in medical school, when "body as cultural construct met body on the dissecting table. . . . For all of my awareness of how deeply our understanding of what we saw [on the dissecting table] was historically contingent—the product of institutional, political, and epistemological contingencies—the flesh in its simplicity seemed always to shine through" (pp. 14–15).

16. Norbert Elias, *The History of Manners: The Civilizing Process*, trans. Edmund Jephcott (New York: Pantheon Books, 1982).
17. See Elizabeth Aldrich, *From the Ballroom to Hell: Grace and Folly in Nineteenth-Century Dance* (Evanston, Ill.: Northwestern University Press, 1991).
18. Aldrich, pp. 83–85.
19. For instance, see Lawrence Vincent, *Competing with the Sylph: Dancers and the Pursuit of the Ideal Body Form* (Kansas City, Mo.: Andrews and McMeel, 1979). Jowitt does briefly discuss pregnancy and diet, in regard to Romantic ballet dancers (pp. 46–47).
20. Tim Armstrong, "The electrification of the body at the turn of the century," *Textual Practice* 5/3 (Winter 1991): 303–25.
21. See Sally Sommer, "Loïe Fuller," *The Drama Review* 19/1 (T-65; March 1975), and Jowitt, pp. 90–91.
22. For instance, one could profitably examine the historical moment when weddings changed from being the *occasions for* ballets into being the *subject of* ballets. Too, it would be instructive to analyze the changing representations of weddings, from the interrupted ones of the Romantic era to the triumphant ones of the Russian Imperial era to the somewhat brutal one depicted in Nijinska's *Les Noces*.

6. Balanchine and Black Dance (53–69)

1. Deborah Jowitt, "A Gem Remounted," *Village Voice*, December 13, 1983, reprinted in Deborah Jowitt, *The Dance in Mind* (Boston: David Godine, 1985), p. 22.
2. *Partisan Review*, Fall 1968, quoted in Nancy Reynolds, *Repertory in Review* (New York: The Dial Press, 1977), p. 249.
3. Quoted in Reynolds, p. 250.
4. In my telephone interview with him on August 14, 1991, Villella remarked, "There's one step that's now lost in the opening movement, when the man does four steps to the woman—it's all thirties jazz."
5. Merlin, *Le Monde*, June 24, 1969, quoted in Reynolds, p. 250.
6. *New York Times*, April 14, 1967, quoted in Reynolds, p. 248.
7. Joseph H. Mazo, "Jazzdance: Art Not Art?," *Dance Magazine* 65/9 (September 1991): 62.
8. Arlene Croce argues that "*Rubies* has always seemed to me recherché neoclassicism and jazz-ism, and deliberately so. It was 1967 and GB wasn't hip to the new era of rock and he knew it. The fact that *Rubies* hit the

audience so hard and seemed so *new* is a tribute to his genius" (personal communication, February 29, 1992).

9. I should note that although some might argue that the terms "jazz dancing," tapdancing," or "show-biz dancing" might be used by the critics and the dancers without consciously associating these genres with the African-American Tradition, I have taken these references to support my claims for several reasons. First, any historical investigation of all these genres shows that they are rooted in black vernacular dance styles (see Marshall and Jean Stearns, *Jazz Dance* [New York: Schirmer Books, 1968]). Second, my own viewing of some of the dances and movements that have been described this way corroborates the African-American connection. Third, as I intend to show, Balanchine was exposed to the black practice in all these genres and learned them from African-American experts. Fourth, as we shall see, he referred to the steps that way himself.
10. In this respect I differ with Brenda Dixon, who has argued that Balanchine and other white choreographers "without crediting sources . . . used Afrocentric influences at will from their Broadway choreography to their ballets." Dixon suggests that such appropriation may have taken place "with malicious intent" ("Up from Under: The Afrocentric Tradition in American Concert Dance," *The Hong Kong International Dance Conference July 15–28, 1990, Conference Papers*, 1 (A–J): 179). I do not disagree, however, with Dixon's list of African-American elements in Balanchine's style, several of which correspond to features I have often noted myself. In 1985, for instance, attending the Dance Critics Association Conference on *The Four Temperaments*, I was surprised that, although there were some references to "jazzy" movements and to Balanchine's choreography on Broadway and in Hollywood dancing, the deep connections in this ballet to black dance style were not plumbed further. That event inspired the present article (see especially "Celebrating *The Four Temperaments*—II," *Ballet Review* 15/1 [Spring 1987]: 39–43).
11. For instance, tapdancing is a hybrid form, mixing European (primarily Irish) and African elements, and since the nineteenth century it has been performed by both blacks and whites. Tapdancing, as well as other dance forms—like the cakewalk and the soft-shoe—that originated in African-American cultural practice, all have a history of appropriation by whites on the minstrel stage and reappropriation on the black minstrel circuit. The racism of the minstrel show portrayal of African-Americans is undeniable and inexcusable. But to speak, as some commentators have, of certain dances or steps as "belonging" to one "race" or another, or of being "stolen," seems to be missing the point in regard to cultural production. (I put the term "race" in quotation marks because, following such writers as Henry Louis Gates, Jr., and Kwame Anthony Appiah, I view this category as a cultural, not a "natural," construction. See, for instance, Henry Louis Gates, Jr., Introduction, *"Race," Writing, and Difference* [Chicago: University of Chicago Press, 1986], pp. 1–20.) Vernacular culture is produced by people, but it is not private property. What made minstrel shows racist was the disparaging, parodic context in which these dances were performed.

Both African-American and Euro-American concert dance choreographers have used "black dance" and "white dance" elements in their work.

12. Edwin Denby, "Some Thoughts About Classicism and George Balanchine," *Dancers, Buildings, and People in the Streets* (New York: Curtis Books, 1965), p. 68. The article was first published in *Dance Magazine* (February 1953) and is reprinted in Edwin Denby, *Dance Writings*, edited by Robert Cornfield and William MacKay (New York: Knopf, 1986), pp. 433–40. All citations here from Denby reviews and articles, whether or not they were published in previous collections, refer to the definitive *Dance Writings*.
13. Telephone conversation with Elizabeth Kendall, September 1991.
14. Frederick Starr *Red and Hot: The Fate of Jazz in the Soviet Union 1917–1980* (New York: Oxford University Press, 1983), pp. 31–34; Bronislava Nijinska, *Bronislava Nijinska: Early Memoirs*, translated and edited by Irina Nijinska and Jean Rawlinson, with an introduction by Anna Kisselgoff (New York: Holt, Rinehart, and Winston, 1981), p. 25. Ruthanna Boris remembers that when she choreographed *Cakewalk* for the New York City Ballet in 1951, Lincoln Kirstein suggested using music by the white New Orleans composer Louis Gottschalk, "whom nobody had hear of then—except for Balanchine, because Gottschalk had been famous in Russia" (in Reynolds, p. 121).
15. See Starr, pp. 43–53; also, Valentin Parnakh, "Novye tantsy" and "Dzhaz-Band," *Veshch*, nos. 1–2 (Berlin 1922), p. 25.
16. Starr gives a lively account and an informative sociological analysis of "Russia's Roaring Twenties," pp. 54–62.
17. The foxtrot, popularized by Vernon and Irene Castle, spread rapidly throughout Euro-American culture, and its origins may be untraceable. However, like other dances with animal names it seems to be rooted in African-American practice. As well, it has a semisyncopated rhythm. Irene Castle attributed the "invention" of the foxtrot to James Europe, the well-known African-American Jazz musician who was the Castle's musical director: "It was Jim Europe . . . who suggested the foxtrot to us, and for all I know he invented it" ("Swing Music and Popular Dance," *Dance Herald* [February 1938], quoted in Stearns and Stearns, p. 98). Katrina Hazzard-Gordon's interviews with African-American vaudeville performers confirm this view of the black origins of the foxtrot (personal communication, March 1, 1992).
18. *Choreography by Balanchine: A Catalogue of Works* (New York: Viking, 1984; An Eakins Press Foundation Book), pp. 54–55. The second foxtrot was reviewed in *Krasnaya Gazeta*, May 20, 1924. On Balanchine's Russian years, see Elizabeth Suritz, "The Young Balanchine in Russia," *Ballet Review* 18/2 (Summer 1990): 66–71; Souritz, *Soviet Choreographers in the 1920s*, translated by Lynn Visson and edited with an introduction and additional translation by Sally Banes (Durham N.C.: Duke University Press, 1990), pp. 73–78; Yuri Slonimsky, "Balanchine: The Early Years," *Ballet Review* 5/3 (1875–76), reprinted in abridged form in Francis Mason, *I Remember Balanchine: Recollections of the Ballet Master by Those Who*

Knew Him (New York: Doubleday, 1991), pp. 19–78; and Bernard Taper, *Balanchine: A Biography* (New York: Times Books, 1984), pp. 53–73. The two quotes from eyewitnesses to Balanchine's work at the Maly are taken from Slonimsky, pp. 58–59 (in *Ballet Review*).

19. Darius Milhaud, *Ma Vie heureuse* (Paris: Belfond, 1973), pp. 124–25.
20. These dances are described in Sally Banes, "An Introduction to the Ballets Suédois," *Ballet Review* 7/2 & 3 (1978–79): 28–59, and are documented in Bengt Häger, *The Swedish Ballet* (New York: Harry N. Abrams, 1990), pp. 189–219.
21. Phyllis Rose, *Jazz Cleopatra: Josephine Baker in Her Time* (New York: Doubleday, 1989), p. 70.
22. Bryan Hammond and Patrick O'Connor, *Josephine Baker* (Boston: Little, Brown, 1988), p. 118; Lincoln Kirstein, personal communication, November 18, 1991.
23. Cyril W. Beaumont, *The Diaghilev Ballet in London* (London: Black, 1951), p. 269. The information about Snowball comes from Edward Ricco, "The Sitwells at the Ballet," *Ballet Review* 6/2 (1977–78): 87.
24. *Choreography by Balanchine*, pp. 90, 100–101.
25. On Buddy Bradley's work, see Stearns and Stearns, pp. 160–169; Mary Clarke and David Vaughan, eds., *The Encyclopedia of Dance & Ballet* (New York: G. P. Putnam's Sons, 1977), s.v. "Bradley, Buddy"; on Bradley's collaborations with the British ballet choreographer Frederick Ashton, see David Vaughan, *Frederick Ashton and His Ballets* (New York: Knopf, 1977).
26. Lincoln Kirstein, Letter to A. Everett Austin, July 16, 1933, reprinted in Mason, pp. 116, 118.
27. Denby, "A Letter on New York City's Ballet," *Ballet* (August 1952), reprinted in Denby, *Dance Writings*, p. 429.
28. Both before and during Mitchell's tenure, however, several African-American dancers appeared as guests. For the Ballet Society production of Lew Christensen's *Blackface*, in 1947, Betty Nichols and Talley Beatty appeared as "The Colored Couple." In 1950, Arthur Bell had danced in Ashton's *Illuminations*, and, in 1952, Louis Johnson danced in Robbins's *Ballade*. In 1960, Mary Hinkson, from Martha Graham's company, appeared in *The Figure in the Carpet*, and John Jones danced in *Modern Jazz: Variants* (see Reynolds, pp. 81, 136, 203, 212). (I am grateful to David Vaughan for pointing out several of these guest appearances.) Two more African-American dancers were to dance with the company after Mitchell's departure while Balanchine was still alive — Debra Austin in the 1970s and Mel Tomlinson in the 1980s. In 1992 there were three African-American dancers in the company and about twelve African-American students in the School of American Ballet.
29. The music for the revue was by Vernon Duke, the lyrics by Ira Gershwin. For a description of Baker's numbers and an account of her critical reception, see Rose, pp. 165–70. Also see Gerald Bordman, *American Musical Theatre: A Chronicle* (New York: Oxford University Press, 1978), pp. 497–98.
30. "Celebrating *The Four Temperaments* — II," p. 43. Harper had been Buddy

Bradley's studio assistant in the 1920s and 1930s. About *On Your Toes*, see Bordman, p. 498.

31. See *Choreography by Balanchine*, pp. 135–36 and Bordman, pp. 501–502. The Nicholas quote is from Stearns and Stearns, pp. 280–81.
32. Balanchine's tap consultant for the film was the white tapdancer Sammy Lee. See *Choreography by Balanchine*, p. 142.
33. I want to thank Robert Cornfield for raising this and other points.
34. According to *Choreography by Balanchine*, "Balanchine combined classical ballet technique with [the Dunham company's] own highly developed dance forms and choreographed special dances for the leading players." Also see Bordman, pp. 521–22. Dunham's reminiscences are published in Mason, pp. 190–93.
35. The show premiered in Philadelphia; Balanchine quit the production team before the New York opening, and Herbert Ross rechoreographed some of the dances, while others were cut. It was Ross who brought Ailey into the cast. See *Choreography by Balanchine*, p. 214–15.
36. Interview with Edward Villella.
37. See *Choreography by Balanchine*, pp. 208, 252–53, 257; Reynolds, pp. 255, 274–275. In my telephone interview with Arthur Mitchell, September 20, 1991, he described the collaborative process.
38. However, Balanchine was criticized for featuring his own company in the more classical sections and Mitchell's company in the more "black" sections. Indeed, John Gruen has chronicled how Clive Barnes responded to the piece in the *New York Times* by calling for more "black faces" in the New York City Ballet. Karel Shook, associate artistic director of Dance Theater of Harlem, complained to Gruen that "our dancers were presented as the cliché idea of all-black dancers — All they can do is jazz." Mitchell, however, was more forgiving: "One must remember that we were working with a man who is a genius — a genius who comes out of another era. . . . I felt that my kids learned a great deal by working with the New York City Ballet. . . . Of course, it was fantastic for me, because it was the first time I worked with Balanchine in another capacity [than as a dancer]. . . . Just the association of the two companies established The Dance Theater of Harlem" (John Gruen, *The Private World of Ballet* [New York: Viking, 1975], pp. 441–42).
39. *Choreography by Balanchine*, pp. 119, 285, 145, 152–53, 170–71, 235–36, 249, 243–44, 255–56; Reynolds, pp. 39, 71, 199–201, 211, 246, 212–13, 227, 268–70; Edwin Denby, "A Letter on New York City's Ballet," p. 420; Edwin Denby, "Balanchine Choreographing," *Kulchur* (1962), reprinted in *Dance Writings*, pp. 474, 476; David Vaughan, personal communication, January 1992.
40. These two African-American features of dance style were discussed by John Szwed and Robert Farris Thompson, respectively, at the Dance Black America conference, April 21–24, 1983, presented by the Brooklyn Academy of Music and the State University of New York.
41. Denby, "A Letter on New York City's Ballet," pp. 423–24. Denby complains, however, that the company couldn't muster up the proper style for Jerome Robbins's *Pied Piper*.

42. Interview with Mitchell.
43. "Forces of Harlem," *The New Yorker*, May 13, 1974, reprinted in Arlene Croce, *Afterimages* (New York: Knopf, 1977, p. 60. David Vaughan notes that "When I first saw *Barocco*—in 1948 by Grand Ballet de Monte Carlo—it was *much* jazzier than it is now, even by Dance Theater of Harlem" (personal communication).
44. Arlene Croce, "News from the Muses," *The New Yorker*, September 11, 1978, reprinted in *Going to the Dance* (New York: Knopf, 1982), p. 112; interview with Villella; Reynolds, pp. 47–49. The term "multi-unit" torso is taken from Alan Lomax and the Choreometrics project. It refers to the use of a flexible torso, as seen, for instance, in traditional African dance and African-American dance, not only in twisting but also in isolating shoulders or hips or moving different parts of the torso to different rhythms.
45. Reynolds, p. 66; Edwin Denby, "The Rockettes and Rhythm," *New York Herald Tribune*, February 20, 1944, and " 'Concerto Barocco' at Needle Trades High School," *New York Herald Tribune*, November 1, 1943, reprinted in Denby, *Dance Writings*, pp. 201, 167.
46. Reynolds, p. 68; "Celebrating *The Four Temperaments*—II," p. 42; interview with Villella. (I am grateful to Arlene Croce for sharing this information, which Villella repeated to me.) Regarding Danieli's comment, however, David Vaughan notes that no other dancer remembers the finger-snapping (personal communication).
47. The term "angular archaisms" comes from a review in the *New York Herald Tribune*, October 16, 1965, and is quoted in Reynolds, p. 73; Edwin Denby, "The Four Temperaments," *Dance News* (December 1946), reprinted in Denby, *Dance Writings*, p. 415; Mitchell is quoted in Reynolds, p. 72.
48. See Robert Farris Thompson, *African Art in Motion* (Berkeley: University of California Press, 1974), pp. 13–14, for a discussion of the "get-down" posture in black dance; Arlene Croce, "Momentous," *The New Yorker*, Dec. 8, 1975, reprinted in Arlene Croce, *Afterimages* (New York: Knopf, 1977), p. 188. On what I am labeling "ecstatic arms," see Robert Farris Thompson, *The Four Moments of the Sun*, exhibition catalogue (Washington: The National Gallery of Art, 1981), pp. 176–77. My own descriptions and interpretations of this ballet are based on my live viewings of its performance by the New York City Ballet and a close study of the 1977 Dance in America recording, directed by Merrill Brockway and broadcast by PBS as part of *Choreography by Balanchine I*.
49. Flash acts combine jazz dancing with acrobatics. The Nicholas Brothers were an outstanding example of this genre. See Stearns and Stearns, pp. 276–82.
50. Mitchell in Reynolds, p. 72; Croce, "Momentous," p. 189; Thompson, *The Four Moments of the Sun*, pp. 122–24, 172–76. Thompson expands on this gesture in "Kongo Influences on African-American Artistic Culture," in Joseph E. Holloway, *Africanisms in American Culture* (Bloomington: University of Indiana Press, 1990), pp. 161–64, and cites John Szwed, "Introduction," Arthur Huff Fauset, *Black Gods of the Metropolis* (Philadelphia:

University of Pennsylvania Press, 1971), p. vii. On "stepping it down," see Bessie Jones and Bess Lomax Hawes, *Step It Down: Games, Plays, Songs, and Stories from the African Heritage* (New York: Harper and Row, 1972). For other characteristic features, see Joann W. Kealiinohomoku, "A Comparative Study of Dance as a Constellation of Motor Behaviors Among African and United States Negroes [1965]," in Adrienne L. Kaeppler, ed., *Reflections and Perspectives on Two Anthropological Studies of Dance*, CORD Dance Research Annual VII (New York: CORD, 1976), pp. 15–179; Margaretta Bobo Goines, "African Retentions in the Dance of the Americas," *Dance Research Monograph One, 1971–1972* (New York: CORD, 1972), pp. 209–29; Gertrude P. Kurath and Nadia Chilkovsky, "Jazz Choreology," in A. Wallace, ed., *Man and Cultures*, Papers from the Fifth International Congress of Anthropological and Ethnological Sciences (Philadelphia, 1960), pp. 152–59; Stearns and Stearns; and Katrina Hazzard-Gordon, *Jookin': The Rise of Social Dance Formations in African-American Culture* (Philadelphia: Temple University Press, 1990).

51. Hence, perhaps, the references by various critics, notably Thompson on the mambo, to cubism in describing black dance. Of course cubism was itself influenced by the African aesthetic.
52. See Goines and also Nadia Chilkovsky, "Analysis and Notation of Basic Afro-American Movements," in Stearns and Stearns, p. 423, diagram 1.
53. Edwin Denby, "Three Sides of 'Agon,' " *Evergreen Review* (Winter 1959); reprinted in *Dance Writings*, p. 462; Edwin Denby, "In the Abstract," New York City Ballet Souvenir Program (1959–1960), reprinted in *Dance Writings*, p. 466; Denby, "Three Sides of 'Agon,' " p. 463; Denby, "Balanchine Choreographing," p. 478. Denby's complaint that Balanchine was old-fashioned when it came to current jazz dancing corresponds to Croce's point in n. 8 above.
54. This, according to John Willett (in *Art and Politics in the Weimar Period: The New Sobriety, 1917–1933* [New York: Pantheon, 1978], p. 90), was the term the German music critic Heinrich Strobel used to describe the impact of the European tour by Sam Wooding on Hindemith and others.
55. Interviews with Mitchell and Villella. On the process of modernizing ballet by incorporating and abstracting "exotic" folkdances, see Lynn Garafola, *Diaghilev's Ballets Russes* (New York: Oxford University Press, 1989), especially ch. 3, "The Making of Ballet Modernism."
56. I am grateful to Ramsay Burt for making this point (personal communication, February 25, 1992).
57. According to Kirstein, "He never could find a black composer who could give him an authentic black jazz ballet. He loved jazz, but it was George Gershwin and the popular Broadway tunesters that really moved him in this genre" (personal communication).
58. Nancy Reynolds, however, argues that although Balanchine may have had "exoticism" in mind at times when casting Mitchell, the role of Puck was not one of those times. "In that uncanny way GB had of zeroing in and highlighting individual movement idiosyncrasies in dancers, he picked up on Mitchell's essential fleetness and lightness and made it part of the Puck

character. . . . All the effects were dance effects" (personal communication, January 10, 1992).

59. See Jack Slater, "They Told Us Our Bodies Were Wrong for Ballet," *New York Times*, April 27, 1975, and "Black Bodies vs. Classic Symmetry," *New York Times*, May 18, 1975.
60. Balanchine told John Gruen in 1971,

    The fact is, we have black children in our school. But they don't stay in the school long enough. It's always like that, with whites or blacks. Mothers would come to me and ask how long it will take her child of eight to become a ballerina. I say it takes about eight to ten years. Then it takes another ten years. So it's about twenty years' work. . . . Well, the mothers say, "Oh no, that's too long." Then they take their children away.

    Years ago Arthur Mitchell and I made a big campaign. We went to Harlem to find children. We offered them scholarships. But you see, they didn't want to stay. (Gruen, p. 443.)

    Kirstein, writing to me recently about the African-American students in the company and at the School of American Ballet, claims, "It's very hard to find black boys who want to learn classic ballet. They think it unmanly, affected, and inappropriate. . . . They work doubly hard, but so many luckless factors stand in their way, having nothing to do with racial prejudice or physical ability" (personal communication).

    It seems to me that the issue of recruiting African-American students is a complicated one that neither Balanchine nor Kirstein fully addresses, and one that *does* have to do with racial prejudice, from which the school and its students, as part of a culture at large permeated with institutional racism, could not be immune.
61. For help on this article, thanks go first to Joan Acocella. I would also like to thank Mindy Aloff, Valerie Briginshaw, Virginia Brooks, Ramsay Burt, Noël Carroll, Selma Jeanne Cohen, Robert Cornfield, Arlene Croce, Ann Daly, Susan Foster, Lynn Garafola, Katrina Hazzard-Gordon, Stephanie Jordan, Deborah Jowitt, Elizabeth Kendall, Judy Kinberg, Woody McGriff, Nancy Reynolds, John Szwed, David Vaughan, and, at Dance Theater of Harlem, Sharon Williams and Ed Scholwer. I am indebted to Arthur Mitchell and Edward Villella for graciously permitting me to interview them and to Lincoln Kirstein for his prompt correspondence.

7. Ballets Suédois (pp. 70–81)

Unless otherwise indicated, quotations from the French or Swedish are translated by S. Banes.

1. Arnold Haskell with Walter Nouvel, *Diaghileff: His Artistic and Private Life* (New York, 1935; reprint ed. Da Capo Press, 1978), pp. 278–301.
2. Bengt Häger, "The Wise Fools," in *Modern Swedish Ballet* (London: Victoria and Albert Museum, 1970), p. 6; Rolf de Maré, "Naissance et Évolution des Ballets Suédois," *Les Ballets Suédois dans l'Art Contemporain* (Paris: Éditions du Trianon, 1931), pp. 19–26.
3. The biographical information comes from Börlin's cousin, Hedvig Nenzén-Haquinius, in "Le Petit Garçon Qui Ne Demandait Qu'à Danser," *Les Ballets Suédois dans l'Art Contemporain* (hereafter referred to as *LBS*),

pp. 144–48, and from Pierre Tugal, "L'Art de Jean Börlin," *LBS*, pp. 154–56.

Fokine, in his memoir "Börlin, Mon Élève . . ." (*LBS*, p. 148), gives 1911 as the date when he first saw Börlin. However, Bengt Häger corrects this date to 1913 in "The Wise Fools," p. 6, and Anna Greta Ståhle, in "Sweden, Ballet in," *The Dance Encyclopedia*, ed. Anatole Chujoy and P. W. Manchester (New York: Simon and Schuster, 1967), s.v., gives 1913 as the date for Fokine's first visit to Sweden.

4. Fokine, "Börlin, Mon Élève . . . ," pp. 148–49.
5. Haquinius, "Le Petit Garçon," p. 148.
6. Ståhle, "Sweden, Ballet in," s.v.
7. Tugal, "L'Art de Jean Börlin," p. 156.
8. Mikhail Fokine, "The New Russian Ballet," *The Times* (London), July 6, 1914.
9. de Maré, "Naissance et Évolution," p. 26.
10. "Next the Swedish Ballet," *The New York Times Magazine*, November 11, 1923.
11. de Maré, "Naissance et Évolution," p. 27.
12. Häger, "The Wise Fools," p. 7.
13. "Histoire Critique et Analytique des Ballets Suédois," *LBS*, pp. 39–40.
14. de Maré, "Naissance et Évolution," p. 45; Victor I. Seroff, *Maurice Ravel* (New York: Henry Holt, 1953), p. 206.
15. de Maré, "Naissance et Évolution," p. 37; "Histoire Critique et Analytique," pp. 43–44.
16. Cyril W. Beaumont, "Jean Börlin," *Complete Book of Ballets* (New York: Grosset and Dunlap), pp. 672–73.
17. "Swedish Ballet Out of Paris," *New York Telegram*, November 26, 1923; see also various other American Reviews of the same date.
18. [Florence Gilliam?], "The Swedish Ballet: Its Repertory and Its Accomplishment," *Boston Evening Transcript*, September 1, 1923.
19. "Varia," *LBS*, p. 194.
20. Dansmuseet, Stockholm, *Svenska Baletten* (Stockholm: Moderna Museet, 1969), p. 25.
21. "Varia," p. 194.
22. Paul Claudel, *Claudel on the Theatre*, ed. Jacques Petit and Jean-Pierre Kempf, trans. Christine Trollope (Coral Gables, Florida: University of Miami Press, 1972), p. 45.
23. Darius Milhaud, *Ma Vie Heureuse* (Paris: Belfond, 1973), pp. 92–93.
24. Claudel, *Claudel on the Theatre*, p. xvii.
25. Ibid., pp. 45–47. However, Claudel's scenario, in Paul Claudel, *Théâtre* (Paris: Gallimard, 1956), p. 635, only calls for three levels.
26. Neal Oxenhandler, *Scandal and Parade* (New Brunswick, New Jersey: Rutgers University Press, 1957), p. 49.
27. Jean Cocteau, "The Wedding on the Eiffel Tower," trans. Michael Benedikt, in *Modern French Theatre*, ed. Michael Benedikt and George E. Wellwarth (New York: E. P. Dutton, 1966), pp. 99–100.
28. Beaumont, "Jean Börlin," p. 677.

29. Milhaud, *Ma Vie Heureuse*, pp. 124–25.
30. Robert Kimball, ed., *Cole* (New York: Holt, Rinehart and Winston, 1971), pp. 67–68; Charles Schwartz, *Cole Porter* (New York, 1977; reprint ed. Da Capo Press, 1979), pp. 79–82; Calvin Tomkins, *Living Well Is the Best Revenge* (New York: Viking, 1971), pp. 39–40.
31. "Histoire Critique et Analytique," pp. 65–66.
32. Noël Carroll, "Entr'acte, Paris and Dada," *Millennium Film Journal* 1 (Winter 1977–78): 11. The descriptions of the ballet come from "Histoire Critique et Analytique," pp. 73–79; Roger Shattuck, *The Banquet Years*, revised ed. (New York: Random House, Vintage Books, 1968), pp. 172–74; and James Harding, *The Ox on the Roof* (London: Macdonald, 1962), pp. 161–71.
33. *Francis Picabia* (Paris: Galeries Nationales du Grand Palais, 1976), p. 124.
34. Beaumont, "Jean Börlin," p. 683, gives December 4 as the opening date, as does "Histoire Critique et Analytique," p. 76.
35. René Dumesnil, quoted in Shattuck, *The Banquet Years*, p. 174.
36. Ibid.
37. "Pourquoi J'ai Écrit 'Relâche,' " quoted in "Histoire Critique et Analytique," p. 74.
38. Häger, "The Wise Fools," p. 6.

8. Soirée de Paris (pp. 82–91)

1. Both the souvenir program and the poster for the event call it Soirée de Paris (singular) and give the dates for the season as 17 May–30 June 1924. Some reviews and almost all the autobiographies or biographies consulted call it Soirées de Paris (plural). Paul Collaer, *Darius Milhaud* (Antwerp: N. V. de Nederlandsche Boekhandel, 1947), p. 111, and various others report that the season was named after Guillaume Apollinaire's prewar magazine of the same name (plural). I have kept the singular, choosing to agree with the program and the poster. However, I have disagreed with the dates, following instead the daily theater listings in *Le Figaro*.
2. Soirée de Paris, Souvenir Program, Paris, 1924, n. p.
3. Francis Steegmuller, *Cocteau* (Boston and Toronto: Little, Brown, 1970), pp. 326–27; Richard Buckle, *Diaghilev* (New York: Atheneum, 1979), passim.
4. Léonide Massine, *My Life in Ballet*, ed. Phyllis Hartnoll and Robert Rubens (London: Macmillan, 1968), p. 158.
5. Le Comte Étienne de Beaumont, Preface, Souvenir Program.
6. Arthur Gold and Robert Fizdale, *Misia* (New York: Alfred A. Knopf, 1980), p. 238.
7. Ibid., p. 239.
8. Reginald Bridgeman, quoted in Steegmuller, p. 227 note.
9. Steegmuller, p. 284.
10. Gold and Fizdale, p. 239.
11. Jean Hugo, quoted in Steegmuller, p. 308. Gold and Fizdale say, p. 239, that it was Marie Laurencin who came as "La Malade Imaginaire," but agree that Radiguet came as measles.

12. Gold and Fizdale, p. 239.
13. But, for instance, in "Figaro-Théâtre" of 2 June 1924, the *répétition générale* for *Romeo et Juliette* is announced for 9 o'clock in the column "Répétitions générales," while under "Spectacles et Concerts: Ce Soir," the dance program of the preceding week is still listed for 9 P.M. Similarly, a new dance program is announced in Maxime Girard's column "Courrier des Théâtres" (*Le Figaro*, 7 June 1924, p. 3) for June 8 and 9, but on June 8 *Romeo et Juliette* is still listed under "Spectacles et Concerts: Ce Soir," and the dance program is listed respectively in the issues of June 9 and 10.
14. "Spectacles et Concerts: Ce Soir," *Le Figaro*, 18 May 1924, p. 4; 19 May 1924, p. 4; 20 May 1924, p. 4; 21 May 1924, p. 3; 22 May 1924, p. 3; 23 May 1924, p. 5.
15. Souvenir Program. the program gives *Vogues* as the title on one page and *Vogue* on another. The same problem exists in regard to the spelling of dancers' names.
16. Maurice Boucher, " 'Soirées de Paris,' à la Cigale: 'Mercure' de Erik Satie," *Le Monde Musical* 35 (June 1924): 215.
17. Souvenir Program.
18. Tristan Tzara, "Author's Introduction, *Mouchoir de Nuages*," *The Drama Review* 16 (T-56; December 1972): 112.
19. Tzara, "*Mouchoir de Nuages*," p. 118.
20. Souvenir Program.
21. C. Allix, "Soirée de Paris, à la Cigale," *Le Monde Musical* 35 (May 1924): 167.
22. Massine, p. 158.
23. Souvenir Program.
24. Gilson MacCormack, "Pavlova in Paris; Massine's New Productions," *The Dancing Times*, no. 164 (June 1924): 896–97.
25. Darius Milhaud, *Ma Vie heureuse* (Paris: Belfond, 1973), p. 131.
26. Collaer, p. 113. Allix counts five singers.
27. Massine, p. 159.
28. Collaer, p. 114. Translation mine.
29. MacCormack, "Pavlova in Paris," p. 896.
30. Allix.
31. Souvenir Program. Maxime Girard, "Courrier des Théâtres," *Le Figaro*, 23 May 1924, p. 5, announces that the exhibition will open on 24 May; in his column of 24 May, p. 5, he reports that the exhibition is open that evening for the first time.
32. As mentioned above, *Le Figaro* gives conflicting information. The dance program may have run through June 4, as it is listed every day under "Spectacles et Concerts: Ce Soir," from May 25 through June 4. However, *Romeo et Juliette* is listed under "Répétitions générales" for 2 June, p. 4, and under "Premières Representations" for 3 June, p. 3, and finally under "Spectacles et Concerts: Ce Soir," for 5 June, p. 3.
33. Massine, p. 159.
34. Maxime Girard, "Courrier des Théâtres," *Le Figaro*, 22 May 1924, p. 3.
35. Massine, ibid.

36. Souvenir Program.
37. See note 32 above.
38. Steegmuller, passim.
39. Steegmuller, p. 327 note.
40. Neal Oxenhandler, *Scandal and Parade: The Theater of Jean Cocteau* (New Brunswick, N.J.: Rutgers University Press, 1957), p. 54.
41. Steegmuller, pp. 327–28; Jean Cocteau, *Journal d'un inconnu*, p. 222, quoted in Steegmuller, p. 328.
42. Cocteau, Lettre à Jacques Maritain, *Oeuvres completes* IX, pp. 277–78, quoted in Steegmuller, p. 330.
43. "Romeo et Juliette," *Le Théâtre* 27 (15 June 1924): 525.
44. Jean Hugo, quoted in Steegmuller, p. 329.
45. "Romeo et Juliette," translation mine.
46. "Spectacles et Concerts: Ce Soir," *Le Figaro*, 14 June 1924, p. 3; Boucher; MacCormack, "The Russian Ballet in Paris; Les Soirées de Paris," *The Dancing Times*, no. 165 (July 1924): 999.
47. MacCormack, ibid.
48. Boucher.
49. Souvenir Program.
50. Steegmuller identifies the poster for the season, reproduced in his book (p. 375) as by Marie Laurencin. It is the same image as the sketch entitled "Amazon" in the Souvenir Program.
51. Boucher.
52. MacCormack, "The Russian Ballet in Paris," p. 999.
53. "The Sitter Out," *The Dancing Times*, no. 168 (October 1924): 4.
54. Maxime Girard, "Courrier des Théâtres," *Le Figaro*, 11 June 1924, p. 6.
55. Maxime Girard, "Courrier des Théâtres," *Le Figaro*, 12 June 1924, p. 5.
56. Erik Satie, interview with Pierre de Massot, *Paris-Journal*, 30 May 1924, quoted in Douglas Cooper, *Picasso Theatre* (New York: Harry N. Abrams, 1967), p. 56.
57. Cooper, p. 56.
58. Ornella Volta, *L'Ymagier d'Erik Satie* (Paris: Francis van de Velde, 1979), p. 81.
59. Cooper, pp. 56–57.
60. Cooper, p. 59 note 160. I have not changed the spellings of the dancers' names to be consistent with the Souvenir Program.
61. Cooper, p. 58; see plates 322–47.
62. Cooper, pp. 59–61. The letter from André Breton, et al., "Hommage à Picasso," *Paris-Journal*, 20 June 1924, is reprinted on p. 60.
63. Boucher.
64. MacCormack, "The Russian Ballet in Paris," p. 999.
65. Cyril W. Beaumont, *The Diaghilev Ballet in London* (London: Adam and Charles Black, 1951), pp. 280–81.
66. Cooper, p. 59; Buckle, p. 434; Cooper says that the event described by Lifar was the opening night; Buckle says that it was on June 18, which would make it the closing night.
67. Buckle, p. 426.

68. Milhaud, p. 131.
69. Collaer, p. 111, my translation.
70. Massine, conversations with Buckle, quoted in Buckle, p. 446.
71. Buckle, p. 450.

9. Kasyan Goleizovsky's Ballet Manifestos (pp. 92–103)

In transliterating titles and names of authors of Russian works, I have used the Library of Congress system. However, both in the text and in the notes I have left names familiar to the American reader in their more popular form of transliteration — e.g., Alexander Gorsky rather than Aleksandr Gorskii.

1. Mary Clarke and David Vaughan, *Encyclopedia of Dance and Ballet* (New York: G. P. Putnam's Sons, 1977), s.v. "Goleizovsky, Kasyan," by Janet Sinclair and Natalia Roslavleva. Lydia Joffe, in "Kasian Goleizovsky," *The Dancing Times* 56/669 (June 1966): 461, gives 1882 for his birthdate, but I suspect that this is an error, since this would make him twenty-seven at the time of his graduation from the Ballet Academy. Yuri Grigorovich, *Balet: Entsiklopediia* (Moscow: Sovietskaia Entsiklopediia, 1981), s.v. "Goleizovsky, Kasyan Yaroslavich," gives 1892 as his birthdate and Moscow as his birthplace (so does Joffe). Sinclair and Roslavleva give Königgratz, Bohemia, as his birthplace. The rest of the information in this paragraph comes from Elizabeth Souritz, "The Beginning of the Journey: Moscow and Leningrad Ballet in 1917–1927," in Vera Krasovskaya, ed., *Sovietskii Baletnyi Teatr: 1917–1967* (*Soviet Ballet Theater: 1917–1967*) (Moscow: Iskussivo, 1976), p. 36, and from Natalia Roslavleva, *Era of the Russian Ballet* (London: Victor Gollancz, 1966), p. 214. For more information on Goleizovsky's career, see Elizabeth Souritz, *Soviet Choreographers in the 1920s*, trans. Lynn Visson, ed. with additional translation by Sally Banes (Durham, N.C.: Duke University Press, 1991).

   Selma Jeanne Cohen first called my attention to Souritz's essay and showed me her translation of the passage about Goleizovsky. However, the extracts from Souritz quoted in this Introduction are my own translations.
2. Souritz, "The Beginning . . . ," p. 37; Souritz, *Khoreograficheskoe iskusstvo dvadtsatykh godov* (*Choreographic Art of the Twenties*) (Moscow: Iskusstvo, 1979), pp. 158–62.
3. Roslavleva, p. 212; Souritz, "The Beginning . . . ," pp. 43–44.
4. Souritz, *Choreographic Art*, p. 168; Souritz, "The Beginning . . . ," p. 40; Truvit (A. I. Abramov), "The Latest Goleizovsky," *Hermitage* 15 (22–28 August 1922): 9, quoted in Souritz "The Beginning . . . ," p. 40.
5. Souritz, *Choreographic Art*, p. 168; Yuri Slonimsky, "Balanchine: The Early Years," *Ballet Review* 5/3 (1975–76): 37–38.
6. [B. Chmury (?), "Anatol Petrizky,"] *Theatre Arts Monthly* 14 (March 1930): 255. This article gives 1922 as the year for *Eccentric Dances*, but this may be the date of the design rather than the production. Souritz gives 1923 as the date both in "The Beginning . . ." (p. 52) and in *Choreographic Art* (p. 168). For an account of Goleizovsky's work in the 1930s, see Si-Lan Chen Leyda, *Footnote to History*, ed. Sally Banes (New York: Dance Horizons, 1983). On *D. E.*, see Valentine Parnakh, "Notes on the Dance in

the Soviet Union," *Soviet Travel* 4 (1933): 34; James M. Symons, *Meyerhold's Theater of the Grotesque* (Coral Gables, Florida: University of Miami Press, 1971), p. 121; Souritz, "The Beginning . . . ," p. 52; and Llewellyn H. Hedgbeth, "Meyerhold's *D.E.*," *The Drama Review* 19 (T-66; June 1975): 23–36.

7. John E. Bowit, *Stage Designs and the Russian Avant-Garde (1911–1929)* (Washington, D.C.: International Exhibitions Foundation, 1976–78), p. 79.
8. Zakhary L. McLove, "Russian Ballet Has Risen in Revolt," the *New York Times Magazine*, 15 November 1925.
9. Souritz, "The Beginning . . . ," p. 46.
10. Souritz, *Choreographic Art*, p. 200.
11. Souritz, "The Beginning . . . ," p. 73; Mary Grace Swift, *The Art of the Dance in the U.S.S.R.* (Notre Dame, Indiana: University of Notre Dame Press, 1968), p. 311; Kasyan Goleizovsky, "*The Whirlwind* [*Smerch*]," *Sovremennyi Teatr* 7 (18 October 1927): 106, quoted in Souritz, "The Beginning . . . ," p. 76.
12. "*The Whirlwind* at the Bolshoi Theater (Conversation with Goleizovsky)," *Novyi Zritel'* 40 (4 October 1927): 15, quoted in Souritz, "The Beginning . . . ," p. 74; Goleizovsky, "*The Whirlwind*," p. 106; Souritz, "The Beginning . . . ," p. 76; Goleizovsky, "*The Whirlwind*," p. 107, quoted in Souritz, "The Beginning . . . ," p. 77.
13. A. Gidoni, "Ballet at the Breaking Point (On the Performance of the Ballet *The Whirlwind*)," *Sovremennyi Teatr* 17 (27 December 1927): 265; Vik (V. Iving), "*The Whirlwind*," *Pravda* 296 (25 December 1927); both quoted in Souritz, "The Beginning . . . ," p. 77.
14. Souritz, "Goleizovsky Dies," *Dance News* 55 (June 1970): 20; *Encyclopedia of Dance and Ballet*, "Kasyan Goleizovsky"; my conversations with Si-Lan Chen and Jay Leyda, New York City, 1979–82.
15. Joffe, p. 465; Chen; *Ekran*. The first manifesto appeared in *Ekran* 31 (4 May 1922): 3; the second in *Ekran* 32 (15 May 1922): 3–4. The translation is mine. For their help on the research and translation, I wish to thank Irina Belodedova, Thomas Beyer, Selma Jeanne Cohen, Mel Gordon, Michael Kirby, Edward Lee, Jay Leyda, and and Si-Lan Chen Leyda.
16. Nijinsky was dismissed from the Imperial Ballet after he appeared on the Maryinsky stage in a production of *Giselle* (not *Les Sylphides*), in an allegedly revealing costume that Alexandre Benois had designed for Diaghilev's production of *Giselle* the previous year in Europe. Nijinsky was not forced to leave Russia, but, rather, chose to work with Diaghilev outside of Russia. (See Richard Buckle, *Nijinsky* [London: Penguin Books, 1980], pp. 191–93.)
17. *Vain Precautions* is the title used in Russia for the ballet *La Fille mal gardée*.
18. Isadora Duncan had arrived in Moscow in 1921 to open a school, at the invitation of the Soviet government. The first issue of *Ekran*, in the fall of 1921, features an article by Duncan ("My Goal"), and subsequent issues carry articles about the dancer and her performances. On 7 November

1921, Duncan performed an evening of dances at the Bolshoi Theater in celebration of the fourth anniversary of the October Revolution.

19. Goleizovsky probably refers here to Alexander Gorsky's ballet *Eunice and Petronius* (choreographed in 1915 to music by Chopin), which was said to be influenced by Isadora Duncan's style.

    Another possible reference is to Michel Fokine's 1907 ballet *Eunice*, which according to Beaumont was a transition between the old and the new ballets, in which Fokine attempted to create a ballet in antique Greek style, without yet achieving the freedom from ballet tradition he would later, for instance, achieve in *Narcisse* (Cyril Beaumont, *Michel Fokine and His Ballets* [New York: Dance Horizons, 1981], pp. 28–29, 72).
20. Gorsky (1871–1924), trained at the Imperial Ballet School in St. Petersburg, became the leading choreographer at the Bolshoi Theater in Moscow after 1900. He experimented with new forms and with dramatic realism and, in addition, reworked several classic ballets in the repertory, such as *Giselle*, *Swan Lake*, and *The Little Humpbacked Horse*.
21. *Princess Brambilla* (a "capriccio" based on the story by E. T. A. Hoffmann) and Racine's *Phèdre* were two productions of the 1921–22 season at the Moscow Kamerny (literally, Chamber) Theater. Founded in 1914 by an experimental theater collective under the directorship of Alexander Tairov, after the revolution the Kamerny became one of the most important theaters in Moscow. Like Meyerhold, Tairov was opposed to the naturalism practiced by Stanislavsky; he called for a "synthetic" theater that drew on every aspect of theatrical spectacle, including popular forms such as acrobatics, juggling, and pantomime. He rejected the literariness of most theater and substituted a coherence based on a rhythmic musicality.
22. *King Harlequin* was one of the most successful of the Kamerny Theater's productions; Tseretelli was an actor at the Kamerny.

10. Merce Cunningham's *Story* (pp. 103–109)

1. "Chronology," *Robert Rauschenberg*, exhibition catalog (Washington, D.C.: National Collection of Fine Arts, Smithsonian Institution, 1967), pp. 33–37; interview with Trisha Brown, Alex Hay, and Robert Rauschenberg, New York, 17 February 1980.
2. Interview with Barbara Dilley [Lloyd], New York, 15 November 1979.
3. Merce Cunningham, *Changes: Notes on Choreography*, ed. Frances Starr (New York: Something Else Press, 1968), p. [141]; Merce Cunningham, "Two Questions and Five Dances," *Time to Walk in Space, Dance Perspectives* 34 (Summer 1968): 52.
4. Cunningham, "Two Questions and Five Dances," p. 52; film of *Story*, produced by the Finnish Broadcasting Company, 1964.
5. Cunningham, *Changes*, pp. [138–41].
6. Ibid.; Cunningham, "Two Questions and Five Dances," pp. 52–53; interview with Dilley; film of *Story*.
7. Interview with Dilley; interview with Reid.
8. Carolyn Brown, "On Chance," *Ballet Review* 2/2 (1968): 21–22.
9. Interview with Albert Reid, New York, 16 May 1980.

10. Merce Cunningham, "Music and Dance, and Chance Operations: A Forum Discussion," with Robert Stern, Marianne Simon, Anita Page, WFCR, Amherst, Massachusetts, 16 February 1970; interview with William Davis, New York, 3 March 1980; interview with Reid; interview with Dilley; Brown, "On Chance," p. 21.
11. Interview with Dilley; interview with Brown, Hay, Rauschenberg.
12. Interview with Brown, Hay, Rauschenberg.
13. Rauschenberg in Kostelanetz, *The Theatre of Mixed Means*, p. 81.
14. Carolyn Brown, guest lecture, seminar on Merce Cunningham, New York University, New York, 10 May 1979; Cunningham, "Two Questions and Five Dances," p. 52; interview with Dilley.
15. Interview with Brown, Hay, Rauschenberg.
16. Ichiyanagi has written a description of this composition, which is published in Cunningham, *Changes*, pp. [165–66].
17. Unidentified article, *Przekroj*.
18. Interview with Brown, Hay, Rauschenberg.
19. Brown, guest lecture, Cunningham seminar.
20. I would like to thank David Vaughan, who read and commented on an earlier version of this paper, described the dance to me, and generously provided many research materials.

20. The Moscow Charleston (pp. 161–167)

1. Following Marshall and Jean Stearns, I am defining "jazz dance" here as "*American dancing that is performed to and with the rhythms of jazz* [*music*]—that is, dancing that *swings*." Jazz music and dance are intertwined and evolved out of African-American folk culture. Building on older forms of African-American music, jazz emerged in New Orleans in the late nineteenth century and became more widespread (with centers in New Orleans, Chicago, New York, and Kansas City) by 1917. In the twenties, it became an international phenomenon. Jazz music is characterized by "swing," or rhythmic propulsion, accentuated weak beats, blue tonality, open sonority, and improvisation, among other elements. I am using jazz dance, in the Stearnses's sense, to refer to African-American vernacular dancing that can be traced back much earlier than jazz music as we know it, to the earliest days of African-American slave culture. See Marshall and Jean Stearns, *Jazz Dance: The Story of American Vernacular Dance* (New York: Macmillan, 1968); Marshall W. Stearns, *The Story of Jazz* (New York: Oxford University Press, 1958); and Gunther Schuller, *early Jazz: Its Roots and Musical Development* (New York: Oxford University Press, 1968).
2. On Soviet jazz, see S. Frederick Starr, *Red and Hot: The Fate of Jazz in the Soviet Union* (New York: Oxford University Press, 1983), and Aleksei N. Batashev, *Sovetskii dzhaz* (Moscow: Muzyka, 1972).
3. However, Eubie Blake later noted that he felt *Chocolate Dandies*, of all his scores, showed most clearly the influence of Victor Herbert, one of his inspirations.
4. Ads in *Izvestiia*, February–March 1926.
5. Wooding, p. 233.

6. Allen Woll, *Black Musical Theatre: From Coontown to Dreamgirls* (Baton Rouge and London: Louisiana State University Press, 1989), p. 91.
7. *Variety*, 24 September 1924, p. 12, quoted in Woll, pp. 91–92.
8. Quoted in Gerald Bordman, *American Musical Theatre: A Chronicle* (New York: Oxford University Press, 1978), p. 391.
9. Interview with Josephine Baker by Tineri Murari, *Guardian*, 26 August 1974; quoted in Bryan Hammond and Patrick O'Connor, *Josephine Baker* (Boston: Little, Brown, 1988), pp. 11–12.
10. On *The Chocolate Dandies*, see Woll, pp. 91–92; Henry T. Sampson, *Blacks in Blackface: A Source Book on Early Black Musical Shows* (Metuchen, N.J., and London: Scarecrow Press, 1980), pp. 180–82; and Hammond and O'Connor, pp. 11–13, 23–25.
11. See Starr, pp. 31–33, and Batashev, p. 7.
12. See Starr, pp. 43–53.
13. Batashev, pp. 17, 20.
14. Vladimir I. Blum, "The Negro-Operetta," *Zhizn' Iskusstva*, no. 12, (23 March 1926): 14–15.
15. Robert Thompson has traced this pose through African-American and Haitian usage to Kongo origins, and John Szwed sees it in the African Kongo derived baton-twirling pose of American majorettes. See Robert Thompson, *The Four Moments of the Sun*, exhibition catalogue (Washington: The National Gallery of Art, 1981), pp. 122–24, 172–76. Thompson expands on this gesture in "Kongo Influences on African-American Artistic Culture," in Joseph E. Holloway, *Africanisms in American Culture* (Bloomington: University of Indiana Press, 1990), pp. 161–64, and cites John Szwed, "Introduction," Arthur Huff Fauset, *Black Gods of the Metropolis* (Philadelphia: University of Pennsylvania Press, 1971), p. vii.
16. See E. D. Uvarova, "Teatry malykh form," *Russkaia sovetskaia estrada, 1917–1929* (Moscow: Iskusstvo, 1976), pp. 327–44.
17. See Elizabeth Souritz, *Soviet Choreographers in the 1920s*, trans. Lynn Visson, ed., with an introduction and additional translation, Sally Banes (Durham, N.C.: Duke University Press, 1990).
18. N. E. Sheremetevskaya, "Tanets na estrade," *Russkaia sovetskaia estrade, 1917–1929*, pp. 249–50.
19. On the ubiquitous Charleston, see, for instance, Alfred H. Barr, "Russian Diary, 1927–28," *October* 7 (Winter 1978): 18. Barr describes a party at Herzen House as "boringly bourgeois—bad jazz, no room for dancing, ostentatious Charlestoning, good food." A graduate student in art history at Harvard, Barr became the first director of the Museum of Modern Art in New York on his return to the U.S. in 1928 and was active in introducing the American public to the Soviet avant-garde, in his exhibitions, acquisitions, writing, and lectures. In a section called "The Fast Life During the NEP," *Red and Hot*, pp. 57–62, Starr gives a good account of the new popularity of black jazz dances in Soviet culture and the debates about their role in the leisure of Soviet youth.
20. By 1928, Soviet policy had begun to shift and the bourgeois, individualist ethic of jazz was utterly denounced; by 1932 socialist realism was the only

possibility onstage. However, in terms of nightlife, after 1932, jazz dancing was reborn. Because of the new Soviet policy pronouncing African-Americans a distinct nationality with revolutionary potential, jazz was rehabilitated as the expression of the coming proletarian American revolution. A new officially underwritten jazz era, though again short-lived (it lasted until 1936), was ushered in. (On these abrupt oscillations of Soviet policy on jazz music, see Starr, pp. 79–80.)

21. Stepping High (pp. 171–183)

1. Mike Lewington, "Alcoholism in the Movies: An Overview," in Jim Cook and Mike Lewington, eds., *Images of Alcoholism* (London: British Film Institute and the Alcohol Education Centre, 1979), pp. 22–23. Also, Arnold S. Linsky, "Theories of Behavior and the Image of the Alcoholic in Popular Magazines, 1900–1966," *Public Opinion Quarterly* 30 (Winter 1970–71): 573–81.
2. Andrew Tudor, "On Alcohol and the Mystique of Media Effects," in Cook and Lewington, p. 6.
3. John Durang, *The Memoir of John Durang: American Actor, 1785–1816*, ed. Alan S. Downer (Pittsburgh: University of Pittsburgh Press, 1966). Quoted in John H. Towsen, *Clowns* (New York: Hawthorn Books, 1976), p. 108.
4. Towsen, p. 114.
5. Ibid., p. 184.
6. Program, *The Midnight Sons*, Broadway Theater, 1909. Also, clippings files on Vernon Castle, Jack Donahue, and Nick Long, Jr., in Lincoln Center Library for the Performing Arts, Billy Rose Theater Collection. Barbara N. Cohen suggested this connection.
7. Cyril Beaumont, *Complete Book of Ballets* (New York: Grosset and Dunlap, 1938), p. 795.
8. Idem, *Supplement to Complete Book of Ballets* (London: Putnam, 1942), p. 125.
9. On *A Wedding Bouquet*, see David Vaughan, *Frederick Ashton and his Ballets* (New York: Alfred Knopf, 1977), p. 150. On *The New Yorker*, see Beaumont, *Supplement*, pp. 63–64.
10. Raoul Sobel and David Francis, *Chaplin: Genesis of a Clown* (London: Quartet Books, 1977), provide an excellent discussion of Chaplin's music-hall background and the cultural context of music-hall gags and early silent films.
11. Milbourne Christopher, *The Illustrated History of Magic* (New York: Thomas Y. Crowell, 1973), p. 279.
12. Ibid.
13. Robert Sklar, *Movie-Made America: A Cultural History of American Movies* (New York: Random House, Vintage Books, 1976), pp. 253–55.
14. Tudor, pp. 11–13.
15. Barbara Deming, *Running Away from Myself: A Dream Portrait of American Drawn from the Films of the 40's* (New York: Grossman, 1969), pp. 3–71.
16. "Liminality" is a term used by anthropologist Victor Turner, which he

borrows from Arnold van Gennep's analysis of *rites de passage*. Turner describes as liminal that period during transition rites when the status of the ritual subject becomes ambiguous—when he or she is on a threshold (real or symbolic), or *limen*. The betwixt-and-between state can be brought about in a number of ways, including intoxication with alcohol or other drugs. For a discussion of liminality, see Victor Turner, *The Ritual Process* (Chicago: Aldine, 1969), and Turner, "Passages, Margins and Poverty: Religious Symbols of Communitas," *Dramas Fields, and Metaphors: Symbolic Action in Human Society* (Ithaca, N.Y., and London: Cornell University Press, paperback edition, 1975), pp. 231–71.

17. It would be interesting in this regard to analyze other dances about the difficulties of dancing, such as "I'm Putting All My Eggs in One Basket," the number about rehearsal mishaps in *Follow the Fleet*; "Let's Call the Whole Thing Off," on roller skates, in *Shall We Dance*; or "Where Did You Get That Girl," in which Astaire tests an injured knee, in *Three Little Words*.

22. The Men at John Allen's Dance House (pp. 184–199)

1. Oliver Dyer, "The Shady Side of Metropolitan Life. No. One. The Wickedest Man in New York," *Packard's Monthly* 1 (July 1868): 39.
2. Charles Townsend Harris, *Memories of Manhattan in the Sixties and Seventies* (The Derrydale Press, 1928), p. 117.
3. John H. Warren, Jr., *Thirty Years' Battle with Crime* (Poughkeepsie, New York: A. J. White, 1875; reprint, New York: Arno Press and The New York Times, 1970), p. 121.
4. Richard Henry Dana, Jr., *Two Years Before the Mast* (New York: Dodd, Mead and Company, 1946), pp. 1–2.
5. Heber Smith, "Sailors As Propagators of Disease," in *Migrants and Sailors Considered in Their Relation to the Public Health* (Cambridge: Riverside Press, 1875), p. 19.
6. A. B. Judson, "Report upon Sanitary Condition of the Waterside and Seamen," *Report of Metropolitan Board of Health*, New York, 1869, pp. 142–51, cited by Smith, pp. 17–19.
7. Smith, p. 21.
8. Robert Bennett Forbes, *An Appeal to Merchants and Ship Owners on the Subject of Seamen*. A lecture delivered at the request of the Boston Marine Society, 7 March 1854, p. 7.
9. Ibid., p. 14.
10. Ibid., p. 6.
11. Ibid., p. 15.
12. Stan Hugill, *Shanties and Sailors Songs* (New York: Praeger, 1969) pp. 159–60.
13. Ibid., pp. 190–91.
14. Walter McIntosh Merrill, ed., *Behold Me Once More: The Confessions of James Holley Garrison* (Boston: Houghton Mifflin and Cambridge: Riverside Press, 1954), p. 55.
15. Ibid., p. 43.

16. Edward Van Every, *Sins of New York* (New York: Benjamin Blom, 1972; reprint of 1930 edition), p. 288. Van Every's book is based on and quotes extensively from articles from the *Police Gazette*, but unfortunately he never gives references to individual issues.
17. George G. Foster, *New York by Gaslight: With Here and There a Streak of Sunshine* (New York: Dewitt and Davenport, 1850), pp. 75–76.
18. Liminality is a term anthropologist Victor Turner borrows from Arnold van Gennep's *Rites de Passages* and develops in his own essay, "Passages, Margins, and Poverty," in *Dramas, Fields, and Metaphors* (Ithaca, N.Y., and London: Cornell University Press, 1974; Cornell paperbacks, 1975), pp. 231–71. Turner refers to the liminal period of the ritual process as that which takes place after separation, in which the state of the ritual subject "becomes ambiguous, neither here nor there, betwixt and between all the fixed points of classification; he passes through a symbolic domain that has few or none of the attributes of his past or coming state" (p. 232). Liminality also implies "the state of outsiderhood, referring to the condition of being either permanently and by ascription set outside the structural arrangements of a given social system, or being situationally or temporarily set apart, or voluntarily setting oneself apart from the behavior of status-occupying, role-playing members of that system" (pp. 232–33). In liminal situations, time is often experienced as an "eternal now," nature is stressed over culture; rules, structures, and hierarchies are eliminated; social statuses are leveled and stripped.
19. Eric P. Russell and Mark Lovewell, *Songs of South Street—Street of Ships* (Woodbridge, N.J.: Chanteyman Press, 1977), pp. 16–17.
20. Ibid., pp. 14–15.
21. Frederick Pease Harlow, *The Making of a Sailor; or Life Aboard a Yankee Square-Rigger* (Salem, Mass.: Marine Research Society, 1928), p. 221.
22. Ibid., pp. 223–26.
23. Ibid., p. 235.
24. George Sidney Webster. *The Seamen's Friend* (New York: The American Seamen's Friend Society, 1932), p. 41.
25. Ibid., pp. 73–74.
26. *Seamen's Narratives* (New York: American Tract Society, [1860]), pp. 12–13.
27. Ibid., p. 93.
28. Ibid., pp. 252–55.
29. "The Water-street Prayer Meetings—Allen's and Hadden's," *New York Times*, 17 September 1868, p. 8.
30. Foster, p. 73.
31. Ibid., p. 75.
32. Junius Henri Browne, *The Great Metropolis: A Mirror of New York* (Hartford: American Publishing Co., 1869), p. 279.
33. Herbert Asbury, *The Gangs of New York: An Informal History of the Underworld* (New York: Garden City Publishing Company, 1927), pp. 48, 56.
34. Ibid., pp. 49–63.
35. Van Every, p. 290.

36. Foster, p. 73.
37. Warren, p. 124.
38. James D. McCabe, *Lights and Shadows of New York Life; or, the Sights and Sensations of the Great City* (Philadelphia, Cincinnati, Chicago, and St. Louis: National Publishing Company, 1872), p. 598.
39. Dyer, p. 37–38.
40. Browne, p. 278.
41. Ibid., p. 279.

25. Choreographic Methods of the Judson Dance Theater (pp. 211–226)

1. The sources for the information in this paper not otherwise footnoted will be found in the text and footnotes of my book *Democracy's Body: Judson Dance Theater 1962–1964* (Ann Arbor, Mich.: UMI Research Press, 1983). Page numbers from *Democracy's Body* are in parentheses following the quotations.
2. Yvonne Rainer, *Work 1961–73* (Halifax: The Press of the Novia Scotia College of Art and Design; New York: New York University Press, 1974), p. 7.
3. Sally Banes, "Dance," in Stanley Trachtenberg, ed., *The Postmodern Moment: A Handbook of Contemporary Innovation in the Arts* (Westport, Conn., and London: Greenwood Press, 1985), pp. 81–100.
4. A program of Judson reconstructions, curated by Wendy Perron and Cynthia Hedstrom, was produced at St. Mark's Church Danspace in April 1982, as part of the Bennington College Judson Project. The reconstructions were recorded on videotape by the Lincoln Center Library Dance Research Collection and may be viewed there.

26. Vital Signs (pp. 227–239)

1. Steve Paxton with Liza Béar, "Like the Famous Tree . . . ," *Avalanche* 11 (Summer 1975): 26.
2. Marcel Mauss, "Techniques of the Body," *Economy and Society* 2 (Feb. 1973): 70–88; Gordon Hewes, "The Anthropology of Posture," *Scientific American* 196 (Feb. 1957): 123–33, and "World Distribution of Certain Postural Habits," *American Anthropologist* 57 (April 1955): 231–44.
3. See Noël Carroll and Sally Banes, "Working and Dancing," ch. 2, for a discussion of the kind of movements used in postmodern dance and their theoretical relationship to current practices in the visual arts.
4. See Sally Banes, *Democracy's Body: Judson Dance Theater 1962–1964* (Ann Arbor: UMI Research Press, 1983), and *Terpsichore in Sneakers: Post-Modern Dance* (Boston: Houghton Mifflin, 1980); second ed. Middletown, Conn.: Wesleyan University Press, 1987).
5. Petr Bogatyrev, *The Functions of Folk Costume in Moravian Slovakia*, Approaches to Semiotics No. 5 (The Hague and Paris: Mouton, 1971).
6. I have put quotation marks around the word "language" here as a kind of shorthand because, although I do not believe that dance is a language, it is useful here to assume for the moment that it functions like one. To

expound upon this very complicated and important issue is beyond the scope of this essay.

7. Petr Bogatyrev, "Semiotics in the Folk Theater," in L. Matejka and I. R. Titunik, eds., *Semiotics of Arts* (Cambridge, Mass.: MIT Press, 1976), 33, n. 2.
8. For descriptions of all these dances, see Banes (1980, 1983) and the chronology of Paxton and Béar (1975).
9. See Noël Carroll, "Expression and Post-Modern Dance," in G. Fancher and G. Myers, eds., *Philosophical Essays on Dance* (New York: Dance Horizons, 1981), for a discussion of the expressiveness of "lack of expression."

33. Happily Ever After? (pp. 280–290)

1. By the postmodern choreographers of the 1960s and 1970s, I mean such people as Simone Forti, Yvonne Rainer, Steve Paxton, Trisha Brown, David Gordon, Lucinda Childs, et al. For an account of the postmodern choreographers work in the sixties and seventies, see Sally Banes, *Terpsichore in Sneakers: Post-Modern Dance* (Boston: Houghton Mifflin, 1980; reprint ed., Middletown, Conn.: Wesleyan University Press, 1987). In the new introduction to the reprint edition, I discuss the problem of nomenclature for the generations of avant-garde dance, since the concerns of the "moderns" were never really modernist, while those of the "postmoderns" very often were, leaving us without a proper label for the most recent group (whose work I am discussing in part here), who could easily be grouped in terms of themes and styles with "postmodernists" in other art forms.

   On the new narrative, see Marcia Pally, "The Rediscovery of Narrative: Dance in the 1980s," New Wave Festival Catalog (Brooklyn: Brooklyn Academy of Music, 1984): 11–15, for a brief but suggestive study.

   On the new issues cropping up in eighties dance generally, see Sally Banes, "New Dance New York," Festival International de Nouvelle Danse Catalog (Montreal: Festival International de Nouvelle Danse, 1985); Noël Carroll, "The Return of the Repressed: The Re-emergence of Expression in Contemporary American Dance," *Dance Theatre Journal* 2/1 (1984): 16–19, 27; and Deborah Jowitt, "The Return of Drama: New Developments in American Dance," *Dance Theatre Journal* 2/2 (1984): 28–31.
2. I am not claiming here that these generational repudiations and rebuttals necessarily happen in a premeditated, theoretically elaborated, or even conscious way, though in some cases (e.g., the choreography and writing of Yvonne Rainer) they certainly have.
3. Of course, even a dance putatively shorn of expressive meaning still says something—that is, its very "inexpressivity" is an expression of an idea. See Noël Carroll, "Post-Modern Dance and Expression," in Gordon Fancher and Gerald Myers, ed., *Philosophical Essays in Dance* (Brooklyn: Dance Horizons, 1981), pp. 95–104.
4. The fate of the fairytale in the ballet, as opposed to modern or postmodern dance, is of course a quite different, and more continuous story; it is not my purpose to explicate it here. However, it should be noted that there is a

conspicuous return of the fairytale to the ballet stage as well. In spring 1987, the Boston Ballet added three Hans Christian Andersen tales to their repertory; American Ballet Theater opened Kenneth MacMillan's new *Sleeping Beauty*, and both Rudolph Nureyev's and Maguy Marin's *Cinderellas* played in New York.

5. Quoted in Max Lüthi, in *The European Folktale: Form and Nature* (1947; English translation, Bloomington: Indiana University Press, 1986), p. 92.
6. See Bruno Bettelheim, *The Uses of Enchantment: The Meaning and Importance of Fairy Tales* (New York: Alfred A. Knopf, 1976).
7. Roger Abrahams suggests that "we are in a post-modern or at least post-structuralist period in folkloristics, . . . insofar as we seek to add both historical and ethnographic specificity to the way in which we present our collections." He cites Henry Glassie, *Passing the Time in Ballymenone* (Philadelphia: University of Pennsylvania Press, 1982); Alessandro Falassi, *Folklore by the Fireside* (Austin: University of Texas Press, 1980); and Elizabeth Mathias and Richard Raspa, *Italian Folktales in America* (Detroit: Wayne State University Press) as examples of folklore studies that "show that even fairytales must have specific audiences who are able to relate the particulars of narrated experience to the ways in which lives are lived within a specific group, even by specific individuals" (personal communication, May 1987).
8. I am distinguishing here between the larger category of the folktale and the subcategory of folk narrative known in English as the fairytale. Also called the *Márchen*, magic tale, or wondertale, the fairytale has come down to us primarily as a literary form, though based on oral texts, that arose in seventeenth-century Europe; it is a literary genre, even though (as in the case of the Grimm brothers) the writers may claim to be simply collectors of oral texts. See Linda Dégh, "Folk Narrative," in Richard M. Dorson, ed., *Folklore and Folklife* (Chicago: University of Chicago Press, 1972), 53–83; Antti Aarne and Stith Thompson, *The Types of the Folk-Tale: A Classification and Bibliography* (Helsinki: Folklore Fellows Communications 184, 1961); and William Bascom, "The Forms of Folklore: Prose Narratives," *Journal of American Folklore* 78 (1965): 3–20. Jack Zipes, in *Breaking the Magic Spell: Radical Theories of Folk & Fairy Tales* (Austin: University of Texas Press, 1979; reprint ed. New York: Methuen, 1984), makes the distinction between the folktale as "part of a *pre-capitalist people's oral tradition*" and the fairytale as "of *bourgeois coinage* . . . a new literary form" (p. 27). One can also make distinctions between the fairytale's traffic with the supernatural and other forms of the folktale such as the tall tale and the legend.
9. Israel Nestyev, *Sergei Prokofiev: His Musical Life*, trans. Rose Prokofieva, with an introduction by Sergei Eisenstein (New York: Alfred A. Knopf, 1946), p. 131.
10. Cyril W. Beaumont, *Supplement to Complete Book of Ballets* (London: C. W. Beaumont, 1942), p. 159.
11. See Iona and Peter Opie, *The Classic Fairy Tales* (Oxford: Oxford University Press, 1974), and Jack Zipes, *Fairy Tales and the Art of Subversion* (New

York: Wildman Press, 1983), especially the chapter entitled "Setting Standards for Civilization through Fairy Tales."

12. The exhibition, organized by Curt Belshe, Ana Busto, Sarah Drury, Hilary Kliros, Lise Prown, and Steven Schiff, included work by twenty-nine artists, among them Vito Acconci, Ericka Beckman, Mary Kelly, and Perry Hoberman. A catalog for the exhibition is available, and these essays were later supplemented by additional essays and photographs of works in the exhibition, in a special issue of *New Observations* 45 (1987), available from New Observations Ltd., 142 Greene St., New York, N.Y. 10012. The quote here is from the introduction, by the organizers of the exhibition, to the catalog, p. 4, and was reprinted in *New Observations*, p. 2.
13. Related to this revaluing of prerealist conventions by modernists is David Gordon's comment on a section of his *The Matter* (*Plus and Minus*) that quotes The Entrance of the Shades from Petipa's ballet *La Bayadère*. Above all, he praises the repetitive quality of all those shades' entries (*Beyond the Mainstream*, "Dance in America," 1979).
14. Pace Harold Rosenberg, who termed the modernist avant-garde's obsession *The Tradition of the New* (New York: Horizon, 1959). Alluding to Rosenberg, I titled a column about the new postmodern interest in theater traditions (from Shakespeare to vaudeville) "The Tradition of the Old" (*Village Voice*, 27 April 1982).
15. Linda Dégh, "Folk Narrative," p. 63.
16. I discuss the phenomenon of postmodern ballet in ch. 34.
17. Andrew Lang, *The Blue Fairy Book*, revised edition (Middlesex: Kestrel, 1975), p. 354. Quoted in Betsy Hearne, "*Beauty and the Beast*: The Survival of a Story," *New Observations* 45 (1987): 27. Jakob and Wilhelm Grimm, *Grimms Tales for Young and Old*, trans. Ralph Manheim (Garden City, New York: Anchor Press/Doubleday, 1977), pp. 1–2. Of course, the very notion of children's culture is itself a recent invention; hence fairytales, before the nineteenth century, were not considered part of children's domain.
18. Noël Carroll, "The Return of the Repressed," pp. 18, 27.
19. I would like to thank Roger Abrahams, Joan Acocella, Noël Carroll, and John Szwed for their helpful discussions in the writing of this essay.

36. Terpsichore in Sneakers, etc. (pp. 301–310)

1. Jean-François Lyotard, *The Postmodern Condition: A Report on Knowledge* (Minneapolis: University of Minnesota Press, 1984).
2. Charles Jencks, *What is Post-Modernism?* (London: Academy Editions; New York: St. Martin's Press, 1986).
3. See John Barth, "The Literature of Replenishment, Postmodernist Fiction," *The Atlantic* (January 1980): 65–71; Umberto Eco, "Postmodernism, Irony, the Enjoyable," *Postscript to The Name of the Rose* (New York and London: Harcourt Brace Jovanovich, 1984); Charles Newman, *The Post-Modern Aura: The Act of Fiction in an Age of Inflation* (Evanston, Ill.: Northwestern University Press, 1985); Fredric Jameson, "Postmodernism, or The Cultural Logic of Late Capitalism," *New Left Review* 146 (July–

August 1984): 53–92; the various essays in Hal Foster, ed., *The Anti-Aesthetic: Essays on Postmodern Culture* (Port Townsend, Wash.: Bay Press, 1983); Elinor Fuchs, "The Death of Character," *Theater Communications* 5/3 (March 1983). See also Noël Carroll, "Illusions of Postmodernism," *Raritan* 7/2 (Fall 1987): 143–55 for criticisms of some of these positions.

4. See Sally Banes, introduction to the Wesleyan paperback edition, *Terpsichore in Sneakers: Post-Modern Dance* (Middletown, Conn.: Wesleyan University Press, 1987).
5. Michael Kirby, introduction to the Post-Modern Dance Issue, *The Drama Review* 19 (T-65; March 1975).
6. See, for instance, Clement Greenberg, "The New Sculpture," originally published 1948, revised in 1958, and reprinted in Greenberg, *Art and Culture* (Boston: Beacon Press, 1961), pp. 139–45.
7. In the introduction to the Wesleyan paperback edition of *Terpsichore in Sneakers.*
8. I saw a reconstruction of this dance, directed by Rainer, at Bennington College, Bennington, Vermont, 18 April 1980.
9. Mikhail Bakhtin, *Rabelais and His World*, trans. Helene Iswolsky (Cambridge, Mass.: MIT Press, 1968; reprint edition Bloomington, Ind.: Indiana University Press, 1984).
10. See Robert Morris, "Notes on Dance," *The Drama Review* 10/2 (T-30; Winter 1965): 179–86.
11. Yvonne Rainer, "A Quasi Survey of Some 'Minimalist' Tendencies in the Quantitatively Minimal Dance Activity Midst the Plethora, or an Analysis of *Trio A*," first published in Gregory Battcock, ed., *Minimal Art* (New York: E. P. Dutton, 1968), pp. 263–73. It also appears in Yvonne Rainer, *Work 1961–73* (Halifax, Nova Scotia: The Press of The Nova Scotia College of Art and Design; New York: New York University Press, 1974), pp. 63–69.
12. Rainer, "A Quasi Survey," p. 68.
13. In the film *Retracing Steps: American Dance since Postmodernism*, directed by Michael Blackwood, 1988.

37. Dancing [with . . .] the Music (pp. 310–326)

1. Roland John Wiley, *Tchaikovsky's Ballets* (New York: Oxford University Press, 1985), passim.
2. See David Vaughan, "Cunningham, Cage, and Joyce: 'this longawaited messaigh of roaratorios,'" *Choreography and Dance* 1/4 (1992): 79–89.
3. Roger Copeland, "A Community of Originals: Models of Avant-Garde Collaboration," *Next Wave Festival* catalog (Brooklyn Academy of Music, 1983), pp. 10, 12.
4. I will be looking only at American dance here. This is not meant to imply that interesting and important developments have not taken place outside the American situation. I have also concentrated on the New York dance world, where most of the activity is concentrated and where non-New York choreographers showcase their work.
5. Louis Horst and Carroll Russell, *Modern Dance Forms in Relation to the Other Modern Arts* (San Francisco: Impulse Publications, 1961), pp. 81–82.

6. Ibid., p. 140.
7. For descriptions of these and other Judson Dance Theater works, see Sally Banes, *Democracy's Body: Judson Dance Theater 1962–1964* (Ann Arbor, Mich.: UMI Research Press, 1983; reprint ed. Durham, N.C.: Duke University Press, 1993).
8. Simone Forti, *Handbook in Motion* (Halifax: Press of the Nova Scotia College of Art and Design; New York: New York University Press, 1974).
9. See, for instance, the dance reviews in *Artforum*; Yvonne Rainer, "A Quasi Survey of Some 'Minimalist' Tendencies in the Quantitatively Minimal Dance Activity Midst the Plethora, or an Analysis of *Trio A*," in Gregory Battcock, ed., *Minimal Art* (New York: E. P. Dutton, 1968), pp. 263–73; Kenneth King, "Toward a Trans-Literal and Trans-Technical Dance Theater," in Gregory Battcock, ed., *The New Art* (New York: E. P. Dutton, 1973), pp. 119–26.
10. Rainer, "A Quasi Survey," p. 263.
11. Forti; for descriptions of these and other dances, see Sally Banes, *Terpsichore in Sneakers: Post-Modern Dance* (Boston: Houghton Mifflin, 1980; second ed. Middletown, Conn.: Wesleyan University Press, 1987).
12. Yvonne Rainer, *Work 1961–73* (Halifax: Press of the Nova Scotia College of Art and Design; New York: New York University Press, 1974), pp. 111–12.
13. For descriptions of works from the metaphoric phases of postmodern dance, see Banes, *Terpsichore in Sneakers*. For information on Laura Dean, see Noël Carroll, "Introducing Laura Dean's Choreography," *Dance and Dancers* (May 1983).
14. See Richard Colton's account of this aspect of Tharp's choreographic process in John Mueller and Don McDonagh, "Making Musical Dance," *Ballet Review* 13/4 (1986): 23–44.
15. Charles Jencks, *The Language of Post-Modern Architecture* (New York: Rizzoli, 1977); Charles Jencks, *What Is Post-Modernism?* (London: Academy Editions; New York: St. Martin's Press, 1987).
16. On Brown's collaborative process for *Set and Reset*, and on several other postmodern collaborations of the early eighties, see Roselee Goldberg, "Dance from the Music: Performance in the Age of Communications," *Next Wave Festival* catalog (Brooklyn Academy of Music, 1983), pp. 17–22.
17. Jon Pareles, "Reprise for 'Secret Pastures,' a Populist Score," *New York Times*, 11 January 1985.
18. Sally Banes, " 'Drive, She Said: The Dance of Molissa Fenley," ch. 29.
19. Noël Carroll notes this in regard to baroque dance, in "The Return of the Repressed: The Re-Emergence of Expression in Contemporary American Dance," *Dance Theatre Journal* 2/1.
20. Mueller and McDonagh, pp. 40–41.
21. On Mark Morris, see Joan Acocella, "Morris Dances," *Art in America* (October 1988): 178–82.
22. Michael Blackwood, *Retracing Steps: American Dance Since Postmodernism*, 16mm film (New York: Blackwood Productions, 1988).

38. La Onda Próxima (pp. 327—333)

1. Xavier X. Totti, "Latinos in New York," *The Portable Lower East Side* 1/1 & 2 (1988): 7.
2. Ibid., pp. 1—8.
3. Joan Acocella, "Loisaida Story," *7 Days*, November 9, 1988, p. 62.

Index

Page numbers for illustrations are in boldface.

Abrahams, Roger, 381n7
abstract dance, 4–5, 63, 64, 68, 295, 298, 305, 312, 333
Accompaniment for La Monte's "2 sounds" and La Monte's "2 sounds" (Forti and Young), 315
Accumulation (Brown), 15–16, 281
Accumulation Pieces (Brown), 307, 317
Acocella, Joan, 38, 329
acrobatics and gymnastics, 60, 97, 101, 172, 364n49; in breakdancing, 122, 124, 125, 128, 134, 138, 143, 145, 151, 157
aerial dance, 88, 279
aesthetic evaluation, 42
African-American: composers, 69, 365n57; dance style, 63, 64, 65–67; folklore, 57, 79, influence on breakdancing, 126, 128, 129, 132, 136, 149–50
Afternoon (Paxton), 221, 238
"Against Interpretation" (Sontag), 21, 29
agit-prop, 54, 95–96, 165, 201, 358n9
Agon (Balanchine), 64, 67
Ahearn, Charles, 128, 131, 139
Ailey, Alvin, Dance Theater, 61, 327, 363n35
alcoholism, 171–72
Aldrich, Elizabeth, 31–32, 47
Alenikoff, Frances, 275
Alexopoulos, Helene, **54**
Alf, Fe, 200
Alfven, Hugo, 74
Allard, Lynne, **265**, 266
allegory, 92, 95
Allegro, il Penseroso ed il Moderato, L' (Morris), 38
Allen, Barbara, 332, 335
Allen, John, dance house, 184, 194, 195, 196, 197–99
Allen, Robert C., 358n15
Allix, G., 86
Alma Mater (Balanchine), 62
Alonso, Alicia, 39–40
Alston, Richard, 293, 300
Alvarez, Albert, 21
American Ballet Theatre, 92, 285, 291, 297, 309, 322, 326, 380n4
American Seamen's Friend Society, 194
analytic postmodern dance, 217, 226, 254, 255, 282, 295–96, 303, 307, 308, 309, 312–13, 318, 319–20, 321
Andersen, Hans Christian, 75, 286, 288, 380n4
Anderson, Jack, 27–28
Anderson, Laurie, 254, 294, 308, 320, 321, 323, 334
Andres, Jo, 335
Angelos, Maureen, **331**
Angolan dance, 150
animal imitation dances, 134
animal movements, 255, 335
"Anthropologist Looks at Ballet as a Form of Ethnic Dance, An" (Kealiinohomoku), 23

Index

anthropology, 22
Anthropology as Cultural Critique (Marcus and Fischer), 18
Antic Meet (Cunningham), 5
anti-illusionism, 12, 13, 14, 15, 29, 63, 84, 253, 268, 307
Anti-War Cycle (Sokolow), 202
Apollo (Balanchine), 64, 65
Appiah, Kwame Anthony, 360n11
Après-midi d'un faune, L' (Nijinsky), **93**–94, 97
Aragon, Louis, 90
Archer, Kenneth, 324
Archives Internationales de la Danse (Paris), 81
Arden Court (Taylor), 26–27
Arevalo, Carlos, 286
Ari, Carina, 72, 74, 81
Arizona (Morris), 218, 223
Armitage, Karole, **293**, 297–300, 301, 308, 309, 323, 325, 334, 336; *Drastic-Classicism*, 254–55, 291, 298, 321; *The Elizabethan Phrasing of the Late Albert Ayler*, 298, 322; *The Mollino Room*, 291–92, 300, 322; *The Watteau Duets*, 298, 321–22
Armour, Toby, 221
arms and hands, use of, 66, 260–62, 264
Armstrong, Tim, 48–49
Arnold, Becky, 256
Artaud, Antonin, 9, 354n21
Artists Space exhibition, 288
art-rock, 322, 323
Ashbury, Herbert, 196
Ashley, Robert, 254, 320, 334
Ashton, Frederick, 173, 362n28
Astaire, Fred, 61, 171, 174–83, **175**
Astor, Patty, 131
Atlas, Charles, 115n, 254, 294
Attenberg, Kurt, 75
Auric, George, 78
Austin, Debra, 362n28
autobiography, 335
automatism, 216, 287
avant-garde, 12, 230, 256, 267, 319, 320, 327; and Balanchine, 57, 64, 65; and ballet, 64, 65, 70, 73, 75, 76, 291–92, 293–94, 295; and breakdancing, 131, 133, 134; and Jill Johnston, 3, 8; and Judson Dance Theater, 207, 208, 211, 217; and multimedia spectacle, 294, 297, 308, 309; and narrative, 280, 281–82, 304; and ordinary body movements, 253–54, 267, 296; and pop culture, 133, 305, 309, 321, 323–24, 336; and post-modernism, 309–10; in the Soviet Union, 57, 96, 167, 375n19; and theatricality, 252, 253, 300, 333, 334; and the Workers' Dance League, 199, 200
Aviles, Arthur, 329
Ayler, Albert and Don, 299

B-Boys. *See* Breakdancing
Babes in Arms (Rogers and Hart), 60
Bahr, Donald, 21
Bailey, Pearl, 61
Baker, Josephine, 58, 60, 81, 163–64, 362n29
Baker, Rob, 39–40
Bakhtin, Mikhail, 306
Balanchine, George, 53–69, 110, 291, 293, 297–98, 309, 319, 325; abstract ballets, 63, 64, 68; and African-American/Latin American dance themes, 62–63; *Agon*, 64, 67; *Apollo*, 64, 65; and the avant-garde, 57, 64, 65; and *Babes in Arms*' dream ballet "Peter's Journey," 60; and Baker, Josephine, 58, 60; and the black community, 61–62; and Bradley, Buddy, 59, 61; and *Cabin in the Sky* collaboration with Dunham, 59, 61, 64–65, 363n34; *Concerto Barocco*, 64–65, 364n43; and Cunningham, Merce, 110, 253; and the Dance Theater of Harlem, 62, 64, 69; and Diaghilev's Ballets Russes, 58; and Duke, Vernon, 58–59; *The Four Temperaments*, 40, **54**, 63, 65–67, 360n10,

364n48; and *The Goldwyn Follies'* Romeo and Juliet ballet, 60–61; Goleizovsky's influence on, 94, 97; and Graham, Martha, collaboration on *Episodes*, 292; and Harper, Herbert, 60, 61; and *House of Flowers*, 61, 363n35; *Jewels*, 53–54, 55, 359n8; and Kirstein, Lincoln, 59–60; *Modern Jazz: Variants*, 61, 62–63, 67–68, 362n28; and modernism, 54–55, 63, 65, 69, 253; and musicals, 61; neo-classical technique, 53, 63–64; and racial integration of ballet, 60, 62, 63, 69, 363n38; in Russia, 57; and the School of American Ballet, 59, 366n60; *Slaughter on Tenth Avenue*, 59, 60, 68; as Snowball in *The Triumph of Neptune*, 58, 66, 172–73, 362n23; and *Uncle Tom's Cabin* plans, 59–60; and variety shows, 59
"Balanchine Woman: Of Hummingbirds and Channel Swimmers, The" (Daly), 40
Ballade (Robbins), 362n28
ballet: and the avant-garde, 64, 65, 70, 73, 75, 76, 291–92, 293–94, 295; drunk scenes in, 172–73; and the fairytale, 281–90, 380n4; pantomime in, 75, 256, 288; and rock, 135; social dances in, 311, 324, 325; solos, 349
ballet américain, 58, 73, 79
Ballet Espagnol (Sert), 87
Ballet Hispanico, 327
Ballet Nacional de Cuba, 39–40
ballet nègre, 57, 58
Ballet Rambert, 285, 293, 297, 300
Ballet West, 293
Ballets 1933, Les, 59
Ballets Russes, 48, 57, 58, 70, 73, 75, 82, 89, 91
Ballets Suédois, 57, 70–81
ballroom dancing, 31–32, 44, 47, 56, 324, 336
Banda dance, 61
Bank, Lyubov, 95
Banks, Jennifer, 28
Barnes, Clive, 26–27, 53, 363n38
baroque dance, 324, 384n19
Barr, Alfred H., 375n19
Barr, Burt, 29–30
Barth, John, 302
Barthes, Roland, 309
Baryshnikov, Mikhail, 291, 292, 293, 297, 309
Barzel, Ann, 258
Basil, Toni, 133–35, 151–52
Bausch, Pina, 287
Bayadère, La (Petipa), 320, 382n13
Bayou (Balanchine), 62
Bazin, André, 112
Beals, Jennifer, 48, 138
Beardsley, Monroe C., 10–16, 42, 354n1, 357n20
Beat Street (film), 131, 132, 140, 143, 145, 156, 158
Beatty, Talley, 69, 362n28
Beau Danube, Le (Massine), 85, 91
Beaumont, Cyril, 58, 66, 91, 285
Beaumont, Étienne de, 82–83, 85, 87, 89, 91
Becker, M.J., 279
Beckman, Ericka, 288
Beehive (Self and Moore), 290, 338
Beer, Boris, 95
Behrman, David, 115
Bell, Arthur, 362n28
Bells, The (Rainer), 7, 215
Bengis, Ingrid, 276
Bennington College, 208, 275, 276
Benois, Alexandre, 372n16
Berenson, Paulus, 212
Berners, Lord, 58
Berry, Fred, 151–52
Bhartonn, Edward, 209, 210
Bigot, Eugene, 74–75
Bissell, Patrick, 33–34
Bitter Tongue (Zollar), 344
Black and White (Segal), 202
black choreographers, 308, 327, 334
Black Ritual (de Mille), 68
black women dancers, 159–61
Blackface (Christensen), 62, 362n28

Blair, Shareen, 104
Blake, Eubie, 162–63, 374n3
Blauvelt Mountain (Jones and Zane), 322
Blecher, Miriam, 201
Blinx, Andy, 323
Blue Fairy Book, The (Lang), 289–90
Blue Skies (film), 171, 177, 178, 181–83
Bluebeard (Bausch), 287
Blum, Vladimir, 165–66
body culture, 279, 296, 336
Body Rock (film), 132
Boca Raton (Fenley), 264
Boeuf sur le toit, Le (Cocteau/Milhaud), 57, 79
Bogatyrev, Petr, 238
Boîte à Joujoux, La (Börlin), 73, 74
Bolger, Ray, 60
Bolm, Adolph, 285
Bolshoi Theater, 92, 93, 95, 96–97, 99
Bonnard, Pierre, 73
Boothe, Power, 254
Bordo, Susan, 46, 358n9/10
Boris, Ruthanna, 62, 361n14
Börlin, Jean, 70, 71–81; *La Création du monde*, 57–58, 79–80; *El Greco*, 73, 74; *L'Homme et son Désir*, 76–77; *Maison de fous*, 73, 74; *Les Mariés de la Tour Eiffel*, 77–79; *Offerlunden*, 75; *Relâche*, 80–81; *Le Tombeau de Couperin*, 73, 74; *Les Vierges Folles*, 73, 75; *Within the Quota*, 57, 58, 73, 79
Bosho, 323
Boston, the, 56, 164
Boston Ballet, 292, 293, 294, 380n14
Boston shag, the, 65
Boucher, Maurice, 89, 90–91
Bound (Paxton), 238–39
Bournonville technique, 71
Boutique Fantasque, La (Massine), 74
Bowden, Sally, 269
Bowery, Leigh, 300
Boyce, Johanna, 258, 279, 290, 294, 308, 324, 334, 335
Bradley, Buddy, 59, 61, 362n25/30
Braithwaite, Fred, 128, 139, 149
Braque, Georges, 85, 86, 91
Brazilian folkdances, 62, 128, 149–50
Bread to the Bone series (Knitting Factory), 347
Breakdance/You Can Do It! (videotape), 142
breakdancing, 23, 44, 48, 61, 121–58, **123**, **130**, 336; and acrobatics, 122, 124, 125, 128, 134, 138, 143, 145, 146, 151, 157; in advertising, 138, 143, 156–57; and African-American folkdancing, 126, 128, 129, 132, 136, 149–50; the Baby, 121, 124; and "break"/"breakdown," 122, 129, 149; the Bus Stop, 136; claiming territory and status, 122, 150–51, 155, 158; clubs, 131, 132, 133–34, 151, 153–56, 157; code of ethics, 148, 158; competitive element, changes in, 126, 131, 135, 138, 143, 144, 145, 151, 152, 157–58; costume, 128, 129, 132, 134–35, 136, 138, 148, 158; crew/crew leader, 148; the Egyptian, 152; the elbow walk, 124, 147; and electric boogie, 131, 138, 140, 141, 143, 151, 152, 157; exploration of body states, 122, 147; and fashion design, 156, 157; films and videotapes, 44, 48, 61, 128, 130, 131, 132, 138–42, 143, 145, 146, 149, 151, 152, 156, 157, 158; the float, 151, 157; the Football, 134; format, 122, 123–24, 146–47; the freeze, 124, 125, 128, 138, 146, 147–48, 150, 151, 157; the Funky Chicken, 134; girls and, 132, 135, 148; and graffiti, 122–57 *passim*; the Graffiti Rock show, 128, 129, 145–46; the Helicopter, 121, 124, 146; how-to books and videos, 137, 140–42, 157; the Hustle, 136; the King Tut, 151, 152, 157; locking, 134–35, 151–52, 157; and the martial arts, 122, 127, 128, 131, 132, 141, 147, 149, 158; and media hype, 126, 129–32, 138, 143–44, 145–46, 151, 156, 157, 158; the moon-

walk, 138, 140, 141, 142, 152; at the Olympics, 138, 143; on point, 124, 146; "opening up the circle," 130, 151, 157; pantomime in, 124, 128, 136, 138, 140, 143, 147, 148, 152; and pop culture, 128, 132, 150, 157, 158; popping, 140, 141, 151, 152, 157; professionalization of, 131, 144, 151, 157; and rapping, 122–56 *passim*; and robotics, 131, 152; as ritual combat, 122, 123, 124, 128, 138, 145, 147; and roller disco, 127, 130, 143, 151, 157; the rope pull, 41; and "scratching" records, 126, 128, 129, 131, 150, 156; spectator interaction, 132, 158; the Spider walk, 139; the swipe, 121, 146; ticking, 151, 157; the Tidal Wave, 136; unison movement, 134, 135, 136, 147, 157; and uprock, 124, 141, 143, 148; the W, 125, 147; at the Wheels of Steel hiphop nights, 151, 153–56
Breakdancing (Mr. Fresh and the Supreme Rockers), 158
Breakin' (film), 131, 132, 139–40, 142, 143, 145, 152, 156, 158
Breakin' in the USA (videotape), 142
Breaking Bett (Steve Durham), 140
Breaking with the Mighty Poppalots (videotape), 140–41
Breakmasters, 124, 125, 128, 147
Breaux, David "Mr. Fantastik," 142
Breton, André, 90
Bridgeman, Reginald, 82
Brisbane, Betty, 159
Brockway, Merrill, 364n48
Bromberg, Craig, 323
Brown, Carolyn, 104, 105, 106, 108, 115, 116, 117, 220
Brown, David, 264
Brown, Louise (Li'l Bits), 159
Brown, Trisha, 6, 7, 253, 256, 257, 269, 276, 278, 294, 303, 315, 320, 334, 344, 348; *Accumulation*, 15–16, 281; Accumulation Pieces, 307, 317; Equipment Pieces, 12, 354n4; *Glacial Decoy*, 254, 320; and the Judson Dance Theater, 208, 212, 213, 222, 295; *Set and Reset*, 294, 308, 320, 321, 384n16; *Son of Gone Fishin*, 254, 320
Browne, Junius, 196
Buchwald, Nathaniel, 203
Buckley, Timothy, 334, 350–52
Burt, Ramsay, 365n56

Cabin in the Sky (Duke and Root), 59, 61
Caesar and Cleopatra (Shaw), 57
Café Society (Littlefield), 173
Cage, John, 3, 108, 217, 219, 278, 281, 302; *Cartridge Music*, 314; Cunningham-Cage model of discrete dance and music channels, 110, 285, 295, 312, 313, 322; influence of, 212, 213, 214, 314, 316, 352; and Zen philosophy, 112, 113
cakewalk, the, 56, 58, 66, 67, 164
Cakewalk (Boris), 361n14
Calico Mingling (Childs), 307, 317
Campbell, Donald (Campbellock), 134
Campbellock, Greg, Jr., 134
Candela (Tropicana/Troyano/Parnes), **331**–332
Canfield (Cunningham), 111
Canudo, Riciotto, 73
capoeira, 128, 149–50
Cardini, 173–74
Caribbean folkdances and ritual, 61, 149, 150, 167
Carlin, John, 192
Carnation (Childs), 210, 223, 306
Carroll, Diahann, 61
Carroll, Noël, 34–35, 80, 290, 355n7, 356n10, 384n19
Carruthers, Tony, 208
Carter, Angela, 288
Casella, Alfredo, 80
cassé-ko, 129, 149
Castle, Irene, 361n17
Castle, Vernon, 172, 361n17
Cats, The (Fenley), 262
causality, absence of, 111–12

Caution to the Wind (Van Tieghem), 324–25
Cendrars, Blaise, 57, 79
Certain Distilling Processes (Corner), 315
Chacon (Monk and Chong), 240–52, **250**
Chaikin, Joseph, 343
Chalfant, Henry, 126, 128, 130, 131, 145, 151, 157
chance techniques, 103, 109, 111, 210–22 *passim*, 278, 305, 345
Chant du rossignol, Le (Balanchine), 58
Chaplin, Charlie, 173
Charles B. Cochran's 1931 Revue, 59
Charleston, the, 53, 63, 65; in breakdancing, 124, 128, 147, 149, 150, 158; in the Soviet Union, 163–64, 166, 167
Charlip, Remy, 208, 209, 212, 215
Chatham, Rhys, 254, 291, 298, 321, 325
Chatte, La (Balanchine), 58
Chief Rocker Busy Bee, 139
children's culture, 290
Childs, Lucinda, 7, 208, 225, 253, 292, 295, 303, 309, 314–15, 321, 326, 334, 336; *Calico Mingling*, 307, 317; *Carnation*, 210, 223, 306; *Dance*, 32, 254, 294, 308, 320; and Fenley, Molissa, compared, 263–64; and Glass' *Einstein on the Beach*, 294, 320
Chirico, Giorgio de, 80
Chocolate Dandies, The (Sissle and Blake), 162–64, 274n3
Chocolate Kiddies, The, 161, 162–67
choice, 103, 214–15, 224
Chong, Ping, 240–52, **250**
Chopiniana (Folkine/Börlin), 73–74
choreographers: black, 308, 327, 334; Latina, 327–33; "new dance," 296; pattern, 263, 307, 317; solo, 348–52
choreographic methods, alternative, 211–26, 308; chance, 210–22 *passim*; choice, 214–15, 224; collage, 215, 217, 222; control, 213, 214, 217, 219, 224; games, 215, 219, 222, 278; improvisation, 219, 221, 224, 278, 341; indeterminacy, 212, 219; media mixing, 224–25; minimalism, 210, 215, 217; number sequences, 212–13; object manipulation, 218, 222–23; repetition, 214, 215, 222; scores, use of, 212, 213, 215, 217–18, 314; space constraints, use of, 220–21; task dances, 218, 222, 223; time structures, 212, 225; verbal analysis, 213–14
Choreometrics project, 364n44
Chout (Larionov), 70
Christensen, Lew, 62, 362n28
Chuma, Yoshiko, 255, 308, 323
Cinderella (Beckman), 288
Cinderella (Marin), 380n4
Cinderella (Nureyev), 380n4
Circle Dances (Hay), 261
circus acts, 94, 99–100, 172
civil rights movement, 28, 54
Clair, René, 80
Clarinade (Balanchine), 63
Clark, Michael, 293–94, 297, **299**, 300–301
Clements, Carol, 335
Cléopâtre (Fokine), 71
clown acts, 172
Cocteau, Jean, 57, 73, 82, 91; *Les Mariés de la Tour Eiffel*, 77–79; *Romeo et Juliette*, 87–89
cognitive evaluation, 41–42
Colin, Paul, 166
Collaer, Paul, 86, 91
collage techniques, 215, 217, 222, 270, 284, 290, 315–16, 332, 337
Comanche, 160
"combine-dance," 6, 215
Common Ground loft, 128, 145
Communist party, 200, 203
Concerto Barocco (Balanchine), 64–65, 364n43
Concerto for Jazz Band and Orchestra (Mitchell and Balanchine), 62, 363n38

constructivism, 94
contact improvisation, 335, 341, 342, 344, 345, 350, 355n10, 357n4
contextualization, 32
Continuous Project—Altered Daily (Rainer), 222
control, 103, 109, 213, 214, 217, 219, 224, 296
Conway, Carol, 260
Cooper, Douglas, 90
Cooper, Martha, 126–28, 144, 145, 154, 156
Copeland, Roger, 312
Coppélia, 99
Corbin, Patrick, 28
Corner, Philip, 208, 209, 225, 314–15
Cornfield, Ellen, 37
Cornfield, Robert, 363n33
Corpus Delecti (Foster), 335
Cost of Living (Miller), 256
costume balls, 82–83
costumes, 106; in breakdancing, 128, 129, 132, 134–35, 136, 138, 148, 158; changes of, on stage, 116, 238; cross-dressing, 300, 336; Paxton, Steve, discusses, 237–39; unisex, 287
Cranky Destroyers (Skura), 326
Crayon (Davis), 219, 314
Crazy Legs, 121–22, 125, 130, 138, 147, 151, 153, 154, 157
Crazzy Leggs (Jerry Cooper), 140
Creach and Koester, 335
Création du monde, La (Börlin), 57–58, 79–80
critical operations, 24–43
Croce, Arlene, 31, 64, 66, 291, 298, 359n8
cross-dressing, 300, 336
cubism, 63, 86, 365n51
cultural pluralism, 304, 308, 309, 324, 327
Cummings, Blondell, 244, 249, 250, 251, 308, 334, 349, **351**, 352
Cunningham, Merce, 4, 9, 41, 103–18, 254, 269, 294, 300, 333; Armitage, Karole, danced with, 291, 298, 321; and Balanchine, George, 110, 253; and causation, absence of, 111–12; and chance, use of, 103, 109, 111, 219, 278, 308; discrete channels model (with John Cage), 110, 285, 295, 312, 313, 322; and Duchamp, Marcel, 109–18; and essentialism, 280–81; Events, 104, 108, 111; and the intelligence of the body, 110; and the Judson Dance Theater, 207, 214, 219; and the "meaning" of dance, 28–29; and mechanical action, 116–17; O'Connor, Dennis, danced with, 349; partnering techniques, 117; Paxton, Steve, danced with, 350; principle of separability, 110–11; *Rune*, *Summerspace*, and *Winterbranch*, 5–6; Self, Jim, influence on, 270, 271, 337–38; and sets, 107, 110–11; slowness and stillness, use of, 117–18; *Sounddance*, 37–38; *Story*, 103–109, 111, 219; *Walkaround Time*, **114**, 115–118
Cunningham-Cage model of discrete channels, 110, 285, 295, 312, 313, 322
cup/saucer/two dancers/radio (King), **223**, 306
Currier, Ruth, 4
Curry, John, 279

D.E. (Give Us Europe!), 56–57, 94, 95, 96, 164
dada, 7, 63, 80, 147, 215, 217, 305, 312
Dada Painters and Poets, The (Motherwell), 217
Dahl, Viking, 74
Daily Mirror, The (Perron), 275
Daily Wake, The (Summers), 218
Dallas Ballet, 294
Daly, Ann, 40
d'Amboise, Jacques, 62, 64
Dana, Richard Henry, Jr., 185
Dance (Childs/LeWitt/Glass), 32, 254, 294, 308, 320
dance clubs, 131, 132, 133–34, 151, 153–56, 157, 323, 324

dance criticism, 24–43; contextual, 32; descriptive, 28–30; evaluative, 25–27, 39–43; interpretive, 27–28
Dance for Lots of People (Summers), 209
Dance for 3 People and 6 Arms (Rainer), 219, 222, 314
dance genre conflict, 60–61, 132, 140
dance houses, 184, 189–99 *passim*
Dance Is a Contact Sport (Mazo), 23
dance "language," 238, 379n6
dance-music collaboration, 310–13; dance-music hierarchy, 311, 325, 336–37; dance without music, 312, 314, 321, 332; in the eighties, 319–26; in the late sixties and seventies, 316–19; in the sixties, 313–16
Dance Theater of Harlem, 62, 64, 69, 291, 327
Dance Theater Workshop, 322
dance's role in society, 43–50
Danceteria, 131, 153–55, 156, 323, 336
Danieli, Fred, 60, 65, 364n46
Danielian, Leon, 62
Daniels, Jeffrey, 151–52
Danilova, Alexandra, 58
Danses Actuelles (Wills), 87
Dansgille (Börlin), 74–75
Dansmuseet (Stockholm), 81
Danspace project, 207, 208–209
Dardel, Nils von, 74
Dare, Donald, 61
Davis, Anthony, 322
Davis, Pat, 135
Davis, William, 104, 219, 306, 314
Days on Earth (Siegel), 21
Dean, Laura, 261, 264, 292, 303, 309, 318, 320, 324, 334, 336
deconstruction, 287, 291, 298, 302, 309
Defense of Paradise, The, 44–45
Dégh, Linda, 289
de Groat, Andrew, 260, 261
de Maré, Rolf, 70–71, 72, 73, 74, 76, 78, 79, 81
de Mille, Agnes, 60, 68, 293
Deming, Barbara, 176
Denby, 18, 24, 55, 60, 62–63, 65, 67–68, 361n12, 363n41, 365n53
Denishawn, 200
De Palma, Brian, 209
Derviche (Börlin), 73
dervish dance, 73, 264, 318
descriptive criticism, 28–30
Deuce Coupe (Tharp), 292, 308
Dewhorse (Dunn), 209, 210
De Wolfe, Billy, 183
Diaghilev, Serge, 48, 57, 58, 70, 71, 72, 73, 76, 82, 91, 92, 172, 292, 297, 312
Dialogues, The (Kovich and King), 324
Diamond, Dennis, 254
Dickey, Lucinda, 140
Dido and Aeneas (Morris), 336
Dieu Bleu, Le (Fokine), 71
disco, 136, 336
Divertissement (Perron and Van Tieghem), 322–23, 324
Divertissement (Rainer), 219
Dixon, Bill, 209
Dixon, Brenda, 360n10
documentary films, 97, 105, 106, 115n, 165, 208, 227; on breakdancing (*Style Wars*), 130, 143, 151, 157
Dollar, William, 66
Dolls (Mendez), 39
Domestic Interlude, A (Self), 272–73
Donahue, Jack, 172
Doone, Rupert, 84
"double coding," 296, 302, 319
Douglas, Mary, 44
Drama Review, The, 29–30, 356n8
Drastic-Classicism (Armitage and Chatham), 254–55, 291, 298, 321
dream ballets, 60
Dream Maker/Heart Breaker (Self), 337, 339–40
Drink to Me Only with Thine Eyes (Morris), 326
Drinkers, Drummers, and Decent Folk (Stewart), 21
drunk dances and acts, 172–174; Fred Astaire, 171, 174–83; striptease, 159–60

Duchamp, Marcel, 109–18, 215
Dudley, Jane, 201
Duke, Vernon, 58–59, 60, 61, 62, 362n29
Dunas, William, 275
Duncan, Isadora, 45, 49, 71, 72, 100, 248, 252, 281, 312, 348, 349, 372n18
Dunham, Katherine, 61, 68, 69, 149, 363n34
Dunn, Douglas, 256, 269
Dunn, Judith, 7, 104, 208, 209, 210, 212, 221, 225, 278, 315
Dunn, Robert, 6, 207, 212–15, 220, 221, 314, 315
Durang, John, 172
Dwyer, Kevin, 21
Dyer, Oliver, 198
Dynamite Rockers *or* Dynamite Breakers, 130, 151, 157

Eccentric Dances (Goleizovsky), 94
Eco, Umberto, 302
Edge (Herko), 6–7
Education of the Girlchild (Monk), 242, 248, 249
Efimov, Nicholas, 57
Efimov, V., 101
Eglevsky, André, 64
Eight Jelly Rolls (Tharp), 308
Eikhenbaum, Boris, 57
Eiko and Koma, 308
Einstein on the Beach (Glass and Wilson), 256, 294, 320
Eisenberg, Emanuel, 202, 203
Eisenstein, Sergei, 164
El Greco (Börlin), 73, 74
electric boogie, 131, 138, 140, 141, 143, 151, 152, 157
Electric Bugaloos, 134, 135–36
"electrification of the body at the turn of the century, The" (Armstrong), 48–49
electronic music, 265, 322, 323
Elias, Norbert, 47
Elizabethan Phrasing of the Late Albert Ayler, The (Armitage and Salle), 298, 322
Elovich, Richard, 258, 271
Emerson, 6, 7, 208, 212, 213, 214, 217, 314; *Narrative* and *Timepiece*, 216
Endred, Haan, 241–51 *passim*
Energizer (Fenley and Freedman), **265**–67, 322
English (Paxton), 238
English music hall, 172, 173
English New Dance movement, 293, 300, 304
English pantomime, 58, 172, 300
Ensminger, Morgan, 37
"environmental" dances, 220
Epic (Taylor), 5
Episodes (Balanchine and Graham), 292
Equipment Pieces (Brown), 12
Erdman, Boris, 94
Ernst, Max, 90
eroticism, 94, 96, 97
essentialism, 280–81, 282, 309, 312, 324
ethnic identity, 308, 327, 328, 329, 330, 332
"Ethnicity and the Post-Modern Arts of Memory" (Fischer), 20
ethnography, 16–24, 102
Eugen the Unfortunate (Toller), 57
Eunice (Fokine), 101, 373n19
Eunice and Petronius (Gorsky), 101, 373n19
Eureka (Fenley), 254
Euro-American culture: sexual power masked in dance, 160; wedding dance, 49–50, 359n22
Europe, James, 361n17
evaluation, 25–27, 39–43; aesthetic, 42; cognitive, 41–42; political, 39–41
Evans, Albert, 28
exhibition dancing, 56, 167
exotic dance, 159–61
exoticism, 69, 365n58
experimental theater movement, 253, 258
expressiveness: lack of, 239, 282, 380n3; superfluity of, 10–11, 15

Fab Five Freddy, 122, **123**, 125, 128, 129, 139, 149, 153
facial expression, 230, 239
Factory of the Experimental Actor, 57
Fairy Tale: Politics, Desire, and Everyday Life, The (Artists Space exhibition), 288, 382n12
fairytale, 281–90, 335, 381n8
Fall, the, 300
Fantasia Brasiliera (Balanchine), 62
Fantastic Gardens (Summers), 209, 225, 315
Farber, Viola, 104, 105, 106, 269
Farrell, Suzanne, 62
Faun (Goleizovsky), 93–94, 97
February Fun at Bucharest (McDowell), 314
Federal Theater Project dance wing, 203
feet, sixth position, 97, 101
femininity, 235
feminism, 21, 40, 45–46, 288, 306, 308, 334, 335, 343, 358n9/10
Fenley, Molissa, 44, 254, 259–68, **265**, 292, 308, 309, 326, 334, 336, 348–49; arms and hands, use of, 260–62, 264; *Boca Raton*, 264; and Childs, Lucinda, compared, 263–64; *Energizer*, **265**–67, 322; *Mix*, 263–64, 322, 324; *Planets*, 260–61; speed and virtuosity, 259, 260, 265–68; "wall of dance," 267, 278, 322, 336; *The Willies*, 262
Fever Swamp (Jones and Gordon), 322
Field, Chair and Mountain (Gordon), 291
Figure in the Carpet, The (Balanchine), 69, 362n28
Fille mal gardée, La. *See Vain Precautions*.
Film About a Woman Who . . . (Rainer), 269
films. *See also* documentary films; about breakdancing, 44, 48, 61, 128, 130, 131, 132, 138–42, 143, 145, 146, 149, 151, 152, 156, 157, 158; drinking in, 171, 172, 173, 174–83; "new talkies," 256, 320, 335; and the spectator, 112–13; use of, in ballet and dance, 80, 224–25; Westerns, 331, 332
Fine, Elizabeth C., 41
Fischer, Michael, M.J., 18, 20
Fisher, Ellen, 335
Fisk University choir, 164
Fiske, John, 46
Fitzdale, Robert, 82
Five Things (Hay), 219
Flamenco dancing, 260, 322, 330
Flament, Albert, 85
Flares (Corner), 209
flash acts, 66, 128, 364n49
Flashdance (film), 44, 48, 61, 131, 132, 138–39, 143, 146, 156
Flat (Paxton), 227–39
Fleming, Donald, 347
Flit, Alexander, 57
Fluky Luke, 134
Fluxus, 3, 7–8, 212, 278
Fogarty, Thom, 286
Fokine, Irine, 275
Fokine, Mikhail, 70–71, 72, 73–74, 92, 95, 97, 98; *Eunice*, 101, 373n19
Fokine, Vera, 70–71
folkdances, 102, 133, 263, 287, 346; Angolan, 150; Brazilian capoeira, 128, 149–50; and breakdancing, 126, 128, 129, 132, 136, 149–50; Caribbean, 61; Danube Slavic, 94; "exotic," 365n55; French Guiana *cassé-ko*, 129, 149; Goleizovsky's interest in, 94, 96; Haitian, 68; Jamaican ska, 128; Nigerian ritual dance, 259, 260, 322; political, 201; Spanish, 74, 94; Swedish, 74–75; vodun, 129, 136, 149
folklore studies, 381n7
folktales, 381n8
Folktales (Lemon), 283–84
Fontana Mix (Cage), 212
. . . for nearly an hour . . . (Behrman), 115
Forbes, Robert Bennett, 186–87
Foregger, Nikolai, 116

formalism, 253, 282, 292, 333
Forti, Simone, 208, 212, 215, 217, 261, 277, 305, 306, 315, 317; *Slant Board*, 12, 209, 278, 354n4
Foster, George, 190, 196
Foster, Susan, 287, 309, 335
Foucault, Michel, 45, 309, 358n10
Four Moments of the Sun, The (Thompson), 364n48/50
Four Temperaments, The (Balanchine), 40, **54**, 63, 65–67, 360n10, 364n48
foxtrot, 56, 57, 58, 79, 94, 95, 96, 164, 361n17
Fraad, Julie, 131
Fraleigh, Sondra, 41–42
Frank, Andrew, 135
Frankie and Johnny (Page), 69
Freedman, Mark, 265, 322
Freeman, Damita Jo, 135
Freire, Paulo, 343
French danse actuelle, 304
French Guiana *cassé-ko*, 129, 149
Friedman, Gene, 212, 216
From Keyboard Dances (Corner), 315
Frosty Freeze, **123**, 133, 139, 146
Fuller, Loïe, 48, 49, 83, 84, 252
Fun House, The, 131
funding agencies, 294

GV-10 (Armitage), **293**
Gallopade (Cunningham), 112
games. *See* play, games, and sports, use of
Garafola, Lynn, 365n55
Garis, Robert, 53
Garrison, James Holley, 189
Gasteazoro, Eva, 329
Gates, Henry Louis, Jr., 360n11
Gautier, Théophile, 18, 25–26
gay identity, 28, 135, 308, 327, 334, 335, 340
Geertz, Clifford, 20
gender codes, 46, 292, 327, 335, 350
Geneva Ballet, 291, 297, 321
Gennaro, Peter, 158
geometrical patterns, 263, 307, 317
George, Yvonne, 88
Gerdt, Pavel, 92
German: expressionist dance, 209, 312; poor dance, 304
Gershwin, George, 63, 365n57
Gershwin, Ira, 362n29
"get-down" posture, 66, 364n48
Geva, Tamara, 60
Giarra, La (Börlin), 80
Gibb, Linda, 324
Gibson, Jon, 254
Gift/No God Logic, The (Zane), 326
Gigue (Massine), 86, 87, 89
Gillerman, Hope, 287
Girard, Maxime, 87
Giselle, 39–40, 372n16, 373n20
Glacial Decoy (Brown and Rauschenberg), 254, 320
Glass, Philip, 291, 295, 321, 334, 336; *Dance* (with Childs), 32, 254, 294, 308, 320; *Einstein on the Beach* (with Wilson), 256, 294, 320
Go Go Ballerina (Armitage), 325
Going Solo (Kraus), 323
Gold, Arthur, 82
Goldberg Variations (Paxton), 326, 350, 352
Goldstein, Malcolm, 208, 225, 314–15
Goldwyn Follies, The (film), 59, 60–61
Goleizovsky, Kasyan, 92–103, 167; Balanchine, influence on, 94, 97; *Faun*, **93**–94, 97; folkdances and folklore, use of, 94, 96, 102; *Joseph the Beautiful*, 94–95; manifestos, 97–103; and the sixth position, 97, 101; *Whirlwind*, 95–96
Goodman, Benny, 63
Gordon, David, 7, 208, 212, 219, 225, 256, 295, 303, 309, 321, 326, 334, 336; *Mannequin Dance*, 217, 314; *The Matter (plus and minus)*, 320, 382n13; *Murder*, 291, 326; *T.V. Reel*, 254; *Trying Times*, 257; *What Happened*, 29–30, 281, 320
Gordon, Peter, 321, 322
Gorey, Edward, 291
Gorsky, Alexander, 92–93, 97, 101, 373n19/20

Gottschalk, Louis Moreau, 255, 361n14
Graf, Patricia, **265**, 266
graffiti, 292; and breakdancing, 122–57 *passim*
Graham, Martha, 41, 110, 200, 203, 204, 252, 260, 275, 281, 295, 303, 306, 312, 316; *Episodes* (with Balanchine), 292
Grand Union, 44, 256–57, 269, 303, 319, 342
Grandmaster Flash, 139
Grave Digger, The (Buckley), 350–51
Gray, Spalding, 335
Green Table, The (Jooss), 36–37, 39, 81
Greenberg, Clement, 303, 304–305, 312
Gregorio, Juan, 21
Greskovic, Robert, 322
Gries, Lance, 347
Grimes, Chinki, 160
Grimm brothers, 282, 288, 290
Gross, Sally, 208
Grotowski, Jerzy, 253
Gruen, John, 363n8
Guergué, Marga, 347
Guerin, Isabelle, **293**
Guiablesse, La (Page/Dunham/Beatty), 69
Guillem, Sylvie, **293**
Guimond, Rick, 262
Guy-Stéphan, Marie, 25–26

Häger, Bengt, 73
Hager, Steve, 158
Haitian folkdances, 68
Hallström, Gunnar, 75
Halprin, Ann[a], 212, 315, 342
Hanlon-Lees acrobatic team, 172
"happenings," 212, 213, 253, 278, 305
Haquinius, Algot, 75
Harlow, Frederick Pease, 192–94
Harper, Herbert, 60, 61, 362n30
Harper, Meg, 37
Hasselquist, Jenny, 72
Hawitt, Jane, 83
Hay, Alex, 7, 104, 106, 107, 208, 212, 219
Hay, Deborah, 7, 104, 210, 212, 219, 226, 261, 317, 350
Hayden, Melissa, 67
Hayes, Alfred, 202
Hayman-Chaffey, Susana, 117
Hayn, Sybille, 241–51 *passim*
Hays Office, 172
Hazzard-Gordon, Katrina, 361n17
H'Doubler, Margaret, 342
Healy, Sophie, 274
"Heat Wave" (*Blue Skies*), 171, 178, 181–82
Hedstrom, Cynthia, 209
Helen's Dance (Gordon), 219
Hellé, André, 74
Herko, Fred, 208, 209, 212, 215; *Edge*, 6–7; *Once or Twice a Week I Put on Sneakers to Go Uptown*, 217, 219, 314
Heroic Action, 95
Herrand, Marcel, 84, 85, 88
Hewes, Gordon, 234, 235
High Times, 121–22, 126–27, 144, 145
Highlife, the, 260
Hinkson, Mary, 362n28
hiphop culture, 126–58 *passim*, 323, 336
History of Manners: The Civilizing Process, The (Elias), 47
Hodson, Millicent, 324
Hoffbauer, Patricia, 329
Holah, David, 300
Holder, Geoffrey, 61
Holiday Inn (film), 171, **175**–76, 177, 178–79
Holland, Fred, 294, 308, 323, 334
Holm, Hanya, 200, 252
Holman, Michael, 131
Holst, Spencer, 222
Home Life of a Wild Girl (Kaye), **255**
Homme et son Désir, L' (Börlin and Milhaud), 76–77
Horrible Prettiness: Burlesque and American Culture (Allen), 358n15
Horst, Louis, 15, 27, 212, 260, 313–14, 316
Hot Chocolate (*The Nutcracker*), 69
House, The, 240

House of Flowers (Capote and Arlen), 61, 363n35
Houston, Kipling, **54**
Houston-Jones, Ishmael, 294, 308, **331**, 334
Huddle (Forti), 277, 306
Hugo, Jean, 77–78, 82, 83, 88
Hugo, Valentine, 82, 83, 88
humor, 54, 58, 66, 91, 223, 272, 285, 338, 340
Humphrey, Doris, 21, 33, 200, 203, 212, 252, 260, 295, 303, 312
Hundreds, The (Tharp), 275
Hunerberg, Don, 323
Huot, Robert, 220
Huperbody, 269

I Flew to Fiji; You Went South (Chong), 249
Iberia (Börlin), 73
Ichiyanagi, Toshi, 107
Ida, Cousin, 160
identity, 239
Idzikowski, Stanislas, 85, 87, 89, 90
Illuminations (Ashton), 362n28
illusionism. *See* anti-illusionism
Images of Russian Folk Choreography (Goleizovsky), 96
Imperial Russian ballet, 70, 71, 72, 92, 97, 281, 287–88, 293
improvisation, 103–104, 108, 109, 135, 142, 151, 157, 201, 341–47, 350; as amateurism, 341–42; contact improvisation, 335, 341, 342, 344, 345, 350, 355n10, 357n4; at the Judson Dance Theater, 219, 221, 224, 278
Index I/Index II (Dunn and Dunn), 315
infantile movements, 255, 335
Instant Chance (Summers), 216–17
intelligence, 110
interpretation, 27–28, 217
irony, 290, 302, 305, 316, 331, 332–33, 338
Irwin, Bill, 256
Isolations (Scothorn), 217, 314
Italian academic method, 71
Ivanov, Lev, 311
Iver, Lydia, 167
Iving, V., 96

Jack in the Box, 58
Jack London Rebel Dancers, 202
Jackson, Michael, 44, 47, 143, 152
Jackson and Johnson, 56
Jacob's Pillow, 293, 309, 348
Jag ville görna telefonera (Paxton), 210, 238
Jahan, Marine, 138
Jamaican ska, 128
Jameson, Fredric, 302
Japanese dance: butoh, 304, 308
Japanese dancers, 308
Jaroslow, Risa, 275, 276
Jasperse, John, 345, 347
jazz: in the Soviet Union, 56–57, 161–67
jazz ballet, 73, 79
jazz bands, use of, 56–57, 94
jazz dance, 53, 56, 58, 60, 61, 63, 65, 66, 67, 69, 360n9; defined, 374n1
jazz music, 160, 299; defined, 374n1
Jencks, Charles, 296, 302, 304, 308, 319
Jeux (Nijinsky, Börlin), 73
Jewels (Balanchine), 53–54
Joffrey, Robert, Ballet, 275, 292, 294, 308, 309, 324
Johns, Jasper, 12–13, 115
Johnson, Louis, 362n28
Johnson, Ray, 212
Johnson, Scott, 323
Johnston, Jill, 3–10, 21, 42, 207, 212, 215, 217, 224, 225, 240
Jonas, Joan, 282
Jones, Bill T., **257**, 308, 322, 334
Jones, John, 63, 362n28
Jooss, Kurt, 36–37, 39, 81
Joseph the Beautiful (Goleizovsky), 94–95
Jowitt, Deborah, 21, 37–38, 43, 45, 53
Judd, Donald, 254, 295, 334
Judson Dance Theater, 4, 6, 7, 8, 9, 108, 113, 240, 295, 303, 314–15, 334, 341, 353n12; alternative

Judson Dance Theater (*continued*)
choreographic methods, 211–26; reconstructions, 207, 208–10, 226; weekly workshop, 207–208, 211, 219–21, 253
Judson Nights (Summers' film collage), 209
Junior Red Dancers, 202
Juniper Tree, The (Jonas), 282

Kamerny Ballet, 93, 97
Kamerny Theatre, 94, 101, 373n21
Kammerdisco (Armitage and Lohn), 325
Karno, Fred, troupe, 173
Kaye, Pooh, **255**, 294, 335
Kealiinohomoku, Joann, 23, 356n6
Keen, Elizabeth, 208
Ken (a Breakmaster), 124, 147
Kendall, Elizabeth, 55
Keyboard Dances (Corner), 209
Kid Smooth, 152
Kimoto, Kumiko, 324, 334
Kinder, Küche, and Kirche, 202
Kinematic, **286**–87, 309, 323, 335
King, B.B., 275
King, John, 324
King, Kenneth, 208, 221, **223**, 255, 256, 261, 269, 275, 303, 318; *cup/saucer/two dancers/radio*, **223**, 306; *Wor(l)d (T)raid*, 34–35
King Harlequin, 101, 373n22
Kip Dee, 124, 125
Kirby, Michael, 29, 303
Kirkland, Gelsey, 33–34
Kirstein, Lincoln, 44–45, 58, 59–60, 203, 365n57, 366n60
Kitchen, The, 131, 133–34, 263
Knitting Factory, 347
Kogan, Petr, 165
Kongo pose, 66, 167, 364n50, 375n15
Kool Lady Blue, 131, 153
Kotoske, Tamar, 286
Kovich, Robert, 324
Kraus, Lisa, 323
Kruger, Barbara, 358n9
Kurchin, Al, 212

Laban, Rudolf, 14, 21, 110, 213
Lac des Signes (Foster), 287, 309
Lacey, Jennifer, 347
Lagut, Irène, 78
Laibach band, 300
Lakis, Maria, 286
Lancaster, Mark, 37
Lang, Andrew, 289–90
Lang, Pearl, 4
Langer, Susanne, 41, 112
Langevin, Karen, 329
Lanvin, Jeanne, 83, 84
Laqueur, Thomas, 358n15
Large Glass, The (Duchamp), 110–18 *passim*
Larionov, Mikhail, 70
Lashchilin, Lev, 95
Last Point (Dunn), 225
Lateral Splay (Schneemann), 210
Lathan, Stan, 140
Latina choreographers, 327–33
Laurencin, Marie, 89
League of Workers' Theaters, 201, 203
Le Clerc, Tanaquil, 62
Lee, Deborah, 221
Lee, Sammy, 363n32
"leftist" choreography, 95–96, 97
Legend of Joseph (Fokine), 95
Léger, Fernand, 58, 73, 79
Leili and Mejnun (Goleizovsky), 97
Lemon, Ralph, 309, 326; "Tar Baby" (*Folktales*), 283–84
Lennon, Joseph, 298
Leroy, A., 323
Les Six, 78
Let's Break (videotape), 141
Lévi-Strauss, Claude, 20, 21, 282
Levine, Dick, 212, 213
Lewis, Nancy, 256
LeWitt, Sol, 32, 225, 254, 294, 308, 320, 334
Liebermann, Rolf, 62
Lifar, Serge, 91
Life and Times of Joseph Stalin, The (Wilson), 256
LifeDance I . . . The Magician (Zollar), **342**
lighting, 106–107

Like Most People (Herko and Taylor), 219, 314
Lilienstein, Cheryl, 209
liminal state, 177, 191, 376n16, 378n18
Limón, José, 4, 5, 9, 294, 303, 306
lindy, the, 62–63, 66, 149, 150, 158
linguistic models, 20
Linton, David, band, 298, 321, 323
list (choreographic structure), 222, 226, 307
Little Humpbacked Horse, The (Gorsky), 100, 101, 373n20
Littlefield, Catherine, 173
Litz, Katherine, 4, 7, 208
"live décor," 104, 107, 111
Living Theater, 212, 253, 315
Lloyd, Barbara Dilley, 104, 106, 256, 269
Lock, Janet, 135
Lockers, the, 134–35, 151–52
Lohn, Jeffrey, 325
Lomax, Alan, 364n44
Long, Nick, Jr., 172
Lookout (Self and Elovich), 258
Loose Bruce, 154, 155
Lopez, David, 21
Lopokova, Lydia, 85, 89, 90
Lopukhov, Feodor, 167
Louis, Murray, 5
Luecht, Joel, 271–77
Lutin de la Vallée, Le, 25–26
Lyne, Adrian, 139

MTV videodance, 323, 332, 335, 336
Ma, Yo-Yo, 299
Mabou Mines, 253
McAuley, Jerry, 196
McBride, Patricia, 64
MacCormack, Gilson, 85, 86, 89, 91
McCoy, Terry, 156
machine references, 116–17
McDonagh, Don, 316
McDowell, John Herbert, 208, 209, 212, 216, 314, 315, 316
MacLane, Gretchen, 212, 219
Mac Low, Clarinda, 345
McLove, Zakhary, 94–95
MacMillan, Kenneth, 380n4
McRae, Edna, 135
Macunias, George, 8
Madonna, 46
magicians, 173–74
Magnificent Force, 131, 140
Mahaffay, Marni, 212, 214
Maison de fous (Börlin), 73, 74
Making Sex: Body and Gender from the Greeks to Freud (Laqueur), 358n15
mambo, 62, 181, 365n51
Mangrove group, 335
Manheim, Ralph, 290
Mannequin Dance (Gordon), 217, 314
Manning, Susan, 357n2
Märchen, 282, 289, 381n8
Marclay, Christian, 323
Marcus, George E., 18
Marcy, Carol, 221
Mariès de la Tour Eiffel, Les (Börlin), 77–79
Marin, Maguy, 380n4
Marking Time (Self), 271–72
Marks, Bruce, 293
Marks, Victoria, 335
Marra, Eleanor, 85, 86
Marranca, Bonnie, 256
Marshall, Susan, 294, 324, 334, 335, 336
Marsicano, Merle, 4, 7
Martel, Diane, 287, 324, 335, 336
Martin, John, 18
Martin, Steve, 152
Marxism, 202, 288, 343
Maryinsky Theater school (St. Petersburg), 92
Mascando Inglés (Vázquez), 329–30
masculine beauty, 235
masks, use of, 77, 79, 112
Maslow, Sophie, 4, 201
Masque of the Red Death, The (Goleizovsky), 92, 95
massacre of St. Bartholomew, 44–45
Massine, Léonide, 70, 73, 74, 82, 173; *Le Beau Danube*, 85, 87, 91; *Gigue*, 86, 87, 89; *Mercure*, 89–91; *Salade*, 85–86, 89, 91

Index

" 'Material Girl': The Effacements of Postmodern Culture" (Bordo), 358n9/10
mathematical system, 307, 317
Matons, Bill, 201
Matter (plus and minus), The (Gordon), 320, 382n13
Matthews, Jessie, 59
Mauss, Marcel, 234
Maxfield, Richard, 316
May, Elaine, 291, 292
Mayakovsky, Vladimir, 96n
Mazo, Joseph, 23, 53–54
Me and Mayakovsky (Miller), 335
Meat Joy (Schneemann), 306
mechanical action, 116–17, 136
media, the: and breakdancing, 126, 129–32, 143–44, 145–46
medical studies, 47–48
Meditation (Charlip), 209
Medley, Odis, 142
Meier, Yvonne, 345–46, 347
Mendez, Alberto, 39
Mercure (Massine), 89–91
metaphoric postmodern dance, 255, 256, 303, 318, 319–20, 329, 384n18
Meyerhold, Vsevolod, 56, 94, 96, 164–65, 373n21
Miami Beach (Self), 268
Middleman (Buckley), 351
Midsummer Night's Dream, A (Balanchine), 69, 365n58
Mignone, Francisco, 62
Milhaud, Darius, 57–58, 68, 76, 78, 79, 85, 86, 91
Miller, Bebe, 308, 323, 324, 334, 347
Miller, Tim, 256, 294, 324, 335
Miller and Lyles, 163
Mind is a Muscle, Part 1, The or *Trio A* (Rainer), 34, 42, 209–10, 222, 307, 352
minimalism, 27, 32, 210, 215, 217, 290, 292, 295, 303, 307, 316–17, 318, 320, 333
minstrel shows, 45, 156, 360n11
Mr. Freeze, 121, 124, 125, 139
Mr. Fresh, 158
Mitchell, Arthur, 60, 61, 62, 63–64, 65, 66, 68, 69, 363n38, 365n58
Mix (Fenley), 263–64, 322, 324
modern dance, 4, 7, 9, 16, 72, 103, 108, 259, 304–305, 312–13; historically rooted styles, 313–14; and the Judson Dance Theater, 212, 213, 218, 295; and modernism, 304–305, 312; professionalism and improvisation, 341–42; solo choreography, 349; and theatricality, 253, 317; vocabulary, 252, 295; and the Workers' Dance League, 199, 200, 201, 203
Modern Jazz Quartet, 62
Modern Jazz Variants (Balanchine), 61, 62–63, 67–68, 362n28
modernism, 13, 17, 55, 63, 65, 70, 72, 113, 115, 292, 295–96, 309, 324, 380n1
Mollino Room, The (Armitage and Salle), 291–92, 300, 322
MoMing Dance Center (Chicago), 269
Monk, Meredith, 208, 221, 225, 255–56, 261, 269, 282, 294, 303, 318, 324, 336, 345, 348; *Chacon* (with Chong), 240–52, **250**
monkey, the, 339
Monkey Run Road (Jones and Zane), 322
Monson, Jennifer, 345, 346, 347
Monte, Elisa, 264, 323
Moore, Frank, 271, 272, 290, **338**
Morand, Paul, 83, 88
Mordine, Shirley, 269
Mordkin, Mikhail, Ballet Company, 92
Moroccan Dialogues (Dwyer), 21
Morphology of the Folktale (Propp), 282
Morris, Mark, 292, 294, 304, 309, 325–26, 335, 336; *L'Allegro, il Penseroso ed il Moderato*, 38
Morris, Marnee, 53
Morris, Robert, 3, 7, 111, 208, 212, 218, 220, 278, 295, 302, 306, 307, 315; and the manipulation of objects, 222–23

Moschen, Michael, 323
Moseley, Monica, 241–51 *passim*
Motherwell, Robert, 217
Mouchoir de Nuages (Tzara), 84–85
Moulton, Charles, 278, 294, 323
Mouveau, Georges, 74
movements: animal, 255, 335; of arms and hands, 66, 260–62, 264; masculine and feminine poses, 235; mechanical, 116–17, 136; ordinary, 11–12, 13–15, 108, 234–36, 239, 253–54, 267, 277, 278, 296, 307, 332; pure, 113, 115, 295, 317, 333; refraining, 16, 355n8
Movie-Made America (Sklar), 174
Mueller, John, 33
¡Muévete!, 328, 329
Muller, Jennifer, 323
multimedia spectacles, 224–25, 254–56, 294, 308, 309, 331–32, 334
"multi-unit" torso, 64, 364n44
Mulvihill, Colleen, 279
Mumma, Gordon, 317
Munson, Richard, 324
Murder (Gordon), 291, 326
Murphy, Gerald, 73, 79
music: absence of, 312, 314, 321; collage of, 222, 315–16; commissioned, 312, 322; Cunningham's use of, 107–108, 110, 117; electronic, 265, 322, 323; produced by dancers, 265, 322; Rainer against the use of, 317–18
Music (Dean), 320
music-dance collaboration, 310–13; Cunningham-Cage model, 110, 285, 295, 312, 313, 322; in the eighties, 319–26; and the hierarchy of dance and music, 311, 325, 336–37; in the late sixties and seventies, 316–19; in the sixties, 313–16
Music for Word Words (Paxton), 238, 315
musicals, 61, 172
My Son, the Nurse (Nichols and May), 292
Nagrin, Lee, 241–51 *passim*
Narrative (Emerson), 216
narrative structure, 273–74, 280–81, 304, 309, 332, 337
National Choreography Project, 294
Nature Friends Dance Group, 201, 202
Ne (Armitage), 298
Neels, Sandra, 104, 115
Negril, 131, 151, 153, 155–56
Negro Sculpture (Börlin), 73
Neimanas, John, 270, 337
Nelson, Arkady, 167
Nelson, Lisa, 349, 352
Nemchinova, Nina, 87
Nemirovich-Danchenko, Vladimir, 92–93
neo-classical ballet, 53, 63–64
Nerman, Einar, 75
Neuman, Natanya, 4
Neville, Phoebe, 208, 221, **223**
"new dance" choreographers, 296
New Dance Group, 201–202
New Dance League, 203
New Duncan Dancers, 202
New Masses, 200
"new talkies" cinema, 256, 320, 335
New Theater, 202, 203
New Theater League, 203
new wave music, 254, 291, 298, 321, 323
New York by Gaslight (Foster), 190
New York City Ballet, 23, 60, 292, 362n28; collaboration with the Dance Theater of Harlem, 62, 69
New York City Breakers, 131, 144, 157
New York Export: Op. Jazz (Robbins), 68
New Yorker, The (Massine), 173
Newman, Charles, 302
Newspaper Event (Schneemann), 225
Newsweek cover, 137, 143
Next Wave Festival (BAM), 291, 294, 308, 324, 334
Nicholas Brothers (Fayard and Harold), 60, 364n49
Nichols, Betty, 362n28
Nichols, Mike, 291, 292

Nicks, Walter, 61
Nigeria, 259, 260, 322
Night Shadow (Balanchine), 62
Nijinska, Bronislava, 56, 92, 359n22
Nijinsky Vaslav, 71, 73, 75, 76, 93, 98
Nikolais, Alwin, 4; *Totem*, 5
No Fire Escape in Hell (Clark), 301
No Regrets (Soto and Osorio), 330–31
Noces, Les (Lemon), 326
Noces, Les (Nijinska), 359n22
North Carolina Dance Theater, 294
Novack, Cynthia, 23, 341, 355n10, 357n4
Nuchtern, Jean, 33–34
nudity, 48, 101, 238
Nuit de Saint-Jean, La (Börlin), 73, 74–75
Nureyev, Rudolph, 380n4
Nutcracker, The, 31, 69

Oath (Perron), 275
Oberlin College, 240, 252
objecthood, 113, 237, 238
objects, manipulation of, 218, 222–23, 236–37
Obukhov, Mikhail, 92
O'Connor, Dennis, 349
O'Connor, Patrick, 58
O'Connor, Tere, 335
Octandre (Waring), 210
Offerlunden (Börlin), 75
Ohio Ballet, 292
Olitski, Jules, 15, 113
Olympics, 138, 143, 201
On Your Toes (Rogers and Hart), 60, 61
Once or Twice a Week I Put on Sneakers to Go Uptown (Herko), 217, 219, 314
"One for My Baby (and One More for the Road)" (*The Sky's the Limit*), 171, 179–81
One-Sixth of the World (Vertov), 165
one-step, the, 56, 164
Ono, Yoko, 3, 209
Open Theater, 253
Ordinary Dance (Rainer), 219, 222, 314
ordinary movement, 108, 253–54, 267, 277, 278, 296, 307, 332; Paxton's *Flat*, 234, 236, 239; Rainer's *Room Service*, 11–12, 13–15
Osorio, Pepón, 329, 330–31
Östör, Ákos, 21
Other, 18, 19, 20, 23, 324
Our Lady of Late (Monk), 318
outdoor performance, 221, 238
Oxenhandler, Neal, 88

PBS, 130, 143, 364n48
Pacific Northwest Ballet, 292
Page, Ruth, 69
Palestine, Charlemagne, 317
pantomime: in ballet, 75, 256, 288; in breakdancing, 124, 128, 136, 138, 140, 143, 147, 148, 152; English, 58, 172, 300
Parade (Massine), 73, 79, 87
"Paranarrative" festivals (P.S. 1), 258
Paris, Livia Daza, 329
Paris (Monk), 247–48, 250, 251
Paris Opera Ballet, 292, 297, 326
Paris Sciences, The (Perron), 273–75
Parish, Ed, 269
Parnakh, Valentin, 56–57, 164
Parnes, Uzi, **331**
parody, 85, 222, 225, 285, 300, 333, 335
Parr, Andrée, 76
partnering techniques, 117, 298, 321, 335, 340, 350
Parts of Some Sextets (Rainer), 354n2, 356n5
Pas de Deux—Blues (Balanchine), 62
Pascal, Andrée, 84, 85, 88
Passacaglia (Humphrey), 33
Passloff, Aileen, 4, 7, 208, 210, 220, 221
Pastime (Childs and Corner), 314–15
pattern choreographers, 263, 307, 317
Paulie Gee, 154, 155
Pavlova, Anna, 71, 89, 92
Pavlova, Nadezhda, 31
Paxton, Steve, 7, 9, 104, 208, 212, 215, 219, 220, 253, 256, 278, 294, 295, 303, 306; body movement and poses, 234–36; on clothing/

costumes, 237–39; facial expression, 230, 239; *Flat*, 227–39; *Goldberg Variations*, 326, 350, 352; *Jag ville görna telefonera*, 210, 238; and the objecthood of the body, 237, 238; and objects, 236–37; *Proxy*, 217–18; and time, 234; use of space, 230–34; *Word Words* and *Music for Word Words*, 238, 315
Payton, Lew, 163
Pelican (Rauschenberg), 220
Pennsylvania Ballet, 294
Penguin, 134
Pentland, Joe, 172
Percelay, James L., 142
Perez, Rudy, 275
Performance Group, 253
Perrault, Charles, 287, 288
Perrault, John, 21
Perron, Wendy, 208–209, 273–77, **274**, 279, 322–23, 324, 326, 348, 352; *The Paris Sciences*, 273–75
Persephone (Balanchine), 69
Peter and the Wolf (Bolm), 285
Peter and the Wolf (Staff), 285
Peter and the Wolf (Zane), 284–85
Peters, Sally, 44
"Peter's Journey" from *Babes in Arms* (Balanchine), 60
Petipa, 5, 45, 53, 72, 97, 99, 133, 281, 283, 287, 311; *La Bayadère*, 320, 382n13
Petrizky, Anatol, 94
Petronio, Stephen, 309, 323, 335, 343–45
Petsch, Robert, 282
Peyton, Benny, Jazz Kings, 164
Phase Two, 154
Phèdre (Racine), 101, 373n21
Photographer, The (Glass), 291
Phrasing (Armitage), 299
physical dissociation, 136
Physical Things (Paxton), 306
Piano Movers (Gordon), 291
Picabia, Francis, 80, 81
Picasso, Pablo, 63, 73, 74, 86, 113; and *Mercure*, 89–91
Pickett, Lenny, 323
Pied Piper (Robbins), 363n41
Pietro, Vera, 90
Piman Shamanism and Staying Sickness (Bahr, Gregorio, Lopez, and Alvarez), 21
Pirandello, Luigi, 80
Planets (Fenley), 260–61
play, games, and sports, use of, 73, 258, 277–79, 290, 323; and the Judson Dance Theater, 215, 219, 222, 225
pluralism, 302, 309
Pluto (*Persephone*), 69
Poiret, Paul, 48
Police Gazette, 189
political dance, 308, 309, 327, 333, 334–35, 343, 345–46; proletarian dance, 95–96, 203; and the Workers' Dance League, 199–204
political evaluation, 39–41
Polunin, Vladimir and Elizabeth, 85
Pop #1/Pop #2 (Bhartonn), 209
pop art, 212, 222, 305
pop culture, 308, 309, 323; and breakdancing, 128, 132, 150, 157, 158; and "high" art, 133, 283, 292, 298, 316, 319, 321, 325, 336; and Latino dance, 330, 331, 332, 333
pop music, 304
POPism (Warhol), 275
Poppalots, 140–41
Porcher, Le (Börlin), 75–76
Porter, Esther, 201
poses, masculine/feminine, 235
possession dances, 129, 136, 149
posters, 96, 165, 166–67
postmodern dance, 3, 8, 15, 16, 17, 28–29, 35, 44, 46, 108, 133, 240, 259, 263, 269, 301–304, 356n8, 380n1; analytic, 217, 226, 254, 255, 282, 295–96, 303, 307, 308, 309, 312–13, 318, 319–20, 321; and the artworld, 303, 305, 317, 319; and ballet, 297–98, 299–300, 309, 325–26; and children's culture, 290; collaboration with music, 310–313; "double coding," 296,

postmodern dance (*continued*) 302, 319; eclecticism of, 281, 284, 290, 292, 296, 297, 302, 333–34; in the eighties, 308–10, 319–26; and the fairytale, 281–90, 291, 309, 335; *Flat* (Paxton), analysis of, 227, 230–39; interdisciplinary mingling with the other arts, 302–303, 309, 319–20, 321, 324–25; and the Judson Dance Theater, 208, 210, 217, 222; Latino, 327–33; metaphoric, 255, 256, 303, 318, 319–20, 384n13; play, games, and sports, use of, 277–78, 297; reflexive, 303, 305; ritual forms, 261; in the seventies, 307–308, 316–19; in the sixties, 304–306, 313–16; and social dancing, 296, 323–24, 336; theatricality of, 252, 253–58, 294, 297, 301, 308, 319, 320, 333–34, 337; and verbal language, 256–58; virtuosity of, 267–68, 278–79, 296–97, 326, 336
poststructuralism, 20, 21, 280, 282, 288, 309, 381n7
Pratt, Tina, 159
Premier Amour, 89
Première Orage (Childs), 326
Preston, Don, 318
primitivism, 312, 324, 335
Prince Ken Swift, 139
Princess Brambilla, 101, 373n21
Princess Story, The (Gillerman), 287
Prohibition, 171, 172
Prokofiev, Sergei, 284–85
proletarian dance, 95–96, 203
propaganda posters, 95, 96
Propp, Vladimir, 282
Proxy (Paxton), 217–18
"Psychedelic Six Pack" (Corbin), 28
psychoanalysis, 171–72
Puck (*A Midsummer Night's Dream*), 69, 365n58
punk, 133, 135, 155, 254–55, 284, 287, 291, 298, 321, 336
pure dance, 253, 281, 311
pure movement, 113, 115, 295, 317, 333
Pure Pre-Scenes (Clark), 300
Queen Walks in the Garden, The (Tamiris), 312
Quibic (MacLane), 219

racism, 45, 360n11
Radiguet, Raymond, 83, 87, 88
Rafladan (Hay, Hay, and Rotmil), 219
ragtime, 56, 79
Ragtime I/Ragtime II (Balanchine), 57, 62
Rain Fur (Hay), 219
Rainer, Yvonne, 29, 238, 253, 256, 269, 278, 281, 301, 320, 326, 333, 335; *Dance for 3 people and 6 arms* and *Ordinary Dance*, 219, 222, 314; and the Judson Dance Theater, 4, 6, 7, 8, 208, 212, 214–15, 216, 220, 295, 303, 315, 334, 341; *The Mind is a Muscle, Part 1* or *Trio A*, 34, 42, 209–210, 222, 307, 352; *Parts of Some Sextets*, 12, 354n2, 356n5; *Performance Demonstration*, 317–18; *Room Service*, 11–12, 13–15, 277–78, 354n2; *Some Thoughts on Improvisation*, 224; *Terrain*, 222, 306; *We Shall Run*, 9, 306, 316
Rammellzee, 124, 128
Random Breakfast (Gordon), 225
Rankin, Kay, 200
rap groups, 154–55, 325
Rauschenberg, Robert, 6, 208, 212, 215, 334; and Brown's *Glacial Decoy*, 254, 320; and Brown's *Set and Reset*, 294, 308, 320; and Cunningham's *Story*, 104, 105, 106–107, 108, 111; *Pelican*, 220
Raw Recital (Monk), 318
Reagan, Ronald, 144, 157
Red and Hot: The Fate of Jazz in the Soviet Union 1917–1980 (Starr), 361n14/15/16, 375n19
Red Art Screen (Fenley), 262
Red Dancers, 201, 202
Red Poppy, The (Lashchilin and Tikhomirov), 95
Red Rooster (Dale Hurd), 140
reductive style, 208, 303

reflexivity, 303, 305, 312
refraining movements, 16, 355n8
reggae, 128, 131, 153, 154
regional ballet movement, 309
Reich, Steve, 295, 318
Reid, Albert, 104, 105–106, 108
Relâche (Börlin), 80–81, 116
Relative Calm (Childs), 254
Reliquary (Nikolais), 5
Renzi, Marta, 323, 332, 335
repetition, use of, 7, 214, 215, 222, 242, 307, 318, 382n13
Requiem Canticles (Balanchine), 62
Rethorst, Susan, 276
Retracing Steps (Self), 326
"return of the repressed," 335, 384n19
Reuben Gallery, 305
Revolutionary Dancers, 202
Revue Négre, La, 163, 166
Reynolds, Nancy, 64, 365n58
rhumba, 62
Rialto (Paxton), 238
Rice, Dan, 172
Richter, Mary, 286
Riefenstahl, Leni, 42
Rinker, Kenneth, 321
ritual dance, 259, 260, 322, 323
ritual forms, 261
Ritz, 132, 324
Robbins, Jerome, 61, 68–69, 292, 293, 362n28, 363n4
Robertson, Allen, 32
Robinson, David "Fresh Jome," 142
rock music, 133, 210, 299, 314, 317, 322, 324, 325, 335, 336
Rock Steady, **123**, 124, 125, 128, 129–30, 131, 138, 140, 146, 151, 153, 157
"rocking"/"rocking down". *See* breakdancing
Rodriguez, Tony, 141
Rogers, Ginger, 61
Rogers, Jaime, 140
roller disco, 127, 130, 143, 151, 157, 220
Rollers (Forti), 277
Romano, U. Roberto, 141
Romeo and Juliet story, 59–60
Romeo et Juliette (Cocteau), 87–89
Room Service (Rainer), 11–12, 13–15, 277–78, 354n2
Rooms (Sokolow), 11
Rose, Phyllis, 58
Rose Fractions (Rainer), 318
Roseau, Le (Börlin), 80
Rosén, Gunhild, 71
Roses, Les (Massine), 89
Roslavleva, Natalia, 45
Ross, Charles, 210, 221, 278, 354n2
Ross, Herbert, 363n35
Rotary Action (Jones and Zane), **257**, 322
Rotmil, Charles, 219
Roxy, 131, 132, 157, 324
Rubenstein, Ida, 87
Rudner, Sara, 275, 276, 308, 321, 334
rule games, 215, 222, 278, 350
Rulegame 5 (Brown), 12
Rune (Cunningham), 5, 6
Running Away from Myself: A Dream Portrait of America Drawn from the Films of the 40's (Deming), 176

Sacra Conversazione (O'Connor), 349
Sacre du Printemps (Nijinsky), 75, 324
St. Denis, Ruth, 252, 312, 349
Salade (Massine), 85–86, 89, 91
Salle, David, 291, 298, 322
Salome (Goleizovsky), 93
Salon Waltzes (Aldrich), 31–32
salsa, 323, 330
samba, 62
San Andreas (Uchizono), **346**
San Juan, Olga, 181–82
Sanctum (Nikolais), 5
Sapporo (Ichiyanagi), 107
Satie, Erik, 73, 80, 89–90, 212–13, 314, 317
Satie for Two (Rainer), 7, 215
Satisfyin Lover (Paxton), 238
Sauguet, Henri, 89
Savina, Vera, 89
Schéhérazade (Fokine), 71
Schick, Vicky, 347
Schlichter, Joseph, 212
Schmidt, Beverly, 225

Schmidt, Lisa, 347
Schneemann, Carolee, 7, 208, 210, 225, 306, 315
Schorer, Suki, 53, 65
Schumann, Peter, 212
Schumann Op. 102 (Perron), 326
scores, use of, 212, 213, 215, 217–18, 314, 317, 350
Scothorn, Carol, 212, 217, 314
Scott, Lincoln, 256
Scraping Bottoms (Self), 272
Scriabiniana (Goleizovsky), 96–97
sculpture, use of, 221
seamen, 184–95
Seamen's Narratives (American Tract Society), 194–95
Seasons, The (Schmidt), 225
Secret Pastures (Jones and Zane), 322
Segal, Edith, 201, 202
Self, Jim, 258, 268–73, 292, 308, 309, 323, 332, 336, 337–40, **338**; *Beehive*, with Frank Moore, 290, **338**; Cunningham's influence on, 270, 271, 337–38; *A Domestic Interlude*, 272–73; *Dream Maker/Heart Breaker*, 337, 339–40; *Marking Time*, 271–72; *Miami Beach*, 268; Neimanas, John, influence of, 270, 337; and Rainer, Yvonne, attitudes contrasted, 326, 334; *Scraping Bottoms*, 272; *Tuscaloosa*, 270; *White on White*, 270–71
Self Studies (Self), 269
separability, principle of, 110–11
Serenade (Balanchine), 69
Sert, José-Maria, 87
set, 107, 110–11
Set and Reset (Brown/Rauschenberg/Anderson), 294, 308, 320, 321, 384n18
Setterfield, Valda, 115, 212
Seven Deadly Sins, The (Brecht and Weill/Balanchine), 59
Severinsen, "Doc," 62
sexual power, masked/flaunted, 160
Shabba-doo (Adolfo Quinones), 134, 135, 140, 152
shag, the, 63, 65
shake dance, 159–61
shanties, 188, 191–92
Sharing the Dance: Contact Improvisation and American Culture (Novack), 341, 355n10, 357n4
Shawn, Ted, 252
Shearer, Sybil, 4
Sherman, Stuart, 290
Shields and Yarnell, 152
shimmy, the, 58, 67, 79, 94, 164, 339
Shook, Karel, 363n38
Shorts (Perry and King), 275
shoulder r (Scothorn), 217, 314
"show-biz dancing," 56, 64, 360n9
Shuffle Along (Sissle and Blake), 163
Siegel, Marcia B., 21, 36–37, 39
Silbert, Joel, 140
silence, use of, 117–18, 214, 236, 332
Silver, Tony, 130, 151, 157
Silver Star, 154–55
Silvers, Sally, 344
Simpleton's Guide to the World's Greatest Music, The (Linton), 321–22
Simulacrum Reels (Petronio), 309
Sissle, Noble, 162–63
Sister Carrie (Dreiser), 49
Site (Morris), 306
Sitwell, Sacheverell, 58
Sixteen Millimeter Earrings (Monk), 225
Skaggs, Sarah, 347
Skating Rink (Börlin), 73
Sklar, Robert, 174
Skura, Stephanie, 326, 344
Sky's the Limit, The (film), 171, 176–78, 179–81
Slant Board (Forti), 12, 209, 278, 354n4
Slaughter on MacDougal Street (Armitage and Chatham), 325
Slaughter on Tenth Avenue (from *On Your Toes*) (Balanchine), 59, 60, 68
Sleeping Beauty, The, (MacMillan), 380n4
Sleeping Beauty, The, (Petipa), 9, 42, 45, 72, 117, 281, 311

Slim the Robot, 134
Slonimsky, Yuri, 94
slow motion, 116, 117–18, 141
Sly C (Donny Walker), 140
Smith, Heber, 186
Smith, Jack, 331
Smith, Kaj, 58
Snow Queen, The (Kinematic), 286–87, 335
Snowball (*The Triumph of Neptune*), 58, 66, 172–73, 362n23
social dancing, 136, 137, 167; the Nigerian Highlife, 260, 322; and postmodern dance, 296, 323–24, 336; and theatrical dance, 311, 324, 325
soft-shoe dance, 63, 66
Soirée de Paris, 82–91
Sokolow, Anna, 4, 11, 202
solo choreography, 348–52
Solomons, Gus, 31–32
Some Thoughts on Improvisation (Rainer), 221
Son of Gone Fishin' (Brown and Ashley), 254, 320
Sontag, Susan, 21, 29
Soto, Merián, 329; *No Regrets*, with Osorio, 330–31
Soul Train (TV), 151
Sounddance (Cunningham), 37–38
Souritz, Elizabeth, 92, 95, 96, 371n1
Soviet Union, 200; avant-garde in, 57, 96, 167, 375n19; Blue Blouse movement, 167; *Chocolate Kiddies* tour in, 161–67; gymnastics and dance, 45; jazz in, 56–57, 161–67; New Economic Policy, 94, 162, 164; Rosfil (Russian Philharmonic Society), 162; ROSTA (Russian Telegraph Agency) propaganda posters, 96; social realism in the jazz era, 375n20; State Institute of Theatrical Art, 94
space, use of: Judson Dance Theater, 220–21; Paxton's *Flat*, 230–34
Spanish dances, 74, 94; flamenco, 260, 322, 330; stepping dance, 329
Specimen Days (Monk), 255
spectator, role of, 112–13, 220; in breakdancing, 132, 158
Spector, Phil, 322
speed and motion: Molissa Fenley, 259, 260, 265–67
Speedlimit (Dunn), 225
spontaneity, 103–104, 109
sports. *See* play, games, and sports, use of
Spy, 121–22
Staff, Frank, 285
Stanislavsky, Konstantin, 93, 165, 373n21
Star, 135
Star-Spangled Rhythm (film), 61
Starr, Frederick, 361n14/15/16, 375n19
State of Darkness (Fenley), 326
Stebbins, Genevieve, 49
Steegmuller, Francis, 82, 87
Stein, Gertrude, 7, 173, 215
Steinlen, T.A., 74
stepdancing, 41, 329
"stepping it down," 67, 364n50
stereotyped roles, 69, 159, 167, 333, 365n58
Stevens, Ashton, 163
Stewart, John O., 21
Stockholm Royal Opera ballet company, 71, 72
Stoll, Sir Oswald, 59
Story (Cunningham), 103–109, 111, 219
Strandin, Ebon, 72
Stravinsky, Igor, 53, 57, 62, 63, 64, 75, 299, 324, 326
Stravinsky Violin Concerto (Balanchine), 63
Streb, Elizabeth, 264, 278
Street Dreams (Gennaro), 158
street subculture, 122, 126, 131, 133, 134, 156
striptease dancing, 159–61
Strobel, Heinrich, 365n54
structuralism, 20, 282, 307
Structures (Passloff), 307
Style Wars (documentary film), 130, 143, 151, 157
subcultures, 308, 323

Subway Art (Cooper), 126
Suleiman, Susan Rubin, 46
Summers, Elaine, 7, 208, 212, 219; *Fantastic Gardens*, 209, 225, 315; *Instant Chance*, 216–17, 218
Summerspace (Cunningham), 5, 6
Supreme Rockers, 158
Surplus Dance Theater, 9
surrealism, 60, 90, 134, 147, 216, 217, 306, 331
Susie, 141
Sverdlik, Daniel Ira, 241–51 *passim*
Swan Lake (Basil), 133
Swan Lake (Foster), 287, 309
Swan Lake (Gorsky), 101, 373n20
Swan Lake (Petipa), 45, 133, 311
Swedish folklore, 73, 74–76
Swift, Kay, 62
symbolism, 20, 302, 305
Symphony in Three Movements (Balanchine), 63, 65
syncopation, 63, 64, 65, 124, 128, 143, 146, 299
Szwed, John, 66, 363n40, 375n15

Tadjik folkore, 96
Taglioni, Marie, 48, 98, 99
Tailleferre, Germaine, 78
Tairov, Alexander, 94, 165, 373n21
Take One, 153, 154
Takei, Kei, 308
Talking Heads videos, 134, 152
Tamiris, Helen, 200, 203, 252, 312
tango, 62, 164, 336
Tango (Balanchine), 62
tapdancing, 55, 56, 59, 60, 61, 65, 66, 67, 360n9/11
"Tar Baby" (*Folktales*) (Lemon), 283–284
Tarantella (Balanchine), 68
task dances, 12, 16, 218, 222, 223, 278, 307, 317
Taylor, Cecil, 219, 314
Taylor, Paul, 4, 5, 117, 292, 319; *Arden Court*, 26–27
Taylor, Robert, 140
Tchaikovsky, 311
Tchernicheva, Lyubov, 92
television, 97, 129, 130, 134, 135, 137, 146, 152, 286–87, 294, 323, 336, 364n48
Ten (Hay), 210, 317
Ten Thoughts Sleeping (Perron), 352
Tenney, James, 208, 314, 315
Teolinda (Goleizovsky), 95
Terminal Defense (Nelson), 352
Terrain (Rainer), 222, 306
Tharp, Twyla, 41, 133, 244, 279, 296, 304, 307–308, 309, 321, 323, 326, 334; *The Big Pieces*, 319; *Deuce Coupe*, 292, 308; *Eight Jelly Rolls*, 308, 319; *The Hundreds*, 275
Theater Laboratory (Grotowski), 253
Theater Union Dance Group, 202
theatricality, 252, 253–58, 294, 301, 333, 334, 337
Third Eye, 317
Thompson, Liz, 293
Thompson, Robert Farris, 66, 363n40, 364n48/50, 365n51, 375n15
Thomson, David, 347
Thomson, Virgil, 62, 326
Thorington, Helen, 322
Three Epitaphs (Taylor), 5
Three Piece (Childs and Goldstein), 314–15
Three-Piece Suite, A (Perron), **274**
Three Seascapes (Rainer), 7
Tikhomirov, Vassily, 95
Tiller in the Fields, The (Tudor), 33–34
Time and the Dancing Image (Jowitt), 21, 43
time structure, 212, 225, 234, 272
Timepiece (Emerson), 216
Tinker, 135
Tombeau de Couperin, Le (Börlin), 73, 74
Tomlinson, Mel, 69, 362n28
Torres, Julio, 340
Torse (Cunningham), 111
Totem (Nikolais), 5
Totti, Xavier, 328
Tour de Fuerza, 328, 329, 331
Tournoi singulier, Le (Börlin), 80
Towsen, John, 172

Transit (Paxton), 219
transvestite imagery, 135
Tricorne, Le (Massine), 74
Trio A or *The Mind is a Muscle, Part 1* (Rainer), 34, 42, 209–10, 222, 307, 352
Triumph of Neptune, The (Sitwell and Berners), 58, 66, 172–73, 362n23
Triumph of the Will (Riefenstahl), 42
Trois Gymnopédies (Satie), 212–13
Tropicana, Carmelita, 329, **331**; *Candela*, with Troyano and Parnes, **331**–32
Troyano, Ela, **331**
Truvit (A.I. Abramov), 93–94
Trying Times (Gordon), 257
Tudor, Andrew, 174
Tudor, Antony, 33–34, 293
Tudor, David, 37
Tugal, Pierre, 72
Turner, Victor, 23, 376n16, 378n18
Tuscaloosa (Self), 270
twist, the, 44, 143
Two Roses (Goleizovsky), 96
two-step, the, 164
Two Years Before the Mast (Dana), 185
Tyler, Edwina Lee, 323
Tzara, Tristan, 84, 217

Uchizono, Donna, 343–44, **346**–47
Unknown Solo (Paxton), 350
Untitled Solo (Cunningham), 111
uprock, 124, 141, 143, 148
Upside Down and Backwards (Jonas), 282
Urban Bush Women, 287, 324, 335, 343, **344**

Vain Precautions (*La Fille mal gardée*), 99, 101, 372n17
Valley Cottage (Jones and Zane), 322
Van der Lubbe's Head, 202
Van Riper, Peter, 317
van Schuylenburch, Ellen, 271–72
Van Tieghem, David, 322–23, 324–25
Vanover, Harmony, 141
Vassilenko, Sergei, 94
vaudeville, 361n17
Vaughan, David, 212, 362n28, 364n43/46
Vázquez, Viveca: *Mascando Inglés*, 329–30
Vega, Ana, 329
Vega, Frank, 141
Vélez, Evelyn, 329
verbal text: in ballet, 288–89; in dance, 222, 224, 230, 256–58
Vernon, Charlie, 258
Vertige, 298
Vertov, Dziga, 165
Vespers (Miller and Gibb), 324
Vessel (Monk), 249, 345
Video Clones (Fenley), 262
Vierges Folles, Les (Börlin), 73, 75
Villella, Edward, 53, 61, 64, 65, 68
Vincent, Mark, 142
virtuosity, 277, 278–79, 296–97, 326, 336; Fenley, Molissa, 267–68
vodun, 129, 136, 149
Vogue (cover), 156
Vogue ("three danced pages"), 83–84, 89
"Vogues," the, 134, 135
Volta, Ornella, 90
Vsevolozhsky, I.A., 312

WBGH, 323
Wake up and Dream! (Porter), 59
Walkaround Time (Cunningham), **114**, 115–18
waltz, the, 31–32, 47
War (Huot and Morris), 220
Warhol, Andy, 13, 133, 209, 275
Waring, James, 4, 7, 208, 210, 220, 221, 314, 315–16
Warren, John H., Jr., 184, 197–98
Water Study (Humphrey), 312
Watteau Duets, The (Armitage and Linton), 298, 321–22
Wayne, Gerri, 159–60
We Shall Run (Rainer), 9, 306, 316
Wedding Bouquet, A (Ashton/Stein), 173
wedding dance, the, 49–50
Weidman, Charles, 200, 203, 252
Weiss, Susana, **265**, 266

West Side Story (Bernstein/Robbins), 61, 68, 135
What Happened (Gordon), 29–30, 281, 320
"What Is Going on in a Dance?" (Beardsley), 10–16, 354n1
What is Post-Modernism? (Jencks), 302
Whirlwind, The (Goleizovsky), 95–96
White Mass (Goleizovsky), 93
White on White (Self), 270–71
Who Cares? (Balanchine), 63
Wiener, Nina, 294, 308, 321, 334
Wigman, Mary, 303, 312
Wild Style (film), 128, 131, 139, 140, 143, 149, 156, 157
Willett, John, 365n54
Willies, The (Fenley), 262
Wills, Harry, 83, 87
Wilson, Robert, 254, 256, 294, 320, 339
Winfield, Hemsley, 202
Winterbranch (Cunningham), 5, 6
Within the Quota (Porter/Börlin), 57, 58, 73, 79
women rappers, 154–55, 323
Women, Water, and a Waltz (Boyce), 324
Wood, Marilyn, 104
Woodard, Stephanie, 276
Wooding, Sam, jazz band, 162, 365n54
Wooster Group, The, 253
Word of Mouth (Basil), 134
Word Words (Paxton), 238, 315
Workers' Dance League, 199, 201, 202–203
Workers' Theater, 201, 203
workers' theater movement, 200–201, 203
World, The, 323, 336
Wor(l)d (T)raid (King), 34–35
Wortham, Tomi, 321
Woton's Wake (De Palma film), 209
Wylie, Grace, 202

You Little Wild Heart (Renzi), 323
Young, La Monte, 220, 315
Young Ballet, 57
Young Pioneers of America, 200

Zaloom, Paul, 290
Zambrano, David, 329, 347
Zamir, Batya, 279
Zane, Arnie, 308, 322, 326, 334; *Peter and the Wolf*, 284–85; *Rotary Action*, with Bill T. Jones, 257
zarzuela, 331, 332
Zeitland, Steven, 157
Ziegfeld Follies of 1936, 59, 60, 362n29
Ziff, Paul, 355n8
Zipes, Jack, 288
Zollar, Jawole Willa Jo, 287, 323, 324, 334, **342**, 343; *Bitter Tongue*, **344**; *LifeDance I . . . The Magician*, **342**

University Press of New England
publishes books under its own imprint and is the publisher for Brandeis University Press, Brown University Press, University of Connecticut, Dartmouth College, Middlebury College Press, University of New Hampshire, University of Rhode Island, Tufts University, University of Vermont, and Wesleyan University Press.

About the Author

SALLY BANES is Professor of Dance and Theater History and Chair of the Dance Program at University of Wisconsin-Madison. She is the author of *Greenwich Village 1963: Avant-Garde Performance and the Effervescent Body; Writing Dancing in the Age of Postmodernism; Terpsichore in Sneakers: Post-Modern Dance*; and *Democracy's Body: Judson Dance Theater, 1962–1964*. She has written on dance, theater, film, and performance for numerous publications and she edited *Footnote to History* by Si-lan Chen Leyda and *Soviet Choreographers in the 1920s* by Elizabeth Souritz. She also contributed the chapter on breakdancing to *Fresh: Hip Hop Don't Stop*. She was consultant/writer for the film *Retracing Steps: American Dance since Postmodernism* and co-consultant for *Dancing with the Camera* and *Style Wars*. She has curated the Megadance program, part of the Serious Fun! Festival at Lincoln Center. She has received fellowships from the National Endowment for the Humanities and the John Simon Guggenheim Foundation. She is currently President of the Society of Dance History Scholars.

Library of Congress Cataloging-in-Publication Data

Banes, Sally.
Writing dancing in the age of postmodernism / Sally Banes.
p. cm.
Includes index.
ISBN 0–8195–5266–6. — ISBN 0–8195–6268–8 (pbk.)
1. Ballet — United States — History — 20th century. 2. Dancing — United States — History — 20th century. I. Title.
GV1623.B36 1993
792.8′0973 — dc20 93–8225
♾

Structure & Function of the Body

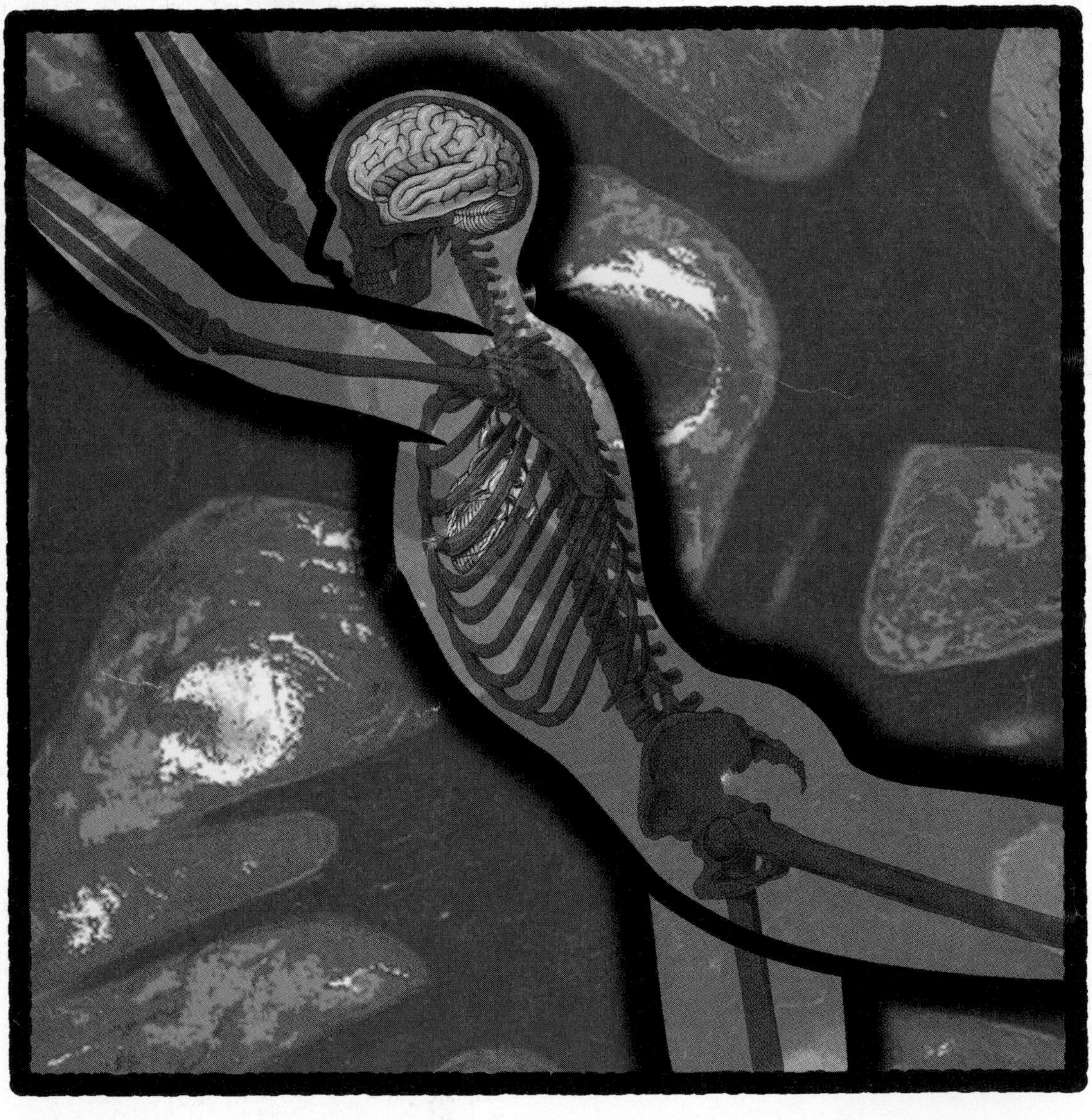

Structure & Function OF THE BODY

GARY A. THIBODEAU, PhD
Chancellor and Professor of Biology,
University of Wisconsin—River Falls,
River Falls, Wisconsin

KEVIN T. PATTON, PhD
Professor, Department of Life Sciences,
St. Charles County Community College,
St. Peters, Missouri

TENTH EDITION

Mosby

St. Louis Baltimore Boston Carlsbad Chicago Naples New York Philadelphia Portland
London Madrid Mexico City Singapore Sydney Tokyo Toronto Wiesbaden

Mosby
Dedicated to Publishing Excellence

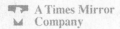

A Times Mirror Company

Vice President and Publisher: James M. Smith
Senior Acquisitions Editor: Ronald E. Worthington, PhD
Developmental Editor: Kristin M. Shahane
Project Manager: Carol Sullivan Weis
Production Editor: Karen M. Rehwinkel
Design Manager: Sheilah Barrett
Design: Rose Design
Manufacturing Manager: Karen Lewis
Cover Illustration: William C. Andrea, CMI

TENTH EDITION

Printed in the United States of America
Composition by The Clarinda Company
Lithography/color film by Color Associates, Inc.
Printing/binding by Von Hoffmann Press, Inc.

Mosby-Year Book, Inc.
11830 Westline Industrial Drive
St. Louis, Missouri 63146

Library of Congress Cataloging in Publication Data

Thibodeau, Gary A.,
Structure & function of the body / Gary A. Thibodeau, Kevin T. Patton.—10th ed.
p. cm.
Includes index.
ISBN 0-8151-8714-9 (HC). — ISBN 0-8151-8713-0 (SC)
1. Human physiology. 2. Human anatomy. I. Patton, Kevin T. II. Title.
[DNLM: 1. Anatomy. 2. Physiology. QS 4 T427s 1997]
QP34.5.T5 1997
612—dc20
DNLM/DLC
for Library of Congress 96-17642
CIP

97 98 99 00 / 9 8 7 6 5 4 3 2

Preface

We have been privileged to teach human anatomy and physiology for several decades. Each time we interact with students in the classroom or laboratory we become more aware of the challenges of teaching—and learning—about a body of knowledge that is not only fascinating and complex but ever-growing.

Advances in many areas of science have an impact on anatomy and physiology, perhaps more than other biological disciplines. Classroom instructors in the late 1990s are faced with the growing dilemma of selecting the most appropriate information for inclusion in introductory but nonetheless rigorous and demanding anatomy and physiology courses. New information is constantly being published describing advances in areas such as medicine, laboratory and clinical instrumentation, physiological chemistry, biotechnology, immunology, and molecular genetics. The result is an information explosion of incredible magnitude that makes it more and more difficult for teachers to select appropriate material and to give an up-to-date, contemporary presentation of anatomy and physiology that is accurate and user friendly for students. This edition of *Structure & Function of the Body* retains many features that have proved successful in over 35 years of classroom use; yet as a new text it presents a wealth of carefully selected new content, as well as pedagogical enhancements that will better serve the needs of today's instructors and students. The writing style and depth of coverage are intended to challenge, reward, and reinforce introductory students as they grasp and assimilate important concepts.

During the revision of this text, each change in the selection, sequencing, or method of presentation of material was evaluated by anatomy and physiology teachers working in the field—teachers currently assisting students to learn about human structure and function for the first time. The result is a text that students will read—one designed to help the teacher teach and the student learn. It is particularly suited to introductory anatomy and physiology courses in nursing and allied health-related programs. Emphasis is on material required for entry into more advanced courses, completion of professional licensing examinations, and successful application of information in a practical work-related environment.

Dr. Kevin Patton, who contributed significantly to the previous edition of this book, joins now as a coauthor to form a dynamic new writing team. We are confident that you will agree that our teamwork has resulted in a synergistic blend of talents evident throughout the book.

Special Features

UNIFYING THEMES

Anatomy and physiology encompass a body of knowledge that, because of its sheer magnitude, can easily discourage and overwhelm the introductory student. There is no question, however, that competency in both anatomy and physiology is essential for student success in almost every clinical or advanced course in a health-related or science curriculum. If a textbook is to be successful as a teaching tool in such a complex and important learning environment, it must assist and complement the efforts of instructor and student. It must help unify information, stimulate critical thinking, and motivate students to master a new vocabulary as they learn about the beauty and connectedness of human structure and function.

Structure & Function of the Body is dominated by two major unifying themes: the *complementarity of normal structure and function* and *homeostasis.* In every chapter of the book the student is shown how organized anatomical structures of a particular size, shape, form, or placement serve unique and specialized functions. Repeated emphasis of this principle encourages students to integrate otherwise isolated factual information into a cohesive and understandable whole. As a result, anatomy and physiology emerge as living and dynamic topics of personal interest and importance to the student. The integrating principle of homeostasis is used to show how the "normal" interaction of structure and function is achieved and maintained by dynamic counterbalancing forces within the body.

PRESENTATION OF CLINICAL AND PATHOLOGICAL INFORMATION

Highly selective clinical and pathological examples are included in each chapter of the book to help students understand that the disease process is a disruption in homeostasis and a breakdown of the normal integration of form and function. In the use of clinical examples the intent is to reinforce the normal mechanisms of body defense and adaptation and to stimulate student interest. The unifying themes are based on the need for introductory students in anatomy and physiology to have a firm foundation in the normal state before primary learning emphasis is focused on the diseased state. This text deals primarily with normal anatomy and physiology. An alternate text, *The Human Body in Health & Disease,* emphasizes pathology in addition to normal structure and function and is intended as an introduction to structural anomaly and pathophysiology.

ORGANIZATION AND CONTENT

The 20 chapters of *Structure & Function of the Body* present the core material of anatomy and physiology most *important* for introductory students. The selection of appropriate information in both disciplines was designed to eliminate the confusing mix of nonessential and overly specialized material that unfortunately accompanies basic information in many introductory textbooks. Information is presented so that students know and understand what is *important.* Further, pedagogical aids in each chapter identify learning objectives and then reinforce successful mastery of this clearly identified core material. As a result, students and instructors can interact more effectively as active participants in the learning experience. The sequencing of chapters in the book follows a course organization most commonly used in teaching at the undergraduate level. Because each chapter is self-contained, instructors have the flexibility to alter the sequence of material to fit personal teaching preferences or the special content or time constraints of their courses or students.

At every level of organization, both within and between chapters, care has been taken to couple structural information with important functional concepts. Students are presented with a conceptual framework and the necessary information on which to build. In each chapter of the text, appropriate physiological content balances the anatomical information that is presented. As a result, the student has a more integrated understanding of human structure and function. Throughout the text, examples that stress the complementarity of structure and function have been consciously selected to emphasize the importance of homeostasis as a unifying concept.

Acquiring and *using* the terms so necessary for any study of anatomy and physiology can be difficult for many students. To assist students in this area, new terms are introduced, defined, and incorporated into a working vocabulary. In addition to vocabulary development, every chapter incorporates skillfully designed visuals to reinforce written information with sensory input. Information related to body structure and function is presented in ways designed to help students develop the ability to integrate conceptual material and reinforce the normal integration of form and function.

The style of presentation of material in this text and its readability, accuracy, and level of coverage have been carefully developed to meet the needs of undergraduate students taking an introductory course in anatomy and physiology. *Structure & Function of the Body* remains an introductory textbook—a teaching book and not a reference text. No textbook can replace the direction and stimulation provided by an enthusiastic teacher to a curious and involved student. A good textbook, however, can and should be enjoyable to read and helpful to both.

PEDAGOGICAL FEATURES

Structure & Function of the Body is a student-oriented text. Written in a very readable style, it has numerous pedagogical aids that maintain interest and motivation. Every chapter contains the following elements that facilitate learning and the retention of information in the most effective manner.

Chapter Outline: An overview outline introduces each chapter and enables the student to preview the content and direction of the chapter at the major concept level before the detailed reading.

Chapter Objectives: Each chapter opening page contains approximately five measurable objectives for the student. Each objective clearly identifies for the student, before he or she reads the chapter, what the key goals should be and what information should be mastered.

Key Terms and Pronunciation Guide: Key terms, when introduced and defined in the text body, are identified in **boldface** to highlight their importance. A pronunciation guide follows each new term that students may find difficult to pronounce correctly.

Boxed Inserts and Essays: Brief boxed inserts or longer essays appear in every chapter. These inserts include information ranging from clinical applications to sidelights on recent research or related topics to exercise and fitness. Pathological conditions are sometimes explained in essay format to help students better understand the relationship between normal structure and function. Examples include AIDS, ulcers, and shingles. New boxed essays on Home Health Care issues have been added to this edition and reflect the growing trend in home based health care. Due to this trend, many students using this text will at some point encounter some of the issues discussed in the boxes. Topics reflect the diversity and wide range of conditions and problems a home health care worker must be prepared to deal with, including procedures, assessments, and administration. All boxed material is highlighted with an easily recognized symbol so that students can see at a glance whether the box contains clinical, general, fitness, or home health care information.

Outline Summaries: Extensive and detailed end-of-chapter summaries in outline format provide excellent guides for students as they review the text materials when preparing for examinations. Many students also find these detailed guides useful as a chapter preview in conjunction with the chapter outline.

Chapter Tests: Objective-type Chapter Test questions are included at the end of each chapter. They serve as quick checks for the recall and mastery of important subject matter. They are also designed as aids to increase the retention of information. Answers to all Chapter Test questions are provided at the end of the text.

Review Questions: Subjective review questions at the end of each chapter allow students to use a narrative format to discuss concepts and synthesize important chapter information for review by the instructor. The answers to these review questions are available in the Instructor's Manual that accompanies the text.

Critical Thinking Questions: Review questions that encourage students to use critical thinking skills are highlighted at the end of the Review Questions section. Answers to these questions are found in the Instructor's Manual along with the answers to the other Review Questions.

Chemistry Appendix: Recognizing that some students may need to review basic chemistry, we have added a new fully-illustrated Chemistry of Life appendix. This section discusses in simple, straightforward terms the concepts needed to understand basic anatomy and physiology with *concept summaries* to emphasize key points. As an appendix, this information will be readily available to students who need it, but it won't burden the text itself with unnecessary detail for those who do not. References within the chapters point students exactly to the appropriate coverage in the Appendix.

Additional learning and study aids at the end of the text include **Common Medical Abbreviations, Prefixes,** and **Suffixes;** an extensive **Glossary** of terms to assist students in mastering the vocabulary of anatomy and physiology; and a detailed **Index** that serves as a ready reference for locating information.

ILLUSTRATIONS

A major strength of *Structure & Function of the Body* is the exceptional quality, accuracy, and beauty of the illustration program. The truest test of any illustration is how effectively it can complement and strengthen written information found in the text and how successfully it can be used by the student as a learning tool. Extensive use has been made of full-color illustrations, micrographs, and dissection photographs throughout the text. Illustrations proven pedagogically effective in previous editions of *Structure & Function of the Body* have been retained or updated in appearance to provide accurate information and visual appeal. Each illustration is carefully referred to in the text and is designed to support the text discussion. The illustrations are an integral part of the learning process and should be carefully studied by the student.

Supplements

The supplements package has been carefully planned and developed to assist instructors and to enhance their use of the text. Each supplement, including the test items and study guide, has been thoroughly reviewed by many of the same instructors who reviewed the text.

INSTRUCTOR'S RESOURCE MANUAL AND TEST BANK

The Instructor's Resource Manual and Test Bank, prepared by Judith Diehl of Reid State Technical College, provides text adopters with substantial support in teaching from the text. The following features are included in every chapter:

Sample lecture outlines based on student objectives

Transparency masters for duplication or overhead projection

Outlines and **worksheets** for class demonstrations

Suggestions for student activities and assignments

Sources of audiovisual support

Information on current topics for distribution to students

Answers to the Chapter Test and Review Questions in the textbook

Critical Thinking Exercises for each chapter provide a step-by-step problem-solving opportunity for students

A **computerized test bank** is also available for Windows and MacIntosh users.

TRANSPARENCY ACETATES

A set of full-color transparency acetates—all with large, easy-to-read labels—is available to adopters of the text for use as a teaching aid.

STUDY GUIDE

The Study Guide, written by Linda Swisher of Sarasota County Vocational Technical Center, provides students with additional self-study aids, including chapter overviews, topic reviews, review questions keyed to specific pages in the text, and application and labeling exercises, as well as answers to the questions in the Study Guide.

MULTIMEDIA

Exciting new software is now available to facilitate the learning of difficult concepts in anatomy and physiology using the power of interactive media. **The Dynamic Human CD-ROM** uses animations, interactive anatomy and histology images, clinical illustrations and movies, and three-dimensional rotating viewers to bring the 10 major body systems to life for the student to explore and learn.

Mosby is pleased to bring to the scientific community a remarkable series of multimedia and print products made possible the National Library of Medicine's Visible Human Project (VHP) and innovative software technology developed by EAI. The first of these products is the **Dissectable Human CD-ROM,** which uses segmented, volume rendered VHP data to present systems-based human anatomy and digital dissection of major organs, both for the first time. Body systems can be studied in isolation or in context with other organs and tissues, with rotational viewing in three dimensions. Labeling can be toggled on or off, and authoring capability allows users to create customized presentations and study programs.This software will change the way anatomy is taught, and the way it is understood. Images from the Mosby-EAI image library are also available in a four color atlas, **Mosby's Systems Atlas of Anatomy**.

In addition to these exciting products, Mosby offers **Body Spectrum** software. The software provides reinforcement of anatomy with computerized coloring and labeling exercises.

A WORD OF THANKS

Many people have contributed to the development and success of *Structure & Function of the Body*. We extend our thanks and deep appreciation to the various students and classroom instructors who have provided us with helpful suggestions following their use of earlier editions of this text.

A specific "thank you" goes to the following instructors who critiqued in detail the ninth and tenth editions of this text or various drafts of the revision. Their invaluable comments were instrumental in the development of this new edition.

Patricia Laing-Arie
Meridian Technology Center
Stillwater, Oklahoma

Bert Atsma
Union County College
Cranford, New Jersey

Ethel J. Avery
Trenholm State Technical College
Montgomery, Alabama

Barbara Barger
Clarion County Career Center
Shippenville, Pennsylvania

Lydia R. Chavana
South Texas Vo-Tech Institute
McAllen, Texas

Marie Conn
Mayo State Vo-Tech School
Pikeville, Kentucky

Joseph Devine
Allied Health Careers
Austin, Texas

Edna M. Dilmore
Bessemer State Technical College
Bessemer, Alabama

Sally Flesch
Black Hawk College
Moline, Illinois

Denise L. Kampfhenkel
Schreiner College
Kerrville, Texas

Anne Lilly
Santa Rosa Junior College
Santa Rosa, California

Richard E. McKeeby
Union County College
Cranford, New Jersey

Keith R. Orloff
California Paramedical and Technical College
Long Beach, California

Christine Payne
Sarasota County Vocational Technical Center
Sarasota, Florida

Ann Senisi Scott
Nassau Tech VOCES
Westbury, New York

Anna M. Strand
Gogebic Community College
Ironwood, Michigan

Eugene R. Volz
Sacramento City College
Sacramento, California

Iris Wilkelhake
Southeast Community College
Lincoln, Nebraska

At Mosby–Year Book, Inc., thanks are due all who have worked with us on this new edition. We wish especially to acknowledge the support and effort of Ronald E. Worthington, PhD, senior editor; Kristin Shahane, developmental editor; Carol Sullivan Weis, project manager; Karen Rehwinkel, production editor; and Sheilah Barrett, design manager, all of whom were instrumental in bringing this edition to successful completion.

GARY A. THIBODEAU
KEVIN T. PATTON

Contents in Brief

1
An Introduction to the Structure and Function of the Body, 1

2
Cells and Tissues, 16

3
Organ Systems of the Body, 46

4
The Integumentary System and Body Membranes, 62

5
The Skeletal System, 80

6
The Muscular System, 110

7
The Nervous System, 136

8
The Senses, 172

9
The Endocrine System, 190

10
Blood, 214

11
The Circulatory System, 228

12
The Lymphatic System and Immunity, 258

13
The Respiratory System, 278

14
The Digestive System, 304

15
Nutrition and Metabolism, 328

16
The Urinary System, 340

17
Fluid and Electrolyte Balance, 358

18
Acid-Base Balance, 370

19
The Reproductive Systems, 382

20
Growth and Development, 406

Appendix A
The Chemistry of Life, 426

Appendix B
Medical Abbreviations, 441

Chapter Test Answers, 443

Glossary, G-1

Contents

CHAPTER 1

An Introduction to the Structure and Function of the Body, 1

Structural Levels of Organization, 1
Anatomical Position, 1
Anatomical Directions, 3
Planes or Body Sections, 3
Body Cavities, 5
Body Regions, 8
The Balance of Body Functions, 8

CHAPTER 2

Cells and Tissues, 16

Cells, 17
  Size and Shape, 17
  Composition, 17
  Parts of the Cell, 17
  Relationship of Cell Structure and Function, 22
Movement of Substances Through Cell Membranes, 22
  Passive Transport Processes, 23
  Active Transport Processes, 25
Cell Reproduction and Heredity, 26
  DNA Molecule and Genetic Information, 27
  Cell Division, 29
Tissues, 31
  Epithelial Tissue, 31
  Connective Tissue, 36
  Muscle Tissue, 38
  Skeletal Muscle Tissue, 38
  Nervous Tissue, 40

CHAPTER 3

Organ Systems of the Body, 46

Organ Systems of the Body, 47
  Integumentary System, 47
  Skeletal System, 47
  Muscular System, 50
  Nervous System, 50
  Endocrine System, 51
  Circulatory System, 52
  Lymphatic System, 52
  Respiratory System, 54
  Digestive System, 54
  Urinary System, 54
  Reproductive System, 54

CHAPTER 4

The Integumentary System and Body Membranes, 62

Classification of Body Membranes, 63
  Epithelial Membranes, 63
  Connective Tissue Membranes, 65
The Skin, 65
  Structure of the Skin, 65
  Appendages of the Skin, 68
  Functions of the Skin, 73
  Burns, 73

CHAPTER 5

The Skeletal System, 80

Functions of the Skeletal System, 81
  Support, 81
  Protection, 81
  Movement, 81
  Hemopoiesis, 81
Types of Bones, 81

Structure of Long Bones, 82
Microscopic Structure of Bone and Cartilage, 82
Bone Formation and Growth, 84
Divisions of Skeleton, 87
Axial Skeleton, 87
Appendicular Skeleton, 94
Differences Between a Man's and a Woman's Skeleton, 100
Joints (Articulations), 101
Kinds of Joints, 102

CHAPTER 6

The Muscular System, 110

Muscle Tissue, 111
Structure of Skeletal Muscle, 111
Microscopic Structure, 113
Functions of Skeletal Muscle, 113
Movement, 113
Posture, 115
Heat Production, 115
Fatigue, 115
Role of Other Body Systems in Movement, 116
Motor Unit, 116
Muscle Stimulus, 117
Types of Skeletal Muscle Contraction, 117
Twitch and Tetanic Contractions, 117
Isotonic Contraction, 117
Isometric Contraction, 117
Effects of Exercise on Skeletal Muscles, 117
Skeletal Muscle Groups, 119
Muscles of the Head and Neck, 123
Muscles That Move the Upper Extremities, 123
Muscles of the Trunk, 124
Muscles That Move the Lower Extremities, 125
Movements Produced by Skeletal Muscle Contractions, 127

CHAPTER 7

The Nervous System, 136

Organs and Divisions of the Nervous System, 137
Cells of the Nervous System, 137
Neurons, 137
Glia, 138
Nerves, 140
Reflex Arcs, 141
Nerve Impulses, 143
The Synapse, 145
Central Nervous System, 146
Divisions of the Brain, 146
Spinal Cord, 150
Coverings and Fluid Spaces of the Brain and Spinal Cord, 154
Peripheral Nervous System, 156
Cranial Nerves, 156
Spinal Nerves, 156
Autonomic Nervous System, 159
Functional Anatomy, 160
Autonomic Conduction Paths, 162
Sympathetic Nervous System, 163
Parasympathetic Nervous System, 163
Autonomic Neurotransmitters, 164
Autonomic Nervous System as a Whole, 164

CHAPTER 8

The Senses, 172

Classification of Sense Organs, 173
Converting a Stimulus Into a Sensation, 173
General Sense Organs, 173
Special Sense Organs, 176
The Eye, 176
The Ear, 180
The Taste Receptors, 184
The Smell Receptors, 185

CHAPTER 9

The Endocrine System, 190

Mechanisms of Hormone Action, 191
Protein Hormones, 191
Steroid Hormones, 192
Regulation of Hormone Secretion, 194
Prostaglandins, 195
Pituitary Gland, 196
Anterior Pituitary Gland Hormones, 196
Posterior Pituitary Gland Hormones, 198
Hypothalamus, 198
Thyroid Gland, 200
Parathyroid Glands, 202
Adrenal Glands, 203
Adrenal Cortex, 204
Adrenal Medulla, 205
Pancreatic Islets, 207
Female Sex Glands, 208
Male Sex Glands, 208
Thymus, 209

Placenta, 209
Pineal Gland, 209
Other Endocrine Structures, 209

CHAPTER 10

Blood, 214

Blood Composition, 215
Blood Plasma, 215
Formed Elements, 215
Red Blood Cells, 217
White Blood Cells, 219
Platelets and Blood Clotting, 220
Blood Types, 222
ABO System, 222
RH System, 223

CHAPTER 11

The Circulatory System, 228

Heart, 229
Location, Size, and Position, 229
Anatomy, 229
Heart Sounds, 232
Blood Flow Through the Heart, 234
Blood Supply to the Heart Muscle, 234
Cardiac Cycle, 235
Conduction System of the Heart, 236
Electrocardiogram, 238
Blood Vessels, 238
Kinds, 238
Structure, 238
Functions, 241
Circulation, 241
Systemic and Pulmonary Circulation, 241
Hepatic Portal Circulation, 245
Fetal Circulation, 247
Blood Pressure, 248
Understanding Blood Pressure, 248
Factors That Influence Blood Pressure, 248
Fluctuations in Blood Pressure, 251
Pulse, 251

CHAPTER 12

The Lymphatic System and Immunity, 258

The Lymphatic System, 259
Lymph and Lymph Vessels, 259
Lymph Nodes, 261
Thymus, 262
Tonsils, 263
Spleen, 263
The Immune System, 263
Function of the Immune System, 263
Nonspecific Immunity, 263
Specific Immunity, 264
Immune System Molecules, 265
Antibodies, 265
Complement Proteins, 267
Immune System Cells, 268
Phagocytes, 268
Lymphocytes, 268

CHAPTER 13

The Respiratory System, 278

Structural Plan, 279
Respiratory Tracts, 279
Respiratory Mucosa, 282
Nose, 283
Pharynx, 284
Larynx, 284
Trachea, 284
Bronchi, Bronchioles, and Alveoli, 287
Lungs and Pleura, 290
Respiration, 290
Mechanics of Breathing, 290
Exchange of Gases in Lungs, 293
Exchange of Gases in Tissues, 295
Volumes of Air Exchanged in Pulmonary Ventilation, 295
Regulation of Respiration, 297
Cerebral Cortex, 298
Receptors Influencing Respiration, 299
Types of Breathing, 299

CHAPTER 14

The Digestive System, 304

Wall of the Digestive Tract, 305
Mouth, 307
Teeth, 309
Typical Tooth, 310
Salivary Glands, 311
Pharynx, 312
Esophagus, 312

Stomach, 312
Small Intestine, 314
Liver and Gallbladder, 316
Pancreas, 317
Large Intestine, 318
Appendix, 320
Peritoneum, 320
  Extensions, 321
Digestion, 322
  Carbohydrate Digestion, 322
  Protein Digestion, 322
  Fat Digestion, 322
Absorption, 322

CHAPTER 15

Nutrition and Metabolism, 328

Role of the Liver, 329
Nutrient Metabolism, 329
  Carbohydrate Metabolism, 329
  Fat Metabolism, 332
  Protein Metabolism, 332
Vitamins and Minerals, 333
Metabolic Rates, 334
Body Temperature, 336

CHAPTER 16

The Urinary System, 340

Kidneys, 341
  Location, 341
  Internal Structure, 341
  Microscopic Structures, 341
  Function, 345
Formation of Urine, 346
  Control of Urine Volume, 348
Ureters, 349
Urinary Bladder, 352
Urethra, 353
Micturition, 353

CHAPTER 17

Fluid and Electrolyte Balance, 358

Body Fluids, 359
Mechanisms That Maintain Fluid Balance, 359
  Regulation of Fluid Intake, 362
  Importance of Electrolytes in Body Fluids, 362
  Capillary Blood Pressure and Blood Proteins, 367
Fluid Imbalances, 367

CHAPTER 18

Acid-Base Balance, 370

pH of Body Fluids, 371
  Mechanisms That Control pH of Body Fluids, 371
  Buffers, 371
  Respiratory Mechanism of pH Control, 375
  Urinary Mechanism of pH Control, 375
pH Imbalances, 377
  Metabolic and Respiratory Disturbances, 377
  Vomiting, 378

CHAPTER 19

The Reproductive Systems, 382

Common Structural and Functional Characteristics Between the Sexes, 383
Male Reproductive System, 383
  Structural Plan, 383
  Testes, 384
  Reproductive Ducts, 389
  Accessory or Supportive Sex Glands, 389
  External Genitals, 390
Female Reproductive System, 391
  Structural Plan, 391
  Ovaries, 392
  Reproductive Ducts, 394
  Accessory or Supportive Sex Glands, 396
  External Genitals, 396
  Menstrual Cycle, 397
Summary of Male and Female Reproductive System, 401

CHAPTER 20

Growth and Development, 406

Prenatal Period, 407
  Fertilization to Implantation, 407
  Periods of Development, 412
  Formation of the Primary Germ Layers, 412
  Histogenesis and Organogenesis, 414

Birth or Parturition, 414
Stages of Labor, 414
Postnatal Period, 416
Infancy, 417
Childhood, 419
Adolescence and Adulthood, 419
Older Adulthood, 420
Effects of Aging, 420
Skeletal System, 420
Integumentary System (Skin), 420
Urinary System, 420
Respiratory System, 420
Cardiovascular System, 420
Special Senses, 422

APPENDIX A

Chemistry of Life, 426

Levels of Chemical Organization, 426
Atoms, 426
Elements, Molecules, and Compounds, 427
Chemical Bonding, 429
Ionic Bonds, 429
Covalent Bonds, 430
Inorganic Chemistry, 431
Water, 431
Acids, Bases, and Salts, 433
Organic Chemistry, 434
Carbohydrates, 434
Lipids, 435
Proteins, 436
Nucleic Acids, 438

APPENDIX B

Common Medical Abbreviations, Prefixes, and Suffixes, 441

An Introduction to the Structure and Function of the Body

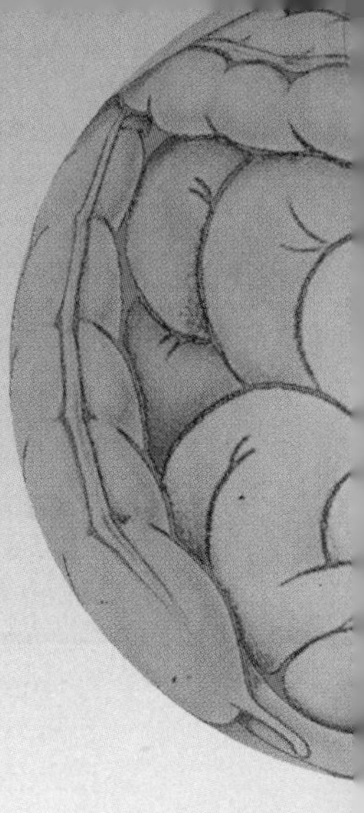

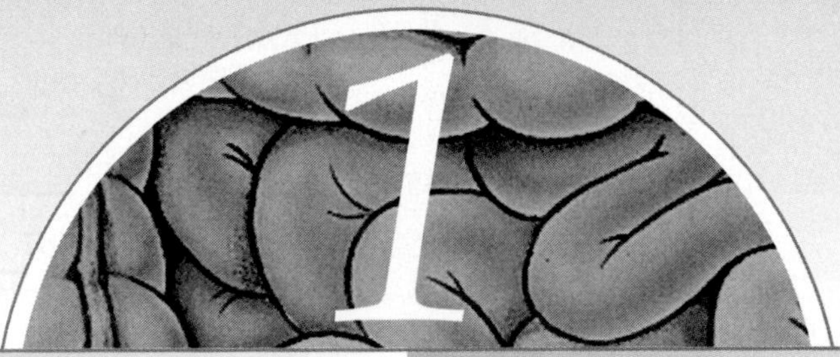

1

OUTLINE

Structural Levels of Organization
Anatomical Position
Anatomical Directions
Planes or Body Sections
Body Cavities
Body Regions
The Balance of Body Functions

BOXED ESSAY

Exercise Physiology

OBJECTIVES

After you have completed this chapter, you should be able to:

1. Define the terms *anatomy* and *physiology*.
2. List and discuss in order of increasing complexity the levels of organization of the body.
3. Define the term *anatomical position*.
4. List and define the principal directional terms and sections (planes) used in describing the body and the relationship of body parts to one another.
5. List the nine abdominopelvic regions and the abdominopelvic quadrants.
6. List the major cavities of the body and the subdivisions of each.
7. Discuss and contrast the axial and the appendicular subdivisions of the body. Identify a number of specific anatomical regions in each area.
8. Explain the meaning of the term *homeostasis* and give an example of a typical homeostatic mechanism.

There are many wonders in our world, but none is more wondrous than the human body. This is a textbook about that incomparable structure. It deals with two very distinct and yet interrelated sciences: **anatomy** and **physiology.** As a science, anatomy is often defined as the study of the structure of an organism and the relationships of its parts. The word *anatomy* is derived from two Greek words that mean "a cutting up." Anatomists learn about the structure of the human body by cutting it apart. This process, called **dissection,** is still the principal technique used to isolate and study the structural components or parts of the human body. Physiology is the study of the functions of living organisms and their parts. It is a dynamic science that requires active experimentation. In the chapters that follow, you will see again and again that anatomical structures seem designed to perform specific functions. Each has a particular size, shape, form, or position in the body related directly to its ability to perform a unique and specialized activity.

Structural Levels of Organization

Before you begin the study of the structure and function of the human body and its many parts, it is important to think about how those parts are organized and how they might logically fit together into a functioning whole. Examine Figure 1-1. It illustrates the differing levels of organization that influence body structure and function. Note that the levels of organization progress from the least complex (chemical level) to the most complex (body as a whole).

Organization is one of the most important characteristics of body structure. Even the word *organism,* used to denote a living thing, implies organization.

Although the body is a single structure, it is made up of trillions of smaller structures. Atoms and molecules are often referred to as the **chemical level** of organization (see Appendix A). The existence of life depends on the proper levels and proportions of many chemical substances in the cells of the body. Many of the physical and chemical phenomena that play important roles in the life process will be reviewed in the next chapter. Such information provides an understanding of the physical basis for life and for the study of the next levels of organization so important in the study of anatomy and physiology—cells, tissues, organs, and systems.

Cells are considered to be the smallest "living" units of structure and function in our body. Although long recognized as the simplest units of living matter, cells are far from simple. They are extremely complex, a fact you will discover in Chapter 2.

Tissues are somewhat more complex than cells. By definition a tissue is an organization of many similar cells that act together to perform a common function. Cells are held together and surrounded by varying amounts and varieties of gluelike, nonliving intercellular substances.

Organs are more complex than tissues. An organ is a group of several different kinds of tissues arranged so that they can together act as a unit to perform a special function. For instance, the lungs shown in Figure 1-1 are an example of organization at the organ level.

Systems are the most complex units that make up the body. A system is an organization of varying numbers and kinds of organs arranged so that they can together perform complex functions for the body. The organs of the respiratory system shown in Figure 1-1 permit air to enter the body and travel to the lungs, where the eventual exchange of oxygen and carbon dioxide occurs. Organs of the respiratory system include the nose, the windpipe or trachea, and the complex series of bronchial tubes that permit passage of air into the lungs.

The **body as a whole** is all the atoms, molecules, cells, tissues, organs, and systems that you will study in subsequent chapters of this text. Although capable of being dissected or broken down into many parts, the body is a unified and complex assembly of structurally and functionally interactive components, each working together to ensure healthy survival.

Anatomical Position

Discussions about the body, the way it moves, its posture, or the relationship of one area to another

FIGURE 1–1 ***Structural Levels of Organization in the Body.***

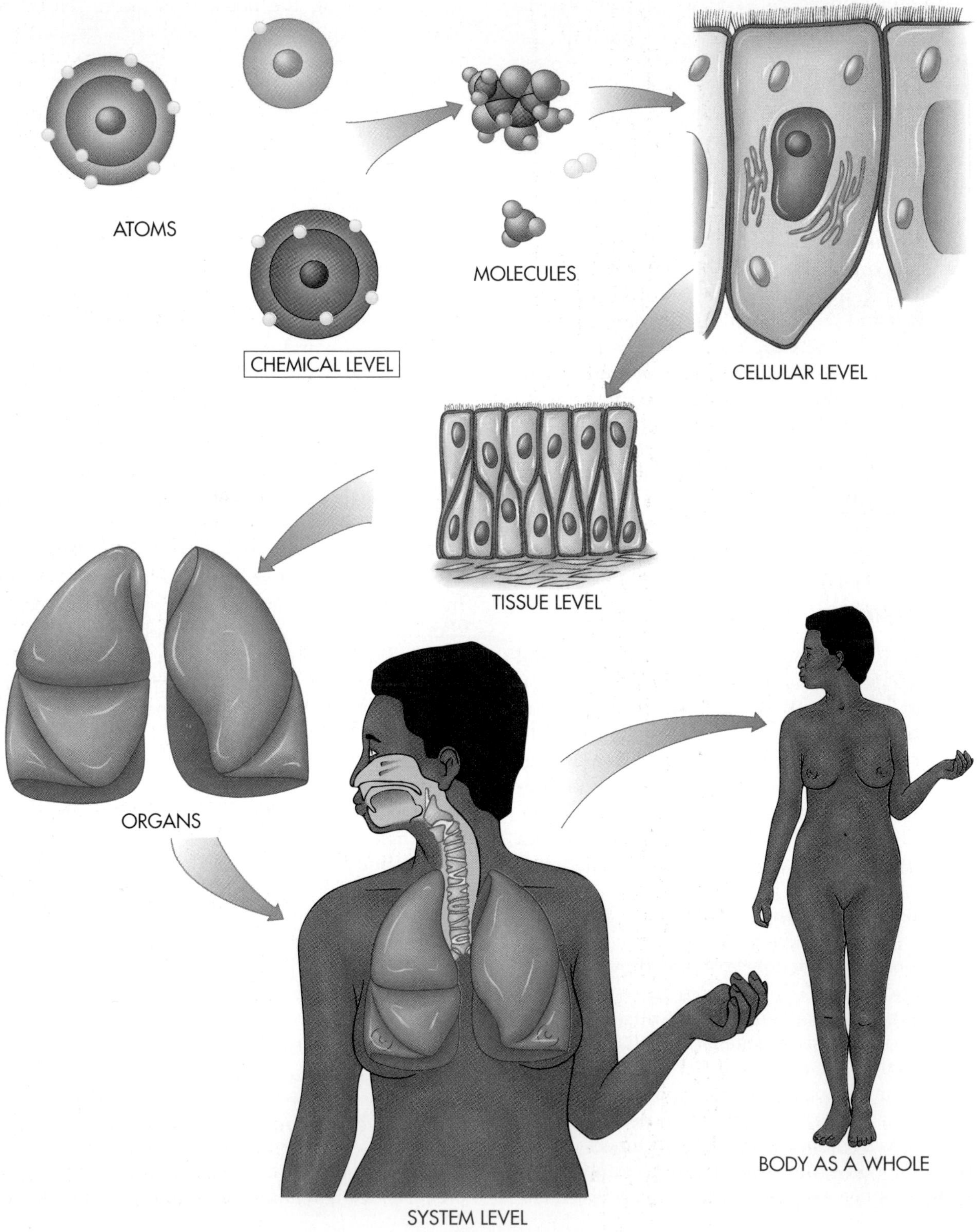

FIGURE 1–2 *Anatomical Position.* The body is in an erect or standing posture with the arms at the sides and the palms forward. The head and feet also point forward.

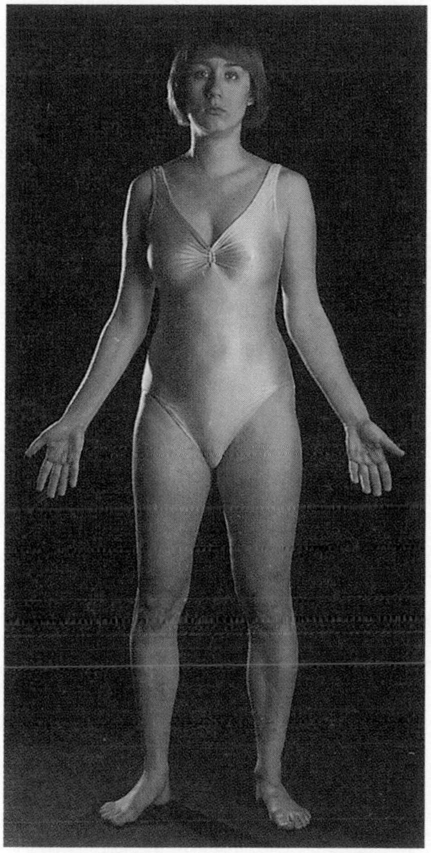

assume that the body as a whole is in a specific position called the **anatomical position.** In this reference position (Figure 1-2) the body is in an erect or standing posture with the arms at the sides and palms turned forward. The head and feet also point forward. The anatomical position is a reference position that gives meaning to the directional terms used to describe the body parts and regions.

Supine and **prone** are terms used to describe the position of the body when it is not in the anatomical position. In the supine position the body is lying face upward, and in the prone position the body is lying face downward.

Anatomical Directions

When studying the body, it is often helpful to know where an organ is in relation to other structures. The following directional terms are used in describing relative positions of body parts:

1. Superior and **inferior** (Figure 1-3)—*superior* means "toward the head," and *inferior* means "toward the feet." *Superior* also means "upper" or "above," and *inferior* means "lower" or "below." For example, the lungs are located superior to the diaphragm, whereas the stomach is located inferior to it.

2. Anterior and **posterior** (Figure 1-3)—*anterior* means "front" or "in front of"; *posterior* means "back" or "in back of." In humans, who walk in an upright position, *ventral* (toward the belly) can be used in place of anterior, and *dorsal* (toward the back) can be used for posterior. For example, the nose is on the anterior surface of the body, and the shoulder blades are on its posterior surface.

3. Medial and **lateral** (Figure 1-3)—*medial* means "toward the midline of the body"; *lateral* means "toward the side of the body or away from its midline." For example, the great toe is at the medial side of the foot, and the little toe is at its lateral side. The heart lies medial to the lungs, and the lungs lie lateral to the heart.

4. Proximal and **distal** (Figure 1-3)—*proximal* means "toward or nearest the trunk of the body, or nearest the point of origin of one of its parts"; *distal* means "away from or farthest from the trunk or the point of origin of a body part." For example, the elbow lies at the proximal end of the lower arm, whereas the hand lies at its distal end.

5. Superficial and **deep**—*superficial* means nearer the surface; *deep* means farther away from the body surface. For example, the skin of the arm is superficial to the muscles below it, and the bone of the upper arm is deep to the muscles that surround and cover it.

Planes or Body Sections

To facilitate the study of individual organs or the body as a whole, it is often useful to subdivide or "cut" it into smaller segments. To do this, body planes or sections have been identified by special

FIGURE 1–3 ***Directions and Planes of the Body.***

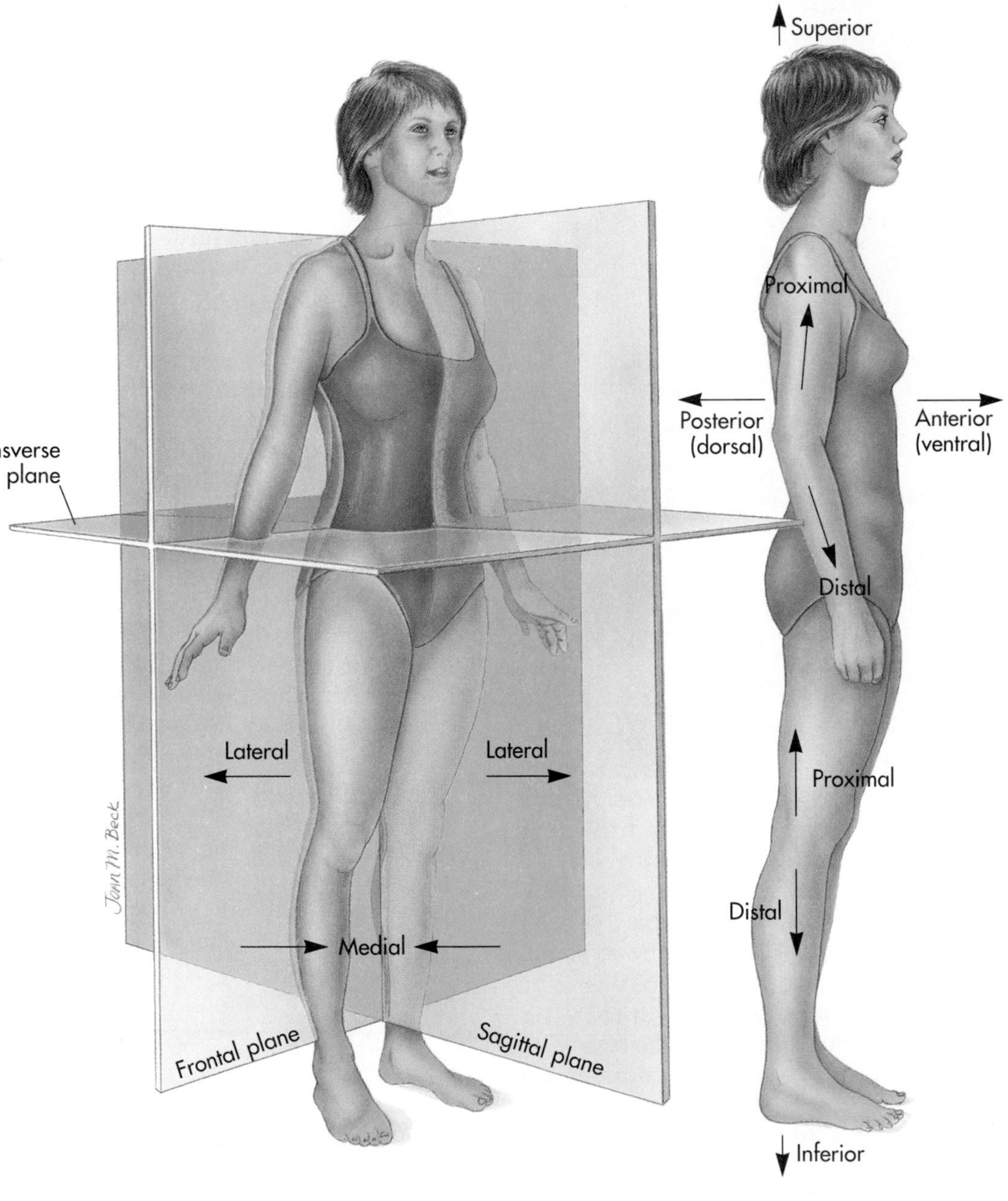

names. Read the following definitions and identify each term in Figure 1-3.

1. Sagittal—a sagittal cut or section is a lengthwise plane running from front to back. It divides the body or any of its parts into right and left sides. The sagittal plane shown in Figure 1-3 divides the body into two *equal halves.* This unique type of sagittal plane is called a **midsagittal plane.**

2. Frontal—a frontal (*coronal*) plane is a lengthwise plane running from side to side. As you can see in Figure 1-3, a frontal plane divides the body or any of its parts into anterior and posterior (front and back) portions.

3. Transverse—a transverse plane is a horizontal or crosswise plane. Such a plane (Figure 1-3) divides the body or any of its parts into upper and lower portions.

Body Cavities

Contrary to its external appearance, the body is not a solid structure. It is made up of open spaces or cavities that in turn contain compact, well-ordered arrangements of internal organs. The two major body cavities are called the **ventral** and **dorsal body cavities.** The location and outlines of the body cavities are illustrated in Figure 1-4. The ventral cavity includes the **thoracic cavity,** a space that you may think of as your chest cavity. Its midportion is a subdivision of the thoracic cavity, called the **mediastinum;** its other subdivisions are called the right and left **pleural cavities.** The ventral cavity in Figure 1-4 is broken down into an **abdominal cavity** and a **pelvic cavity.** Actually, they form only one cavity, the **abdominopelvic cavity,** because no physical partition separates them. In Figure 1-4 a dotted line shows the approximate point of separation between the abdominal and pelvic subdivisions. Notice, however, that an actual physical partition, represented in the figure as a wide band, separates the thoracic cavity from the abdominal cavity. This muscular partition is the **diaphragm.** It is dome-shaped and is the most important muscle for breathing.

To make it easier to locate organs in the large abdominopelvic cavity, anatomists have divided the abdominopelvic cavity into the nine regions shown in Figure 1-5 and defined them as follows:

FIGURE 1–4 ***Body Cavities.*** Location and subdivisions of the dorsal and ventral body cavities as viewed from the front (anterior) and from the side (lateral).

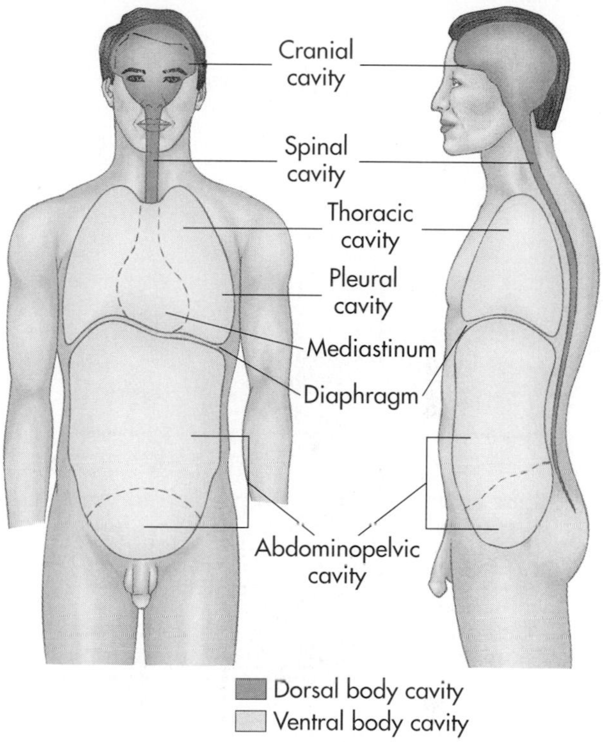

1. Upper abdominopelvic regions—the right and left hypochondriac regions and the epigastric region lie above an imaginary line across the abdomen at the level of the ninth rib cartilages.

2. Middle regions—the right and left lumbar regions and the umbilical region lie below an imaginary line across the abdomen at the level of the ninth rib cartilages and above an imaginary line across the abdomen at the top of the hip bones.

3. Lower regions—the right and left iliac (or inguinal) regions and the hypogastric region lie below an imaginary line across the abdomen at the level of the top of the hip bones.

FIGURE 1–5 ***The Nine Regions of the Abdominopelvic Cavity.*** The most superficial organs are shown.

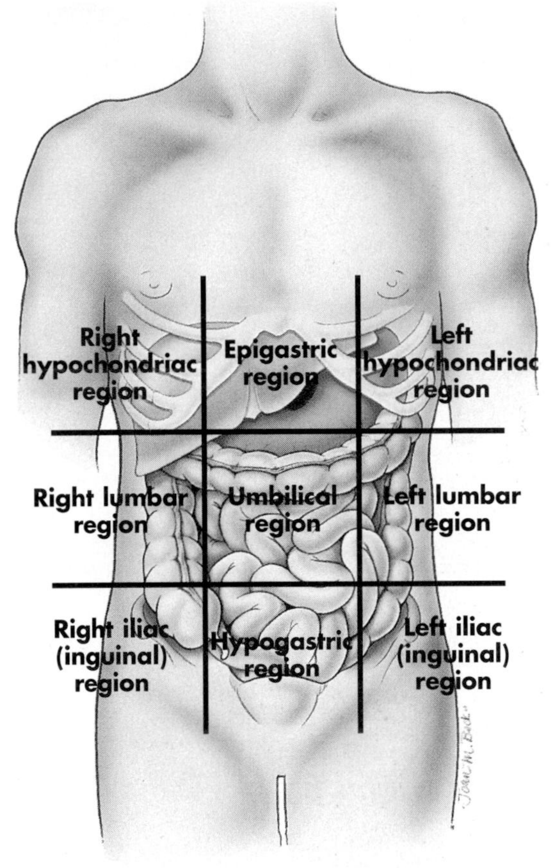

FIGURE 1–6 ***Division of the Abdominopelvic Cavity into Four Quadrants.*** Diagram showing relationship of internal organs to the four abdominal quadrants.

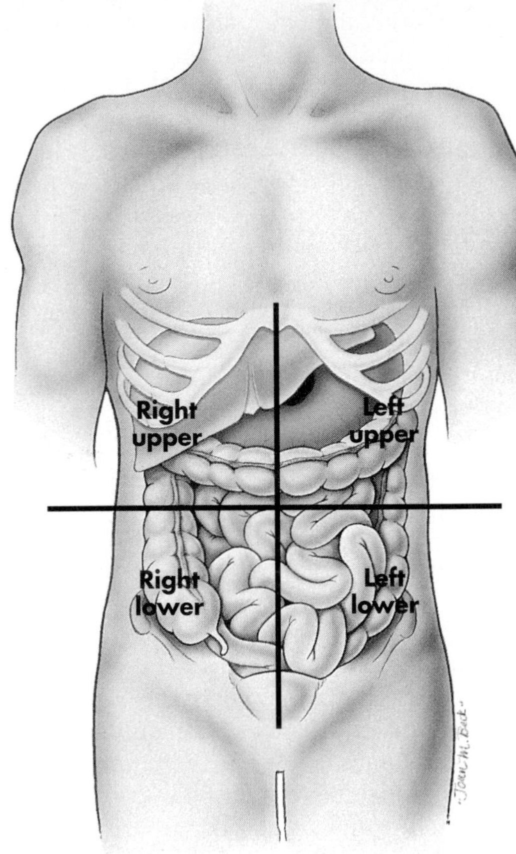

Another and perhaps easier way to divide the abdominopelvic cavity is shown in Figure 1-6. This method is frequently used by health professionals and is useful for locating pain or describing the location of a tumor. As you can see in Figure 1-6, the midsagittal and transverse planes, which were described in the previous section, pass through the navel (umbilicus) and divide the abdominopelvic region into the following **four quadrants:** right upper or superior, right lower or inferior, left upper or superior, and left lower or inferior.

The dorsal cavity shown in Figure 1-4 includes the space inside the skull that contains the brain; it is called the **cranial cavity.** The space inside the spinal column is called the **spinal cavity;** it contains the spinal cord. The cranial and spinal cavities are **dorsal cavities,** whereas the thoracic and abdominopelvic cavities are **ventral cavities.**

Some of the organs in the largest body cavities are visible in Figure 1-7 and are listed in Table 1-1. Find each body cavity in a model of the human body if you have access to one. Try to identify the organs in each cavity, and try to visualize their locations in your own body. Study Figures 1-4 and 1-7.

FIGURE 1–7 ***Organs of the Major Body Cavities.*** A view from the front.

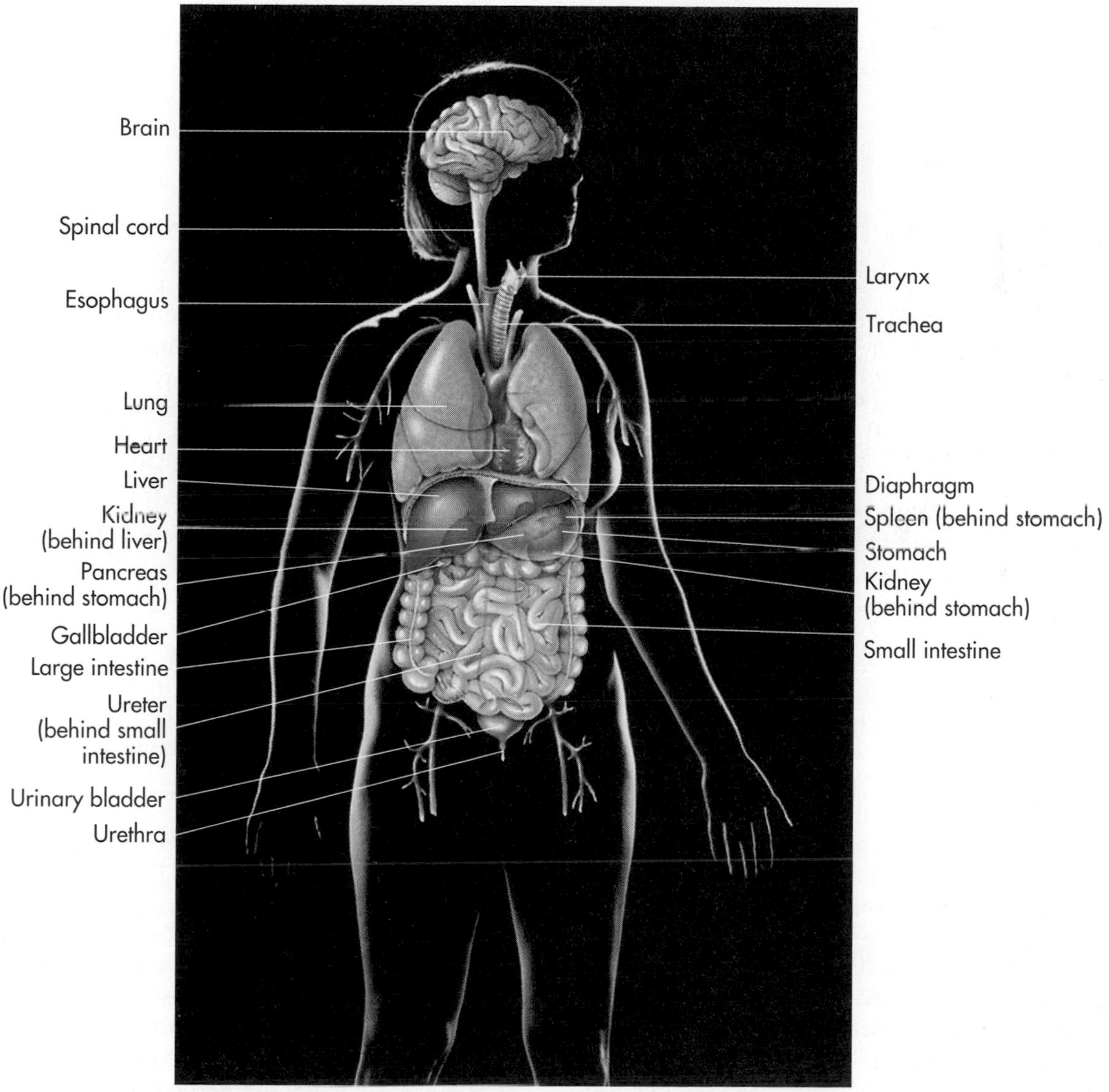

TABLE 1–1 Body Cavities

BODY CAVITY	ORGAN(S)
Ventral Body Cavity	
Thoracic cavity	
Mediastinum	Trachea, heart, blood vessels
Pleural cavities	Lungs
Abdominopelvic cavity	
Abdominal cavity	Liver, gallbladder, stomach, spleen, pancreas, small intestine, parts of large intestine
Pelvic cavity	Lower (sigmoid) colon, rectum, urinary bladder, reproductive organs
Dorsal Body Cavity	
Cranial cavity	Brain
Spinal cavity	Spinal cord

Body Regions

To recognize an object, you usually first notice its overall structure and form. For example, a car is recognized as a car before the specific details of its tires, grill, or wheel covers are noted. Recognition of the human form also occurs as you first identify overall shape and basic outline. However, for more specific identification to occur, details of size, shape, and appearance of individual body areas must be described. Individuals differ in overall appearance because specific body areas such as the face or torso have unique identifying characteristics. Detailed descriptions of the human form require that specific regions be identified and appropriate terms be used to describe them.

The ability to identify and correctly describe specific body areas is particularly important in the health sciences. For a patient to complain of pain in the head is not as specific and therefore not as useful to a physician or nurse as a more specific and localized description. Saying that the pain is facial provides additional information and helps to more specifically identify the area of pain. By using correct anatomical terms such as forehead, cheek, or chin to describe the area of pain, attention can be focused even more quickly on the specific anatomical area that may need attention. Familiarize yourself with the more common terms used to describe specific body regions identified in Figure 1-8 and listed in Table 1-2.

The body as a whole can be subdivided into two major portions or components: **axial** and **appendicular.** The axial portion of the body consists of the head, neck, and torso or trunk; the appendicular portion consists of the upper and lower extremities. Each major area is subdivided as shown in Figure 1-8. Note, for example, that the torso is composed of thoracic, abdominal, and pelvic areas, and the upper extremity is divided into arm, forearm, wrist, and hand components. Although most terms used to describe gross body regions are well understood, misuse is common. The word *leg* is a good example: it refers to the area of the lower extremity between the knee and ankle and not to the entire lower extremity.

The structure of the body changes in many ways and at varying rates during a lifetime. Before young adulthood, it develops and grows; after young adulthood, it gradually undergoes degenerative changes. With advancing age, there is a generalized decrease in size or a wasting away of many body organs and tissues that affects the structure and function of many body areas. This degenerative process is called **atrophy.** Nearly every chapter of this book will refer to a few of these changes.

The Balance of Body Functions

Although they may have very different structures, all living organisms maintain mechanisms that ensure survival of the body and success in propagating its genes through its offspring.

Survival depends on the body maintaining relatively constant conditions within the body. **Homeostasis** is what physiologists call the relative constancy of the internal environment. The cells of the body live in an internal environment made up mostly of water combined with salts and other dissolved substances. Like fish in a fish-

FIGURE 1–8 ***Axial and Appendicular Divisions of the Body.*** Specific body regions are labeled.

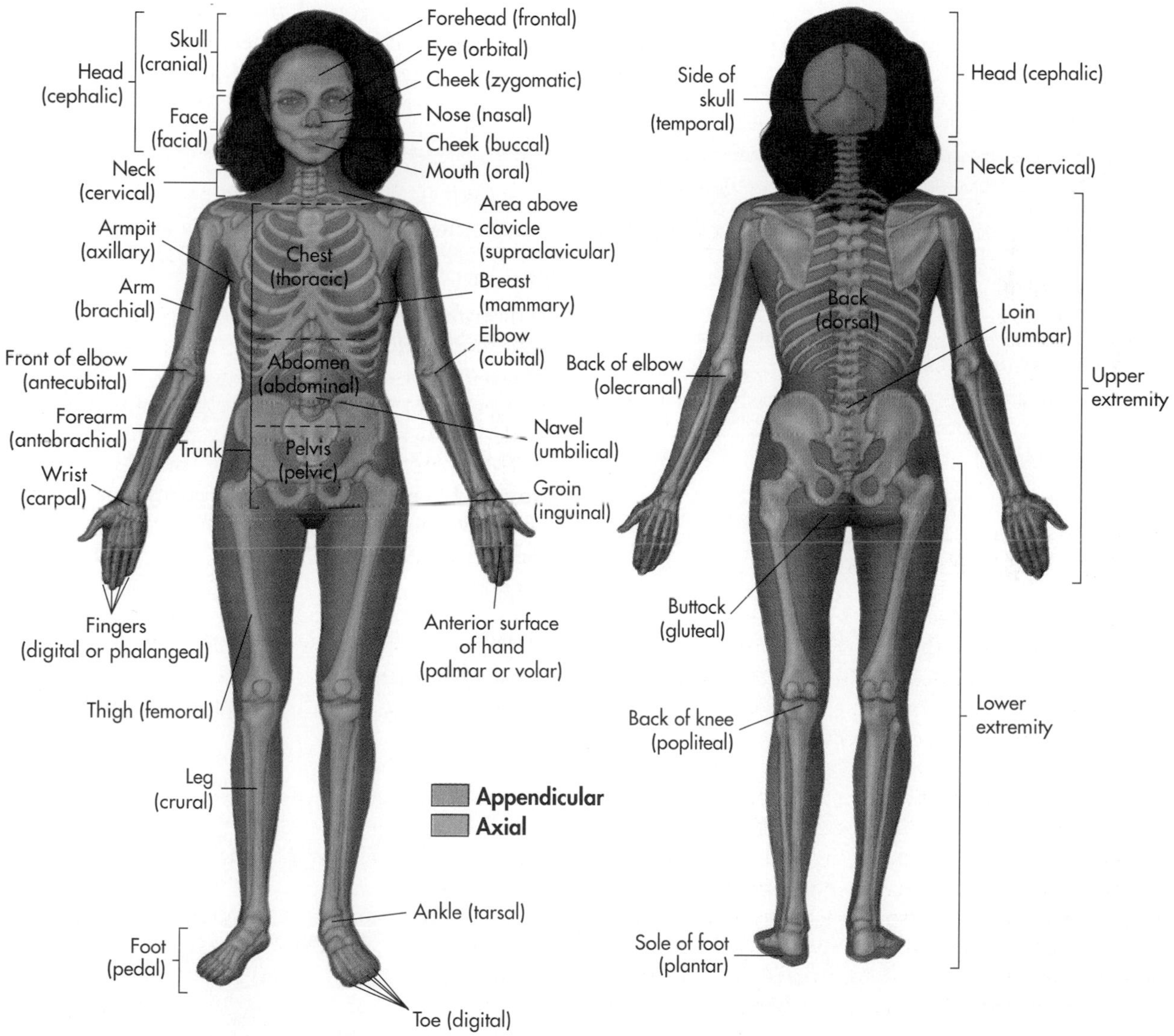

bowl, the cells are able to survive only if the conditions of their watery environment remain stable. The temperature, salt content, acid level (pH), fluid volume and pressure, oxygen concentration, and other vital conditions must remain within acceptable limits. To maintain constant water conditions in a fishbowl, one may add a heater, an air pump, and filters. Likewise, the body has mechanisms that act as heaters, air pumps, and the like, to maintain conditions of its internal fluid environment.

Because the activities of cells and external disturbances are always threatening internal stability, or homeostasis, the body must constantly work to maintain or restore that stability. To accomplish this self-regulation, a highly complex and integrated communication control system is required. The basic type of control system in the body is called a **feedback loop.** The idea of a feedback loop is borrowed from engineering. Figure 1-9, *A,* shows how an engineer would describe the feedback loop that maintains stability of tempera-

TABLE 1–2 Descriptive Terms for Body Regions

BODY REGION	AREA OR EXAMPLE	BODY REGION	AREA OR EXAMPLE
Abdominal (ab-DOM-in-al)	Anterior torso below diaphragm	**Facial, cont'd**	
Antebrachial (an-tee-BRAY-kee-al)	Forearm	**Zygomatic** (zye-go-MAT-ik)	Upper cheek
Antecubital (an-tee-KYOO-bi-tal)	Depressed area just in front of elbow	**Femoral** (FEM-or-al)	Thigh
Axillary (AK-si-lair-ee)	Armpit	**Gluteal** (GLOO-tee-al)	Buttock
Brachial (BRAY-kee-al)	Arm	**Inguinal** (ING-gwi-nal)	Groin
Buccal (BUK-al)	Cheek	**Lumbar** (LUM-bar)	Lower back between ribs and pelvis
Carpal (KAR-pal)	Wrist	**Mammary** (MAM-er-ee)	Breast
Cephalic (se-FAL-ik)	Head	**Occipital** (ok-SIP-i-tal)	Back of lower skull
Cervical (SER-vi-kal)	Neck	**Olecranal** (oh-LEK-kra-nal)	Back of elbow
Cranial (KRAY-nee-al)	Skull	**Palmar** (PAHL-mar)	Palm of hand
Crural (KROOR-al)	Leg	**Pedal** (PED-al)	Foot
Cubital (KYOO-bi-tal)	Elbow	**Pelvic** (PEL-vik)	Lower portion of torso
Cutaneous (kyoo-TANE-ee-us)	Skin (or body surface)	**Perineal** (pair-i-NEE-al)	Area (perineum) between anus and genitals
Digital (DIJ-i-tal)	Fingers or toes	**Plantar** (PLAN-tar)	Sole of foot
Dorsal (DOR-sal)	Back	**Popliteal** (pop-li-TEE-al)	Area behind knee
Facial (FAY-shal)	Face	**Supraclavicular** (soo-pra-kla-VIK-yoo-lar)	Area above clavicle
Frontal (FRON-tal)	Forehead	**Tarsal** (TAR-sal)	Ankle
Nasal (NAY-zal)	Nose	**Temporal** (TEM-por-al)	Side of skull
Oral (OR-al)	Mouth	**Thoracic** (tho-RAS-ik)	Chest
Orbital or **ophthalmic** (OR-bi-tal or op-THAL-mik)	Eyes	**Umbilical** (um-BILL-ih-kal)	Area around navel or umbilicus
		Volar (VO-lar)	Palm or sole

ture in a building. Cold winds outside a building may cause a decrease in building temperature below normal. A **sensor,** in this case a thermometer, detects the change in temperature. Information from the sensor *feeds back* to a **control center**—a thermostat in this example—that compares the actual temperature to the normal temperature and responds by activating the building's furnace. The furnace is called an **effector** because it has an effect on the controlled condition (temperature). Because the sensor continually feeds information back to the control center, the furnace will be automatically shut off when the temperature has returned to normal.

As you can see in Figure 1-9, *B,* the body uses a similar feedback loop in restoring body temperature when we become chilled. Nerve endings that act as temperature sensors feed information to a control center in the brain that compares actual body temperature to normal body temperature. In

FIGURE 1–9 ***Negative Feedback Loops.*** **A,** An engineer's diagram showing how a relatively constant room temperature (*controlled condition*) can be maintained. A thermostat (*control center*) receives feedback information from a thermometer (*sensor*) and responds by counteracting a change from normal by activating a furnace (*effector*). **B,** A physiologist's diagram showing how a relatively constant body temperature (*controlled condition*) can be maintained. The brain (*control center*) receives feedback information from nerve endings called cold receptors (*sensors*) and responds by counteracting a change from normal by activating shivering by muscles (*effectors*).

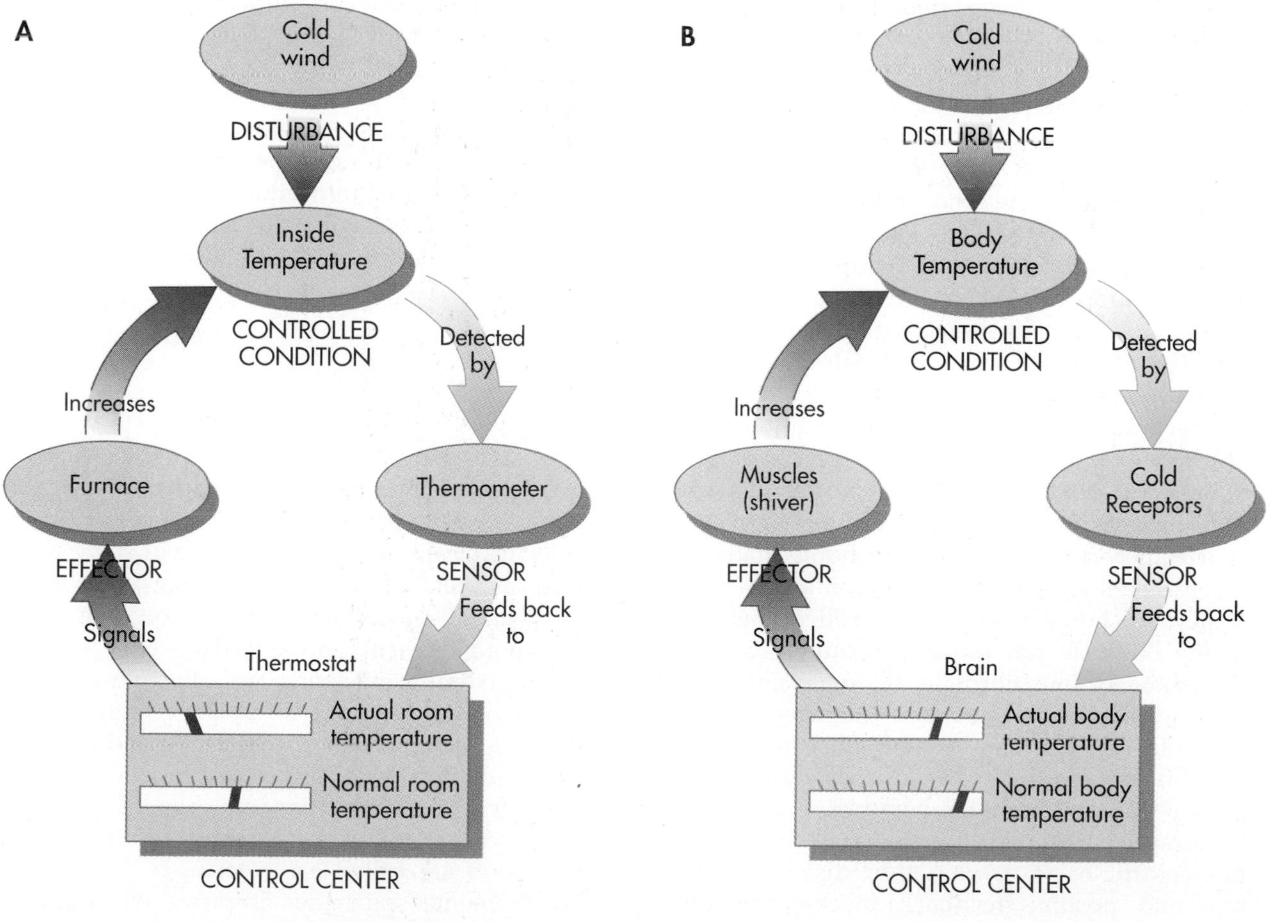

response to a chill, the brain sends nerve signals to muscles that shiver. Shivering produces heat that increases our body temperature. We stop shivering when feedback information tells the brain that body temperature has increased to normal.

Feedback loops such as those shown in Figure 1-9 are called **negative feedback** loops because they oppose, or negate, a change in a controlled condition. Most homeostatic control loops in the body involve negative feedback because reversing changes back toward a normal value tends to stabilize conditions—exactly what homeostasis is all about. An example of a negative feedback loop occurs when decreasing blood oxygen concentration caused by muscles using oxygen during exercise is counteracted by an increase in breathing to bring the blood oxygen level back up to normal. Another example is the excretion of larger than usual volumes of urine when the volume of fluid in the body is greater than the normal, ideal amount.

Although not common, **positive feedback** loops exist in the body and are involved in normal function. Positive feedback control loops are stimulatory. Instead of opposing a change in the internal environment and causing a "return to normal," positive feedback loops amplify or reinforce the change that is occurring. This type of feedback loop causes an ever-increasing rate of events to occur until something stops the process. An example of a positive feedback loop includes the events that cause rapid increases in uterine contractions before the birth of a baby. Another example is the increasingly rapid sticking together of blood cells called *platelets* to form a plug that begins formation of a blood clot.

It is important to realize that homeostatic control mechanisms can only maintain a *relative* constancy. All homeostatically controlled conditions in the body do not remain absolutely constant. Rather, conditions normally fluctuate near a normal, ideal value. Thus body temperature, for example, rarely remains exactly the same for very long; it usually fluctuates up and down near a person's normal body temperature.

Because all organs function to help maintain homeostatic balance, we will be discussing negative and positive feedback mechanisms often throughout the remaining chapters of this book.

Exercise Physiology

Exercise physiologists study the effects of exercise on the body organ systems. They are especially interested in the complex control mechanisms that preserve or restore homeostasis during or immediately after periods of strenuous physical activity. Exercise, defined as any significant use of skeletal muscles, is a normal activity with beneficial results. However, exercise disrupts homeostasis. For example, when muscles are worked, the core body temperature rises and blood CO_2 levels increase. These and many other body functions quickly deviate from "normal ranges" that exist at rest. Complex control mechanisms must then "kick in" to restore homeostasis.

As a scientific discipline, exercise physiology attempts to explain many body processes in terms of how they maintain homeostasis. Exercise physiology has many practical applications in therapy and rehabilitation, athletics, occupational health, and general wellness. This specialty concerns itself with the function of the whole body, not just one or two body systems.

Before leaving this brief introduction to physiology, we must pause to state the important principle that maintaining the balance of body functions is related to age. During childhood, homeostatic functions gradually become more and more efficient and effective. They operate with maximum efficiency and effectiveness during young adulthood. During late adulthood and old age, they gradually become less and less efficient and effective. Changes and functions occurring during the early years are called *developmental processes;* those occurring after young adulthood are called *aging processes.* In general, developmental processes improve efficiency of functions; aging processes usually diminish it.

OUTLINE SUMMARY

STRUCTURAL LEVELS OF ORGANIZATION (Figure 1-1)

A Organization is an outstanding characteristic of body structure

B The body is a unit constructed of the following smaller units:

- **1** Cells—the smallest structural units; organizations of various chemicals
- **2** Tissues—organizations of similar cells
- **3** Organs—organizations of different kinds of tissues
- **4** Systems—organizations of many different kinds of organs

ANATOMICAL POSITION (Figure 1-2)

Standing erect with the arms at the sides and palms turned forward

ANATOMICAL DIRECTIONS

A Superior—toward the head, upper, above
Inferior—toward the feet, lower, below

B Anterior—front, in front of (same as ventral in humans)
Posterior—back, in back of (same as dorsal in humans)

C Medial—toward the midline of a structure
Lateral—away from the midline or toward the side of a structure

D Proximal—toward or nearest the trunk, or nearest the point of origin of a structure
Distal—away from or farthest from the trunk, or farthest from a structure's point of origin

E Superficial—nearer the body surface
Deep—farther away from the body surface

PLANES OR BODY SECTIONS (Figure 1-3)

A Sagittal plane—lengthwise plane that divides a structure into right and left sections

B Midsagittal—sagittal plane that divides the body into two equal halves

C Frontal (coronal) plane—lengthwise plane that divides a structure into anterior and posterior sections

D Transverse plane—horizontal plane that divides a structure into upper and lower sections

BODY CAVITIES (Figure 1-4):

A Ventral cavity

- **1** Thoracic cavity
  - **a** Mediastinum—midportion of thoracic cavity; heart and trachea located in mediastinum
  - **b** Pleural cavities—right lung located in right pleural cavity, left lung in left pleural cavity
- **2** Abdominopelvic cavity
  - **a** Abdominal cavity contains stomach, intestines, liver, gallbladder, pancreas, and spleen
  - **b** Pelvic cavity contains reproductive organs, urinary bladder, and lowest part of intestine
  - **c** Abdominopelvic regions (Figures 1-5 and 1-6)
    - **(1)** Nine regions
    - **(2)** Four quadrants

B Dorsal cavity

- **1** Cranial cavity contains brain
- **2** Spinal cavity contains spinal cord

BODY REGIONS (Figure 1-8)

A Axial region—head, neck, and torso or trunk

B Appendicular region—upper and lower extremities

THE BALANCE OF BODY FUNCTIONS

A Survival of the individual and of the genes is the body's most important business

B Survival depends on the maintenance or restoration of homeostasis (relative constancy of the internal environment; Figure 1-9); the body uses negative feedback loops and, less often, positive feedback loops to maintain or restore homeostas is

C All organs function to maintain homeostasis

D Body functions are related to age; peak efficiency is during young adulthood, diminishing efficiency occurs after young adulthood

NEW WORDS

abdominopelvic quadrants (4)
abdominopelvic regions (9)
anatomical position
anatomy
atrophy
cavities
- abdominal
- cranial
- pelvic
- pleural
- spinal

thoracic
control center
directional terms
- superior
- inferior
- anterior
- posterior
- ventral
- dorsal
- medial
- lateral
- proximal
- distal
- superficial
- deep

effector loop
feedback
homeostasis
mediastinum
negative feedback
organization (structural levels)
- chemical
- cellular
- tissue
- organ
- system

physiology
planes of section
- sagittal
- midsagittal
- frontal
- transverse

positive feedback
prone
sensor
supine

CHAPTER TEST

1. The study of the structure of an organism and the relationship of its parts is called ______________; the study of the functions of that organism is called ______________.
2. An organization of many similar cells that together perform a common function is called a ______________.
3. The term ______________ means "toward the side of the body."
4. A frontal plane divides the body or any of its parts into ______________ and ______________ portions.
5. The body as a whole can be subdivided into two major portions: ______________ and ______________.
6. The relative constancy of the body's internal environment is described by the term ______________.

Match the body area in column B with the area or example in column A. (Only one answer is correct.)

COLUMN A	COLUMN B
7. ______ Skull	a. Mammary
8. ______ Groin	b. Thoracic
9. ______ Breast	c. Digital
10. ______ Sole of foot	d. Carpal
11. ______ Chest	e. Inguinal
12. ______ Wrist	f. Axillary
13. ______ Fingers or toes	g. Gluteal
14. ______ Armpit	h. Cranial
15. ______ Mouth	i. Oral
16. ______ Buttock	j. Plantar

17. The mediastinum is a subdivision of the:
    a. Thoracic cavity
    b. Pleural cavity
    c. Abdominal cavity
    d. Pelvic cavity
18. Which of the following is an example of a lower abdominal region?
    a. Epigastric region
    b. Umbilical region
    c. Right hypochondriac region
    d. Hypogastric region
19. Which of the following represents the least complex of the structural levels of organization?
    a. System
    b. Tissue
    c. Cell
    d. Organ
20. The diaphragm separates the:
    a. Right and left pleural cavities
    b. Abdominal and pelvic cavities
    c. Thoracic and abdominal cavities
    d. Mediastinum and pleural cavities

REVIEW QUESTIONS

1. Name the four kinds of structural units of the body. Define each briefly.
2. In one word, what is the one dominant function of the body or of any living thing?
3. Explain briefly what *homeostasis* means.
4. What do *proximal* and *distal* mean?
5. On what surface of the foot are the toenails located?
6. What structures lie lateral to the bridge of the nose?
7. Which joint—hip or knee—lies at the distal end of the thigh?
8. Define *anatomical position.*
9. List the major subdivisions of the axial and appendicular areas of the body.
10. List and define the four major planes of section.

CRITICAL THINKING

11. In what cavity could you find each of the following?
    brain
    esophagus
    gallbladder
    heart
    liver
12. Identify and discuss the mechanisms of negative and positive feedback loops in homeostasis.

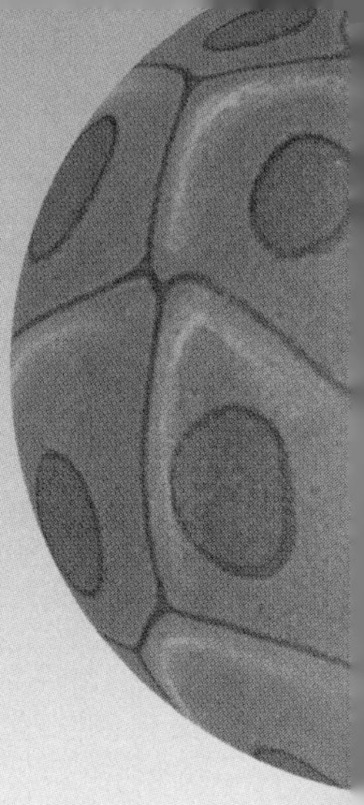

Cells and Tissues

2

OUTLINE

Cells
- Size and Shape
- Composition
- Parts of the Cell
- Relationship of Cell Structure and Function

Movement of Substances Through Cell Membranes
- Passive Transport Processes
- Active Transport Processes

Cell Reproduction and Heredity
- DNA Molecule and Genetic Information
- Cell Division

Tissues
- Epithelial Tissue
- Connective Tissue
- Muscle Tissue
- Nervous Tissue

BOXED ESSAYS

Tonicity
Tissues and Fitness

OBJECTIVES

After you have completed this chapter, you should be able to:

1. Identify and discuss the basic structure and function of the three major components of a cell.
2. List and briefly discuss the functions of the primary cellular organelles.
3. Compare the major passive and active transport processes that act to move substances through cell membranes.
4. Compare and discuss DNA and RNA and their function in protein synthesis.
5. Discuss the stages of mitosis and explain the importance of cellular reproduction.
6. Explain how epithelial tissue is grouped according to shape and arrangement of cells.
7. List and briefly discuss the major types of connective and muscle tissue.
8. List the three structural components of a neuron.

About 300 years ago Robert Hooke looked through his microscope—one of the very early, somewhat primitive ones—at some plant material. What he saw must have surprised him. Instead of a single magnified piece of plant material, he saw many small pieces. Because they reminded him of miniature prison cells, that is what he called them—cells. Since Hooke's time, thousands of individuals have examined thousands of plant and animal specimens and found them all, without exception, to be composed of cells. This fact, that cells are the smallest structural units of living things, has become the foundation of modern biology. Many living things are so simple that they consist of just one cell. The human body, however, is so complex that it consists not of a few thousand or millions or even billions of cells but of many trillions of them. This chapter discusses cells first and then tissues.

Cells

SIZE AND SHAPE

Human cells are microscopic in size; that is, they can be seen only when magnified by a microscope. However, they vary considerably in size. An ovum (female sex cell), for example, has a diameter of a little less than 1000 micrometers (about 1⁄25 of an inch), whereas red blood cells have a diameter of only 7.5 micrometers. Cells differ even more notably in shape than in size. Some are flat, some are brick shaped, some are threadlike, and some have irregular shapes.

COMPOSITION

Cells contain **cytoplasm** (SI-to-plazm), or "living matter," a substance that exists only in cells. The term *cyto-* is a Greek combining form and denotes a relationship to a cell. Each cell in the body is surrounded by a thin membrane, the **plasma membrane**. This membrane separates the cell contents from the dilute salt water solution called **interstitial** (in-ter-STISH-al) **fluid,** or simply **tissue fluid,** that bathes every cell in the body. Numerous specialized structures called **organelles** (or-gan-ELZ), which will be described in subsequent sections, are contained within the cytoplasm of each cell. A small, circular body called the **nucleus** (NOO-kle-us) is also inside the cell.

Important information related to body composition is included in Appendix A. You are encouraged to review this material, which includes a discussion of the chemical elements and compounds important to body structure and function.

PARTS OF THE CELL

The three main parts of a cell are:

1. Plasma membrane
2. Cytoplasm
3. Nucleus

The plasma membrane surrounds the entire cell, forming its outer boundary. The cytoplasm is all the living material inside the cell (except the nucleus). The nucleus is a large, membrane-bound structure in most cells that contains the genetic code.

Plasma Membrane

As the name suggests, the **plasma membrane** is the membrane that encloses the cytoplasm and forms the outer boundary of the cell. It is an incredibly delicate structure—only about 7 nm (nanometers) or 3/10,000,000 of an inch thick! Yet it has a precise, orderly structure (Figure 2-1). Two layers of phosphate-containing fat molecules called **phospholipids** form a fluid framework for the plasma membrane. Another kind of fat molecule called *cholesterol* is also a component of the plasma membrane. Cholesterol helps stabilize the phospholipid molecules to prevent breakage of the plasma membrane. Note in Figure 2-1 that protein molecules dot the surfaces of the membrane and extend all the way through the phospholipid framework.

Despite its seeming fragility, the plasma membrane is strong enough to keep the cell whole and intact. It also performs other life-preserving functions for the cell. It serves as a well-guarded gateway between the fluid inside the cell and the fluid around it. Certain substances move through it, but it bars the passage of others. The plasma membrane even functions as a communication device. How? Some protein molecules on the membrane's outer surface serve as receptors for certain other molecules when the other molecules contact them. In other words, certain molecules bind to certain receptor proteins. For example, some hormones (chemicals secreted into blood from ductless glands) bind to membrane receptors, and a change in cell functions follows. We might therefore think of such hormones as chemical messages, communicated to cells by binding to their cytoplasmic membrane receptors.

The plasma membrane also identifies a cell as coming from one particular individual. Its surface proteins serve as positive identification tags because they occur only in the cells of that individual. A practical application of this fact is made in *tissue typing,* a procedure performed before an organ from one individual is transplanted into another. Carbohydrate chains attached to the surface of cells often play a role in the identification of cell types.

Cytoplasm

Cytoplasm is the specialized living material of cells. It lies between the plasma membrane and the nucleus, which can be seen in Figure 2-2 as a round or spherical structure in the center of the cell. Numerous small structures are part of the cytoplasm, along with the fluid that serves as the interior environment of each cell. As a group, the small structures that make up much of the cytoplasm are called **organelles.** This name means "little organs," an appropriate name because they function like organs function for the body.

Look again at Figure 2-2. Notice how many different kinds of structures you can see in the cytoplasm of this cell. A little more than a generation ago, almost all of these organelles were

FIGURE 2–1 ***Structure of the Plasma Membrane.*** Note that protein molecules may penetrate completely through the two layers of phospholipid molecules.

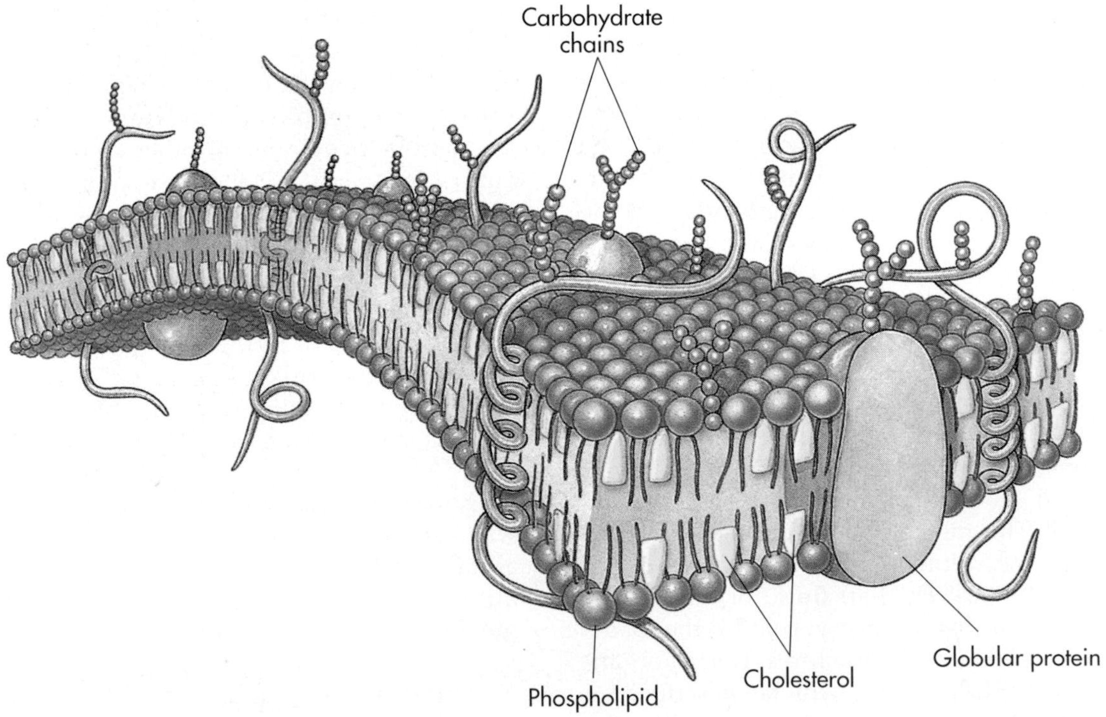

FIGURE 2–2 ***General Characteristics of the Cell.*** Artist's interpretation of cell structure.

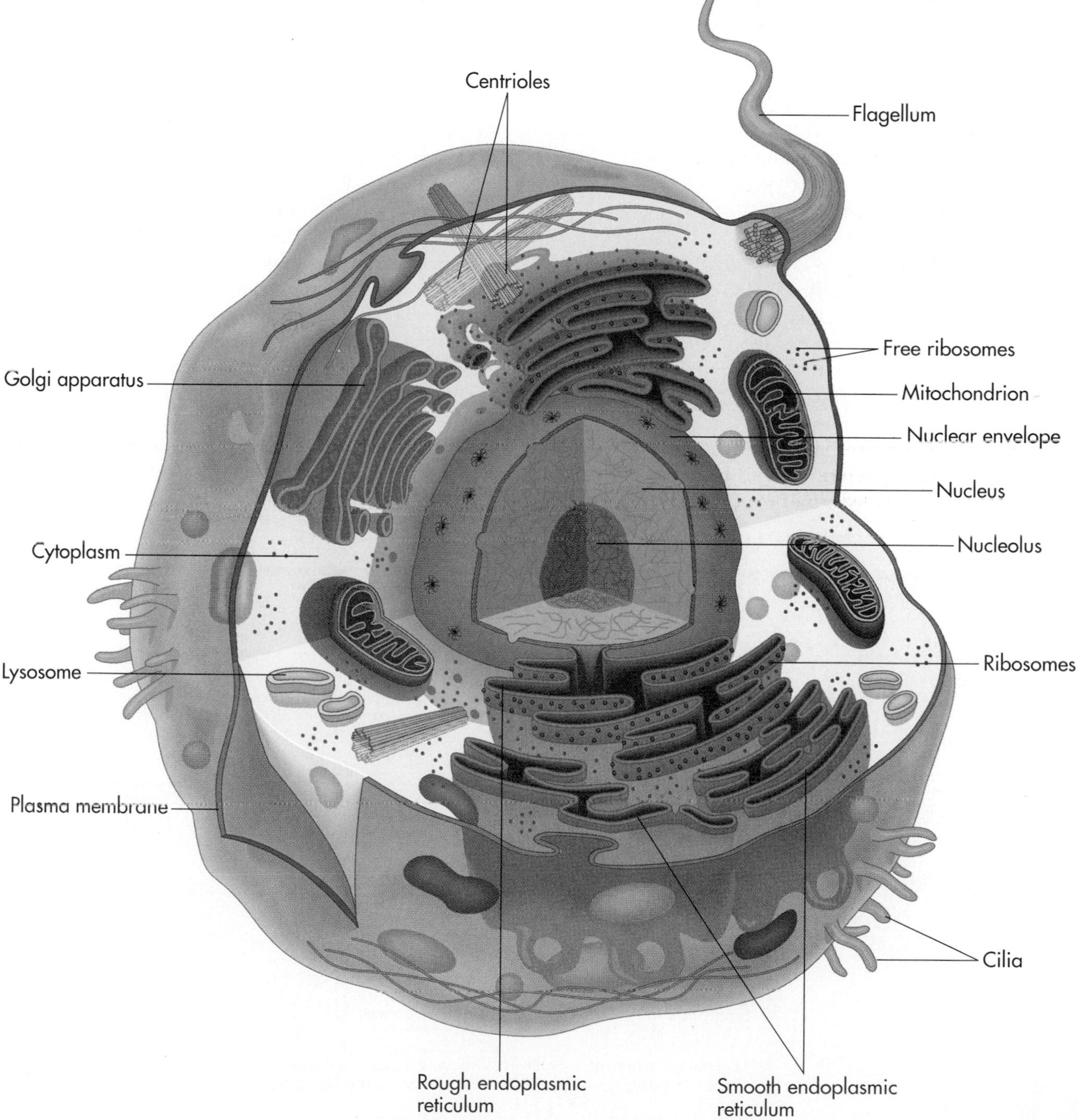

unknown. They are so small that they are invisible even when magnified 1000 times by a light microscope. Electron microscopes brought them into view by magnifying them many thousands of times. We shall briefly discuss the following organelles, which are found in cytoplasm (see also Table 2-1):

1. Ribosomes
2. Endoplasmic reticulum
3. Golgi apparatus
4. Mitochondria
5. Lysosomes
6. Centrioles
7. Cilia
8. Flagella

Ribosomes. Organelles called **ribosomes** (RI-bo-sohms), shown as dots in Figure 2-2, are very tiny particles found throughout the cell. Some ribosomes are found temporarily attached to a network of membranous canals called *endoplasmic reticulum (ER)*—another type of organelle described in the next paragraph. Ribosomes may also be free in the cytoplasm. Ribosomes perform a very complex function; they make enzymes and other protein compounds. Their nickname, "protein factories," indicates this function.

Endoplasmic reticulum. An **endoplasmic reticulum** (en-doe-PLAZ-mik ree-TIK-yoo-lum) **(ER)** is a system of membranes forming a network of connecting sacs and canals that wind back and forth through a cell's cytoplasm, all the way from the nucleus and almost to the plasma membrane. The tubular passageways or canals in the ER carry proteins and other substances through the cytoplasm of the cell from one area to another. There are two types of ER: *rough* and *smooth.* Rough ER gets its name from the fact that many ribosomes are attached to its outer surface, giving it a rough texture similar to sandpaper. As ribosomes make their proteins, they may attach to the rough ER and drop the protein into the interior of the ER. The ER then transports the proteins to areas where chemical processing takes place. These areas of the ER are so full that ribosomes do not attach to pass their proteins, giving this type of ER a smooth texture. Fats, carbohydrates, and proteins that make up cellular membrane material are manufactured in smooth ER. Thus the smooth ER makes new membrane for the cell. To sum up:

TABLE 2–1 Some Major Cell Structures and Their Functions

CELL STRUCTURE	FUNCTION(S)
Plasma membrane	Serves as the boundary of the cell; protein and carbohydrate molecules on outer surface of plasma membrane perform various functions; for example, they serve as markers that identify cells of each individual or as receptor molecules for certain hormones
Ribosomes	Synthesize proteins; a cell's "protein factories"
Endoplasmic reticulum (ER)	Ribosomes attached to rough ER synthesize proteins; smooth ER synthesizes lipids and certain carbohydrates
Golgi apparatus	Chemically processes, then packages substances from the ER
Mitochondria	ATP synthesis; a cell's "powerhouses"
Lysosomes	A cell's "digestive system"
Centrioles	Function in cell reproduction
Cilia	Short, hairlike extensions on the free surfaces of some cells capable of movement
Flagella	Single and much larger projections of cell surfaces than cilia; the only example in humans is the "tail" of a sperm cell
Nucleus	Dictates protein synthesis, thereby playing an essential role in other cell activities, namely active transport, metabolism, growth, and heredity
Nucleoli	Play an essential role in the formation of ribosomes

rough ER receives and transports newly made proteins and smooth ER makes new membrane.

Golgi Apparatus. The **Golgi** (GOL-jee) **apparatus** consists of tiny, flattened sacs stacked on one another near the nucleus. Little bubbles, or sacs, break off the smooth ER and carry new proteins and other compounds to the sacs of the Golgi apparatus. These little sacs, also called **vesicles,** fuse with the Golgi sacs and allow the contents of both to mingle. The Golgi apparatus chemically processes the molecules from the ER, then packages them into little vesicles that break away from the Golgi apparatus and move slowly outward to the plasma membrane. Each vesicle fuses with the plasma membrane, opens to the outside of the cell, and releases its contents. An example of a Golgi apparatus product is the slippery substance called mucus. If we wanted to nickname the Golgi apparatus, we might call it the cell's "chemical processing and packaging center."

Mitochondria. Mitochondria (my-toe-KON-dree-ah) are another kind of organelle in all cells. Mitochondria are so tiny that a lineup of 15,000 or more of them would fill a space only about 2.5 cm or 1 inch long. Two membranous sacs, one inside the other, compose a mitochondrion. The inner membrane forms folds that look like miniature incomplete partitions. Within a mitochondrion's fragile walls, complex, energy-releasing chemical reactions occur continuously. Because these reactions supply most of the power for cellular work, mitochondria have been nicknamed the cell's "power plants." The survival of cells and therefore of the body depends on mitochondrial chemical reactions. Enzymes (molecules that promote specific chemical reactions), which are found in mitochondrial walls and inner substance, use oxygen to break down glucose and other nutrients to release energy required for cellular work. The process is called *aerobic* or *cellular respiration.*

Lysosomes. The **lysosomes** (LYE-so-sohms) are membranous-walled organelles that in their active stage look like small sacs, often with tiny particles in them (Figure 2-2). Because lysosomes contain chemicals (enzymes) that can digest food compounds, one of their nicknames is "digestive bags." Lysosomal enzymes can also digest substances other than foods. For example, they can digest and thereby destroy microbes that invade the cell. Thus lysosomes can protect cells against destruction by microbes. Yet, paradoxically, lysosomes sometimes kill cells instead of protecting them. If their powerful enzymes escape from the lysosome sacs into the cytoplasm, they kill the cell by digesting it. This fact has earned lysosomes their other nickname, which is "suicide bags."

Centrioles. The **centrioles** (SEN-tree-olz) are paired organelles. Two of these rod-shaped structures exist in every cell. They are arranged so that they lie at right angles to each other (Figure 2-2). Each centriole is composed of fine tubules that play an important role during cell division.

Cilia. Cilia (SIL-ee-ah) are extremely fine, almost hairlike extensions on the exposed or free surfaces of some cells. Cilia are organelles capable of movement. One cell may have a hundred or more cilia capable of moving together in a wave-like fashion over the surface of a cell. They often have highly specialized functions. For example, by moving as a group in one direction, they propel mucus upward over the cells that line the respiratory tract.

Flagella. A **flagellum** (flah-JEL-um) is a single projection extending from the cell surface. Flagella are much larger than cilia. In the human, the only example of a flagellum is the "tail" of the male sperm cell. Propulsive movements of the flagellum make it possible for sperm to "swim" or move toward the ovum after they are deposited in the female reproductive tract (Figure 2-3).

Nucleus

Viewed under a light microscope, the **nucleus** of a cell looks like a very simple structure—just a small sphere in the central portion of the cell. However, its simple appearance belies the complex and critical role it plays in cell function. The nucleus ultimately controls every organelle in the cytoplasm. It also controls the complex process of cell reproduction. In other words, the nucleus must function properly for a cell to accomplish its normal activities and be able to duplicate itself.

Note that the cell nucleus in Figure 2-2 is surrounded by a **nuclear envelope.** The envelope, made up of two separate membranes, encloses a special type of cell material in the nucleus called **nucleoplasm.** Nucleoplasm contains a number of specialized structures; two of the most important

FIGURE 2–3 ***Human Sperm.*** Note the tail-like flagellum on each sperm cell. The flagella are so long that they do not fit into the photograph at this magnification.

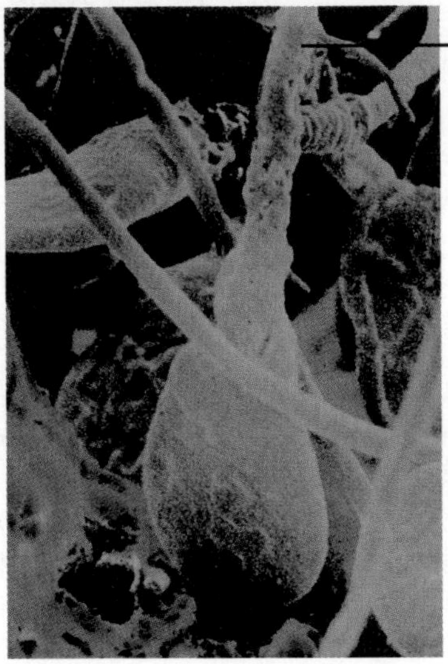

are shown in Figure 2-2. They are the **nucleolus** (noo-KLEE-oh-lus) and the **chromatin** (KRO-mah-tin) **granules.**

Nucleolus. The nucleolus is critical in protein formation because it "programs" the formation of ribosomes in the nucleus. The ribosomes then migrate through the nuclear envelope into the cytoplasm of the cell and produce proteins.

Chromatin and Chromosomes. Chromatin granules in the nucleus are threadlike structures made of proteins and hereditary material called **DNA** or **deoxyribonucleic** (dee-OK-see-rye-bo-noo-KLEE-ik) **acid.** DNA is the genetic material often described as the chemical "blueprint" of the body. It determines everything from gender to body build and hair color in every human being. During cell division, DNA molecules become tightly coiled. They then look like short, rodlike structures and are called **chromosomes.** The importance and function of DNA will be explained in greater detail in the section on cell reproduction later in this chapter. Information about DNA can also be found in *Appendix A: Chemistry of Life,* which begins on p. 426.

RELATIONSHIP OF CELL STRUCTURE AND FUNCTION

Every human cell performs certain functions; some maintain the cell's survival, and others help maintain the body's survival. In many instances, the number and type of organelles allow cells to differ dramatically in terms of their specialized functions. For example, cells that contain large numbers of mitochondria, such as heart muscle cells, are capable of sustained work. Why? Because the numerous mitochondria found in these cells supply the necessary energy required for rhythmic and ongoing contractions. Movement of the flagellum of a sperm cell is another example of the way a specialized organelle has a specialized function. The sperm's flagellum propels it through the reproductive tract of the female, thus increasing the chances of successful fertilization. This is how and why organizational structure at the cellular level is so important for function in living organisms. There are examples in every chapter of the text to illustrate how structure and function are intimately related at every level of body organization.

Movement of Substances Through Cell Membranes

The plasma membrane in every healthy cell separates the contents of the cell from the tissue fluid that surrounds it. At the same time the membrane must permit certain substances to enter the cell and allow others to leave. Heavy traffic moves continuously in both directions through cell membranes. Molecules of water, foods, gases, wastes, and many other substances stream in and out of all cells in endless procession. A number of processes allow this mass movement of substances into and out of cells. These transport processes are classified under two general headings:

1. Passive transport processes
2. Active transport processes

As implied by their name, active transport processes require the expenditure of energy by the cell, and passive transport processes do not. The energy required for active transport processes is obtained from a very important chemical substance called **adenosine triphosphate** (ah-DEN-o-sen tri-FOS-fate) or **ATP.** ATP is produced in the mitochondria using energy from nutrients and is capable of releasing that energy to do work in the cell. For active transport processes to occur, the breakdown of ATP and the use of the released energy are required.

The details of active and passive transport of substances across cell membranes are much easier to understand if you keep in mind the following two key facts: (1) in passive transport processes, no cellular energy is required to move substances from a high concentration to a low concentration; and (2) in active transport processes, cellular energy is required to move substances from a low concentration to a high concentration.

PASSIVE TRANSPORT PROCESSES

The primary passive transport processes that move substances through the cell membranes include the following:

1. Diffusion
   a. Osmosis
   b. Dialysis
2. Filtration

Scientists describe the movement of substances in passive systems as going "down a concentration gradient." This means that substances in passive systems move from a region of high concentration to a region of low concentration until they reach equal proportions on both sides of the membrane. As you read the next few paragraphs, refer to Table 2-2, which summarizes important information about passive transport processes.

Diffusion

Diffusion is a good example of a passive transport process. Diffusion is the process by which substances scatter themselves evenly throughout an available space. The system does not require additional energy for this movement. To demon-

TABLE 2–2 Passive Transport Processes

PROCESS	DESCRIPTION		EXAMPLES
Diffusion	Movement of particles through a membrane from an area of high concentration to an area of low concentration—that is, down the concentration gradient	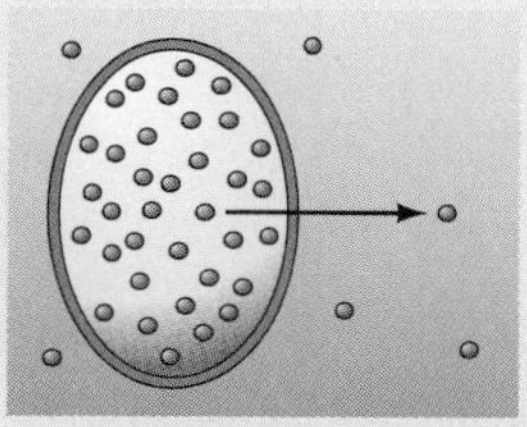	Movement of carbon dioxide out of all cells; movement of sodium ions into nerve cells as they conduct an impulse
Osmosis	Diffusion of water through a selectively permeable membrane in the presence of at least one impermeant solute	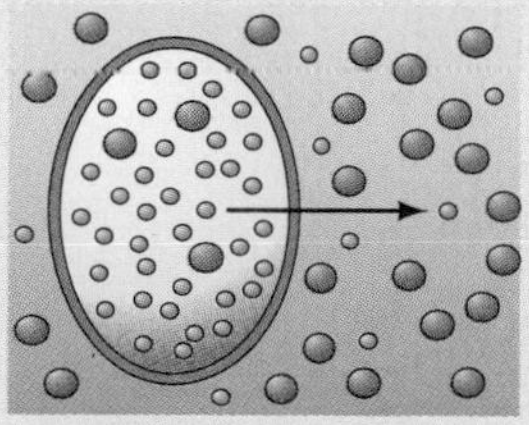	Diffusion of water molecules into and out of cells to correct imbalances in water concentration
Filtration	Movement of water and small solute particles, but not larger particles, through a filtration membrane; movement occurs from area of high pressure to area of low pressure	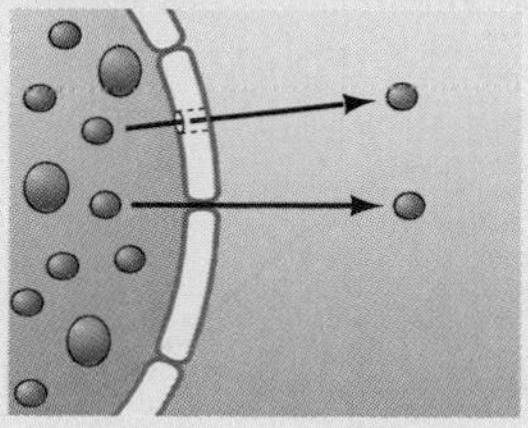	In the kidney, water and small solutes move from blood vessels but blood proteins and blood cells do not, thus beginning the formation of urine

FIGURE 2–4 ***Diffusion.*** Note that the membrane is permeable to glucose and water and that it separates a 10% glucose solution from a 20% glucose solution. The container on the left shows the two solutions separated by the membrane at the start of diffusion. The container on the right shows the result of diffusion after time.

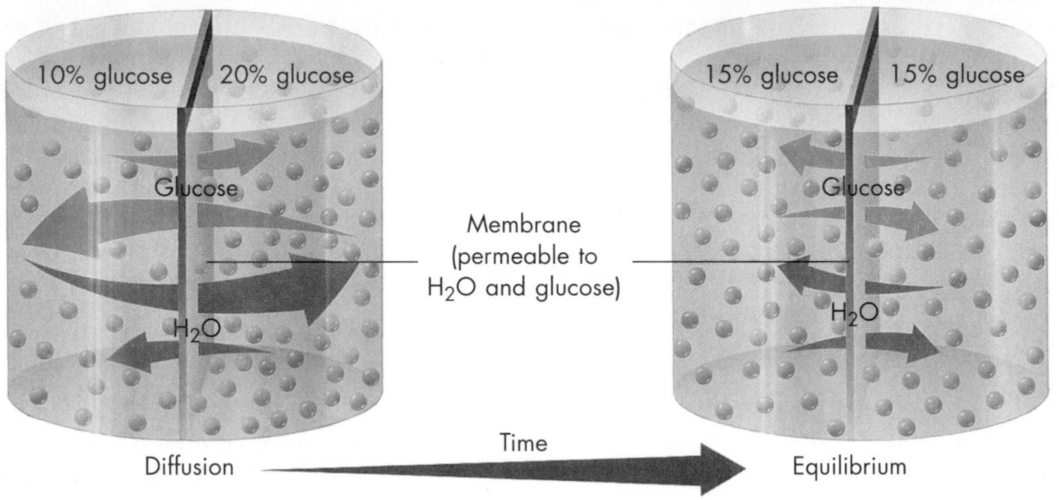

Tonicity

A salt (NaCl) solution is said to be **isotonic** (*iso* = equal) if it contains the same concentration of salt normally found in a living red blood cell. A 0.9% NaCl solution is isotonic; that is, it contains the same level of NaCl as found in red cells. A solution that contains a higher level of salt (above 0.9%) is said to be **hypertonic** (*hyper* = above) and one containing less (below 0.9%) is hypotonic (*hypo* = below). With what you now know about filtration, diffusion, and osmosis, can you predict what would occur if red blood cells were placed in isotonic, hypotonic, and hypertonic solutions?

Examine the figures. Note that red blood cells placed in isotonic solution remain unchanged because there is no effective difference in salt or water concentrations. The movement of water into and out of the cells is about equal. This is not the case with red cells placed in hypertonic salt solution; they immediately lose water from their cytoplasm into the surrounding salty solution, and they shrink. This process is called **crenation.**

The opposite occurs if red cells are placed in a hypotonic solution; they swell as water enters the cell from the surrounding dilute solution. Eventually the cells break or **lyse,** and the hemoglobin they contain is released into the solution.

strate diffusion of particles throughout a fluid, perform this simple experiment the next time you pour yourself a cup of coffee or tea. Place a cube of sugar on a teaspoon and lower it gently to the bottom of the cup. Let it stand for 2 or 3 minutes, and then, holding the cup steady, take a sip off the top. It will taste sweet. Why? Because some of the sugar molecules will have diffused from the area of high concentration near the sugar cube at the bottom of the cup to the area of low concentration at the top of the cup.

The process of diffusion is shown in Figure 2-4. Note that both substances diffuse rapidly through the membrane in both directions. However, as indicated by the green arrows, more glucose moves out of the 20% solution, where the concentration is higher, into the 10% solution, where the concentration is lower, than in the opposite direction. This is an example of movement down a concentration gradient. Simultaneously, more water moves from the 10% solution, where there are more water molecules, into the 20% solution, where there are fewer water molecules. This is also an example of movement down a concentration gradient. Water moves from high to low concentration. The result? Equilibration (balancing) of the concentrations of the two solutions after an interval of time. From then on, equal amounts of glucose will diffuse in both directions, as will equal amounts of water.

Osmosis and dialysis. Osmosis (os-MO-sis) and **dialysis** (dye-AL-i-sis) are specialized examples of diffusion. In both cases, diffusion occurs across a selectively permeable membrane. The plasma membrane of a cell is said to be selectively permeable because it permits the passage of certain substances but not others. This is a necessary property if the cell is to permit some substances, such as nutrients, to gain entrance to the cell while excluding others. Osmosis is the diffusion of *water* across a selectively permeable membrane. However, in the case of dialysis, substances called **solutes,** which are dissolved particles in water, move across a selectively permeable membrane by diffusion.

Filtration

Filtration is the movement of water and solutes through a membrane because of a greater pushing force on one side of the membrane than on the other side. The force is called *hydrostatic pressure,* which is simply the force or weight of a fluid pushing against some surface. A principle about filtration that is of great physiological importance is that it always occurs *down* a hydrostatic pressure gradient. This means that when two fluids have unequal hydrostatic pressures and are separated by a membrane, water and diffusible solutes or particles (those to which the membrane is permeable) filter out of the solution that has the higher hydrostatic pressure into the solution that has the lower hydrostatic pressure. Filtration is the process responsible for urine formation in the kidney; wastes are filtered out of the blood into the kidney tubules because of a difference in hydrostatic pressure.

ACTIVE TRANSPORT PROCESSES

Active transport is the uphill movement of a substance through a living cell membrane. *Uphill* means "up a concentration gradient" (that is, from a lower to a higher concentration). The energy required for this movement is obtained from ATP. Because the formation and breakdown of ATP requires complex cellular activity, active transport mechanisms can take place only through living membranes. Table 2-3 summarizes active transport processes.

Ion Pumps

A specialized cellular component called the ion pump makes possible a number of active transport mechanisms. An ion pump is a protein structure in the cell membrane called a *carrier.* The ion pump uses energy from ATP to actively move ions across cell membranes *against* their concentration gradients. "Pump" is an appropriate term because it suggests that active transport moves a substance in an uphill direction just as a water pump, for example, moves water uphill.

Ion pumps are very specific, and different ion pumps are required to move different types of ions. For example, sodium pumps move sodium ions only. Likewise, calcium pumps move calcium ions and potassium pumps move potassium ions.

Some ion pumps are "coupled" to one another so that two or more different substances may be moved through the cell membrane at one time. For example, the **sodium-potassium pump** is an ion pump that pumps sodium ions out of a cell

TABLE 2–3 Active Transport Processes

PROCESS	DESCRIPTION		EXAMPLES
Ion Pump	Movement of solute particles from an area of low concentration to an area of high concentration (up the concentration gradient) by means of a carrier protein structure	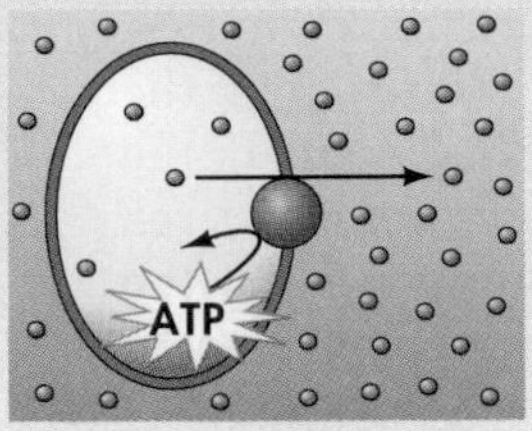	In muscle cells, pumping of nearly all calcium ions to special compartments—or out of the cell
Phagocytosis	Movement of cells or other large particles into cell by trapping it in a section of plasma membrane that pinches off inside the cell	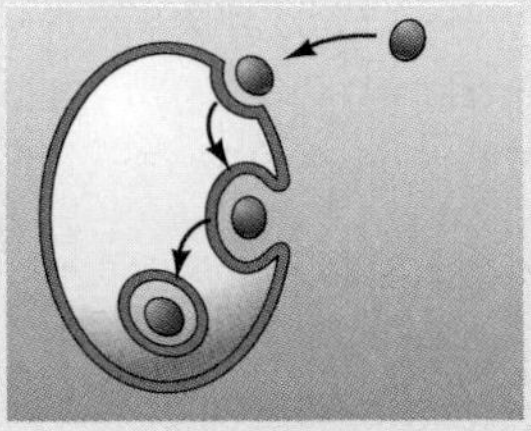	Trapping of bacterial cells by phagocytic white blood cells
Pinocytosis	Movement of fluid and dissolved molecules into a cell by trapping them in a section of plasma membrane that pinches off inside the cell	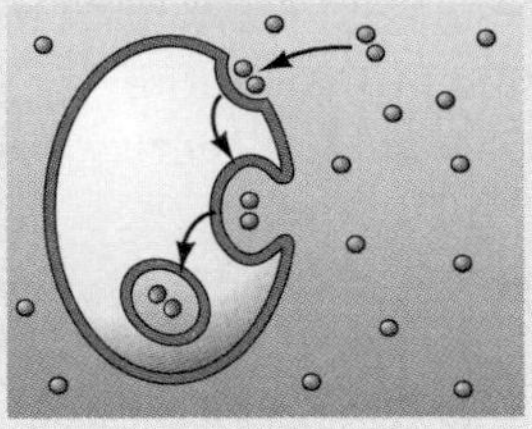	Trapping of large protein molecules by some body cells

while it pumps potassium ions into the cell. Because both ions are moved against their concentration gradients, this pump creates a high sodium concentration outside the cell and a high potassium concentration inside the cell. Such a pump is required to remove sodium from the inside of a nerve cell after it has rushed in as a result of the passage of a nerve impulse. Some ion pumps are coupled with other specific carriers that transport glucose, amino acids, and other substances.

Phagocytosis and Pinocytosis

Phagocytosis (fag-o-sye-TOE-sis) is another example of how a cell can use its active transport mechanism to move an object or substance through the plasma membrane and into the cytoplasm. The term *phagocytosis* comes from a Greek word meaning "to eat." The word is appropriate because the process permits a cell to engulf and literally "eat" foreign material (Figure 2-5). Certain white blood cells destroy bacteria in the body by phagocytosis. During this process the cell membrane forms a pocket around the material to be moved into the cell and, by expenditure of energy from ATP, the object is moved to the interior of the cell. Once inside the cytoplasm, the bacterium fuses with a lysosome and is destroyed.

Pinocytosis (pin-o-sye-TOE-sis) is an active transport mechanism used to incorporate fluids or dissolved substances into cells. Again, the term is appropriate because it comes from the Greek word meaning "drink."

Cell Reproduction and Heredity

All human cells that reproduce do so by a process called **mitosis** (my-TOE-sis). During this process a cell divides to multiply; one cell divides to form two cells. Cell reproduction and ultimately the transfer of heritable traits is closely tied to the production of proteins. Two *nucleic acids,* **ribonucleic acid** or **RNA** in the cytoplasm and **deoxyribonucleic acid** or **DNA** in the nucleus play crucial roles in protein synthesis.

DNA MOLECULE AND GENETIC INFORMATION

Chromosomes, which are composed largely of DNA, make heredity possible. The "genetic information" contained in DNA molecules ultimately determines the transmission and expression of heritable traits such as skin color and blood group from each generation of parents to their children.

FIGURE 2–5 ***Phagocytosis of Bacteria by a White Blood Cell.*** Phagocytosis is an active transport mechanism that requires expenditure of energy. Note how an extension of cytoplasm envelops the bacteria, which are drawn through the cell membrane and into the cytoplasm.

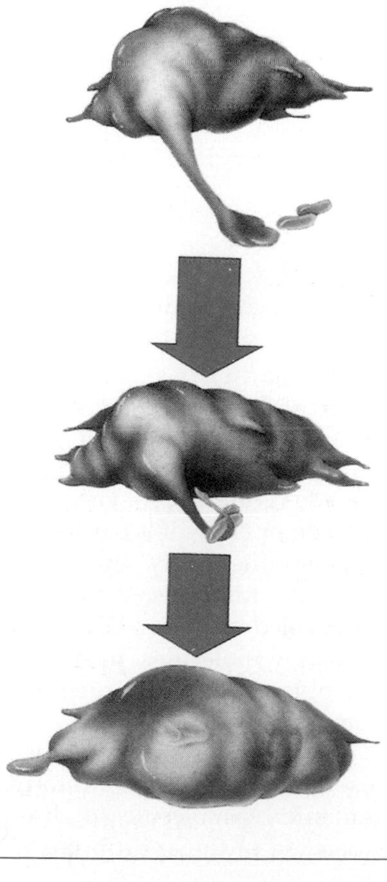

Structurally, the DNA molecule resembles a long, narrow ladder made of a pliable material. It is twisted round and round its axis, taking on the shape of a double helix. Each DNA molecule is made of many smaller units, namely, a sugar, bases, and phosphate units. The bases are adenine, thymine, guanine, and cytosine. As you can see in Figure 2-6, *A,* each step in the DNA ladder consists of a pair of bases. Only two combinations of bases occur, and the same two bases invariably pair off with each other in a DNA molecule. Adenine always binds to thymine, and cytosine always binds to guanine. This characteristic of DNA structure is called **complementary base pairing.**

A **gene** is a specific segment of base pairs in a chromosome. Although the types of base pairs in all chromosomes are the same, the order or *sequence* of base pairs is not the same. This fact has tremendous functional importance because it is the sequence of base pairs in each gene of each chromosome that determines heredity. Each gene directs the synthesis of one kind of protein molecule that may function, for example, as an enzyme, a structural component of a cell, or a specific hormone. In humans having 46 chromosomes in each body cell, the nuclear DNA represents a total genetic information package or **genome** (JEE-nohm) of over 3 *billion* base pairs in about 100,000 genes that make up the 23 pairs of chromosomes received from both parents. Is it any wonder, then, with such vast amounts of genetic information in each of our cells, that no two of us inherit exactly the same traits?

Genetic Code

How do genes bring about heredity? There is, of course, no short and easy answer to that question. We know that the genetic information contained in each gene is capable of "directing" the synthesis of a specific protein. The unique sequence of a thousand or so base pairs in a gene determines the sequence of specific building blocks required to form a particular protein. This store of information in each gene is called the *genetic code.* In summary, the coded information in genes controls protein and enzyme production, enzymes facilitate cellular chemical reactions, and cellular chemical reactions determine cell structure and function and therefore heredity.

FIGURE 2–6 ***Protein Synthesis.*** **A,** The DNA molecule contains a sequence of base pairs, or gene, that represents a sequence of amino acids. **B,** During transcription, the DNA code is "transcribed" as an mRNA molecule forms. **C,** During translation, the mRNA code is "translated" at the ribosome and the proper sequence of amino acids is assembled. The amino acid strand coils or folds as it is formed. **D,** The coiled amino acid strand folds again to form a protein molecule with a specific, complex shape.

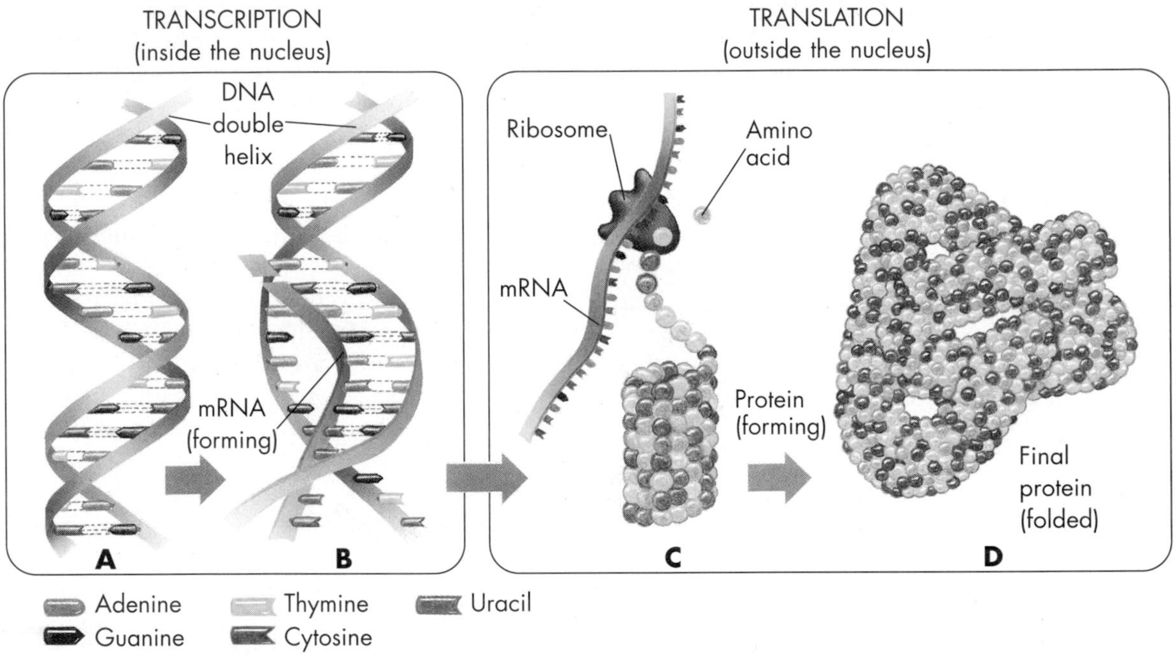

RNA Molecules and Protein Synthesis

DNA, with its genetic code that dictates directions for protein synthesis, is contained in the nucleus of the cell. The actual process of protein synthesis, however, occurs in ribosomes and on ER. Another specialized nucleic acid, ribonucleic acid or RNA, transfers this genetic information from the nucleus to the cytoplasm. (Note: if you are not familiar with the chemical structure of proteins or nucleic acids, you may want to review *Appendix A: Chemistry of Life*, p. 426, before reading further.)

Both RNA and DNA are composed of four bases, a sugar, and phosphate. RNA, however, is a single- rather than a double-stranded molecule, and it contains a different sugar and base component. The base uracil replaces thymine.

The process of transferring genetic information from the nucleus into the cytoplasm where proteins are actually produced requires completion of two specialized steps called **transcription** and **translation.**

Transcription. During *transcription* the double-stranded DNA molecule separates or unwinds, and a special type of RNA called **messenger RNA** or **mRNA** is formed (Figure 2-6, *B*). Each strand of mRNA is a duplicate or copy of a particular gene sequence along one of the newly separated DNA spirals. The messenger RNA is said to have been "transcribed" or copied from its DNA mold or template. The mRNA molecules pass from the nucleus to the cytoplasm to direct protein synthesis in the ribosomes and ER.

Translation. *Translation* is the synthesis of a protein by ribosomes, which use the information contained in an mRNA molecule to direct the choice and sequencing of the appropriate chemical building blocks called *amino acids* (Figure 2-6, C). As amino acids are assembled into their proper sequence by a ribosome, a protein strand forms. This strand then folds on itself and perhaps even combines with another strand to form a complete protein molecule. The specific, complex shape of each type of protein molecule allows the molecule to perform specific functions in the cell. It is clear that because DNA directs the shape of each protein, DNA also directs the function of each protein in a cell.

CELL DIVISION

The process of cell reproduction involves the division of the nucleus (mitosis) and the cytoplasm. After the process is complete, two daughter cells result; both have the same genetic material as the cell that preceded them. As you can see in Figure 2-7, the specific and visible stages of cell division are preceded by a period called **interphase** (IN-ter-faze). During interphase the cell is said to be "resting." However, it is resting only from the standpoint of active cell division. In all other

FIGURE 2–7 ***Mitosis.*** For simplicity, only four chromosomes are shown in the diagram.

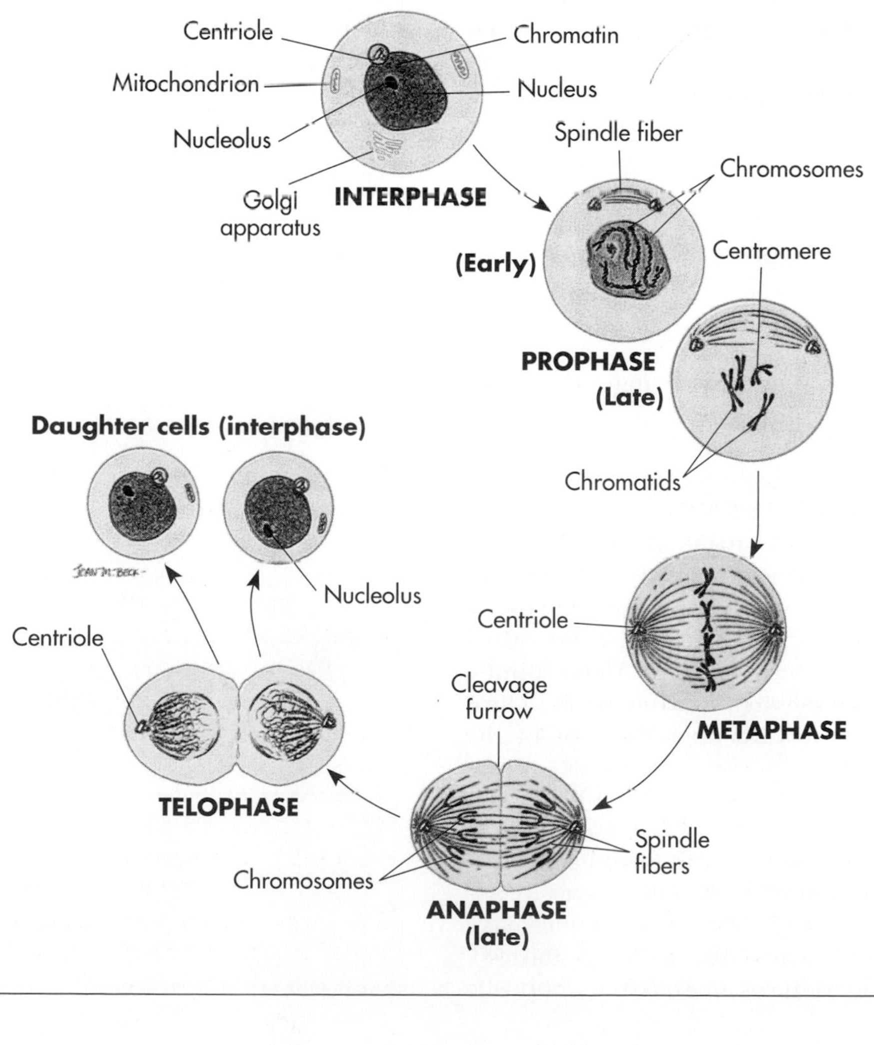

aspects it is exceedingly active. During interphase and just before mitosis begins, the DNA of each chromosome replicates itself.

DNA Replication

DNA molecules possess a unique ability that no other molecules in the world have. They can make copies of themselves, a process called **DNA replication.** Before a cell divides to form two new cells, each DNA molecule in its nucleus forms another DNA molecule just like itself. When a DNA molecule is not replicating, it has the shape of a tightly coiled double helix. As it begins replication, short segments of the DNA molecule uncoil and the two strands of the molecule pull apart between their base pairs. The separated strands therefore contain unpaired bases. Each unpaired base in each of the two separated strands attracts its complementary base (in the nucleoplasm) and binds to it. Specifically, each adenine attracts and binds to a thymine, and each cytosine attracts and binds to a guanine. These steps are repeated over and over throughout the length of the DNA molecule. Thus each half of a DNA molecule becomes a whole DNA molecule identical to the original DNA molecule. After DNA replication is complete, the cell continues to grow until it is ready for the first phase of mitosis.

Prophase

Look at Figure 2-7 and note the changes that identify the first stage of mitosis, prophase (PRO-faze). The chromatin becomes "organized." Chromosomes in the nucleus have formed two strands called **chromatids** (KRO-mah-tids). Note that the two chromatids are held together by a beadlike structure called the **centromere** (SEN-tro-meer). In the cytoplasm the centrioles are moving away from each other as a network of tubules called **spindle fibers** forms between them. These spindle fibers serve as "guidewires" and assist the chromosomes to move toward opposite ends of the cell later in mitosis.

Metaphase

By the time metaphase (MET-ah-faze) begins, the nuclear envelope and nucleolus have disappeared. Note in Figure 2-7 the chromosomes have aligned themselves across the center of the cell. Also, the centrioles have migrated to opposite ends of the cell, and spindle fibers are attached to each chromatid.

Anaphase

As anaphase (AN-ah-faze) begins, the beadlike centromeres, which were holding the paired chromatids together, break apart. As a result, the individual chromatids, identified once again as chromosomes, move away from the center of the cell. Movement of chromosomes occurs along spindle fibers toward the centrioles. Note in Figure 2-7 that chromosomes are being pulled to opposite ends of the cell. A **cleavage furrow** that begins to divide the cell into two daughter cells can be seen for the first time at the end of anaphase.

Telophase

During telophase (TEL-o-faze) cell division is completed. Two nuclei appear, and chromosomes become less distinct and appear to break up. As the nuclear envelope forms around the chromatin,

TABLE 2–4 Stages of Cell Division

STAGE	CHARACTERISTICS
Prophase	The chromatin condenses into visible chromosomes
	Chromatids become attached at the centromere
	Spindle fibers appear
	The nucleolus and nuclear envelope disappear
Metaphase	Spindle fibers attach to each chromatid
	Chromosomes align across the center of the cell
Anaphase	Centromeres break apart
	Chromosomes move away from the center of the cell
	The cleavage furrow appears
Telophase	The nuclear envelope and both nuclei appear
	The cytoplasm and organelles divide equally
	The process of cell division is completed

the cleavage furrow completely divides the cell into two parts. Before division is complete, each nucleus is surrounded by cytoplasm in which organelles have been equally distributed. By the end of telophase, two separate daughter cells, each having identical genetic characteristics, are formed. Each cell is fully functional and will perhaps itself undergo mitosis in the future.

Results of Cell Division

Mitosis results in the production of identical new cells. In the adult, mitosis replaces cells that have become less functional with age or have been damaged or destroyed by illness or injury. During periods of body growth, mitosis allows groups of similar cells to develop into **tissues.**

If the body loses its ability to control mitosis, an abnormal mass of proliferating cells develops. This mass is a **neoplasm** (NEE-o-plazm). Neoplasms may be relatively harmless growths called *benign* (be-NINE) *tumors* or dangerous and *malignant* (mah-LIG-nant) cancerous growths. The stages of mitosis are listed in Table 2-4 with descriptions of changes that occur during each stage.

Tissues

The four main kinds of tissues that compose the body's many organs follow:

1. Epithelial tissue
2. Connective tissue
3. Muscle tissue
4. Nervous tissue

Tissues differ from each other in the size and shape of their cells, in the amount and kind of material between the cells, and in the special functions they perform to help maintain the body's survival. In Table 2-5, you will find a listing of the four major tissues and the various subtypes of each. The table also includes examples of the location of the tissues and a primary function of each tissue type.

EPITHELIAL TISSUE

Epithelial (ep-i-THEE-lee-al) **tissue** covers the body and many of its parts. It also lines various parts of the body. Because epithelial cells are packed close together with little or no intercellular material between them, they form continuous sheets that contain no blood vessels. Examine Figure 2-8. It illustrates how this large group of tissues can be subdivided according to the **shape** and **arrangement** of the cells found in each type.

Shape of Cells

If classified according to *shape*, epithelial cells are:

1. Squamous (flat and scalelike)
2. Cuboidal (cube shaped)
3. Columnar (higher than they are wide)

Arrangement of Cells

If categorized according to *arrangement* of cells, epithelial tissue can be classified as the following:

1. Simple (a single layer of cells of the same shape)
2. Stratified (many layers of cells of the same shape)
3. Transitional (several layers of cells of differing shapes)

Several types of epithelium are described in the paragraphs that follow and are illustrated in Figures 2-9 to 2-12.

Simple Squamous Epithelium

Simple squamous (SKWAY-mus) **epithelium** consists of a single layer of very thin and irregularly shaped cells. Because of its structure, substances can readily pass through simple squamous epithelial tissue, making absorption its special function. Absorption of oxygen into the blood, for example, takes place through the simple squamous epithelium that forms the tiny air sacs in the lungs (Figure 2-9).

Stratified Squamous Epithelium

Stratified squamous epithelium (Figure 2-10) consists of several layers of closely packed cells, an arrangement that makes this tissue a specialist at protection. For instance, stratified squamous epithelial tissue protects the body against invasion by microorganisms. Most microbes cannot work their way through a barrier of stratified squamous tissue such as that which composes the surface of skin and of mucous membranes.

TABLE 2–5 Tissues

TISSUE	LOCATION(S)	FUNCTION(S)
Epithelial		
Simple squamous	Alveoli of lungs	Absorption by diffusion of respiratory gases between alveolar air and blood
	Lining of blood and lymphatic vessels	Absorption by diffusion, filtration, and osmosis
Stratified squamous	Surface of lining of mouth and esophagus	Protection
	Surface of skin (epidermis)	Protection
Simple columnar	Surface layer of lining of stomach, intestines, parts of respiratory tract	Protection; secretion; absorption
Stratified transitional	Urinary bladder	Protection
Pseudostratified	Surface of lining of trachea	Protection
Simple cuboidal	Glands; kidney tubules	Secretion, absorption
Connective (most widely distributed of all tissues)		
Areolar	Area between other tissues and organs	Connection
Adipose (fat)	Area under skin	Protection
	Padding at various points	Insulation; support; nutrient reserve
Dense fibrous	Tendons; ligaments; fascia; scar tissue	Flexible but strong connection
Bone	Skeleton	Support; protection
Cartilage	Part of nasal septum; area covering articular surfaces of bones; larynx; rings in trachea and bronchi	Firm but flexible support
	Disks between vertebrae	Withstand pressure
	External ear	Flexible support
Blood	Blood vessels	Transportation
Hemopoietic	Red bone marrow	Blood cell formation
Muscle		
Skeletal (striated voluntary)	Muscles that attach to bones	Maintenance of posture; movement of bones
	Eyeball muscles	Eye movements
	Upper third of esophagus	First part of swallowing
Cardiac (striated involuntary)	Wall of heart	Contraction of heart
Smooth (nonstriated involuntary or visceral)	Walls of tubular viscera of digestive, respiratory, and genitourinary tracts	Movement of substances along respective tracts
	Walls of blood vessels and large lymphatic vessels	Changing of diameter of vessels
	Ducts of glands	Movement of substances along ducts
	Intrinsic eye muscles (iris and ciliary body)	Changing of diameter of pupils and shape of lens
	Arrector muscles of hairs	Erection of hairs (goose pimples)
Nervous		
	Brain; spinal cord; nerves	Irritability; conduction

FIGURE 2–8 ***Classification of Epithelial Tissues.*** The tissues are classified according to the shape and arrangement of cells.

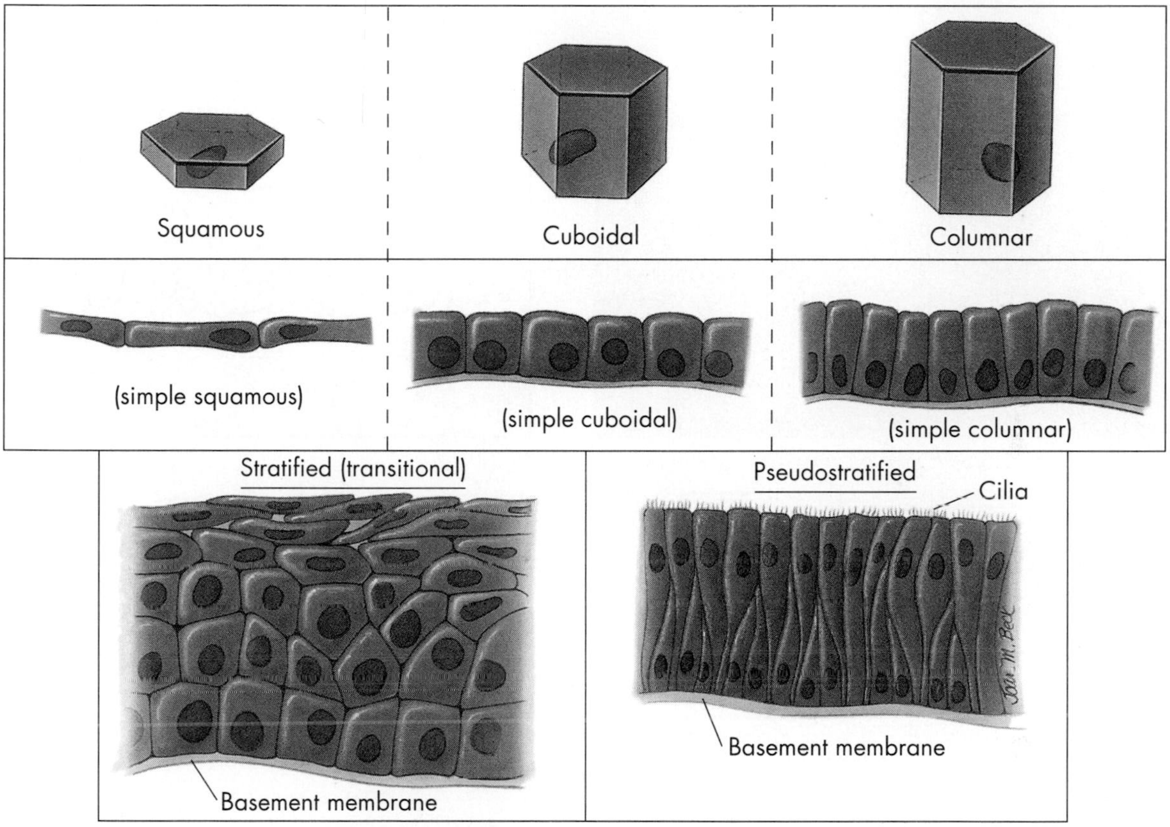

FIGURE 2–9 ***Simple Squamous Epithelium.*** **A,** Photomicrograph of lung tissue shows thin simple squamous epithelium lining the alveolar air sacs. **B,** Sketch of photomicrograph.

A

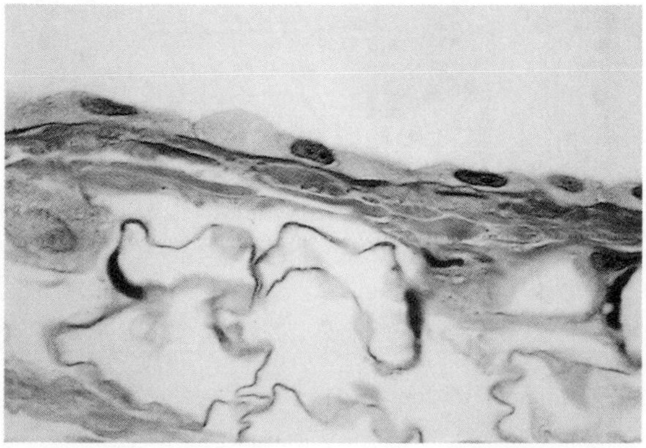

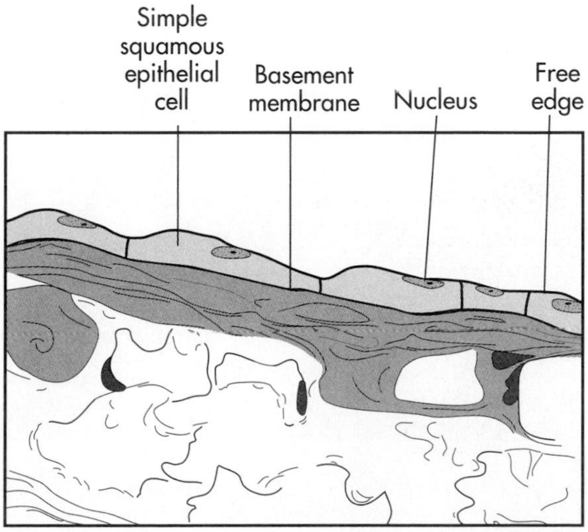

B

FIGURE 2–10 ***Stratified Squamous Epithelium.*** **A,** Photomicrograph. **B,** Sketch of the photomicrograph. Note the many layers of epithelial cells that have been stained yellow.

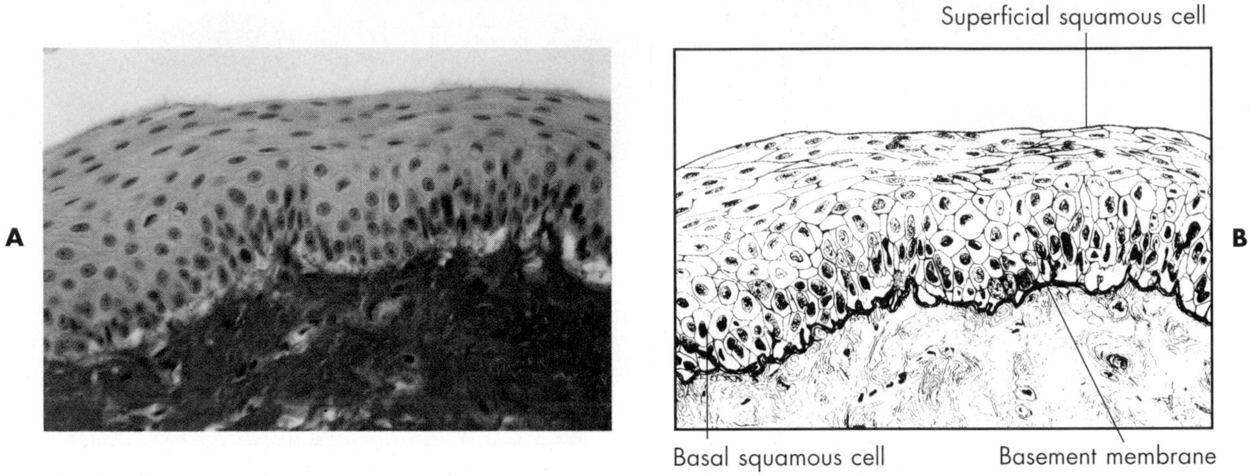

FIGURE 2–11 ***Simple Columnar Epithelium.*** **A,** Photomicrograph. **B,** Sketch of the photomicrograph. Note the goblet or mucus-producing cells that are present.

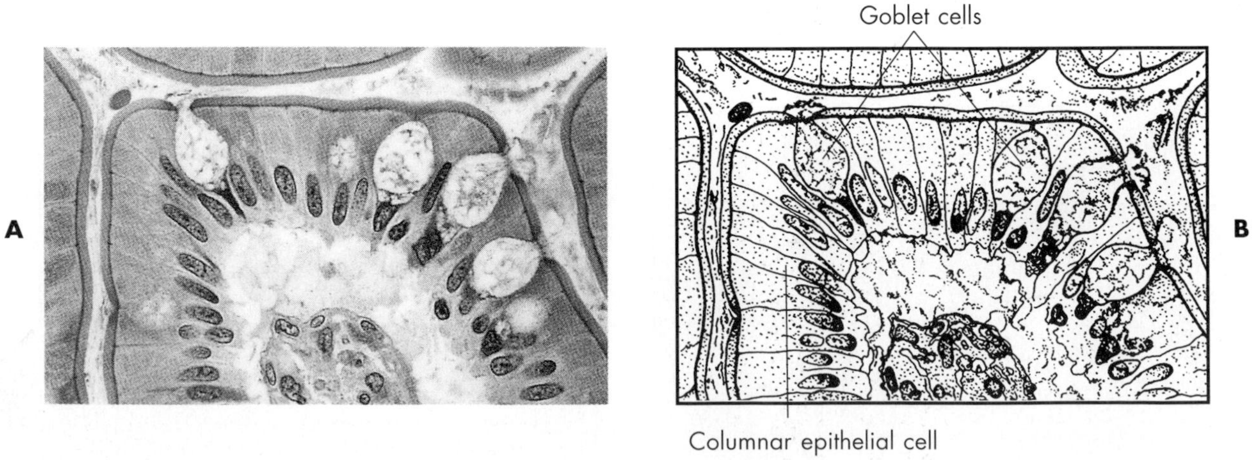

One way of preventing infections, therefore, is to take good care of your skin. Don't let it become cracked from chapping, and guard against cuts and scratches.

Simple Columnar Epithelium

Simple columnar epithelium can be found lining the inner surface of the stomach, intestines, and some areas of the respiratory and reproductive tracts. In Figure 2-11 the simple columnar cells are arranged in a single layer lining the inner surface of the colon or large intestine. These epithelial cells are higher than they are wide, and the nuclei are located toward the bottom of each cell. The "open spaces" among the cells are specialized **goblet cells** that produce mucus. The regular columnar-shaped cells specialize in absorption.

Stratified Transitional Epithelium

Stratified transitional epithelium is typically found in body areas subjected to stress and must be able to stretch; an example would be the wall of the urinary bladder. In many instances, up to 10 layers of cuboidal-shaped cells of varying sizes are present in the absence of stretching. When stretching occurs, the epithelial sheet expands, the number of cell layers decreases, and cell shape changes from cuboidal to squamous (flat) in appearance. The fact that transitional epithelium has this ability keeps the bladder wall from tearing under the pressures of stretching. Stratified transitional epithelium is shown in Figures 2-8 and 2-12.

Pseudostratified Epithelium

Pseudostratified epithelium, illustrated in Figure 2-8, is typical of that which lines the trachea or windpipe. Look carefully at the illustration. Note that each cell actually touches the gluelike **basement membrane** that lies under all epithelial tissues. Although the epithelium in Figure 2-8 (pseudostratified) appears to be two cell layers thick, it is not. This is the reason it is called *pseudo* (or false) stratified epithelium. The cilia that extend from the cells are capable of moving in unison. In doing so, they move mucus along the lining surface of the trachea, thus affording protection against entry of dust or foreign particles into the lungs.

Cuboidal Epithelium

Simple cuboidal epithelium does not form protective coverings but instead forms tubules or other groupings specialized for secretory activity

FIGURE 2–12 ***Stratified Transitional Epithelium.*** **A,** Photomicrograph of tissue lining the urinary bladder wall. **B,** Sketch of the photomicrograph. Note the many layers of epithelial cells of various shapes.

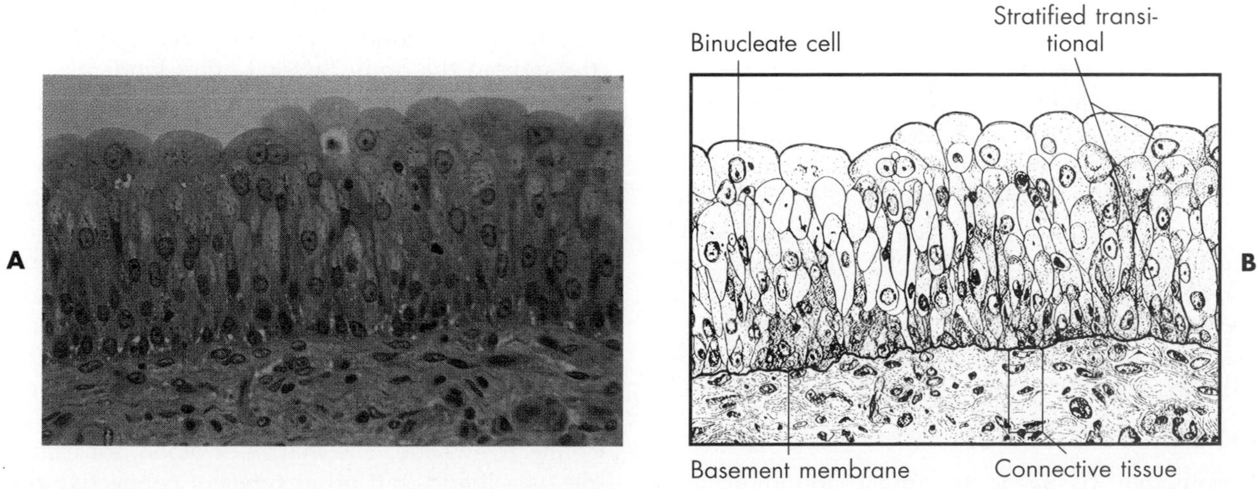

FIGURE 2–13 ***Simple Cuboidal Epithelium.*** This scanning electron micrograph shows how a single layer of cuboidal cells can form glands. The secreting cells arrange themselves into single or branched tubules that open onto a surface—the lining of the stomach in this case.

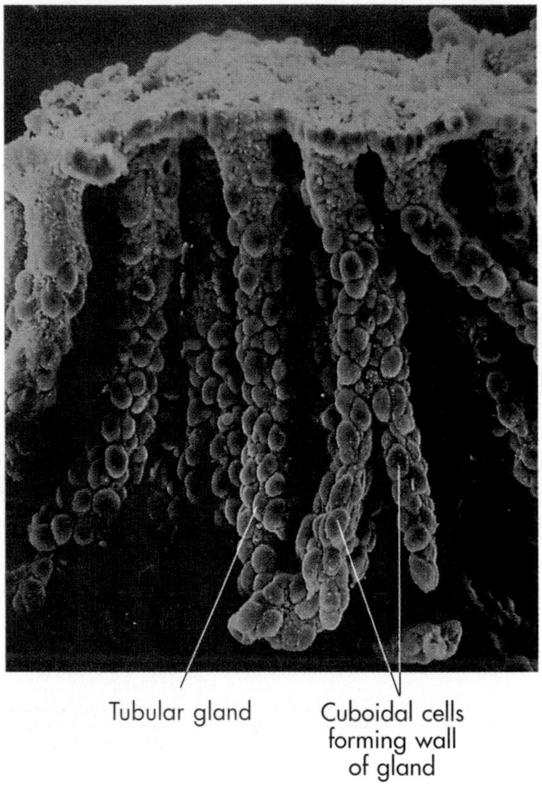

(Figure 2-13). Secretory cuboidal cells usually function in clusters or tubes of secretory cells commonly called glands. Glands of the body may be classified as exocrine if they release their secretion through a duct or as endocrine if they release their secretion directly into the bloodstream. Examples of glandular secretions include saliva produced by the salivary glands, digestive juices, sweat or perspiration, and hormones such as those secreted by the pituitary or thyroid glands. Simple cuboidal epithelium also forms the tubules that form urine in the kidneys.

CONNECTIVE TISSUE

Connective tissue is the most abundant and widely distributed tissue in the body. It also exists

FIGURE 2–14 ***Adipose Tissue.*** Photomicrograph showing the large storage spaces for fat inside the adipose tissue cells.

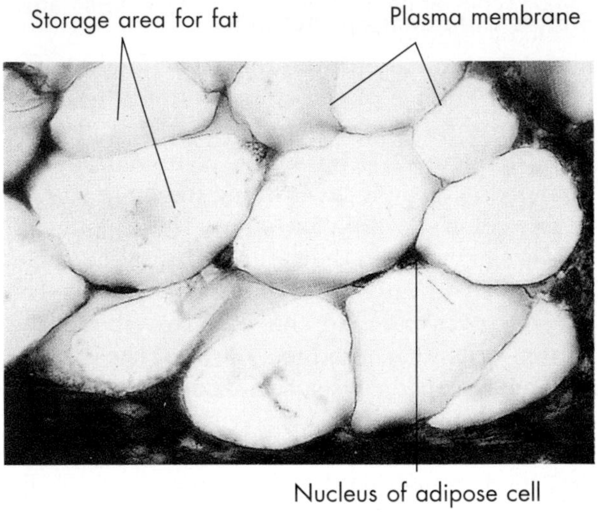

in more varied forms than any of the other tissue types. It is found in skin, membranes, muscles, bones, nerves, and all internal organs. Connective tissue exists as delicate, paper-thin webs that hold internal organs together and give them shape. It also exists as strong and tough cords, rigid bones, and even in the form of a fluid—blood.

The functions of connective tissue are as varied as its structure and appearance. It connects tissues to each other and forms a supporting framework for the body as a whole and for its individual organs. As blood, it transports substances throughout the body. Several other kinds of connective tissue function to defend us against microbes and other invaders.

Connective tissue differs from epithelial tissue in the arrangement and variety of its cells and in the amount and kinds of intercellular material, called **matrix,** found between its cells. In addition to the relatively few cells embedded in the matrix of most types of connective tissue, varying numbers and kinds of fibers are also present. The structural quality and appearance of the matrix and fibers determine the qualities of each type of connective tissue. The matrix of blood, for example, is a liquid, but other types of connective tissue, such as cartilage, have the consistency of firm rubber. The matrix of bone is hard and rigid, although the matrix of connective tissues such as tendons and ligaments is strong and flexible.

The following list identifies a number of the major types of connective tissue in the body. Photomicrographs of several are also shown.

1. Areolar connective tissue
2. Adipose or fat tissue
3. Fibrous connective tissue
4. Bone
5. Cartilage
6. Blood
7. Hemopoietic tissue

Areolar and Adipose Connective Tissue

Areolar (ah-REE-o-lar) **connective tissue** is the most widely distributed of all connective tissue types. It is the "glue" that gives form to the internal organs. It consists of delicate webs of fibers and of a variety of cells embedded in a loose matrix of soft, sticky gel.

Adipose (AD-i-pose) or **fat tissue** is specialized to store lipids. In Figure 2-14, numerous spaces have formed in the tissue so that large quantities of fat can accumulate inside cells.

Fibrous Connective Tissue

Fibrous connective tissue (Figure 2-15) consists mainly of bundles of strong, white **collagen** fibers arranged in parallel rows. This type of connective tissue composes tendons. It provides great strength and flexibility but it does not stretch. Such characteristics are ideal for these structures that anchor our muscles to our bones.

Bone and Cartilage

Bone is one of the most highly specialized forms of connective tissue. The matrix of bone is hard and calcified. It forms numerous structural building blocks called **osteons** (AHS-tee-onz), or *Haversian* (ha-VER-shan) *systems.* When bone is viewed under a microscope, we can see these circular arrangements of calcified matrix and cells that give bone its characteristic appearance (Figure 2-16). Bones are a storage area for calcium and provide support and protection for the body.

Cartilage differs from bone in that its matrix is the consistency of a firm plastic or a gristlelike gel. Cartilage cells, which are called **chondrocytes** (KON-dro-sites), are located in many tiny spaces distributed throughout the matrix (Figure 2-17).

FIGURE 2–15 ***Dense Fibrous Connective Tissue.*** Photomicrograph of tissue in the tendon. Note the multiple bundles of collagenous fibers in a parallel arrangement.

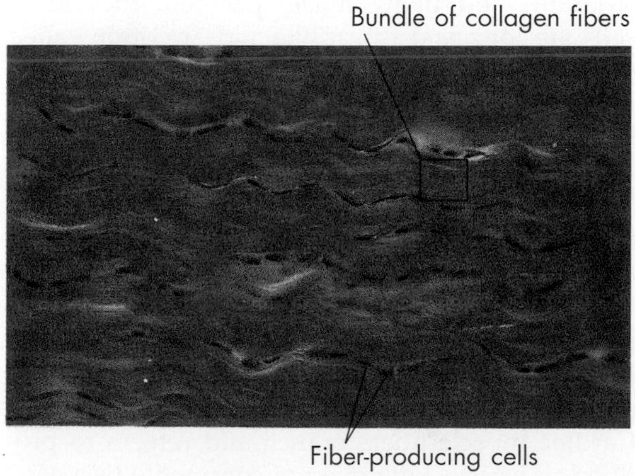

FIGURE 2–16 ***Bone Tissue.*** Photomicrograph of dried, ground bone. Many wheel-like structural units of bone, known as osteons (Haversian systems), are apparent in this section.

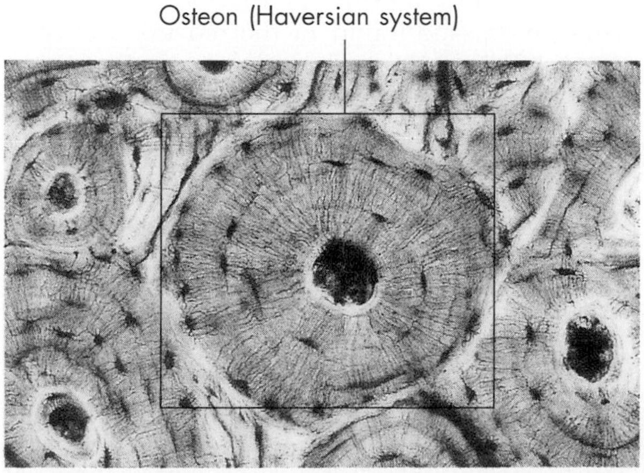

FIGURE 2–17 ***Cartilage.*** Photomicrograph showing the chondrocytes distributed throughout the gel-like matrix.

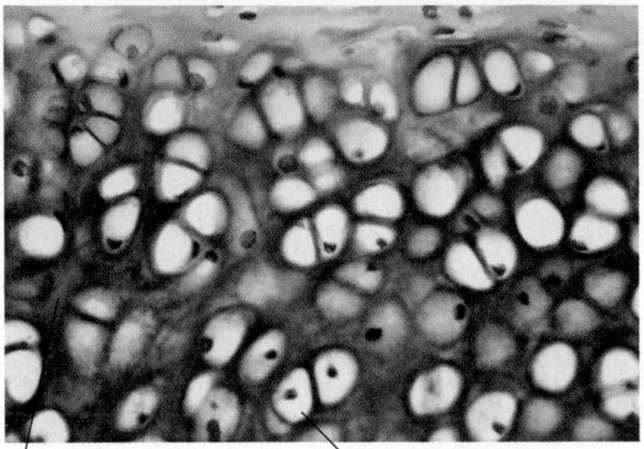

FIGURE 2–18 ***Blood.*** Photomicrograph of a human blood smear. This smear shows two white blood cells surrounded by a number of smaller red blood cells. The liquid matrix of this tissue is also called *plasma.*

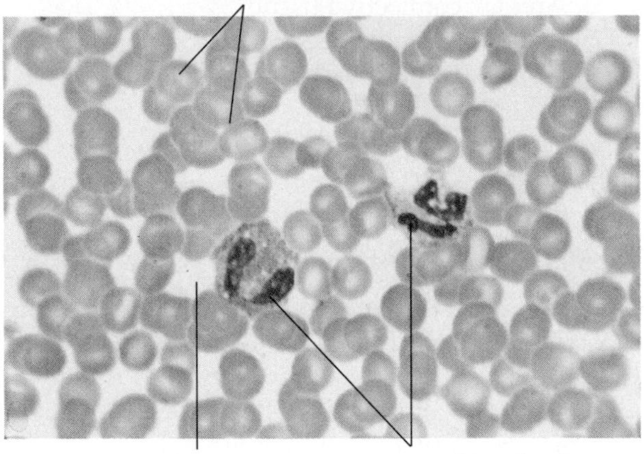

Blood and Hemopoietic Tissue

Because its matrix is liquid, blood is perhaps the most unusual form of connective tissue. It has transportational and protective functions in the body. Red and white blood cells are the cell types common to blood (Figure 2-18).

Hemopoietic (hee-mo-poy-ET-ik) **tissue** is the connective tissue found in the red marrow cavities of bones and in organs such as the spleen, tonsils, and lymph nodes. This type of tissue is responsible for the formation of blood cells and lymphatic system cells important in our defense against disease.

MUSCLE TISSUE

Muscle cells are the movement specialists of the body. They have a higher degree of contractility (ability to shorten or contract) than any other tissue cells. Unfortunately, injured muscle cells are often slow to heal and are frequently replaced by scar tissue if injured. There are three kinds of muscle tissue: **skeletal, cardiac,** and **smooth.**

Skeletal Muscle Tissue

Skeletal or striated muscle is called *voluntary* because willed or voluntary control of skeletal muscle contractions is possible. Note in Figure 2-19 that, when viewed under a microscope, skeletal muscle is characterized by many cross striations and many nuclei per cell. Individual cells are long and threadlike and are often called *fibers.* Skeletal muscles are attached to bones and when contracted produce voluntary and controlled body movements.

Cardiac Muscle Tissue

Cardiac muscle forms the walls of the heart, and the regular but involuntary contractions of cardiac muscle produce the heartbeat. Under the light microscope (Figure 2-20), cardiac muscle fibers have cross striations (like skeletal muscle) and thicker dark bands called *intercalated disks.* Cardiac muscle fibers branch and reform to produce an interlocking mass of contractile tissue.

FIGURE 2–19 ***Skeletal Muscle.*** Photomicrograph showing the striations of the muscle cell fibers in longitudinal section.

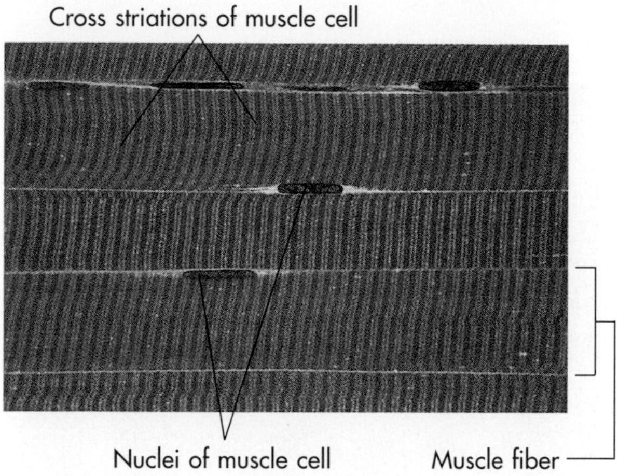

FIGURE 2–20 ***Cardiac Muscle.*** Photomicrograph showing the branched, lightly striated fibers. The darker bands, called *intercalated disks,* which are characteristic of cardiac muscle, are easily identified in this tissue section.

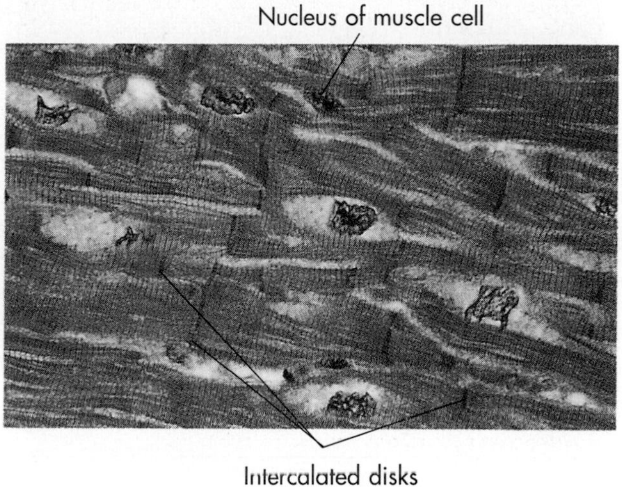

Tissues and Fitness

Achieving and maintaining an ideal body weight is a health-conscious goal. However, a better indicator of health and fitness is **body composition.** Exercise physiologists assess body composition to identify the percentage of the body made of lean tissue and the percentage made of fat. Body-fat percentage is often determined by using calipers to measure the thickness of skin folds at certain places on the body. A person with low body weight may still have a high ratio of fat to muscle, an unhealthy condition. In this case the individual is "underweight" but "overfat." In other words, fitness depends more on the percentage and ratio of specific tissue types than the overall amount of tissue present.

Therefore one goal of a good fitness program is a desirable body-fat percentage. For men, the ideal is 15% to 18%, and for women, the ideal is 20% to 22%. Because fat contains stored energy (measured in calories), a low-fat percentage means a low-energy reserve. High body-fat percentages are associated with several life-threatening conditions, including cardiovascular disease. A balanced diet and an exercise program ensure that the ratio of fat to muscle tissue stays at a level appropriate for maintaining homeostasis.

FIGURE 2–21 ***Smooth Muscle.*** Photomicrograph, longitudinal section. Note the central placement of nuclei in the spindle-shaped smooth muscle fibers.

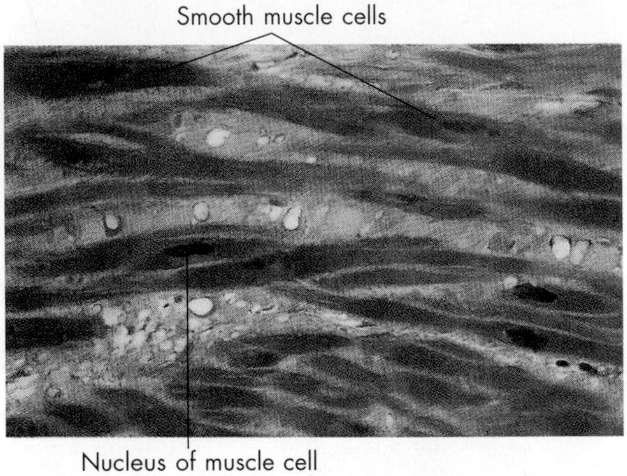

FIGURE 2–22 ***Nervous Tissue.*** Photomicrograph of neurons in a smear of the spinal cord. Both neurons in this slide show characteristic cell bodies and multiple cell processes.

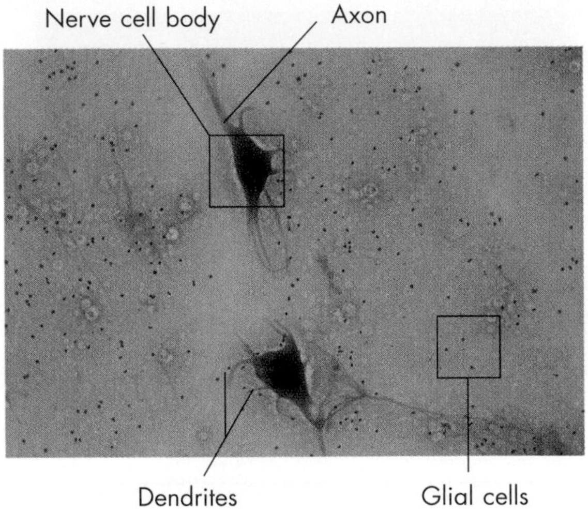

Smooth Muscle Tissue

Smooth (visceral) muscle is said to be *involuntary* because it is not under conscious or willful control. Under a microscope (Figure 2-21), smooth muscle cells are seen as long, narrow fibers but not nearly as long as skeletal or striated fibers. Individual smooth muscle cells appear smooth (that is, without cross striations) and have only one nucleus per fiber. Smooth muscle helps form the walls of blood vessels and hollow organs such as the intestines and other tube-shaped structures in the body. Contractions of smooth (visceral) muscle propel food material through the digestive tract and help regulate the diameter of blood vessels. Contraction of smooth muscle in the tubes of the respiratory system, such as the bronchioles in the lungs, can impair breathing and result in asthma attacks and labored respiration.

NERVOUS TISSUE

The function of **nervous tissue** is rapid communication between body structures and control of body functions. Nervous tissue consists of two kinds of cells: nerve cells, or **neurons** (NOO-rons), which are the functional or conducting units of the system, and special connecting and supporting cells called **glia** (GLEE-ah) or *neuroglia.*

All neurons are characterized by a **cell body** and two types of processes: one **axon,** which transmits a nerve impulse away from the cell body, and one or more **dendrites** (DEN-drites), which carry impulses toward the cell body. Both neurons in Figure 2-22 have many dendrites extending from the cell body.

OUTLINE SUMMARY

CELLS

A Size and shape
  1 Human cells vary considerably in size
  2 All are microscopic
  3 Cells differ notably in shape
B Composition
  1 Cytoplasm containing specialized organelles surrounded by a plasma membrane
  2 Organization of cytoplasmic substances important for life
C Structural parts
  1 Plasma membrane (Figure 2-1)
    a Forms outer boundary of cell
    b Thin, two-layered membrane of phospholipids containing proteins
    c Is selectively permeable
  2 Cytoplasm (Figure 2-2)
    a Organelles
      (1) Ribosomes
        (a) May attach to rough ER or lie free in cytoplasm
        (b) Manufacture proteins
        (c) Often called *protein factories*
      (2) Endoplasmic reticulum (ER)
        (a) Network of connecting sacs and canals
        (b) Carry substances through cytoplasm
        (c) Types are rough and smooth
        (d) Rough ER collects and transports proteins made by ribosomes
        (e) Smooth ER synthesizes chemicals; makes new membrane
      (3) Golgi apparatus
        (a) Group of flattened sacs near nucleus
        (b) Collect chemicals that move from the smooth ER in vesicles
        (c) Called the *chemical processing and packaging center*
      (4) Mitochondria
        (a) Composed of inner and outer membranes
        (b) Involved with energy-releasing chemical reactions
        (c) Often called *power plants* of the cell
      (5) Lysosomes
        (a) Membranous-walled organelles
        (b) Contain digestive enzymes
        (c) Have protective function (eat microbes)
        (d) Often called *suicide bags*
      (6) Centrioles
        (a) Paired organelles
        (b) Lie at right angles to each other near nucleus
        (c) Function in cell reproduction
      (7) Cilia
        (a) Fine, hairlike extensions found on free or exposed surfaces of some cells
        (b) Capable of moving in unison in a wavelike fashion
      (8) Flagella
        (a) Single projections extending from cell surfaces
        (b) Much larger than cilia
        (c) "Tails" of sperm cells only example of flagella in humans
  3 Nucleus
    a Controls cell because it contains the genetic code—instructions for making proteins, which in turn determine cell structure and function
    b Component structures include nuclear envelope, nucleoplasm, nucleolus, and chromatin granules
    c Chromosomes contain DNA
D Relationship of cell structure and function
  1 Regulation of life processes
  2 Survival of species through reproduction of the individual
  3 Relationship of structure to function apparent in number and type of organelles seen in different cells
    a Heart muscle cells contain many mitochondria required to produce adequate energy needed for continued contractions
    b Flagellum of sperm cell gives motility, allowing movement of sperm through female reproductive tract, thus increasing chances for fertilization (Figure 2-3)

MOVEMENTS OF SUBSTANCES THROUGH CELL MEMBRANES

A Passive transport processes do not require added energy and result in movement "down a concentration gradient"
  1 Diffusion (Figure 2-4)
    a Substances scatter themselves evenly throughout an available space
    b It is unnecessary to add energy to the system
    c Movement is from high to low concentration
    d Osmosis and dialysis are specialized examples of diffusion across a selectively permeable membrane
    e Osmosis is diffusion of water
    f Dialysis is diffusion of solutes
  2 Filtration
    a Movement of water and solutes caused by hydrostatic pressure on one side of membrane
    b Responsible for urine formation

B Active transport processes occur only in living cells; movement of substances is "up the concentration gradient"; requires energy from ATP
  1 Ion pumps
    a An ion pump is protein complex in cell membrane
    b Ion pumps use energy from ATP to move substances across cell membranes against their concentration gradients
    c Examples: sodium-potassium pump, calcium pump
    d Some ion pumps work with other carriers so that glucose or amino acids are transported along with ions
  2 Phagocytosis and pinocytosis
    a Both are active transport mechanisms because they require cell energy
    b Phagocytosis is a protective mechanism often used to destroy bacteria (Figure 2-5)
    c Pinocytosis is used to incorporate fluids or dissolved substances into cells

CELL REPRODUCTION

A DNA structure—large molecule shaped like a spiral staircase; sugar (deoxyribose), and phosphate units compose sides of the molecule; base pairs (adenine-thymine or guanine-cytosine) compose "steps"; base pairs always the same but sequence of base pairs differs in different DNA molecules; a gene is a specific sequence of base pairs within a DNA molecule; genes dictate formation of enzymes and other proteins by ribosomes, thereby indirectly determining a cell's structure and functions; in short, genes are heredity determinants (Figure 2-6)
B Genetic code
  1 Genetic information—stored in base-pair sequences on genes—expressed through protein synthesis
  2 RNA molecules and protein synthesis
    a DNA—contained in cell nucleus
    b Protein synthesis—occurs in cytoplasm, thus genetic information must pass from the nucleus to the cytoplasm
    c Process of transferring genetic information from nucleus to cytoplasm where proteins are produced requires completion of *transcription* and *translation* (Figure 2-6).
  3 Transcription
    a Double-stranded DNA separates to form messenger RNA or mRNA
    b Each strand of mRNA duplicates a particular gene (base-pair sequence) from a segment of DNA
    c mRNA molecules pass from the nucleus to the cytoplasm where they direct protein synthesis in ribosomes and ER
  4 Translation
    a Involves synthesis of proteins in cytoplasm by ribosomes
    b Requires use of information contained in mRNA
C Cell Division—reproduction of cell involving division of the nucleus (mitosis) and the cytoplasm; period when the cell is not actively dividing is called interphase
D DNA replication—process by which each half of a DNA molecule becomes a whole molecule identical to the original DNA molecule; precedes mitosis
E Mitosis—process in cell division that distributes identical chromosomes (DNA molecules) to each new cell formed when the original cell divides; enables cells to reproduce their own kind; makes heredity possible
F Stages of mitosis (Figure 2-7)
  1 Prophase—first stage
    a Chromatin granules become organized
    b Chromosomes (pairs of linked chromatids) appear
    c Centrioles move away from nucleus
    d Nuclear envelope disappears, freeing genetic material
    e Spindle fibers appear
  2 Metaphase—second stage
    a Chromosomes align across center of cell
    b Spindle fibers attach themselves to each chromatid
  3 Anaphase—third stage
    a Centromeres break apart
    b Separated chromatids now called *chromosomes*
    c Chromosomes are pulled to opposite ends of cell
    d Cleavage furrow develops at end of anaphase
  4 Telophase—fourth stage
    a Cell division is completed
    b Nuclei appear in daughter cells
    c Nuclear envelope and nucleoli appear
    d Cytoplasm is divided (cytokinesis)
    e Daughter cells become fully functional

TISSUES

A Epithelial tissue
  1 Covers body and lines body cavities
  2 Cells packed closely together with little matrix
  3 Classified by shape of cells (Figure 2-8)
    a Squamous
    b Cuboidal
    c Columnar

- **4** Classified by arrangement of cells
  - **a** Simple
  - **b** Stratified
  - **c** Transitional
- **5** Simple squamous epithelium (Figure 2-9)
  - **a** Single layer of scalelike cells
  - **b** Absorption is function
- **6** Stratified squamous epithelium (Figure 2-10)
  - **a** Several layers of closely packed cells
  - **b** Protection is primary function
- **7** Simple columnar epithelium (Figure 2–11)
  - **a** Columnar cells arranged in a single layer
  - **b** Line stomach and intestines
  - **c** Contain mucus-producing goblet cells
  - **d** Specialized for absorption
- **8** Stratified transitional epithelium (Figure 2-12)
  - **a** Found in body areas, such as urinary bladder, that stretch
  - **b** Up to 10 layers of cuboidal-shaped cells that distort to squamous shape when stretched
- **9** Pseudostratified epithelium
  - **a** Each cell touches basement membrane
  - **b** Lines the trachea
- **10** Simple cuboidal epithelium (Figure 2-13)
  - **a** Often specialized for secretory activity
  - **b** Cuboidal cells may be grouped into glands
  - **c** May secrete into ducts, directly into blood, and on body surface
  - **d** Examples of secretions include saliva, digestive juice, and hormones
  - **e** Cuboidal epithelium also forms the urine-producing tubules of the kidney

B Connective tissue
- **1** Most abundant tissue in body
- **2** Most widely distributed tissue in body
- **3** Multiple types, appearances, and functions
- **4** Relatively few cells in intercellular matrix
- **5** Types
  - **a** Areolar—glue that holds organs together
  - **b** Adipose (fat)—lipid storage is primary function (Figure 2-14)
  - **c** Fibrous—strong fibers; example is tendon (Figure 2-15)
  - **d** Bone—matrix is calcified; function in support and protection (Figure 2-16)
  - **e** Cartilage—chondrocyte is cell type (Figure 2-17)
  - **f** Blood—matrix is fluid; function is transportation (Figure 2-18)

C Muscle tissue (Figures 2-19 to 2-21)
- **1** Types
  - **a** Skeletal—attaches to bones; also called *striated* or *voluntary;* control is voluntary; striations apparent when viewed under a microscope (Figure 2-19)
  - **b** Cardiac—also called *striated involuntary;* composes heart wall; ordinarily cannot control contractions (Figure 2-20)
  - **c** Smooth—also called *nonstriated (visceral)* or *involuntary;* no cross striations; found in blood vessels and other tube-shaped organs (Figure 2-21)

D Nervous tissue (Figure 2-22)
- **1** Cell types
  - **a** Neurons—conducting cells
  - **b** Glia (neuroglia)—supportive and connecting cells
- **2** Neurons
  - **a** Cell components
    - **(1)** Cell body
    - **(2)** Axon (one) carries nerve impulse away from cell body
    - **(3)** Dendrites (one or more) carry nerve impulse toward the cell body
- **3** Function—rapid communication between body structures and control of body functions

NEW WORDS

adenosine triphosphate (ATP)
adipose
areolar
axon
centriole
centromere
chondrocyte
chromatid
chromatin
collagen
columnar
crenation
cuboidal
cytoplasm
dendrite
deoxyribonucleic acid (DNA)
glia
goblet cell
hemopoietic
hypertonic
hypotonic
interphase
lyse
matrix
mitosis
  prophase
  metaphase
  anaphase
  telophase
neuron
nucleoplasm
organelle
  cilia
  endoplasmic reticulum (ER)
  flagellum
  Golgi apparatus
  lysosome
  mitochondria
  nucleolus
  nucleus
  plasma membrane
  ribosome
osteon
ribonucleic acid (RNA)
spindle fiber
squamous
transcription
translation
transport
  dialysis
  diffusion
  filtration
  osmosis
  phagocytosis
  pinocytosis

CHAPTER TEST

1. Which of the following groups represents the three principal parts of a cell?
   a. Plasma membrane, nucleus, cytoplasm
   b. Ribosomes, plasma membrane, mitochondria
   c. Lysosomes, centrioles, plasma membrane
   d. Nucleus, Golgi apparatus, mitochondria
2. Which of the following is considered an active transport process?
   a. Osmosis
   b. Ion pump
   c. Filtration
   d. Dialysis
3. Deoxyribonucleic acid or DNA:
   a. Is exactly the same as RNA
   b. Contains the compound uracil
   c. Is sometimes called the "heredity molecule"
   d. Is not involved with genes or chromosomes
4. The stage of mitosis in which the chromosomes align themselves across the center of the cell is called:
   a. Prophase
   b. Anaphase
   c. Telophase
   d. Metaphase
5. Which of the following terms describes flat, plate-like cells that permit substances to readily pass through them?
   a. Squamous
   b. Stratified
   c. Transitional
   d. Columnar
6. Osteons are associated with which of the following?
   a. Adipose or fat tissue
   b. Bone
   c. Fibrous connective tissue
   d. Cartilage
7. Which of the following types of muscle is considered voluntary?
   a. Cardiac
   b. Smooth
   c. Visceral
   d. Skeletal

Select the most appropriate answer in column B for each item in Column A. (Only one answer is correct.)

COLUMN A	COLUMN B
8. ______ Cellular organelles	a. Osmosis
9. ______ Example of diffusion	b. Blood
10. ______ Active transport mechanism	c. Mitochondria
11. ______ Characteristic of DNA	d. Anaphase
12. ______ Stage of mitosis	e. Complementary base pairing
13. ______ Type of connective tissue	f. Pinocytosis
14. ______ Composed of epithelial tissue	g. Dendrite
15. ______ Component of a nerve cell	h. Glands

16. The nickname, "protein factories," is often used to describe ______________.
17. Substances move "up a concentration gradient" in ______________ transport processes.
18. The first stage of mitosis is called ______________.
19. Absorption, protection, and secretion are important functions of ______________ tissue.
20. No blood vessels are found in ______________ tissue.

REVIEW QUESTIONS

1. Identify the three main parts of a cell.
2. Describe the structure and functions of the plasma membrane.
3. What and where are the following? What functions do they perform?
   nucleolus
   endoplasmic reticulum
   ribosomes
   chromatin
4. Discuss the genetic code and its relationship to protein synthesis.
5. What is a gene? How does a gene differ from a chromosome?
6. Compare and contrast active and passive transport systems. List by name the major active and passive transport processes.
7. List the stages of mitosis and briefly describe what occurs during each period.
8. When does DNA replication occur with respect to mitosis?
9. Identify the stage of mitosis that could be described as "prophase in reverse."
10. Explain how epithelial tissue can be classified according to the shape and arrangement of the cells.
11. Compare the matrix found in bone, areolar connective tissue, and blood.
12. What is the most widely distributed tissue in the body? What tissue exists in more varied forms than any other tissue type? In what type of tissue is appearance most determined by the nature of the matrix?
13. Compare and contrast the three major types of muscle tissue.
14. Identify the two basic types of cells found in nervous tissue. What is the difference between an axon and a dendrite?

CRITICAL THINKING

15. Discuss the importance of the following three chemical substances: DNA, RNA, and ATP. Where in the cell would you expect to find the largest quantity of each?
16. What actually moves during osmosis? During dialysis? What is required for both osmosis and dialysis to occur that is not required for diffusion?
17. How is ATP involved in active transport processes?
18. Explain how the structure of stratified transitional epithelium is related to its function.

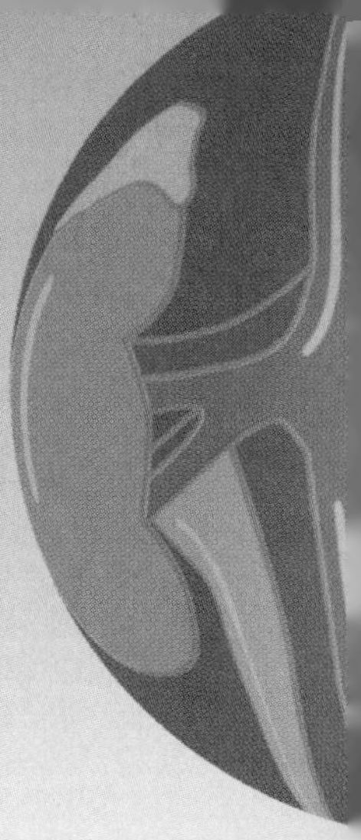

Organ Systems of the Body

3

OUTLINE

Organ Systems of the Body
- Integumentary System
- Skeletal System
- Muscular System
- Nervous System
- Endocrine System
- Circulatory System
- Lymphatic System
- Respiratory System
- Digestive System
- Urinary System
- Reproductive System

OBJECTIVES

After you have completed this chapter, you should be able to:

1. Define and contrast the terms *organ* and *organ system.*
2. List the 11 major organ systems of the body.
3. Identify and locate the major organs of each major organ system.
4. Briefly describe the major functions of each major organ system.
5. Identify and discuss the major subdivisions of the reproductive system.

BOXED ESSAYS

Cancer Screening Tests
Paired Organs

The words *organ* and *system* were discussed in Chapter 1 as having special meanings when applied to the body. An **organ** is a structure made up of two or more kinds of tissues organized in such a way that the tissues can together perform a more complex function than can any tissue alone. A **system** is a group of organs arranged in such a way that they can together perform a more complex function than can any organ alone. This chapter gives an overview of the 11 major organ systems of the body.

In the chapters that follow, the presentation of information on individual organs and an explanation of how they work together to accomplish complex body functions will form the basis for the discussion of each organ system. For example, a detailed description of the skin as the primary organ of the integumentary system will be covered in Chapter 4, and information on the bones of the body as organs of the skeletal system will be presented in Chapter 5. A knowledge of individual organs and how they are organized into groups makes much more meaningful the understanding of how a particular organ system functions as a unit in the body.

When you have completed your study of the major organ systems in the chapters that follow, it will be possible to view the body not as an assembly of individual parts but as an integrated and functioning whole. This chapter names the systems of the body and the major organs that compose them, and it briefly describes the functions of each system. It is intended to provide a basic "road map" to help you anticipate and prepare for the more detailed information that follows in the remainder of the text.

Organ Systems of the Body

In contrast to cells, which are the smallest structural units of the body, organ systems are its largest and most complex structural units. The 11 major organ systems that compose the human body are listed below.

1. Integumentary
2. Skeletal
3. Muscular
4. Nervous
5. Endocrine
6. Circulatory
7. Lymphatic
8. Respiratory
9. Digestive
10. Urinary
11. Reproductive
    a. Male subdivision
    b. Female subdivision

Examine Figure 3-1 to find a diagrammatical listing of the body systems and the major organs in each. In addition to the information contained in Figure 3-1, each system is presented in visual form in Figures 3-2 through 3-13. Visual presentation of material is often useful in understanding the interrelationships that are so important in anatomy and physiology.

INTEGUMENTARY SYSTEM

Note in Figure 3-2 that the skin is the largest and most important organ in the **integumentary** (in-teg-yoo-MEN-tar-ee) **system.** Its weight in most adults is 20 pounds or more, accounting for about 16% of total body weight and making it the body's heaviest organ. The integumentary system includes the skin and its **appendages,** which include the hair, nails, and specialized sweat- and oil-producing glands. In addition, a number of microscopic and highly specialized sense organs are embedded in the skin. They permit the body to respond to pain, pressure, touch, and changes in temperature.

The integumentary system is crucial to survival. Its primary function is *protection.* The skin protects underlying tissue against invasion by harmful bacteria, bars entry of most chemicals, and minimizes the chances of mechanical injury to underlying structures. In addition, the skin regulates body temperature by sweating, synthesizes important chemicals, and functions as a sophisticated sense organ.

SKELETAL SYSTEM

The sternum or breastbone, the humerus, and the femur shown in Figure 3-3 are examples of the 206 individual organs (bones) found in the **skeletal system.** The system includes not only bones but also related tissues such as cartilage and liga-

FIGURE 3–1 ***Body Systems and Their Organs.***

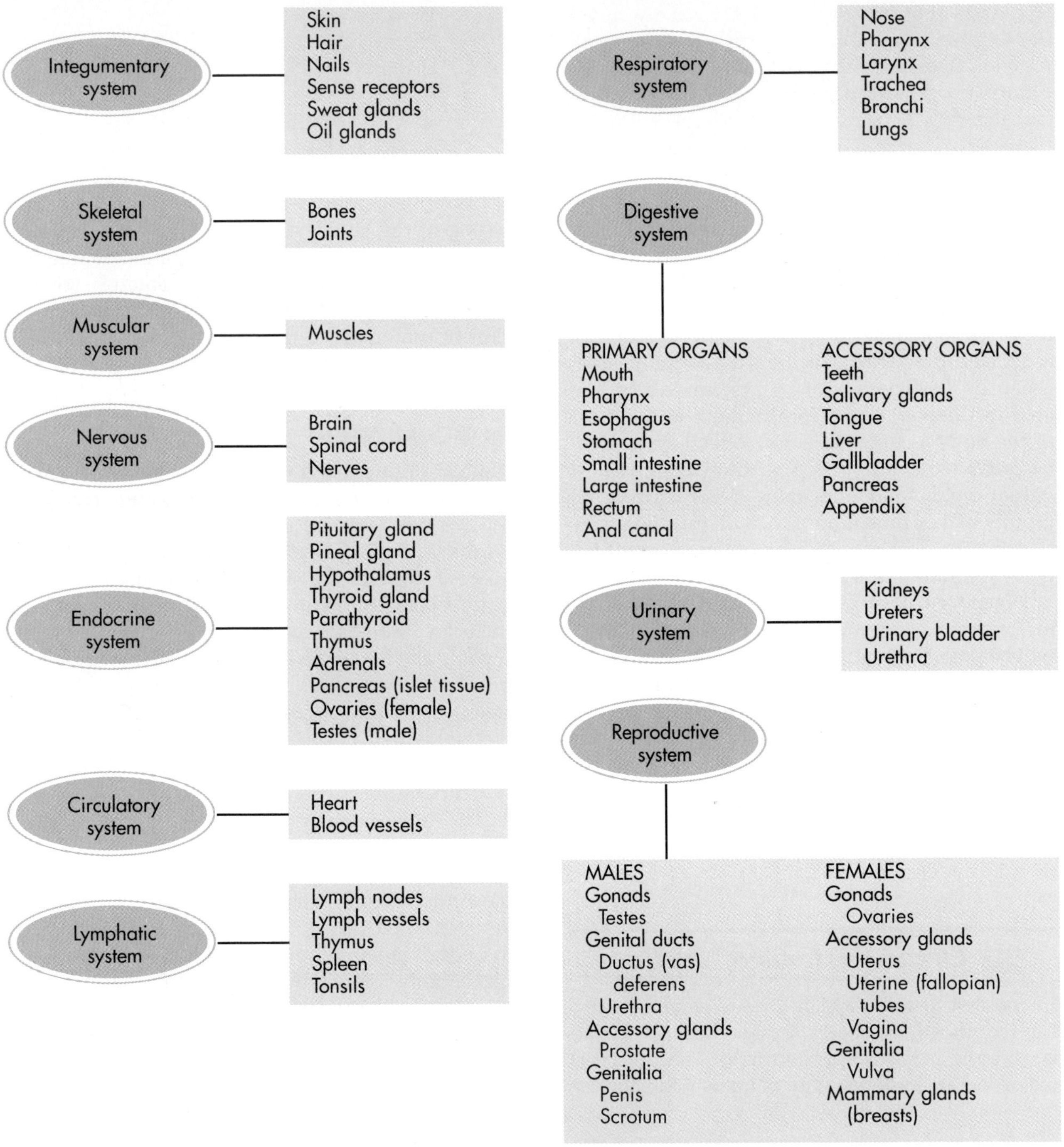
Integumentary system
Skin
Hair
Nails
Sense receptors
Sweat glands
Oil glands
Skeletal system
Bones
Joints
Muscular system
Muscles
Nervous system
Brain
Spinal cord
Nerves
Endocrine system
Pituitary gland
Pineal gland
Hypothalamus
Thyroid gland
Parathyroid
Thymus
Adrenals
Pancreas (islet tissue)
Ovaries (female)
Testes (male)
Circulatory system
Heart
Blood vessels
Lymphatic system
Lymph nodes
Lymph vessels
Thymus
Spleen
Tonsils
Respiratory system
Nose
Pharynx
Larynx
Trachea
Bronchi
Lungs
Digestive system
PRIMARY ORGANS
Mouth
Pharynx
Esophagus
Stomach
Small intestine
Large intestine
Rectum
Anal canal
ACCESSORY ORGANS
Teeth
Salivary glands
Tongue
Liver
Gallbladder
Pancreas
Appendix
Urinary system
Kidneys
Ureters
Urinary bladder
Urethra
Reproductive system
MALES
Gonads
Testes
Genital ducts
Ductus (vas) deferens
Urethra
Accessory glands
Prostate
Genitalia
Penis
Scrotum
FEMALES
Gonads
Ovaries
Accessory glands
Uterus
Uterine (fallopian) tubes
Vagina
Genitalia
Vulva
Mammary glands (breasts)

FIGURE 3–2 *Integumentary System.*

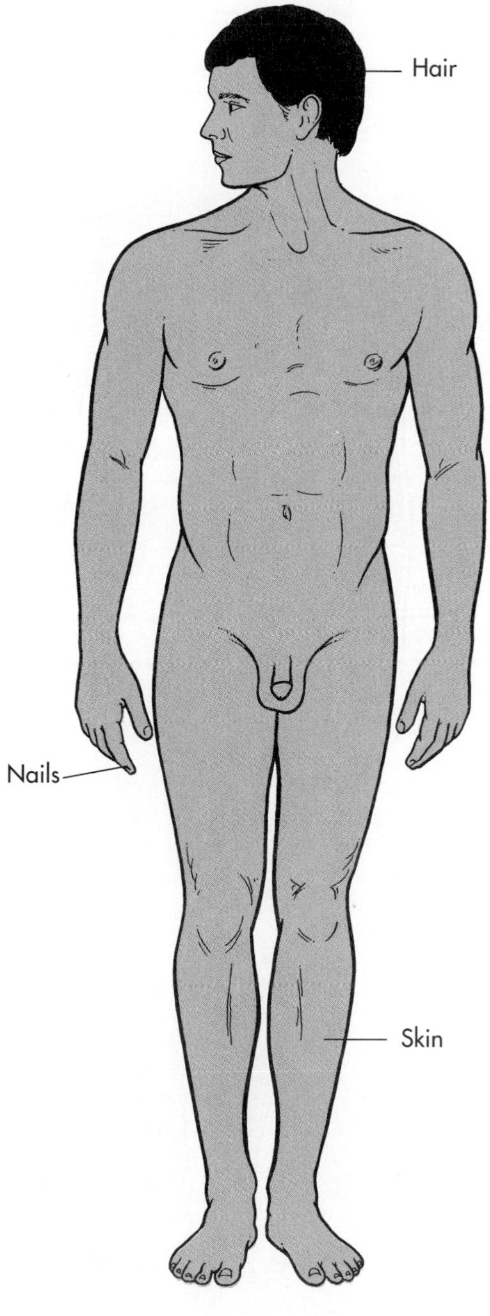

FIGURE 3–3 *Skeletal System.*

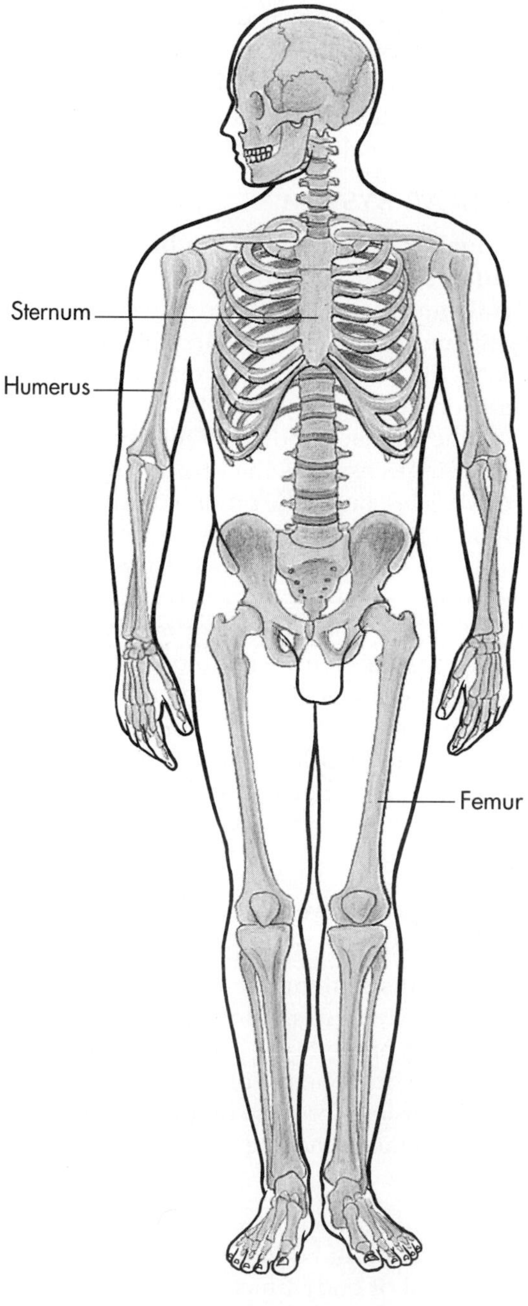

ments that together provide the body with a rigid framework for support and protection. In addition, the skeletal system, through the existence of **joints** between bones, makes possible the movements of body parts. Without joints, we could make no movements; our bodies would be rigid, immobile hulks. Bones also serve as storage areas for important minerals such as calcium and phosphorus. The formation of blood cells in the red marrow of certain bones is another crucial function of the skeletal system.

MUSCULAR SYSTEM

Individual skeletal muscles are the organs of the **muscular system.** In addition to **voluntary** or **skeletal** muscles, which have the ability to contract when stimulated and are under conscious control, the muscular system also contains **smooth** or **involuntary** muscles found in organs such as the stomach and small intestine. The third type of muscle tissue is the **cardiac muscle** of the heart. Muscles not only produce movement and maintain body posture but also generate the heat required for maintaining a constant core body temperature.

The tendon labeled in Figure 3-4 represents how tendons attach muscles to bones. When stimulated by a nervous impulse, muscle tissue shortens or contracts. Voluntary movement occurs when skeletal muscles contract because of the way muscles are attached to bones and the way bones articulate or join together with one another in joints.

NERVOUS SYSTEM

The brain, spinal cord, and nerves are the organs of the **nervous system.** As you can see in Figure 3-5, nerves extend from the brain and spinal cord to every area of the body. The extensive networking of the components of the nervous system makes it possible for this complex system to perform its primary functions. These include the following:

1. Communication between body functions
2. Integration of body functions
3. Control of body functions
4. Recognition of sensory stimuli

These functions are accomplished by specialized signals called **nerve impulses.** In general, the

FIGURE 3–4 *Muscular System.*

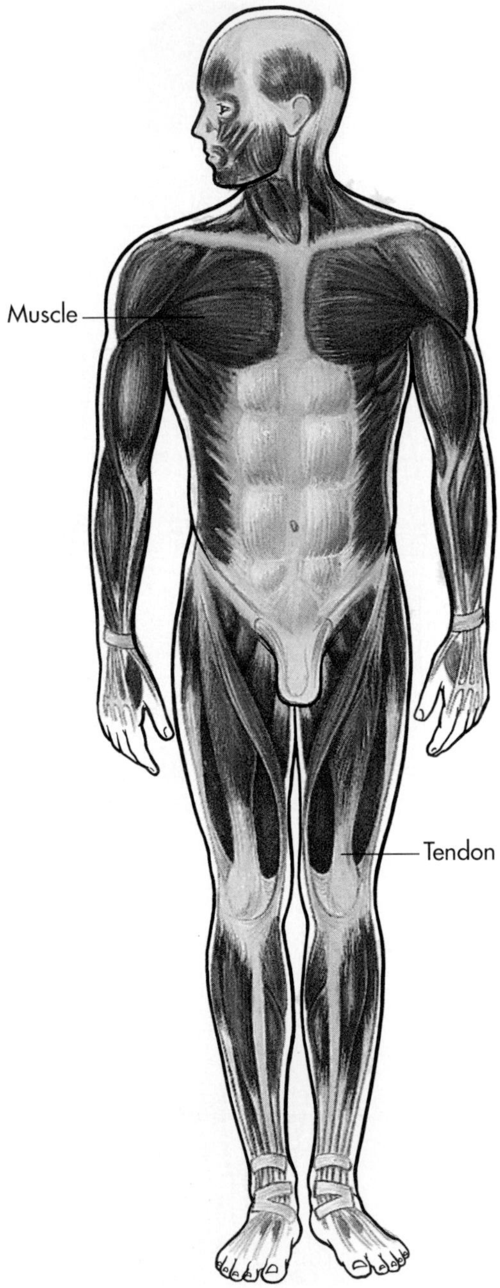

FIGURE 3–5 *Nervous System.*

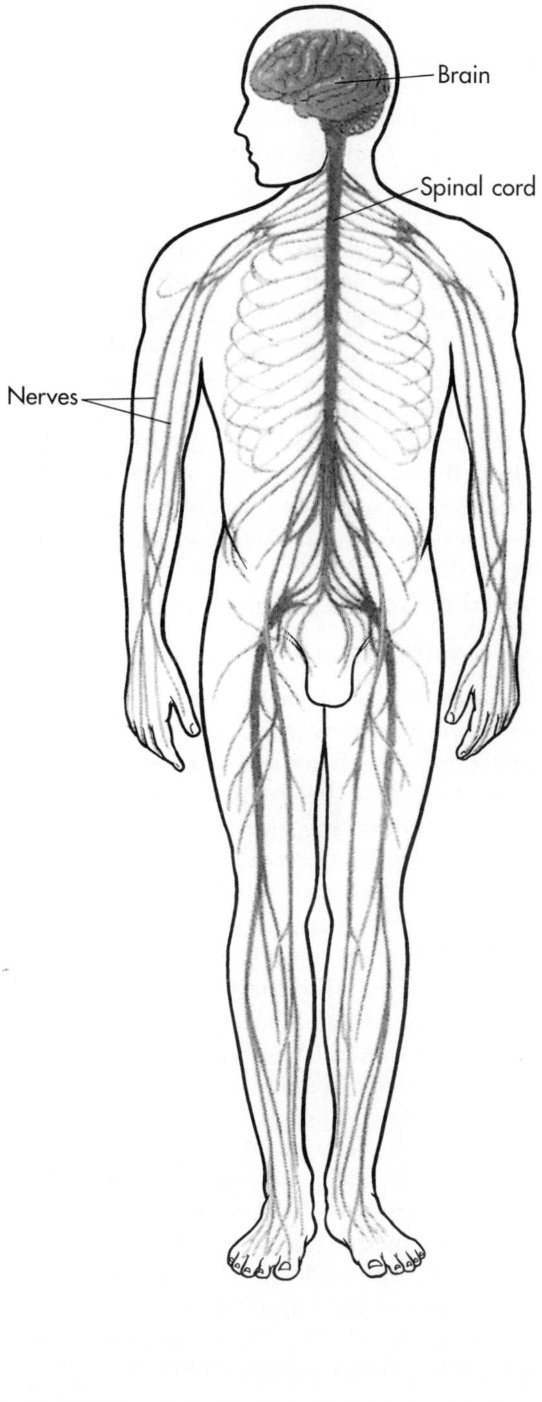

functions of the nervous system result in rapid activity that lasts usually for a short duration. For example, we can chew our food normally, walk, and perform coordinated muscular movements only if our nervous system functions properly. The nerve impulse permits the rapid and precise control of diverse body functions. Other types of nerve impulses cause glands to secrete fluids. In addition, elements of the nervous system can recognize certain **stimuli** (STIM-yoo-lye), such as heat, light, pressure, or temperature, that affect the body. When stimulated, these specialized components of the nervous system, called **sense organs** (discussed in Chapter 8), generate nervous impulses that travel to the brain or spinal cord where analysis or relay occurs and, if needed, appropriate action is initiated.

ENDOCRINE SYSTEM

The **endocrine system** is composed of specialized glands that secrete chemicals known as **hormones** directly into the blood. Sometimes called *ductless glands,* the organs of the endocrine system perform the same general functions as the nervous system: communication, integration, and control. The nervous system provides rapid, brief control by fast-traveling nerve impulses. The endocrine system provides slower but longer-lasting control by hormone secretion; for example, secretion of growth hormone controls the rate of development over long periods of gradual growth.

In addition to controlling growth, hormones are the main regulators of metabolism, reproduction, and other body activities. They play important roles in fluid and electrolyte balance, acid-base balance, and energy metabolism.

As you can see in Figure 3-6, the endocrine glands are widely distributed throughout the body. The **pituitary** (pi-TOO-i-TAIR-ee) **gland, pineal** (PIN-e-al) **gland,** and **hypothalamus** (hi-po-THAL-ah-mus) are located in the skull. The **thyroid** (THY-roid) and **parathyroid** (PAIR-ah-THY-roid) **glands** are in the neck, and the **thymus** (THY-mus) **gland** is in the thoracic cavity, specifically in the mediastinum (see Figure 1-4, p. 5). The **adrenal** (ah-DRE-nal) **glands** and **pancreas** (PAN-kree-as) are found in the abdominal cavity. Note in Figure 3-6 that the ovaries in the female and the testes in the male also function as endocrine glands.

FIGURE 3–6 *Endocrine System.*

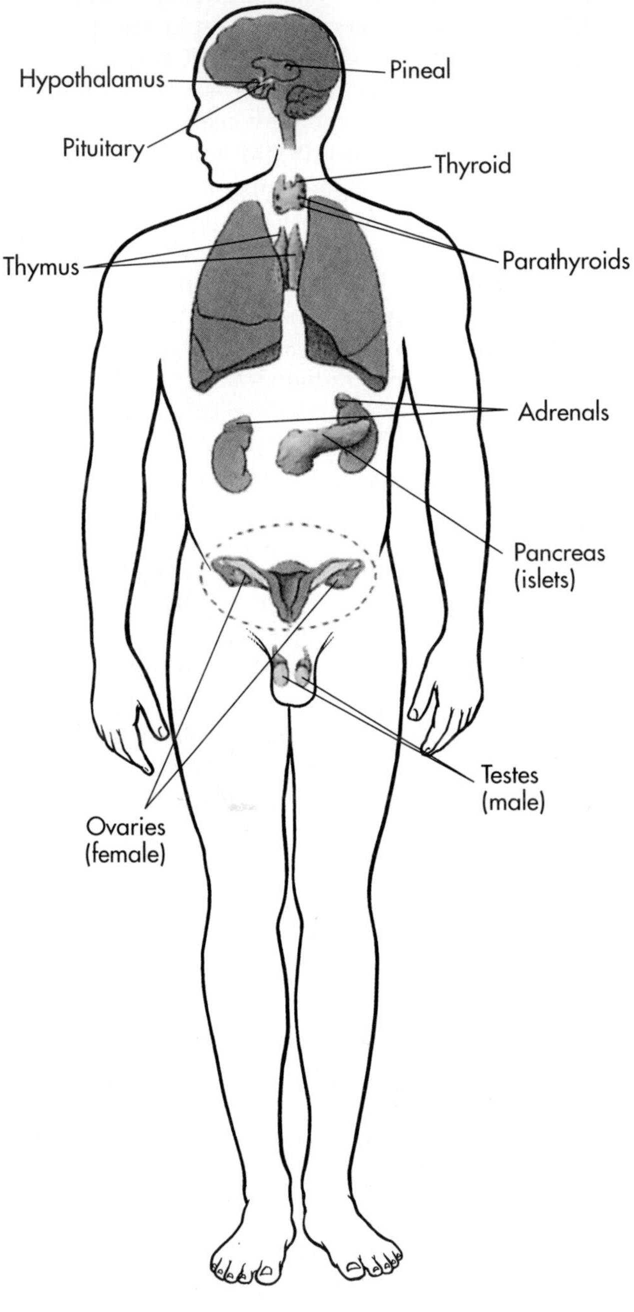

CIRCULATORY SYSTEM

The **circulatory system** consists of the heart, which is a muscular pumping device as shown in Figure 3-7, and a closed system of vessels made up of **arteries, veins,** and **capillaries.** As the name implies, blood contained in the circulatory system is pumped by the heart around a closed circle or circuit of vessels as it passes through the body. The term **cardiovascular** refers to the system of the heart and blood vessels.

The primary function of the circulatory system is *transportation.* The need for an efficient transportation system in the body is critical. Transportation needs include continuous movement of oxygen and carbon dioxide, nutrients, hormones, and other important substances. Wastes produced by the cells are released into the bloodstream on an ongoing basis and are transported by the blood to the excretory organs. The circulatory system also helps regulate body temperature by distributing heat throughout the body and by assisting in retaining or releasing heat from the body by regulating blood flow near the body surface. Certain cells of the circulatory system can also become involved in the defense of the body or immunity.

LYMPHATIC SYSTEM

The **lymphatic system** is composed of **lymph nodes, lymphatic vessels,** and specialized lymphatic organs such as the **tonsils, thymus,** and **spleen.** Note that the thymus in Figure 3-8 functions as an endocrine and as a lymphatic gland. Instead of containing blood, the lymphatic vessels are filled with lymph, a whitish, watery fluid that contains lymphocytes, proteins, and some fatty molecules. No red blood cells are present. The lymph is formed from the fluid around the body cells and diffuses into the lymph vessels. However, unlike blood, lymph does not circulate repeatedly through a closed circuit or loop of vessels. Instead, lymph flowing through lymphatic vessels eventually enters the circulatory system by passing through large ducts, including the **thoracic duct** shown in Figure 3-8, which in turn connect with veins in the upper area of the thoracic cavity. Collections of lymph nodes can be seen in the axillary (armpit) and in the inguinal (groin) areas of the body in Figure 3-8. The formation and movement of lymph are discussed in Chapter 11.

FIGURE 3–7 *Circulatory System.*

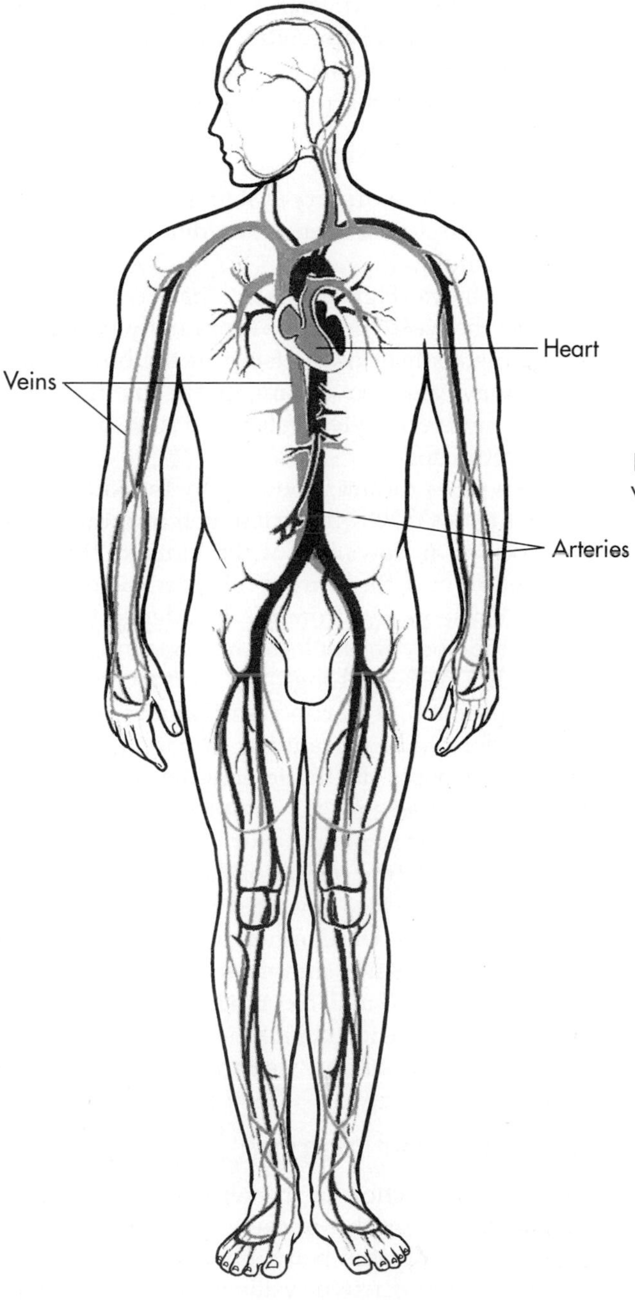

FIGURE 3–8 *Lymphatic System.*

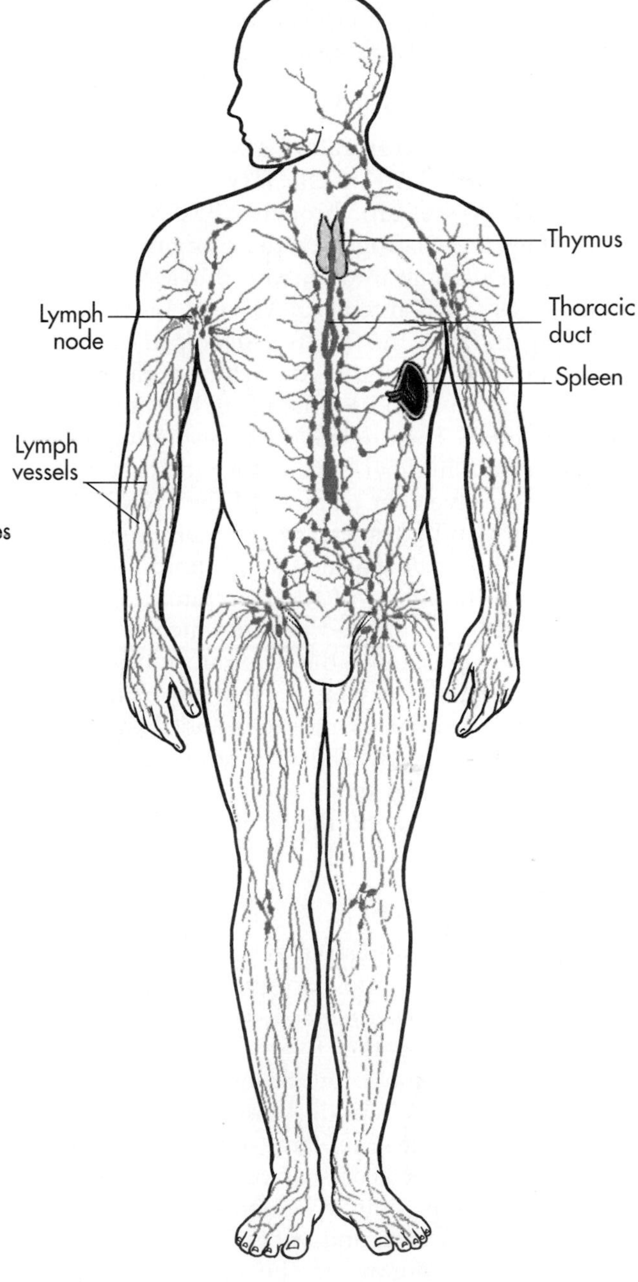

The functions of the lymphatic system include movement of fluids and certain large molecules from the tissue spaces around the cells and movement of fat-related nutrients from the digestive tract back to the blood. The lymphatic system is also involved in the functioning of the immune system, which plays a critical role in the defense mechanism of the body against disease.

RESPIRATORY SYSTEM

The organs of the **respiratory system** include the nose, **pharynx** (FAIR-inks), **larynx** (LAR-inks), **trachea** (TRAY-kee-ah), **bronchi** (BRON-ki), and lungs (Figure 3-9). Together these organs permit the movement of air into the tiny, thin-walled sacs of the lungs called **alveoli** (al-VE-o-li). In the alveoli, oxygen from the air is exchanged for the waste product carbon dioxide, which is carried to the lungs by the blood so that it can be eliminated from the body. The organs of the respiratory system perform a number of functions in addition to permitting movement of air into the alveoli. For example, if you live in a cold or dry environment, incoming air can be warmed and humidified as it passes over the lining of the respiratory air passages. In addition, inhaled irritants such as pollen or dust passing through the respiratory tubes can be trapped in the sticky mucus that covers the lining of many respiratory passages and then eliminated from the body. The respiratory system is also involved in regulating the acid-base balance of the body—a function that will be discussed in Chapter 18.

DIGESTIVE SYSTEM

The organs of the **digestive system** (Figure 3-10) are often separated into two groups: the *primary organs* and the *secondary* or *accessory organs* (Figure 3-1). They work together to ensure proper digestion and absorption of nutrients. The primary organs include the mouth, pharynx, esophagus, stomach, small intestine, large intestine, rectum, and anal canal. The accessory organs of digestion include the teeth, salivary glands, tongue, liver, gallbladder, pancreas, and appendix.

The primary organs of the digestive system form a tube, open at both ends, called the **gastrointestinal** (GAS-tro-in-TES-ti-nal) or **GI tract.** Food that enters the tract is digested, its nutrients are absorbed, and the undigested residue is eliminated from the body as waste material called **feces** (FEE-seez). The accessory organs assist in the mechanical or chemical breakdown of ingested food. The appendix, although classified as an accessory organ of digestion and physically attached to the digestive tube, is not functionally important in the digestive process. However, inflammation of the appendix, called **appendicitis** (ah-PEN-di-SYE-tis) is a very serious clinical condition and frequently requires surgery.

URINARY SYSTEM

The organs of the **urinary** system include the **kidneys, ureters** (u-REE-ters), **bladder,** and **urethra** (yoo-RE-thrah).

The kidneys (Figure 13-11) "clear" or clean the blood of the waste products continually produced by the metabolism of foodstuff in the body cells. The kidneys also play an important role in maintaining the electrolyte, water, and acid-base balances in the body.

The waste product produced by the kidneys is called **urine** (YOOR-in). After it is produced by the kidneys, it flows out of the kidneys through the ureters into the urinary bladder, where it is stored. Urine passes from the bladder to the outside of the body through the urethra. In the male the urethra passes through the penis, which has a double function; it transports urine and semen or seminal fluid. Therefore it has urinary and reproductive purposes. In the female the urinary and reproductive passages are completely separate, so the urethra performs only a urinary function.

In addition to the organs of the urinary system, other organs are also involved in the elimination of body wastes. Undigested food residues and metabolic wastes are eliminated from the intestinal tract as feces, and the lungs rid the body of carbon dioxide. The skin also serves an excretory function by eliminating water and some salts in sweat.

REPRODUCTIVE SYSTEM

The normal function of the **reproductive system** is different from the normal function of other organ systems of the body. The proper functioning of the reproductive systems ensures survival, not of the individual but of the species—the human race. In addition, production of the hormones that permit the development of sexual characteristics occurs as a result of normal reproductive system activity.

FIGURE 3–9 *Respiratory System.*

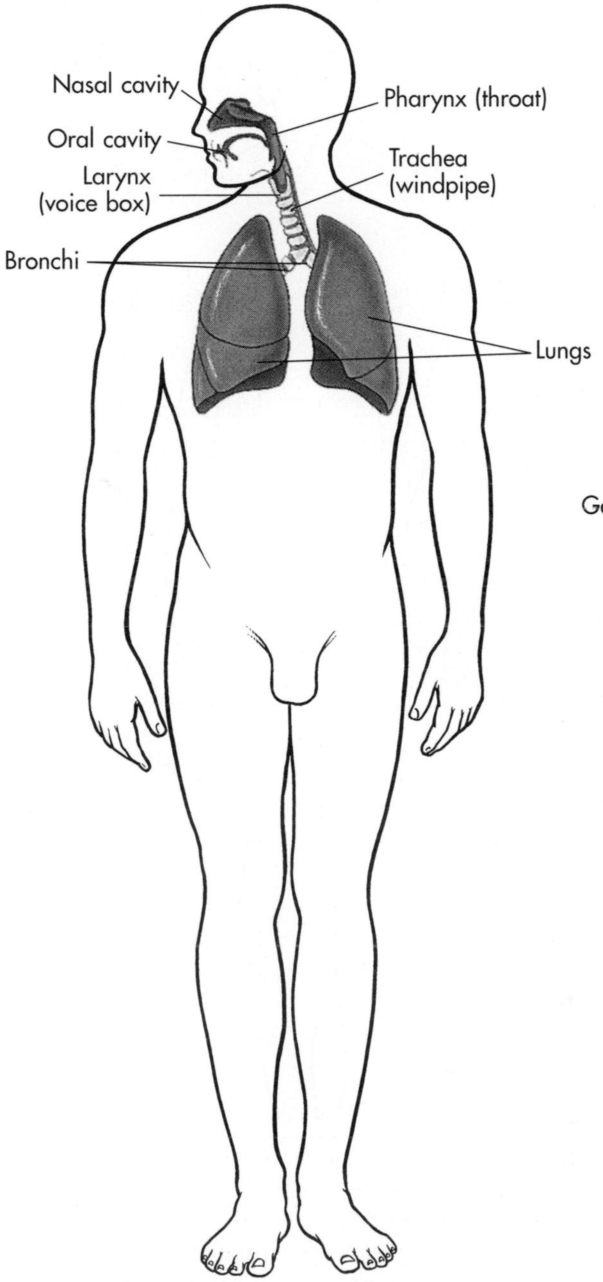

FIGURE 3–10 *Digestive System.*

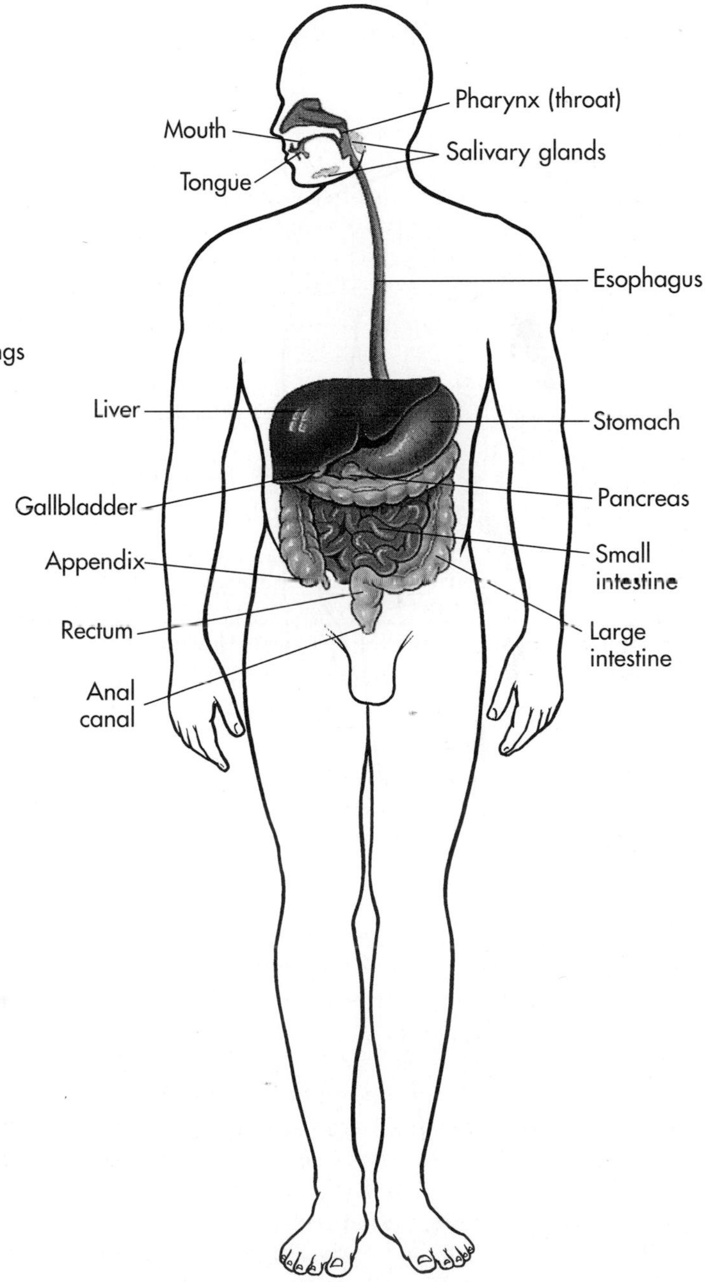

FIGURE 3–11 *Urinary System.*

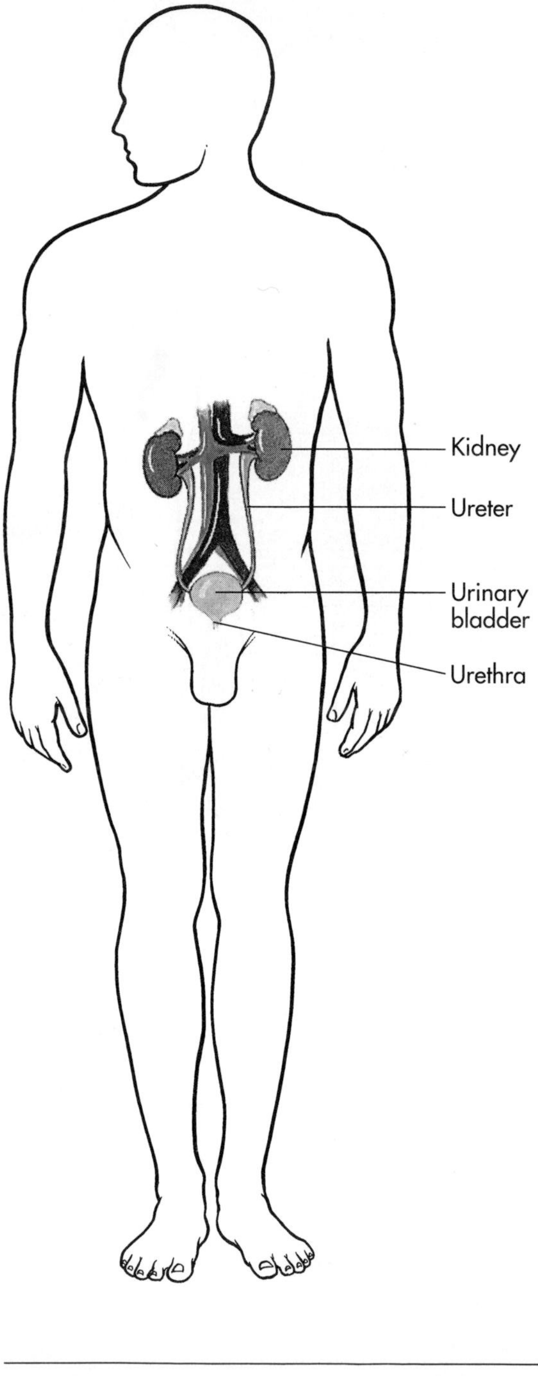

FIGURE 3–12 *Male Reproductive System.*

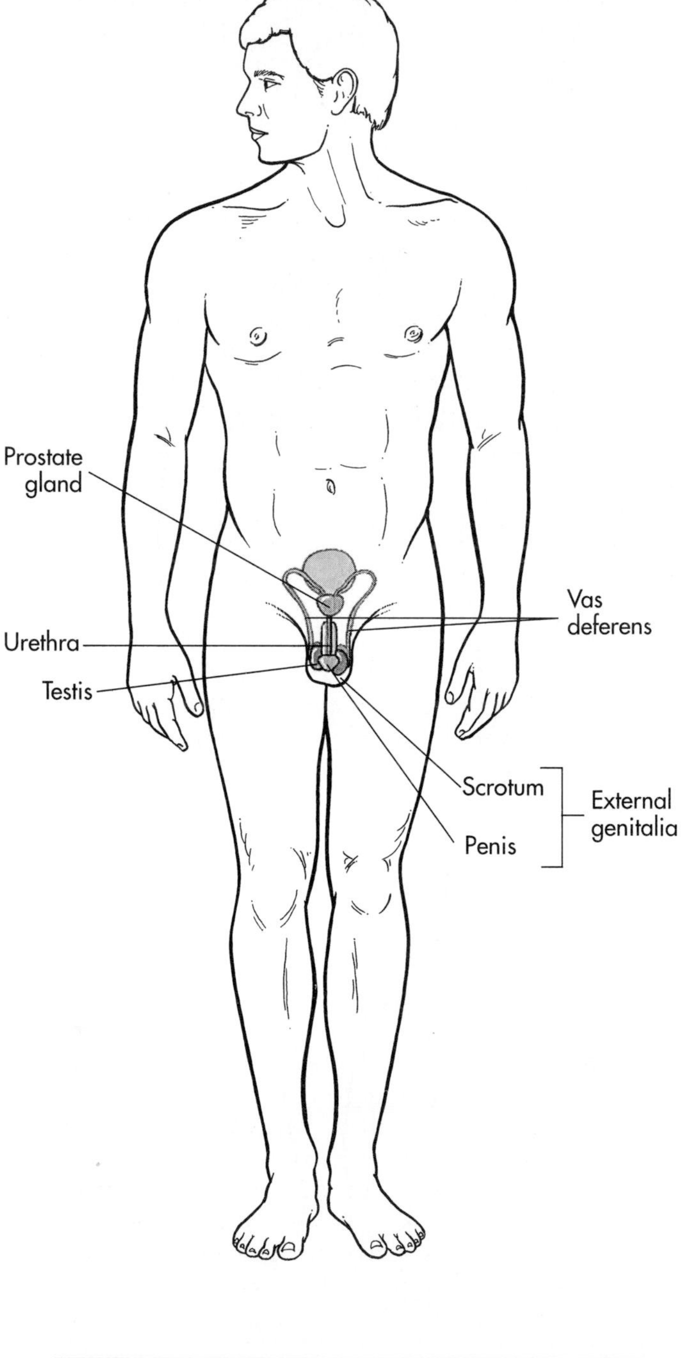

Male Reproductive System

The male reproductive structures shown in Figure 3-12 include the **gonads** (GO-nads), called **testes** (TES-teez), which produce the sex cells or **sperm**; one of the important **genital ducts,** called the **vas deferens** (vas DEF-er-enz); and the **prostate** (PROSS-tate), which is classified as an **accessory gland** in the male. The **penis** (PEE-nis) and **scrotum** (SKRO-tum) are supporting structures and together are known as the **genitalia** (jen-i-TAIL-yah). The urethra, which is identified in Figure 3-11 as part of the urinary system, passes through the penis. It serves as a genital duct that carries sperm to the exterior and as a passageway for the elimination of urine. Functioning together, these structures produce, transfer, and ultimately introduce sperm into the female reproductive tract, where fertilization can occur. Sperm produced by the testes travel through a number of genital ducts, including the vas deferens, to exit the body. The prostate and other accessory glands, which add fluid and nutrients to the sex cells as they pass through the ducts and the supporting structures (especially the penis), permit transfer of sex cells into the female reproductive tract.

Female Reproductive System

The female **gonads** are the **ovaries.** The **accessory organs** shown in Figure 3-13 include the **uterus** (YOO-ter-us), **uterine** (YOO-ter-in) or **fallopian tubes,** and the **vagina** (vah-JYE-nah). In the female the term **vulva** (VUL-vah) is used to describe the external genitalia. The breasts or **mammary glands** are also classified as external accessory sex organs in the female.

The reproductive organs in the female produce the sex cells or **ova;** receive the male sex cells (sperm); permit fertilization and transfer of the sex cells to the uterus; and allow for the development, birth, and nourishment of offspring.

As you study the more detailed structure and function of the organ systems in the chapters that follow, always relate the system and its component organs to the body as a whole. No one body system functions entirely independently of other systems. Instead, you will find that they are structurally and functionally interrelated and interdependent.

FIGURE 3–13 *Female Reproductive System.*

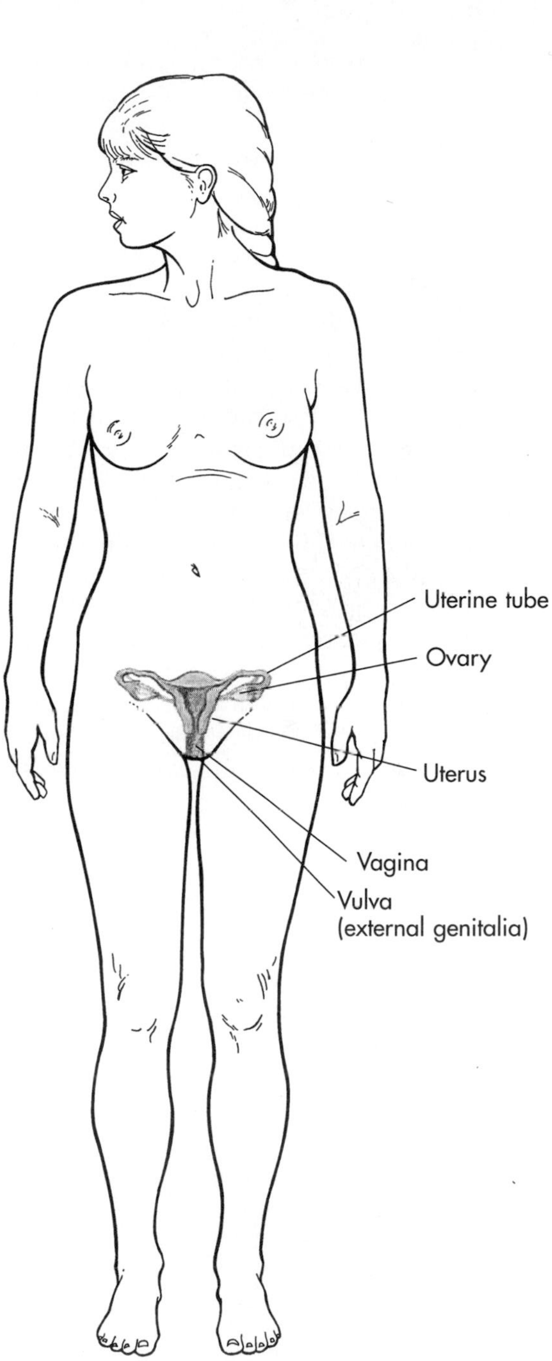

Cancer Screening Tests

A knowledge of the structure and function of the body organ systems is a critically important "first step" in understanding and using information that empowers us to become more sophisticated guardians of our own health and well-being. For example, a better understanding of the reproductive system helps individuals participate in a more direct and personal way in cancer prevention screening techniques.

Breast and testicular self-examinations to detect cancer are two important ways that women and men can participate directly in protecting their own health. Instruction in these techniques is an important part of many home health care educational outreach services. Although specific instructions for these self-tests lie beyond the scope of a textbook of normal anatomy and physiology, it is important to note that this information is readily available from the American Cancer Society and from most hospitals, clinics, and health care providers.

Paired Organs

Have you ever wondered what advantage there might be in having two kidneys, two lungs, two eyes, and two of many other organs? Although the body could function well with only one of each, most of us are born with a pair of these organs. For paired organs that are vital to survival, such as the kidneys, this arrangement allows for the accidental loss of one organ without immediate threat to the survival of the individual. Athletes who have lost one vital organ through injury or disease are often counseled against participating in contact sports that carry the risk of damaging the remaining organ. If the second organ is damaged, total loss of a vital function, such as sight, or even death may result.

OUTLINE SUMMARY

DEFINITIONS AND CONCEPTS

A Organ—a structure made up of two or more kinds of tissues organized in such a way that they can together perform a more complex function than can any tissue alone
B Organ system—a group of organs arranged in such a way that they can together perform a more complex function than can any organ alone
C A knowledge of individual organs and how they are organized into groups makes more meaningful the understanding of how a particular organ system functions as a whole

ORGAN SYSTEMS

A Integumentary system
  1 Structure—organs
    a Skin
    b Hair
    c Nails
    d Sense receptors
    e Sweat glands
    f Oil glands
  2 Functions
    a Protection
    b Regulation of body temperature
    c Synthesis of chemicals
    d Sense organ
B Skeletal system
  1 Structure
    a Bones
    b Joints
  2 Functions
    a Support
    b Movement (with joints and muscles)
    c Storage of minerals
    d Blood cell formation
C Muscular system
  1 Structure
    a Muscles
      (1) Voluntary or striated
      (2) Involuntary or smooth
      (3) Cardiac
  2 Functions
    a Movement
    b Maintenance of body posture
    c Production of heat
D Nervous system
  1 Structure
    a Brain
    b Spinal cord
    c Nerves
    d Sense organs
  2 Functions
    a Communication
    b Integration
    c Control
    d Recognition of sensory stimuli
  3 System functions by production of nerve impulses caused by stimuli of various types
  4 Control is fast-acting and of short duration
E Endocrine system
  1 Structure
    a Pituitary gland
    b Pineal gland
    c Hypothalamus
    d Thyroid gland
    e Parathyroid glands
    f Thymus gland
    g Adrenal glands
    h Pancreas
    i Ovaries (female)
    j Testes (male)
  2 Functions
    a Secretion of special substances called *hormones* directly into the blood
    b Same as nervous system—communication, integration, control
    c Control is slow and of long duration
    d Examples of hormone regulation:
      (1) Growth
      (2) Metabolism
      (3) Reproduction
      (4) Fluid and electrolyte balance
F Circulatory system
  1 Structure
    a Heart
    b Blood vessels
  2 Functions
    a Transportation
    b Regulation of body temperature
    c Immunity (body defense)
G Lymphatic system
  1 Structure
    a Lymph nodes
    b Lymphatic vessels
    c Thymus
    d Spleen
  2 Functions
    a Transportation
    b Immunity (body defense)
H Respiratory system
  1 Structure
    a Nose
    b Pharynx

c Larynx
d Trachea
e Bronchi
f Lungs
2 Functions
a Exchange of waste gas (carbon dioxide) for oxygen in the lungs
b Area of gas exchange in the lungs called *alveoli*
c Filtration of irritants from inspired air
d Regulation of acid-base balance

I Digestive system
1 Structure
a Primary organs
(1) Mouth
(2) Pharynx
(3) Esophagus
(4) Stomach
(5) Small intestine
(6) Large intestine
(7) Rectum
(8) Anal canal
b Accessory organs
(1) Teeth
(2) Salivary glands
(3) Tongue
(4) Liver
(5) Gallbladder
(6) Pancreas
(7) Appendix
2 Functions
a Mechanical and chemical breakdown (digestion) of food
b Absorption of nutrients
c Undigested waste product that is eliminated is called *feces*
d Appendix is a structural but not a functional part of digestive system
e Inflammation of appendix is called *appendicitis*

J Urinary system
1 Structure
a Kidneys
b Ureters
c Urinary bladder
d Urethra
2 Functions
a "Clearing" or cleaning blood of waste products—waste product excreted from body is called *urine*
b Electrolyte balance
c Water balance
d Acid-base balance
e In male, urethra has urinary and reproductive functions

K Reproductive system
1 Structure
a Male
(1) Gonads—testes
(2) Genital ducts—vas deferens, urethra
(3) Accessory gland—prostate
(4) Supporting structures—genitalia (penis and scrotum)
b Female
(1) Gonads—ovaries
(2) Accessory organs—uterus, uterine (fallopian) tubes, vagina
(3) Supporting structures—genitalia (vulva), mammary glands (breasts)
2 Functions
a Survival of species
b Production of sex cells (male: sperm; female: ova)
c Transfer and fertilization of sex cells
d Development and birth of offspring
e Nourishment of offspring
f Production of sex hormones

NEW WORDS

Review the names of organ systems and individual organs in Figures 3-1 through 3-13.

appendix
cardiovascular
endocrine
feces
gastrointestinal (GI) tract
genitalia
hormone
integumentary
lymphatic
nerve impulse
stimuli
urine

CHAPTER TEST

1. The largest and most important organ of the integumentary system is the ______________.
2. The 206 individual organs of the skeletal system are called ______________.
3. The four primary functions of the nervous system are ______________, ______________, ______________, and ______________.
4. The organs of the endocrine system secrete substances called ______________ into the blood.
5. The thymus and spleen are classified as ______________ organs.
6. The waste product produced by the kidneys is called ______________.
7. The tongue, liver, and gallbladder are classified as ______________ organs of digestion.
8. Oxygen from the air is exchanged for the waste product carbon dioxide in thin-walled sacs in the lungs called ______________.

Select the most appropriate answer in column B for each item in column A. (Only one answer is correct.)

COLUMN A		COLUMN B
9.	______Appendage of skin	a. Lymphatic system
10.	______Storage site for calcium	b. Muscles
11.	______Function to generate heat	c. Feces
12.	______Permit rapid communication	d. Hair
13.	______Important in body defense mechanism	e. Vulva
		f. Testes
14.	______Undigested residue in GI tract	g. Bones
15.	______Female external genitalia	h. Nerve impulses
16.	______Male gonads	

REVIEW QUESTIONS

1. Give brief definitions of the terms *organ* and *organ system*.
2. List the 11 major organ systems of the body.
3. Discuss the structure and generalized functions of the integumentary system.
4. What is the relationship between a stimulus and a nerve impulse?
5. Define the term *hormone*.
6. List and discuss the structural and functional components of the circulatory system.
7. Identify the waste products associated with the urinary and digestive systems.
8. List the primary and accessory organs of the digestive system.
9. Compare and contrast the structure and function of the male and female reproductive systems.

CRITICAL THINKING

10. Explain the functional interaction that occurs between the skeletal, muscular, and nervous systems.
11. Compare the generalized functions of the nervous and endocrine systems. How are they similar? How do they differ?

The Integumentary System and Body Membranes

4

OUTLINE

Classification of Body Membranes
- Epithelial Membranes
- Connective Tissue Membranes

The Skin
- Structure of the Skin
- Appendages of the Skin
- Functions of the Skin
- Burns

BOXED ESSAYS

Subcutaneous Injection
Depilatories
Decubitus Ulcers
Exercise and the Skin

OBJECTIVES

After you have completed this chapter, you should be able to:

1. Classify, compare the structure of, and give examples of each type of body membrane.
2. Describe the structure and function of the epidermis and dermis.
3. List and briefly describe each accessory organ of the skin.
4. List and discuss the three primary functions of the integumentary system.
5. Classify burns and describe how to estimate the extent of a burn injury.

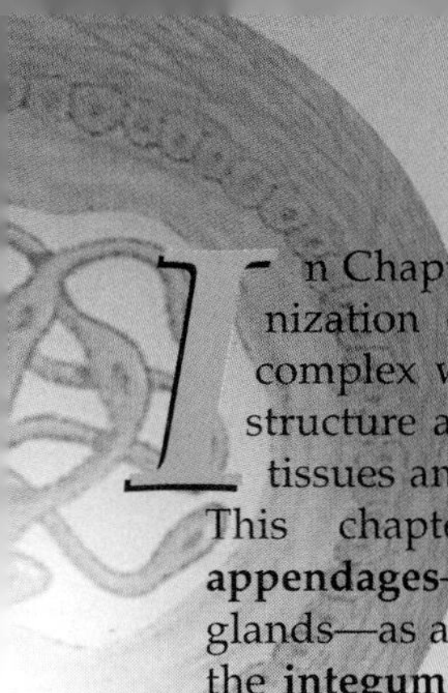

In Chapter 1 the concept of progressive organization of body structures from simple to complex was established. Complexity in body structure and function progresses from cells to tissues and then to organs and organ systems. This chapter discusses the skin and its **appendages**—the hair, the nails, and the skin glands—as an organ system. This system is called the **integumentary system. Integument** (in-TEG-yoo-ment) is another name for the skin, and the skin itself is the principal organ of the integumentary system. The skin is one of a group of anatomically simple but functionally important sheetlike structures called **membranes.** This chapter will begin with classification and discussion of the important body membranes. Study of the structure and function of the integument will follow. Ideally, you should study the skin and its appendages before proceeding to the more traditional organ systems in the chapters that follow to improve your understanding of how structure is related to function.

Classification of Body Membranes

The term **membrane** refers to a thin, sheetlike structure that may have many important functions in the body. Membranes cover and protect the body surface, line body cavities, and cover the inner surfaces of the hollow organs such as the digestive, reproductive, and respiratory passageways. Some membranes anchor organs to each other or to bones, and others cover the internal organs. In certain areas of the body, membranes secrete lubricating fluids that reduce friction during organ movements such as the beating of the heart or lung expansion and contraction. Membrane lubricants also decrease friction between bones in joints. There are two major categories or types of body membranes:

1. **Epithelial membranes,** composed of epithelial tissue and an underlying layer of specialized connective tissue
2. **Connective tissue membranes,** composed exclusively of various types of connective tissue; no epithelial cells are present in this type of membrane

EPITHELIAL MEMBRANES

There are three types of epithelial tissue membranes in the body:

1. Cutaneous membrane
2. Serous membranes
3. Mucous membranes

Cutaneous Membrane

The **cutaneous** (kyoo-TAY-nee-us) **membrane** or **skin** is the primary organ of the integumentary system. It is one of the most important and certainly one of the largest and most visible organs. In most individuals the skin composes some 16% of the body weight. It fulfills the requirements necessary for an epithelial tissue membrane in that it has a superficial layer of epithelial cells and an underlying layer of supportive connective tissue. Its structure is uniquely suited to its many functions. The skin will be discussed in depth later in the chapter.

Serous Membranes

Like all epithelial membranes, a **serous** (SE-rus) **membrane** is composed of two distinct layers of tissue. The epithelial sheet is a thin layer of simple squamous epithelium. The connective tissue layer forms a very thin, gluelike **basement membrane** that holds and supports the epithelial cells.

The serous membrane that lines body cavities and covers the surfaces of organs in those cavities is in reality a single, continuous sheet of tissue covering two different surfaces. The name of the serous membrane is determined by its location. Using this criterion results in two types of serous membranes; the first type lines body cavities, and the second type covers the organs in those cavities. The serous membrane, which lines the walls of a body cavity much like wallpaper covers the walls of a room, is called the **parietal** (pah-RYE-i-tal) **portion.** The other type of serous membrane, which covers the surface of organs found in body cavities, is called the **visceral** (VIS-er-al) **portion.**

The serous membranes of the thoracic and abdominal cavities are identified in Figure 4-1. In the thoracic cavity the serous membranes are called **pleura** (PLOOR-ah), and in the abdominal cavity, they are called **peritoneum** (pair-i-toe-NEE-um). Look again at Figure 4-1 to note the placement of the **parietal** and **visceral pleura** and

FIGURE 4–1 ***Types of Body Membranes.*** **A,** Epithelial membranes, including cutaneous membrane (skin), serous membranes (parietal and visceral pleura and peritoneum), and mucous membranes. **B,** Connective tissue membranes, including synovial membranes. See text for explanation.

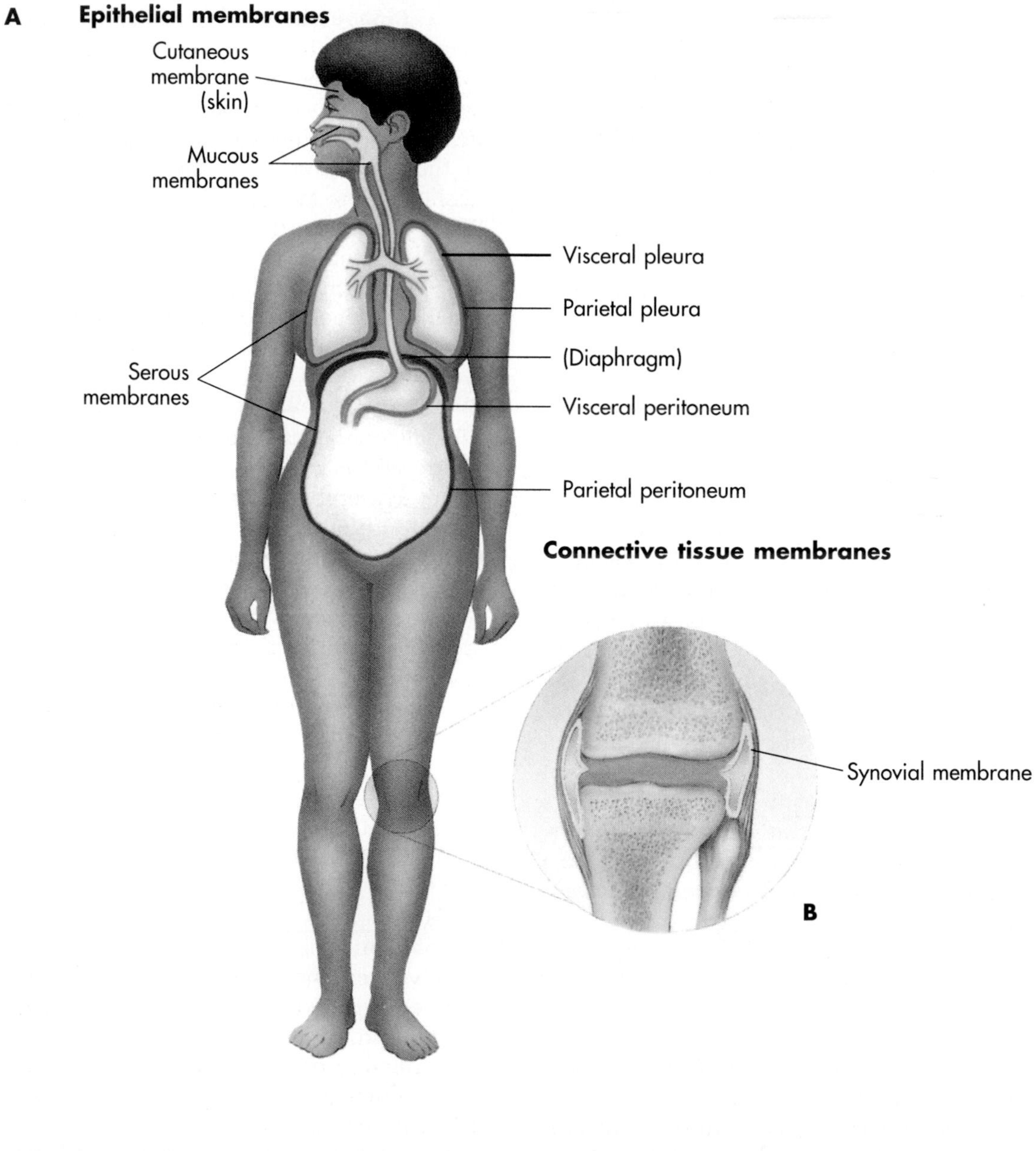

the **parietal** and **visceral peritoneum.** In both cases the parietal layer forms the lining of the bodycavity, and the visceral layer covers the organs found in that cavity.

Serous membranes secrete a thin, watery fluid that helps reduce friction and serves as a lubricant when organs rub against one another and against the walls of the cavities that contain them. **Pleurisy** (PLOOR-i-see) is a very painful pathological condition characterized by inflammation of the serous membranes (pleura) that line the chest cavity and cover the lungs. Pain is caused by irritation and friction as the lungs rub against the walls of the chest cavity. In severe cases the inflamed surfaces of the pleura fuse, and permanent damage may develop. The term **peritonitis** (pair-i-toe-NYE-tis) is used to describe inflammation of the serous membranes in the abdominal cavity. Peritonitis is sometimes a serious complication of an infected appendix.

Mucous Membranes

Mucous (MYOO-kus) **membranes** are epithelial membranes that line body surfaces opening directly to the exterior. Examples of mucous membranes include those lining the respiratory, digestive, urinary, and reproductive tracts. The epithelial component of a mucous membrane varies, depending on its location and function. In the esophagus, for example, a tough, abrasion-resistant stratified squamous epithelium is found. A thin layer of simple columnar epithelium covers the walls of the lower segments of the digestive tract.

The epithelial cells of most mucous membranes secrete a thick, slimy material called **mucus** that keeps the membranes moist and soft.

The term **mucocutaneous** (myoo-ko-kyoo-TAY-nee-us) **junction** is used to describe the transitional area that serves as a point of "fusion" where skin and mucous membranes meet. Such junctions lack accessory organs such as hair or sweat glands that characterize skin. These transitional areas are generally moistened by mucous glands within the body orifices or openings where these junctions are located. The eyelids, nasal openings, vulva, and anus have mucocutaneous junctions that may become sites of infection or irritation.

CONNECTIVE TISSUE MEMBRANES

Unlike cutaneous, serous, and mucous membranes, connective tissue membranes do not contain epithelial components. The **synovial** (si-NO-vee-al) **membranes** lining the spaces between bones and joints that move are classified as connective tissue membranes. These membranes are smooth and slick and secrete a thick and colorless lubricating fluid called **synovial fluid.** The membrane itself, with its specialized fluid, helps reduce friction between the opposing surfaces of bones in movable joints. Synovial membranes also line the small, cushionlike sacs called **bursae** (BER-see) found between moving body parts.

The Skin

The brief description of the skin in Chapter 3 (see p. 47) identified it not only as the primary organ of the integumentary system but also as the largest and one of the most important organs of the body. Architecturally the skin is a marvel. Consider the incredible number of structures fitting into 1 square inch of skin: 500 sweat glands; over 1000 nerve endings; yards of tiny blood vessels; nearly 100 oil or **sebaceous** (se-BAY-shus) glands; 150 sensors for pressure, 75 for heat, 10 for cold; and millions of cells.

STRUCTURE OF THE SKIN

The skin or cutaneous membrane is a sheetlike organ composed of the following layers of distinct tissue (Figure 4-2):

1. The **epidermis** is the outermost layer of the skin. It is a relatively thin sheet of stratified squamous epithelium.
2. The **dermis** is the deeper of the two layers. It is thicker than the epidermis and is made up largely of connective tissue.

As you can see in Figure 4-2, the layers of the skin are supported by a thick layer of loose connective tissue and fat called **subcutaneous** (sub-kyoo-TAY-nee-us) **tissue.** Fat in the subcutaneous layer insulates the body from extremes of heat and cold. It also serves as a stored source of energy for the body and can be used as a food source if required. In addition, the subcutaneous

FIGURE 4–2 ***Microscopic View of the Skin.*** The epidermis, shown in longitudinal section, is raised at one corner to reveal the ridges in the dermis.

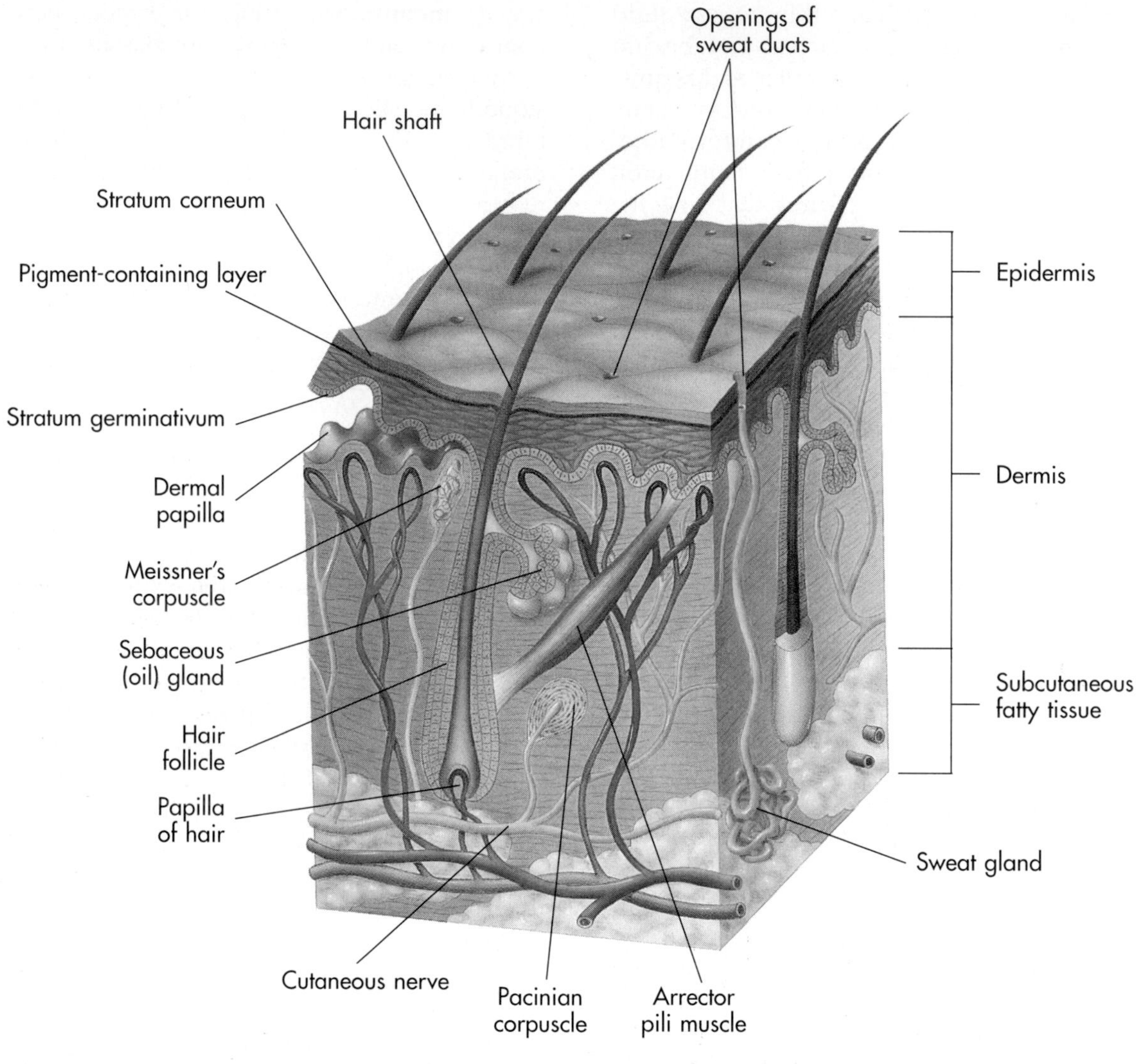

tissue acts as a shock-absorbing pad and helps protect underlying tissues from injury caused by bumps and blows to the body surface.

Epidermis

The tightly packed epithelial cells of the epidermis are arranged in many distinct layers. The cells of the innermost layer, called the **stratum germinativum,** undergo mitosis and reproduce themselves (Figure 4-2). As they move toward the surface of the skin, these new cells "specialize" in ways that increase their ability to provide protection for the body tissues that lie below them. This ability is of critical clinical significance. It enables the skin to repair itself if it is injured. The self-repairing characteristic of normal skin makes it possible for the body to maintain an effective barrier against infection, even when it is subjected to injury and normal wear and tear. As new cells are produced in the deep layer of the epidermis, they

FIGURE 4–3 ***Photomicrograph of the Skin.*** Many dead cells of the stratum corneum have flaked off from the surface of the epidermis. Note that the epidermis is very cellular. The dermis has fewer cells and more connective tissue.

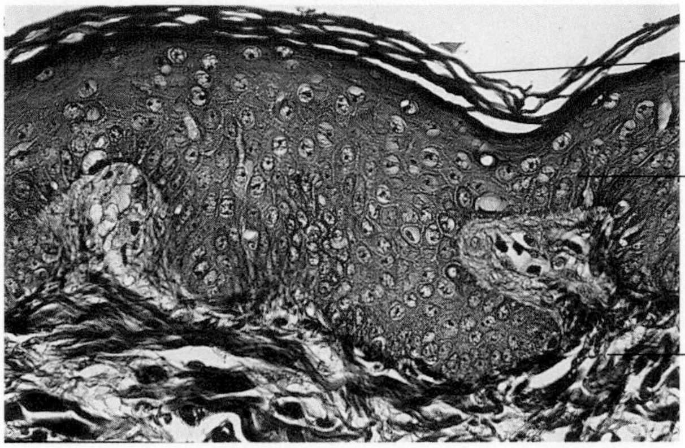

move upward through additional layers, or "strata" of cells. As they approach the surface, the cytoplasm is replaced by one of nature's most unique proteins, a substance called **keratin** (KARE-ah-tin). Keratin is a tough, waterproof material that provides cells in the outer layer of the skin with a horny, abrasion-resistant, and protective quality. The tough outer layer of the epidermis is called the **stratum corneum** (KOR-nee-um). Cells filled with keratin are continually pushed to the surface of the epidermis. In the photomicrograph of the skin shown in Figure 4-3, many of the outermost cells of the stratum corneum have been dislodged. These dry, dead cells filled with keratin "flake off" by the thousands onto our clothes, our bathwater, and things we handle. Millions of epithelial cells reproduce daily to replace the millions shed—just one example of the work our bodies do without our knowledge, even when we seem to be resting.

The deepest cell layer of the epidermis identified in Figure 4-2 is responsible for the production of a specialized **pigment** substance that gives color to the skin. The term *pigment* comes from a Latin word meaning "paint." It is this epidermal layer that gives color to the skin. The brown pigment **melanin** (MEL-ah-nin) is produced by specialized cells in this layer. These cells are called **melanocytes** (MEL-ah-no-sites). The higher the concentration of melanin, the deeper the color of skin. The amount of melanin in your skin depends first on the skin color genes you have inherited. That is, heredity determines how dark or light your basic skin color is. However, other factors such as sunlight can modify this hereditary effect. Prolonged exposure to sunlight in light-skinned people darkens the exposed area because it leads to increased melanin deposits in the epidermis. If the skin contains little melanin, a change in color can occur if the volume of blood in the skin changes significantly or if the amount of oxygen in the blood is increased or decreased. In these individuals increased blood flow to the skin or increased blood oxygen levels can cause a pink flush to appear. However, if blood oxygen levels decrease or if actual blood flow is reduced dramatically, the skin turns a bluish gray color—a condition called **cyanosis** (SYE-ah-NO-sis). In general, the less abundant the melanin deposits in the skin, the more visible the changes in color caused by the change in skin blood volume or oxygen level. Conversely, the richer the skin's pigmentation, the less noticeable such changes will be.

The cells of the epidermis are packed tightly together. They are held firmly to one another and to the dermis below by specialized junctions between the membranes of adjacent cells. If these specialized links, sometimes described as "spot welds," are weakened or destroyed, the skin falls apart. When this occurs because of burns, friction injuries, or exposure to irritants, **blisters** may result.

The junction that exists between the thin epidermal layer of the skin above and the dermal layer below is called the **dermal-epidermal junction.** The area of contact between dermis and epidermis "glues" them together and provides support for the epidermis, which is attached to its upper surface. Blister formation also occurs if this junction is damaged or destroyed. The junction is visible in Figure 4-2, which shows the epidermis raised on one corner to reveal the underlying dermis more clearly.

Dermis

The dermis is the deeper of the two primary skin layers and is much thicker than the epidermis. It is composed largely of connective tissue. Instead of cells being crowded close together like the epithelial cells of the epidermis, they are scattered far apart, with many fibers in between. Some of the fibers are tough and strong (collagen or white fibers), and others are stretchable and elastic (elastic or yellow fibers).

The upper region of the dermis is characterized by parallel rows of peglike projections called **dermal papillae** (pah-PIL-ee), which are visible in Figure 4-2. These upward projections are interesting and useful features. They form an important part of the dermal-epidermal junction that helps bind the skin layers together. In addition, they form the ridges and grooves that make possible fingerprinting as a means of identification.

You can observe these ridges on the tips of the fingers and on the skin covering the palms of your hands. Observe in Figure 4-2 how the epidermis follows the contours of the dermal papillae. These ridges develop sometime before birth. Not only is their pattern unique in each individual, but also it never changes except to grow larger—two facts that explain why our fingerprints or footprints positively identify us. Many hospitals identify newborn babies by footprinting them soon after birth.

The deeper area of the dermis is filled with a dense network of interlacing fibers. Most of the fibers in this area are collagen that gives toughness to the skin. However, elastic fibers are also present. These make the skin stretchable and elastic (able to rebound). As we age, the number of elastic fibers in the dermis decreases, and the amount of fat stored in the subcutaneous tissue is reduced. Wrinkles develop as the skin loses elasticity, sags, and becomes less soft and pliant.

In addition to connective tissue elements, the dermis contains a specialized network of nerves and nerve endings to process sensory information such as pain, pressure, touch, and temperature. At various levels of the dermis, there are muscle fibers, hair follicles, sweat and sebaceous glands, and many blood vessels.

APPENDAGES OF THE SKIN

Hair

The human body is covered with millions of hairs. Indeed, at the time of birth most of the specialized structures called **follicles** (FOL-li-kuls) that are required for hair growth are already present. They develop early in fetal life and by birth are present in most parts of the skin. The hair of a newborn infant is extremely fine and soft; it is called **lanugo** (lah-NOO-go) from the Latin word meaning "down." In premature infants, lanugo may be noticeable over most of the body, but soon after birth the lanugo is lost and replaced by new hair that is stronger and more pigmented. Although only a few areas of the skin are hair-

Subcutaneous Injection

Although the subcutaneous layer is not part of the skin, it carries the major blood vessels and nerves to the skin above it. The rich blood supply and loose, spongy texture of the subcutaneous layer make it an ideal site for the rapid and relatively pain-free absorption of injected material. Liquid medicines such as insulin and pelleted implant materials are often administered by **subcutaneous injection** into this spongy and porous layer beneath the skin.

FIGURE 4–4 *Hair Follicle.* Relationship of a hair follicle and related structures to the epidermal and dermal layers of the skin.

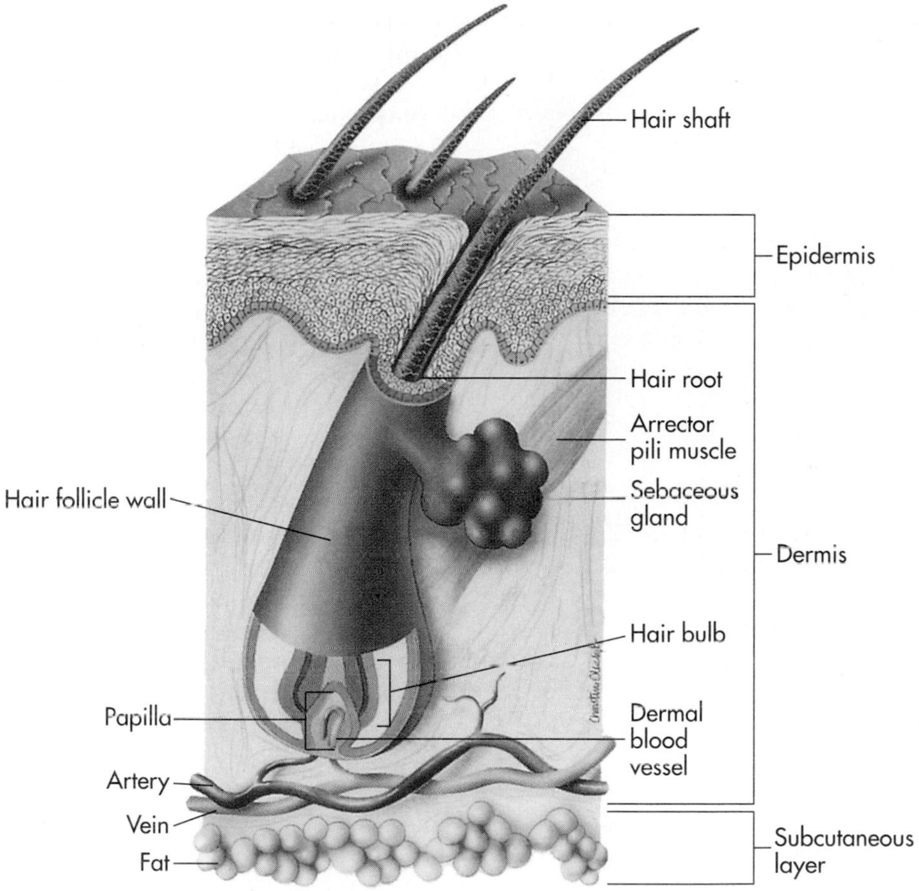

less—notably the lips, the palms of the hands, and the soles of the feet—most body hair remains almost invisible. Hair is most visible on the scalp, eyelids, and eyebrows. The coarse hair that first appears in the pubic and axillary regions at the time of puberty develops in response to the secretion of hormones.

Hair growth begins when cells of the epidermal layer of the skin grow down into the dermis, forming a small tube called the **hair follicle.** The relationship of a hair follicle and its related structures to the epidermal and dermal layers of the skin is shown in Figure 4-4. Hair growth begins from a small, cap-shaped cluster of cells called the **hair papilla** (pah-PIL-ah), which is located at the base of the follicle. The papilla is nourished by a dermal blood vessel. Note in Figure 4-4 that part of the hair, namely the **root,** lies hidden in the follicle. The visible part of a hair is called the **shaft.** Figure 4-5 shows shafts of hair extending from their follicles.

As long as cells in the papilla of the hair follicle remain alive, new hair will replace any that is cut or plucked. Contrary to popular belief, frequent cutting or shaving does not make hair grow faster or become coarser. Why? Because neither process affects the epithelial cells that form the hairs, since they are embedded in the dermis.

FIGURE 4–5 ***Hair Shaft and Follicle.*** Scanning electron micrograph showing shafts of hair extending from their follicles.

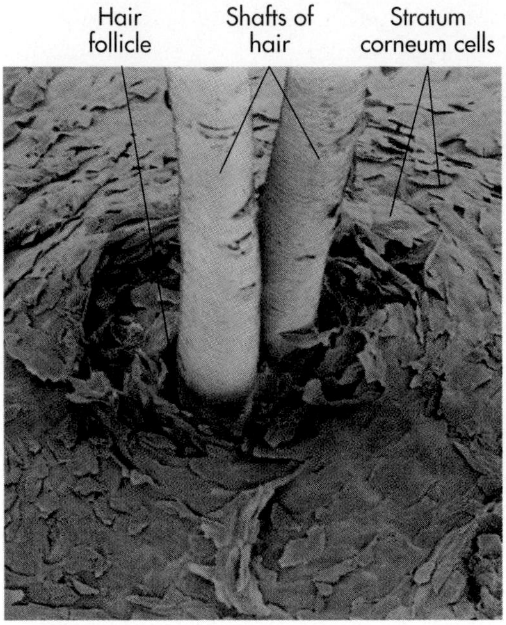

A tiny, smooth (involuntary) muscle can be seen in Figure 4-4. It is called an **arrector pili** (ah-REK-tor PYE-lie) muscle. It is attached to the base of a dermal papilla above and to the side of a hair follicle below. Generally, these muscles contract only when we are frightened or cold. When contraction occurs, each muscle simultaneously pulls on its two points of attachment (that is, up on a hair follicle but down on a part of the skin). This produces little raised places, called *goose pimples,* between the depressed points of the skin and at the same time pulls the hairs up until they are more or less straight. The name *arrector pili* describes the function of these muscles; it is Latin for "erectors of the hair." We unconsciously recognize these facts in expressions such as "I was so frightened my hair stood on end."

Receptors

Receptors in the skin make it possible for the body surface to act as a sense organ, relaying messages to the brain concerning sensations such as touch, pain, temperature, and pressure. Receptors differ in structure from the highly complex to the very simple. Figure 4-6 shows enlarged views of a **Meissner's** (MIZE-ners) **corpuscle** and a **Pacin-**

FIGURE 4–6 ***Skin Receptors.*** Receptors are specialized nerve endings that make it possible for the skin to act as a sense organ. **A,** Meissner's corpuscle. **B,** Pacinian corpuscle. (See also Figure 4-2.)

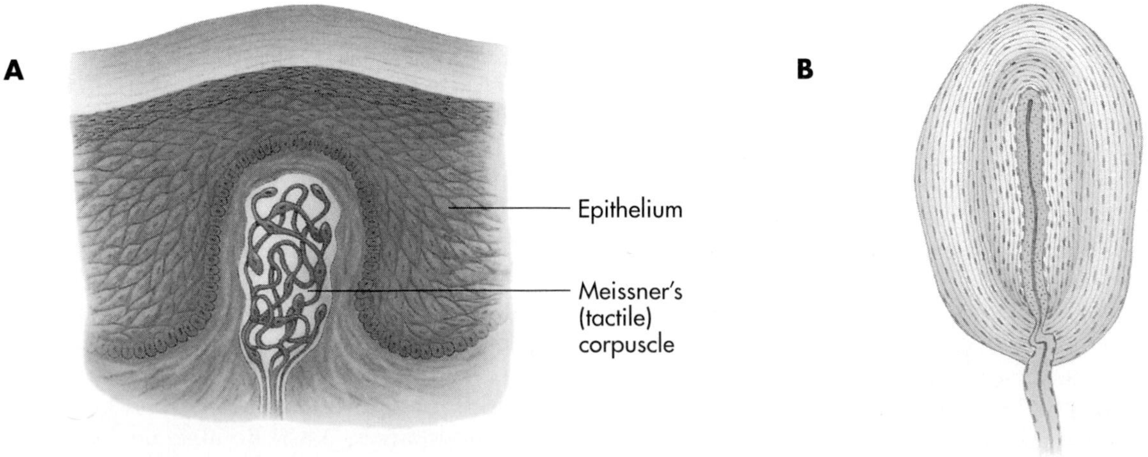

ian (pah-SIN-ee-an) **corpuscle.** Look again at Figure 4-2 and find these receptors. The Pacinian corpuscle is deep in the dermis. It is capable of detecting *pressure* on the skin surface. The Meissner's corpuscle is generally located close to the skin surface. It is capable of detecting sensations of *light touch.* Both specialized receptors are widely distributed in skin. Additional receptors in the skin respond to other types of stimuli. For example, **free nerve endings** respond to pain, and receptors called **Krause's end bulbs** detect sensations of touch, low frequency vibration, and possibly cold. Other receptors mediate sensations of heat, crude touch, and vibration.

Nails

Nails are classified as accessory organs of the skin and are produced by cells in the epidermis. They form when epidermal cells over the terminal ends of the fingers and toes fill with keratin and become hard and platelike. The components of a typical fingernail and its associated structures are shown in Figure 4-7. In this illustration the fingernail of the index finger is viewed from above and in sagittal section. (Recall that a sagittal section divides a body part into right and left portions.) Look first at the nail as seen from above. The visible part of the nail is called the **nail body.** The rest of the nail, namely, the **root,** lies in a groove and is hidden by a fold of skin called the **cuticle** (KYOO-ti-kul). In the sagittal section you can see the nail root from the side and note its relationship to the cuticle, which is folded back over its upper surface. The nail body nearest the root has a crescent-shaped white area known as the **lunula** (LOO-nyoo-lah), or "little moon." You should be able to identify this area easily on your own nails; it is most noticeable on the thumbnail. Under the nail lies a layer of epithelium called the **nail bed,** which is labeled on the sagittal section in Figure 4- 7. Because it contains abundant blood vessels, it appears pink in color through the translucent nail bodies. If blood oxygen levels drop and cyanosis develops, the nail bed will turn blue.

Depilatories

All **depilatories** (de-PIL-ah-toe-rees) are used to remove unwanted hair. They dissolve the protein in hair shafts that extend above the skin surface. Because the follicle is not affected, regrowth of hair continues at a normal rate. Unfortunately, use of depilatories sometimes results in allergic reactions producing irritation and rash. If used to remove body hair before surgery, reactions to depilatories may delay healing of the surgical incision.

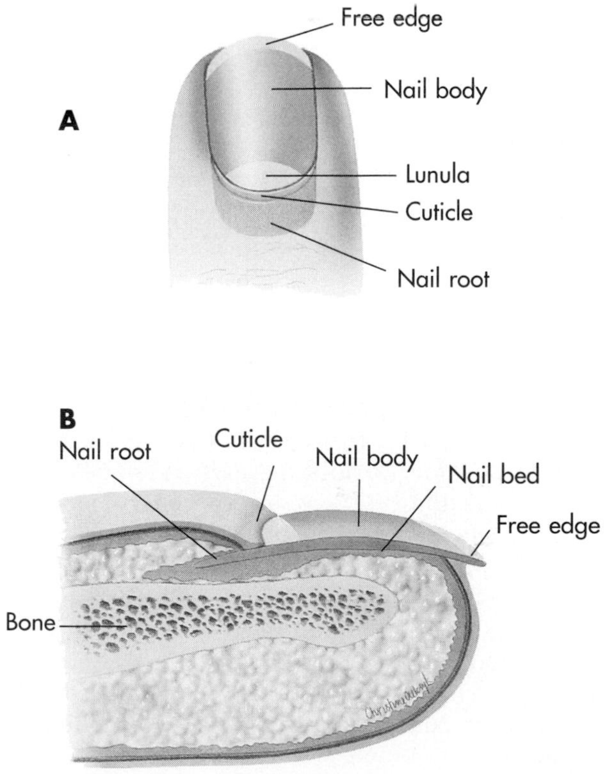

FIGURE 4–7 ***Structure of Nails.*** **A,** Fingernail viewed from above. **B,** Sagittal section of fingernail and associated structures.

Skin Glands

The skin glands include the two varieties of **sweat** or **sudoriferous** (soo-doe-RIF-er-us) **glands** and the microscopic **sebaceous glands.**

Sweat (sudoriferous) glands. Sweat glands are the most numerous of the skin glands. They can be classified into two groups—**eccrine** (EK-rin) and **apocrine** (AP-o-krin)—based on type of secretion and location. **Eccrine sweat glands** are by far the more numerous, important, and widespread sweat glands in the body. They are quite small and, with few exceptions, are distributed over the total body surface. Throughout life they produce a transparent, watery liquid called **perspiration,** or **sweat.** Sweat assists in the elimination of waste products such as ammonia and uric acid. In addition to elimination of waste, sweat plays a critical role in helping the body maintain a constant temperature. Anatomists estimate that a single square inch of skin on the palms of the hands contains about 3000 eccrine sweat glands. With a magnifying glass you can locate the pinpoint-size openings on the skin that you probably call **pores.** The pores are outlets of small ducts from the eccrine sweat glands.

Apocrine sweat glands are found primarily in the skin in the armpit (axilla) and in the pigmented skin areas around the genitals. They are larger than the eccrine glands, and instead of watery sweat, they secrete a thicker, milky secretion. The odor associated with apocrine gland secretion is not caused by the secretion itself. Instead, it is caused by the contamination and decomposition of the secretion by skin bacteria. Apocrine glands enlarge and begin to function at puberty.

Sebaceous glands. Sebaceous glands secrete oil for the hair and skin. Oil or sebaceous glands grow where hairs grow. Their tiny ducts open into hair follicles (Figure 4-4) so that their secretion, called **sebum** (SEE-bum), lubricates the hair and skin. Someone aptly described sebum as "nature's skin cream" because it prevents drying and cracking of the skin. Sebum secretion increases during adolescence, stimulated by the increased blood levels of the sex hormones. Frequently sebum

Decubitus Ulcers

Family members, nurses, or other professionals who provide home health care services for bedridden or otherwise immobilized individuals need to be aware of the causes and nature of **decubitus** (de-KU-bi-tus) **ulcers** or pressure sores. Decubitus means "lying down," a name that hints at a common cause of pressure sores: lying in one position for long periods. Also called *bedsores,* these lesions appear after blood flow to a local area of skin slows because of pressure on skin covering a bony prominence such as the heel (see illustration). Ulcers form and infections develop as lack of blood flow causes tissue damage. Frequent changes in body position and soft support cushions help prevent decubitus ulcers.

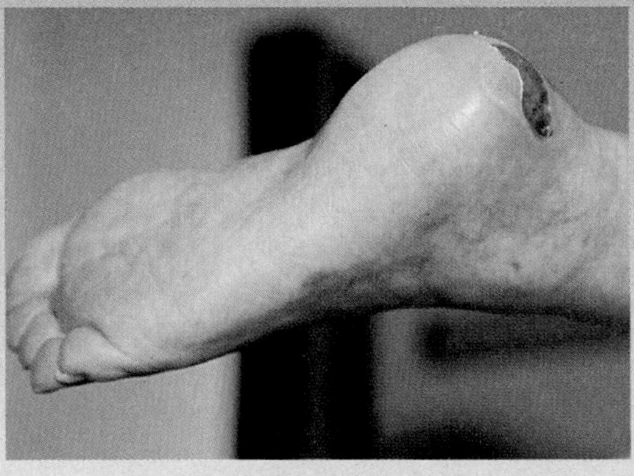

accumulates in and enlarges some of the ducts of the sebaceous glands, forming white pimples. This sebum often darkens, forming a **blackhead.** Sebum secretion decreases in late adulthood, contributing to increased wrinkling and cracking of the skin.

FUNCTIONS OF THE SKIN

The skin or cutaneous membrane serves three important functions that contribute to survival. The most important functions are:

1. Protection
2. Temperature regulation
3. Sense organ activity

Protection

The skin as a whole is often described as our "first line of defense" against a multitude of hazards. It protects us against the daily invasion of deadly microbes. The tough, keratin-filled cells of the stratum corneum also resist the entry of harmful chemicals and protect against physical tears and cuts. Because it is waterproof, **keratin** also protects the body from excessive fluid loss. Melanin in the pigment layer of the skin prevents the sun's harmful ultraviolet rays from penetrating the interior of the body.

Temperature Regulation

The skin plays a key role in regulating the body's temperature. Incredible as it seems, on a hot and humid day the skin can serve as a means for releasing almost 3000 calories of body heat—enough heat energy to boil over 20 liters of water! It accomplishes this feat by regulating sweat secretion and by regulating the flow of blood close to the body surface. When sweat evaporates from the body surface, heat is also lost. The principle of heat loss through evaporation is basic to many cooling systems. When increased quantities of blood are allowed to fill the vessels close to the skin, heat is also lost by radiation. Blood supply to the skin far exceeds the amount needed by the skin. Such an abundant blood supply primarily enables the regulation of body temperature.

Sense Organ Activity

The skin functions as an enormous sense organ. Its millions of nerve endings serve as antennas or receivers for the body, keeping it informed of changes in its environment. The specialized receptors shown in Figures 4-2 and 4-6 make it possible for the body to detect sensations of light touch (Meissner's corpuscles) and pressures (Pacinian corpuscles). Other receptors make it possible for us to respond to the sensations of pain, heat, and cold.

BURNS

Burns constitute one of the most serious and frequent problems that affect the skin. Typically, we think of a burn as an injury caused by fire or by contact of the skin with a hot surface. However, overexposure to ultraviolet light (sunburn) or contact of the skin with an electric current or a harmful chemical such as an acid can also cause burns.

Exercise and the Skin

Excess heat produced by the skeletal muscles during exercise increases the core body temperature far beyond the normal range. Because blood in vessels near the skin's surface dissipates heat well, the body's control centers adjust blood flow so that more warm blood from the body's core is sent to the skin for cooling. During exercise, blood flow in the skin can be so high that the skin takes on a redder coloration.

To help dissipate even more heat, sweat production increases to as high as 3 L per hour during exercise. Although each sweat gland produces very little of this total, over 3 million individual sweat glands are found throughout the skin. Sweat evaporation is essential to keeping body temperature in balance, but excessive sweating can lead to a dangerous loss of fluid. Because normal drinking may not replace the water lost through sweating, it is important to increase fluid consumption during and after any type of exercise to avoid **dehydration.**

FIGURE 4–8 *The "Rule of Nines."* Dividing the body into 11 areas of 9% each helps one to estimate the amount of skin surface burned in an adult.

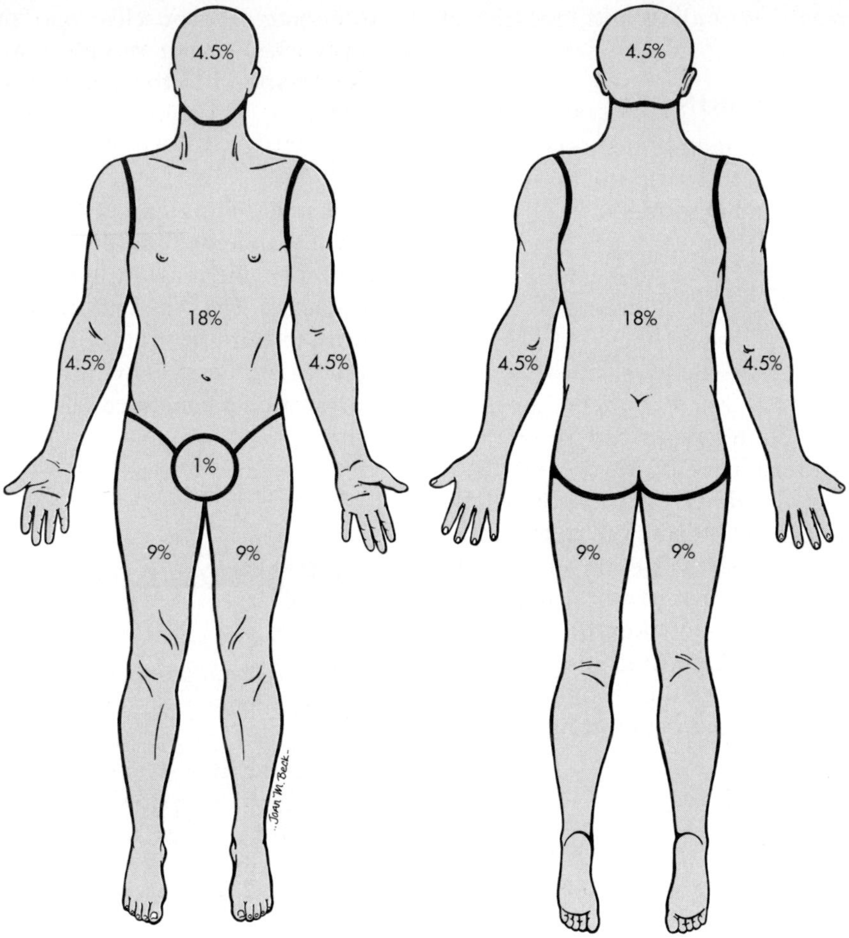

Estimating Body Surface Area

When burns involve large areas of the skin, treatment and the possibility for recovery depend in large part on the **total area involved** and the **severity of the burn.** The severity of a burn is determined by the depth of the injury, as well as by the amount of body surface area affected.

The "**rule of nines**" is one of the most frequently used methods of determining the extent of a burn injury. With this technique (Figure 4-8) the body is divided into 11 areas of 9% each, with the area around the genitals representing the additional 1% of body surface area. As you can see in Figure 4-8, in the adult 9% of the skin covers the head and each upper extremity, including front and back surfaces. Twice as much, or 18%, of the total skin area covers the front and back of the trunk and each lower extremity, including front and back surfaces.

Classification of Burns

The classification system used to describe the severity of burns is based on the number of tissue layers involved. The most severe burns destroy not only layers of the skin and subcutaneous tissue but underlying tissues, as well.

First-degree burns. A **first-degree burn** (for example, a typical sunburn) causes minor discomfort and some reddening of the skin. Although the surface layers of the epidermis may peel in 1 to 3 days, no blistering occurs, and actual tissue destruction is minimal.

Second-degree burns. A **second-degree burn** involves the deep epidermal layers and always causes injury to the upper layers of the dermis. Although deep second-degree burns damage sweat glands, hair follicles, and sebaceous glands, complete destruction of the dermis does not occur. Blisters, severe pain, generalized swelling, and fluid loss characterize this type of burn. Scarring is common. First- and second-degree burns are called **partial-thickness burns.**

Third-degree burns. A **third-degree,** or **full-thickness burn** is characterized by complete destruction of the epidermis and dermis. In addition, tissue death extends below the primary skin layers into the subcutaneous tissue. Third-degree burns often involve underlying muscles and even bone. One distinction between second- and third-degree burns is that third-degree lesions are insensitive to pain immediately after injury because of the destruction of nerve endings. The fluid loss that results from third-degree burns is a very serious problem.

OUTLINE SUMMARY

CLASSIFICATION OF BODY MEMBRANES

A Classification of body membranes (Figure 4-1)
- **1** Epithelial membranes—composed of epithelial tissue and an underlying layer of connective tissue
- **2** Connective tissue membranes—composed largely of various types of connective tissue

B Epithelial membranes
- **1** Cutaneous membrane—the skin
- **2** Serous membranes—simple squamous epithelium on a connective tissue basement membrane
  - **a** Types
    - **(1)** Parietal—line walls of body cavities
    - **(2)** Visceral—cover organs found in body cavities
  - **b** Examples
    - **(1)** Pleura—parietal and visceral layers line walls of thoracic cavity and cover the lungs
    - **(2)** Peritoneum—parietal and visceral layers line walls of abdominal cavity and cover the organs in that cavity
  - **c** Diseases
    - **(1)** Pleurisy—inflammation of the serous membranes that line the chest cavity and cover the lungs
    - **(2)** Peritonitis—inflammation of the serous membranes in the abdominal cavity that line the walls and cover the abdominal organs
- **3** Mucous membranes
  - **a** Line body surfaces that open directly to the exterior
  - **b** Produce mucus, a thick secretion that keeps the membranes soft and moist

C Connective tissue membranes
- **1** Do not contain epithelial components
- **2** Produce a lubricant called *synovial fluid*
- **3** Examples are the synovial membranes in the spaces between joints and in the lining of bursal sacs

THE SKIN

A Structure (Figure 4-2)—two primary layers called *epidermis* and *dermis*
- **1** Epidermis
  - **a** Outermost and thinnest primary layer of skin
  - **b** Composed of several layers of stratified squamous epithelium
  - **c** Stratum germinativum—innermost layer of cells that continually reproduce, and new cells move toward the surface
  - **d** As cells approach surface, they are filled with a tough, waterproof protein called *keratin* and eventually flake off
  - **e** Stratum corneum—outermost layer of keratin-filled cells
  - **f** Pigment-containing layer—epidermal layer that contains pigment cells called *melanocytes,* which produce the brown pigment melanin
  - **g** Blisters—caused by breakdown of union between cells or primary layers of skin
  - **h** Dermal-epidermal junction—specialized area between two primary skin layers
- **2** Dermis
  - **a** Deeper and thicker of the two primary skin layers and composed largely of connective tissue
  - **b** Upper area of dermis characterized by parallel rows of peglike dermal papillae
  - **c** Ridges and grooves in dermis form pattern unique to each individual (basis of fingerprinting)
  - **d** Deeper areas of dermis filled with network of tough collagenous and stretchable elastic fibers
  - **e** Number of elastic fibers decreases with age and contributes to wrinkle formation
  - **f** Dermis also contains nerve endings, muscle fibers, hair follicles, sweat and sebaceous glands, and many blood vessels

B Appendages of the skin
- **1** Hair (Figures 4-4 and 4-5)
  - **a** Soft hair of fetus and newborn called *lanugo*
  - **b** Hair growth requires epidermal tubelike structure called *hair follicle*
  - **c** Hair growth begins from hair papilla
  - **d** Hair root lies hidden in follicle and visible part of hair called *shaft*
  - **e** Arrector pili—specialized smooth muscle that produces "goose pimples" and causes hair to stand up straight
- **2** Receptors (Figure 4-6)
  - **a** Specialized nerve endings—make it possible for skin to act as a sense organ
  - **b** Meissner's corpuscle—capable of detecting light touch
  - **c** Pacinian corpuscle—capable of detecting pressure
- **3** Nails (Figure 4-7)
  - **a** Produced by epidermal cells over terminal ends of fingers and toes
  - **b** Visible part called *nail body*
  - **c** Root lies in a groove and is hidden by cuticle
  - **d** Crescent-shaped area nearest root called *lunula*
  - **e** Nail bed may change color with change in blood flow

- **4** Skin glands
  - **a** Types
    - **(1)** Sweat or sudoriferous
    - **(2)** Sebaceous
  - **b** Sweat or sudoriferous glands
    - **(1)** Types
      - **(a)** Eccrine sweat glands
        - Most numerous, important, and widespread of the sweat glands
        - Produce perspiration or sweat, which flows out through pores on skin surface
        - Function throughout life and assist in body heat regulation
      - **(b)** Apocrine sweat glands
        - Found primarily in axilla and around genitalia
        - Secrete a thicker, milky secretion quite different from eccrine perspiration
        - Breakdown of secretion by skin bacteria produces odor
  - **c** Sebaceous glands
    - **(1)** Secrete oil or sebum for hair and skin
    - **(2)** Level of secretion increases during adolescence
    - **(3)** Amount of secretion regulated by sex hormones
    - **(4)** Sebum in sebaceous gland ducts may darken to form a blackhead

C Functions of the skin

- **1** Protection—first line of defense
  - **a** Against infection by microbes
  - **b** Against ultraviolet rays from sun
  - **c** Against harmful chemicals
  - **d** Against cuts and tears
- **2** Temperature regulation
  - **a** Skin can release almost 3000 calories of body heat per day
    - **(1)** Mechanisms of temperature regulation
      - **(a)** Regulation of sweat secretion
      - **(b)** Regulation of flow of blood close to the body surface
- **3** Sense organ activity
  - **a** Skin functions as an enormous sense organ
  - **b** Receptors serve as receivers for the body, keeping it informed of changes in its environment

D Burns

- **1** Treatment and recovery or survival depend on total area involved and severity or depth of the burn
- **2** Estimating body surface area using the "rule of nines" (Figure 4-8) in adults
  - **a** Body divided into 11 areas of 9% each
  - **b** Additional 1% of body surface area around genitals
- **3** Classification of burns
  - **a** First-degree (partial-thickness) burns—only surface layers of epidermis involved
  - **b** Second-degree (partial-thickness) burns—involve the deep epidermal layers and always cause injury to the upper layers of the dermis
  - **c** Third-degree (full-thickness) burns—characterized by complete destruction of the epidermis and dermis
    - **(1)** May involve underlying muscle and bone
    - **(2)** Lesion is insensitive to pain because of destruction of nerve endings immediately after injury—intense pain is soon experienced

NEW WORDS

apocrine sweat gland
arrector pili
blister
bursa
cutaneous
cuticle
cyanosis
dehydration
depilatories
dermis
eccrine sweat gland
epidermis
follicle
keratin
Krause's end bulb
lanugo
lunula
Meissner's corpuscle
melanin
melanocyte
mucocutaneous junction
mucous membrane
mucus
Pacinian corpuscle
papilla
parietal
peritoneum
peritonitis
pleura
pleurisy
sebaceous gland
serous membrane
stratum corneum
subcutaneous
sudoriferous gland
synovial membrane
visceral portion

C H A P T E R T E S T

1. There are two major categories of body membranes called ______________ membranes and ______________ membranes.
2. The membrane that lines the walls of a body cavity is called the ______________ portion of the membrane, and the portion that covers the surface of organs found in body cavities is called the ______________ portion of that membrane.
3. The connective tissue membranes that line joint spaces are called ______________ membranes.
4. The principal organ of the integumentary system is the ______________.
5. The skin is classified as a ______________ membrane.
6. The two principal layers of the skin are called the ______________ and the ______________.
7. The tough waterproof material that provides cells in the outer layer of the skin with a protective quality is called ______________.
8. The brown pigment that gives color to the skin is known as ______________.
9. The part of a hair that lies hidden in the follicle is called the ______________.
10. The Pacinian corpuscle is capable of detecting ______________ on the skin surface.
11. Sweat or sudoriferous glands are classified into two groups, ______________ and ______________, based on type of secretion and location.
12. Specialized glands that secrete oil for the hair and skin are known as ______________ glands.
13. The "rule of nines" is used in the treatment and prognosis of ______________.

Select the most correct answer from Column B for each statement in Column A. (Only one answer is correct.)

COLUMN A	COLUMN B
14.______Another name for skin	a. Lanugo
15.______Outermost layer of skin	b. Arrector pili
16.______Contains melanocytes	c. Shaft
17.______Fine, soft hair of newborn	d. Integument
18.______Visible part of a hair	e. Pigment-containing layer
19.______Produce "goose pimples"	f. Bursae
20.______Lined with synovial membrane	g. Epidermis

REVIEW QUESTIONS

1. Define the term *membrane* and discuss a variety of functions that membranes serve in the body.
2. Classify body membranes.
3. Discuss the two types of serous membranes and give examples of each.
4. Compare mucous and synovial membranes.
5. How do the terms *integument* and *integumentary system* differ in meaning?
6. List the appendages of the skin.
7. Discuss the three primary functions of the skin.
8. What are the two major factors that determine the treatment of and possibility for recovery from burn injuries?

CRITICAL THINKING

9. Identify and compare the two main layers of the skin. How are these layers related to the subcutaneous layer?
10. Classify the skin glands. Locate each type of gland and compare the secretions of each.
11. Classify and compare the three major types of burn injuries.

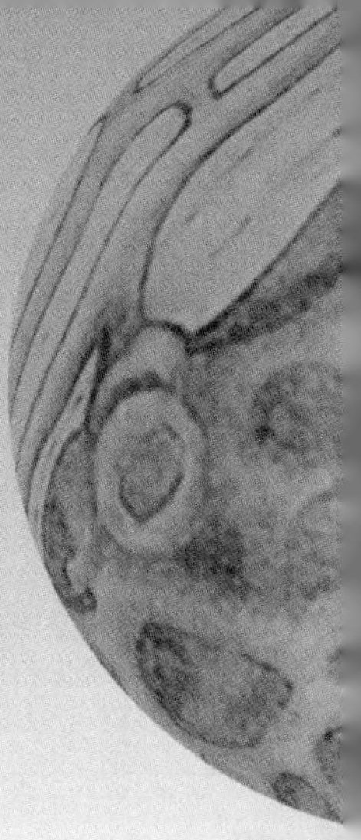

The Skeletal System

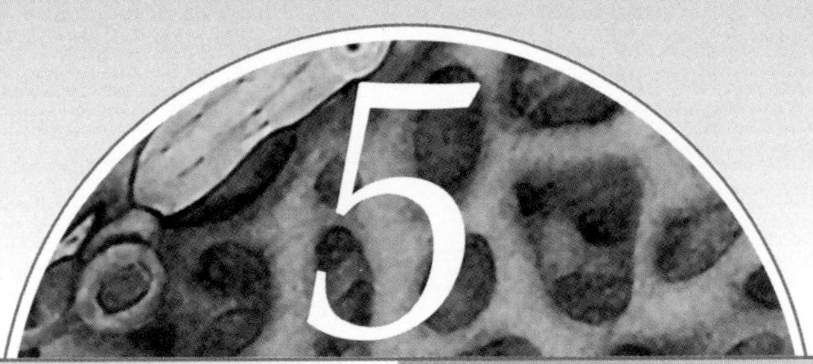

OUTLINE

Functions of the Skeletal System
- Support
- Protection
- Movement
- Storage
- Hemopoiesis

Types of Bones

Structure of Long Bones

Microscopic Structure of Bone and Cartilage

Bone Formation and Growth

Divisions of Skeleton
- Axial Skeleton
- Appendicular Skeleton

Differences Between a Man's and a Woman's Skeleton

Joints (Articulations)
- Kinds of Joints

BOXED ESSAYS

Osteoporosis
Epiphyseal Fracture
Palpable Bony Landmarks
Total Hip Replacement
The Knee Joint

OBJECTIVES

After you have completed this chapter, you should be able to:

1. List and discuss the generalized functions of the skeletal system.
2. Identify the major anatomical structures found in a typical long bone.
3. Discuss the microscopic structure of bone and cartilage, including the identification of specific cell types and structural features.
4. Explain how bones are formed, how they grow, and how they are remodeled.
5. Identify the two major subdivisions of the skeleton and list the bones found in each area.
6. List and compare the major types of joints in the body and give an example of each.

The primary organs of the skeletal system, bones, lie buried within the muscles and other soft tissues, providing a rigid framework and support structure for the whole body. In this respect the skeletal system functions like steel girders in a building; however, unlike steel girders, bones can be moved. Bones are also living organs. They can change and help the body respond to a changing environment. This ability of bones to change allows our bodies to grow and change.

Our study of the skeletal system will begin with an overview of its function. We will then classify bones by their structure and describe the characteristics of a typical bone. After discussing the microscopic structure of skeletal tissues, we will briefly outline bone growth and formation. With this information, the study of specific bones and the way they are assembled in the skeleton will be more meaningful. The chapter will end with a discussion of skeletal functions and an overview of joints or **articulations** (ar-tick-yoo-LAY-shuns).

An understanding of how bones articulate with one another in joints and how they relate to other body structures provides a basis for understanding the functions of many other organ systems. Coordinated movement, for example, is possible only because of the way bones are joined to one another and because of the way muscles are attached to those bones. In addition, knowing where specific bones are in the body will assist you in locating other body structures that will be discussed later.

Functions of the Skeletal System

SUPPORT

Bones form the body's supporting framework. All the softer tissues of the body literally hang from the skeletal framework.

PROTECTION

Hard, bony "boxes" protect delicate structures enclosed within them. For example, the skull protects the brain. The breastbone and ribs protect vital organs (heart and lungs) and also a vital tissue (red bone marrow, the blood cell–forming tissue).

MOVEMENT

Muscles are anchored firmly to bones. As muscles contract and shorten, they pull on bones and thereby move them.

STORAGE

Bones play an important part in maintaining homeostasis of blood calcium, a vital substance required for normal nerve and muscle function. They serve as a safety-deposit box for calcium. When the amount of calcium in blood increases above normal, calcium moves out of the blood and into the bones for storage. Conversely, when blood calcium decreases below normal, calcium moves in the opposite direction. It comes out of storage in bones and enters the blood.

HEMOPOIESIS

The term **hemopoiesis** (hee-mo-poy-EE-sis) is used to describe the process of blood cell formation. It is a combination of two Greek words: *hemo* (HEE-mo) meaning "blood" and *poiesis* (poy-EE-sis) meaning "to make." Blood cell formation is a vital process carried on in **red bone marrow.** Red bone marrow is soft connective tissue inside the hard walls of some bones.

Types of Bones

There are four types of bones. Their names suggest their shapes: *long* (for example, humerus or upper arm bone), *short* (for example, carpals or wrist bones), *flat* (for example, frontal or skull bone), and *irregular* (for example, vertebrae or spinal bones). Many important bones in the skeleton are classified as long bones, and all have several common characteristics. By studying a typical long bone, you can become familiar with the structural features of the entire group.

Structure of Long Bones

Figure 5-1 will help you learn the names of the main parts of a long bone. Identify each of the following:

1. **Diaphysis** (dye-AF-i-sis) or shaft—a hollow tube made of hard compact bone, hence a rigid and strong structure light enough in weight to permit easy movement
2. **Medullary cavity**—the hollow area inside the diaphysis of a bone; contains soft **yellow bone marrow,** an inactive, fatty form of marrow found in the adult skeleton
3. **Epiphyses** (e-PIF-i-sees) or the ends of the bone—red bone marrow fills in small spaces in the spongy bone composing the epiphyses
4. **Articular cartilage**—a thin layer of cartilage covering each epiphysis; functions like a small rubber cushion would if it were placed over the ends of bones where they form a joint
5. **Periosteum**—a strong fibrous membrane covering a long bone except at joint surfaces, where it is covered by articular cartilage
6. **Endosteum**—a fibrous membrane that lines the medullary cavity

FIGURE 5–1 *Longitudinal Section of a Long Bone.*

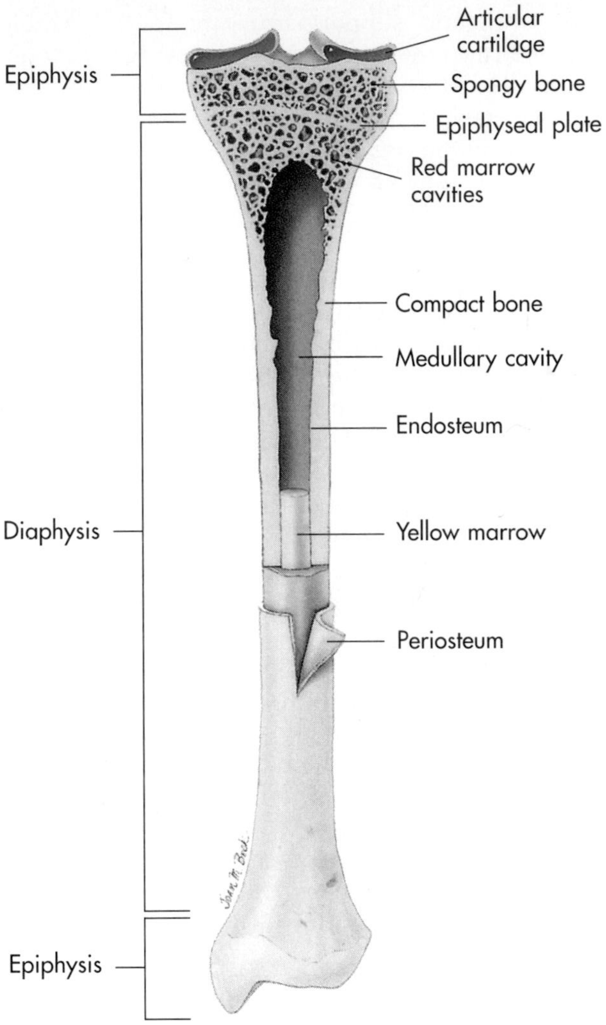

Microscopic Structure of Bone and Cartilage

The skeletal system contains two major types of connective tissue: **bone** and **cartilage.** Bone has different appearances and textures, depending on its location. In Figure 5-2, *A,* the outer layer of bone is hard and dense. Bone of this type is called **dense** or **compact bone.** The porous bone in the end of the long bone is called *spongy bone.* As the name implies, spongy bone contains many spaces that may be filled with marrow. Compact or dense bone appears solid to the naked eye. Figure 5-2, *B,* shows the microscopic appearance of spongy and compact bone. The needlelike threads of spongy bone that surround a network of spaces are called **trabeculae** (trah-BEK-yoo-lee).

As you can see in Figures 5-2 and 5-3, compact or dense bone does not contain a network of open spaces. Instead, the matrix is organized into numerous structural units called **osteons** or *Haversian systems.* Each circular and tubelike osteon is composed of calcified matrix arranged in multiple layers resembling the rings of an onion. Each ring is called a **concentric lamella** (lah-MEL-ah). The circular rings or lamellae surround the **central canal,** which contains a blood vessel.

Bones are not lifeless structures. Within their hard, seemingly lifeless matrix are many living bone cells called **osteocytes** (OS-tee-o-sites).

FIGURE 5–2 ***Microscopic Structure of Bone.*** Longitudinal section of a long bone **(A)** shows the location of the microscopic section illustrated in **B.** Note that the compact bone forming the hard shell of the bone is constructed of cylindrical units called *osteons*. Spongy bone is constructed of bony projections called *trabeculae*.

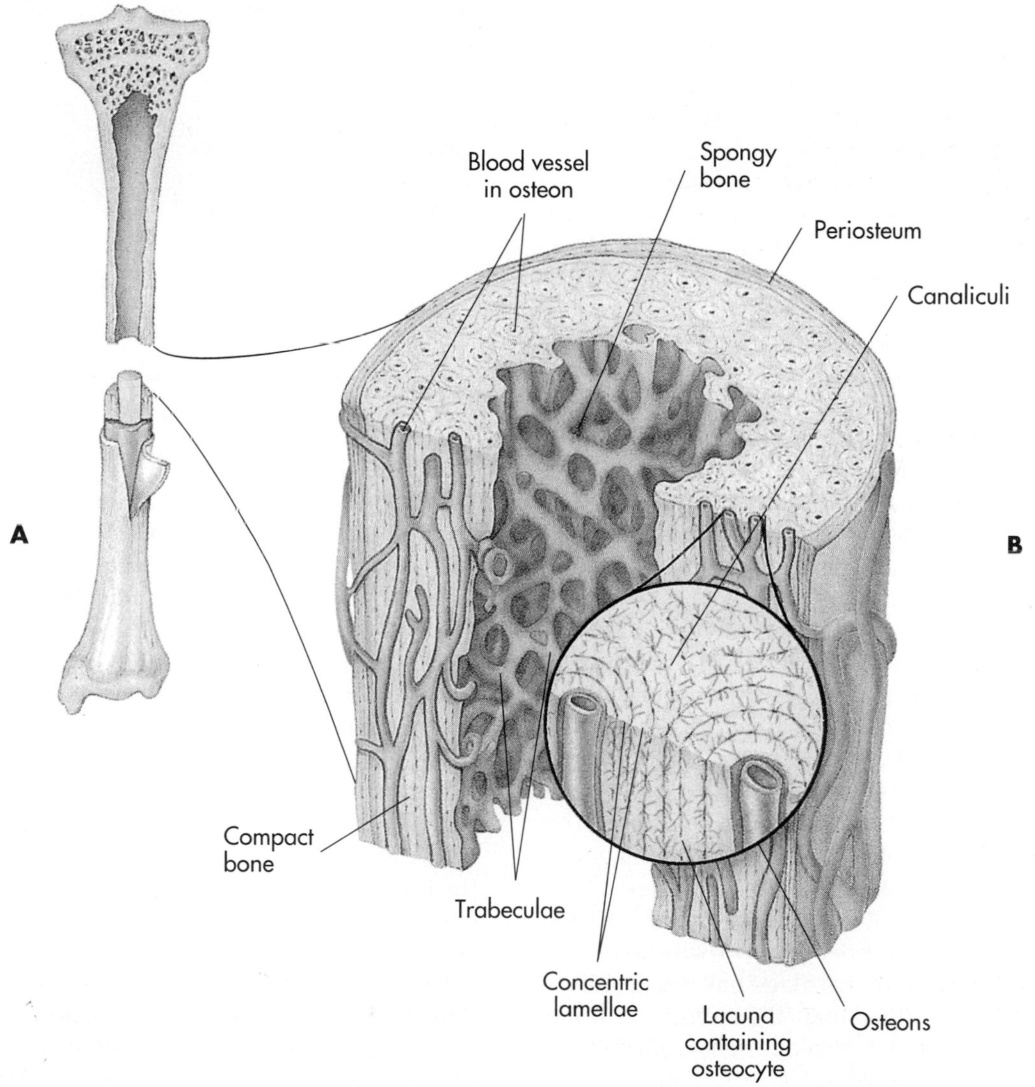

FIGURE 5–3 *Compact Bone.* Photomicrograph shows osteon system of organization.

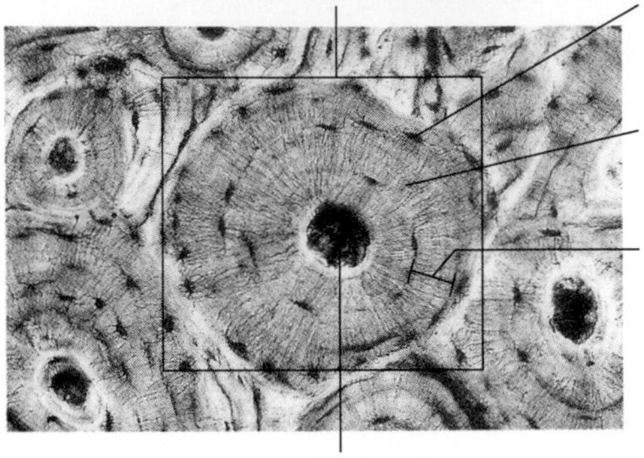

FIGURE 5–4 *Cartilage Tissue.* Photomicrograph shows chondrocytes scattered around the tissue in spaces called lacunae.

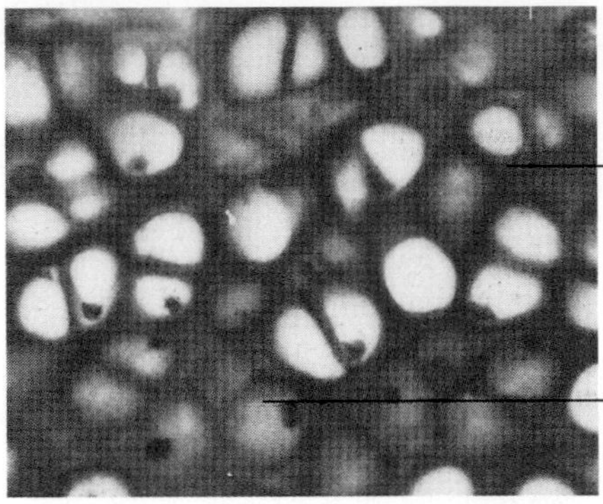

Osteocytes lie between the hard layers of the lamellae in little spaces called **lacunae** (lah-KOO-nee). In Figures 5-2, *B*, and 5-3, note that tiny passageways or canals called **canaliculi** (kan-ah-LIK-yoo-lye) connect the lacunae with one other and with the central canal in each Haversian system. Nutrients pass from the blood vessel in the Haversian canal through the canaliculi to the osteocytes. Note also in Figure 5-2, *B*, that numerous blood vessels from the outer **periosteum** (pair-ee-OS-tee-um) enter the bone and eventually pass through the Haversian canals.

Cartilage both resembles and differs from bone. Like bone, it consists more of intercellular substance than of cells. Innumerable collagenous fibers reinforce the matrix of both tissues. However, in cartilage the fibers are embedded in a firm gel instead of in a calcified cement substance like they are in bone; hence cartilage has the flexibility of a firm plastic rather than the rigidity of bone. Note in Figure 5-4 that cartilage cells, called **chondrocytes** (KON-dro-sites), like the osteocytes of bone, are located in lacunae. In cartilage, lacunae are suspended in the cartilage matrix much like air bubbles in a block of firm gelatin. Because there are no blood vessels in cartilage, nutrients must diffuse through the matrix to reach the cells. Because of this lack of blood vessels, cartilage rebuilds itself very slowly after an injury.

Bone Formation and Growth

When the skeleton begins to form in a baby before its birth, it consists not of bones but of cartilage and fibrous structures shaped like bones. Gradually these cartilage "models" become transformed into real bones when the cartilage is replaced with calcified bone matrix. This process of constantly "remodeling" a growing bone as it changes from a small cartilage model to the characteristic shape and proportion of the adult bone requires continuous activity by bone-forming cells called **osteoblasts** (OS-tee-o-blasts) and bone-resorbing cells called **osteoclasts** (OS-tee-o-clasts). The laying down of calcium salts in the gel-like matrix of the forming bones is an ongoing process. This calcification process is what makes bones as "hard as bone." The combined action of the osteoblasts and osteoclasts sculpts bones into their adult shapes (Figure 5-5). The process of "sculpting" by the bone-forming and -resorbing cells allows bones to respond to stress or injury by changing size, shape, and density. The stresses placed on certain bones during exercise increase the rate of bone deposition. For this reason, athletes or dancers may have denser, stronger bones than less active people.

Most bones of the body are formed from cartilage models as illustrated in Figures 5-5 and 5-6.

FIGURE 5–5 ***Endochondral Ossification.*** **A,** Bone formation begins with a cartilage model. **B** and **C,** Invasion of the diaphysis (shaft) by blood vessels and the combined action of osteoblast and osteoclast cells result in cavity formation, calcification, and the appearance of bone tissue. **D** and **E,** centers of ossification also appear in the epiphyses (ends) of the bone. **F,** Note the epiphyseal plate, indications that this bone is not yet mature and that additional growth is possible. **G,** In a mature bone, only a faint epiphyseal line marks where the cartilage has disappeared and the centers of ossification have fused together.

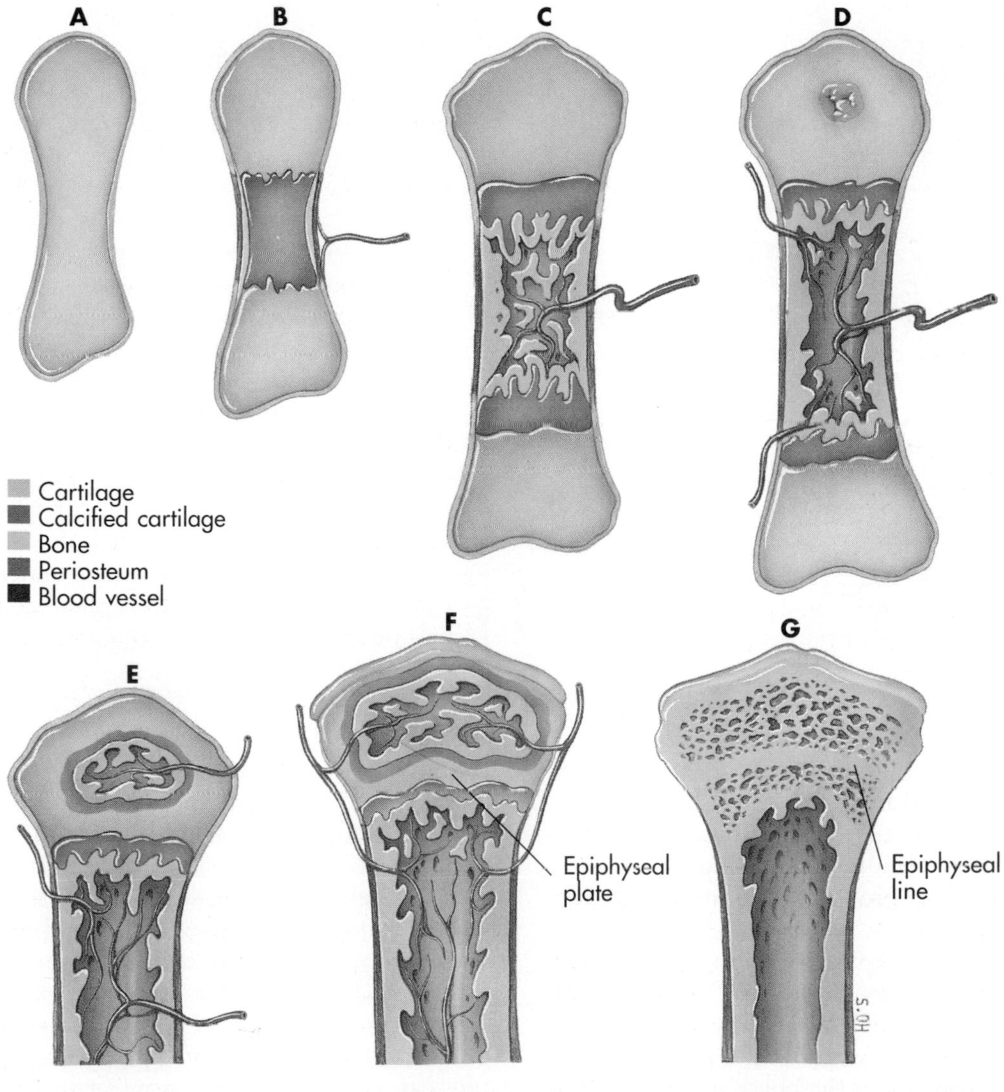

FIGURE 5–6 ***Bone Development in a Newborn.*** An infant's skeleton has many bones that are not yet completely ossified.

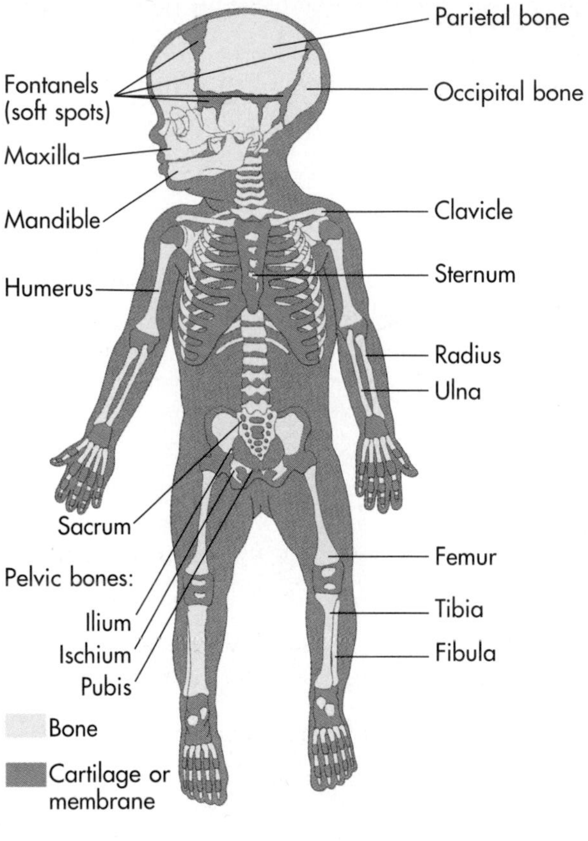

Osteoporosis

Osteoporosis (os-tee-o-po-RO-sis) is one of the most common and serious of all bone diseases. It is characterized by excessive loss of calcified matrix and collagenous fibers from bone. Osteoporosis occurs most frequently in elderly white females. Although white and black males are also susceptible, black women are seldom affected by it.

Because sex hormones play important roles in stimulating osteoblast activity after puberty, decreasing levels of these hormones in the blood of elderly persons reduces new bone growth and the maintenance of existing bone mass. Therefore some resorption of bone and subsequent loss of bone mass is an accepted consequence of advancing years. However, bone loss in osteoporosis goes far beyond the modest decrease normally seen in old age. The result is a dangerous pathological condition resulting in bone degeneration, increased susceptibility to "spontaneous fractures," and pathological curvature of the spine. Treatment may include sex hormone therapy and dietary supplements of calcium and vitamin D to replace deficiencies or to offset intestinal malabsorption.

This process is called **endochondral** (en-doe-KON-dral) **ossification** (os-i-fi-KAY-shun), meaning "formed in cartilage." A few flat bones, such as the skull bones illustrated in Figure 5-6, are formed by another process in connective tissue membranes.

As you can see in Figure 5-5, a long bone grows and ultimately becomes "ossified" from small centers located in both ends of the bone, called **epiphyses,** and from a larger center located in the shaft or the **diaphysis** of the bone. As long as any cartilage, called an **epiphyseal plate,** remains between the epiphyses and the diaphysis, growth continues. Growth ceases when all epiphyseal cartilage is transformed into bone. All that remains is an *epiphyseal line* that marks the location where the two centers of ossification have fused together. Physicians sometimes use this knowledge to determine whether a child is going to grow any more. They have an x-ray study performed on the child's wrist, and if it shows a layer of epiphyseal cartilage, they know that additional growth will occur. However, if it shows no epiphyseal cartilage, they know that growth has stopped and that the individual has attained adult height.

Epiphyseal Fracture

The point of articulation between the epiphysis and diaphysis of a growing long bone is susceptible to injury if overstressed, especially in the young child or preadolescent athlete. In these individuals the epiphyseal plate can be separated from the diaphysis or epiphysis, causing an **epiphyseal fracture.** This x-ray study shows such a fracture in a young boy

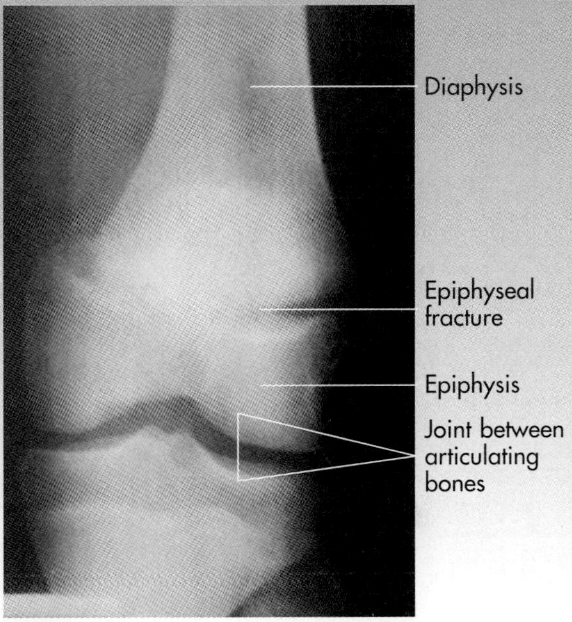

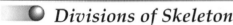

Divisions of Skeleton

The human skeleton has two divisions: the **axial skeleton** and the **appendicular skeleton.** Bones of the center or axis of the body make up the axial skeleton. The bones of the skull, spine, and chest and the hyoid bone in the neck are all in the axial skeleton. The bones of the upper and lower extremities or appendages make up the appendicular skeleton. The appendicular skeleton consists of the bones of the upper extremities (shoulder, pectoral girdles, arms, wrists, and hands) and the lower extremities (hip, pelvic girdles, legs, ankles, and feet) (Table 5-1). Locate the various parts of the axial skeleton and the appendicular skeleton in Figure 5-7.

AXIAL SKELETON

Skull

The skull consists of 8 bones that form the **cranium,** 14 bones that form the **face,** and 6 tiny bones in the **middle ear.** You will probably want to learn the names and locations of these bones.

TABLE 5–1 Main Parts of the Skeleton*

AXIAL SKELETON†	APPENDICULAR SKELETON‡
Skull	Upper Extremities
Cranium	Shoulder (pectoral) girdle
Ear bones	Arm
Face	Wrists
	Hands
Spine	Lower Extremities
Vertebrae	Hip (pelvic) girdle
Thorax	Legs
Ribs	Ankles
Sternum	Feet
Hyoid Bone	

*Total bones = 206.
†Total = 80 bones.
‡Total = 126 bones.

FIGURE 5–7 ***Human Skeleton.*** The axial skeleton is distinguished by its bluer tint. **A,** Anterior view.

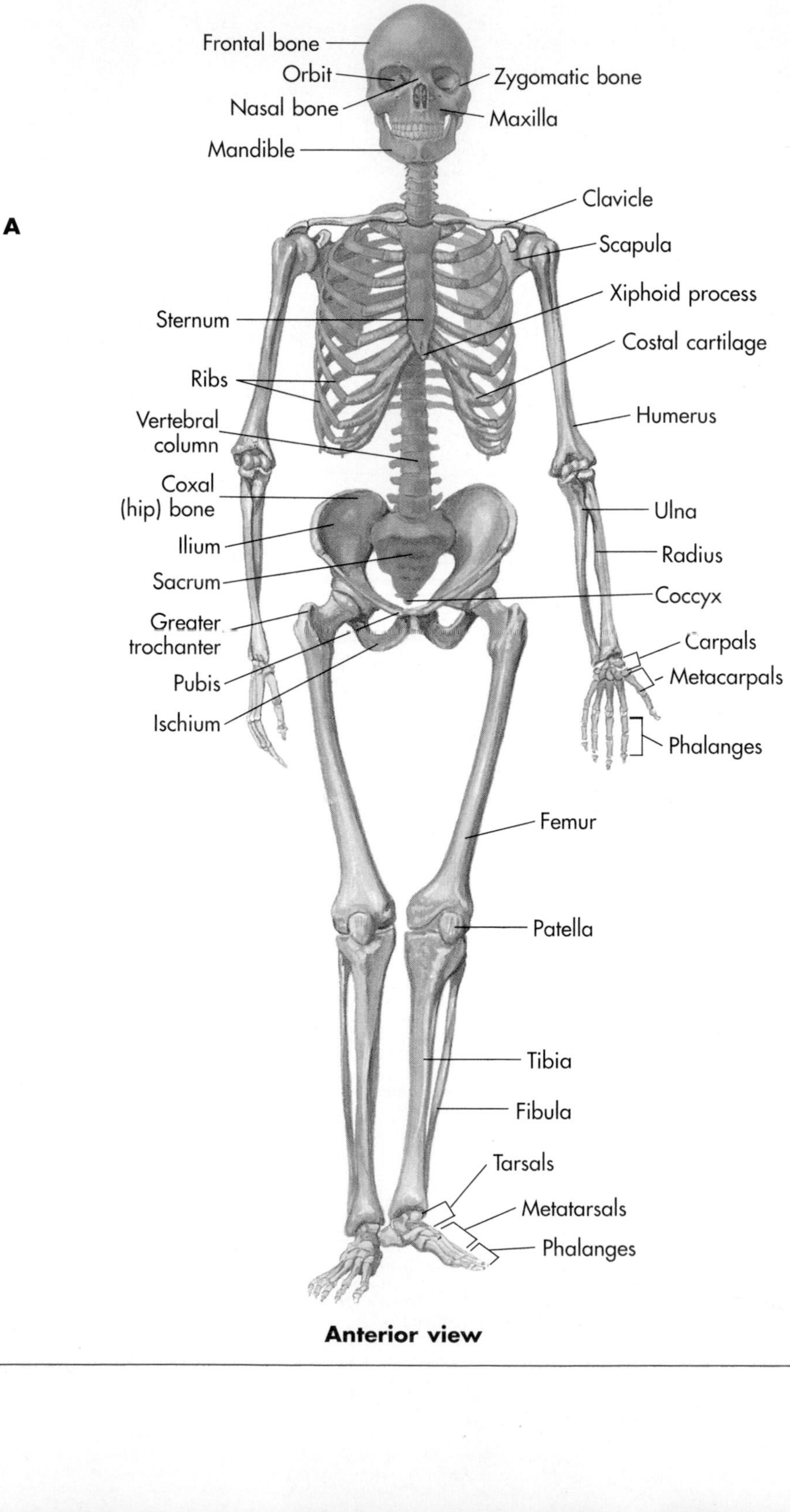

FIGURE 5–7 cont'd **B,** Posterior view

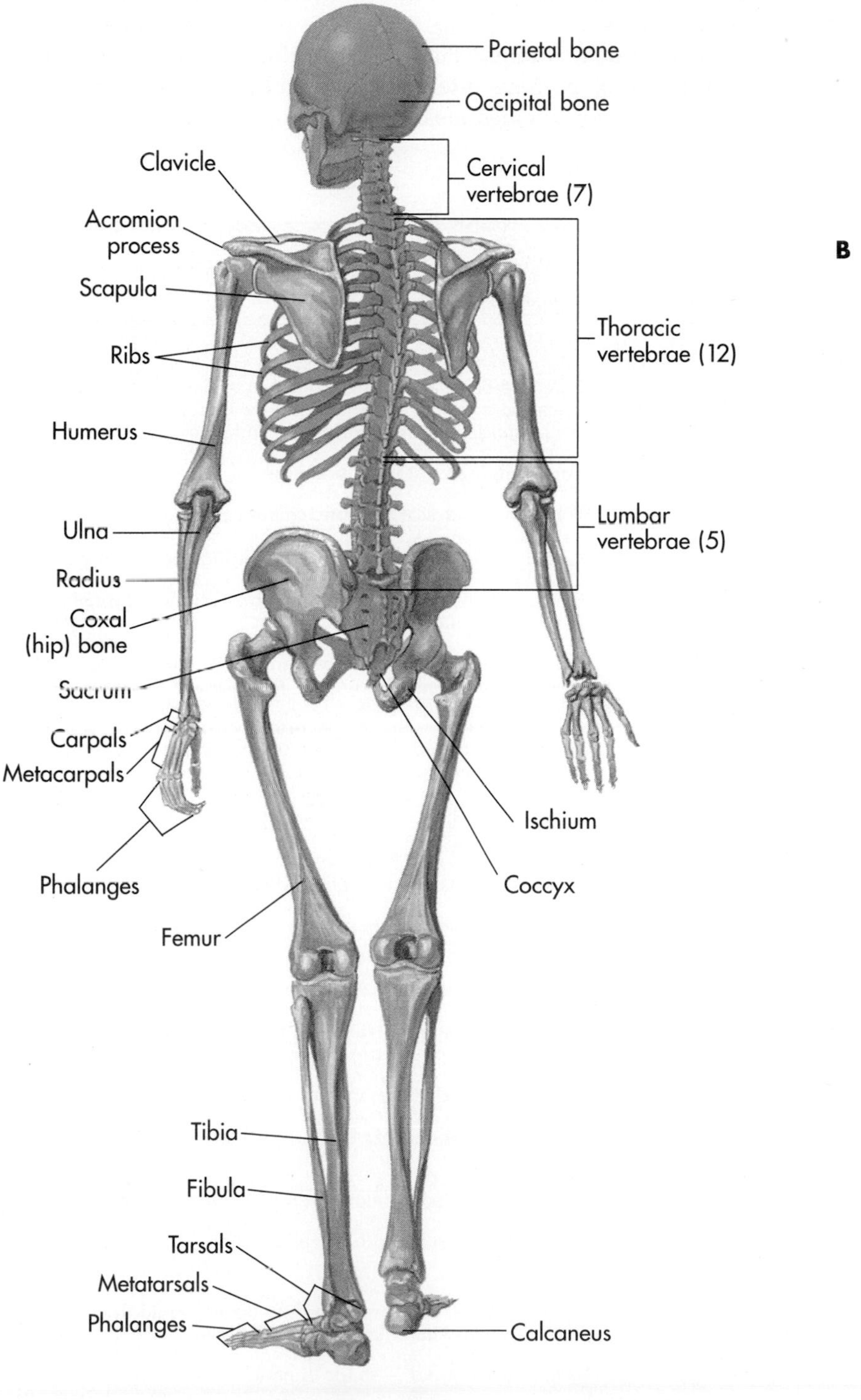

Posterior view

These are given in Table 5-2. Find as many of them as you can on Figure 5-8. Feel their outlines in your own body where possible. Examine them on a skeleton if you have access to one.

"My sinuses give me so much trouble." Have you ever heard this complaint or perhaps uttered it yourself? **Sinuses** are spaces or cavities inside some of the cranial bones. Four pairs of them (those in the frontal, maxillary, sphenoid, and ethmoid bones) have openings into the nose and thus are referred to as **paranasal sinuses.** Sinuses give trouble when the mucous membrane that lines them becomes inflamed, swollen, and painful. For example, inflammation in the frontal sinus *(frontal*

TABLE 5–2 Bones of the Skull

NAME	NUMBER	DESCRIPTION
Cranial Bones		
Frontal	1	Forehead bone; also forms front part of floor of cranium and most of upper part of eye sockets; cavity inside bone above upper margins of eye sockets (orbits) called *frontal sinus;* lined with mucous membrane
Parietal	2	Form bulging topsides of cranium
Temporal	2	Form lower sides of cranium; contain *middle* and *inner ear structures; mastoid sinuses* are mucosa-lined spaces in *mastoid process,* the protuberance behind ear; *external auditory canal* is tube leading into temporal bone; muscles attach to *styloid process*
Occipital	1	Forms back of skull; spinal cord enters cranium through large hole *(foramen magnum)* in occipital bone
Sphenoid	1	Forms central part of floor of cranium; pituitary gland located in small depression in sphenoid called *sella turcica (Turkish saddle),* muscles attach to *pterygoid process*
Ethmoid	1	Complicated bone that helps form floor of cranium, side walls and roof of nose and part of its middle partition (nasal septum—made up of the *vomer* and the *perpendicular plate*), and part of orbit; contains honeycomb-like spaces, the *ethmoid sinuses; superior* and *middle conchae* are projections of ethmoid bone; form "ledges" along side wall of each nasal cavity
Face Bones		
Nasal	2	Small bones that form upper part of bridge of nose
Maxilla	2	Upper jawbones; also help form roof of mouth, floor, and side walls of nose and floor of orbit; large cavity in maxillary bone is *maxillary sinus*
Zygomatic	2	Cheek bones; also help form orbit
Mandible	1	Lower jawbone articulates with temporal bone at *condyloid process;* small anterior hole for passage of nerves and vessels is the *mental foramen*
Lacrimal	2	Small bones; help form medial wall of eye socket and side wall of nasal cavity
Palatine	2	Form back part of roof of mouth and floor and side walls of nose and part of floor of orbit
Inferior concha	2	Form curved "ledge" along inside of side wall of nose, below middle concha
Vomer	1	Forms lower, back part of nasal septum
Ear Bones		
Malleus	2	Malleus, incus, and stapes are tiny bones in middle ear cavity in temporal bone; *malleus* means "hammer"—shape of bone
Incus	2	*Incus* means "anvil"—shape of bone
Stapes	2	*Stapes* means "stirrup"—shape of bone

FIGURE 5–8 ***The Skull.*** **A,** Right side. **B,** Front.

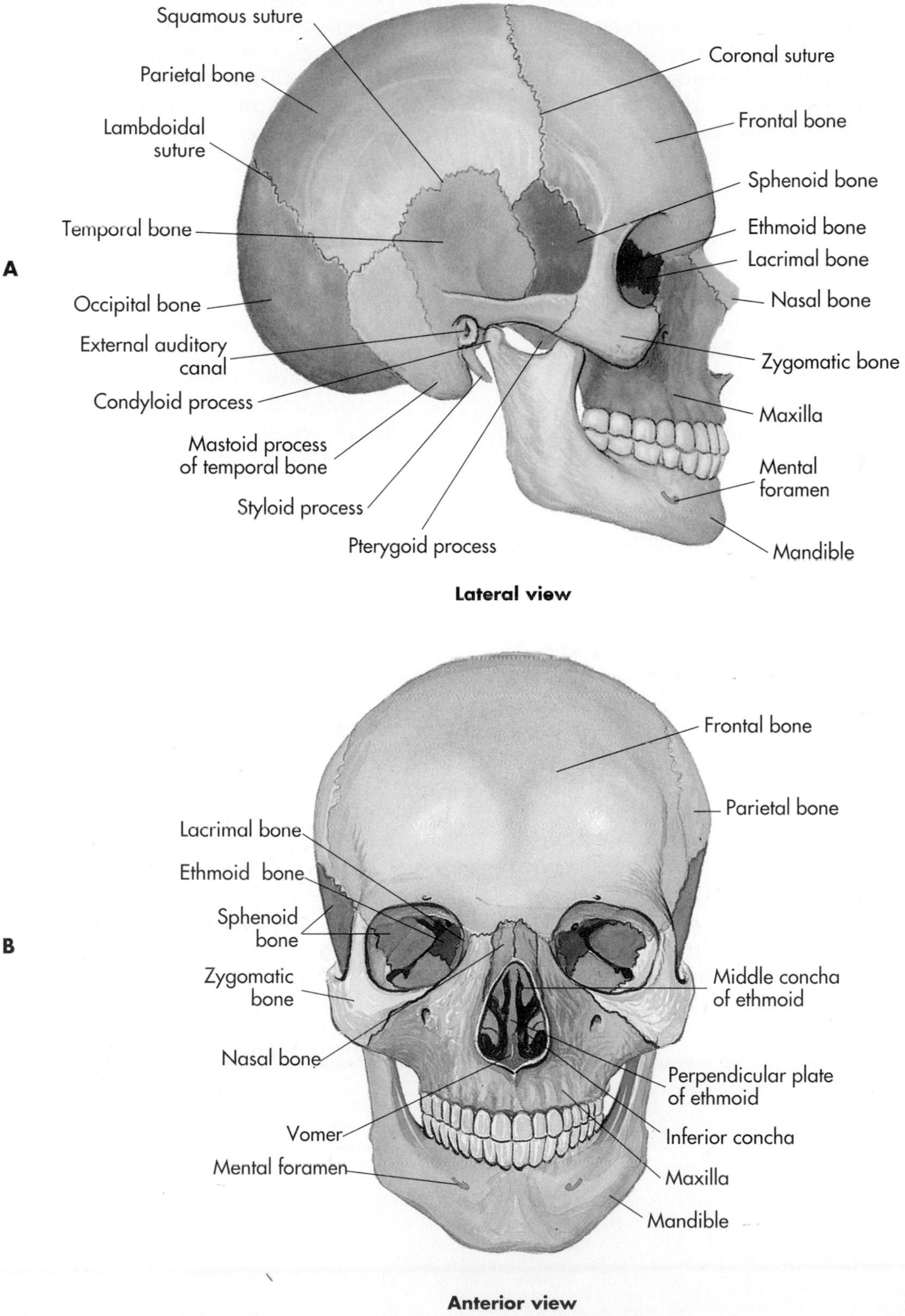
A
Squamous suture
Parietal bone
Lambdoidal suture
Temporal bone
Occipital bone
External auditory canal
Condyloid process
Mastoid process of temporal bone
Styloid process
Pterygoid process
Coronal suture
Frontal bone
Sphenoid bone
Ethmoid bone
Lacrimal bone
Nasal bone
Zygomatic bone
Maxilla
Mental foramen
Mandible
Lateral view
B
Frontal bone
Parietal bone
Lacrimal bone
Ethmoid bone
Sphenoid bone
Zygomatic bone
Nasal bone
Vomer
Mental foramen
Middle concha of ethmoid
Perpendicular plate of ethmoid
Inferior concha
Maxilla
Mandible
Anterior view

sinusitis) often starts from a common cold. The letters *-itis* added to a word mean "inflammation of."

Note in Figure 5-8 that the two parietal bones, which give shape to the bulging topside of the skull, form immovable joints called **sutures** with several bones: the *lambdoidal suture* with the occipital bone, the *squamous suture* with the temporal bone and part of the sphenoid, and the *coronal suture* with the frontal bone.

You may be familiar with the "soft spots" on a baby's skull. These are six **fontanels,** or areas where ossification is incomplete at birth. You can see them in Figure 5-6. Fontanels allow some compression of the skull during birth without much risk of breaking the skull bones. They may also be important in determining the position of the baby's head before delivery. The fontanels fuse to form sutures before a baby is 2 years old.

Spine (Vertebral Column)

The term *vertebral column* may conjure up a mental picture of the spine as a single long bone shaped like a column in a building, but this is far from true. The vertebral column consists of a series of separate bones or **vertebrae** connected in such a way that they form a flexible curved rod (see Figure 5-9). Different sections of the spine have different names: cervical region, thoracic region, lumbar region, sacrum, and coccyx. They are illustrated in Figure 5-9 and described in Table 5-3.

Although individual vertebrae are small bones, irregular in shape, they have several well-defined parts. Note, for example, in Figure 5-10, the body of the lumbar vertebra shown there, its spinous process (or spine), its two transverse processes, and the hole in its center, called the *vertebral foramen.* The superior and inferior articular processes permit limited and controlled movement between adjacent vertebrae. To feel the tip of the spinous process of one of your vertebrae, simply bend your head forward and run your fingers down the back of your neck until you feel a projection of bone at shoulder level. This is the tip of the seventh cervical vertebra's long spinous process. The seven cervical vertebrae form the supporting framework of the neck.

Have you ever noticed the four curves in your spine? Your neck and the small of your back curve slightly inward or forward, whereas the chest region of the spine and the lowermost portion curve in the opposite direction (Figure 5-9). The cervical and lumbar curves of the spine are called *concave curves,* and the thoracic and sacral curves are called *convex curves.* This is not true, however, of a newborn baby's spine. It forms a continuous convex curve from top to bottom (Figure 5-11). Gradually, as the baby learns to hold up his or her head, a reverse or concave curve develops in his or her neck, (cervical region). Later, as the baby learns to stand, the lumbar region of his or her spine also becomes concave.

The normal curves of the spine have important functions. They give it enough strength to support the weight of the rest of the body. They also provide the balance necessary for us to stand and walk on two feet instead of having to crawl on all fours. A curved structure has more strength than a straight one of the same size and materials. (The next time you pass a bridge, look to see whether or not its supports form a curve.) Clearly the spine needs to be a strong structure. It supports the head that is balanced on top of it, the ribs and internal organs that are suspended from it in front, and the hips and legs that are attached to it below.

TABLE 5–3 Bones of the Vertebral Column

NAME	NUMBER	DESCRIPTION
Cervical	7	Upper seven vertebrae, in neck region; first cervical vertebra called *atlas;* second, *axis*
Thoracic vertebrae	12	Next twelve vertebrae; ribs attach to these
Lumbar vertebrae	5	Next five vertebrae; are in small of back
Sacrum	1	In child, five separate vertebrae; in adult, fused into one
Coccyx	1	In child, three to five separate vertebrae; in adult, fused into one

FIGURE 5–9 ***The Spinal Column.*** View shows the 7 cervical vertebrae, the 12 thoracic vertebrae, the 5 lumbar vertebrae, the sacrum, and the coccyx. **A,** Lateral view. **B,** Anterior view. **C,** Posterior view.

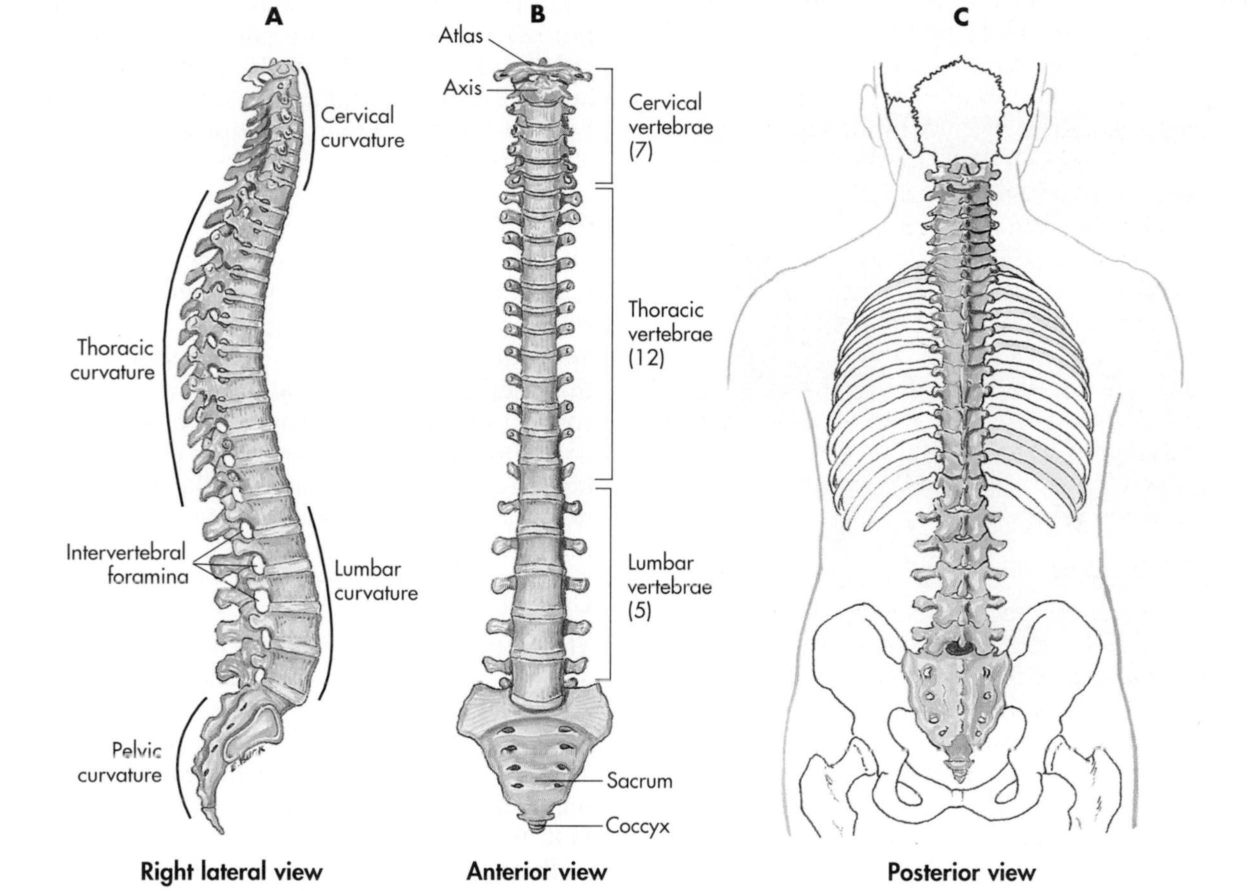

FIGURE 5–10 ***The Third Lumbar Vertebra.*** **A,** From above. **B,** From the side.

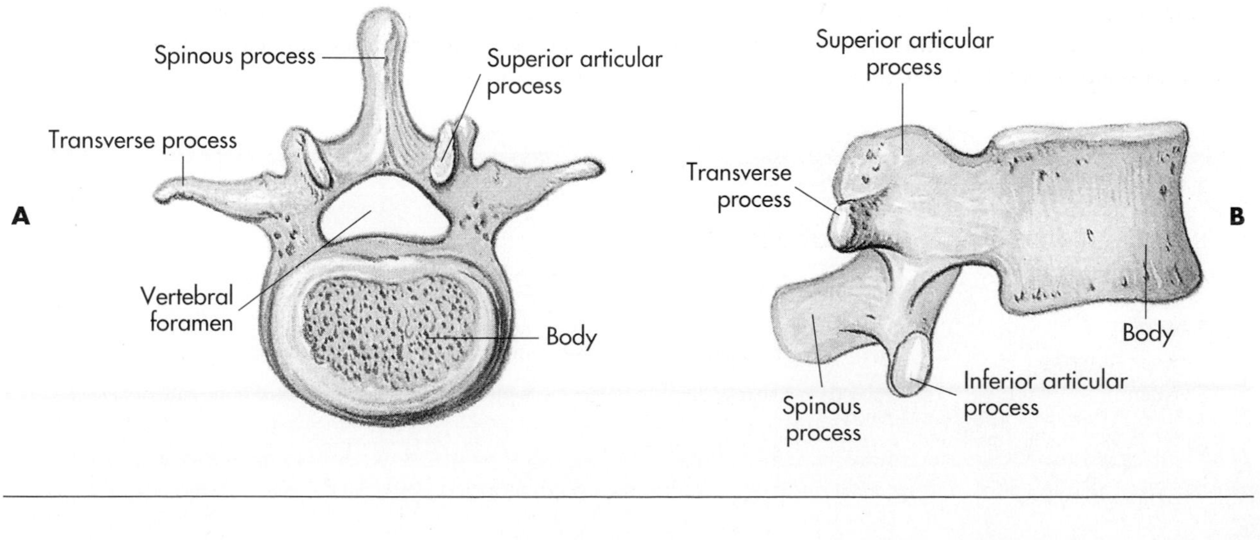

FIGURE 5–11 ***Spinal Curvature of an Infant.*** The spine of the newborn baby forms continuous convex curve.

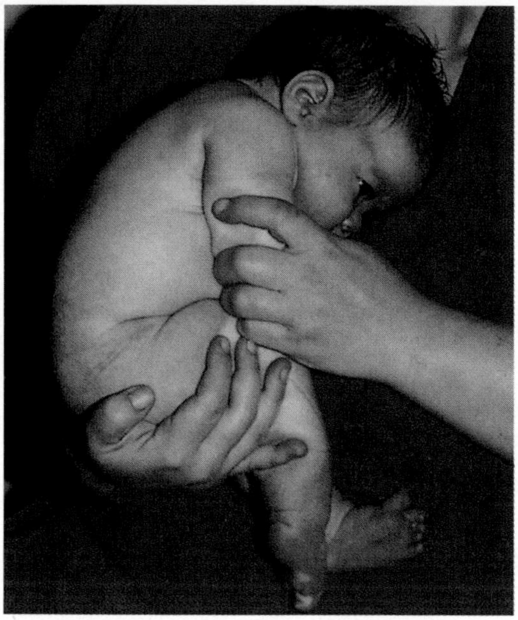

Thorax

Twelve pairs of ribs, the sternum (breastbone), and the thoracic vertebrae form the bony cage known as the **thorax** or **chest.** Each of the 12 pairs of ribs is attached posteriorly to a vertebra. Also, all the ribs except the lower two pairs are attached to the sternum and so have anterior and posterior anchors. Look closely at Figure 5-12, and you can see that the first seven pairs of ribs (sometimes referred to as the *true ribs*) are attached to the sternum by costal cartilage. The eighth, ninth, and tenth pairs of ribs are attached to the cartilage of the seventh ribs and are sometimes called *false ribs.* The last two pairs of ribs, in contrast, are not attached to any costal cartilage but seem to float free in front, hence their descriptive name, *floating ribs* (Table 5-4).

APPENDICULAR SKELETON

Of the 206 bones that form the skeleton as a whole, 126 are contained in the appendicular subdivision. Look again at Figure 5-7 to identify the appendicular components of the skeleton. Note that the bones in the shoulder or pectoral girdle connect the bones of the arm, forearm, wrist, and hands to the axial skeleton of the thorax, and the hip or pelvic girdle connects the bones of the thigh, leg, ankle, and foot to the axial skeleton of the pelvis.

Upper Extremity

The **scapula** (SKAP-yoo-lah) or shoulder blade and the **clavicle** (KLAV-ik-kul) or collar bone compose the *shoulder* or *pectoral girdle.* This connects the upper extremity to the axial skeleton. The only direct point of attachment between bones occurs at the **sternoclavicular** (ster-no-klah-VIK-yoo-lar) **joint** between the clavicle and the sternum or breastbone. As you can see in Figures 5-7 and 5-12, this joint is very small. Because the upper extremity is capable of a wide range of motion, great pressures can occur at or near the joint. As a result, fractures of the clavicle are very common.

The **humerus** (HYOO-mer-us) is the long bone of the arm and the second longest bone in the body. It is attached to the scapula at its proximal end and articulates with the two bones of the fore-

TABLE 5–4 Bones of the Thorax

NAME	NUMBER	DESCRIPTION
True ribs	14	Upper seven pairs; attached to sternum by *costal cartilages*
False ribs	10	Lower five pairs; lowest two pairs do not attach to sternum, therefore, called *floating ribs;* next three pairs attached to sternum by costal cartilage of seventh ribs
Sternum	1	Breastbone; shaped like a dagger; piece of cartilage at lower end of bone called *xiphoid process*

FIGURE 5–12 ***Bones of the Thorax.*** Rib pairs 1 through 7, the true ribs, are attached by cartilage to the sternum. Rib pairs 8 through 10, the false ribs, are attached to the cartilage of the seventh pair. Rib pairs 11 and 12 are called floating ribs because they have no anterior cartilage attachments.

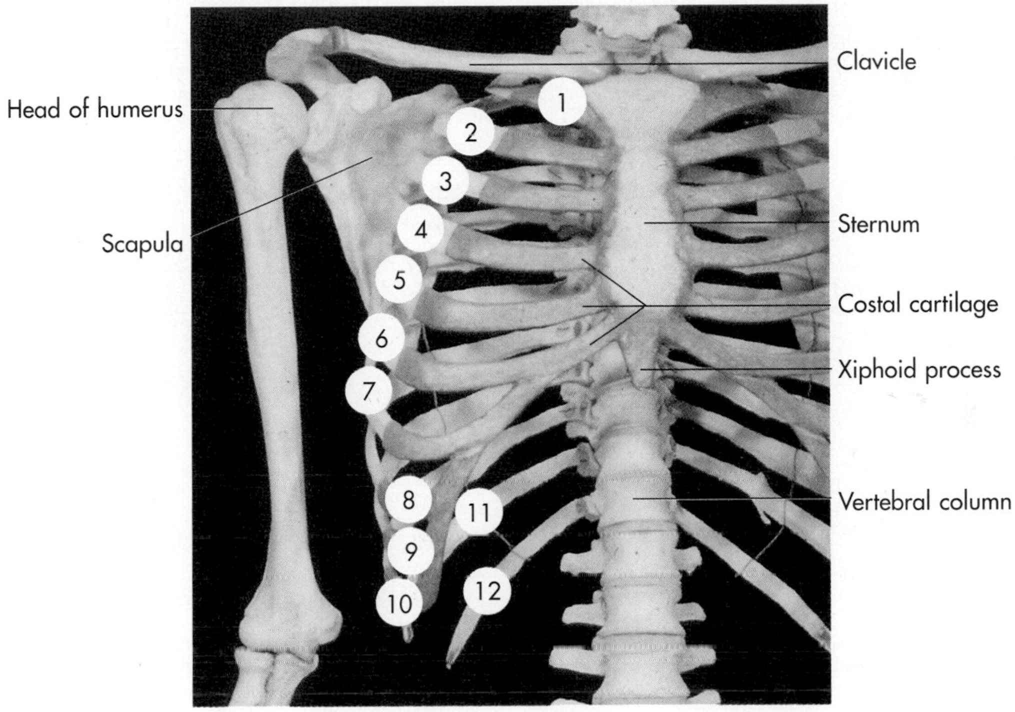

arm at the elbow joint. The bones of the forearm are the **radius** and the **ulna.** The anatomy of the elbow is a good example of how structure determines function. Note in Figure 5-13 that the large bony process of the ulna, called the **olecranon** (o-LEK-rah-non) **process,** fits nicely into a large depression on the posterior surface of the humerus, called the **olecranon fossa.** This structural relationship makes possible movement at the joint.

The radius and the ulna of the forearm articulate with each other and with the distal end of the humerus at the elbow joint. In addition, they also touch each another distally where they articulate with the bones of the wrist. In the anatomical position, with the arm at the side and the palm facing forward, the radius runs along the lateral side of the forearm, and the ulna is located along the medial border.

The wrist and the hand have more bones in them for their size than any other part of the body—8 **carpal** (KAR-pal) or wrist bones, 5 **metacarpal** (met-ah-KAR-pal) bones that form the support structure for the palm of the hand, and 14 **phalanges** (fah-LAN-jeez) or finger bones—27 bones in all (Table 5-5). This composition is very important structurally. The presence of many small bones in the hand and wrist and the many movable joints between them makes the human hand highly maneuverable. Some anatomists refer to the hand and wrist as the functional "reason" for the upper extremity. Figure 5-14 shows the relationships between the bones of the wrist and hand.

FIGURE 5–13 ***Bones of the Arm, Elbow Joint, and Forearm.*** Posterior aspect of right humerus **(A)**, right radius and ulna **(B)**, and right elbow **(C)**.

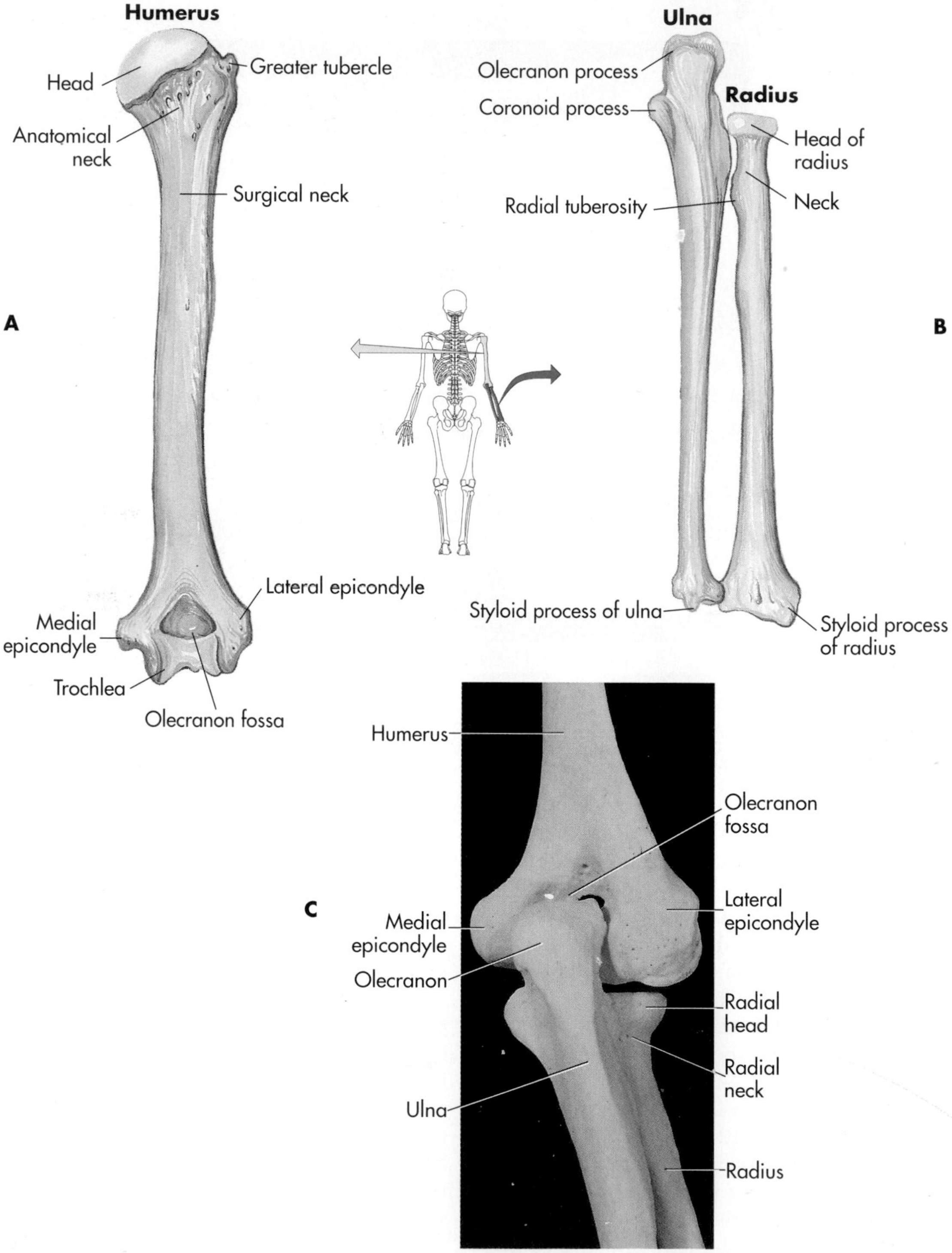

FIGURE 5–14 ***Bones of the Right Hand and Wrist.*** There are 14 phalanges in each hand. Each of these bones is called a phalanx.

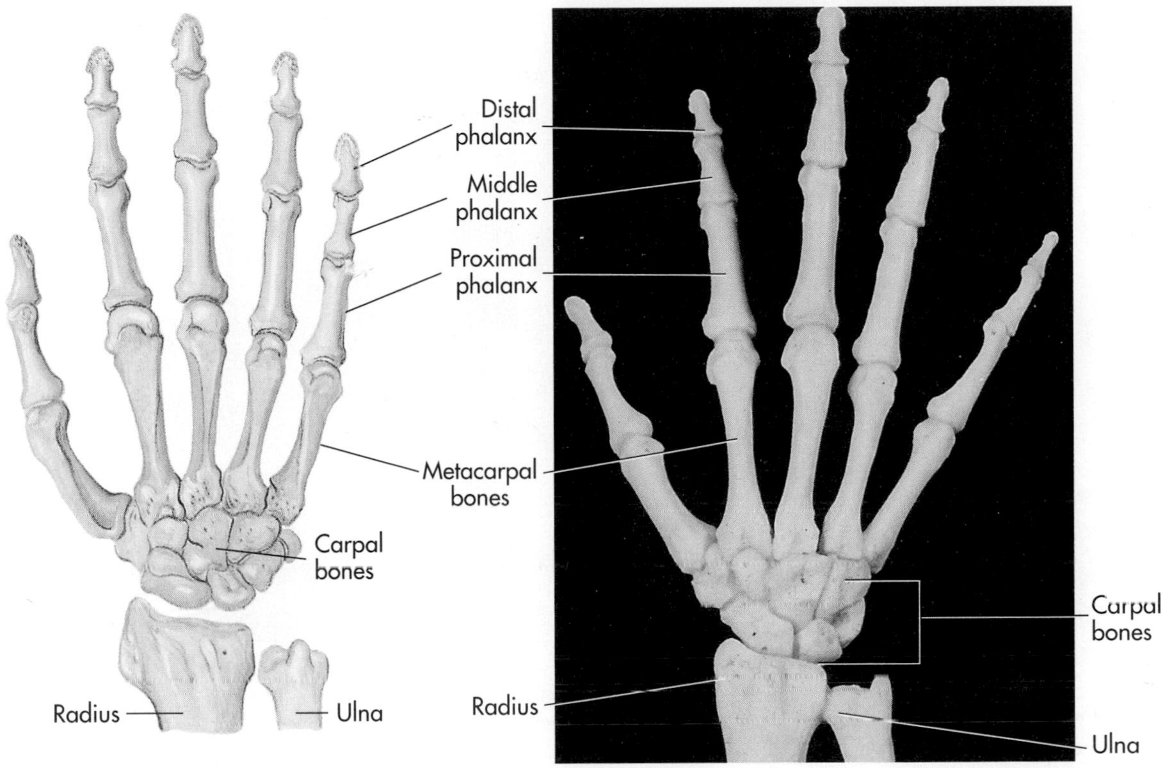

TABLE 5–5 Bones of the Upper Extremities

NAME	NUMBER	DESCRIPTION
Clavicle	2	Collarbones; only joints between shoulder girdle and axial skeleton are those between each clavicle and sternum *(sternoclavicular joints)*
Scapula	2	Shoulder blades; scapula plus clavicle forms *shoulder girdle; acromion process*—tip of shoulder that forms joint with clavicle; *glenoid cavity*—arm socket
Humerus	2	Upper arm bone (Muscles are attached to the *greater tubercle* and to the *medial* and *lateral epicondyles;* the *trochlea* articulates with the ulna; the *surgical neck* is a common fracture site.)
Radius	2	Bone on thumb side of lower arm (Muscles are attached to the *radial tuberosity* and to the *styloid process.*)
Ulna	2	Bone on little finger side of lower arm; *olecranon process*—projection of ulna known as elbow or "funny bone" (Muscles are attached to the *coronoid process* and to the *styloid process.*)
Carpal bones	16	Irregular bones at upper end of hand; anatomical wrist
Metacarpals	10	Form framework of palm of hand
Phalanges	28	Finger bones; three in each finger, two in each thumb

FIGURE 5–15 ***Bones of the Thigh, Knee Joint, and Leg.*** Anterior aspect of right femur **(A)**, anterior aspect of the knee **(B)**, right tibia and fibula **(C)**, and posterior aspect of the right knee **(D)**.

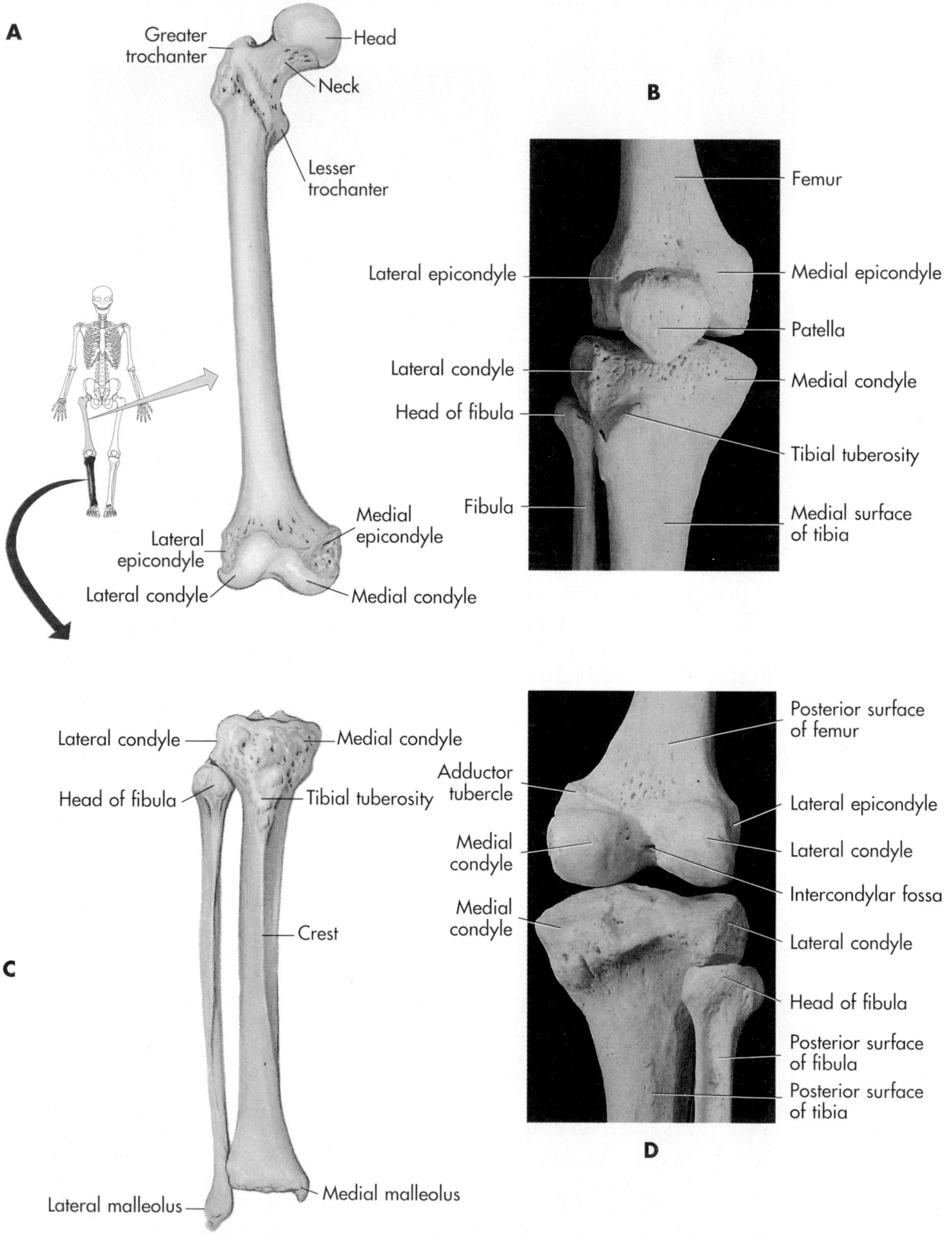

Lower Extremity

The *hip* or *pelvic girdle* connects the legs to the trunk. The hip girdle as a whole consists of two large **coxal** or pelvic bones, one located on each side of the pelvis. These two bones, with the sacrum and coccyx behind, provide a strong base of support for the torso and connect the lower extremities to the axial skeleton. In an infant's body each coxal bone consists of three separate bones—the **ilium** (ILL-ee-um), the **ischium** (IS-kee-um), and the **pubis** (PYOO-bis) (Figure 5-6). These bones grow together to become one bone in an adult (Figures 5-7 and 5-18).

Just as the humerus is the only bone in the arm, the **femur** (FEE-mur) is the only bone in the thigh (Figure 5-15). It is the longest bone in the body and articulates proximally (toward the hip) with the coxal bone in a deep, cup-shaped socket called the **acetabulum** (as-e-TAB-yoo-lum). The articulation of the head of the femur in the acetabulum is more stable than the articulation of the head of the humerus with the scapula in the upper extremity. As a result, dislocation of the hip occurs less often than does disarticulation of the shoulder. Distally, the femur articulates with the knee cap or **patella** (pah-TEL-ah) and the **tibia** or "shinbone." The tibia forms a rather sharp edge or crest along the front of your lower leg. A slender, non–weight-bearing, and rather fragile bone named the **fibula** lies along the outer or lateral border of the lower leg.

Toe bones have the same name as finger bones—**phalanges.** There are the same number of toe bones as finger bones, a fact that might surprise you because toes are shorter than fingers. Foot bones comparable to the metacarpals and carpals of the hand have slightly different names. They are called **metatarsals** and **tarsals** in the foot (Figure 5-16). Just as each hand contains five metacarpal bones, each foot contains five metatarsal bones. However, the foot has only seven tarsal bones, in contrast to the hand's eight carpals. The largest tarsal bone is the **calcaneus** or heel bone. The bones of the lower extremities are summarized in Table 5-6.

You stand on your feet, so certain features of their structure make them able to support the body's weight. The great toe, for example, is considerably more solid and less mobile than the thumb. The foot bones are held together in such a way as to form springy lengthwise and crosswise arches. These provide great supporting strength and a highly stable base. Strong ligaments and leg muscle tendons normally hold the foot bones firmly in their arched positions. Frequently, however, the foot ligaments and tendons weaken. The arches then flatten, a condition appropriately called *fallen arches* or *flatfeet.*

Two arches extend in a lengthwise direction in the foot (Figure 5-17, *A*). One lies on the inside part of the foot and is called the **medial longitudinal arch.** The other lies along the outer edge of the foot and is named the **lateral longitudinal arch.** Another arch extends across the ball of the foot; this arch is called the **transverse** or **metatarsal arch** (Figure 5-17, *B*).

FIGURE 5–16 ***Bones of the Right Foot.*** Compare the names and numbers of foot bones (viewed here from above) with those of the hand bones shown in Figure 5–14.

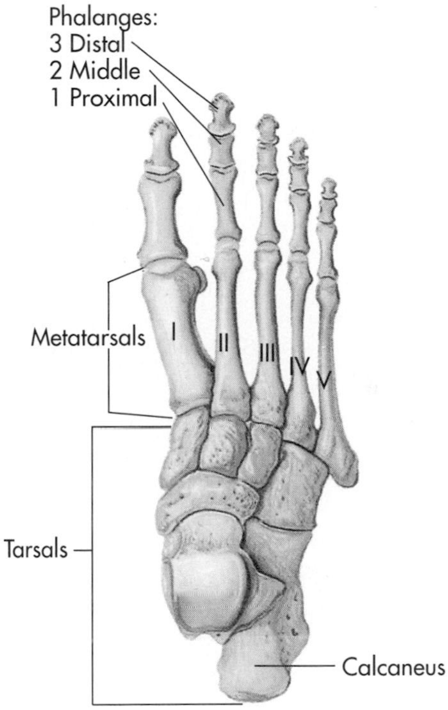

TABLE 5–6 Bones of the Lower Extremities

NAME	NUMBER	DESCRIPTION
Coxal bone	2	Hipbones; *ilium*—upper flaring part of pelvic bone; *ischium*—lower back part; *pubic bone*—lower front part; *acetabulum*—hip socket; *symphysis pubis*—joint in midline between two pubic bones; *pelvic inlet*—opening into *true pelvis* or pelvic cavity; if pelvic inlet is misshapen or too small, infant skull cannot enter true pelvis for natural birth
Femur	2	Thigh or upper leg bones; *head of femur*—ball-shaped upper end of bone; fits into acetabulum (Muscles are attached to the *greater* and *lesser trochanters* and to the *lateral* and *medial epicondyles;* the *lateral* and *medial condyles* form articulations at the knee.)
Patella	2	Kneecap
Tibia	2	Shinbone; *medial malleolus*—rounded projection at lower end of tibia commonly called *inner anklebone;* muscles are attached to the *tibial tuberosity*
Fibula	2	Long slender bone of lateral side of lower leg; *lateral malleolus*—rounded projection at lower end of fibula commonly called *outer anklebone*
Tarsal bones	14	Form heel and back part of foot; anatomical ankle; largest is the *calcaneus*
Metatarsals	10	Form part of foot to which toes are attached; tarsal and metatarsal bones arranged so that they form three arches in foot; *inner longitudinal arch* and *outer longitudinal arch,* which extend from front to back of foot, and transverse or *metatarsal arch,* which extends across foot
Phalanges	28	Toe bones; three in each toe, two in each great toe

FIGURE 5–17 *Arches of the Foot.* **A,** Medial and lateral longitudinal arches. **B,** Transverse arch.

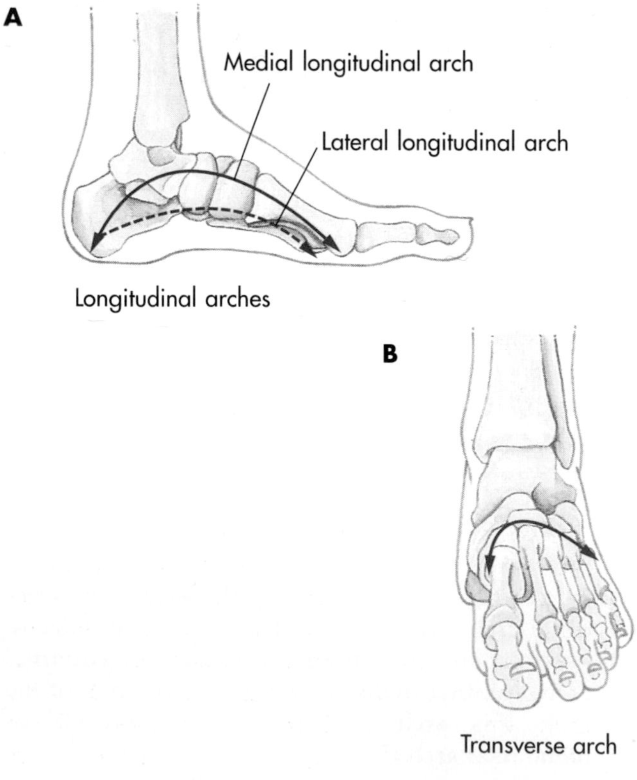

Differences Between a Man's and a Woman's Skeleton

A man's skeleton and a woman's skeleton differ in several ways. If you were to examine a male skeleton and a female skeleton placed side by side, you would probably first notice the difference in their sizes. Most male skeletons are larger than most female skeletons, a structural difference that seems to have no great functional importance. Structural differences between the male and female hipbones, however, do have functional importance. The female pelvis is made so that the body of a baby can be cradled in it before birth and can pass through it during birth. Although the individual male hipbones (coxal bones) are generally larger than the individual female hipbones, together the male hipbones form a narrower structure than do the female hipbones. A man's pelvis is shaped something like a funnel, but a woman's pelvis has a broader, shallower shape, more like a basin. (Incidentally, the word *pelvis* means "basin.") Another difference is that the pelvic inlet and pelvic outlet are both normally much wider in the female than in the male. Figure 5-18 shows this difference clearly. The angle at the front of the female pelvis where the two pubic bones join is wider than it is in the male.

FIGURE 5–18 ***Comparison of the Male and Female Pelvis.*** Notice the narrower width of the male pelvis, giving it a more funnel-like shape than the female pelvis.

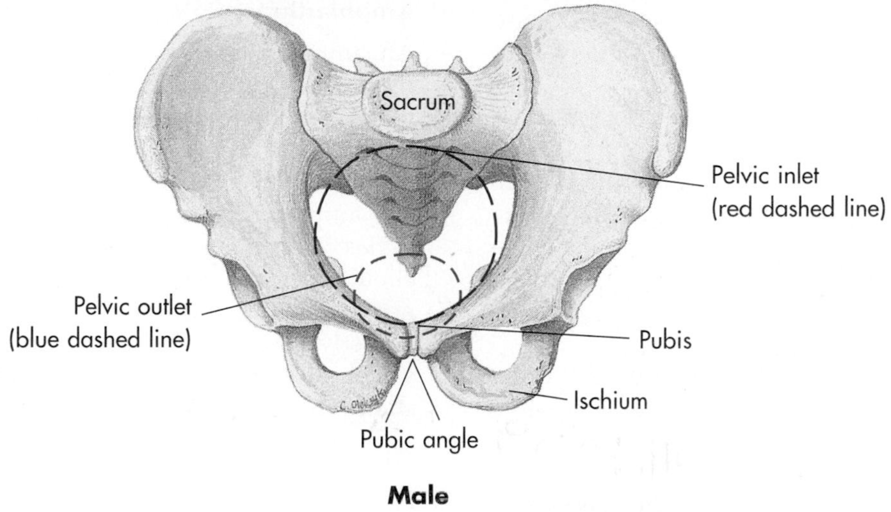

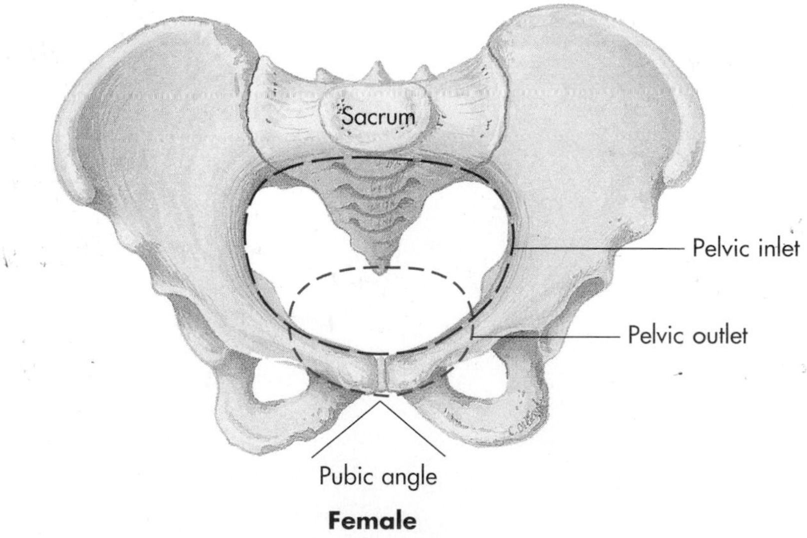

Joints (Articulations)

Every bone in the body, except one, connects to at least one other bone. In other words, every bone but one forms a joint with some other bone. (The exception is the hyoid bone in the neck, to which the tongue anchors.) Most of us probably never think much about our joints unless something goes wrong with them and they do not function properly. Then their tremendous importance becomes painfully clear. Joints hold our bones together securely and at the same time make it possible for movement to occur between the bones—between most of them, that is. Without joints we could not move our arms, legs, or any other of our body parts. Our bodies would, in short, be rigid, immobile hulks. Try, for example, to move your arm at your shoulder joint in as many directions as you can. Try to do the same thing at your elbow joint. Now examine the shape of the bones at each of these joints on a skeleton or in Figure 5-7. Do you see why you cannot move your arm at your elbow in nearly as many directions as you can at your shoulder?

KINDS OF JOINTS

One method classifies joints into three types according to the degree of movement they allow:

1. Synarthroses (no movement)
2. Amphiarthroses (slight movement)
3. Diarthroses (free movement)

Differences in joint structure account for differences in the degree of movement that is possible.

Synarthroses

A synarthrosis is a joint in which fibrous connective tissue grows between the articulating (joining) bones holding them close together. The joints between cranial bones are synarthroses, commonly called *sutures* (Figure 5-19, *A*).

Amphiarthroses

An amphiarthrosis is a joint in which cartilage connects the articulating bones. The symphysis pubis, the joint between the two pubic bones, is an amphiarthrosis (Figure 5-19, *B*).

Joints between the bodies of the vertebrae are also amphiarthroses. These joints make it possible to flex the trunk forward or sideways and even to circumduct and rotate it. Strong ligaments connect the bodies of the vertebrae, and fibrous disks lie between them. The central core of these intervertebral disks consists of a pulpy, elastic substance that loses some of its resiliency with age.

Diarthroses

Fortunately most of our joints by far are diarthroses. Such joints allow considerable move-

FIGURE 5–19 ***Joints of the Skeleton.*** **A,** Synarthrotic joint. **B,** Amphiarthrotic joint.

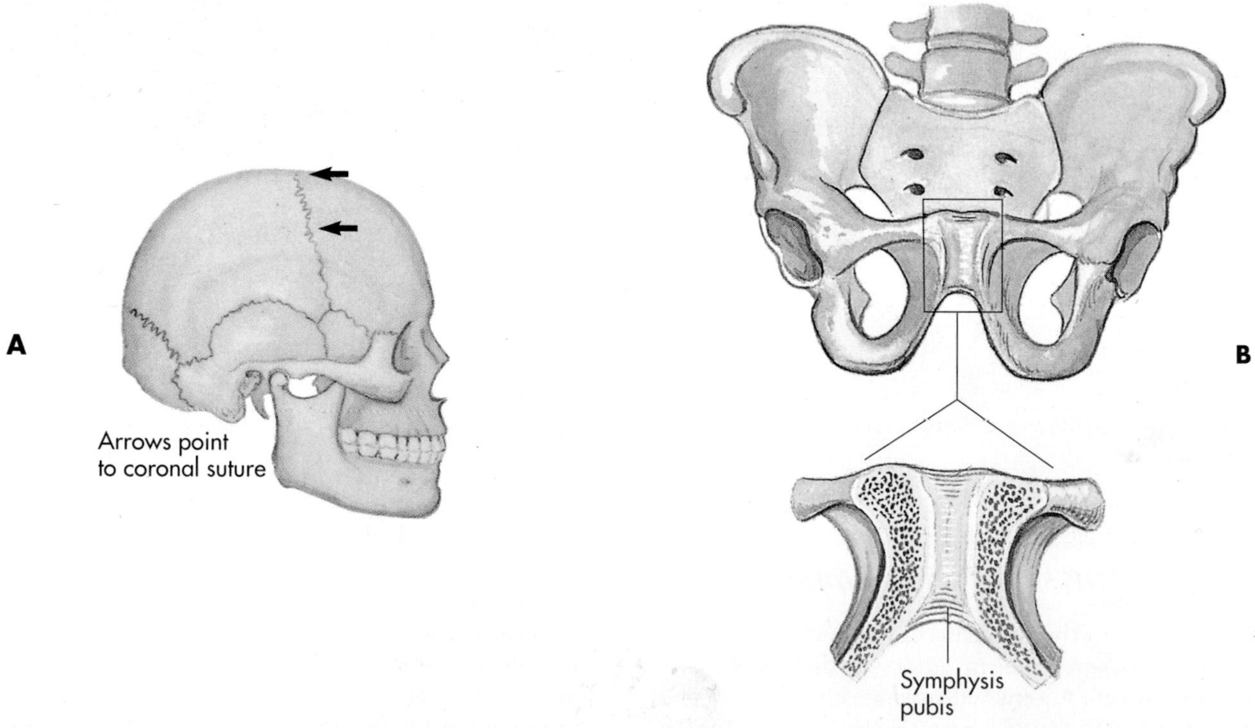

Palpable Bony Landmarks

Health professionals often identify externally palpable bony landmarks when dealing with the sick and injured. **Palpable** bony landmarks are bones that can be touched and identified through the skin. They serve as reference points in identifying other body structures.

There are externally palpable bony landmarks throughout the body. Many skull bones such as the zygomatic bone, can be palpated. The medial and lateral epicondyles of the humerus, the olecranon process of the ulna, and the styloid process of the ulna and the radius at the wrist can be palpated on the upper extremity. The highest corner of the shoulder is the acromion process of the scapula.

When you put your hands on your hips, you can feel the superior edge of the ilium called the *iliac crest*. The anterior end of the crest, called the *anterior superior iliac spine*, is a prominent landmark used often as a clinical reference. The medial malleolus of the tibia and the lateral malleolus of the fibula are prominent at the ankle. The calcaneus or heel bone is easily palpated on the posterior aspect of the foot. On the anterior aspect of the lower extremity, examples of palpable bony landmarks include the patella or knee cap, the anterior border of the tibia or shin bone, and the metatarsals and phalanges of the toes. Try to identify as many of the externally palpable bones of the skeleton as possible on your own body. Using these as points of reference will make it easier for you to visualize the placement of other bones that cannot be touched or palpated through the skin.

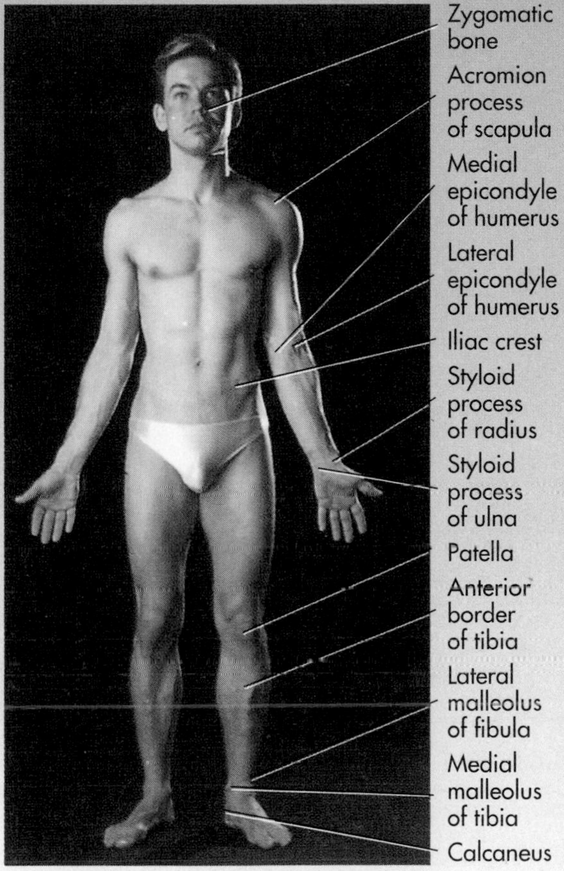

ment, sometimes in many directions and sometimes in only one or two directions.

Structure. Diarthroses (freely movable joints) are made alike in certain ways. All have a joint capsule, a joint cavity, and a layer of cartilage over the ends of two joining bones (Figure 5-20). The **joint capsule** is made of the body's strongest and toughest material, fibrous connective tissue, and is lined with a smooth, slippery synovial membrane. The capsule fits over the ends of the two bones somewhat like a sleeve. Because it attaches firmly to the shaft of each bone to form its covering (called the *periosteum; peri* means "around," and *osteon* means "bone"), the joint capsule holds the bones securely together but at the same time permits movement at the joint. The structure of the joint capsule, in other words, helps make possible the joint's function.

FIGURE 5–20 ***Structure of a Diarthrotic Joint.*** Each diarthrosis has a joint capsule, a joint cavity, and a layer of cartilage over the ends of the joined bones.

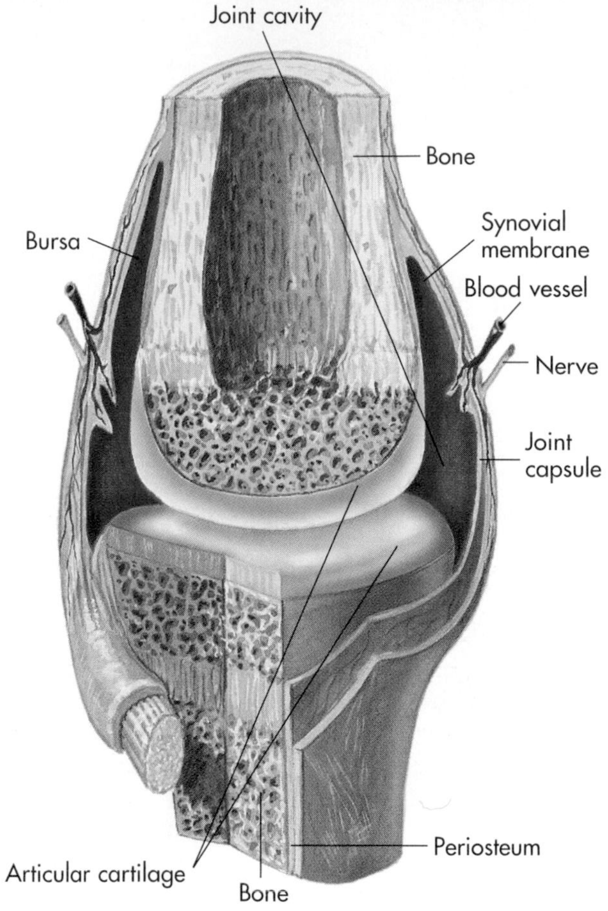

Total Hip Replacement

Because total hip replacement (THR) is the most common orthopedic operation performed on older persons (over 200,000 procedures per year in the U.S.), home health care professionals often work with patients recovering from THR surgery.

The THR procedure involves replacement of the femoral head by a metal prosthesis and the acetabular socket by a polyethylene cup. The prostheses are usually coated with a porous material that allows natural growth of bone to mesh with the artificial material. Such meshing of tissue and prostheses ensures stability of the parts without the loosening that the use of glues in the past often allowed. First introduced in 1953, THR technique has advanced to the state that the procedure has a success rate of about 85%.

Patients at home after THR surgery should progress through proper surgical healing and recovery, including stabilization of the prostheses as new tissue grows into their porous surfaces. THR patients should also expect some improvement in regained use of the affected hip, including weight-bearing and walking movements.

Ligaments (cords or bands made of the same strong fibrous connective tissue as the joint capsule) also grow out of the periosteum and lash the two bones together even more firmly.

The layer of **articular cartilage** over the joint ends of bones acts like a rubber heel on a shoe—it absorbs jolts. The **synovial membrane** secretes a lubricating fluid (synovial fluid) that allows easier movement with less friction.

There are several types of diarthroses, namely, ball-and-socket, hinge, pivot, saddle, gliding, and condyloid (Figure 5-21). Because they differ in structure, they differ also in their possible range of movement. In a ball-and-socket joint, a ball-shaped head of one bone fits into a concave socket of another bone. Shoulder and hip joints, for example, are ball-and-socket joints. Of all the joints in our bodies, these permit the widest range of movements. Think for a moment about how many ways you can move your upper arms. You can move them forward, you can move them backward, you can move them away from the sides of your body, and you can move them back down to your sides. You can also move them around so as to describe a circle with your hands.

FIGURE 5–21 ***Types of Diarthrotic Joints.*** Notice that the structure of each type dictates its function (movement).

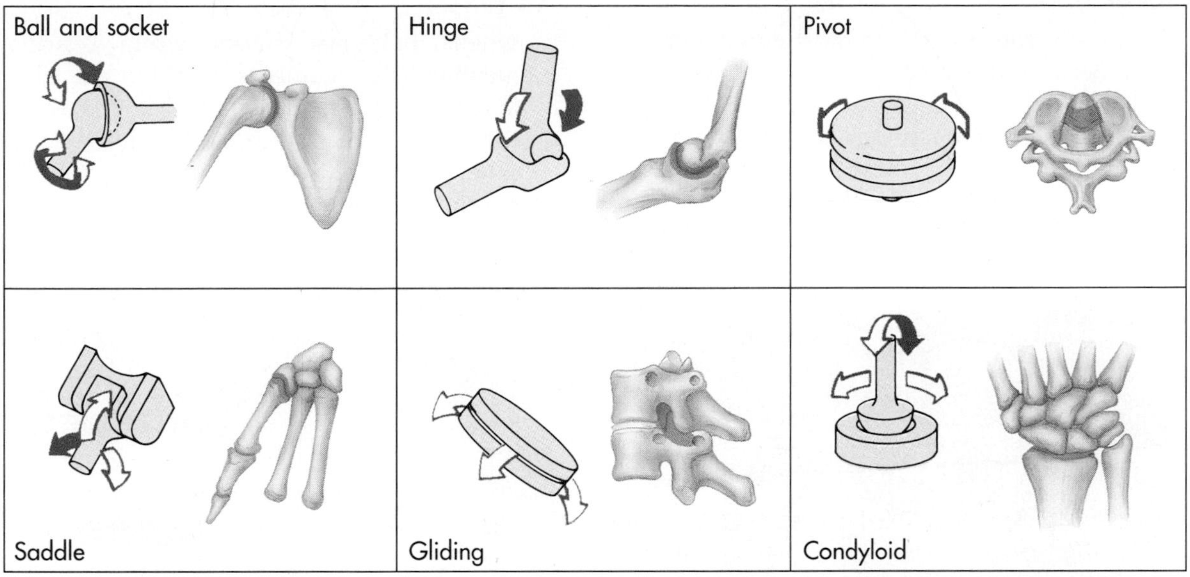

Hinge joints, like the hinges on a door, allow movements in only two directions, namely, flexion and extension. Flexion is bending a part; extension is straightening it out. Elbow and knee joints and the joints in the fingers are hinge joints.

Pivot joints are those in which a small projection of one bone pivots in an arch of another bone. For example, a projection of the axis, the second vertebra in the neck, pivots in an arch of the atlas, the first vertebra in the neck. This rotates the head, which rests on the atlas.

Only one pair of saddle joints exists in the body—between the metacarpal bone of each thumb and a carpal bone of the wrist (the name of this carpal bone is the *trapezium*). Because the articulating surfaces of these bones are saddle-shaped, they make possible the human thumb's great mobility, a mobility no animal's thumb possesses. We can flex, extend, abduct, adduct, and circumduct our thumbs, and most important of all, we can move our thumbs to touch the tip of any one of our fingers. (This movement is called *opposing the thumb to the fingers.*) Without the saddle joints at the base of each of our thumbs, we could not do such a simple act as picking up a pin or grasping a pencil between thumb and forefinger.

Gliding joints are the least movable diarthrotic joints. Their flat articulating surfaces allow limited gliding movements, such as that at the superior and inferior articulating processes between successive vertebrae.

Condyloid joints are those in which a condyle (an oval projection) fits into an elliptical socket. An example is the fit of the distal end of the radius into depressions in the carpal bones.

The Knee Joint

The knee is the largest and most vulnerable joint. Because the knee is often subjected to sudden, strong forces during athletic activity, knee injuries are among the most common type of athletic injury. Sometimes, the articular cartilages on the tibia become torn when the knee twists while bearing weight. The ligaments holding the tibia and femur together can also be injured in this way. Knee injuries may also occur when a weight-bearing knee is hit by another person.

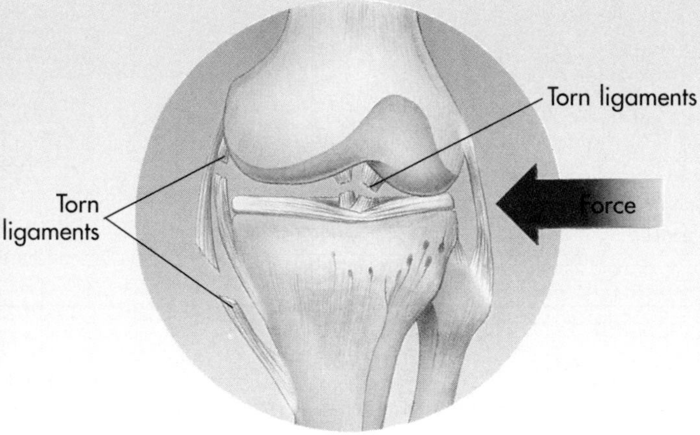

OUTLINE SUMMARY

FUNCTIONS OF BONE

A Supports and gives shape to the body
B Protects internal organs
C Helps make movements possible
D Stores calcium
E Hemopoiesis or blood cell formation

TYPES OF BONES

A Long—Example: humerus (upper arm)
B Short—Example: carpals (wrist)
C Flat—Example: frontal (skull)
D Irregular—Example: vertebrae (spinal cord)

STRUCTURE OF LONG BONES

A Structural components (Figure 5-1)
  1 Diaphysis or shaft
  2 Medullary cavity containing yellow marrow
  3 Epiphyses or ends of the bone; spongy bone contains red bone marrow
  4 Articular cartilage—covers epiphyses as a cushion
  5 Periosteum—strong membrane covering bone except at joint surfaces
  6 Endosteum—lines medullary cavity

MICROSCOPIC STRUCTURE OF BONE AND CARTILAGE

A Bone types (Figure 5-2)
  1 Spongy
    a Texture results from needlelike threads of bone called *trabeculae* surrounded by a network of open spaces
    b Found in epiphyses of bones
    c Spaces contain red bone marrow
  2 Compact
    a Structural unit is Haversian system—composed of concentric lamella, lacunae containing osteocytes, and canaliculi, all covered by periosteum
B Cartilage (Figure 5-4)
  1 Cell type called *chondrocyte*
  2 Matrix is gel-like and lacks blood vessels

BONE FORMATION AND GROWTH

(Figures 5-5 and 5-6)
A Sequence of development early—cartilage models replaced by calcified bone matrix
B Osteoblasts form new bone, and osteoclasts resorb bone

DIVISIONS OF SKELETON

Skeleton composed of the following divisions and their subdivisions:
A Axial skeleton
  1 Skull
  2 Spine
  3 Thorax
  4 Hyoid bone
B Appendicular skeleton
  1 Upper extremities, including shoulder girdle
  2 Lower extremities, including hip girdle
C Location and description of bones—see Figures 5-7 to 5-17 and Tables 5-2 to 5-6

DIFFERENCES BETWEEN A MAN'S AND A WOMAN'S SKELETON

A Size—male skeleton generally larger
B Shape of pelvis—male pelvis deep and narrow, female pelvis broad and shallow
C Size of pelvic inlet—female pelvic inlet generally wider, normally large enough for baby's head to pass through it (Figure 5-18)
D Pubic angle—angle between pubic bones of female generally wider

JOINT (ARTICULATIONS)

A Kinds of joints (Figures 5-19 to 5-21)
  1 Synarthroses (no movement)—fibrous connective tissue grows between articulating bones; for example, sutures of skull
  2 Amphiarthroses (slight movement)—cartilage connects articulating bones; for example, symphysis pubis
  3 Diarthroses (free movement)—most joints belong to this class
    a Structures of freely movable joints—joint capsule and ligaments hold adjoining bones together but permit movement at joint
    b Articular cartilage—covers joint ends of bones and absorbs joints
    c Synovial membrane—lines joint capsule and secretes lubricating fluid
    d Joint cavity—space between joint ends of bones
B Types of freely movable joints—ball-and-socket, hinge, pivot, saddle, gliding, and condyloid

NEW WORDS

amphiarthroses	diaphysis	osteoblasts	sinus
appendicular skeleton	diarthroses	osteoclasts	skull
articular cartilage	epiphyses	osteocytes	spine
articulation	fontanels	osteon	synarthroses
axial skeleton	hemopoiesis	pectoral girdle	synovial membrane
canaliculi	lacunae	pelvic girdle	thorax
chondrocytes	lamella	periosteum	trabeculae
compact bone	medullary cavity	red bone marrow	yellow bone marrow

CHAPTER TEST

1. Spongy bone contains needlelike threads of bone known as ______________.

2. The structural units of compact bone are called ______________.

3. Bone-forming cells are called ______________, whereas bone-resorbing cells are called ______________.

4. The hollow shaft of a long bone is also known as the______________.

5. The human skeleton has two main divisions, the ______________ skeleton and the ______________ skeleton.

6. Spaces or cavities located inside some of the cranial bones are called ______________.

7. The supporting framework of the neck is formed by the seven ______________ vertebrae.

8. The shoulder blade is also known as the ______________, and the collar bone is called the ______________.

9. The long bones of the forearm are the ______________ and the ______________.

10. The large bony process of the ulna that forms the elbow is called the ______________ process.

11. There are 8 ______________ bones in the wrist and 14 ______________ or finger bones in each hand.

12. Each hip bone consists of three separate bones called the ______________, ______________, and ______________, which fuse in the adult to become one bone.

13. The femur of the leg articulates distally with the knee cap or ______________ and the shinbone or ______________.

14. The metatarsal and tarsal bones are located in the ______________.

15. Joints that permit free movement are called ______________ joints.

Circle the "T" before each true statement and the "F" before each false statement.

T F 16. Adult bones do not contain living cells.

T F 17. Red bone marrow functions in hemopoiesis or blood cell formation.

T F 18. The hollow cylindrical portion of a long bone is called the *epiphysis.*

T F 19. Haversian systems are components of spongy bone.

T F 20. Lacunae are found in compact bone and cartilage.

T F 21. There are more bones in the axial than in the appendicular skeleton.

T F 22. The term *phalanges* is used to describe the bones of the fingers and the toes.

T F 23. "Soft spots" in the skull at birth are called *fontanels.*

T F 24. Synarthroses are freely movable joints.

T F 25. Synovial membranes are found in diarthrotic joints.

REVIEW QUESTIONS

1. Discuss the mechanism of bone formation and growth.
2. Compare the structures of compact and spongy bone.
3. Discuss the following cell types: osteocyte, osteoblast, osteoclast, chondrocyte.
4. List the major structural components of a typical long bone, and briefly describe the function of each.
5. List and discuss the generalized functions of the skeletal system.
6. What are the two major subdivisions of the skeleton? What are the major body areas in each subdivision?
7. Give the correct anatomical name for each of the following: collarbone, breastbone, wrist bones, finger bones, forearm bones, thigh bone, hip bone, knee cap, ankle bones, and neck vertebrae.
8. Compare the structures and functions of the arms and legs, pectoral and pelvic girdles, shoulder and hip joints, and hands and feet.
9. Classify the major types of joints.
10. List and compare the types of freely movable joints.

CRITICAL THINKING

11. Is it possible to tell whether a child is going to grow taller? If so, how?
12. Describe one functionally important difference between a male and a female adult skeleton. Why is this difference important?

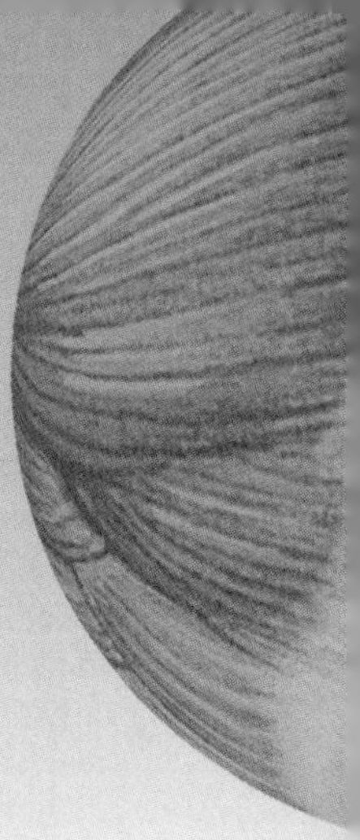

The Muscular System

6

OUTLINE

Muscle Tissue

Structure of Skeletal Muscle
- Microscopic Structure

Functions of Skeletal Muscle
- Movement
- Posture
- Heat Production

Fatigue

Role of Other Body Systems in Movement

Motor Unit

Muscle Stimulus

Types of Skeletal Muscle Contraction
- Twitch and Tetanic Contractions
- Isotonic Contraction
- Isometric Contraction

Effects of Exercise on Skeletal Muscles

Skeletal Muscle Groups
- Muscles of the Head and Neck
- Muscles That Move the Upper Extremities
- Muscles of the Trunk
- Muscles That Move the Lower Extremities

Movements Produced by Skeletal Muscle Contractions

BOXED ESSAYS

Carpal Tunnel Syndrome
Intramuscular Injections

OBJECTIVES

After you have completed this chapter, you should be able to:

1. List, locate in the body, and compare the structure and function of the three major types of muscle tissue.
2. Discuss the microscopic structure of a skeletal muscle sarcomere and motor unit.
3. Discuss how a muscle is stimulated and compare the major types of skeletal muscle contractions.
4. Name, identify on a model or diagram, and give the function of the major muscles of the body discussed in this chapter.
5. List and explain the most common types of movement produced by skeletal muscles.

Although we will initially review the three types of muscle tissue introduced earlier (see Chapter 3), the plan for this chapter is to focus on skeletal or voluntary muscle—those muscle masses that attach to bones and actually move them about when contraction or shortening of muscle cells, or muscle fibers, occurs. If you weigh 120 pounds, about 50 pounds of your weight comes from your skeletal muscles, the "red meat" of the body that is attached to your bones.

Movements caused by skeletal muscle contraction vary in complexity from blinking an eye to the coordinated and fluid movements of a gifted athlete. Not many of our body structures can claim as great an importance for happy, useful living as can our voluntary muscles, and only a few can boast of greater importance for life itself. Our ability to survive often depends on our ability to adjust to the changing conditions of our environment. Movements frequently constitute a major part of this adjustment.

Muscle Tissue

Under the microscope, threadlike and cylindrical skeletal muscle cells appear in bundles. They are characterized by many crosswise stripes and multiple nuclei (Figure 6-1, *A*). Each fine thread is a muscle cell or, as it is usually called, a *muscle fiber.* This type of muscle tissue has three names: *skeletal muscle,* because it attaches to bone; *striated muscle,* because of its cross stripes or striations; and *voluntary muscle,* because its contractions can be controlled voluntarily.

In addition to **skeletal muscle,** the body also contains two other kinds of muscle tissue: cardiac muscle and nonstriated, smooth, or involuntary muscle. **Cardiac muscle** composes the bulk of the heart. Cells in this type of muscle are also cylindrical, branch frequently, (Figure 6-1, *B*) and then recombine into a continuous mass of interconnected tissue. Like skeletal muscle cells, they have cross striations. They also have unique dark bands called *intercalated disks* where the plasma membranes of adjacent cardiac fibers come in contact with each other. Cardiac muscle tissue demonstrates the principle that "form follows function." The interconnected nature of cardiac muscle fibers helps the tissue to contract as a unit and increases the efficiency of the heart muscle in pumping blood.

Nonstriated or **smooth muscle** cells are tapered at each end, have a single nucleus, and lack the cross stripes or striations of skeletal muscle cells (Figure 6-1, C). They have a smooth, even appearance when viewed through a microscope. They are called *involuntary* because we normally do not have control over their contractions. Smooth or involuntary muscle forms an important part of blood vessel walls and of many hollow internal organs (viscera) such as the gut, urethra, and ureters. Because of its location in many visceral structures, it is sometimes called *visceral muscle.* Although we cannot willfully control the action of smooth muscle, its contractions are highly regulated so that, for example, food is passed through the digestive tract or urine is pushed through the ureters into the bladder.

Muscle cells specialize in contraction or shortening. Every movement we make is produced by contractions of skeletal muscle cells. Contractions of cardiac muscle cells keep the blood circulating, and smooth muscle contractions do many things; for instance, they move food into and through the stomach and intestines and make a major contribution to the maintenance of normal blood pressure.

Structure of Skeletal Muscle

A skeletal muscle is an organ composed mainly of striated muscle cells and connective tissue. Most skeletal muscles attach to two bones that have a movable joint between them. In other words, most muscles extend from one bone across a joint to another bone. Also, one of the two bones is usually more stationary in a given movement than the other. The muscle's attachment to this more stationary bone is called its **origin.** Its attachment to the more movable bone is called the muscle's **insertion.** The rest of the muscle (all of it except its two ends) is called the *body* of the muscle (Figure 6-2).

Tendons anchor muscles firmly to bones. Made of dense fibrous connective tissue in the shape of

FIGURE 6–1 ***Muscle Tissue.*** **A,** Skeletal muscle. **B,** Cardiac muscle. **C,** Smooth muscle.

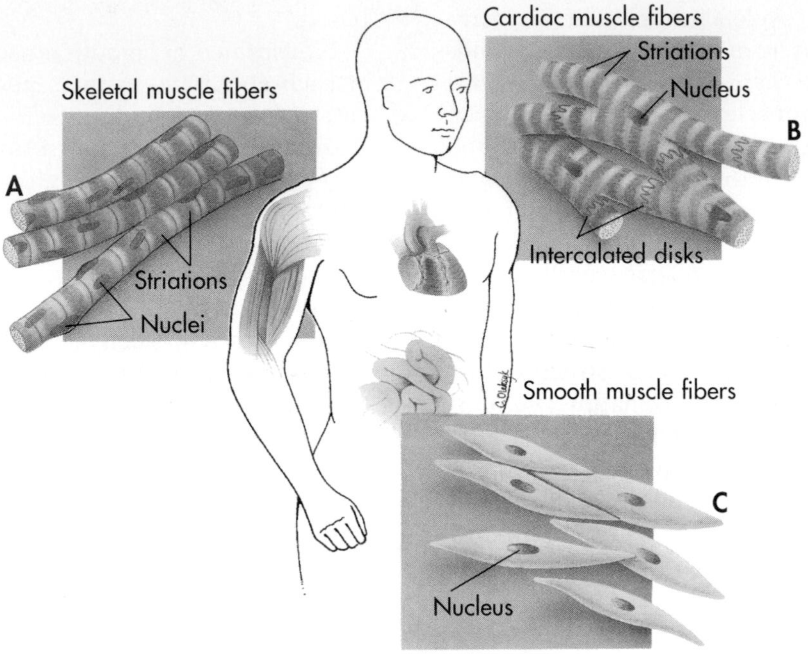

FIGURE 6–2 ***Attachments of a Skeletal Muscle.*** A muscle originates at a relatively stable part of the skeleton (origin) and inserts at the skeletal part that is moved when the muscle contracts (insertion).

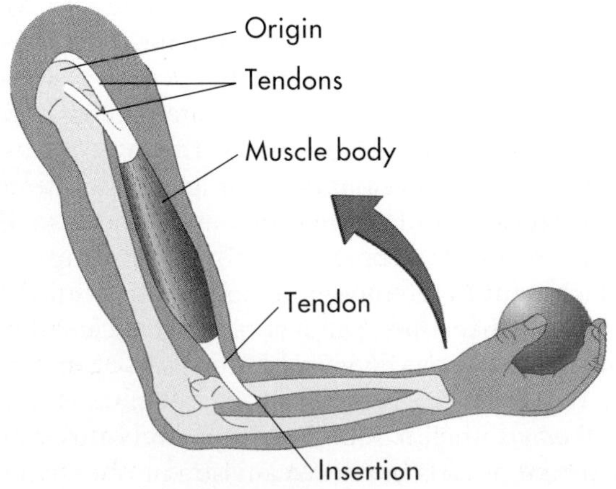

heavy cords, tendons have great strength. They do not tear or pull away from bone easily. Yet any emergency room nurse or physician sees many tendon injuries—severed tendons and tendons torn loose from bones.

Small fluid-filled sacs called **bursae** lie between some tendons and the bones beneath them (see Figure 5-20). These small sacs are made of connective tissue and are lined with **synovial membrane.** The synovial membrane secretes a slippery lubricating fluid (synovial fluid) that fills the bursa. Like a small, flexible cushion, a bursa makes it easier for a tendon to slide over a bone when the tendon's muscle shortens. **Tendon sheaths** enclose some tendons. Because these tube-shaped structures are also lined with synovial membrane and are moistened with synovial fluid, they, like the bursae, facilitate body movement.

MICROSCOPIC STRUCTURE

Muscle tissue consists of specialized contractile cells or **muscle fibers** that are grouped together and arranged in a highly organized way. Each skeletal muscle fiber is itself filled with two kinds of very fine and threadlike structures called **thick** and **thin myofilaments** (my-o-FIL-a-ments). The thick myofilaments are formed from a protein called **myosin,** and the thin myofilaments are composed mostly of the protein **actin.** Find the label **sarcomere** (SAR-ko-meer) in Figure 6-3. Think of the sarcomere as the basic functional or *contractile unit* of skeletal muscle. Recall that the osteon (Haversian system) serves as the basic building block of compact bone; the sarcomere serves that function in skeletal muscle. The submicroscopic structure of a sarcomere consists of numerous actin and myosin myofilaments arranged so that, when viewed under a microscope, dark and light stripes or cross striations are seen. The repeating units or sarcomeres are separated from each other by dark bands called *Z lines.*

Although the sarcomeres in the upper portion (Figure 6-3, *A*) and in the electron photomicrograph (EM) of Figure 6-3, *B,* are in a relaxed state, the thick and thin myofilaments, which are lying parallel to each other, still overlap. Now look at the diagrams in the lower portion of Figure 6-3, *A.* Note that contraction of the muscle causes the two types of myofilaments to slide toward each other and shorten the sarcomere and thus the entire muscle. When the muscle relaxes, the sarcomeres can return to resting length, and the filaments resume their resting positions.

An explanation of how a skeletal muscle contracts is provided by the **sliding filament model.** According to this model, during contraction, the thick and thin myofilaments in a muscle fiber first attach to one another by forming "bridges" that then act as levers to ratchet or pull the myofilaments past each other. The connecting bridges between the myofilaments form properly only if calcium is present. During the relaxed state, calcium is within the endoplasmic reticulum (see Chapter 2) in the muscle cell. It is released into the cytoplasm when the muscle is stimulated to contract. The shortening of a muscle cell also requires energy. This is supplied by the breakdown of adenosine triphosphate (ATP) molecules, the energy storage molecules of the cell.

Functions of Skeletal Muscle

The three primary functions of the muscular system are:

1. Movement
2. Posture or muscle tone
3. Heat production

MOVEMENT

Muscles move bones by pulling on them. Because the length of a skeletal muscle becomes shorter as its fibers contract, the bones to which the muscle attaches move closer together. As a rule, only the insertion bone moves. Look again at Figure 6-2. As the ball is lifted, the shortening of the muscle body pulls the insertion bone toward the origin bone. The origin bone stays put, holding firm, while the insertion bone moves toward it. One tremendously important function of skeletal muscle contractions therefore is to produce body movements. Remember this simple rule: a muscle's insertion bone moves toward its origin bone. It can help you understand muscle actions.

Voluntary muscular movement is normally smooth and free of jerks and tremors because skeletal muscles generally work in coordinated teams, not singly. Several muscles contract while others relax to produce almost any movement that you can imagine. Of all the muscles contracting simultaneously, the one that is mainly responsible for producing a particular movement is called the **prime mover** for that movement. The other muscles that help in producing the movement are called **synergists** (SIN-er-jists). As prime movers and synergist muscles at a joint contract, other muscles, called **antagonists** (an-TAG-o-nists), relax. When antagonist muscles contract, they produce a movement opposite to that of the prime movers and their synergist muscles.

Locate the biceps brachii, brachialis, and triceps brachii muscles in Figure 6-6. All the muscles in these figures are involved in bending and straightening the forearm at the elbow joint. The biceps brachii is the prime mover during bending, and the brachialis is its helper or synergist muscle. When the biceps brachii and brachialis muscles bend the forearm, the triceps brachii relaxes. Therefore while the forearm bends, the triceps brachii is the antagonistic muscle. While the fore-

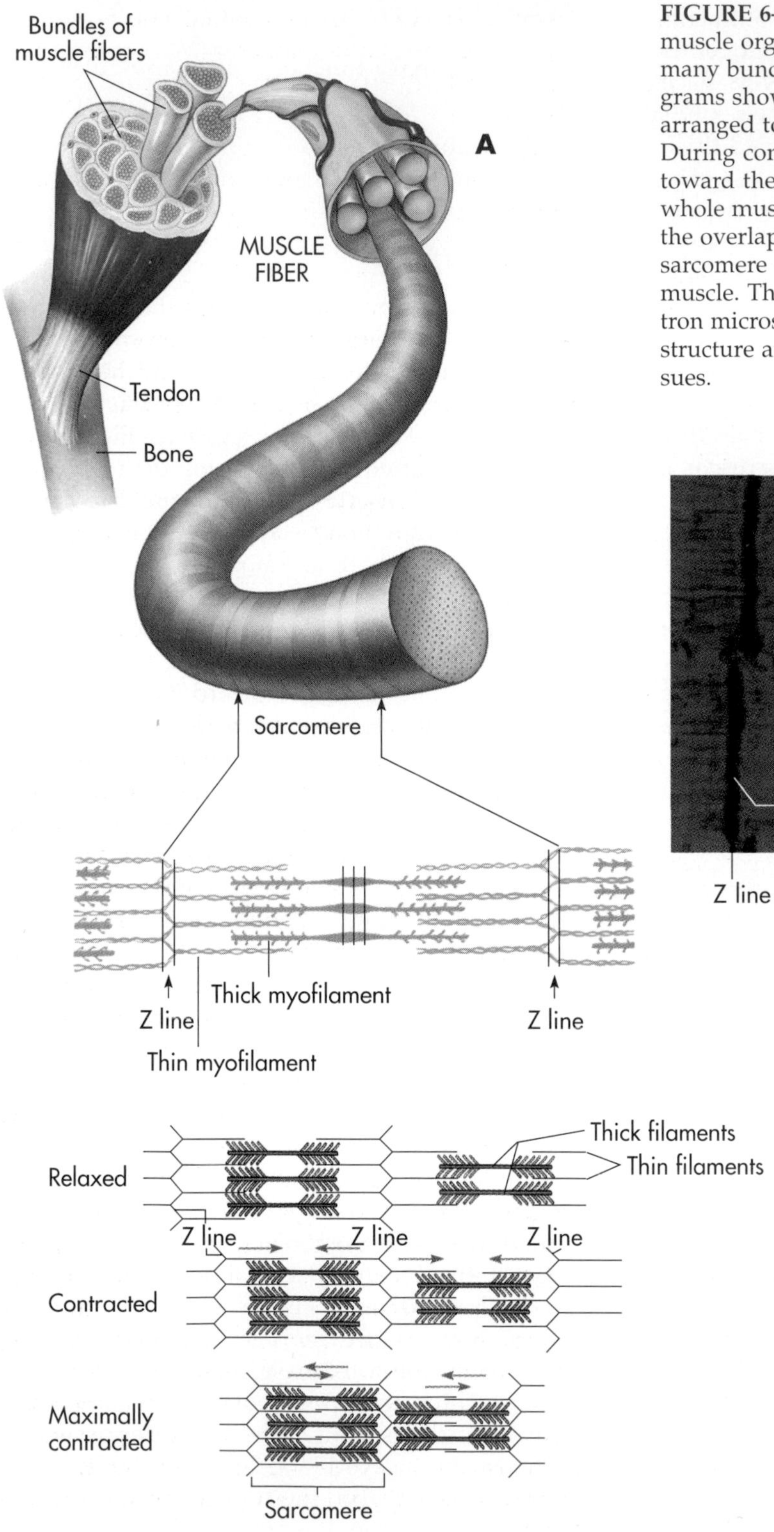

FIGURE 6–3 ***Structure of Skeletal Muscle.*** **A,** Each muscle organ has many muscle fibers, each containing many bundles of thick and thin filaments. The diagrams show the overlapping thick and thin filaments arranged to form adjacent segments called *sarcomeres.* During contraction, the thin filaments are pulled toward the center of each sarcomere, shortening the whole muscle. **B,** This electron micrograph shows that the overlapping thick and thin filaments within each sarcomere create a pattern of dark striations in the muscle. The extreme magnification allowed by electron microscopy has revolutionized our concept of the structure and function of skeletal muscle and other tissues.

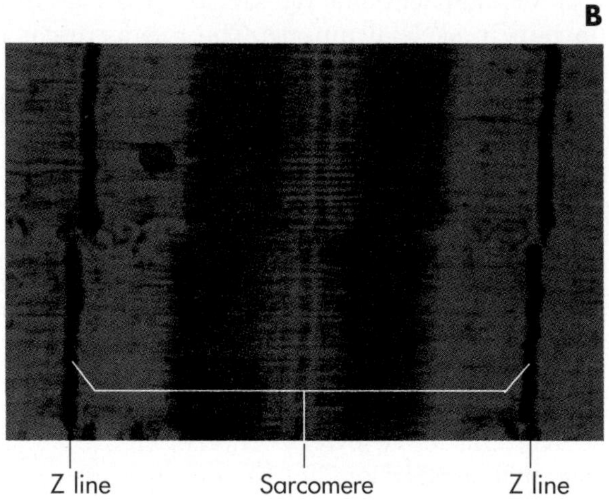

arm straightens, these three muscles continue to work as a team. However, during straightening, the triceps brachii becomes the prime mover and the biceps brachii and brachialis become the antagonistic muscles. This combined and coordinated activity is what makes our muscular movements smooth and graceful.

POSTURE

We are able to maintain our body position because of a specialized type of skeletal muscle contraction called **tonic contraction.** Because relatively few of a muscle's fibers shorten at one time in a tonic contraction, the muscle as a whole does not shorten, and no movement occurs. Consequently, tonic contractions do not move any body parts. They do hold muscles in position, however. In other words, muscle tone maintains **posture.** Good posture means that body parts are held in the positions that favor best function. These positions balance the distribution of weight and therefore put the least strain on muscles, tendons, ligaments, and bones. To have good posture in a standing position, for example, you must stand with your head and chest held high, your chin, abdomen, and buttocks pulled in, and your knees bent slightly.

To judge for yourself how important good posture is, consider some of the effects of poor posture. Besides detracting from appearance, poor posture makes a person tire more quickly. It puts an abnormal pull on ligaments, joints, and bones and sometimes leads to deformities. Poor posture crowds the heart, making it harder for it to contract. Poor posture also crowds the lungs, decreasing their breathing capacity.

Skeletal muscle tone maintains posture by counteracting the pull of gravity. Gravity tends to pull the head and trunk down and forward, but the tone in certain back and neck muscles pulls just hard enough in the opposite direction to overcome the force of gravity and hold the head and trunk erect. The tone in thigh and leg muscles puts just enough pull on thigh and leg bones to counteract the pull of gravity on them that would otherwise collapse the hip and knee joints and cause us to fall in a heap.

HEAT PRODUCTION

Healthy survival depends on our ability to maintain a constant body temperature. A fever or elevation in body temperature of only a degree or two above 37° C (98.6° F) is almost always a sign of illness. Just as serious is a fall in body temperature. Any decrease below normal, a condition called **hypothermia** (hy-po-THER-mee-ah), drastically affects cellular activity and normal body function. The contraction of muscle fibers produces most of the heat required to maintain body temperature. Energy required to produce a muscle contraction is obtained from ATP. Most of the energy released during the breakdown of ATP during a muscular contraction is used to shorten the muscle fibers; however, some of the energy is lost as heat during the reaction. This heat helps us to maintain our body temperature at a constant level.

Fatigue

If muscle cells are stimulated repeatedly without adequate periods of rest, the strength of the muscle contraction decreases, resulting in **fatigue.** If repeated stimulation occurs, the strength of the contraction continues to decrease, and eventually the muscle loses its ability to contract.

During exercise, the stored ATP required for muscle contraction becomes depleted. Formation of more ATP results in a rapid consumption of oxygen and nutrients, often outstripping the ability of the muscle's blood supply to replenish them. When oxygen supplies run low, the muscle cells switch to a type of energy conversion that does not require oxygen. This process produces lactic acid that may result in muscle soreness after exercise. The term **oxygen debt** describes the continued increased metabolism that must occur in a cell to remove excess lactic acid that accumulates during prolonged exercise. Thus the depleted energy reserves are replaced. Labored breathing after the cessation of exercise is required to "pay the debt" of oxygen required for the metabolic effort. This mechanism is a good example of homeostasis at work. The body returns the cells' energy and oxygen reserves to normal, resting levels.

FIGURE 6–4 *Motor Neuron.* A motor unit consists of one motor neuron and the muscle fibers supplied by its branches.

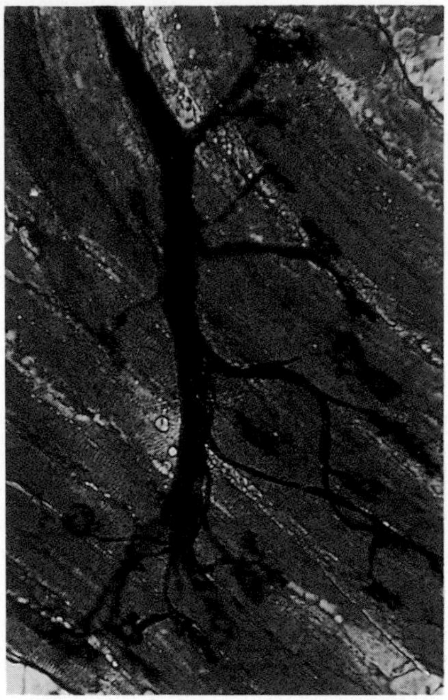

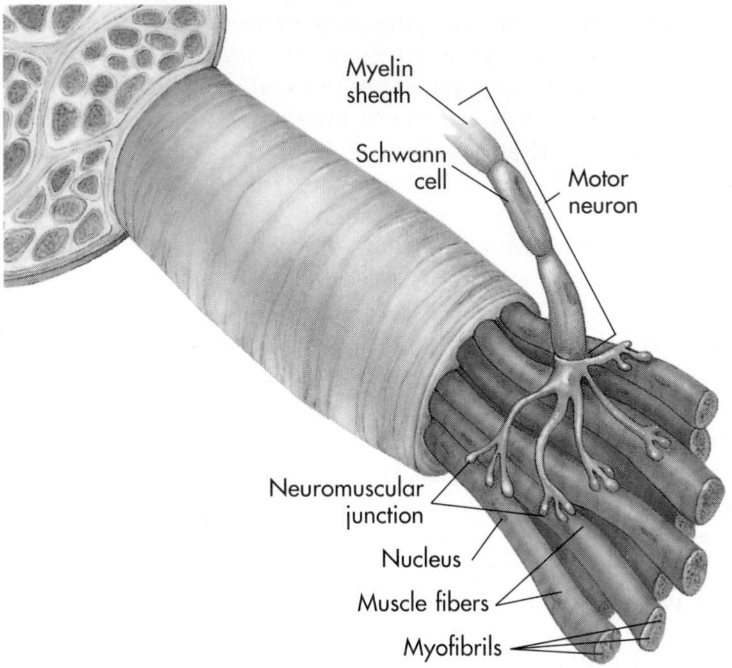

Role of Other Body Systems in Movement

Remember that muscles do not function alone. Other structures such as bones and joints must function with them. Most skeletal muscles cause movements by pulling on bones across movable joints.

The respiratory, circulatory, nervous, muscular, and skeletal systems play essential roles in producing normal movements. This fact has great practical importance. For example, a person might have perfectly normal muscles and still not be able to move normally. He might have a nervous system disorder that shuts off impulses to certain skeletal muscles and thereby results in **paralysis.** Multiple sclerosis acts in this way, but so do some other conditions such as a brain hemorrhage, a brain tumor, or a spinal cord injury. Skeletal system disorders, especially arthritis, have disabling effects on body movement. Muscle functioning, then, depends on the functioning of many other parts of the body. This fact illustrates a principle that is repeated often in this book. It can be simply stated: Each part of the body is one of many components in a large, interactive system. The normal function of one part depends on the normal function of the other parts.

Motor Unit

Before a skeletal muscle can contract and pull on a bone to move it, the muscle must first be stimulated by nerve impulses. Muscle cells are stimulated by a nerve fiber called a **motor neuron** (Figure 6-4). The point of contact between the nerve ending and the muscle fiber is called a **neuromuscular junction.** Specialized chemicals are released by the motor neuron in response to a nervous impulse. These chemicals then generate events within the muscle cell that result in contraction or shortening of the muscle cell. A single motor neuron, with the muscle cells it innervates, is called a **motor unit** (Figure 6-4).

Muscle Stimulus

In a laboratory setting a single muscle fiber can be isolated and subjected to stimuli of varying intensities so that it can be studied. Such experiments show that a muscle fiber does not contract until an applied stimulus reaches a certain level of intensity. The minimal level of stimulation required to cause a fiber to contract is called the **threshold stimulus.**

When a muscle fiber is subjected to a threshold stimulus, it contracts completely. Because of this, muscle cells are said to respond **"all or none."** However, a muscle is composed of many muscle cells that are controlled by different motor units and that have different threshold-stimulus levels. Although each fiber in a muscle such as the biceps brachii responds all or none when subjected to a threshold stimulus, the muscle as a whole does not. This fact has tremendous importance in everyday life. It allows you to pick up a 2-liter bottle of soda or a 20 kg weight by stimulating the same muscle but executing contractions of varying strength. This is possible because different numbers of motor units can be activated for different loads. Once activated, however, each fiber always responds all or none.

Types of Skeletal Muscle Contraction

In addition to the specialized tonic contraction of muscle that maintains muscle tone and posture, other types of contraction also occur. Additional types of muscle contraction include the following:

1. **Twitch contraction**
2. **Tetanic contraction**
3. **Isotonic contraction**
4. **Isometric contraction**

TWITCH AND TETANIC CONTRACTIONS

A **twitch** is a quick, jerky response to a stimulus. Twitch contractions can be seen in isolated muscles during research, but they play a minimal role in normal muscle activity. To accomplish the coordinated and fluid muscular movements needed for most daily tasks, muscles must contract not in a jerky but in a smooth and sustained way.

A **tetanic contraction** is a more sustained and steady response than a twitch. It is produced by a series of stimuli bombarding the muscle in rapid succession. Contractions "melt" together to produce a sustained contraction or *tetanus.* About 30 stimuli per second, for example, evoke a tetanic contraction in certain types of skeletal muscle. Tetanic contraction is not necessarily a maximal contraction in which each muscle fiber responds at the same time. In most cases, only a few areas of the muscle undergo contractions at any time.

ISOTONIC CONTRACTION

In most cases, isotonic contraction of muscle produces movement at a joint. With this type of contraction the muscle shortens, and the insertion end moves toward the point of origin (Figure 6-5, *A*). Walking, running, breathing, lifting, and twisting are examples of isotonic contraction.

ISOMETRIC CONTRACTION

Contraction of a skeletal muscle does not always produce movement. Sometimes, it increases the tension within a muscle but does not shorten the muscle. When the muscle does not shorten and no movement results, it is called an *isometric contraction.* The word *isometric* comes from Greek words that mean "equal measure." In other words, a muscle's length during an isometric contraction and during relaxation is about equal. Although muscles do not shorten (and thus produce no movement) during isometric contractions, tension within them increases (Figure 6-5, *B*). Because of this, repeated isometric contractions make muscles grow larger and stronger—hence the popularity in recent years of isometric exercises. Pushing against a wall or other immovable object is a good example of isometric exercise. Although no movement occurs and the muscle does not shorten, its internal tension increases dramatically.

Effects of Exercise on Skeletal Muscles

We know that exercise is good for us. Some of the benefits of regular, properly practiced exercise are greatly improved muscle tone, better posture, more efficient heart and lung function, less fatigue, and looking and feeling better.

FIGURE 6–5 ***Types of Muscle Contraction.*** **A,** In isotonic contraction the muscle shortens, producing movement. **B,** In isometric contraction the muscle pulls forcefully against a load but does not shorten.

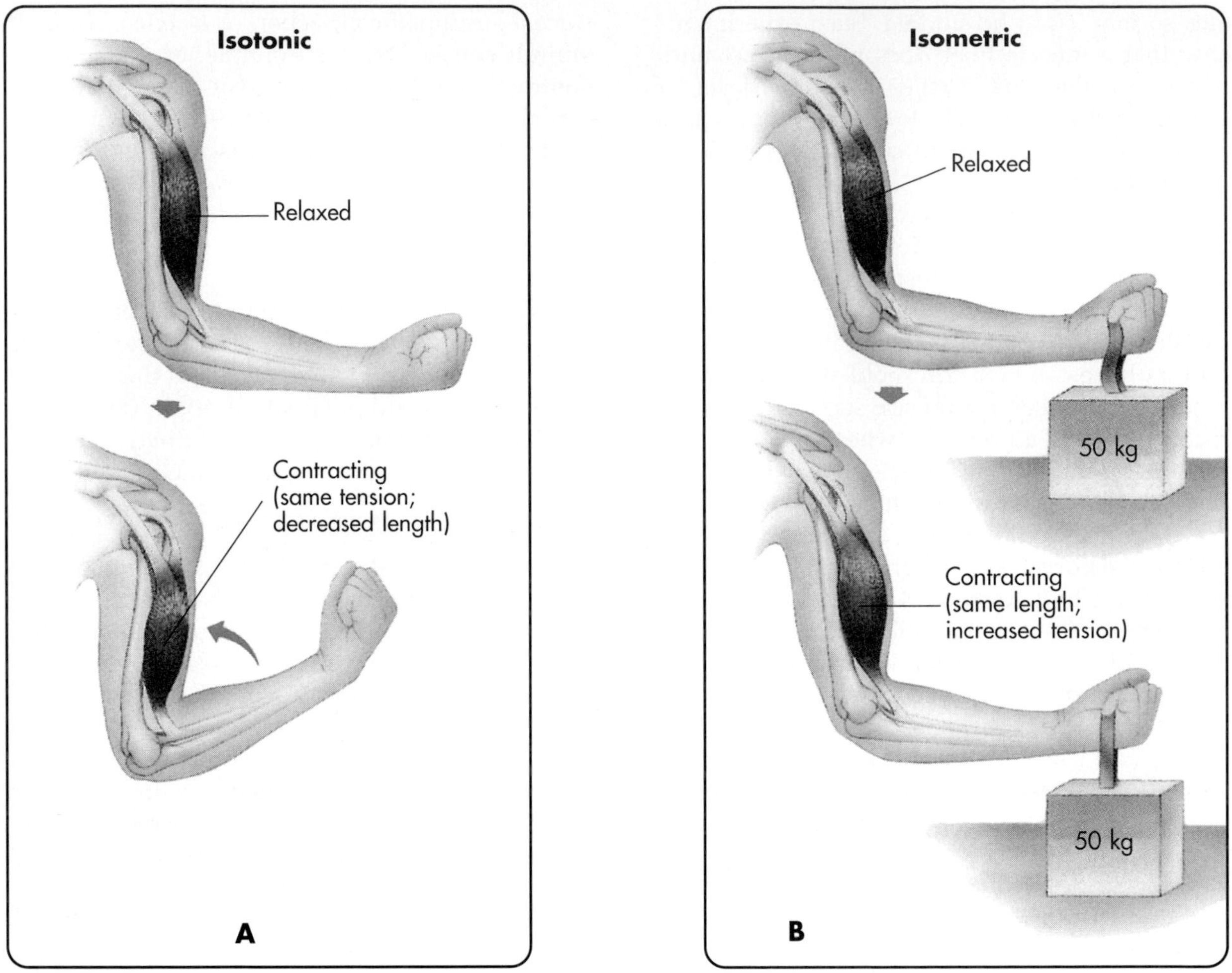

Skeletal muscles undergo changes that correspond to the amount of work that they normally do. During prolonged inactivity, muscles usually shrink in mass, a condition called **disuse atrophy.** Exercise, on the other hand, may cause an increase in muscle size called **hypertrophy**.

Muscle hypertrophy can be enhanced by **strength training,** which involves contracting muscles against heavy resistance. Isometric exercises and weight lifting are common strength-training activities. This type of training results in increased numbers of myofilaments in each muscle fiber. Although the number of muscle fibers stays the same, the increased number of myofilaments greatly increases the mass of the muscle.

Endurance training, often called **aerobic training,** does not usually result in muscle hypertrophy. Instead, this type of exercise program increases a muscle's ability to sustain moderate exercise over a long period. Aerobic activities such as running, bicycling, or other primarily isotonic movements increase the number of blood vessels in a muscle without significantly increasing its size. The increased blood flow allows a more efficient delivery of oxygen and glucose to muscle fibers during exercise. Aerobic training

Carpal Tunnel Syndrome

Some physicians specialize in the field of occupational health, the study of health matters related to work or the workplace. Many problems seen by occupational health experts are caused by repetitive motions of the wrists or other joints. Word processors (typists) and meat cutters, for example, are at risk of developing conditions caused by repetitive motion injuries.

One common problem often caused by such repetitive motion is **tenosynovitis** (ten-o-sin-o-VYE-tis)—inflammation of the tendon sheath. Tenosynovitis can be painful, and the swelling characteristic of this condition can limit movement in affected parts of the body. For example, swelling of the tendon sheath around tendons in an area of the wrist known as the *carpal tunnel* can limit movement of the wrist, hand, and fingers. The figure shows the relative positions of the tendon sheath and medial nerve within the carpal tunnel. If this swelling, or any other lesion in the carpal tunnel, presses on the *median nerve,* a condition called **carpal tunnel syndrome** may result. Because the median nerve connects to the palm and radial side (thumb side) of the hand, carpal tunnel syndrome is characterized by weakness, pain, and tingling in this part of the hand. The pain and tingling may also radiate to the forearm and shoulder. Prolonged and severe cases of carpal tunnel syndrome may be relieved by injection of inflammatory agents. A permanent cure is sometimes accomplished by surgical cutting or removal of the swollen tissue pressing on the median nerve.

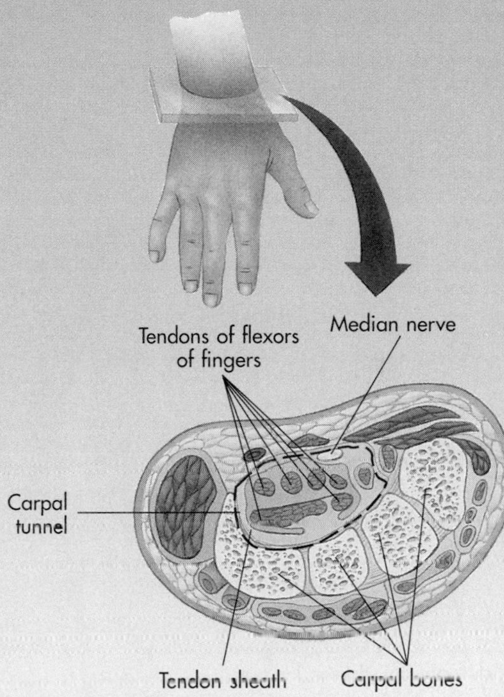

also causes an increase in the number of mitochondria in muscle fibers. This allows production of more ATP as a rapid energy source.

Skeletal Muscle Groups

In the paragraphs that follow, representative muscles from the most important skeletal muscle groups will be discussed. Refer to Figure 6-6 often so that you will be able to see a muscle as you read about its placement on the body and its function. Table 6-1 identifies and groups muscles according to function and provides information about muscle action and points of origin and insertion. Keep in mind that muscles move bones, and the bones that they move are their insertion bones.

FIGURE 6–6 ***General Overview of the Body Musculature.*** **A,** Anterior view.

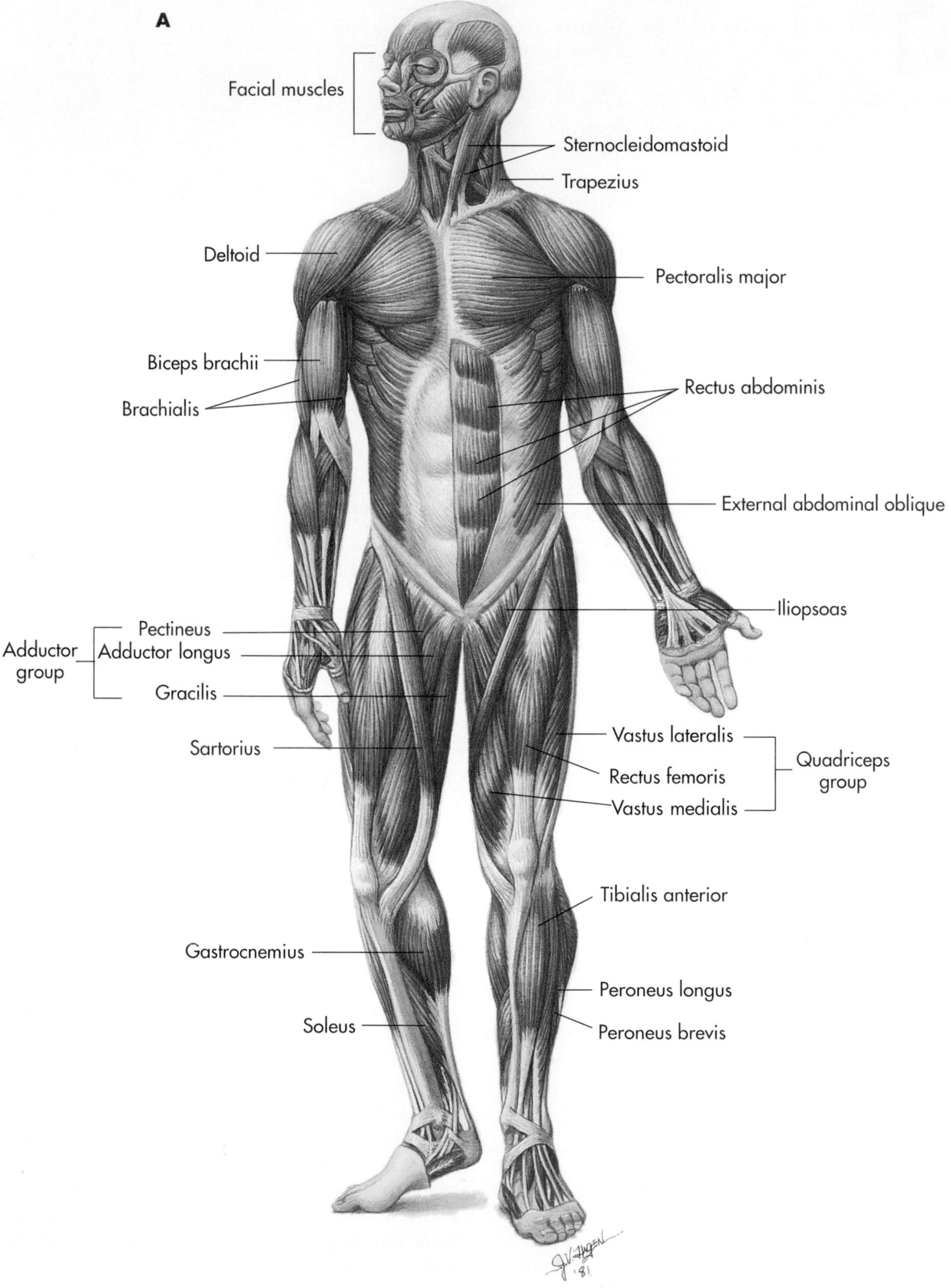

FIGURE 6–6, cont'd. B, Posterior view.

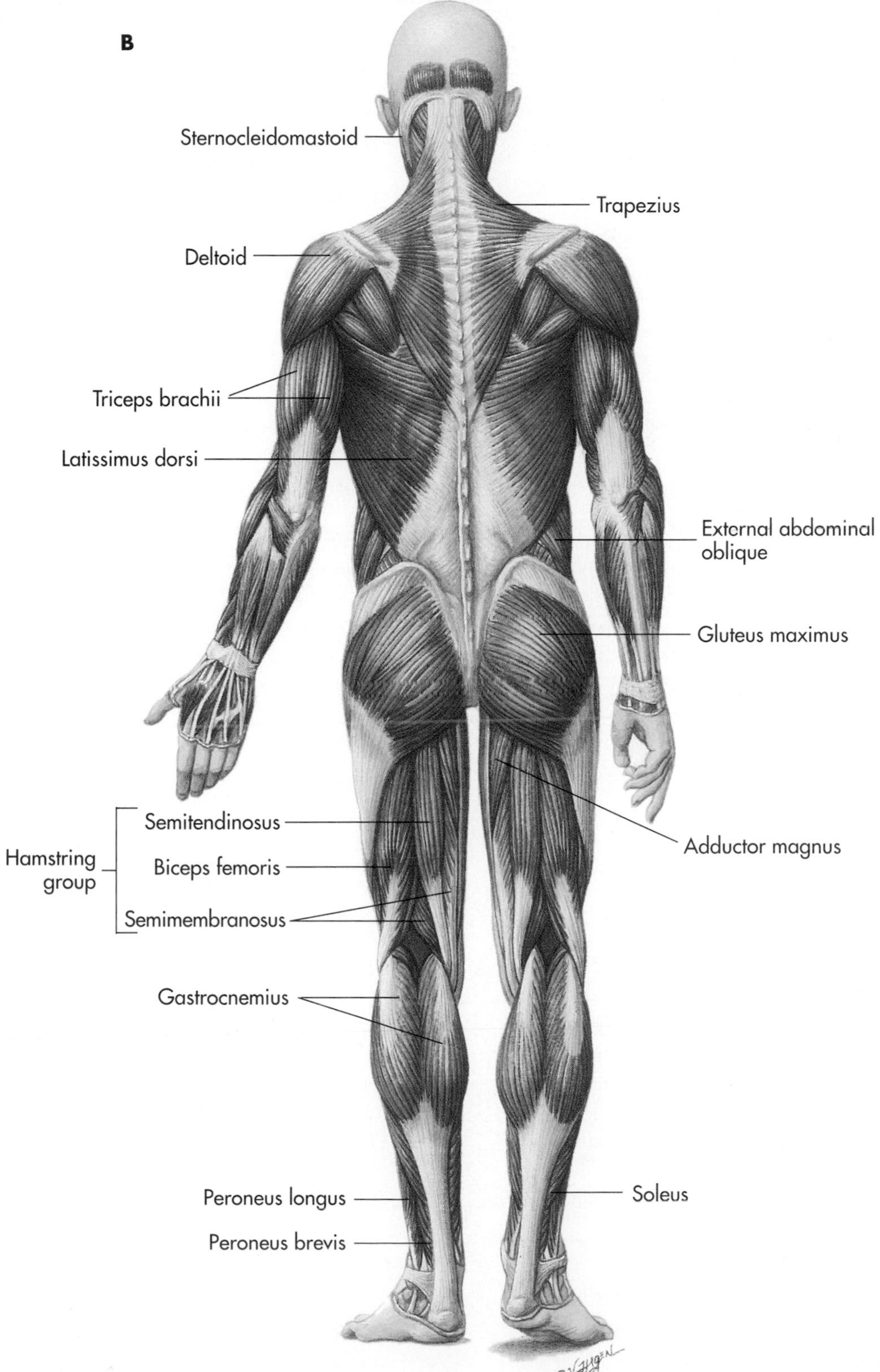

TABLE 6–1 Principal Muscles of the Body

MUSCLE	FUNCTION	INSERTION	ORIGIN
Muscles of the Head and Neck			
Frontal	Raises eyebrow	Skin of eyebrow	Occipital bone
Orbicularis oculi	Closes eye	Maxilla and frontal bone	Maxilla and frontal bone (encircles eye)
Orbicularis oris	Draws lips together	Encircles lips	Encircles lips
Zygomaticus	Elevates corners of mouth and lips	Angle of mouth and upper lip	Zygomatic
Masseter	Closes jaws	Mandible	Zygomatic arch
Temporal	Closes jaw	Mandible	Temporal region of the skull
Sternocleidomastoid	Rotates and extends head	Mastoid process	Sternum and clavicle
Trapezius	Extends head and neck	Scapula	Skull and upper vertebrae
Muscles That Move the Upper Extremities			
Pectoralis major	Flexes and helps adduct upper arms	Humerus	Sternum, clavicle, and upper rib cartilages
Latissimus dorsi	Extends and helps adduct upper arm	Humerus	Vertebrae and ilium
Deltoid	Abducts upper arm	Humerus	Clavicle and scapula
Biceps brachii	Flexes lower arm	Radius	Scapula
Triceps brachii	Extends lower arm	Ulna	Scapula and humerus
Muscles of the Trunk			
External oblique	Compresses abdomen	Midline of abdomen	Lower thoracic cage
Internal oblique	Compresses abdomen	Midline of abdomen	Pelvis
Transversus abdominis	Compresses abdomen	Midline of abdomen	Ribs, vertebrae, and pelvis
Rectus abdominis	Flexes trunk	Lower rib cage	Pubis
Muscles That Move the Lower Extremities			
Iliopsoas	Flexes thigh or trunk	Femur	Ilium and vertebrae
Sartorius	Flexes thigh and rotates lower leg	Tibia	Ilium
Gluteus maximus	Extends thigh	Femur	Ilium, sacrum, and coccyx
Adductor group			
Adductor longus	Adducts thigh	Femur	Pubis
Gracilis	Adducts thigh	Tibia	Pubis
Pectineus	Adducts thigh	Femur	Pubis

TABLE 6–1 Principal Muscles of the Body—Cont'd

MUSCLE	FUNCTION	INSERTION	ORIGIN
Muscles That Move the Lower Extremities (cont'd)			
Hamstring group			
Semimembranosus	Flexes lower leg	Tibia	Ischium
Semitendinosus	Flexes lower leg	Tibia	Ischium
Biceps femoris	Flexes lower leg	Fibula	Ischium and femur
Quadriceps group			
Rectus femoris	Extends lower leg	Tibia	Ilium
Vastus lateralis, intermedius, and medialus	Extend lower leg	Tibia	Femur
Tibialis anterior	Dorsiflexes foot	Metatarsals (foot)	Tibia
Gastrocnemius	Plantar flexes foot	Calcaneus (heel)	Femur
Soleus	Plantar flexes foot	Calcaneus (heel)	Tibia and fibula
Peroneus group			
Peroneus longus and brevis	Plantar flex foot	Tarsal and metatarsals (ankle and foot)	Tibia and fibula

MUSCLES OF THE HEAD AND NECK

The **muscles of facial expression** (Figure 6-7) allow us to communicate many different emotions nonverbally. Contraction of the **frontal** muscle, for example, allows you to raise your eyebrows in surprise and furrow the skin of your forehead into a frown. The **orbicularis** (or-bik-yoo-LAIR-is) **oris** (OR-iss), called the *kissing muscle,* puckers the lips. The **zygomaticus** (zye-go-MAT-ik-us) elevates the corners of the mouth and lips and has been called the *smiling muscle.*

The **muscles of mastication** are responsible for closing the mouth and producing chewing movements. As a group, they are among the strongest muscles in the body. The two largest muscles of the group, identified in Figure 6-7, are the **masseter** (mas-SEE-ter), which elevates the mandible, and the **temporal** (TEM-po-ral), which assists the masseter in closing the jaw.

The **sternocleidomastoid** (stern-o-kli-doe-MAS-toyd) and **trapezius** (tra-PEE-zee-us) muscles are easily identified in Figures 6-6 and 6-7. The two sternocleidomastoid muscles are located on the anterior surface of the neck. They originate on the sternum and then pass up and cross the neck to insert on the mastoid process of the skull. Working together, they flex the head on the chest. If only one contracts, the head is both flexed and tilted to the opposite side. The triangular-shaped trapezius muscles form the line from each shoulder to the neck on its posterior surface. They have a wide line of origin extending from the base of the skull down the spinal column to the last thoracic vertebra. When contracted, the trapezius muscles help elevate the shoulders and extend the head backwards.

MUSCLES THAT MOVE THE UPPER EXTREMITIES

The upper extremity is attached to the thorax by the fan-shaped **pectoralis** (pek-tor-RAL-is) **major** muscle, which covers the upper chest, and by the **latissimus** (la-TIS-i-mus) **dorsi** muscle, which takes its origin from structures over the lower

FIGURE 6–7 ***Muscles of the Head and Neck.*** Muscles that produce most facial expressions surround the eyes, nose, and mouth. Large muscles of mastication stretch from the upper skull to the lower jaw. These powerful muscles produce chewing movements. The neck muscles connect the skull to the trunk of the body, rotating the head or bending the neck.

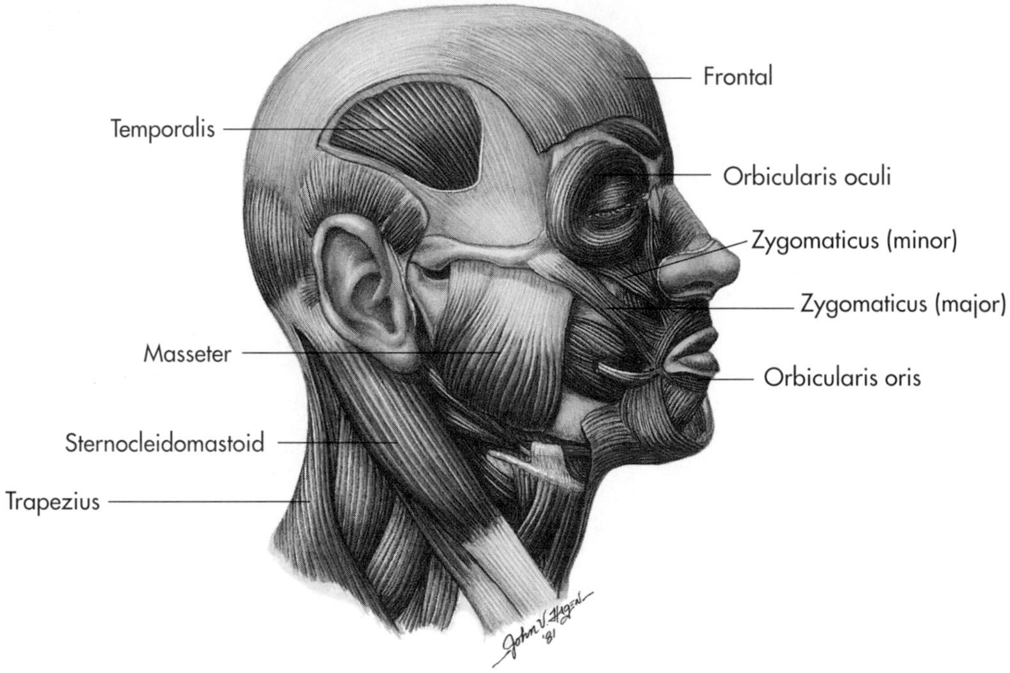

back (Figures 6-6 and 6-8). Both muscles insert on the humerus. The pectoralis major is a flexor, and the latissimus dorsi is an extensor of the upper arm.

The deltoid muscle forms the thick, rounded prominence over the shoulder and upper arm (Figure 6-6). The muscle takes its origin from the scapula and clavicle and inserts on the humerus. It is a powerful abductor of the upper arm.

As the name implies, the biceps brachii (BRAY-kee-eye) is a two-headed muscle that serves as a primary flexor of the forearm (Figure 6-6). It originates from the bones of the shoulder girdle and inserts on the radius in the forearm.

The **triceps brachii** is on the posterior or back surface of the upper arm. It has three heads of origin from the shoulder girdle and inserts into the olecranon process of the ulna. The triceps is an extensor of the elbow and thus performs a straightening function. Because this muscle is responsible for delivering blows during fights, it is often called the *boxer's muscle.*

MUSCLES OF THE TRUNK

The muscles of the anterior or front side of the abdomen are arranged in three layers, with the fibers in each layer running in different directions much like the layers of wood in a sheet of plywood (Figure 6-8). The result is a very strong "girdle" of muscle that covers and supports the abdominal cavity and its internal organs.

The three layers of muscle in the anterolateral (side) abdominal walls are arranged as follows: the outermost layer or **external oblique;** a middle layer or **internal oblique;** and the innermost layer or **transversus abdominis.** In addition to these sheetlike muscles, the band- or strap-shaped **rectus abdominis** muscle runs down the midline of

FIGURE 6–8 ***Muscles of the Trunk.*** **A,** Anterior view showing superficial muscles. **B,** Anterior view showing deeper muscles.

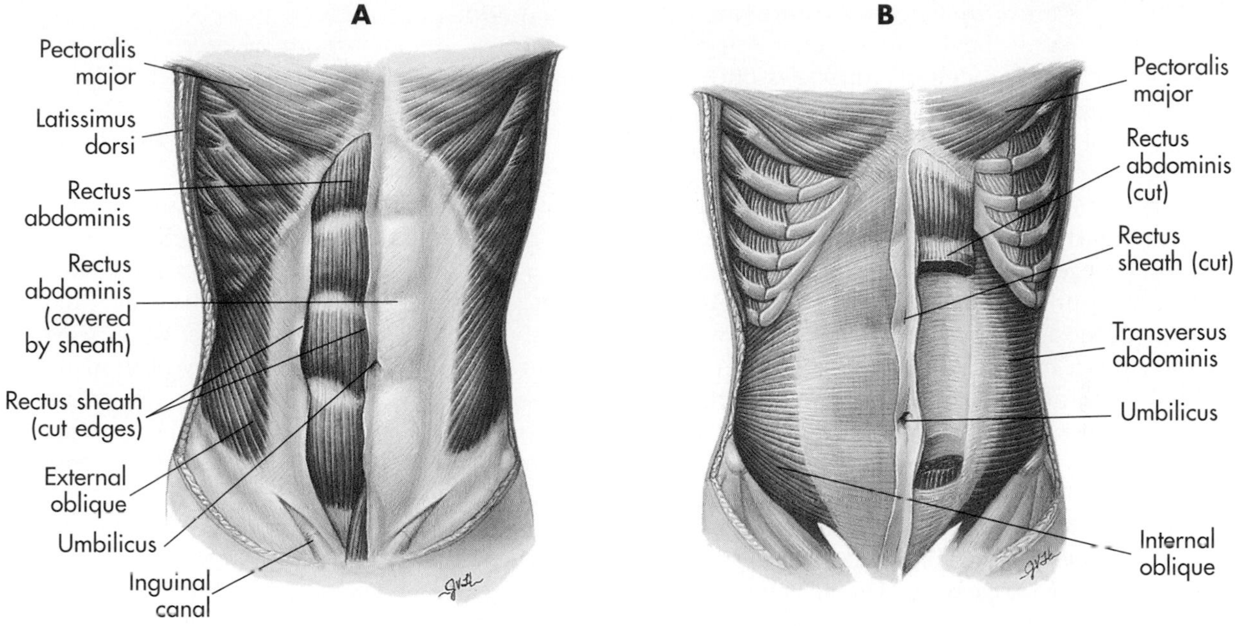

the abdomen from the thorax to the pubis. The rectus abdominis and external oblique muscles can be seen in Figure 6-8. In addition to protecting the abdominal viscera, the rectus abdominis flexes the spinal column.

The *respiratory muscles* will be discussed in Chapter 13. **Intercostal muscles,** located between the ribs, and the sheetlike **diaphragm** separating the thoracic and abdominal cavities change the size and shape of the chest during breathing. As a result, air is moved into or out of the lungs.

MUSCLES THAT MOVE THE LOWER EXTREMITIES

The **iliopsoas** (il-ee-o-SO-us) originates from deep within the pelvis and the lower vertebrae to insert on the lesser trochanter of the femur and capsule of the hip joint. It is generally classified as a flexor of the thigh and an important postural muscle that stabilizes and keeps the trunk from falling over backward when you stand. However, if the thigh is fixed so that it cannot move, the iliopsoas flexes the *trunk.* An example would be doing sit-ups.

The **gluteus** (GLOO-tee-us) **maximus** (MAX-i-mus) forms the outer contour and much of the substance of the buttock. It is an important extensor of the thigh (Figure 6-6) and supports the torso in the erect position.

The **adductor muscles** originate on the bony pelvis and insert on the femur. They are located on the inner or medial side of the thighs. These muscles adduct or press the thighs together.

The three **hamstring muscles** are called the *semimembranosus, semitendinosus,* and *biceps femoris.* Acting together, they serve as powerful flexors of the lower leg (Figure 6-6). They originate on the ischium and insert on the tibia or fibula.

The **quadriceps** (KWOD-re-seps) **femoris** muscle group covers the upper thigh. The four thigh muscles—the *rectus femoris* and three *vastus* muscles—extend the lower leg (Figure 6-6 and Table 6-1). One component of the quadriceps group has its origin on the pelvis, and the remaining three originate on the femur; all four insert on the tibia. Only two of the vastus muscles are visible in Figure 6-6. The vastus intermedius is covered by the rectus femoris and is not visible.

Intramuscular Injections

Many drugs are administered by intramuscular injection. If the amount to be injected is 2 ml or less, the deltoid muscle is often selected as the site of injection. Note in Figure *A* that the needle is inserted into the muscle about two-fingers' breadth below the acromion process of the scapula and lateral to the tip of the acromion. If the amount of medication to be injected is 2 to 3 ml, the gluteal area shown in Figure *B* is often used. Injections are made into the gluteus medius muscle near the center of the upper outer quadrant, as shown in the illustration. Another technique of locating the proper injection site is to draw an imaginary diagonal line from a point of reference on the back of the bony pelvis (posterior superior iliac spine) to the greater trochanter of the femur. The injection is given about three-fingers' breadth above and one third of the way down the line. It is important that the sciatic nerve and the superior gluteal blood vessels be avoided during the injection. Proper technique requires a knowledge of the underlying anatomy.

In addition to intramuscular injections, which are generally administered by a health care provider in an institutional setting, many individuals must self-administer injections of needed medications, such as insulin, on a regular basis in their homes. Educating these patients or their care givers on how to correctly administer medication by injection is an important issue in the delivery of home health care services. Topics that must be covered include instruction on proper injection techniques, selection of needle length and gauge, identification of important anatomic landmarks in making injection site selections, and the preparation and rotation of selected injection sites.

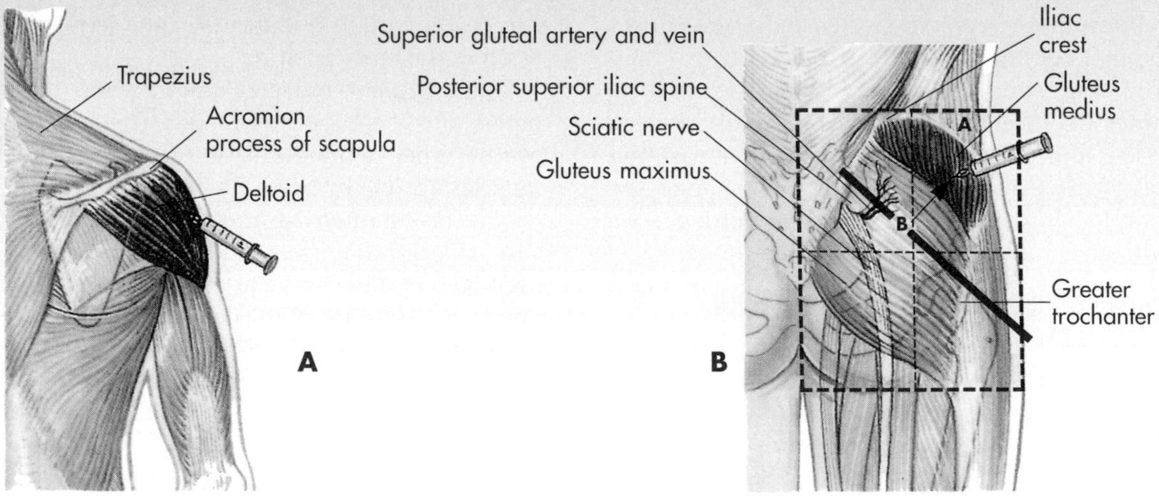

The **tibialis** (tib-ee-AL-is) **anterior** muscle (Figure 6-6) is located on the anterior or front surface of the leg. It dorsiflexes the foot. The **gastrocnemius** (gas-trok-NEE-mee-us) is the primary calf muscle. Note in Figure 6-6 that it has two fleshy components arising from both sides of the femur. It inserts through the Achilles tendon into the heel bone or calcaneus. The gastrocnemius is responsible for plantar flexion of the foot; because it is used to stand on tiptoe, it is sometimes called the *toe dancer's muscle.* A group of three muscles called the **peroneus** (pair-o-NEE-us) **group** (Figure 6-6) is found along the sides of the lower leg. As a group, these muscles plantar flex the foot. A long tendon from one component of the group—the *peroneus longus* muscle tendon—forms a support arch for the foot (see Figure 5-17).

Movements Produced by Skeletal Muscle Contractions

The types of movement that may produce a muscle contraction at any joint depend largely on the shapes of the bones involved and the joint type (see Chapter 5). Muscles acting on some joints produce movement in several directions, whereas only limited movement is possible at other joints. The terms most often used to describe body movements are:

1. **Flexion**
2. **Extension**
3. **Abduction**
4. **Adduction**
5. **Rotation**
6. **Supination** and **pronation**
7. **Dorsiflexion** and **plantar flexion**

Flexion is a movement that makes the angle between two bones at their joint smaller than it was at the beginning of the movement. Most flexions are movements commonly described as bending. If you bend your lower arm at the elbow or your lower leg at the knee, you flex the lower arm and leg. **Extension** movements are the opposite of flexions. They make the angle between two bones at their joint larger than it was at the beginning of the movement. Therefore, extensions are straightening or stretching movements rather than bending movements. Figures 6-9 and 6-10 illustrate flexion and extension of the lower arm and leg.

Abduction means moving a part away from the midline of the body, such as moving your arm out to the side. **Adduction** means moving a part toward the midline, such as bringing your arms down to your sides from an elevated position. Figure 6-11, *A,* shows abduction and adduction.

Rotation is movement around a longitudinal axis. You rotate your head by moving your skull from side to side as in shaking your head "no" (Figure 6-11, *B*).

Supination and **pronation** refer to hand positions that result from rotation of the forearm. (The term *prone* refers to the body as a whole lying face down. *Supine* means lying face up.) Supination results in a hand position with the palm turned to the anterior position (as in the anatomical position), and pronation occurs when you turn the palm of your hand so that it faces posteriorly (Figure 6-11, C).

Dorsiflexion and **plantar flexion** refer to foot movements. In dorsiflexion the dorsum or top of the foot is elevated with the toes pointing upward. In plantar flexion the bottom of the foot is directed downward so that you are in effect standing on your toes (Figure 6-11, *D*).

As you study the illustrations and learn to recognize the muscles discussed in this chapter, you should attempt to group them according to function, as in Table 6-2. You will note, for example, that flexors produce many of the movements used for walking, sitting, swimming, typing, and many other activities. Extensors also function in these activities but perhaps play their most important role in maintaining an upright posture.

FIGURE 6–9 ***Flexion and Extension of the Lower Arm.*** **A** and **B,** When the lower arm is flexed at the elbow, the biceps brachii contracts while its antagonist, the triceps brachii, relaxes. **B** and **C,** When the lower arm is extended, the biceps brachii relaxes while the triceps brachii contracts.

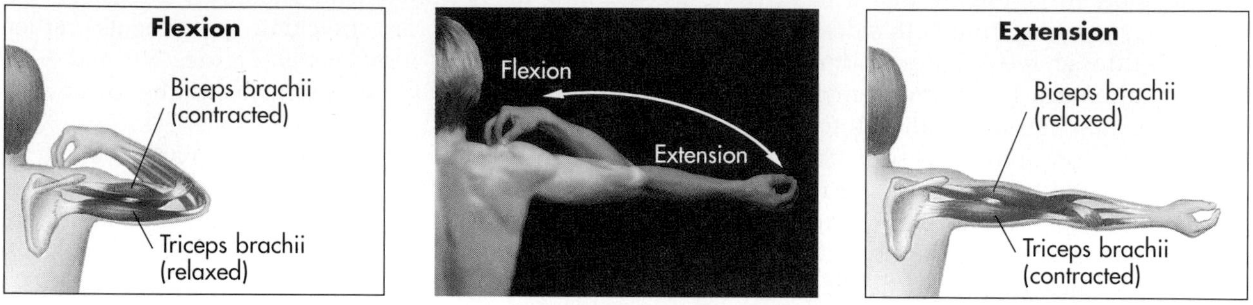

A B C

FIGURE 6–10 ***Flexion and Extension of the Lower Leg.*** **A** and **B,** When the lower leg flexes at the knee, muscles of the hamstring group contract while their antagonists in the quadriceps femoris group relax. **B** and **C,** When the lower leg extends, the hamstring muscles relax while the quadriceps femoris muscle contracts.

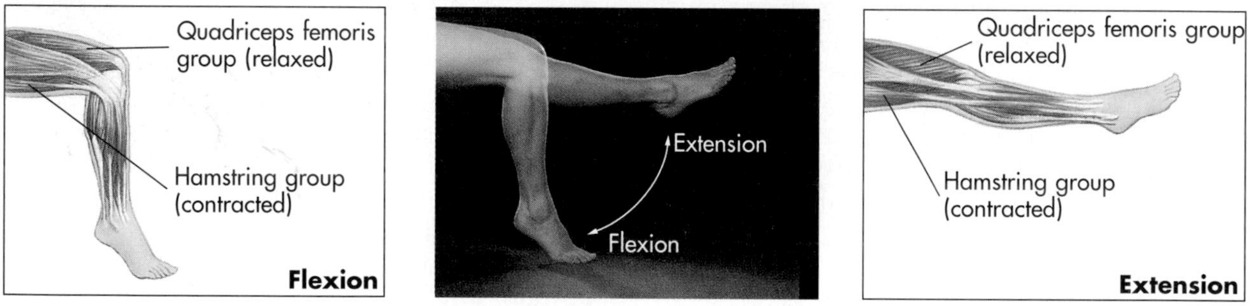

A B C

TABLE 6–2 Muscles Grouped According to Function

PART MOVED	FLEXORS	EXTENSORS	ABDUCTORS	ADDUCTORS
Upper arm	Pectoralis major	Latissimus dorsi	Deltoid	Pectoralis major and latissimus dorsi contracting together
Lower arm	Biceps brachii	Triceps brachii	None	None
Thigh	Iliopsoas and sartorius	Gluteus maximus	Gluteus medius	Adductor group
Lower leg	Hamstrings	Quadriceps group	None	None
Foot	Tibialis anterior	Gastrocnemius and soleus	Peroneus longus	Tibialis anterior

FIGURE 6–11 *Examples of Body Movements.* **A,** Adduction and abduction. **B,** Rotation. **C,** Pronation and supination. **D,** Dorsiflexion and plantar flexion.

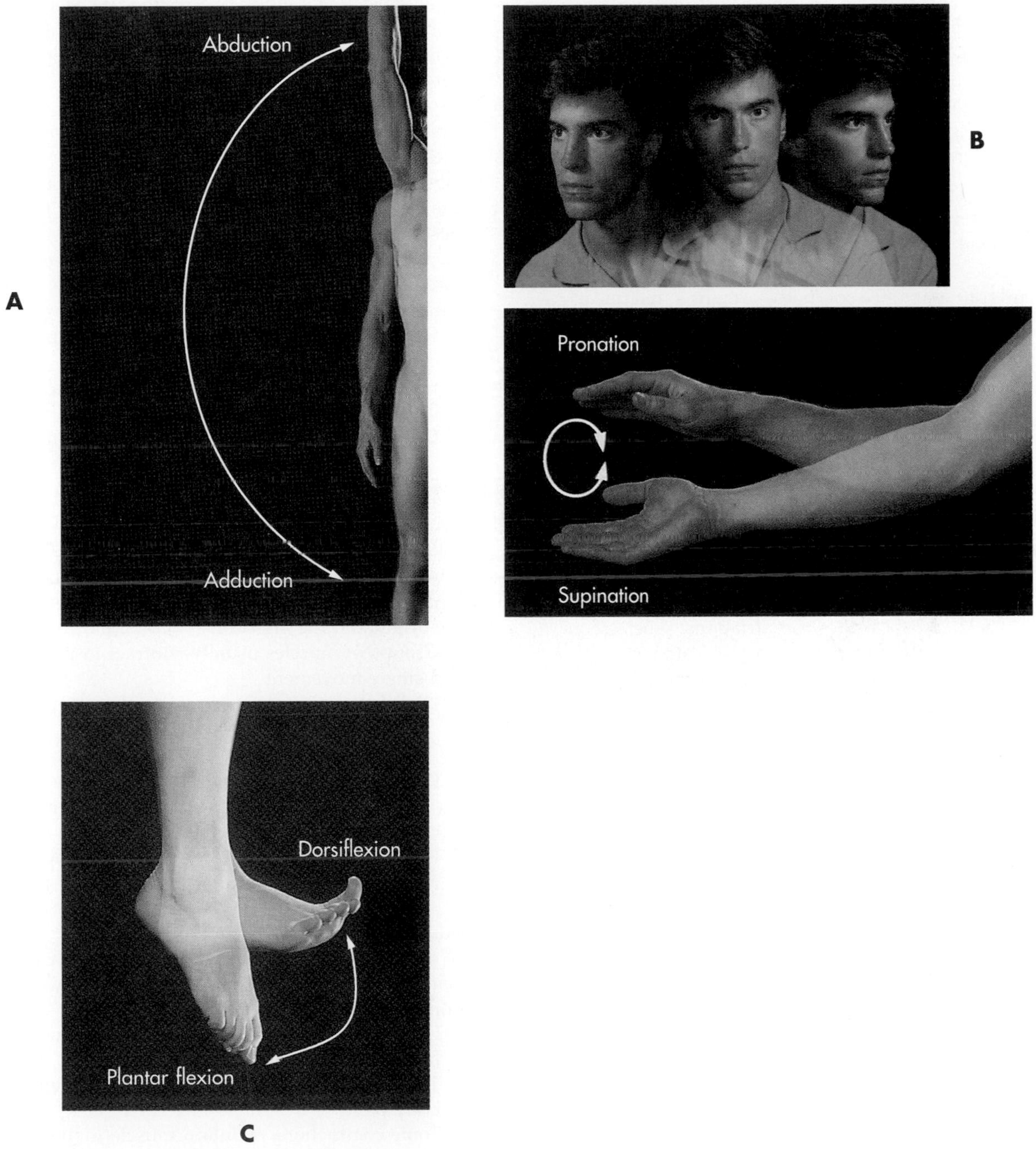

OUTLINE SUMMARY

INTRODUCTION

A Muscular tissue enables the body and its parts to move
   1 Movement caused by ability of muscle cells (called *fibers*) to shorten or contract
   2 Muscle cells shorten by converting chemical energy (obtained from food) into mechanical energy, which causes movement
   3 Three types of muscle tissue exist in body (see Chapter 2)

MUSCLE TISSUE

A Types of muscle tissue (Figure 6-1)
   1 Skeletal muscle—also called *striated* or *voluntary muscle*
      a Is 40% to 50% of body weight ("red meat" attached to bones)
      b Microscope reveals crosswise stripes or striations
      c Contractions can be voluntarily controlled
   2 Cardiac muscle—composes bulk of heart
      a Cardiac muscle cells branch frequently
      b Characterized by unique dark bands called *intercalated disks*
      c Interconnected nature of cardiac muscle cells allows heart to contract efficiently as a unit
   3 Nonstriated muscle or involuntary muscle—also called *smooth* or *visceral* muscle
      a Lacks cross stripes or striations when seen under a microscope; appears smooth
      b Found in walls of hollow visceral structures such as digestive tract, blood vessels, and ureters
      c Contractions not under voluntary control; movement caused by contraction is involuntary

B Function—all muscle cells specialize in contraction (shortening)

STRUCTURE OF SKELETAL MUSCLE

A Structure
   1 Each skeletal muscle is an organ composed mainly of skeletal muscle cells and connective tissue
   2 Most skeletal muscles extend from one bone across a joint to another bone
   3 Parts of a skeletal muscle
      a Origin—attachment to the bone that remains relatively stationary or fixed when movement at the joint occurs
      b Insertion—point of attachment to the bone that moves when a muscle contracts
      c Body—main part of the muscle
   4 Muscles attach to bone by tendons—strong cords of fibrous connective tissue; some tendons enclosed in synovial-lined tubes and are lubricated by synovial fluid; tubes called *tendon sheaths*
   5 Bursae—small synovial-lined sacs containing a small amount of synovial fluid; located between some tendons and underlying bones

B Microscopic structure (Figure 6-3)
   1 Contractile cells called *fibers*—grouped into bundles
   2 Fibers contain thick myofilaments (containing protein myosin) and thin myofilaments (composed of actin)
   3 Basic functional (contractile) unit called *sarcomere;* sarcomeres separated from each other by dark bands called *Z lines*
      a Sliding filament model explains mechanism of contraction
         (1) Thick and thin myofilaments slide past each other as a muscle contracts
         (2) Contraction requires calcium and energy-rich ATP molecules

FUNCTIONS OF SKELETAL MUSCLE

A Movement
   1 Muscles produce movement; as a muscle contracts, it pulls the insertion bone closer to the origin bone; movement occurs at the joint between the origin and the insertion
      a Groups of muscles usually contract to produce a single movement
         (1) Prime mover—muscle whose contraction is mainly responsible for producing a given movement
         (2) Synergist—muscle whose contractions help the prime mover produce a given movement
         (3) Antagonist—muscle whose actions oppose the action of a prime mover in any given movement

B Posture
   1 A specialized type of muscle contraction, called *tonic contraction,* enables us to maintain body position
      a In tonic contraction, only a few of a muscle's fibers shorten at one time
      b Tonic contractions produce no movement of body parts
      c Tonic contractions maintain muscle tone called *posture*

(1) Good posture reduces strain on muscles, tendons, ligaments, and bones
(2) Poor posture causes fatigue and may lead to deformity

C Heat production
1 Survival depends on the body's ability to maintain a constant body temperature
a Fever—an elevated body temperature—often a sign of illness
b Hypothermia—a reduced body temperature
2 Contraction of muscle fibers produces most of the heat required to maintain normal body temperature

FATIGUE

A Reduced strength of muscle contraction
B Caused by repeated muscle stimulation without adequate periods of rest
C Repeated muscular contraction depletes cellular ATP stores and outstrips the ability of the blood supply to replenish oxygen and nutrients
D Contraction in the absence of adequate oxygen produces lactic acid, which contributes to muscle soreness
E *Oxygen debt*—term used to describe the metabolic effort required to burn excess lactic acid that may accumulate during prolonged periods of exercise; the body is attempting to return the cells' energy and oxygen reserves to pre-exercise levels

ROLE OF OTHER BODY SYSTEMS IN MOVEMENT

A Muscle functioning depends on the functioning of many other parts of the body
1 Most muscles cause movements by pulling on bones across movable joints
2 Respiratory, circulatory, nervous, muscular, and skeletal systems play essential roles in producing normal movements
3 Multiple sclerosis, brain hemorrhage, and spinal cord injury are examples of how pathological conditions in other body organ systems can dramatically affect movement

MOTOR UNIT (Figure 6-4)

A Stimulation of a muscle by a nerve impulse is required before a muscle can shorten and produce movement
B A motor neuron is the specialized nerve that transmits an impulse to a muscle, causing contraction
C A neuromuscular junction is the specialized point of contact between a nerve ending and the muscle fiber it innervates
D A motor unit is the combination of a motor neuron with the muscle cell or cells it innervates

MUSCLE STIMULUS

A A muscle will contract only if an applied stimulus reaches a certain level of intensity
1 A threshold stimulus is the minimal level of stimulation required to cause a muscle fiber to contract
B Once stimulated by a threshold stimulus, a muscle fiber will contract completely, a response called *all or none*
C Different muscle fibers in a muscle are controlled by different motor units having different threshold-stimulus levels
1 Although individual muscle fibers always respond all or none to a threshold stimulus, the muscle as a whole does not
2 Different motor units responding to different threshold stimuli permit a muscle as a whole to execute contractions of graded force

TYPES OF SKELETAL MUSCLE CONTRACTION

A Twitch and tetanic contractions
1 Twitch contractions are laboratory phenomena and do not play a significant role in normal muscular activity; they are a single contraction of muscle fibers caused by a single threshold stimulus
2 Tetanic contractions are sustained and steady muscular contractions caused by a series of stimuli bombarding a muscle in rapid succession
B Isotonic contractions
1 Contraction of a muscle that produces movement at a joint
2 During isotonic contractions, the muscle shortens, causing the insertion end of the muscle to move toward the point of origin
3 Most types of body movements such as walking and running are caused by isotonic contractions
C Isometric contractions
1 Isometric contractions are muscle contractions that do not produce movement; the muscle as a whole does not shorten
2 Although no movement occurs during isometric contractions, tension within the muscle increases

EFFECTS OF EXERCISE ON SKELETAL MUSCLES

A Exercise, if regular and properly practiced, improves muscle tone and posture, results in more efficient heart and lung functioning, and reduces fatigue
B Effects of exercise on skeletal muscles
1 Muscles undergo changes related to the amount of work they normally do
a Prolonged inactivity causes disuse atrophy
b Regular exercise increases muscle size, called *hypertrophy*

2 Strength training is exercise involving contraction of muscles against heavy resistance
  a Strength training increases the numbers of myofilaments in each muscle fiber, and as a result, the total mass of the muscle increases
  b Strength training does not increase the number of muscle fibers
3 Endurance training is exercise that increases a muscle's ability to sustain moderate exercise over a long period; it is sometimes called *aerobic training*
  a Endurance training allows more efficient delivery of oxygen and nutrients to a muscle via increased blood flow
  b Endurance training does not usually result in muscle hypertrophy

SKELETAL MUSCLE GROUPS (Table 6-1)

A Muscles of the head and neck (Figure 6-7)
  1 Facial muscles
    a Orbicularis oculi
    b Orbicularis oris
    c Zygomaticus
  2 Muscles of mastication
    a Masseter
    b Temporal
  3 Sternocleidomastoid—flexes head
  4 Trapezius—elevates shoulders and extends head
B Muscles that move the upper extremities
  1 Pectoralis major—flexes upper arm
  2 Latissimus dorsi—extends upper arm
  3 Deltoid—abducts upper arm
  4 Biceps brachii—flexes forearm
  5 Triceps brachii—extends forearm
C Muscles of the trunk (Figure 6-8)
  1 Abdominal muscles
    a Rectus abdominis
    b External oblique
    c Internal oblique
    d Transversus abdominis
  2 Respiratory muscles
    a Intercostal muscles
    b Diaphragm
D Muscles that move the lower extremities
  1 Iliopsoas—flexes thigh
  2 Gluteus maximus—extends thigh
  3 Adductor muscles—adduct thighs
  4 Hamstring muscles—flex lower leg
    a Semimembranosus
    b Semitendinosus
    c Biceps femoris
  5 Quadriceps femoris group—extend lower leg
    a Rectus femoris
    b Vastus muscles
  6 Tibialis anterior—dorsiflexes foot
  7 Gastrocnemius—plantar flexes foot
  8 Peroneus group—flex foot

TYPES OF MOVEMENTS PRODUCED BY SKELETAL MUSCLE CONTRACTIONS

(Figures 6-9 through 6-11)

A Flexion—movement that decreases the angle between two bones at their joint: bending
B Extension—movement that increases the angle between two bones at their joint: straightening
C Abduction—movement of a part away from the midline of the body
D Adduction—movement of a part toward the midline of the body
E Rotation—movement around a longitudinal axis
F Supination and pronation—hand positions that result from rotation of the forearm; supination results in a hand position with the palm turned to the anterior position; pronation occurs when the palm faces posteriorly
G Dorsiflexion and plantar flexion—foot movements; dorsiflexion results in elevation of the dorsum or top of the foot; during plantar flexion, the bottom of the foot is directed downward

NEW WORDS

abduction
actin
adduction
all or none
antagonist
atrophy
bursa
dorsiflexion
extension
fatigue
flexion
hypertrophy
hypothermia
insertion
isometric
isotonic
motor neuron
motor unit
myofilaments
myosin
neuromuscular junction
origin
oxygen debt
paralysis
plantar flexion
posture
prime mover
pronation
rotation
sarcomere
sliding filament theory
stimulus
supination
synergist
tendon
tenosynovitis
tetanic contraction
tonic contraction

CHAPTER TEST

1. Cardiac muscle:
   - **a.** Cells have no nuclei
   - **b.** Is composed of cells that branch frequently
   - **c.** Lines many hollow internal organs
   - **d.** All of the above are correct
2. The term *origin* refers to:
   - **a.** The attachment of a muscle to a bone that does not move when contraction occurs
   - **b.** Attachment of a muscle to a bone that moves when contraction occurs
   - **c.** The body of a muscle
   - **d.** None of the above are correct
3. A sarcomere:
   - **a.** Is the basic functional or contractile unit of skeletal muscle
   - **b.** Contains only actin myofilaments
   - **c.** Contains only myosin myofilaments
   - **d.** Is found only in smooth or involuntary muscle
4. The muscle mainly responsible for producing a particular movement is called a:
   - **a.** Synergist
   - **b.** Prime mover
   - **c.** Antagonist
   - **d.** Fixator
5. A motor unit consists of:
   - **a.** Only a motor neuron
   - **b.** A motor neuron and the muscle cells it innervates
   - **c.** Only contracting muscle cells
   - **d.** None of the above are correct
6. Which of the following types of muscle contraction does not produce movement?
   - **a.** Isotonic contraction
   - **b.** Tetanic contraction
   - **c.** Twitch contraction
   - **d.** Isometric contraction
7. Which of the following terms refers to moving a part away from the midline of the body?
   - **a.** Abduction
   - **b.** Adduction
   - **c.** Supination
   - **d.** Flexion

8. Many hollow internal organs and blood vessel walls contain _____________ muscle.
9. Muscles are anchored firmly to bones by _____________.
10. Thick myofilaments are formed from a protein called _____________.
11. The explanation of muscle contraction resulting from movement of thick and thin myofibrils toward one another is called the _____________ theory.
12. The muscles that assist prime movers in producing a particular movement are called _____________.
13. Skeletal muscle tone maintains _____________ by counteracting the pull of gravity.
14. Depletion of oxygen in a muscle during vigorous and prolonged exercise is called _____________.
15. Walking and running are examples of _____________ muscle contraction.
16. Standing on your toes is an example of _____________ flexion.
17. The term _____________ is used to describe shrinkage or decrease in the size of a muscle.
18. The major flexor muscles of the lower leg are the _____________.

Select the most correct answer from Column B for each statement in Column A. (Only one answer is correct.)

COLUMN A	COLUMN B
19. _____ Contractile unit of muscle	a. Biceps brachii
20. _____ Flexes lower arm	b. Masseter
21. _____ Extends lower leg	c. Sarcomere
22. _____ Closes jaw	d. Quadriceps group
23. _____ Movable point of attachment	e. Pectoralis major
24. _____ Flexes upper arm	f. Gluteus maximus
25. _____ Extends thigh	g. Insertion

REVIEW QUESTIONS

1. Compare the three kinds of muscle tissue regarding location, microscopic appearance, and nerve control.
2. Explain flexion, extension, abduction, and adduction; give an example of each.
3. Explain how skeletal muscles, bones, and joints work together to produce movements.
4. What two kinds of muscle contractions do not produce movement?
5. What is the name of the main muscle or muscles that
   - **a.** Flex the upper arm?
   - **b.** Flex the lower leg?
   - **c.** Extend the lower arm?
   - **d.** Extend the thigh?
   - **e.** Abduct the upper arm?
   - **f.** Elevate the mandible?
   - **g.** Flex the spinal column?
   - **h.** Dorsiflex the foot?
6. Give the approximate location of the biceps brachii, hamstrings, deltoid, pectoralis major, quadriceps femoris group, latissimus dorsi, trapezius, rectus abdominis, and gastrocnemius; tell what movement each produces.
7. What is meant by the term *tetanus?*
8. Discuss the microscopic structure of skeletal muscle tissue.
9. Explain good posture, hypertrophy, sarcomere, muscle tone, isometric contractions, isotonic contractions, tonic contractions, tetanus, threshold, and all or none.

CRITICAL THINKING

10. Why can a spinal cord injury be followed by muscle paralysis?
11. Can a muscle contract very long if its blood supply is shut off? Give a reason for your answer.
12. Briefly describe changes that gradually take place in bones, joints, and muscles if a person habitually gets too little exercise.

The Nervous System

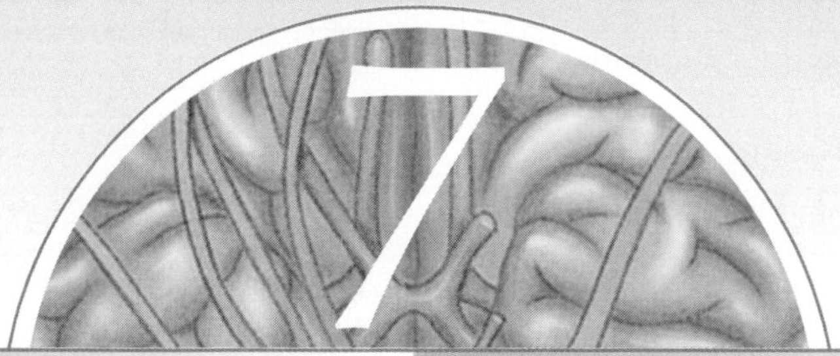

OUTLINE

Organs and Divisions of the Nervous System

Cells of the Nervous System
- Neurons
- Glia

Nerves

Reflex Arcs

Nerve Impulses

The Synapse

Central Nervous System
- Divisions of the Brain
- Spinal Cord
- Coverings and Fluid Spaces of the Brain and Spinal Cord

Peripheral Nervous System
- Cranial Nerves
- Spinal Nerves

Autonomic Nervous System
- Functional Anatomy
- Autonomic Conduction Paths
- Sympathetic Nervous System
- Parasympathetic Nervous System
- Autonomic Neurotransmitters
- Autonomic Nervous System as a Whole

BOXED ESSAYS

Multiple Sclerosis (MS)
Suppressing Pain During Exercise
Lumbar Puncture
Herpes Zoster or Shingles

OBJECTIVES

After you have completed this chapter, you should be able to:

1. List the organs and divisions of the nervous system and describe the generalized functions of the system as a whole.
2. Identify the major types of cells in the nervous system and discuss the function of each.
3. Identify the anatomical and functional components of a three-neuron reflex arc. Compare and contrast the propagation of a nerve impulse along a nerve fiber and across a synaptic cleft.
4. Identify the major anatomical components of the brain and spinal cord and briefly comment on the function of each.
5. Compare and contrast spinal and cranial nerves.
6. Discuss the anatomical and functional characteristics of the two divisions of the autonomic nervous system.

The normal body must accomplish a gigantic and enormously complex job—keeping itself alive and healthy. Each one of its billions of cells performs some activity that is a part of this function. Control of the body's billions of cells is accomplished mainly by two communication systems: the nervous system and the endocrine system. Both systems transmit information from one part of the body to another, but they do it in different ways. The nervous system transmits information very rapidly by nerve impulses conducted from one body area to another. The endocrine system transmits information more slowly by chemicals secreted by ductless glands into the bloodstream and circulated from the glands to other parts of the body. Nerve impulses and hormones communicate information to body structures, increasing or decreasing their activities as needed for healthy survival. In other words, the communication systems of the body are also its control and integrating systems. They weld the body's hundreds of functions into its one overall function of keeping itself alive and healthy.

Recall that homeostasis is the balanced and controlled internal environment of the body that is basic to life itself. Homeostasis is possible only if our physiological control and integration systems function properly. Our plan for this chapter is to name the cells, organs, and divisions of the nervous system; discuss the generation of nervous impulses; and then discover how these impulses move between one area of the body and another. We will study not only the major components of the nervous system, such as the brain, spinal cord, and nerves, but also learn about how they function to maintain and regulate homeostasis. In Chapter 8, we will consider the special senses.

Organs and Divisions of the Nervous System

The organs of the nervous system as a whole include the brain and spinal cord, the numerous nerves of the body, the specialized sense organs such as the eyes and ears, and the microscopic sense organs such as those found in the skin. The system as a whole consists of two principal divisions called the central nervous system and the peripheral nervous system (Figure 7-1). Because the brain and spinal cord occupy a midline or central location in the body, they are together called the **central nervous system** or **CNS.** Similarly, the usual designation for the nerves of the body is the **peripheral nervous system** or **PNS.** Use of the term *peripheral* is appropriate because nerves extend to outlying or peripheral parts of the body. A subdivision of the peripheral nervous system, called the **autonomic nervous system** or **ANS,** consists of structures that regulate the body's automatic or involuntary functions (for example, the heart rate, the contractions of the stomach and intestines, and the secretion of chemical compounds by glands).

Cells of the Nervous System

The two types of cells found in the nervous system are called **neurons** (NOO-rons) or nerve cells and **glia** (GLEE-ah), which are specialized connective tissue cells. Neurons conduct impulses, whereas glia support neurons.

NEURONS

Each neuron consists of three parts: a main part called the neuron **cell body,** one or more branching projections called **dendrites** (DEN-drites), and one elongated projection known as an **axon.** Identify each part on the neuron shown in Figure 7-2. Dendrites are the processes or projections that transmit impulses to the neuron cell bodies or axons, and axons are the processes that transmit impulses away from the neuron cell bodies or dendrites.

The three types of neurons are classified according to the direction in which they transmit impulses: **sensory neurons, motor neurons,** and **interneurons.** Sensory neurons transmit impulses to the spinal cord and brain from all parts of the body. Motor neurons transmit impulses in the opposite direction—away from the brain and spinal cord. They do not conduct impulses to all parts of the body but only to two kinds of tissue—muscle and glandular epithelial tissue. Interneurons conduct impulses from sensory neurons to motor neurons. Sensory neurons are also called *afferent* neurons; motor neurons are called *efferent* neurons, and interneurons are called *central* or *connecting* neurons.

FIGURE 7–1 *Divisions of the Nervous System.*

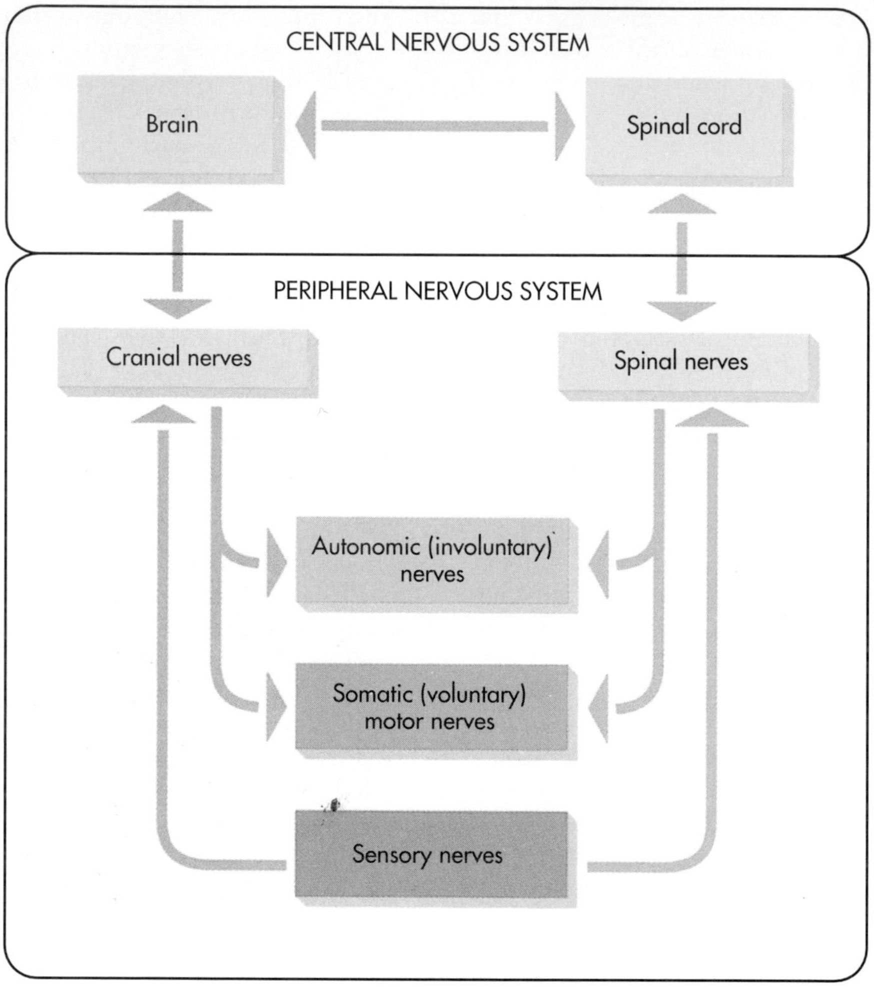

The axon shown in Figure 7-2, *B*, is surrounded by a segmented wrapping of a material called **myelin** (MY-e-lin). Myelin is a white, fatty substance formed by **Schwann cells** that wrap around some axons outside the central nervous system. Such fibers are called **myelinated fibers.** In Figure 7-2, *B*, one such axon has been enlarged to show additional detail. **Nodes of Ranvier** (rahn-vee-AY) are indentations between adjacent Schwann cells.

The outer cell membrane of a Schwann cell is called the **neurilemma** (noo-ri-LEM-mah). The fact that axons in the brain and cord have no neurilemma is clinically significant because it plays an essential part in the regeneration of cut and injured axons. Therefore the potential for regeneration in the brain and spinal cord is far less than it is in the peripheral nervous system.

GLIA

Glia—or *neuroglia* (noo-ROG-lee-ah)—do not specialize in transmitting impulses. Instead, they are special types of connective tissue cells. Their name is appropriate because it is derived from the Greek word *glia* meaning "glue." One function of glia cells is to hold the functioning neurons

FIGURE 7–2 ***Neuron.*** **A,** Diagram of a typical neuron showing dendrites, a cell body, and an axon. **B,** Segment of a myelinated axon cut to show detail of the concentric layers of the Schwann cell filled with myelin. **C,** Photomicrograph of neuron.

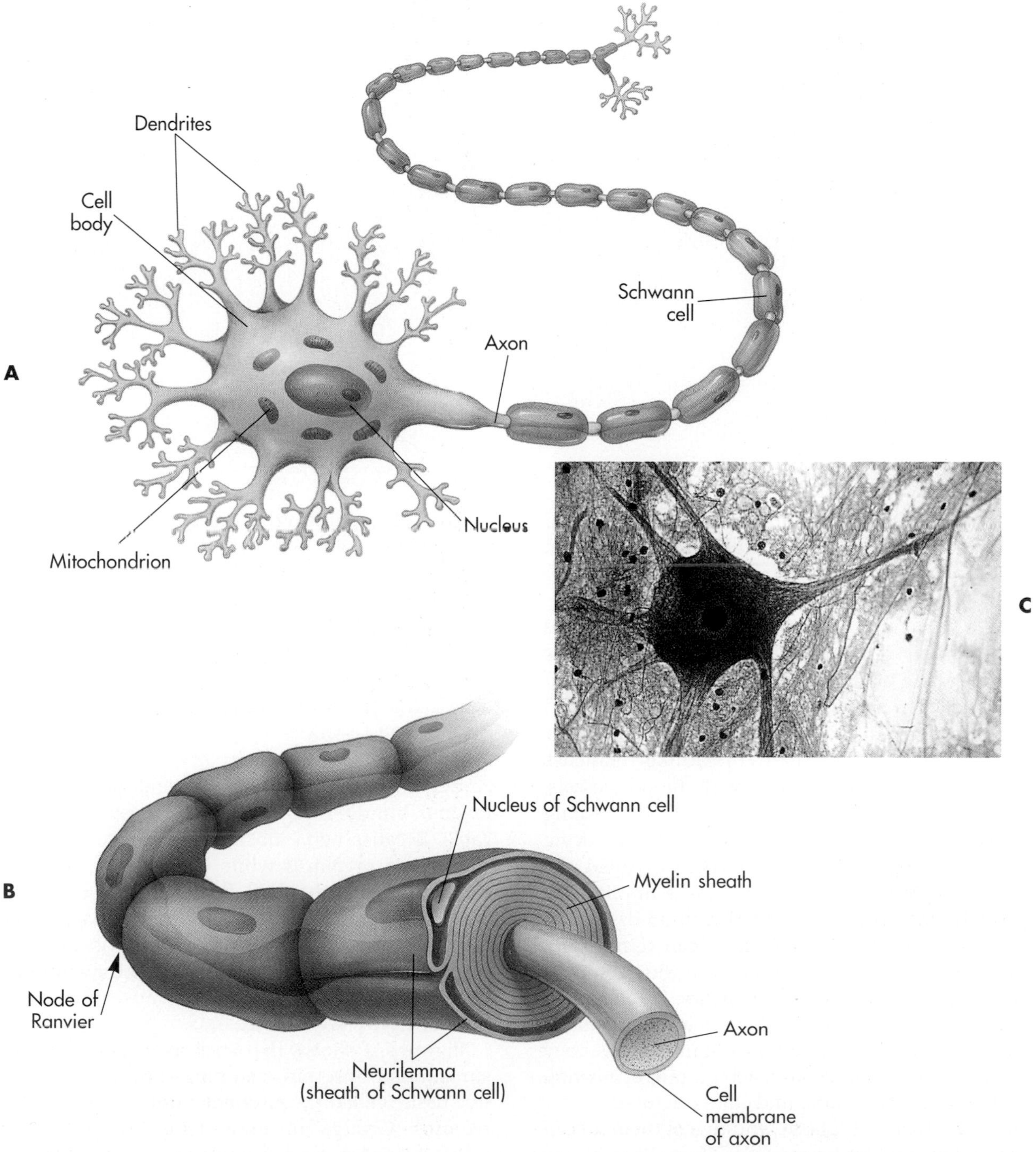

FIGURE 7–3 *Glia.* **A,** Astrocytes have extensions attached to blood vessels in the brain. **B,** Microglia within the central nervous system can enlarge and consume microbes by phagocytosis. **C,** Oligodendroglia have extensions that form myelin sheaths around axons in the central nervous system.

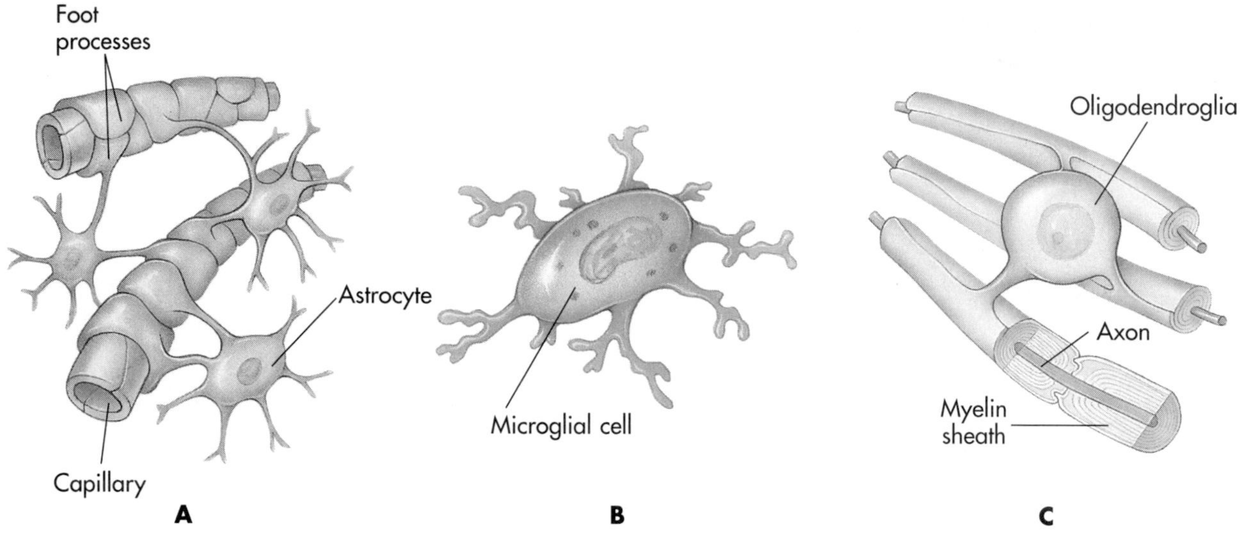

together and protect them. An important reason for discussing glia is that one of the most common types of brain tumor—called **glioma** (glee-O-mah)—develops from them.

Glia vary in size and shape (Figure 7-3). Some are relatively large cells that look somewhat like stars because of the threadlike extensions that jut out from their surfaces. These glia cells are called **astrocytes** (AS-tro-sites), a word that means "star cells" (Figure 7-3). Their threadlike branches attach to neurons and to small blood vessels, holding these structures close to each other. Along with the walls of the blood vessels, astrocyte branches form a two-layer structure called the *blood-brain barrier (BBB).* As its name implies, the blood-brain barrier separates the blood tissue and nervous tissue to protect vital brain tissue from harmful chemicals that might be in the blood.

Microglia (my-KROG-lee-ah) are smaller than astrocytes. They usually remain stationary, but in inflamed or degenerating brain tissue, they enlarge, move about, and act as microbe-eating scavengers. They surround the microbes, draw them into their cytoplasm, and digest them. Recall from Chapter 2 that phagocytosis is the scientific name for this important cellular process.

The **oligodendroglia** (ol-i-go-den-DROG-lee-ah) help to hold nerve fibers together and also serve another and probably more important function; they produce the fatty myelin sheath that envelops nerve fibers located in the brain and spinal cord.

Nerves

A **nerve** is a group of peripheral nerve fibers (axons) bundled together like the strands of a cable. Because nerve fibers usually have a myelin sheath and myelin is white, nerves are called the **white matter** of the PNS. Bundles of axons in the CNS, called **tracts,** may also be myelinated and thus form this system's white matter. Tissue comprised of cell bodies and unmyelinated axons and dendrites is called **gray matter** because of its characteristic gray appearance.

Figure 7-4 shows that each axon in a nerve is surrounded by a thin wrapping of fibrous connective tissue called the **endoneurium** (en-doe-NOO-ree-um). Groups of these wrapped axons are called **fascicles.** Each fascicle is surrounded by a thin, fibrous **perineurium** (pair-i-NOO-ree-um). A

FIGURE 7–4 ***The Nerve.*** Each nerve contains axons bundled into fascicles. A connective tissue epineurium wraps the entire nerve. Perineurium surrounds each fascicle. Inset shows a scanning electron micrograph of a cross section of a nerve. From Kessel RG, Kardong RH: Tissues and organs: A text-atlas of scanning electron microscopy, WH Freeman, 1979.

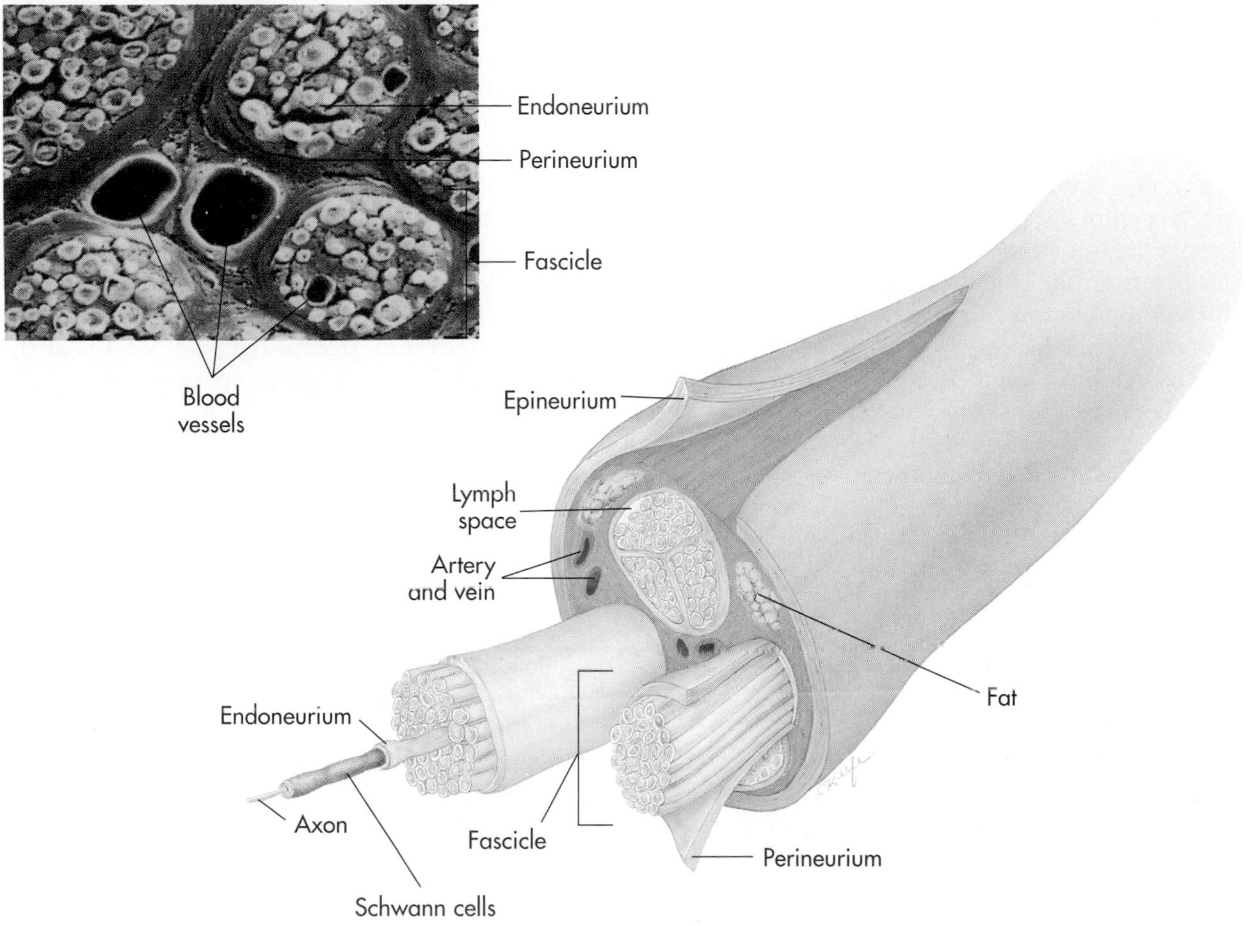

tough, fibrous sheath called the **epineurium** (ep-i-NOO-ree-um) covers the whole nerve.

Reflex Arcs

During every moment of our lives, nerve impulses speed over neurons to and from our spinal cords and brains. If all impulse conduction ceases, life itself ceases. Only neurons can provide the rapid communication between cells that is necessary for maintaining life. Hormonal messages are the only other kind of communications the body can send, and they travel much more slowly than impulses. They can move from one part of the body to another only via circulating blood. Compared with impulse conduction, circulation is a very slow process.

Nerve impulses, sometimes called *action potentials,* can travel over trillions of routes—routes made up of neurons because they are the cells that conduct impulses. Hence the routes traveled by nerve impulses are sometimes spoken of as *neuron pathways.* A specialized type of neuron pathway, called a **reflex arc,** is important to nervous system functioning. The simplest kind of reflex arc is a two-neuron arc, so called because it consists of only two types of neurons: sensory neurons and motor neurons. Three-neuron arcs are the next simplest kind. They, of course, consist of all three kinds of neurons: sensory neurons, interneurons, and motor neurons. Reflex arcs are like one-way streets; they allow impulse conduction in only one direction. The next paragraph describes this direction in detail. Look frequently at Figure 7-5 as you read it.

Impulse conduction normally starts in receptors. **Receptors** are the beginnings of dendrites of sensory neurons. They are often located at some distance from the spinal cord (in tendons, skin, or mucous membranes, for example). In Figure 7-5 the sensory receptors are located in the quadriceps muscle group and in the patellar tendon. In the reflex that is illustrated there, stretch receptors are stimulated as a result of a tap on the patellar tendon from a rubber hammer used by a physician to elicit a reflex during a physical examination. The nerve impulse that is generated, its neurologic pathway, and its ultimate "knee-jerk" effect is an example of the simplest form of a two-neuron reflex arc. In this reflex, only sensory and motor neurons are involved. The nerve impulse that is generated by stimulation of the stretch receptors travels along the length of the sensory neuron's dendrite to its cell body located in the **posterior (dorsal) root ganglion** (GANG-lee-on). A **ganglion** is a group of nerve-cell bodies located in the PNS. This ganglion is located near the spinal cord. Each spinal ganglion contains not one sensory neuron cell body as shown in Figure 7-5 but hundreds of them. The axon of the sensory neuron travels from the cell body in the dorsal root ganglion and ends near the dendrites of another neuron located in the gray matter of the spinal cord. A microscopic space separates the axon ending of one neuron from the dendrites of another neuron. This space is called a **synapse.** The nerve impulse stops at the synapse, chemical signals are sent across the gap, and the impulse then continues along the dendrites, cell body, and

FIGURE 7–5 ***Patellar Reflex.*** The neural pathway involved in the patellar ("knee-jerk") reflex.

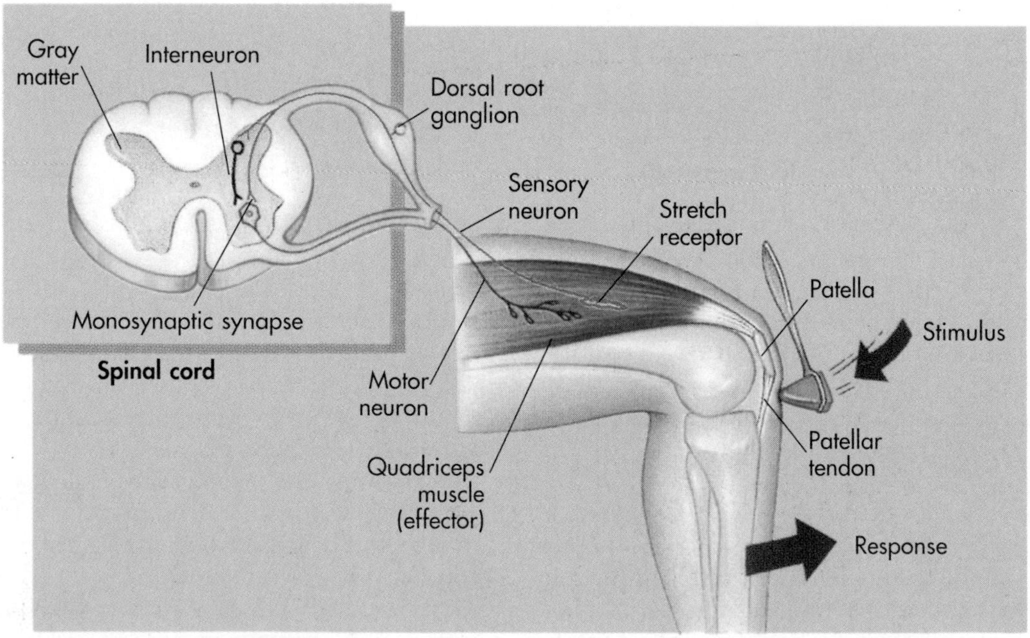

Multiple Sclerosis (MS)

Many diseases are associated with disorders of the oligodendroglia. Because these glia cells are involved in myelin formation, these diseases are called **myelin disorders.** The most common primary disease of the CNS is a myelin disorder called **multiple sclerosis** or **MS.** It is characterized by myelin loss and destruction accompanied by varying degrees of oligodendroglial cell injury and death. The result is demyelination of the white matter of the CNS. Hard, plaquelike lesions replace the destroyed myelin, and affected areas are invaded by inflammatory cells. As the myelin around axons is lost, nerve conduction is impaired, and weakness, incoordination, visual impairment, and speech disturbances occur. Although the disease occurs in both sexes and all age groups, it is most common in women between 20 and 40 years.

The cause may be related to autoimmunity and viral infections in some individuals. It is relapsing and chronic in nature, but some cases of acute and unremitting disease have been reported. In most cases, MS is prolonged, with remissions and relapses occurring over many years. There is no known cure.

axon of the motor neuron. The motor neuron axon forms a synapse with a structure called an *effector,* an organ that puts nerve signals "into effect."

Effectors are muscles or glands, and muscle contractions and gland secretion are the only kinds of reflexes. The response to impulse conduction over a reflex arc is called a **reflex.** In short, impulse conduction by a reflex arc causes a reflex to occur. In a patellar reflex, the nerve impulses that reach the quadriceps muscle (the effector) result in the "knee-jerk" response.

Now turn your attention to the *interneuron* shown in Figure 7-5. Some reflexes involve three rather than two neurons. In these more complex types of responses, an interneuron, in addition to a sensory and motor neuron, is involved. In three-neuron reflexes, the end of the sensory neuron's axon synapses first with an interneuron before chemical signals are sent across a second synapse, resulting in conduction through the motor neuron. For example, application of an irritating stimulus to the skin of the thigh initiates a three-neuron reflex response that causes contraction of muscles to pull the leg away from the irritant—a three-neuron arc reaction called the *withdrawal reflex.* All interneurons lie entirely within the gray matter of the brain or spinal cord. Gray matter forms the H-shaped inner core of the spinal cord. Because of the presence of an interneuron, three-neuron reflex arcs have two synapses. A two-neuron reflex arc, however, has only a sensory neuron and a motor neuron with one synapse between them.

Identify the motor neuron in Figure 7-5. Observe that its dendrites and cell body, like those of an interneuron, are located in the spinal cord's gray matter. The axon of this motor neuron, however, runs through the anterior (ventral) root of the spinal nerve and terminates in a muscle.

Nerve Impulses

What are nerve impulses? Here is one widely accepted definition: a nerve impulse is a self-propagating wave of electrical disturbance that travels along the surface of a neuron's plasma membrane. You might visualize this as a tiny spark sizzling its way along a fuse. Nerve impulses do not continually race along every nerve cell's surface. First they have to be initiated by a stimulus, a change in the neuron's environment. Pressure, temperature, and chemical changes are the usual stimuli. The membrane of

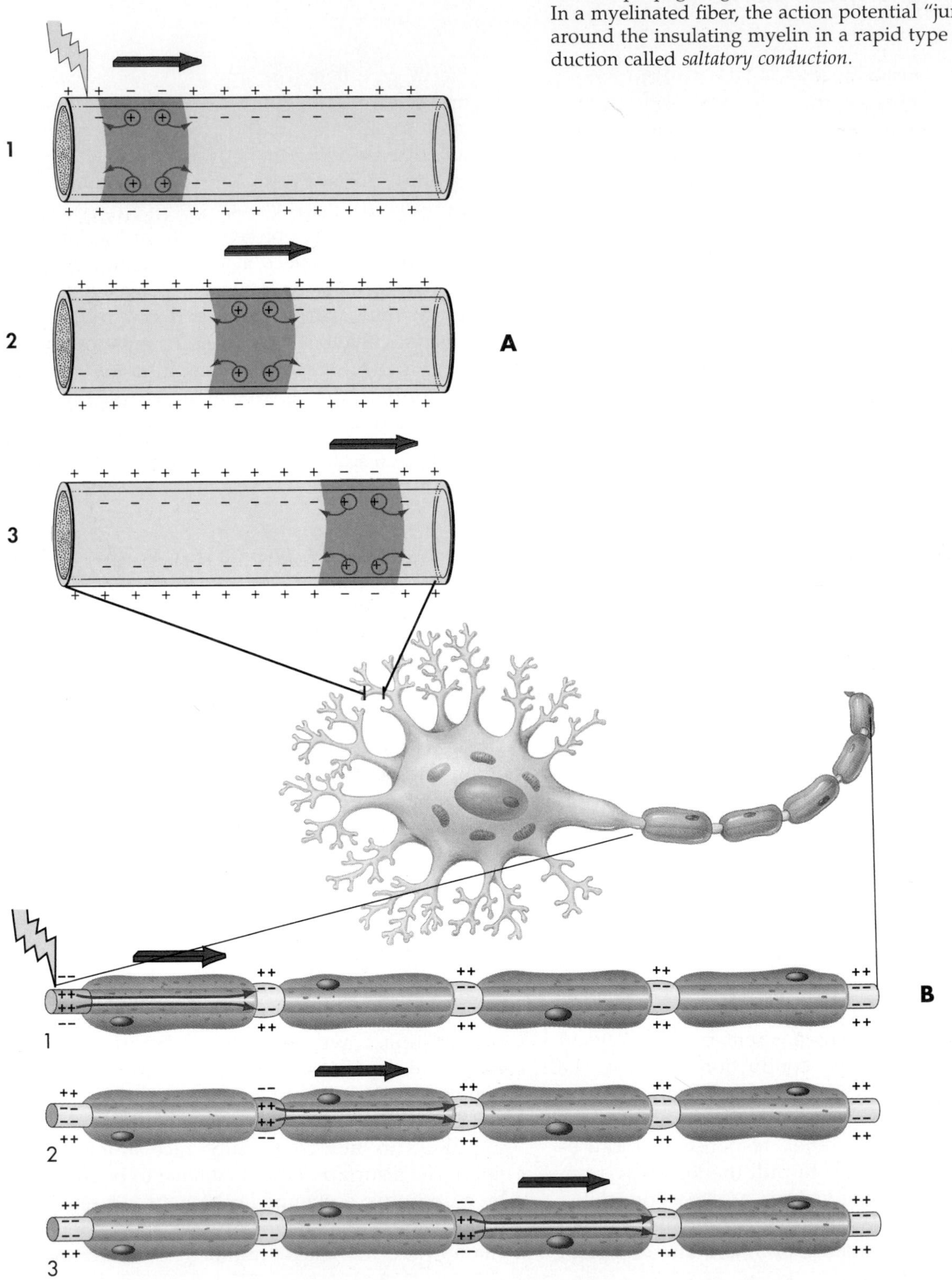

FIGURE 7–6 ***Conduction of Nerve Impulses.*** **A,** In an unmyelinated fiber, a nerve impulse (action potential) is a self-propagating wave of electrical disturbance. **B,** In a myelinated fiber, the action potential "jumps" around the insulating myelin in a rapid type of conduction called *saltatory conduction.*

each resting neuron has a slight positive charge on the outside and a negative charge on the inside, as shown in Figure 7-6. This occurs because there is normally an excess of sodium ions (Na^+) on the outside of the membrane. When a section of the membrane is stimulated, its Na^+ channels suddenly open, and Na^+ rushes inward. The inside of the membrane temporarily becomes positive, and the outside becomes negative. Although this section of the membrane immediately recovers, the electrical disturbance stimulates Na^+ channels in the next section of the membrane to open. Thus a self-propagating wave of disturbance—a nerve impulse—travels in one direction across the neuron's surface (Figure 7-6, *A*). If the traveling impulse encounters a section of membrane covered with insulating myelin, it simply "jumps" around the myelin. Called **saltatory conduction,** this type of impulse travel is much faster than is possible in nonmyelinated sections. Saltatory conduction is illustrated in Figure 7-6, *B*.

The Synapse

Transmission of signals from one neuron to the next—across the synapse—is an important part of the nerve conduction process. By definition, a synapse is the place where impulses are transmitted from one neuron, called the **presynaptic neuron,** to another neuron, called the **postsynaptic neuron.** Three structures make up a synapse: a synaptic knob, a synaptic cleft, and the plasma membrane of a postsynaptic neuron. A **synaptic knob** is a tiny bulge at the end of a terminal branch of a presynaptic neuron's axon (Figure 7-7). Each synaptic knob contains many small sacs or vesi-

FIGURE 7–7 *Components of a Synapse.* Diagram shows synaptic knob or axon terminal of presynaptic neuron, the plasma membrane of a postsynaptic neuron, and a synaptic cleft. On the arrival of an action potential at a synaptic knob, neurotransmitter molecules are released from vesicles in the knob into the synaptic cleft. The combining of neurotransmitter and receptor molecules in the plasma membrane of the postsynaptic neuron opens ion channels and thereby initiates impulse conduction in the postsynaptic neuron.

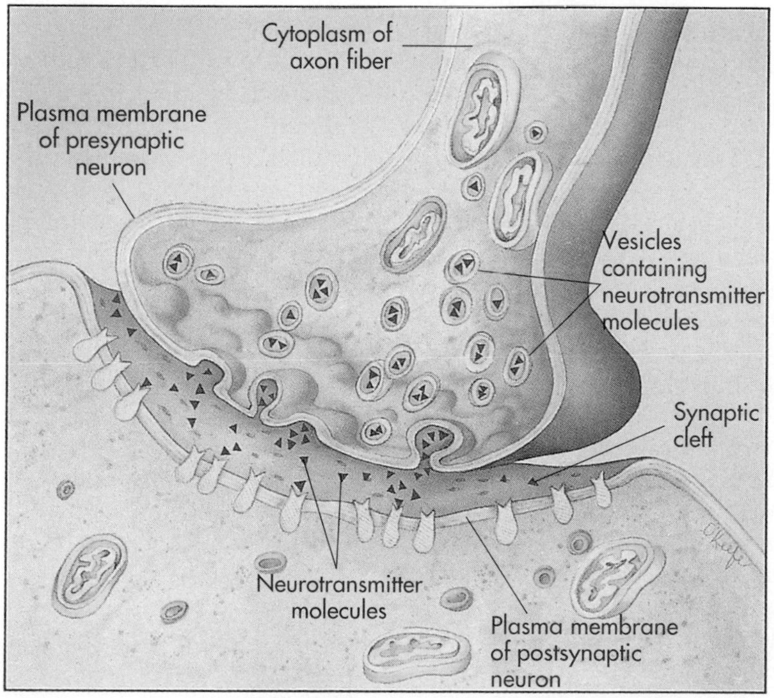

cles. Each vesicle contains a very small quantity of a chemical compound called a **neurotransmitter.** When a nerve impulse arrives at the synaptic knob, neurotransmitter molecules are released from the vesicles into the **synaptic cleft.** The synaptic cleft is the space between a synaptic knob and the plasma membrane of a *postsynaptic neuron.* It is an incredibly narrow space—only about two millionths of a centimeter in width. Identify the synaptic cleft in Figure 7-7. The plasma membrane of a postsynaptic neuron has protein molecules embedded in it opposite each synaptic knob. These serve as receptors to which neurotransmitter molecules bind. This binding can initiate an impulse in the postsynaptic neuron by opening ion channels in the postsynaptic membrane.

After impulse conduction by postsynaptic neurons is initiated, neurotransmitter activity is rapidly terminated. Either one or both of two mechanisms cause this. Some neurotransmitter molecules diffuse out of the synaptic cleft back into synaptic knobs. Other neurotransmitter molecules are metabolized into inactive compounds by specific enzymes.

Neurotransmitters are chemicals by which neurons communicate. As previously noted, at trillions of synapses in the CNS, presynaptic neurons release neurotransmitters that assist, stimulate, or inhibit postsynaptic neurons. At least 30 different compounds have been identified as neurotransmitters. They are not distributed randomly through the spinal cord and brain. Instead, specific neurotransmitters are localized in discrete groups of neurons and released in specific pathways.

For example, the substance named **acetylcholine** (as-e-til-KO-leen) is released at some of the synapses in the spinal cord and at neuromuscular (nerve-muscle) junctions. Other well-known neurotransmitters include **norepinephrine** (nor-ep-i-NEF-rin), **dopamine** (DOE-pa-meen), and **serotonin** (sair-o-TOE-nin). They belong to a group of compounds called **catecholamines** (kat-e-kol-AM-eens), which may play a role in sleep, motor function, mood, and pleasure recognition.

Two morphinelike neurotransmitters called **endorphins** (en-DOR-fins) and **enkephalins** (en-KEF-a-lins) are released at various spinal cord and brain synapses in the pain conduction pathway. These neurotransmitters inhibit conduction of pain impulses. They are natural pain killers.

Suppressing Pain During Exercise

Research shows that the release of endorphins increases during heavy exercise. Endorphins inhibit pain, so it is no wonder that pain associated with muscle fatigue decreases when endorphins are present. Normally, pain is a warning signal that calls attention to injuries or dangerous circumstances. However, it is better to inhibit severe pain if it stops us from continuing an activity that may be necessary for survival. Athletes and others who exercise heavily have even reported a unique feeling of well-being or euphoria associated with elevated endorphin levels.

Central Nervous System

The CNS, as its name implies, is centrally located. Its two major structures, the brain and spinal cord, are found along the midsagittal plane of the body (Figure 7-8). The brain is protected in the cranial cavity of the skull, and the spinal cord is surrounded in the spinal cavity by the vertebral column. In addition, the brain and spinal cord are covered by protective membranes called **meninges** (me-NIN-jeez), which are discussed in a later section of the chapter.

DIVISIONS OF THE BRAIN

The brain, one of our largest organs, consists of the following major divisions, named in ascending order beginning with most inferior part:

I Brain stem
- **A Medulla oblongata**
- **B Pons**
- **C Midbrain**

II Cerebellum

III Diencephalon
- **A Hypothalamus**
- **B Thalamus**

IV Cerebrum

Observe in Figure 7-9 the location and relative sizes of the medulla, pons, cerebellum, and cerebrum. Also identify the midbrain.

Brain Stem

The lowest part of the brain stem is the medulla oblongata. Immediately above the medulla lies the pons and above that the midbrain. Together these three structures are called the *brain stem* (Figure 7-9).

The **medulla oblongata** (ob-long-GAH-tah) is an enlarged, upward extension of the spinal cord. It lies just inside the cranial cavity above the large hole in the occipital bone called the *foramen magnum.* Like the spinal cord, the medulla consists of gray and white matter, but their arrangement differs in the two organs. In the medulla, bits of gray matter mix closely and intricately with white matter to form the *reticular formation* (*reticular* means "netlike"). In the spinal cord, gray and white matter do not intermingle; gray matter forms the interior core of the cord, and white matter surrounds it. The **pons** and **midbrain,** like the medulla, consist of white matter and scattered bits of gray matter.

All three parts of the brain stem function as two-way conduction paths. Sensory fibers conduct impulses up from the cord to other parts of the brain, and motor fibers conduct impulses down from the brain to the cord. In addition, many important reflex centers lie in the brain stem. The cardiac, respiratory, and vasomotor centers (collectively called the *vital centers*), for example, are located in the medulla. Impulses from these centers control heartbeat, respirations, and blood vessel diameter (which is important in regulating blood pressure).

Diencephalon

The **diencephalon** (dye-en-SEF-ah-lon) is a small but important part of the brain located between the midbrain below and the cerebrum above. It consists of two major structures: the hypothalamus and the thalamus.

Hypothalamus. The **hypothalamus** (hye-po-THAL-ah-mus), as its name suggests, is located below the thalamus. The posterior pituitary gland, the stalk that attaches it to the undersurface of the brain, and areas of gray matter located in the side walls of a fluid-filled space called the

FIGURE 7–8 ***The Nervous System.*** The brain and spinal cord constitute the *central nervous system* (CNS), and the nerves make up the *peripheral nervous system* (PNS).

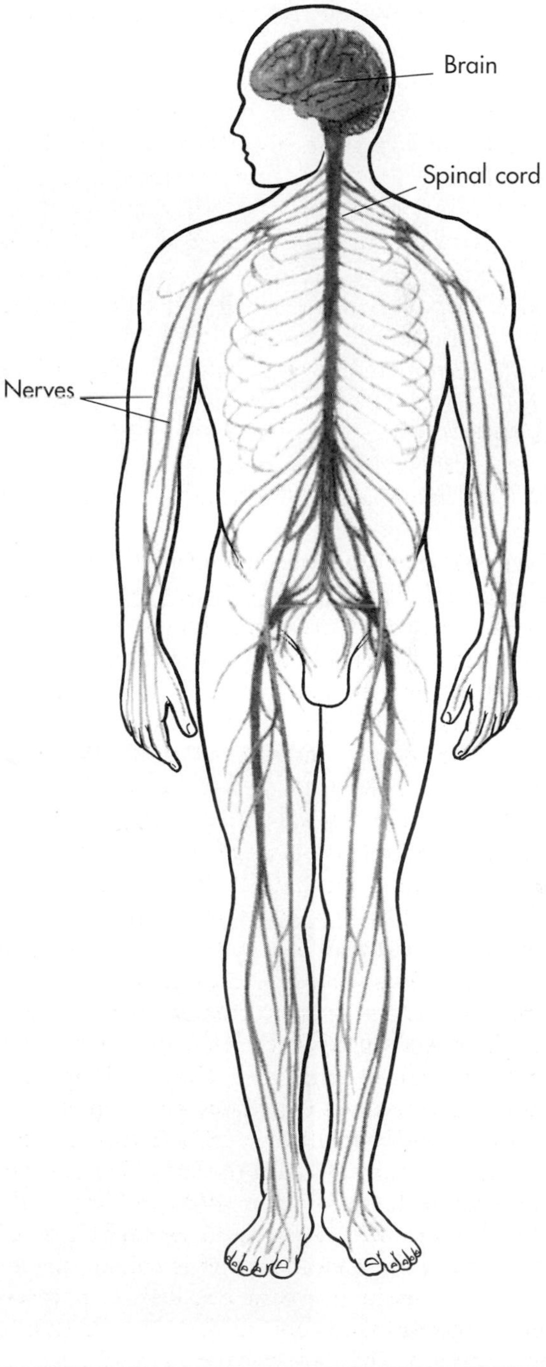

FIGURE 7–9 ***Major Regions of the Central Nervous System.*** **A,** Sagittal sections of the brain and spinal cord. **B,** Section of preserved brain.

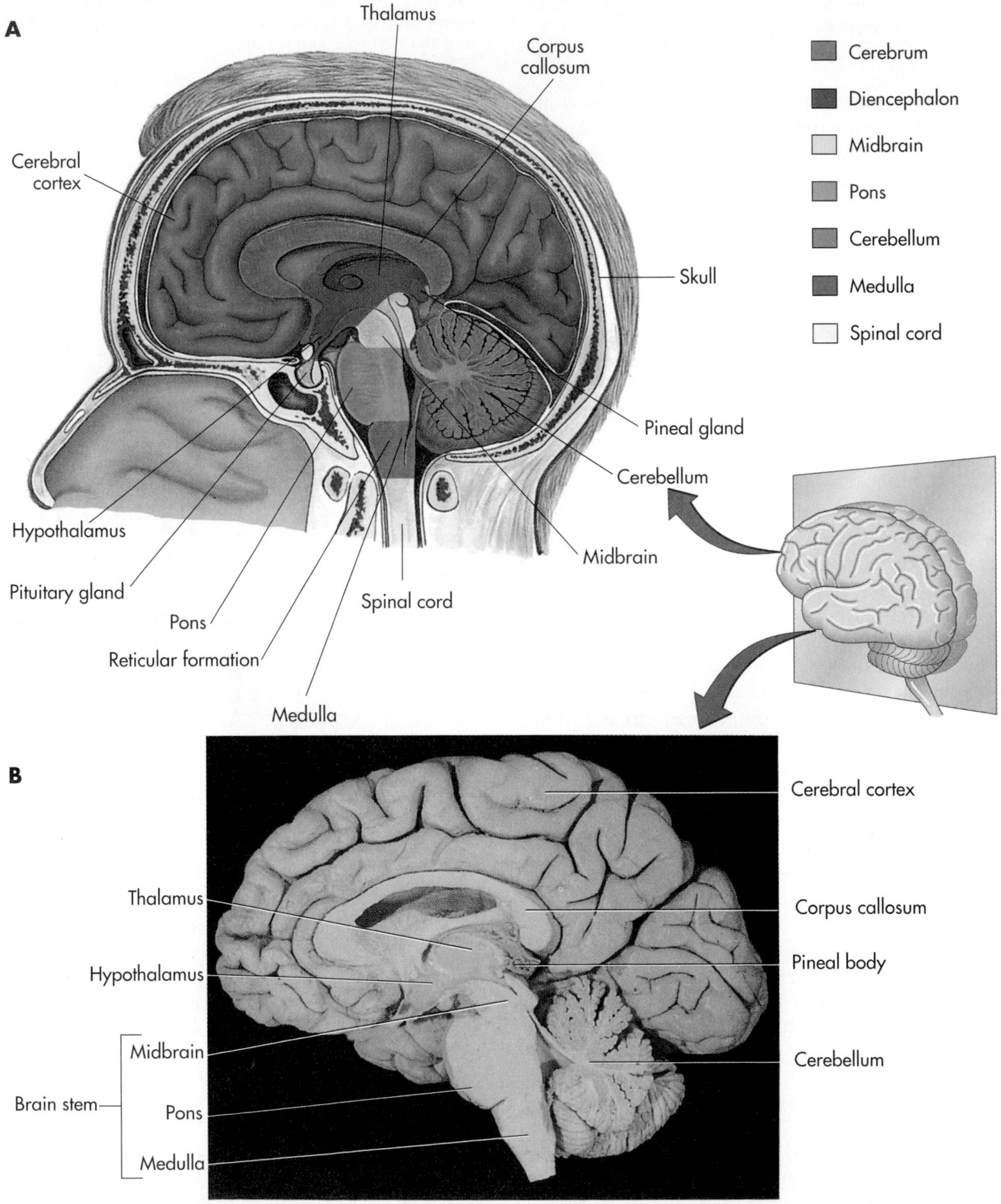

third ventricle are extensions of the hypothalamus. Identify the pituitary gland and the hypothalamus in Figure 7-9.

The old adage, "Don't judge by appearances," applies well to appraising the importance of the hypothalamus. Measured by size, it is one of the least significant parts of the brain, but measured by its contribution to healthy survival, it is one of the most important brain structures. Impulses from neurons whose dendrites and cell bodies lie in the hypothalamus are conducted by their axons to neurons located in the spinal cord, and many of these impulses are then relayed to muscles and glands all over the body. Thus the hypothalamus exerts a major control over virtually all internal organs. Among the vital functions that it helps control are the heart beat, constriction and dilation of blood vessels, and contractions of the stomach and intestines.

Some neurons in the hypothalamus function in a surprising way; they make the hormones that the posterior pituitary gland secretes into the blood. Because one of these hormones (called *antidiuretic hormone* or *ADH*) affects the volume of urine excreted, the hypothalamus plays an essential role in maintaining the body's water balance.

Some of the neurons in the hypothalamus function as endocrine (ductless) glands. Their axons secrete chemicals called *releasing hormones* into the blood, which then carries them to the anterior pituitary gland. Releasing hormones, as their name suggests, control the release of certain anterior pituitary hormones. These in turn influence the hormone secretion of other endocrine glands. Thus the hypothalamus indirectly helps control the functioning of every cell in the body.

The hypothalamus is a crucial part of the mechanism for maintaining body temperature. Therefore marked elevation in body temperature in the absence of disease frequently characterizes injuries or other abnormalities of the hypothalamus. In addition, this important center is involved in functions such as the regulation of water balance, sleep cycles, and the control of appetite and many emotions involved in pleasure, fear, anger, sexual arousal, and pain.

Thalamus. Just above the hypothalamus is a dumbbell-shaped section of gray matter called the **thalamus** (THAL-ah-mus). Each enlarged end of the dumbbell lies in a lateral wall of the third ventricle. The thin center section of the thalamus passes from left to right through the third ventricle. The thalamus is composed chiefly of dendrites and cell bodies of neurons that have axons extending up toward the sensory areas of the cerebrum. The thalamus performs the following functions:

1. It helps produce sensations. Its neurons relay impulses to the cerebral cortex from the sense organs of the body.
2. It associates sensations with emotions. Almost all sensations are accompanied by a feeling of some degree of pleasantness or unpleasantness. The way that these pleasant and unpleasant feelings are produced is unknown except that they seem to be associated with the arrival of sensory impulses in the thalamus.
3. It plays a part in the so-called arousal or alerting mechanism.

Cerebellum

Structure. Look at Figure 7-9 to find the location, appearance, and size of the cerebellum. The cerebellum is the second largest part of the human brain. It lies under the occipital lobe of the cerebrum. In the cerebellum, gray matter composes the outer layer, and white matter composes the bulk of the interior.

Function. Most of our knowledge about cerebellar functions has come from observing patients who have some sort of disease of the cerebellum and from animals who have had the cerebellum removed. From such observations, we know that the cerebellum plays an essential part in the production of normal movements. Perhaps a few examples will make this clear. A patient who has a tumor of the cerebellum frequently loses his balance and topples over; he may reel like a drunken man when he walks. He cannot coordinate his muscles normally. He may complain, for instance, that he is clumsy about everything he does—that he cannot even drive a nail or draw a straight line. With the loss of normal cerebellar functioning, he has lost the ability to make precise movements. The general functions of the cerebellum, then, are to produce smooth coordinated movements, maintain equilibrium, and sustain normal postures.

Cerebrum

The **cerebrum** (SAIR-e-brum) is the largest and uppermost part of the brain. If you were to look at the outer surface of the cerebrum, the first features you would notice might be its many ridges and grooves. The ridges are called *convolutions* or *gyri* (JYE-rye), and the grooves are called *sulci* (SUL-kye). The deepest sulci are called *fissures;* the longitudinal fissure divides the cerebrum into right and left halves or hemispheres. These halves are almost separate structures except for their lower midportions, which are connected by a structure called the **corpus callosum** (COR-pus kal-LO-sum) (Figure 7-9). Two deep sulci subdivide each cerebral hemisphere into four major lobes and each lobe into numerous convolutions. The lobes are named for the bones that lie over them: the frontal lobe, the parietal lobe, the temporal lobe, and the occipital lobe. Identify these in Figure 7-10, *A.*

A thin layer of gray matter, made up of neuron dendrites and cell bodies, composes the surface of the cerebrum. Its name is the *cerebral cortex.* White matter, made up of bundles of nerve fibers (tracts), composes most of the interior of the cerebrum. Within this white matter, however, are a few islands of gray matter known as the **cerebral nuclei** or *basal ganglia,* whose functioning is essential for producing automatic movements and postures. Parkinson's disease is a disease of the cerebral nuclei. Because shaking or tremors are common symptoms of Parkinson's disease, it is also called "shaking palsy."

What functions does the cerebrum perform? This is a hard question to answer briefly because the neurons of the cerebrum do not function alone. They function with many other neurons in many other parts of the brain and in the spinal cord. Neurons of these structures continually bring impulses to cerebral neurons and continually transmit impulses away from them. If all other neurons were functioning normally and only cerebral neurons were not functioning, here are some of the things that you could not do. You could not think or use your will. You could not remember anything that has ever happened to you. You could not decide to make the smallest movement, nor could you make it. You would not see or hear. You could not experience any of the sensations that make life so rich and varied. Nothing would anger or frighten you, and nothing would bring you joy or sorrow. You would, in short, be unconscious. These terms sum up cerebral functions: consciousness, thinking, memory, sensations, emotions, and willed movements. Figure 7-10, *B,* shows the areas of the cerebral cortex essential for willed movements, general sensations, vision, hearing, and normal speech.

Injury or disease can destroy neurons. A common example is the destruction of neurons of the motor area of the cerebrum that results from a **cerebrovascular accident (CVA),** which is a hemorrhage from or cessation of blood flow through cerebral blood vessels. When this happens, the victim can no longer voluntarily move the parts of his body on the side opposite to the side on which the CVA occurred. In nontechnical language, he has suffered a stroke. Note in Figure 7-10, *B,* the location of the motor area in the frontal lobe of the cerebrum.

It is important to understand that very specific areas of the cortex have very specific functions. For example, the temporal lobe's auditory areas interpret incoming nervous signals from the ear as very specific sounds. The visual area of the cortex in the occipital lobe helps you identify and understand specific images. Localized areas of the cortex are directly related to specific functions, as shown in Figure 7-10, *B.* This explains the very specific symptoms associated with an injury to localized areas of the cerebral cortex after a stroke or traumatic injury to the head. Table 7-1 summarizes the major components of the brain and their main functions.

SPINAL CORD

Structure

If you are of average height, your spinal cord is about 17 or 18 inches long (Figure 7-11). It lies inside the spinal column in the spinal cavity and extends from the occipital bone down to the bottom of the first lumbar vertebra. Place your hands on your hips, and they will line up with your fourth lumbar vertebra. Your spinal cord ends just above this level.

Look now at Figure 7-12. Notice the H-shaped core of the spinal cord. It consists of gray matter and so is composed mainly of dendrites and cell bodies of neurons. Columns of white matter form the outer portion of the spinal cord, and bundles

FIGURE 7–10 ***The Cerebrum.*** **A,** The lobes of the cerebrum. **B,** Functional regions of the cerebral cortex. *Association areas* are so named because they put together (associate) information from many different parts of the brain.

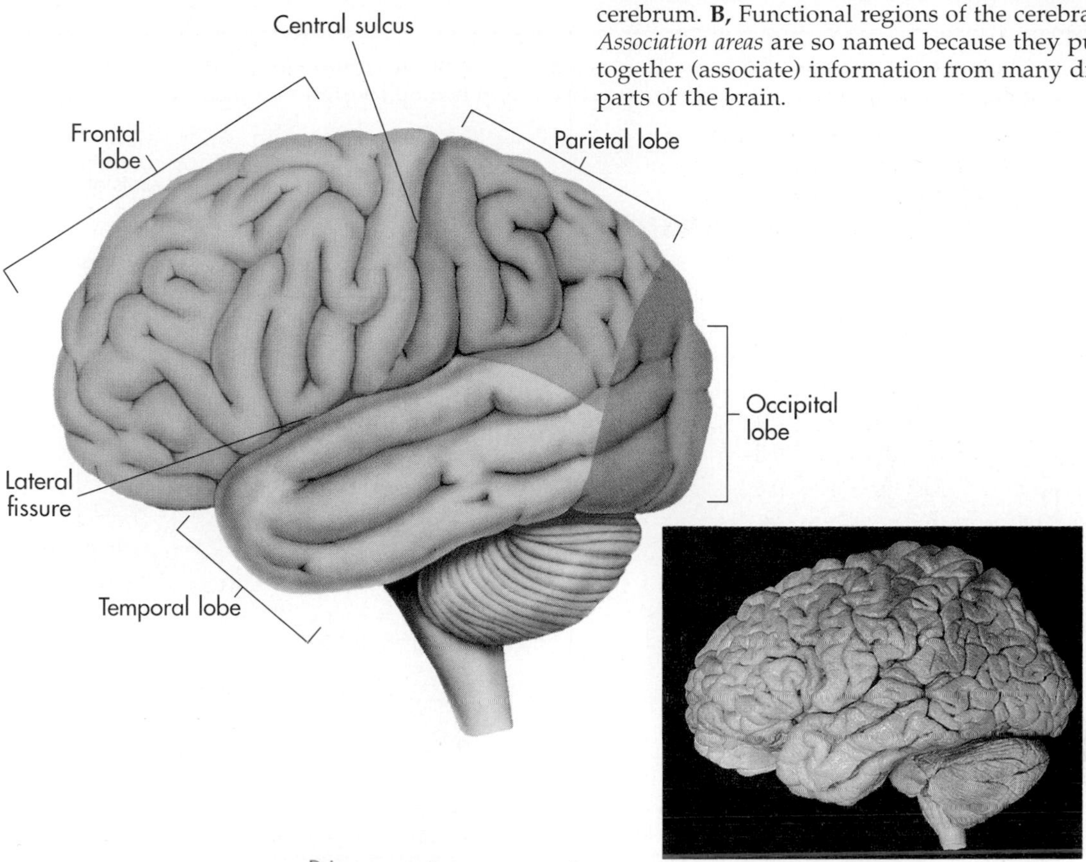

A

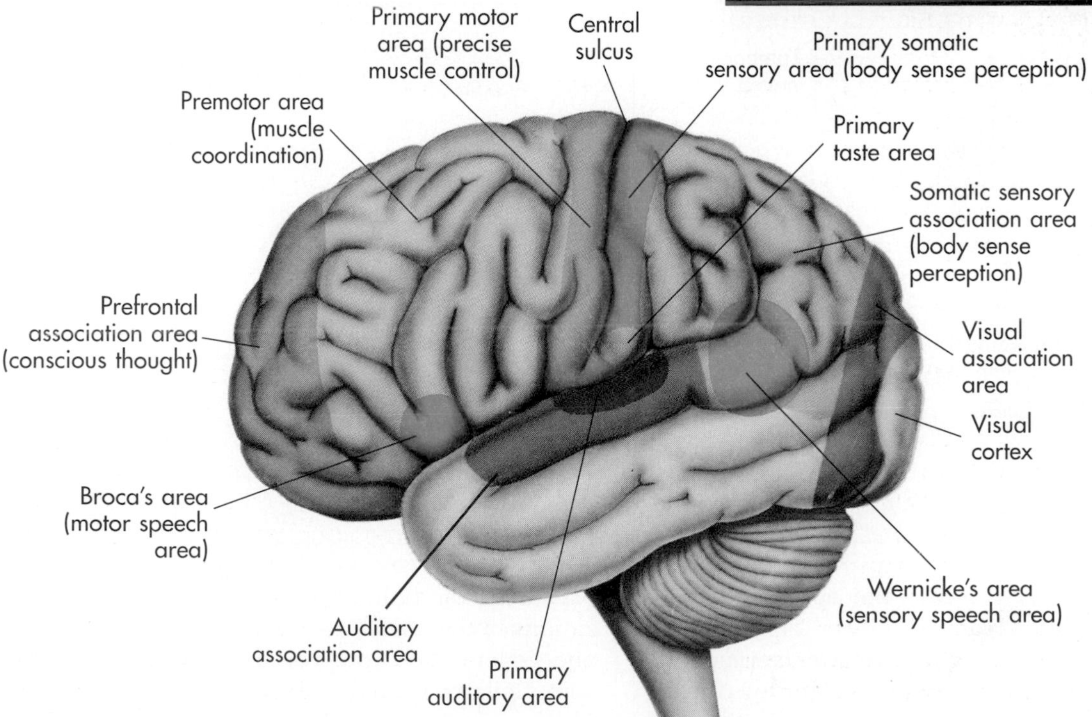

B

FIGURE 7–11 ***Spinal Cord and Spinal Nerves.*** Inset is a dissection of the cervical segment of the spinal cord showing emerging cervical nerves. The spinal cord is viewed from behind (posterior aspect).

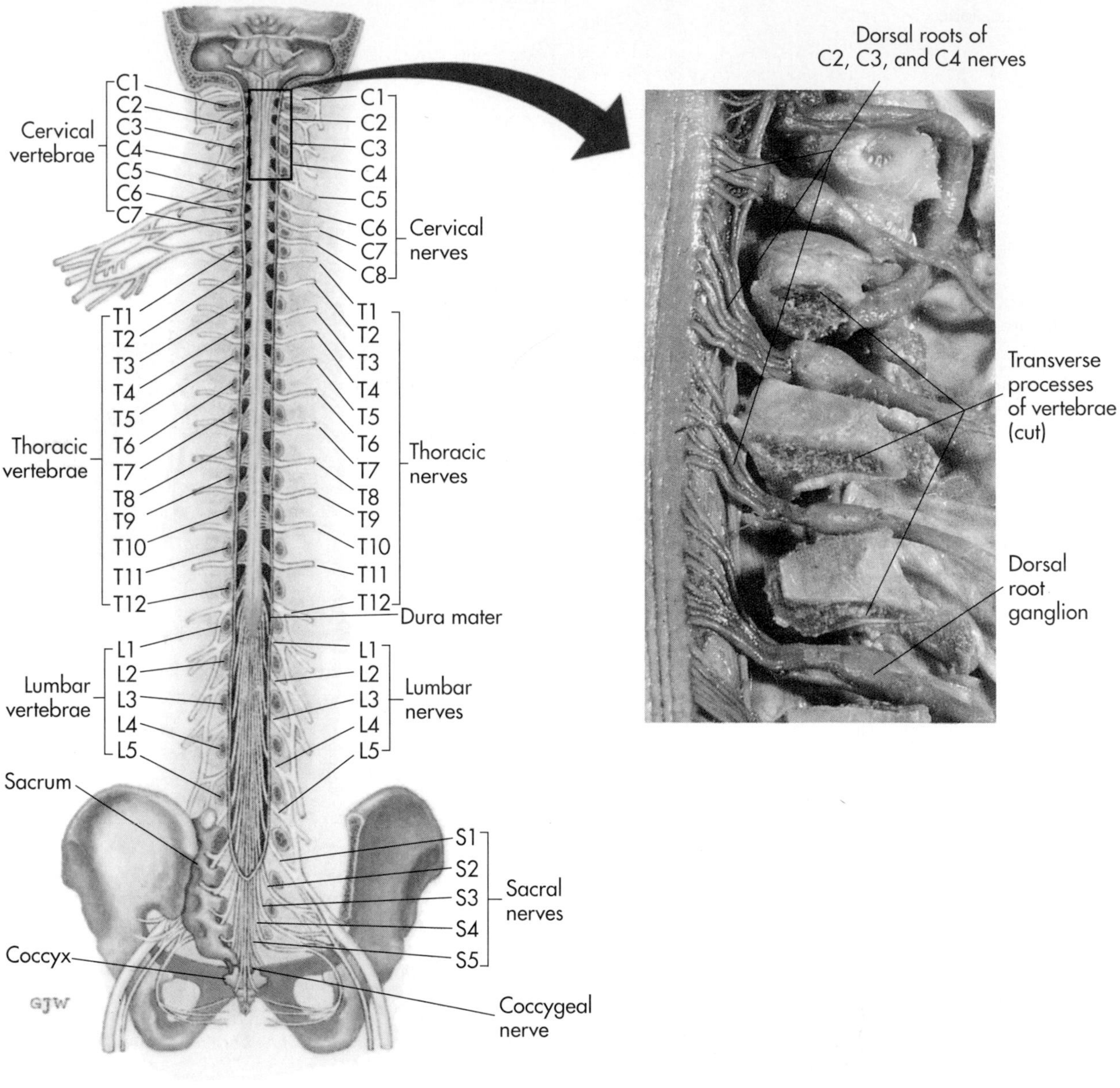

of myelinated nerve fibers—the **spinal tracts**—make up the white columns.

Spinal cord tracts provide two-way conduction paths to and from the brain. **Ascending tracts** conduct impulses up the cord to the brain. **Descending tracts** conduct impulses down the cord from the brain. Tracts are functional organizations in that all axons composing one tract serve one general function. For instance, fibers of the spinothalamic tracts serve a sensory function. They transmit impulses that produce sensations of crude touch, pain, and temperature. Other

TABLE 7–1 Functions of Major Divisions of the Brain

BRAIN AREA	FUNCTION
Brain stem	
Medulla oblongata	Two-way conduction pathway between the spinal cord and higher brain centers; cardiac, respiratory, and vasomotor control center
Pons	Two-way conduction pathway between areas of the brain and other regions of the body; influences respiration
Midbrain	Two-way conduction pathway; relay for visual and auditory impulses
Diencephalon	
Hypothalamus	Regulation of body temperature, water balance, sleep-cycle control, appetite, and sexual arousal
Thalamus	Sensory relay station from various body areas to cerebral cortex; emotions and alerting or arousal mechanisms
Cerebellum	Muscle coordination; maintenance of equilibrium and posture
Cerebrum	Sensory perception, emotions, willed movements, consciousness, and memory

FIGURE 7–12 ***Spinal Cord.*** Cross section of the spinal cord showing the horns, pathways (nerve tracts), and roots.

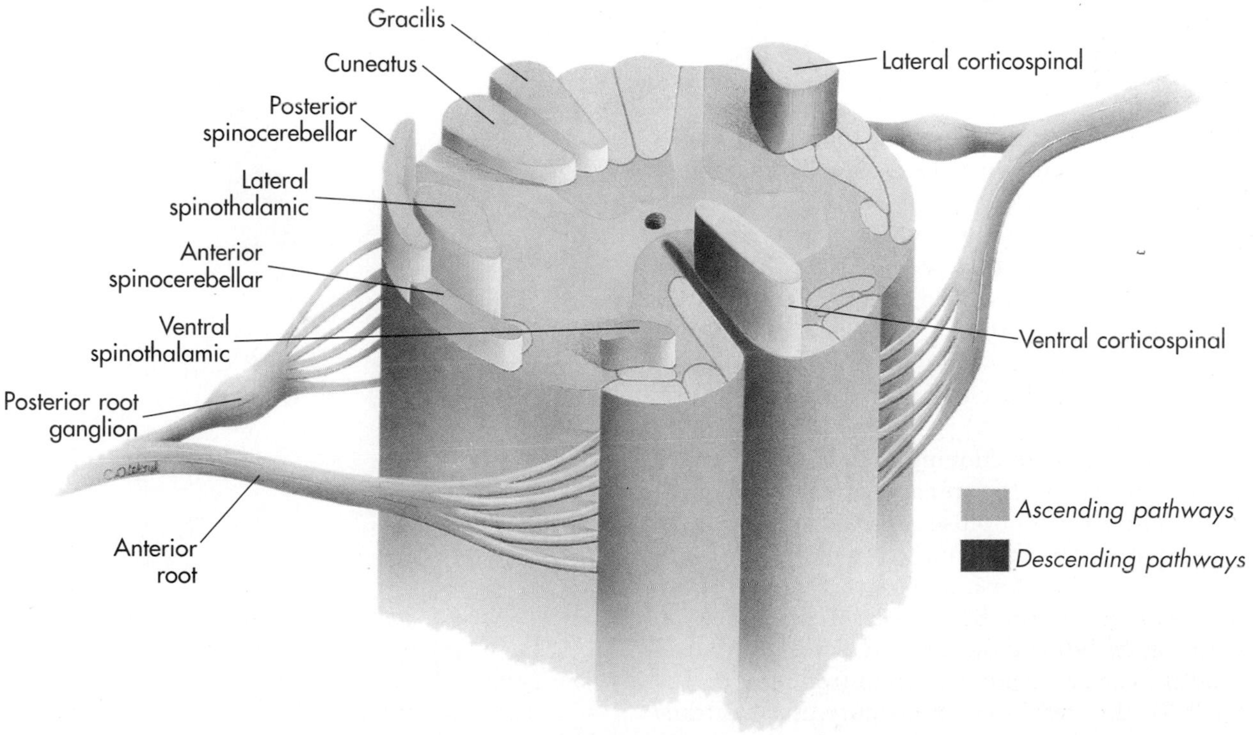

ascending tracts shown in Figure 7-12 include the gracilis and cuneatus tracts, which transmit sensations of touch and pressure up to the brain, and the anterior and posterior spinocerebellar tracts, which transmit information about muscle length to the cerebellum. Descending tracts include the lateral and ventral corticospinal tracts, which transmit impulses controlling many voluntary movements.

Functions

To try to understand spinal cord functions, think about a hotel telephone switching system. Suppose a guest in Room 108 calls the switching system and keys in the extension number for Room 520, and in a second or so, someone in that room answers. Very briefly, three events took place: a message traveled into the switching system, the system routed the message along the proper path, and the message traveled out from the switching system toward Room 520. The telephone switching system provided the network of connections that made possible the completion of the call. We might say that the switching system transferred the incoming call to an outgoing line. The spinal cord functions similarly. It contains the centers for thousands and thousands of reflex arcs. Look back at Figure 7-5. The interneuron shown there is an example of a spinal cord reflex center. It switches or transfers incoming sensory impulses to outgoing motor impulses, thereby making it possible for a reflex to occur. Reflexes that result from conduction over arcs whose centers lie in the spinal cord are called *spinal cord reflexes.* Two common kinds of spinal cord reflexes are withdrawal and jerk reflexes. An example of a withdrawal reflex is pulling one's hand away from a hot surface. The familiar knee jerk is an example of a jerk reflex.

In addition to functioning as the primary reflex center of the body, the spinal cord tracts, as previously noted, carry impulses to and from the brain. Sensory impulses travel up to the brain in ascending tracts, and motor impulses travel down from the brain in descending tracts. Therefore if an injury cuts the cord all the way across, impulses can no longer travel to the brain from any part of the body located below the injury, nor can they travel from the brain down to these parts. In short, this kind of spinal cord injury produces a loss of sensation, which is called **anesthesia** (an-es-THEE-zee-ah), and a loss of the ability to make voluntary movements, which is called **paralysis** (pah-RAL-i-sis).

COVERINGS AND FLUID SPACES OF THE BRAIN AND SPINAL CORD

Nervous tissue is not a sturdy tissue. Even moderate pressure can kill nerve cells, so nature safeguards the chief organs made of this tissue—the spinal cord and the brain—by surrounding them with a tough, fluid-containing membrane called the **meninges** (me-NIN-jeez). The meninges are then surrounded by bone. The spinal meninges

FIGURE 7–13 *Spinal Cord.* The meninges, spinal nerves, and sympathetic trunk are visible.

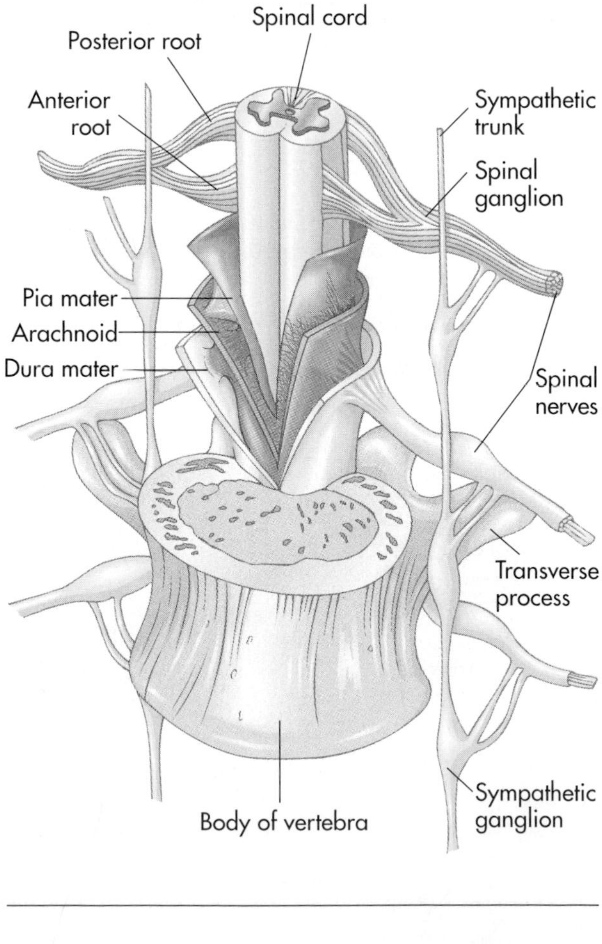

form a tubelike covering around the spinal cord and line the bony vertebral foramen of the vertebrae that surround the cord. Look at Figure 7-13, and you can identify the three layers of the spinal meninges. They are the **dura mater** (DOO-rah MA-ter), which is the tough outer layer that lines the vertebral canal, the **pia** (PEE-ah) **mater,** which is the innermost membrane covering the spinal cord itself, and the **arachnoid** (ah-RAK-noyd), which is the membrane between the dura and the pia mater. The arachnoid resembles a cobweb with fluid in its spaces. The word *arachnoid* means "cobweblike." It comes from *arachne,* the Greek word for spider. Arachne is the name of the girl who was changed into a spider by Athena because she boasted of the fineness of her weaving—at least, so an ancient Greek myth tells us.

The meninges that form the protective covering around the spinal cord also extend up and around the brain to enclose it completely (Figure 7-13). Fluid fills the subarachnoid spaces between the pia mater and arachnoid in the brain and spinal cord. This fluid is called **cerebrospinal fluid (CSF).**

Cerebrospinal (ser-e-bro-SPI-nal) **fluid** also fills spaces in the brain called cerebral **ventricles.** In Figure 7-14, you can see the irregular shapes of the ventricles of the brain. These illustrations can also help you visualize the location of the ventricles if you remember that these large spaces lie deep inside the brain and that there are two lateral ventricles. One lies inside the right half of the cerebrum (the largest part of the human brain), and the other lies inside the left half.

FIGURE 7-14 ***Fluid Spaces of the Brain.*** The large figure shows the ventricles highlighted within the brain in a left lateral view. The small figure shows the ventricles from above.

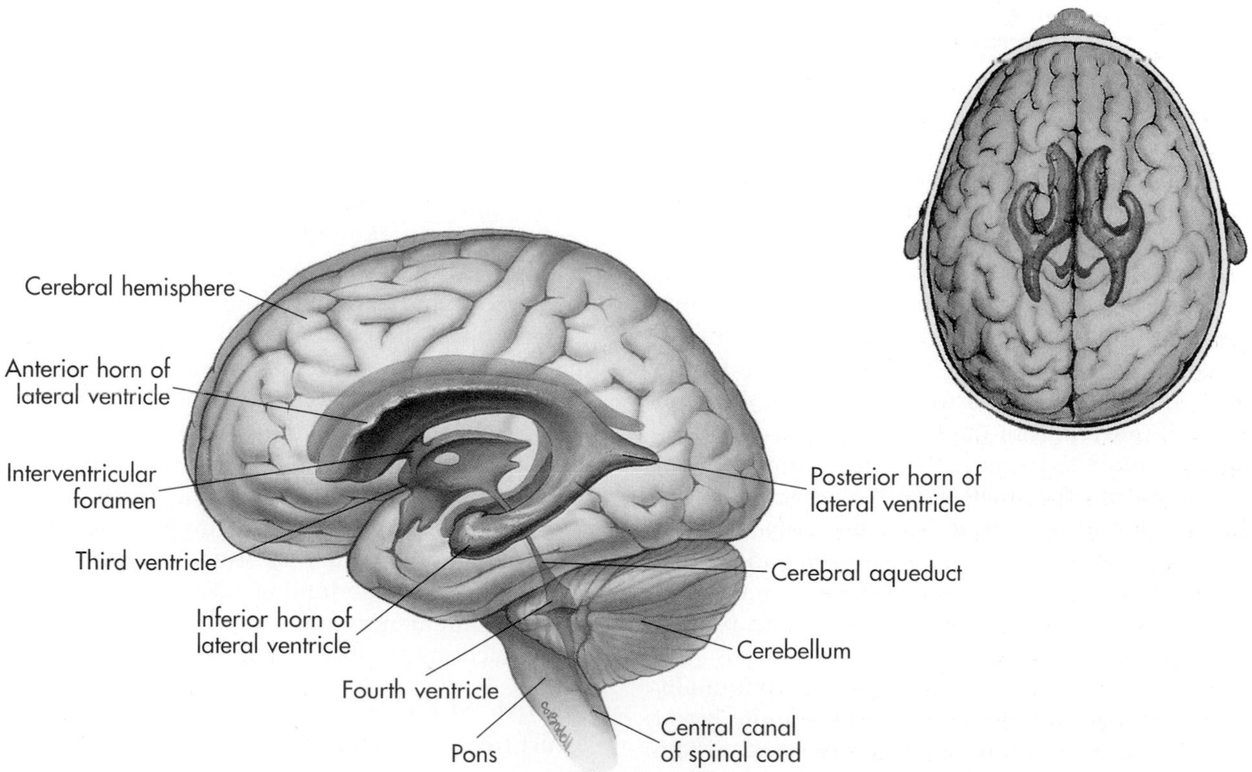

Lumbar Puncture

The extension of the meninges beyond the spinal cord is convenient for performing lumbar punctures without danger of injuring the spinal cord. A **lumbar puncture** is the withdrawal of some CSF from the subarachnoid space in the lumbar region of the spinal cord. The physician inserts a needle just above or below the fourth lumbar vertebra, knowing that the spinal cord ends an inch or more above the level. The fourth lumbar vertebra can be easily located because it lies on a line with the iliac crest. Placing a patient on his side and arching his back by drawing the knees and chest together separates the vertebrae sufficiently to introduce the needle. Lumbar punctures are often performed to withdraw CSF for analysis or to reduce pressure caused by swelling of the brain or spinal cord after injury or disease.

CSF is one of the body's circulating fluids. It forms continually from fluid filtering out of the blood in a network of brain capillaries known as the **choroid plexus** (KO-royd PLEK-sus) and into the ventricles. CSF seeps from the lateral ventricles into the third ventricle and flows down through the cerebral aqueduct (find this in Figure 7-14 and 7-15) into the fourth ventricle. Most of the CSF moves from the fourth ventricle into the subarachnoid space near the cerebellum. Some of it moves into the small, tubelike central canal of the cord and then out into the subarachnoid spaces. Then it moves leisurely down and around the cord and up and around the brain (in the subarachnoid spaces of their meninges) and returns to the blood (in the veins of the brain).

Remembering that this fluid forms continually from blood, circulates, and is resorbed into blood can be useful. It can help you understand certain abnormalities. Suppose a person has a brain tumor that presses on the cerebral aqueduct. This blocks the way for the return of CSF to the blood. Because the fluid continues to form but cannot drain away, it accumulates in the ventricles or in the meninges. Other conditions can cause an accumulation of CSF in the ventricles. An example is **hydrocephalus** (hye-dro-SEF-ah-lus) or "water on the brain." One form of treatment involves surgical placement of a hollow tube or catheter through the blocked channel so that CSF can drain into another location in the body.

Peripheral Nervous System

The nerves connecting the brain and spinal cord to other parts of the body constitute the **peripheral nervous system (PNS).** This system includes **cranial** and **spinal nerves** that connect the brain and spinal cord, respectively, to peripheral structures such as the skin surface and the skeletal muscles. In addition, other structures in the **autonomic nervous system** or **ANS** are considered part of the PNS. These connect the brain and spinal cord to various glands in the body and to the cardiac and smooth muscle in the thorax and abdomen.

CRANIAL NERVES

Twelve pairs of cranial nerves are attached to the undersurface of the brain, mostly from the brain stem. Figure 7-16 shows the attachments of these nerves. Their fibers conduct impulses between the brain and structures in the head and neck and in the thoracic and abdominal cavities. For instance, the second cranial nerve (optic nerve) conducts impulses from the eye to the brain, where these impulses produce vision. The third cranial nerve (oculomotor nerve) conducts impulses from the brain to muscles in the eye, where they cause contractions that move the eye. The tenth cranial nerve (vagus nerve) conducts impulses between the medulla oblongata and structures in the neck and thoracic and abdominal cavities. The names of each cranial nerve and a brief description of their functions are listed in Table 7-2.

SPINAL NERVES

Structure

Thirty-one pairs of nerves are attached to the spinal cord in the following order: eight pairs are attached

FIGURE 7–15 ***Flow of Cerebrospinal Fluid.*** The fluid produced by filtration of blood by the choroid plexus of each ventricle flows inferiorly through the lateral ventricles, interventricular foramen, third ventricle, cerebral aqueduct, fourth ventricle, and subarachnoid space and to the blood.

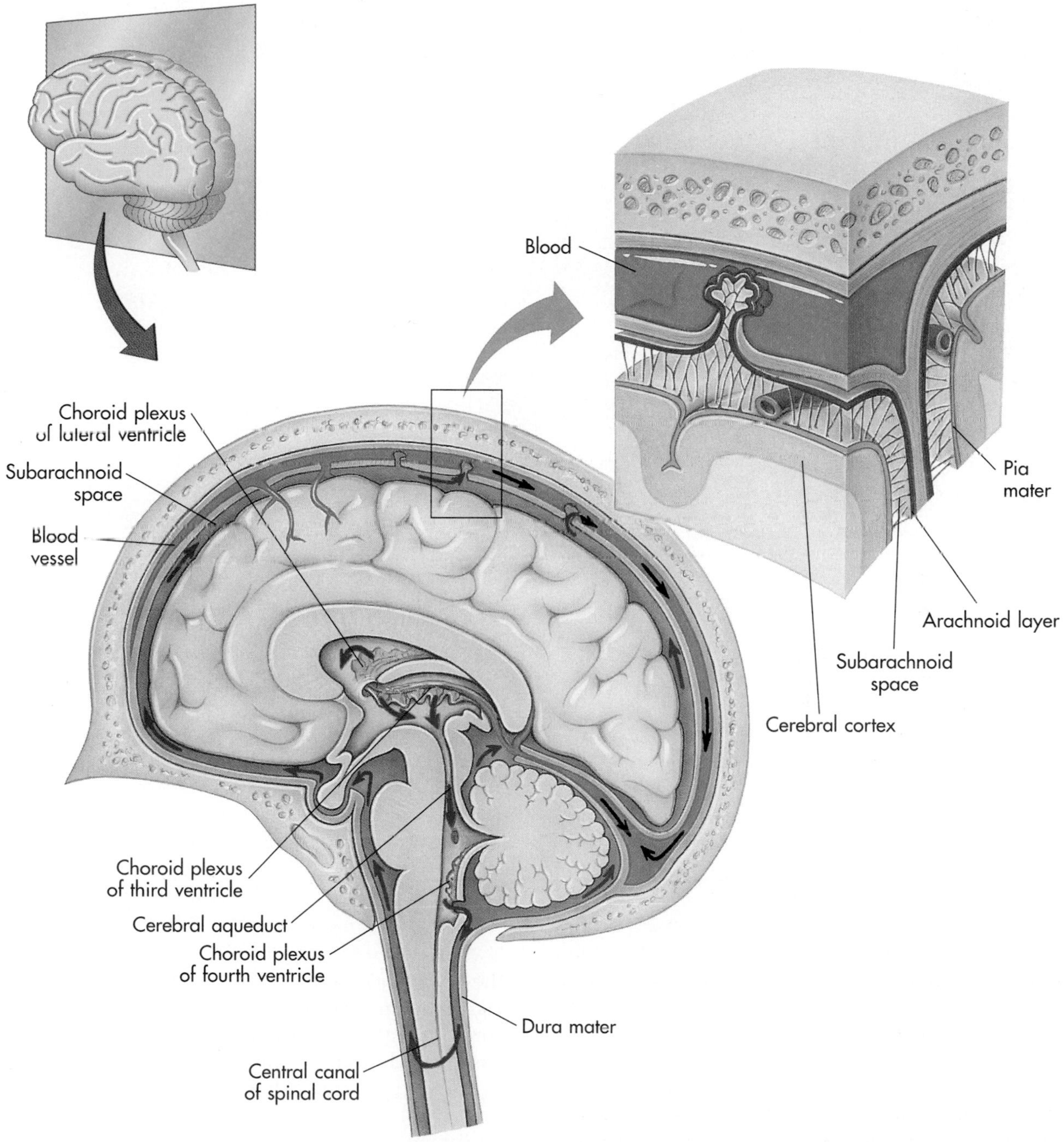

FIGURE 7–16 ***Cranial Nerves.*** View of the undersurface of the brain shows attachments of the cranial nerves.

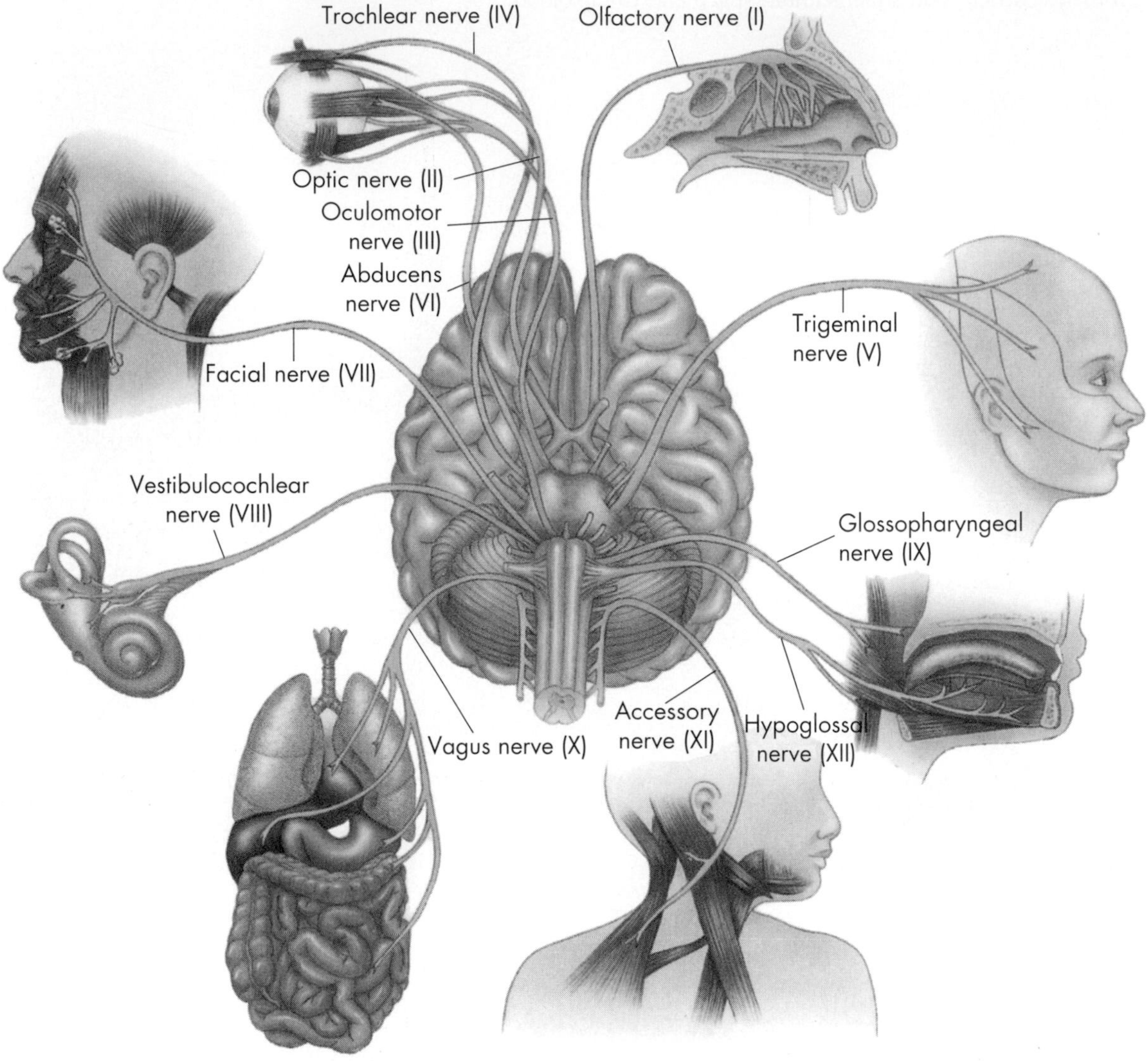

to the cervical segments, twelve pairs are attached to the thoracic segments, five pairs are attached to the lumbar segments, five pairs are attached to the sacrospinal segments, and one pair is attached to the coccygeal segment (Figure 7-11). Unlike cranial nerves, spinal nerves have no special names; instead, a letter and number identify each one. C1, for example, indicates the pair of spinal nerves attached to the first segment of the cervical part of the cord, and T8 indicates nerves attached to the eighth segment of the thoracic part of the spinal cord. In Figure 7-11 the cervical area of the spine has been dissected to show the emerging spinal nerves in that area. After spinal nerves exit from the spinal cord, they branch to form the many peripheral nerves of the trunk and limbs. Sometimes, nerve fibers from several spinal nerves are reorganized to form a single peripheral nerve.

TABLE 7–2 Cranial Nerves

NERVE*	CONDUCT IMPULSES	FUNCTIONS
I Olfactory	From nose to brain	Sense of smell
II Optic	From eye to brain	Vision
III Oculomotor	From brain to eye muscles	Eye movements
IV Trochlear	From brain to external eye muscles	Eye movements
V Trigeminal	From skin and mucous membrane of head and from teeth to brain; also from brain to chewing muscles	Sensations of face, scalp, and teeth, chewing movements
VI Abducens	From brain to external eye muscles	Turning eyes outward
VII Facial	From taste buds of tongue to brain; from brain to face muscles	Sense of taste; contraction of muscles of facial expression
VIII Vestibulocochlear	From ear to brain	Hearing; sense of balance
IX Glossopharyngeal	From throat and taste buds of tongue to brain; also from brain to throat muscles and salivary glands	Sensations of throat, taste, swallowing movements, secretion of saliva
X Vagus	From throat, larynx, and organs in thoracic and abdominal cavities to brain; also from brain to muscles of throat and to organs in thoracic and abdominal cavities	Sensations of throat and larynx and of thoracic and abdominal organs; swallowing, voice production, slowing of heartbeat, acceleration of peristalsis (gut movements)
XI Accessory	From brain to certain shoulder and neck muscles	Shoulder movements; turning movements of head
XII Hypoglossal	From brain to muscles of tongue	Tongue movements

*The first letter of the words in the following sentence are the first letters of the names of the cranial nerves, in the correct order. Many anatomy students find that using this sentence, or one like it, helps in memorizing the names and numbers of the cranial nerves. It is "**O**n **O**ld **O**lympus' **T**iny **T**ops, **A** **F**riendly **V**iking **G**rew **V**ines **A**nd **H**ops."

This reorganization can be seen as a network of intersecting or "braided" branches called a **plexus.** Figure 7-11 shows several plexuses.

Functions

Spinal nerves conduct impulses between the spinal cord and the parts of the body not supplied by cranial nerves. The spinal nerves shown in Figure 7-11 contain, as do all spinal nerves, sensory and motor fibers. Spinal nerves therefore function to make possible sensations and movements. A disease or injury that prevents conduction by a spinal nerve thus results in a loss of feeling and a loss of movement in the part supplied by that nerve.

Detailed mapping of the skin's surface reveals a close relationship between the source on the spinal cord of each spinal nerve and the part of the body that it innervates (Figure 7-17). Knowledge of the segmental arrangement of spinal nerves is useful to physicians. For instance, a neurologist can identify the site of a spinal cord or nerve abnormality from the area of the body that is insensitive to a pinprick. Skin surface areas that are supplied by a single spinal nerve are called **dermatomes** (DER-mah-tomes). A dermatome "map" of the body is shown in Figure 7-17.

Autonomic Nervous System

The **autonomic nervous system (ANS)** consists of certain motor neurons that conduct impulses from

FIGURE 7–17 ***Dermatomes.*** Segmental dermatome distribution of spinal nerves to the front, back, and side of the body. *C,* Cervical segments; *T,* thoracic segments; *L,* lumbar segments; *S,* sacral segments; *CX,* coccygeal segment.

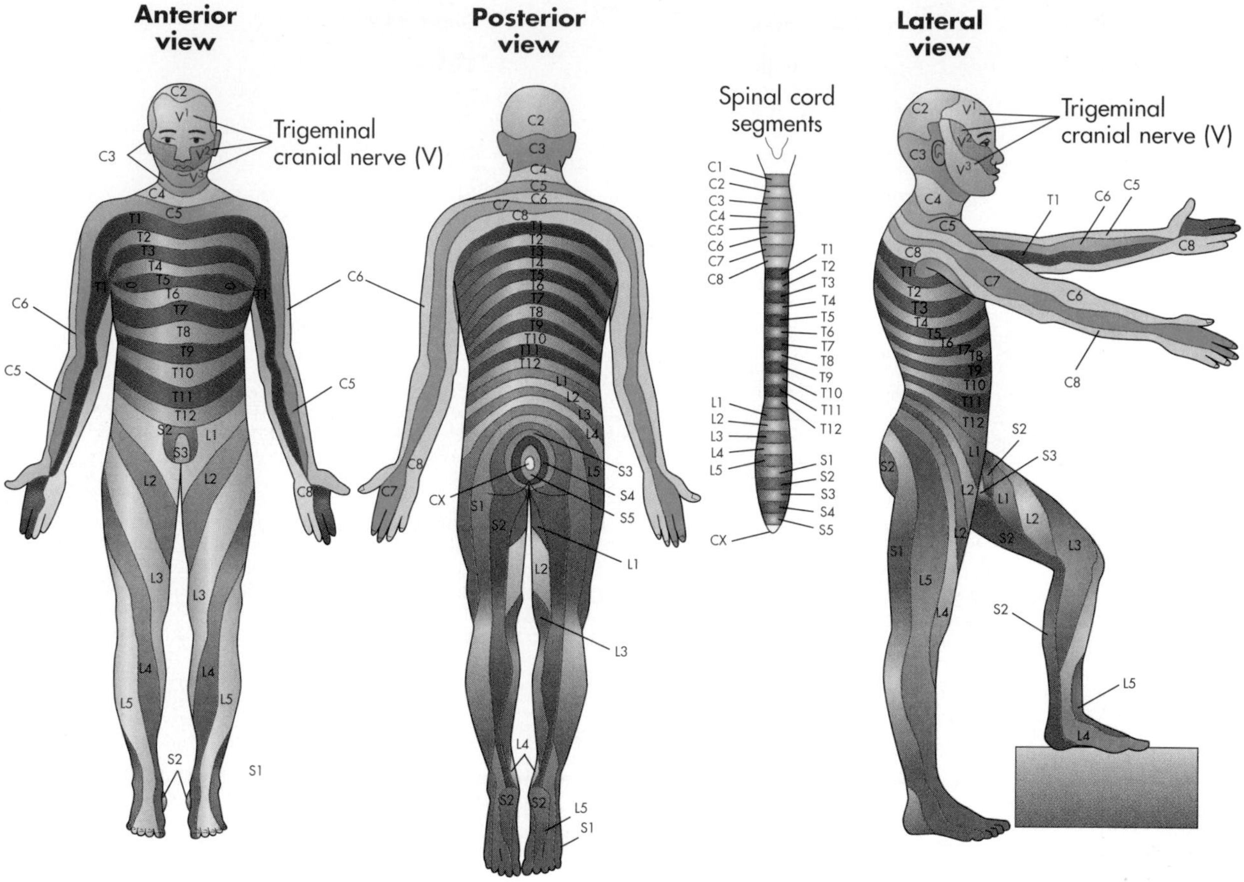

the spinal cord or brain stem to the following kinds of tissues:

1. Cardiac muscle tissue
2. Smooth muscle tissue
3. Glandular epithelial tissue

The ANS consists of the parts of the nervous system that regulate involuntary functions (for example, the heartbeat, contractions of the stomach and intestines, and secretions by glands). On the other hand, motor nerves that control the voluntary actions of skeletal muscles are sometimes called the *somatic nervous system.*

The autonomic nervous system consists of two divisions called the **sympathetic nervous system** and the **parasympathetic nervous system** (Figure 7-18).

FUNCTIONAL ANATOMY

Autonomic neurons are the motor neurons that make up the ANS. The dendrites and cell bodies of some autonomic neurons are located in the gray matter of the spinal cord or brain stem. Their axons extend from these structures and terminate in ganglia. These autonomic neurons are called **preganglionic neurons** because they conduct

FIGURE 7–18 ***Innervation of the Major Target Organs by the Autonomic Nervous System.*** The sympathetic pathways are highlighted with red, and the parasympathetic pathways are highlighted with blue.

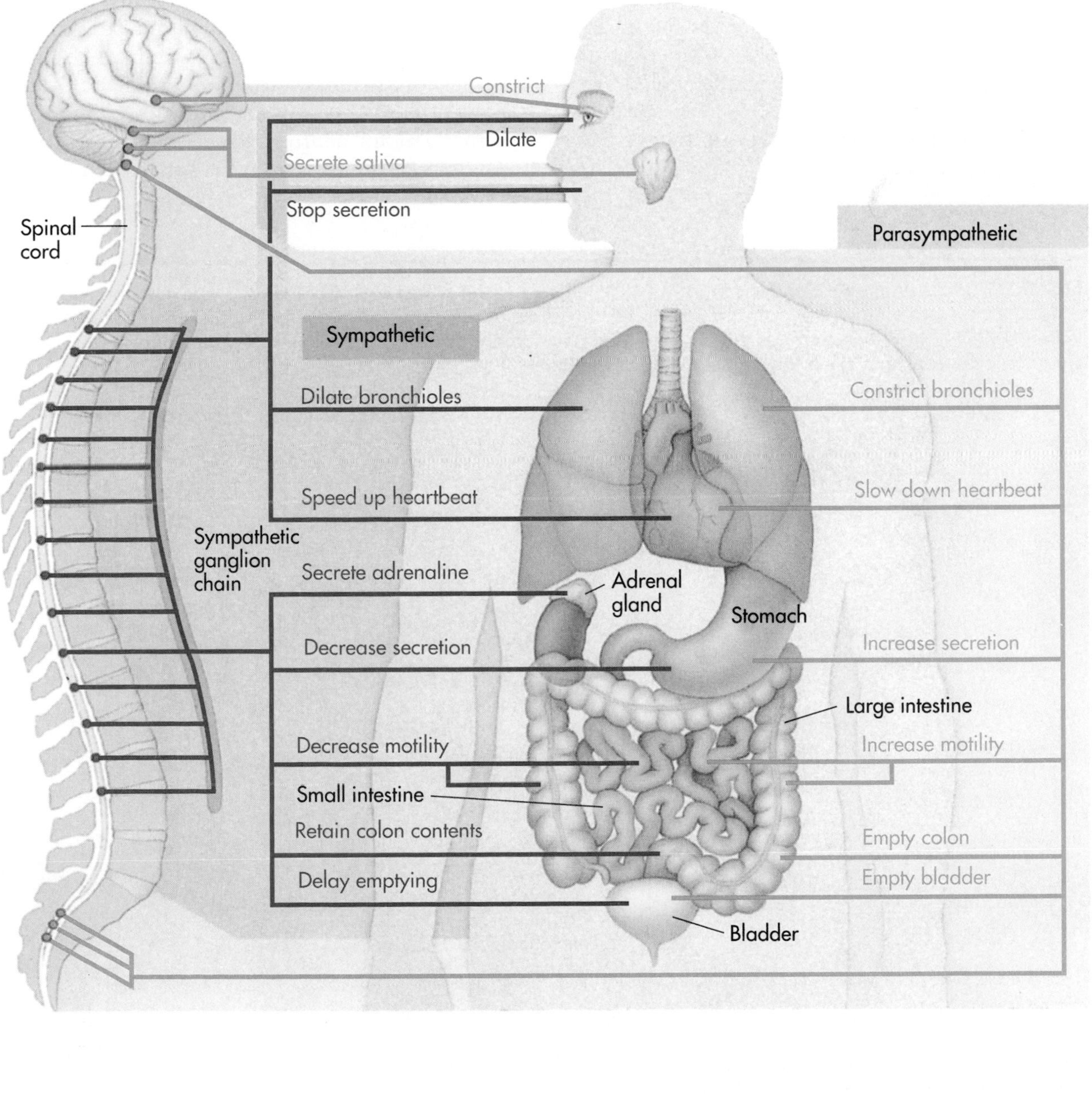

impulses between the spinal cord and a ganglion. In the ganglia the axon endings of preganglionic neurons synapse with the dendrites or cell bodies of postganglionic neurons. **Postganglionic neurons,** as their name suggests, conduct impulses from a ganglion to cardiac muscle, smooth muscle, or glandular epithelial tissue.

Autonomic or **visceral effectors** are the tissues to which autonomic neurons conduct impulses. Specifically, visceral effectors are cardiac muscle that makes up the wall of the heart, smooth muscle that partially makes up the walls of blood vessels and other hollow internal organs, and glandular epithelial tissue that makes up the secreting part of glands.

AUTONOMIC CONDUCTION PATHS

Conduction paths to visceral and somatic effectors from the CNS (spinal cord or brain stem) differ somewhat. Autonomic paths to visceral effectors, as the right side of Figure 7-19 shows, consist of two-neuron relays. Impulses travel over preganglionic neurons from the spinal cord or brain stem to autonomic ganglia. There, they are relayed across synapses to postganglionic neurons, which then conduct the impulses from the ganglia to visceral effectors. Compare the autonomic conduction path with the somatic conduction path illustrated on the left side of Figure 7-19. Somatic motor neurons, like the ones shown here, conduct all the way from the spinal cord or brain

FIGURE 7–19 ***Autonomic Conduction Paths.*** The left side of the diagram shows that one somatic motor neuron conducts impulses all the way from the spinal cord to a somatic effector. Conduction from the spinal cord to any visceral effector, however, requires a relay of at least two autonomic motor neurons—a preganglionic and a postganglionic neuron, shown on the right side of the diagram.

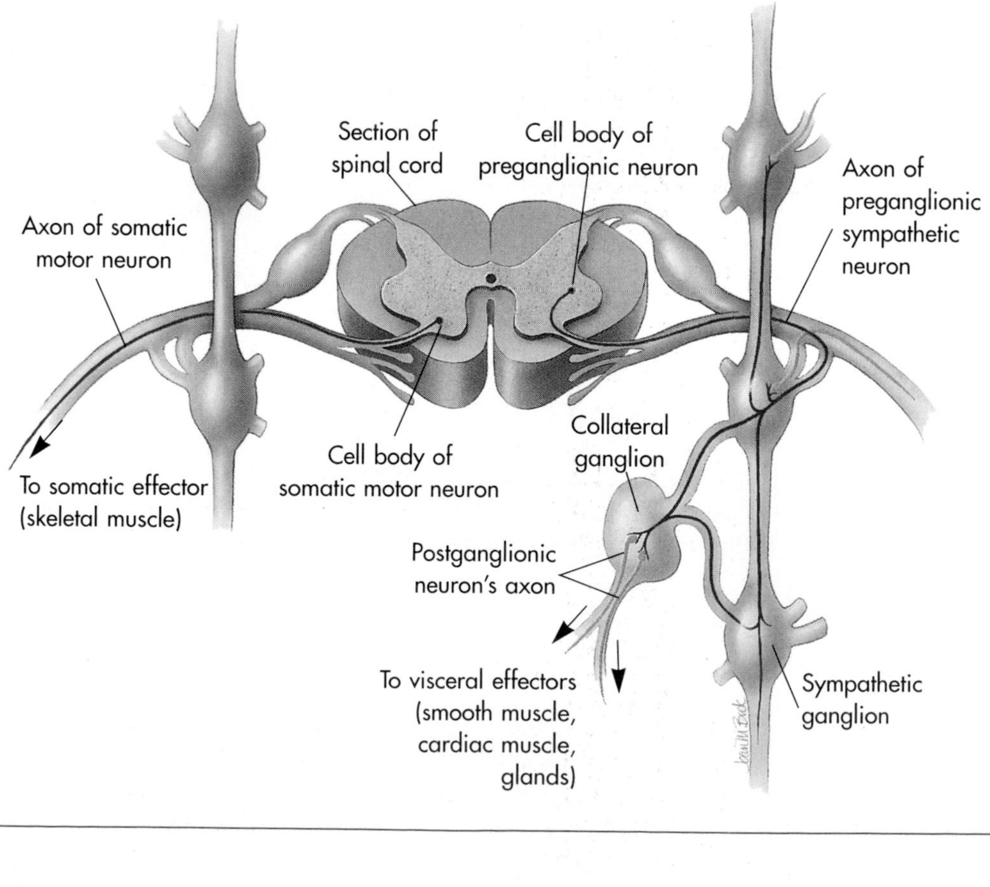

stem to somatic effectors with no intervening synapses.

SYMPATHETIC NERVOUS SYSTEM

Structure

Sympathetic preganglionic neurons have dendrites and cell bodies in the gray matter of the thoracic and upper lumbar segments of the spinal cord. The sympathetic system has also been referred to as the *thoracolumbar system.* Look now at the right side of Figure 7-19. Follow the course of the axon of the sympathetic preganglionic neuron shown there. It leaves the spinal cord in the anterior (ventral) root of a spinal nerve. It next enters the spinal nerve but soon leaves it to extend to and through a sympathetic ganglion and terminate in a collateral ganglion. There, it synapses with several postganglionic neurons whose axons extend to terminate in visceral effectors. Also shown in Figure 7-19, branches of the preganglionic axon may ascend or descend to terminate in ganglia above and below their point of origin. All sympathetic preganglionic axons therefore synapse with many postganglionic neurons, and these frequently terminate in widely separated organs. Hence sympathetic responses are usually wide-spread, involving many organs and not just one.

Sympathetic postganglionic neurons have dendrites and cell bodies in sympathetic ganglia. Sympathetic ganglia are located in front of and at each side of the spinal column. Because short fibers extend between the sympathetic ganglia, they look a little like two chains of beads and are often referred to as the *sympathetic chain ganglia.* Axons of sympathetic postganglionic neurons travel in spinal nerves to blood vessels, sweat glands, and arrector hair muscles all over the body. Separate autonomic nerves distribute many sympathetic postganglionic axons to various internal organs.

Functions of the Sympathetic Nervous System

The sympathetic nervous system functions as an emergency system. Impulses over sympathetic fibers take control of many internal organs when we exercise strenuously and when strong emotions—anger, fear, hate, anxiety—are elicited. In short, when we must cope with stress of any kind, sympathetic impulses increase to many visceral effectors and rapidly produce widespread changes within our bodies. The middle column of Table 7-3 indicates many sympathetic responses. The heart beats faster. Most blood vessels constrict, causing blood pressure to increase. Blood vessels in skeletal muscles dilate, supplying the muscles with more blood. Sweat glands and adrenal glands secrete more abundantly. Salivary and other digestive glands secrete more sparingly. Digestive tract contractions (peristalsis) become sluggish, hampering digestion. Together, these sympathetic responses make us ready for strenuous muscular work, or they prepare us for *fight or flight.* The group of changes induced by sympathetic control is known as the **fight-or-flight response.**

PARASYMPATHETIC NERVOUS SYSTEM

Structure

The dendrites and cell bodies of parasympathetic preganglionic neurons are located in the gray matter of the brain stem and the sacral segments of the spinal cord. The parasympathetic system has also been referred to as the *craniosacral system.* The preganglionic parasympathetic axons extend some distance before terminating in the parasympathetic ganglia located in the head and in the thoracic and abdominal cavities close to the visceral effectors that they control. The dendrites and cell bodies of parasympathetic postganglionic neurons lie in these outlying parasympathetic ganglia, and their short axons extend into the nearby structures. Therefore each parasympathetic preganglionic neuron synapses only with postganglionic neurons to a single effector. For this reason, parasympathetic stimulation frequently involves response by only one organ. This is not true of sympathetic responses; as noted, sympathetic stimulation usually results in responses by numerous organs.

Functions of the Parasympathetic Nervous System

The parasympathetic system dominates control of many visceral effectors under normal, everyday conditions. Impulses over parasympathetic fibers, for example, tend to slow heartbeat, increase peristalsis, and increase secretion of digestive juices and insulin (Table 7-3).

TABLE 7–3 Autonomic Functions

VISCERAL EFFECTORS	SYMPATHETIC CONTROL	PARASYMPATHETIC CONTROL
Heart muscle	Accelerates heartbeat	Slows heartbeat
Smooth muscle		
Of most blood vessels	Constricts blood vessels	None
Of blood vessels in skeletal muscles	Dilates blood vessels	None
Of the digestive tract	Decreases peristalsis; inhibits defecation	Increases peristalsis
Of the anal sphincter	Stimulates—closes sphincter	Inhibits—opens sphincter for defecation
Of the urinary bladder	Inhibits—relaxes bladder	Stimulates—contracts bladder
Of the urinary sphincters	Stimulates—closes sphincter	Inhibits—opens sphincter for urination
Of the eye		
Iris	Stimulates radial fibers—dilation of pupil	Stimulates circular fibers—constriction of pupil
Ciliary	Inhibits—accomodation for far vision (flattening of lens)	Stimulates—accomodation for near vision (bulging of lens)
Of hairs (pilomotor muscles)	Stimulates—"goose pimples"	No parasympathetic fibers
Glands		
Adrenal medulla	Increases epinephrine secretion	None
Sweat glands	Increases sweat secretion	None
Digestive glands	Decreases secretion of digestive juices	Increases secretion of digestive juices

AUTONOMIC NEUROTRANSMITTERS

Turn your attention now to Figure 7-20. It reveals information about autonomic neurotransmitters, the chemical compounds released from the axon terminals of autonomic neurons. Observe that three of the axons shown in Figure 7-20—the sympathetic preganglionic axon, the parasympathetic preganglionic axon, and the parasympathetic postganglionic axon—release acetylcholine. These axons are therefore classified as **cholinergic fibers.** Only one type of autonomic axon releases the neurotransmitter norepinephrine (noradrenaline). This is the axon of a sympathetic postganglionic neuron, and such neurons are classified as **adrenergic fibers.** The fact that each division of the ANS signals its effectors with a different neurotransmitter explains how an organ can tell which division is stimulating it. The heart, for example, responds to acetylcholine from the parasympathetic division by slowing down. The presence of norepinephrine at the heart, on the other hand, is a signal from the sympathetic division, and the response is an increase in heart activity.

AUTONOMIC NERVOUS SYSTEM AS A WHOLE

The function of the **autonomic nervous system** is to regulate the body's automatic, involuntary functions in ways that maintain or quickly restore homeostasis. Many internal organs are doubly innervated by the ANS. In other words, they receive fibers from parasympathetic and sympathetic divisions. Parasympathetic and sympathetic impulses continually bombard them

FIGURE 7–20 ***Autonomic Neurotransmitters.*** Three of the four fiber types are cholinergic, secreting the neurotransmitter acetylcholine (Ach) into a synapse. Only the sympathetic postganglionic fiber is adrenergic, secreting norepinephrine (NE) into a synapse.

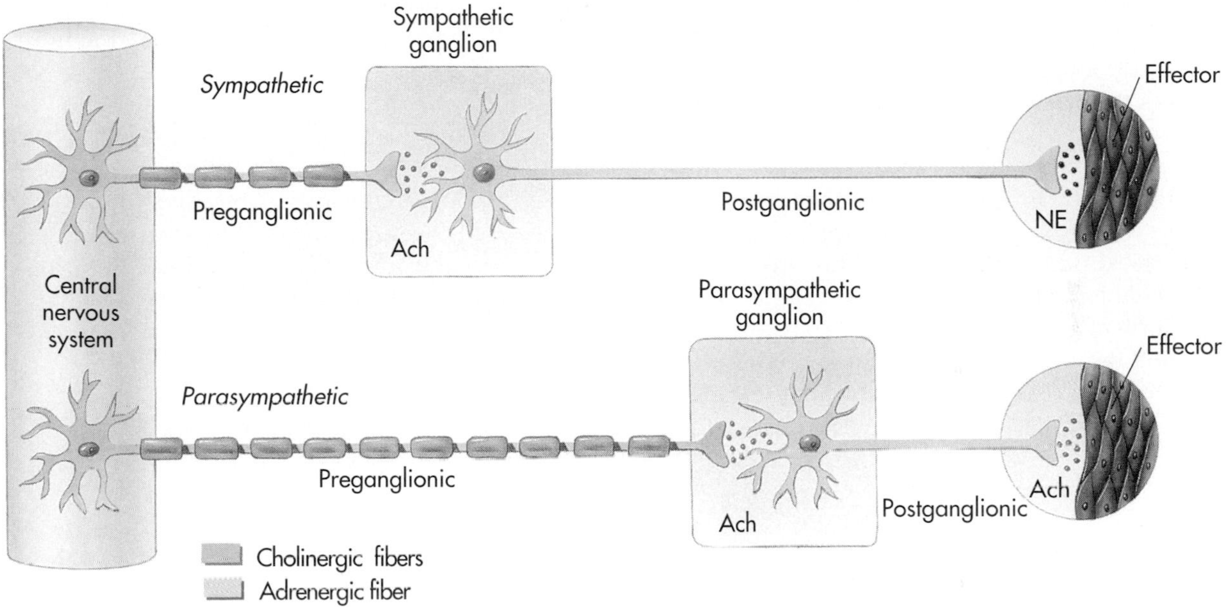

and, as Table 7-3 indicates, influence their function in opposite or antagonistic ways. For example, the heart continually receives sympathetic impulses that make it beat faster and parasympathetic impulses that slow it down. The ratio between these two antagonistic forces, determined by the ratio between the two different autonomic neurotransmitters, determines the actual heart rate.

The name *autonomic nervous system* is something of a misnomer. It seems to imply that this part of the nervous system is independent from other parts. This is not true. Dendrites and cell bodies of preganglionic neurons are located, as observed, in the spinal cord and brain stem. They are continually influenced directly or indirectly by impulses from neurons located above them, notably by some in the hypothalamus and in the parts of the cerebral cortex called the *emotional brain*. Through conduction paths from these areas, emotions can produce widespread changes in the automatic functions of our bodies, in cardiac and smooth muscle contractions, and in secretion by glands. Anger and fear, for example, lead to increased sympathetic activity and the fight-or-flight response. According to some physiologists, the altered state of consciousness known as *meditation* leads to decreased sympathetic activity and a group of changes opposite to those of the fight-or-flight response.

Herpes Zoster or Shingles

Herpes zoster or **shingles** is a unique viral infection that almost always affects the skin of a single dermatome. It is caused by a varicella zoster virus of chickenpox. About 3% of the population will suffer from shingles at some time in their lives. In most cases the disease results from reactivation of the varicella virus. The virus probably traveled through a cutaneous nerve and remained dormant in a dorsal root ganglion for years after an episode of the chickenpox. If the body's immunological protective mechanism becomes diminished in the elderly after stress, or in individuals undergoing radiation therapy or taking immunosuppressive drugs, the virus may reactivate. If this occurs, the virus travels over the sensory nerve to the skin of a single dermatome. The result is a painful eruption of red, swollen plaques or vesicles that eventually rupture and crust before clearing in 2 to 3 weeks. In severe cases, extensive inflammation, hemorrhagic blisters, and secondary bacterial infection may lead to permanent scarring. In most cases, the eruption of vesicles is preceded by 4 to 5 days of preeruptive pain, burning, and itching in the affected dermatome. Unfortunately, an attack of herpes zoster does not confer lasting immunity. Many individuals suffer three or four episodes in a lifetime.

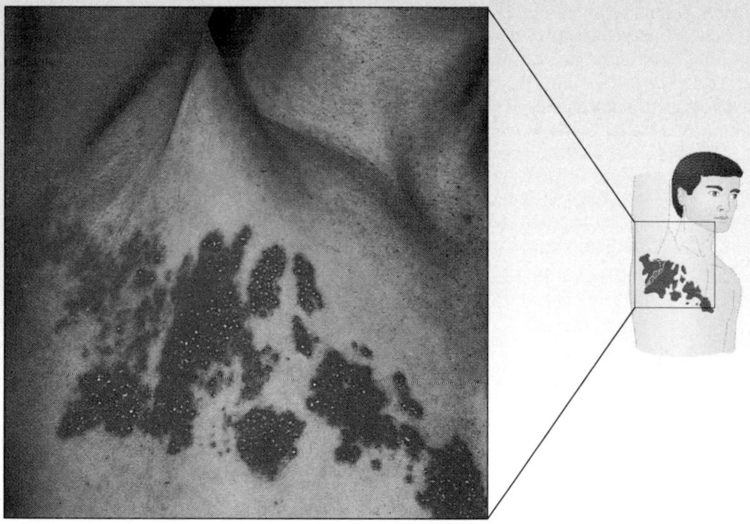

OUTLINE SUMMARY

ORGANS AND DIVISIONS OF THE NERVOUS SYSTEM (Figure 7-1)

A Central nervous system (CNS)—brain and spinal cord
B Peripheral nervous system (PNS)—all nerves
C Autonomic nervous system (ANS)

CELLS OF THE NERVOUS SYSTEM

A Neurons
  1 Consist of three main parts—dendrites: conduct impulses to cell body of neuron; cell body of neuron; and axon: conducts impulses away from cell body of neuron (Figure 7-2)
  2 Neurons classified according to function—sensory: conduct impulses to the spinal cord and brain; motor: conduct impulses away from brain and spinal cord to muscles and glands; and interneurons: conduct impulses from sensory neurons to motor neurons
B Glia—three main types of connective tissue cells of the CNS (Figure 7-3)
  1 Astrocytes—star-shaped cells that anchor small blood vessels to neurons
  2 Microglia—small cells that move in inflamed brain tissue carrying on phagocytosis
  3 Oligodendroglia—form myelin sheaths on axons in the CNS

NERVES (Figure 7-4)

A Nerve—bundle of peripheral axons
  1 Tract—bundle of central axons
  2 White matter—tissue composed primarily of myelinated axons (nerves or tracts)
  3 Gray matter—tissue composed primarily of cell bodies and unmyelinated fibers
B Nerve coverings—fibrous connective tissue
  1 Endoneurium—surrounds individual fibers within a nerve
  2 Perineurium—surrounds a group (fascicle) of nerve fibers
  3 Epineurium—surrounds the entire nerve

REFLEX ARCS

A Nerve impulses are conducted from receptors to effectors over neuron pathways or reflex arcs; conduction by a reflex arc results in a reflex (that is, contraction by a muscle or secretion by a gland)
B Simplest reflex arcs are two-neuron arcs—consist of sensory neurons synapsing in the spinal cord with motor neurons; three-neuron arcs consist of sensory neurons synapsing in the spinal cord with interneurons that synapse with motor neurons (Figure 7-5)

NERVE IMPULSES

A Definition—self-propagating wave of electrical disturbance that travels along the surface of a neuron membrane
B Mechanism
  1 A stimulus triggers the opening of Na^+ channels in the plasma membrane of the neuron
  2 Inward movement of positive sodium ions leaves a slight excess of negative ions outside at a stimulated point; marks the beginning of a nerve impulse

THE SYNAPSE

A Definition—chemical compounds released from axon terminals (of a presynaptic neuron) into a synaptic cleft
B Neurotransmitters bind to specific receptor molecules in the membrane of a postsynaptic neuron, opening ion channels and thereby stimulating impulse conduction by the membrane
C Names of neurotransmitters—acetylcholine, catecholamines (norepinephrine, dopamine, and serotonin), and other compounds

CENTRAL NERVOUS SYSTEM

A Divisions of the brain (Figure 7-9 and Table 7-1)
  1 Brain stem
    a Consists of three parts of brain; named in ascending order, they are the medulla oblongata, pons, and midbrain
    b Structure—white matter with bits of gray matter scattered through it
    c Function—gray matter in the brain stem functions as reflex centers (for example, for heartbeat, respirations, and blood vessel diameter); sensory tracts in the brain stem conduct impulses to the higher parts of the brain; motor tracts conduct from the higher parts of the brain to the spinal cord
  2 Diencephalon
    a Structure and function of the hypothalamus
      (1) Consists mainly of the posterior pituitary gland, pituitary stalk, and gray matter
      (2) Acts as the major center for controlling the ANS; therefore helps control the functioning of most internal organs
      (3) Controls hormone secretion by anterior and posterior pituitary glands; therefore indirectly helps control hormone secretion by most other endocrine glands
      (4) Contains centers for controlling appetite, wakefulness, pleasure, etc.

- **b** Structure and function of the thalamus
  - **(1)** Dumbbell-shaped mass of gray matter in each cerebral hemisphere
  - **(2)** Relays sensory impulses to cerebral cortex sensory areas
  - **(3)** In some way produces the emotions of pleasantness or unpleasantness associated with sensations
- **3** Cerebellum
  - **a** Second largest part of the human brain
  - **b** Helps control muscle contractions to produce coordinated movements so that we can maintain balance, move smoothly, and sustain normal postures
- **4** Cerebrum
  - **a** Largest part of the human brain
  - **b** Outer layer of gray matter is the cerebral cortex; made up of lobes; composed mainly of dendrites and cell bodies of neurons
  - **c** Interior of the cerebrum composed mainly of white matter (that is nerve fibers arranged in bundles called *tracts*)
  - **d** Functions of the cerebrum—mental processes of all types, including sensations, consciousness, memory, and voluntary control of movements

B Spinal cord (Figure 7-11)
- **1** Outer part is composed of white matter made up of many bundles of axons called *tracts;* interior composed of gray matter made up mainly of neuron dendrites and cell bodies
- **2** Functions as the center for all spinal cord reflexes; sensory tracts conduct impulses to the brain, and motor tracts conduct impulses from the brain

C Coverings and fluid spaces of the brain and spinal cord
- **1** Coverings
  - **a** Cranial bones and vertebrae
  - **b** Cerebral and spinal meninges—the dura mater, the pia mater, and the arachnoid (Figure 7-13)
- **2** Fluid spaces—subarachnoid spaces of meninges, central canal inside cord, and ventricles in brain (Figure 7-14)

PERIPHERAL NERVOUS SYSTEM

A Cranial nerves (Figure 7-16 and Table 7-2)
- **1** Twelve pairs—attached to undersurface of the brain
- **2** Connect brain with the neck and structures in the thorax and abdomen

B Spinal nerves
- 1 Structure—contain dendrites of sensory neurons and axons of motor neurons
- **2** Functions—conduct impulses necessary for sensations and voluntary movements

AUTONOMIC NERVOUS SYSTEM

A Autonomic nervous system—motor neurons that conduct impulses from the central nervous system to cardiac muscle, smooth muscle, and glandular epithelial tissue; regulates the body's automatic or involuntary functions (Figure 7-18)

B Autonomic neurons—preganglionic autonomic neurons conduct from spinal cord or brain stem to an autonomic ganglion; postganglionic neurons conduct from autonomic ganglia to cardiac muscle, smooth muscle, and glandular epithelial tissue

C Autonomic or visceral effectors—tissues to which autonomic neurons conduct impulses (that is, cardiac and smooth muscle and glandular epithelial tissue)

D Composed of two divisions—the sympathetic system and the parasympathetic system

E Autonomic conduction paths
- **1** Consist of two-neuron relays (that is, preganglionic neurons from the central nervous system to autonomic ganglia, synapses, postganglionic neurons from ganglia to visceral effectors)
- **2** In contrast, somatic motor neurons conduct all the way from the CNS to somatic effectors with no intervening synapses

F Sympathetic nervous system
- **1** Structure
  - **a** Dendrites and cell bodies of sympathetic preganglionic neurons are located in the gray matter of the thoracic and upper lumbar segments of the spinal cord
  - **b** Axons leave the spinal cord in the anterior roots of spinal nerves, extend to sympathetic or collateral ganglia, and synapse with several postganglionic neurons whose axons extend to spinal or autonomic nerves to terminate in visceral effectors
  - **c** A chain of sympathetic ganglia is in front of and at each side of the spinal column
- **2** Functions
  - **a** Serves as the emergency or stress system, controlling visceral effectors during strenuous exercise and strong emotions (anger, fear, hate, or anxiety)
  - **b** Group of changes induced by sympathetic control is called the *fight-or-flight response*

G Parasympathetic nervous system
- **1** Structure
  - **a** Parasympathetic preganglionic neurons have dendrites and cell bodies in the gray matter of the brain stem and the sacral segments of the spinal cord

  - **b** Parasympathetic preganglionic neurons terminate in parasympathetic ganglia located in the head and the thoracic and abdominal cavities close to visceral effectors
  - **c** Each parasympathetic preganglionic neuron synapses with postganglionic neurons to only one effector
- **2** Function—dominates control of many visceral effectors under normal, everyday conditions

H Autonomic neurotransmitters
- **1** Cholinergic fibers—preganglionic axons of parasympathetic and sympathetic systems and parasympathetic postganglionic axons release acetylcholine
- **2** Adrenergic fibers—axons of sympathetic postganglionic neurons release norepinephrine (noradrenaline)

I Autonomic nervous system as a whole
- **1** Regulates the body's automatic functions in ways that maintain or quickly restore homeostasis
- **2** Many visceral effectors are doubly innervated (that is, they receive fibers from parasympathetic and sympathetic divisions and are influenced in opposite ways by the two divisions)

NEW WORDS

acetylcholine
anesthesia
arachnoid
astrocytes
axon
catecholamines
dendrite
dopamine
dura mater
effectors
endorphins
enkephalins
fight-or-flight response
ganglion
glia
hydrocephalus
interneuron
meninges
microglia
motor neuron
multiple sclerosis
myelin
neurons
neurotransmitter
node of Ranvier
norepinephrine
oligodendroglia
parasympathetic system
pia mater
postganglionic neurons
postsynaptic neuron
preganglionic neuron
presynaptic neuron
receptors
reflex arc
saltatory conduction
sensory neuron
serotonin
sympathetic system
synapse
synaptic cleft
tract

CHAPTER TEST

1. The nervous system as a whole is divided into two principal divisions: the ______________ and ______________ nervous systems.
2. The tough, fluid-containing membrane surrounding the brain and spinal cord is called the ______________.
3. The medical name describing an accumulation of CSF in the ventricles of the brain is ______________.
4. The two principal types of specialized cells found in the nervous system are ______________ and ______________.
5. Nervous system cells that form the myelin sheaths around nerve fibers in the brain and spinal cord are called ______________.
6. Nervous impulses travel ______________ from a nerve cell body in a single process called the ______________.
7. The microscopic space that separates the axon endings of one neuron from the dendrites of another neuron is called a ______________.
8. Chemical compounds released from axon terminals into synaptic clefts are called ______________.
9. An area of skin supplied by a single spinal nerve is called a ______________.
10. Two natural, morphinelike painkillers produced in the brain are called ______________ and ______________.
11. The two major structures that make up the diencephalon are called the ______________ and ______________.
12. There are ______________ pairs of cranial nerves and ______________ pairs of spinal nerves.
13. Motor neurons in the ANS conduct impulses to three kinds of tissues: ______________, ______________, and ______________.
14. The ANS consists of two divisions called the ______________ and ______________ divisions.
15. Strong emotions and strenuous exercise activate the ______________ division of the ANS.

Select the most correct answer from Column B for each statement in Column A. (Only one answer is correct.)

COLUMN A	COLUMN B
16. ______ Meninges	a. Microglia
17. ______ Transmit impulses to a neuron	b. Schwann cells
18. ______ Capable of phagocytosis	c. Pia mater
19. ______ Produce myelin	d. Response to stress
20. ______ Natural pain killer	e. Endorphin
21. ______ Brain tumor	f. Gray matter
22. ______ Nerve cell bodies	g. Cerebrum
23. ______ Largest part of the brain	h. Dendrites
24. ______ Fight-or-flight response	i. Glioma

REVIEW QUESTIONS

1. What general function does the nervous system perform?
2. What other system performs the same general function as the nervous system?
3. What general functions does the spinal cord perform?
4. What does *CNS* mean? *PNS?*
5. What are the meninges?
6. What general functions does the cerebellum perform?
7. What general functions does the cerebrum perform?
8. What general functions do spinal nerves perform?
9. Define briefly each of the terms listed under "New Words."
10. Identify interneuron, motor neuron, reflex center, sensory neuron, somatic motor neuron, and synapse.
11. Compare parasympathetic and sympathetic functions.

CRITICAL THINKING

12. Why is the medulla considered the most vital part of the brain?
13. Explain the fight-or-flight response.
14. Contrast visceral and somatic effectors.

The Senses

OUTLINE

Classification of Sense Organs

Converting a Stimulus Into a Sensation

General Sense Organs

Special Sense Organs

- The Eye
- The Ear
- The Taste Receptors
- The Smell Receptors

BOXED ESSAYS

Focusing Problems
Color Blindness
Swimmer's Ear

OBJECTIVES

After you have completed this chapter, you should be able to:

1. Classify sense organs as special or general and explain the basic differences between the two groups.
2. Discuss how a stimulus is converted into a sensation.
3. Discuss the general sense organs and their functions.
4. List the major senses.
5. Describe the structure of the eye and the functions of its components.
6. Discuss the anatomy of the ear and its sensory function in hearing and equilibrium.
7. Discuss the chemical receptors and their functions.

If you were asked to name the sense organs, what organs would you name? Can you think of any besides the eyes, ears, nose, and taste buds? Actually there are millions of other sense organs throughout the body in our skin, internal organs, and muscles. They constitute the many **sensory receptors** that allow us to respond to stimuli such as touch, pressure, temperature, and pain. These microscopic receptors are located at the tips of dendrites of sensory neurons.

Our ability to "sense" changes in our external and internal environments is a requirement for maintaining homeostasis and for survival itself. We can initiate protective reflexes important to homeostasis only if we can sense a change or danger. External dangers may be detected by sight or hearing. If the danger is internal, such as overstretching a muscle, detecting an increase in body temperature (fever), or sensing the pain caused by an ulcer, other receptors make us aware of the problem and permit us to take appropriate action to maintain homeostasis.

Classification of Sense Organs

The sense organs are often classified as **special** sense organs and **general** sense organs. Special sense organs, such as the eye, are characterized by large and complex organs or by localized groupings of specialized receptors in areas such as the nasal mucosa or tongue. The general sense organs for detecting stimuli such as pain and touch are microscopic receptors widely distributed throughout the body.

Receptors are often classified according to the types of stimuli that activate them and whether or not they are *encapsulated* or *unencapsulated*, that is, whether or not they are covered by some sort of capsule or are "free" or "naked" of any such covering. Receptors in the retina of the eye are stimulated by light *(photoreceptors)*, whereas taste and smell are activated by chemical stimuli *(chemoreceptors)*. Still other receptors respond to physical damage or injury *(pain receptors)*, changes in temperature *(thermoreceptors)*, or to mechanical stimuli that change their position or in some way deform the capsule that surrounds them *(mechanoreceptors)*. Table 8-1 classifies the general sense organs and Table 8-2 on p. 176 classifies the special sense organs.

Converting a Stimulus Into a Sensation

All sense organs, regardless of size, type, or location, have in common some important functional characteristics. First, they must be able to sense or detect a stimulus in their environment. Of course, different sense organs detect different types of stimuli. Whether it is light, sound, temperature change, mechanical pressure, or the presence of chemicals ultimately identified as taste or smell, the stimulus must be changed into an electrical signal or nerve impulse. This signal is then transmitted over a nervous system "pathway" to the brain, where the sensation is actually perceived.

General Sense Organs

Groups of highly specialized and localized receptors are typically associated with the special senses. In the general sense organs, however, receptors are found in almost every part of the body, but are concentrated in the skin (Figure 8-1). To demonstrate this fact, try touching any point of your skin with the tip of a toothpick. You can hardly miss stimulating at least one receptor and almost instantaneously experiencing a sensation of touch. Stimulation of some receptors leads to the sensation of vibration; stimulation of others gives the sensation of pressure, and stimulation of still others gives the sensation of pain or temperature. General sense receptors are listed in Table 8-1 and illustrated in Figure 8-1.

Some specialized receptors found near the point of junction between tendons and muscles and others found deep within skeletal muscle tissue are called *proprioceptors*. When stimulated, they provide us with information concerning the position or movement of the different parts of the body as well as the length and the extent of contraction of our muscles. The Golgi tendon receptors and muscle spindles identified in Table 8-1 are important proprioceptors.

TABLE 8–1 General Sense Organs

TYPE	MAIN LOCATIONS	GENERAL SENSES	
Free nerve endings (naked nerve endings)	Skin and mucosa (epithelial layers)	Pain, crude touch, and possibly temperature	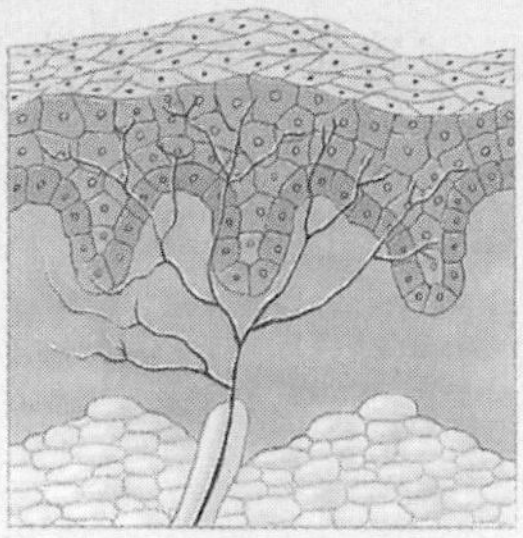
Encapsulated nerve endings			
Meissner's corpuscles	Skin (in papillae of dermis) and fingertips and lips (numerous)	Fine touch and vibration	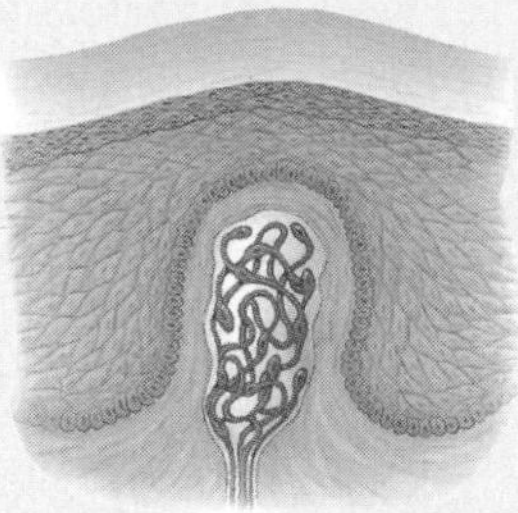
Ruffini's corpuscles	Skin (dermal layer) and subcutaneous tissue of fingers	Touch and pressure	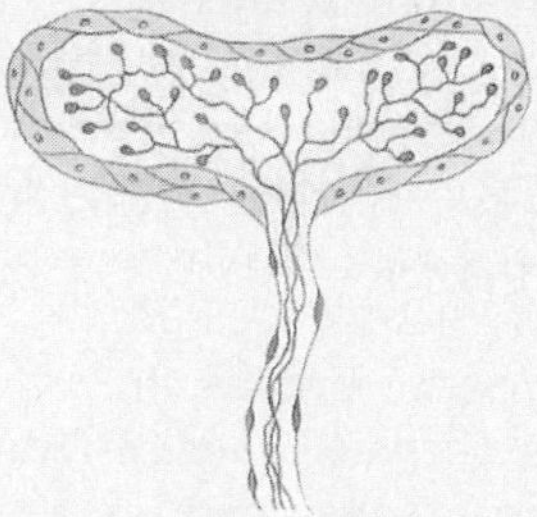
Pacinian corpuscles	Subcutaneous, submucous, and subserous tissues; around joints; in mammary glands and external genitals of both sexes	Pressure and vibration	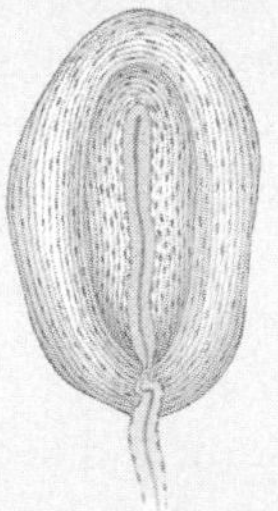
Krause's end-bulbs	Skin (dermal layer), subcutaneous tissue, mucosa of lips and eyelids, and external genitals	Touch and possibly cold	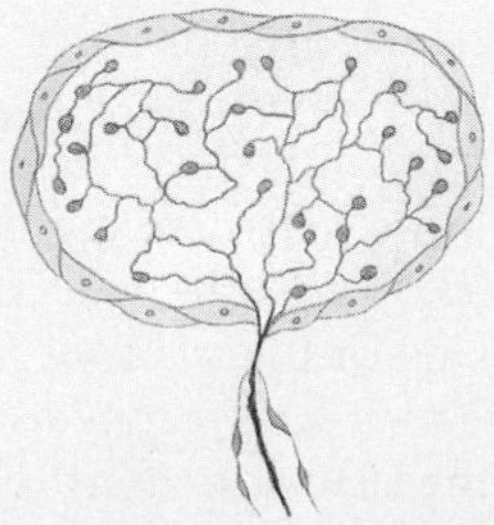

TABLE 8–1 General Sense Organs—cont'd

TYPE	MAIN LOCATIONS	GENERAL SENSES	
Encapsulated nerve endings—cont'd			
Golgi tendon receptors	Near junction of tendons and muscles	Proprioception	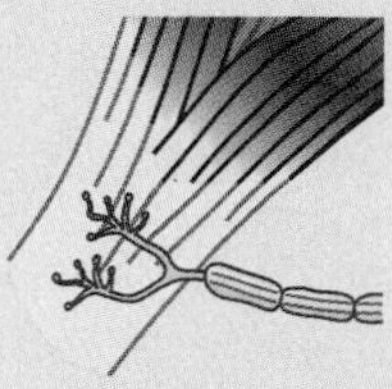
Muscle spindles	Skeletal muscles	Proprioception	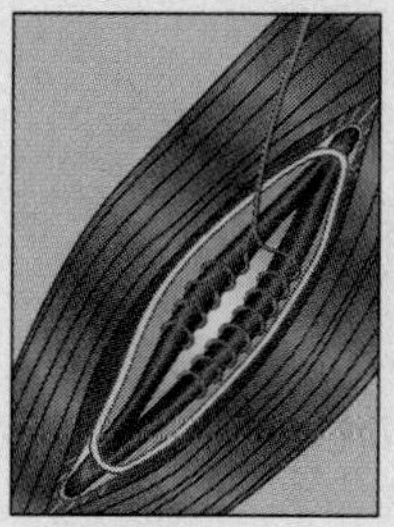

FIGURE 8–1 *General Sense Receptors.* This section of skin shows the placement of a number of receptors described in Table 8-1.

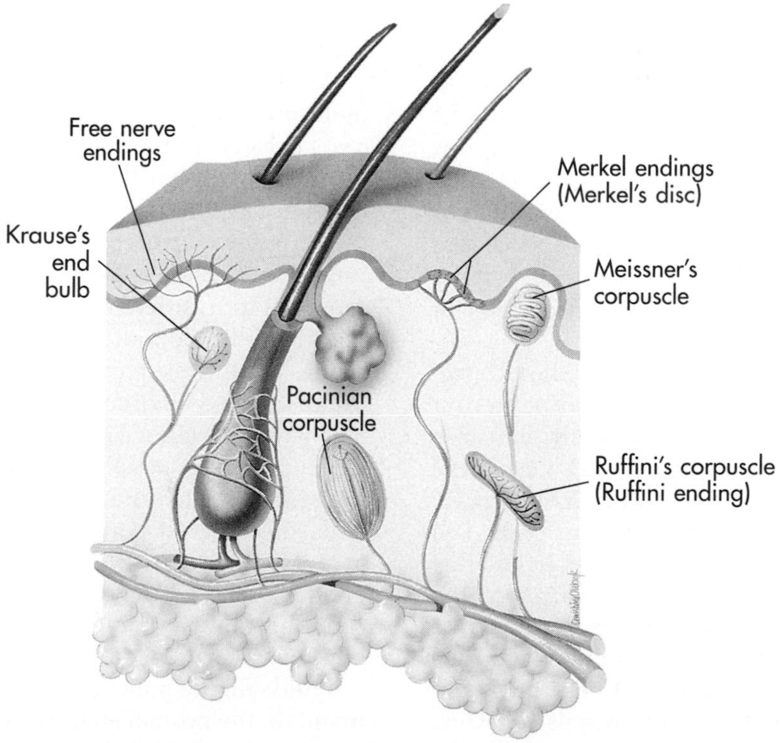

TABLE 8–2 Special Sense Organs

SENSE ORGAN	SPECIFIC RECEPTOR	TYPE OF RECEPTOR	SENSE
Eye	Rods and cones	Photoreceptor	Vision
Ear	Organ of Corti	Mechanoreceptor	Hearing
	Cristae ampullares	Mechanoreceptor	Balance
Nose	Olfactory cells	Chemoreceptor	Smell
Taste buds	Gustatory cells	Chemoreceptor	Taste

Special Sense Organs

THE EYE

When you look at a person's eye, you see only a small part of the whole eye. Three layers of tissue form the eyeball: the **sclera** (SKLE-rah), the **choroid** (KO-royd), and the **retina** (RET-i-nah) (Figure 8-2). The outer layer of sclera consists of tough fibrous tissue. The "white" of the eye is part of the front surface of the sclera. The other part of the front surface of the sclera is called the *cornea* and is sometimes spoken of as the window of the eye because of its transparency. At a casual glance, however, it does not look transparent but appears blue, brown, gray, or green because it lies over the **iris,** the colored part of the eye. A mucous membrane known as the **conjunctiva** (kon-junk-TEE-vah) lines the eyelids and covers the sclera in front. The conjunctiva is kept moist by tears formed in the **lacrimal gland** located in the upper lateral portion of the orbit.

The middle layer of the eyeball, the *choroid,* contains a dark pigment to prevent the scattering of incoming light rays. Two involuntary muscles make up the front part of the choroid. One is the *iris,* the colored structure seen through the cornea, and the other is the *ciliary muscle* (Figure 8-2). The black center of the iris is really a hole in this doughnut-shaped muscle; it is the **pupil** of the eye. Some of the fibers of the iris are arranged like spokes in a wheel. When they contract, the pupils dilate, letting in more light rays. Other fibers are circular. When they contract, the pupils constrict, letting in fewer light rays. Normally, the pupils constrict in bright light and dilate in dim light. When we look at distant objects, the ciliary muscle is relaxed, and the lens has only a slightly curved shape. To focus on near objects, however, the ciliary muscle must contract. As it contracts, it pulls the choroid coat forward toward the lens, thus causing the lens to bulge and curve even more. Most of us become more farsighted as we grow older and lose the ability to focus on close objects because our lenses lose their elasticity and can no longer bulge enough to bring near objects into focus. **Presbyopia** or "oldsightedness" is the name for this condition.

The *retina* or innermost layer of the eyeball contains microscopic receptor cells, called *rods* and *cones* because of their shapes. Dim light can stimulate the rods, but fairly bright light is necessary to stimulate the cones. In other words, **rods** are the receptors for night vision and **cones** for daytime vision. There are three kinds of cones; each is sensitive to a different color: red, green, or blue. Scattered throughout the central portion of the retina, these three types of cones allow us to distinguish between different colors.

There is a yellowish area near the center of the retina called the *macula lutea.* It surrounds a small depression, called the **fovea centralis,** which contains the greatest concentration of cones of any area of the retina (Figure 8-2). In good light, greater *visual acuity,* or sharpness of visual perception, can be obtained if we look directly at an object and focus the image on the fovea.

Fluids fill the hollow inside of the eyeball. They maintain the normal shape of the eyeball and help refract light rays; that is, the fluids bend light rays

FIGURE 8–2 ***Horizontal Section Through the Left Eyeball.*** The eye is viewed from above.

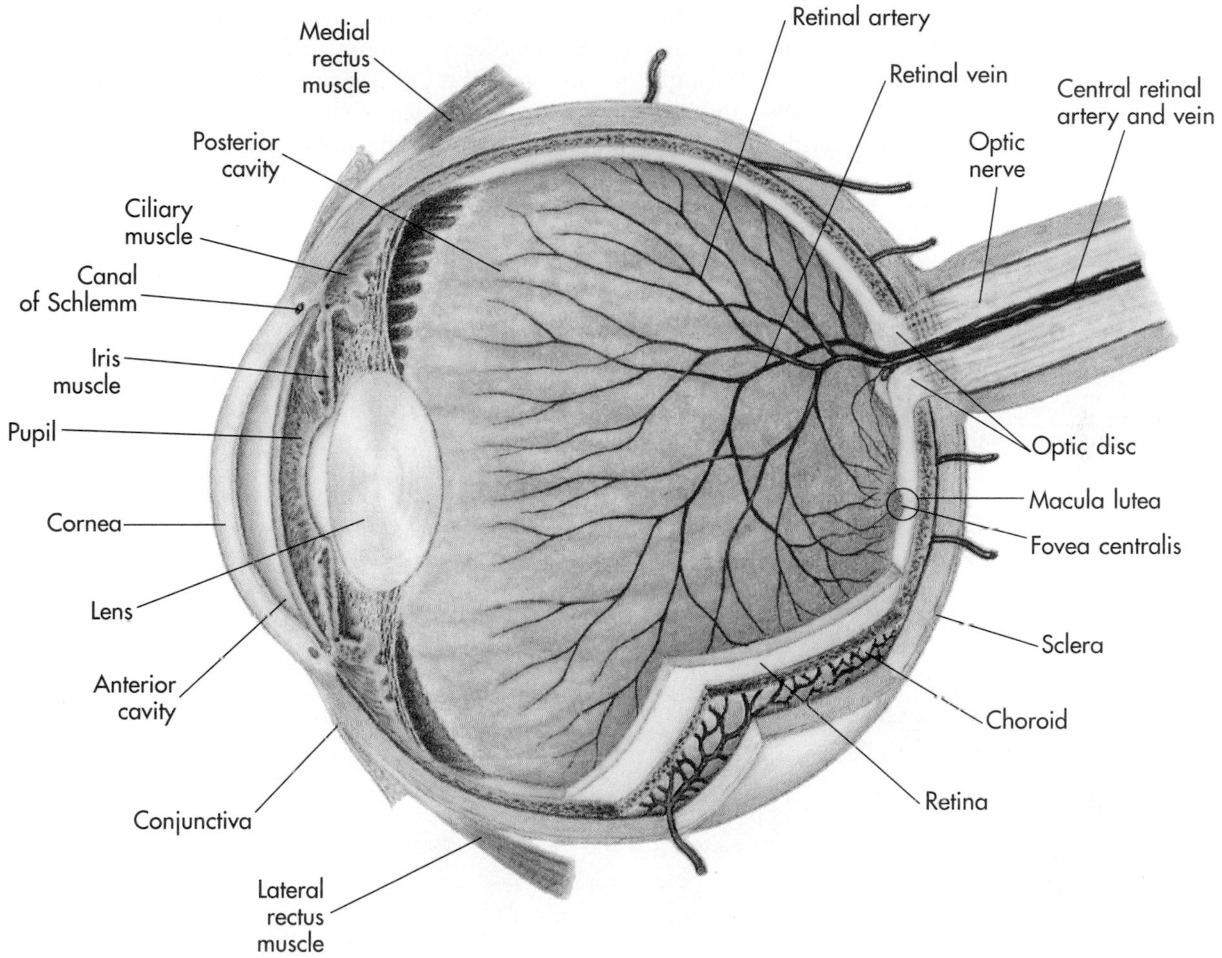

to bring them to focus on the retina. **Aqueous humor** is the name of the watery fluid in front of the lens (in the anterior cavity of the eye), and **vitreous humor** is the name of the jellylike fluid behind the lens (in the posterior cavity). Aqueous humor is constantly being formed, drained, and replaced in the anterior cavity. If drainage is blocked for any reason, the internal pressure within the eye will increase, and damage that could lead to blindness will occur. This condition is called **glaucoma** (glaw-KO-mah).

The **lens** of the eye lies directly behind the pupil. It is held in place by a ligament attached to the ciliary muscle. In most young people, the lens is transparent and somewhat elastic so that it is capable of changing shape. Exposure to ultraviolet (UV) radiation in sunlight causes the lens to become hard and milky. Over the years, repeated exposure to sunlight may cause **cataracts** or milky spots on the lens. Large or numerous cataracts may cause blindness. Cataracts can be removed surgically and replaced with artificial lenses. Many scientists believe that wearing sunglasses that filter UV radiation from an early age will help prevent the formation of cataracts.

Visual Pathway

Light is the stimulus that results in vision (that is, our ability to see objects as they exist in our environment). Light enters the eye through the pupil and is *refracted* or bent so that it is focused on the retina. Refraction occurs as light passes through the cornea, the aqueous humor, the lens, and the vitreous humor on its way to the retina.

The innermost layer of the retina contains the rods and cones, which are the *photoreceptor* cells of the eye (Figure 8-3). They respond to a light stimulus by producing a nervous impulse. The rod and cone photoreceptor cells synapse with neurons in the bipolar and ganglionic layers of the retina. Nervous signals eventually leave the retina and exit the eye through the optic nerve on the posterior surface of the eyeball. No rods or cones are present in the area of the retina where the optic nerve fibers exit. The result is a "blind spot" known as the *optic disc* (Figure 8-2).

FIGURE 8–3 ***Cells of the Retina.*** Photoreceptors called *rods* and *cones* (notice their shapes) detect changes in light and relay the information to bipolar neurons. The bipolar cells, in turn, conduct the information to ganglion cells. The information eventually leaves the eye by way of the optic nerve.

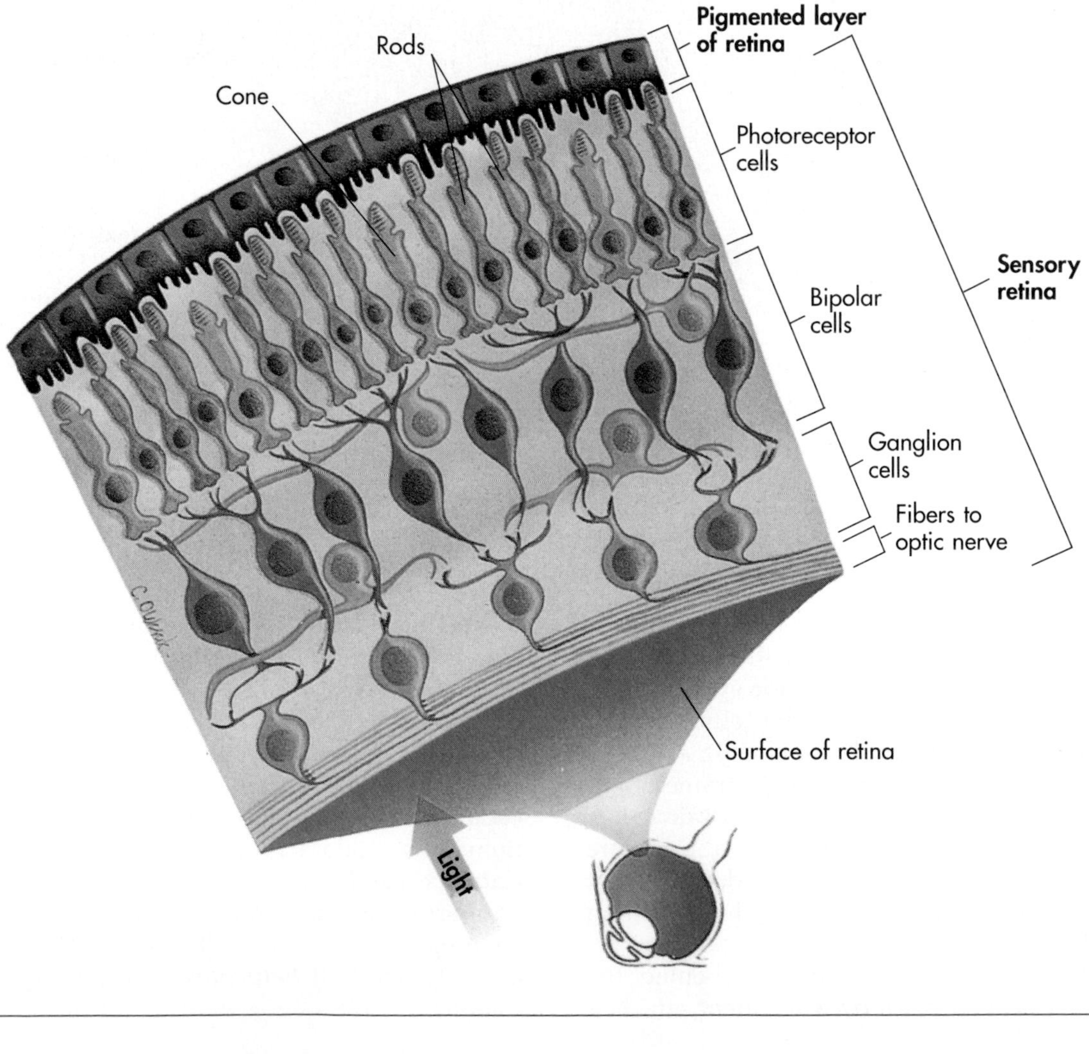

Focusing Problems

Focusing a clear image on the retina is essential for good vision. In the normal eye *(A)*, light rays enter the eye and are focused into a clear, upside-down image on the retina. The brain can easily right the upside-down image in our conscious perception but cannot fix an image that is not sharply focused. If our eyes are elongated *(B)*, the image focuses in front of the retina rather than on it. The retina receives only a fuzzy image. This condition, called **myopia** or *nearsightedness*, can be corrected by using contact lenses or glasses *(C)*. If our eyes are shorter than normal *(D)*, the image focuses behind the retina, also producing a fuzzy image. This condition, called **hyperopia** or *farsightedness*, can also be corrected by lenses *(E)*.

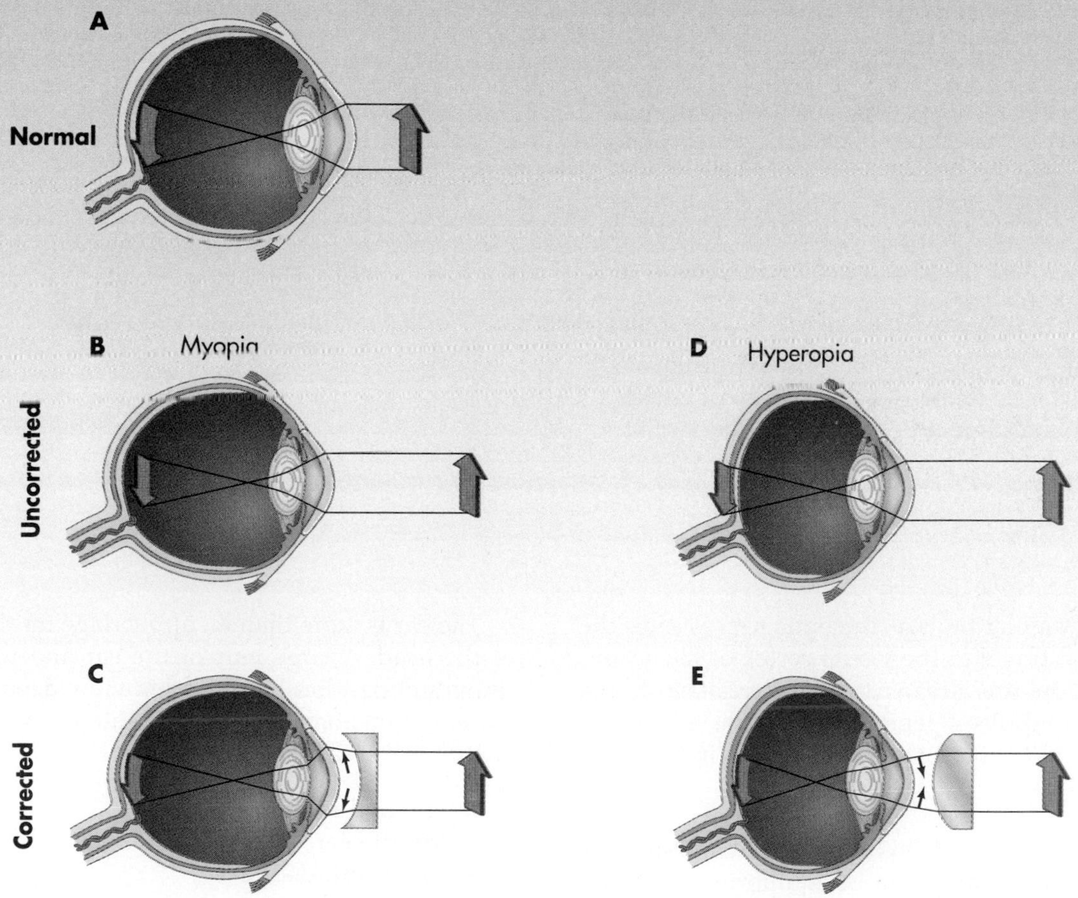

Color Blindness

Color blindness, usually an inherited condition, is caused by mistakes in producing three chemicals called *photopigments* in the cones. Each photopigment is sensitive to one of the three primary colors of light: green, blue, and red. In many cases, the green-sensitive photopigment is missing or deficient; other times, the red-sensitive photopigment is abnormal. (Deficiency of the blue-sensitive photopigment is very rare.) Color-blind individuals see colors, but they cannot distinguish between them normally.

Figures such as those shown here are often used to screen individuals for color blindness. A person with red-green blindness cannot see the *74* in Figure *A*, whereas a person with normal vision can. To determine which photopigment is deficient, a color-blind person may try a figure similar to *B*. Persons with a deficiency of red-sensitive photopigment can distinguish only the *2*; those deficient in green-sensitive photopigment can only see the *4*.

A

B

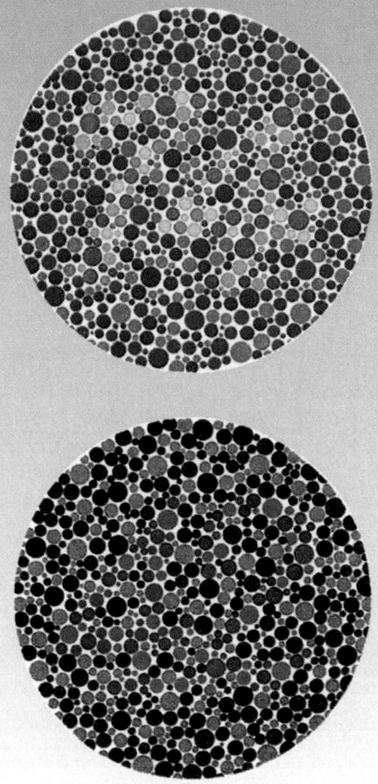

After leaving the eye, the optic nerves enter the brain and travel to the visual cortex of the occipital lobe. In this area, *visual interpretation* of the nervous impulses generated by light stimuli in the rods and cones of the retina result in "seeing."

THE EAR

In addition to its role in hearing, the ear also functions as the sense organ of equilibrium and balance. As we shall later see, the stimulation or "trigger" that activates receptors involved with hearing and equilibrium is mechanical, and the receptors themselves are called *mechanoreceptors* (mek-an-o-ree-SEP-tors). Physical forces that involve sound vibrations and fluid movements are responsible for initiating nervous impulses eventually perceived as sound and balance.

The ear is more than an appendage on the side of the head. A large part of the ear and its most important part lies hidden from view deep inside the temporal bone. It is divided into the following anatomical areas (Figure 8-4):

1. **External ear**
2. **Middle ear**
3. **Inner (internal) ear**

External Ear

The external ear has two parts: the **auricle** (AW-ri-kul) or pinna and the **external auditory canal.** The auricle is the appendage on the side of the head surrounding the opening of the external auditory canal. The canal itself is a curving tube about 2.5 cm (1 inch) in length. It extends into the temporal

like a "tube within a tube." This is the **membranous labyrinth,** and it is filled with a thicker fluid called **endolymph** (EN-doe-limf).

The specialized mechanoreceptors for balance and equilibrium are located in the three semicircular canals and the vestibule. The three half-circle semicircular canals are oriented at right angles to one another (Figure 8-5). Within each canal is a dilated area called the *ampulla* that contains a specialized receptor called a **crista** (KRIS-tah) **ampullaris** (am-pyoo-LAIR-is), which generates a nerve impulse when you move your head. The sensory cells in the cristae ampullares have hairlike extensions that are suspended in the endolymph. The sensory cells are stimulated when movement of the head causes the endolymph to move, thus causing the hairs to bend. Nerves from other receptors in the vestibule join those from the semicircular canals to form the **vestibular nerve,** which joins with the cochlear nerve to form the acoustic nerve or cranial nerve VIII (Figure 8-5). Eventually, nervous impulses passing through this nerve reach the cerebellum and medulla. Other connections from these areas result in impulses reaching the cerebral cortex.

The organ of hearing, which lies in the snail-shaped cochlea, is the **organ of Corti** (KOR-tie). It is surrounded by endolymph, filling the membranous cochlea or **cochlear duct,** which is the membranous tube within the bony cochlea. Specialized hair cells on the organ of Corti generate nerve impulses when they are bent by the movement of endolymph set in motion by sound waves (Figures 8-5 and 8-6).

FIGURE 8–6 ***Effect of Sound Waves on Cochlear Structures.*** Sound waves strike the tympanic membrane and cause it to vibrate. This vibration causes the membrane of the oval window to vibrate. This vibration causes the perilymph in the bony labyrinth of the cochlea to move, which causes the endolymph in the membranous labyrinth of the cochlea or cochlear duct to move. This movement of endolymph stimulates hair cells on the organ of Corti to generate a nerve impulse. The nerve impulse travels over the cochlear nerve, which becomes a part of the eighth cranial nerve. Eventually, nerve impulses reach the auditory cortex and are interpreted as sound.

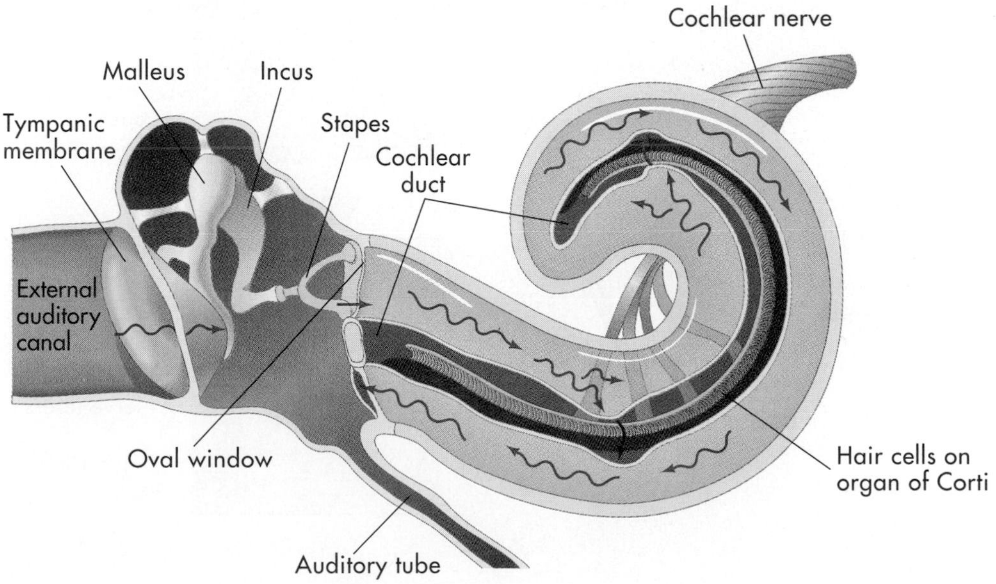

Swimmer's Ear

External otitis or *swimmer's ear* is a common infection of the external ear in athletes. It can be bacterial or fungal in origin and is usually associated with prolonged exposure to water. The infection generally involves, at least to some extent, the auditory canal and auricle. The ear as a whole is tender, red, and swollen. Treatment of swimmer's ear usually involves antibiotic therapy and prescription analgesics.

THE TASTE RECEPTORS

The chemical receptors, or chemoreceptors, that generate nervous impulses resulting in the sense of taste are called **taste buds.** About 10,000 of these microscopic receptors are found on the sides of much larger structures on the tongue called **papillae** (pah-PIL-ee) and also as portions of other tissues in the mouth and throat. Nervous impulses are generated by specialized cells in taste buds, called **gustatory** (GUS-tah-toe-ree) **cells.** They respond to dissolved chemicals in the saliva that bathe the tongue and mouth tissues (Figure 8-7).

Only four kinds of taste sensations—sweet, sour, bitter, and salty—result from stimulation of

FIGURE 8-7 *The Tongue.* **A,** Dorsal surface and regions sensitive to various tastes. **B,** Section through a papilla with taste buds on the side. **C,** Enlarged view of a section through a taste bud.

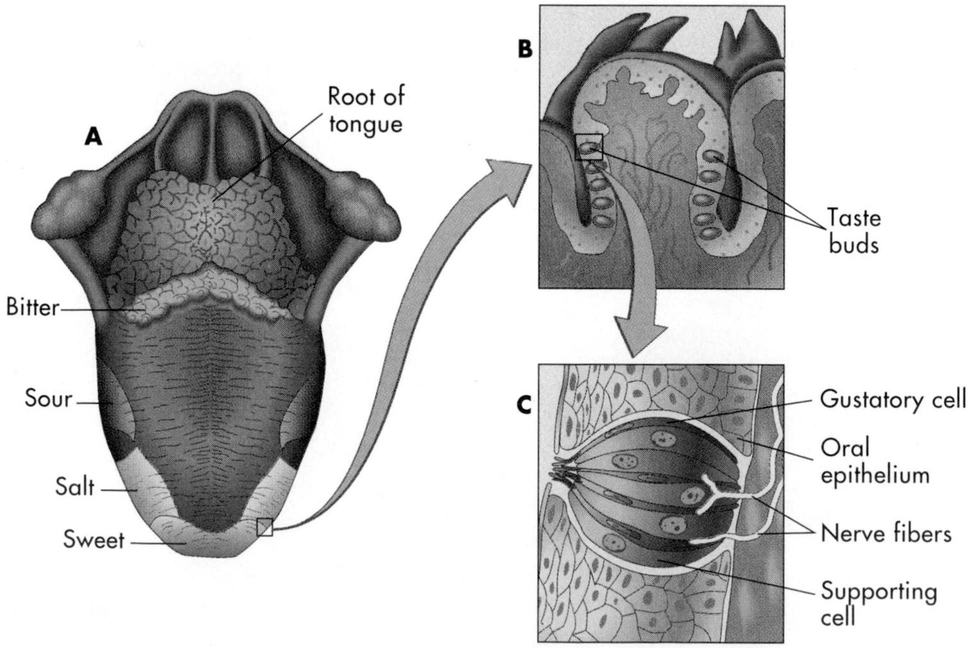

taste buds. All other flavors result from a combination of taste bud and olfactory receptor stimulation. In other words, the myriads of tastes recognized are not tastes alone but tastes plus odors. For this reason a cold that interferes with the stimulation of the olfactory receptors by odors from foods in the mouth markedly dulls taste sensations. Nervous impulses that are generated by stimulation of taste buds travel primarily through two cranial nerves (VII and IX) to end in the specialized taste area of the cerebral cortex.

THE SMELL RECEPTORS

The chemoreceptors responsible for the sense of smell are located in a small area of epithelial tissue in the upper part of the nasal cavity (Figure 8-8). The location of the **olfactory receptors** is somewhat hidden, and we are often forced to forcefully sniff air to smell delicate odors. Each olfactory cell has a number of specialized cilia that sense different chemicals and cause the cell to respond by generating a nervous impulse. To be detected by olfactory receptors, chemicals must be dissolved in the watery mucus that lines the nasal cavity.

Although the olfactory receptors are extremely sensitive (that is, stimulated by even very slight odors), they are also easily fatigued—a fact that explains why odors that are at first very noticeable are not sensed at all after a short time. After the olfactory cells are stimulated by odor-causing chemicals, the resulting nerve impulse travels through the olfactory nerves in the olfactory bulb and tract and then enters the thalamic and olfactory centers of the brain, where the nervous impulses are interpreted as specific odors. The pathways taken by olfactory nerve impulses and the areas where these impulses are interpreted are closely associated with areas of the brain important in memory and emotion. For this reason, we may retain vivid and long-lasting memories of particular smells and odors.

FIGURE 8–8 ***Olfactory Structures.*** Gas molecules stimulate olfactory cells in the nasal epithelium. Sensory information is then conducted along nerves in the olfactory bulb and olfactory tract to sensory processing centers in the brain.

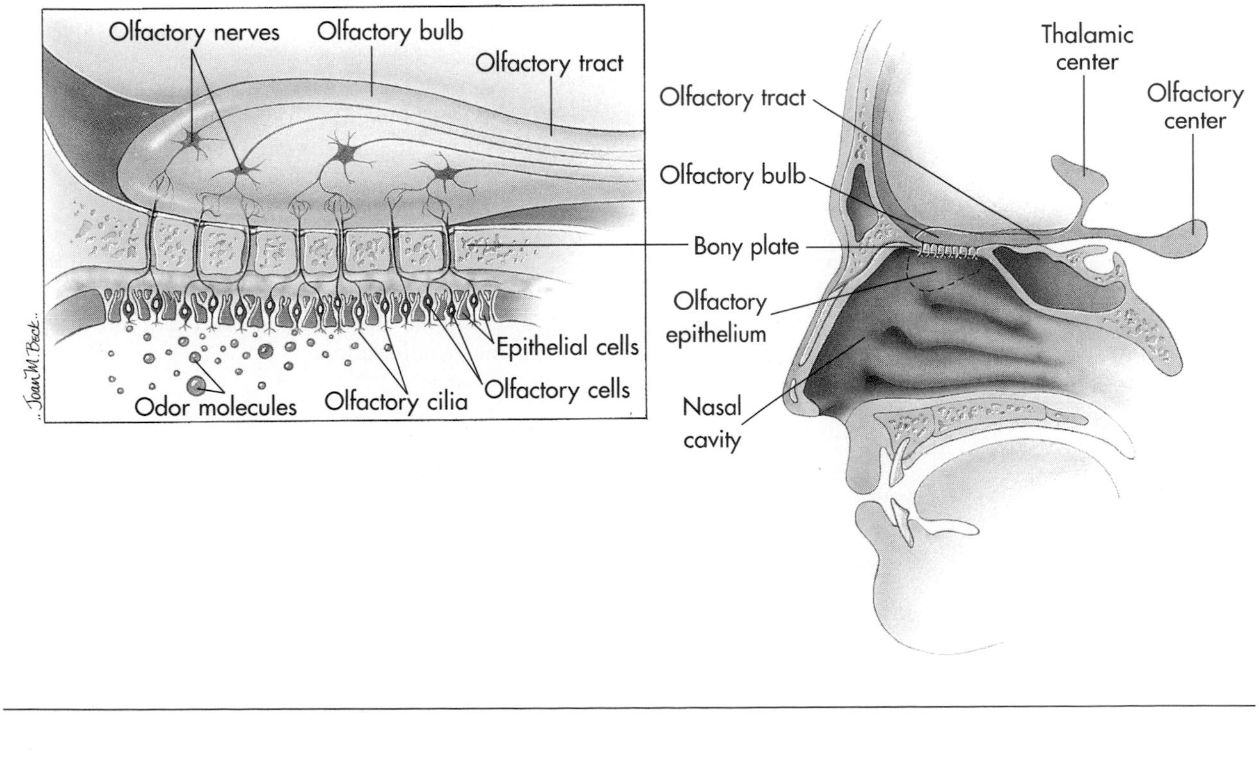

OUTLINE SUMMARY

CLASSIFICATION OF SENSE ORGANS

A General sense organs (Table 8-1)
  1 Often exist as individual cells or receptor units
  2 Widely distributed throughout the body
B Special sense organs (Table 8-2)
  1 Large and complex organs
  2 Localized grouping of specialized receptors
C Classification by presence or absence of covering capsule
  1 Encapsulated
  2 Unencapsulated ("free" or "naked")
D Classification by type of stimuli required to activate receptors
  1 Photoreceptors (light)
  2 Chemoreceptors (chemicals)
  3 Pain receptors (injury)
  4 Thermoreceptors (temperature change)
  5 Mechanoreceptors (movement or deforming of capsule)
  6 Proprioceptors (position of body parts or changes in muscle length or tension)

CONVERTING A STIMULUS INTO A SENSATION

A All sense organs have common functional characteristics
  1 All are able to detect a particular stimulus
  2 A stimulus is converted into a nerve impulse
  3 A nerve impulse is perceived as a sensation in the CNS

GENERAL SENSE ORGANS (Table 8-1)

A Distribution is widespread; single-cell receptors are common
B Examples (Figure 8-1, Table 8-1)
  1 Free nerve endings—pain and crude touch
  2 Meissner's corpuscles—fine touch and vibration
  3 Ruffini's corpuscles—touch and pressure
  4 Pacinian corpuscles—pressure and vibration
  5 Krause's end-bulbs—touch
  6 Golgi tendon receptors—proprioception
  7 Muscle spindles—proprioception

SPECIAL SENSE ORGANS

A The eye (Figure 8-2)
  1 Layers of eyeball
    a Sclera—tough outer coat; "white" of eye; cornea is transparent part of sclera over iris
    b Choroid—pigmented vascular layer prevents scattering of light; front part of this layer made of ciliary muscle and iris, the colored part of the eye; the pupil is the hole in the center of the iris; contraction of iris muscle dilates or constricts pupil
    c Retina (Figure 8-3)—innermost layer of the eye; contains rods (receptors for night vision) and cones (receptors for day vision and color vision)
  2 Conjunctiva—mucous membrane covering the front surface of the sclera and lining the eyelid
  3 Lens—transparent body behind the pupil; focuses light rays on the retina
  4 Eye fluids
    a Aqueous humor—in the anterior cavity in front of the lens
    b Vitreous humor—in the posterior cavity behind the lens
  5 Visual pathway
    a Innermost layer of retina contains rods and cones
    b Impulse travels from the rods and cones through the bipolar and ganglionic layers of retina (Figure 8-3)
    c Nerve impulse leaves the eye through the optic nerve; the point of exit is free of receptors and is therefore called a *blind spot*
    d Visual interpretation occurs in the visual cortex of the cerebrum
B The ear
  1 The ear functions in hearing and in equilibrium and balance
    a Receptors for hearing and equilibrium are mechanoreceptors

2 Divisions of the ear (Figure 8-4)
  a External ear
    (1) Auricle (pinna)
    (2) External auditory canal
      (a) Curving canal 2.5 cm (1 inch) in length
      (b) Contains ceruminous glands
      (c) Ends at the tympanic membrane
  b Middle ear
    (1) Houses ear ossicles—malleus, incus, and stapes
    (2) Ends in the oval window
    (3) The auditory (eustachian) tube connects the middle ear to the throat
    (4) Inflammation called *otitis media*
  c Inner ear (Figure 8-5)
    (1) Bony labyrinth filled with perilymph
    (2) Subdivided into the vestibule, semicircular canals, and cochlea
    (3) Membranous labyrinth filled with endolymph
    (4) The receptors for balance in the semicircular canals are called *cristae ampullaris*
    (5) Specialized hair cells on the organ of Corti respond when bent by the movement of surrounding endolymph set in motion by sound waves (Figure 8-6)

C The taste receptors (Figure 8-7)
  1 Receptors are chemoreceptors called *taste buds*
  2 Cranial nerves VII and IX carry gustatory impulses
  3 Only four kinds of taste sensations—sweet, sour, bitter, salty
  4 Gustatory and olfactory senses work together

D The smell receptors (Figure 8-8)
  1 Receptors for fibers of olfactory or cranial nerve I lie in olfactory mucosa of nasal cavity
  2 Olfactory receptors are extremely sensitive but easily fatigued
  3 Odor-causing chemicals initiate a nervous signal that is interpreted as a specific odor by the brain

N E W W O R D S

aqueous humor	crista ampullaris	organ of Corti	pupil
auricle	endolymph	ossicles	retina
cataract	glaucoma	papillae	sclera
chemoreceptor	gustatory cells	perilymph	semicircular canals
choroid	lacrimal gland	photoreceptor	tympanic membrane
cochlea	lens	presbyopia	vitreous humor
conjunctiva	mechanoreceptor	proprioception	

CHAPTER TEST

1. ______________ sense organs are widely distributed throughout the body.
2. The receptors involved in vision are called ______________ and ______________.
3. The three layers of tissue that form the eyeball are the ______________, the ______________, and the ______________.
4. The colored structure seen through the cornea of the eye is called the ______________.
5. The fluid found in the anterior cavity of the eye is called ______________.
6. The loss of lens transparency is a condition called ______________.
7. The area of the retina that helps to reduce light scattering is called the ______________ retina.
8. The type of receptors involved with hearing and equilibrium are called ______________.
9. The major anatomical areas of the ear are called: ______________ ear; ______________ ear; and ______________ ear.
10. The ear ossicle attached to the tympanic membrane is called the ______________.
11. The bony labyrinth is filled with fluid called ______________.
12. The hearing sense organ is called the organ of ______________.
13. Sense receptors of the type used in taste and smell are called ______________.
14. Receptor cells in the taste buds are called ______________ cells.

Select the most correct answer from Column B for each statement in Column A. (Only one answer is correct.)

COLUMN A	COLUMN B
15. ______ White portion of eyeball	**a.** Rods
16. ______ Receptors for night vision	**b.** Auricle
17. ______ Sense of position	**c.** Optic disk
18. ______ Blind spot	**d.** Otitis media
19. ______ External ear	**e.** Olfactory cell
20. ______ Ear drum	**f.** Crista ampullaris
21. ______ Middle ear infection	**g.** Sclera
22. ______ Receptor for equilibrium	**h.** Tympanic membrane
23. ______ Receptor for smell	**i.** Proprioception

REVIEW QUESTIONS

1. List, compare, and contrast special and general sense organs.
2. What are the functional characteristics required for a sense organ to convert a stimulus into a sensation?
3. How do rods and cones differ in terms of their ability to serve as receptors for vision?
4. Which pair or pairs of cranial nerves would you nickname "seeing nerves," "hearing nerves," "smelling nerves," and "tasting nerves"?
5. Explain the anatomical relationship between the bony and the membranous labyrinths.
6. Explain how photoreceptors, mechanoreceptors, and chemoreceptors differ in function.
7. What is the function of the ear ossicles?
8. Discuss the sense of balance or equilibrium, including the name, location, and mechanism of action of the specialized receptors involved.
9. Discuss the organ of Corti. Where is it located? How is it stimulated?
10. Discuss how odors are detected and perceived.
11. Identify and give the functions of five general sense organs.

CRITICAL THINKING

12. How does a cataract cause a problem with visual quality?
13. Trace and discuss the path of a sound wave as it influences the structures involved in hearing.
14. Briefly explain why most elderly people have difficulty in seeing objects close to their eyes.
15. Explain the difference between a tongue papilla, a taste bud, and a gustatory cell.

The Endocrine System

9

OUTLINE

Mechanisms of Hormone Action
- Protein Hormones
- Steroid Hormones

Regulation of Hormone Secretion

Prostaglandins

Pituitary Gland
- Anterior Pituitary Gland Hormones
- Posterior Pituitary Gland Hormones

Hypothalamus

Thyroid Gland

Parathyroid Glands

Adrenal Glands
- Adrenal Cortex
- Adrenal Medulla

Pancreatic Islets

Female Sex Glands

Male Sex Glands

Thymus

Placenta

Pineal Gland

Other Endocrine Structures

BOXED ESSAYS

Steroid Abuse
Growth Hormone Abnormalities
Thyroid Hormone Abnormalities
Adrenal Hormone Abnormalities
Exercise and Diabetes Mellitus

OBJECTIVES

After you have completed this chapter, you should be able to:

1. Distinguish between endocrine and exocrine glands and define the terms *hormone* and *prostaglandin*.
2. Identify and locate the primary endocrine glands and list the major hormones produced by each gland.
3. Describe the mechanisms of steroid and protein hormone action.
4. Explain how negative and positive feedback mechanisms regulate the secretion of endocrine hormones.
5. Identify the principal functions of each major endocrine hormone and describe the conditions that may result from hyposecretion or hypersecretion.
6. Define *diabetes insipidus, diabetes mellitus, gigantism, goiter, cretinism, glycosuria.*

Have you ever seen a giant or a dwarf? Have you ever known anyone who had "sugar diabetes" or a goiter? If so, you have had visible proof of the importance of the endocrine system for normal development and health.

The **endocrine system** performs the same general functions as the nervous system: communication and control. The nervous system provides rapid, brief control by fast-traveling nerve impulses. The endocrine system provides slower but longer-lasting control by **hormones** (chemicals) secreted into and circulated by the blood.

The organs of the endocrine system are located in widely separated parts of the body—in the neck; the cranial, thoracic, abdominal, and pelvic cavities; and outside of the body cavities. Note the names and locations of the endocrine glands shown in Figure 9-1.

All organs of the endocrine system are glands, but not all glands are organs of the endocrine system. Of the two types of glands in the body—**exocrine glands** and **endocrine glands**—only endocrine glands belong to this system. Exocrine glands secrete their products into ducts that empty onto a surface or into a cavity. For example, sweat glands produce a watery secretion that empties onto the surface of the skin. Salivary glands are also exocrine glands, secreting saliva that flows into the mouth. Endocrine glands are ductless glands. They secrete chemicals known as **hormones** into intercellular spaces. From there, the hormones diffuse directly into the blood and are carried throughout the body. Each hormone molecule may then bind to a cell that has specific receptors for that hormone, triggering a reaction in the cell. Such a cell is called a **target organ** cell. The list of endocrine glands and their target organs continues to grow. The names, locations, and functions of the well-known endocrine glands are given in Figure 9-1 and Table 9-1.

In this chapter you will read about the functions of the main endocrine glands and discover why their importance is almost impossible to exaggerate. Hormones are the main regulators of metabolism, growth and development, reproduction, and many other body activities. They play important roles in maintaining homeostasis—fluid and electrolyte, acid-base, and energy balances, for example. Hormones make the difference between normalcy and many kinds of abnormalities such as dwarfism, gigantism, and sterility. They are important not only for the healthy survival of each one of us but also for the survival of the human species.

Diseases of the endocrine glands are numerous, varied, and sometimes spectacular. Tumors or other abnormalities frequently cause a gland to secrete too much or too little hormone. Production of too much hormone by a diseased gland is called **hypersecretion.** If too little hormone is produced, the condition is called **hyposecretion.**

Mechanisms of Hormone Action

A hormone causes its target cells to respond in particular ways; this has been the subject of intense interest and research. The two major classes of hormones—**protein hormones** and **steroid hormones**—differ in the mechanisms by which they influence target organ cells.

PROTEIN HORMONES

The most widely accepted theory of protein hormone action is called the **second messenger hypothesis.** A *hypothesis* (hye-POTH-e-sis) is a proposed explanation that explains observed phenomena. The second messenger hypothesis attempts to explain why protein hormones cause specific effects in target organs but do not "recognize" or act on other organs of the body. According to this concept, a protein hormone, such as thyroid-stimulating hormone, acts as a "first messenger" (that is, it delivers its chemical message from the cells of an endocrine gland to highly specific membrane receptor sites on the cells of a target organ). This interaction between a hormone and its specific receptor site on the cell membrane of a target organ cell is often compared to the fitting of a unique key into a lock. After the hormone is attached to its specific receptor site, a number of chemical reactions occur. These reactions activate molecules within the cell called *second messengers.* One example of this mechanism occurs when the hormone-receptor interaction changes energy-rich ATP molecules inside the cell into **cyclic AMP** (adenosine monophosphate). Cyclic AMP serves as the second messenger,

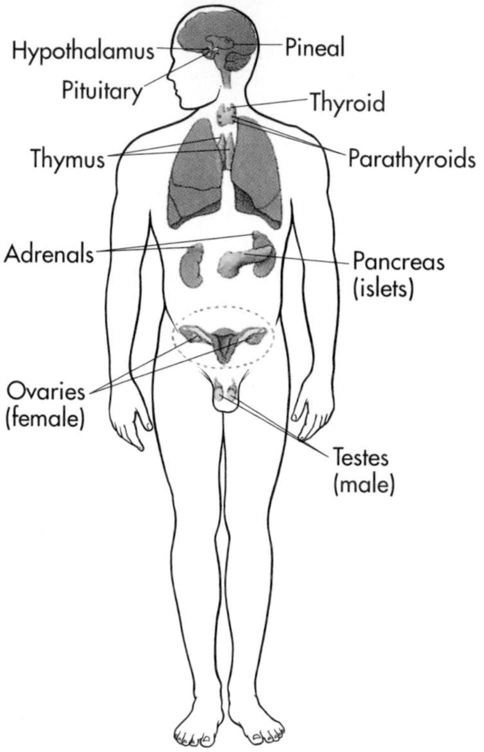

FIGURE 9–1 ***Location of the Endocrine Glands.*** Thymus gland is shown at maximum size at puberty.

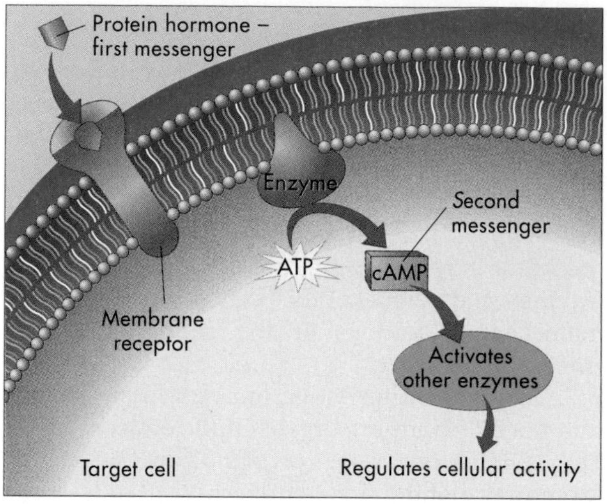

FIGURE 9–2 ***Mechanism of Protein Hormone Action.*** The hormone acts as "first messenger," delivering its message via the bloodstream to a membrane receptor in the target organ cell much like a key fits into a lock. The "second messenger" causes the cell to respond and perform its specialized function.

delivering information inside the cell that regulates the cell's activity. For example, cyclic AMP causes thyroid cells to respond to thyroid-stimulating hormone by secreting a thyroid hormone such as thyroxine. Cyclic AMP is only one of several second messengers that have been discovered.

In summary, protein hormones serve as first messengers, providing communication between endocrine glands and target organs. Another molecule, such as cyclic AMP, then acts as the second messenger, providing communication within a hormone's target cells. Figure 9-2 summarizes the mechanism of protein hormone action as explained by the second messenger hypothesis.

STEROID HORMONES

The action of small, lipid-soluble steroid hormones such as estrogen is not explained by the

Steroid Abuse

Some steroid hormones are called **anabolic steroids** because they stimulate the building of large molecules (anabolism). Specifically, they stimulate the building of proteins in muscle and bone. Steroids such as testosterone and its synthetic derivatives are often abused by athletes and others who want to increase their performance. The anabolic effects of the hormones increase the mass and strength of skeletal muscles.

Unfortunately, steroid abuse has other consequences. It disrupts the normal negative feedback control of hormones throughout the body and may result in tissue damage, sterility, mental imbalance, and many life-threatening metabolic problems.

TABLE 9–1 Endocrine Glands, Hormones, and Their Functions

GLAND/HORMONE	FUNCTION
Anterior Pituitary	
Thyroid-stimulating hormone (TSH)	Tropic hormone Stimulates secretion of thyroid hormones
Adrenocorticotropic hormone (ACTH)	Tropic hormone Stimulates secretion of adrenal cortex hormones
Follicle-stimulating hormone (FSH)	Tropic hormone *Female:* stimulates development of ovarian follicles and secretion of estrogens *Male:* stimulates seminiferous tubules of testes to grow and produce sperm
Luteinizing hormone (LH)	Tropic hormone *Female:* stimulates maturation of ovarian follicle and ovum; stimulates secretion of estrogen; triggers ovulation; stimulates development of corpus luteum (luteinization) *Male:* stimulates interstitial cells of the testes to secrete testosterone
Melanocyte-stimulating hormone (MSH)	Stimulates synthesis and dispersion of melanin pigment in the skin
Growth hormone (GH)	Stimulates growth in all organs; mobilizes food molecules, causing an increase in blood glucose concentration
Prolactin (lactogenic hormone)	Stimulates breast development during pregnancy and milk secretion after pregnancy
Posterior Pituitary*	
Antidiuretic hormone (ADH)	Stimulates retention of water by the kidneys
Oxytocin	Stimulates uterine contractions at the end of pregnancy; stimulates the release of milk into the breast ducts
Hypothalamus	
Releasing hormones (several)	Stimulate the anterior pituitary to release hormones
Inhibiting hormones (several)	Inhibit the anterior pituitary's secretion of hormones
Thyroid	
Thyroxine (T_4) and triiodothyronine (T_3)	Stimulate the energy metabolism of all cells
Calcitonin	Inhibits the breakdown of bone; causes a decrease in blood calcium concentration
Parathyroid	
Parathyroid hormone (PTH)	Stimulates the breakdown of bone; causes an increase in blood calcium concentration
Adrenal Cortex	
Mineralocorticoids: aldosterone	Regulate electrolyte and fluid homeostasis
Glucocorticoids: cortisol (hydrocortisone)	Stimulate gluconeogenesis, causing an increase in blood glucose concentration; also have antiinflammatory and antiimmunity, antiallergy effects
Sex hormones (androgens)	Stimulate sexual drive in the female but have negligible effects in the male
Adrenal/Medulla	
Epinephrine (adrenaline) and norepinephrine	Prolong and intensify the sympathetic nervous response during stress

Continued.

TABLE 9–1, cont'd Endocrine Glands, Hormones, and Their Functions

GLAND/HORMONE	FUNCTION
Pancreatic Islets	
Glucagon	Stimulates liver glycogenolysis, causing an increase in blood glucose concentration
Insulin	Promotes glucose entry into all cells, causing a decrease in blood glucose concentration
Ovary	
Estrogens	Promotes development and maintenance of female sexual characteristics (see Chapter 19)
Progesterone	Promotes conditions required for pregnancy (see Chapter 19)
Testis	
Testosterone	Promotes development and maintenance of male sexual characteristics (see Chapter 19)
Thymus	
Thymosin	Promotes development of immune-system cells
Placenta	
Chorionic gonadotropin, estrogens, progesterone	Promote conditions required during early pregnancy
Pineal	
Melatonin	Inhibits tropic hormones that affect the ovaries; may be involved in the body's internal clock
Heart (atria)	
Atrial natriuretic hormone (ANH)	Regulates fluid and electrolyte homeostasis

*Posterior pituitary hormones are synthesized in the hypothalamus but released from axon terminals in the posterior pituitary.

second messenger hypothesis. Because they are lipid soluble, steroid hormones can pass intact directly through the cell membrane of the target organ cell. Once inside the cell, steroid hormones pass through the cytoplasm and enter the nucleus where they bind with a receptor to form a hormone-receptor complex. This complex acts on DNA, which utimately causes the formation of a new protein in the cytoplasm that then produces specific effects in the target cell. In the case of estrogen, that effect might be breast development in the female adolescent. Figure 9-3 summarizes the mechanism of steroid hormone action.

Regulation of Hormone Secretion

The regulation of hormone levels in the blood depends on a highly specialized homeostatic mechanism called *negative feedback.* The principle of **negative feedback** can be illustrated by using the hormone insulin as an example. When released from endocrine cells in the pancreas, insulin lowers blood sugar levels. Normally, elevated blood sugar levels occur after a meal, after the absorption of sugars from the digestive tract takes place. The elevated blood sugar stimulates the release of insulin from the pancreas. Insulin then assists in the transfer of sugar from the blood into cells, and blood sugar levels drop. Low blood sugar levels then cause endocrine cells in the pancreas to cease the production and release of insulin. These responses are *negative.* Therefore the homeostatic mechanism is called a negative feedback control mechanism because it reverses the change in blood sugar level (Figure 9-4).

Positive feedback mechanisms, which are uncommon, amplify changes rather than reverse them. Usually, such amplification threatens homeostasis, but in some situations it can help the body maintain its stability. For example, during labor,

FIGURE 9–3 ***Mechanism of Steroid Hormone Action.*** Steroid hormones pass through the plasma membrane and enter the nucleus to form a hormone receptor complex that acts on DNA. As a result, a new protein is formed in the cytoplasm that produces specific effects in the target cell.

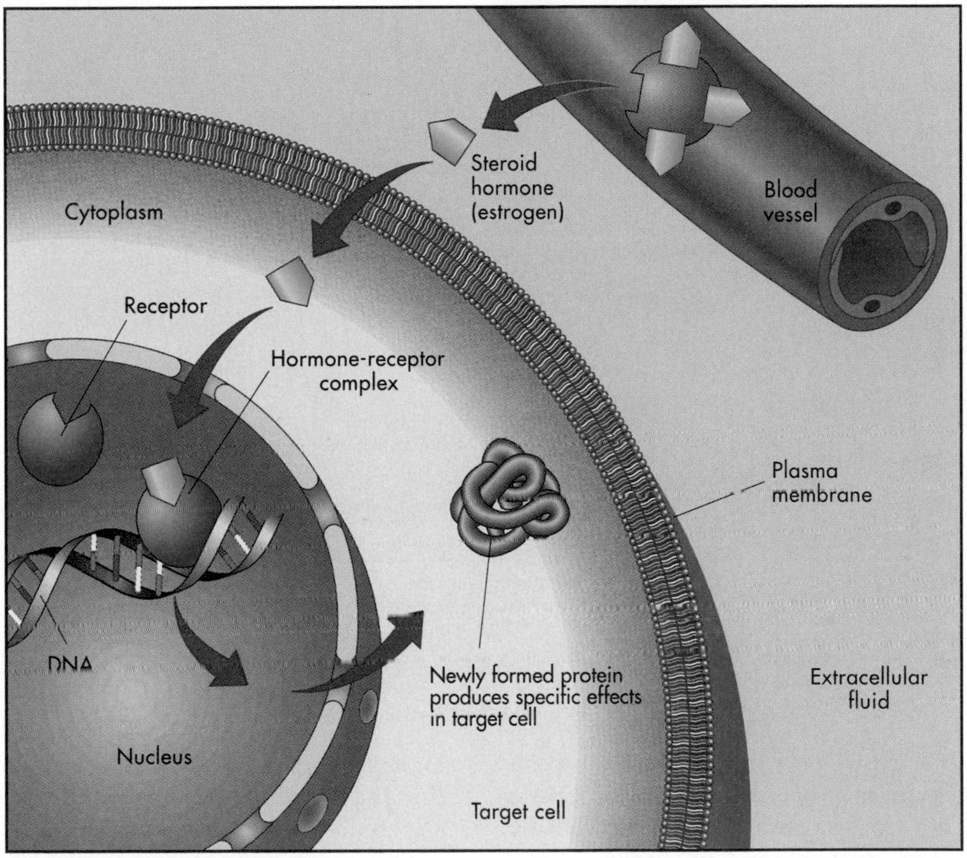

the muscle contractions that push the baby through the birth canal become stronger and stronger by means of a positive feedback mechanism that regulates secretion of the hormone oxytocin.

Prostaglandins

Prostaglandins (PGs) or tissue hormones are important and extremely powerful substances found in a wide variety of tissues. They play an important role in communication and the control of many body functions but do not meet the definition of a typical hormone. The term *tissue hormone* is appropriate because in many instances a prostaglandin is produced in a tissue and diffuses only a short distance to act on cells within that tissue. Typical hormones influence and control activities of widely separated organs; typical prostaglandins influence activities of neighboring cells.

The prostaglandins in the body can be divided into several groups. Three classes of prostaglandins—prostaglandin A (PGA), prostaglandin E (PGE), and prostaglandin F (PGF)—are among the best known. Prostaglandins have profound effects on many body functions. They influence

FIGURE 9–4 ***Negative Feedback.*** The secretion of most hormones is regulated by negative feedback mechanisms that tend to reverse any deviations from normal. In this example, an increase in blood glucose triggers secretion of insulin. Since insulin promotes glucose uptake by cells, the blood glucose level is restored to its lower, normal level.

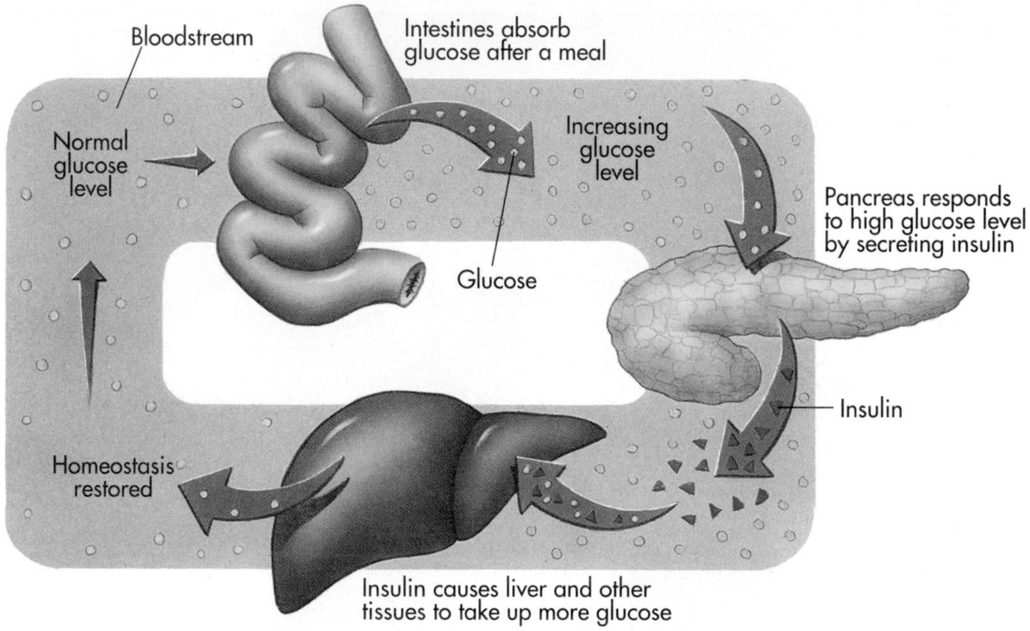

respiration, blood pressure, gastrointestinal secretions, and the reproductive system. Researchers believe that most prostaglandins regulate cells by influencing the production of cyclic AMP. Although much research is yet to be done, prostaglandins are already playing an important role in the treatment of conditions such as high blood pressure, asthma, and ulcers.

Pituitary Gland

The **pituitary** (pi-TOO-i-tair-ee) **gland** is a small but mighty structure. Although no larger than a pea, it is really two endocrine glands. One is called the **anterior pituitary gland** or *adenohypophysis* (ad-e-no-hye-POF-i-sis), and the other is called the **posterior pituitary gland** or *neurohypophysis* (noo-ro-hye-POF-i-sis). Differences between the two glands are suggested by their names—*adeno* means "gland," and *neuro* means "nervous." The adenohypophysis has the structure of an endocrine gland, whereas the neurohypophysis has the structure of nervous tissue. Hormones secreted by the adenohypophysis serve very different functions from those released from the neurohypophysis.

The protected location of this dual gland suggests its importance. The pituitary gland lies buried deep in the cranial cavity, in the small depression of the sphenoid bone that is shaped like a saddle and called the *sella turcica* (Turkish saddle). A stemlike structure, the pituitary stalk, attaches the gland to the undersurface of the brain. More specifically, the stalk attaches the pituitary body to the hypothalamus.

ANTERIOR PITUITARY GLAND HORMONES

The anterior pituitary gland secretes several major hormones. Each of the four hormones listed as a **tropic** (TRO-pik) **hormone** in Table 9-1 stimulates another endocrine gland to grow and secrete its hormones. Because the anterior pitu-

Growth Hormone Abnormalities

Hypersecretion of growth hormone during the early years of life produces a condition called **gigantism** (jye-GAN-tizm). The name suggests the obvious characteristics of this condition. The child grows to giant size. Hyposecretion of the growth hormone produces pituitary **dwarfism** (DWARF-izm).

If the anterior pituitary gland secretes too much growth hormone after the normal growth years, then the disease called **acromegaly** (ak-ro-MEG-ah-lee) develops. Characteristics of this disease are enlargement of the bones of the hands, feet, jaws, and cheeks. The facial appearance typical of acromegaly results from the combination of bone and soft tissue overgrowth. A prominent forehead and large nose are characteristic. In addition, the skin is characterized by large, widened pores, and the mandible grows in length so that separation of the lower teeth commonly occurs.

itary gland exerts this control over the structure and function of the thyroid gland, the adrenal cortex, the ovarian follicles, and the corpus luteum, it is sometimes referred to as the *master gland*.

Thyroid-stimulating hormone (TSH) acts on the thyroid gland. As its name suggests, it stimulates the thyroid gland to increase secretion of thyroid hormone.

The **adrenocorticotropic** (ad-re-no-kor-ti-ko-TRO-pik) **hormone (ACTH)** acts on the adrenal cortex. It stimulates the adrenal cortex to increase in size and to secrete larger amounts of its hormones, especially larger amounts of cortisol (hydrocortisone).

Follicle-stimulating hormone (FSH) stimulates the primary ovarian follicles in an ovary to start growing and to continue developing to maturity (that is, to the point of ovulation). FSH also stimulates follicle cells to secrete estrogens. In the male, FSH stimulates the seminiferous tubules to grow and form sperm.

Luteinizing (LOO-te-nye-zing) **hormone (LH)** acts with FSH to perform several functions. It stimulates a follicle and ovum to complete their growth to maturity, it stimulates follicle cells to secrete estrogens, and it causes ovulation (rupturing of the mature follicle with expulsion of its ripe ovum). Because of this function, LH is sometimes called the *ovulating hormone.* Finally, LH stimulates the formation of a golden body, the corpus luteum, in the ruptured follicle; the process is called *luteinization.* This function, of course, is the one that earned LH its title of *luteinizing hormone.* The male pituitary gland also secretes LH; it was formerly called *interstitial cell-stimulating hormone (ICSH)* because it stimulates interstitial cells in the testes to develop and secrete testosterone, the male sex hormone.

The **melanocyte-stimulating hormone (MSH)** causes a rapid increase in the synthesis and dispersion of melanin (pigment) granules in specialized skin cells.

Another important hormone secreted by the anterior pituitary gland is **growth hormone.** Growth hormone (GH) speeds up the movement of digested proteins (amino acids) out of the blood and into the cells, and this accelerates the cells' anabolism (build up) of amino acids to form tissue proteins; hence this action promotes normal growth. Growth hormone also affects fat and carbohydrate metabolism; it accelerates fat catabolism (breakdown) but slows glucose catabolism. This means that less glucose leaves the blood to enter cells, and therefore the amount of glucose in the blood increases. Thus growth hormone and insulin have opposite effects on blood glucose. Insulin decreases blood glucose, and growth hormone increases it. Too much insulin in the blood produces **hypoglycemia** (hye-po-glye-SEE-me-ah) (lower than normal blood glucose concentration). Too much growth hormone produces **hyperglycemia** (higher than normal blood glucose concentration).

The anterior pituitary gland also secretes **prolactin** (pro-LAK-tin) or lactogenic hormone. During pregnancy, prolactin stimulates the breast development necessary for eventual lactation (milk secretion). Also, soon after delivery of a baby, prolactin stimulates the breasts to start secreting milk, a function suggested by prolactin's other name, lactogenic hormone.

For a brief summary of anterior pituitary hormone target organs and functions, see Figure 9-5.

POSTERIOR PITUITARY GLAND HORMONES

The posterior pituitary gland releases two hormones—**antidiuretic** (an-tie-dye-yoo-RET-ik) **hormone (ADH)** and **oxytocin** (ok-see-TOE-sin). ADH accelerates the reabsorption of water from urine in kidney tubules back into the blood. With more water moving out of the tubules into the blood, less water remains in the tubules, and therefore less urine leaves the body. The name *antidiuretic hormone* is appropriate because *anti-* means "against" and *diuretic* means "increasing the volume of urine excreted." Therefore antidiuretic means "acting against an increase in urine volume"; in other words, ADH acts to decrease urine volume. Hyposecretion of ADH results in **diabetes insipidus** (dye-ah-BEE-tes in-SIP-i-dus), a condition in which large volumes of urine are formed. Dehydration and electrolyte imbalances may cause serious problems unless the sufferer is treated with injections or nasal sprays containing ADH.

The posterior pituitary hormone oxytocin is secreted by a woman's body before and after she has a baby. Oxytocin stimulates contraction of the smooth muscle of the pregnant uterus and is believed to initiate and maintain labor. This is why physicians sometimes prescribe oxytocin injections to induce or increase labor. Oxytocin also performs a function important to a newborn baby. It causes the glandular cells of the breast to release milk into ducts from which a baby can obtain it by sucking. The right side of Figure 9-5 summarizes posterior pituitary functions.

Hypothalamus

In discussing ADH and oxytocin, we noted that these hormones were *released* from the posterior lobe of the pituitary. Actual production of these two hormones occurs in the hypothalamus. Two groups of specialized neurons in the hypothala-

FIGURE 9–5 ***Pituitary Hormones.*** Principal anterior and posterior pituitary hormones and their target organs.

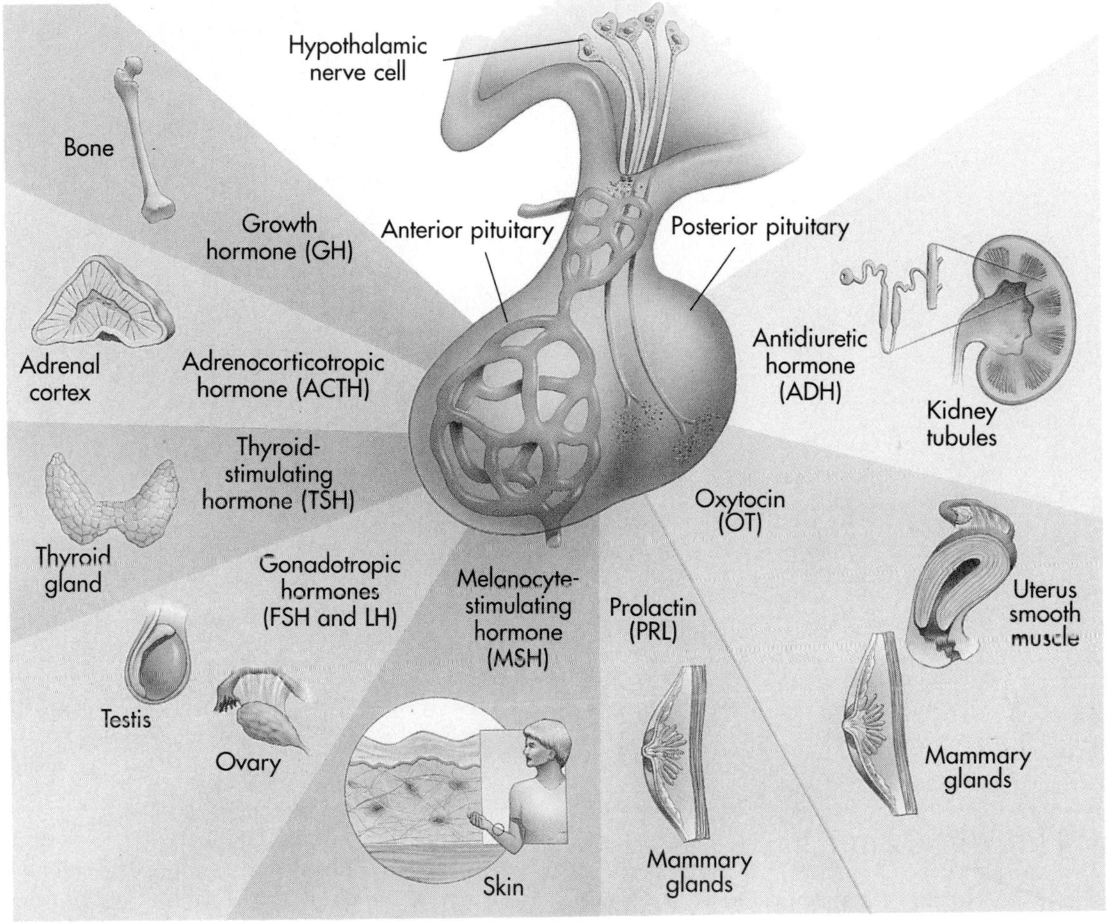

mus synthesize the posterior pituitary hormones, which then pass down along axons into the pituitary gland. Release of ADH and oxytocin into the blood is controlled by nervous stimulation.

In addition to oxytocin and ADH, the hypothalamus also produces substances called **releasing** and **inhibiting hormones.** These substances are produced in the hypothalamus and then travel directly through a specialized blood capillary system to the anterior pituitary gland, where they cause the release of anterior pituitary hormones or, in a number of instances, inhibit their production and their release into the general circulation.

The combined nervous and endocrine functions of the hypothalamus allow it to play a dominant role in the regulation of many body functions related to homeostasis. Examples include the regulation of body temperature, appetite, and thirst.

FIGURE 9–6 *Thyroid and Parathyroid Glands.* Note their relationship to each other and to the larynx (voice box) and trachea.

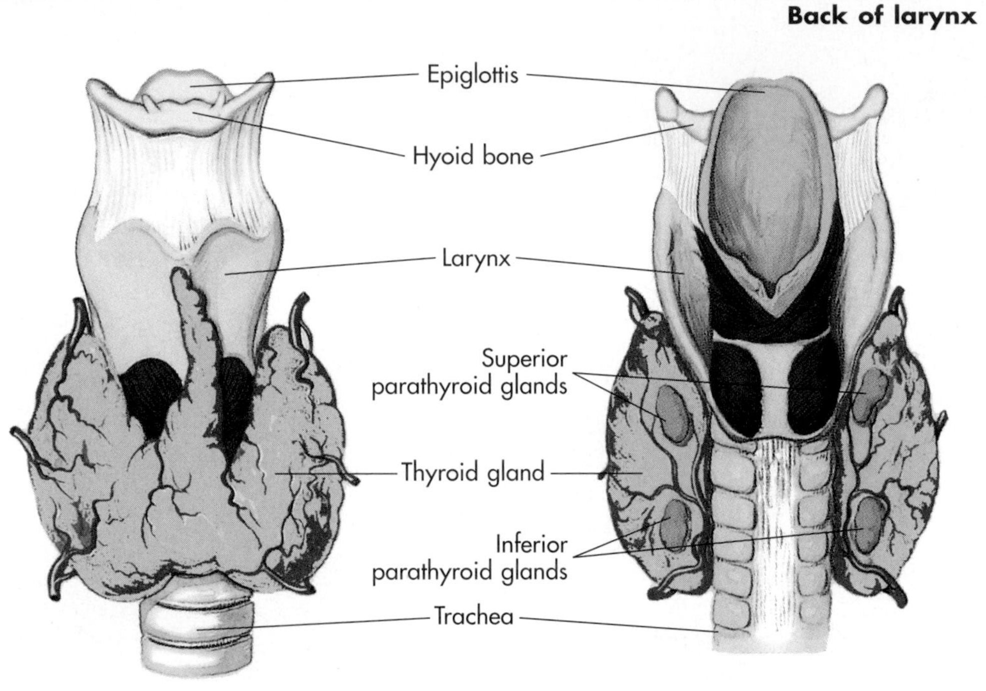

Thyroid Gland

Earlier in this chapter, we mentioned that some endocrine glands are not located in a body cavity. The thyroid is one of these. It lies in the neck just below the larynx (Figure 9-6).

The thyroid gland secretes two thyroid hormones, **thyroxine** (thye-ROK-sin) or $\mathbf{T_4}$ and **triiodothyronine** (try-eye-o-doe-THY-ro-neen) or $\mathbf{T_3}$. It also secretes the hormone **calcitonin** (kal-si-TOE-nin). Of the two thyroid hormones, T_4 is the more abundant; however, T3 is the more potent and is considered by physiologists to be the principal thyroid hormone. One molecule of T_4 contains four atoms of iodine, and one molecule of T_3, as its name suggests, contains three iodine atoms. For T_4 to be produced in adequate amounts, the diet must contain sufficient iodine.

Most endocrine glands do not store their hormones but secrete them directly into the blood as they are produced. The thyroid gland is different

FIGURE 9–7 *Thyroid Gland Tissue.* Note that each of the follicles is filled with colloid. The colloid serves as a storage medium for the thyroid hormones.

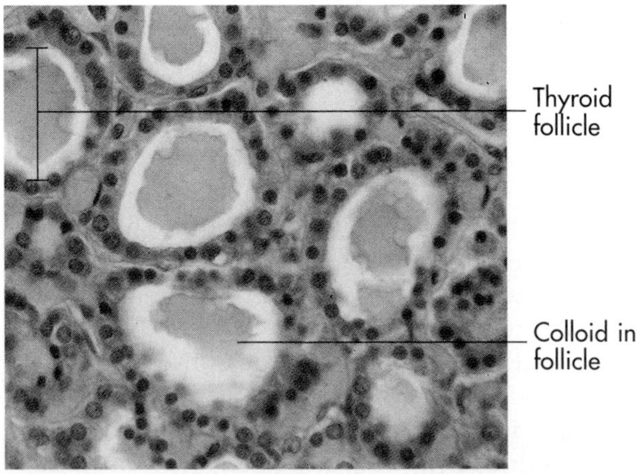

Thyroid Hormone Abnormalities

Hyperthyroidism (hye-per-THY-royd-izm) or oversecretion of the thyroid hormones dramatically increases the metabolic rate. Food material is burned by the cells at an excessive rate, and individuals who suffer from this condition lose weight, are irritable, have an increased appetite, and often show protrusion of the eyeballs due in part to edema of tissue at the back of the eye socket; see Figure *A*.

Hypothyroidism (hye-po-THY-royd-izm) or undersecretion of thyroid hormones can be caused by and result in a number of different conditions. Low dietary intake of iodine causes a painless enlargement of the thyroid gland called **simple goiter** (GOY-ter), shown in Figure *B*. This condition was once common in areas of the United States where the iodine content of the soil and water is inadequate. The use of iodized salt has dramatically reduced the incidence of simple goiter caused by low iodine intake. In simple goiter the gland enlarges to compensate for the lack of iodine in the diet necessary for the synthesis of thyroid hormones.

Hyposecretion of thyroid hormones during the formative years leads to a condition called **cretinism** (KREE-tin-izm). It is characterized by a low metabolic rate, retarded growth and sexual development, and, frequently, mental retardation. Later in life, deficient thyroid hormone secretion produces the disease called **myxedema** (mik-se-DEE-mah). The low metabolic rate that characterizes myxedema leads to lessened mental and physical vigor, weight gain, loss of hair, and swelling of tissues.

A

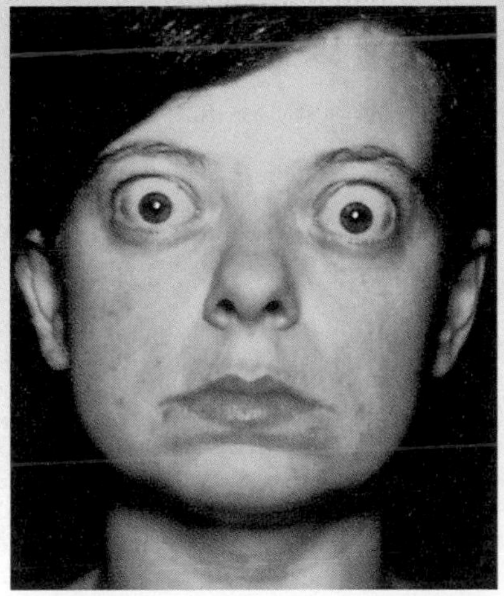

B

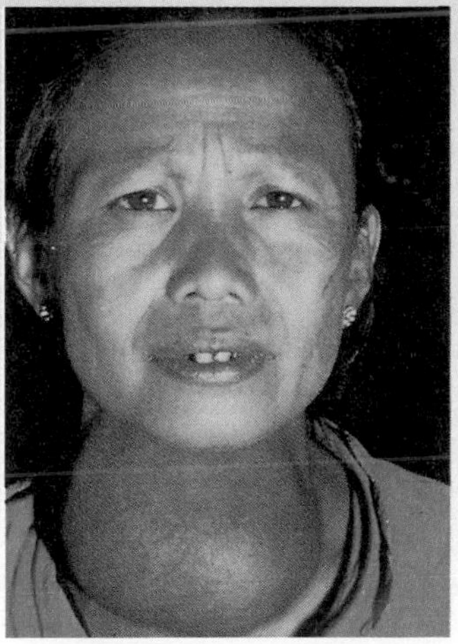

in that it stores considerable amounts of the thyroid hormones in the form of a colloid compound seen in Figure 9-7. The colloid material is stored in the follicles of the gland, and when the thyroid hormones are needed, they are released from the colloid and secreted into the blood.

T_4 and T_3 influence every one of the trillions of cells in our bodies. They make them speed up their release of energy from foods. In other words, these thyroid hormones stimulate cellular metabolism. This has far-reaching effects. Because all body functions depend on a normal supply of

FIGURE 9–8 ***Regulation of Blood Calcium Levels.*** Calcitonin and parathyroid hormones have antagonistic (opposite) effects on calcium concentration in the blood.

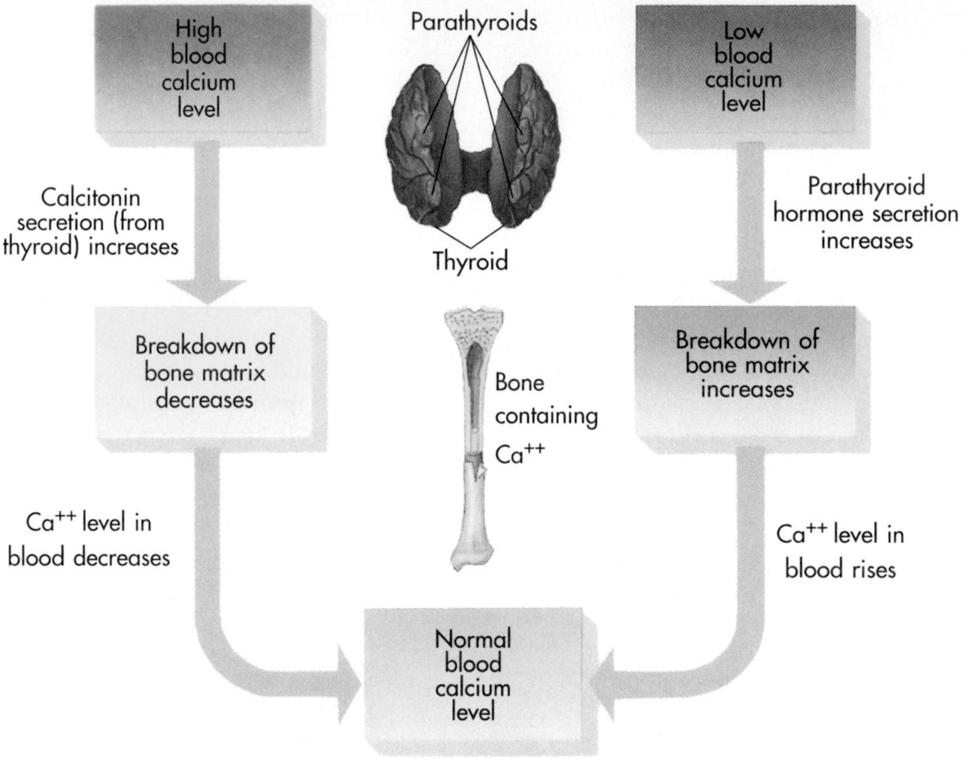

energy, they all depend on normal thyroid secretion. Even normal mental and physical growth and development depend on normal thyroid functioning.

Calcitonin decreases the concentration of calcium in the blood by first acting on bone to inhibit its breakdown. With less bone being resorbed, less calcium moves out of bone into blood, and, as a result, the concentration of calcium in blood decreases. An increase in calcitonin secretion quickly follows any increase in blood calcium concentration, even if it is a slight one. This causes blood calcium concentration to decrease to its normal level. Calcitonin thus helps maintain homeostasis of blood calcium. It prevents a harmful excess of calcium in the blood, a condition called **hypercalcemia** (hye-per-kal-SEE-me-ah), from developing.

Parathyroid Glands

The **parathyroid glands** are small glands. There are usually four of them, and they are found on the back of the thyroid gland (Figure 9-6). The parathyroid glands secrete **parathyroid hormone (PTH).**

Parathyroid hormone increases the concentration of calcium in the blood—the opposite effect of the thyroid gland's calcitonin. Whereas calcitonin acts to decrease the amount of calcium being resorbed from bone, parathyroid hormone acts to increase it. Parathyroid hormone stimulates bone-resorbing cells or osteoclasts to increase their breakdown of bone's hard matrix, a process that frees the calcium stored in the matrix. The released calcium then moves out of bone into

FIGURE 9–9 ***The Adrenal Gland.*** The three cell layers of the adrenal cortex are shown. The zona glomerulosa cells secrete mineralocorticoids (aldo-sterone). The zona fasciculata cells secrete glucocorticoids (hydorcortisone). The zona reticularis cells secrete sex hormones (androgens).

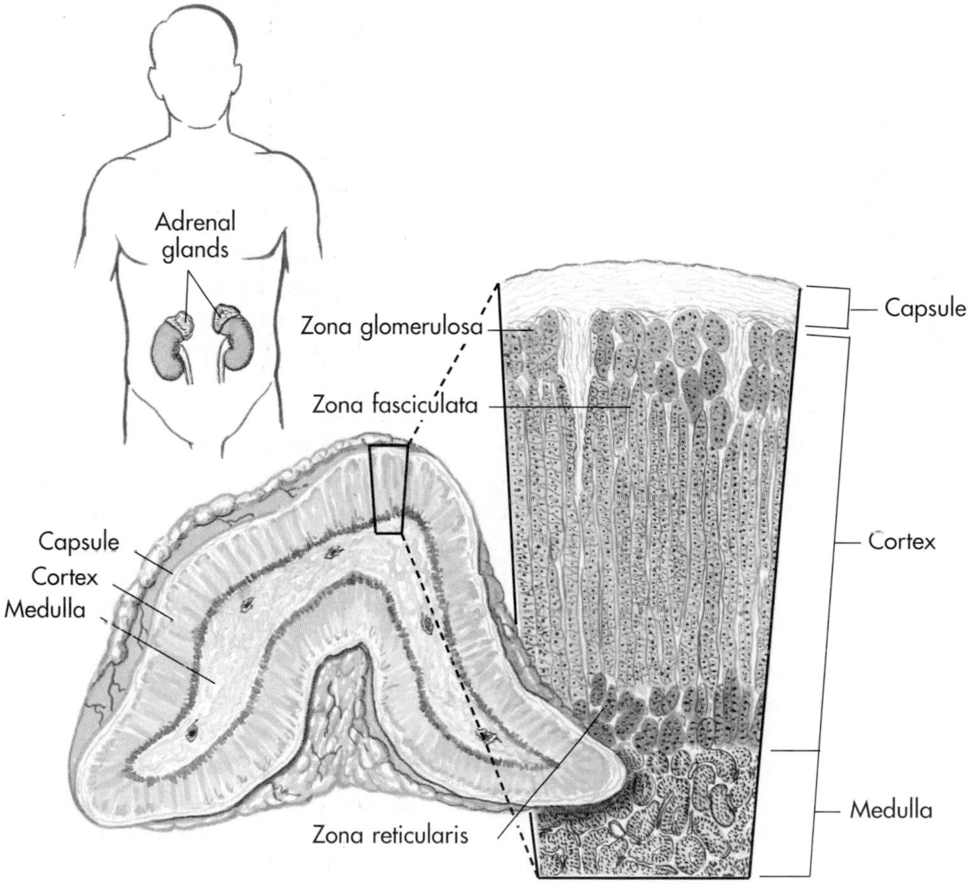

blood, and this in turn increases the blood's calcium concentration. For a summary of the antagonistic effects of calcitonin and parathyroid hormone, see Figure 9-8. This is a matter of life-and-death importance because our cells are extremely sensitive to changing amounts of blood calcium. They cannot function normally with too much or too little calcium. For example, with too much blood calcium, brain cells and heart cells soon do not function normally; a person becomes mentally disturbed, and the heart may stop. However, with too little blood calcium, nerve cells become overactive, sometimes to such a degree that they bombard muscles with so many impulses that the muscles go into spasms.

Adrenal Glands

As you can see in Figures 9-1 and 9-9, an adrenal gland curves over the top of each kidney. From the surface an adrenal gland appears to be only one organ, but it is actually two separate endocrine glands: the **adrenal cortex** and the **adrenal medulla.** Does this two-glands-in-one structure remind you of another endocrine organ? (See pp. 196-198). The adrenal cortex is the outer part of an adrenal gland, and the medulla is its inner part. Adrenal cortex hormones have different names and quite different actions from adrenal medulla hormones.

ADRENAL CORTEX

Three different zones or layers of cells make up the **adrenal cortex** (Figure 9-9). Starting with the zone or layer directly under the outer capsule of the gland and proceeding toward the center (that is, going from superficial to deep), their names are:

1. Zona (ZO-nah) glomerulosa (glo-mare-yoo-LO-sah)
2. Zona (ZO-nah) fasciculata (fas-ik-yoo-LAH-tah)
3. Zona (ZO-nah) reticularis (re-tic-yoo-LAIR-is)

Hormones secreted by the three cell layers or zona of the adrenal cortex are called **corticoids** (KOR-ti-koyds). The outer zone of adrenal cortex cells or zona glomerulosa secretes hormones called **mineralocorticoids** (min-er-al-o-KOR-ti-koyds) or **MCs** for short. The main mineralocorticoid is the hormone **aldosterone** (al-DOS-ste-rone). The middle zone or zona fasciculata secretes **glucocorticoids** (gloo-ko-KOR-ti-koyds) or **GCs. Cortisol** or **hydrocortisone** is the chief glucocorticoid. The innermost or deepest zone of the cortex or zona reticularis secretes small amounts of **sex hormones.** Sex hormones secreted by the adrenal cortex resemble testosterone. We shall now discuss briefly the functions of these three kinds of adrenal cortical hormones.

As their name suggests, **mineralocorticoids** help control the amount of certain mineral salts (mainly sodium chloride) in the blood. Aldosterone is the chief mineralocorticoid. Remember its main functions—to increase the amount of sodium and decrease the amount of potassium in the blood—because these changes lead to other profound changes. Aldosterone increases blood sodium and decreases blood potassium by influencing the kidney tubules. It causes them to speed up their reabsorption of sodium back into the blood so that less of it will be lost in the urine. At the same time, aldosterone causes the tubules to increase their secretion of potassium so that more of this mineral will be lost in the urine. The effects of aldosterone speed up kidney reabsorption of water.

One of the important functions of glucocorticoids is to help maintain normal blood glucose concentration. Glucocorticoids increase **gluconeogenesis** (gloo-ko-nee-o-JEN-e-sis), a process that converts amino acids or fatty acids to glucose and that is performed mainly by liver cells. Glucocorticoids act in several ways to increase gluconeogenesis. They promote the breakdown of tissue proteins to amino acids, especially in muscle cells. Amino acids thus formed move out of the tissue cells into blood and circulate to the liver. Liver cells then change them to glucose by the process of gluconeogenesis. The newly formed glucose leaves the liver cells and enters the blood. This action increases blood glucose concentration.

In addition to performing these functions that are necessary for maintaining normal blood glucose concentration, glucocorticoids also play an essential part in maintaining normal blood pressure. They act in a complicated way to make it possible for two other hormones secreted by the adrenal medulla to partially constrict blood vessels, a condition necessary for maintaining normal blood pressure. Also, glucocorticoids act with these hormones from the adrenal medulla to produce an antiinflammatory effect. They bring about a normal recovery from inflammations produced by many kinds of agents. The use of hydrocortisone to relieve skin rashes, for example, is based on the antiinflammatory effect of glucocorticoids.

Another effect produced by glucocorticoids is called their *antiimmunity, antiallergy effect.* Glucocorticoids bring about a decrease in the number of certain cells that produce antibodies, substances that make us immune to some factors and allergic to others.

When extreme stimuli act on the body, they produce an internal state or condition known as *stress.* Surgery, hemorrhage, infections, severe burns, and intense emotions are examples of extreme stimuli that bring on stress. The normal adrenal cortex responds to the condition of stress by quickly increasing its secretion of glucocorticoids. This fact is well established. What is still not known, however, is whether the increased amount of glucocorticoids helps the body cope successfully with stress. Increased glucocorticoid secretion is only one of many ways in which the body responds to stress, but it is one of the first stress responses, and it brings about many of the other stress responses. Examine Figure 9-10 to discover what stress responses are produced by a high concentration of glucocorticoids in the blood.

FIGURE 9–10 *Stress Responses Induced by High Concentrations of Glucocorticoids in Blood.*

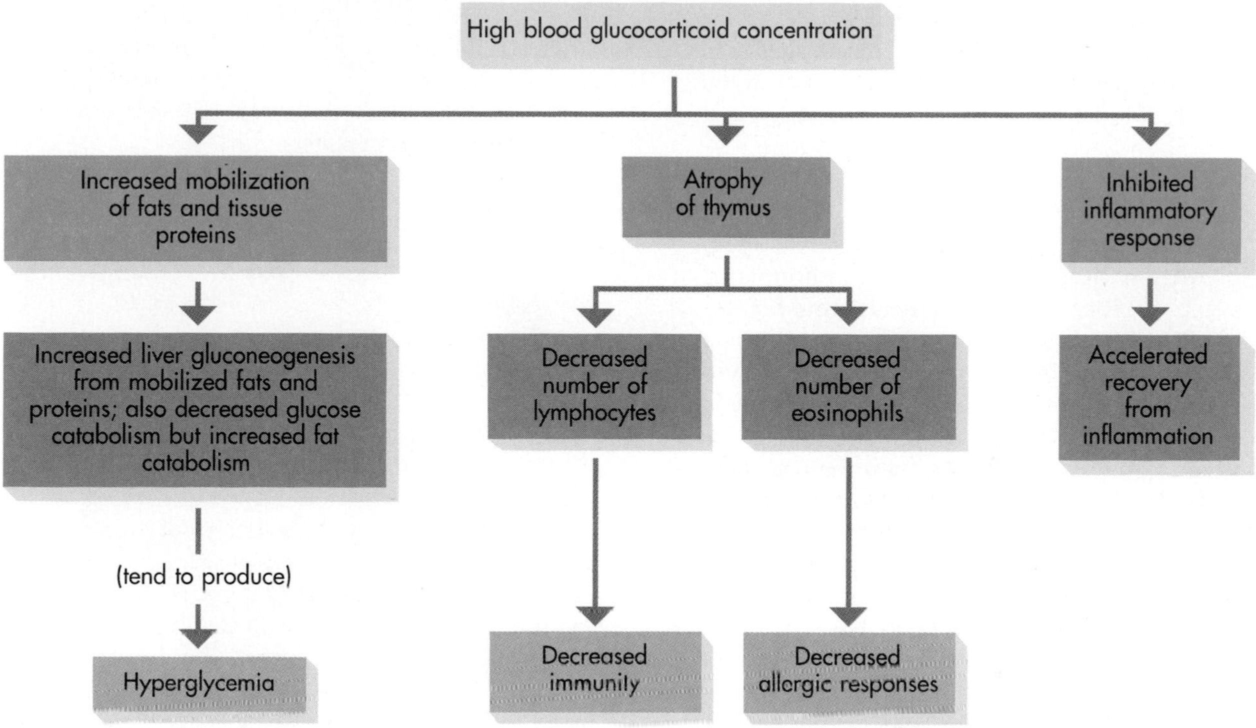

The sex hormones that are secreted by the zona reticularis are weak male hormones **(androgens)** similar to testosterone. These hormones are secreted in small amounts in both males and females. In females, these androgens stimulate the female sexual drive. In males, so much testosterone is secreted by the testes that adrenal androgens are physiologically insignificant.

ADRENAL MEDULLA

The **adrenal medulla,** or inner portion of the adrenal gland shown in Figure 9-9, secretes the hormones **epinephrine** (ep-i-NEF-rin) and **norepinephrine** (nor-ep-i-NEF-rin).

Our bodies have many ways to defend themselves against enemies that threaten their well-being. A physiologist might say that the body resists stress by making many stress responses. We have just discussed increased glucocorticoid secretion. An even faster-acting stress response is increased secretion by the adrenal medulla. This occurs very rapidly because nerve impulses conducted by sympathetic nerve fibers stimulate the adrenal medulla. When stimulated, it literally squirts epinephrine and norepinephrine into the blood. Like glucocorticoids, these hormones may help the body resist stress. Unlike glucocorticoids, they are not essential for maintaining life. On the other hand, glucocorticoids, the hormones from the adrenal cortex, may help the body resist stress and are essential for life.

Suppose you suddenly faced some threatening situation. Imagine that a gunman threatened to kill you or that your doctor told you that you had to have a dangerous operation. Almost instantaneously, the medullas of your two adrenal glands would be galvanized into feverish activity. They would quickly secrete large amounts of epinephrine (adrenaline) into your blood. Many of your body functions would seem to be supercharged.

Adrenal Hormone Abnormalities

Injury, disease states, or malfunction of the adrenal glands can result in hypersecretion or hyposecretion of several different hormones.

Tumors of the adrenal cortex located in the zona fasciculata often result in the production of abnormally large amounts of glucocorticoids. The medical name for this is **Cushing's syndrome.** Figure *A* shows a boy just diagnosed with Cushing's syndrome. Figure *B* shows the same boy 4 months later after treatment. For some reason many more women than men develop Cushing's syndrome. Its most noticeable features are the so-called moon face and the buffalo hump on the upper back that develop because of redistribution of body fat. These individuals also have elevated blood sugar levels and suffer frequent infections. Surgical removal of a glucocorticoid-producing tumor may result in dramatic improvement of the moon-face symptom within 6 months.

Deficiency or hyposecretion of adrenal cortex hormones results in a condition called **Addison's disease.** Reduced cortical hormone levels result in muscle weakness, reduced blood sugar, nausea, loss of appetite, and weight loss.

A

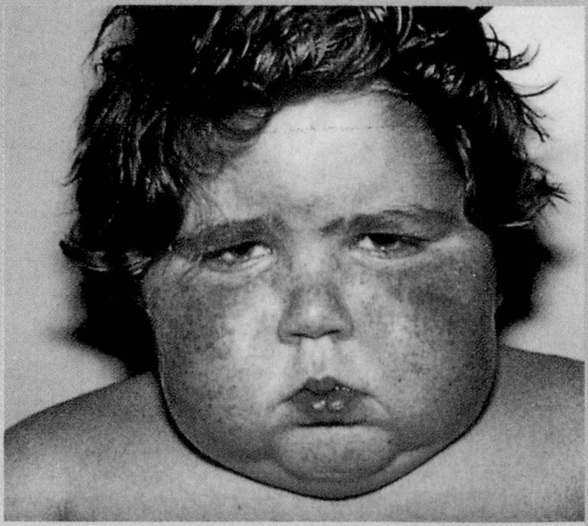

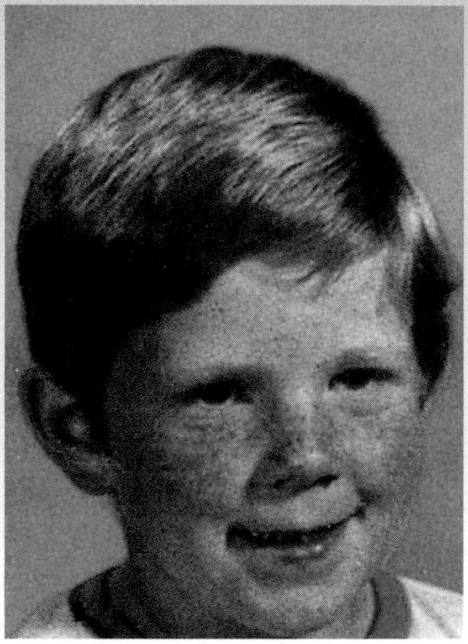

B

Your heart would beat faster; your blood pressure would rise; more blood would be pumped to your skeletal muscles; your blood would contain more glucose for more energy, and so on. In short, you would be geared for strenuous activity, for "fight or flight." Epinephrine prolongs and intensifies changes in body function brought about by the stimulation of the sympathetic subdivision of the autonomic nervous system. Recall from Chapter 7 that sympathetic or adrenergic nerve fibers release epinephrine and norepinephrine as neurotransmitter substances.

The close functional relationship between the nervous and the endocrine systems is perhaps most noticeable in the body's response to stress. The term **general-adaptation syndrome** or **GAS** is often used to describe how the body mobilizes different defense mechanisms when threatened by harmful stimuli. In generalized stress conditions the hypothalamus acts on the anterior pituitary gland to cause the release of ACTH, which stimulates the adrenal cortex to secrete glucocorticoids. In addition, the sympathetic subdivision of the autonomic nervous system is stimulated with

FIGURE 9–11 ***Pancreas.*** Two pancreatic islets (of Langerhans) or hormone-producing areas are evident among the pancreatic cells that produce the pancreatic digestive juice.

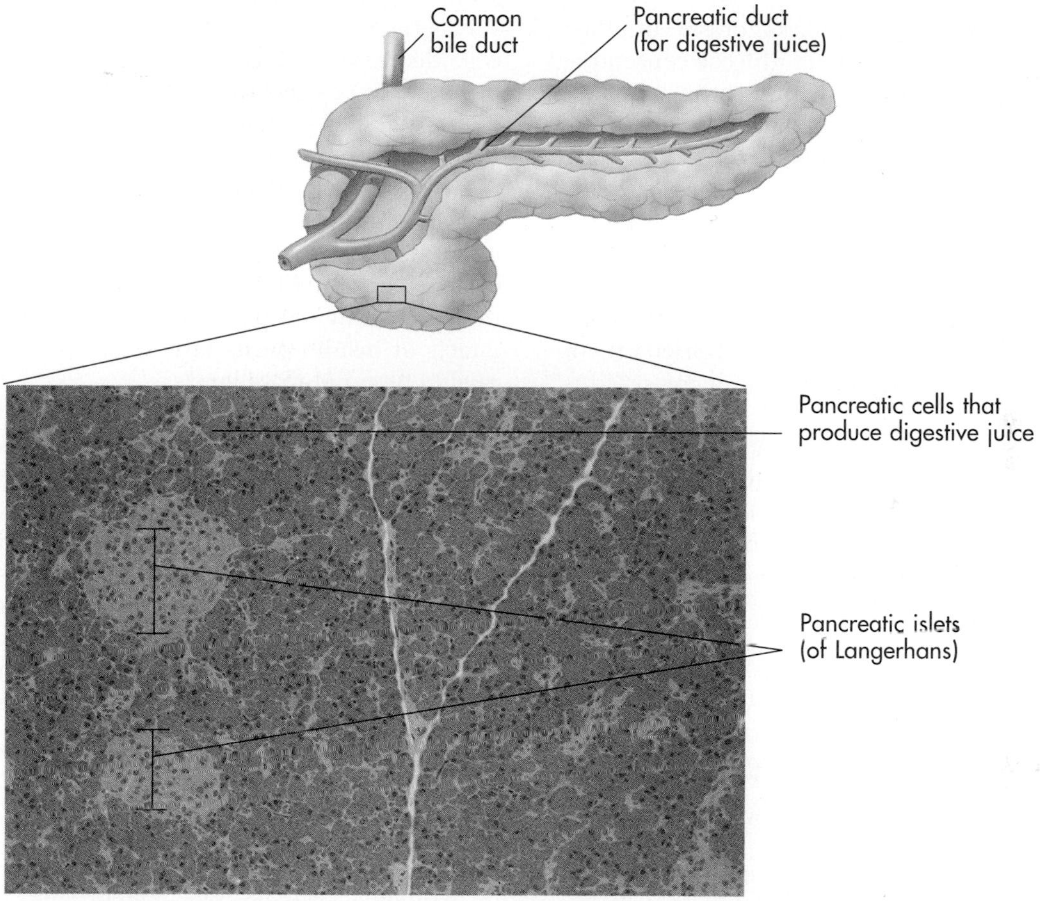

the adrenal medulla, so the release of epinephrine and norepinephrine occurs to assist the body in responding to the stressful stimulus. Unfortunately, during periods of prolonged stress, glucocorticoids may have harmful side effects because they are antiinflammatory and cause blood vessels to constrict. For example, decreased immune activity in the body may promote the spread of infections, and prolonged blood vessel constriction may lead to increased blood pressure.

Pancreatic Islets

All the endocrine glands discussed so far are big enough to be seen without a magnifying glass. The **pancreatic islets** or **islets of Langerhans,** in contrast, are too tiny to be seen without a microscope. These glands are merely little clumps of cells scattered like islands in a sea among the pancreatic cells that secrete the pancreatic digestive juice (Figure 9-11).

There are two kinds of cells in the pancreatic islets: the *alpha cells* and *beta cells.* Alpha cells secrete a hormone called **glucagon,** whereas beta cells secrete one of the most famous of all hormones, **insulin.** Glucagon accelerates a process called **liver glycogenolysis** (glye-ko-jen-OL-i-sis). Glycogenolysis is a chemical process by which the glucose stored in the liver cells in the form of glycogen is converted to glucose. This glucose then leaves the liver cells and enters the blood.

Glucagon therefore increases blood glucose concentration.

Insulin and glucagon are antagonists. In other words, insulin decreases blood glucose concentration; glucagon increases it. Insulin is the only hormone that can decrease blood glucose concentration. Other hormones, however, increase its concentration, including glucocorticoids, growth hormone, and glucagon. Insulin decreases blood glucose by accelerating its movement out of the blood, through cell membranes, and into cells. As glucose enters the cells at a faster rate, the cells increase their metabolism of glucose. Briefly then, insulin decreases blood glucose and increases glucose metabolism.

If the pancreatic islets secrete a normal amount of insulin, a normal amount of glucose enters the cells, and a normal amount of glucose stays behind in the blood. ("Normal" blood glucose is about 80 to 120 mg of glucose in every 100 ml of blood.) If the pancreatic islets secrete too much insulin, as they sometimes do when a person has a tumor of the pancreas, more glucose than usual leaves the blood to enter the cells, and blood glucose decreases. If the pancreatic islets secrete too little insulin, as they do in type I (insulin-dependent) **diabetes** (dye-ah-BEE-tes) **mellitus** (mell-EYE-tus), less glucose leaves the blood to enter the cells, so the blood glucose increases, sometimes to even three or more times the normal amount. Most cases of type II (insulin-independent) diabetes mellitus result from an abnormality of the insulin receptors, preventing the normal effects of insulin on its target cells and thus also raising blood glucose levels.

Screening tests for all types of diabetes mellitus rely on the fact that the blood glucose level is elevated in this condition. Today, most screening is done with a simple test with a drop of blood. Subjects with a high blood glucose level are suspected of having diabetes mellitus. Testing for sugar in the urine is another common screening procedure. In diabetes mellitus, excess glucose is filtered out of the blood by the kidneys and lost in the urine, producing the condition **glycosuria** (glye-ko-SOO-ree-ah).

Exercise and Diabetes Mellitus

Type I (insulin-dependent) diabetes mellitus is characterized by high blood glucose concentration because the lack of sufficient insulin prevents glucose from entering cells. However, exercise physiologists have found that aerobic training increases the number of insulin receptors in target cells and the insulin affinity (attraction) of the receptors. This condition allows a small amount of insulin to have a greater effect than it would have otherwise had. Thus exercise reduces the severity of the diabetic condition.

All forms of diabetes benefit from properly planned exercise therapy. Not only is this form of treatment natural and cost effective, but it also helps reduce or prevent other problems such as obesity and heart disease.

Female Sex Glands

A woman's primary sex glands are her two ovaries. Each ovary contains two different kinds of glandular structures: the ovarian follicles and the corpus luteum. **Ovarian follicles** secrete estrogen, the "feminizing hormone." Estrogen is involved in the development and maturation of the breasts and external genitals. This hormone is also responsible for development of adult female body contours and initiation of the mentrual cycle. The **corpus luteum** chiefly secretes progesterone but also some estrogen. We shall save our discussion of the structure of these endocrine glands and the functions of their hormones for Chapter 19.

Male Sex Glands

Some of the cells of the testes produce the male sex cells called **sperm.** Other cells in the testes, male reproductive ducts, and glands produce the liquid portion of the male reproductive fluid called *semen.* The interstitial cells in the testes secrete the male sex hormone called **testosterone** directly into the blood. These cells of the testes are therefore the male endocrine glands. Testosterone is the "masculinizing hormone." It is responsible for the maturation of the external genitals, beard growth, changes in voice at puberty, and for the muscular development and body contours typical of the male. Chapter 19 contains more information about the structure of the testes and the functions of testosterone.

Thymus

The thymus is located in the mediastinum (Figure 9-1), and in infants it may extend up into the neck as far as the lower edge of the thyroid gland. Like the adrenal gland, the thymus has a cortex and medulla. Both portions are composed largely of lymphocytes (white blood cells). As part of the body's immune system, the endocrine function of the thymus is not only important but essential. This small structure (it weighs at most less than a gram) plays a critical part in the body's defenses against infections—its vital immunity mechanism.

The hormone **thymosin** (THY-mo-sin) has been isolated from thymus tissue and is considered responsible for its endocrine activity. Thymosin is actually a group of several hormones that together play an important role in the development and function of the body's immune system.

Suppression of the immune system sometimes occurs in certain disease states and in patients who are undergoing massive chemotherapy or radiotherapy for the treatment of cancer. Such individuals are said to be "immunosuppressed" and are extremely susceptible to infections. Thymosin may prove useful as an activator of the immune system in such patients.

Placenta

The placenta functions as a temporary endocrine gland. During pregnancy, it produces **chorionic** (KO-ree-on-ik) **gonadotropins** (gon-ah-doe-TRO-pins), so called because they are tropic hormones secreted by cells of the **chorion** (KO-ree-on), the outermost membrane that surrounds the baby during development in the uterus. In addition to chorionic gonadotropins, the placenta also produces estrogen and progesterone. During pregnancy, the kidneys excrete large amounts of chorionic gonadotropins in the urine. This fact, discovered more than a half century ago, led to the development of the now-familiar pregnancy tests.

Pineal Gland

The pineal gland is a small, pine-cone-shaped gland near the roof of the third ventricle of the brain (see Figure 7-9). It is easily located in a child but becomes fibrous and encrusted with calcium deposits as a person ages. The pineal gland produces a number of hormones in very small quantities, with **melatonin** being the most significant. Melatonin inhibits the tropic hormones that affect the ovaries, and it is thought to be involved in regulating the onset of puberty and the menstrual cycle in women. Because the pineal gland receives and responds to sensory information from the optic nerves, it is sometimes called the *third eye.* The pineal gland uses information regarding changing light levels to adjust its output of melatonin; melatonin levels increase during the night and decrease during the day. This cyclic variation is thought to be an important timekeeping mechanism for the body's internal clock.

Other Endocrine Structures

Continuing research into the endocrine system has shown that nearly every organ and system has an endocrine function. Tissues in the kidneys, stomach, intestines, and other organs secrete hormones that regulate a variety of essential human functions. One of the most recently discovered hormones is **atrial natriuretic hormone (ANH).** Secreted by cells in the wall of the heart's atria (upper chambers), ANH is an important regulator of fluid and electrolyte homeostasis. ANH is an antagonist to aldosterone. Aldosterone stimulates the kidney to retain sodium ions and water, whereas ANH stimulates loss of sodium ions and water.

OUTLINE SUMMARY

MECHANISMS OF HORMONE ACTION

A Endocrine glands secrete chemicals (hormones) into the blood (Figure 9-1)
B Hormones perform general functions of communication and control but a slower, longer-lasting type of control than that provided by nerve impulses
C Cells acted on by hormones are called *target organ cells*
D Protein hormones (first messengers) bind to receptors on the target cell membrane, triggering second messengers to affect the cell's activities (Figure 9-2)
E Steroid hormones bind to receptors within the target cell nucleus and influence cell activity by acting on DNA (Figure 9-3)

REGULATION OF HORMONE SECRETION

A Hormone secretion is controlled by homeostatic feedback
B Negative feedback—mechanisms that reverse the direction of a change in a physiological system (Figure 9-4)
C Positive feedback—(uncommon) mechanisms that amplify physiological changes

PROSTAGLANDINS

A Prostaglandins (PGs) are powerful substances found in a wide variety of body tissues
B PGs are often produced in a tissue and diffuse only a short distance to act on cells in that tissue
C Several classes of PGs include prostaglandin A (PGA), prostaglandin E (PGE), and prostaglandin F (PGF)
D PGs influence many body functions, including respiration, blood pressure, gastrointestinal secretions, and reproduction

PITUITARY GLAND (Figure 9-5)

A Anterior pituitary gland (adenohypophysis)
  1 Names of major hormones
    a Thyroid-stimulating hormone (TSH)
    b Adrenocorticotropic hormone (ACTH)
    c Follicle-stimulating hormone (FSH)
    d Luteinizing hormone (LH)
    e Melanocyte-stimulating hormone (MSH)
    f Growth hormone (GH)
    g Prolactin (lactogenic hormone)
  2 Functions of major hormones
    a TSH—stimulates growth of the thyroid gland; also stimulates it to secrete thyroid hormone
    b ACTH—stimulates growth of the adrenal cortex and stimulates it to secrete glucocorticoids (mainly cortisol)
    c FSH—initiates growth of ovarian follicles each month in the ovary and stimulates one or more follicles to develop to the stage of maturity and ovulation; FSH also stimulates estrogen secretion by developing follicles; stimulates sperm production in the male
    d LH—acts with FSH to stimulate estrogen secretion and follicle growth to maturity; causes ovulation; causes luteinization of the ruptured follicle and stimulates progesterone secretion by corpus luteum; causes interstitial cells in the testes to secrete testosterone in the male
    e MSH—causes a rapid increase in the synthesis and spread of melanin (pigment) in the skin
    f GH—stimulates growth by accelerating protein anabolism; also accelerates fat catabolism and slows glucose catabolism; by slowing glucose catabolism, tends to increase blood glucose to higher than normal level (hyperglycemia)
    g Prolactin or lactogenic hormone—stimulates breast development during pregnancy and secretion of milk after the delivery of the baby
B Posterior pituitary gland (neurohypophysis)
  1 Names of hormones
    a Antidiuretic hormone (ADH)
    b Oxytocin
  2 Functions of hormones
    a ADH—accelerates water reabsorption from urine in the kidney tubules into the blood, thereby decreasing urine secretion
    b Oxytocin—stimulates the pregnant uterus to contract; may initiate labor; causes glandular cells of the breast to release milk into ducts

HYPOTHALAMUS

A Actual production of ADH and oxytocin occurs in the hypothalamus
B After production in the hypothalamus, hormones pass along axons into the pituitary gland
C The secretion and release of posterior pituitary hormones is controlled by nervous stimulation
D The hypothalamus controls many body functions related to homeostasis (temperature, appetite, and thirst)

THYROID GLAND (Figure 9-6)

A Names of hormones
  1 Thyroid hormone—thyroxine (T_4) and triiodothyronine (T_3)
  2 Calcitonin

B Functions of hormones
  1 Thyroid hormones—accelerate catabolism (increase the body's metabolic rate)
  2 Calcitonin—decreases the blood calcium concentration by inhibiting breakdown of bone, which would release calcium into the blood

PARATHYROID GLANDS (Figure 9-6)

A Name of hormone—parathyroid hormone (PTH)
B Function of hormone—increases blood calcium concentration by increasing the breakdown of bone with the release of calcium into the blood

ADRENAL GLANDS (Figure 9-9)

A Adrenal cortex
  1 Names of hormones (corticoids)
    a Glucocorticoids (GCs)—chiefly cortisol (hydrocortisone)
    b Mineralocorticoids (MCs)—chiefly aldosterone
    c Sex hormones—small amounts of male hormones (androgens) secreted by adrenal cortex of both sexes
  2 Cell layers (zonae)
    a Zona glomerulosa—outermost layer, secretes mineralocorticoids
    b Zona fasciculata—middle layer, secretes glucocorticoids
    c Zona reticularis—deepest or innermost layer, secretes sex hormones
  3 Mineralocorticoids—increase blood sodium and decrease body potassium concentrations by accelerating kidney tubule reabsorption of sodium and excretion of potassium
  4 Functions of glucocorticoids
    a Help maintain normal blood glucose concentration by increasing gluconeogenesis—the formation of "new" glucose from amino acids produced by the breakdown of proteins, mainly those in muscle tissue cells; also the conversion to glucose of fatty acids produced by the breakdown of fats stored in adipose tissue cells
    b Play an essential part in maintaining normal blood pressure—make it possible for epinephrine and norepinephrine to maintain a normal degree of vasoconstriction, a condition necessary for maintaining normal blood pressure
    c Act with epinephrine and norepinephrine to produce an antiinflammatory effect, to bring about normal recovery from inflammations of various kinds
    d Produce antiimmunity, antiallergy effect; bring about a decrease in the number of lymphocytes and plasma cells and therefore a decrease in the amount of antibodies formed
    e Secretion of glucocorticoid quickly increases when the body is thrown into a condition of stress; high blood concentration of glucocorticoids, in turn, brings about many other stress responses (Figure 9-10)

B Adrenal medulla
  1 Names of hormones—epinephrine (adrenaline) and norepinephrine
  2 Functions of hormones—help the body resist stress by intensifying and prolonging the effects of sympathetic stimulation; increased epinephrine secretion is the first endocrine response to stress

PANCREATIC ISLETS (Figure 9-11)

A Names of hormones
  1 Glucagon—secreted by alpha cells
  2 Insulin—secreted by beta cells
B Functions of hormones
  1 Glucagon increases the blood glucose level by accelerating liver glycogenolysis (conversion of glycogen to glucose)
  2 Insulin decreases the blood glucose by accelerating the movement of glucose out of the blood into cells, which increases glucose metabolism by cells

FEMALE SEX GLANDS

The ovaries contain two structures that secrete hormones—the ovarian follicles and the corpus luteum; see Chapter 19

A Effects of estrogen (feminizing hormone)
  1 Development and maturation of breasts and external genitals
  2 Development of adult female body contours
  3 Initiation of menstrual cycle

MALE SEX GLANDS

The interstitial cells of testes secrete the male hormone testosterone; see Chapter 19

A Effects of testosterone (masculinizing hormone)
  1 Maturation of external genitals
  2 Beard growth
  3 Voice changes at puberty
  4 Development of musculature and body contours typical of the male

THYMUS

A Name of hormone—thymosin
B Function of hormone—plays an important role in the development and function of the body's immune system

PLACENTA

A Name of hormones—chorionic gonadotropins, estrogens, and progesterone

B Functions of hormones—maintain the corpus luteum during pregnancy

PINEAL GLAND

A A cone-shaped gland near the roof of the third ventricle of the brain

  1 Glandular tissue predominates in children and young adults

  2 Becomes fibrous and calcified with age

B Called *third eye* because its influence on secretory activity is related to the amount of light entering the eyes

C Secretes melatonin, which

  1 Inhibits ovarian activity

  2 Regulates the body's internal clock

OTHER ENDOCRINE STRUCTURES

A Many organs (for example, the stomach, intestines, and kidney) produce endocrine hormones

B The atrial wall of the heart secretes atrial natriuretic hormone (ANH), which stimulates sodium loss from the kidneys

NEW WORDS

corticoids
cretinism
Cushing's syndrome
diabetes insipidus
diabetes mellitus
diuresis
endocrine
exocrine
gigantism
glucocorticoids
gluconeogenesis
glycogenolysis
goiter
hormone
hypercalcemia
hyperglycemia
hypoglycemia
luteinization
mineralocorticoids
myxedema
negative feedback
prostaglandins
second messenger
steroids
stress
target organ cell

CHAPTER TEST

1. Chemicals secreted directly into the blood by endocrine glands are called ______________.
2. Glands that discharge their secretions into ducts are called ______________ glands.
3. Cyclic AMP is said to serve as a ______________, providing communication within the cells acted on by protein hormones.
4. The regulation of hormone levels in the blood depends on a homeostatic mechanism that reverses physiological changes, called ______________ feedback.
5. Another name for the group of powerful "tissue hormones" found in many body tissues is ______________ .
6. Production of too much hormone by a diseased gland is called ______________ .
7. The hormone that acts on the thyroid gland and is produced by the pituitary gland is called ______________ hormone.
8. Growth hormone and prolactin are both secreted by the ______________ gland.
9. The letters ADH stand for ______________ hormone.
10. One of the primary thyroid hormones is called T_4 or ______________.
11. Low dietary intake of iodine may cause an enlargement of the thyroid gland, called simple ______________.
12. The layer of the adrenal cortex that secretes mineralocorticoids is called the zona ______________ .
13. Epinephrine and norepinephrine are secreted by the adrenal ______________.
14. The alpha cells of the pancreatic islets secrete ______________.
15. Inadequate insulin secretion is associated with the disease ______________.
16. The corpus luteum of the ovary secretes chiefly ______________.
17. The male sex hormone is called ______________.
18. The hormone of the thymus gland is called ______________.
19. The hormone melatonin is secreted by the ______________ gland.
20. In the female the ovarian follicles secrete the hormone ______________.

Circle the T before each true statement and the F before each false statement.

T F 21. Endocrine and exocrine glands discharge their secretions directly into the blood.

T F 22. Hormones act on target organ cells.

T F 23. The placenta is considered an endocrine gland.

T F 24. The second messenger hypothesis is used to explain the action of steroid hormones.

T F 25. Prostaglandins are also called *tissue hormones.*

T F 26. The term *adenohypophysis* is used to describe the posterior pituitary gland.

T F 27. Hyposecretion of antidiuretic hormone causes diabetes insipidus.

T F 28. Oxytocin and ADH are produced in the anterior pituitary gland.

T F 29. Parathyroid hormone stimulates breakdown of bone with release of calcium into the blood.

T F 30. The zona fasciculata of the adrenal cortex secretes sex hormones.

T F 31. High blood glucocorticoid concentration inhibits the inflammatory response.

T F 32. Hyposecretion of glucocorticoids results in Addison's disease.

T F 33. Beta cells of the pancreatic islets secrete insulin.

T F 34. Glycogenolysis converts glycogen to glucose.

T F 35. The thymus does not function as an endocrine gland.

REVIEW QUESTIONS

1. What endocrine glands are located in the abdominal cavity, cranial cavity, mediastinum, neck, and pelvic cavity?
2. How are the prostaglandins similar or dissimilar to regular hormones?
3. What endocrine gland secretes ACTH, aldosterone, calcitonin, chorionic gonadotropins, epinephrine, growth hormone, insulin, oxytocin, and progesterone?
4. What hormone is called the *water-retaining hormone* because it decreases the amount of urine formed?
5. What hormone causes potassium loss from the body through the urine?
6. What hormone is called the *salt-retaining hormone* because it makes the kidneys resorb sodium into the blood more rapidly so that less sodium is lost in the urine?
7. Name two or more hormones that increase blood glucose.
8. What hormone speeds up the rate of catabolism (that is, makes you burn up your foods faster)?
9. What is the main function of ACTH, ADH, calcitonin, epinephrine, insulin, parathyroid hormone, thyroid hormone, and testosterone?
10. Which hormone stimulates ovulation?
11. Cretinism results from abnormal secretion of what hormone?
12. Does diabetes insipidus result from abnormal secretion of ADH or insulin?
13. What endocrine disorder produces gigantism?
14. What hormone or hormones prepare the body for strenuous activity—for "fight or flight," in other words?
15. What hormone is important in the development and function of the immune system?
16. Name the hormone found at high levels only in the urine of pregnant women.

CRITICAL THINKING

17. Many changes occur in the body when it is in a condition of stress (for example, after a person has had major surgery). Name two endocrine glands that greatly increase their secretion of hormones in times of stress. Name the hormones they secrete.
18. Metabolism changes when the body is in a condition of stress. How does the metabolism of proteins, of fats, and of carbohydrates change, and what hormones cause the changes?
19. What hormones, with a high concentration present in the blood, make us less immune to infectious diseases?
20. What hormone decreases blood calcium concentration? What effect does this have on bone breakdown?

Blood

10

OUTLINE

Blood Composition
- Blood Plasma
- Formed Elements
- Red Blood Cells
- White Blood Cells
- Platelets and Blood Clotting

Blood Types
- ABO System
- Rh System

BOXED ESSAYS

Sickle Cell Anemia
Blood Doping

OBJECTIVES

After you have completed this chapter, you should be able to:

1. Describe the primary functions of blood.
2. Describe the characteristics of blood plasma.
3. List the formed elements of blood and identify the most important function of each.
4. Discuss anemia in terms of red blood cell numbers and hemoglobin content.
5. Explain the steps involved in blood clotting.
6. Describe ABO and Rh blood typing.
7. Define the following medical terms associated with blood: *hematocrit, leukocytosis, leukopenia, polycythemia, sickle cell, phagocytosis, acidosis, thrombosis, erythroblastosis fetalis, serum, fibrinogen, Rh factor, anemia.*

The next few chapters deal with **transportation** and **protection,** two of the body's most important functions. Have you ever thought of what would happen if the transportation ceased in your city or town? Or what would happen if the police, firefighters, and armed services stopped doing their jobs? Food would become scarce, garbage would pile up, and no one would protect you or your property. Stretch your imagination just a little, and you can imagine many disastrous results. Similarly, lack of transportation and protection for the cells—the "individuals" of the body—threatens the homeostasis of the body. The systems that provide these vital services for the body are the **circulatory system** and **lymphatic system.** In this chapter, we will discuss the primary transportation fluid—blood. Blood not only performs vital pickup and delivery services, but it also provides much of the protection necessary to withstand foreign "invaders." Blood vessels and the heart are discussed in Chapter 11. The lymphatic system is discussed in Chapter 12.

Blood Composition

Blood is a fluid tissue that has many kinds of chemicals dissolved in it and millions upon millions of cells floating in it (Figure 10-1). The liquid (extracellular) part is called **plasma.** Suspended in the plasma are many different types of cells and cell fragments, which make up the **formed elements** of blood.

BLOOD PLASMA

Blood plasma is the liquid part of the blood or blood minus its formed elements. It consists of water with many substances dissolved in it. All of the chemicals needed by cells to stay alive—food, oxygen, and salts, for example—have to be brought to them by the blood. Food and salts are dissolved in plasma; so, too, is a small amount of oxygen. (Most of the oxygen in the blood is carried in the RBCs as oxyhemoglobin.) Wastes that cells must get rid of are dissolved in plasma and transported to the excretory organs. The hormones and other regulatory chemicals that help control cells' activities are also dissolved in plasma. As Figure 10-1 shows, the most abundant type of solute in the plasma is a group of **plasma proteins.** These proteins include *albumins,* which help thicken the blood, *globulins,* which include the antibodies that help protect us from infections, and *fibrinogen,* which is necessary for blood clotting.

Blood **serum** is plasma minus its clotting factors such as fibrinogen. Serum is obtained from whole blood by allowing it to clot in the bottom of a tube and then pouring off the liquid serum. Serum still contains antibodies, so it can be used to treat patients that have a need for specific antibodies.

Many people seem curious about how much blood they have. The amount depends on how big they are and whether they are male or female. A big person has more blood than a small person, and a man has more blood than a woman. But as a general rule, most adults probably have between 4 and 6 L of blood. It normally accounts for about 7% to 9% of the total body weight.

The volume of the plasma part of blood is usually a little more than half the volume of whole blood. Examples of normal volumes are plasma—2.6 L; blood cell—2.4 L; total blood—5 L.

Blood is alkaline with a pH between 7.35 and 7.45; it rarely reaches even the neutral point (see Appendix A). If the alkalinity of your blood decreases toward neutral, you are a very sick person; in fact, you have **acidosis.** But even in this condition, blood almost never becomes the least bit acid; it just becomes less alkaline than normal.

FORMED ELEMENTS

There are three main types and several subtypes of formed elements:

1. Red blood cells (RBCs) or **erythrocytes** (e-RITH-ro-sites)
2. White blood cells (WBCs) or **leukocytes** (LOO-ko-sites)
   a. Granular leukocytes (have granules in their cytoplasm)
      (1) Neutrophils
      (2) Eosinophils
      (3) Basophils
   b. Nongranular leukocytes (do not have granules in their cytoplasm)
      (1) Lymphocytes
      (2) Monocytes
3. Platelets or **thrombocytes** (THROM-bo-sites)

FIGURE 10–1 ***Components of Blood.*** Approximate values for the components of blood in a normal adult.

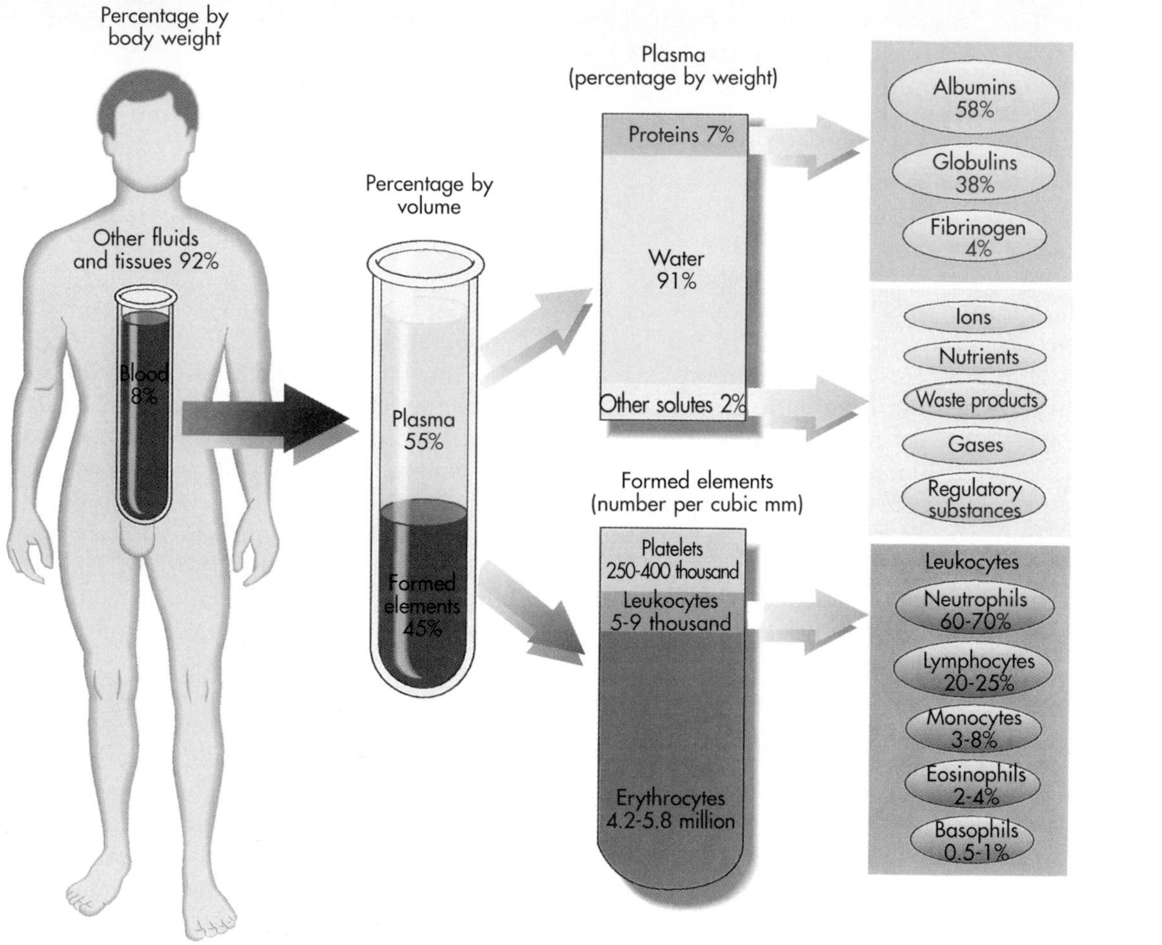

Figure 10-1 shows the breakdown of numbers and percentages of the formed elements. Table 10-1 lists the functions of these different kinds of blood cells and shows what each looks like under the microscope.

It is difficult to believe how many blood cells and cell fragments there are in the body. For instance, 5,000,000 RBCs, 7500 WBCs, and 300,000 platelets in 1 cubic millimeter (mm^3) of blood (approximately 1 drop) would be considered normal RBC, WBC, and platelet counts. Because RBCs, WBCs, and platelets are continually being destroyed, the body must continually make new ones to take their place at a really staggering rate; a few million RBCs are manufactured *each second!*

Two kinds of connective tissue—**myeloid tissue** and **lymphatic tissue**—make blood cells for the body. Recall that formation of new blood cells is called *hemopoiesis.* Myeloid tissue is better known as *red bone marrow.* In the adult, it is chiefly in the sternum, ribs, and hipbones. A few other bones such as the vertebrae, clavicles, and cranial bones also contain small amounts of this valuable substance. Red bone marrow forms all types of blood cells except some lymphocytes and monocytes. Most of these others are formed by lymphatic tissue, which is located chiefly in the lymph nodes, thymus, and spleen.

As blood cells mature, they move into the circulatory vessels. Erythrocytes circulate up to 4

TABLE 10–1 Classes of Blood Cells

BODY CELL		FUNCTION	BODY CELL		FUNCTION
Erythrocyte	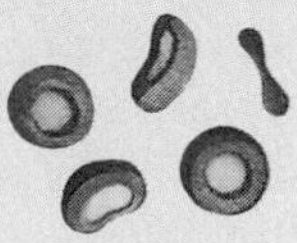	Oxygen and carbon dioxide transport	B-lymphocyte	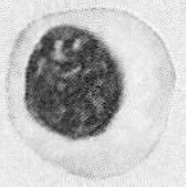	Antibody production (precursor of plasma cells)
Neutrophil	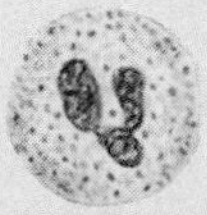	Immune defense (phagocytosis)	T-lymphocyte		Cellular immune response
Eosinophil	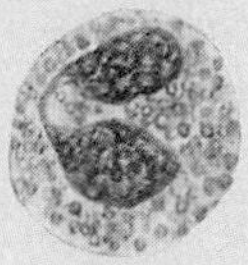	Defense against parasites	Monocyte	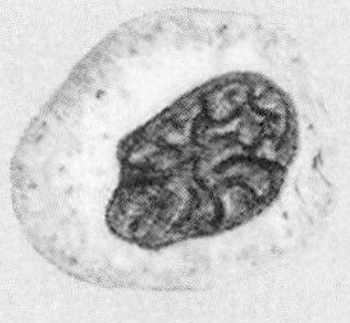	Immune defenses (phagocytosis)
Basophil	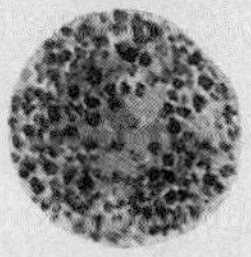	Inflammatory response	Platelet	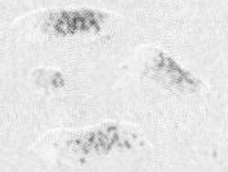	Blood clotting

months before they break apart and their components are removed from the bloodstream by the liver. Granular leukocytes often have a lifespan of only a few days, but nongranular leukocytes may live over 6 months.

RED BLOOD CELLS

As you can see in Figure 10-2, RBCs have an unusual shape. The cell is "caved in" on both sides so that each one has a thin center and thicker edges. Notice also that mature RBCs have no nucleus. Figure 10-2 shows RBCs photographed with a scanning electron microscope. With this instrument, extremely small objects can be enlarged far more than is possible with a standard light microscope, and, as you can see in the illustration, objects appear more three-dimensional. Because of the large numbers of RBCs and their unique shape, their total surface area is enormous. It provides an area larger than a football field for the exchange of oxygen and carbon dioxide between the blood and the body's cells.

RBCs perform several important functions. One essential function is to help transport carbon dioxide. Carbon dioxide (CO_2) is a harmful waste produced by the energy-producing processes of all living cells. It must be carried away from cells

FIGURE 10–2 ***RBCs.*** Color-enhanced scanning electron micrograph shows the detailed structure of normal RBCs.

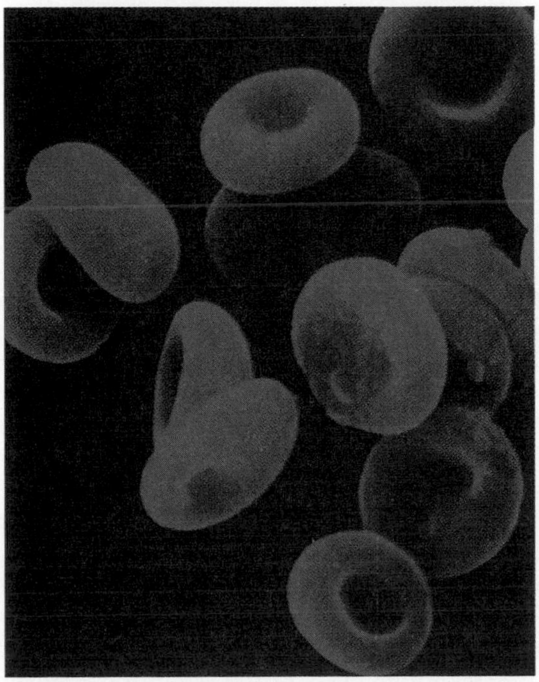

Sickle Cell Anemia

Sickle cell anemia is a severe and sometimes fatal hereditary disease caused by an abnormal type of hemoglobin. A person who inherits only one defective gene develops a form of the disease called *sickle cell trait*. In this condition, RBCs contain a small amount of a type of hemoglobin that is less soluble than normal. It forms solid crystals when the blood oxygen level is low, causing distortion of the RBC. If two defective genes are inherited (one from each parent), more of the defective hemoglobin is produced, and the distortion of red blood cells becomes severe. The figure shows the characteristic sickle shape of many of the cells. Interestingly, this condition provides resistance to the parasite that causes malaria, an often fatal disease. Thus sickle cell conditions persist in areas in which malaria is prevalent.

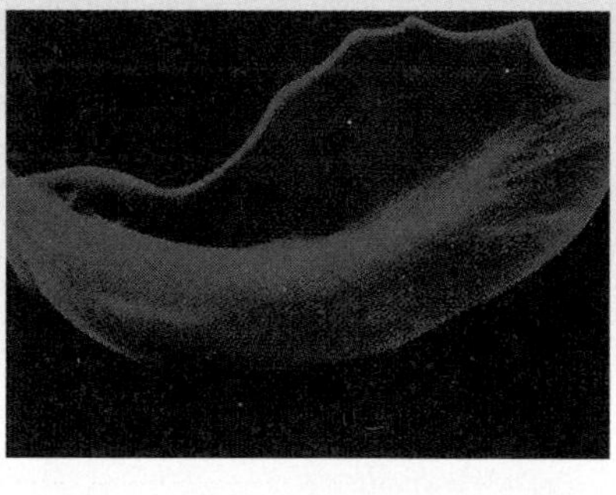

and to the lungs for disposal into the external environment. RBCs also transport oxygen from the lungs to other cells in the body. A red pigment called **hemoglobin** (HEE-mo-glo-bin) in RBCs unites with oxygen to form **oxyhemoglobin** (ok-see-HEE-mo-glo-bin). This combined oxygen-hemoglobin complex makes possible the efficient transport of large quantities of oxygen to body cells. Hemoglobin can also carry a small proportion of the CO_2 carried by the blood.

The term **anemia** (ah-NEE-me-ah) is used to describe a number of different disease conditions caused by an inability of the blood to carry sufficient oxygen to the body cells. Anemias can result from inadequate numbers of RBCs or a deficiency of hemoglobin. Thus anemia can occur if the hemoglobin in RBCs is inadequate, even if adequate numbers of RBCs are present. Anemias caused by an actual decrease in the number of RBCs can occur if blood is lost by hemorrhage, as with accidents or bleeding ulcers, or if the blood-forming tissues cannot maintain normal numbers of blood cells. Such failures occur because of cancer, radiation (x-ray) damage, and certain types of infections. The term **pernicious** (per-NISH-us) **anemia** is used to describe a deficiency of RBCs caused by the lack of vitamin B_{12}. If bone marrow produces an *excess* of RBCs, the result is a condition called **polycythemia** (pol-ee-sye-THEE-me-ah). The blood in individuals suffering from this condition may contain so many RBCs that it may become too thick to flow properly.

Iron is a critical component of the hemoglobin molecule. Without adequate iron in the diet, the body cannot manufacture enough hemoglobin. The result is **iron deficiency anemia**—a worldwide medical problem. If hemoglobin falls below the normal level, as it does in this type of anemia, it starts an unhealthy chain reaction; less hemoglobin, less oxygen transported to cells, slower breakdown and use of nutrients by cells, less energy produced by cells, decreased cellular functions. If you understand this relationship between hemoglobin and energy, you can correctly guess that an anemic person's chief complaint will probably be that he or she feels "so tired all the time."

A common laboratory test called the **hematocrit** can tell a physician a great deal about the volume of RBCs in a blood sample. If whole blood is placed in a special hematocrit tube and then "spun down" in a centrifuge, the heavier formed elements will quickly settle to the bottom of the tube. During the hematocrit procedure, RBCs are forced to the bottom of the tube first. The WBCs and platelets then settle out in a layer called the **buffy coat.** In Figure 10-3 the buffy coat can be seen between the packed RBCs on the bottom of the hematocrit tube and the liquid layer of plasma above. Normally about 45% of the blood volume consists of RBCs. For a patient with anemia, the percentage of RBCs drops, and for a patient with polycythemia, it increases dramatically (Figure 10-3).

FIGURE 10–3 ***Hematocrit Tubes Showing Normal Blood, Anemia, and Polycythemia.*** Note the buffy coat located between the packed RBCs and the plasma. **A,** A normal percent of RBCs. **B,** Anemia (a low percent of RBCs). **C,** Polycythemia (a high percent of RBCs).

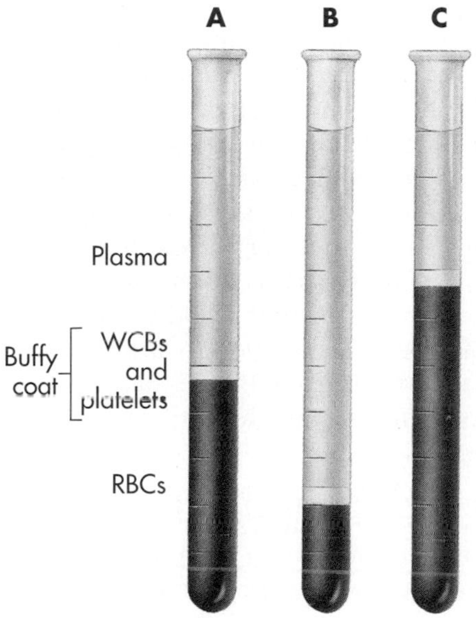

FIGURE 10–4 ***Leukocytes in Human Blood Smears.*** Each light micrograph shows a different type of stained WBC surrounded by several smaller RBCs.

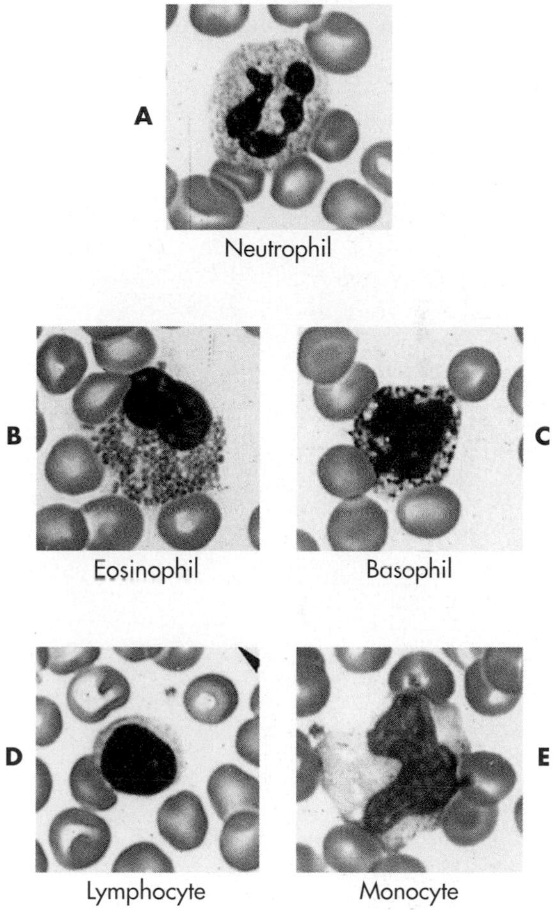

WHITE BLOOD CELLS

WBCs have a function that is just as vital as that of RBCs. They defend the body from microorganisms that have succeeded in invading the tissues or bloodstream. For example, **neutrophils** (NOO-tro-fils) (Figure 10-4, *A*) and **monocytes** (MON-o-sites) (Figure 10-4, *E*) engulf microbes. They actually take them into their own cell bodies and digest them in the process of **phagocytosis** (see p. 27), and the cells that carry on this process are called **phagocytes** (FAG-o-sites) (Figure 10-5). The neutrophils are the most numerous of the phagocytes.

WBCs of the type called **lymphocytes** (LIM-fo-sites) (Figure 10-4, *D*) also help protect us against infections, but they do it by a process different from phagocytosis. Lymphocytes function in the immune mechanism, the complex process that makes us immune to infectious diseases. The immune mechanism starts to operate, for example, when microbes invade the body. In some way, their presence stimulates lymphocytes to start multiplying and become active immune cells. Lymphocytes called *B-lymphocytes* begin to actively produce specific antibodies that inhibit the microbes. Other lymphocytes, called *T-lymphocytes,* may also become involved, directly attacking the microbes or aiding in the function of B-lymphocytes. Details of the immune system are discussed in Chapter 12.

FIGURE 10–5 ***Phagocytosis.*** This transmission electron micrograph shows a phagocytic cell consuming a foreign particle in a manner similar to that used by human WBCs. Extensions of the plasma membrane literally reach out and grab a particle, and then digest the particle within an intracellular vesicle. (Courtesy of *A. Arlan Hinchee*)

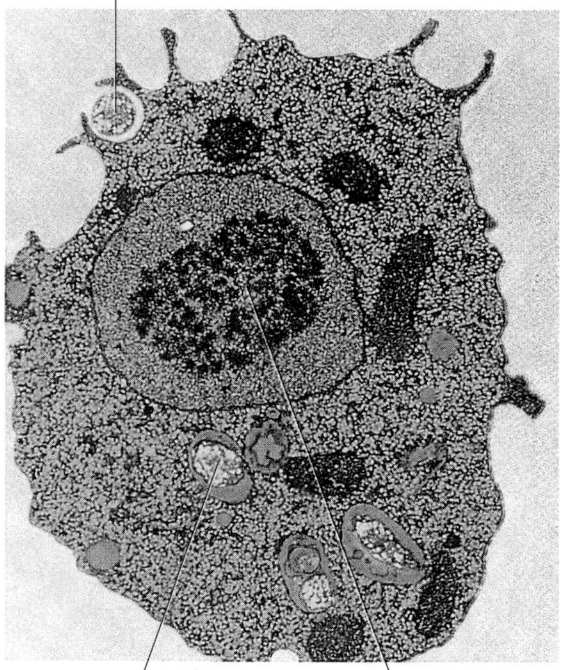

Eosinophils (ee-o-SIN-o-fils) (Figure 10-4, *B*) are granulocytic WBCs that help protect the body from the numerous irritants that cause allergies. They are also capable of phagocytosis. **Basophils** (BAY-so-fils) (Figure 10-4, *C*) also function in allergic reactions. These leukocytes, which are less abundant than other types, also secrete a number of important substances. For example, they secrete the potent chemical **heparin,** which helps prevent the clotting of blood as it flows through the blood vessels of the body.

The term **leukopenia** (loo-ko-PEE-nee-ah) refers to an abnormally low WBC count (under 5000 WBCs/mm^3 of blood). A number of disease conditions may affect the immune system and decrease the amount of circulating WBCs. **Acquired immunodeficiency syndrome** or **AIDS,** which will be discussed in Chapter 12, is one example of a disease characterized by marked leukopenia. **Leukocytosis** (loo-ko-SYE-toe-sis) refers to an abnormally high WBC count (over 10,000 WBCs/mm^3 of blood). It is a much more common problem than leukopenia and almost always accompanies infections. There is also a malignant disease, **leukemia** (loo-KEE-mee-ah), in which the number of WBCs increases tremendously. The buffy coat is thicker and more noticeable in the hematocrit of blood from patients with leukemia because of the elevated WBC counts. You may have heard of this disease as "blood cancer." As in all cancers, the extra cells do not function properly.

PLATELETS AND BLOOD CLOTTING

Platelets, the third main type of formed element, play an essential part in blood clotting. Your life might someday be saved just because your blood can clot. A clot plugs up torn or cut vessels and stops bleeding that otherwise might prove fatal.

The story of how blood clots is the story of a chain of rapid-fire reactions. The first step in the chain is some kind of an injury to a blood vessel that makes a rough spot in its lining. (Normally the lining of blood vessels is extremely smooth.) Almost immediately, damaged tissue cells release certain clotting factors into the plasma. These factors rapidly react with other factors already present in the plasma to form **prothrombin activator** (pro-THROM-bin AK-tiv-ayt-or). At the same time this is happening, platelets become "sticky" at the point of injury and soon accumulate near the opening in the broken blood vessel, forming a soft, temporary *platelet plug*. As the platelets accumulate, they release additional clotting factors, forming even more prothrombin activator. If the normal amount of blood calcium is present, prothrombin activator triggers the next step of clotting by converting **prothrombin** (a protein in normal blood) to **thrombin** (THROM-bin). In the last step, thrombin reacts with **fibrinogen** (fi-BRIN-o-jen) (a normal plasma protein) to change it to a

FIGURE 10–6 ***Blood Clotting.*** The extremely complex clotting mechanism can be distilled into three basic steps: **1,** release of clotting factors from both injured tissue cells and sticky platelets at the injury site; **2,** formation of thrombin; and **3,** formation of fibrin and trapping of red blood cells to form a clot.

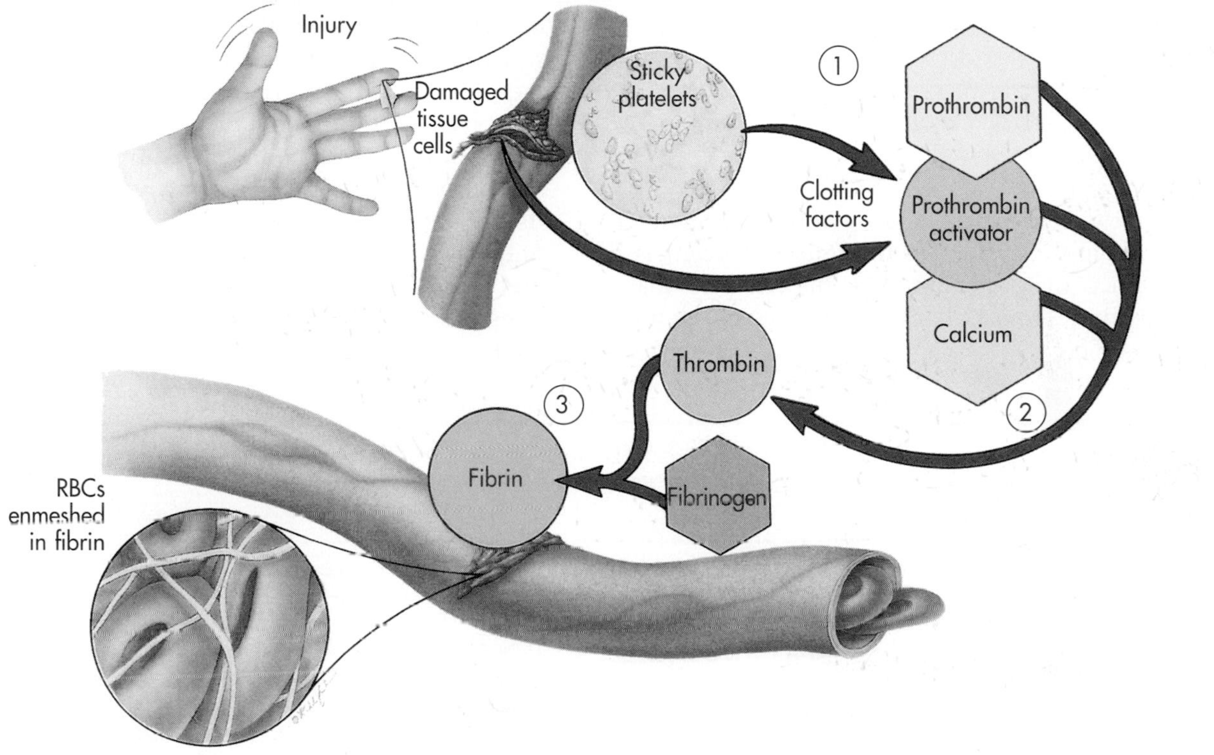

fibrous gel called **fibrin.** Under the microscope, fibrin looks like a tangle of fine threads with RBCs caught in the tangle. Figure 10-6 illustrates the steps in the blood-clotting mechanism.

The clotting mechanism contains clues for ways to stop bleeding by speeding up blood clotting. For example, you might simply apply gauze to a bleeding surface. Its slight roughness would cause more platelets to stick together and release more clotting factors. These additional factors would then make the blood clot more quickly.

Physicians sometimes prescribe vitamin K before surgery to make sure that the patient's blood will clot fast enough to prevent hemorrhage. Vitamin K stimulates liver cells to increase the synthesis of prothrombin. More prothrombin in blood allows faster production of thrombin during clotting and thus faster clot formation.

Unfortunately, clots sometimes form in unbroken blood vessels of the heart, brain, lungs, or some other organ—a dreaded thing because clots may produce sudden death by shutting off the blood supply to a vital organ. When a clot stays in the place where it formed, it is called a **thrombus** (THROM-bus) and the condition is spoken of as **thrombosis** (throm-BO-sus). If part of the clot dislodges and circulates through the bloodstream, the dislodged part is then called an **embolus** (EM-bo-lus), and the condition is called an **embolism** (EM-bo-lizm). Suppose that your doctor told you that you had a clot in one of your coronary arteries. Which diagnosis would he make—coronary thrombosis or coronary embolism—if he thought that the clot had formed originally in the coronary artery as a result of the accumulation of fatty material in the vessel wall? Physicians now have some drugs that they can use to help prevent thrombosis and embolism. Heparin, for example, can be used to prevent excessive blood clotting. Heparin inhibits the conversion of prothrombin to thrombin, thus preventing formation of a thrombus.

Blood Types

ABO SYSTEM

Blood types are identified by certain antigens in RBCs (Figure 10-7). An **antigen** (AN-ti-jen) is a substance that can stimulate the body to make antibodies. Almost all substances that act as antigens are foreign proteins. That is, they are not the body's own natural proteins but are proteins that have entered the body from the outside by infection, transfusion, or some other method.

The word *antibody* can be defined in terms of what causes its formation or in terms of how it functions. Defined the first way, an **antibody** (AN-ti-bod-ee) is a substance made by the body in response to stimulation by an antigen. Defined according to its functions, an antibody is a substance that reacts with the antigen that stimulated its formation. Many antibodies react with their antigens to clump or **agglutinate** (ah-GLOO-tin-ate) them. In other words, they cause their antigens to stick together in little clusters.

FIGURE 10–7 ***Results of Different Combinations of Donor and Recipient Blood.*** The left columns show the recipient's blood characteristics and the top row shows the donor's blood type.

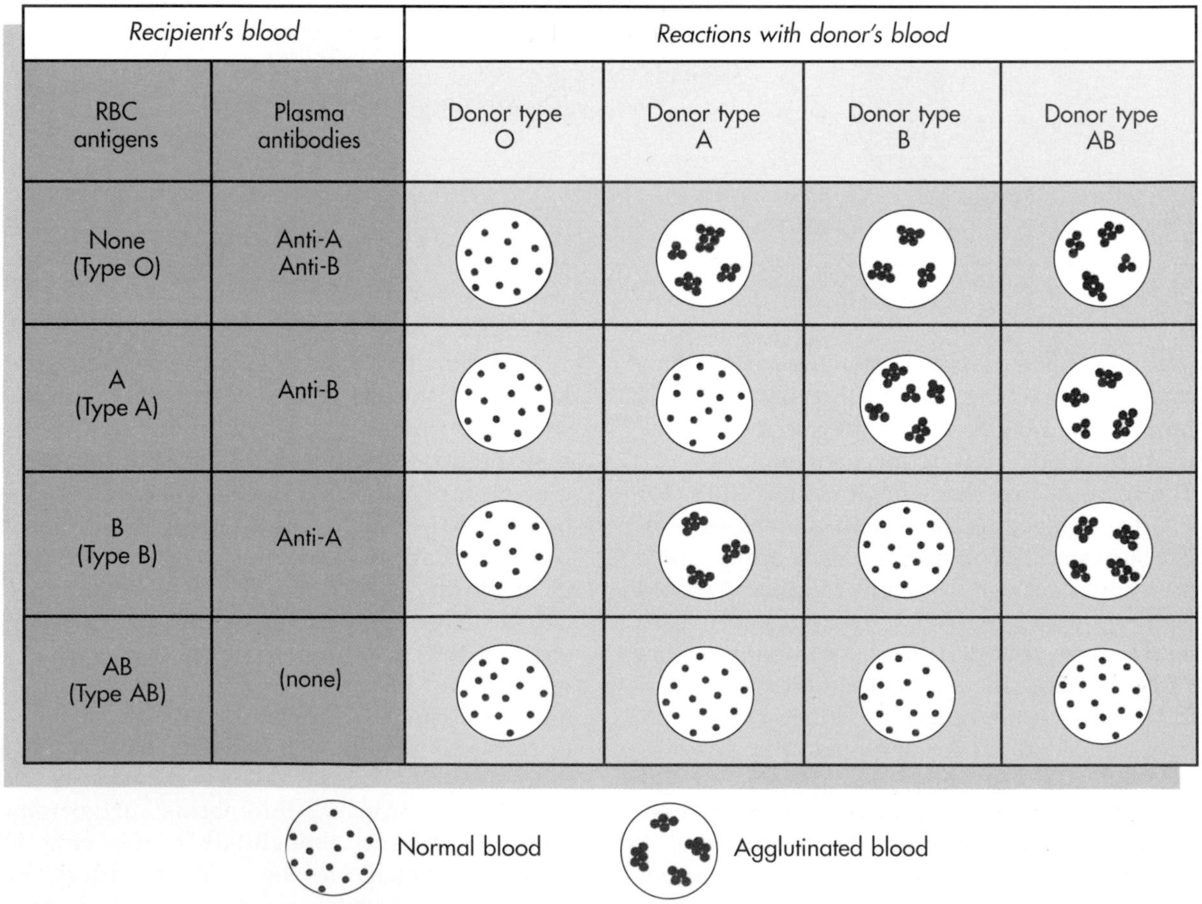
Recipient's blood
Reactions with donor's blood
RBC antigens
Plasma antibodies
Donor type O
Donor type A
Donor type B
Donor type AB
None (Type O)
Anti-A Anti-B
A (Type A)
Anti-B
B (Type B)
Anti-A
AB (Type AB)
(none)
Normal blood
Agglutinated blood

Every person's blood is one of the following blood types in the ABO system of typing:

1. Type A
2. Type B
3. Type AB
4. Type O

Suppose that you have type A blood (as do about 41% of Americans). The letter *A* stands for a certain type of antigen (a protein) in the plasma membrane of your RBCs since birth. Because you were born with type A antigen, your body does not form antibodies to react with it. In other words, your blood plasma contains no anti-A antibodies. It does, however, contain anti-B antibodies. For some unknown reason, these antibodies are present naturally in type A blood plasma. The body did not form them in response to the presence of the B antigen. In summary, in type A blood the RBCs contain type A antigen and the plasma contains anti-B antibodies.

Similarly, in type B blood, the RBCs contain type B antigen, and the plasma contains anti-A antibodies. In type AB blood, as its name indicates, the RBCs contain both type A and type B antigens, and the plasma contains neither anti-A nor anti-B antibodies. The opposite is true of type O blood; its RBCs contain neither type A nor type B antigens, and its plasma contains both anti-A and anti-B antibodies.

Harmful effects or even death can result from a blood transfusion if the donor's RBCs become agglutinated by antibodies in the recipient's plasma. If a donor's RBCs do not contain any A or B antigen, they of course cannot be clumped by anti-A or anti-B antibodies. For this reason the type of blood that contains neither A nor B antigens—namely, type O blood—can be used in an emergency as donor blood without the danger of anti-A or anti-B antibodies clumping its RBCs. Type O blood has therefore been called **universal donor** blood. Similarly, blood type AB has been called **universal recipient** blood because it contains neither anti-A nor anti-B antibodies in its plasma. Therefore it does not clump any donor's RBCs containing A or B antigens. In a normal clinical setting, however, all blood intended for transfusion is matched carefully to the blood of the recipient for a variety of factors.

Figure 10-7 shows the results of different combinations of donor and recipient blood.

Blood Doping

A number of athletes have reportedly improved their performance by a practice called **blood doping.** A few weeks before an important event, an athlete has some blood drawn. The RBCs are separated and frozen. Just before competition, the RBCs are thawed and injected into the athlete. The increased hematocrit that results slightly improves the oxygen-carrying capacity of the blood, which theoretically improves performance. This method is judged to be an unfair and unwise practice in athletics.

RH SYSTEM

You may be familiar with the term **Rh-positive** blood. It means that the RBCs of this type of blood contain an antigen called the Rh factor. If, for example, a person has type AB, Rh-positive blood, his red blood cells contain type A antigen, type B antigen, and the Rh factor antigen. The term *Rh* is used because this important blood cell antigen was first discovered in the blood of Rhesus monkeys.

In **Rh-negative** blood the RBCs do not contain the Rh factor. Plasma never naturally contains anti-Rh antibodies. But if Rh-positive blood cells are introduced into an Rh-negative person's body, anti-Rh antibodies soon appear in the blood plasma. In this fact lies the danger for a baby born to an Rh-negative mother and an Rh-positive father. If the baby inherits the Rh-positive trait from his father, the Rh factor on his RBCs may stimulate the mother's body to form anti-Rh antibodies. Then, if she later carries another Rh-positive fetus, he may develop a disease called **erythroblastosis** (e-rith-ro-blas-TOE-sis) **fetalis** (fe-TAL-is), caused by the mother's Rh antibodies reacting with the baby's Rh-positive cells (Figure 10-8).

Some Rh-negative mothers who carry an Rh-positive baby are treated with a protein marketed as RhoGAM. RhoGAM stops the mother's body from forming anti-Rh antibodies and thus prevents the possibility of harm to the next Rh-positive baby.

FIGURE 10–8 ***Erythroblastosis Fetalis.*** **A,** Rh-positive blood cells enter the mother's blood stream during delivery of an Rh-positive baby. If not treated, the mother's body will produce anti-Rh antibodies. **B,** A later pregnancy involving an Rh-negative baby is normal because there are no Rh antigens in the baby's blood. **C,** A later pregnancy involving an Rh-positive baby may result in erythroblastosis fetalis. Anti-Rh antibodies enter the baby's blood supply and cause agglutination of RBCs with the Rh antigen.

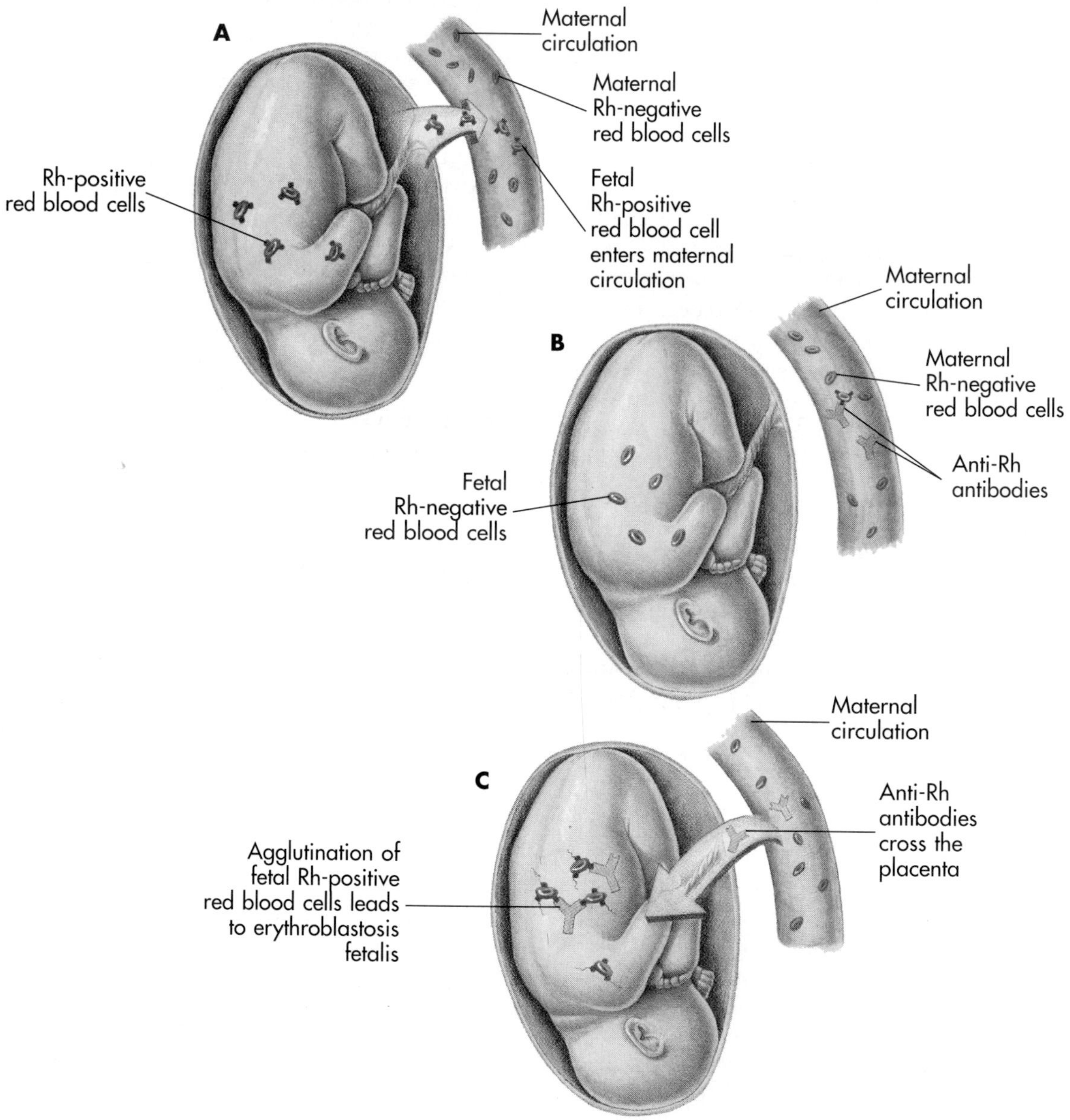

OUTLINE SUMMARY

BLOOD COMPOSITION (Table 10-1)

A Blood plasma
  1 Definition—blood minus its cells
  2 Composition—water containing many dissolved substances (for example, foods, salts, and hormones)
  3 Amount of blood—varies with size and sex; 4 to 6 L about average; about 7% to 9% of body weight
  4 Slightly alkaline

B Formed elements
  1 Kinds
    a RBCs (erythrocytes)
    b WBCs (leukocytes)
      (1) Granular leukocytes—neutrophils, eosinophils, and basophils
      (2) Nongranular leukocytes—lymphocytes and monocytes
    c Platelets or thrombocytes
  2 Numbers
    a RBCs—4½ to 5 million per mm^3 of blood
    b WBCs—5000 to 10,000 per mm^3 of blood
    c Platelets—300,000 per mm^3 of blood
  3 Formation—red bone marrow (myeloid tissue) forms all blood cells except some lymphocytes and monocytes, which are formed by lymphatic tissue in the lymph nodes, thymus, and spleen

C RBCs
  1 Structure—disk-shaped, without nuclei
  2 Functions—transport oxygen and carbon dioxide
  3 Anemia—inability of blood to carry adequate oxygen to tissues; caused, for example, by:
    a Inadequate RBC numbers
    b Deficiency of hemoglobin
    c Pernicious anemia—deficiency of vitamin B_{12}
  4 Hematocrit—medical test in which a centrifuge is used to separate whole blood into formed elements and liquid fraction (Figure 10-3)
    a Buffy coat is WBC and platelet fraction
    b Normal RBC level is about 45%
    c Polycythemia—abnormally high RBC count

D WBCs
  1 General function—defense
  2 Neutrophils and monocytes carry out phagocytosis
  3 Lymphocytes produce antibodies (B-lymphocytes) or directly attack foreign cells (T-lymphocytes)
  4 Eosinophils protect against irritants that cause allergies
  5 Basophils produce heparin, which inhibits clotting
  6 Clinical conditions related to blood:
    a Leukopenia—abnormally low WBC count
    b Leukocytosis—abnormally high WBC count
    c Leukemia—cancer: elevated WBC count; cells do not function properly

E Platelets and blood clotting (Figure 10-6)
  1 Platelets play an essential role in blood clotting
  2 Blot clot formation
    a Clotting factors released at the injury site produce prothrombin activator
    b Prothrombin activator and calcium convert prothrombin to thrombin
    c Thrombin triggers formation of fibrin, which traps RBC to form a clot

BLOOD TYPES

A ABO system (Figure 10-7)
  1 Type A blood—type A antigens in RBCs; anti-B type antibodies in plasma
  2 Type B blood—type B antigens in RBCs; anti-A type antibodies in plasma
  3 Type AB blood—type A and type B antigens in RBCs; no anti-A or anti-B antibodies in plasma
  4 Type O blood—no type A or type B antigens in RBCs; both anti-A and anti-B antibodies in plasma

B Rh system
  1 Rh-positive blood—Rh factor antigen present in RBCs
  2 Rh-negative blood—no Rh factor present in RBCs; no anti-Rh antibodies present naturally in plasma; anti-Rh antibodies, however, appear in the plasma of Rh-negative persons if Rh-positive RBCs have been introduced into their bodies
  3 Erythroblastosis fetalis—may occur when Rh-negative mother carries a second Rh-positive fetus; caused by mother's Rh antibodies reacting with baby's Rh-positive cells

NEW WORDS

acidosis
anemia
antibodies
antigens
basophil
buffy coat
embolism
embolus
eosinophil
erythroblastosis fetalis
erythrocyte
fibrin
fibrinogen
hematocrit
hemoglobin
heparin
leukemia
leukocyte
leukocytosis
leukopenia
lymphocyte
monocyte
neutrophil
oxyhemoglobin
pernicious anemia
phagocyte
plasma
plasma protein
polycythemia
prothrombin
prothrombin activator
serum
thrombin
thrombocyte
thrombosis
thrombus

CHAPTER TEST

1. Erythrocytes is another name for:
a. WBCs
b. RBCs
c. Platelets
d. Thrombocytes

2. Which of the following is classified as a granular leukocyte?
a. Monocyte
b. Neutrophil
c. Lymphocyte
d. None of the above are correct

3. Which of the following terms refers to an abnormally low WBC count?
a. Anemia
b. Leukemia
c. Leukocytosis
d. Leukopenia

4. The most numerous of the phagocytes are the:
a. Neutrophils
b. RBCs
c. Basophils
d. Lymphocytes

5. Heparin secretion is a function of:
a. Monocytes
b. Neutrophils
c. Basophils
d. Eosinophils

6. Vitamin K:
a. Increases prothrombin levels in blood
b. Is necessary for normal blood clotting
c. Stimulates liver cells
d. All of the above are correct

7. A thrombus:
a. Is a stationary blood clot
b. Is a moving blood clot
c. Is seldom serious
d. Is a normal component of plasma

8. Erythroblastosis fetalis is caused by:
a. Anti-Rh antibodies in the father's blood
b. Anti-Rh antibodies in the mother's blood
c. Both of the above are correct
d. None of the above are correct

9. The liquid part of blood that has not clotted is called ______________.

10. A better-known name for myeloid tissue is ______________.

11. An excess of RBCs is called ______________.

12. A moving blood clot is called an ______________.

13. A substance that can stimulate the body to produce antibodies is called an ______________.

14. Type ______________ blood contains both A and B antigens and neither anti-A nor anti-B antibodies.

15. The blood cell antigen first discovered in the blood of Rhesus monkeys is the ______________ factor.

REVIEW QUESTIONS

1. What is the normal number of RBCs per mm^3 of blood? WBCs? Platelets?
2. Name the granular and nongranular leukocytes.
3. What two kinds of connective tissue make blood cells for the body?
4. What does the hematocrit blood test measure? What is the normal value for this test?
5. Your circulatory system is the transportation system of your body. Mention some of the substances it transports and tell whether each is carried in blood cells or in the blood plasma.
6. Briefly describe three ways in which blood cells defend the body against foreign cells.
7. Briefly explain what happens when blood clots, including what makes it start to clot.
8. You hear that a friend has a "coronary thrombosis." What does this mean to you?
9. Define *antibody* and *antigen* as they apply to blood typing.
10. Identify the four blood types.
11. What is the difference between ABO blood type and the Rh blood type?

CRITICAL THINKING

12. Suppose that your doctor told you that your "red count was 3 million." What does "red count" mean? Might the doctor say that you had any of the following conditions—anemia, leukocytosis, leukopenia, or polycythemia—with an RBC count of this amount? If so, which one?
13. If you had appendicitis or some other acute infection, would your WBC count be more likely to be 2000, 7000, or 15,000 per mm^3? Give a reason for your answer.
14. Why might a physician prescribe vitamin K before surgery for a patient with a history of bleeding problems?

The Circulatory System

11

OUTLINE

Heart
- Location, Size, and Position
- Anatomy
- Heart Sounds
- Blood Flow Through the Heart
- Blood Supply to the Heart Muscle
- Cardiac Cycle
- Conduction System of the Heart
- Electrocardiogram

Blood Vessels
- Kinds
- Structure
- Functions

Circulation
- Systemic and Pulmonary Circulation
- Hepatic Portal Circulation
- Fetal Circulation

Blood Pressure
- Understanding Blood Pressure
- Factors That Influence Blood Pressure
- Fluctuations in Blood Pressure

Pulse

BOXED ESSAYS

Changes in Blood Flow During Exercise
Blood Pressure Readings

OBJECTIVES

After you have completed this chapter, you should be able to:

1. Discuss the location, size, and position of the heart in the thoracic cavity and identify the heart chambers, sounds, and valves.
2. Trace blood through the heart and compare the functions of the heart chambers on the right and left sides.
3. List the anatomical components of the heart conduction system and discuss the features of a normal electrocardiogram.
4. Explain the relationship between blood vessel structure and function.
5. Trace the path of blood through the systemic, pulmonary, hepatic portal, and fetal circulations.
6. Identify and discuss the primary factors involved in the generation and regulation of blood pressure and explain the relationships between these factors.

Differing amounts of nutrients and waste products enter and leave the fluid surrounding each body cell continually. In addition, requirements for hormones, body salts, water, and other critical substances constantly change. However, homeostasis or constancy of the body fluid contents surrounding the billions of cells that make up our bodies is required for survival. The system that supplies our cells' transportation needs is the **circulatory system.** The levels of dozens of substances in the blood can remain constant even though the absolute amounts that are needed or produced may change because we have this extremely effective system that transports these substances to or from each cell as circumstances change.

We will begin the study of the circulatory system with the heart—the pump that keeps blood moving through a closed circuit of blood vessels. Details related to heart structure will be followed by a discussion of how the heart functions. This chapter concludes with a study of the vessels through which blood flows as a result of the pumping action of the heart. As a group, these vessels are multipurpose structures. Some allow for rapid movement of blood from one body area to another. Others, such as the microscopic capillaries, permit the movement or exchange of many substances between the blood and fluid surrounding body cells. Chapter 12 will cover the lymphatic system and immunity topics that relate in many ways to the structure and functions of the circulatory system.

Heart

LOCATION, SIZE, AND POSITION

No one needs to be told where the heart is or what it does. Everyone knows that the heart is in the chest, that it beats night and day to keep the blood flowing, and that if it stops, life stops.

Most of us probably think of the heart as located on the left side of the body. As you can see in Figure 11-1, the heart is located between the lungs in the lower portion of the mediastinum. Draw an imaginary line through the middle of the trachea in Figure 11-1 and continue the line down through the thoracic cavity to divide it into right and left halves. Note that about two thirds of the mass of the heart is to the left of this line and one third to the right.

The heart is often described as a triangular organ, shaped and sized roughly like a closed fist. In Figure 11-1 you can see that the **apex** or blunt point of the lower edge of the heart lies on the diaphragm, pointing toward the left. Doctors and nurses often listen to the heart sounds by placing a stethoscope on the chest wall directly over the apex of the heart. Sounds of the so-called apical beat are easily heard in this area (that is, in the space between the fifth and sixth ribs on a line even with the midpoint of the left clavicle).

The heart is positioned in the thoracic cavity between the sternum in front and the bodies of the thoracic vertebrae behind. Because of this placement, it can be compressed or squeezed by application of pressure to the lower portion of the body of the sternum using the heel of the hand. Rhythmic compression of the heart in this way can maintain blood flow in cases of cardiac arrest and, if combined with effective artificial respiration, the resulting procedure, called **cardiopulmonary resuscitation (CPR)**, can be lifesaving.

ANATOMY

Heart Chambers

If you cut open a heart, you can see many of its main structural features (Figure 11-2). This organ is hollow, not solid. A partition divides it into right and left sides. The heart contains four cavities or hollow chambers. The two upper chambers are called **atria** (AY-tree-ah), and the two lower chambers are called **ventricles** (VEN-tri-kuls). The atria are smaller than the ventricles, and their walls are thinner and less muscular. Atria are often called *receiving chambers* because blood enters the heart through veins that open into these upper cavities. Eventually, blood is pumped from the heart into arteries that exit from the ventricles; therefore the ventricles are sometimes referred to as the *discharging chambers* of the heart. Each heart chamber is named according to its location. Thus there is a right and left atrial chamber above and a right and left ventricular chamber below. The wall of each heart chamber is composed of cardiac muscle tissue usually referred to as the **myocardium** (my-o-KAR-dee-um). The septum

FIGURE 11–1 *The Heart.* The heart and major blood vessels viewed from the front (anterior). Inset shows the relationship of the heart to other structures in the thoracic cavity.

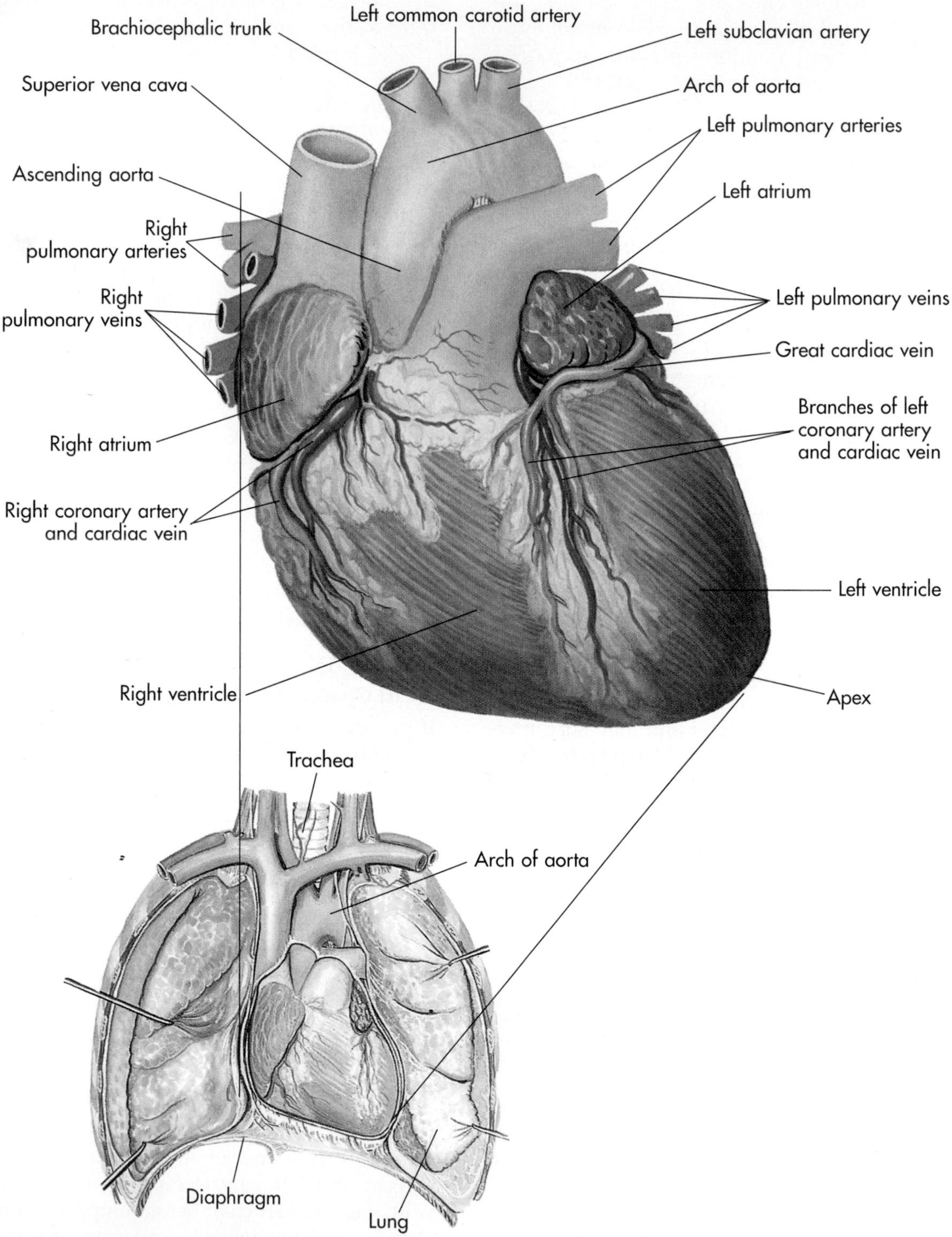

FIGURE 11–2 ***An Internal View of the Heart.*** The inset shows a cross section of the heart wall, including the pericardium.

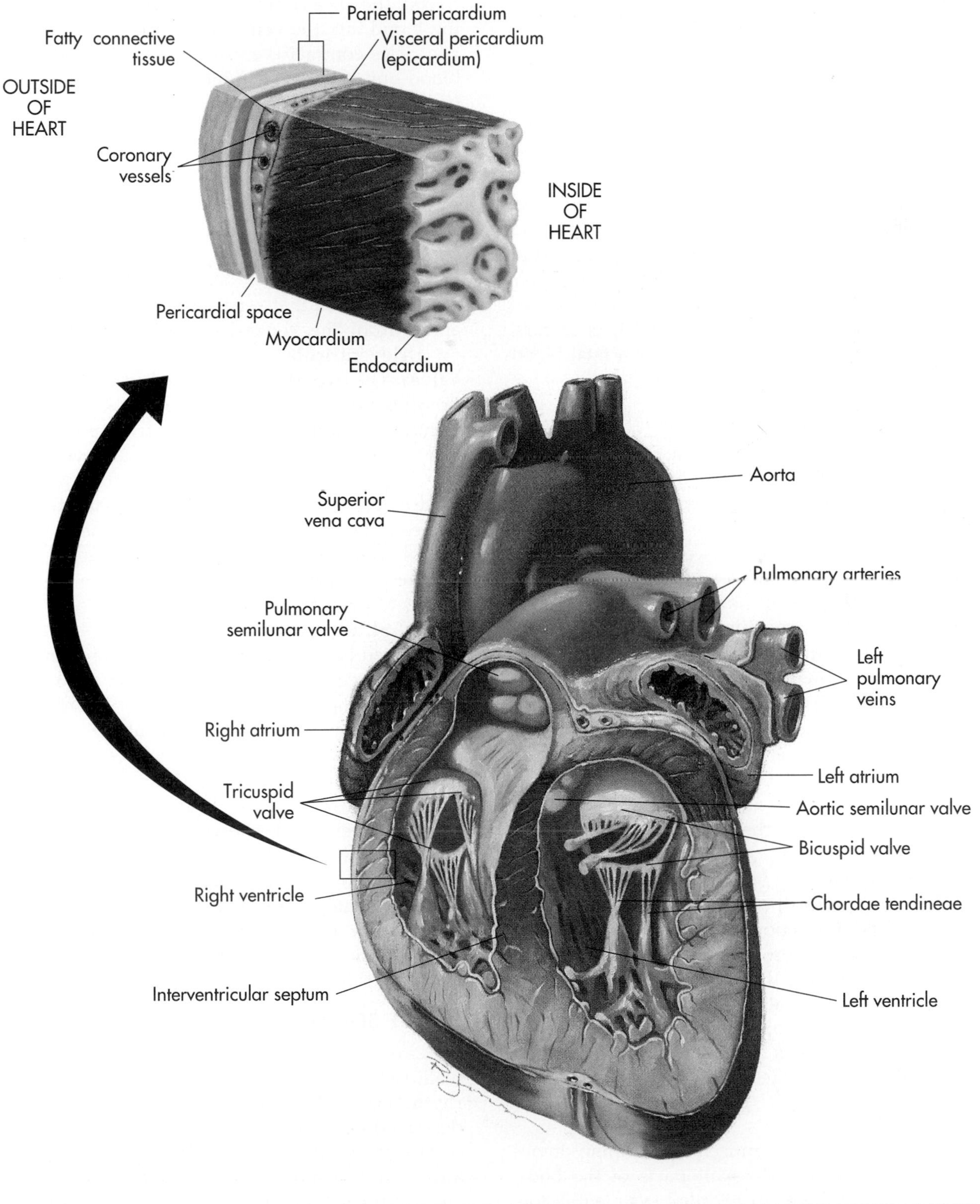

between the atrial chambers is called the *interatrial septum;* the *interventricular septum* separates the ventricles.

Each chamber of the heart is lined by a thin layer of very smooth tissue called the **endocardium** (en-doe-KAR-dee-um) (Figure 11-2). Inflammation of this lining is referred to as **endocarditis** (en-doe-kar-DYE-tis). If inflamed, the endocardial lining can become rough and abrasive to RBCs passing over its surface. Blood flowing over a rough surface is subject to clotting, and a **thrombosis** (throm-BO-sis) or clot may form (see Chapter 10). Unfortunately, rough spots caused by endocarditis or injuries to blood vessel walls often cause the release of platelet factors. The result is often the formation of a fatal blood clot.

Covering Sac or Pericardium

The heart has a covering and a lining. Its covering, called the **pericardium** (pair-i-KAR-dee-um), consists of two layers of fibrous tissue with a small space in between. The inner layer of the pericardium is called the **visceral pericardium** or **epicardium** (ep-i-KAR-dee-um). It covers the heart the way an apple skin covers an apple. The outer layer of pericardium is called the **parietal pericardium.** It fits around the heart like a loose-fitting sack, allowing enough room for the heart to beat. It is easy to remember the difference between the *endocardium,* which lines the heart chambers, and the *epicardium,* which covers the surface of the heart (Figure 11-2), if you understand the meaning of the prefixes *endo-* and *epi-*. *Endo-* comes from the Greek word meaning "inside" or "within," and *epi-* comes from the Greek word meaning "upon" or "on."

The two pericardial layers slip against each other without friction when the heart beats because these are serous membranes with moist, not dry, surfaces. A thin film of pericardial fluid furnishes the lubricating moistness between the heart and its enveloping pericardial sac. If the pericardium becomes inflamed, a condition called **pericarditis** (pair-i-kar-DYE-tis) results.

Heart Action

The heart serves as a muscular pumping device for distributing blood to all parts of the body. Contraction of the heart is called **systole** (SIS-toe-lee), and relaxation is called **diastole** (dye-AS-toe-lee). When the heart beats (that is, when it contracts), the atria contract first (atrial systole), forcing blood into the ventricles. Once filled, the two ventricles contract (ventricular systole) and force blood out of the heart (Figure 11-3). For the heart to be efficient in its pumping action, more than just the rhythmic contraction of its muscular fibers is required. The direction of blood flow must be directed and controlled. This is accomplished by four sets of valves located at the entrance and near the exit of the ventricles.

Heart Valves

The two valves that separate the atrial chambers above from the ventricles below are called **AV** or **atrioventricular** (ay-tree-o-ven-TRIK-yoo-lar) **valves.** The two AV valves are called the **bicuspid** or **mitral** (MY-tral) **valve,** located between the left atrium and ventricle, and the **tricuspid valve,** located between the right atrium and ventricle. The AV valves prevent backflow of blood into the atria when the ventricles contract. Locate the AV valves in Figures 11-2 and 11-3. Note that a number of stringlike structures called **chordae tendineae** (KOR-dee ten-DIN-ee) attach the AV valves to the wall of the heart.

The **SL** or **semilunar** (sem-i-LOO-nar) **valves** are located between the two ventricular chambers and the large arteries that carry blood away from the heart when contraction occurs (Figure 11-3). The ventricles, like the atria, contract together. Therefore the two semilunar valves open and close at the same time. The **pulmonary semilunar valve** is located at the beginning of the pulmonary artery and allows blood going to the lungs to flow out of the right ventricle but prevents it from flowing back into the ventricle. The **aortic semilunar valve** is located at the beginning of the aorta and allows blood to flow out of the left ventricle up into the aorta but prevents backflow into this ventricle.

HEART SOUNDS

If a stethoscope is placed on the anterior chest wall, two distinct sounds can be heard. They are rhythmical and repetitive sounds that are often described as **lub dup.**

The first or *lub* sound is caused by the vibration and abrupt closure of the AV valves as the ventricles contract. Closure of the AV valves prevents blood from rushing back up into the atria during

FIGURE 11–3 ***Heart Action.*** **A,** During atrial systole (contraction) cardiac muscle in the atrial wall contracts, forcing blood through the AV valves and into the ventricles. Bottom illustration shows superior view of all four valves, with SL valves closed and AV valves open. **B,** During ventricular systole that follows, the AV valves close, and blood is forced out of the ventricles through the semilunar valves and into the arteries. Bottom illustration shows superior view of SL valves open and AV valves closed.

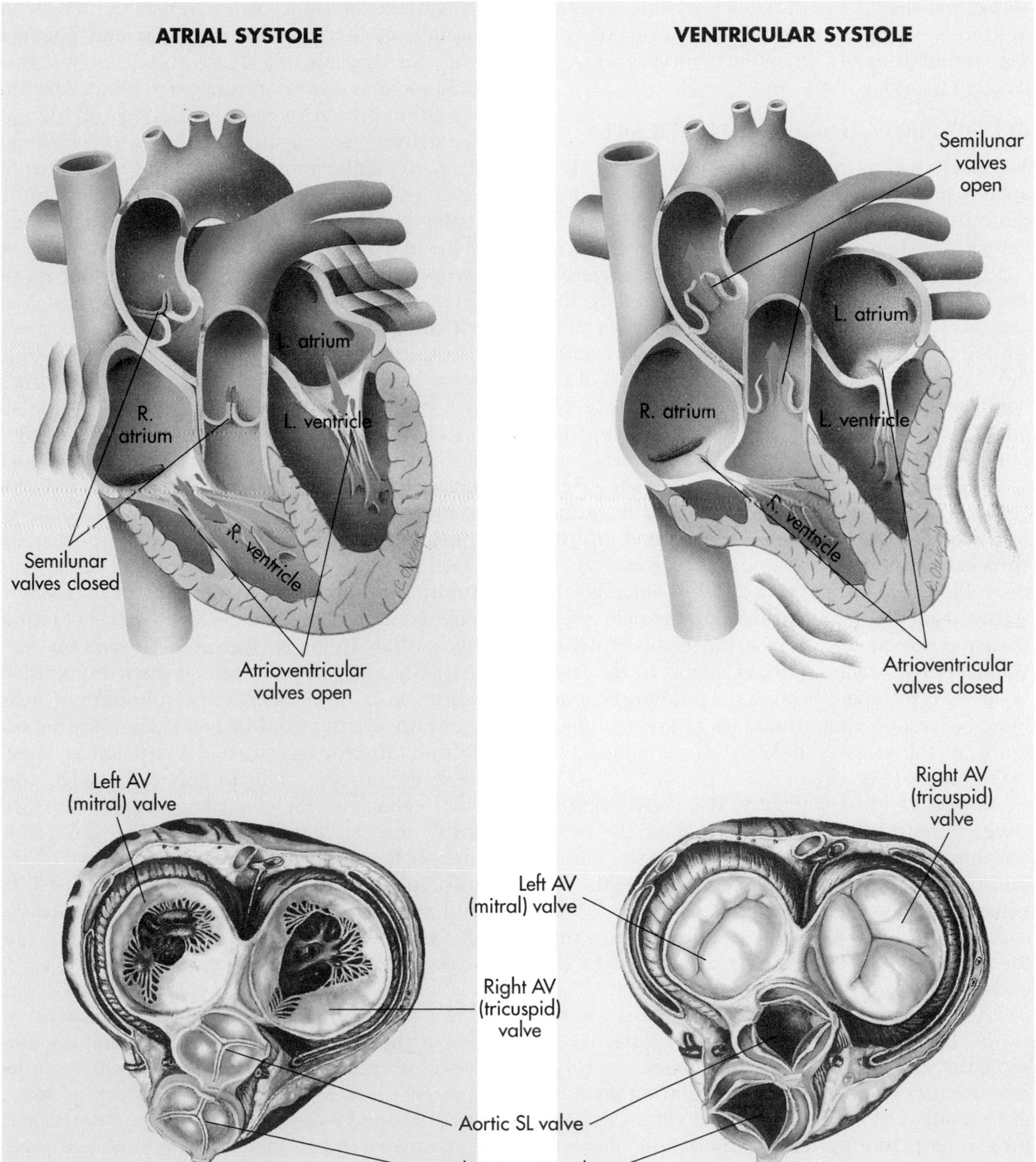

contraction of the ventricles. This first sound is of longer duration and lower pitch than the second. The pause between this first sound and the *dup* or second sound is shorter than that after the second sound and the *lub dup* of the next systole. The second heart sound is caused by the closing of both the semilunar valves when the ventricles undergo diastole (relax).

BLOOD FLOW THROUGH THE HEART

The heart acts as two separate pumps. The right atrium and the right ventricle perform a task quite different from the left atrium and the left ventricle. When the heart "beats," first the atria contract simultaneously. This is atrial systole. Then the ventricles fill with blood, and they, too, contract together during ventricular systole. Although the atria contract as a unit followed by the ventricles below, the right and left sides of the heart act as separate pumps. As we study the blood flow through the heart, the separate functions of the two pumps will become clearer.

Note in Figure 11-3 that blood enters the right atrium through two large veins called the **superior vena** (VEE-nah) **cava** (KAY-vah) and **inferior vena cava.** The right heart pump receives oxygen-poor blood from the veins. After entering the right atrium, it is pumped through the right AV or tricuspid valve and enters the right ventricle. When the ventricles contract, blood in the right ventricle is pumped through the pulmonary semilunar valve into the **pulmonary artery** and eventually to the lungs, where oxygen is added and carbon dioxide is lost.

As you can see in Figure 11-3, blood rich in oxygen returns to the left atrium of the heart through four **pulmonary veins.** It then passes through the left AV or bicuspid valve into the left ventricle. When the left ventricle contracts, blood is forced through the aortic semilunar valve into the **aorta** (ay-OR-tah) and is distributed to the body as a whole.

As you can tell from Figure 11-4, the two sides of the heart actually pump blood through two separate "circulations" and function as two separate pumps. The **pulmonary circulation** involves movement of blood from the right ventricle to the lungs, and the **systemic circulation** involves movement of blood from the left ventricle throughout the body as a whole. The pulmonary and systemic circulations are discussed later in the chapter.

BLOOD SUPPLY TO THE HEART MUSCLE

To sustain life, the heart must pump blood throughout the body on a regular and ongoing basis. As a result, the heart muscle or myocardium requires a constant supply of blood containing nutrients and oxygen to function effectively. The delivery of oxygen and nutrient-rich arterial blood to cardiac muscle tissue and the return of oxygen-poor blood from this active tissue to the venous system is called the **coronary circulation.**

Blood flows into the heart muscle by way of two small vessels that are surely the most famous of all the blood vessels—the **right** and **left coronary arteries**—famous because coronary heart disease kills many thousands of people every year. The coronary arteries are the aorta's first branches. The openings into these small vessels lie behind the flaps of the aortic semilunar valves. In both coronary thrombosis and coronary **embolism** (EM-bo-lizm), a blood clot occludes or plugs up some part of a coronary artery. Blood cannot pass through the occluded vessel and so cannot reach the heart muscle cells it normally supplies. Deprived of oxygen, these cells soon die or are damaged. In medical terms, **myocardial** (my-o-KAR-dee-al) **infarction** (in-FARK-shun) or tissue death occurs. Myocardial infarction or "heart attack" is a common cause of death during middle and late adulthood. Recovery from a myocardial infarction is possible if the amount of heart tissue damaged was small enough so that the remaining undamaged heart muscle can pump blood effectively enough to supply the needs of the rest of the heart and the body. The term **angina** (an-JYE-nah) **pectoris** (PEK-tor-is) is used to describe the severe chest pain that occurs when the myocardium is deprived of adequate oxygen. It is often a warning that the coronary arteries are no longer able to supply enough blood and oxygen to the heart muscle. **Coronary bypass surgery** is a frequent treatment for those who suffer from severely restricted coronary artery blood flow. In this procedure, veins are "harvested" or removed from other areas of the body and used to bypass partial blockages in coronary arteries.

FIGURE 11–4 ***Blood Flow Through the Circulatory System.*** In the pulmonary circulatory route, blood is pumped from the right side of the heart to the gas-exchange tissues of the lungs. In the systemic circulation, blood is pumped from the left side of the heart to all other tissues of the body.

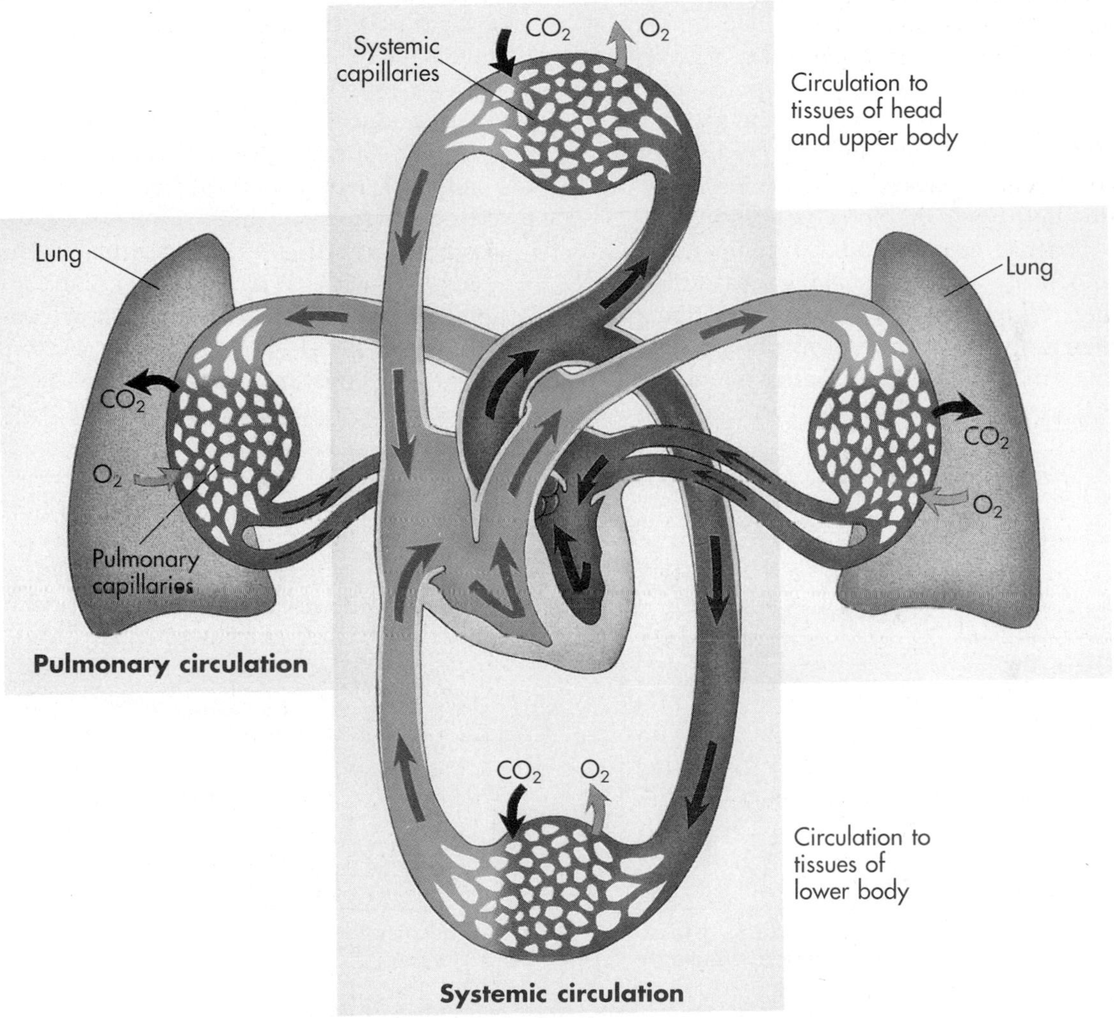

After blood has passed through the capillary beds in the myocardium, it flows into **cardiac veins,** which empty into the **coronary sinus** and finally into the right atrium.

CARDIAC CYCLE

The beating of the heart is a regular and rhythmic process. Each complete heart beat is called a **cardiac cycle** and includes the contraction (systole) and relaxation (diastole) of atria and ventricles. Each cycle takes about 0.8 seconds to complete if the heart is beating at an average rate of about 72 beats per minute. The term **stroke volume** refers to the volume of blood ejected from the ventricles during each beat. **Cardiac output,** or the volume of blood pumped by one ventricle per minute, averages about 5 L in a normal, resting adult.

Changes in Blood Flow During Exercise

Not only does the overall rate of blood flow increase during exercise, but the relative blood flow through the different organs of the body also changes. During exercise, blood is routed away from the kidneys and digestive organs and toward the skeletal muscles, cardiac muscle, and skin. Rerouting of blood is accomplished by contracting precapillary sphincters in some tissues (thus reducing blood flow) while relaxing precapillary sphincters in other tissues (thus increasing blood flow). How can homeostasis be better maintained by these changes? One reason is because glucose and oxygen levels are dropping rapidly in muscles as they use up these substances to produce energy. Increased blood flow restores normal levels of glucose and oxygen rapidly. Blood warmed up in active muscles flows to the skin for cooling. This helps keep the body temperature from getting too high. Can you think of other ways this situation helps maintain homeostasis? Typical changes in organ blood flow with exercise are shown in the illustration. The green bar in each pair shows the resting blood flow; the blue bar shows the flow during exercise.

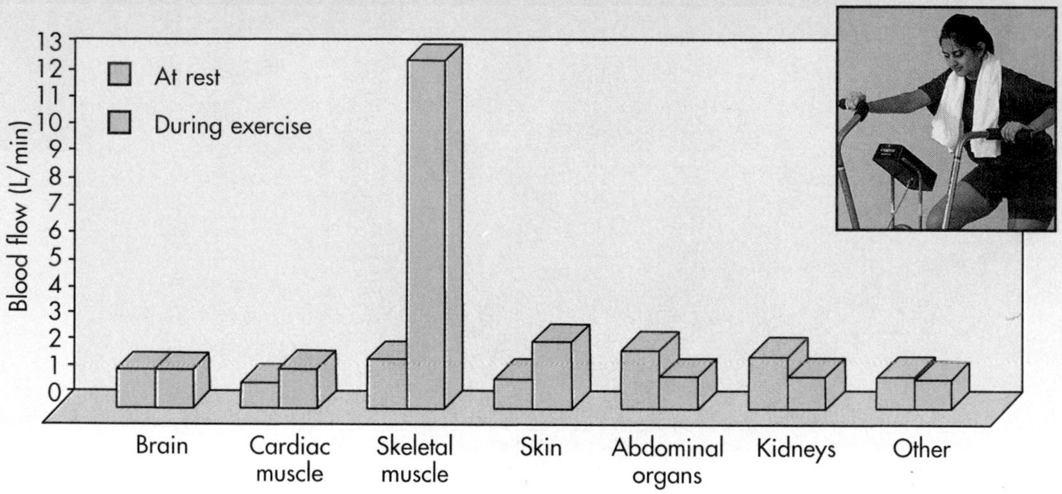

CONDUCTION SYSTEM OF THE HEART

Cardiac muscle fibers can contract rhythmically on their own. However, they must be coordinated by electrical signals (impulses) if the heart is to pump effectively. Although the rate of the cardiac muscle's rhythm is controlled by autonomic nerve signals, the heart has its own built-in conduction system for coordinating contractions during the cardiac cycle. The most important thing to realize about this conduction system is that all of the cardiac muscle fibers in each region of the heart are electrically linked together. The *intercalated disks* that were first introduced in Chapter 2 (see Figure 2-20, p. 39) are actually electrical connectors that join muscle fibers into a single unit that can conduct an impulse through the entire wall of a heart chamber without stopping. Thus both atrial walls will contract at about the same time because all their fibers are electrically linked. Likewise, both ventricular walls will contract at about the same time.

FIGURE 11–5 ***Conduction System of the Heart.*** Specialized cardiac muscle cells in the wall of the heart rapidly conduct an electrical impulse throughout the myocardium. The signal is initiated by the SA node (pacemaker) and spreads to the rest of the atrial myocardium and to the AV node. The AV node then initiates a signal that is conducted through the ventricular myocardium by way of the AV bundle (of His) and Purkinje fibers.

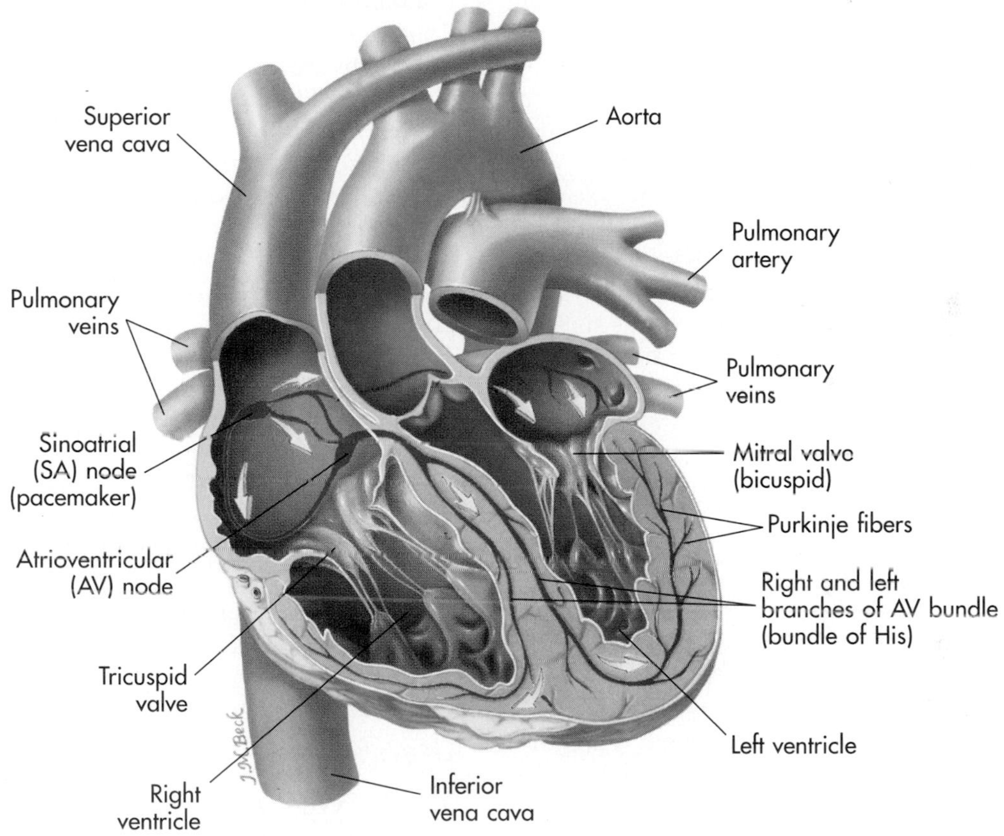

Four structures embedded in the wall of the heart are specialized to generate strong impulses and conduct them rapidly to certain regions of the heart wall. Thus they make sure that the atria contract and then the ventricles contract in an efficient manner. The names of the structures that make up this conduction system of the heart follow:

1. **Sinoatrial** (sye-no-AY-tree-al) **node,** which is sometimes called the SA node or the *pacemaker*
2. **Atrioventricular** (ay-tree-o-ven-TRIK-yoo-lar) **node** or **AV node**
3. **AV bundle** or **bundle of His**
4. **Purkinje** (pur-KIN-jee) **fibers**

Impulse conduction normally starts in the heart's pacemaker, namely, the SA node. From there, it spreads, as you can see in Figure 11-5, in all directions through the atria. This causes the atrial fibers to contract. When impulses reach the AV node, it relays them by way of the bundle of His and Purkinje fibers to the ventricles, causing them to contract. Normally, therefore, a ventricular beat follows each atrial beat. Various conditions such as endocarditis or myocardial infarction, however, can damage the heart's conduction system and thereby disturb its rhythmical beating. One such disturbance is the condition commonly called *heart block.* Impulses are blocked from getting through to the ventricles, resulting in the heart beating at a much slower rate than normal. A physician may treat heart block by implanting in the heart an **artificial pacemaker,** an electrical device that causes ventricular contractions at a rate fast enough to maintain an adequate circulation of blood.

ELECTROCARDIOGRAM

The specialized structures of the heart's conduction system generate tiny electrical currents that spread through surrounding tissues to the surface of the body. This fact is of great clinical significance because these electrical signals can be picked up from the body surface and transformed into visible tracings by an instrument called an **electrocardiograph** (e-lek-tro-KAR-dee-o-graf).

The **electrocardiogram** (e-lek-tro-KAR-dee-o-gram) or **ECG** is the graphic record of the heart's electrical activity. Skilled interpretation of these ECG records may sometimes make the difference between life and death. A normal ECG tracing is shown in Figure 11-6.

A normal ECG tracing has three very characteristic deflections or waves called the **P wave,** the **QRS complex,** and the **T wave.** These deflections represent the electrical activity that regulates the contraction or relaxation of the atria or ventricles. The term *depolarization* describes the electrical activity that triggers contraction of the heart muscle. *Repolarization* begins just before the relaxation phase of cardiac muscle activity. In the normal ECG shown in Figure 11-6, the small P wave occurs with depolarization of the atria. The QRS complex occurs as a result of depolarization of the ventricles, and the T wave results from electrical activity generated by repolarization of the ventricles. You may wonder why no visible record of atrial repolarization is noted in a normal ECG. The reason is simply that the deflection is very small and is hidden by the large QRS complex that occurs at the same time.

Damage to cardiac muscle tissue that is caused by a myocardial infarction or disease affecting the heart's conduction system results in distinctive changes in the ECG. Therefore ECG tracings are extremely valuable in the diagnosis and treatment of heart disease.

Blood Vessels

KINDS

Arterial blood is pumped from the heart through a series of large distribution vessels—the **arteries.** The largest artery in the body is the aorta. Arteries subdivide into vessels that become progressively smaller and finally become tiny **arterioles** (ar-TEER-ee-ols) that control the flow into microscopic exchange vessels called **capillaries** (KAP-i-lair-ees). In the so-called **capillary beds,** the exchange of nutrients and respiratory gases occurs between the blood and tissue fluid around the cells. Blood exits or is drained from the capillary beds and then enters the small **venules** (VEN-yools), which join with other venules and increase in size, becoming **veins.** The largest veins are the superior vena cava and the inferior vena cava.

As noted before (Figure 11-4), arteries carry blood away from the heart toward capillaries. Veins carry blood toward the heart away from capillaries, and capillaries carry blood from the tiny arterioles into tiny venules. The aorta carries blood out of the left ventricle of the heart, and the venae cavae return blood to the right atrium after the blood has circulated through the body.

STRUCTURE

Arteries, veins, and capillaries differ in structure. Three coats or layers are found in both arteries and veins (Figure 11-7). The outermost layer is called the **tunica adventitia.** Note that smooth muscle tissue is found in the middle layer or **tunica media** of arteries and veins. However, the muscle layer is much thicker in arteries than in veins. Why is this important? Because the thicker muscle layer in the artery wall is able to resist great pressures generated by ventricular systole. In arteries, the tunica media plays a critical role in maintaining blood pressure and controlling blood distribution. This is a smooth muscle, so it is controlled by the autonomic nervous system. The tunica media also includes a thin layer of elastic fibrous tissue.

An inner layer of endothelial cells called the **tunica intima** lines arteries and veins. The tunica intima is actually a single layer of squamous epithelial cells called **endothelium** (en-doe-THEE-lee-um) that lines the inner surface of the entire circulatory system.

FIGURE 11–6 ***Events Represented by the Electrocardiogram (ECG).*** **A** through **C,** The P wave represents the depolarization of cardiac muscle tissue in the SA node and atrial walls. **C** and **D,** Before the QRS complex is observed, the AV node and AV bundle depolarize. **E** and **F,** The QRS complex occurs as the atrial walls repolarize and the ventricular walls depolarize. **G,** The T wave is observed as the ventricular walls repolarize. Depolarization triggers contraction in the affected muscle tissue. Thus cardiac muscle contraction occurs *after* depolarization begins.

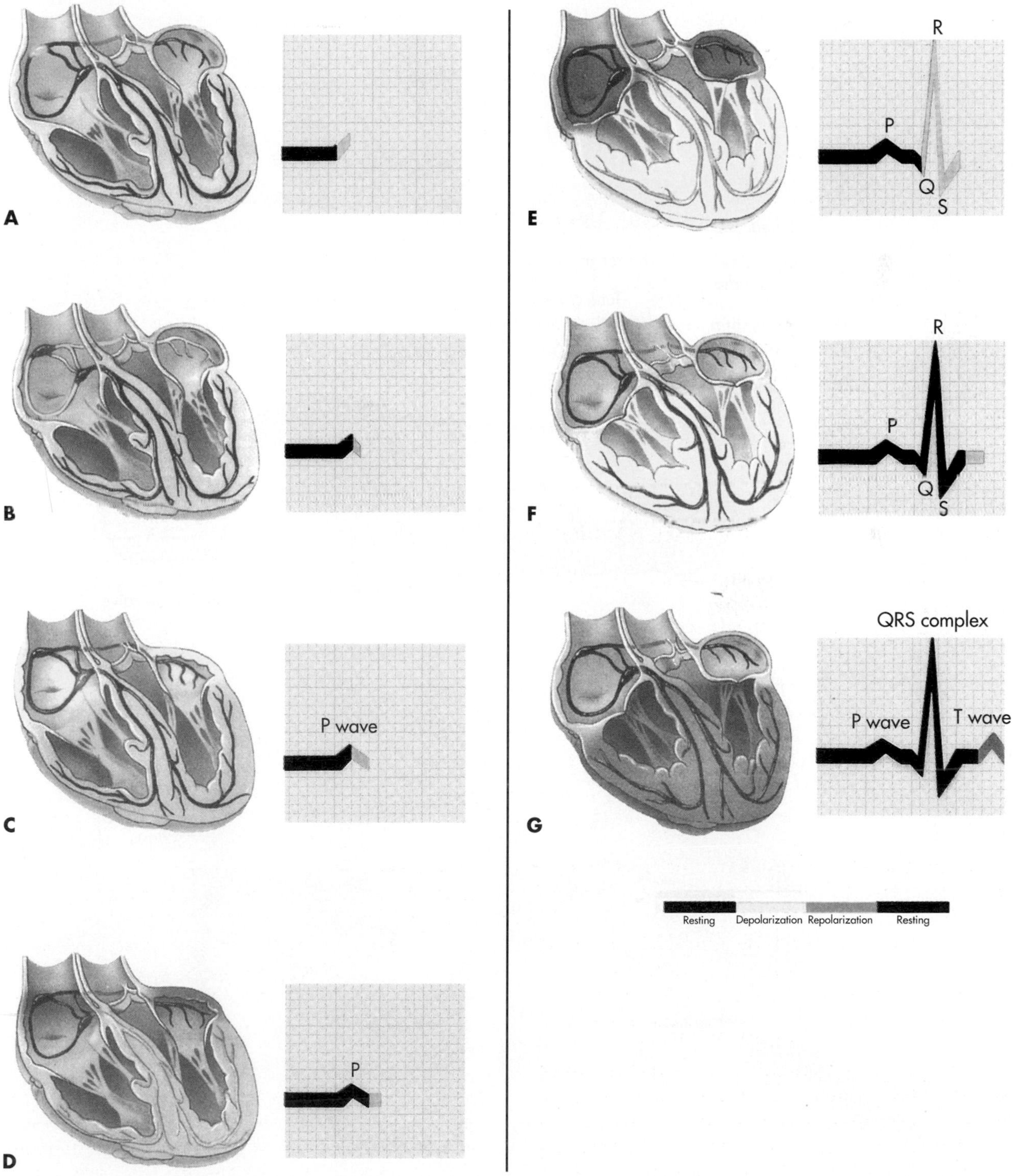

FIGURE 11–7 ***Artery and Vein.*** **A,** Schematic drawings of an artery and a vein show comparative thicknesses of the three layers: the outer layer or tunica adventitia, the muscle layer or tunica media, and the tunica intima made of endothelium. Note that the muscle and outer layer are much thinner in veins than in arteries and that veins have valves. **B,** Photomicrograph of artery and vein.

A

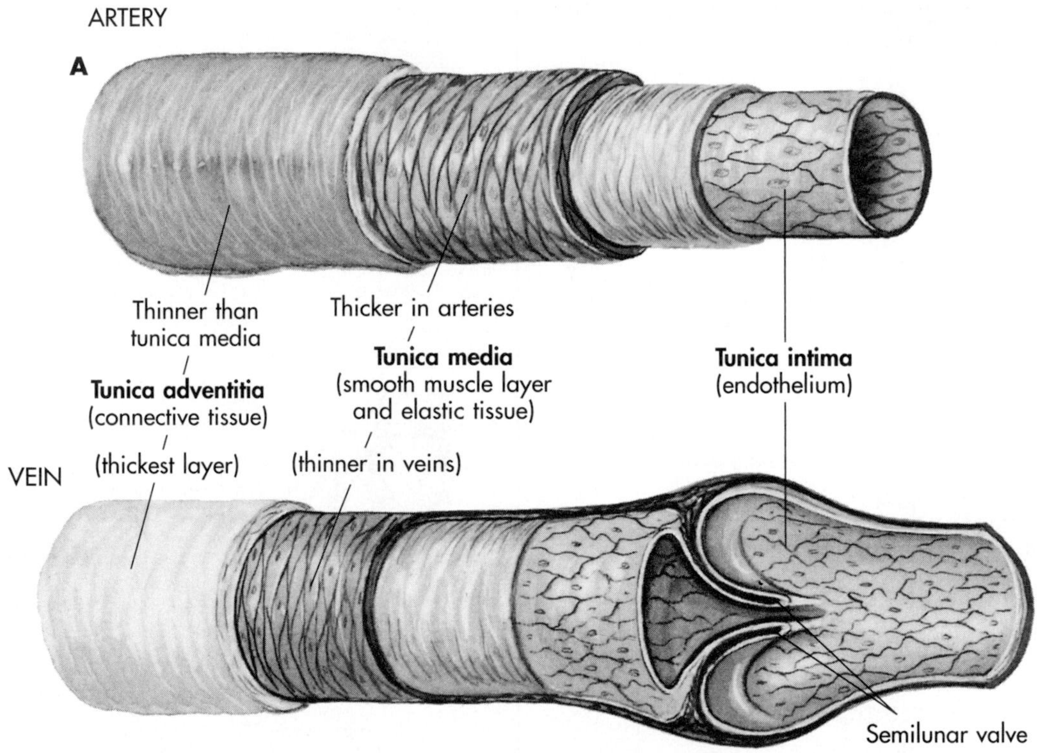

B

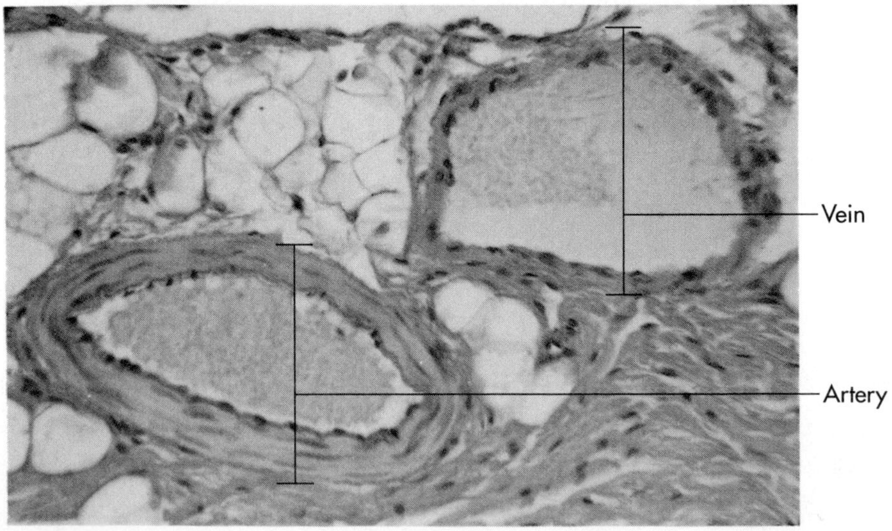

As you can see in Figure 11-7, veins have a unique structural feature not present in arteries. They are equipped with one-way valves that prevent the backflow of blood. When a surgeon cuts into the body, only arteries, arterioles, veins, and venules can be seen. Capillaries cannot be seen because they are microscopic. The most important structural feature of capillaries is their extreme thinness—only one layer of flat, endothelial cells composes the capillary membrane. Instead of three layers or coats, the capillary wall is composed of only one—the tunica intima. Substances such as glucose, oxygen, and wastes can quickly pass through it on their way to or from cells. Smooth muscle cells called **precapillary sphincters** guard the entrance to the capillary and determine into which capillary blood will flow.

FUNCTIONS

Arteries, veins, and capillaries have different functions. Arteries and arterioles distribute blood from the heart to capillaries in all parts of the body. In addition, by constricting or dilating, arterioles help maintain arterial blood pressure at a normal level. Venules and veins collect blood from capillaries and return it to the heart. They also serve as blood reservoirs because they can expand to hold a larger volume of blood or constrict to hold a much smaller amount. Capillaries function as exchange vessels. For example, glucose and oxygen move out of the blood in capillaries into interstitial fluid and on into cells. Carbon dioxide and other substances move in the opposite direction (that is, into the capillary blood from the cells). Fluid is also exchanged between capillary blood and interstitial fluid (see Chapter 18).

Study Figure 11-8 and Table 11-1 to learn the names of the main arteries of the body and Figures 11-9 and 11-10 and Table 11-2 for the names of the main veins.

Circulation

SYSTEMIC AND PULMONARY CIRCULATION

The term **circulation of blood** is self-explanatory, meaning that blood flows through vessels that are arranged to form a circuit or circular pattern. Blood flow from the left ventricle of the heart

TABLE 11–1 The Major Arteries

ARTERY	TISSUES SUPPLIED
Head and Neck	
Occipital	Posterior head and neck
Facial	Mouth, pharynx, and face
Internal carotid	Anterior brain and meninges
External carotid	Superficial neck, face, eyes, and larynx
Right common carotid	Right side of the head and neck
Left common carotid	Left side of the head and neck
Thorax	
Left subclavian	Left upper extremity
Brachiocephalic	Head and arm
Arch of aorta	Branches to head, neck, and upper extremities
Right and left coronary	Heart muscle
Abdomen	
Celiac	Stomach, spleen, and liver
Splenic	Spleen
Renal	Kidneys
Superior mesenteric	Small intestine; first half of the large intestine
Inferior mesenteric	Lower half of the large intestine
Upper Extremity	
Axillary	Axilla (armpit)
Brachial	Arm
Radial	Lateral side of the hand
Ulnar	Medial side of the hand
Lower Extremity	
Internal iliac	Pelvic viscera and rectum
External iliac	Genitalia and lower trunk muscles
Deep femoral	Deep thigh muscles
Femoral	Thigh
Popliteal	Leg and foot
Anterior tibial	Leg

FIGURE 11–8 ***Principal Arteries of the Body.***

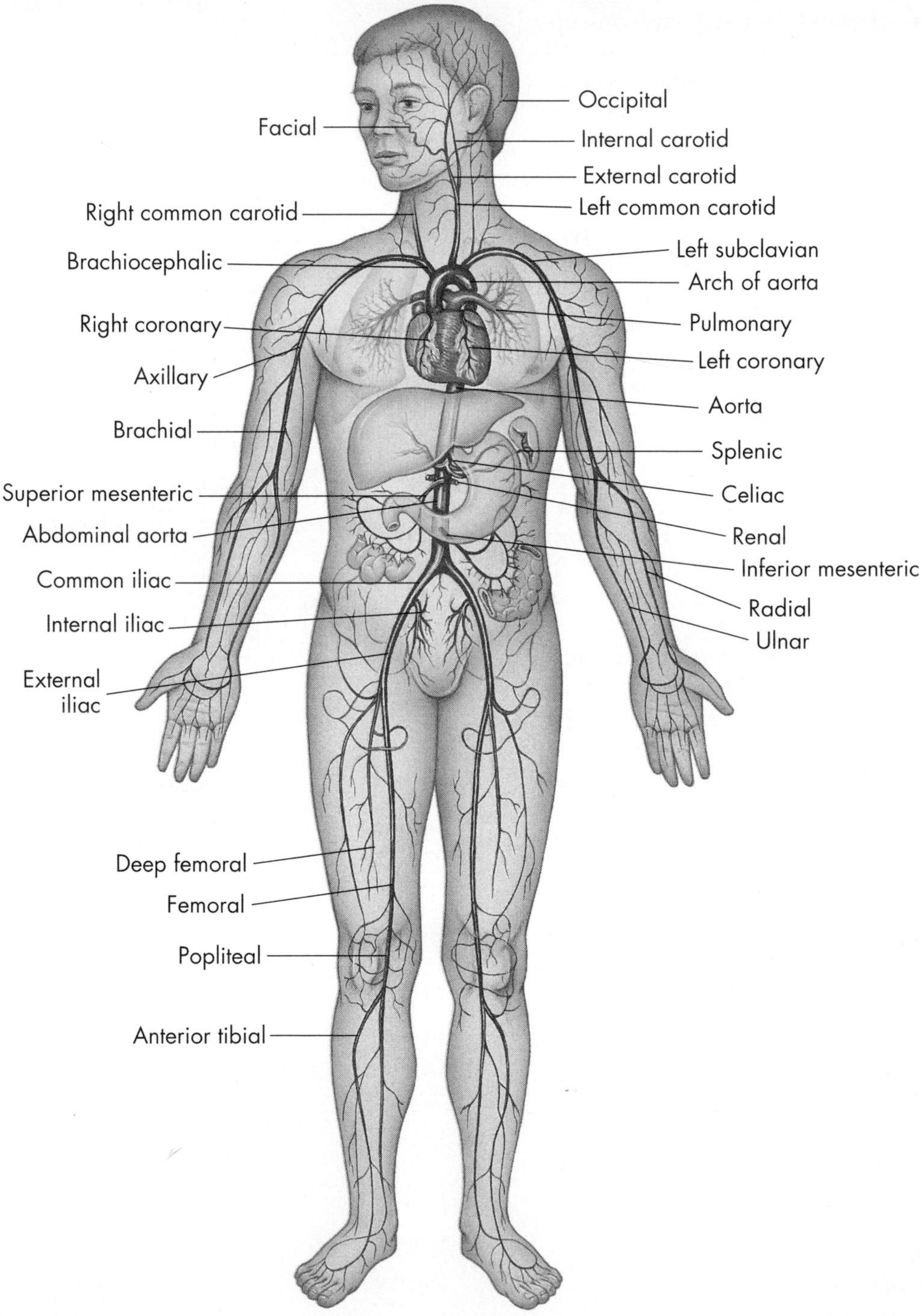

FIGURE 11–9 *Principal Veins of the Body.*

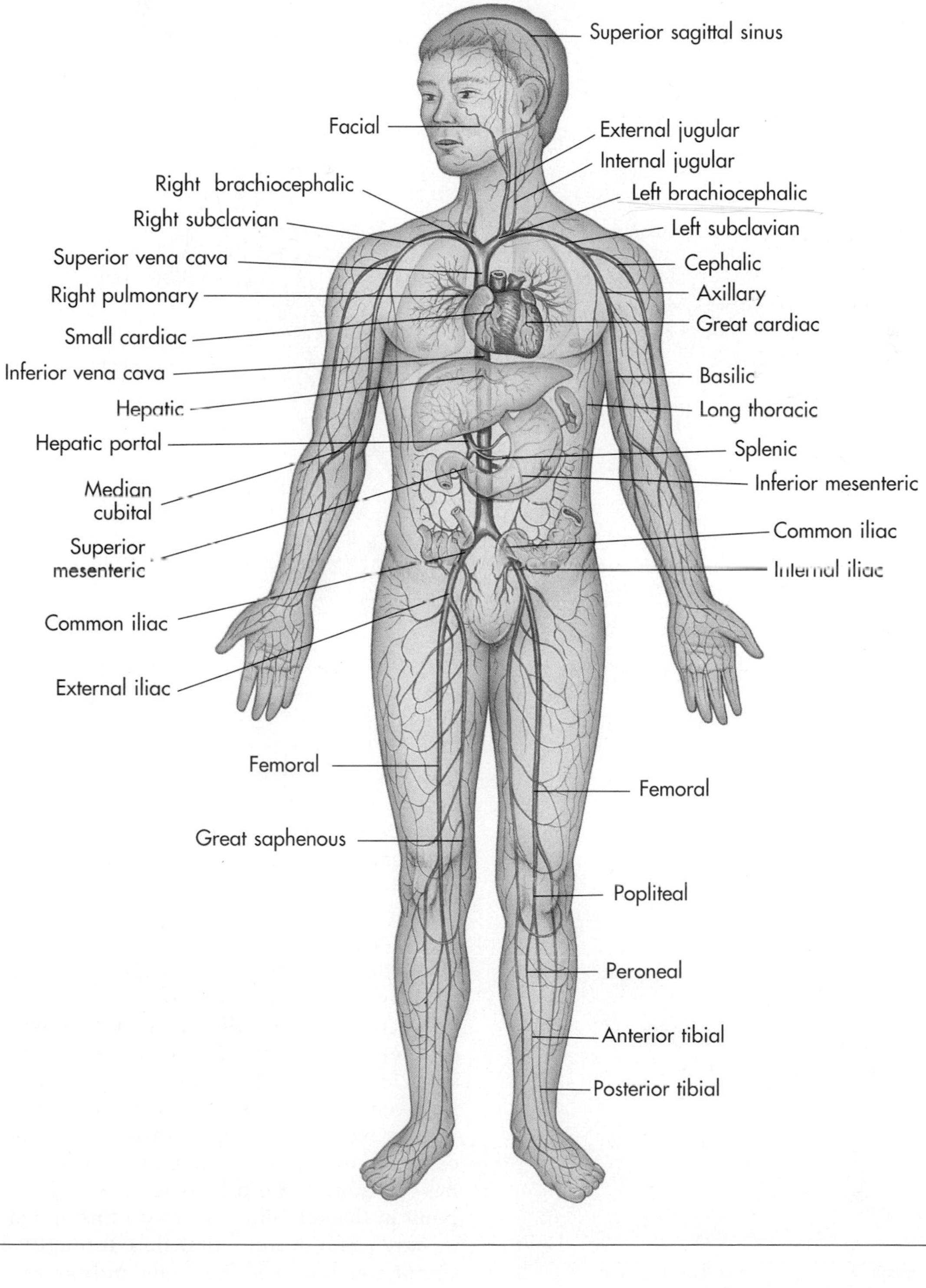

TABLE 11–2 The Major Veins

VEIN	TISSUES DRAINED
Head and Neck	
Superior sagittal sinus	Brain
Anterior facial	Anterior and superficial face
External jugular	Superficial tissues of the head and neck
Internal jugular	Sinuses of the brain
Thorax	
Brachiocephalic	Viscera of the thorax
Subclavian	Upper extremities
Superior vena cava	Head, neck, and upper extremities
Pulmonary	Lungs
Right and left coronary	Heart
Inferior vena cava	Lower body
Abdomen	
Hepatic	Liver
Long thoracic	Abdominal and thoracic muscles
Hepatic portal	Liver and gallbladder
Splenic	Spleen
Superior mesenteric	Small intestine and most of the colon
Inferior mesenteric	Descending colon and rectum
Upper Extremity	
Cephalic	Lateral arm
Axillary	Axilla and arm
Basilic	Medial arm
Median cubital	Cephalic vein (to basilic vein)
Lower Extremity	
External iliac	Lower limb
Internal iliac	Pelvic viscera
Femoral	Thigh
Great saphenous	Leg
Popliteal	Lower leg
Peroneal	Foot
Anterior tibial	Deep anterior leg and dorsal foot
Posterior tibial	Deep posterior leg and plantar aspect of foot

FIGURE 11–10 *Main Superficial Veins of the Arm.*

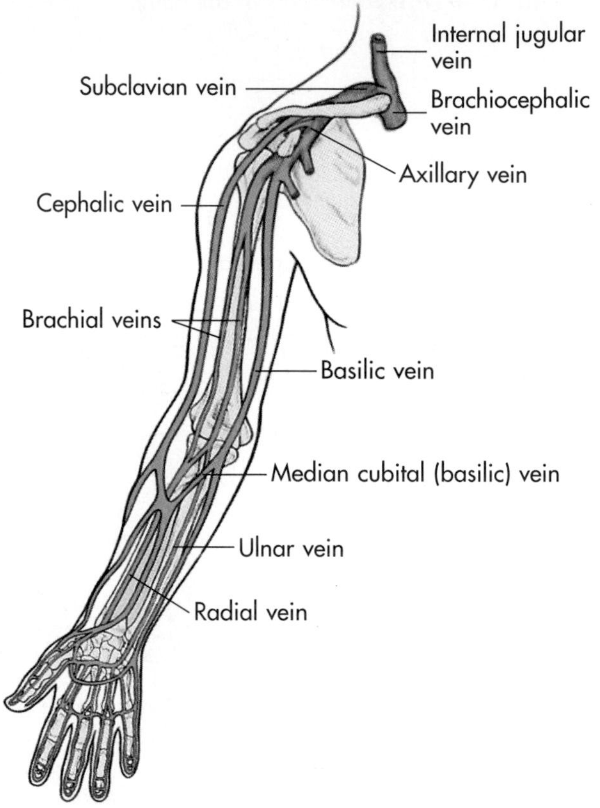

through blood vessels to all parts of the body and back to the right atrium of the heart has already been described as the **systemic circulation.** The left ventricle pumps blood into the aorta. From there, it flows into arteries that carry it into the tissues and organs of the body. As indicated in Figure 11-11, within each structure, blood moves from arteries to arterioles to capillaries. There, the vital two-way exchange of substances occurs between blood and cells. Next, blood flows out of each organ by way of its venules and then its veins to drain eventually into the inferior or superior vena cava. These two great veins return venous blood to the right atrium of the heart to complete the systemic circulation. But the blood has not quite come full circle back to its starting point in the left ventricle. To do this and start on its way again, it must first flow through another circuit, referred to earlier as the **pulmonary circulation.** Observe in Figure 11-11 that venous blood

FIGURE 11–11 ***Diagram of Blood Flow in the Circulatory System.*** Blood leaves the heart through arteries, then travels through arterioles, capillaries, venules, and veins before returning to the opposite side of the heart. Compare this figure with Figure 11-4.

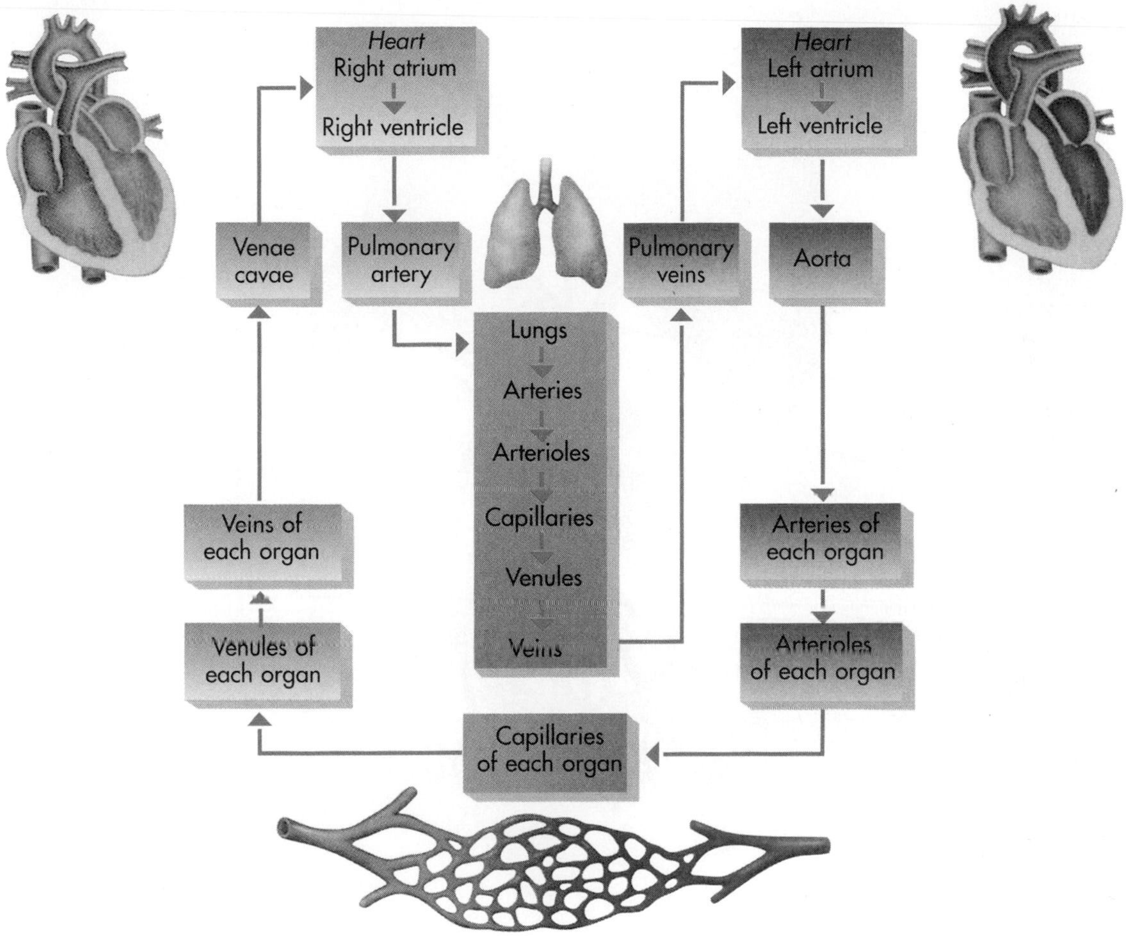

moves from the right atrium to the right ventricle to the pulmonary artery to lung arterioles and capillaries. There, the exchange of gases between the blood and air takes place, converting the deep crimson typical of venous blood to the scarlet of arterial blood. This oxygenated blood then flows through lung venules into four pulmonary veins and returns to the left atrium of the heart. From the left atrium, it enters the left ventricle to be pumped again through the systemic circulation.

HEPATIC PORTAL CIRCULATION

The term **hepatic portal circulation** refers to the route of blood flow through the liver. Veins from the spleen, stomach, pancreas, gallbladder, and intestines do not pour their blood directly into the inferior vena cava as do the veins from other abdominal organs. Instead, they send their blood to the liver by means of the hepatic portal vein (Figure 11-12). The blood then must pass through the liver before it reenters the regular venous

FIGURE 11–12 ***Hepatic Portal Circulation.*** In this very unusual circulation, a vein is located between two capillary beds. The hepatic portal vein collects blood from capillaries in visceral structures located in the abdomen and empties it into the liver. Hepatic veins return blood to the inferior vena cava. (Organs are not drawn to scale.)

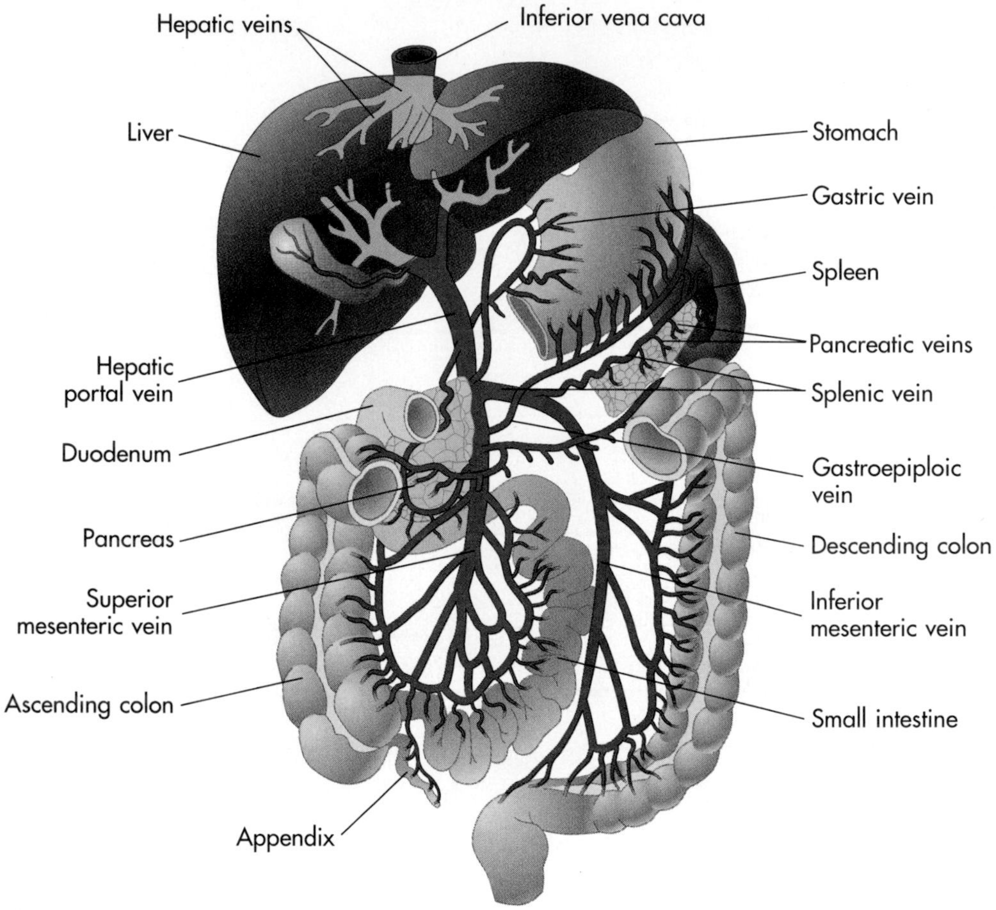

return to the heart. Blood leaves the liver by way of the hepatic veins, which drain into the inferior vena cava. As noted in Figure 11-11, blood normally flows from arteries to arterioles to capillaries to venules to veins and back to the heart. Blood flow in the hepatic portal circulation, however, does not follow this typical route. Venous blood, which would ordinarily return directly to the heart, is sent instead through a second capillary bed in the liver. The hepatic portal vein shown in Figure 11-12 is located between two capillary beds—one set in the digestive organs and the other in the liver. From the liver capillary beds, the path of blood returns to its normal route.

The detour of venous blood through a second capillary bed in the liver before its return to the heart serves some valuable purposes. For example, when a meal is being absorbed, the blood in the portal vein contains a higher-than-normal concentration of glucose. Liver cells remove the excess glucose and store it as glycogen; therefore blood leaving the liver usually has a normal blood glucose concentration. Liver cells also

FIGURE 11–13 *The Fetal Circulation.*

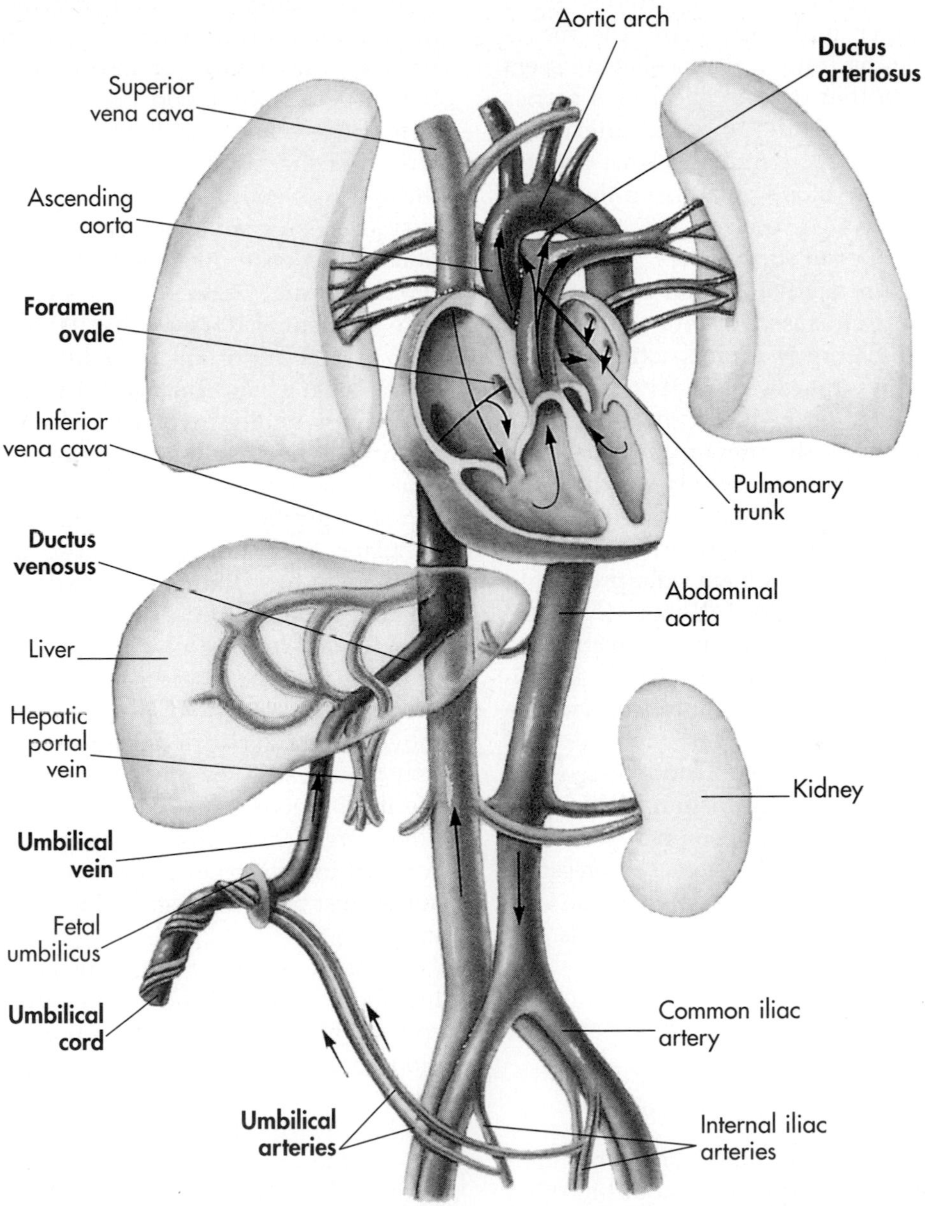

remove and detoxify various poisonous substances that may be present in the blood. The hepatic portal system is an excellent example of how "structure follows function" in helping the body maintain homeostasis.

FETAL CIRCULATION

Circulation in the body before birth differs from circulation after birth because the fetus must secure oxygen and food from maternal blood instead of from its own lungs and digestive organs. For the exchange of nutrients and oxygen to occur between fetal and maternal blood, specialized blood vessels must carry the fetal blood to the **placenta** (plah-SEN-tah), where the exchange occurs, and then return it to the fetal body. Three vessels (shown in Figure 11-13 as part of the **umbilical cord**) accomplish this purpose.

They are the two small **umbilical arteries** and a single, much larger **umbilical vein.** The movement of blood in the umbilical vessels may seem unusual at first in that the umbilical vein carries oxygenated blood, and the umbilical artery carries oxygen-poor blood. Remember that arteries are vessels that carry blood away from the heart, whereas veins carry blood toward the heart, regardless of the oxygen supply they may have.

Another structure unique to fetal circulation is called the **ductus venosus** (DUK-tus ve-NO-sus). As you can see in Figure 11-13, it is actually a continuation of the umbilical vein. It serves as a shunt, allowing most of the blood returning from the placenta to bypass the immature liver of the developing baby and empty directly into the inferior vena cava. Two other structures in the developing fetus allow most of the blood to bypass the developing lungs, which remain collapsed until birth. The **foramen ovale** (fo-RAY-men o-VAL-ee) shunts blood from the right atrium directly into the left atrium, and the **ductus arteriosus** (DUK-tus ar-teer-ee-O-sus) connects the aorta and the pulmonary artery.

At birth, the specialized fetal blood vessels and shunts must be rendered nonfunctional. When the newborn infant takes its first deep breaths, the circulatory system is subjected to increased pressure. The result is closure of the foramen ovale and rapid collapse of the umbilical blood vessels, the ductus venosus, and ductus arteriosus.

Blood Pressure

UNDERSTANDING BLOOD PRESSURE

A good way to understand blood pressure might be to try to answer a few questions about it. What is blood pressure? Just what the words say—blood pressure is the pressure or push of blood.

Where does blood pressure exist? It exists in all blood vessels, but it is highest in the arteries and lowest in the veins. In fact, if we list blood vessels in order according to the amount of blood pressure in them and draw a graph, as in Figure 11-14, the graph looks like a hill, with aortic blood pressure at the top and vena caval pressure at the bottom. This blood pressure "hill" is spoken of as the *blood pressure gradient.* More precisely, the blood pressure gradient is the difference between two blood pressures. The blood pressure gradient for the entire systemic circulation is the difference between the average or mean blood pressure in the aorta and the blood pressure at the termination of the venae cavae where they join the right atrium of the heart. The mean blood pressure in the aorta, given in Figure 11-14, is 100 mm of mercury (mm Hg), and the pressure at the termination of the venae cavae is 0. Therefore, with these typical normal figures, the systemic blood pressure gradient is 100 mm Hg (100 minus 0).

Why is it important to understand blood pressure? What is its function? The blood pressure gradient is vitally involved in keeping the blood flowing. When a blood pressure gradient is present, blood circulates; conversely, when a blood pressure gradient is not present, blood does not circulate. For example, suppose that the blood pressure in the arteries were to decrease so that it became equal to the average pressure in arterioles. There would no longer be a blood pressure gradient between arteries and arterioles, and therefore there would no longer be a force to move blood out of arteries into arterioles. Circulation would stop, in other words, and very soon life itself would cease. This is why when arterial blood pressure is observed to be falling rapidly, whether in surgery or elsewhere, emergency measures must be quickly started to try to reverse this fatal trend.

What we have just said may start you wondering about why high blood pressure (meaning, of course, high arterial blood pressure) and low blood pressure are bad for circulation. High blood pressure is bad for several reasons. For one thing, if it becomes too high, it may cause the rupture of one or more blood vessels (for example, in the brain, as happens in a stroke). But low blood pressure also can be dangerous. If arterial pressure falls low enough, circulation and life cease. Massive hemorrhage, which dramatically reduces blood pressure, kills in this way.

FACTORS THAT INFLUENCE BLOOD PRESSURE

What causes blood pressure, and what makes blood pressure change from time to time? Factors such as blood volume, the strength of each heart contraction, heart rate, and the thickness of blood are all discussed in the following paragraphs.

FIGURE 11–14 ***Pressure Gradients in Blood Flow.*** Blood flows down a "blood pressure hill" from arteries, where blood pressure is highest, into arterioles, where it is somewhat lower, into capillaries, where it is still lower, and so on. All numbers on the graph indicate blood pressure measured in millimeters of mercury. The broken line, starting at 100 mm, represents the average pressure in each part of the circulatory system.

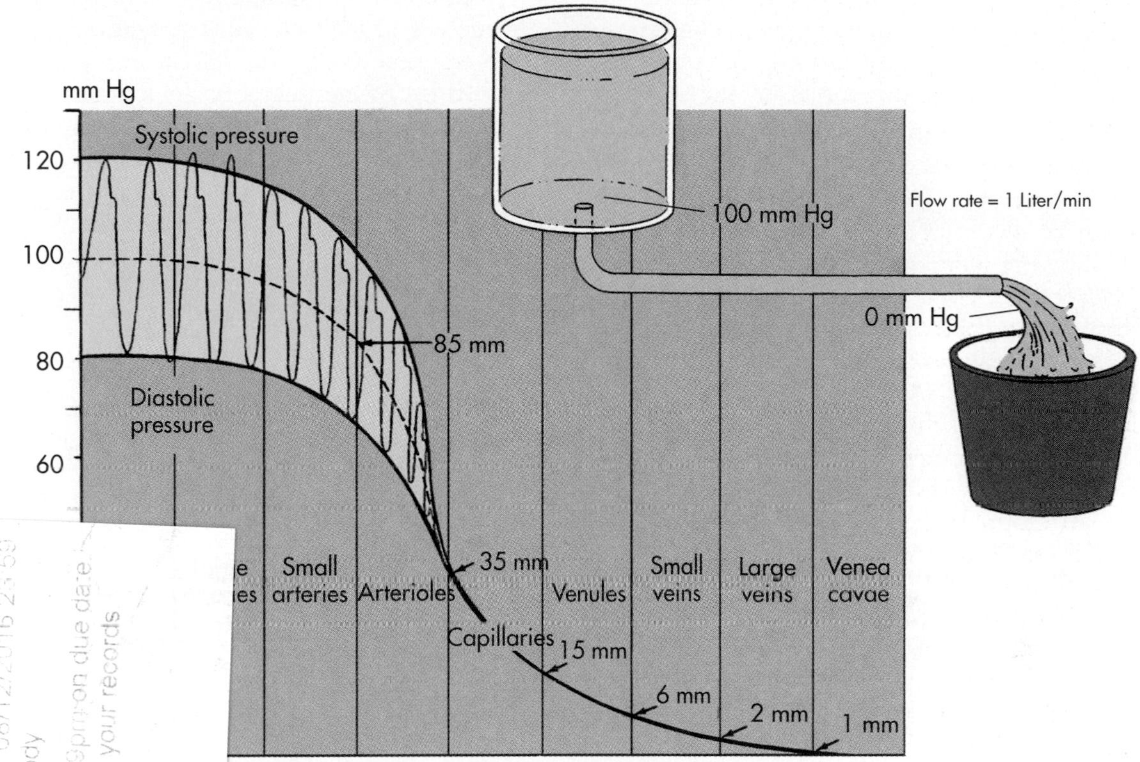

…od pressure is the volume …. The larger the volume of …or example, the more pressure the blood exerts on the walls of the arteries, or the higher the arterial blood pressure.

Conversely, the less blood in the arteries, the lower the blood pressure tends to be. Hemorrhage demonstrates this relation between blood volume and blood pressure. In hemorrhage a pronounced loss of blood occurs, and this decrease in the volume of blood causes blood pressure to drop. In fact, the major sign of hemorrhage is a rapidly falling blood pressure.

The volume of blood in the arteries is determined by how much blood the heart pumps into the arteries and how much blood the arterioles drain out of them. The diameter of the arterioles plays an important role in determining how much blood drains out of arteries into arterioles.

Strength of Heart Contractions

The strength and the rate of the heartbeat affect cardiac output and therefore blood pressure. Each time the left ventricle contracts, it squeezes a certain volume of blood (the stroke volume) into the aorta and on into other arteries. The stronger that

Blood Pressure Readings

A device called a **sphygmomanometer** (sfig-mo-ma-NAH-me-ter) is often used to measure blood pressures in both clinical and home health care situations. The traditional sphygmomanometer is an inverted tube of mercury (Hg) with a balloonlike air cuff attached via an air hose. The air cuff is placed around a limb, usually the subject's upper arm as shown in the figure. A stethoscope sensor is placed over a major artery (the *brachial artery* in the figure) to listen for the arterial pulse. A hand-operated pump fills the air cuff, increasing the air pressure and pushing the column of mercury higher. While listening through the stethoscope, the operator opens the air cuff's outlet valve and slowly reduces the air pressure around the limb. Loud, tapping *Korotkoff sounds* suddenly begin when the cuff pressure measured by the mercury column equals the systolic pressure—usually about 120 mm. As the air pressure surrounding the arm continues to decrease, the Korotkoff sounds disappear. The pressure measurement at which the sounds disappear is equal to the diastolic pressure—usually about 80 mm. The subject's blood pressure is then expressed as **systolic pressure** (the maximum arterial pressure during each cardiac cycle) over the **diastolic pressure** (the minimum arterial pressure), such as 120/80. Mercury sphygmomanometers have been replaced in many clinical settings by nonmercury devices that similarly measure the maximum and minimum arterial blood pressures. In home health care settings, patients can often learn to monitor their own blood pressure.

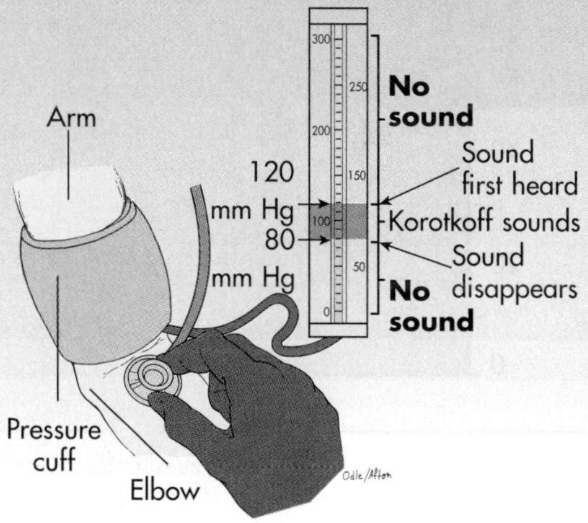

each contraction is, the more blood it pumps into the aorta and arteries. Conversely, the weaker that each contraction is, the less blood it pumps. Suppose that one contraction of the left ventricle pumps 70 ml of blood into the aorta, and suppose that the heart beats 70 times a minute; 70 ml × 70 equals 4900 ml. Almost 5 L of blood would enter the aorta and arteries every minute (the cardiac output). Now suppose that the heartbeat were to become weaker and that each contraction of the left ventricle pumps only 50 ml instead of 70 ml of blood into the aorta. If the heart still contracts 70 times a minute, it will obviously pump much less blood into the aorta—only 3500 ml instead of the more normal 4900 ml per minute. This decrease in the heart's output decreases the volume of blood in the arteries, and the decreased arterial blood volume decreases arterial blood pressure. In summary, the strength of the heartbeat affects blood pressure in this way: a stronger heartbeat increases blood pressure, and a weaker beat decreases it.

Heart Rate

The rate of the heartbeat may also affect arterial blood pressure. You might reason that when the heart beats faster, more blood enters the aorta, and therefore the arterial blood volume and blood pressure increase. This is true only if the stroke volume does not decrease sharply when the heart rate increases. Often, however, when the heart beats faster, each contraction of the left ventricle takes place so rapidly that it has little time to fill, and it squeezes out much less blood than usual into the aorta. For example, suppose that the heart rate speeded up from 70 to 100 times a minute and that at the same time its stroke volume decreased from 70 ml to 40 ml. Instead of a cardiac output of 70 × 70 or 4900 ml per minute, the cardiac output would have changed to 100 × 40 or 4000 ml per minute. Arterial blood volume decreases under these conditions, and therefore blood pressure also decreases, even though the heart rate has increased. What generalization, then, can we make? We can only say that an increase in the rate of the heartbeat increases blood pressure, and a decrease in the rate decreases blood pressure. But whether a change in the heart rate actually produces a similar change in blood pressure depends on whether the stroke volume also changes and in which direction.

Blood Viscosity

Another factor that we ought to mention in connection with blood pressure is the viscosity of blood, or in plainer language, its thickness. If blood becomes less viscous than normal, blood pressure decreases. For example, if a person suffers a hemorrhage, fluid moves into the blood from the interstitial fluid. This dilutes the blood and decreases its viscosity, and blood pressure then falls because of the decreased viscosity. After hemorrhage, whole blood or plasma is preferred to saline solution for transfusions. The reason is that saline solution is not a viscous liquid and so cannot keep blood pressure at a normal level.

FLUCTUATIONS IN BLOOD PRESSURE

No one's blood pressure stays the same all the time. It fluctuates, even in a perfectly healthy individual. For example, it goes up when a person exercises strenuously. Not only is this normal, but the increased blood pressure serves a good purpose. It increases circulation to bring more blood to muscles each minute and thus supplies them with more oxygen and food for more energy.

A normal average arterial blood pressure is about 120/80, or 120 mm Hg systolic pressure (as the ventricles contract) and 80 mm Hg diastolic pressure (as the ventricles relax). Remember, however, that what is "normal" varies somewhat among individuals and also with age.

The venous blood pressure, as you can see in Figure 11-14, is very low in the large veins and falls almost to 0 by the time blood leaves the venae cavae and enters the right atrium. The venous blood pressure within the right atrium is called the **central venous pressure.** This pressure level is important because it influences the pressure that exists in the large peripheral veins. If the heart beats strongly, the central venous pressure is low as blood enters and leaves the heart chambers efficiently. However, if the heart is weakened, central venous pressure increases, and the flow of blood into the right atrium is slowed. As a result, a person suffering heart failure, who is sitting at rest in a chair, often has distended external jugular veins as blood "backs up" in the venous network.

Five mechanisms help to keep venous blood moving back through the circulatory system and into the right atrium. They include a strongly beating heart, an adequate arterial blood pressure, valves in veins, the "milking action" of skeletal muscles as they contract, and changing pressures in the chest cavity caused by breathing.

Pulse

What you feel when you take a pulse is an artery expanding and then recoiling alternately. To feel a pulse, you must place your fingertips over an artery that lies near the surface of the body and over a bone or other firm base. The pulse is a valuable clinical sign. It can provide information, for example, about the rate, strength, and rhythmicity of the heart beat. It is also easily determined with little or no danger or discomfort. There are nine major "pulse points" named after the arteries where they are felt. Locate each pulse point on Figure 11-15 and on your own body.

FIGURE 11–15 ***Pulse Points.*** Each pulse point is named after the artery with which it is associated.

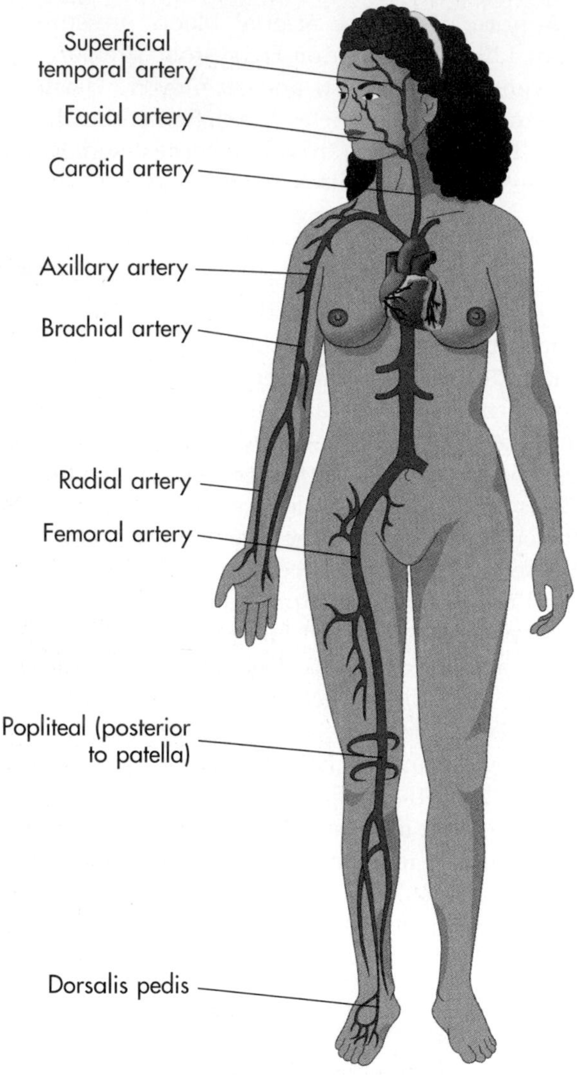

The following pulse points are located on each side of the head and neck: (1) over the superficial temporal artery in front of the ear, (2) the common carotid artery in the neck along the front edge of the sternocleidomastoid muscle, and (3) over the facial artery at the lower margin of the mandible at a point below the corner of the mouth.

A pulse is also detected at three points in the upper limb: (1) in the axilla over the axillary artery; (2) over the brachial artery at the bend of the elbow along the inner or medial margin of the biceps brachii muscle, and (3) at the radial artery at the wrist. The so-called radial pulse is the most frequently monitored and easily accessible in the body.

The pulse can also be felt at three locations in the lower extremity: (1) over the femoral artery in the groin, (2) at the popliteal artery behind and just proximal to the knee, and (3) at the dorsalis pedis artery on the front surface of the foot, just below the bend of the ankle joint.

OUTLINE SUMMARY

HEART

A Location, size, and position
 1 Triangular organ located in mediastinum with two thirds of the mass to the left of the body midline and one third to the right; the apex on the diaphragm; shape and size of a closed fist (Figure 11-1)
 2 Cardiopulmonary resuscitation (CPR)—heart lies between the sternum in front and the bodies of the thoracic vertebrae behind; rhythmic compression of the heart between the sternum and vertebrae can maintain blood flow during cardiac arrest; if combined with artificial respiration procedure, it can be life saving

B Anatomy
 1 Heart chambers (Figure 11-2)
  a Two upper chambers are called *atria* (receiving chambers)—right and left atria
  b Two lower chambers called *ventricles* (discharging chambers)—right and left ventricles
  c Wall of each heart chamber is composed of cardiac muscle tissue called *myocardium*
  d Endocardium—smooth lining of heart chambers—inflammation of endocardium called *endocarditis*
 2 Covering sac or pericardium
  a Pericardium is a two-layered fibrous sac with a lubricated space between the two layers
  b Inner layer is called *visceral pericardium* or *epicardium*
  c Outer layer called *parietal pericardium*
 3 Heart action
 Contraction of the heart is called *systole;* relaxation is called *diastole.*
 4 Heart valves (Figure 11-3)
 Four valves keep blood flowing through the heart; prevent backflow (two atrioventricular or AV and two semilunar valves)
  a Tricuspid—at the opening of the right atrium into the ventricle
  b Bicuspid (mitral)—at the opening of the left atrium into the ventricle
  c Pulmonary semilunar—at the beginning of the pulmonary artery
  d Aortic semilunar—at the beginning of the aorta

C Heart sounds
 1 Two distinct heart sounds in every heartbeat or cycle—"lub-dup"
 2 First (lub) sound is caused by the vibration and closure of AV valves during contraction of the ventricles
 3 Second (dup) sound is caused by the closure of the semilunar valves during relaxation of the ventricles

D Blood flow through the heart (Figure 11-4)
 1 Heart acts as two separate pumps—the right atrium and ventricle performing different functions from the left atrium and ventricle
 2 Sequence of blood flow: venous blood enters the right atrium through the superior and inferior venae cavae—passes from the right atrium through the tricuspid valve to the right ventricle; from the right ventricle it passes through the pulmonary semilunar valve to the pulmonary artery to the lungs—blood moves from the lungs to the left atrium, passing through the bicuspid (mitral) valve to the left ventricle; blood in the left ventricle is pumped through the aortic semilunar valve into the aorta and is distributed to the body as a whole

E Blood supply to the heart muscle
 1 Blood, which supplies oxygen and nutrients to the myocardium of the heart, flows through the right and left coronary arteries
 2 Blockage of blood flow through the coronary arteries is called *myocardial infarction (heart attack)*
 3 Angina pectoris—chest pain caused by inadequate oxygen to the heart

F Cardiac cycle
 1 Heart beat is regular and rhythmic—each complete beat called a *cardiac cycle*—average is about 72 beats per minute
 2 Each cycle, about 0.8 seconds long, subdivided into systole (contraction phase) and diastole (relaxation phase)
 3 Stroke volume—volume of blood ejected from one ventricle with each beat
 4 Cardiac output—amount of blood that one ventricle can pump each minute; average is about 5 L per minute at rest

G Conduction system (Figure 11-5)
- **1** Intercalated disks are electrical connectors that join all the cardiac muscle fibers in a region together so that they receive their impulse, and thus contract, at about the same time
- **2** SA (sinoatrial) node, the pacemaker—located in the wall of the right atrium near the opening of the superior vena cava
- **3** AV (atrioventricular) node—located in the right atrium along the lower part of the interatrial septum
- **4** AV bundle (bundle of His)—located in the septum of the ventricle
- **5** Purkinje fibers—located in the walls of the ventricles

H Electrocardiogram (Figure 11-6)
- **1** Specialized conduction system structures generate and transmit the electrical impulses that result in contraction of the heart
- **2** These tiny electrical impulses can be picked up on the surface of the body and transformed into visible tracings by a machine called an electrocardiograph
- **3** The visible tracing of these electrical signals is called an *electrocardiogram* or *ECG*
- **4** The normal ECG has three deflections or waves called the *P wave*, the *QRS complex*, and the *T wave*
  - **a** P wave—associated with depolarization of the atria
  - **b** QRS complex—associated with depolarization of the ventricles
  - **c** T wave—associated with repolarization of the ventricles

BLOOD VESSELS

A Kinds
- **1** Arteries—carry blood away from the heart
- **2** Veins—carry blood toward the heart
- **3** Capillaries—carry blood from the arterioles to the venules

B Structure (Figure 11-7)
- **1** Arteries
  - **a** Tunica intima—inner layer of endothelial cells
  - **b** Tunica media—smooth muscle with some elastic tissue, thick in arteries; important in blood pressure regulation
  - **c** Tunica adventitia—thin layer of elastic tissue
- **2** Capillaries—microscopic vessels
  - **a** Only layer is the tunica intima
- **3** Veins
  - **a** Tunica intima—inner layer; valves prevent retrograde movement of blood
  - **b** Tunica media—smooth muscle; thin in veins
  - **c** Tunica adventitia—heavy layer in many veins

C Functions
- **1** Arteries—distribution of nutrients, gases, etc., with movement of blood under high pressure; assist in maintaining the arterial blood pressure
- **2** Capillaries—serve as exchange vessels for nutrients, wastes, and fluids
- **3** Veins—collect blood for return to the heart; low pressure vessels

D Names of main arteries—see Figure 11-8 and Table 11-1

E Names of main veins—see Figure 11-9 and Table 11-2

CIRCULATION

A Plan of circulation—refers to the blood flow through the vessels arranged to form a circuit or circular pattern (Figure 11-11)

B Types of circulation
- **1** Systemic circulation
  - **a** Carries blood throughout the body
  - **b** Path goes from left ventricle through aorta, smaller arteries, arterioles, capillaries, venules, venae cavae, to right atrium
- **2** Pulmonary circulation
  - **a** Carries blood to and from the lungs; arteries deliver deoxygenated blood to the lungs for gas exchange
  - **b** Path goes from right ventricle through pulmonary arteries, lungs, pulmonary veins, to left atrium
- **3** Hepatic portal circulation (Figure 11-12)
  - **a** Unique blood route through the liver
  - **b** Vein (hepatic portal vein) exists between two capillary beds
  - **c** Assists with homeostasis of blood glucose levels

4 Fetal circulation (Figure 11-13)
  a Refers to circulation before birth
  b Modifications required for fetus to efficiently secure oxygen and nutrients from the maternal blood
  c Unique structures include the placenta, umbilical arteries and vein, ductus venosus, ductus arteriosus, and foramen ovale

BLOOD PRESSURE

A Blood pressure is push or force of blood in the blood vessels
B Highest in arteries, lowest in veins (Figure 11-14)
C Blood pressure gradient causes blood to circulate—liquids can flow only from the area where pressure is higher to where it is lower
D Blood volume, heartbeat, and blood viscosity are main factors that produce blood pressure
E Blood pressure varies within normal range from time to time

PULSE

A Definition—alternate expansion and recoil of the blood vessel wall
B Places where you can count the pulse easily (Figure 11-15)

N E W W O R D S

angina pectoris
arteriole
artery
atrioventricular (AV) valve
atrium
bicuspid valve
capillary
cardiac output
cardiopulmonary resuscitation (CPR)
coronary circulation
diastolic pressure
ductus arteriosus
ductus venosus
electrocardiogram (ECG)
endocarditis
endocardium
epicardium
foramen ovale
hepatic portal circulation
mitral valve
myocardial infarction
myocardium
P wave
pacemaker
pericardium
pulmonary circulation
pulse
Purkinje fibers
QRS complex
semilunar valve
sinoatrial node
systemic circulation
T wave
tricuspid valve
umbilical
vein
ventricle
venule

CHAPTER TEST

1. The two upper chambers of the heart are called ______________, and the two lower chambers are called ______________.
2. Cardiac muscle tissue, which forms the wall of each heart chamber, is called the ______________.
3. The covering sac around the heart is called the ______________.
4. The two valves that separate the upper from the lower chambers of the heart are called ______________ valves.
5. The valve located between the right atrium and ventricle is called the ______________ valve.
6. Blood enters the right atrium through two large veins called the superior and inferior ______________.
7. Blood passing through the pulmonary semilunar valve enters the ______________ artery.
8. Severe chest pain caused by inadequate blood flow to the myocardium is called ______________.
9. The sinoatrial or SA node is often called the ______________ of the heart.
10. A graphic recording of the heart's electrical activity is called an ______________.
11. In a normal electrocardiogram the QRS complex occurs as a result of depolarization of the ______________.
12. Blood is carried toward the heart by large vessels called ______________.
13. The muscular middle layer of both arteries and veins is called the ______________.
14. Blood flow from the left ventricle of the heart to all parts of the body and back to the right atrium of the heart is called the ______________ circulation.
15. In portal circulation a portal vein is located between two ______________ beds.
16. In fetal circulation, blood is shunted from the right atrium directly into the left atrium by passing through the ______________ ______________ of the heart.
17. The volume of blood pumped into the arteries from one ventricle in 1 minute is called the ______________ ______________.
18. The ______________ ______________ is a continuation of the umbilical vein.
19. In the fetus the ______________ ______________ connects the aorta and pulmonary artery.
20. Contraction of the heart is called ______________.
21. Each complete heart beat is called a ______________.
22. The venous blood pressure within the right atrium is called the ______________ ______________ ______________.

Select the most correct answer from Column B for each statement in Column A. (Only one answer is correct.)

COLUMN A	COLUMN B
23. ______ Receiving chambers of heart	**a.** P wave
24. ______ Attach valves to heart wall	**b.** Coronary arteries
25. ______ Supply blood to heart muscle	**c.** Portal circulation
26. ______ Myocardial infarction	**d.** Heart attack
27. ______ Depolarization of atria	**e.** Ductus arteriosus
28. ______ Vein between two capillary beds	**f.** Chordae tendinea
29. ______ Fetal circulation	**g.** Systole
30. ______ Heart contraction	**h.** Atria

REVIEW QUESTIONS

1. Describe the position of the heart in the mediastinum.
2. What is cardiopulmonary resuscitation (CPR)?
3. What is meant by the term *cardiac cycle?*
4. A patient has had an operation to repair the bicuspid valve. Where is the valve, and what is its function?
5. What are some differences between an artery, a vein, and a capillary?
6. The right ventricle of the heart pumps blood to and through only one organ. Which one?
7. What part of the heart pumps blood through the systemic circulation (that is, to and through all organs other than the lungs)?
8. All blood returns from the systemic circulation to what part of the heart?
9. Blood returning from the pulmonary circulation (from the lungs, in other words) enters what part of the heart?
10. How do arterial blood and venous blood differ with regard to their oxygen and carbon dioxide contents?
11. How does cardiac output influence blood pressure?
12. Explain what causes a pulse in an arterial vessel.

CRITICAL THINKING

13. Outline the path of blood flow through the heart. Explain the function of the valves as you proceed.
14. Considering that the function of the circulatory system is to transport substances to and from the cells, do you think it is true that in one sense capillaries are our most important blood vessels? Give a reason for your answer.
15. Does every artery carry oxygenated blood and every vein carry deoxygenated blood? If not, what exceptions are there?

The Lymphatic System and Immunity

OUTLINE

The Lymphatic System
- Lymph and Lymph Vessels
- Lymph Nodes
- Thymus
- Tonsils
- Spleen

The Immune System
- Functions of the Immune System
- Nonspecific Immunity
- Specific Immunity

Immune System Molecules
- Antibodies
- Complement Proteins

Immune System Cells
- Phagocytes
- Lymphocytes

OBJECTIVES

After you have completed this chapter, you should be able to:

1. Describe the generalized functions of the lymphatic system and list the primary lymphatic structures.
2. Define and compare nonspecific and specific immunity, inherited and acquired immunity, and active and passive immunity.
3. Discuss the major types of immune system molecules and indicate how antibodies and complements function.
4. Discuss and contrast the development and functions of B and T cells.
5. Compare and contrast humoral and cell-mediated immunity.

BOXED ESSAYS

Effects of Exercise on Immunity
Allergy
Monoclonal Antibodies
Interferon
AIDS

All of us live in a hostile and dangerous environment. Each day we are faced with potentially harmful toxins, disease-causing bacteria, viruses, and even cells from our own bodies that have been transformed into cancerous invaders. Fortunately, we are protected from this staggering variety of differing biological enemies by a remarkable set of defense mechanisms. We refer to this protective "safety net" as the **immune system.**

This chapter deals with the immune system. This system is characterized by structural components, many of them lymphatic organs, and by a functional group of specialized cells and molecules that protect us from infection and disease. This chapter begins with an overview of the lymphatic system, discussing vessels that help maintain fluid balance and lymphoid tissues that help protect the internal environment. We will then discuss the concept of immunity and the ways that highly specialized cells and molecules provide us with effective and very specific resistance to disease.

The Lymphatic System

LYMPH AND LYMPH VESSELS

Maintaining the constancy of the fluid around each body cell is possible only if numerous homeostatic mechanisms function effectively together in a controlled and integrated response to changing conditions. We know from Chapter 11 that the circulatory system provides a key role in bringing many needed substances to cells and then removing the waste products that accumulate as a result of metabolism. This exchange of substances between blood and tissue fluid occurs in capillary beds. Many additional substances that cannot enter or return through the capillary walls, including excess fluid and protein molecules, are returned to the blood as **lymph.** Lymph is a specialized fluid formed in the tissue spaces that is transported by way of specialized **lymphatic vessels** to eventually reenter the circulatory system. In addition to lymph and the lymphatic vessels, the lymphatic system includes lymph nodes and specialized lymphatic organs such as the thymus and spleen (Figure 12-1).

Lymph forms in this way: blood plasma filters out of the capillaries into the microscopic spaces between tissue cells because of the pressure generated by the pumping action of the heart. There, the liquid is called **interstitial fluid** or tissue fluid. Much of the interstitial fluid goes back into the blood by the same route it came out (that is, through the capillary membrane). The remainder of the interstitial fluid enters the lymphatic system before it returns to the blood. The fluid, now called *lymph,* enters a network of tiny blind-ended tubes distributed in the tissue spaces. These tiny vessels, called *lymphatic capillaries,* permit excess tissue fluid and some other substances such as dissolved protein molecules to leave the tissue spaces. Figure 12-2 shows the role of the lymphatic system in fluid homeostasis.

Lymphatic and blood capillaries are similar in many ways. Both types of vessels are microscopic and both are formed from sheets consisting of a cell layer of simple squamous epithelium called *endothelium* (en-doe-THEE-lee-um). The flattened endothelial cells that form blood capillaries, however, fit tightly together so that large molecules cannot enter or exit from the vessel. The "fit" between endothelial cells forming the lymphatic capillaries is not as tight. As a result, they are more porous and allow larger molecules, including proteins and other substances, as well as the fluid itself, to enter the vessel and eventually return to the general circulation. The movement of lymph in the lymphatic vessels is one way. Unlike blood, lymph does not flow over and over again through vessels that form a circular route.

Lymph flowing through the lymphatic capillaries next moves into successively larger and larger vessels called *lymphatic venules* and *veins* and eventually empties into two terminal vessels called the **right lymphatic duct** and the **thoracic duct,** which empty their lymph into the blood in veins in the neck region. Lymph from about three fourths of the body eventually drains into the thoracic duct, which is the largest lymphatic vessel in the body. Lymph from the right upper extremity and from the right side of the head, neck, and upper torso flows into the right lymphatic duct (Figure 12-3). The lymphatic vessels have a "beaded" appearance caused by the presence of valves that assist in maintaining a one-way flow of lymph. Note in Fig-

FIGURE 12–1 ***Principal Organs of the Lymphatic System.***

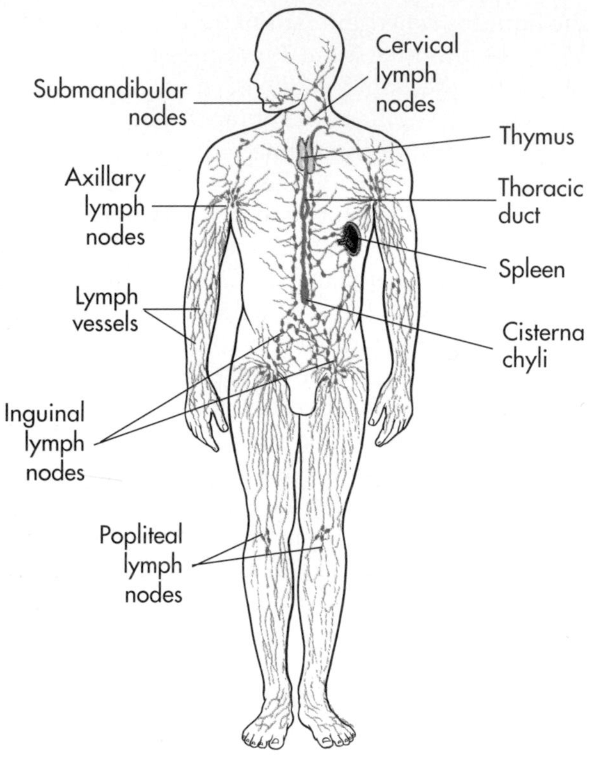

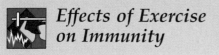

Effects of Exercise on Immunity

Exercise physiologists have found that moderate exercise increases the number of WBCs, specifically granular leukocytes and lymphocytes. Not only is the number of circulating immune cells higher after exercise, but the activity of sensitized T cells is also increased. But at the same time, research also shows that strenuous exercise may actually inhibit immune function. Nevertheless, immediate moderate exercise such as walking after a trauma such as surgery is often encouraged because of its immunity-strengthening effects.

FIGURE 12–2 ***Role of Lymphatic System in Fluid Homeostasis.*** Fluid from blood plasma that is not reabsorbed by blood vessels drains into lymphatic vessels. Lymphatic drainage prevents accumulation of too much tissue fluid.

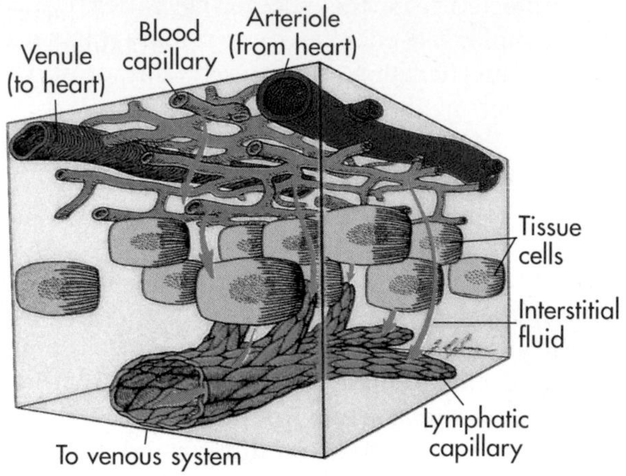

FIGURE 12–3 ***Lymph Drainage.*** The right lymphatic duct drains lymph from the upper right quarter of the body into the right subclavian vein. The thoracic duct drains lymph from the rest of the body into the left subclavian vein.

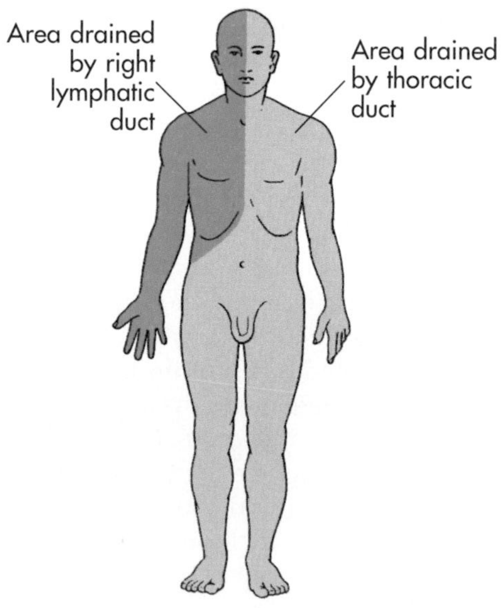

ure 12-1 that the thoracic duct in the abdomen has an enlarged pouchlike structure called the **cisterna chyli** (sis-TER-nah KI-li) that serves as a storage area for lymph moving toward its point of entry into the venous system.

Lymphatic capillaries in the wall of the small intestine are given the special name of **lacteals** (LAK-tee-als). They transport fats obtained from food to the bloodstream and are discussed in Chapter 14.

LYMPH NODES

As lymph moves from its origin in the tissue spaces toward the thoracic or right lymphatic ducts and then into the venous blood, it is filtered by moving through **lymph nodes,** which are located in clusters along the pathway of lymphatic vessels. Some of these nodes may be as small as a pinhead, and others may be as large as a lima bean. With the exception of a comparatively few single nodes, most lymph nodes occur in groups or clusters in certain areas. Figure 12-1 shows the locations of the clusters of greatest clinical importance. You may have experienced swelling of the submandibular nodes during a "sore throat" or as a result of an infected tooth. The structure of the lymph nodes makes it possible for them to perform two important functions: defense and white blood cell formation.

Defense Function: Biological Filtration

Figure 12-4 shows the structure of a typical lymph node. In this example, a small node located next to an infected hair follicle is shown filtering bacteria from lymph. Lymph nodes perform biological filtration, a process in which cells (phagocytic cells in this case) alter the contents of the filtered fluid. Biological filtration of bacteria and other abnormal cells by phagocytosis prevents local infections from spreading. Note that lymph enters

Figure 12–4 ***Infection of Hair Follicle.*** Diagrammatic representation of a skin section in which an infection surrounds a hair follicle. The yellow areas represent dead and dying cells (pus). The black dots around the yellow areas represent bacteria. Bacteria entering the node via the afferent lymphatics are filtered out.

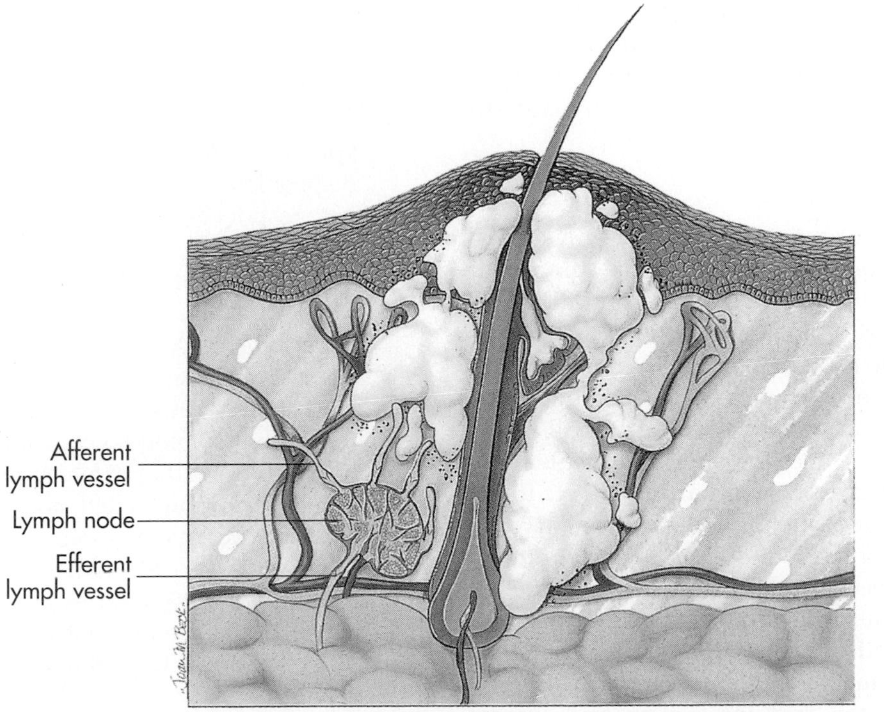

the node through four **afferent** (from the Latin "to carry toward") **lymph vessels.** These vessels deliver lymph to the node. When passing through the node, lymph is filtered so that injurious particles such as bacteria, soot, and cancer cells are removed and prevented from entering the blood and circulating all over the body. Lymph exits from the node through a single **efferent** (from the Latin "to carry away from") **lymph vessel.** Clusters of lymph nodes allow a very effective biological filtration of lymph flowing from specific body areas. A knowledge of lymph node location and function is important in clinical medicine. For example, a school nurse monitoring the progress of a child with an infected finger will watch the elbow and axillary regions for swelling and tenderness of the lymph nodes. These nodes filter lymph returning from the hand and may become infected by the bacteria they trap. A surgeon uses knowledge of lymph node function when removing lymph nodes under the arms (axillary nodes) and in other areas during an operation for breast cancer. These nodes may contain cancer cells filtered out of the lymph drained from the breast. Cancer of the breast is one of the most common forms of this disease in women. Unfortunately, cancer cells from a single tumorous growth in the breast often spread to other areas of the body through the lymphatic system. Figure 12-5 shows how lymph from the breast drains into many different and widely placed nodes.

FIGURE 12–5 ***Lymphatic Drainage of the Breast.*** Note the extensive network of nodes that receive lymph from the breast.

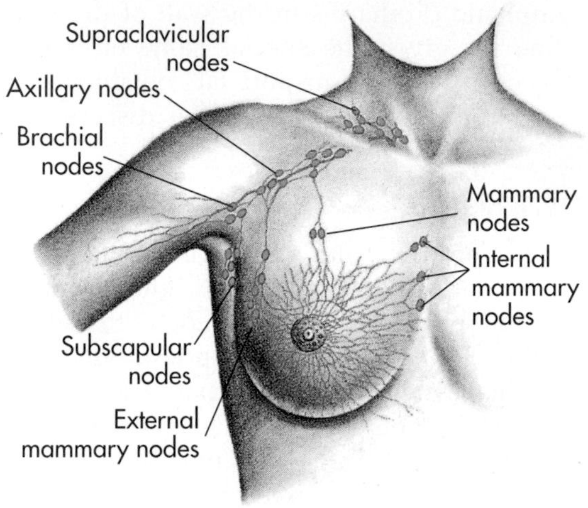

THYMUS

The **thymus** (THYE-mus) (Figure 12-1) is a small lymphoid tissue organ located in the mediastinum, extending upward in the midline of the neck. It is composed of lymphocytes in a unique epithelial tissue framework. The thymus is largest at puberty and even then weighs only about 35 or 40 g—less than an ounce. Although small in size the thymus plays a central and critical role in the body's vital immunity mechanism. First, it is a source of lymphocytes before birth and is then especially important in the "maturation" or development of specialized lymphocytes that then leave the thymus and circulate to the spleen, tonsils, lymph nodes, and other lymphatic tissues. These **T-lymphocytes** or T cells are critical to the functioning of the immune system and are discussed later. They develop under the influence of

Allergy

The term **allergy** is used to describe hypersensitivity of the immune system to relatively harmless environmental antigens. One in six Americans have a genetic predisposition to an allergy. Immediate allergic responses involve antigen-antibody reactions that trigger the release of histamine, kinins, and other inflammatory substances. These responses usually cause symptoms such as a runny nose, conjunctivitis, and hives. In some cases, these substances may cause constriction of airways, relaxation of blood vessels, and irregular heart rhythms that can lead to a life-threatening condition called *anaphylactic shock.* Delayed allergic responses, on the other hand, involve cell-mediated immunity. In contact dermatitis, for example, T-lymphocytes trigger events that lead to local skin inflammation a few hours or days after initial exposure.

a hormone secreted by the thymus, **thymosin** (THYE-mo-sin). The thymus essentially completes its work early in childhood and is then replaced by fat and connective tissue, a process called *involution.*

TONSILS

Masses of lymphoid tissue called tonsils are located in a protective ring under the mucous membranes in the mouth and back of the throat (Figure 12-6). They help protect us against bacteria that may invade tissues in the area around the openings between the nasal and oral cavities. The **palatine tonsils** are located on each side of the throat. The **pharyngeal tonsils,** known as **adenoids** (AD-e-noyds) when they become swollen, are near the posterior opening of the nasal cavity. A third type of tonsil, the **lingual tonsils,** are near the base of the tongue. The tonsils serve as the first line of defense from the exterior and as such are subject to chronic infection. They may have to be removed surgically if antibiotic therapy is not successful or if swelling impairs breathing.

FIGURE 12–6 *Location of the Tonsils.* Small segments of the roof and floor of the mouth have been removed to show the protective ring of tonsils (lymphoid tissue) around the internal opening of the nose and throat.

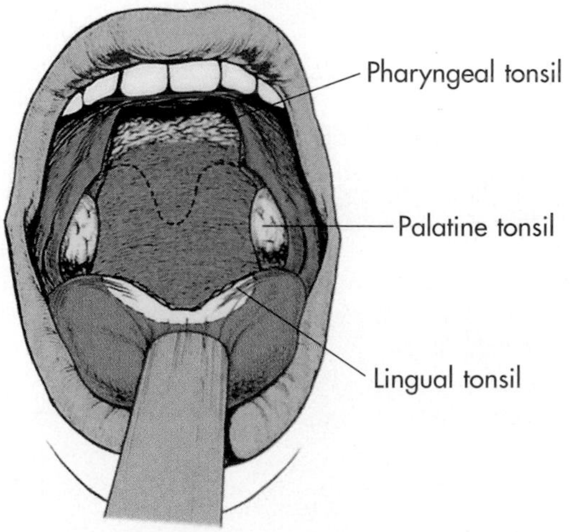

SPLEEN

The spleen is the largest lymphoid organ in the body. It is located high in the upper left quadrant of the abdomen lateral to the stomach (Figures 12-1 and 1-7). Although the spleen is protected by the lower ribs, it can be injured by abdominal trauma. The spleen has a very rich blood supply and may contain over 1 pint of blood. If damaged and bleeding, surgical removal, called a **splenectomy** (splen-NEK-toe-mee), may be required to stop the loss of blood.

After entering the spleen, blood flows through dense, pulplike accumulations of lymphocytes. As blood flows through the pulp, the spleen removes by filtration and phagocytosis many bacteria and other foreign substances, destroys worn out RBCs and salvages the iron found in hemoglobin for future use, and serves as a reservoir for blood that can be returned to the circulatory system when needed.

The Immune System

FUNCTION OF THE IMMUNE SYSTEM

The body's defense mechanisms protect us from disease-causing microorganisms that invade our bodies, foreign tissue cells that may have been transplanted into our bodies, and our own cells that have turned malignant or cancerous. The body's specific defense system is called the **immune system.** The immune system makes us immune (that is, able to resist these enemies). Unlike other systems of the body, which are made up of groups of organs, the immune system is made up of billions of cells and trillions of molecules.

NONSPECIFIC IMMUNITY

Nonspecific immunity is maintained by mechanisms that attack any irritant or abnormal substance that threatens the internal environment. In other words, nonspecific immunity confers general protection rather than protection from certain kinds of invading cells or chemicals. The skin and mucous membranes, for example, are mechanical barriers to prevent entry into the body of bacteria and many other substances such as toxins and harmful chemicals. Tears and mucus also contribute to nonspecific immunity. Tears wash harmful substances from the eyes, and mucus traps foreign material that may enter the respiratory tract. Phagocytosis of bacteria by WBCs is a nonspecific form of immunity.

The **inflammatory response** is a set of nonspecific responses that often occurs in the body. In the example shown in Figure 12-7, bacteria cause tissue damage that, in turn, triggers the release of mediators from any of a variety of immune cells. Some of the mediators attract white blood cells to the area. Many of these factors produce the characteristic signs of inflammation: heat, redness, pain, and swelling. These signs are caused by increased blood flow (resulting in heat and redness) and vascular permeability (resulting in tissue swelling and the pain it causes) in the affected region. Such changes help phagocytic white blood cells reach the general area and enter the affected tissue.

SPECIFIC IMMUNITY

Specific immunity includes protective mechanisms that confer very specific protection against certain types of invading bacteria or other toxic materials. Specific immunity involves memory and the ability to recognize and respond to certain particular harmful substances or bacteria. For example, when the body is first attacked by particular bacteria or viruses, disease symptoms may occur as the body fights to destroy the invading organism. However, if the body is exposed a second time, no symptoms occur because the organism is destroyed quickly—the person is said to be **immune.** Immunity to one type of disease-causing bacteria or virus does not protect the body against others. Immunity can be very selective.

Immunity to disease is classified as **inherited** or **acquired.** If inherited, it is described as **inborn immunity** (Table 12-1). Humans are immune from birth to certain diseases that affect other animals. Distemper, for example, is an often fatal viral disease in dogs. The virus does not produce symptoms in humans; we have an inborn or inherited immunity to the disease.

Acquired immunity may be further classified as "natural" or "artificial" depending on how the body is exposed to the harmful agent. Natural exposure is not deliberate and occurs in the

FIGURE 12–7 ***Inflammatory Response.*** In this example, bacterial infection triggers a set of responses that tend to inhibit or destroy the bacteria.

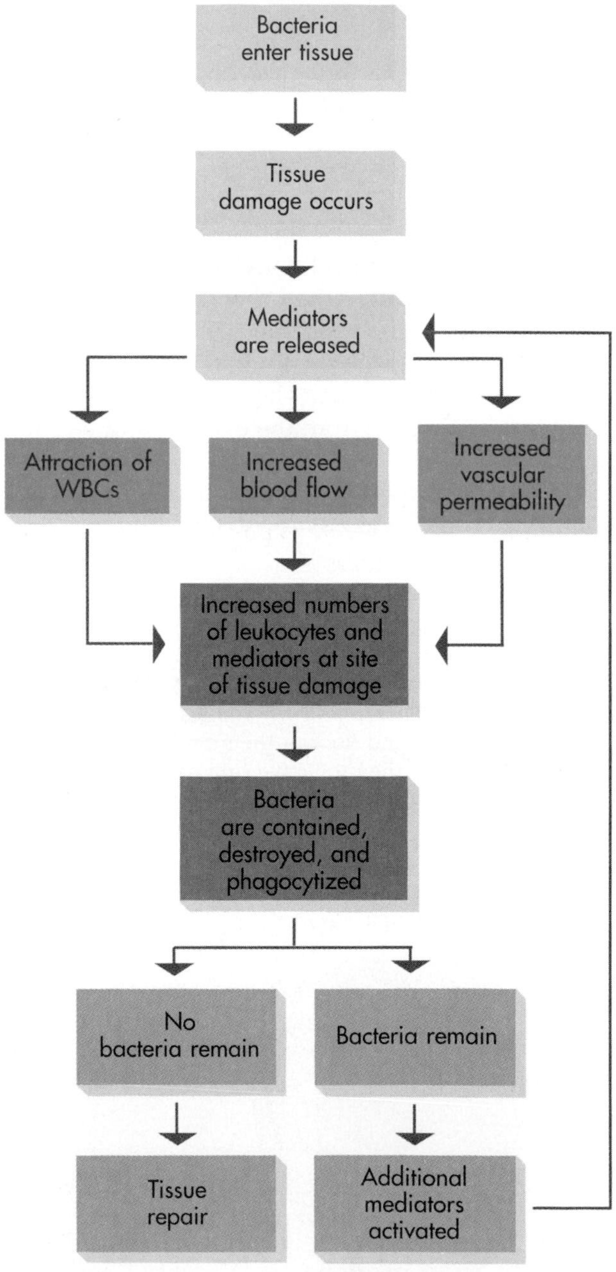

TABLE 12–1 Specific Immunity

TYPE	EXAMPLE
Inborn immunity	Immunity to certain diseases (for example, canine distemper) is inherited.
Acquired immunity	
Natural immunity	Exposure to the causative agent is not deliberate.
Active (exposure)	A child develops measles and acquires an immunity to a subsequent infection.
Passive (exposure)	A fetus receives protection from the mother through the placenta, or an infant receives protection via the mother's milk.
Artificial immunity	Exposure to the causative agent is deliberate.
Active (exposure)	Injection of the causative agent, such as a vaccination against polio, confers immunity.
Passive (exposure)	Injection of protective material (antibodies) that was developed by another individual's immune system is given.

course of everyday living. We are naturally exposed to many disease-causing agents on a regular basis. Artificial exposure is called *immunization* and is the deliberate exposure of the body to a potentially harmful agent.

Natural and artificial immunity may be "active" or "passive." Active immunity occurs when an individual's own immune system responds to a harmful agent, regardless of whether that agent was naturally or artificially encountered. Passive immunity results when immunity to a disease that has developed in another individual or animal is transferred to an individual who was not previously immune. For example, antibodies in a mother's milk confer passive immunity to her nursing infant. Active immunity generally lasts longer than passive immunity. Passive immunity, although temporary, provides immediate protection. Table 12-1 lists the various forms of specific immunity and gives examples of each.

Immune System Molecules

The immune system functions because of adequate amounts of highly specialized protein molecules and unique cells. The protein molecules critical to immune system functioning are called **antibodies** (AN-ti-bod-ees) and **complements** (KOM-ple-ments). Antibody molecules outnumber the cells of the immune system by about 100 million to one.

ANTIBODIES

Definition

Antibodies are protein compounds that are normally present in the body. A defining characteristic of an antibody molecule is the uniquely shaped concave regions called combining sites on its surface. Another defining characteristic is the ability of an antibody molecule to combine with a specific compound called an **antigen** (AN-ti-jen). All antigens are compounds whose molecules have small regions on their surfaces that are uniquely shaped to fit into the combining sites of a specific antibody molecule as precisely as a key fits into a specific lock. Antigens are usually foreign proteins, most often the molecules in the surface membranes of invading or diseased cells such as microorganisms or cancer cells.

Functions

In general, antibodies produce **humoral** or **antibody-mediated immunity** by changing the antigens so that they cannot harm the body (Figure 12-8). To do this, an antibody must first bind to its specific antigen. This forms an antigen-antibody complex. The antigen-antibody complex then acts in one or more ways to make the antigen, or the

FIGURE 12–8 ***Antibody Function.*** Antibodies produce humoral immunity by binding to specific antigens to form antigen-antibody complexes. These complexes produce a variety of changes that inactivate or kill invading cells.

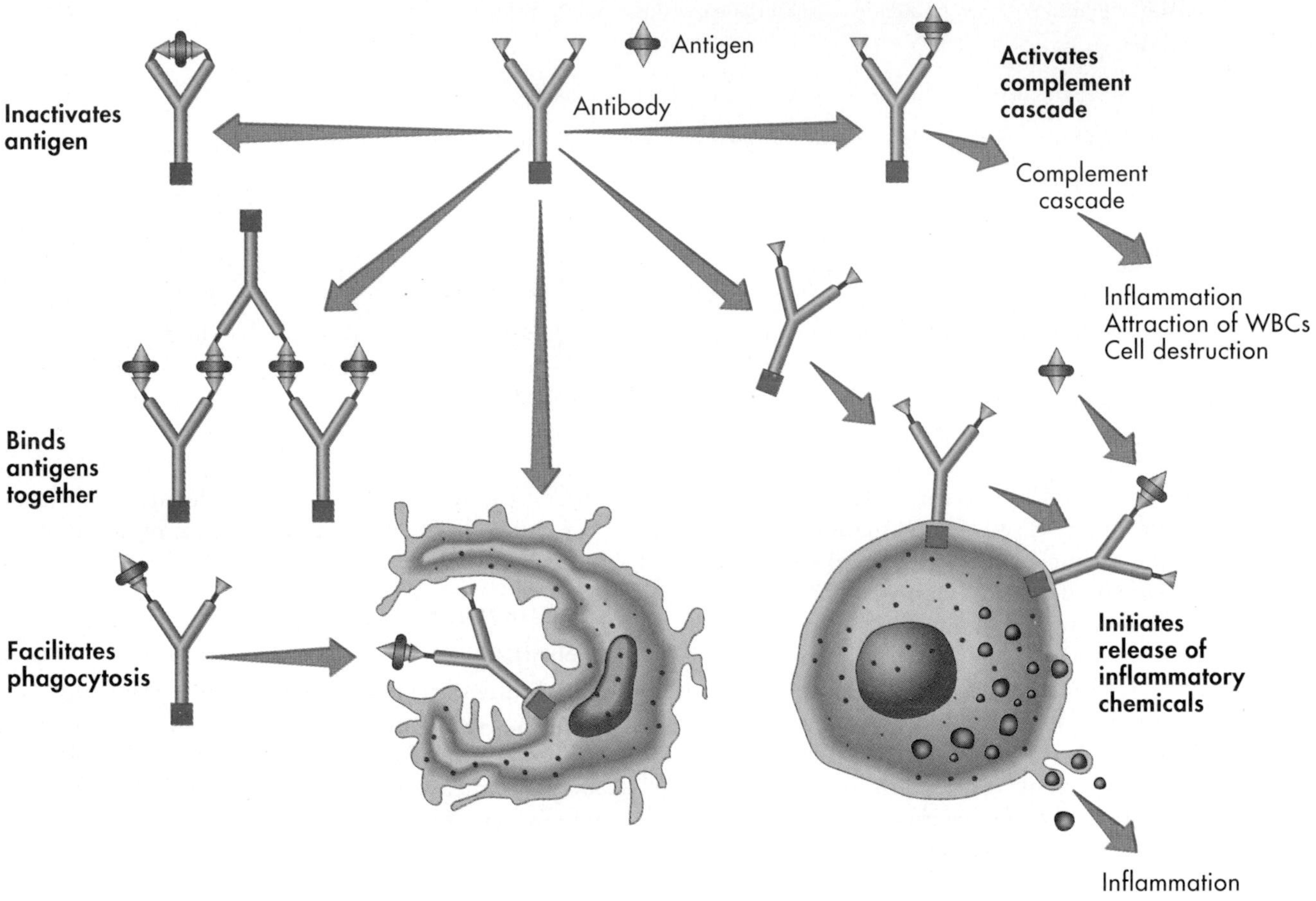

cell on which it is present, harmless. For example, if the antigen is a toxin, a substance poisonous to body cells, the toxin is neutralized or made nonpoisonous by becoming part of an antigen-antibody complex. Or if antigens are molecules in the surface membranes of invading cells, when antibodies combine with them, the resulting antigen-antibody complexes may agglutinate the enemy cells (that is, make them stick together in clumps). Then macrophages or the other phagocytes can rapidly destroy them by ingesting and digesting large numbers of them at one time.

Another important function of antibodies is promotion and enhancement of phagocytosis. Certain antibody fractions help promote the attachment of phagocytic cells to the object they will engulf. As a result, the contact between the phagocytic cell and its victim is enhanced, and the object is more easily ingested. This process contributes to the efficiency of immune system phagocytic cells, which is described on p. 268.

Probably the most important way in which antibodies act is one we will consider last. It is a process called **complement fixation.** In many instances, when antigens that are molecules on an antigenic or foreign cell's surface combine with antibody molecules, they change the shape of the antibody molecule slightly but just enough to

Monoclonal Antibodies

Techniques that have permitted biologists to produce large quantities of pure and very specific antibodies have resulted in dramatic advances in medicine. As a new medical technology, the development of **monoclonal antibodies** has been compared in importance with advances in recombinant DNA or genetic engineering.

Monoclonal antibodies are specific antibodies produced or derived from a population or culture of identical, or **monoclonal,** cells. In the past, antibodies produced by the immune system against a specific antigen had to be "harvested" from serum containing literally hundreds of other antibodies. The total amount of a specific antibody that could be recovered was very limited, so the cost of recovery was high. Monoclonal antibody techniques are based on the ability of immune system cells to produce individual antibodies that bind to and react with very specific antigens. We know, for example, that if the body is exposed to the varicella virus of chickenpox, WBCs will produce an antibody that will react very specifically with that virus and no other. With monoclonal antibody techniques, lymphocytes that are produced by the body after the injection of a specific antigen are "harvested" and then "fused" with other cells that have been transformed to grow and divide indefinitely in a tissue culture medium. These fused or hybrid cells, called *hybridomas* (HYE-brid-o-mahs) continue to produce the same antibody produced by the original lymphocyte. The result is a rapidly growing population of identical or monoclonal cells that produce large quantities of a very specific antibody. Monoclonal antibodies have now been produced against a wide array of different antigens, including disease-producing organisms and various types of cancer cells.

The availability of very pure antibodies against specific disease-producing agents is the first step in the commercial preparation of diagnostic tests that can be used to identify viruses, bacteria, and even specific cancer cells in the blood or other body fluids. The use of monoclonal antibodies may serve as the basis for specific treatment of many human diseases.

expose two previously hidden regions. These are called **complement-binding sites.** Their exposure initiates a series of events that kill the cell on whose surface they take place. The next section describes these events.

COMPLEMENT PROTEINS

Complement is the name used to describe a group of 14 proteins normally present in an inactive state in blood. These proteins are activated by exposure of complement-binding sites. The result is formation of highly specialized antigen-antibody complexes that target foreign cells for destruction. The process is a rapid-fire cascade or sequence of events collectively called **complement fixation.** In this process a doughnut-shaped assemblage complete with a hole in the middle is formed when antibodies, antigens in the invading cell's plasma membrane, and complement molecules combine.

Complement fixation kills invading cells of various types. How? In effect, by drilling a hole in their plasma membranes! The tiny holes allow sodium to rapidly diffuse into the cell; then water follows through osmosis. The cell literally bursts as the internal osmotic pressure increases (Figure 12-9).

FIGURE 12–9 ***Complement Fixation.*** **A,** Complement molecules activated by antibodies form doughnut-shaped complexes in a bacterium's plasma membrane. **B,** Holes in the complement complex allow sodium (Na^+) and then water (H_2O) to diffuse into the bacterium. **C,** After enough water has entered, the swollen bacterium bursts.

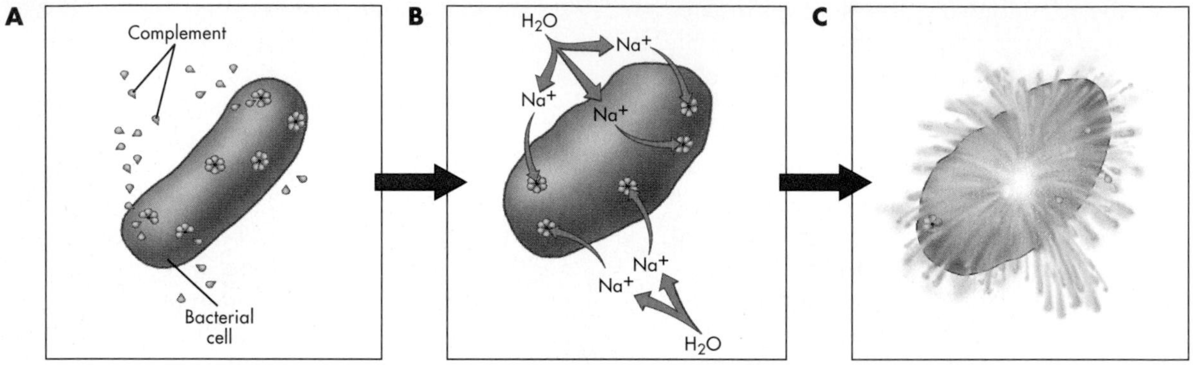

Immune System Cells

The primary cells of the immune system include:

1. Phagocytes
   a. Neutrophils
   b. Monocytes
   c. Macrophages
2. Lymphocytes
   a. T-lymphocytes
   b. B-lymphocytes

PHAGOCYTES

Phagocytic WBCs are an important part of the immune system. In Chapter 10, phagocytes were described as cells derived from the bone marrow that carry on phagocytosis or ingestion and digestion of foreign cells or particles. The most important phagocytes are neutrophils and monocytes (see Figure 10-4, p. 219). These blood phagocytes migrate out of the blood and into the tissues in response to an infection. The neutrophils are functional but short lived in the tissues. Once in the tissues, monocytes develop into phagocytic cells called **macrophages** (MAK-ro-fay-jes). Some macrophages "wander" through the tissues to engulf bacteria wherever they find them. Other macrophages become permanent residents of other organs. Macrophages found in spaces between liver cells, for example, are called *Kupffer's cells,* whereas those that ingest particulate matter in the small air sacs of the lungs are called *dust cells.* Macrophages can also be found in the spleen and lymph nodes and on the lining membranes of the abdominal and thoracic cavities. Specialized antibodies that bind to and coat certain foreign particles help macrophages function effectively. They serve as "flags" that alert the macrophage to the presence of foreign material, infectious bacteria, or cellular debris. They also help bind the phagocyte to the foreign material so that it can be engulfed more effectively (Figure 12-10).

LYMPHOCYTES

The most numerous cells of the immune system are the lymphocytes; they are ultimately responsible for antibody production. Several million strong, lymphocytes continually patrol the body, searching out any enemy cells that may have entered. Lymphocytes circulate in the body's fluids. Huge numbers of them wander vigilantly through most of its tissues. Lymphocytes densely populate the body's widely scattered lymph nodes and its other lymphatic tissues, especially the thymus gland in the chest and the spleen and liver in the abdomen. There are two major types of lymphocytes, designated as *B-* and *T-lymphocytes* but usually called *B cells* and *T cells.*

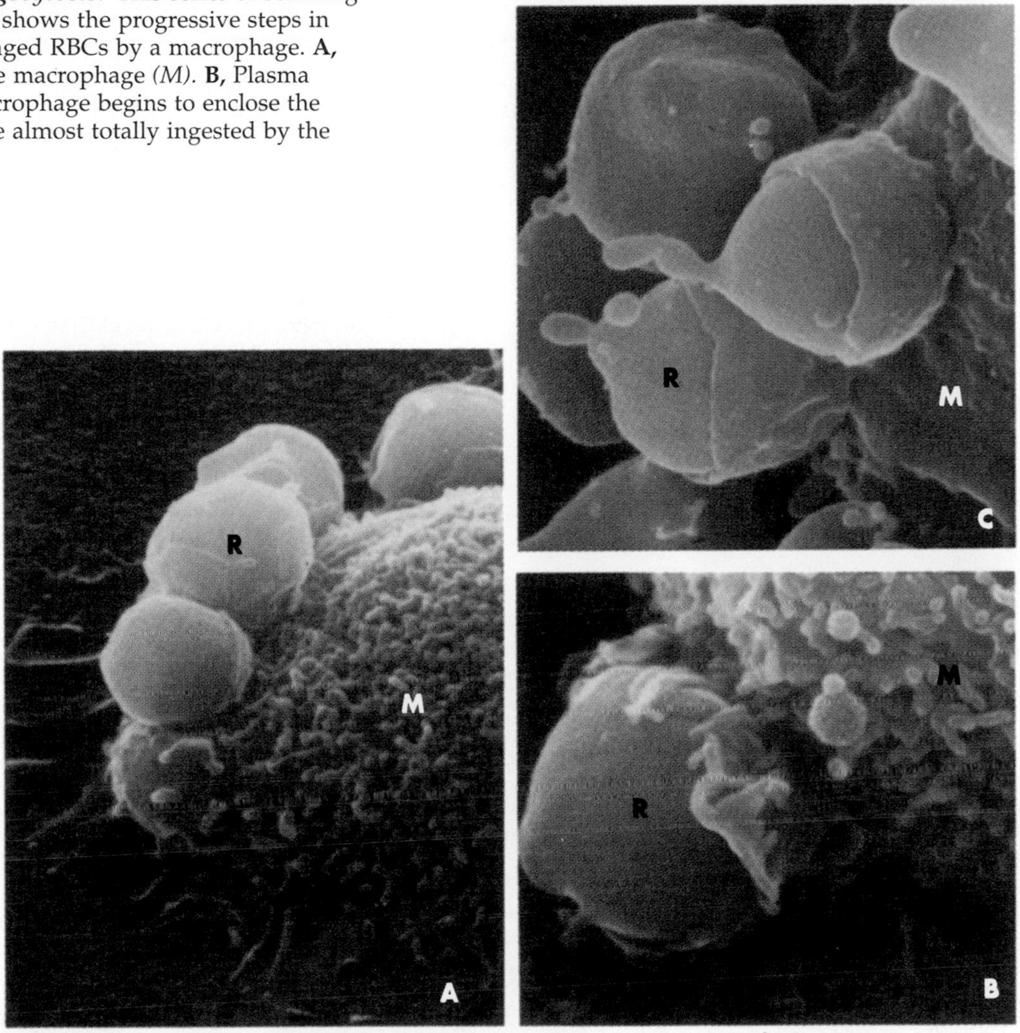

FIGURE 12–10 *Phagocytosis.* This series of scanning electron micrographs shows the progressive steps in phagocytosis of damaged RBCs by a macrophage. **A,** RBCs *(R)* attach to the macrophage *(M).* **B,** Plasma membrane of the macrophage begins to enclose the RBC. **C,** The RBCs are almost totally ingested by the macrophage.

Interferon

Interferon (in-ter-FEER-on) is a small protein compound that plays a very significant role in producing immunity from viral infections. It is produced by T cells within hours after they have been infected by a virus. The interferon released from the T cells protects other cells by interfering with the ability of the virus to reproduce as it moves from cell to cell. In the past, thousands of pints of blood had to be processed to harvest tiny quantities of leukocyte (T cell) interferon for study. Synthetic human interferon is now being "manufactured" in bacteria as a result of gene-splicing techniques and is available in quantities sufficient for clinical use. Synthetic interferon decreases the severity of many virus-related diseases including chickenpox and measles. Interferon also shows promise as an anticancer agent. It has been shown to be effective in treating breast, skin, and other forms of cancer.

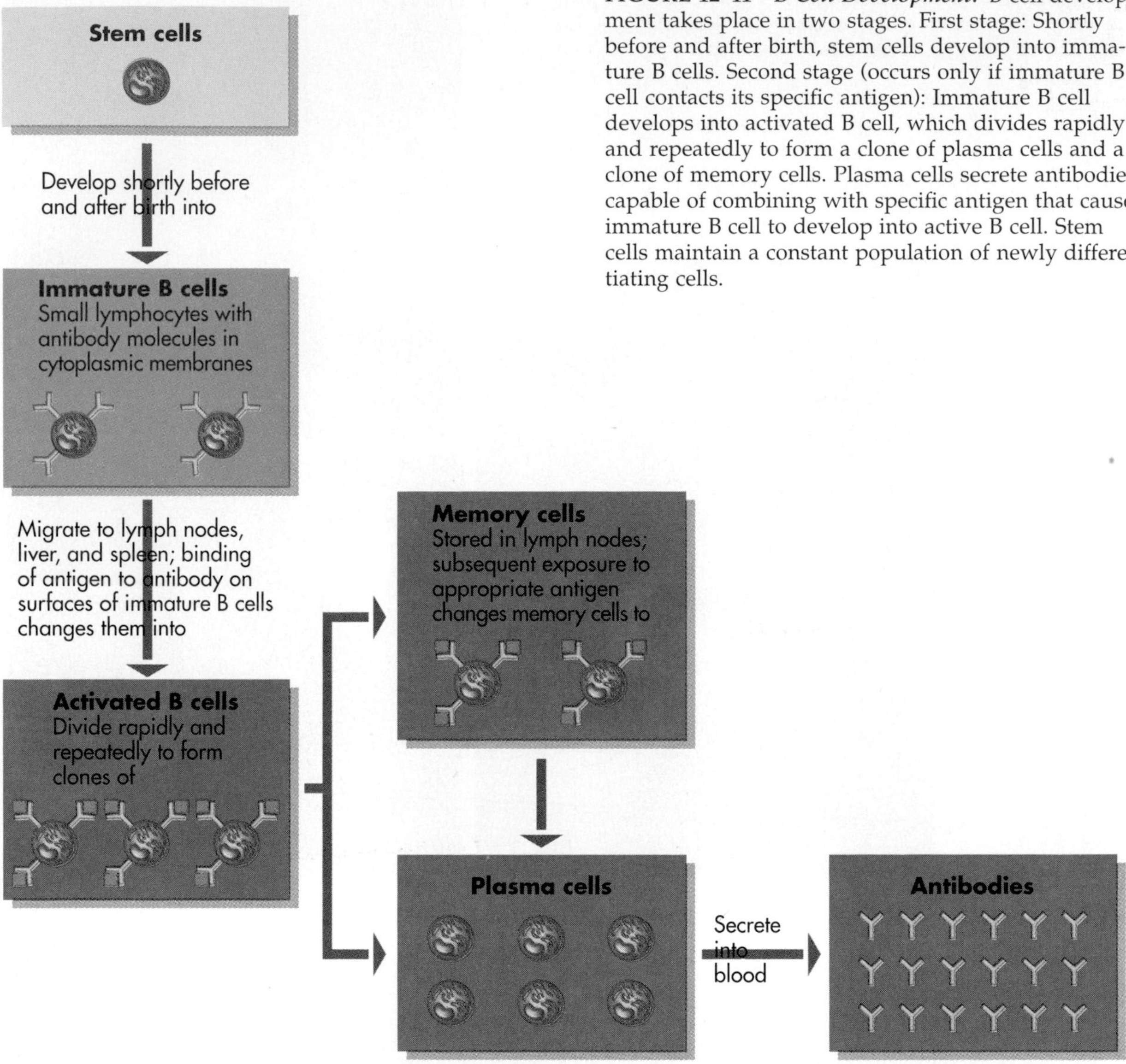

FIGURE 12–11 ***B Cell Development.*** B cell development takes place in two stages. First stage: Shortly before and after birth, stem cells develop into immature B cells. Second stage (occurs only if immature B cell contacts its specific antigen): Immature B cell develops into activated B cell, which divides rapidly and repeatedly to form a clone of plasma cells and a clone of memory cells. Plasma cells secrete antibodies capable of combining with specific antigen that caused immature B cell to develop into active B cell. Stem cells maintain a constant population of newly differentiating cells.

Development of B Cells

All lymphocytes that circulate in the tissues arise from primitive cells in the bone marrow called *stem cells* and go through two stages of development. The first stage of B-cell development, transformation of stem cells into immature B cells, occurs in the liver and bone marrow before birth but only in the bone marrow in adults. Because this process was first discovered in a bird organ called the *bursa,* these cells were named B cells.

Immature B cells are small lymphocytes that have synthesized and inserted into their cytoplasmic membranes numerous molecules of one specific kind of antibody (Figure 12-11). These antibody-bearing immature B cells leave the tissue

AIDS

AIDS or **acquired immunodeficiency syndrome** was first recognized as a new disease by the Centers for Disease Control (CDC) in 1981. This syndrome (collection of symptoms) is caused by the human immunodeficiency virus or HIV. HIV, a retrovirus, contains RNA that undergoes reverse transcription inside infected cells to form its own DNA. The viral DNA often becomes part of the cell's DNA. When the viral DNA is activated, it directs the synthesis of its own RNA and protein coat, thus "stealing" raw materials from the cell. When this occurs in certain T cells, the cell is destroyed, and immunity is impaired. As the T cell dies, it releases new retroviruses that can spread the HIV infection.

Although HIV can invade several types of cells, it has its most obvious effects in certain types of T cells. When T cell function is impaired, infectious organisms and cancer cells can grow and spread much more easily than normal. Unusual conditions, such as pneumocystosis (a protozoan infection) and Kaposi sarcoma (a type of skin cancer), may also appear. Because their immune systems are deficient, AIDS patients usually die from one of these infections or cancers.

After infection with HIV, a person may not show signs of AIDS for months or years. This is because the immune system can hold the infection at bay for a long time before finally succumbing to it.

There are several strategies for controlling AIDS. Many agencies are trying to slow the spread of AIDS by educating people about how to avoid contact with the HIV retrovirus. HIV is spread by means of direct contact of body fluids, so preventing such contact reduces HIV transmission. Sexual relations, contaminated blood transfusions, and intravenous use of contaminated needles are the usual modes of HIV transmission. Several teams of researchers are working on HIV vaccines. Like many viruses, such as those that cause the common cold, HIV changes rapidly enough to make development of a vaccine difficult at best.

Another way to inhibit the disease is by means of chemicals such as azidothymidine (AZT) that block HIV's ability to reproduce within infected cells. At least 80 such compounds are being evaluated for use in halting the progress of HIV infections.

where they were formed, enter the blood, and are transported to their new place of residence, chiefly the lymph nodes. There they act as seed cells. Each immature B cell undergoes repeated mitosis (cell division) and forms a clone of immature B cells. A **clone** is a family of many identical cells all descended from one cell. Because all the cells in a clone of immature B cells have descended from one immature B cell, all of them bear the same surface antibody molecules as did their single ancestor cell.

The second stage of B cell development changes an immature B cell into an activated B cell. Not all immature B cells undergo this change. They do so only if an immature B cell comes in contact with certain protein molecules—antigens—whose shape fits the shape of the immature B cell's surface antibody molecules. If this happens, the antigens lock onto the antibodies and by so doing change the immature B cell into an activated B cell. Then the activated B cell, by dividing rapidly and repeatedly, develops into clones of two kinds of cells, **plasma cells** and **memory cells** (Figure 12-11). Plasma cells secrete copious amounts of antibody into the blood—reportedly, 2000 antibody molecules per second by each plasma cell for every second of the few days that it lives. Antibodies circulating in the blood constitute an enormous, mobile, ever-on-duty army.

FIGURE 12–12 *T Cell Development.* The first stage takes place in the thymus gland shortly before and after birth. Stem cells maintain a constant population of newly differentiating cells as they are needed. The second stage occurs only if a T cell contacts antigen, which combines with certain proteins on the T cell's surface.

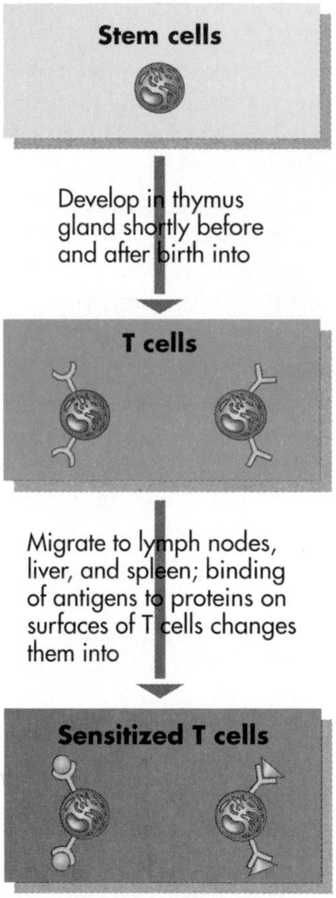

FIGURE 12–13 *T Cells.* The blue spheres seen in this scanning electron microscope view are T cells attacking a much larger cancer cell. The cells are a significant part of our defense against cancer and other types of foreign cells.

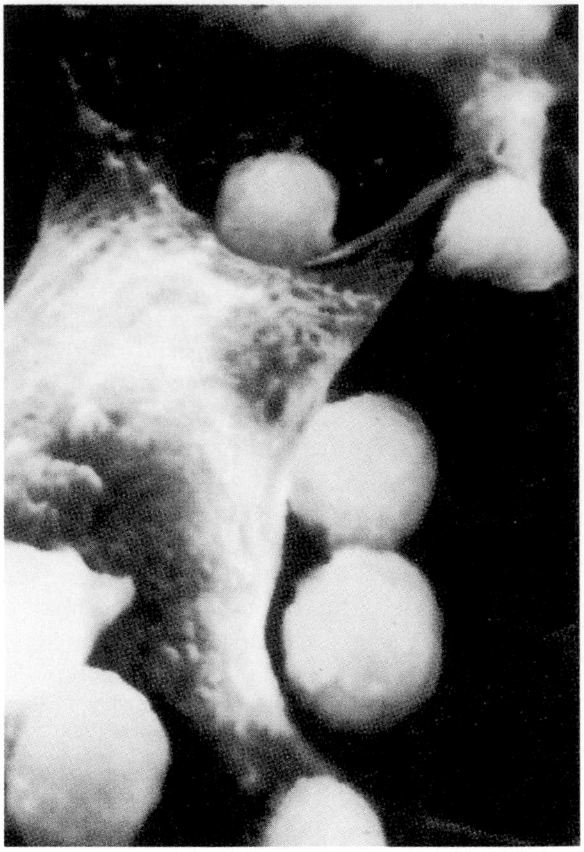

Memory cells can secrete antibodies but do not immediately do so. They remain in reserve in the lymph nodes until they are contracted by the same antigen that led to their formation. Then, very quickly, the memory cells develop into plasma cells and secrete large amounts of antibody. Memory cells, in effect, seem to remember their ancestor-activated B cell's encounter with its appropriate antigen. They stand ready, at a moment's notice, to produce antibody that will combine with this antigen.

Function of B Cells

B cells function indirectly to produce humoral immunity. Recall that humoral immunity is resistance to disease organisms produced by the actions of antibodies binding to specific antigens while circulating in body fluids. Activated B cells develop into plasma cells. Plasma cells secrete antibodies into the blood; they are the "antibody factories" of the body. These antibodies, like other proteins manufactured for extracellular use, are formed on the endoplasmic reticulum of the cell.

FIGURE 12–14 ***T Cell Function.*** Sensitized T cells produce cell-mediated immunity by releasing various compounds in the vicinity of invading cells. Some act directly, and some act indirectly to kill invading cells.

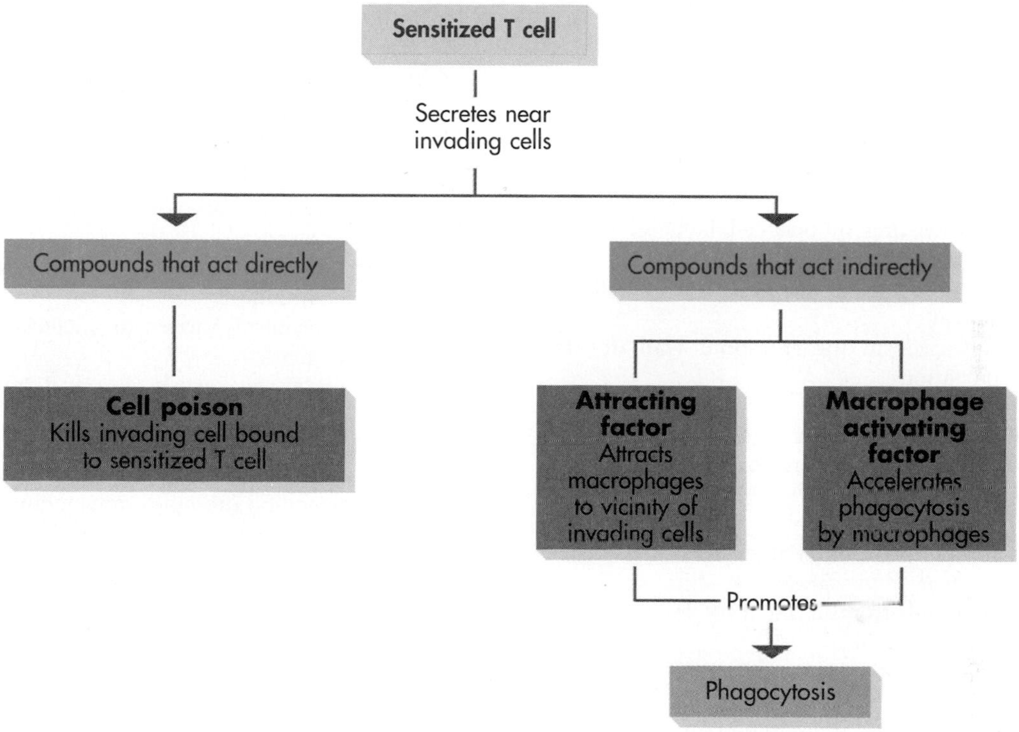

Development of T Cells

T cells are lymphocytes that have undergone their first stage of development in the thymus gland. Stem cells from the bone marrow seed the thymus, and shortly before and after birth, they develop into T cells. The newly formed T cells stream out of the thymus into the blood and migrate chiefly to the lymph nodes, where they take up residence. Embedded in each T cell's cytoplasmic membrane are protein molecules shaped so that they can fit only one specific kind of antigen molecule. The second stage of T-cell development takes place when and if a T cell comes into contact with its specific antigen. If this happens, the antigen binds to the protein on the T cell's surface, thereby changing the T cell into a sensitized T cell (Figure 12-12).

Functions of T Cells

Sensitized T cells produce cell-mediated immunity. As the name suggests, **cell-mediated immunity** is resistance to disease organisms resulting from the actions of cells—chiefly sensitized T cells. Some sensitized T cells kill invading cells directly (Figure 12-13). When bound to antigens on an invading cell's surface, they release a substance that acts as a specific and lethal poison against the bound cell. Many sensitized cells produce their deadly effects indirectly by means of compounds that they release into the area around enemy cells. Among these are a substance that attracts macrophages into the neighborhood of the enemy cells. The assembled macrophages then destroy the cells by phagocytosing (ingesting and digesting) them (Figure 12-14).

OUTLINE SUMMARY

THE LYMPHATIC SYSTEM (Figure 12-1)

A Lymph—fluid in the tissue spaces that carries protein molecules and other substances back to the blood
B Lymphatic vessels—permit only one-way movement of lymph
  1 Lymphatic capillaries—tiny blind-ended tubes distributed in tissue spaces (Figure 12-2)
    a Microscopic in size
    b Sheets consisting of one cell layer of simple squamous epithelium
    c Poor "fit" between adjacent cells results in porous walls
    d Called *lacteals* in the intestinal wall (for fat transportation)
  2 Right lymphatic duct
    a Drains lymph from the right upper extremity and right side of head, neck, and upper torso
  3 Thoracic duct
    a Largest lymphatic vessel
    b Has an enlarged pouch along its course, called *cisterna chyli*
    c Drains lymph from about three fourths of the body (Figure 12-3)
C Lymph nodes
  1 Filter lymph (Figure 12-4)
  2 Located in clusters along the pathway of lymphatic vessels (Figure 12-5)
  3 Functions include defense and WBC formation
  4 Flow of lymph: to node via several afferent lymph vessels and drained from node by a single efferent lymph vessel
D Thymus
  1 Lymphoid tissue organ located in mediastinum
  2 Total weight of 35 to 40 g—less than an ounce
  3 Plays a vital and central role in immunity
  4 Produces T-lymphocytes or T cells
  5 Secretes hormone called *thymosin*
  6 Lymphoid tissue is replaced by fat in the process called *involution*
E Tonsils (Figure 12-6)
  1 Composed of three masses of lymphoid tissue around the openings of the mouth and throat
    a Palatine tonsils ("the tonsils")
    b Pharyngeal tonsils (adenoids)
    c Lingual tonsils
  2 Subject to chronic infection
  3 Enlargement of pharyngeal tonsils may impair breathing
F Spleen
  1 Largest lymphoid organ in body
  2 Located in upper left quadrant of abdomen
  3 Often injured by trauma to abdomen
  4 Surgical removal called *splenectomy*
  5 Functions include phagocytosis of bacteria and old RBCs; acts as a blood reservoir

THE IMMUNE SYSTEM (Table 12-1)

A Protects body from pathological bacteria, foreign tissue cells, and cancerous cells
B Made up of specialized cells and molecules
C Nonspecific immunity
  1 Skin—mechanical barrier to bacteria and other harmful agents
  2 Tears and mucus—wash eyes and trap and kill bacteria
  3 Inflammation—attracts immune cells to site of injury, increases local blood flow, increases vascular permeability; promotes movement of WBCs to site of injury or infection (Figure 12-7)
D Specific immunity—ability of body to recognize, respond to, and remember harmful substances or bacteria
E Inherited or inborn immunity—inherited immunity to certain diseases from birth
F Acquired immunity
  1 Natural immunity—exposure to causative agent is not deliberate
    a Active—active disease produces immunity
    b Passive—immunity passes from mother to fetus through placenta or from mother to child through mother's milk
  2 Artificial immunity—exposure to causative agent is deliberate
    a Active—vaccination results in immunity
    b Passive—protective material developed in another individual's immune system and given to previously nonimmune individual

IMMUNE SYSTEM MOLECULES

A Antibodies
  1 Protein compounds with specific combining sites
  2 Combining sites attach antibodies to specific antigens (foreign proteins), forming an antigen-antibody complex—called *humoral* or *antibody-mediated immunity* (Figure 12-8)
  3 Antigen-antibody complexes may:
    a Neutralize toxins
    b Clump or agglutinate enemy cells
    c Promote phagocytosis

B Complement proteins
  1 Group of 14 proteins normally present in blood in inactive state
  2 Complement fixation
    a Important mechanism of action for antibodies
    b Causes cell lysis by permitting entry of water through a defect created in the plasma membrane (Figure 12-9)

IMMUNE SYSTEM CELLS

A Phagocytes—ingest and destroy foreign cells or other harmful substances via phagocytosis (Figure 12-10)
  1 Types
    a Neutrophils
    b Monocytes
    c Macrophages (Figure 12-10)
      (1) Kupffer's cells (liver)
      (2) Dust cells (lung)

B Lymphocytes
  1 Most numerous of immune system cells
  2 Development of B cells—primitive stem cells migrate from bone marrow and go through two stages of development (Figure 12-11)
    a First stage—stem cells develop into immature B cells; takes place in the liver and bone marrow before birth and in the bone marrow only in adults; immature B cells are small lymphocytes with antibody molecules (which they have synthesized) in their plasma membranes; migrate chiefly to lymph nodes
    b Second stage—immature B cell develops into activated B cell; initiated by immature B cell's contact with antigens, which bind to its surface antibodies; activated B cell, by dividing repeatedly, forms two clones of cells; plasma cells and memory cells; plasma cells secrete antibodies into blood; memory cells stored in lymph nodes; if subsequent exposure to antigen that activated B cell occurs, memory cells become plasma cells and secrete antibodies
  3 Function of B cells—indirectly, B cells produce humoral immunity; activated B cells develop into plasma cells; plasma cells secrete antibodies into the blood; circulating antibodies produce humoral immunity (Figure 12-11)
  4 Development of T cells—stem cells from bone marrow migrate to thymus gland (Figure 12-12)
    a Stage 1—stem cells develop into T cells; occurs in thymus during few months before and after birth; T cells migrate chiefly to lymph nodes
    b Stage 2—T cells develop into sensitized T cells; occurs when, and if, antigen binds to T cell's surface proteins
  5 Functions of T cells—produce cell-mediated immunity; kill invading cells by releasing a substance that poisons cells and also by releasing chemicals that attract and activate macrophages to kill cells by phagocytosis (Figures 12-13 and 12-14)

N E W W O R D S

afferent	cell-mediated immunity	complement fixation	macrophage
AIDS	clone	efferent	memory cells
antibodies	combining sites	humoral immunity	monoclonal antibodies
antigen	complement	inflammatory response	plasma cells
B cells (lymphocytes)		interferon	T cells (lymphocytes)
		lymph	

CHAPTER TEST

1. The largest lymphatic vessel in the body is called the ______________ ______________.

2. Phagocytic cells located in the ______________ ______________ perform biological filtration.

3. Deliberate exposure to a causative agent produces ______________ immunity.

4. The two protein molecules most critical to immune system functioning are called ______________ and ______________.

5. Antibodies are characterized by their ability to combine with very specific compounds called ______________.

6. Antibodies make antigens unable to harm the body—a process called ______________ immunity.

7. Plasma cells produce ______________.

8. The most numerous cells of the immune system are the ______________.

9. The most important phagocytes of the immune system are the ______________ and ______________.

10. B cells and T cells are the two major types of ______________ in the immune system.

11. B cells indirectly produce ______________ immunity in the body.

12. Sensitized T cells produce ______________ immunity in the body.

Circle the T before each true statement and the F before each false statement.

T F 13. Lymphatic vessels permit only one-way movement of lymph.

T F 14. The right lymphatic duct is the largest lymph vessel in the body.

T F 15. Vaccination is an example of active artificial immunity.

T F 16. Cells of the immune system outnumber antibody molecules by about 100 million to one.

T F 17. Antibodies function to produce cell-mediated immunity.

T F 18. After leaving the blood and entering the tissue space, monocytes are called macrophages.

T F 19. Macrophages are capable of phagocytosis.

T F 20. Complement fixation is an important way in which antibodies act.

T F 21. Antigen-antibody complexes may neutralize toxins.

T F 22. Activated B cells develop into Kupffer's cells.

T F 23. Memory cells develop from sensitized T cells.

T F 24. T cells begin as stem cells that develop in the thymus gland.

REVIEW QUESTIONS

1. Discuss two functions of the lymph nodes.
2. Explain nonspecific immunity, specific immunity, inherited immunity, acquired immunity, natural immunity, artificial immunity, active immunity, and passive immunity.
3. Explain the terms *antigen* and *antibody.*
4. What are combining sites? Complement binding sites?
5. Name four kinds of cells that constitute part of the immune system. Which are most numerous? How numerous are they estimated to be?
6. Name the two major immune system molecules.
7. What are the two major types of lymphocytes called? What makes these names appropriate?
8. Describe briefly the two stages of development that B cells undergo.
9. Describe briefly the two stages of development that T cells undergo.
10. What cells secrete antibodies?
11. Explain the function of memory cells.
12. Describe the function of activated B cells.
13. Describe the function of sensitized T cells.

CRITICAL THINKING

14. Sometimes a woman's arm becomes very swollen for a while after removal of a breast and the nearby lymph nodes and lymphatic vessels, including some of those in the upper arm. Can you think of any reason why swelling occurs?
15. How does the "circulation" of lymph differ from that of blood?
16. Outline the inflammatory response and explain its advantages in an infection.

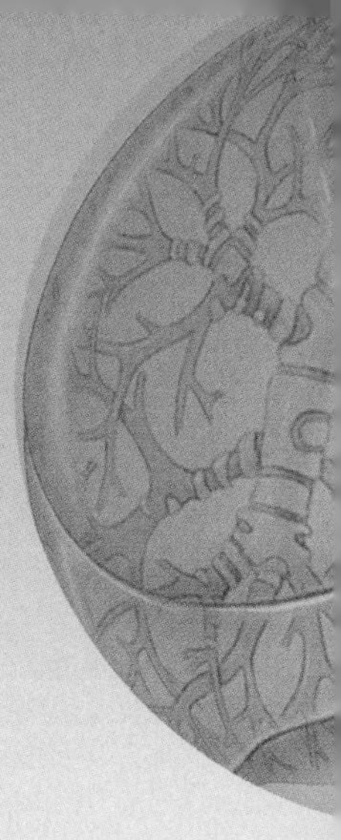

The Respiratory System

OUTLINE

Structural Plan
Respiratory Tracts
Respiratory Mucosa
Nose
Pharynx
Larynx
Trachea
Bronchi, Bronchioles, and Alveoli
Lungs and Pleura
Respiration
- Mechanics of Breathing
- Exchange of Gases in Lungs
- Exchange of Gases in Tissues
- Volumes of Air Exchanged in Pulmonary Ventilation

Regulation of Respiration
- Cerebral Cortex
- Receptors Influencing Respiration

Types of Breathing

BOXED ESSAYS

Heimlich Maneuver
Infant Respiratory Distress Syndrome
Hiccup
Maximum Oxygen Consumption
Oxygen Therapy

OBJECTIVES

After you have completed this chapter, you should be able to:

1. Discuss the generalized functions of the respiratory system.
2. List the major organs of the respiratory system and describe the function of each.
3. Compare, contrast, and explain the mechanism responsible for the exchange of gases that occurs during internal and external respiration.
4. List and discuss the volumes of air exchanged during pulmonary ventilation.
5. Identify and discuss the mechanisms that regulate respiration.

No one needs to be told how important the **respiratory system** is. The respiratory system serves the body much as a lifeline to an oxygen tank serves a deep-sea diver. Think how panicked you would feel if suddenly your lifeline became blocked—if you could not breathe for a few seconds! Of all the substances that cells and therefore the body as a whole must have to survive, oxygen is by far the most crucial. A person can live a few weeks without food, a few days without water, but only a few minutes without oxygen. Constant removal of carbon dioxide from the body is just as important for survival as a constant supply of oxygen.

The organs of the respiratory system are designed to perform two basic functions; they serve as an **air distributor** and as a **gas exchanger** for the body. The respiratory system ensures that oxygen is supplied to and carbon dioxide is removed from the body's cells. The process of respiration therefore is an important **homeostatic mechanism.** By constantly supplying adequate oxygen and by removing carbon dioxide as it forms, the respiratory system helps maintain a constant environment that enables our body cells to function effectively.

In addition to air distribution and gas exchange, the respiratory system effectively **filters, warms,** and **humidifies** the air we breathe. Respiratory organs or organs closely associated with the respiratory system, such as the **sinuses,** also influence speech or sound production and make possible the sense of smell or **olfaction** (ol-FAK-shun). In this chapter the structural plan of the respiratory system will be considered first, then the respiratory organs will be discussed individually, and finally some facts about gas exchange and the nervous system's control of respiration will be discussed.

Structural Plan

Respiratory organs include the **nose, pharynx** (FAIR-inks), **larynx** (LAIR-inks), **trachea** (TRAY-kee-ah), **bronchi** (BRONG-ki), and **lungs.** The basic structural design of this organ system is that of a tube with many branches ending in millions of extremely tiny, very thin-walled sacs called **alveoli** (al-VEE-o-li). Figure 13-1 shows the extensive branching of the "respiratory tree" in both lungs. Think of this air distribution system as an "upside-down tree." The trachea or windpipe then becomes the trunk and the bronchial tubes the branches. This idea will be developed when the types of bronchi and the alveoli are studied in more detail later in the chapter. A network of capillaries fits like a hairnet around each microscopic alveolus. Incidentally, this is a good place for us to think again about a principle already mentioned several times, namely, that structure and function are intimately related. The function of alveoli—in fact, the function of the entire respiratory system—is to distribute air close enough to blood for a gas exchange to take place between air and blood. The passive transport process of **diffusion,** which was described in Chapter 2, is responsible for the exchange of gases that occurs in the respiratory system. You may want to review the discussion of diffusion on pp. 23 to 25 before you study the mechanism of gas exchange that occurs in the lungs and body tissues.

Two characteristics about the structure of alveoli assist in diffusion and make them able to perform this function admirably. First, the wall of each alveolus is made up of a single layer of cells and so are the walls of the capillaries around it. This means that, between the blood in the capillaries and the air in the alveolus, there is a barrier probably less than 1 micron thick! This extremely thin barrier is called the **respiratory membrane** (Figure 13-2). Second, there are millions of alveoli. This means that together they make an enormous surface (approximately 100 square meters, an area many times larger than the surface of the entire body) where larger amounts of oxygen and carbon dioxide can rapidly be exchanged.

Respiratory Tracts

The respiratory system is often divided into upper and lower tracts or divisions to assist in the description of symptoms associated with common respiratory problems such as a cold. The organs of the upper respiratory tract are located outside of the thorax or chest cavity, whereas those in the lower tract or division are located almost entirely within it. The **upper respiratory** tract is composed of the nose, pharynx, and larynx. The **lower res-**

FIGURE 13–1 ***Structural Plan of the Respiratory Organs Showing the Pharynx, Trachea, Bronchi, and Lungs.*** The inset shows the alveolar sacs where the interchange of oxygen and carbon dioxide takes place through the walls of the grapelike alveoli. Capillaries surround the alveoli.

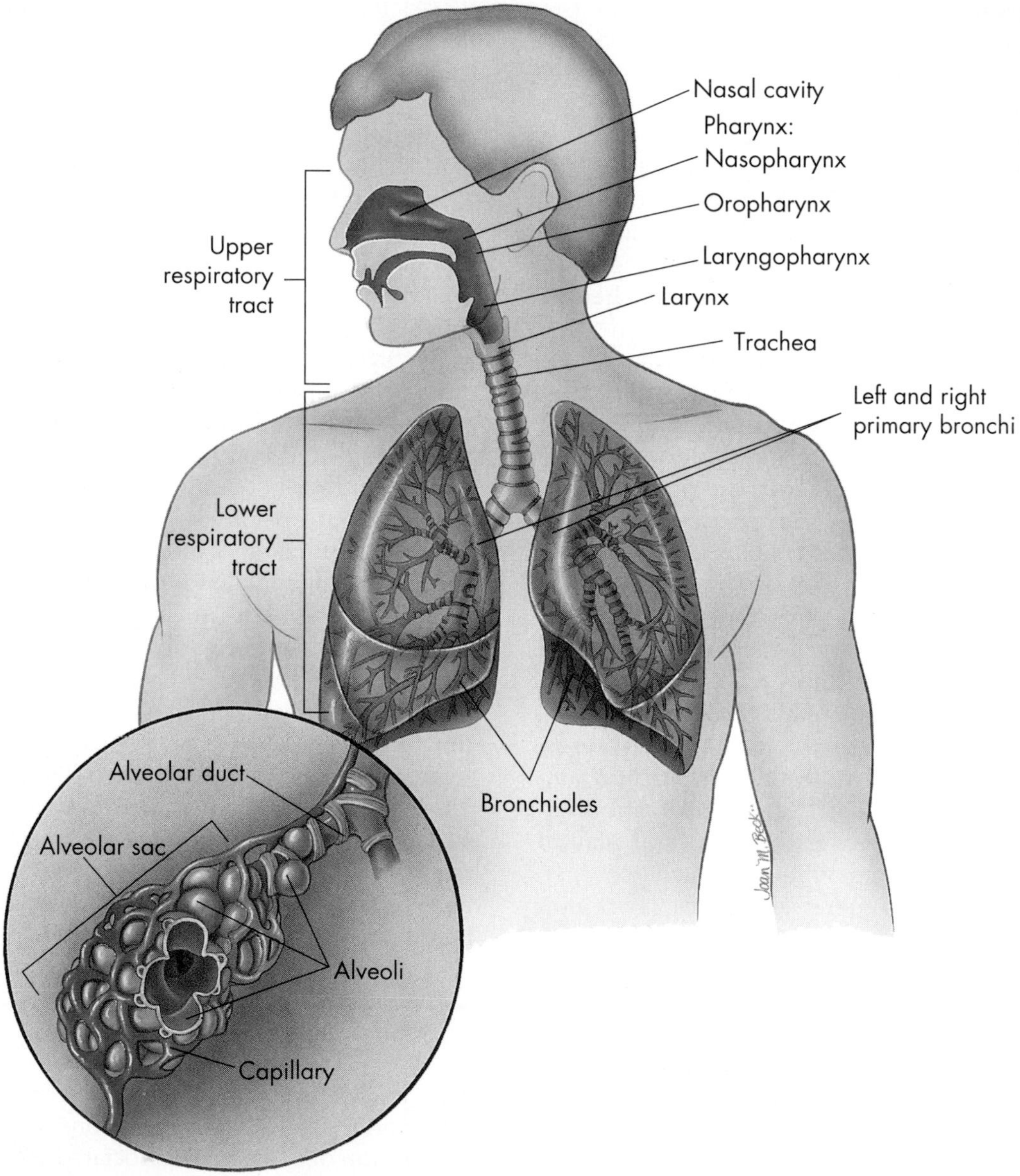

FIGURE 13–2 ***The Gas-Exchange Structures of the Lung.*** Each alveolus is continually ventilated with fresh air. The inset shows a magnified view of the respiratory membrane composed of the alveolar wall (surfactant, epithelial cells, and basement membrane), interstitial fluid, and the wall of a pulmonary capillary (basement membrane and endothelial cells). The gases, CO_2 (carbon dioxide) and O_2 (oxygen), diffuse across the respiratory membrane.

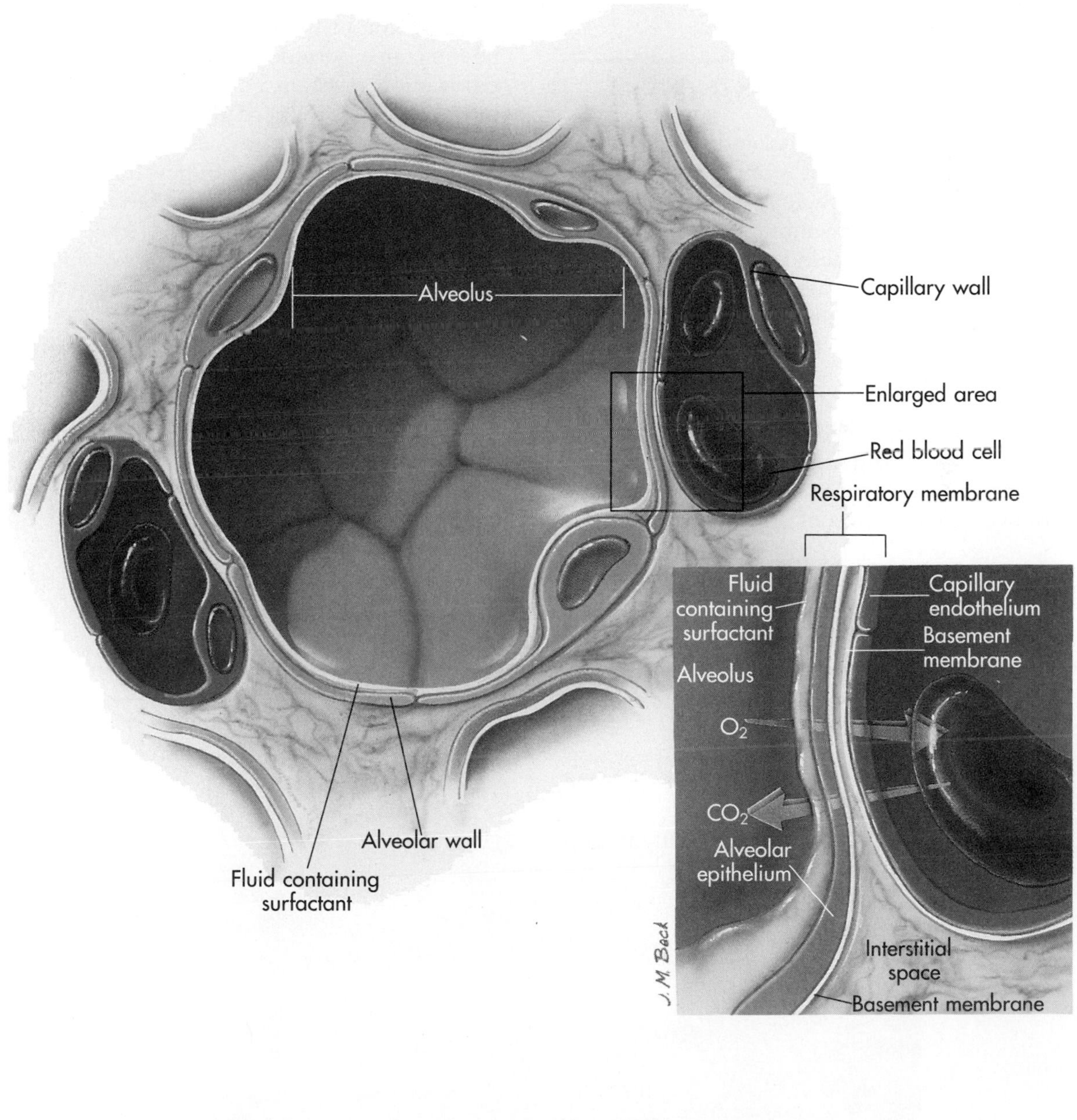

piratory tract or division consists of the trachea, all segments of the bronchial tree, and the lungs. The designation "upper respiratory infection" or URI is often used to describe a head cold. Typically the symptoms of an upper respiratory infection involve the sinuses, nasal cavity, pharynx, and larynx, whereas the symptoms of a chest cold are similar to pneumonia and involve the organs of the lower respiratory tract.

Respiratory Mucosa

Before beginning the study of individual organs in the respiratory system, it is important to review the histology or microscopic anatomy of the **respiratory mucosa**—the membrane that lines most of the air distribution tubes in the system. Do not confuse the respiratory membrane with the respiratory mucosa! The **respiratory membrane** (Figure 13-2) separates the air in the alveoli from the blood in surrounding capillaries. The respiratory mucosa (Figure 13-3) is covered with mucus and lines the tubes of the respiratory tree.

Recall that in addition to serving as air distribution passageways or gas exchange surfaces, the anatomical components of the respiratory tract and lungs cleanse, warm, and humidify inspired air. Air entering the nose is generally contaminated with one or more common irritants; examples include insects, dust, pollen, and bacterial organisms. A remarkably effective air purification mechanism removes almost every form of contaminant before inspired air reaches the alveoli or terminal air sacs in the lungs.

The layer of protective mucus that covers a large portion of the membrane that lines the respiratory tree serves as the most important air purification mechanism. Over 125 ml of respiratory mucus is produced daily. It forms a continuous sheet called a *mucous blanket* that covers the lining of the air distribution tubes in the respiratory tree. This layer of cleansing mucus moves upward to the pharynx from the lower portions of the bronchial tree on millions of hairlike cilia that cover the epithelial cells in the respiratory mucosa (Figure 13-3). The microscopic cilia that cover epithelial cells in the respiratory mucosa beat or move only in one direction. The result is movement of mucus toward the pharynx. Cigarette smoke paralyzes these cilia and results in accumulations of mucus and the typical smoker's cough, which is an effort to clear the secretions.

FIGURE 13–3 *Respiratory Mucosa Lining the Trachea.* A layer of mucus covers the hairlike cilia.

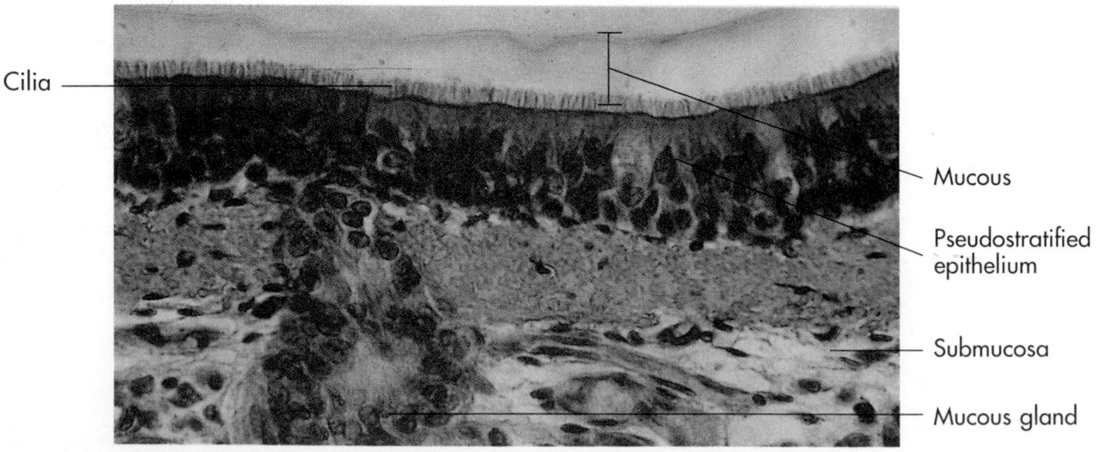

Nose

Air enters the respiratory tract through the **external nares** (NA-rees) or nostrils. It then flows into the right and left **nasal cavities,** which are lined by respiratory mucosa. A partition called the *nasal septum* separates these two cavities.

The surface of the nasal cavities is moist from mucus and warm from blood flowing just under it. Nerve endings responsible for the sense of smell (olfactory receptors) are located in the nasal mucosa. Four **paranasal sinuses**—frontal, maxillary, sphenoidal, and ethmoidal—drain into the nasal cavities (Figure 13-4). Because the mucosa that lines the sinuses is continuous with the mucosa that lines the nose, sinus infections, called **sinusitis** (sye-nyoo-SYE-tis), often develop from colds in which the nasal mucosa is inflamed. The paranasal sinuses are lined with a mucous membrane that assists in the production of mucus for the respiratory tract. In addition, these hollow spaces help to lighten the skull bones and serve as resonant chambers for the production of sound.

FIGURE 13–4 ***The Paranasal Sinuses.*** The anterior view shows the anatomical relationship of the paranasal sinuses to each other and to the nasal cavity. The inset is a lateral view of the position of the sinuses.

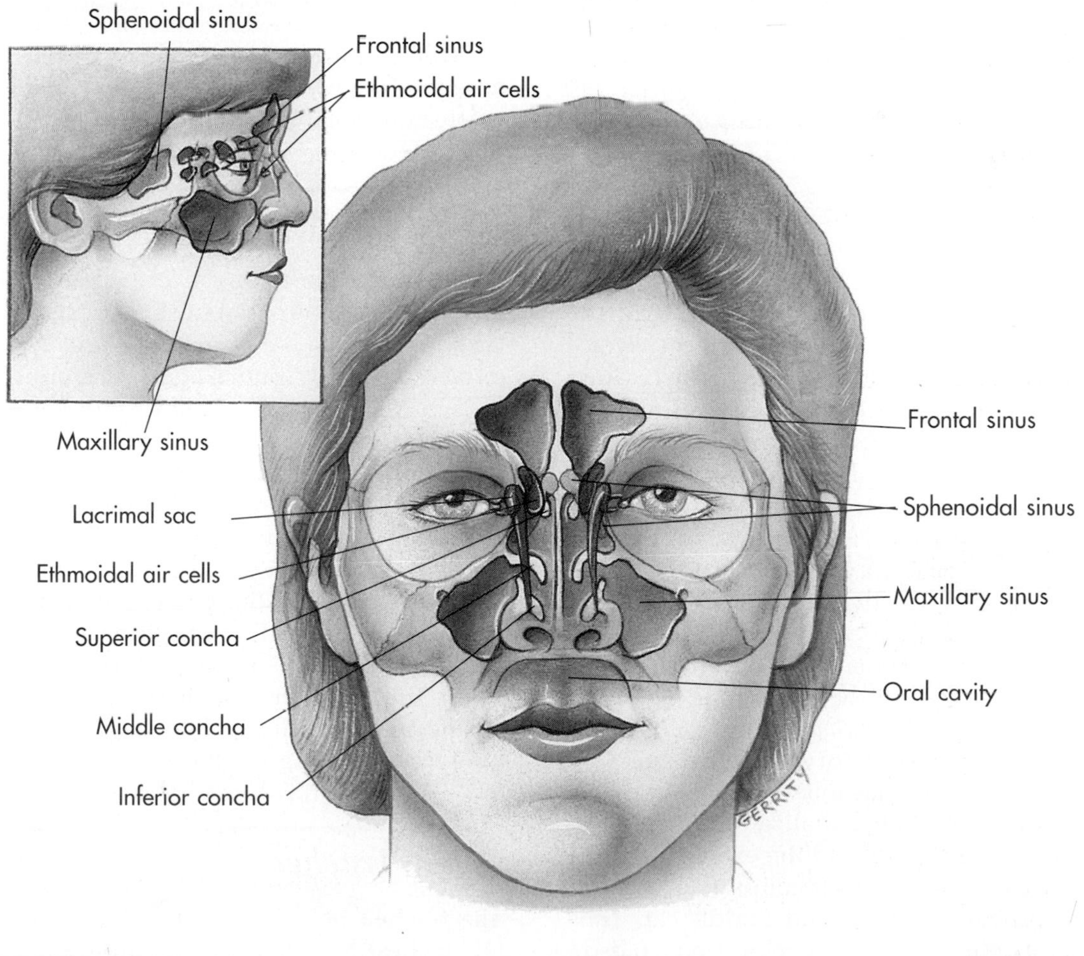

Two ducts from the **lacrimal sacs** (LAK-rim-al saks) also drain into the nasal cavity, as Figure 13-4 shows. The lacrimal sacs collect tears from the corner of the each eyelid and drain them into the nasal cavity.

Note in Figure 13-5 that three shelflike structures called **conchae** (KONG-kee) protrude into the nasal cavity on each side. The mucosa-covered conchae greatly increase the surface over which air must flow as it passes through the naval cavity. As air moves over the conchae and through the nasal cavities, it is warmed and humidified. This helps explain why breathing through the nose is more effective in humidifying inspired air than is breathing through the mouth. If an individual who is ill requires supplemental oxygen, it is first bubbled through water to reduce the amount of moisture that would otherwise have to be removed from the lining of the respiratory tree to humidify it. Administration of "dry" oxygen pulls water from the mucosa and results in respiratory discomfort and irritation.

Pharynx

The **pharynx** is the structure that many of us call the throat. It is about 12.5 cm (5 inches) long and can be divided into three portions (Figure 13-5). The uppermost part of the tube just behind the nasal cavities is called the **nasopharynx** (nay-zo-FAIR-inks). The portion behind the mouth is called the **oropharynx** (o-ro-FAIR-inks). The last or lowest segment is called the **laryngopharynx** (lah-ring-go-FAIR-inks). The pharynx as a whole serves the same purpose for the respiratory and digestive tracts as a hallway serves for a house. Air and food pass through the pharynx on their way to the lungs and the stomach respectively. Air enters the pharynx from the two nasal cavities and leaves it by way of the larynx; food enters it from the mouth and leaves it by way of the esophagus. The right and left **auditory** or *eustachian* (yoo-STAY-she-an) **tubes** open into the nasopharynx; they connect the middle ears with the nasopharynx (Figure 13-5). This connection permits equalization of air pressure between the middle and the exterior ear. The lining of the auditory tubes is continuous with the lining of the nasopharynx and middle ear. Thus just as sinus infections can develop from colds in which the nasal mucosa is inflamed, middle ear infections can develop from inflammation of the nasopharynx.

Masses of lymphatic tissue called **tonsils** are embedded in the mucous membrane of the pharynx (see p. 263). The **pharyngeal** (fa-RIN-jee-al) **tonsils** or **adenoids** (AD-e-noyds) are in the nasopharynx. The **palatine tonsils** are located in the oropharynx (Figure 13-5). Both tonsils are generally removed in a **tonsillectomy** (ton-si-LEK-toe-mee). Although this surgical procedure is still rather common, the number of tonsillectomies reported each year continues to decrease as new and more effective antibiotics become available. Physicians now recognize the value of lymphatic tissue in the body defense mechanism and delay removal of the tonsils—even in cases of inflammation or **tonsillitis—**unless antibiotic treatment is ineffective. When the pharyngeal tonsils become swollen, they are referred to as adenoids. Such swelling caused by infections may make it difficult or impossible for air to travel from the nose into the throat. In these cases the individual is forced to breathe through the mouth.

Larynx

The **larynx** or voice box is located just below the pharynx. It is composed of several pieces of cartilage. You know the largest of these (the *thyroid cartilage*) as the "Adam's apple" (Figure 13-6).

Two short fibrous bands, the **vocal cords,** stretch across the interior of the larynx. Muscles that attach to the larynx cartilages can pull on these cords in such a way that they become tense or relaxed. When they are tense, the voice is high pitched; when they are relaxed, it is low pitched. The space between the vocal cords is the **glottis.** Another cartilage, the **epiglottis** (ep-i-GLOT-is) partially covers the opening of the larynx (Figure 13-6). The epiglottis acts like a trapdoor, closing off the larynx during swallowing and preventing food from entering the trachea.

Trachea

The **trachea** or windpipe is a tube about 11 cm (4½ inches) long that extends from the larynx in

FIGURE 13–5 ***Sagittal Section of the Head and Neck.*** The nasal septum has been removed, exposing the right lateral wall of the nasal cavity so that the nasal conchae can be seen. Note also the divisions of the pharynx and the position of the tonsils.

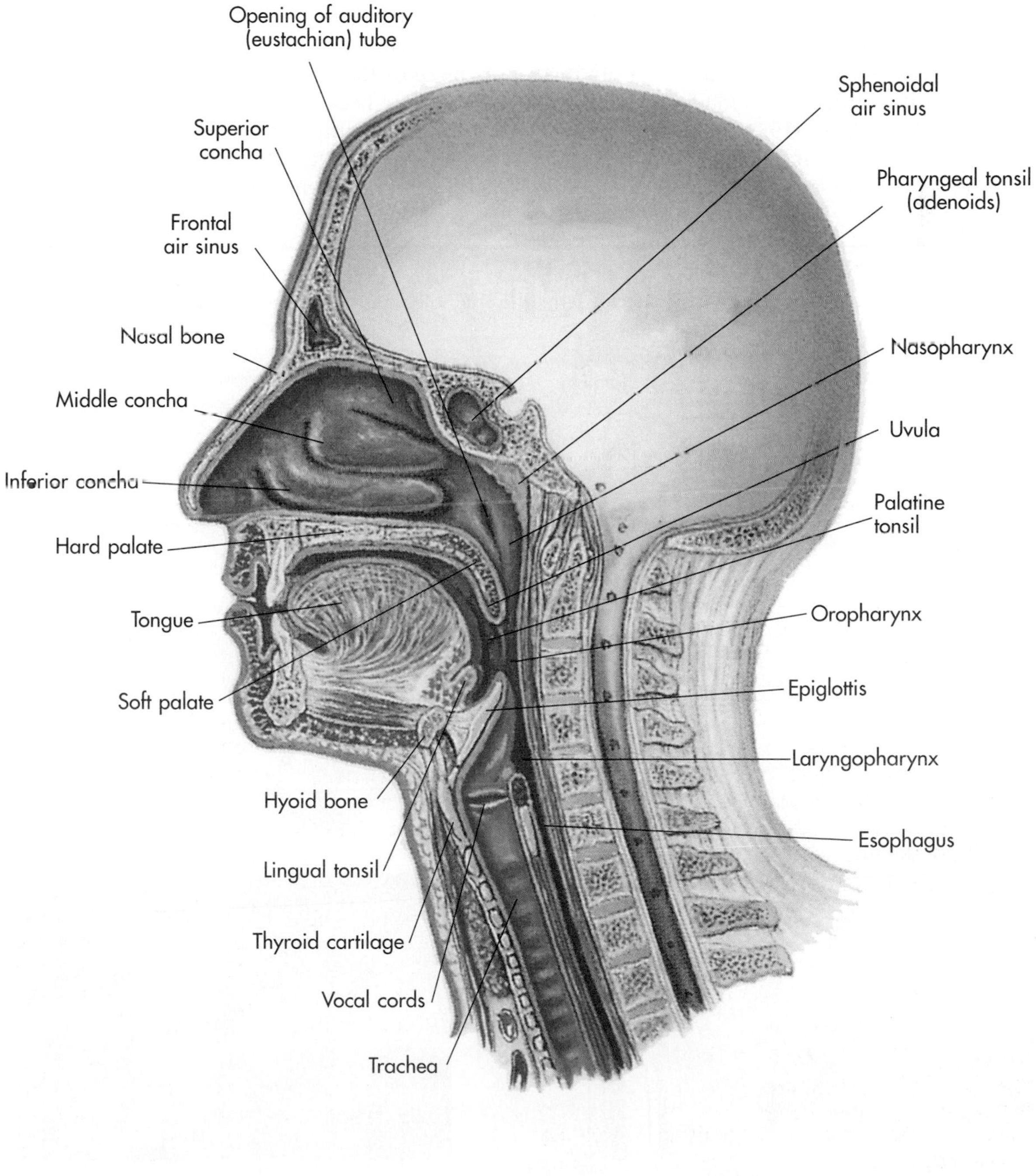

the neck to the bronchi in the chest cavity (Figures 13-1 and 13-7). The trachea performs a simple but vital function; it furnishes part of the open passageway through which air can reach the lungs from the outside.

By pushing with your fingers against your throat about an inch above the sternum, you can feel the shape of the trachea or windpipe. Only if you use considerable force can you squeeze it closed. Nature has taken precautions to keep this lifeline open. Its framework is made of an almost noncollapsible material—15 or 20 C-shaped rings of cartilage placed one above the other with only a little soft tissue between them (Figure 13-7). The trachea is lined by the typical respiratory mucosa. Glands below the ciliated epithelium help produce the blanket of mucus that continually moves upward toward the pharynx.

Despite the structural safeguard of cartilage rings, closing of the trachea sometimes occurs. A tumor or an infection may enlarge the lymph nodes of the neck so much that they squeeze the trachea shut, or a person may aspirate (breathe in) a piece of food or something else that blocks the windpipe. Because air has no other way to get to the lungs, complete tracheal obstruction causes death in a matter of minutes. Choking on food and other substances caught in the trachea kills

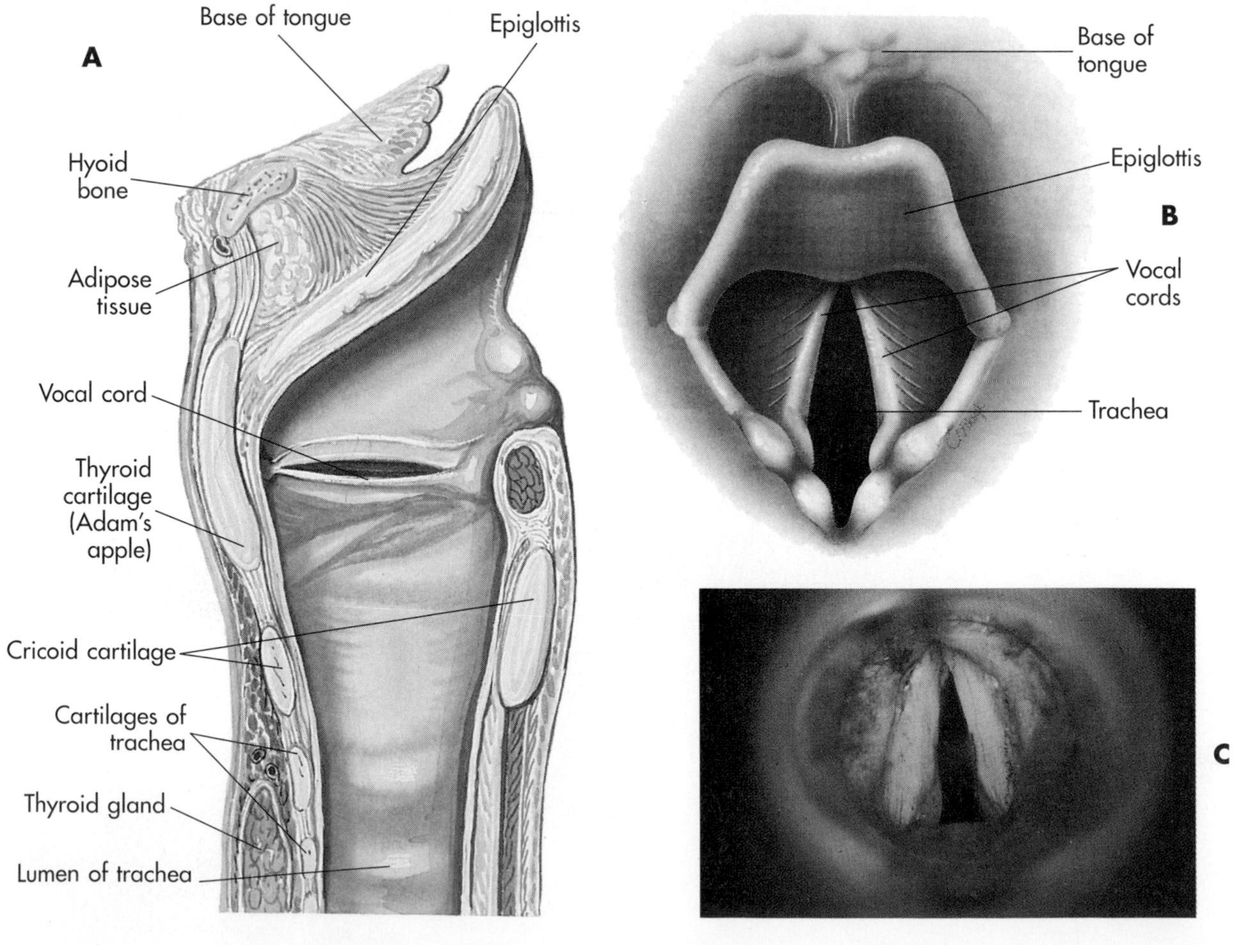

FIGURE 13–6 ***The Larynx.*** **A,** Sagittal section of the larynx. **B,** Superior view of the larynx. **C,** Photograph of the larynx taken with an endoscope (optical device) inserted through the mouth and pharynx to the epiglottis.

over 4000 people each year and is the fifth major cause of accidental deaths in the United States. A lifesaving technique developed by Dr. Henry Heimlich (see p. 288), is now widely used to free the trachea of ingested food or other foreign objects that would otherwise block the airway and cause death in choking victims.

Bronchi, Bronchioles, and Alveoli

Recall that one way to picture the thousands of air tubes that make up the lungs is to think of an upside-down tree. The trachea is the main trunk of this tree; the right bronchus (the tube leading into the right lung) and the left bronchus (the tube leading into the left lung) are the trachea's first branches or **primary bronchi.** In each lung, they branch into smaller or **secondary bronchi** whose walls, like those of the trachea and bronchi, are kept open by rings of cartilage for air passage. These bronchi divide into smaller and smaller tubes, ultimately branching into tiny tubes whose walls contain only smooth muscle. These very small passageways are called **bronchioles.** The bronchioles subdivide into microscopic tubes called **alveolar ducts,** which resemble the main

FIGURE 13–7 ***Cross Section of the Trachea.*** Inset at top shows where the section was cut. The scanning electron micrograph shows the tip of one of the C-shaped cartilage rings.

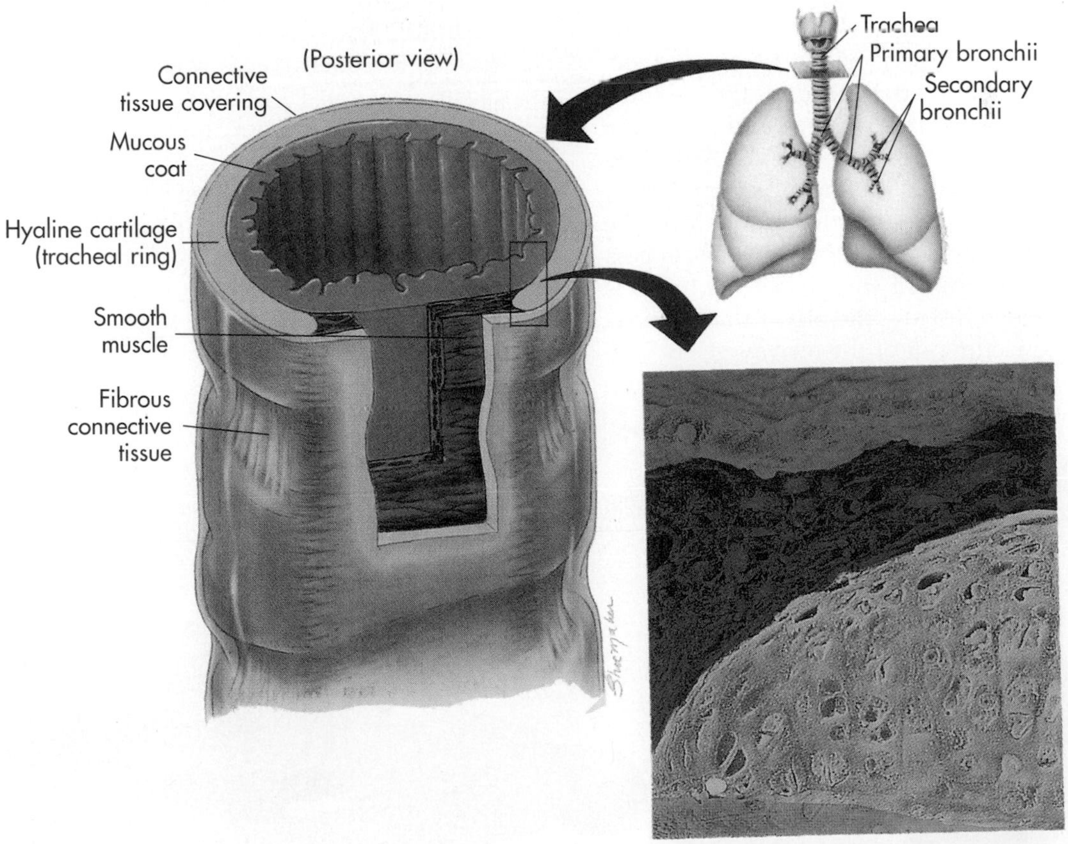

Heimlich Maneuver

The **Heimlich maneuver** is an effective and often lifesaving technique that can be used to open a windpipe that is suddenly obstructed. The maneuver (see figures) uses air already present in the lungs to expel the object obstructing the trachea. Most accidental airway obstructions result from pieces of food aspirated (breathed in) during a meal; the condition is sometimes referred to as a *cafe coronary*. Other objects such as chewing gum or balloons are frequently the cause of obstructions in children.

Individuals trained in emergency procedures must be able to tell the difference between airway obstruction and other conditions such as heart attacks that produce similar symptoms. The key question they must ask the person who appears to be choking is, "Are you choking?" A person with an obstructed airway will not be able to speak, even while conscious. The Heimlich maneuver, if the victim is standing, consists of the rescuer's grasping the victim with both arms around the victim's waist just below the rib cage and above the navel. The rescuer makes a fist with one hand, grasps it with the other, and then delivers an upward thrust against the diaphragm just below the xiphoid process of the sternum. Air trapped in the lungs is compressed, forcing the object that is choking the victim out of the airway.

Technique if victim can be lifted (see *A*)

1. The rescuer stands behind the victim and wraps both arms around the victim's chest slightly below the rib cage and above the navel. The victim is allowed to fall forward with the head, arms, and chest over the rescuer's arms.

2. The rescuer makes a fist with one hand and grasps it with the other hand, pressing the thumb side of the fist against the victim's abdomen just below the end of the xiphoid process and above the navel.

3. The hands only are used to deliver the upward subdiaphragmatic thrusts. It is performed with sharp flexion of the elbows, in an upward rather than inward direction, and is usually repeated four times. It is very important not to compress the rib cage or actually press on the sternum during the Heimlich maneuver.

Technique if victim has collapsed or cannot be lifted (see *B*)

1. Rescuer places victim on floor face up.

2. Facing victim, rescuer straddles the victim's hips.

3. Rescuer places one hand on top of the other, with the bottom hand on the victim's abdomen slightly above the navel and below the rib cage.

4. Rescuer performs a forceful upward thrust with the heel of the bottom hand, repeating several times if necessary.

A

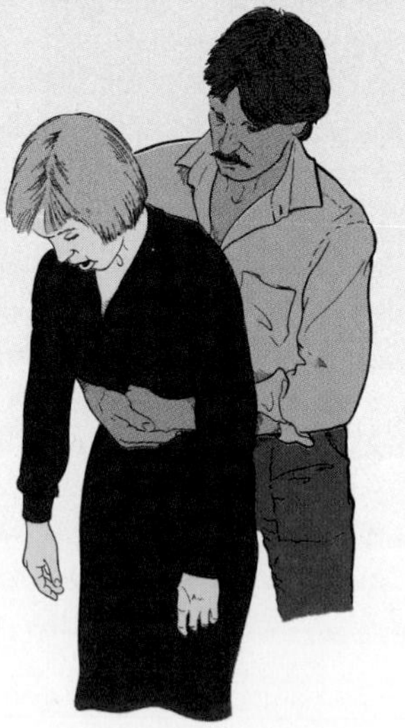

B

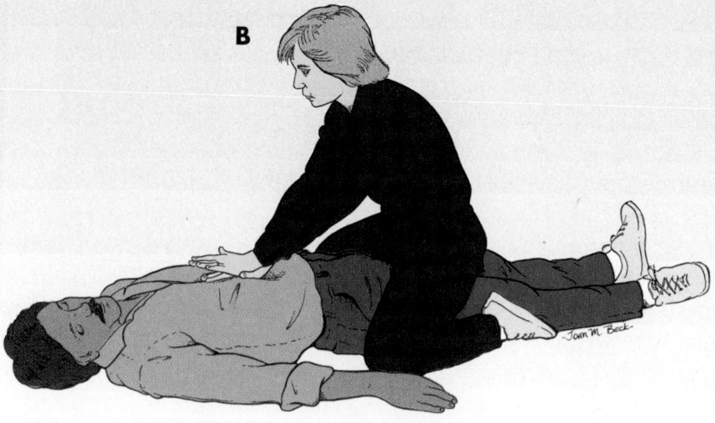

FIGURE 13–8 ***Alveoli.*** Bronchioles subdivide to form tiny tubes called *alveolar ducts,* which end in clusters of alveoli called *alveolar sacs.*

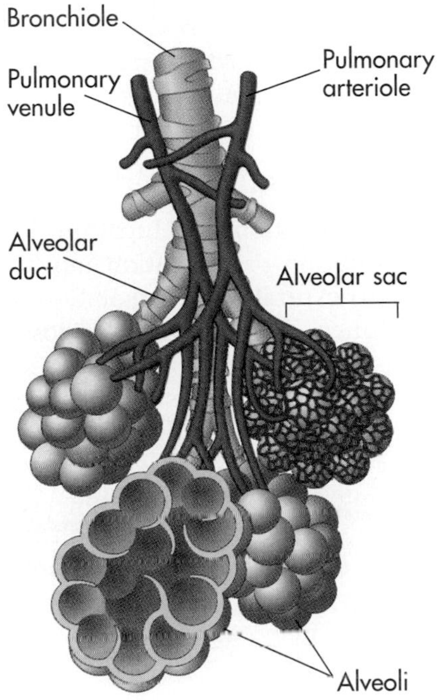

stem of a bunch of grapes (Figure 13-8). Each alveolar duct ends in several **alveolar sacs,** each of which resembles a cluster of grapes, and the wall of each alveolar sac is made up of numerous **alveoli,** each of which resembles a single grape.

Alveoli are very effective in gas exchange, mainly because they are extremely thin walled; each alveolus lies in contact with a blood capillary, and there are millions of alveoli in each lung. The surface of the respiratory membrane inside the alveolus is covered by a substance called **surfactant** (sur-FAK-tant). This important substance helps reduce surface tension in the alveoli and keeps them from collapsing as air moves in and out during respiration.

Infant Respiratory Distress Syndrome

Infant respiratory distress syndrome or **IRDS** is a very serious, life-threatening condition that often affects prematurely born infants of less than 37 weeks' gestation or those who weigh less than 2.2 kg (5 lbs) at birth. IRDS is the leading cause of death among premature infants in the United States, claiming over 5000 premature babies each year. The disease, characterized by a lack of **surfactant** in the alveolar air sacs, affects 50,000 babies annually.

Surfactant is manufactured by specialized cells in the walls of the alveoli. Surfactant reduces the surface tension of the fluid on the free surface of the alveolar walls and permits easy movement of air into and out of the lungs. The ability of the body to manufacture this important substance is not fully developed until shortly before birth—normally about 40 weeks after conception.

In newborn infants who are unable to manufacture surfactant, many air sacs collapse during expiration because of the increased surface tension. The effort required to reinflate these collapsed alveoli is much greater than that needed to reinflate normal alveoli with adequate surfactant. The baby soon develops labored breathing, and symptoms of respiratory distress appear shortly after birth.

In the past, treatment of IRDS was limited to keeping the alveoli open so that delivery and exchange of oxygen and carbon dioxide could occur. To accomplish this, a tube is inserted into the respiratory tract, and oxygen-rich air is delivered under sufficient pressure to keep the alveoli from collapsing at the end of expiration. A newer treatment involves delivering air under pressure and applying prepared surfactant directly into the baby's airways by means of a tube.

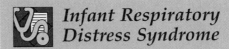

Lungs and Pleura

The **lungs** are fairly large organs. Note in Figure 13-9 that the right lung has three lobes and the left lung has two. Figure 13-9 shows the relationship of the lungs to the rib cage at the end of a normal expiration. The narrow, superior position of each lung, up under the collarbone, is the apex; the broad, inferior portion resting on the diaphragm, is the base.

The **pleura** covers the outer surface of the lungs and lines the inner surface of the rib cage. The pleura resembles other serous membranes in structure and function. Like the peritoneum or pericardium, the pleura is an extensive, thin, moist, slippery membrane. It lines a large, closed cavity of the body and covers the organs located within it. The parietal pleura lines the walls of the thoracic cavity; the visceral pleura covers the lungs, and the intrapleural space lies between the two pleural membranes (Figure 13-10). Pleurisy is an inflammation of the pleura that causes pain when the pleural membranes rub together.

Normally the intrapleural space contains just enough fluid to make both portions of the pleura moist and slippery and able to glide easily against each other as the lungs expand and deflate with each breath. **Pneumothorax** (noo-mo-THO-raks) is the presence of air in the intrapleural space on one side of the chest. The additional air increases the pressure on the lung on that side and causes it to collapse. While collapsed, the lung does not function in breathing.

Respiration

Respiration means exchange of gases (oxygen and carbon dioxide) between a living organism and its environment. If the organism consists of only one cell, gases can move directly between it and the environment. If, however, the organism consists of billions of cells, as do our bodies, most of its cells are too far from the air for a direct exchange of gases. To overcome this difficulty, a pair of organs—the lungs—provides a place where air and a circulating fluid (blood) can come close enough to each other for oxygen to move out of the air into blood while carbon dioxide moves out of the blood into air. Breathing or **pulmonary ventilation** is the process that moves air into and out of the lungs. It makes possible the exchange of gases between air in the lungs and in the blood. This exchange is often called **external respiration.** In addition, exchange of gases occurs between the blood and the cells of the body—a process called **internal respiration.** *Cellular respiration* refers to the actual use of oxygen by cells in the process of metabolism, which is discussed in Chapter 15.

MECHANICS OF BREATHING

Pulmonary ventilation or breathing has two phases. **Inspiration** or inhalation moves air into the lungs, and **expiration** or exhalation moves air out of the lungs. The lungs are enclosed within the thoracic cavity. Thus changes in the shape and size of the thoracic cavity result in changes in the air pressure within that cavity and in the lungs. This difference in air pressure causes the movement of air into and out of the lungs. Air moves from an area where pressure is high to an area where pressure is lower. Respiratory muscles are responsible for the changes in the shape of the thoracic cavity that cause the air movements involved in breathing.

Hiccup

The term **hiccup** (HIK-up) is used to describe an involuntary, spasmodic contraction of the diaphragm. When such a contraction occurs, generally at the beginning of an inspiration, the glottis suddenly closes, producing the characteristic sound.

Hiccups lasting for extended periods of time can be disabling. They may be produced by irritation of the phrenic nerve or the sensory nerves in the stomach or by direct injury or pressure on certain areas of the brain. Fortunately, most cases of hiccups last only a few minutes and are harmless.

FIGURE 13–9 ***Lungs.*** The trachea is an airway that branches to form a treelike formation of bronchi and bronchioles. Note that the right lung has three lobes and that the left lung two lobes.

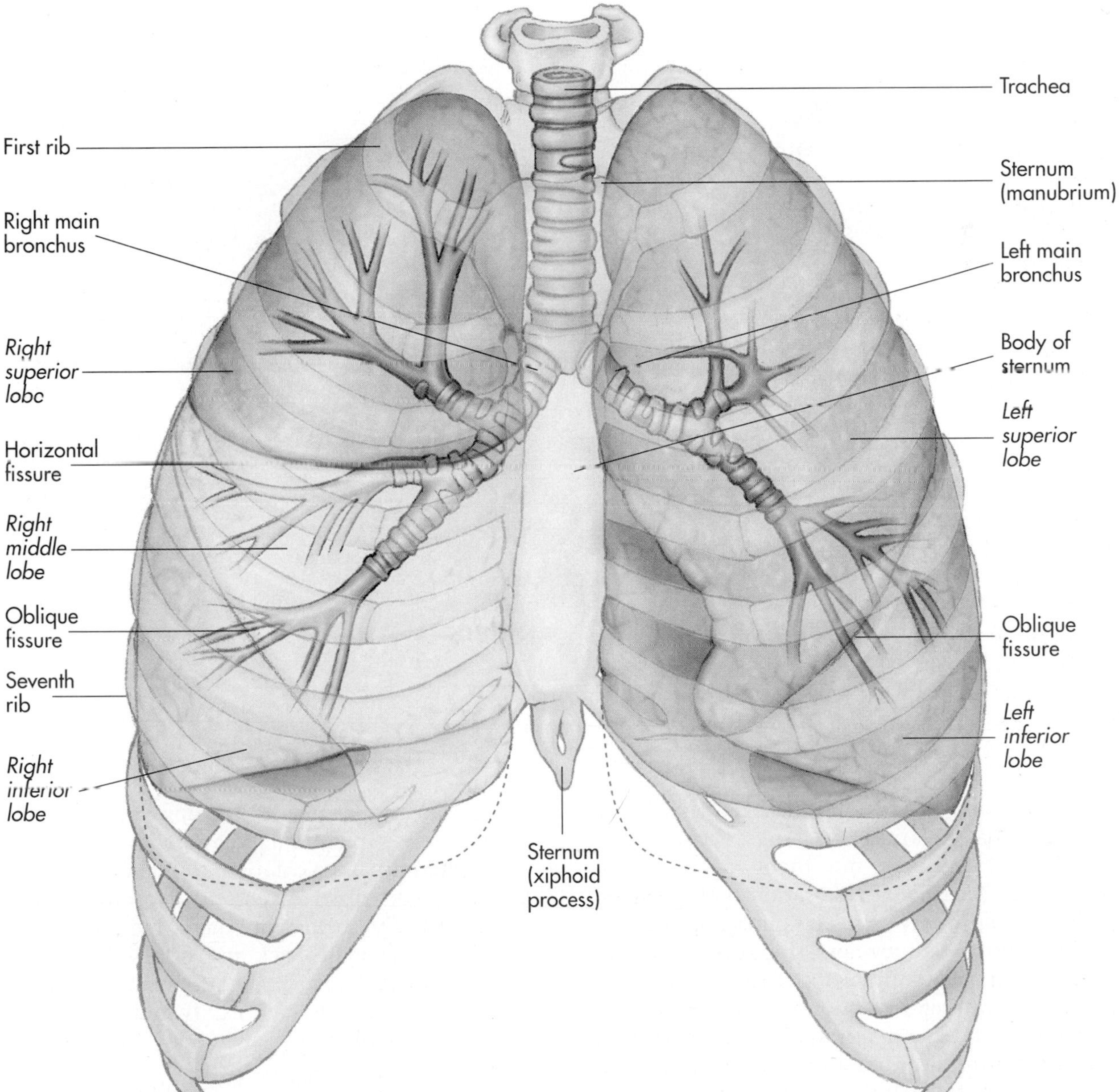

FIGURE 13–10 ***Lungs and Pleura.*** The inset shows where the body was cut to show this transverse section of the thorax. A serous membrane lines the thoracic wall (parietal pleura) and then folds inward near the bronchi to cover the lung (visceral pleura). The intrapleural space contains a small amount of serous pleural fluid.

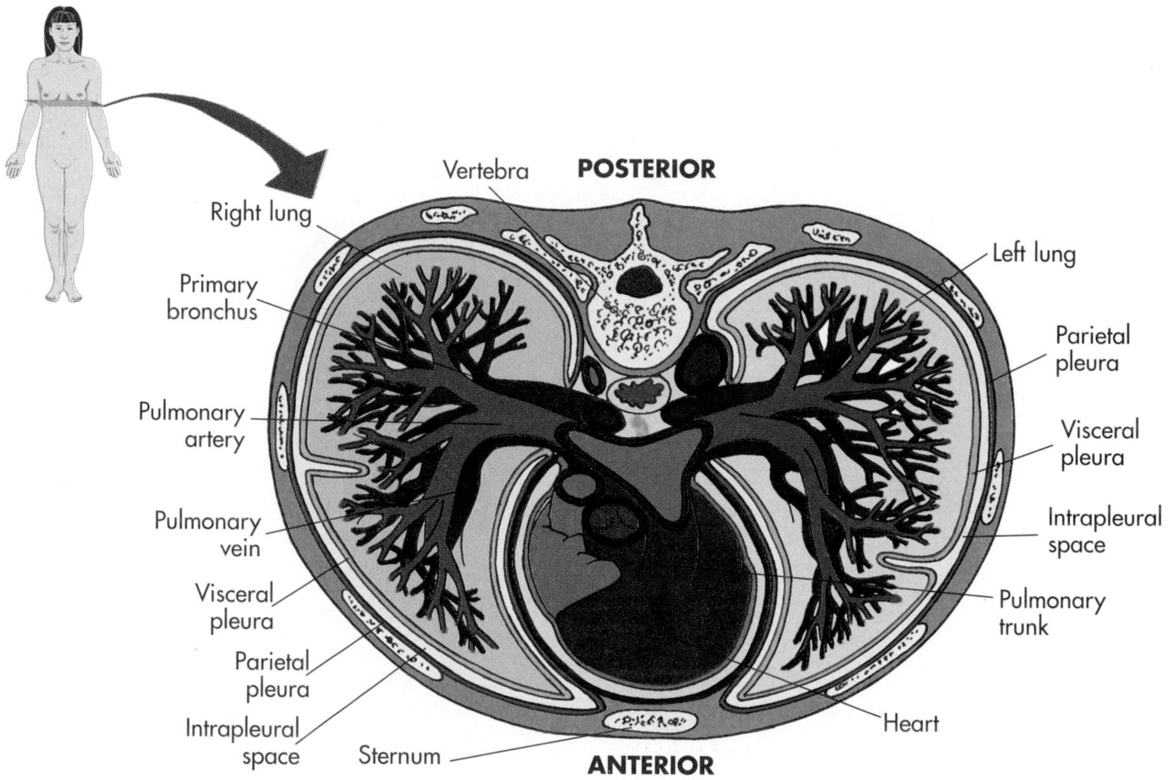

Inspiration

Inspiration occurs when the chest cavity enlarges. As the thorax enlarges, the lungs expand along with it, and air rushes into them and down into the alveoli. Muscles of respiration that are classified as **inspiratory muscles** include the **diaphragm** (DYE-a-fram) and the external intercostals. The diaphragm is the dome-shaped muscle separating the abdominal cavity from the thoracic cavity. The diaphragm flattens out when it contracts during inspiration. Instead of protruding up into the chest cavity, it moves down toward the abdominal cavity. Thus the contraction or flattening of the diaphragm makes the chest cavity longer from top to bottom. The diaphragm is the most important muscle of inspiration. Nerve impulses passing through the *phrenic nerve* stimulate the diaphragm to contract. The external intercostal muscles are located between the ribs. When they contract, they enlarge the thorax by increasing the size of the cavity from front to back and from side to side. Contraction of the inspiratory muscles increases the volume of the thoracic cavity and reduces the air pressure within it, drawing air into the lungs (Figure 13-11).

Expiration

Quiet expiration is ordinarily a passive process that begins when the inspiratory muscles relax. The thoracic cavity then returns to its smaller size.

FIGURE 13–11 ***Mechanics of Breathing.*** During *inspiration,* the diaphragm contracts, increasing the volume of the thoracic cavity. This increase in volume results in a decrease in pressure, which causes air to rush into the lungs. During *expiration,* the diaphragm returns to an upward position, reducing the volume in the thoracic cavity. Air pressure increases then, forcing air out of the lungs. The insets show the classic model in which a jar represents the rib cage, a rubber sheet represents the diaphragm, and a balloon represents the lungs.

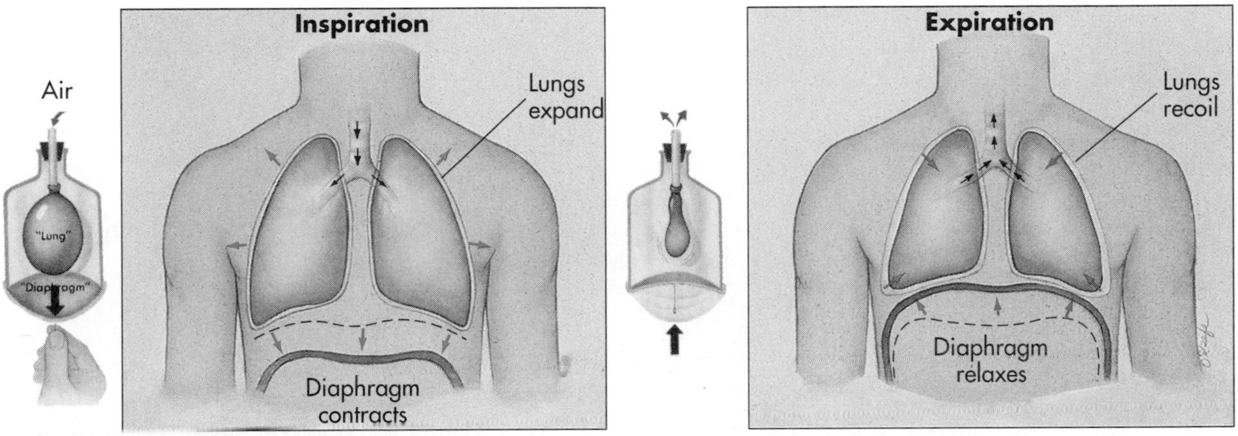

The elastic nature of lung tissue also causes these organs to "recoil" and decrease in size as air leaves the alveoli and flows outward through the respiratory passageways. When we speak, sing, or do heavy work, we may need more forceful expiration to increase the rate and depth of ventilation. During more forceful expiration, the **expiratory muscles** (internal intercostals and abdominal muscles) contract. When contracted, the internal intercostal muscles depress the rib cage and decrease the front-to-back size of the thorax. Contraction of the abdominal muscles pushes the abdominal organs against the underside of the diaphragm, thus elevating it and making it more "domeshaped." The result is to further shorten or decrease the top to bottom size of the thoracic cavity. As the thoracic cavity decreases in size, the air pressure within it increases and air flows out of the lungs (Figure 13-11).

EXCHANGE OF GASES IN LUNGS

Blood pumped from the right ventricle of the heart enters the pulmonary artery and eventually enters the lungs. It then flows through the thousands of tiny lung capillaries that are in close proximity to the air-filled alveoli (Figure 13-1). External respiration or the exchange of gases between the blood and alveolar air occurs by diffusion.

Diffusion is a passive process that results in movement down a concentration gradient; that is, substances move from an area of high concentration to an area of low concentration of the diffusing substance. Blood flowing into lung capillaries is low in oxygen. Oxygen is continually removed from the blood and used by the cells of the body. By the time it enters the lung capillaries, it is low in oxygen content. Because alveolar air is rich in oxygen, diffusion causes movement of oxygen from the area of high concentration (alveolar air) to the area of low concentration (capillary blood). Note in Figure 13-12 that most of the oxygen (O_2) entering the blood combines with hemoglobin (Hb) in the RBCs to form **oxyhemoglobin** (ok-see-HEE-mo-glo-bin) (HbO_2) so that it can be carried to the tissues and used by the body cells.

Diffusion of carbon dioxide (CO_2) also occurs between blood in lung capillaries and alveolar air.

FIGURE 13–12 ***Exchange of Gases in Lung and Tissue Capillaries.*** The left insets show O_2 diffusing out of alveolar air into blood and associating with hemoglobin (Hb) in lung capillaries to form oxyhemoglobin. In tissue capillaries, oxyhemoglobin dissociates, releasing O_2, which diffuses from the RBC and then crosses the capillary wall to reach the tissue cells. As the left insets show, CO_2 diffuses in the opposite direction (into RBCs) and some of it associates with Hb to form carbaminohemoglobin. However, most CO_2 combines with water to form carbonic acid (H_2CO_3), which dissociates to form H^+ and HCO_3^- (bicarbonate) ions. Back in the lung capillaries, CO_2 dissociates from the bicarbonate and carbaminohemoglobin molecules and diffuses out of blood into alveolar air.

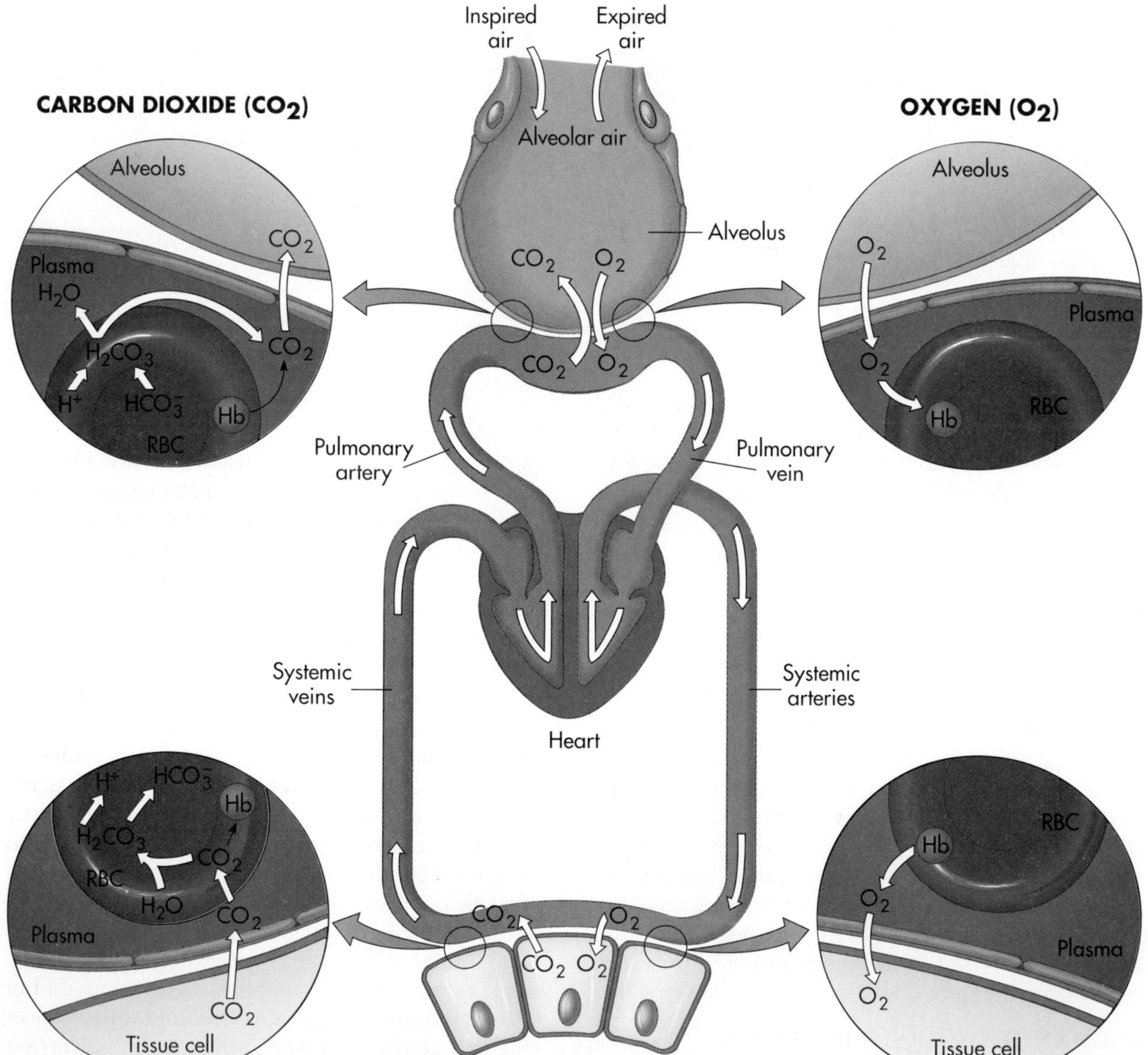

Blood flowing through the lung capillaries is high in carbon dioxide. Most carbon dioxide is carried as bicarbonate ion (HCO_3^-) in the blood. Some, as in Figure 13-12, combines with the hemoglobin in RBCs to form **carbaminohemoglobin** (kar-bam-i-no-HEE-mo-glo-bin) (HbNHCOOH). As cells remove oxygen from circulating blood, they add the waste product carbon dioxide to it. As a result, the blood in pulmonary capillaries eventually becomes low in oxygen and high in carbon dioxide. Diffusion of carbon dioxide results in its movement from an area of high concentration in the pulmonary capillaries to an area of low concentration in alveolar air. Then from the alveoli, carbon dioxide leaves the body in expired air.

EXCHANGE OF GASES IN TISSUES

The exchange of gases that occurs between blood in tissue capillaries and the body cells is called *internal respiration.* As you would expect, the direction of movement of oxygen and carbon dioxide during internal respiration is just the opposite of that noted in the exchange that occurs during external respiration when gases are exchanged between the blood in the lung capillaries and the air in alveoli. As shown in Figure 13-12, oxyhemoglobin breaks down into oxygen and hemoglobin in the tissue capillaries. Oxygen molecules move rapidly out of the blood through the tissue capillary membrane into the interstitial fluid and on into the cells that compose the tissues. The oxygen is used by the cells in their metabolic activities. Diffusion results in the movement of oxygen from an area of high concentration to an area of low concentration in the cells where it is needed. While this is happening, carbon dioxide molecules leave the cells, entering the tissue capillaries where bicarbonate ions are formed and where hemoglobin molecules unite with carbon dioxide to form carbaminohemoglobin. Once again, diffusion is responsible for the movement of carbon dioxide from an area of high concentration in the cells to an area of lower concentration in the capillary blood. In other words, oxygenated blood enters tissue capillaries and is changed into deoxygenated blood as it flows through them. In the process of losing oxygen, the waste product carbon dioxide is picked up and transported to the lungs for removal from the body.

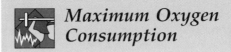

Maximum Oxygen Consumption

Exercise physiologists use **maximum oxygen consumption** ($VO_{2\ max}$) as a predictor of a person's capacity to do aerobic exercise. An individual's $VO_{2\ max}$ represents the amount of oxygen taken up by the lungs, transported to the tissues, and used to do work. $VO_{2\ max}$ is determined largely by hereditary factors, but aerobic (endurance) training can increase it by as much as 35%. Many endurance athletes are now using $VO_{2\ max}$ measurements to help them determine and then maintain their peak condition.

VOLUMES OF AIR EXCHANGED IN PULMONARY VENTILATION

A special device called a **spirometer** is used to measure the amount of air exchanged in breathing. Figure 13-13 illustrates the various pulmonary volumes, which can be measured as a subject breathes into a spirometer. We take 500 ml (about a pint) of air into our lungs with each normal inspiration and expel it with each normal expiration. Because this amount comes and goes regularly like the tides of the sea, it is referred to as the **tidal volume (TV).** The largest amount of air that we can breathe out in one expiration is known as the **vital capacity (VC).** In normal young men, this is about 4800 ml. Tidal volume and vital capacity are frequently measured in patients with lung or heart disease, conditions that often lead to abnormal volumes of air being moved in and out of the lungs.

Observe the area in Figure 13-13 that represents the **expiratory reserve volume (ERV).** This is the amount of air that can be forcibly exhaled after expiring the tidal volume. Compare this with the area in Figure 13-13 that represents the **inspiratory reserve volume (IRV).** The IRV is the amount of air that can be forcibly inspired over and above a normal inspiration. As the tidal volume

FIGURE 13–13 ***Pulmonary Ventilation Volumes.*** The chart in *A* shows a tracing like that produced with a spirometer. The diagram in *B* shows the pulmonary volumes as relative proportions of an inflated balloon (see Figure 13-11). During normal, quiet breathing, about 500 ml of air is moved into and out of the respiratory tract, an amount called the *tidal volume.* During forceful breathing (like that during and after heavy exercise), an extra 3300 ml can be inspired (the inspiratory reserve volume), and an extra 1000 ml or so can be expired (the expiratory reserve volume). The largest volume of air that can be moved in and out during ventilation is called the *vital capacity.* Air that remains in the respiratory tract after a forceful expiration is called the residual volume.

A

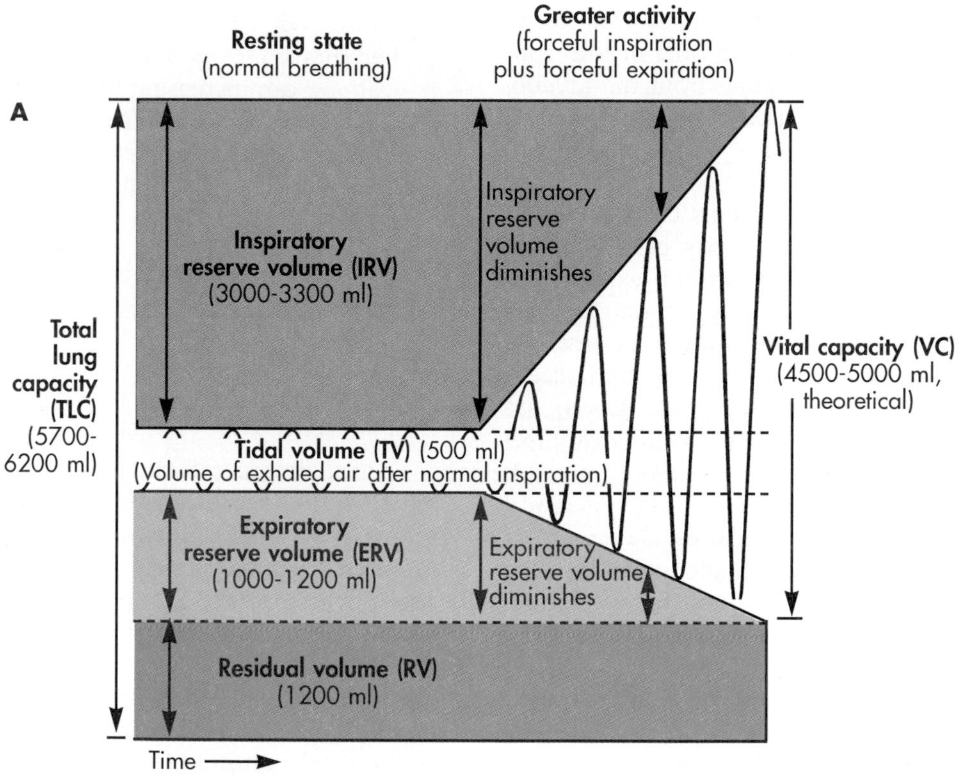

B

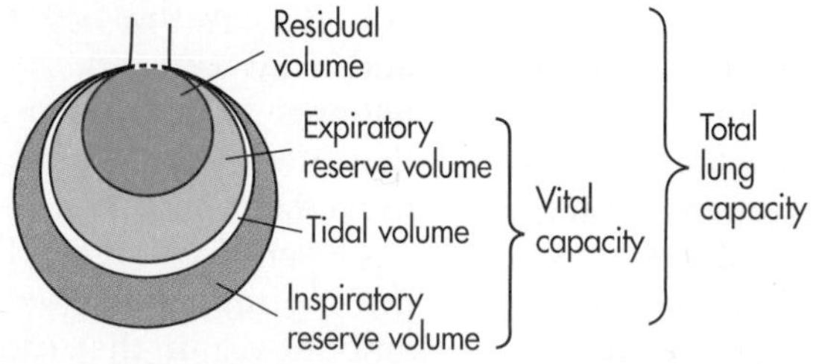

increases, the ERV and IRV decrease. Note in Figure 13-13 that vital capacity (VC) is the total of tidal volume, inspiratory reserve volume, and expiratory reserve volume—or expressed in another way: VC = TV + IRV + ERV. **Residual volume (RV)** is simply the air that remains in the lungs after the most forceful expiration.

Oxygen Therapy

Oxygen therapy is the administration of oxygen, often by a registered *respiratory therapist*, to patients suffering from **hypoxia** (hi-POK-see-a)—an insufficient oxygen supply to the tissues. Respiratory problems that involve a decrease in ventilation or a lack of effecient gas exchange in the lungs often require home treatment with oxygen therapy.

Oxygen (O_2) gas is commonly stored in and dispensed from small, green storage tanks that hold the gas under high pressure until it is used. Because the oxygen dispensed from such tanks is cold and very dry, it must first be warmed and moistened to prevent damage to the respiratory tract. This is usually done by simply bubbling the oxygen through warm water as it leaves the tank. The oxygen gas may then pass through a mask or through tubes that lead into the nasal passage (nasal prongs).

Oxygen therapy is used in a variety of home health situations. For example, the hypoxia that often accompanies chronic pulmonary disease and heart problems such as myocardial infarctions may be treated with oxygen therapy.

Regulation of Respiration

We know that the body uses oxygen to obtain energy for the work it has to do. The more work the body does, the more oxygen that must be delivered to its millions of cells. One way this is accomplished is by increasing the rate and depth of respirations. Although we may take only 12 to 18 breaths a minute when we are not moving about, we take considerably more than this when we are exercising. Not only do we take more breaths, but our tidal volume also increases.

To help supply cells with more oxygen when they are doing more work, automatic adjustments occur not only in respirations but also in circulation. Most notably, the heart beats faster and harder and therefore pumps more blood through the body each minute. This means that the millions of RBCs make more round trips between the lungs and tissues each minute and so deliver more oxygen per minute to tissue cells.

Working cells not only require more oxygen, but they also produce more waste products such as carbon dioxide and certain metabolic acids. The increase in respirations during exercise shows us how the body automatically regulates its vital functions. By increasing the rate and depth of respiration, we can adjust to the varying demands for increased oxygen while increasing the elimination of metabolic waste products in expired air to maintain homeostasis.

Normal respiration depends on proper functioning of the muscles of respiration. These muscles are stimulated by nervous impulses that originate in **respiratory control centers** located in the medulla and pons of the brain. These centers are in turn regulated by a number of inputs from receptors located in varying areas of the body. These receptors can sense the need for changing the rate or depth of respirations to maintain homeostasis. Certain receptors sense carbon dioxide or oxygen levels, whereas others sense blood acid levels or the amount of stretch in lung tissues. The two most important control centers are in the medulla and are called the **inspiratory center** and the **expiratory center.** Centers in the pons have a modifying function. Under rest conditions, neurons in the inspiratory and expiratory centers "fire" at a rate that will produce a normal breathing rate of about 12 to 18 breaths a minute.

The depth and rate of respiration can be influenced by many "inputs" to the respiratory control centers from other areas of the brain or from specialized receptors located outside of the central nervous system (Figure 13-14).

FIGURE 13–14 ***Regulation of Respiration.*** Respiratory control centers in the brain stem control the basic rate and depth of breathing. The brain stem also receives input from other parts of the body; information from chemoreceptors and stretch receptors can alter the basic breathing pattern, as can emotional and sensory input. Despite these controls, the cerebral cortex can override the "automatic" control of breathing to some extent to accomplish activities such as singing or blowing up a balloon. Green arrows show the flow of regulatory information flows into the respiratory control centers. The purple arrow shows the flow of regulatory information from the control centers to the respiratory muscles that drive breathing.

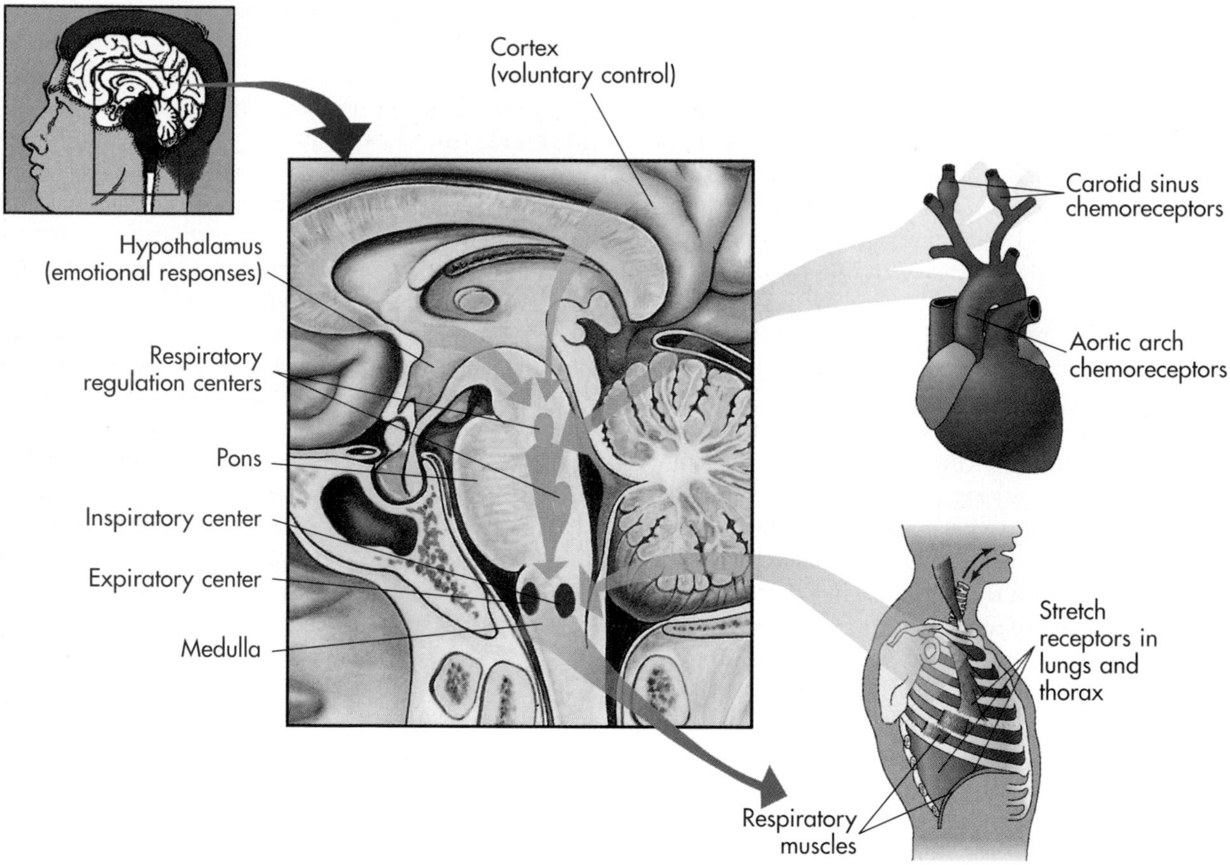

CEREBRAL CORTEX

The cerebral cortex can influence respiration by modifying the rate at which neurons "fire" in the inspiratory and expiratory centers of the medulla. In other words, an individual may voluntarily speed up or slow down the breathing rate or greatly change the pattern of respiration during activities. This ability permits us to change respiratory patterns and even to hold our breath for short periods to accommodate activities such as underwater swimming, speaking, or eating. This voluntary control of respiration, however, has limits. As indicated in a later section, other factors such as blood carbon dioxide levels are much more powerful in controlling respiration than conscious control. Regardless of cerebral intent to the contrary, we resume breathing when our bodies sense the need for more oxygen or if carbon dioxide levels increase to certain levels.

RECEPTORS INFLUENCING RESPIRATION

Chemoreceptors

Chemoreceptors (KEE-mo-ree-SEP-tors) located in the **carotid** and **aortic bodies** are specialized receptors that are sensitive to increases in blood carbon dioxide level and decreases in blood oxygen level. They also can sense and respond to increasing blood acid levels. The carotid body receptors are found at the point where the common carotid arteries divide, and the aortic bodies are small clusters of chemosensitive cells that lie adjacent to the aortic arch near the heart (Figure 13-14). When stimulated by increasing levels of blood carbon dioxide, decreasing oxygen levels, or increasing blood acidity, these receptors send nerve impulses to the respiratory regulatory centers that in turn modify respiratory rates.

Pulmonary Stretch Receptors

Specialized stretch receptors in the lungs are located throughout the pulmonary airways and in the alveoli (Figure 13-14). Nervous impulses generated by these receptors influence the normal pattern of breathing and protect the respiratory system from excess stretching caused by harmful overinflation. When the tidal volume of air has been inspired, the lungs are expanded enough to stimulate stretch receptors that then send inhibitory impulses to the inspiratory center. Relaxation of inspiratory muscles occurs, and expiration follows. After expiration, the lungs are sufficiently deflated to inhibit the stretch receptors, and inspiration is then allowed to start again.

Types of Breathing

A number of terms are used to describe breathing patterns. **Eupnea** (YOOP-nee-ah), for example, refers to a normal respiratory rate. During eupnea, the need for oxygen and carbon dioxide exchange is being met, and the individual is usually not aware of the breathing pattern. The terms **hyperventilation** and **hypoventilation** describe very rapid and deep or slow and shallow respirations, respectively. Hyperventilation sometimes results from a conscious voluntary effort preceding exertion or from psychological factors—"hysterical hyperventilation." **Dyspnea** (DISP-nee-ah) refers to labored or difficult breathing and is often associated with hypoventilation. If breathing stops completely for a brief period, regardless of cause, it is called **apnea** (AP-nee-ah). Failure to resume breathing after a period of apnea is called **respiratory arrest**.

OUTLINE SUMMARY

STRUCTURAL PLAN (Figure 13-1)

Basic plan of respiratory system would be similar to an inverted tree if it were hollow; leaves of the tree would be comparable to alveoli, with the microscopic sacs enclosed by networks of capillaries

RESPIRATORY TRACTS

A Upper respiratory tract—nose, pharynx, and larynx
B Lower respiratory tract—trachea, bronchial tree, and lungs

RESPIRATORY MUCOSA (Figure 13-3)

A Specialized membrane that lines the air distribution tubes in the respiratory tree
B Over 125 ml of mucus produced each day forms a "mucous blanket" over much of the respiratory mucosa
C Mucus serves as an air purification mechanism by trapping inspired irritants such as dust and pollen
D Cilia on mucosal cells beat in only one direction, moving mucus upward to pharynx for removal

NOSE

A Structure
  1 Nasal septum separates interior of nose into two cavities
  2 Mucous membrane lines nose
  3 Frontal, maxillary, sphenoidal, and ethmoidal sinuses drain into nose (Figure 13-4)
B Functions
  1 Warms and moistens inhaled air
  2 Contains sense organs of smell

PHARYNX

A Structure (Figure 13-5)
  1 Pharynx (throat) about 12.5 cm (5 inches) long
  2 Divided into nasopharynx, oropharynx, and laryngopharynx
  3 Two nasal cavities, mouth, esophagus, larynx, and auditory tubes all have openings into pharynx
  4 Pharyngeal tonsils and openings of auditory tubes open into nasopharynx; tonsils found in oropharynx
  5 Mucous membrane lines pharynx
B Functions
  1 Passageway for food and liquids
  2 Air distribution; passageway for air

LARYNX

A Structure (Figure 13-6)
  1 Several pieces of cartilage form framework
    a Thyroid cartilage (Adam's apple) is largest
    b Epiglottis partially covers opening into larynx
  2 Mucous lining
  3 Vocal cords stretch across interior of larynx
B Functions
  1 Air distribution; passageway for air to move to and from lungs
  2 Voice production

TRACHEA

A Structure (Figure 13-7)
  1 Tube about 11 cm ($4\frac{1}{2}$ inches) long that extends from larynx into the thoracic cavity
  2 Mucous lining
  3 C-shaped rings of cartilage hold trachea open
B Function—passageway for air to move to and from lungs
C Obstruction
  1 Blockage of trachea occludes the airway and if complete causes death in minutes
  2 Tracheal obstruction causes over 4000 deaths annually in the United States
  3 Heimlich maneuver (p. 288) is a lifesaving technique used to free the trachea of obstructions

BRONCHI, BRONCHIOLES, AND ALVEOLI

A Structure
  1 Trachea branches into right and left bronchi
  2 Each bronchus branches into smaller and smaller tubes eventually leading to bronchioles
  3 Bronchioles end in clusters of microscopic alveolar sacs, the walls of which are made up of alveoli (Figure 13-8)
B Function
  1 Bronchi and bronchioles—air distribution; passageway for air to move to and from alveoli
  2 Alveoli—exchange of gases between air and blood

LUNGS AND PLEURA

A Structure (Figure 13-9)
  1 Size—large enough to fill the chest cavity, except for middle space occupied by heart and large blood vessels
  2 Apex—narrow upper part of each lung, under collarbone
  3 Base—broad lower part of each lung; rests on diaphragm
  4 Pleura—moist, smooth, slippery membrane that lines chest cavity and covers outer surface of lungs; reduces friction between the lungs and chest wall during breathing (Figure 13-10)
B Function—breathing (pulmonary ventilation)

RESPIRATION

A Mechanics of breathing (Figure 13-11)
  1 Pulmonary ventilation includes two phases called *inspiration* (movement of air into lungs) and *expiration* (movement of air out of lungs)
  2 Changes in size and shape of thorax cause changes in air pressure within that cavity and in the lungs
  3 Air pressure differences actually cause air to move into and out of the lungs

B Inspiration
  1 Active process—air moves into lungs
  2 Inspiratory muscles include diaphragm and external intercostals
    a Diaphragm flattens during inspiration—increases top to bottom length of thorax
    b External intercostals contraction elevates the ribs and increases the size of the thorax from the front to the back and from side to side
  3 The increase in the size of the chest cavity reduces pressure within it, and air enters the lungs

C Expiration
  1 Quiet expiration is ordinarily a passive process
  2 During expiration, thorax returns to its resting size and shape
  3 Elastic recoil of lung tissues aids in expiration
  4 Expiratory muscles used in forceful expiration are internal intercostals and abdominal muscles
    a Internal intercostals—contraction depresses the rib cage and decreases the size of the thorax from the front to back
    b Contraction of abdominal muscles elevates the diaphragm, thus decreasing size of the thoracic cavity from the top to bottom
  5 Reduction in the size of the thoracic cavity increases its pressure and air leaves the lungs

D Exchange of gases in lungs (Figure 13-12)
  1 Carbaminohemoglobin breaks down into carbon dioxide and hemoglobin
  2 Carbon dioxide moves out of lung capillary blood into alveolar air and out of body in expired air
  3 Oxygen moves from alveoli into lung capillaries
  4 Hemoglobin combines with oxygen, producing oxyhemoglobin

E Exchange of gases in tissues
  1 Oxyhemoglobin breaks down into oxygen and hemoglobin
  2 Oxygen moves out of tissue capillary blood into tissue cells
  3 Carbon dioxide moves from tissue cells into tissue capillary blood
  4 Hemoglobin combines with carbon dioxide, forming carbaminohemoglobin

F Volumes of air exchanged in pulmonary ventilation (Figure 13-13)
  1 Volumes of air exchanged in breathing can be measured with a spirometer
  2 Tidal volume (TV)—amount normally breathed in or out with each breath
  3 Vital capacity (VC)—largest amount of air that one can breathe out in one expiration
  4 Expiratory reserve volume (ERV)—amount of air that can be forcibly exhaled after expiring the tidal volume
  5 Inspiratory reserve volume (IRV)—amount of air that can be forcibly inhaled after a normal inspiration
  6 Residual volume (RV)—air that remains in the lungs after the most forceful expiration
  7 Rate—usually about 12 to 18 breaths a minute; much faster during exercise

G Regulation of respiration (Figure 13-14)
  1 Regulation of respiration permits the body to adjust to varying demands for oxygen supply and carbon dioxide removal
  2 Most important central regulatory centers in medulla are called *respiratory control centers* (inspiratory and expiratory centers)
    a Under resting conditions nervous activity in the respiratory control centers produces a normal rate and depth of respirations (12 to 18 per minute)
  3 Respiratory control centers in the medulla are influenced by "inputs" from receptors located in other body areas:
    a Cerebral cortex—voluntary (but limited) control of respiratory activity
    b Chemoreceptors respond to changes in carbon dioxide, oxygen, and blood acid levels—located in carotid and aortic bodies
    c Pulmonary stretch receptors—respond to the stretch in lungs, thus protecting respiratory organs from overinflation

TYPES OF BREATHING

A Eupnea—normal breathing
B Hyperventilation—rapid and deep respirations
C Hypoventilation—slow and shallow respirations
D Dyspnea—labored or difficult respirations
E Apnea—stopped respiration
F Respiratory arrest—failure to resume breathing after a period of apnea

NEW WORDS

alveoli
aortic body
apnea
bronchi
carbaminohemoglobin
carotid body
conchae
dyspnea
eupnea
expiratory reserve volume (ERV)
Heimlich maneuver
hyperventilation
hypoventilation
inspiratory reserve volume (IRV)
larynx
oxyhemoglobin
paranasal sinuses
pharynx
pleurisy
pulmonary ventilation
residual volume (RV)
respiration
respiratory arrest
respiratory membrane
spirometer
surfactant
tidal volume (TV)
tonsillectomy
trachea
vital capacity (VC)

CHAPTER TEST

1. The exchange of gases in the respiratory system depends on the passive transport process of ______________.
2. Surface tension in the alveoli is reduced by a substance called ______________.
3. The trachea is located in the ______________ respiratory tract.
4. The portion of the pharynx located behind the mouth is called the ______________.
5. The adenoids or pharyngeal tonsils are located in the ______________.
6. The voice box is also known as the ______________.
7. During swallowing, food is prevented from entering the trachea by the ______________.
8. The presence of air in the pleural space is called ______________.
9. The exchange of gases between air in the lungs and the blood is called ______________ respiration.
10. Most oxygen entering the blood combines with hemoglobin in the RBCs to form ______________.
11. The largest amount of air we can breathe out in one expiration is known as the ______________.
12. The most important respiratory control centers are located in the ______________.
13. Gas exchange in the lung takes places across the thin, moist membranes of the ______________, which are surrounded by a dense network of capillaries.

Select the most correct answer from Column B for each statement in Column A. (Only one answer is correct.)

COLUMN A	COLUMN B
14. ______ Maximum expiration	a. Diaphragm
15. ______ "Adam's apple"	b. Thyroid cartilage
16. ______ Lines thoracic cavity	c. Chemoreceptor
17. ______ Pulmonary ventilation	d. Breathing
18. ______ Labored breathing	e. Vital capacity
19. ______ Carotid body	f. Dyspnea
20. ______ Major muscle of inspiration	g. Parietal pleura

REVIEW QUESTIONS

1. Discuss the location, microscopic structure, and functions of the respiratory mucosa.
2. List the paranasal air sinuses.
3. Discuss the functions of the nose in respiration.
4. What and where are the pharynx and larynx?
5. What structures open into the pharynx?
6. What are the anatomical subdivisions of the pharynx?
7. Where are the tonsils and adenoids located?
8. What function do the C-shaped rings of cartilage serve in the trachea?
9. What and where is the "Adam's apple"?
10. Define parietal pleura, pleural space, pleurisy, pneumothorax, and visceral pleura.
11. Do breathing and respiration mean the same thing? Define each term.
12. What does *residual volume* mean?
13. Discuss the anatomy of the "respiratory membrane."
14. Compare the structure, location, and functions of the respiratory membrane and the respiratory mucosa.
15. Discuss the Heimlich maneuver.
16. Discuss the respiratory control mechanisms.

CRITICAL THINKING

17. Why does sinusitis or middle ear infection occur so frequently after the common cold?
18. Briefly explain how oxygen and carbon dioxide can move between alveolar air, blood, and tissue cells.
19. Explain the following equation:

$$VC = TV + IRV + ERV$$

20. How can a brain hemorrhage affect the respiratory system?

The Digestive System

14

OUTLINE

Wall of the Digestive Tract

Mouth

Teeth
- Typical Tooth

Salivary Glands

Pharynx

Esophagus

Stomach

Small Intestine

Liver and Gallbladder

Pancreas

Large Intestine

Appendix

Peritoneum
- Extensions

Digestion
- Carbohydrate Digestion
- Protein Digestion
- Fat Digestion

Absorption

BOXED ESSAYS

Dental Diseases
Heartburn
Fractal Geometry of the Body
Ulcers
Exercise and Fluid Uptake
Colostomy

OBJECTIVES

After you have completed this chapter, you should be able to:

1. List in sequence each of the component parts or segments of the alimentary canal from the mouth to the anus and identify the accessory organs of digestion.
2. List and describe the four layers of the wall of the alimentary canal. Compare the lining layer in the esophagus, stomach, small intestine, and large intestine.
3. Discuss the basics of protein, fat, and carbohydrate digestion and give the end products of each process.
4. Define and contrast mechanical and chemical digestion.
5. Define: *peristalsis, bolus, chyme, jaundice, ulcer,* and *diarrhea.*

The principal structure of the **digestive system** is an irregular tube, open at both ends, called the **alimentary** (al-i-MEN-tar-ee) **canal** or the **gastrointestinal** (gas-tro-in-TES-ti-nal) **(GI) tract.** In the adult, this hollow tube is about 9 m (29 feet) long. Although this may seem strange, food or other material that enters the digestive tube is not really inside the body. Most parents of young children quickly learn that a button or pebble swallowed by their child will almost always pass unchanged and with little difficulty through the tract. Think of the tube as a passageway that extends through the body like a hallway through a building. Food must be broken down or **digested** and then absorbed through the walls of the digestive tube before it can actually enter the body and be used by cells. The breakdown or digestion of food material is both mechanical and chemical in nature. The teeth are used to physically break down food material before it is swallowed. The churning of food in the stomach then continues the mechanical breakdown process. Chemical breakdown results from the action of digestive enzymes and other chemicals acting on food as it passes through the GI tract. In chemical digestion, large food molecules are reduced to smaller molecules that can be absorbed through the lining of the intestinal wall and then distributed to body cells for use. This process of altering the chemical and physical composition of food so that it can be absorbed and used by body cells is known as *digestion,* and it is the function of the digestive system. Part of the digestive system, the large intestine, serves also as an organ of elimination, ridding the body of the waste material or **feces** resulting from the digestive process. Table 14-1 names both main and accessory digestive organs. Note that the accessory organs include the teeth, tongue, gallbladder, and appendix, as well as a number of glands that secrete their products into the digestive tube.

Foods undergo three kinds of processing in the body: **digestion, absorption,** and **metabolism.** Digestion and absorption are performed by the organs of the digestive system (Figure 14-1). Metabolism, on the other hand, is performed by all body cells. In this chapter, we shall begin by describing digestive organs and then discuss digestion and absorption. Later, in Chapter 15, we will discuss the metabolism of food after it has been absorbed.

Wall of the Digestive Tract

The digestive tract has been described as a tube that extends from the mouth to the anus. The wall of this digestive tube is fashioned of four layers of tissue (Figure 14-2). The inside or hollow space within the tube is called the **lumen.** The four layers, named from the inside coat to the outside of the tube, follow:

1. Mucosa or mucous membrane
2. Submucosa
3. Muscularis
4. Serosa

Although the same four tissue coats form the organs of the alimentary tract, their structures vary in different organs. The **mucosa** of the esophagus, for example, is composed of tough and stratified abrasion-resistant epithelium. The mucosa of the remainder of the tract is a delicate layer of simple columnar epithelium designed for absorption and secretion. The mucus produced by either type of epithelium coats the lining of the alimentary canal.

The **submucosa,** as the name implies, is a connective tissue layer that lies just below the mucosa. It contains many blood vessels and nerves. The two layers of muscle tissue called the **muscularis** have an important function in the digestive process. By a wavelike, rhythmic contraction of the muscular coat, called **peristalsis** (pair-i-STAL-sis), food material is moved through the digestive tube. In addition, the contraction of the muscularis also assists in the mixing of food with digestive juice and in the further mechanical breakdown of larger food particles.

The **serosa** is the outermost covering or coat of the digestive tube. In the abdominal cavity it is composed of the parietal peritoneum. The loops of the digestive tract are anchored to the posterior wall of the abdominal cavity by a large double fold of peritoneal tissue called the **mesentery** (MEZ-en-tair-ee).

TABLE 14–1 Organs of the Digestive System

MAIN ORGAN	ACCESSORY ORGAN	MAIN ORGAN	ACCESSORY ORGAN
Mouth	Teeth and tongue	Large intestine	Vermiform appendix
Pharynx (throat)	Salivary glands	Cecum	
Esophagus (foodpipe)	Parotid	Colon	
Stomach	Submandibular	Ascending colon	
Small intestine	Sublingual	Transverse colon	
Duodenum	Liver	Descending colon	
Jejunum	Gallbladder	Sigmoid colon	
Ileum	Pancreas	Rectum	
		Anal canal	

FIGURE 14–1 *Location of Digestive Organs.*

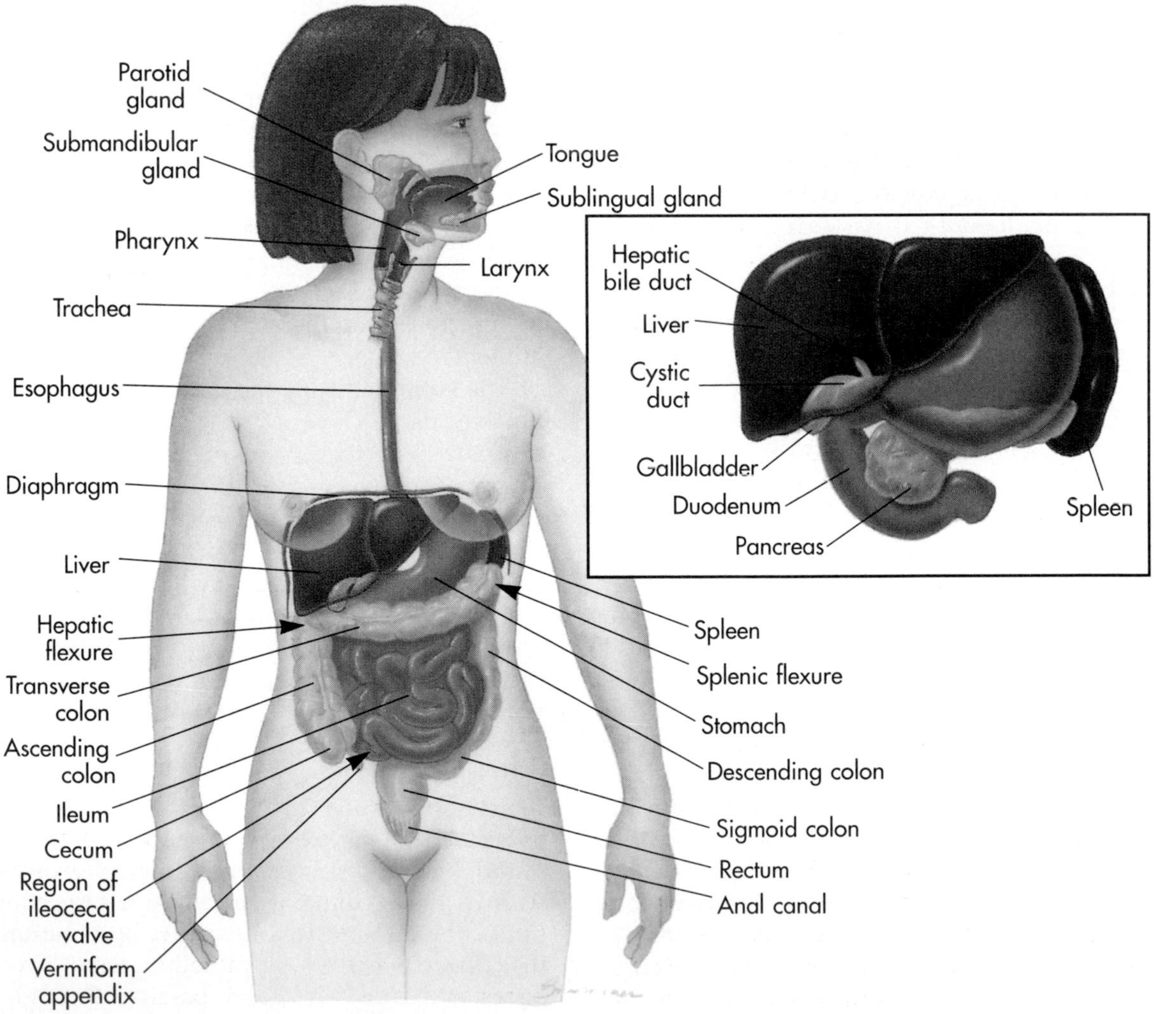

FIGURE 14–2 ***Section of the Small Intestine.*** The four layers typical of walls of the gastrointestinal tract are shown. Circular folds of mucous membrane called *plicae* increase the surface area of the lining coat.

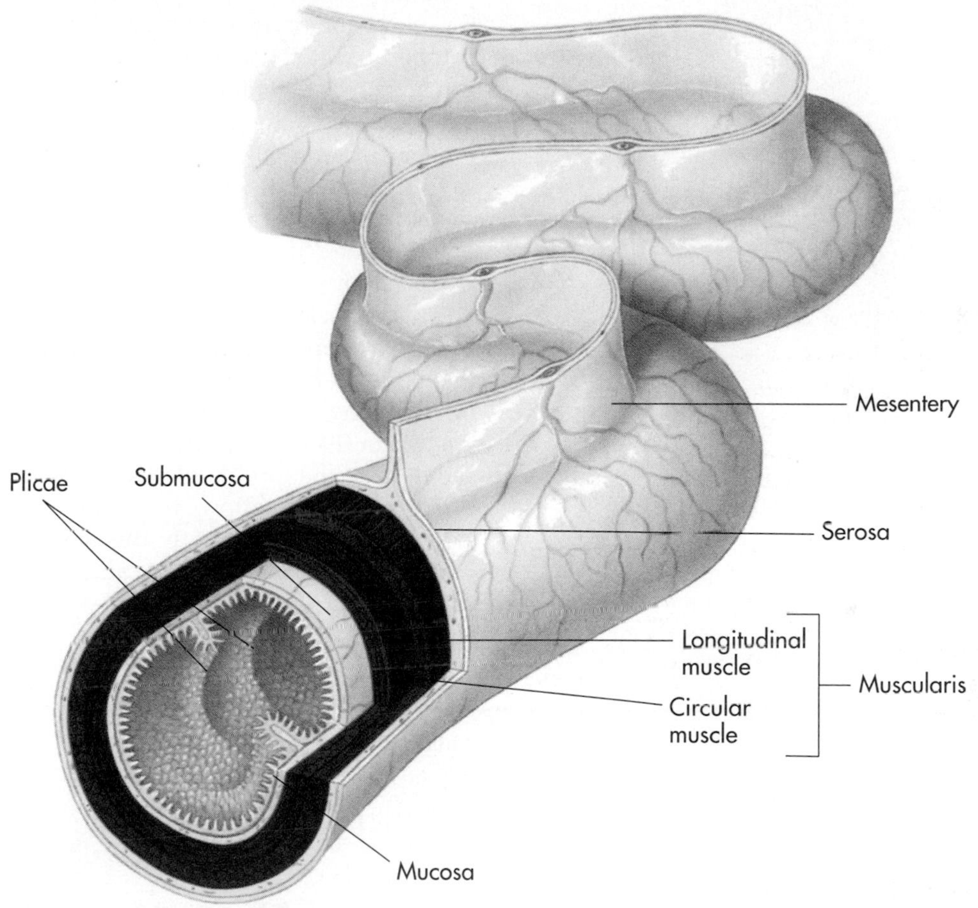

Mouth

The **mouth** or **oral cavity** is a hollow chamber with a roof, a floor, and walls. Food enters or is ingested into the digestive tract through the mouth, and the process of digestion begins immediately. Like the remainder of the digestive tract, the mouth is lined with mucous membrane. It may be helpful if you review the structure and function of mucous membranes in Chapter 4. Typically, mucous membranes line hollow organs, such as the digestive tube, that open to the exterior of the body. Mucus produced by the lining of the GI tract protects the epithelium from digestive juices and lubricates food passing through the lumen.

FIGURE 14–3 *The Mouth Cavity.*

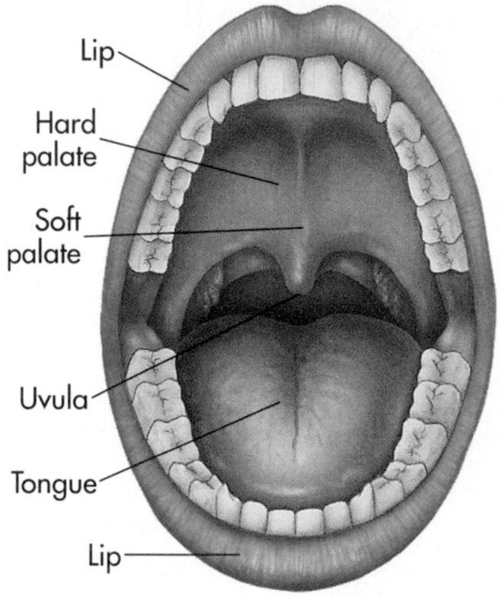

The roof of the mouth is formed by the **hard** and **soft palates** (Figure 14-3). The hard palate is a bony structure in the anterior or front portion of the mouth, formed by parts of the palatine and maxillary bones. The soft palate is located above the posterior or rear portion of the mouth. It is soft because it consists chiefly of muscle. Hanging down from the center of the soft palate is a cone-shaped process, the **uvula** (YOO-vyoo-lah). If you look in the mirror, open your mouth wide, and say "Ah," you can see your uvula. The uvula and the soft palate prevent any food and liquid from entering the nasal cavities above the mouth.

The floor of the mouth consists of the tongue and its muscles. The tongue is made of skeletal muscle covered with mucous membrane. It is anchored to bones in the skull and to the hyoid bone in the neck. A thin membrane called the **frenulum** (FREN-yoo-lum) attaches the tongue to the floor of the mouth. Occasionally the frenulum is too short to allow free movements of the tongue. Individuals with this condition cannot enunciate words normally and are said to be tongue-tied. Note in Figure 14-4 that the tongue

FIGURE 14–4 *The Tongue.* **A,** Surface. **B,** Mouth cavity showing the undersurface of the tongue.

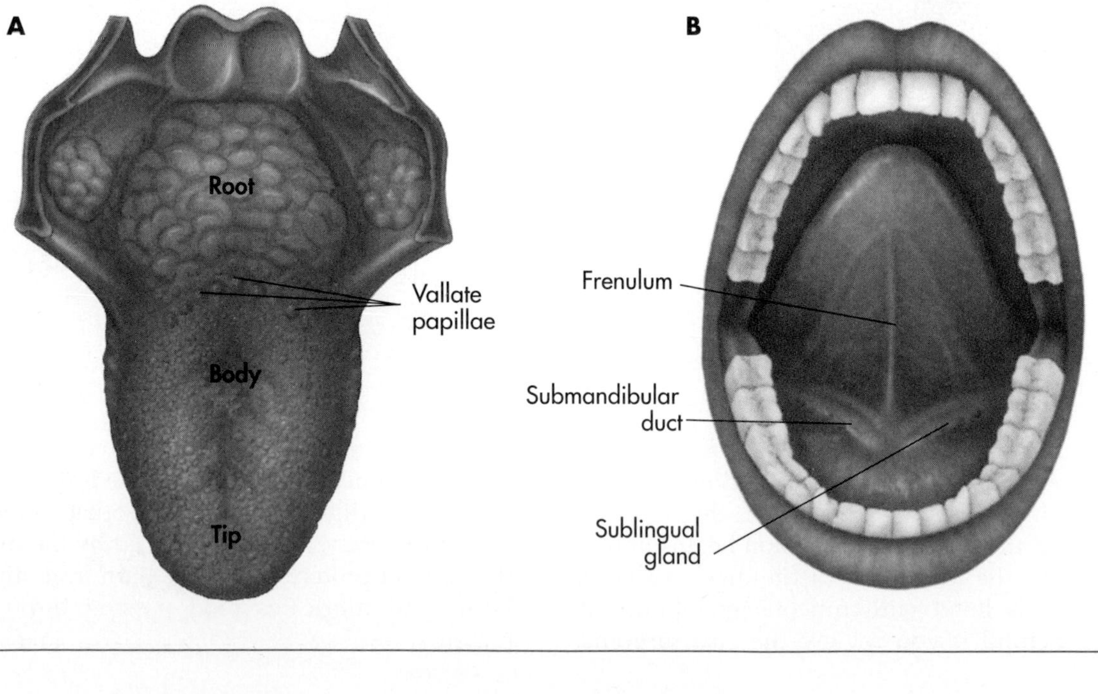

can be divided into a blunt rear portion called the *root,* a pointed *tip,* and a central *body.*

Have you ever noticed the many small elevations on the surface of your tongue? They are **papillae.** The largest are the **vallate** type; as you can see in Figure 14-4, they form an inverted V-shaped row of about 10 to 12 mushroomlike elevations. The taste buds, which contain sensory receptors for salty, sour, sweet, and bitter compounds, are located on the papillae (see Chapter 8).

Teeth

The shape and placement of the teeth assist in their functions. The four major types of teeth follow:

1. Incisors
2. Canines
3. Premolars
4. Molars

Note in Figure 14-5 that the incisors have a sharp cutting edge. They have a cutting function during **mastication** (mas-ti-KAY-shun) or chewing of food. The canine teeth are sometimes called **cuspids.** They pierce or tear the food that is being eaten. This tooth type is particularly apparent in meat-eating mammals such as dogs. Premolars or **bicuspids** and molars or **tricuspids** have rather large, flat surfaces with two or three grinding or crushing "cusps" on their surface. They provide extensive breakdown of food in the mouth. After food has been chewed, it is formed into a small rounded mass called a **bolus** (BO-lus) so that it can be swallowed.

By the time a baby is 2 years old, the child probably has his full set of 20 baby teeth. When a young adult is somewhere between 17 and 24 years old, a full set of 32 permanent teeth is generally present. The average age for cutting the first tooth is about 6 months, and the average age for losing the first baby tooth and starting to cut

FIGURE 14–5 ***The Deciduous (Baby) Teeth and Adult Teeth.*** In the deciduous set, there are no premolars and only two pairs of molars in each jaw. Generally the lower teeth erupt before the corresponding upper teeth.

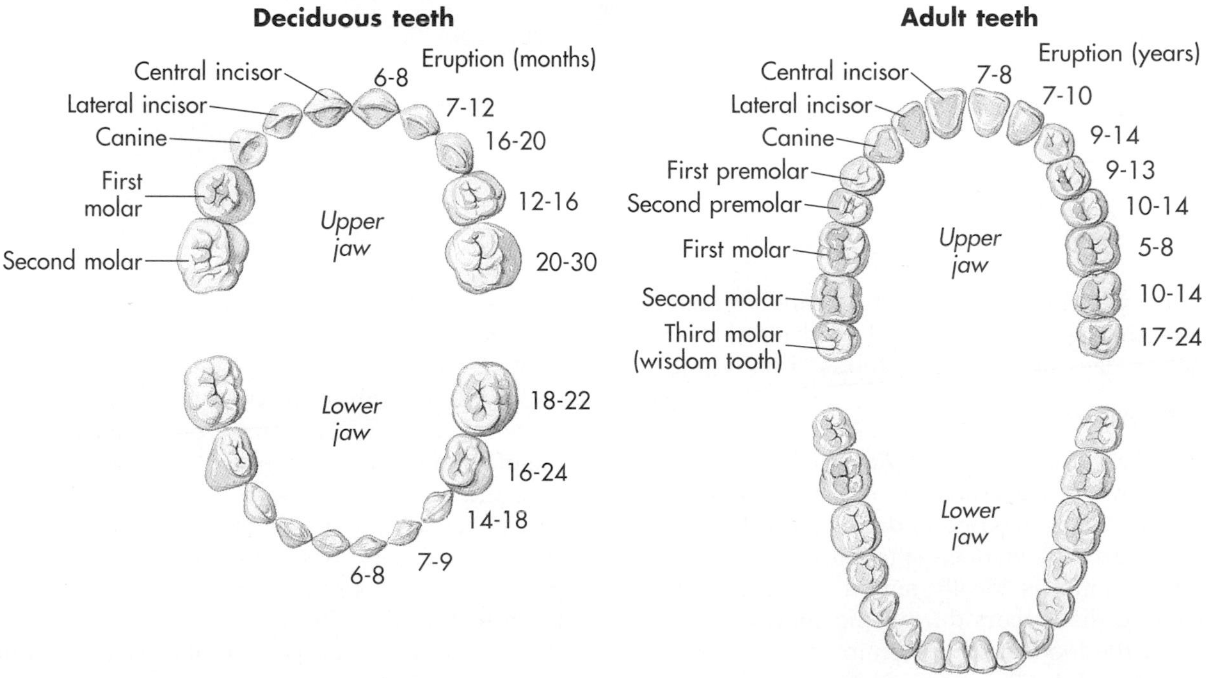

FIGURE 14–6 ***Longitudinal Section of a Tooth.*** A molar is sectioned to show its bony socket and details of its three main parts: crown, neck, and root. Enamel (over the crown) and cementum (over the neck and root) surround the dentin layer. The pulp contains nerves and blood vessels.

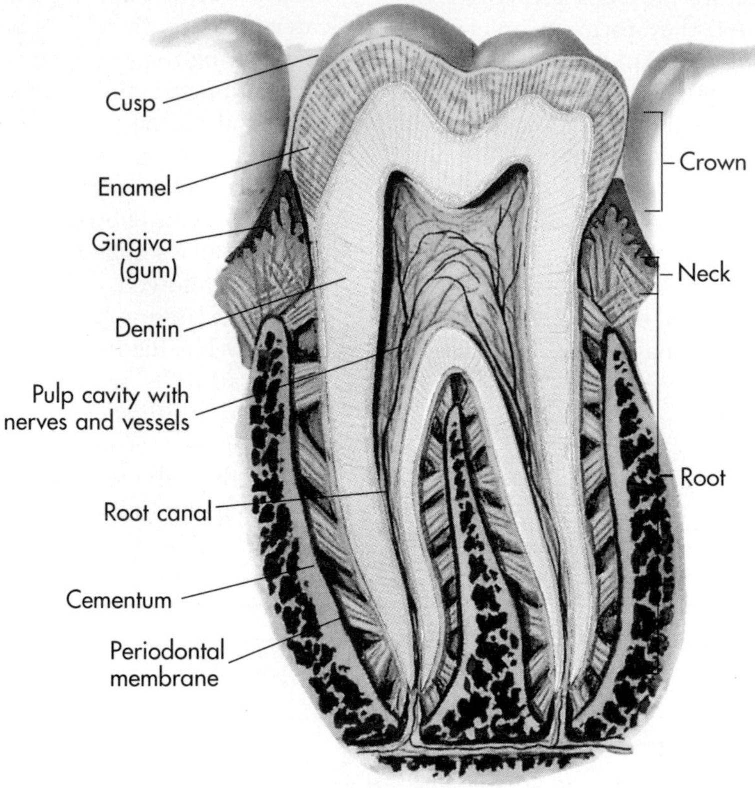

the permanent teeth is about 6 years. Figure 14-5 gives the names of the teeth and shows which ones are lacking in the deciduous or baby set.

TYPICAL TOOTH

A typical tooth can be divided into three main parts: crown, neck, and root. The **crown** is the portion that is exposed and visible in the mouth. It is covered by enamel—the hardest tissue in the body. Enamel is ideally suited to withstand the grinding that occurs during the chewing of hard and brittle foods. In addition to enamel, the outer shell of each tooth is covered by two other dental tissues—dentin and cementum (Figure 14-6). Dentin makes up the greatest proportion of the tooth shell. It is covered by enamel in the crown and by cementum in the neck and root areas. The center of the tooth contains a pulp cavity consisting of connective tissue, blood and lymphatic vessels, and sensory nerves.

The **neck** of a tooth is the narrow portion, shown in Figure 14-6, surrounded by the pink gingiva or gum tissue. It joins the crown of the tooth to the root. The **root** fits into the socket of the upper or lower jaw. A fibrous **periodontal membrane** lines each tooth socket.

Salivary Glands

Three pairs of salivary glands—the parotids, submandibulars, and sublinguals—secrete most (about 1 L) of the saliva produced each day in the adult. The salivary glands (Figure 14-7) are typical of the accessory glands associated with the digestive system. They are located outside of the digestive tube itself and must convey their secretions by way of ducts into the tract.

The **parotid glands,** largest of the salivary glands, lie just below and in front of each ear at the angle of the jaw—an interesting anatomical position because it explains why people who have mumps (an infection of the parotid gland) often complain that it hurts when they open their mouths or chew; these movements squeeze the tender, inflamed gland. To see the openings of the parotid ducts, look in a mirror at the insides of your cheeks opposite the second molar tooth on either side of the upper jaw.

The ducts of the **submandibular glands** open into the mouth on either side of the lingual frenulum (Figure 14-4). The ducts of the **sublingual glands** open into the floor of the mouth.

FIGURE 14–7 *Location of the Salivary Glands.*

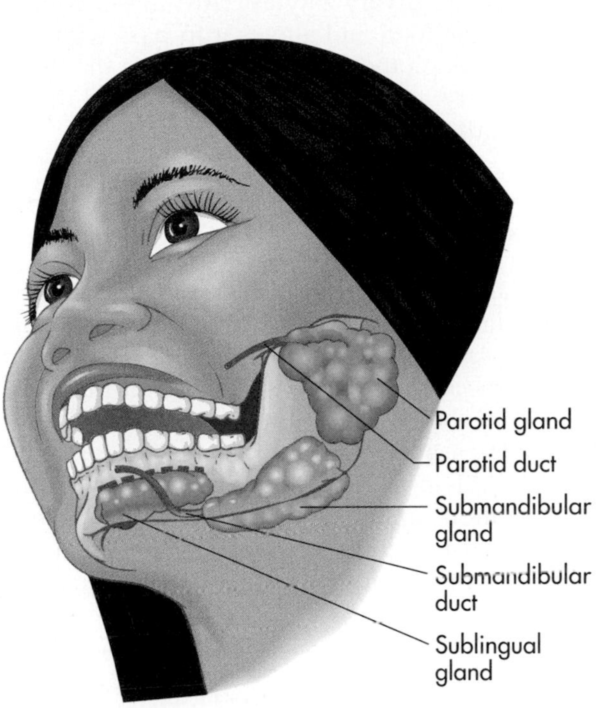

Dental Diseases

Tooth decay or dental caries is one of the most common diseases in the civilized world. It is a disease of the enamel, dentin, and cementum of teeth that results in the formation of a permanent defect called a **cavity.** Most people living in the United States, Canada, and Europe are significantly affected by the disease. Decay occurs on tooth surfaces where food debris, acid-secreting bacteria, and plaque accumulate.

Regular and thorough brushing of the teeth is important in preventing decay. Reducing dietary intake of refined sugars, which promote growth of decay bacteria, also reduces the rate of cavity formation. The introduction of fluoride to water supplies has proved to be the most effective and practical method of reducing the rate of tooth decay in children, and it is considered an important public health measure in many areas of the United States.

If the disease is untreated, tooth decay results in infection, loss of teeth, and inflammation of the soft tissues in the mouth. Bacteria may also invade the paranasal sinuses or extend to the surface of the face and neck, causing serious complications.

Saliva contains mucus and a digestive enzyme that is called **salivary amylase** (AM-i-lase). Mucus moistens the food and allows it to pass with less friction through the esophagus and into the stomach. Salivary amylase begins the chemical digestion of carbohydrates.

Pharynx

The **pharynx** is a tubelike structure made of muscle and lined with mucous membrane. Observe its location in Figure 14-1. Because of its location behind the nasal cavities and mouth, it functions as part of the respiratory and digestive systems. Air must pass through the pharynx on its way to the lungs, and food must pass through it on its way to the stomach. The pharynx as a whole is subdivided into three anatomical components, as described in Chapter 13.

Esophagus

The **esophagus** (e-SOF-ah-gus) or foodpipe is the muscular, mucus-lined tube that connects the pharynx with the stomach. It is about 25 centimeters (10 inches) long. The esophagus serves as a dynamic passageway for food, pushing the food toward the stomach.

Stomach

The **stomach** (Figure 14-8) lies in the upper part of the abdominal cavity just under the diaphragm. It serves as a pouch that food enters after it has been chewed, swallowed, and passed through the esophagus. The stomach looks small after it is emptied, not much bigger than a large sausage, but it expands considerably after a large meal. Have you ever felt so uncomfortably full after eating that you could not take a deep breath? If so, it probably meant that your stomach was so full of food that it occupied more space than usual and pushed up against the diaphragm. This made it hard for the diaphragm to contract and move downward as much as necessary for a deep breath.

Heartburn

Heartburn is often described as a burning sensation characterized by pain and a feeling of fullness beneath the sternum. It is a common problem caused by irritation of esophageal mucosa by acidic stomach contents that reenter the esophagus—a process called **reflux** (REE-fluhks). Even very small quantities of acidic stomach contents regurgitating back into the esophagus through the cardiac sphincter can cause discomfort and even inflammation. Total emptying of stomach contents back through the cardiac sphincter and ultimately up the esophagus and out of the mouth is called **vomiting** or **emesis** (EM-e-sis).

After food has entered the stomach by passing through the muscular **cardiac sphincter** (SFINGK-ter) at the end of the esophagus, the digestive process continues. Sphincters are rings of muscle tissue. The cardiac sphincter keeps food from reentering the esophagus when the stomach contracts.

Contraction of the stomach's muscular walls mixes the food thoroughly with the gastric juice and breaks it down into a semisolid mixture called **chyme** (KIME). Gastric juice contains hydrochloric acid and enzymes that function in the digestive process. Chyme formation is a continuation of the mechanical digestive process that begins in the mouth.

Note in Figure 14-8 that three layers of smooth muscle are in the stomach wall. The muscle fibers that run lengthwise, around, and obliquely make the stomach one of the strongest internal organs—well able to break up food into tiny particles and to mix them thoroughly with gastric juice to form chyme. Stomach muscle contractions result in **peristalsis,** which propels food down the digestive tract. Mucous membrane lines the stomach; it contains thousands of microscopic **gastric glands** that secrete gastric juice and hydrochloric acid into the stomach. When the stomach is empty, its lining lies in folds called **rugae.**

FIGURE 14–8 ***Stomach.*** A portion of the anterior wall has been cut away to reveal the muscle layers of the stomach wall. Notice that the mucosa lining the stomach forms folds called *rugae.*

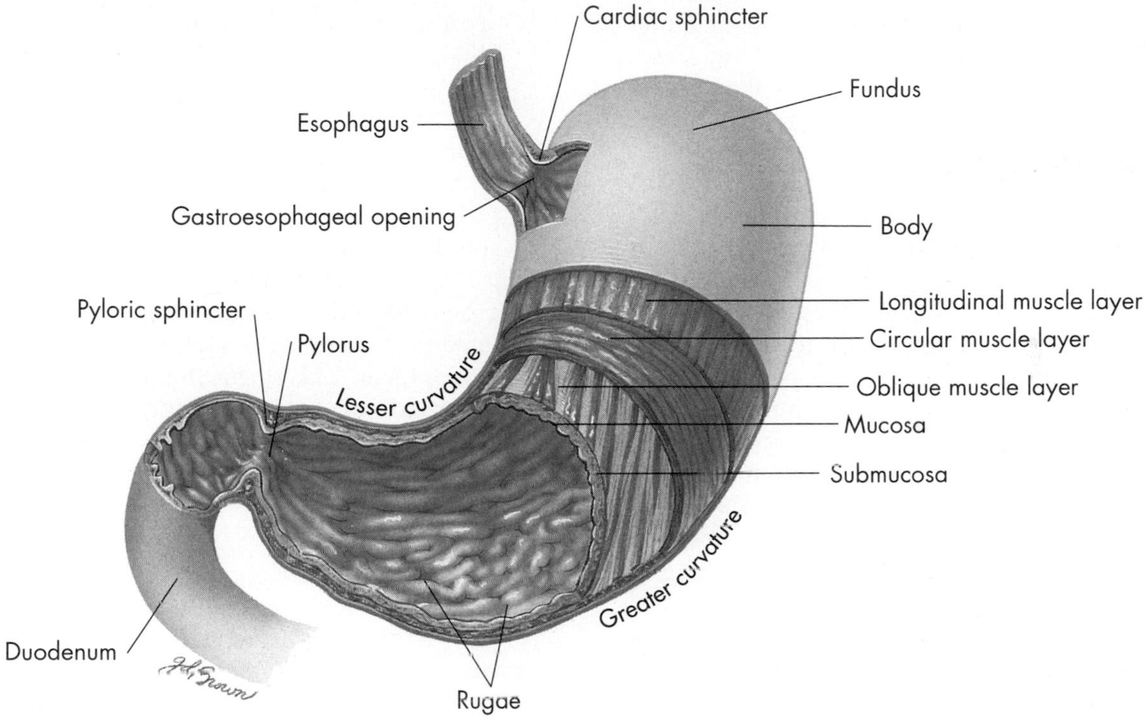

The three divisions of the stomach shown in Figure 14-8 are the **fundus, body,** and **pylorus** (pye-LOR-us). The fundus is the enlarged portion to the left of and above the opening of the esophagus into the stomach. The body is the central part of the stomach, and the pylorus is its lower narrow section, which joins the first part of the small intestine. Partial digestion occurs after food is held in the stomach by the **pyloric** (pi-LOR-ik) **sphincter** muscle. The smooth muscle fibers of the sphincter stay contracted most of the time and thereby close off the opening of the pylorus into the small intestine. Note also in Figure 14-8 that the upper right border of the stomach is known as the **lesser curvature,** and the lower left border is called the **greater curvature.** After food has been mixed in the stomach, chyme begins its passage through the pyloric sphincter into the first part of the small intestine.

Fractal Geometry of the Body

Biologists have just begun applying the principles of the new field of **fractal geometry** to human anatomy. Specialists in fractal geometry study surfaces with a seemingly infinite area, such as the lining of the small intestine. Fractal surfaces have bumps that have bumps that have bumps, and so on. The fractal nature of the intestinal lining is represented in Figure 14-9. The plicae (folds) have villi, the villi have microvilli, and even the microvilli have bumps that cannot be seen in the figure. Thus, the absorptive surface area of the small intestine is almost limitless.

Ulcers

An **ulcer** is a craterlike wound in a membrane caused by tissue destruction. The two most common sites for GI ulcers are the stomach (gastric ulcers) and the duodenum (duodenal ulcers). Both sites are regularly exposed to high levels of hydrochloric acid from the stomach. Excessive secretion of acid or **hyperacidity** is an important factor in the formation of ulcers. If the acid is not neutralized by other substances in chyme or stopped by the protective mucus, it destroys enough tissue to perforate the wall of the stomach or duodenum. This can lead to massive hemorrhage and widespread inflammation of the abdominal cavity and its contents. Even if the ulcer does not perforate the wall, episodes of moderate bleeding can eventually cause anemia. Until recently, drugs such as cimetidine (Tagamet) that reduce secretion of hydrochloric acid were a primary treatment. However, recent research shows that in many cases hyperacidity is only partly to blame. The basic cause seems to be a spiral-shaped bacterium called *Helicobacter pylori*. This bacterium burrows through the protective mucus lining the GI tract and impairs the lining's ability to produce more mucus. This opens the way for stomach acid to begin its ulcer-producing attack. Many ulcer treatments now center around antibiotics that inhibit the *H. pylori* bacterium.

Small Intestine

The **small intestine** seems to be misnamed if you look at its length—it is roughly 7 meters (20 feet) long. However, it is noticeably smaller in diameter than the large intestine, so in this respect its name is appropriate. Different names identify different sections of the small intestine. In the order in which food passes through them, they are the **duodenum** (doo-o-DEE-num), **jejunum**, (je-JOO-num), and **ileum** (IL-ee-um).

The mucous lining of the small intestine, like that of the stomach, contains thousands of microscopic glands. These **intestinal glands** secrete the intestinal digestive juice. Another structural feature of the lining of the small intestine makes it especially well suited to absorption of food and water; it is not perfectly smooth, as it appears to the naked eye. Instead, the intestinal lining is arranged into multiple circular folds called **plicae** (PLYE-kee) (Figures 14-2 and 14-9). These folds are themselves covered with thousands of tiny "fingers" called **villi** (VILL-eye). Under the microscope, the villi can be seen projecting into the hollow interior of the intestine. Inside each villus lies a rich network of blood capillaries that absorb the products of carbohydrate and protein digestion (sugars and amino acids). Millions and millions of villi jut inward from the mucous lining. Imagine the lining as perfectly smooth without any villi; think how much less surface area there would be for contact between capillaries and intestinal lining. Consider what an advantage a large contact area offers for faster absorption of food from the intestine into the blood and lymph—one more illustration that structure and function are intimately related.

Note also in Figure 14-9 that each villus in the intestine contains a lymphatic vessel or **lacteal** that absorbs lipid or fat materials from the chyme passing through the small intestine. In addition to the thousands of villi that increase surface area in the small intestine, each villus is itself covered by epithelial cells, which have a brushlike border composed of **microvilli.** The microvilli further increase the surface area of each villus for absorption of nutrients.

FIGURE 14–9 ***The Small Intestine.*** Note that the folds of mucosa are covered with villi and that each villus is covered with epithelium, which increases the surface area for absorption of food.

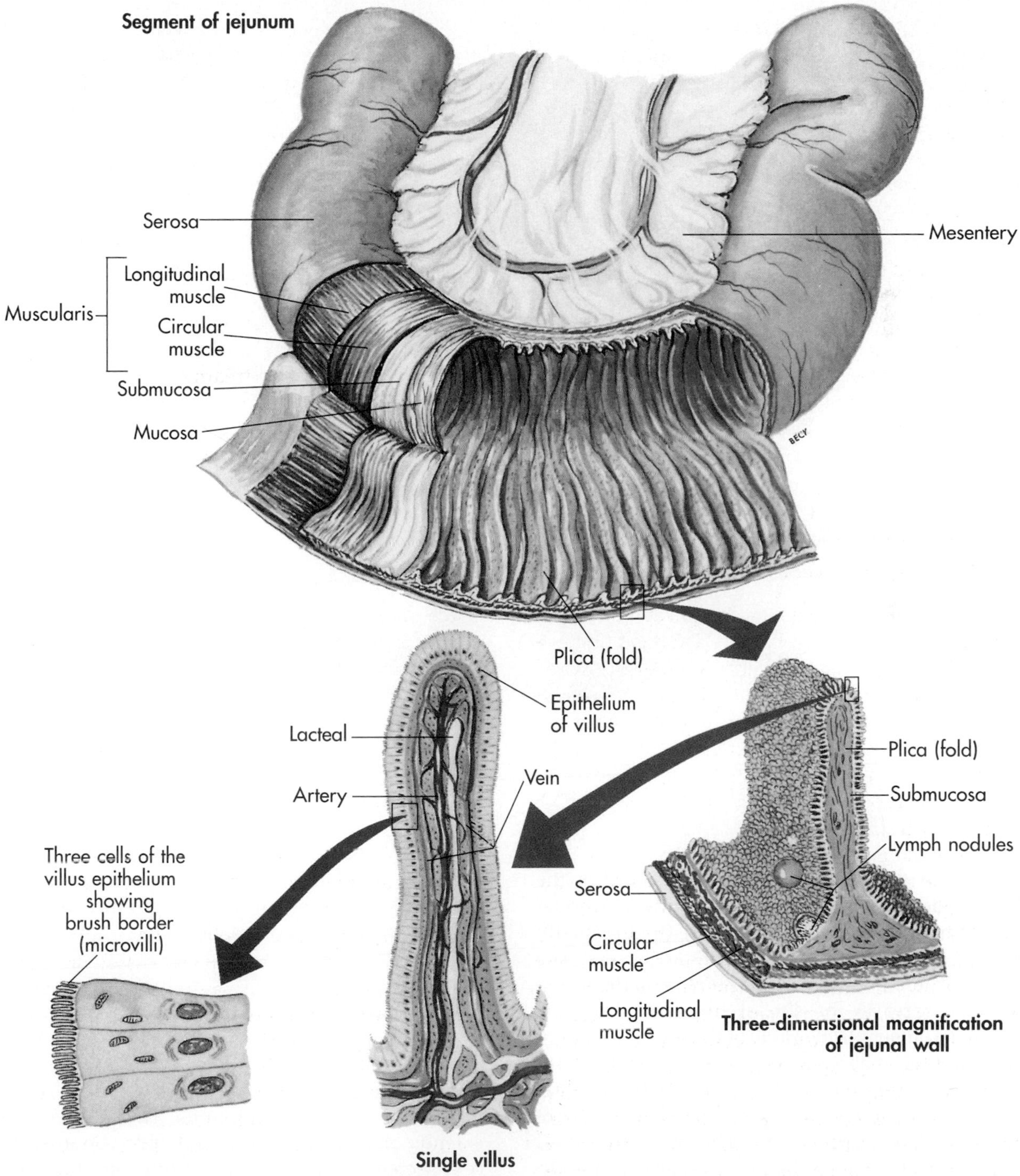

FIGURE 14–10 ***The Gallbladder and Bile Ducts.*** Obstruction of the hepatic or common bile duct by stone or spasm blocks the exit of bile from the liver, where it is formed, and prevents bile from being ejected into the duodenum.

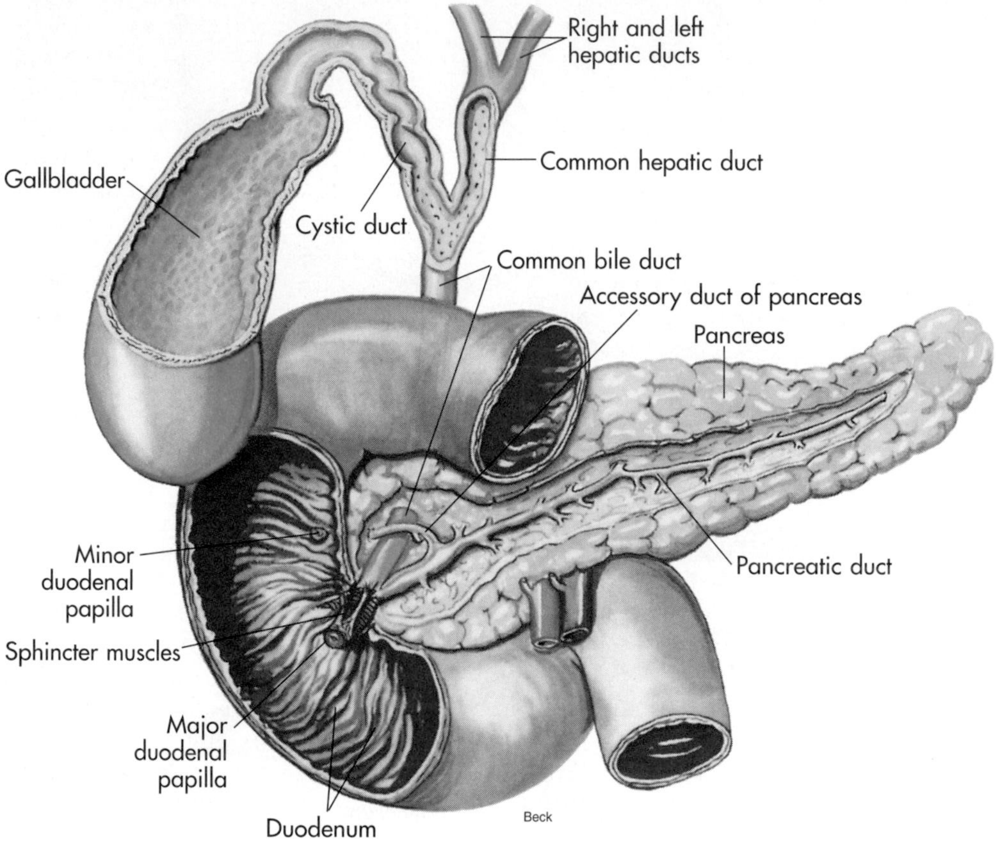

Most of the chemical digestion occurs in the first subdivision of the small intestine or duodenum. The duodenum is C shaped (Figure 14-10) and curves around the head of the pancreas. The acid chyme enters the duodenum from the stomach. This area is the site of frequent ulceration (duodenal ulcers.) The middle third of the duodenum contains the openings of ducts that empty pancreatic digestive juice and bile from the liver into the small intestine. As you can see in Figure 14-10, the two openings are called the **minor** and **major duodenal papillae.** Occasionally a gallstone blocks the major duodenal papilla, causing symptoms such as severe pain, jaundice, and digestive problems. Smooth muscle in the wall of the small intestine contracts to produce peristalsis, the wavelike contraction that moves food through the tract.

Liver and Gallbladder

The liver is so large that it fills the entire upper right section of the abdominal cavity and even extends partway into the left side. Because its cells secrete a substance called **bile** into ducts, the liver is classified as an exocrine gland; in fact, it is the largest gland in the body.

Exercise and Fluid Uptake

Replacement of fluids lost during exercise, primarily through sweating, is essential for maintaining homeostasis. Nearly everyone increases his or her intake of fluids during and after exercise. The main limitation to efficient fluid replacement is how quickly fluid can be absorbed, rather than how much a person drinks. Very little water is absorbed until it reaches the intestines, where it is absorbed almost immediately. Thus the rate of **gastric emptying** into the intestine is critical.

Large volumes of fluid leave the stomach and enter the intestines more rapidly than small volumes. However, large volumes may be uncomfortable during exercise. Cool fluids (8° to 13° C) empty more quickly than warm fluids. Fluids with a high solute concentration empty slowly and may cause nausea or stomach cramps. Thus large amounts of cool, dilute, or isotonic fluids are best for replacing fluids quickly during exercise.

The duration of exercise does not affect gastric emptying, but the intensity can. Strenuous exercise practically shuts down gastric emptying. Thus the harder you work, the harder it is to replace lost fluids.

Look again at Figure 14-10. First, identify the hepatic ducts. They drain bile out of the liver, a fact suggested by the name "hepatic," which comes from the Greek word for liver *(hepar)*. Next, notice the duct that drains bile into the small intestine (duodenum), the common bile duct. It is formed by the union of the common hepatic duct with the cystic duct.

Because fats form large globules, they must be broken down into smaller particles to increase the surface area for digestion. This is the function of bile. It mechanically breaks up or **emulsifies** (e-MUL-se-fi) fats. When chyme containing lipid or fat enters the duodenum, it initiates a mechanism that contracts the gallbladder and forces bile into the small intestine. Fats in chyme stimulate or "trigger" the secretion of the hormone **cholecystokinin** (ko-le-sis-toe-KYE-nin) or **CCK** from the intestinal mucosa of the duodenum. This hormone then stimulates the contraction of the gallbladder, and bile flows into the duodenum. Between meals, a lot of bile moves up the cystic duct into the gallbladder on the undersurface of the liver. The gallbladder thus concentrates and stores bile produced in the liver.

Visualize a gallstone blocking the common bile duct shown in Figure 14-10. Bile could not then drain into the duodenum. Feces would then appear gray-white because the pigments from bile give feces its characteristic color. Furthermore, excessive amounts of bile would be absorbed into the blood. A yellowish skin discoloration called **jaundice** (JAWN-dis) would result. Obstruction of the common hepatic duct also leads to jaundice. Because bile cannot then drain out of the liver, excessive amounts of it are absorbed. Because bile is not resorbed from the gallbladder, no jaundice occurs if the cystic duct is blocked.

Pancreas

The pancreas lies behind the stomach in the concavity produced by the C shape of the duodenum. It is an exocrine gland that secretes pancreatic juice into ducts and an endocrine gland that secretes hormones into the blood. Pancreatic juice is the most important digestive juice. It contains enzymes that digest all three major kinds of foods. It also contains sodium bicarbonate, an alkaline substance that neutralizes the hydrochloric acid in the gastric juice that enters the intestines. Pancreatic juice enters the duodenum of the small intestine at the same place that bile enters. As you can see in Figure 14-10, the common bile and pancreatic ducts open into the duodenum at the major duodenal papilla.

FIGURE 14–11 ***Horizontal (Transverse) Section of the Abdomen.*** The photograph of a cadaver section shows the relative position of some of the major digestive organs of the abdomen. Such a view is typical in newer imaging methods such as computed tomography (CT) scanning and magnetic resonance imaging (MRI).

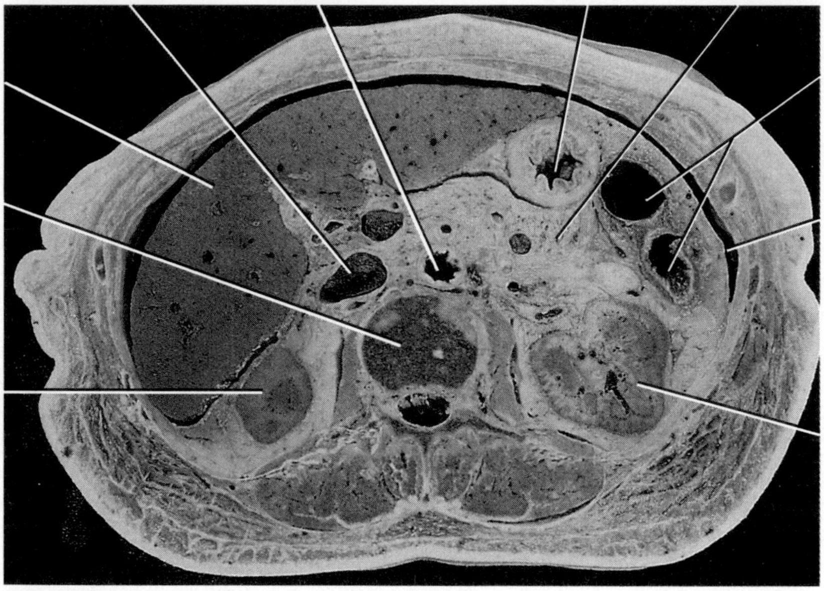

Between the cells that secrete pancreatic juice into ducts lie clusters of cells that have no contact with any ducts. These are the pancreatic islets (of Langerhans), which secrete the hormones of the pancreas described in Chapter 9. Locate the pancreas and nearby structures in Figure 14-11, which shows a transverse section of a human cadaver.

Large Intestine

The **large intestine** is only about 1.5 meters (5 feet) in length. As the name implies, it has a much larger diameter than the small intestine. It forms the lower or terminal portion of the digestive tract. Undigested and unabsorbed food material enters the large intestine after passing through a sphincterlike structure (Figure 14-12) called the **ileocecal** (il-ee-o-SEE-kal) **valve.** The word *chyme* is no longer appropriate in describing the contents of the large intestine. Chyme, which has the consistency of soup and is found in the small intestine, changes to the consistency of fecal matter as water and salts are reabsorbed during its passage through the small intestine. During its movement through the large intestine, material that escaped digestion in the small intestine is acted upon by bacteria. As a result of this bacterial action, additional nutrients may be released from cellulose and other fibers and absorbed. In addition to their digestive role, bacteria in the large intestine have other important functions. They are responsible for the synthesis of vitamin K needed for normal blood clotting and for the production of some of the B-complex vitamins. Once formed, these vitamins are absorbed from the large intestine and enter the blood.

FIGURE 14–12 *Divisions of the Large Intestine.*

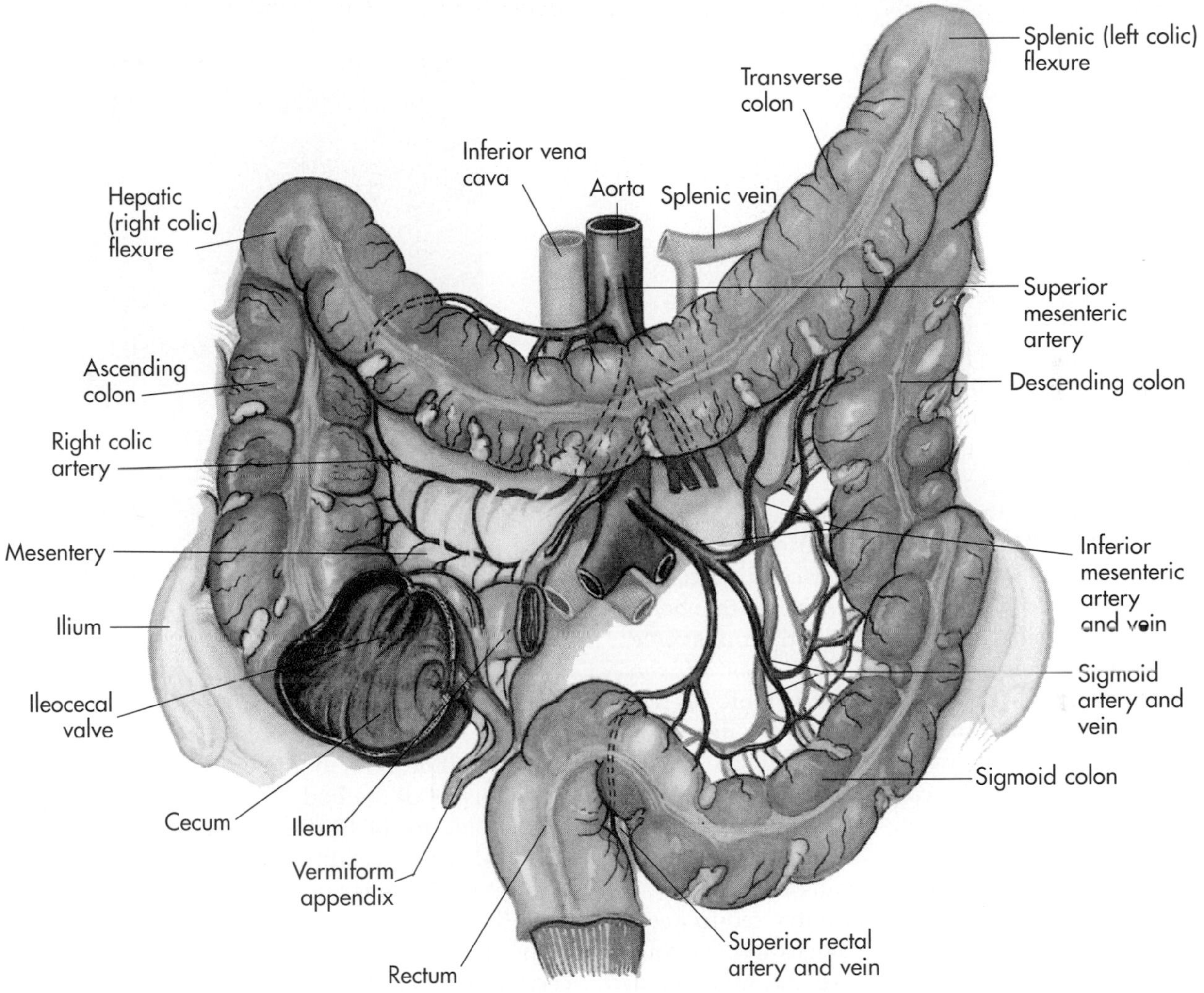

Although some absorption of water, salts, and vitamins occurs in the large intestine, this segment of the digestive tube is not as well suited for absorption as is the small intestine. Salts, especially sodium, are absorbed by active transport, and water is moved into the blood by osmosis. No villi are present in the mucosa of the large intestine. As a result, much less surface area is available for absorption, and the efficiency and speed of movement of substances through the wall of the large intestine is lower than in the small intestine. Normal passage of material through the large intestine takes about 3 to 5 days. If the rate of passage of material quickens, the consistency of the stools or fecal material becomes more and more fluid, and **diarrhea** (dye-ah-REE-ah) results. If the time of passage through the large intestine is prolonged beyond 5 days, the feces lose volume and becomes more solid because of excessive water absorption. This reduces stimulation of the bowel emptying reflex, resulting in retention of feces, a condition called **constipation.**

The subdivisions of the large intestine are listed below in the order in which food passes through them.

1. Cecum
2. Ascending colon
3. Transverse colon
4. Descending colon
5. Sigmoid colon
6. Rectum
7. Anal canal

These areas can be studied and identified by tracing the passage of material from its point of entry into the large intestine at the ileocecal valve to its elimination from the body through the external opening called the **anus.**

Note in Figure 14-12 that the ileocecal valve opens into a pouchlike area called the **cecum** (SEE-kum). The opening itself is about 5 or 6 cm (2 inches) above the beginning of the large intestine. Food residue in the cecum flows upward on the right side of the body in the **ascending colon.** The **hepatic** or **right colic flexure** is the bend between the ascending colon and the **transverse colon,** which extends across the front of the abdomen from right to left. The **splenic** or **left colic flexure** marks the point where the **descending colon** turns downward on the left side of the abdomen. The **sigmoid colon** is the S-shaped segment that terminates in the **rectum.** The terminal portion of the rectum is called the **anal canal,** which ends at the external opening or anus.

Two sphincter muscles stay contracted to keep the anus closed except during defecation. Smooth or involuntary muscle composes the **inner anal sphincter,** but striated, or voluntary, muscle composes the outer one. This anatomical fact sometimes becomes highly important from a practical standpoint. For example, often after a person has had a stroke, the voluntary anal sphincter at first becomes paralyzed. This means, of course, that the individual has no control at this time over bowel movements.

Appendix

The **vermiform appendix** (Latin *vermiformis* from *vermis* "worm" and *forma* "shape") is, as the name implies, a wormlike, tubular structure. Although

FIGURE 14–13 ***The Large Intestine.*** A special x-ray technique produces a clear image of the large intestine and its position relative to the skeleton.

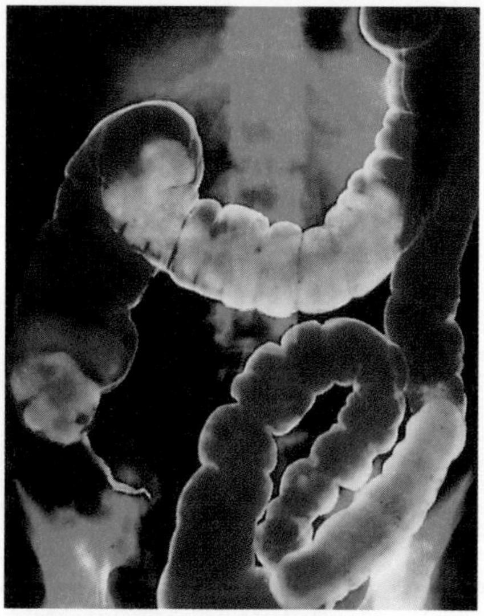

it serves no important digestive function in humans, it contains lymphatic tissue and may play a minor role in the immunologic defense mechanisms of the body described in Chapter 12. Note in Figure 14-12 that the appendix is directly attached to the cecum. The appendix contains a blind, tubelike interior lumen that communicates with the lumen of the large intestine 3 cm (1 inch) below the opening of the ileocecal valve into the cecum. If the mucous lining of the appendix becomes inflamed, the resulting condition is the well-known affliction, **appendicitis.** As you can see in Figures 14-12 and 14-13, the appendix is very close to the rectal wall. For patients with suspected appendicitis, a physician often evaluates the appendix by a digital rectal examination.

Peritoneum

The **peritoneum** is a large, moist, slippery sheet of serous membrane that lines the abdominal cavity and covers the organs located in it, including most of the digestive organs. The parietal layer of the peritoneum lines the abdominal cavity. The

FIGURE 14–14 ***The Peritoneum.*** The parietal layer of the peritoneum lines the abdominopelvic cavity, and then extends as a series of mesenteries to form the visceral layer that covers abdominal organs.

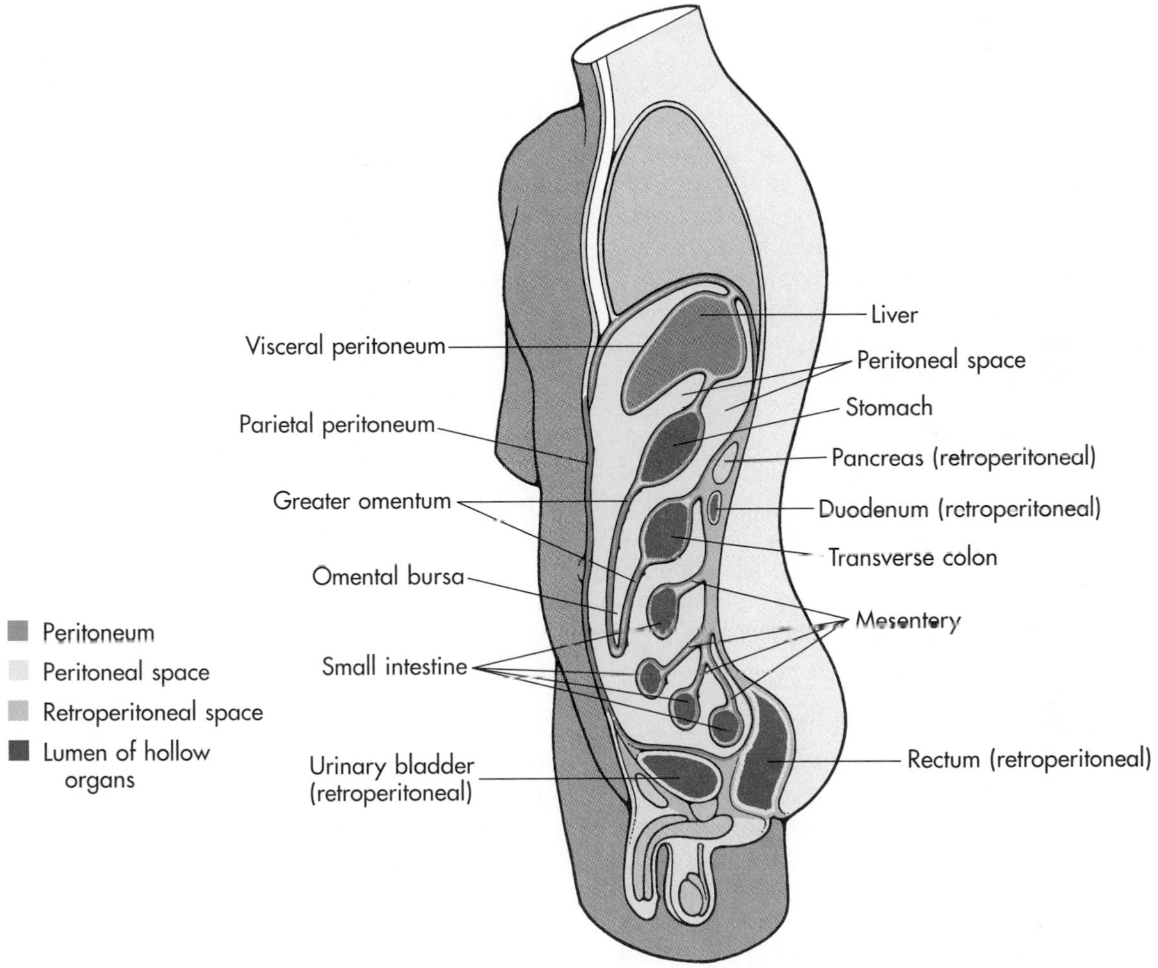

visceral layer of the peritoneum forms the outer or covering layer of each abdominal organ. The small space between the parietal and visceral layers is called the *peritoneal space.* It contains just enough peritoneal fluid to keep both layers of the peritoneum moist and able to slide freely against each other during breathing and digestive movements (Figure 14-14). Organs outside of the peritoneum are said to be retroperitoneal.

EXTENSIONS

The two most prominent extensions of the peritoneum are the mesentery and the greater omentum. The **mesentery,** an extension between the parietal and visceral layers of the peritoneum, is shaped like a giant, pleated fan. Its smaller edge attaches to the lumbar region of the posterior abdominal wall, and its long, loose outer edge encloses most of the small intestine, anchoring it to the posterior abdominal wall. The **greater omentum** is a pouchlike extension of the visceral peritoneum from the lower edge of the stomach, part of the duodenum, and the transverse colon. Shaped like a large apron, it hangs down over the intestines, and because spotty deposits of fat give it a lacy appearance, it has been nicknamed the *lace apron.* It usually envelops a badly inflamed appendix, walling it off from the rest of the abdominal organs.

Digestion

Digestion, a complex process that occurs in the alimentary canal, consists of physical and chemical changes that prepare food for absorption. **Mechanical digestion** breaks food into tiny particles, mixes them with digestive juices, moves them along the alimentary canal, and finally eliminates the digestive wastes from the body. Chewing or mastication, swallowing or **deglutition** (deg-loo-TISH-un), peristalsis, and defecation are the main processes of mechanical digestion. **Chemical digestion** breaks down large, nonabsorbable food molecules into smaller, absorbable molecules—molecules that are able to pass through the intestinal mucosa into blood and lymph. Chemical digestion consists of numerous chemical reactions catalyzed by enzymes in saliva, gastric juice, pancreatic juice, and intestinal juice.

CARBOHYDRATE DIGESTION

Very little digestion of carbohydrates (starches and sugars) occurs before food reaches the small intestine. Salivary amylase usually has little time to do its work because so many of us swallow our food so fast. Gastric juice contains no carbohydrate-digesting enzymes. But after the food reaches the small intestine, pancreatic and intestinal juice enzymes digest the starches and sugars. A pancreatic enzyme (amylase) starts the process by changing starches into a double sugar, namely, maltose. Three intestinal enzymes—maltase, sucrase, and lactase—digest double sugars by changing them into simple sugars, chiefly glucose (dextrose). Maltase digests maltose (malt sugar), sucrase digest sucrose (ordinary cane sugar), and lactase digests lactose (milk sugar). The end products of carbohydrate digestion are the so-called simple sugars; the most abundant is glucose.

PROTEIN DIGESTION

Protein digestion starts in the stomach. Two enzymes (rennin and pepsin) in the gastric juice cause the giant protein molecules to break up into somewhat simpler compounds. Pepsinogen, a component of gastric juice, is converted into active pepsin enzyme by hydrochloric acid (also in gastric juice). In the intestine, other enzymes (trypsin in the pancreatic juice and peptidases in the intestinal juice) finish the job of protein digestion. Every protein molecule is made up of many amino acids joined together. When enzymes have split up the large protein molecule into its separate amino acids, protein digestion is completed. Hence the end product of protein digestion is amino acids. For obvious reasons, the amino acids are also referred to as *protein building blocks.*

FAT DIGESTION

Very little carbohydrate and fat digestion occurs before food reaches the small intestine. Most fats are undigested until after emulsification by bile in the duodenum (that is, fat droplets are broken into very small droplets). After this takes place, pancreatic lipase splits up the fat molecules into fatty acids and glycerol (glycerin). The end products of fat digestion, then, are fatty acids and glycerol.

Table 14-2 summarizes the main facts about chemical digestion. Enzyme names indicate the type of food digested by the enzyme. For example, the name *amylase* indicates that the enzyme digests carbohydrates (starches and sugars), *protease* indicates a protein-digesting enzyme, and *lipase* means a fat-digesting enzyme. When carbohydrate digestion has been completed, starches (polysaccharides) and double sugars (disaccharides) have been changed mainly to glucose, a simple sugar (monosaccharide). The end products of protein digestion, on the other hand, are amino acids. Fatty acid and glycerol are the end products of fat digestion.

Absorption

After food is digested, it is absorbed; that is, it moves through the mucous membrane lining of the small intestine into the blood and lymph. In other words, food absorption is the process by which molecules of amino acids, glucose, fatty acids, and glycerol go from the inside of the

TABLE 14–2 Chemical Digestion

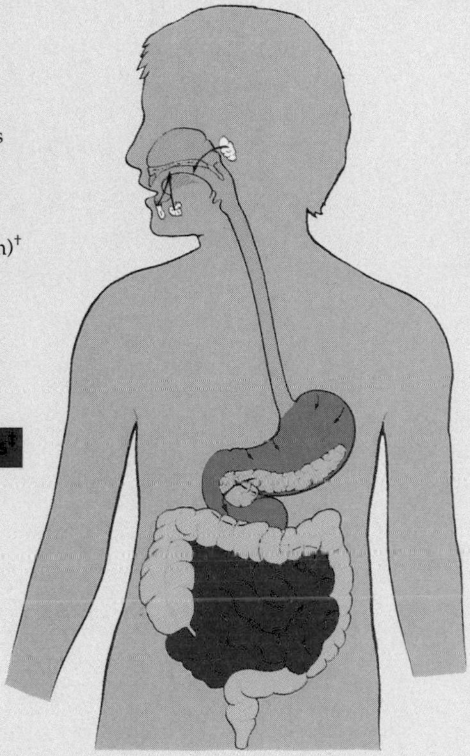

DIGESTIVE JUICES AND ENZYMES	SUBSTANCE DIGESTED (OR HYDROLYZED)	RESULTING PRODUCT*
Saliva		
Amylase	Starch (polysaccharide)	Maltose (a double sugar, or disaccharide)
Gastric Juice		
Protease (pepsin) plus hydrochloric acid	Proteins	Partially digested proteins
Pancreatic Juice		
Proteases (e.g., trypsin)†	Proteins (intact or partially digested)	Peptides and **amino acids**
Lipases	Fats emulsified by bile	**Fatty acids, monoglycerides, and glycerol**
Amylase	Starch	Maltose
Intestinal Enzymes‡		
Peptidases	Peptides	**Amino acids**
Sucrase	Sucrose (cane sugar)	**Glucose and fructose§** (simple sugars, or monosaccharides)
Lactase	Lactose (milk sugar)	**Glucose and galactose** (simple sugars)
Maltase	Maltose (malt sugar)	**Glucose**

*Substances in boldface type are end products of digestion (that is, completely digested nutrients ready for absorption).
†Secreted in inactive form (trypsinogen); activated by enterokinase, an enzyme in the intestinal brush order.
‡Brush-border enzymes.
§Glucose is also called *dextrose;* fructose is also called *levulose.*

intestines into the circulating fluids of the body. Absorption of foods is just as essential as digestion of foods. The reason is fairly obvious. As long as food stays in the intestines, it cannot nourish the millions of cells that compose all other parts of the body. Their lives depend on the absorption of digested food and its transportation to them by the circulating blood.

Structural adaptations of the digestive tube, including folds in the lining mucosa, villi, and microvilli, increase the absorptive surface and the efficiency and speed of transfer of materials from the intestinal lumen to body fluids. Many salts such as sodium are actively transported through the intestinal mucosa. Water follows by osmosis. Other nutrients are also actively transported into the blood of capillaries in the intestinal villi. Fats enter the lymphatic vessels or lacteals found in intestinal villi.

Colostomy

Colostomy (ko-LAH-sto-me) is a surgical procedure in which an artificial anus is created on the abdominal wall by cutting the colon and bringing the cut end or ends out to the surface to form an opening called a *stoma* (see the figure). In the home health care situation, patients are helped to accept the change in body image that may cause emotional discomfort. The patient or caregiver is also trained in the regular changing of the disposable bag, including cleaning of the stoma and preventing of irritation, chapping, or infection. Irrigation of the colon with isotonic solutions is sometimes necessary. Deodorants may be added to the fresh bag to prevent unpleasant odors. Patients are also taught to manage their diet to include low-residue food and to avoid foods that produce gas or cause diarrhea. Fluid intake is also carefully managed.

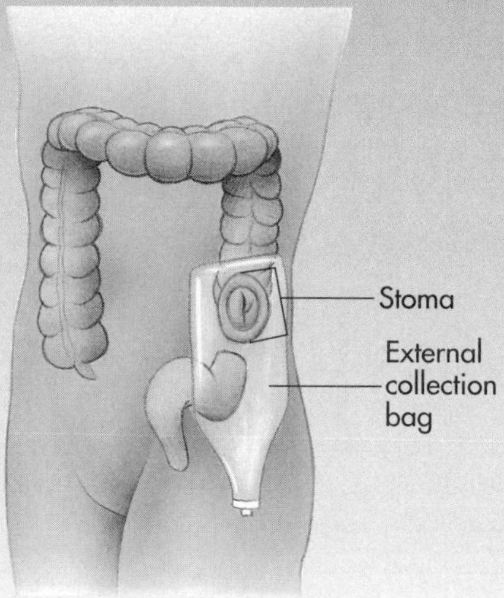

WALL OF THE DIGESTIVE TRACT (Figure 14-2)

The wall of the digestive tube is formed by four layers of tissue:

A Mucosa—mucous epithelium
B Submucosa—connective tissue
C Muscularis—two or three layers of smooth muscle
D Serosa—serous membrane that covers the outside of abdominal organs; it attaches the digestive tract to the wall of the abdominopelvic cavity by forming folds called *mesenteries*

MOUTH

A Roof—formed by hard palate (parts of maxillary and palatine bones) and soft palate, an arch-shaped muscle separating mouth from pharynx; uvula, a downward projection of soft palate (Figure 14-3)
B Floor—formed by tongue and its muscles; papillae, small elevations on mucosa of tongue; taste buds, found in many papillae; lingual frenulum, fold of mucous membrane that helps anchor tongue to floor of mouth (Figure 14-4)

TEETH

A Names of teeth—incisors, cuspids, bicuspids, and tricuspids
B Twenty teeth in temporary set; average age for cutting first tooth about 6 months; set complete at about 2 years of age
C Thirty-two teeth in permanent set; 6 years about average age for starting to cut first permanent tooth; set complete usually between ages of 17 and 24 years (Figure 14-5)
D Structures of a typical tooth—crown, neck, and root (Figure 14-6)

SALIVARY GLANDS (Figure 14-7)

A Parotid glands
B Submandibular glands
C Sublingual glands

PHARYNX

ESOPHAGUS

STOMACH (Figure 14-8)

A Size—expands after large meal; about size of large sausage when empty
B Pylorus—lower part of stomach; pyloric sphincter muscle closes opening of pylorus into duodenum
C Wall—many smooth muscle fibers; contractions produce churning movements (peristalsis)
D Lining—mucous membrane; many microscopic glands that secrete gastric juice and hydrochloric acid into stomach; mucous membrane lies in folds (rugae) when stomach is empty

SMALL INTESTINE (Figure 14-9)

A Size—about 7 meters (20 feet) long but only 2 cm or so in diameter
B Divisions
  1 Duodenum
  2 Jejunum
  3 Ileum
C Wall—contains smooth muscle fibers that contract to produce peristalsis
D Lining—mucous membrane; many microscopic glands (intestinal glands) secrete intestinal juice; villi (microscopic finger-shaped projections from surface of mucosa into intestinal cavity) contain blood and lymph capillaries

LIVER AND GALLBLADDER

A Size and location—liver is largest gland; fills upper right section of abdominal cavity and extends over into left side
B Liver secretes bile
C Ducts (Figure 14-10)
  1 Hepatic—drains bile from liver
  2 Cystic—duct by which bile enters and leaves gallbladder
  3 Common bile—formed by union of hepatic and cystic ducts; drains bile from hepatic or cystic ducts into duodenum
D Gallbladder
  1 Location—undersurface of the liver
  2 Function—concentrates and stores bile produced in the liver

PANCREAS

A Location—behind stomach
B Functions
  1 Pancreatic cells secrete pancreatic juice into pancreatic ducts; main duct empties into duodenum
  2 Pancreatic islets (of Langerhans)—cells not connected with pancreatic ducts; secrete hormones glucagon and insulin into the blood

LARGE INTESTINE (Figure 14-12)

A Divisions
  1 Cecum
  2 Colon—ascending, transverse, descending, and sigmoid
  3 Rectum
B Opening to exterior—anus
C Wall—contains smooth muscle fibers that contract to produce churning, peristalsis, and defecation
D Lining—mucous membrane

APPENDIX

Blind tube off cecum; no important digestive functions in humans

PERITONEUM (Figure 14-14)

A Definitions—peritoneum, serous membrane lining abdominal cavity and covering abdominal organs; parietal layer of peritoneum lines abdominal cavity; visceral layer of peritoneum covers abdominal organs; peritoneal space lies between parietal and visceral layers

B Extensions—largest ones are the mesentery and greater omentum; mesentery is extension of parietal peritoneum, which attaches most of small intestine to posterior abdominal wall; greater omentum, or "lace apron," hangs down from lower edge of stomach and transverse colon over intestines

DIGESTION (Table 14-2)

Meaning—changing foods so that they can be absorbed and used by cells

A Mechanical digestion—chewing, swallowing, and peristalsis break food into tiny particles, mix them well with digestive juices, and move them along the digestive tract

B Chemical digestion—breaks up large food molecules into compounds having smaller molecules; brought about by digestive enzymes

C Carbohydrate digestion—mainly in small intestine

- **1** Pancreatic amylase—changes starches to maltose
- **2** Intestinal juice enzymes
  - **a** Maltase—changes maltose to glucose
  - **b** Sucrase—changes sucrose to glucose
  - **c** Lactase—changes lactose to glucose

D Protein digestion—starts in stomach; completed in small intestine

- **1** Gastric juice enzymes, rennin and pepsin, partially digest proteins
- **2** Pancreatic enzyme, trypsin, completes digestion of proteins to amino acids
- **3** Intestinal enzymes, peptidases, complete digestion of partially digested proteins to amino acids

E Fat digestion

- **1** Bile contains no enzymes but emulsifies fats (breaks fat droplets into very small droplets)
- **2** Pancreatic lipase changes emulsified fats to fatty acids and glycerol in small intestine

ABSORPTION

A Meaning—digested food moves from intestine into blood or lymph

B Where absorption occurs—foods and most water from small intestine; some water also absorbed from large intestine

NEW WORDS

absorption
alimentary canal
appendicitis
bolus
cavity
chyme
diarrhea
digestion
emesis
feces
frenulum
jaundice
lumen
mastication
mesentery
papilla
peristalsis
peritoneum
plica
rugae
ulcer
uvula
villus

CHAPTER TEST

1. In the digestive system the breakdown of food material is ______________ and ______________ in nature.
2. Undigested waste material resulting from the digestive process is called ______________.
3. The liver and gallbladder are classified as ______________ organs of digestion.
4. The hollow space within the digestive tube is called the ______________.
5. The inside or lining coat of the digestive tube is called the ______________.
6. The roof of the mouth is formed by the hard and soft ______________.
7. The portion of a tooth that is exposed and visible is called the ______________.
8. The teeth serve cutting and grinding functions during the chewing of food—a process called ______________.
9. Saliva contains the enzyme called salivary ______________.
10. Food moves from the pharynx to the stomach by passing through the ______________.
11. The semisolid mixture of food and gastric juice in the stomach is called ______________.
12. The movement of food through the digestive tract results from contractions called ______________.
13. The middle segment of the small intestine is called the ______________.

Select the most correct answer from Column B for each statement in Column A. (Only one answer is correct.)

COLUMN A	COLUMN B
14. _____ Waste material	a. Liver
15. _____ Accessory organ of digestion	b. Enamel
16. _____ Double fold of peritoneum	c. Fundus
17. _____ Hardest tissue in body	d. Feces
18. _____ Semisolid mixture	e. Jaundice
19. _____ Division of stomach	f. Mesentery
20. _____ Yellowish skin condition	g. Lipase
21. _____ Digestive enzyme	h. Chyme

Circle the T before each true statement and the F before each false statement.

T F 22. The salivary glands are considered accessory organs of digestion.

T F 23. The ileum is the portion of the small intestine found between the duodenum and jejunum.

T F 24. The large intestine is classified as an accessory organ of digestion.

T F 25. The serosa is the outermost coat of the digestive tube.

T F 26. The uvula is attached to the soft palate.

T F 27. In humans there are 32 deciduous (baby) teeth and 20 permanent teeth.

T F 28. No chemical digestion can occur in the mouth.

T F 29. The pyloric sphincter is located between the esophagus and stomach.

T F 30. Plica, villi, and microvilli all increase the surface area of the small intestine.

REVIEW QUESTIONS

1. What organs form the gastrointestinal tract?
2. Identify the jejunum, cecum, colon, duodenum, and ileum.
3. How many teeth should an adult have?
4. Identify the pancreatic islets, parotid glands, pylorus, rugae, and villi.
5. In what organ does the digestion of starches begin?
6. What digestive juice contains no enzymes?
7. Only one digestive juice contains enzymes for digesting all three kinds of food. Which juice is this? In what organ does it do its work?
8. Which digestive juice emulsifies fats?
9. What three digestive juices act on foods in the small intestine?
10. What juices digest carbohydrates? Proteins? Fats?
11. Where are simple sugars and amino acids absorbed into blood capillaries? Where are lipids absorbed into lacteals?
12. Where is most of the water absorbed from the lumen of the digestive tract?

CRITICAL THINKING

13. If you inserted 9 inches of an enema tube through the anus, the tip of the tube would probably be in what structure?
14. How many teeth should a child 2½ years old have? Would he have some of each of the following teeth: incisors, canines, premolars, and molars? If not, which ones would he not have?
15. What kinds of food are not digested in the stomach?

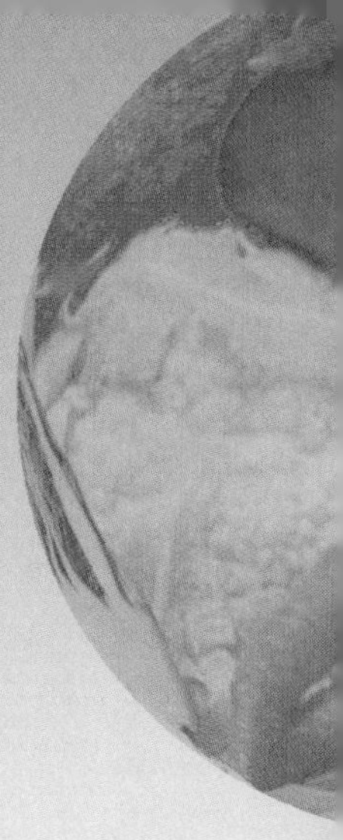

Nutrition and Metabolism

OUTLINE

Role of the Liver

Nutrient Metabolism
- Carbohydrate Metabolism
- Fat Metabolism
- Protein Metabolism

Vitamins and Minerals

Metabolic Rates

Body Temperature

BOXED ESSAYS

Carbohydrate Loading
Vitamin Supplements for Athletes
Measuring Energy

OBJECTIVES

After you have completed this chapter, you should be able to:

1. Define and contrast *catabolism* and *anabolism.*
2. Describe the metabolic roles of carbohydrates, fats, proteins, vitamins, and minerals.
3. Define basal metabolic rate and list some factors that affect it.
4. Discuss the physiological mechanisms that regulate body temperature.

Nutrition and *metabolism* are words that are often used together—but what do they mean? *Nutrition* is a term that refers to the food (nutrients) that we eat. Proper nutrition requires a balance of the three basic food types, *carbohydrates, fats,* and *proteins,* plus essential *vitamins* and *minerals.* Malnutrition is a deficiency or imbalance in the consumption of food, vitamins, and minerals.

A good phrase to remember in connection with the word metabolism is "use of foods" because basically this is what metabolism is—the use the body makes of foods after they have been digested, absorbed, and circulated to cells. It uses them in two ways: as an energy source and as building blocks for making complex chemical compounds. Before they can be used in these two ways, foods have to be *assimilated.* Assimilation occurs when food molecules enter cells and undergo many chemical changes there. All the chemical reactions that release energy from food molecules make up the process of catabolism, a vital process because it is the only way that the body has of supplying itself with energy for doing any work. The many chemical reactions that build food molecules into more complex chemical compounds constitute the process of anabolism. Catabolism and anabolism make up the process of metabolism.

This chapter explores many of the basic ideas about why certain nutrients are necessary for survival and how they are used by the body.

Role of the Liver

As we discussed in Chapter 14, the liver plays an important role in the mechanical digestion of lipids because it secretes *bile.* As you recall, bile breaks large fat globules into smaller droplets of fat that are more easily broken down. In addition, liver cells perform other functions necessary for healthy survival. They play a major role in the metabolism of all three kinds of foods. They help maintain a normal blood glucose concentration by carrying on complex and essential chemical reactions. Liver cells also carry on the first steps of protein and fat metabolism and synthesize several kinds of protein compounds. They release them into the blood, where they are called the *blood proteins* or *plasma proteins.* Prothrombin and fibrinogen, two of the plasma proteins formed by liver cells, play essential parts in blood clotting (see pp. 220 and 221). Another protein made by liver cells, albumin, helps maintain normal blood volume. Liver cells detoxify various poisonous substances such as bacterial products and certain drugs. Liver cells store several substances, notably iron and vitamins A and D.

The liver is assisted by an interesting structural feature of the blood vessels that supply it. As you may recall from Chapter 11, the hepatic portal vein delivers blood directly from the gastrointestinal tract to the liver (see Figure 11-12). This arrangement allows blood that has just absorbed nutrients and other substances to be processed by the liver before being distributed throughout the body. Thus excess nutrients and vitamins can be stored and toxins can be removed from the bloodstream.

Nutrient Metabolism

CARBOHYDRATE METABOLISM

Carbohydrates are the preferred energy food of the body. They are composed of smaller "building blocks"—primarily *glucose.* (See Appendix A). Human cells catabolize (break down) glucose rather than other substances as long as enough glucose enters them to supply their energy needs. Three series of chemical reactions, occurring in a precise sequence, make up the process of glucose catabolism. **Glycolysis** (glye-KOL-i-sis) is the name given the first series of reactions; **citric acid cycle** is the name of the second series, and **electron transfer system** is the third. Glycolysis, as Figure 15-1 shows, changes glucose to pyruvic acid. The citric acid cycle changes the pyruvic acid to carbon dioxide. Glycolysis takes place in the cytoplasm of a cell, whereas the citric acid cycle goes on in the mitochondria, the cell's miniature power plants. Glycolysis uses no oxygen; it is an **anaerobic** (an-er-O-bik) process. The citric acid cycle, in contrast, is an oxygen-using or **aerobic** (aer-O-bik) process.

While the chemical reactions of glycolysis and the citric acid cycle occur, energy stored in the glucose molecule is being released. Over half the released energy is in the form of high-energy elec-

FIGURE 15–1 ***Catabolism of Glucose.*** Glycolysis splits one molecule of glucose (six carbon atoms) into two molecules of pyruvic acid (three carbon atoms each). The citric acid cycle converts each pyruvic acid molecule into three carbon dioxide molecules (one carbon atom each).

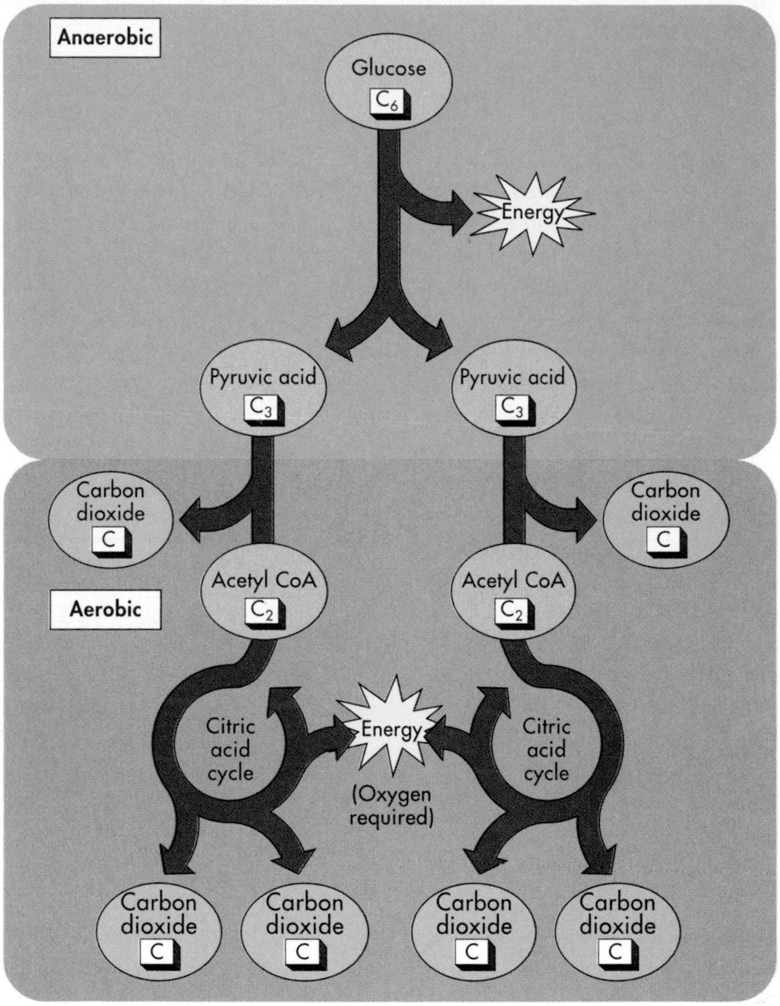

trons. The electron transport system, located in the mitochondria, almost immediately transfers the energy to molecules of adenosine triphosphate (ATP). The rest of the energy originally stored in the glucose molecule is released as heat. ATP serves as the direct source of energy for doing cellular work in all kinds of living organisms from one-cell plants to billion-cell animals, including man. Among biological compounds, therefore, ATP ranks as one of the most important. The energy transferred to ATP molecules differs in two ways from the energy stored in food molecules; the energy in ATP molecules is not stored but is released almost instantaneously, and it can be used directly to do cellular work. Release of energy from food molecules occurs much more slowly because it accompanies the long series of chemical reactions that make up the process of catabolism. Energy released from food molecules cannot be used directly for doing cellular work. It must first be transferred to ATP molecules and be released explosively from them.

FIGURE 15–2 *ATP.* **A,** The structure of ATP. A single adenosine group *(A)* has three attached phosphate groups *(P)*. The high-energy bonds between the phosphate groups can release chemical energy to do cellular work. **B,** ATP energy cycle. ATP stores energy in its last high-energy phosphate bond. When that bond is later broken, energy is released to do cellular work. The ADP and phosphate groups that result can be resynthesized into ATP capturing additional energy from nutrient catabolism.

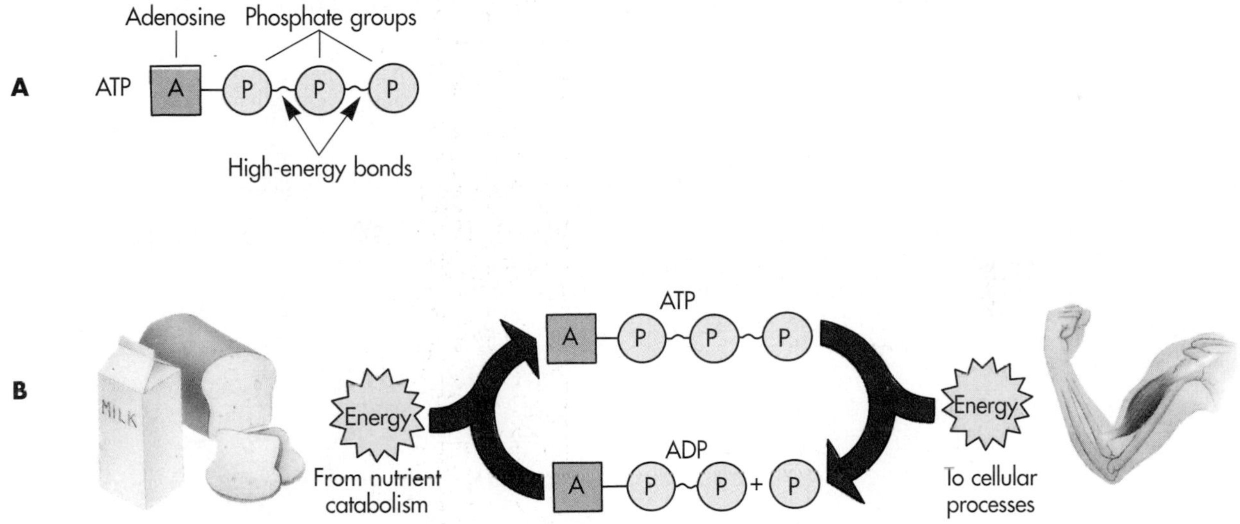

As Figure 15-2 shows, ATP comprises an adenosine group and three phosphate groups. The capacity of ATP to store large amounts of energy is found in the high-energy bonds that hold the phosphate groups together, illustrated as curvy lines. When a phosphate group breaks off the molecule, an adenosine diphosphate (ADP) molecule and free phosphate group result. Energy that had been holding the phosphate bond together is freed to do cellular work (muscle fiber contractions, for example). As you can see in Figure 15-2, the ADP and phosphate are reunited by the energy produced by carbohydrate catabolism, making ATP a reusable energy-storage molecule. Only enough ATP for immediate cellular requirements is made at any one time. Glucose that is not needed is anabolized into larger molecules that are stored for later use.

Glucose anabolism is called **glycogenesis** (glye-ko-JEN-e-sis). Carried on chiefly by liver and muscle cells, glycogenesis consists of a series of reactions that join glucose molecules together, like many beads in a necklace, to form *glycogen,* a compound sometimes called *animal starch.*

Something worth noticing is that the amount of nutrients in the blood normally does not change very much, not even when we go without food for many hours, when we exercise and use a lot of food for energy, or when we sleep and use little food for energy. The amount of glucose in our blood, for example, usually stays at about 80 to 120 mg in 100 ml of blood.

Several hormones help regulate carbohydrate metabolism to keep blood glucose normal. **Insulin** is one of the most important of these. It acts in some way not yet definitely known to make glucose leave the blood and enter the cells at a more rapid rate. As insulin secretion increases, more glucose leaves the blood and enters the cells. The amount of glucose in the blood therefore decreases as the rate of glucose metabolism in cells increases (see p. 207). Too little insulin secretion, such as that which occurs with diabetes mellitus, produces the opposite effects. Less glucose leaves the blood and enters the cells; more glucose therefore remains in the blood, and less glucose is metabolized by cells. In other words, high blood glucose (hyperglycemia)

Carbohydrate Loading

A number of athletes and others who must occasionally sustain endurance exercise for a significant period practice **carbohydrate loading** or **glycogen loading.** Like liver cells, some skeletal muscle fibers can take up and store glucose in the form of glycogen. By ceasing intense exercise and switching to a diet high in carbohydrates 2 or 3 days before an endurance event, an athlete can cause the skeletal muscles to store almost twice as much glycogen as usual. This allows the muscles to sustain aerobic exercise for up to 50% longer than usual.

and a low rate of glucose metabolism characterize insulin deficiency. Insulin is the only hormone that lowers the blood glucose level. Several other hormones, on the other hand, increase it. Growth hormone secreted by the anterior pituitary gland, hydrocortisone secreted by the adrenal cortex, epinephrine secreted by the adrenal medulla, and glucagon secreted by the pancreatic islets are four of the most important hormones that increase blood glucose. More information about these hormones appears in Chapter 9.

FAT METABOLISM

Fats, like carbohydrates, are primarily energy foods. If cells have inadequate amounts of glucose to catabolize, they immediately shift to the catabolism of fats for energy. They are simply converted into a form of glucose that can enter the citric acid cycle. This happens normally when a person goes without food for many hours. It happens abnormally in diabetic individuals. Because of an insulin deficiency, too little glucose enters the cells of a diabetic person to supply all energy needs. Result? The cells catabolize fats to make up the difference (Figure 15-3). In all persons, fats not needed for catabolism are anabolized to form tryglycerides and stored in adipose tissue.

FIGURE 15–3 ***Catabolism of Nutrients.*** Fats, carbohydrates, and proteins can be converted to products that enter the citric acid cycle to yield energy.

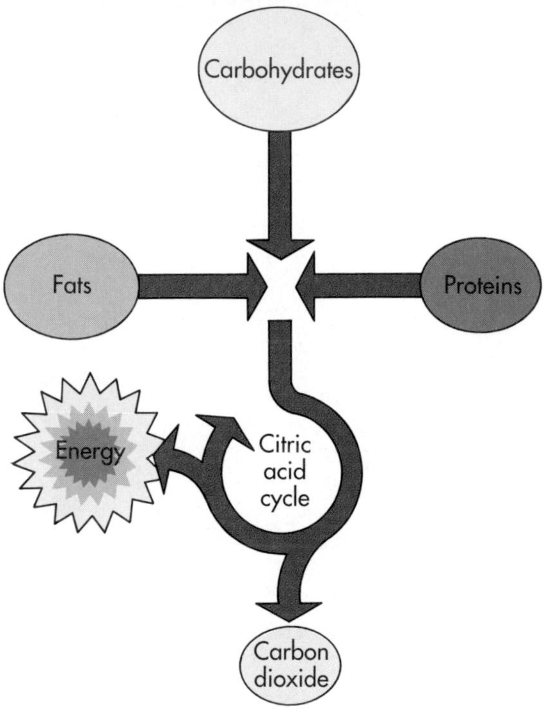

PROTEIN METABOLISM

In a healthy person, proteins are catabolized to release energy to a very small extent. When fat reserves are low, as they are in the starvation that accompanies certain eating disorders such as anorexia nervosa, the body can start to use its protein molecules as an energy source. Specifically, the amino acids that make up proteins are each broken apart to yield an amine group that is converted to a form of glucose that can enter the citric acid cycle. After a shift to reliance on protein catabolism as a major energy source occurs, death may quickly follow because vital proteins in the muscles and nerves are catabolized (Figure 15-3).

A more common situation in normal bodies is protein anabolism, the process by which the body builds amino acids into complex protein compounds (for example, enzymes and proteins that form the structure of the cell). Proteins are assembled from a pool of 20 different kinds of amino acids. If any one type of amino acid is deficient, vital proteins cannot be synthesized—a serious health threat. One way your body maintains a constant supply of amino acids is by making them from other compounds already present in the body. Only about half of the required 20 types of amino acids can be made by the body, however. The remaining types of amino acids must be supplied in the diet. **Essential amino acids** are those that must be in the diet. **Nonessential amino acids** can be missing from the diet because they can be made by the body. See Table 15-1.

Vitamins and Minerals

One glance at the label of any packaged food product reveals the importance we place on vitamins and minerals. We know that carbohydrates, fats, and proteins are used by our bodies to build important molecules and to provide energy. So why do we need vitamins and minerals?

First, let's discuss the importance of vitamins. Vitamins are organic molecules needed in small quantities for normal metabolism throughout the body. Vitamin molecules attach to enzymes and help them work properly. Many enzymes are totally useless without the appropriate vitamins to activate them. Most vitamins cannot be made by the body, so we must eat them in our food. The body can store fat-soluble vitamins—A, D, E, and K—in the liver for later use. Because the body cannot store water-soluble vitamins such as B vitamins and vitamin C, they must be continually supplied in the diet. Vitamin deficiencies can lead to severe metabolic problems. Table 15-2 lists some of the more well-known vitamins, their sources, functions, and symptoms of deficiency.

Minerals are just as important as vitamins. Minerals are inorganic elements or salts found naturally in the earth. Like vitamins, mineral ions can attach to enzymes and help them work. Minerals also function in a variety of other vital chemical reactions. For example, sodium, calcium, and other minerals are required for nerve conduction and for contraction in muscle fibers. Without these minerals, the brain, heart, and respiratory tract would cease to function. Information about some of the more important minerals is summarized in Table 15-3.

TABLE 15–1 Amino Acids

ESSENTIAL (INDISPENSABLE)	NONESSENTIAL (DISPENSABLE)
Histidine*	Alanine
Isoleucine	Arginine
Leucine	Asparagine
Lysine	Aspartic acid
Methionine	Cysteine
Phenylalanine	Glutamic acid
Threonine	Glutamine
Tryptophan	Glycine
Valine	Proline
	Serine
	Tyrosine†

*Essential in infants and, perhaps, adult males.
†Can be synthesized from phenylalanine; therefore is nonessential as long as phenylalanine is in the diet.

Vitamin Supplements for Athletes

Because a deficiency of vitamins **(avitaminosis)** can cause poor athletic performance, many athletes regularly consume vitamin supplements. However, research suggests that vitamin supplementation has little or no effect on athletic performance. A reasonably well-balanced diet supplies more than enough vitamins for even the elite athlete. The use of vitamin supplements therefore has fueled somewhat of a controversy among exercise experts. Opponents of vitamin supplements cite the cost and the possibility of liver damage associated with some forms of **hypervitaminosis,** whereas supporters cite the benefit of protecting against vitamin deficiency.

TABLE 15–2 Major Vitamins

VITAMIN	DIETARY SOURCE	FUNCTIONS	SYMPTOMS OF DEFICIENCY
Vitamin A	Green and yellow vegetables, dairy products, and liver	Maintains epithelial tissue and produces visual pigments	Night blindness and flaking skin
B-complex vitamins			
B_1 (thiamine)	Grains, meat, and legumes	Helps enzymes in the citric acid cycle	Nerve problems (beriberi), heart muscle weakness, and edema
B_2 (riboflavin)	Green vegetables, organ meats, eggs, and dairy products	Aids enzymes in the citric acid cycle	Inflammation of skin and eyes
B_3 (niacin)	Meat and grains	Helps enzymes in the citric acid cycle	Pellagra (scaly dermatitis and mental disturbances) and nervous disorders
B_5 (pantothenic acid)	Organ meat, eggs, and liver	Aids enzymes that connect fat and carbohydrate metabolism	Loss of coordination (rare)
B_6 (pyridoxine)	Vegetable, meats, and grains	Helps enzymes that catabolize amino acids	Convulsions, irritability, and anemia
B_{12} (cyanocobalamin)	Meat and dairy products	Involved in blood production and other processes	Pernicious anemia
Biotin	Vegetables, meat, and eggs	Helps enzymes in amino acid catabolism and fat and glycogen synthesis	Mental and muscle problems (rare)
Folic acid	Vegetables	Aids enzymes in amino acid catabolism and blood production	Digestive disorders and anemia
Vitamin C (ascorbic acid)	Fruits and green vegetables	Helps in manufacture of collagen fibers	Scurvy and degeneration of skin, bone, and blood vessels
Vitamin D (calciferol)	Dairy products and fish liver oil	Aids in calcium absorption	Rickets and skeletal deformity
Vitamin E (tocopherol)	Green vegetable and seeds	Protects cell membranes from being catabolized	Muscle and reproductive disorders (rare)

Metabolic Rates

The **basal metabolic rate (BMR)** is the rate at which food is catabolized under basal conditions (that is, when the individual is resting but awake, is not digesting food, and is not adjusting to a cold external temperature). Or, stated differently, the BMR is the number of calories of heat that must be produced per hour by catabolism just to keep the body alive, awake, and comfortably warm. To provide energy for muscular work and digestion and absorption of food, an additional amount of food must be catabolized. The amount of additional food depends mainly on how much work the individual does. The more active he or she is, the more food the body must catabolize and the higher the total metabolic rate will be. The **total metabolic rate (TMR)** is the total amount of energy used by the body per day (Figure 15-4).

When the number of calories in your food intake equals your TMR, your weight remains constant (except for possible variations resulting from water retention or water loss). When your food intake provides more calories than your TMR, you gain weight; when your food intake

TABLE 15–3 Major Minerals

MINERAL	DIETARY SOURCE	FUNCTIONS	SYMPTOMS OF DEFICIENCY
Calcium (Ca)	Dairy products, legumes, and vegetables	Helps blood clotting, bone formation, and nerve and muscle function	Bone degeneration and nerve and muscle malfunction
Chlorine (Cl)	Salty foods	Aids in stomach acid production and acid-base balance	Acid-base imbalance
Cobalt (Co)	Meat	Helps vitamin B_{12} in blood cell production	Pernicious anemia
Copper (Cu)	Seafood, organ meats, and legumes	Involved in extracting energy from the citric acid cycle and in blood production	Fatigue and anemia
Iodine (I)	Seafood and iodized salt	Aids in thyroid hormone synthesis	Goiter (thyroid enlargement) and decrease of metabolic rate
Iron (Fe)	Meat, eggs, vegetables, and legumes	Involved in extracting energy from the citric acid cycle and in blood production	Fatigue and anemia
Magnesium (Mg)	Vegetables and grains	Helps many enzymes	Nerve disorders, blood vessel dilation, and heart rhythm problems
Manganese (Mn)	Vegetables, legumes, and grains	Helps many enzymes	Muscle and nerve disorders
Phosphorus (P)	Dairy products and meat	Aids in bone formation and is used to make ATP, DNA, RNA, and phospholipids	Bone degeneration and metabolic problems
Potassium (K)	Seafood, milk, fruit, and meats	Helps muscle and nerve function	Muscle weakness, heart problems, and nerve problems
Sodium (Na)	Salty foods	Aids in muscle and nerve function and fluid balance	Weakness and digestive upset
Zinc (Zn)	Many foods	Helps many enzymes	Metabolic problems

FIGURE 15–4 *Factors That Determine the Basal and Total Metabolic Rates.*

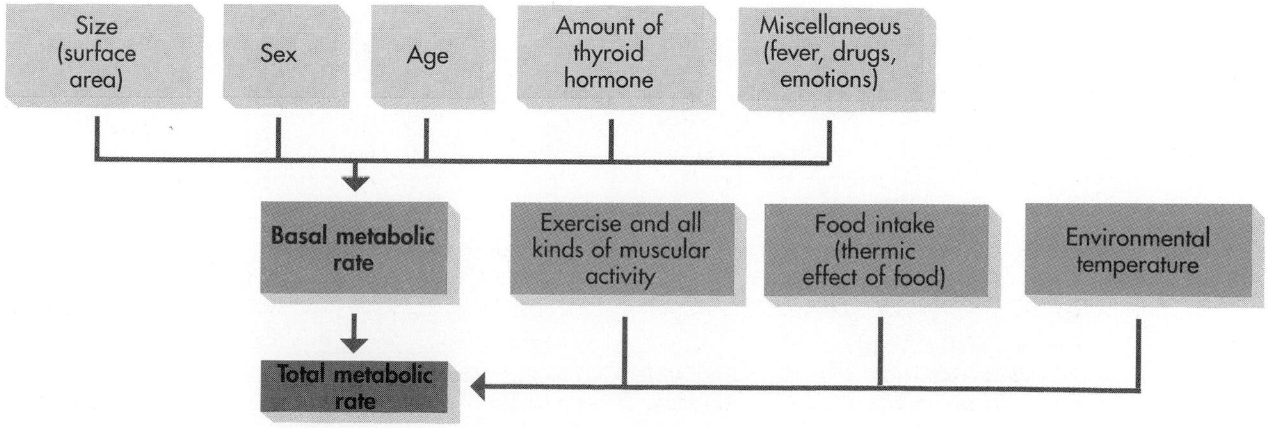

Measuring Energy

Physiologists studying metabolism must be able to express a quantity of energy in mathematical terms. The unit of energy measurement most often used is the calorie (cal). A calorie is the amount of energy needed to raise the temperature of 1 g of water 1° C. Because physiologists often deal with very large amounts of energy, the larger unit, *kilocalorie* (kcal) or *Calorie* (notice the upper-case C), is used. There are 1000 cal in 1 kcal or Calorie. Nutritionists prefer to use *Calorie* when they express the amount of energy stored in a food.

provides fewer calories than your TMR, you lose weight. These weight control principles rarely fail to operate. Nature does not forget to count calories. Reducing diets make use of this knowledge. They contain fewer calories than the TMR of the individual eating the diet.

Body Temperature

Considering the fact that over 60% of the energy released from food molecules during catabolism is converted to heat rather than being transferred to ATP, it is no wonder that maintaining a constant body temperature is a challenge. Maintaining homeostasis of body temperature or thermoregulation is the function of the hypothalamus. The hypothalamus operates a variety of negative-feedback mechanisms that keep body temperature in its normal range (36.2° to 37.6° C or 97° to 100° F).

The skin is often involved in negative-feedback loops that maintain body temperature. When the body is overheated, blood flow to the skin increases (Figure 15-5). Warm blood from the body's core can then be cooled by the skin, which acts as a radiator. At the skin, heat can be lost from blood by the following mechanisms:

1. Radiation—flow of heat waves away from the blood
2. Conduction—transfer of heat energy to the skin and then the external environment
3. Convection—transfer of heat energy to air that is continually flowing away from the skin
4. Evaporation—absorption of heat by water (sweat) vaporization

When necessary, heat can be conserved by reducing blood flow in the skin (Figure 15-5).

A number of other mechanisms can be called on to help maintain the homeostasis of body temperature. Heat-generating muscle activity such as shivering and secretion of metabolism-regulating hormones are two of the body's processes that can be altered to adjust the body's temperature. The concept of using feedback control loops in homeostatic mechanisms was introduced in Chapter 1.

FIGURE 15–5 ***The Skin as a Thermoregulatory Organ.*** When homeostasis requires that the body conserve heat, blood flow in the warm organs of the body's core increases *(left)*. When heat must be lost to maintain the stability of the internal environment, flow of warm blood to the skin increases *(right)*. Heat can be lost from the blood and skin by means of radiation, conduction, convection, and evaporation.

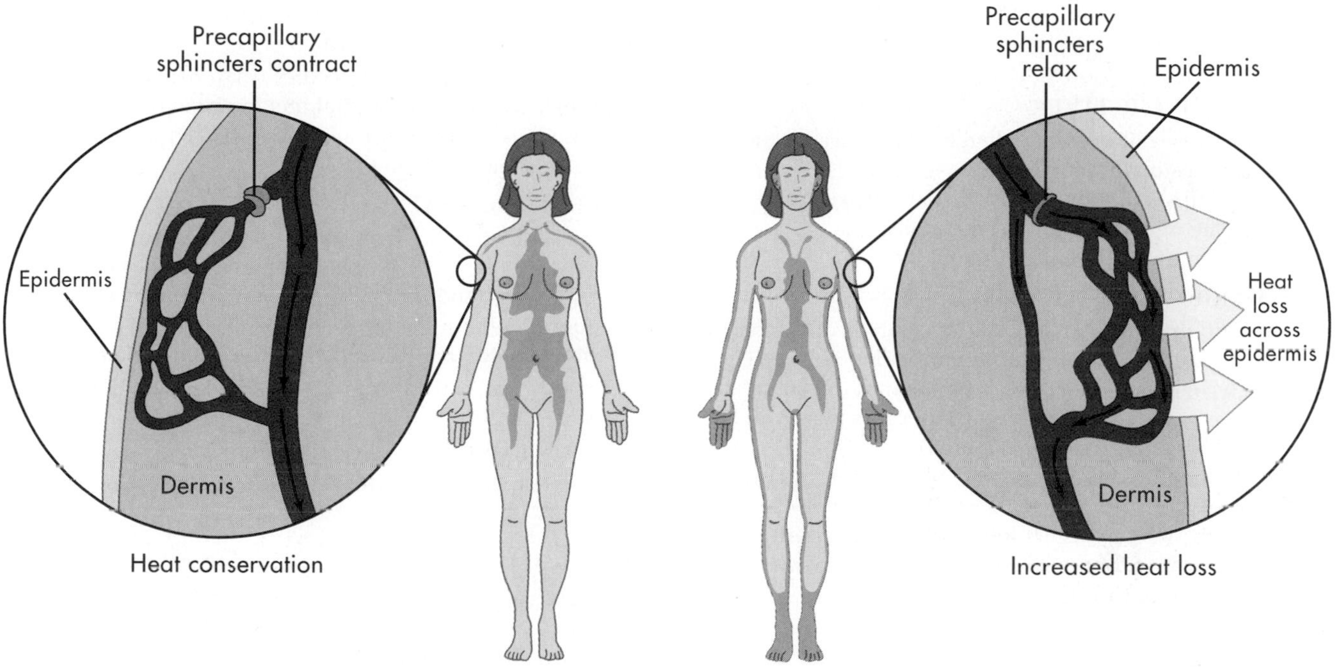

OUTLINE SUMMARY

DEFINITIONS

A Nutrition—food, vitamins, and minerals that are ingested and assimilated into the body

B Metabolism—process of using food molecules as energy sources and as building blocks for our own molecules

C Catabolism—breaks food molecules down, releasing their stored energy; oxygen used in catabolism

D Anabolism—builds food molecules into complex substances

ROLE OF THE LIVER

A Processes blood immediately after it leaves the gastrointestinal tract
  1 Helps maintain normal blood glucose level
  2 Site of protein and fat metabolism
  3 Removes toxins from the blood

NUTRIENT METABOLISM

A Carbohydrates are primarily catabolized for energy (Figure 15-1), but small amounts are anabolized by glycogenesis (a series of chemical reactions that changes glucose to glycogen—occurs mainly in liver cells where glycogen is stored)

B Blood glucose (imprecisely, blood sugar)—normally stays between about 80 and 120 mg per 100 ml of blood; insulin accelerates the movement of glucose out of the blood into cells, therefore decreases blood glucose and increases glucose catabolism

C Adenosine triphosphate (ATP)—molecule in which energy obtained from breakdown of foods is stored; serves as a direct source of energy for cellular work (Figure 15-2)

D Fats catabolized to yield energy and anabolized to form adipose tissue (Figure 15-3)

E Proteins primarily anabolized and secondarily catabolized

VITAMINS AND MINERALS

A Vitamins—organic molecules that are needed in small amounts for normal metabolism (Table 15-2)

B Minerals—inorganic molecules required by the body for normal function (Table 15-3)

METABOLIC RATES

A Basal metabolic rate (BMR)—rate of metabolism when a person is lying down but awake and not digesting food and when the environment is comfortably warm

B Total metabolic rate (TMR)—the total amounts of energy, expressed in calories, used by the body per day (Figure 15-4)

BODY TEMPERATURE

A Hypothalamus—regulates the homeostasis of body temperature through a variety of processes

B Skin—can cool the body by losing heat from the blood through four processes: radiation, conduction, convection, evaporation (Figure 15-5)

NEW WORDS

anabolism
basal metabolic rate (BMR)
calorie
catabolism
citric acid cycle
electron transport system
glycogenesis
glycolysis
kilocalorie
thermoregulation
total metabolic rate (TMR)
vitamin

CHAPTER TEST

1. The type of metabolism that involves the breakdown of food molecules is called ______________.
2. The type of metabolism that involves the synthesis of large molecules is called ______________.
3. *Nutrition* refers to the food that we eat, whereas ______________ refers to the use of foods after they have entered the cells.
4. The ______________ vein delivers blood from the gastrointestinal tract directly to the liver.
5. The chemical process that changes glucose into pyruvic acid, producing energy, is called ______________.
6. The series of reactions in liver cells that joins glucose molecules together to form glycogen is called ______________.
7. When the body runs low on carbohydrates several hours after a meal, it begins catabolizing ______________ instead.
8. ______________ are organic molecules needed in small quantities for normal metabolism throughout the body.
9. The molecule in which energy from catabolism is stored until it is used by the cell is called ______________.
10. The rate at which food is catabolized in a resting individual who is not digesting a meal is called the ______________.
11. Thermoregulation is controlled mainly by the ______________ in the brain.

Circle the T before each true statement and the F before each false statement.

T F 12. The citric acid cycle changes glucose into pyruvic acid, releasing energy for the cell's use.

T F 13. Insulin promotes the entry of glucose into body cells.

T F 14. Anorexia nervosa can result in death.

T F 15. Minerals can also be called vitamins.

T F 16. Sodium is a mineral that is found in only a few types of food.

T F 17. Measuring oxygen consumption or blood concentration of protein-bound iodine can be used to determine a person's rate of metabolism.

T F 18. The skin is an important organ for maintaining the body's temperature homeostasis.

REVIEW QUESTIONS

1. Briefly and clearly explain anabolism, catabolism, metabolism, and nutrition.
2. In words or in a sketched diagram, describe the metabolic pathway taken by a glucose molecule when energy is extracted from it.
3. Liver cells perform a process that prevents the blood glucose level from getting too high just after a large meal. What is it?
4. How are fats used by the body? Proteins?
5. Explain the metabolic roles of vitamins and minerals.
6. Explain what is meant by the term *metabolic rate.*
7. What is the difference between basal metabolic rate and total metabolic rate?
8. How does the body maintain the body temperature within a normal range?
9. Name the four mechanisms by which the skin removes heat from the body.

CRITICAL THINKING

10. What adaptive advantage is gained by detouring blood from the gastrointestinal tract to the liver before returning it to the heart?
11. How does the body get energy during fasting?
12. Explain why you think the following statement is true or false: "If you do not want to gain or lose weight but just stay the same, you must eat just enough food to supply the kilocalories of your BMR. If you eat more than this, you will gain; if you eat less than this, you will lose."

The Urinary System

OUTLINE

Kidneys
- Location
- Internal Structure
- Microscopic Structure
- Function

Formation of Urine
- Control of Urine Volume

Ureters

Urinary Bladder

Urethra

Micturition

BOXED ESSAYS

Proteinuria After Exercise
Artificial Kidney
Urinary Catheterization
Removal of Kidney Stones Using Ultrasound

OBJECTIVES

After you have completed this chapter, you should be able to:

1. Identify the major organs of the urinary system and give the generalized function of each.
2. Name the parts of a nephron and describe the role each component plays in the formation of urine.
3. Explain the importance of filtration, tubular reabsorption, and tubular secretion in urine formation.
4. Discuss the mechanisms that control urine volume.
5. Explain how the kidneys act as vital organs in maintaining homeostasis.

As you might guess from its name, the urinary system performs the functions of producing and excreting urine from the body. What you might not guess so easily is how essential these functions are for the maintenance of homeostasis and healthy survival. The constancy of body fluid volumes and the levels of many important chemicals depend on normal urinary system function. Unless the urinary system operates normally, the normal composition of blood cannot be maintained long, and serious consequences soon follow. The kidneys "clear" or clean the blood of the many waste products continually produced as a result of metabolism of foodstuffs in the body cells. As nutrients are burned for energy, the waste products produced must be removed from the blood, or they quickly accumulate to toxic levels—a condition called **uremia** (yoo-REE-mee-ah) or **uremic poisoning.** The kidneys also play a vital role in maintaining electrolyte, water, and acid-base balances in the body. In this chapter, we will discuss the structure and function of each organ of the urinary system. There are two kidneys, two ureters, one bladder, and one urethra (Figure 16-1). We will also briefly mention disease conditions produced by abnormal functioning of the urinary system.

Kidneys

LOCATION

To locate the kidneys on your own body, stand erect and put your hands on your hips with your thumbs meeting over your backbone. When you are in this position, your kidneys lie just above your thumb; in short, the kidneys lie just above the waistline. Usually the right kidney is a little lower than the left. They are located under the muscles of the back and behind the parietal peritoneum (the membrane that lines the abdominal cavity). Because of this retroperitoneal location, a surgeon can operate on a kidney without cutting through the peritoneum. A heavy cushion of fat normally encases each kidney and helps hold it in place.

Note the relatively large diameter of the renal arteries in Figure 16-1. Normally a little over 20% of the total blood pumped by the heart each minute enters the kidneys. The rate of blood flow through this organ is among the highest in the body. This is understandable because one of the main functions of the kidney is to remove waste products from the blood. Maintenance of a high rate of blood flow and normal blood pressure in the kidneys is essential for the formation of urine.

INTERNAL STRUCTURE

If you were to slice through a kidney from side to side and open it like the pages of a book, you would see the structures shown in Figure 16-2. Identify each of the following parts:

1. **Cortex** (KOR-teks)—the outer part of the kidney (The word *cortex* comes from the Latin word for "bark" or "rind," so the cortex of an organ is its outer layer; each kidney and adrenal gland, as well as the brain, has a cortex.)
2. **Medulla** (me-DUL-ah)—the inner portion of the kidney
3. **Pyramids** (PIR-ah-mids)—the triangular divisions of the medulla of the kidney
4. **Papilla** (pah-PIL-ah) (pl. *papillae*)—narrow, innermost end of a pyramid
5. **Pelvis**—(the kidney or renal pelvis) an expansion of the upper end of a ureter (the tube that drains urine into the bladder)
6. **Calyx** (KAY-liks) (pl. *calyces*)—a division of the renal pelvis (The papilla of a pyramid opens into each calyx.)

MICROSCOPIC STRUCTURE

More than a million microscopic units called **nephrons** (NEF-rons) make up each kidney's interior. The shape of a nephron is unique, unmistakable, and admirably suited to its function of producing urine. It looks a little like a tiny funnel with a very long stem, but it is an unusual stem in that it is highly convoluted (that is, it has many bends in it). The nephron is composed of two principle components: the **renal corpuscle** and the **renal tubule.** The renal corpuscle can be subdivided still further into two parts and the renal tubule into four regions or segments. Identify each part of the renal corpuscle and renal tubule described below in Figures 16-3 and 16-4.

FIGURE 16–1 ***Urinary System.*** **A,** Location of urinary system organs. **B,** X-ray film of the urinary organs.

A

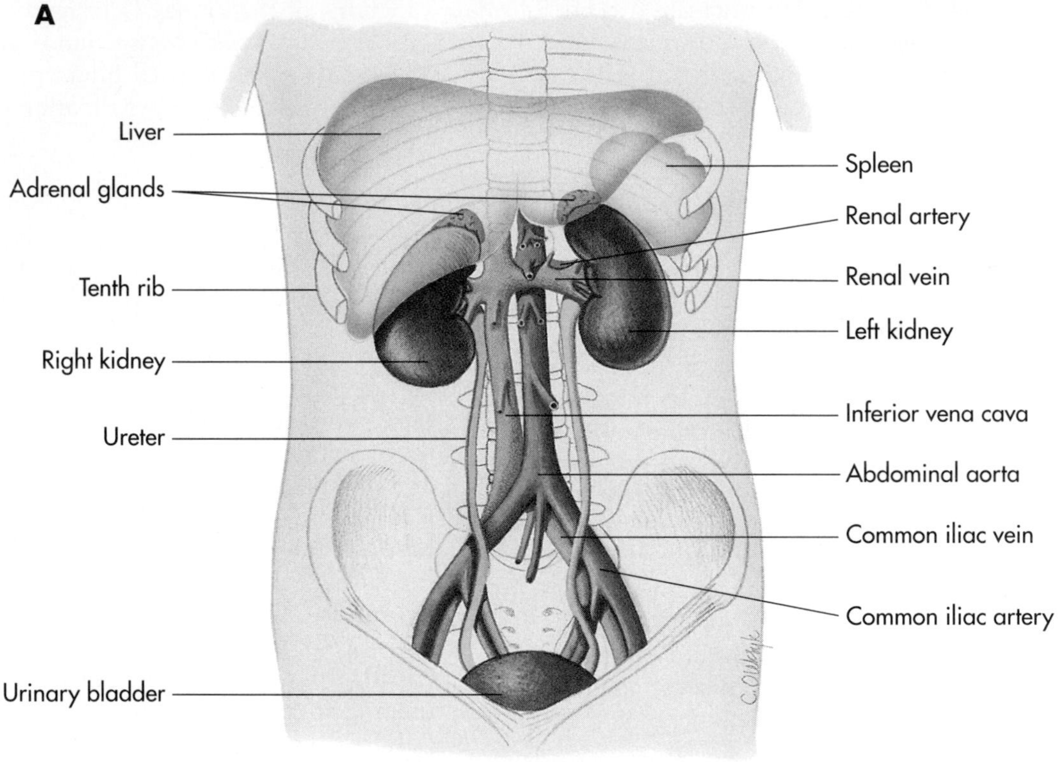

B

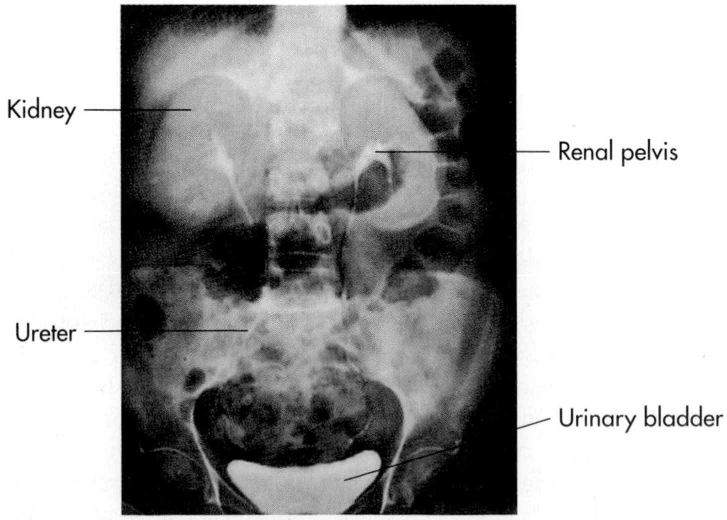

FIGURE 16–2 ***Kidney.*** Coronal section through the right kidney.

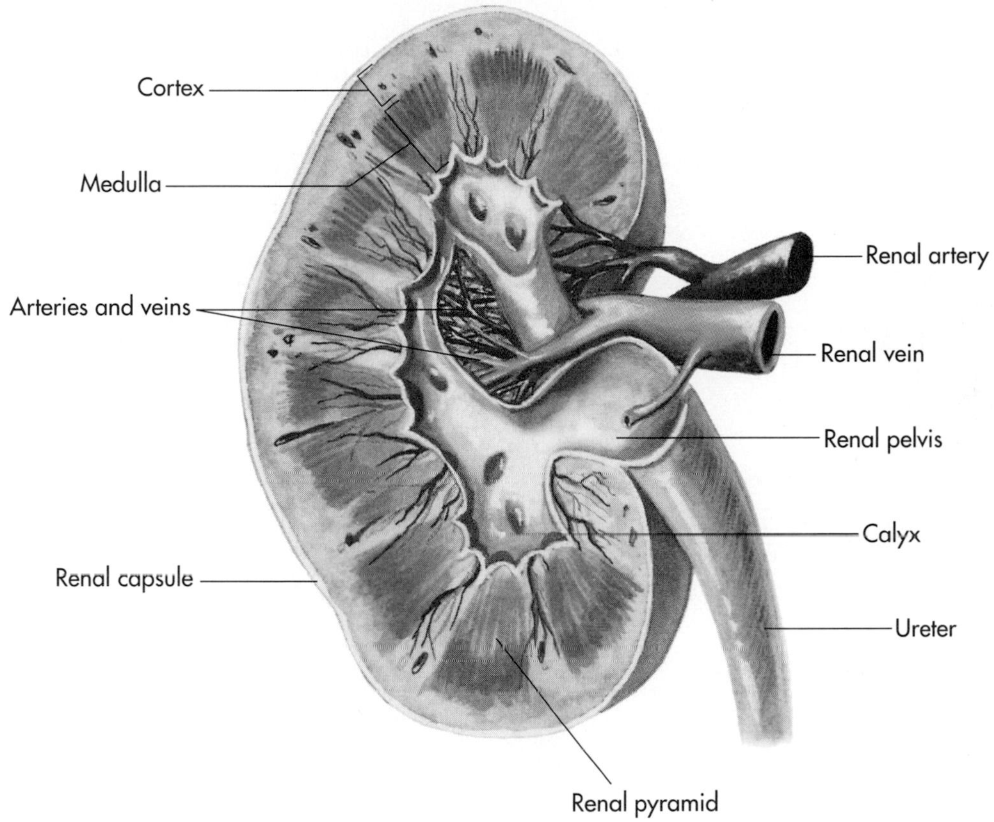

1. **Renal corpuscle**
   a. **Bowman's capsule**—the cup-shaped top of a nephron (The saclike Bowman's capsule surrounds the glomerulus.)
   b. **Glomerulus** (glo-MAIR-yoo-lus) (pl. *glomeruli*)—a network of blood capillaries tucked into Bowman's capsule (Note in Figure 16-3 that the small artery that delivers blood to the glomerulus, **[afferent arteriole]** is larger in diameter than the blood vessel that drains blood from it **[efferent arteriole]** and that it is relatively short. This explains the high blood pressure that exists in the glomerular capillaries. This high pressure is required to filter wastes from the blood.)
2. **Renal tubule**
   a. **Proximal convoluted tubule**—the first segment of a renal tubule (It is called *proximal* because it lies nearest the tubule's origin from Bowman's capsule, and it is called *convoluted* because it has several bends.)
   b. **Loop of Henle** (HEN-lee)—the extension of the proximal tubule (Observe that the loop of Henle consists of a straight descending limb, a hairpin loop, and a straight ascending limb.)
   c. **Distal convoluted tubule**—the part of the tubule distal to the ascending limb of the loop of Henle (It is the extension of the ascending limb.)
   d. **Collecting tubule**—a straight (that is, not convoluted) part of a renal tubule (Distal tubules of several nephrons join to form a single collecting tubule or duct.)

FIGURE 16–3 ***Location of the Nephron.*** **A,** Magnified wedge cut from a renal pyramid. **B,** Scanning electron micrograph showing several glomeruli and their associated blood vessels.

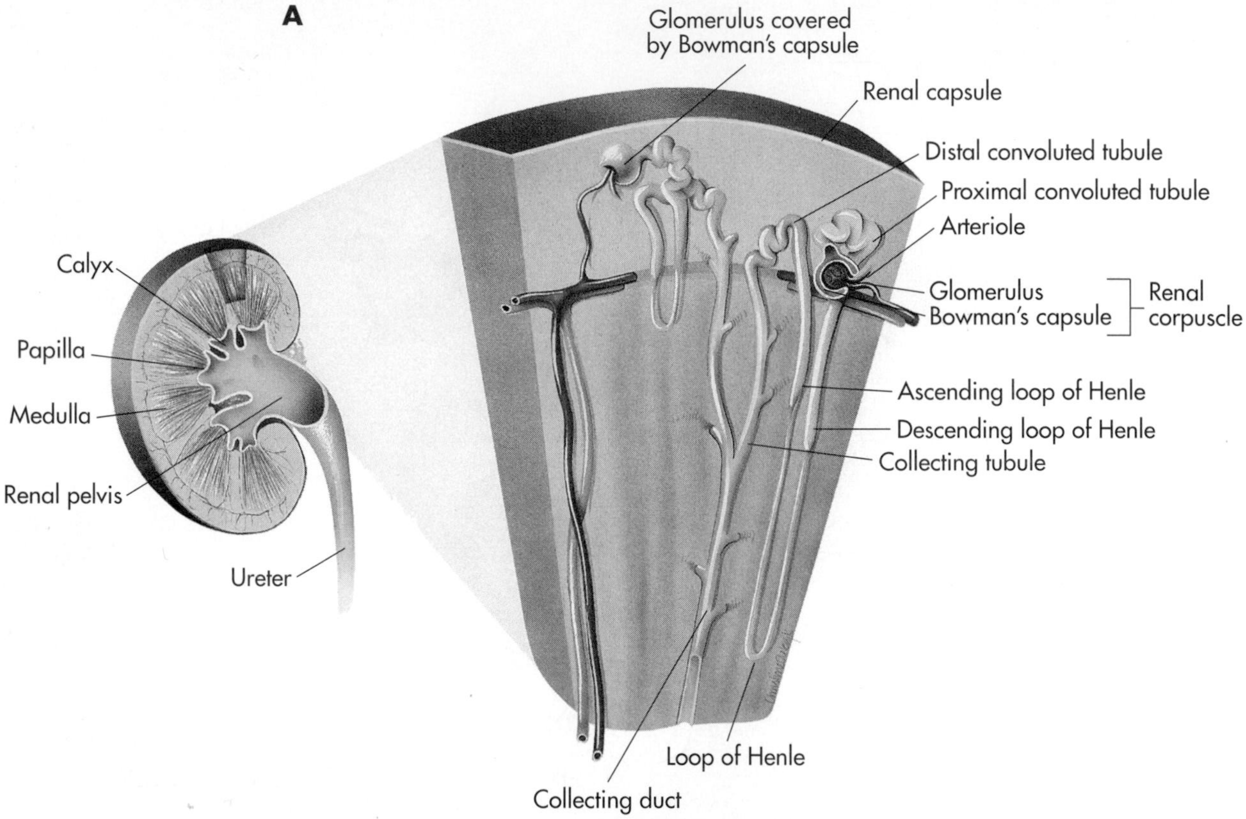

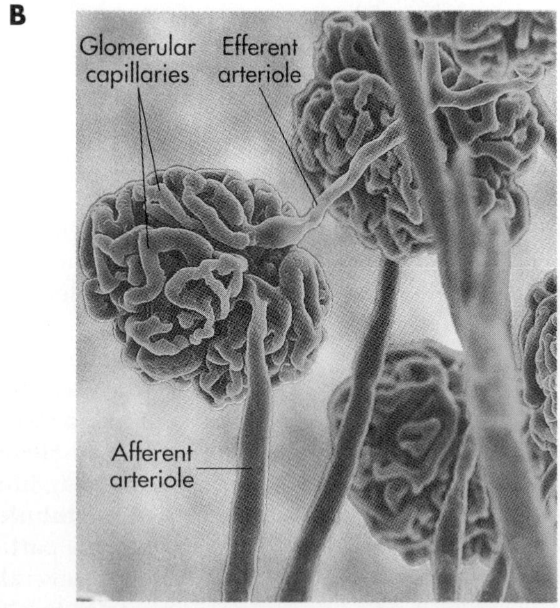

FIGURE 16–4 ***The Nephron Unit.*** Cross sections from the four segments of the renal tubule are shown. The differences in appearance in tubular cells seen in a cross section reflect the differing functions of each nephron segment.

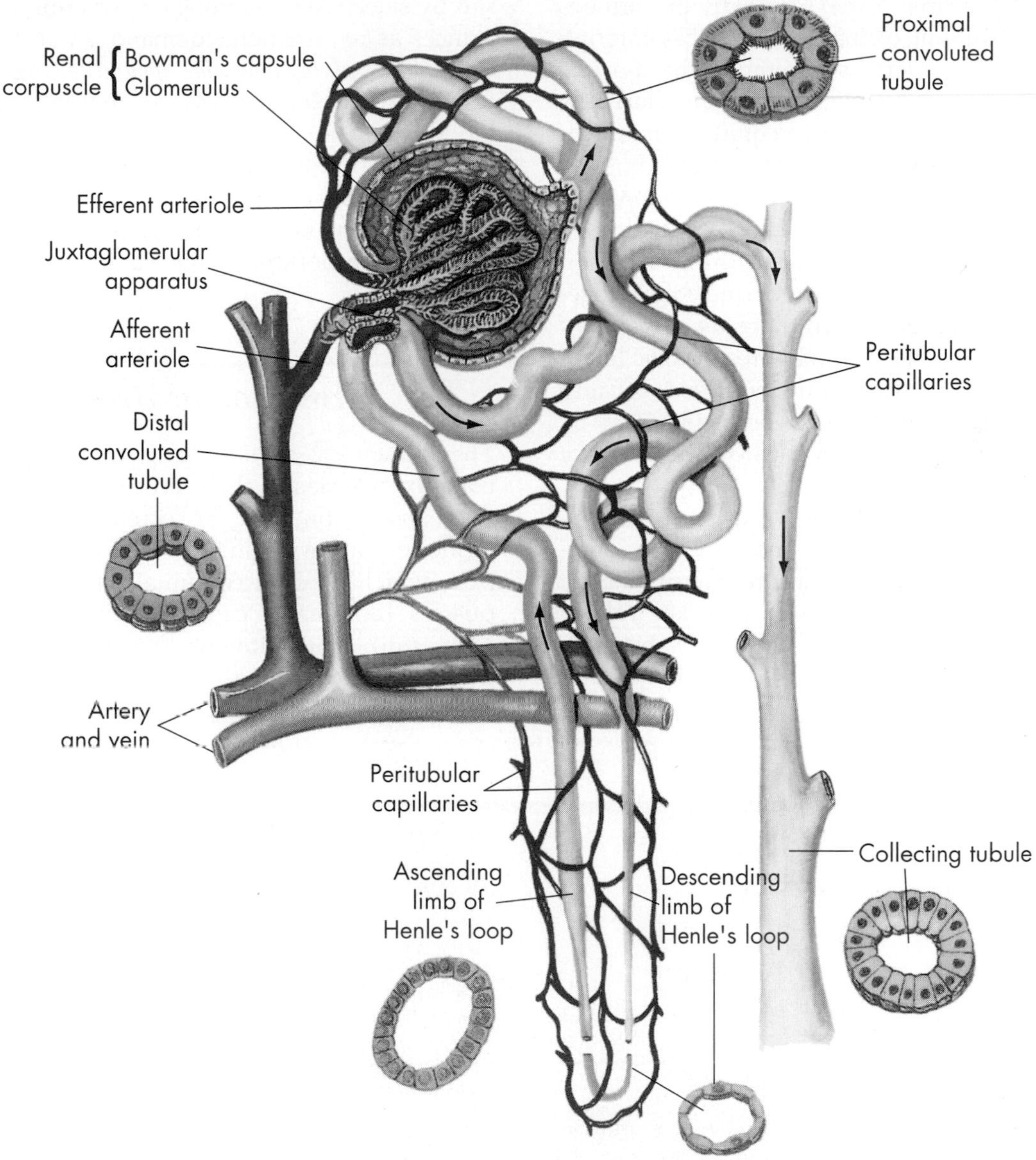

Look again at Figure 16-3. Note that the renal corpuscles (glomeruli surrounded by Bowman's capsule) and both proximal and distal convoluted tubules are located in the cortex of the kidney. The medulla contains the loop of Henle and collecting tubules. Urine from the collecting tubules exits from the pyramid through the papilla and enters the calyx and renal pelvis before flowing into the ureter.

FUNCTION

The kidneys are vital organs. The function they perform, that of forming urine, is essential for homeostasis and maintenance of life. Early in the process of urine formation, fluid, electrolytes, and wastes from metabolism are *filtered* from the blood and enter the nephron. Additional wastes may be *secreted* into the tubules of the nephron as substances useful to the body are reabsorbed into the blood. Table 16-1 lists the components of normal versus abnormal urine. Normally the kidneys balance the amount of many substances entering and leaving the blood over time so that normal concentrations can be maintained. In short, the kidneys adjust their output to equal the intake of the body. By eliminating wastes and adjusting fluid balance, the kidneys play an essential part in maintaining homeostasis. Homeostasis cannot be maintained—nor can life itself—if the kidneys fail and the condition is not soon corrected. Nitrogenous waste products accumulate as a result of protein breakdown and quickly reach toxic levels if not excreted. If kidney function ceases because of injury or disease, life can be maintained by using an artificial kidney to cleanse the blood of wastes.

Excretion of toxins and of waste products containing nitrogen such as urea and ammonia represents only one of the important responsibilities of the kidney. The kidney also plays a key role in regulating the levels of many chemical substances in the blood such as chloride, sodium, potassium, and bicarbonate. The kidneys also regulate the proper balance between body water content and salt by selectively retaining or excreting both substances as requirements demand. In addition, the cells of the *juxtaglomerular apparatus* (Figure 16-4) function in blood pressure regulation. When blood pressure is low, these cells secrete a hormone that initiates constriction of blood vessels and thus raises blood pressure. It is easy to understand why the kidneys are often considered to be the most important homeostatic organs in the body.

Formation of Urine

The kidney's 2 million or more nephrons form urine by a series of three processes: (1) filtration, (2) reabsorption, and (3) secretion (Figure 16-5). Urine formation begins with the process of **filtration,** which goes on continually in the renal corpuscles (Bowman's capsules plus their encased glomeruli). Blood flowing through the glomeruli exerts pressure, and this glomerular blood pressure is high enough to push water and dissolved

TABLE 16–1 Characteristics of Urine

NORMAL CHARACTERISTICS	ABNORMAL CHARACTERISTICS
Color	
Transparent yellow, amber, or straw colored	Abnormal colors or cloudiness, which may indicate presence of blood, bile, bacteria, drugs, food pigments, or high-solute concentration
Compounds	
Mineral ions (for example, Na, Cl, K)	Acetone
Nitrogenous wastes: ammonia, creatinine, urea, uric acid	Albumin
Suspended solids (sediment)*: bacteria, blood cells, casts (solid matter)	Bile
Urine pigments	Glucose
Odor	
Slight odor	Acetone odor, which is common in diabetes mellitus
pH	
4.6-8.0	High in alkalosis; low in acidosis
Specific Gravity	
1.001-1.035	High specific gravity can cause precipitation of solutes and formation of kidney stones

*Occasional trace amounts.

substances out of the glomeruli into the Bowman's capsule. Briefly, glomerular blood pressure causes filtration through the glomerular-capsular membrane. If the glomerular blood pressure drops below a certain level, filtration and urine formation cease. Hemorrhage, for example, may cause a precipitous drop in blood pressure followed by kidney failure.

Glomerular filtration normally occurs at the rate of 125 ml per minute. As a result, about 180 liters (almost 190 quarts) of **glomerular filtrate** is produced by the kidneys every day.

Obviously no one ever excretes anywhere near 180 L of urine per day. Why? Because most of the fluid that leaves the blood by glomerular filtration, the first process in urine formation, returns to the blood by the second process—reabsorption.

Reabsorption is the movement of substances out of the renal tubules into the blood capillaries located around the tubules (peritubular capillaries). Water, glucose and other nutrients, and sodium and other ions are substances that are reabsorbed. Reabsorption begins in the proximal convoluted tubules and continues in the loop of Henle, distal convoluted tubules, and collecting tubules.

FIGURE 16–5 *Formation of Urine.* Diagram shows the steps in urine formation in successive parts of a nephron: filtration, reabsorption, and secretion.

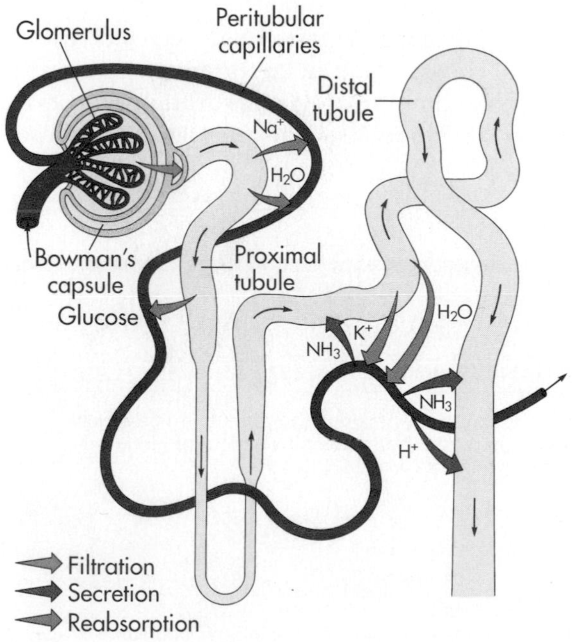

Large amounts of water—approximately 178 L per day—are reabsorbed by osmosis from the proximal tubules. In other words, nearly 99% of the 180 L of water that leave the blood each day by glomerular filtration returns to the blood by proximal tubule reabsorption.

The nutrient glucose is only reabsorbed from the proximal tubules. It is actively transported out of them into peritubular capillary blood. None of this valuable nutrient is wasted by being lost in the urine. However, exceptions occur. For example, in *diabetes mellitus,* if blood glucose concentration increases above a certain level, the tubular filtrate then contains more glucose than kidney tubule cells can reabsorb. Some of the glucose therefore remains behind in the urine. Glucose in the urine—**glycosuria** (glye-ko-SOO-ree-ah)—is a well-known sign of the condition, diabetes mellitus (Figure 16-6).

Sodium ions and other ions are only partially reabsorbed from renal tubules. For the most part, sodium ions are actively transported back into blood from the tubular urine. The amount of sodium reabsorbed varies from time to time; it

FIGURE 16–6 *Glycosuria.* Using a reagent strip to check the level of glucose in the urine of a diabetic patient.

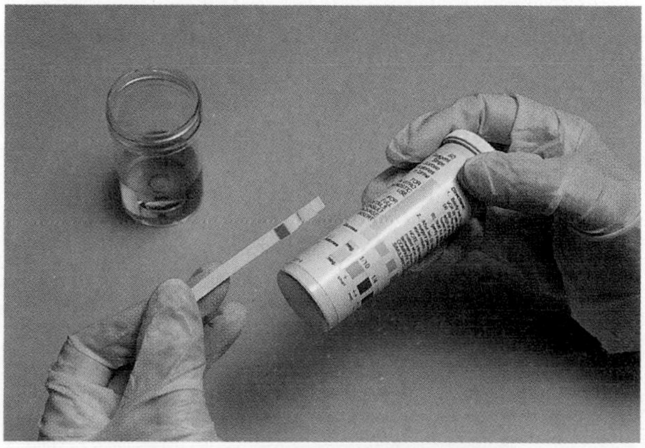

depends largely on salt intake. In general the greater the amount of salt intake, the less the amount of salt reabsorption and therefore the greater the amount of salt excreted in the urine. Also, the less the salt intake, the greater the salt reabsorption and the less salt excreted in the urine. By varying the amount of salt reabsorbed, the body usually can maintain homeostasis of the blood's salt concentration. This is an extremely important matter because cells are damaged by either too much or too little salt in the fluid around them (see box about tonicity, p. 24).

Secretion is the process by which substances move into urine in the distal and collecting tubules from blood in the capillaries around these tubules. In this respect, secretion is reabsorption in reverse. Whereas reabsorption moves substances out of the urine into the blood, secretion moves substances out of the blood into the urine. Substances secreted are hydrogen ions, potassium ions, ammonia, and certain drugs. Hydrogen ions, potassium ions, and drugs are secreted by being actively transported out of the blood into tubular urine. Ammonia is secreted by diffusion. Kidney tubule secretion plays a crucial role in maintaining the body's acid-base balance (see Chapter 18).

In summary, the following processes occurring in successive portions of the nephron accomplish the function of urine formation (Table 16-2):

1. **Filtration**—of water and dissolved substances out of the blood in the glomeruli into Bowman's capsule
2. **Reabsorption**—of water and dissolved substances out of kidney tubules back into blood (This prevents substances needed by the body from being lost in urine. Usually, 97% to 99% of water filtered out of glomerular blood is retrieved from tubules.)
3. **Secretion**—of hydrogen ions, potassium ions, and certain drugs

CONTROL OF URINE VOLUME

The body has ways to control the amount and composition of the urine that it excretes. It does this mainly by controlling the amount of water and dissolved substances that are reabsorbed by the convoluted tubules. For example, a hormone (antidiuretic hormone or ADH) from the posterior pituitary gland decreases the amount of urine by making collecting tubules permeable to water. If no ADH is present, the tubules are practically impermeable to water, so little or no water is reabsorbed from them. When ADH is present in the blood, collecting tubules are permeable to water and water is reabsorbed from them. As a result, less water is lost from the body as urine, or more water is retained from the tubules—whichever way you wish to say it. At any rate, for this reason ADH is accurately described as the "water-retaining hormone." You might also think of it as the "urine-decreasing hormone."

The hormone aldosterone, secreted by the adrenal cortex, plays an important part in controlling the kidney tubules' reabsorption of salt. Primarily it stimulates the tubules to reabsorb

TABLE 16–2 Functions of Parts of Nephron in Urine Formation

PART OF NEPHRON	PROCESS IN URINE FORMATION	SUBSTANCES MOVED
Glomerulus	Filtration	Water and solutes (for example, sodium and other ions, glucose and other nutrients filtering out of glomeruli into Bowman's capsules)
Probimal tubule	Reabsorption	Water and solutes
Loop of Henle	Reabsorption	Sodium and chloride ions
Distal and collecting tubules	Reabsorption	Water, sodium, and chloride ions
	Secretion	Ammonia, potassium ions, hydrogen ions, and some drugs

sodium salts at a faster rate. Secondarily, aldosterone also increases tubular water reabsorption. The term *salt- and water-retaining hormone* therefore is a descriptive nickname for aldosterone. This mechanism is discussed in the next chapter.

Another hormone, atrial natriuretic hormone (ANH) secreted from the heart's atrial wall, has the opposite effect of aldosterone. ANH stimulates kidney tubules to secrete more sodium and thus lose more water. Thus ANH is a *salt- and water-losing hormone.* The body secretes ADH, aldosterone, and ANH in different amounts, depending on the homeostatic balance of body fluids at any particular moment.

Sometimes the kidneys do not excrete normal amounts of urine as a result of kidney disease, cardiovascular disease, or stress. Here are some terms associated with abnormal amounts of urine:

1. **Anuria** (ah-NOO-ree-ah)—absence of urine
2. **Oliguria** (ol-i-GOO-ree-ah)—scanty amounts of urine
3. **Polyuria** (pol-e-YOO-ree-ah)—an unusually large amount of urine

Proteinuria After Exercise

Proteinuria is the presence of abnormally large amounts of plasma proteins in the urine. Proteinuria usually indicates kidney disease **(nephropathy)** because only damaged nephrons consistently allow many plasma protein molecules to leave the blood. However, intense exercise causes temporary proteinuria in many individuals. Some exercise physiologists believed that intense athletic activities cause kidney damage, but subsequent research has ruled out that explanation. One current hypothesis is that hormonal changes during strenuous exercise increase the permeability of the nephron's filtration membrane, allowing more plasma proteins to enter the filtrate. Some postexercise proteinuria is usually considered normal.

Ureters

Urine drains out of the collecting tubules of each kidney into the renal pelvis and down the ureter into the urinary bladder (Figure 16-1). The **renal pelvis** is the basinlike upper end of the ureter located inside the kidney. Ureters are narrow tubes less than 6 mm (¼ inch) wide and 25 to 30 cm (10 to 12 inches) long. Mucous membranes line both ureters and each renal pelvis. Note in Figure 16-7 that the ureter has a thick, muscular wall. Contraction of the muscular coat produces peristaltic-type movements that assist in moving urine down the ureters into the bladder. The lining membrane of the ureters is richly supplied with sensory nerve endings.

FIGURE 16–7 ***Ureter Cross Section.*** Note the thick layer of muscle around the tube.

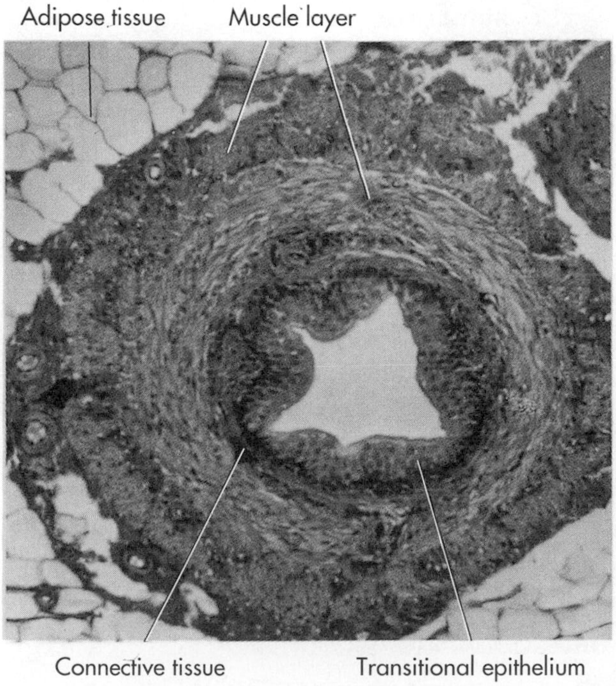

Artificial Kidney

The artificial kidney is a mechanical device that uses the principle of dialysis to remove or separate waste products from the blood. In the event of kidney failure, the process, appropriately called **hemodialysis** (Greek *haima* "blood" and *lysis* "separate"), is a reprieve from death for the patient. During a hemodialysis treatment, a semipermeable membrane is used to separate large (nondiffusible) particles such as blood cells from small (diffusible) ones such as urea and other wastes. Figure *A* shows blood from the radial artery passing through a porous (semipermeable) cellophane tube that is housed in a tanklike container. The tube is surrounded by a bath or dialyzing solution containing varying concentrations of electrolytes and other chemicals. The pores in the membrane are small and allow only very small molecules, such as urea, to escape into the surrounding fluid. Larger molecules and blood cells cannot escape and are returned through the tube to reenter the patient via a wrist vein. By constantly replacing the bath solution in the dialysis tank with freshly mixed solution, levels of waste materials can be kept at low levels. As a result, wastes such as urea in the blood rapidly pass into the surrounding wash solution. For a patient with complete kidney failure, two or three hemodialysis treatments a week are required.

Dialysis treatments are now being monitored and controlled by sophisticated com-

A

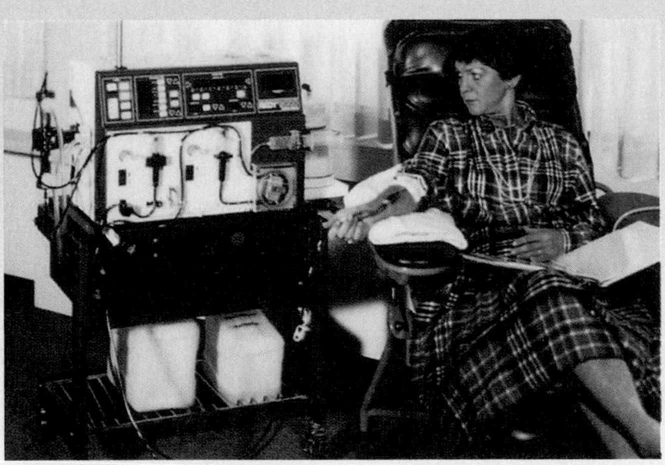

puter components and software integrated into modern hemodialysis equipment. New and dramatic advances in both treatment techniques and equipment are expected to continue. Although most hemodialysis treatments occur in hospital or clinical settings, equipment designed for use in the home is now available and appropriate for some individuals. Patients and their families using this equipment are initially instructed in its use and then monitored and supported on an ongoing basis by home health care professionals.

Another technique used in the treatment of renal failure is called **continuous ambulatory peritoneal dialysis (CAPD).** In this procedure, 1 to 3 L of sterile dialysis fluid is introduced directly into the peritoneal cavity through an opening in the abdominal wall (Figure *B*). Peritoneal membranes in the abdominal cavity transfer waste products from the blood into the dialysis fluid, which is then drained back into a plastic container after about 2 hours. This technique is less expensive than hemodialysis and does not require the use of complex equipment. CAPD is the more frequently used home-based dialysis treatment for patients with chronic renal failure. Successful longterm treatment is greatly enhanced by support from professionals trained in home health care services.

B

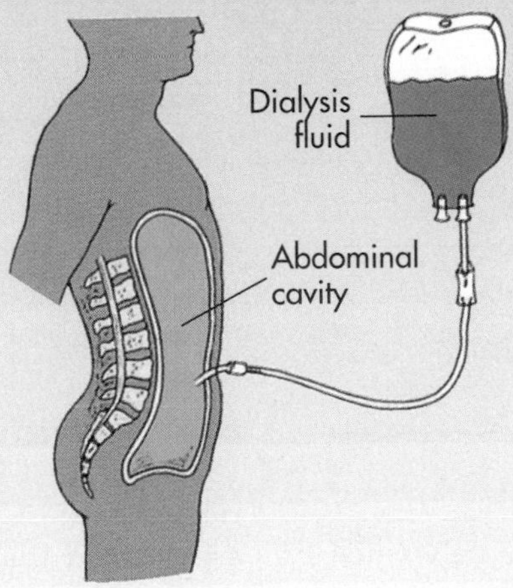

FIGURE 16–8 ***The Male Urinary Bladder.*** This view (with bladder cut to show the interior) shows how the prostate gland surrounds the urethra as it exits from the bladder. The glands associated with the male reproductive system are further discussed in Chapter 19.

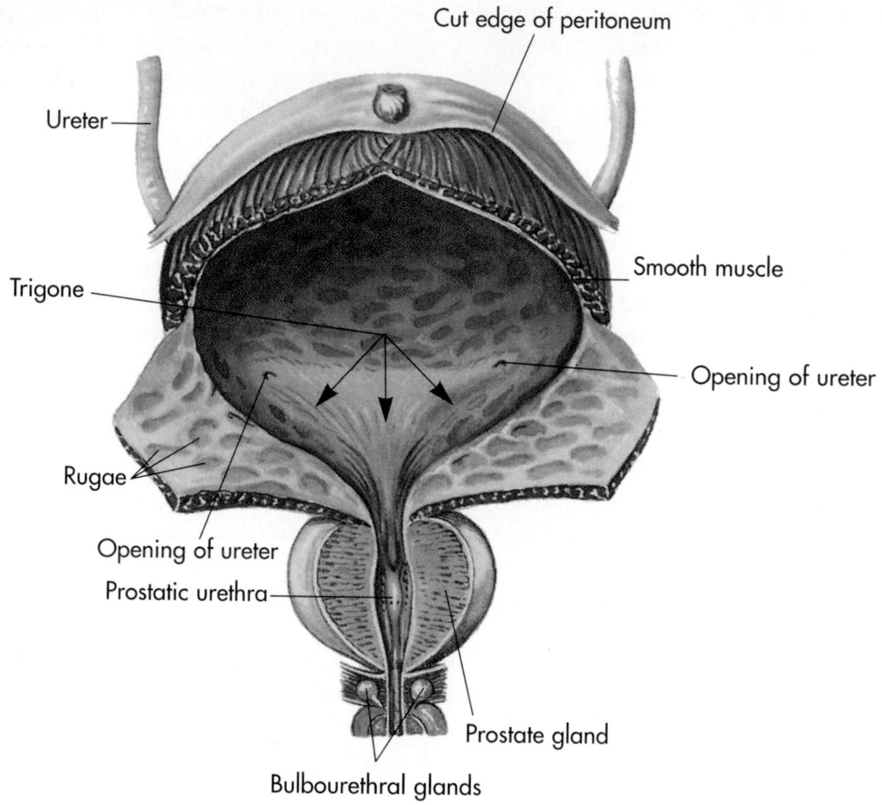

Urinary Bladder

The empty urinary bladder lies in the pelvis just behind the pubic symphysis. When full of urine, it projects upward into the lower portion of the abdominal cavity.

Elastic fibers and involuntary muscle fibers in the wall of the urinary bladder make it well suited for expanding to hold variable amounts of urine and then contracting to empty itself. Mucous membrane lines the urinary bladder. The lining is loosely attached to the deeper muscular layer so that the bladder is very wrinkled and lies in folds called *rugae* when it is empty. When the bladder is filled, its inner surface is smooth. Note in Figure 16-8 that one triangular area on the back or posterior surface of the bladder is free of rugae. This area, called the *trigone,* is always smooth. There, the lining membrane is tightly fixed to the deeper muscle coat. The trigone extends between the openings of the two ureters above and the point of exit of the urethra below.

Attacks of *renal colic*—pain caused by the passage of a kidney stone—have been described in medical writings since antiquity. Kidney stones cause intense pain if they have sharp edges or are large enough to distend the walls or cut the lining of the ureters or urethra as they pass from the kidneys to the exterior of the body.

Urinary Catheterization

Urinary catheterization is the passage or insertion of a hollow tube or catheter through the urethra into the bladder for the withdrawal of urine. It is a medical procedure commonly performed on many patients who undergo prolonged surgical or diagnostic procedures or who experience problems with urinary retention.

Correct catheterization procedures require aseptic techniques to prevent the introduction of infectious bacteria into the urinary system. Clinical studies have proved that improper catheterization techniques cause bladder infections (cystitis) in hospitalized patients. One landmark study confirmed the high percentage of catheterized patients who develop cystitis (almost 8%) and found that, of those who developed such infections, a significant number died. The results of the study are sobering and point out the need for extensive training of health professionals in this area.

Urethra

To leave the body, urine passes from the bladder, down the urethra, and out of its external opening, the **urinary meatus.** In other words, the urethra is the lowest part of the urinary tract. The same sheet of mucous membrane that lines each renal pelvis, the ureters, and the bladder extends down into the urethra, too; this is a structural feature worth noting because it accounts for the fact that an infection of the urethra may spread upward through the urinary tract. The urethra is a narrow tube; it is only about 4 cm (1½ inches) long in a woman, but it is about 20 cm (8 inches) long in a man. In a man, the urethra has two functions: (1) it is the terminal portion of the urinary tract, and (2) it is the passageway for movement of the reproductive fluid (semen) from the body. In a woman, the urethra is a part of only the urinary tract.

Micturition

The terms **micturition** (mik-too-RISH-un), **urination** (yoor-i-NAY-shun), and **voiding** refer to the passage of urine from the body or the emptying of the bladder. This is a reflex action in infants or very young children. Although there is considerable variation between individuals, most children between 2 and 3 years of age learn to urinate voluntarily and also to inhibit voiding if the urge comes at an inconvenient time.

Two **sphincters** (SFINGK-ters) or rings of muscle tissue guard the pathway leading from the bladder. The **internal urethral sphincter** is located at the bladder exit, and the **external urethral sphincter** circles the urethra just below the neck of the bladder. When contracted, both sphincters seal off the bladder and allow urine to accumulate without leaking to the exterior. The internal urethral sphincter is involuntary, and the external urethral sphincter is composed of striated muscle and is under voluntary control.

The muscular wall of the bladder permits this organ to accommodate a considerable volume of urine with very little increase in pressure until a volume of 300 to 400 ml is reached. As the volume of urine increases, the need to void may be noticed at volumes of 150 ml, but micturition in adults does not normally occur much below volumes of 350 ml. As the bladder wall stretches, nervous impulses are transmitted to the second, third, and fourth sacral segments of the spinal cord, and an **emptying reflex** is initiated. The reflex causes contraction of the muscle of the bladder wall and relaxation of the internal sphincter. Urine then enters the urethra. If the external sphincter, which is under voluntary control, is relaxed, micturition occurs. Voluntary contraction of the external sphincter suppresses the emptying reflex until the bladder is filled to capacity with urine and loss of control occurs. Contraction of this powerful sphincter also abruptly terminates urination voluntarily.

Higher centers in the brain also function in micturition by integrating bladder contraction and internal and external sphincter relaxation, with the cooperative contraction of pelvic and abdominal muscles. Urinary **retention** is a condition in which no urine is voided. The kidneys produce urine, but the bladder for one reason or

Removal of Kidney Stones Using Ultrasound

Statistics suggest that approximately 1 in every 1000 adults in the United States suffers from kidney stones or **renal calculi** (KAL-kyoo-lye) at some point in their life. Although symptoms of excruciating pain are common, many kidney stones are small enough to pass out of the urinary system spontaneously. If this is possible, no therapy is required other than treatment for pain and antibiotics if the calculi are associated with infection. Larger stones, however, may obstruct the flow of urine and are much more serious and difficult to treat.

Until recently, only traditional surgical procedures were effective in removing relatively large stones that formed in the calyces and renal pelvis of the kidney. In addition to the risks that always accompany major medical procedures, surgical removal of stones from the kidneys frequently requires rather extensive hospital and home recovery periods, lasting 6 weeks or more.

A technique that uses ultrasound to pulverize the stones so that they can be flushed out of the urinary tract without surgery is used in hospitals across the United States. The specially designed ultrasound generator required for the procedure is called a **lithotriptor** (li-tho-TRIP-ter). Using a lithotriptor, physicians break up the stones with ultrasound waves without making an incision. Recovery time is minimal and patient risk and costs are reduced.

another cannot empty itself. In urinary **suppression** the opposite is true. The kidneys do not produce any urine, but the bladder retains the ability to empty itself.

Incontinence (in-KON-ti-nens) is a condition in which the patient voids urine involuntarily. It frequently occurs in patients who have suffered a stroke or spinal cord injury. If the sacral segments of the spinal cord are injured, some loss of bladder function always occurs. Although the voiding reflex may be reestablished to some degree, the bladder does not empty completely. In these individuals the residual urine is often the cause of repeated bladder infections or **cystitis** (sis-TIE-tis). Complete destruction or transection of the sacral cord produces a condition called an *automatic bladder.* Totally cut off from spinal innervation, the bladder musculature acquires some automatic action and periodic but unpredictable voiding occurs.

OUTLINE SUMMARY

KIDNEYS

A Location—under back muscles, behind parietal peritoneum, just above waistline; right kidney usually a little lower than left (Figure 16-1)

B Internal structure (Figure 16-2)
- **1** Cortex—outer layer of kidney substance
- **2** Medulla—inner portion of kidney
- **3** Pyramids—triangular divisions of medulla
- **4** Papilla—narrow, innermost end of pyramid
- **5** Pelvis—expansion of upper end of ureter; lies inside kidney
- **6** Calyces—divisions of renal pelvis

C Microscopic structure—nephrons are microscopic units of kidneys; consist of (Figure 16-3):
- **1** Renal corpuscle—Bowman's capsule with its glomerulus
  - **a** Bowman's capsule—the cup-shaped top
  - **b** Glomerulus—network of blood capillaries surrounded by Bowman's capsule
- **2** Renal tubule
  - **a** Proximal convoluted tubule—first segment
  - **b** Loop of Henle—extension of proximal tubule; consists of descending limb, loop, and ascending limb
  - **c** Distal convoluted tubule—extension of ascending limb of loop of Henle
  - **d** Collecting tubule—straight extension of distal tubule

D Functions
- **1** Excretes toxins and nitrogenous wastes
- **2** Regulates levels of many chemicals in blood
- **3** Maintains water balance
- **4** Helps regulate blood pressure via secretion of renin

FORMATION OF URINE (Figure 16-5)

A Occurs by a series of three processes that take place in successive parts of nephron
- **1** Filtration—goes on continually in renal corpuscles; glomerular blood pressure causes water and dissolved substances to filter out of glomeruli into Bowman's capsule; normal glomerular filtration rate 125 ml per minute
- **2** Reabsorption—movement of substances out of renal tubules into blood in peritubular capillaries; water, nutrients, and ions are reabsorbed; water is reabsorbed by osmosis from proximal tubules
- **3** Secretion—movement of substances into urine in the distal and collecting tubules from blood in peritubular capillaries; hydrogen ions, potassium ions, and certain drugs are secreted by active transport; ammonia is secreted by diffusion

B Control of urine volume—mainly by posterior pituitary hormone's ADH, which decreases it

URETERS

A Structure—narrow long tubes with expanded upper end (renal pelvis) located inside kidney and lined with mucous membrane

B Function—drain urine from renal pelvis to urinary bladder

URINARY BLADDER

A Structure (Figure 16-8)
- **1** Elastic muscular organ, capable of great expansion
- **2** Lined with mucous membrane arranged in rugae, like stomach mucosa

B Functions
- **1** Storage of urine before voiding
- **2** Voiding

URETHRA

A Structure
- **1** Narrow tube from urinary bladder to exterior
- **2** Lined with mucous membrane
- **3** Opening of urethra to the exterior called *urinary meatus*

B Functions
- **1** Passage of urine from bladder to exterior of the body
- **2** Passage of male reproductive fluid (semen) from the body

MICTURITION

A Passage of urine from body (also called *urination* or *voiding*)

B Regulatory sphincters
- **1** Internal urethral sphincter (involuntary)
- **2** External urethral sphincter (voluntary)

C Bladder wall permits storage of urine with little increase in pressure

D Emptying reflex
- **1** Initiated by stretch reflex in bladder wall
- **2** Bladder wall contracts
- **3** Internal sphincter relaxes
- **4** External sphincter relaxes, and urination occurs

E Urinary retention—urine produced but not voided

F Urinary suppression—no urine produced but bladder is normal

G Incontinence—urine is voided involuntarily
- **1** May be caused by spinal injury or stroke
- **2** Retention of urine may cause cystitis

NEW WORDS

anuria
atrial natriuretic hormone (ANH)
Bowman's capsule
calyx
catheterization
cystitis
glomerulus
glycosuria
incontinence
lithotriptor
micturition
oliguria
papilla
polyuria
pyramid
renal colic
trigone
uremia
urination
voiding

CHAPTER TEST

1. Failure of the urinary system results in rapid accumulation of toxic wastes, a condition called ______________.
2. Normally a little over ______________ of the total blood pumped by the heart enters the kidneys.
3. The outer portion of the kidney is called the ______________, and the inner portion is called the ______________.
4. The functional unit of the kidney is called the ______________.
5. The renal corpuscle is composed of the cup-shaped ______________, and a network of blood capillaries called the ______________.
6. The first segment of the renal tubule is called the ______________ convoluted tubule.
7. Urine formation begins with the process of ______________ of wastes from the blood.
8. Water is reabsorbed from the proximal convoluted tubules by ______________.
9. Glucose is entirely reabsorbed from the ______________ tubules.
10. Production of unusually large amounts of urine is called ______________.
11. The basinlike upper end of the ureter located inside the kidney is called the renal ______________.
12. Attacks of pain caused by the passage of a kidney stone are called ______________ ______________.
13. Urine passes from the bladder down the ______________ and out its external opening, called the urinary ______________.
14. Voiding urine involuntarily is called ______________.
15. The medical term for bladder infection is ______________.
16. Glomerular filtration normally occurs at the rate of about ______________ ml per minute.

Select the most correct answer from Column B for each statement in Column A. (Only one answer is correct.)

COLUMN A	COLUMN B
17. ______ High waste levels	a. Glycosuria
18. ______ Contain renal corpuscles	b. Glomerulus
19. ______ Functional unit of kidney	c. ADH
20. ______ Tuft of capillaries	d. Nephron
21. ______ Glucose in urine	e. Uremia
22. ______ Absence of urine	f. Renal calculi
23. ______ Water-retaining hormone	g. Anuria
24. ______ Kidney stones	h. Micturition
25. ______ Urination	i. Cortex

REVIEW QUESTIONS

1. What organs form the urinary system?
2. Name the parts of a nephron.
3. What and where are the glomeruli and Bowman's capsules?
4. Explain briefly the functions of the glomeruli and Bowman's capsules.
5. Explain briefly the function of the renal tubules.
6. What kind of membrane lines the urinary tract?
7. Explain briefly the function of ADH. What is the full name of this hormone? What gland secretes it?
8. What hormone might appropriately be nicknamed the "water-retaining hormone"?
9. What hormone might appropriately be nicknamed the "salt- and water-retaining hormone"?
10. What hormone might be called the "salt- and water-losing hormone"?
11. What is the urinary meatus?
12. What and where are the ureters and the urethra?

CRITICAL THINKING

13. To operate on a kidney, does a surgeon have to cut through the peritoneum? Explain your answer.
14. Suppose that ADH secretion increases noticeably. Would this increase or decrease urine volume? Why?
15. Explain the process of micturition.

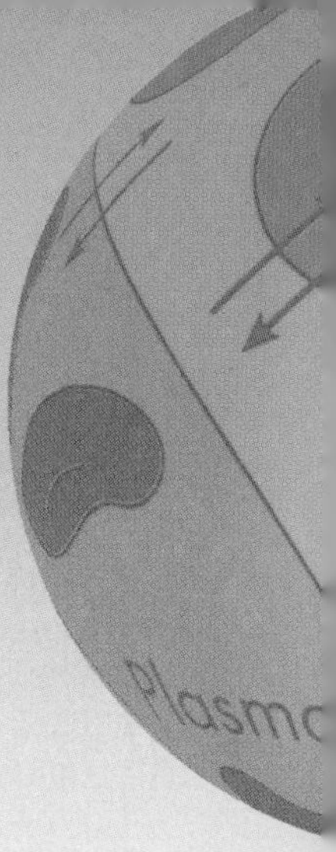

Fluid and Electrolyte Balance

17

OUTLINE

Body Fluids

Mechanisms That Maintain Fluid Balance

- Regulation of Fluid Intake
- Importance of Electrolytes in Body Fluids
- Capillary Blood Pressure and Blood Proteins

Fluid Imbalances

BOXED ESSAYS

Making Weight
Diuretics
Edema

OBJECTIVES

After you have completed this chapter, you should be able to:

1. List, describe, and compare the body fluid compartments and their subdivisions.
2. Discuss avenues by which water enters and leaves the body and the mechanisms that maintain fluid balance.
3. Discuss the nature and importance of electrolytes in body fluids and explain the aldosterone mechanism of extracellular fluid volume control.
4. Explain the interaction between capillary blood pressure and blood proteins.
5. Give examples of common fluid imbalances.

Have you ever wondered why you sometimes excrete great volumes of urine and sometimes excrete almost none at all? Why sometimes you feel so thirsty that you can hardly get enough to drink and other times you want no liquids at all? These conditions and many more relate to one of the body's most important functions—that of maintaining its **fluid** and **electrolyte balance.**

The term *fluid balance* means several things. Of course, it means the same thing as homeostasis of fluids. To say that the body is in a state of fluid balance is to say that the total amount of water in the body is normal and that it remains relatively constant. Electrolytes are substances such as salts that dissolve or break apart in water solution. Health and sometimes even survival itself depend on maintaining proper balance of water and the electrolytes within it.

In this chapter you will find a discussion of body fluids and electrolytes, their normal values, the mechanisms that operate to keep them normal, and some of the more common types of fluid and electrolyte imbalances.

Body Fluids

If you are a healthy young person and you weigh 120 pounds, there is a good chance that, of the hundreds of compounds present in your body, one substance alone accounts for about 50% to 60% of your total weight. This, the body's most abundant compound, is water. It occupies three main locations known as **fluid compartments.** Look now at Figure 17-1. Note that the largest volume of water by far lies inside cells and that it is called, appropriately, **intracellular fluid (ICF).** Note, too, that the water outside of cells—**extracellular fluid (ECF)**—is located in two compartments: in the microscopic spaces between cells, where it is called **interstitial fluid (IF),** and in the blood vessels, where it is called **plasma.** Plasma is the liquid part of the blood, constituting a little more than half of the total blood volume (about 55%); blood cells make up the rest of the volume.

A normal body maintains *fluid balance.* The term fluid balance means that the volumes of ICF, IF, and plasma and the total volume of water in the body remain relatively constant. Of course, not all bodies contain the same amount of water. The more a person weighs, the more water the body contains. This is true because, excluding fat or adipose tissue, about 55% of the body weight is water. Because fat is almost water free, the more fat present in the body, the less the total water content is per unit of weight. In other words, fat people have a lower water content per pound of body weight than slender people. The body of a slender adult man, for instance, typically consists of about 60% water. An obese male body, in contrast, may consist of only 50% water or even less.

Sex and age also influence the amount of water in a body. Infants have more water compared to body weight than adults of either sex. In a newborn, water may account for up to 80% of total body weight. There is a rapid decline in the proportion of body water to body weight during the first year of life. Figure 17-2 illustrates the proportion of body weight represented by water in newborn infants, men, and women. The female body contains slightly less water per pound of weight because it contains slightly more fat than the male body. Age and the body's water content are inversely related. In general, as age increases, the amount of water per pound of body weight decreases.

Mechanisms That Maintain Fluid Balance

Under normal conditions, homeostasis of the total volume of water in the body is maintained or restored primarily by devices that adjust output (urine volume) to intake and secondarily by mechanisms that adjust fluid intake. There is no question about which of the two mechanisms is more important; the body's chief mechanism, by far, for maintaining fluid balance is to adjust its fluid output so that it equals its fluid intake.

Obviously, as long as output and intake are equal, the total amount of water in the body does not change. Figure 17-3 shows the three sources of fluid intake: the liquids we drink, the water in the foods we eat, and the water formed by catabolism of foods. Table 17-1 gives their normal volumes. However, these can vary a great deal and still be considered normal. Table 17-1 also indicates that fluid output from the body occurs through four

FIGURE 17–1 *Fluid Compartments of the Body.* Percentages and volumes are given for young adults weighing 55 kg (120 lbs).

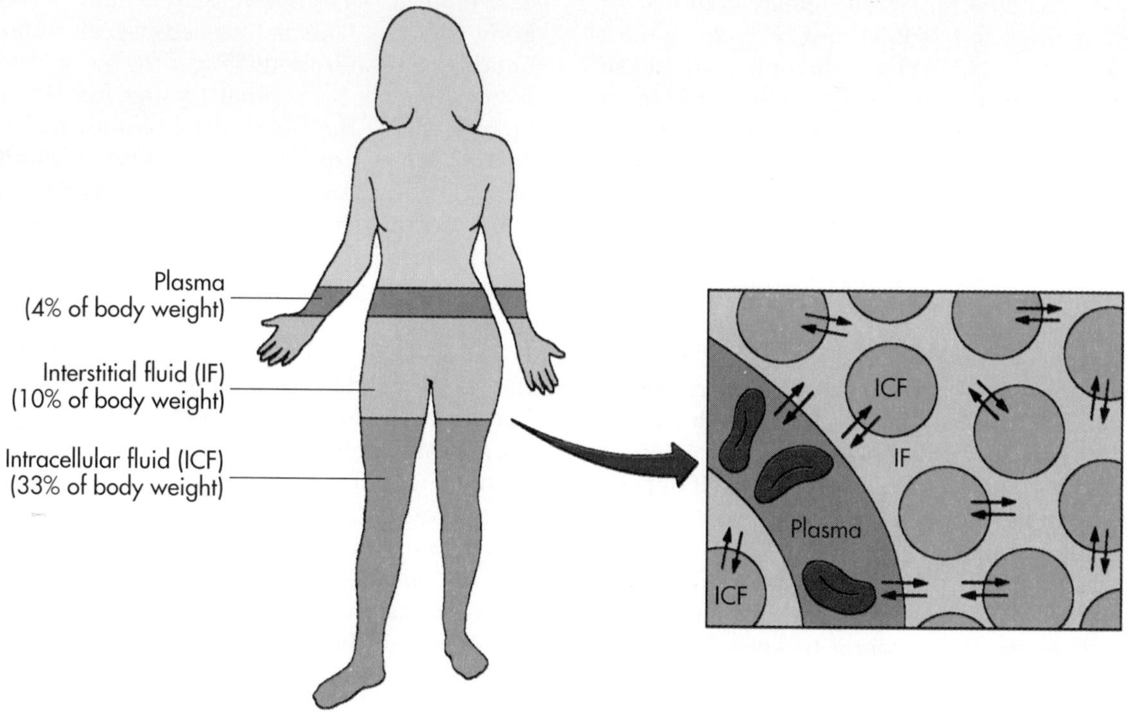

FIGURE 17–2 *Proportion of Body Weight Represented by Water.*

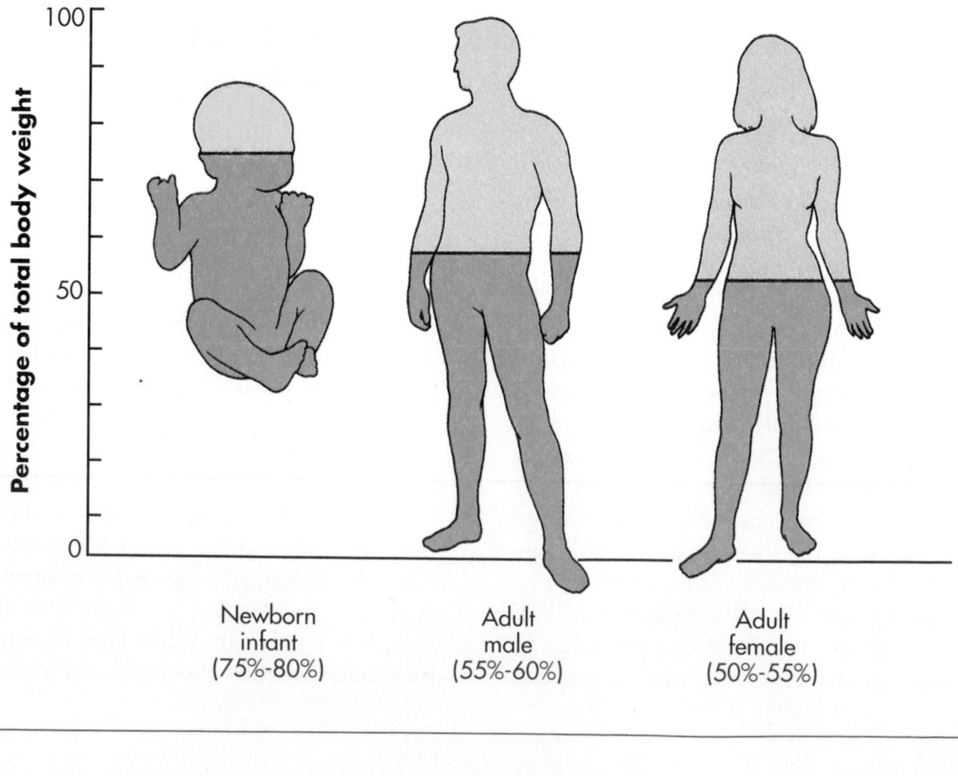

FIGURE 17–3 ***Sources of Fluid Intake and Output.***

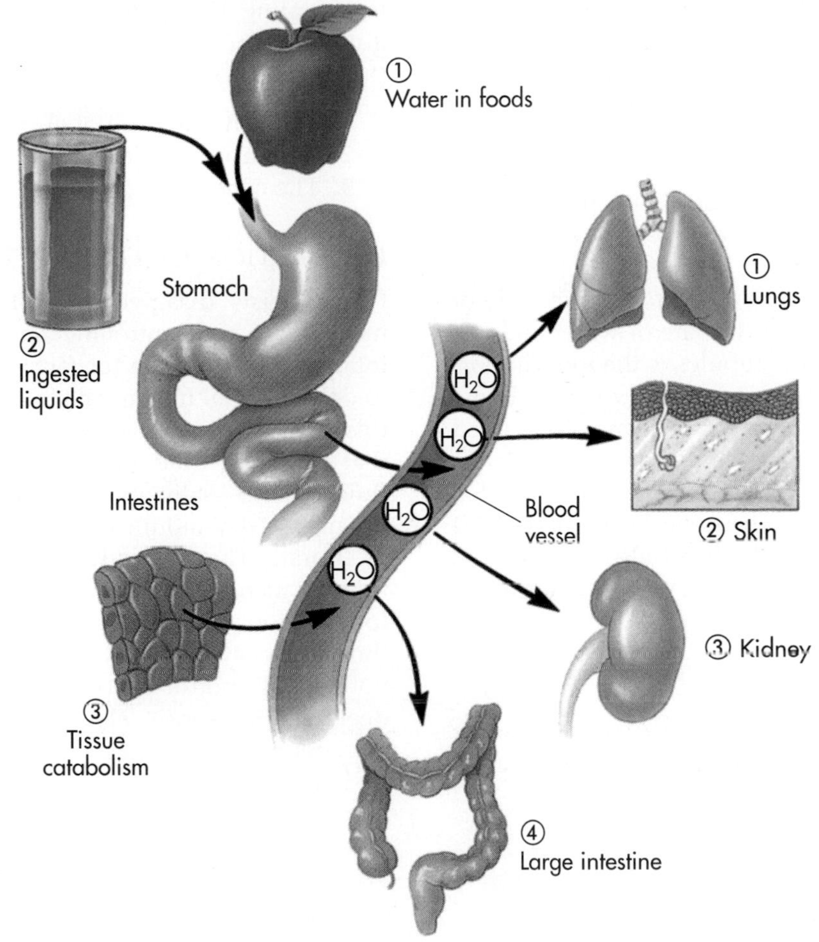

TABLE 17–1 Typical Normal Values for Each Portal of Water Entry and Exit (24 Hours)

INTAKE	AMOUNT*	OUTPUT	AMOUNT*
Water in foods	700 ml	Lungs (water in expired air)	350 ml
Ingested liquids	1500 ml	Skin	
Water formed by catabolism	200 ml	By diffusion	350 ml
		By sweat	100 ml
		Kidneys (urine)	1400 ml
		Intestines (in feces)	200 ml
TOTALS	2400 ml		2400 ml

*Amounts vary widely.

organs: the kidneys, lungs, skin, and intestines. The fluid output that changes the most is that from the kidneys. The body maintains fluid balance mainly by changing the volume of urine excreted to match changes in the volume of fluid intake. Everyone knows this from experience. The more liquid one drinks, the more urine one excretes. Conversely, the less the fluid intake, the less the urine volume. How changes in urine volume come about was discussed on pp. 348–349. This would be a good time to review these paragraphs.

It is important to remember from your study of the urinary system that the rate of water and salt resorption by the renal tubules is the most important factor in determining urine volume. Urine volume is regulated chiefly by hormones secreted by the posterior lobe of the pituitary gland (antidiuretic hormone or ADH) and the adrenal cortex (aldosterone). Atrial natriuretic hormone (ANH) from the atrial wall of the heart also affects urine volume. See p. 348 for a review of the hormonal control of urine volume.

Making Weight

Some sports require athletes to "make weight" or weigh in within certain limits just before a competition. Some athletes add muscle mass until they are over their weight limit and then fast or take diuretics just before weigh-in to lose weight. Their theory is that the increased muscle mass improves their competitive edge. Unfortunately, dehydration and loss of glycogen always result from these techniques. Because water and glycogen cannot possibly be replaced in time for the competition, such an athlete is at a physiological disadvantage. Performance and thus the competitive edge is much greater if an athlete can make weight without resorting to "quick loss" methods.

Several factors act as mechanisms for controlling plasma, IF, and ICF volumes. We shall limit our discussion to naming only three of these factors, stating their effects on fluid volumes, and giving some specific examples of them. Three of the main factors are:

1. The concentration of electrolytes in ECF
2. The capillary blood pressure
3. The concentration of proteins in blood

REGULATION OF FLUID INTAKE

Physiologists disagree about the details of the mechanism for controlling and regulating fluid intake to compensate for factors that would lead to dehydration. In general it appears to operate in this way: when dehydration starts to develop—that is, when fluid loss from the body exceeds fluid intake—salivary secretion decreases, producing a "dry-mouth feeling" and the sensation of thirst. The individual then drinks water, thereby increasing fluid intake and compensating for previous fluid losses. This tends to restore fluid balance (Figure 17-4). If an individual takes nothing by mouth for days, can his fluid output decrease to zero? The answer—no—becomes obvious after reviewing the information in Table 17-1. Despite every effort of homeostatic mechanisms to compensate for zero intake, some output (loss) of fluid occurs as long as life continues. Water is continually lost from the body through expired air and diffusion through skin.

Although the body adjusts fluid intake, factors that adjust fluid output, such as electrolytes and blood proteins, are far more important.

IMPORTANCE OF ELECTROLYTES IN BODY FLUIDS

The bonds that hold together the molecules of certain organic substances such as glucose are such that they do not permit the compound to break up or **dissociate** in water solution. Such compounds are called **nonelectrolytes.** Compounds such as ordinary table salt or sodium chloride (NaCl) that have molecular bonds that permit them to break up or dissociate in water solution into separate particles (Na^+ and Cl^-) are **electrolytes.** The dissociated particles of an electrolyte are **ions** and carry an electrical charge.

FIGURE 17–4 ***Homeostasis of the Total Volume of Body Water.*** A basic mechanism for adjusting intake to compensate for excess output of body fluid is diagrammed.

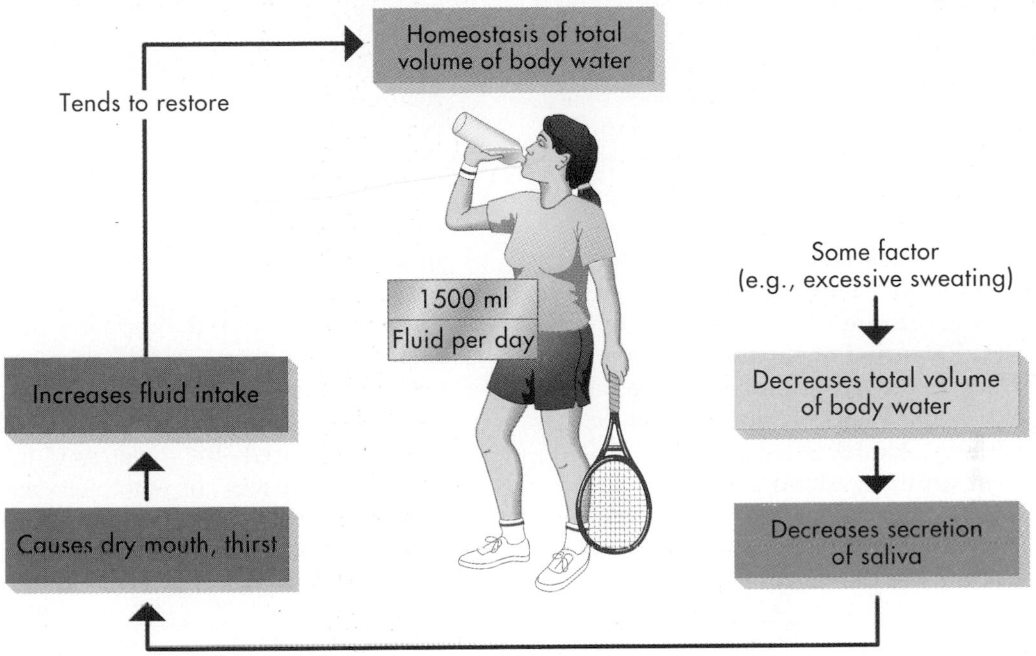

Diuretics

The word **diuretic** is from the Greek word **diouretikos** meaning "causing urine." By definition a diuretic drug is a substance that promotes or stimulates the production of urine.

As a group, diuretics are among the most commonly used drugs in medicine. They are used because of their role in influencing water and electrolyte balance, especially sodium, in the body. Diuretics have their effect on tubular function in the nephron, and the differing types of diuretics are often classified according to their major site of action. Examples would include: (1) *proximal tubule diuretics* such as acetazolamide (Diamox), (2) *loop of Henle diuretics* such as ethacrynic acid (Edecrin) or furosemide (Lasix), and (3) *distal tubule diuretics* such as chlorothiazide (Diuril).

Classification can also be made according to the effect the drug has on the level or concentration of sodium (Na^+), chloride (Cl^-), potassium (K^+), and bicarbonate (HCO_3^-) ions in the tubular fluid.

Nursing implications for caregivers monitoring patients receiving diuretics both in hospitals and home health care environments include keeping a careful record of fluid intake and output and assessing the patient for signs and symptoms of electrolyte and water imbalance. For example, diuretic induced dehydration resulting in a loss of only 6% of initial body weight will cause tingling in the extremities, stumbling gait, headache, fever, and an increase in both pulse and respiratory rates.

Edema

Edema may be defined as the presence of abnormally large amounts of fluid in the intercellular tissue spaces of the body. The condition is a classic example of fluid imbalance and may be caused by disturbances in any factor that governs the interchange between blood plasma and IF compartments. Examples include the following: (1) **Retention of electrolytes (especially Na^+)** in the extracellular fluid as a result of increased aldosterone secretion or after serious kidney disease. (2) **An increase in capillary blood pressure.** Normally, fluid is drawn from the tissue spaces into the venous end of a tissue capillary because of the low venous pressure and the relatively high water-pulling force of the plasma proteins. This balance is upset by anything that increases the capillary hydrostatic pressure. The generalized venous congestion of heart failure is the most common cause of widespread edema. In patients with this condition, blood cannot flow freely through the capillary beds, and therefore the pressure will increase until venous return of blood improves. (3) **A decrease in the concentration of plasma proteins** caused by "leakage" into the interstitial spaces of proteins normally retained in the blood. This may occur as a result of increased capillary permeability caused by infection, burns, or shock.

TABLE 17–2 Common Electrolytes Found in Blood Plasma

POSITIVELY CHARGED IONS	NEGATIVELY CHARGED IONS
142 mEq Na^+	102 mEq Cl^-
4 mEq K^+	26 mEq HCO_3^-
5 mEq Ca^{++}	17 mEq protein$^-$
2 mEq Mg^{++}	6 mEq other
	2 mEq $HPO_4^=$
153 mEq/L plasma	153 mEq/L plasma

Important positively charged ions include sodium (Na^+), calcium (Ca^{++}), potassium (K^+), and magnesium (Mg^{++}). Important negatively charged ions include chloride (Cl^-), bicarbonate (HCO_3^-), phosphate ($HPO_4^=$), and many proteins. Table 17-2 shows that although blood plasma contains a number of important electrolytes, by far the most abundant one is sodium chloride (ordinary table salt, $Na^+ Cl^-$).

A variety of electrolytes have important nutrient or regulatory roles in the body. Many ions are major or important "trace" elements in the body (see Appendix A). Iron, for example, is required for hemoglobin production, and iodine must be available for synthesis of thyroid hormones. Electrolytes are also required for many cellular activities such as nerve conduction and muscle contraction.

Additionally, electrolytes influence the movement of water among the three fluid compartments of the body. To remember how ECF electrolyte concentration affects fluid volumes, remember this one short sentence: where sodium goes, water soon follows. If, for example, the concentration of sodium in blood increases, the volume of blood soon increases. Conversely, if blood sodium concentration decreases, blood volume soon decreases.

Figure 17-5 traces one mechanism that tends to maintain fluid homeostasis. Aldosterone, secreted by the adrenal cortex, increases Na^+ reabsorption by the kidney tubules. Water reabsorption also increases, causing an increase in ECF volume. Begin in the upper right of the diagram and follow, in sequence, each of the informational steps. In summary:

intake. The kidney acts as the chief regulator of sodium levels in body fluids. It is important to know that many electrolytes such as sodium not only pass into and out of the body but also move back and forth between a number of body fluids during each 24-hour period. Figure 17-6 shows the large volumes of sodium-containing internal secretions produced each day. During a 24-hour period, over 8 liters of fluid containing 1000 to 1300 mEq of sodium are poured into the digestive system as part of saliva, gastric secretions, bile, pancreatic juice, and IF secretions. This sodium, along with most of that contained in the diet, is almost completely reabsorbed in the large intestine. Very little sodium is lost in the feces. Precise regulation and control of sodium levels are required for survival.

CAPILLARY BLOOD PRESSURE AND BLOOD PROTEINS

Capillary blood pressure is a "water-pushing" force. It pushes fluid out of the blood in capillaries into the IF. Therefore if capillary blood pressure increases, more fluid is pushed—filtered—out of blood into the IF. The effect of an increase in capillary blood pressure, then, is to transfer fluid from blood to IF. In turn this fluid shift, as it is called, changes blood and IF volumes. It decreases blood volume by increasing IF volume. If, on the other hand, capillary blood pressure decreases, less fluid filters out of blood into IF.

Water continually moves in both directions through the membranous walls of capillaries (Figure 17-1). The amount that moves out of capillary blood into IF depends largely on capillary blood pressure, a water-pushing force. The amount that moves in the opposite direction (that is, into blood from IF) depends largely on the concentration of proteins in blood plasma. Plasma proteins act as a water-pulling or water-holding force. They hold water in the blood and pull it into the blood from IF. If, for example, the concentration of proteins in blood decreases appreciably—as it does in some abnormal conditions such as dietary deficiency—less water moves into blood from IF. As a result, blood volume decreases and IF volume increases. Of the three main body fluids, IF volume varies the most. Plasma volume usually fluctuates only slightly and briefly. If a pronounced change in its volume occurs, adequate circulation cannot be maintained.

Fluid Imbalances

Fluid imbalances are common ailments. They take several forms and stem from a variety of causes, but they all share a common characteristic—that of abnormally low or abnormally high volumes of one or more body fluids.

Dehydration is the fluid imbalance seen most often. In this potentially dangerous condition, IF volume decreases first, but eventually, if treatment has not been given, ICF and plasma volumes also decrease below normal levels. Either too small a fluid intake or too large a fluid output causes dehydration. Prolonged diarrhea or vomiting may result in dehydration due to the loss of body fluids. This is particularly true in infants where the total fluid volume is much smaller than it is in adults. Loss of skin elasticity is a clinical sign of dehydration (Figure 17-7).

Overhydration can also occur but is much less common than dehydration. The grave danger of giving intravenous fluids too rapidly or in too large amounts is overhydration, which can put too heavy a burden on the heart.

FIGURE 17–7 ***Testing for Dehydration.*** Loss of skin elasticity is a sign of dehydration. Skin that does not return quickly to its normal shape after being pinched indicates interstitial water loss.

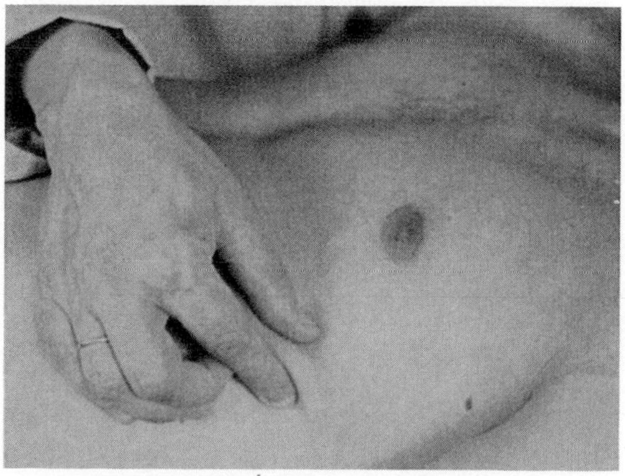

OUTLINE SUMMARY

BODY FLUIDS

A Major locations—inside cells (ICF) and outside of cells in extracellular fluid (ECF) located between the cells as interstitial fluid (IF) and in blood vessels (plasma) (Figure 17-1)

B Total body fluid is approximately 50% to 60% of body weight in a healthy adult.

C Variation in total body water related to:
  1 Total body weight—the more a person weighs, the more water the body contains
  2 Fat content of body—the more fat present, the less total water content per unit of weight (Fat is almost water free.)
  3 Sex—proportion of body weight represented by water is about 10% less in women than in men (Figure 17-2)
  4 Age—in newborn infant water may account for 80% of total body weight

MECHANISMS THAT MAINTAIN FLUID BALANCE

A Fluid output, mainly urine volume, adjusts to fluid intake; ADH from posterior pituitary gland acts to increase kidney tubule reabsorption of sodium and water from tubular urine into blood, thereby tending to increase ECF (and total body fluid) by decreasing urine volume (Figure 17-5)

B ECF electrolyte concentration (mainly Na^+ concentration) influences ECF volume; an increase in ECF Na^+ tends to increase ECF volume by increasing movement of water out of ICF and by increasing ADH secretion, which decreases urine volume, and this, in turn, increases ECF volume

C Capillary blood pressure pushes water out of blood, into IF; blood protein concentration pulls water into blood from IF; hence these two forces regulate plasma and IF volume under usual conditions

D Importance of electrolytes in body fluids
  1 Nonelectrolytes—organic substances that do not break up or dissociate when placed in water solution (for example, glucose)
  2 Electrolytes—compounds that break up or dissociate in water solution into separate particles called ions (for example, ordinary table salt or sodium chloride)
  3 Ions—the dissociated particles of an electrolyte that carry an electrical charge (for example, sodium ion [Na^+])
  4 Positively charged ions (for example, potassium [K^+] and sodium [Na^+]
  5 Negatively charged particles (ions) (for example, chloride [Cl^-] and bicarbonate [HCO_3^-])
  6 Electrolyte composition of blood plasma—Table 17-2
  7 Sodium—most abundant and important positively charged ion of plasma
    a Normal plasma level—142 mEq/L
    b Average daily intake (diet)—100 mEq
    c Chief method of regulation—kidney
    d Aldosterone increases Na^+ reabsorption in kidney tubules (Figure 17-5)
    e Sodium containing internal secretions—Figure 17-6

E Capillary blood pressure and blood proteins

FLUID IMBALANCES

A Dehydration—total volume of body fluids smaller than normal; IF volume shrinks first, and then if treatment is not given, ICF volume and plasma volume decrease; dehydration occurs when fluid output exceeds intake for an extended period

B Overhydration—total volume of body fluids larger than normal; overhydration occurs when fluid intake exceeds output; various factors may cause this (for example, giving excessive amounts of intravenous fluids or giving them too rapidly may increase intake above output)

NEW WORDS

dehydration	edema	interstitial fluid (IF)	ions
dissociate	electrolyte	intracellular fluid (ICF)	overhydration
diuretic	extracellular fluid (ECF)		

CHAPTER TEST

1. The largest volume of water in the body is classified as ______________ fluid.
2. ECF can be subdivided into the fluid between cells, called the ______________ fluid, and the fluid in blood, called ______________.
3. Substances that do not break up or dissociate in water solution are called ______________.
4. The dissociated particles of an electrolyte in water solution are called ______________.
5. The largest quantity of water leaving the body exits as ______________ produced by the kidneys.
6. The most abundant positively charged ion of blood plasma is ______________, and the most abundant negatively charged ion is ______________.
7. A drug that promotes or stimulates the production of urine is called a ______________.
8. The presence of abnormally large amounts of fluid in the intercellular tissue spaces of the body is called ______________.

Circle the "T" before each true statement and the "F" before each false statement.

T F **9.** About 60% of total body weight is water.
T F **10.** Blood plasma is one type of ECF.
T F **11.** There is more IF in the body than ICF.
T F **12.** The more fat in the body the more water per pound of weight.
T F **13.** The chief mechanism for maintaining fluid balance is to adjust fluid output to equal fluid intake.
T F **14.** Capillary blood pressure does not influence ECF or ICF volume.
T F **15.** Water is continually lost from the body by way of expired air and diffusion through the skin.
T F **16.** Electrolytes dissociate in solution to yield charged particles called ions.
T F **17.** Edema is a serious side effect of diuretic drugs.

REVIEW QUESTIONS

1. Suppose a person who had never heard the term *fluid balance* were to ask you what it meant. How would you explain it briefly and simply?
2. Approximately what percentage of a slender man's body weight consists of water? How does that compare to the percentage of body weight consisting of water in a slender woman?
3. The volume of blood plasma in a normal-sized adult weighs approximately what percentage of body weight?
4. The proportion of body weight represented by water is about 10% higher in men than in women. Why?
5. ICF makes up approximately what percentage of adult body weight?
6. IF makes up approximately what percentage of adult body weight?
7. To maintain fluid balance, does output usually change to match intake or does intake usually adjust to output?
8. Explain in words and by a diagram how ADH functions to maintain fluid balance.
9. Define electrolyte, ion, and nonelectrolyte.
10. List the important negatively and positively charged ions that are in blood plasma.
11. List the sodium-containing internal secretions.
12. Explain by words or diagram how capillary blood pressure and blood protein concentration function to maintain fluid balance.
13. If an individual becomes dehydrated, which fluid volume decreases first?

CRITICAL THINKING

14. Use the phrase, *where sodium goes, water soon follows*, to explain how ECF electrolyte concentration affects fluid volumes.
15. Suppose that an individual has suffered a hemorrhage and that, as a result, her capillary blood pressure has decreased below normal. What change would occur in blood and IF volumes as a result of this decrease in capillary blood pressure?
16. Suppose that an individual has a type of kidney disease that allows plasma proteins to be lost in the urine and that, as a result, his plasma protein concentration decreases. How would this tend to change blood and IF volumes?

Acid-Base Balance

18

OUTLINE

pH of Body Fluids

Mechanisms That Control pH of Body Fluids
- Buffers
- Respiratory Mechanism of pH Control
- Urinary Mechanism of pH Control

pH Imbalances
- Metabolic and Respiratory Disturbances
- Vomiting

BOXED ESSAYS

Bicarbonate Loading
Ketosis

OBJECTIVES

After you have completed this chapter, you should be able to:

1. Discuss the concept of pH and define the phrase *acid-base balance.*
2. Define the terms *buffer* and *buffer pair* and contrast strong and weak acids and bases.
3. Contrast the respiratory and urinary mechanisms of pH control.
4. Discuss compensatory mechanisms that may help return blood pH to near-normal levels in cases of pH imbalances.
5. Compare and contrast metabolic and respiratory types of pH imbalances.

One of the requirements for homeostasis and healthy survival is that the body maintain, or quickly restore, the **acid-base balance** of its fluids. Maintaining acid-base balance means keeping the concentration of hydrogen ions in body fluids relatively constant. This is of vital importance. If the hydrogen ion concentration veers away from normal even slightly, cellular chemical reactions cannot take place normally, and survival is thereby threatened.

pH of Body Fluids

Water and all water solutions contain **hydrogen ions (H^+)** and **hydroxide ions (OH^-)** The term *pH* followed by a number indicates a solution's hydrogen ion concentration. More specifically, pH 7.0 means that a solution contains an equal concentration of hydrogen and hydroxide ions. Therefore pH 7.0 also means that a fluid is neutral in reaction (that is, neither acid nor alkaline) (Figure 18-1). The pH of water, for example, is 7.0. A pH higher than 7.0 indicates an alkaline or basic solution (that is, one with a lower concentration of hydrogen than hydroxide ions). The more alkaline a solution, the higher is its pH. A pH lower than 7.0 indicates an acid solution (that is, one with a higher hydrogen ion concentration than hydroxide ion concentration). The higher the hydrogen ion concentration, the lower the pH and the more acid a solution is. With a pH of about 1.6, gastric juice is the most acid substance in the body. Saliva has a pH of 7.7, on the alkaline side. Normally, the pH of arterial blood is about 7.45, and the pH of venous blood is about 7.35. By applying the information given in the last few sentences, you can deduce the answers to the following questions. Is arterial blood slightly acid or slightly alkaline? Is venous blood slightly acid or slightly alkaline? Which is a more accurate statement—venous blood is more acid than arterial blood or venous blood is less alkaline than arterial blood?

Arterial and venous blood are both slightly alkaline because both have a pH slightly higher than 7.0. Venous blood, however, is less alkaline than arterial blood because venous blood's pH of about 7.35 is slightly lower than arterial blood's pH of 7.45.

Mechanisms That Control pH of Body Fluids

The body has three mechanisms for regulating the pH of its fluids. They are (1) the buffer mechanism, (2) the respiratory mechanism, and (3) the urinary mechanism. Together, they constitute the complex pH homeostatic mechanism—the machinery that normally keeps blood slightly alkaline with a pH that stays remarkably constant. Its usual limits are very narrow, about 7.35 to 7.45.

The slightly lower pH of venous blood compared with arterial blood results primarily from carbon dioxide (CO_2) entering venous blood as a waste product of cellular metabolism. As carbon dioxide enters the blood, some of it combines with water (H_2O) and is converted into carbonic acid by **carbonic anhydrase,** an enzyme found in red blood cells. The following chemical equation represents this reaction. If you need to review chemical formulas and equations, please refer to Appendix A.

$$CO_2 + H_2O \xrightarrow{\text{carbonic anhydrase}} H_2CO_3$$

The lungs remove the equivalent of over 30 L of carbonic acid each day from the venous blood by elimination of CO_2. This almost unbelievable quantity of acid is so well buffered that a liter of venous blood contains only about $\frac{1}{100,000,000}$ g more H^+ than does 1 L of arterial blood. What incredible constancy! The pH homeostatic mechanism does indeed control effectively—astonishingly so.

BUFFERS

Buffers are chemical substances that prevent a sharp change in the pH of a fluid when an acid or base is added to it. Strong acids and bases, if added to blood, would "dissociate" almost completely and release large quantities of H^+ or OH^- ions. The result would be drastic changes in blood pH. Survival itself depends on protecting the body from such drastic pH changes.

FIGURE 18–1 ***The pH Range.*** The overall pH range is expressed numerically on what is called a *logarithmic scale* of 1 to 14. This means that a change of 1 pH represents a tenfold difference in actual concentration of hydrogen ions. Note that, as the concentration of H^+ ions increases, the solution becomes increasingly acidic and the pH value decreases. As OH^- concentration increases, the pH value also increases, and the solution becomes more and more basic or alkaline. A pH of 7 is neutral; a pH of 1 is very acidic, and a pH of 13 is very basic.

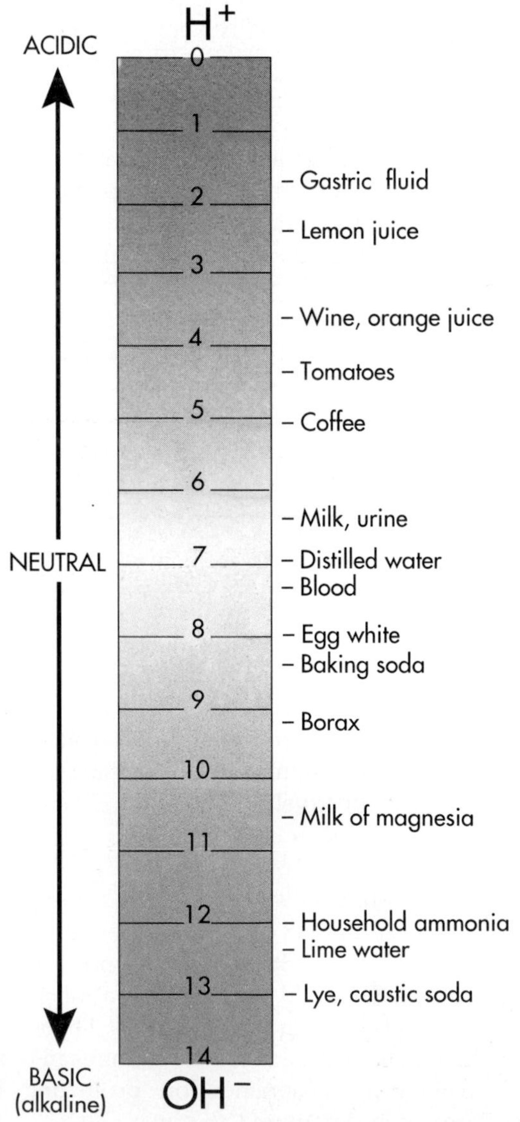

More acids than bases are usually added to body fluids. This is because catabolism, a process that goes on continually in every cell of the body, produces acids that enter blood as it flows through tissue capillaries. Almost immediately, one of the salts present in blood—a buffer, that is—reacts with these relatively strong acids to change them to weaker acids. The weaker acids decrease blood pH only slightly, whereas the stronger acids formed by catabolism would have decreased it greatly if they were not buffered.

Buffers consist of two kinds of substances and are therefore often called **buffer pairs.** One of the main blood buffer pairs is ordinary baking soda (sodium bicarbonate or $NaHCO_3$) and carbonic acid (H_2CO_3).

Let us consider, as a specific example of buffer action, how the $NaHCO_3$ — H_2CO_3 system works with a strong acid or base.

Addition of a strong acid, such as hydrochloric acid (HCl), to the $NaHCO_3$ — H_2CO_3 buffer system would initiate the reaction shown in Figure 18-2. Note how this reaction between HCl and $NaHCO_3$ applies the principle of buffering. As a result of the buffering action of $NaHCO_3$, the weak acid, $H \cdot HCO_3$, replaces the very strong acid, HCl, and therefore the H^+ concentration of the blood increases much less than it would have if HCl were not buffered.

If, on the other hand, a strong base, such as sodium hydroxide (NaOH), were added to the same buffer system, the reaction shown in Figure 18-3 would take place. The H^+ of H_2CO_3 ($H \cdot HCO_3$), the weak acid of the buffer pair, combines with the OH^- of the strong base NaOH to form H_2O. Note what this accomplishes. It decreases the number of OH^- added to the solution, and this in turn prevents the drastic rise in pH that would occur without buffering.

Figure 18-2 shows how a buffer system works with a strong acid. Although useful in demonstrating the principles of buffer action, HCl or similar strong acids are never introduced directly into body fluids under normal circumstances. Instead, the $NaCO_3$ buffer system is most often called on to buffer a number of weaker acids produced during catabolism. Lactic acid is a good example. As a weak acid, it does not "dissociate" as completely as HCl. Incomplete dissociation of lactic acid results in fewer hydrogen ions being

FIGURE 18–2 ***Buffering Action of Sodium Bicarbonate.*** Buffering of acid HCl by $NaHCO_3$. As a result of the buffer action, the strong acid (HCl) is replaced by a weaker acid ($H \cdot HCO_3$). Note that HCl as a strong acid "dissociates" almost completely and releases more H^+ than H_2CO_3. Buffering decreases the number of H^+ in the system.

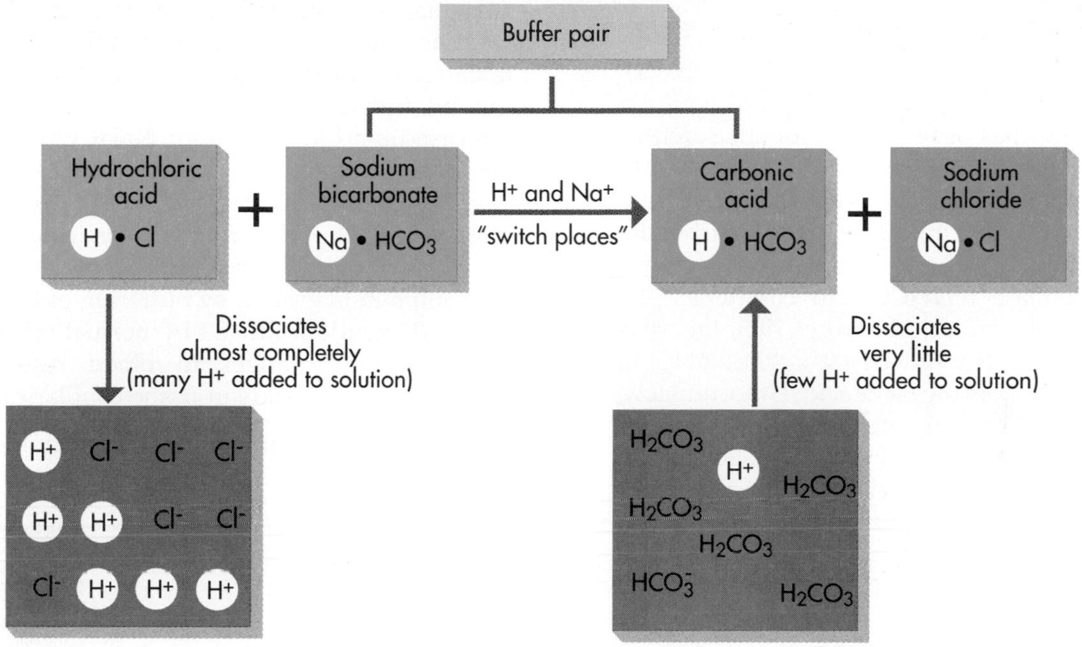

FIGURE 18–3 ***Buffering Action of Carbonic Acid.*** Buffering of base NaOH by H_2CO_3. As a result of buffer action, the strong base (NaOH) is replaced by $NaHCO_3$ and H_2O. As a strong base, NaOH "dissociates" almost completely and releases large quantities of OH^-. Dissociation of H_2O is minimal. Buffering decreases the number of OH^- in the system.

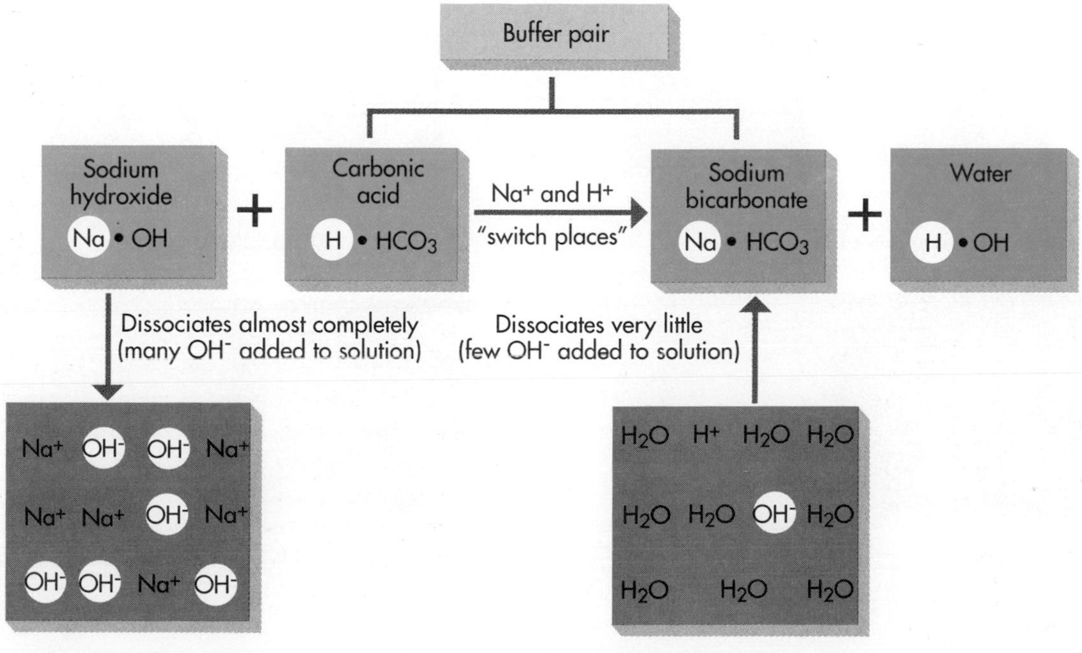

Bicarbonate Loading

The buildup of lactic acid in the blood, released as a waste product from working muscles, has been blamed for the soreness and fatigue that sometimes accompanies strenuous exercise. Some athletes have adopted a technique called **bicarbonate loading,** ingesting large amounts of sodium bicarbonate ($NaHCO_3$) to counteract the effects of lactic acid buildup. Their theory is that fatigue is avoided because the $NaHCO_3$, a base, buffers the lactic acid. Unfortunately, the diarrhea that often results can trigger fluid and electrolyte imbalances. Long-term $NaHCO_3$ abuse can lead to disruption of acid-base balance and its disastrous effects.

added to the blood and a less drastic lowering of blood pH than would occur if HCl were added in an equal amount. Without buffering, however, lactic acid buildup results in significant H^+ accumulation over time. The resulting decrease of pH can produce serious acidosis. Ordinary baking soda (sodium bicarbonate or $NaHCO_3$) is one of the main buffers of the normally occurring "fixed" acids in blood. Lactic acid is one of the most abundant of the "fixed" acids (acids that do not break down to form a gas). Figure 18-4 shows the compounds formed by buffering of lactic acid (a "fixed" acid), produced by normal catabolism. The following changes in blood result from buffering of fixed acids in tissue capillaries:

1. The amount of H_2CO_3 in blood increases slightly because an acid (such as lactic acid) is converted to H_2CO_3.

FIGURE 18–4 ***Lactic Acid Buffered by Sodium Bicarbonate.*** Lactic acid (H • lactate) and other "fixed" acids are buffered by $NaHCO_3$ in the blood. Carbonic acid (H • HCO_3 or H_2CO_3, a weaker acid than lactic acid) replaces lactic acid. As a result, fewer H^+ are added to blood than would be if lactic acid were not buffered.

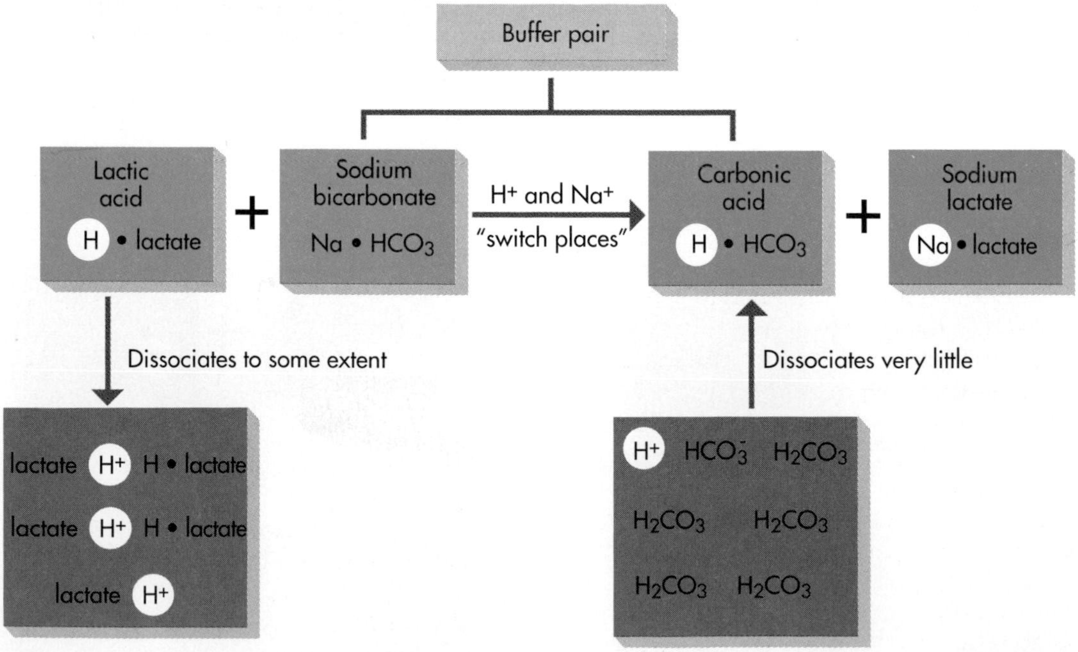

2. The amount of bicarbonate in blood (mainly $NaHCO_3$) decreases because bicarbonate ions become part of the newly formed H_2CO_3. Normal arterial blood with a pH of 7.45 contains 20 times more $NaHCO_3$ than H_2CO_3. If this ratio decreases, blood pH decreases below 7.45.

3. The H^+ concentration of blood increases slightly. H_2CO_3 adds hydrogen ions to blood, but it adds fewer of them than lactic acid would have because it is a weaker acid than lactic acid. In other words the buffering mechanisms do not totally prevent blood hydrogen ion concentration from increasing. It simply minimizes the increase.

4. Blood pH decreases slightly because of the small increase in blood concentration.

H_2CO_3 is the most abundant acid in body fluids because it is formed by the buffering of fixed acids and also because CO_2 forms it by combining with H_2O. Large amounts of CO_2, an end product of catabolism, continually pour into tissue capillary blood from cells. Much of the H_2CO_3 formed in blood diffuses into red blood cells where it is buffered by the potassium salt of hemoglobin. H_2CO_3 breaks down to form the gas, CO_2, and H_2O. This takes place in the blood as it moves through the lung capillaries. Read the next several paragraphs to find out how this affects blood pH.

RESPIRATORY MECHANISM OF pH CONTROL

Respirations play a vital part in controlling pH. With every expiration, CO_2 and H_2O leave the body in the expired air. The CO_2 has diffused out of the venous blood as it moves through the lung capillaries. Less CO_2 therefore remains in the arterial blood leaving the lung capillaries, so less of it is available for combining with water to form H_2CO_3. Hence the arterial blood contains less H_2CO_3 and fewer hydrogen ions and has a higher pH (7.45) than does the venous blood (pH 7.35).

Let us consider now how a change in respirations can change blood pH. Suppose you were to pinch your nose shut and hold your breath for a full minute or a little longer. Obviously, no CO_2 would leave your body by way of the expired air during that time, and the blood's CO_2 content would necessarily increase. This would increase the amount of H_2CO_3 and the hydrogen-ion concentration of blood, which in turn would decrease blood pH. Here then are two useful facts to remember. Anything that causes an appreciable decrease in respirations will in time produce **acidosis**. Conversely, anything that causes an excessive increase in respirations will in time produce **alkalosis.**

URINARY MECHANISM OF pH CONTROL

Most people know that the kidneys are vital organs and that life soon ebbs away if they stop functioning. One reason is that the kidneys are the body's most effective regulators of blood pH. They can eliminate much larger amounts of acid than can the lungs and, if it becomes necessary, they can also excrete excess base. The lungs cannot. In short, the kidneys are the body's last and best defense against wide variations in blood pH. If they fail, homeostasis of pH—acid-base balance—fails.

Because more acids than bases usually enter blood, more acids than bases are usually excreted by the kidneys. In other words, most of the time the kidneys acidify urine; that is, they excrete

Ketosis

An important part of home care for diabetics involves monitoring the level of glucose in the blood and, especially for patients taking insulin, carefully watching for the appearance of **ketone bodies** in the urine. Accumulation of these acidic substances in the blood results from the excessive metabolism of fats in uncontrolled diabetics. These individuals have trouble metabolizing carbohydrates and instead burn fat as a primary energy source. The accumulation of ketone bodies results in a condition called **ketosis** that causes the blood to become dangerously acidic. As blood levels of ketones increase they "spill over" into the urine and can be detected by use of appropriate reagent strips.

FIGURE 18–5 ***Acidification of Urine and Conservation of Base by Distal Renal Tubule Secretion of H^+ Ions.***

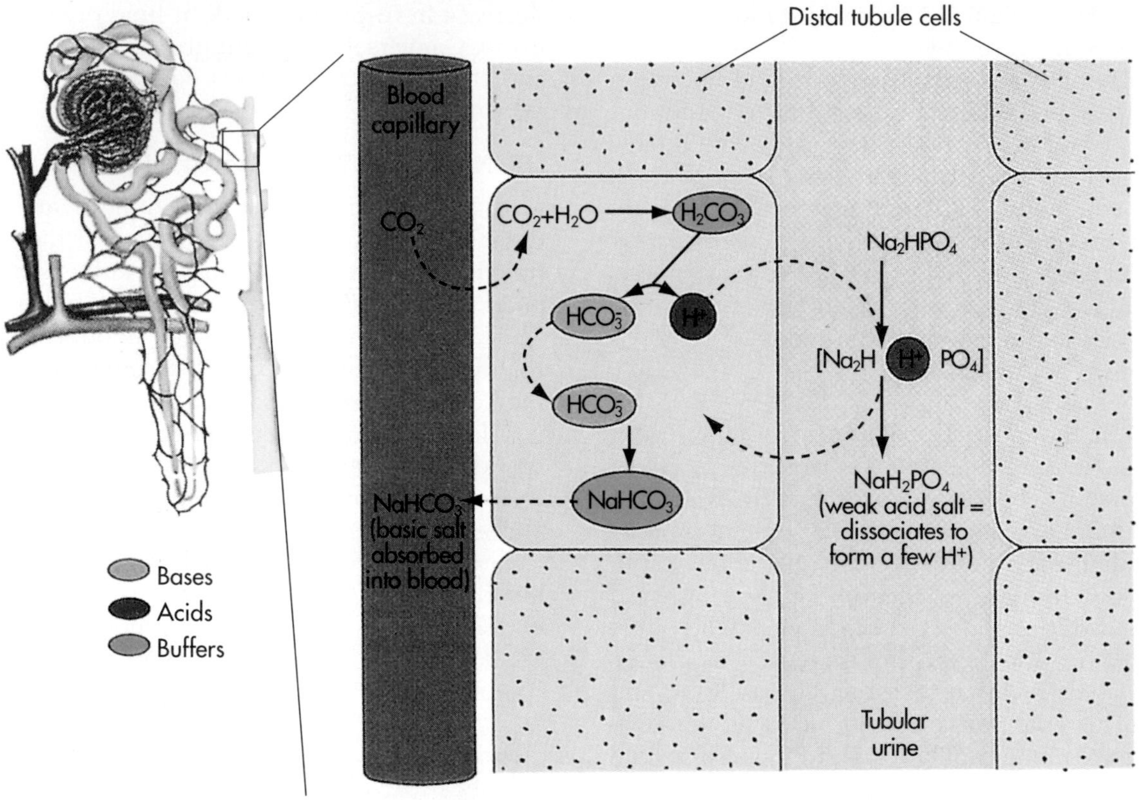

enough acid to give urine an acid pH frequently as low as 4.8. (How does this compare with normal blood pH?) The distal tubules of the kidneys rid the blood of excess acid and at the same time conserve the base present in it by the two mechanisms illustrated by Figures 18-5 and 18-6. To understand these figures fully, you need to have some grasp of basic chemistry. If necessary, refer to Appendix A before proceeding. Then look at Figure 18-5 and find the CO_2 leaving the blood (as it flows through a kidney capillary) and entering one of the cells that helps form the wall of a distal kidney tubule. Note that in this cell the CO_2 combines with water to form H_2CO_3. This occurs rapidly because the cell contains carbonic anhydrase, an enzyme that accelerates this reaction. As soon as H_2CO_3 forms, some of it dissociates to yield hydrogen ions and bicarbonate ions. Note what happens to these ions. Hydrogen ions diffuse out of the tubule cell into the urine trickling down the tubule. There, it replaces one of the sodium ions (Na^+) in a salt (Na_2HPO_4) to form another salt (NaH_2PO_4), which leaves the body in the urine. Notice next that the Na^+ displaced from Na_2HPO_4 by the H^+ moves out of the tubular urine into a tubular cell. Here it combines with a bicarbonate (HCO_3^-) ion to form sodium bicarbonate, which then is resorbed into the blood. What this complex of reactions has accomplished is to add hydrogen ions to the urine—that is, acidify it—and to conserve $NaHCO_3$ by reabsorbing it into the blood.

Figure 18-6 illustrates another method of acidifying urine, as explained in the legend.

FIGURE 18–6 ***Acidification of Urine by Tubule Secretion of Ammonia (NH_3).*** An amino acid (glutamine) moves into the tubule cell and loses an amino group (NH_2) to form ammonia, which is secreted into urine. In exchange, the tubule cell reabsorbs a basic salt (mainly $NaHCO_3$) into blood from urine.

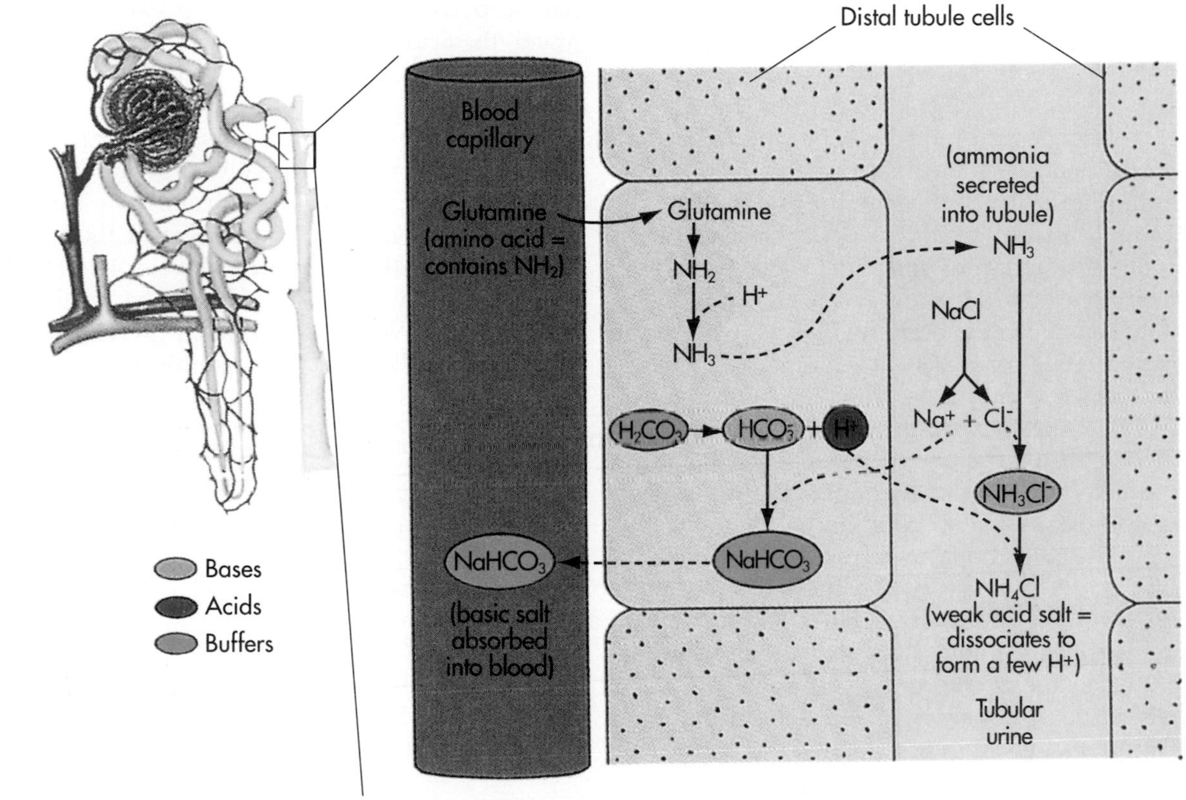

pH Imbalances

Acidosis and **alkalosis** are the two kinds of pH or acid-base imbalance. In acidosis the blood pH falls as H^+ ion concentration increases. Only rarely does it fall as low as 7.0 (neutrality) and almost never does it become even slightly acid, because death usually intervenes before the pH drops this much. In alkalosis, which develops less often than acidosis, the blood pH is higher than normal.

From a clinical standpoint, disturbances in acid-base balance can be considered dependent on the relative quantities (ratio) of H_2CO_3 and $NaHCO_3$ in the blood. Components of this important buffer pair must be maintained at the proper ratio (20 times more $NaHCO_3$ than H_2CO_3) if acid-base balance is to remain normal. It is fortunate that the body can regulate both chemicals in the $NaHCO_3$ — H_2CO_3 buffer system. Blood levels of $NaHCO_3$ can be regulated by the kidneys and H_2CO_3 levels by the respiratory system (lungs).

METABOLIC AND RESPIRATORY DISTURBANCES

Two types of disturbances, metabolic and respiratory, can alter the proper ratio of these components. Metabolic disturbances affect the bicarbonate ($NaHCO_3$) element of the buffer pair, and respiratory disturbances affect the H_2CO_3 element, as follows:

1. **Metabolic disturbances**
   a. *Metabolic acidosis* (bicarbonate deficit)
   b. *Metabolic alkalosis* (bicarbonate excess)
2. **Respiratory disturbances**
   a. *Respiratory acidosis* (H_2CO_3 excess)
   b. *Respiratory alkalosis* (H_2CO_3 deficit)

VOMITING

Vomiting, sometimes referred to as *emesis* (EM-e-sis), is the forcible emptying or expulsion of gastric and occasionally intestinal contents through the mouth (Figure 18-7). It can occur as a result of many stimuli, including foul odors or tastes, irritation of the stomach or intestinal mucosa, and some vomitive (emetic) drugs such as ipecac. A "vomiting center" in the brain regulates the many coordinated (but primarily involuntary) steps involved. Severe vomiting such as the pernicious vomiting of pregnancy or the repeated vomiting associated with pyloric obstruction in infants can be life threatening. One of the most frequent and serious complications of vomiting is metabolic alkalosis. The bicarbonate excess of metabolic alkalosis results because of the massive loss of chloride from the stomach as HCl. The loss of chloride causes a compensatory increase of bicarbonate in the extracellular fluid. The result is metabolic alkalosis. Therapy includes intravenous administration of chloride-containing solutions such as **normal saline**. The chloride ions of the solution replace bicarbonate ions and thus help relieve the bicarbonate excess responsible for the imbalance.

The *ratio* of $NaHCO_3$ to H_2CO_3 levels in the blood is the key to acid-base balance. If the normal ratio (20:1 $NaHCO_3/H_2CO_3$) can be maintained, the acid-base balance and pH remain normal despite changes in the absolute amounts of either component of the buffer pair in the blood.

As a clinical example, in a person suffering from untreated diabetes, abnormally large amounts of acids enter the blood. The normal 20:1 ratio is altered as the $NaHCO_3$ component of the buffer pair reacts with the acids. Blood levels of $NaHCO_3$ decrease rapidly in these patients. The result is a lower ratio of $NaHCO_3$ to H_2CO_3 (perhaps 10:1) and lower blood pH. The condition is called **uncompensated metabolic acidosis.** The body attempts to correct or *compensate* for the acidosis by altering the *ratio* of $NaHCO_3$ to H_2CO_3. Acidosis in a diabetic patient is often accompanied by rapid breathing or hyperventilation. This compensatory action of the respiratory system results in a "blow-off" of CO_2. Decreased blood levels of CO_2 result in lower H_2CO_3 levels. A new compensated ratio of $NaHCO_3$ to H_2CO_3 (perhaps 10:0.5) may result. In such individuals the blood pH returns to normal or near-normal levels. The condition is called **compensated metabolic acidosis.**

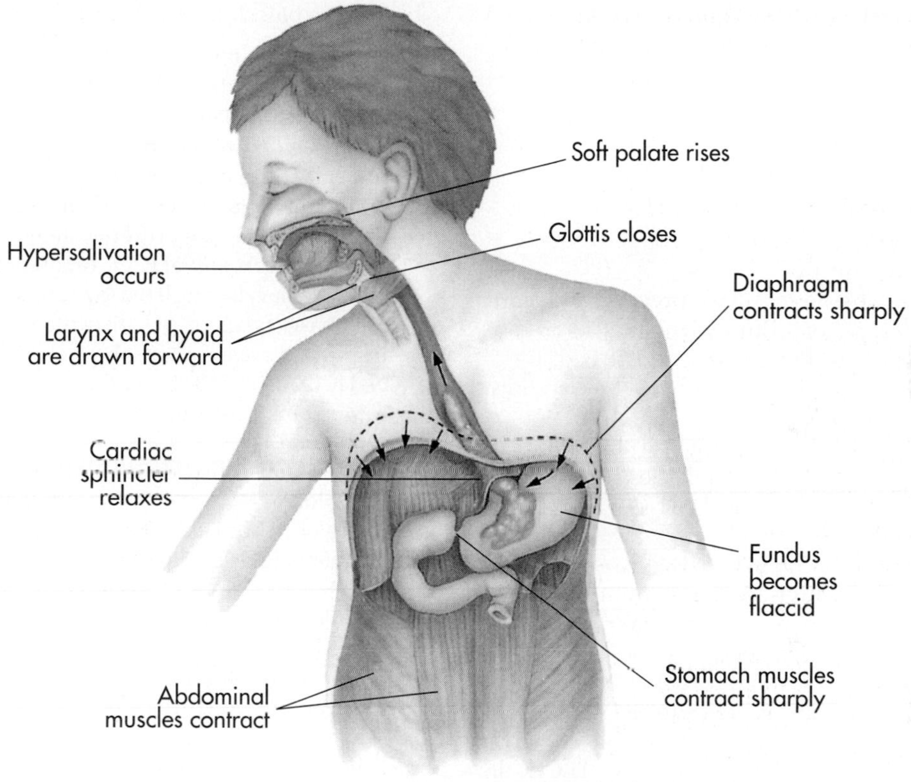

FIGURE 18–7 ***The Vomit Reflex.*** Severe vomiting results in significant loss of HCl and often leads to metabolic alkalosis.

OUTLINE SUMMARY

pH OF BODY FLUIDS

A Definition of pH—a number that indicates the hydrogen ion (H^+) concentration of a fluid; pH 7.0 indicates neutrality, pH higher than 7.0 indicates alkalinity, and pH less than 7.0 indicates acidity—see Figure 18-1

B Normal arterial blood pH—about 7.45

C Normal venous blood pH—about 7.35

MECHANISMS THAT CONTROL pH OF BODY FLUIDS

A Buffers
  1 Definition—substances that prevent a sharp change in the pH of a fluid when an acid or base is added to it—see Figures 18-2 and 18-3
  2 "Fixed" acids are buffered mainly by sodium bicarbonate ($NaHCO_3$)
  3 Changes in blood produced by buffering of "fixed" acids in the tissue capillaries
    a Amount of carbonic acid (H_2CO_3) in blood increases slightly
    b Amount of $NaHCO_3$ in blood decreases; ratio of amount of $NaHCO_3$ to the amount of H_2CO_3 does not normally change; normal ratio is 20:1
    c H^+ concentration of blood increases slightly
    d Blood pH decreases slightly below arterial level

B Respiratory mechanism of pH control—respirations remove some CO_2 from blood as blood flows through lung capillaries, the amount of H_2CO_3 in blood is decreased and thereby its H^+ concentration is decreased, and this in turn increases blood pH from its venous to its arterial level

C Urinary mechanism of pH control—the body's most effective regulator of blood pH, kidneys usually acidify urine by the distal tubules secreting hydrogen ions and ammonia (NH_3) into the urine from blood in exchange for $NaHCO_3$ being reabsorbed into the blood

pH IMBALANCES

A Acidosis and alkalosis are the two kinds of pH or acid-base imbalances

B Disturbances in acid-base balance depend on relative quantities of $NaHCO_3$ and H_2CO_3 in the blood

C Body can regulate both of the components of the $NaHCO_3 — H_2CO_3$ buffer system
  1 Blood levels of $NaHCO_3$ regulated by kidneys
  2 H_2CO_3 levels regulated by lungs

D Two basic types of pH disturbances, metabolic and respiratory, can alter the normal 20:1 ratio of $NaHCO_3$ to H_2CO_3 in blood
  1 Metabolic disturbances affect the $NaHCO_3$ levels in blood
  2 Respiratory disturbances affect the H_2CO_3 levels in blood

E Types of pH or acid-base imbalances
  1 Metabolic disturbances
    a Metabolic acidosis—bicarbonate ($NaHCO_3$) deficit
    b Metabolic alkalosis—bicarbonate ($NaHCO_3$) excess; complication of severe vomiting
  2 Respiratory disturbances
    a Respiratory acidosis (H_2CO_3 excess)
    b Respiratory alkalosis (H_2CO_3 deficit)

F In uncompensated metabolic acidosis, the normal ratio of $NaHCO_3$ to H_2CO_3 is changed; in compensated metabolic acidosis, the ratio remains at 20:1, but the total amount of $NaHCO_3$ and H_2CO_3 changes

NEW WORDS

acid solution	alkaline solution	base	carbonic anhydrase
acidosis (metabolic and respiratory)	alkalosis (metabolic and respiratory)	buffer	emesis
		buffer pairs	pH

CHAPTER TEST

1. A fluid having a pH of 7.0 would be described as ______________ in reaction.
2. A pH higher than 7.0 indicates an ______________ solution, and one with a pH lower than 7.0 indicates an ______________ solution.
3. As CO_2 enters blood, some of it is converted into H_2CO_3 by an enzyme called ______________ found in red blood cells.
4. Substances that prevent a sharp change in pH of a fluid when an acid or base is added are called ______________.
5. The most abundant acid in the body is ______________ acid.
6. Anything that causes an appreciable decrease in respirations will in time produce the condition called ______________.
7. Acidification of urine can occur by renal tubule excretion of ______________.
8. One of the most frequent complications of vomiting is metabolic ______________.
9. A body deficit of $NaHCO_3$ results in metabolic ______________.
10. The ability of the body to maintain a constant blood pH during changing conditions is an example of ______________.

Select the most correct answer from Column B for each statement in Column A. (Only one answer is correct.)

COLUMN A	COLUMN B
11. ______ pH of arterial blood	**a.** Lactic acid
12. ______ Neutral in reaction	**b.** pH 7.0
13. ______ Lost as CO_2	**c.** Excretion of ammonia
14. ______ Prevent pH changes	**d.** Buffers
15. ______ "Fixed" acid	**e.** Metabolic alkalosis
16. ______ Hydrogen ion concentration	**f.** pH 7.45
17. ______ Acidification of urine	**g.** Respiratory acidosis
18. ______ Vomiting	**h.** pH
19. ______ H_2CO_3 excess	**i.** Hyperventilation
20. ______ Compensates for acidosis	**j.** H_2CO_3

REVIEW QUESTIONS

1. Explain briefly what the term *pH* means.
2. What is a typical normal pH for venous blood? For arterial blood?
3. What are the functions of buffers?
4. Explain how respirations affect blood pH.
5. Explain how the kidneys maintain normal blood pH.
6. Which is the most important for maintaining acid-base balance buffers, respirations or kidney functioning?
7. Briefly, how does compensated acidosis differ from uncompensated acidosis?
8. List the types of pH or acid-base imbalances.

CRITICAL THINKING

9. When the body is in acid-base balance, arterial blood contains how many times more sodium bicarbonate than carbonic acid? In other words, what is the normal $NaHCO_3/H_2CO_3$ ratio in blood?
10. How does prolonged hyperventilation (abnormally increased respirations) affect blood pH?

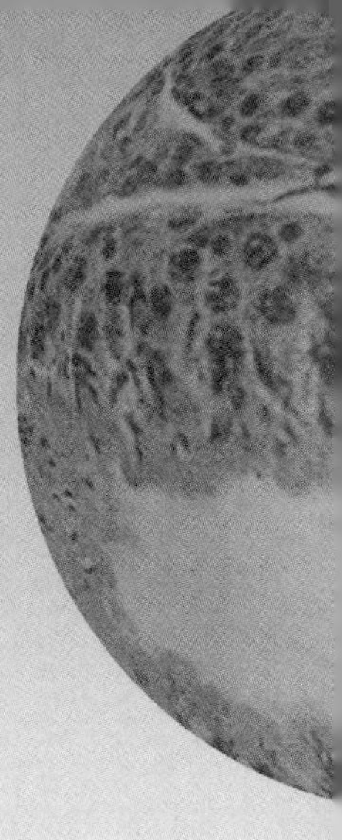

The Reproductive Systems

19

OUTLINE

Common Structural and Functional Characteristics Between the Sexes

Male Reproductive System
- Structural Plan
- Testes
- Reproductive Ducts
- Accessory or Supportive Sex Glands
- External Genitals

Female Reproductive System
- Structural Plan
- Ovaries
- Reproductive Ducts
- Accessory or Supportive Sex Glands
- External Genitals
- Menstrual Cycle

Summary of Male and Female Reproductive Systems

BOXED ESSAYS

Cryptorchidism
Prostatic Hypertrophy
Ectopic Pregnancy
Hysterectomy
Amenorrhea in Female Athletes

OBJECTIVES

After you have completed this chapter, you should be able to:

1. List the essential and accessory organs of the male and female reproductive systems and give the generalized function of each.
2. Describe the gross and microscopic structure of the gonads in both sexes and explain the developmental steps in spermatogenesis and oogenesis.
3. Discuss the primary functions of the sex hormones and identify the cell type or structure responsible for their secretion.
4. Identify and describe the structures that constitute the external genitals in both sexes.
5. Identify and discuss the phases of the endometrial or menstrual cycle and correlate each phase with its occurrence in a typical 28-day cycle.

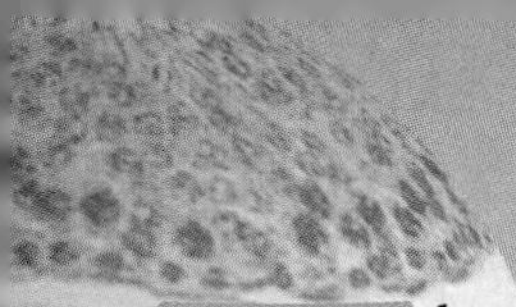

The offspring of many one-celled plants and bacteria come from a single parent. These organisms are said to be *asexual* because they do not produce specialized reproductive or sex cells called **gametes** (GAM-eets). In humans, gametes, called **ova** and **sperm,** fuse during the process of fertilization to produce a cell called the **zygote** (ZYE-gote), which ultimately develops into the new individual. The zygote, which contains an intermingling of genetic messages from the sex cells of both parents, ultimately permits development of new human life. Reproduction in humans therefore is said to be *sexual.* As with all sexually produced offspring, new human life results from the equal contribution of not one but two parent cells—the female ovum and male sperm.

This chapter deals with the structure and function of the reproductive system in men and women. We are truly "fearfully and wonderfully made." Almost any one of the body's organ systems might have inspired this statement, but of them all, perhaps the reproductive systems best deserve such praise. Their awesome achievement is the creation of nature's most complex and beautiful structure—the human body; their ultimate goal is the survival of the human species. After study of the reproductive system in both sexes, Chapter 20 will cover the topic of human development—a process extending from fertilization until death.

Common Structural and Functional Characteristics Between the Sexes

Although the organs and specific functions of the male and female reproductive systems will be discussed separately, it is important to understand that a common general structure and function can be identified between the systems in both sexes and that both sexes contribute in uniquely important ways to overall reproductive success.

In both men and women, the organs of the reproductive system are adapted for the specific sequence of functions that permit development of sperm or ova followed by successful fertilization and then the normal development and birth of a baby. In addition, production of hormones that permits development of secondary sex characteristics, such as breast development in women and beard growth in men, occurs as a result of normal reproductive system activity.

As you study the specifics of each system keep in mind that the male organs function to produce, store, and ultimately introduce mature sperm into the female reproductive tract and that the female system is designed to produce ova, receive the sperm, and permit fertilization. In addition, the highly developed and specialized reproductive system in women permits the fertilized ovum to develop and mature until birth. The complex and cyclic control of reproductive functions in women are particularly crucial to overall reproductive success in humans. The production of sex hormones is required not only for development of the secondary sexual characteristics but also for normal reproductive functions in both sexes. This chapter will end with a table comparing reproductive structures and functions in women and men.

Male Reproductive System

STRUCTURAL PLAN

So many organs make up the male reproductive system that we need to look first at the structural plan of the system as a whole. Reproductive organs can be classified as **essential** or **accessory.**

Essential Organs

The essential organs of reproduction in men and women are called the **gonads.** The gonads of men consist of a pair of main sex glands called the **testes** (TES-teez). The testes produce the male sex cells or **spermatozoa** (sper-ma-toe-ZO-ah).

Accessory Organs

The accessory organs of reproduction in men consist of the following structures:

1. A series of passageways or ducts that carry the sperm from the testes to the exterior
2. Additional sex glands that provide secretions that protect and nurture sperm
3. The external reproductive organs called the external genitals

Table 19-1 lists the names of the essential and accessory organs of reproduction in men, and Figure 19-1 shows the location of most of them. The table and the illustration are included very early in the chapter to provide a preliminary but important overview. Refer back to this table and illustration frequently as you learn about each organ in the pages that follow.

TESTES

Structure and Location

The paired **testes** are the gonads of men. They are located in the pouchlike **scrotum** (SKRO-tum), which is suspended outside of the body cavity behind the penis (Figure 19-1). This exposed location provides an environment about 1°C (3°F) cooler than normal body temperature, an important requirement for the normal production and survival of sperm. Each testis is a small, oval gland about 3.8 cm (1½ inches) long and 2.5 cm (1

TABLE 19–1 Male Reproductive Organs

ESSENTIAL ORGANS	ACCESSORY ORGANS
Gonads: testes (right testis and left testis)	Ducts: epididymis (two), vas deferens (two), ejaculatory duct (two), and urethra
	Supportive sex glands: seminal vesicle (two), bulbourethral or Cowper's gland (two), and prostate gland
	External genitals: scrotum and penis

FIGURE 19–1 *Organization of the Male Reproductive Organs.*

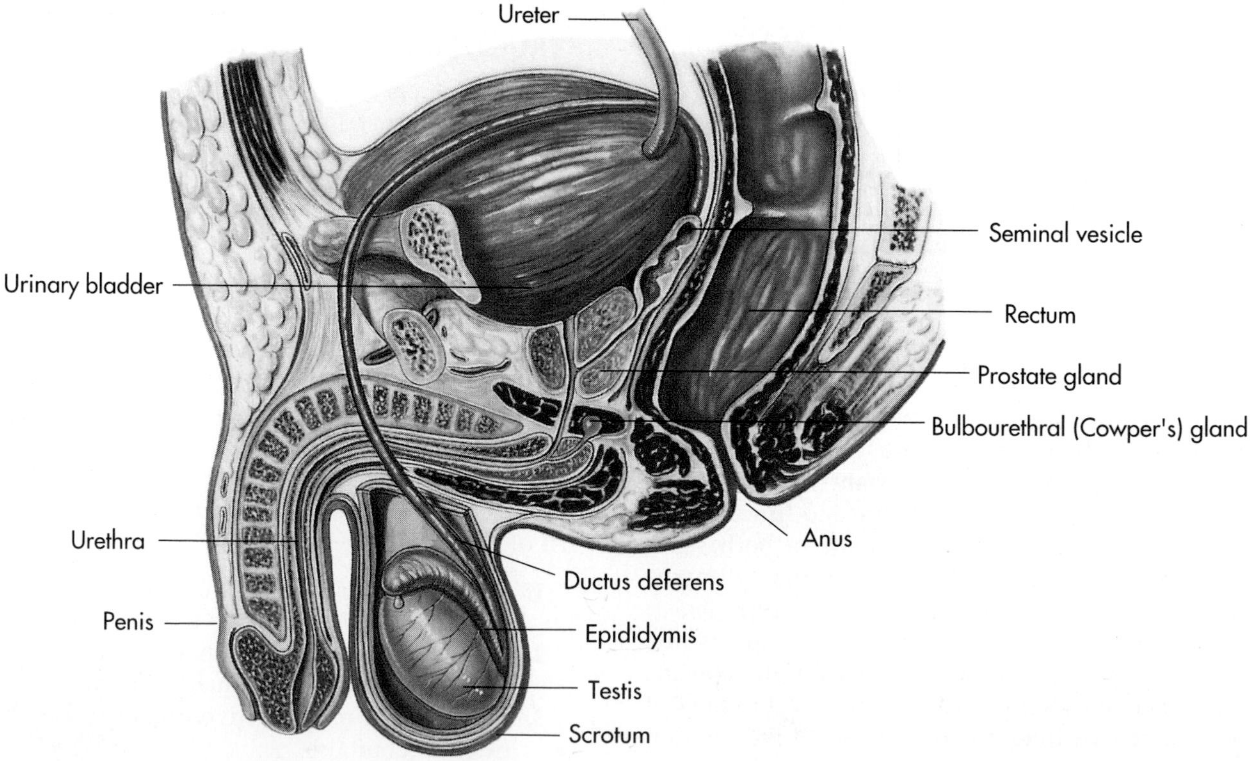

inch) wide. The testis is shaped like an egg that has been flattened slightly from side to side. Note in Figure 19-2 that each testis is surrounded by a tough, whitish membrane called the **tunica** (TOO-ni-kah) **albuginea** (al-byoo-JIN-ee-ah). This membrane covers the testicle and then enters the gland to form the many septa that divide it into sections or lobules. As you can see in Figure 19-2, each lobule consists of a narrow but long and coiled **seminiferous** (se-mi-NIF-er-us) **tubule**. These coiled structures form the bulk of the testicular tissue mass. Small, specialized cells lying near the septa that separate the lobules can be seen in Figure 19-3. These are the **interstitial cells** of the testes that secrete the male sex hormone **testosterone** (tes-TOS-te-rone).

Each seminiferous tubule is a long duct with a central lumen or passageway (Figure 19-3). Sperm develop in the walls of the tubule and are then released into the lumen and begin their journey to the exterior of the body.

FIGURE 19–3 ***Testis Tissue.*** Several seminiferous tubules surrounded by septa containing interstitial cells are shown.

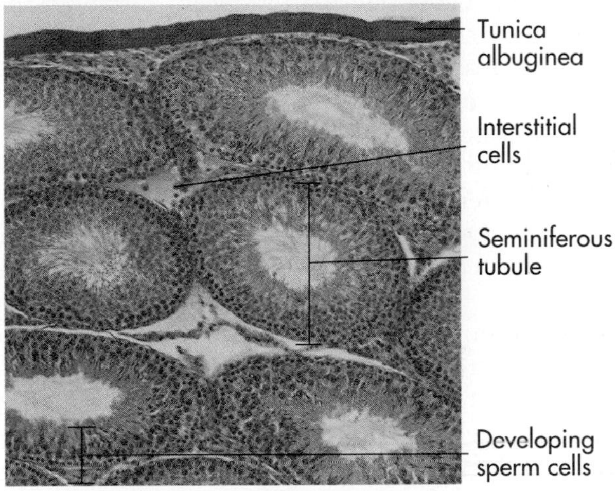

FIGURE 19–2 *Tubules of the Testis and Epididymis.* The ducts and tubules are exaggerated in size. In the photograph, the testicle is the darker sphere in the center.

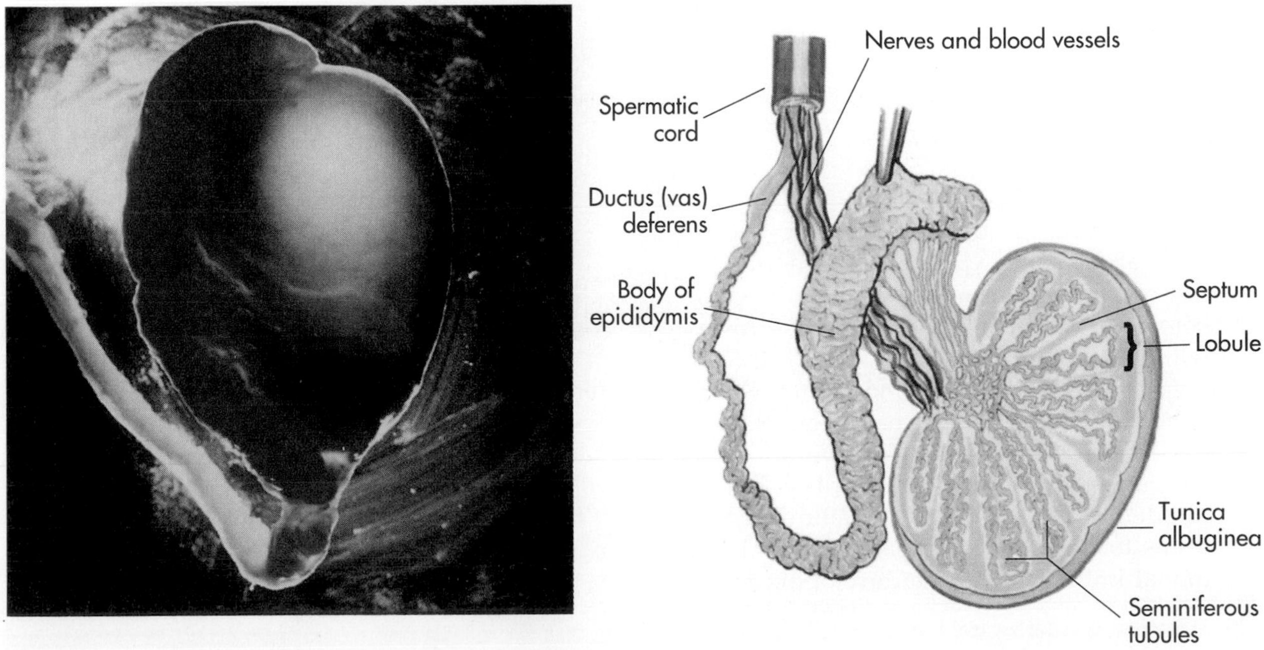

Testis Functions

Spermatogenesis. Sperm production is called **spermatogenesis** (sper-ma-toe-JEN-e-sis). From puberty on, the seminiferous tubules continuously form spermatozoa or sperm. Although the number of sperm produced each day diminish with increasing age, most men continue to produce significant numbers throughout life.

The testes prepare for sperm production before puberty by increasing the numbers of sperm precursor (stem) cells called **spermatogonia** (sperma-toe-GO-nee-ah). These cells are located near the outer edge of each seminiferous tubule (Figure 19-4, *A*). Before puberty, spermatogonia increase in number by the process of mitotic cell division, which was described in Chapter 2. Recall that mitosis results in the division of a "parent" cell into two "daughter" cells, each identical to the parent and each containing a complete copy of the genetic material represented in the normal number of 46 chromosomes.

When a boy enters puberty, circulating levels of follicle-stimulating hormone (FSH) cause a spermatogonium to undergo a unique type of cell division. When the spermatogonium undergoes cell division and mitosis under the influence of FSH, it produces two daughter cells. One of these cells remains as a spermatogonium and the other forms another, more specialized cell called a **primary spermatocyte** (SPER-ma-toe-cyte). These primary spermatocytes then undergo a specialized type of division called **meiosis** (my-O-sis), which ultimately results in sperm formation. Note in Figure 19-4, *B*, that during meiosis two cell divisions occur (not one as in mitosis) and that four daughter cells (not two as in mitosis) are formed. The daughter cells are called **spermatids** (SPER-ma-tids). Unlike the two daughter cells that result from mitosis, the four spermatids, which will develop into spermatozoa, have only half the genetic material and half of the chromosomes (23) of other body cells.

In women, meiosis results in a single ovum, which also has 23 chromosomes. This will be discussed in more detail later in the chapter.

Look again at the diagram of meiosis in Figure 19-4, *B*. It shows that each primary spermatocyte ultimately produces four sperm cells. Note that, in the portion of a seminiferous tubule shown in Figure 19-4, *B*, spermatogonia are found at the outer surface of the tubule, primary and secondary spermatocytes lie deeper in the tubule wall, and mature but immotile sperm are seen about to enter the lumen of the tube and begin their journey through the reproductive ducts to the exterior of the body.

Cryptorchidism

Early in fetal life the testes are located in the abdominal cavity but normally descend into the scrotum about 2 months before birth. Occasionally a baby is born with undescended testes, a condition called **cryptorchidism** (krip-TOR-ki-dizm), which is readily observed by palpation of the scrotum at delivery. The word *cryptorchidism* is from the Greek words *kryptikos* (hidden) and *orchis* (testis). Failure of the testes to descend may be caused by hormonal imbalances in the developing fetus or by a physical deficiency or obstruction. Regardless of cause, in the cryptorchid infant the testes remain "hidden" in the abdominal cavity. Because the higher temperature inside the body cavity inhibits spermatogenesis, measures must be taken to bring the testes down into the scrotum to prevent permanent sterility. Early treatment of this condition by surgery or by injection of testosterone, which stimulates the testes to descend, may result in normal testicular and sexual development.

FIGURE 19–4 ***Spermatogenesis.*** **A,** Cross section of tubule shows progressive meiotic cell types in the wall of a seminiferous tubule. **B,** Diagram of meiotic events and cell types leading to sperm formation.

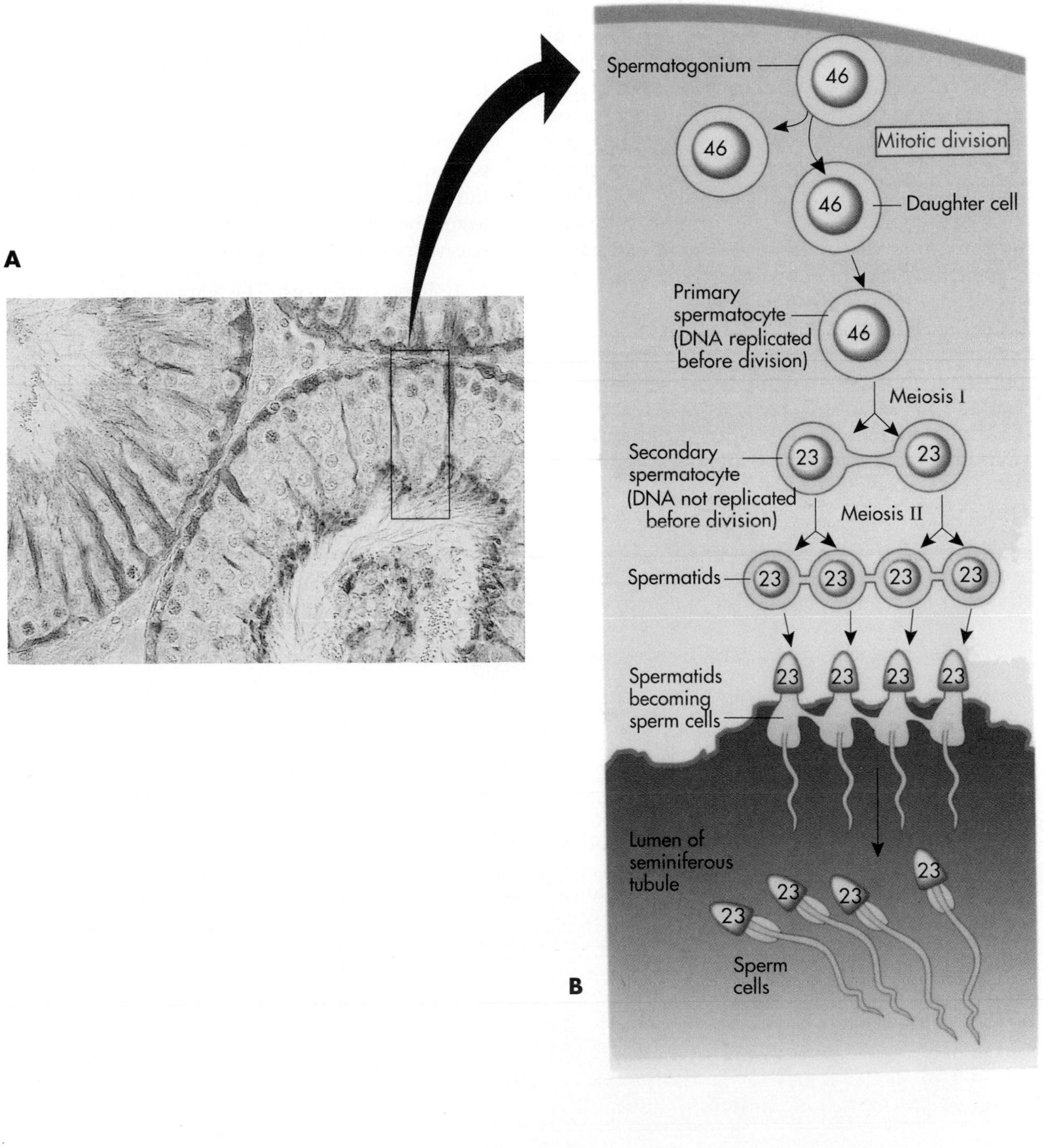

Spermatozoa. Spermatozoa are among the smallest and most highly specialized cells in the body (Figure 19-5, *A*). All of the characteristics that a baby will inherit from its father at fertilization are contained in the condensed nuclear (genetic) material found in each sperm head. However, this genetic information from the father can fuse with genetic material contained in the mother's ovum only if successful fertilization occurs. Ejaculation of sperm into the female vagina during sexual intercourse is only one step in the long journey that these sex cells must make before they can meet and fertilize an ovum. To accomplish their task, these specialized packages of genetic information are equipped with tails for motility and are designed to penetrate the outer membrane of the ovum when contact occurs with it.

The structure of a mature sperm is diagrammed in Figure 19-5, *B*. Note the sperm head containing the nucleus with its genetic material from the father. The nucleus is covered by the **acrosome** (AK-ro-sohm)—a specialized structure containing enzymes that enable the sperm to break down the covering of the ovum and permit entry if contact occurs. In addition to the head with its covering acrosome, each sperm has a midpiece and an elongated tail. Mitochondria in the midpiece break down adenosine triphosphate (ATP) to provide energy for the tail movements required to propel the sperm and allow them to "swim" for relatively long distances through the female reproductive ducts.

Production of testosterone. In addition to spermatogenesis, the other function of the testes is to secrete the male hormone, testosterone. This function is carried on by the interstitial cells of the testes, not by their seminiferous tubules. Testosterone serves the following general functions:

1. It masculinizes. The various characteristics that we think of as "male" develop because of testosterone's influence. For instance, when a young boy's voice changes, it is testosterone that brings this about.
2. It promotes and maintains the development of the male accessory organs (prostate gland, seminal vesicles, and so on).

FIGURE 19–5 ***Human Sperm.*** **A,** Micrograph shows the heads and long, slender tails of several spermatozoa. **B,** Illustration shows the components of a mature sperm cell and an enlargement of a sperm head.

A

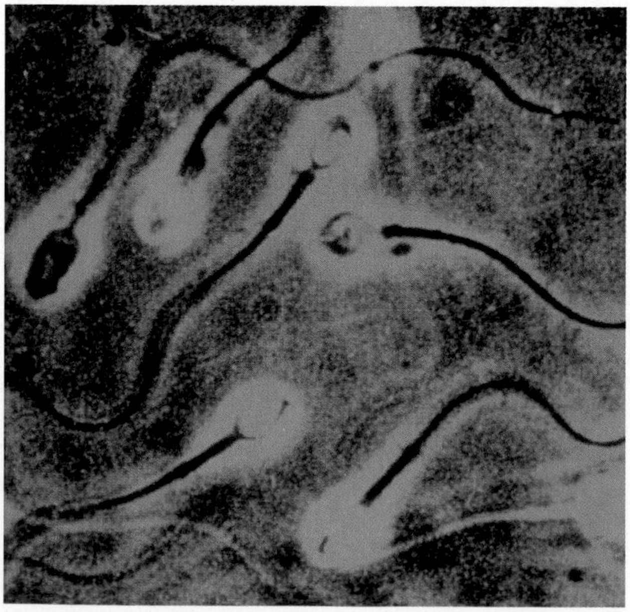

B

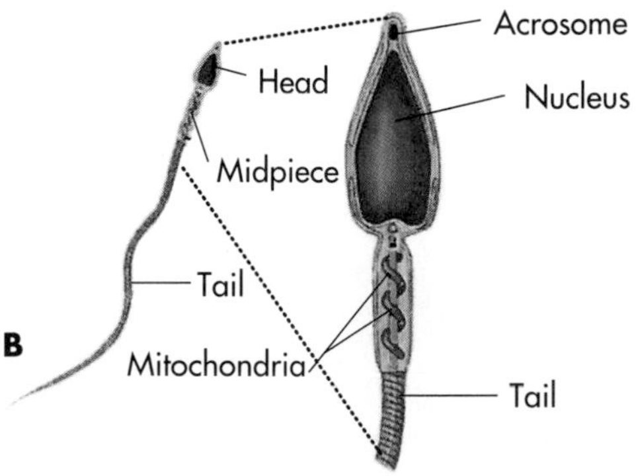

3. It has a stimulating effect on protein anabolism. Testosterone thus is responsible for the greater muscular development and strength of the male.

A good way to remember testosterone's functions is to think of it as "the masculinizing hormone" and the "anabolic hormone."

REPRODUCTIVE DUCTS

The ducts through which sperm must pass after exiting from the testes until they reach the exterior of the body are important components of the accessory reproductive structures. The other two components included in the listing of accessory organs of reproduction in the male—the supportive sex glands and external genitals—will be discussed separately.

Sperm are formed within the walls of the seminiferous tubules of the testes. When they exit from these tubules within the testis, they enter and then pass, in sequence, through the epididymis, ductus (vas) deferens, ejaculatory duct, and the urethra on their journey out of the body.

Epididymis

Each **epididymis** (ep-i-DID-i-mis) consists of a single and very tightly coiled tube about 6 m (20 feet) in length. It is a comma-shaped structure (see Figure 19-2) that lies along the top and behind the testes inside the scrotum. Sperm mature and develop their ability to move or swim as they pass through the epididymis.

Ductus (Vas) Deferens

The **ductus** (DUK-tus) **deferens** (DEF-er-enz) or **vas deferens** is the tube that permits sperm to exit from the epididymis and pass from the scrotal sac upward into the abdominal cavity. Each ductus deferens is a thick, smooth, very muscular, and movable tube that can easily be felt or "palpated" through the thin skin of the scrotal wall. It passes through the inguinal canal into the abdominal cavity as part of the *spermatic cord,* a connective tissue sheath that also encloses blood vessels and nerves.

Ejaculatory Duct and Urethra

Once in the abdominal cavity, the ductus deferens extends over the top and down the posterior surface of the bladder, where it joins the duct from the seminal vesicle to form the **ejaculatory** (ee-JAK-yoo-lah-toe-ree) **duct.** Note in Figure 19-1 that the ejaculatory duct passes through the substance of the prostate gland and permits sperm to empty into the **urethra,** which eventually passes through the penis and opens to the exterior at the external urethral orifice.

ACCESSORY OR SUPPORTIVE SEX GLANDS

The term **semen** (SEE-men) or **seminal fluid** is used to describe the mixture of sex cells or sperm produced by the testes and the secretions of the accessory or supportive sex glands. The accessory glands, which contribute over 95% of the secretions to the gelatinous fluid part of the semen, include the two seminal vesicles, one prostate gland, and two bulbourethral (Cowper's) glands. In addition to the production of sperm, the seminiferous tubules of the testes contribute somewhat less than 5% of the seminal fluid volume. Usually 3 to 5 ml (about 1 teaspoon) of semen is ejaculated at one time, and each milliliter normally contains about 100 million sperm. Semen is alkaline and protects sperm from the acidic environment of the female reproductive tract.

Seminal Vesicles

The paired **seminal vesicles** are pouchlike glands that contribute about 60% of the seminal fluid volume. Their secretions are yellowish, thick, and rich in the sugar fructose. This fraction of the seminal fluid helps provide a source of energy for the highly motile sperm.

Prostate Gland

The **prostate gland** lies just below the bladder and is shaped like a doughnut. The urethra passes through the center of the prostate before traversing the penis to end at the external urinary orifice. The prostate secretes a thin, milk-colored fluid that constitutes about 30% of the total seminal fluid volume. This fraction of the ejaculate helps to activate the sperm and maintain their motility.

Bulbourethral Glands

Each of the two **bulbourethral** (BUL-bo-yoo-REE-thral) glands (also called *Cowper's glands*) resemble peas in size and shape. They are located just

FIGURE 19–6 ***The Penis.*** **A,** In this sagittal section of the penis viewed from above, the urethra is exposed throughout its length and can be seen exiting from the bladder and passing through the prostate gland before entering the penis to end at the external urethral orifice. **B,** Photograph of a cross section of the shaft of the penis showing the three columns of erectile or cavernous tissue. Note the urethra within the substance of the corpus spongiosum.

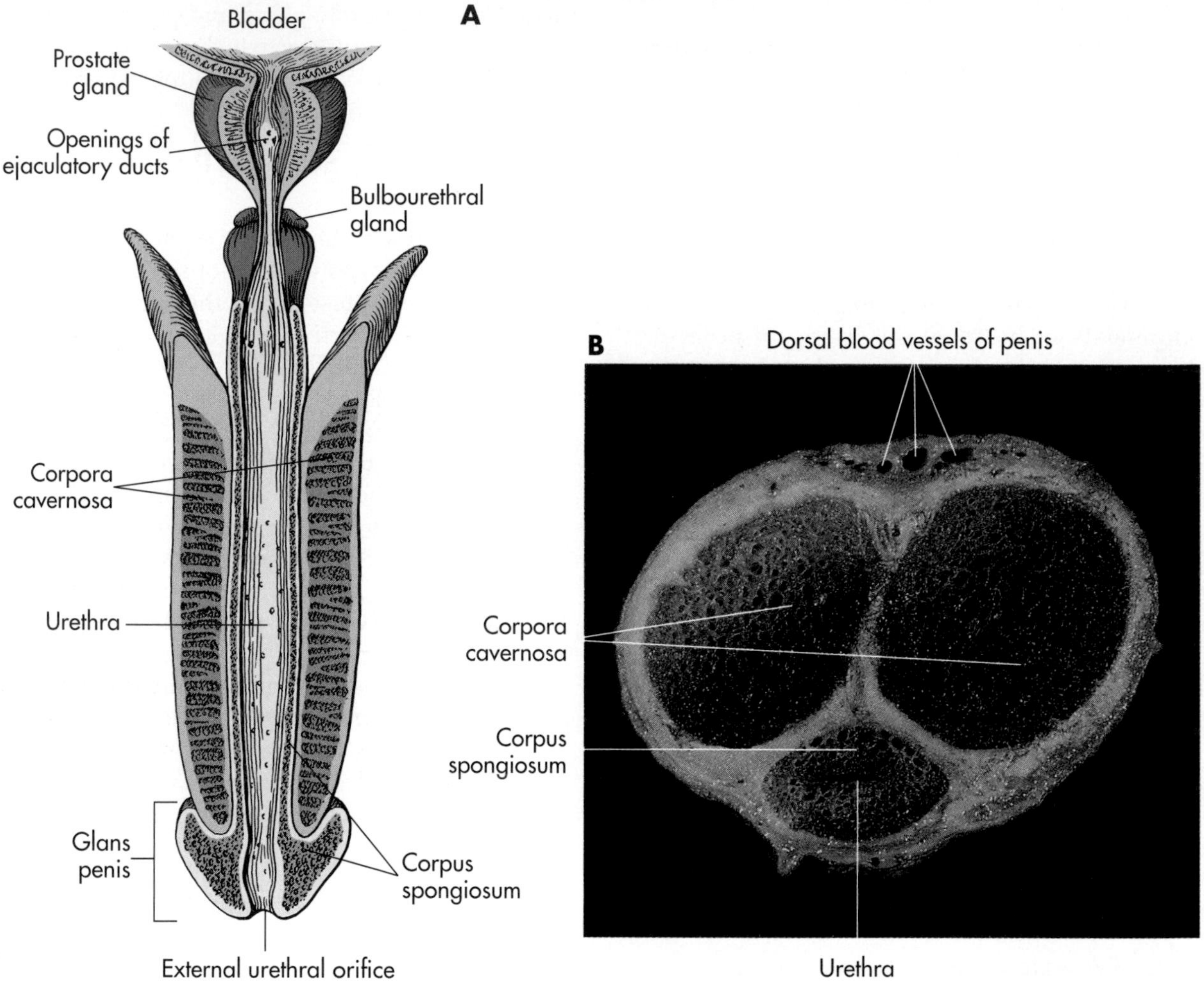

below the prostate gland and empty their secretions into the penile portion of the urethra. The mucus-like secretions of these glands lubricate the terminal portion of the urethra and contribute less than 5% of the seminal fluid volume.

EXTERNAL GENITALS

The **penis** (PEE-nis) and **scrotum** constitute the external reproductive organs or **genitalia** (jen-i-TAL-ee-ah) of men. The penis (Figure 19-6) is the organ that, when made stiff and erect by the filling of its spongy or erectile tissue components with blood during sexual arousal, can enter and deposit sperm in the vagina during intercourse. The penis has three separate columns of erectile tissue in its shaft: one **corpus** (KOR-pus) **spongiosum** (spun-jee-O-sum), which surrounds the urethra, and two **corpora** (KOR-por-ah) **cavernosa** (kav-er-NO-sa), which lie above. The spongy nature of erectile tissue is apparent in Figure 19-6. At the distal end of the shaft of the penis is the enlarged **glans,** over which the skin is folded doubly to form a loose-fitting retractable casing called the **foreskin** or **prepuce** (PRE-pus). If the foreskin

Prostatic Hypertrophy

A noncancerous condition called **benign** (bee-nine) **prostatic hypertrophy** (hye-PER-tro-fee) is a common problem in older men. The condition is characterized by an enlargement or hypertrophy of the prostate gland (see p. 389). The fact that the urethra passes through the center of the prostate after exiting from the bladder is a matter of considerable clinical significance in this condition. As the prostate enlarges, it squeezes the urethra, frequently closing it so completely that urination becomes very difficult or even impossible. In such cases, surgical removal of a part or all of the gland, a procedure called **prostatectomy** (pros-ta-TEC-toe-me), is sometimes performed. Other options, especially for treatment of cancerous prostatic growths, include systemic chemotherapy, cryotherapy (freezing) of prostatic tissue, microwave therapy, hormonal therapy, the placing of radioactive "seeds" directly into the gland, and various types of external beam x-ray radiation treatments.

fits too tightly about the glans, a **circumcision** or surgical removal of the foreskin is usually performed to prevent irritation. The external urethral orifice is the opening of the urethra at the tip of the glans.

The scrotum is a skin-covered pouch suspended from the groin. Internally, it is divided into two sacs by a septum; each sac contains a testis, epididymis, the lower part of the ductus deferens, and the beginning of the spermatic cords.

Female Reproductive System

STRUCTURAL PLAN

The structural plan of the reproductive system in both sexes is similar in that organs are characterized as **essential** or **accessory.**

Essential Organs

The essential organs of reproduction in women, the **gonads,** are the paired **ovaries.** The female sex cells or **ova** are produced here.

Accessory Organs

The accessory organs of reproduction in women consist of the following structures:

1. A series of ducts or modified duct structures that extend from near the ovaries to the exterior
2. Additional sex glands, including the mammary glands, which have an important reproductive function only in women
3. The external reproductive organs or external genitals

Table 19-2 lists the names of the essential and accessory organs of reproduction, and Figure 19-7 shows the location of most of them. Refer back to this table and illustration as you read about each structure in the pages that follow.

TABLE 19–2 Female Reproductive Organs

ESSENTIAL ORGANS	ACCESSORY ORGANS
Gonads: ovaries (right ovary and left ovary)	Ducts: uterine tubes (two), uterus, vagina
	Accessory sex glands: Bartholin's glands (two), breasts (two)
	External genitals: vulva

FIGURE 19–7 *Organization of the Female Reproductive Organs.*

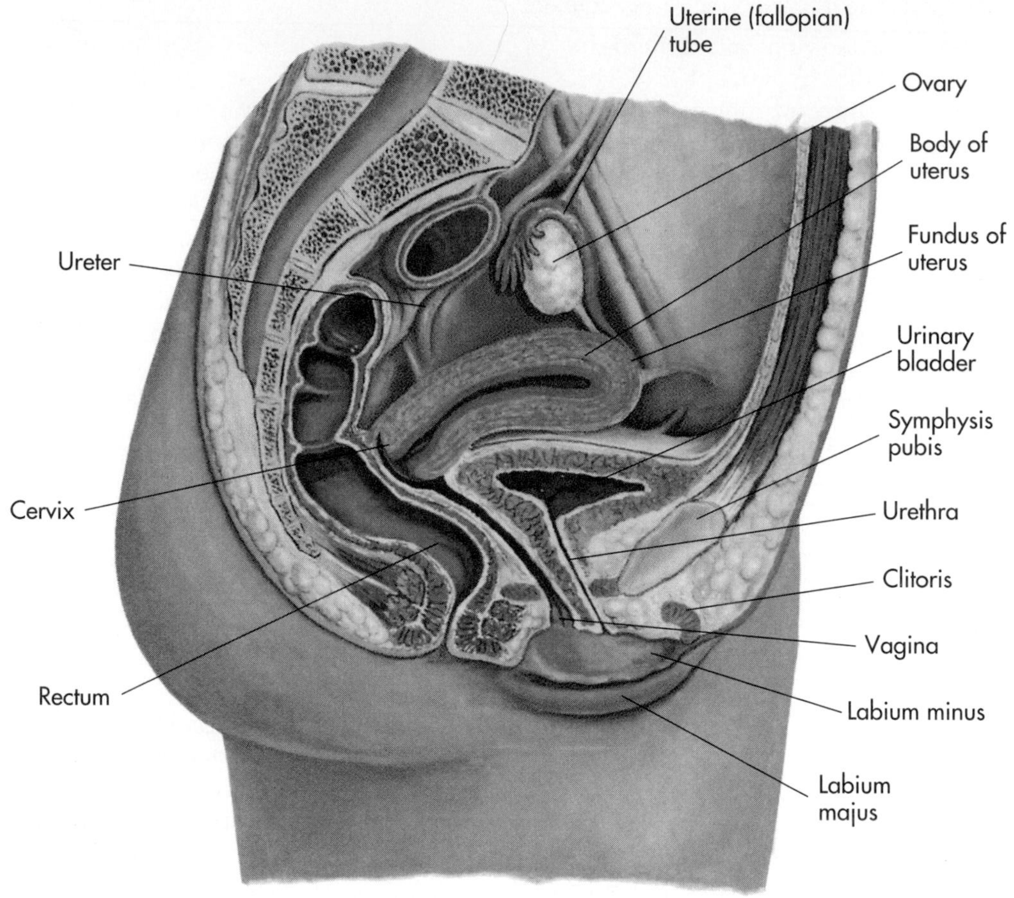

OVARIES

Structure and Location

The paired ovaries are the gonads of women. They have a puckered, uneven surface; each weighs about 3 g. The ovaries resemble large almonds in size and shape and are attached to ligaments in the pelvic cavity on each side of the uterus.

Embedded in a connective tissue matrix just below the outer layer of each ovary in a newborn baby girl are about 1 million **ovarian follicles;** each contains an **oocyte,** an immature stage of the female sex cell. By the time a girl reaches puberty, however, further development has resulted in the formation of a reduced number (about 400,000) of what are now called **primary follicles.** Each primary follicle has a layer of **granulosa cells** around the oocyte. During the reproductive lifetime of most women, only about 350 to 500 of these primary follicles fully develop into **mature follicles,** which ovulate and release an ovum for potential fertilization. Follicles that do not mature degenerate and are reabsorbed into the ovarian tissue. A mature ovum in its sac is sometimes called a **Graafian** (GRAHF-ee-an) **follicle,** in honor of the Dutch anatomist who discovered them some 300 years ago.

The progression of development from primary follicle to ovulation is shown in Figure 19-8. As the thickness of the granulosa cell layer around

FIGURE 19–8 ***Diagram of Ovary and Oogenesis.*** Cross section of mammalian ovary shows successive stages of ovarian (Graafian) follicle and ovum development. Begin with the first stage (primary follicle) and follow around clockwise to the final state (degenerating corpus luteum).

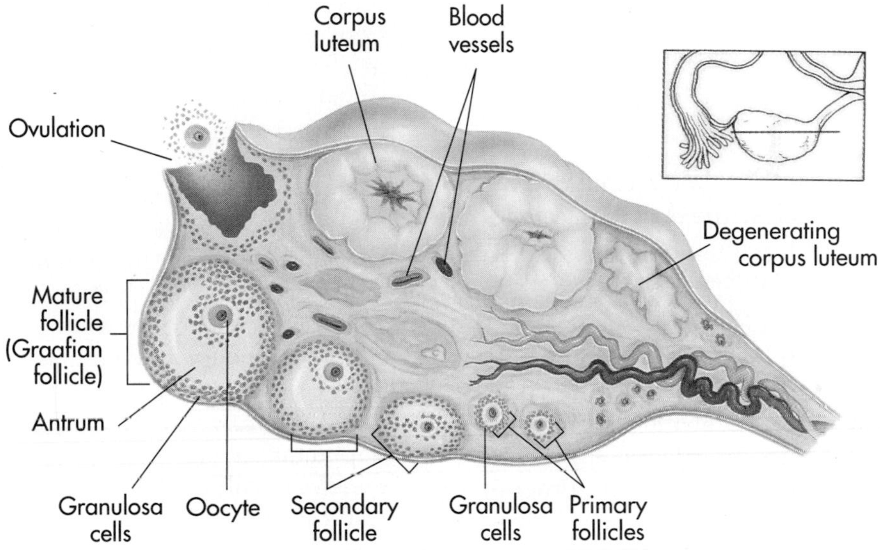

the oocyte increases, a hollow chamber called an *antrum* (AN-trum) appears, and a **secondary follicle** is formed. Development continues, and, after ovulation, the ruptured follicle is transformed into a hormone-secreting glandular structure called the **corpus** (KOR-pus) **luteum** (LOO-tee-um), which is described later. Corpus luteum is from the Latin word meaning "yellow body," an appropriate name to describe the yellow appearance of this glandular structure.

Ovary Functions

Oogenesis. The production of female gametes or sex cells is called **oogenesis** (o-o-JEN-e-sis). The specialized type of cell division that results in sperm formation, meiosis, is also responsible for development of ova. During the developmental phases experienced by the female sex cell from its earliest stage to just after fertilization, two meiotic divisions occur. As a result of meiosis in the female sex cell, the number of chromosomes is reduced equally in each daughter cell to half the number (23) found in other body cells (46). However, the amount of cytoplasm is divided unequally. The result is formation of one large ovum and small daughter cells called *polar bodies* that degenerate.

The ovum, with its large supply of cytoplasm, is one of the body's largest cells and is uniquely designed to provide nutrients for rapid development of the embryo until implantation in the uterus occurs. At fertilization, the sex cells from both parents fuse, and the normal chromosome number (46) is achieved.

Production of estrogen and progesterone. The second major function of the ovary, in addition to oogenesis, is secretion of the sex hormones, **estrogen** and **progesterone.** Hormone production in the ovary begins at puberty with the cyclic development and maturation of the ovum. The granulosa cells around the oocyte in the growing and mature follicle secrete estrogen. The corpus luteum, which develops after ovulation, chiefly secretes progesterone but also some estrogen.

Estrogen is the sex hormone that causes the development and maintenance of the female *secondary sex characteristics* and stimulates growth of the epithelial cells lining the uterus. Some of the actions of estrogen include the following:

1. Development and maturation of female reproductive organs, including the external genitals
2. Appearance of pubic hair and breast development
3. Development of female body contours by deposition of fat below the skin surface and in the breasts and hip region
4. Initiation of the first menstrual cycle

Progesterone is produced by the corpus luteum, which is a glandular structure that develops from a follicle that has just released an ovum. If stimulated by the appropriate anterior pituitary hormone, the corpus luteum produces progesterone for about 11 days after ovulation. Progesterone stimulates proliferation and vascularization of the epithelial lining of the uterus and acts with estrogen to initiate the menstrual cycle in girls entering puberty.

Ectopic Pregnancy

The term **ectopic** (ek-TOP-ic) **pregnancy** is used to describe a pregnancy resulting from the implantation of a fertilized ovum in any location other than the uterus. Occasionally, because the outer ends of the uterine tubes open into the pelvic cavity and are not actually connected to the ovaries, an ovum does not enter an oviduct but becomes fertilized and remains in the abdominal cavity. Although rare, if implantation occurs on the surface of an abdominal organ or on one of the mesenteries, development may continue to term. In such cases delivery by caesarean section is required. Most ectopic pregnancies involve implantation in the uterine tube and are therefore called *tubal pregnancies.* They result in tubal rupture and fetal death.

REPRODUCTIVE DUCTS

Uterine Tubes

The two **uterine tubes,** also called **fallopian** (fal-LO-pee-an) **tubes** or **oviducts** (O-vi-dukts), serve as ducts for the ovaries, even though they are not attached to them. The outer end of each tube terminates in an expanded, funnel-shaped structure that has fringelike projections called **fimbriae** (FIM-bree-ee) along its edge. This part of the tube curves over the top of each ovary (Figure 19-9) and opens into the abdominal cavity. The inner end of each uterine tube attaches to the uterus, and the cavity inside the tube opens into the cavity in the uterus. Each tube is about 10 cm (4 inches) in length.

After ovulation the discharged ovum first enters the abdominal cavity and then enters the uterine tube assisted by the wavelike movement of the fimbriae and the beating of the cilia on their surface. Once in the tube the ovum begins its journey to the uterus. Some ova never find their way into the oviduct and remain in the abdominal cavity where they are reabsorbed. In Chapter 20 the details of fertilization, which normally occurs in the outer one third of the uterine tube, will be discussed.

The mucosal lining of the uterine tubes is directly continuous with the lining of the abdominal cavity on one end and with the lining of the uterus and vagina on the other. This is of great clinical significance because infections of the vagina or uterus such as gonorrhea may pass into the abdominal cavity, where they may become life threatening.

Uterus

The **uterus** (YOO-ter-us) is a small organ—only about the size of a pear—but it is extremely strong. It is almost all muscle or **myometrium** (my-o-ME-tree-um), with only a small cavity inside. During pregnancy the uterus grows many times larger so that it becomes big enough to hold a baby and a considerable amount of fluid. The uterus is composed of two parts: an upper portion, the **body,** and a lower narrow section, the **cervix.** Just above the level where the uterine tubes attach to the body of the uterus, it rounds out to form a bulging prominence called the **fun-**

FIGURE 19–9 ***The Uterus.*** Sectioned view shows muscle layers of the uterus and its relationship to the ovaries and vagina.

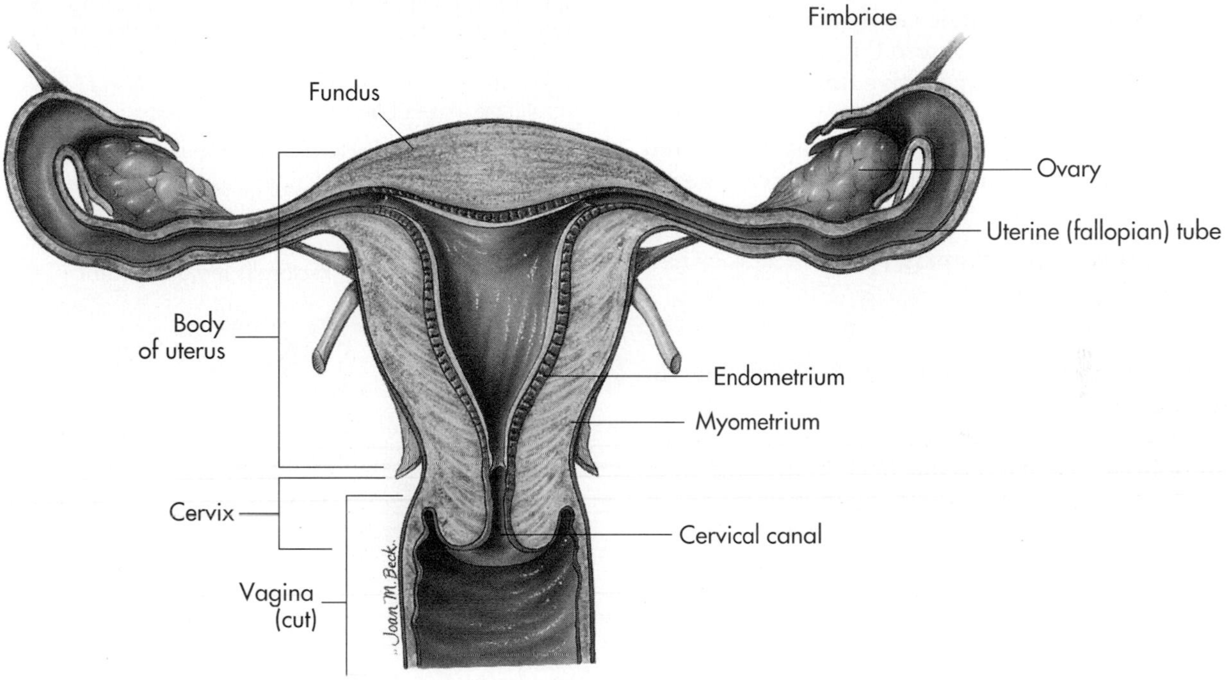

dus (see Figure 19-9). Except during pregnancy, the uterus lies in the pelvic cavity just behind the urinary bladder. By the end of pregnancy, it becomes large enough to extend up to the top of the abdominal cavity. It then pushes the liver against the underside of the diaphragm—a fact that explains such a comment as "I can't seem to take a deep breath since I've gotten so big," made by many women late in their pregnancies.

The uterus functions in three processes—menstruation, pregnancy, and labor. The corpus luteum stops secreting progesterone and decreases its secretion of estrogens about 11 days after ovulation. About 3 days later, when the progesterone and estrogen concentrations in the blood are at their lowest, menstruation starts. Small pieces of the mucous membrane lining of the uterus, or the **endometrium** (en-doe-ME-tree-um) pull loose, leaving torn blood vessels underneath. Blood and bits of endometrium trickle out of the uterus into the vagina and out of the body. Immediately after menstruation the endometrium starts to repair itself. It again grows thick and becomes lavishly supplied with blood in preparation for pregnancy. If fertilization does not take place, the uterus once more sheds the lining made ready for a pregnancy that did not occur. Because these changes in the uterine lining continue to repeat themselves, they are spoken of as the **menstrual cycle** (see p. 397).

If fertilization occurs, pregnancy begins, and the endometrium remains intact. The events of pregnancy are discussed in Chapter 20.

Menstruation first occurs at puberty, often around the age of 12 years. Normally it repeats itself about every 28 days or 13 times a year for some 30 to 40 years before it ceases at *menopause* (MEN-o-pawz), when a woman is somewhere around the age of 50 years.

Vagina

The **vagina** (vah-JYE-nah) is a distensible tube about 10 cm (4 inches) long made mainly of smooth muscle and lined with mucous membrane. It lies in the pelvic cavity between the urinary bladder and the rectum (Figure 19-7). As the part of the female reproductive tract that opens to the exterior, the vagina is the organ that sperm enter during their journey to meet an ovum, and it is also the organ from which a baby emerges to meet its new world.

ACCESSORY OR SUPPORTIVE SEX GLANDS

Bartholin's Glands

One of the small **Bartholin's** (BAR-toe-linz) or **greater vestibular** (ves-TIB-yoo-lar) **glands** lies to the right of the vaginal outlet, and one lies to the left of it. Secretion of a mucuslike lubricating fluid is their function. Their ducts open into the space between the labia minora and the vaginal orifice called the **vestibule** (see Figure 19-11).

Breasts

The **breasts** lie over the pectoral muscles and are attached to them by connective tissue ligaments (of Cooper). Breast size is determined more by the amount of fat around the glandular (milk-secreting) tissue than by the amount of glandular tissue itself. Hence the size of the breast has little to do with its ability to secrete adequate amounts of milk after the birth of a baby.

Each breast consists of 15 to 20 divisions or lobes that are arranged radially (Figure 19-10). Each lobe consists of several lobules, and each lobule consists of milk-secreting glandular cells. The milk-secreting cells are arranged in grapelike clusters called *alveoli.* Small **lactiferous** (lak-TIF-er-us) **ducts** drain the alveoli and converge toward the nipple like the spokes of a wheel. Only one lactiferous duct leads from each lobe to an opening in the nipple. The colored area around the nipple is the **areola** (ah-REE-o-lah).

A knowledge of the lymphatic drainage of the breast is important because cancerous cells from breast tumors often spread to other areas of the body through the lymphatic system. This lymphatic drainage is discussed in Chapter 12 (see also Figure 12-5).

FIGURE 19–10 ***Lateral View of the Breast.*** Sagittal section shows the gland fixed to the overlying skin and the pectoral muscles by the suspensory ligaments of Cooper. Each lobule of secretory tissue is drained by a lactiferous duct that opens through the nipple.

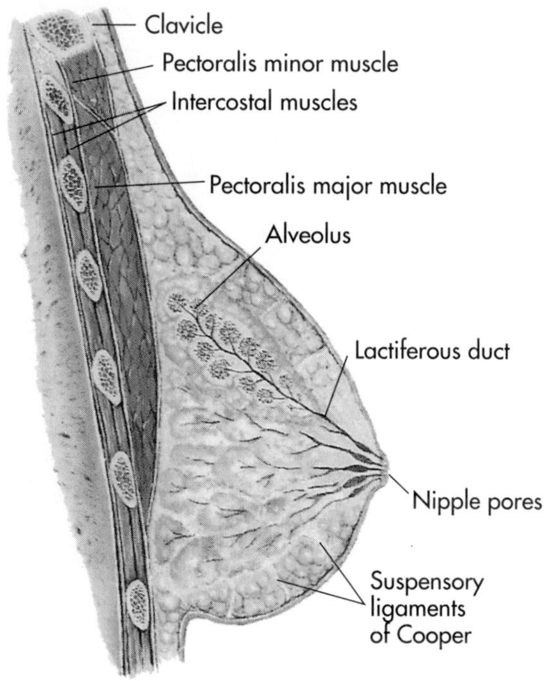

EXTERNAL GENITALS

The **external genitalia** or **vulva** (VUL-vah) of women consist of the following:

1. Mons pubis
2. Clitoris
3. Orifice of urethra
4. Labia minora (singular, *labium minus*) (small lips)
5. Hymen
6. Orifice, duct of Bartholin's gland
7. Orifice of vagina
8. Labia majora (singular, *labium majus*) (large lips)

The **mons pubis** is a skin-covered pad of fat over the symphysis pubis. Hair appears on this structure at puberty and persists throughout life. Extending downward from the elevated mons

FIGURE 19–11 *External Genitals of the Female.*

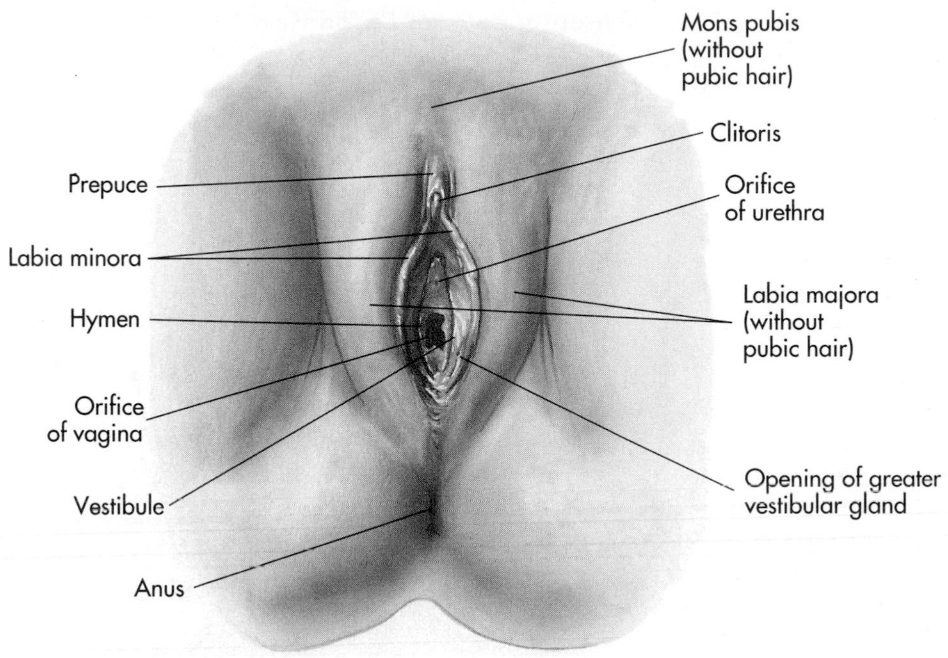

pubis are the **labia** (LAY-bee-ah) **majora** (ma-JO-rah) or "large lips." These elongated folds, which are composed mainly of fat and numerous glands, are covered with pigmented skin and hair on the outer surface and are smooth and free from hair on the inner surface. The **labia minora** or "small lips" are located within the labia majora and are covered with modified skin. These two lips join anteriorly at the midline. The area between the labia minora is the vestibule (Figure 19-11). Several genital structures are located in the vestibule. The **clitoris** (KLIT-o-ris), which is composed of erectile tissue, is located just behind the anterior junction of the labia minora. Situated between the clitoris above and the vaginal opening below is the orifice of the urethra. The vaginal orifice is sometimes partially closed by a membranous **hymen** (HYE-men). The ducts of Bartholin's glands open on either side of the vaginal orifice inside the labia minora.

The term **perineum** (pair-i-NEE-um) is used to describe the area between the vaginal opening and anus. This area is sometimes cut in a surgical procedure called an **episiotomy** (e-piz-ee-OT-o-me) to prevent tearing of tissue during childbirth.

MENSTRUAL CYCLE

Phases and Events

The menstrual cycle consists of many changes in the uterus, ovaries, vagina, and breasts and in the anterior pituitary gland's secretion of hormones (Figure 19-12). In the majority of women, these changes occur with almost precise regularity throughout their reproductive years. The first indication of changes comes with the first menstrual period. The first **menses** (MEN-seez) or menstrual flow is referred to as the **menarche** (me-NAR-kee).

A typical menstrual cycle covers a period of about 28 days. The length of the cycle varies

FIGURE 19–12 *The 28-day Menstrual Cycle.*

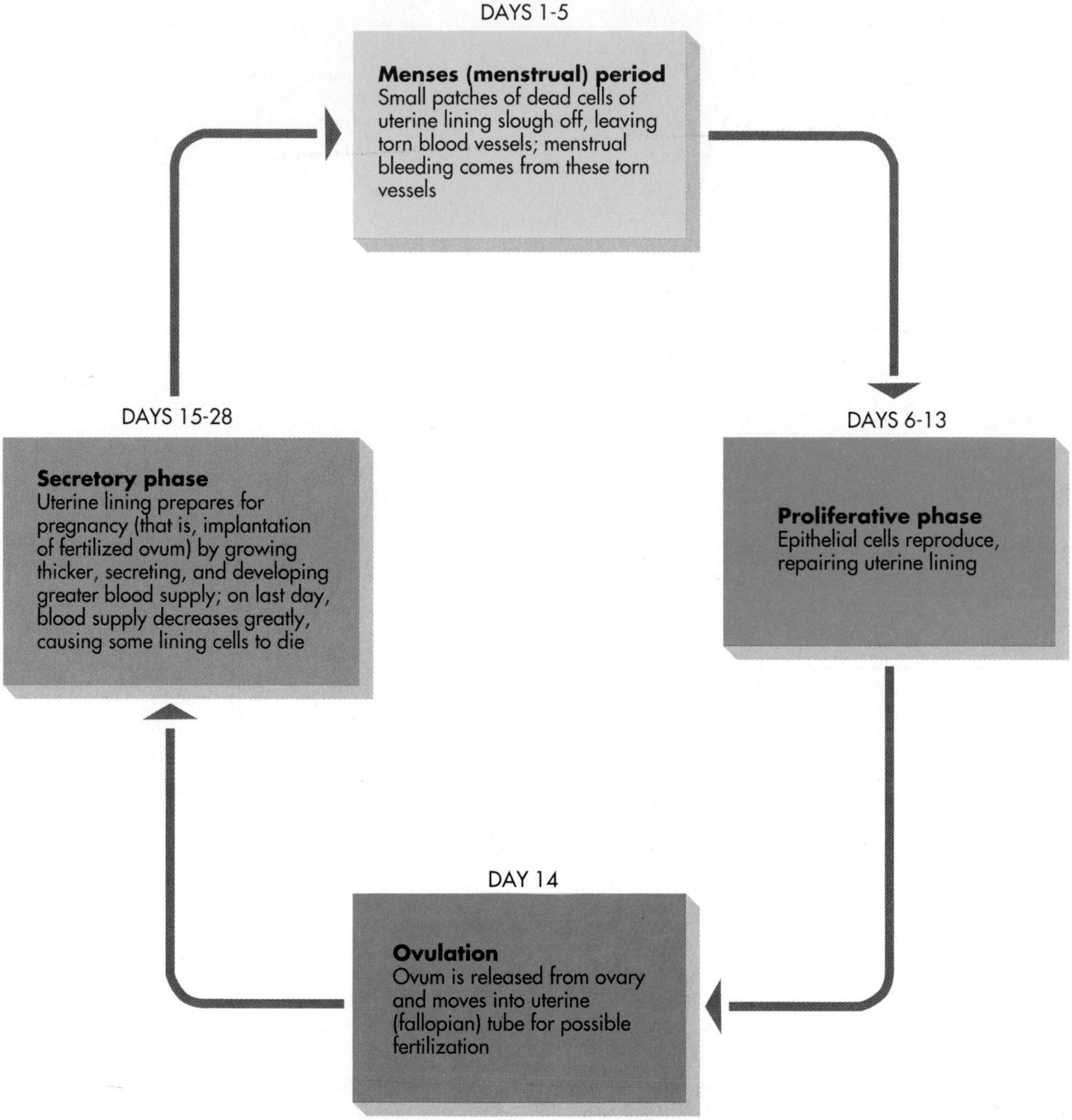
DAYS 1-5
Menses (menstrual) period
Small patches of dead cells of uterine lining slough off, leaving torn blood vessels; menstrual bleeding comes from these torn vessels
DAYS 6-13
Proliferative phase
Epithelial cells reproduce, repairing uterine lining
DAY 14
Ovulation
Ovum is released from ovary and moves into uterine (fallopian) tube for possible fertilization
DAYS 15-28
Secretory phase
Uterine lining prepares for pregnancy (that is, implantation of fertilized ovum) by growing thicker, secreting, and developing greater blood supply; on last day, blood supply decreases greatly, causing some lining cells to die

among women. Some women, for example, may have a regular cycle that covers about 24 days. The length of the cycle also varies within one woman. Some women, for example, may have irregular cycles that range from 21 to 28 days, whereas others may be 2 to 3 months long. Each cycle consists of three phases. The three periods of time in each cycle are called the **menses,** the **proliferative phase,** and the **secretory phase.** Refer often to Figure 19-13 as you read about the events occurring during each phase of the cycle in the pituitary gland, the ovary, and in the uterus. Be sure that you do not overlook the event that occurs around day 14 of a 28-day cycle.

FIGURE 19–13 ***The Human Menstrual Cycle.*** Diagram illustrates the interrelationship of pituitary, ovarian, and uterine functions throughout a usual 28-day cycle. A sharp increase in LH levels causes ovulation, whereas menstruation (sloughing off of the endometrial lining) is initiated by lower levels of progesterone.

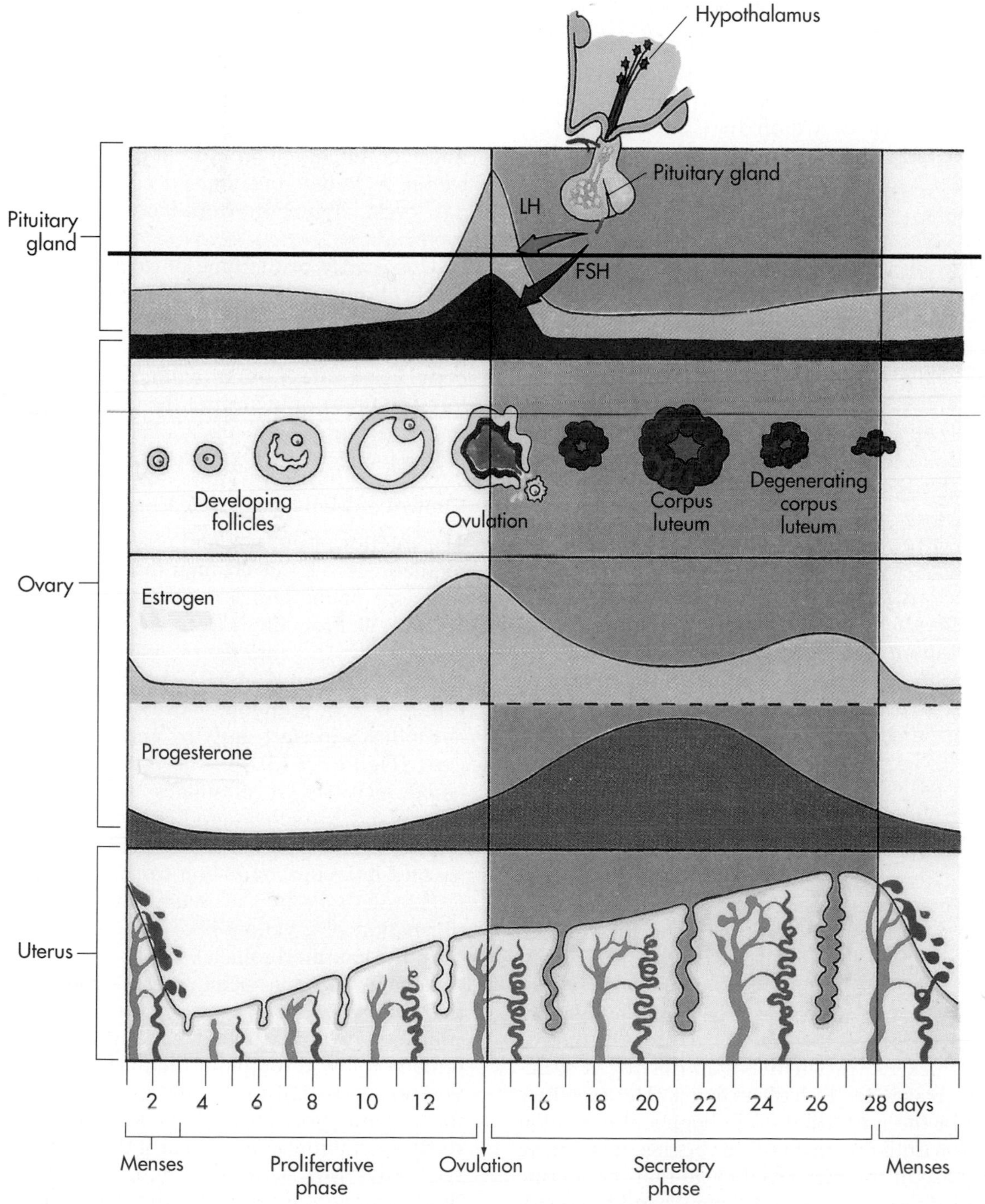

Hysterectomy

The word **hysterectomy** (his-te-REK-toe-me) comes from the combination of two Greek words: *hystera,* meaning "uterus," and *ektome,* meaning "to cut out." By definition it is the surgical removal of the uterus. *Hysterectomy* is a term that is often misused, however, by incorrectly expanding its definition to include the removal of the ovaries or other reproductive structures. Only the uterus is removed in a hysterectomy. If the total uterus, including the cervix, is removed, the terms *total hysterectomy* or *panhysterectomy* may be used. If the cervical portion of the uterus is left in place and only the body of the organ is removed, the term *subtotal hysterectomy* is appropriate. The actual removal of the uterus may be performed through an incision made in the abdominal wall—*abdominal hysterectomy*—or through the vagina—*vaginal hysterectomy.* The term **oophorectomy** (o-off-o-REK-toe-me) is used to describe removal of the ovaries. Although the two surgical procedures may take place during the same operation—for a woman with uterine or ovarian cancer, for example—the terms used to describe them should not be used interchangeably.

The menses is a period of 4 or 5 days characterized by menstrual bleeding. The first day of menstrual flow is considered day 1 of the menstrual cycle. The proliferative phase begins after the menstrual flow ends and lasts until ovulation. During this period the follicles mature, the uterine lining thickens (proliferates), and estrogen secretion increases to its highest level. The secretory phase of the menstrual cycle begins at ovulation and lasts until the next menses begins. It is during this phase of the menstrual cycle that the uterine lining reaches its greatest thickness and the ovary secretes its highest levels of progesterone.

As a general rule, during the 30 or 40 years that a woman has periods, only one ovum matures each month. However, there are exceptions to this rule. Some months, more than one matures, and some months no ovum matures. Ovulation occurs 14 days before the next menses begins. In a 28-day cycle, this means that ovulation occurs around day 14 of the cycle, as shown in Figure 19-12. (Recall that the first day of the menses is considered the first day of the cycle.) In a 30-day cycle, however, ovulation would not occur on the fourteenth cycle day, but the sixteenth. And in a 25-day cycle, ovulation would occur the eleventh cycle day.

This matter of the time of ovulation has great practical importance. An ovum lives only a short time after it is ejected from its follicle, and sperm live only a short time after they enter the female body. Fertilization of an ovum by a sperm therefore can occur only around the time of ovulation. In other words, a woman's fertile period lasts only a few days each month.

Control of Menstrual Cycle Changes

The anterior pituitary gland plays a critical role in regulating the cyclic changes that characterize the functions of the female reproductive system (see Chapter 9). From day 1 to about day 7 of the menstrual cycle, the anterior pituitary gland secretes increasing amounts of FSH. A high blood concentration of FSH stimulates several immature ovarian follicles to start growing and secreting estrogens (Figure 19-13). As the estrogen content of blood increases, it stimulates the anterior pituitary gland to secrete another hormone, luteinizing hormone (LH). LH causes maturing of a follicle and its ovum, ovulation (rupturing of mature follicle with ejection of ovum), and luteinization (formation of a yellow body, the corpus luteum, from the ruptured follicle).

Which hormone—FSH or LH—would you call the "ovulating hormone"? Do you think ovulation could occur if the blood concentration of FSH remained low throughout the menstrual cycle? If you answered LH to the first question and no to the second, you answered both questions correctly. Ovulation cannot occur if the blood level of FSH stays low because a high concentration of this hormone is essential to stimulation of ovarian follicle growth and maturation. With a low level

TABLE 19–3 Analogous Features of the Reproductive Systems

FEATURE	FEMALE	MALE
Essential organs	Ovaries	Testes
Sex cells	Ova (eggs)	Sperm
Hormones	Estrogen and progesterone	Testosterone
Hormone-producing cells	Granulosa cells and corpus luteum	Interstitial cells
Duct systems	Uterine (fallopian) tubes, uterus, and vagina	Epididymis, urethra, and ductus (vas) deferens
External genitals	Clitoris and vulva	Penis and scrotum

of FSH, no follicles start to grow, and therefore none become ripe enough to ovulate. Ovulation is caused by the combined actions of FSH and LH. Birth control pills that contain estrogen substances suppress FSH secretion. This indirectly prevents ovulation.

Ovulation occurs, as we have said, because of the combined actions of the two anterior pituitary hormones, FSH and LH. The next question is: what causes menstruation? A brief answer is this: a sudden, sharp decrease in estrogen and progesterone secretion toward the end of the premenstrual period causes the uterine lining to break down and another menstrual period to begin.

Summary of Male and Female Reproductive Systems

The reproductive systems in both sexes are centered around the production of highly specialized reproductive cells or gametes (sperm and ova), as well as mechanisms to ensure union of these two cells; the fusion of these cells enables transfer of parental genetic information to the next generation. Table 19-3 compares several analogous components of the reproductive systems in both sexes. You can see that men and women have similar structures to accomplish complementary functions. In addition, the female reproductive system permits development and birth of the offspring—and this will be the first subject of our last chapter.

Amenorrhea in Female Athletes

Failure to have a menstrual period is called **amenorrhea**. Amenorrhea occurs in some female athletes, probably resulting from a body fat composition that is too low to sustain normal reproductive function. Although it keeps the hematocrit (RBC level) higher than during menstruation, it is not considered a desirable condition. Besides infertility, amenorrhea may cause other problems. For example, the low blood levels of estrogen associated with long-term amenorrhea may cause osteoporosis (loss of bone mass).

OUTLINE SUMMARY

COMMON STRUCTURAL AND FUNCTIONAL CHARACTERISTICS BETWEEN THE SEXES

- **A** Common general structure and function can be identified between the systems in both sexes
- **B** Systems adapted for development of sperm or ova followed by successful fertilization, development, and birth of offspring
- **C** Sex hormones in both sexes important in development of secondary sexual characteristics and normal reproductive system activity

MALE REPRODUCTIVE SYSTEM

- **A** Structural plan—organs classified as essential or accessory
  - **1** Essential organs of reproduction are the gonads (testes), which produce sex cells (sperm)
  - **2** Accessory organs of reproduction
    - **a** Ducts—passageways that carry sperm from testes to exterior
    - **b** Sex glands—produce protective and nutrient solution for sperm
    - **c** External genitals
- **B** Testes—the gonads of men
  - **1** Structure and location (Figure 19-2)
    - **a** Testes in scrotum—lower temperature
    - **b** Covered by tunica albuginea, which divides testis into lobules containing seminiferous tubules
    - **c** Interstitial cells produce testosterone
  - **2** Functions
    - **a** Spermatogenesis is process of sperm production (Figure 19-4)
      - **(1)** Sperm precursor cells called *spermatogonia*
      - **(2)** Meiosis produces primary spermatocyte, which forms four spermatids with 23 chromosomes
      - **(3)** Spermatozoa—highly specialized cell
        - **(a)** Head contains genetic material
        - **(b)** Acrosome contains enzymes to assist sperm in penetration of ovum
        - **(c)** Mitochondria provide energy for movement
    - **b** Production of testosterone by interstitial cells
      - **(1)** Testosterone "masculinizes" and promotes development of male accessory organs
      - **(2)** Stimulates protein anabolism and development of muscle strength
- **C** Reproductive ducts—ducts through which sperm pass after exiting testes until they exit from the body
  - **1** Epididymis—single, coiled tube about 6 m in length; lies along the top and behind the testis in the scrotum
    - **a** Sperm mature and develop the capacity for motility as they pass through epididymis
  - **2** Ductus (vas) deferens—receives sperm from the epididymis and transports them from scrotal sac through the abdominal cavity
    - **a** Passes through inguinal canal
    - **b** Joins duct of seminal vesicle to form the ejaculatory duct
- **D** Accessory or supportive sex glands—semen: mixture of sperm and secretions of accessory sex glands. Averages 3 to 5 ml per ejaculation, with each milliliter containing about 100 million sperm
  - **1** Seminal vesicles
    - **a** Pouchlike glands that produce about 60% of seminal fluid volume
    - **b** Secretion is yellowish, thick, and rich in fructose to provide energy needed by sperm for motility
  - **2** Prostate gland
    - **a** Shaped like a doughnut and located below bladder
    - **b** Urethra passes through the gland
    - **c** Secretion represents 30% of seminal fluid volume—is thin and milk-colored
    - **d** Activates sperm and is needed for ongoing sperm motility
  - **3** Bulbourethral (Cowper's) glands
    - **a** Resemble peas in size and shape
    - **b** Secrete mucuslike fluid constituting less than 5% of seminal fluid volume
- **E** External genitals
  - **1** Penis and scrotum called *genitalia*
  - **2** Penis has three columns of erectile tissue—two dorsal columns called *corpora cavernosa* and one ventral column surrounding urethra called *corpus spongiosum*
  - **3** Glans penis covered by foreskin
  - **4** Surgical removal of foreskin called *circumcision*

FEMALE REPRODUCTIVE SYSTEM

- **A** Structural plan—organs classified as essential or accessory
  - **1** Essential organs are gonads (ovaries), which produce sex cells (ova)
  - **2** Accessory organs of reproduction
    - **a** Ducts or modified ducts—including oviducts, uterus, and vagina
    - **b** Sex glands—including those in the breasts
    - **c** External genitals

B Ovaries
- **1** Structure and location
  - **a** Paired glands weighing about 3 g each
  - **b** Resemble large almonds
  - **c** Attached to ligaments in pelvic cavity on each side of uterus
  - **d** Microscopic structure (Figure 19-8)
    - **(1)** Ovarian follicles—contain oocyte, which is immature sex cell (about 1 million at birth)
    - **(2)** Primary follicles—about 400,000 at puberty are covered with granulosa cells
    - **(3)** About 350 to 500 mature follicles ovulate during the reproductive lifetime of most women—sometimes called *Graafian follicles*
    - **(4)** Secondary follicles have hollow chamber called *antrum*
    - **(5)** Corpus luteum forms after ovulation
- **2** Functions
  - **a** Oogenesis—this meiotic cell division produces daughter cells with equal chromosome numbers (23) but unequal cytoplasm. Ovum is large; polar bodies are small and degenerate
  - **b** Production of estrogen and progesterone
    - **(1)** Granulosa cells surrounding the oocyte in the mature and growing follicles produce estrogen
    - **(2)** Corpus luteum produces progesterone
    - **(3)** Estrogen causes development and maintenance of secondary sex characteristics
    - **(4)** Progesterone stimulates secretory activity of uterine epithelium and assists estrogen in initiating menses

C Reproductive ducts
- **1** Uterine (fallopian) tubes
  - **a** Extend about 10 cm from uterus into abdominal cavity
  - **b** Expanded distal end surrounded by fimbriae
  - **c** Mucosal lining of tube is directly continuous with lining of abdominal cavity
- **2** Uterus—composed of body, fundus, and cervix (Figure 19-9)
  - **a** Lies in pelvic cavity just behind urinary bladder
  - **b** Myometrium is muscle layer
  - **c** Endometrium lost in menstruation
  - **d** Menopause—end of repetitive menstrual cycles (about 45 years of age)
- **3** Vagina
  - **a** Distensible tube about 10 cm long
  - **b** Located between urinary bladder and rectum in the pelvis
  - **c** Receives penis during sexual intercourse and is birth canal for normal delivery of baby at termination of pregnancy

D Accessory or supportive sex glands
- **1** Bartholin's (greater vestibular) glands
  - **a** Secrete mucuslike lubricating fluid
  - **b** Ducts open between labia minora
- **2** Breasts (Figure 19-10)
  - **a** Located over pectoral muscles of thorax
  - **b** Size determined by fat quantity more than amount of glandular (milk-secreting) tissue
  - **c** Lactiferous ducts drain at nipple, which is surrounded by pigmented areola
  - **d** Lymphatic drainage important in spread of cancer cells to other body areas

E External genitals (Figure 19-11)
- **1** Include mons pubis, clitoris, orifice of urethra, Bartholin's gland, vagina, labia minora and majora, and hymen
- **2** Perineum—area between vaginal opening and anus
  - **a** Surgical cut during birth called *episiotomy*

F Menstrual cycle—involves many changes in the uterus, ovaries, vagina, and breasts (Figures 19-12 and 19-13)
- **1** Length—about 28 days, varies from month to month in individuals and in the same individual
- **2** Phases
  - **a** Menses—about the first 4 or 5 days of the cycle, varies somewhat; characterized by sloughing of bits of endometrium (uterine lining) with bleeding
  - **b** Proliferative phase—days between the end of menses and secretory phase; varies in length; the shorter the cycle, the shorter the proliferative phase; the longer the cycle, the longer the proliferative phase; examples: in 28-day cycle, proliferative phase ends on day 13, but in 26-day cycle, it ends on the 11th day and in 32-day cycle, it ends on day 17; characterized by repair of endometrium
  - **c** Secretory phase—days between ovulation and beginning of next menses; secretory about 14 days before next menses; characterized by further thickening of endometrium and secretion by its glands in preparation for implantation of fertilized ovum; combined actions of the anterior pituitary hormones FSH and LH cause ovulation; sudden sharp decrease in estrogens and progesterone bring on menstruation if pregnancy does not occur.

SUMMARY OF MALE AND FEMALE REPRODUCTIVE SYSTEMS

A In men and women the organs of the reproductive system are adapted for the specific sequence of functions that permit development of sperm or ova followed by the successful fertilization and then the normal development and birth of offspring

B The male organs produce, store, and ultimately introduce mature sperm into the female reproductive tract

C The female system produces ova, receives the sperm, and permits fertilization followed by fetal development and birth, with lactation afterward

D Production of sex hormones is required for development of secondary sex characteristics and for normal reproductive functions in both sexes

NEW WORDS

areola	estrogen	menses	semen
circumcision	fimbriae	oocyte	seminiferous tubule
clitoris	gametes	ovulation	spermatogenesis
corpus luteum	genitals	perineum	spermatozoa
ejaculation	gonads	polar body	testes
endometrium	Graafian follicle	prepuce	testosterone
epididymis	meiosis	progesterone	vulva
episiotomy	menopause	scrotum	zygote

CHAPTER TEST

1. The gonads of the male are the ______________.
2. In men the sex cells are called ______________.
3. The essential organs of reproduction in both sexes are called the ______________.
4. Each lobule of the testis consists of a narrow but long and coiled tube called the ______________ tubule.
5. Testosterone formation is the function of the ______________ cells of the testis.
6. In men the urethra passes through the center of the doughnut-shaped ______________ gland.
7. The narrow section of the uterus that opens into the vagina is called the ______________.
8. The corpus luteum secretes ______________.
9. The mucous membrane lining the uterus is called the ______________.
10. The colored area around the nipple is called the ______________.
11. The scientific name for the beginning of the menses is called ______________.
12. The average length of a typical menstrual cycle is ______________ days.

Select the most correct answer from Column B for each statement in Column A. (Only one answer is correct.)

COLUMN A	COLUMN B
13. ______ Female gonads	**a.** Ovarian follicles
14. ______ External genitals	**b.** Testosterone
15. ______ Secrete estrogen	**c.** LH
16. ______ Corpus luteum	**d.** Secrete progesterone
17. ______ Sperm formation	**e.** Circumcision
18. ______ "Ovulating hormone"	**f.** Ovaries
19. ______ Surgical removal of foreskin	**g.** Estrogen
20. ______ Feminizing hormone	**h.** Spermatogenesis
21. ______ Female sex cell	**i.** Vulva
22. ______ Male sex hormone	**j.** Ovum

REVIEW QUESTIONS

1. Identify the essential and accessory organs of reproduction in men.
2. What organs are included in the external genitals of the male?
3. Discuss the structure of the testes. Explain the function of the seminiferous tubules and the interstitial cells of the testes.
4. What is the name of the masculinizing hormone? What secretes it? What are its general functions?
5. Discuss the anatomy of a sperm cell. Why is it motile? What parts of the sperm cell are designed to provide motility?
6. How many sperm are normally present in one ejaculation of semen? What is the usual volume of semen ejaculated at one time?
7. Discuss the functions of the accessory glands in men.
8. Name the reproductive ducts in men and women.
9. Identify the feminizing hormone by its scientific name. What gland secretes it?
10. Identify the ovulating hormone by its scientific name. What glands secrete it?
11. Identify and locate the alveoli of breast, areola, cervix, clitoris, fundus of uterus, Graafian follicle, labia majora, mons pubis, ovum, and uterine tube.
12. What causes ovulation?
13. What is menstruation? What causes it?

CRITICAL THINKING

14. Trace a sperm cell from its point of formation in the testes through the male reproductive ducts to ejaculation.
15. Castration is an operation that removes the testes. Would this sterilize the male? Why? What other effects would you expect to see as a result of castration? Why?
16. How many female sex cells are usually formed each month? How does this compare with the number of male sex cells formed each month?

Growth and Development

20

OUTLINE

Prenatal Period
- Fertilization to Implantation
- Periods of Development
- Formation of the Primary Germ Layers
- Histogenesis and Organogenesis

Birth or Parturition
- Stages of Labor

Postnatal Period
- Infancy
- Childhood
- Adolescence and Adulthood
- Older Adulthood

Effects of Aging
- Skeletal System
- Integumentary System (Skin)
- Urinary System
- Respiratory System
- Cardiovascular System
- Special Senses

BOXED ESSAYS

In Vitro Fertilization
Quickening
Antenatal Diagnosis and Treatment
Freezing Umbilical Cord Blood
Fetal Alcohol Syndrome

OBJECTIVES

After you have completed this chapter, you should be able to:

1. Discuss the concept of development as a biological process characterized by continuous modification and change.
2. Discuss the major developmental changes characteristic of the prenatal stage of life from fertilization to birth.
3. Discuss the three stages of labor that characterize a normal, vaginal birth.
4. Identify the three primary germ layers and several derivatives in the adult body that develop from each layer.
5. List and discuss the major developmental changes characteristic of the four postnatal periods of life.
6. Discuss the effects of aging on the major body organ systems.

Many of your fondest and most vivid memories are probably associated with your birthdays. The day of birth is an important milestone of life. Most people continue to remember their birthday in some special way each year; birthdays serve as pleasant and convenient reference points to mark periods of transition or change in our lives. The actual day of birth marks the end of one phase of life called the **prenatal period** and the beginning of a second called the **postnatal period.** The prenatal period begins at conception and ends at birth; the postnatal period begins at birth and continues until death. Although important periods in our lives such as childhood and adolescence are often remembered as a series of individual and isolated events, they are in reality part of an ongoing and continuous process. In reviewing the many changes that occur during the cycle of life from conception to death, it is often convenient to isolate certain periods such as infancy or adulthood for study. It is important to remember, however, that life is not a series of stop-and-start events or individual and isolated periods of time. Instead, it is a biological process that is characterized by continuous modification and change.

This chapter discusses some of the events and changes that occur in the development of the individual from conception to death. Study of development during the prenatal period is followed by a discussion of the birth process and a review of changes occurring during infancy and adulthood. Finally some important changes that occur in the individual organ systems of the body as a result of aging are discussed.

Prenatal Period

The **prenatal stage of development** begins at the time of conception or fertilization (that is, at the moment the female ovum and the male sperm cells unite) (Figure 20-1). The period of prenatal development continues until the birth of the child about 39 weeks later. The science of the development of the individual before birth is called **embryology** (em-bree-OL-o-jee). It is a story of miracles, describing the means by which a new human life is started and the steps by which a single microscopic cell is transformed into a complex human being.

FERTILIZATION TO IMPLANTATION

After ovulation the discharged ovum first enters the abdominal cavity and then finds its way into the uterine (fallopian) tubes. Sperm cells "swim" up the uterine tubes toward the ovum. Look at the relationship of the ovary, the two uterine tubes, and the uterus in Figure 20-2. Recall from Chapter 19 that each uterine tube extends outward from the uterus for about 10 cm. It then ends in the abdominal cavity near the ovary, as you can see in Figure 20-2, in an opening surrounded by fringelike processes, the *fimbriae.* Using the uterus as a point of reference, anatomists divide each uterine tube into three parts. The innermost part of the tube actually extends through the uterine wall, the middle third extends out into the abdominal cavity, and the outermost third of the tube ends near the ovary in the dilated, funnel-shaped opening described above.

Sperm cells that are deposited in the vagina must enter and "swim" through the uterus and then move out of the uterine cavity and through the uterine tube to meet the ovum. Fertilization most often occurs in the outer one third of the oviduct as shown in Figure 20-2. The fertilized ovum or **zygote** (ZYE-gote) is genetically complete; it represents a new single-celled individual. Time and nourishment are all that is needed for expression of characteristics such as sex, body build, and skin color that were determined at the time of fertilization. As you can see in the figure, the zygote immediately begins mitotic division, and in about 3 days a solid mass of cells called a **morula** (MOR-yoo-lah) is formed (Figure 20-2). The cells of the morula continue to divide, and by the time the developing embryo reaches the uterus, it is a hollow ball of cells called a **blastocyst** (BLAS-toe-sist).

During the 10 days from the time of fertilization to the time when the blastocyst is completely implanted in the uterine lining, no nutrients from the mother are available. The rapid cell division taking place up to the blastocyst stage occurs with no significant increase in total mass compared to

FIGURE 20–1 ***Fertilization.*** Fertilization is a specific biological event. It occurs when the male and female sex cells fuse. After union between a sperm cell and the ovum has occurred, the cycle of life begins. The scanning electron micrograph shows spermatozoa attaching themselves to the surface of an ovum. Only one will penetrate and fertilize the ovum.

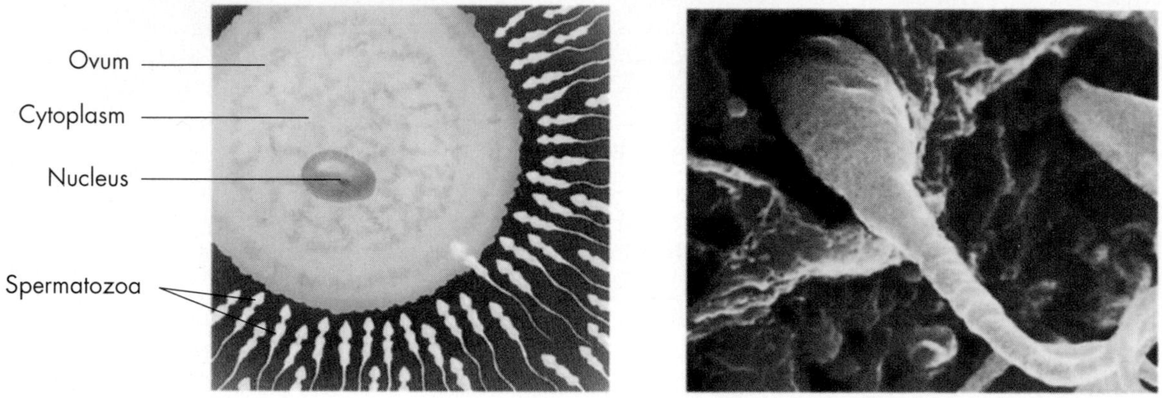

FIGURE 20–2 ***Fertilization and Implantation.*** At ovulation, an ovum is released from the ovary and begins its journey through the uterine tube. While in the tube, the ovum is fertilized by a sperm to form the single-celled zygote. After a few days of rapid mitotic division, a ball of cells called a *morula* is formed. After the morula develops into a hollow ball called a *blastocyst,* implantation occurs.

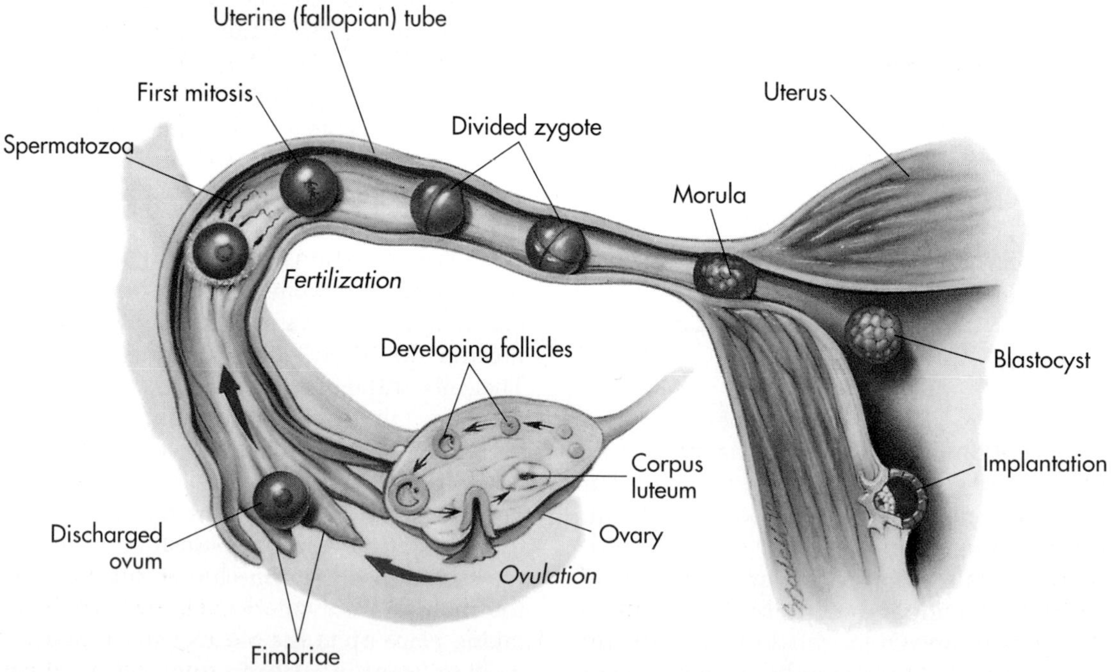

FIGURE 20–3 ***Early Stages of Human Development.*** **A,** Fertilized ovum or zygote. **B** to **D,** Early cell divisions produce more and more cells. The solid mass of cells shown in **D** forms the morula—an early stage in embryonic development.

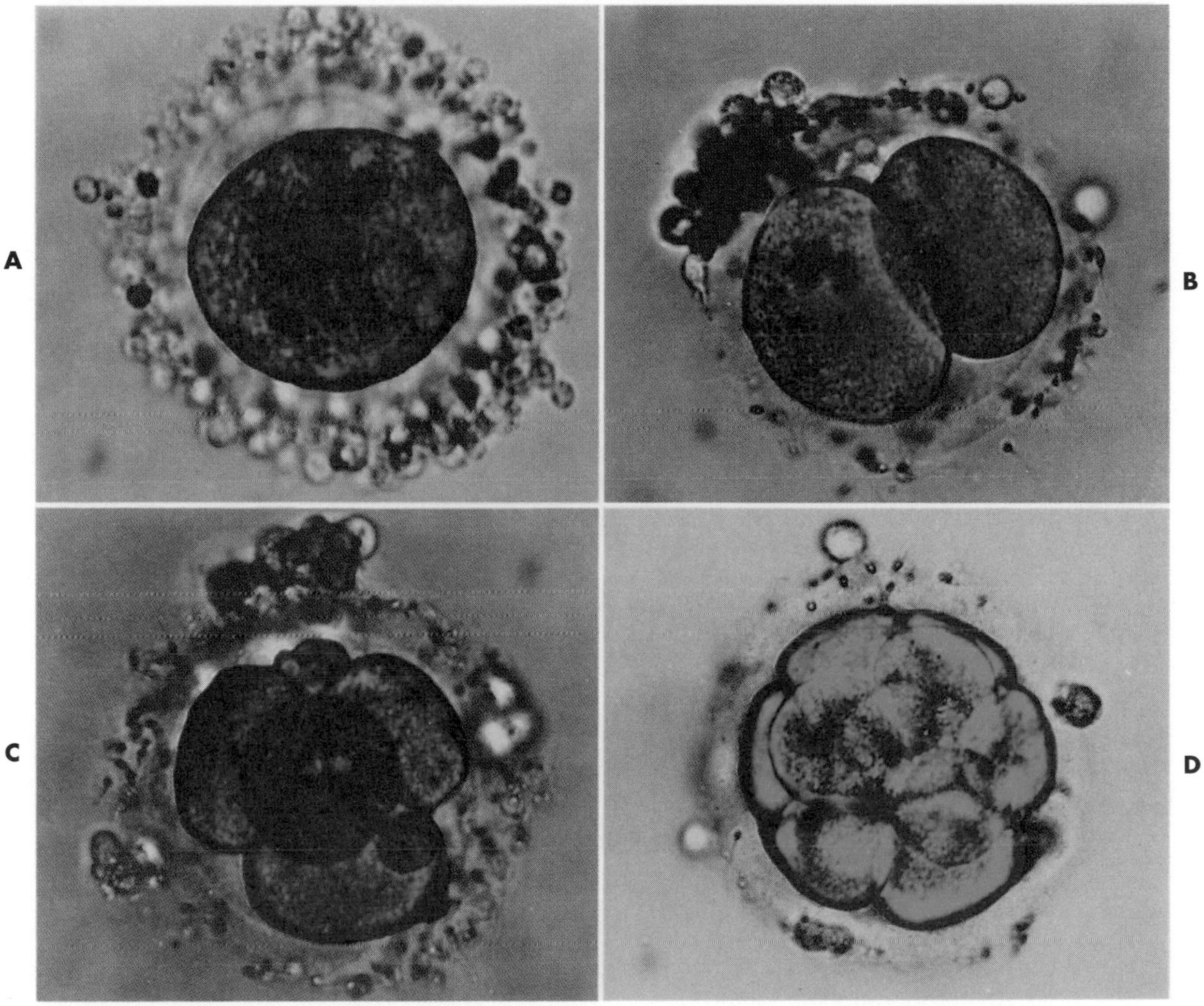

the zygote (Figure 20-3). One of the specializations of the ovum is its incredible store of nutrients that help support this embryonic development until implantation has occurred.

Note in Figure 20-4 that the blastocyst consists of an outer layer of cells and an inner cell mass. As the blastocyst develops, it forms a structure with two cavities, the **yolk sac** and **amniotic** (am-nee-OT-ik) **cavity.** The yolk sac is most important in animals, such as birds, that depend heavily on yolk as the sole source of nutrients for the developing embryo. In these animals the yolk sac digests the yolk and provides the resulting nutrients to the embryo. Because uterine fluids provide nutrients to the developing embryo in humans until the placenta develops, the function of the yolk sac is not a nutritive one. Instead, it has other functions, including production of blood cells.

FIGURE 20–4 ***Implantation and Early Development.*** The hollow blastocyst implants itself in the uterine lining about 10 days after ovulation. Until the placenta is functional, nutrients are obtained by diffusion from uterine fluids. Notice the developing chorion and how the blastocyst eventually forms a yolk sac and amniotic cavity.

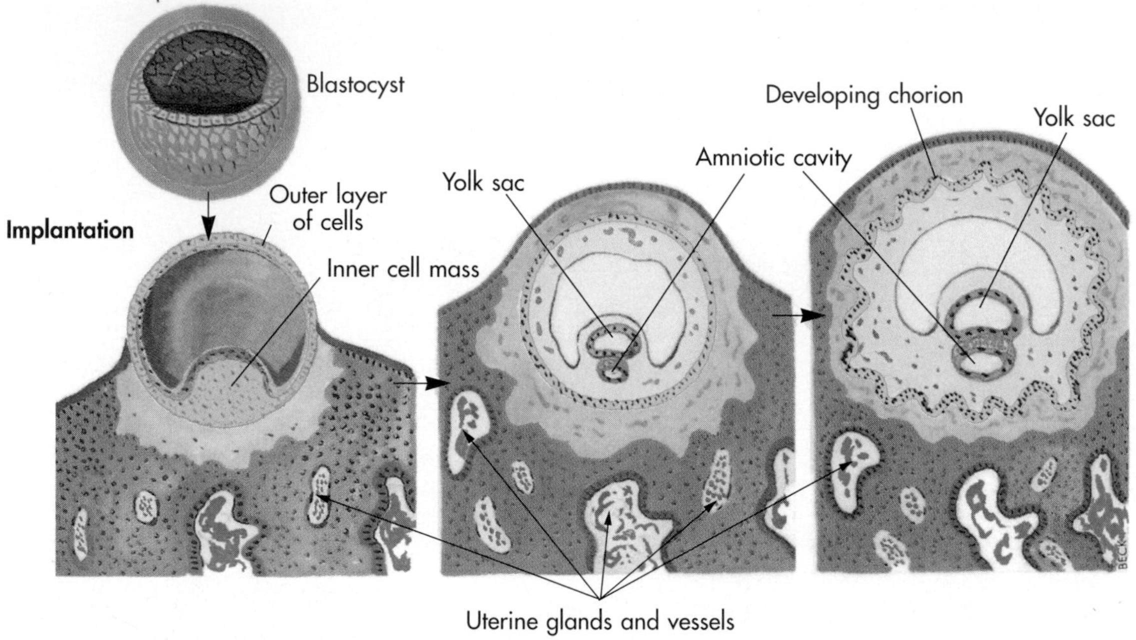

In Vitro Fertilization

The Latin term *in vitro* means, literally, "within a glass." In the case of in vitro fertilization, it refers to the glass laboratory dish where an ovum and sperm are mixed and where fertilization occurs.

In the classic technique, the ovum is obtained from the mother by first inserting a fiberoptic viewing instrument called a **laparoscope** through a very small incision in the woman's abdomen. Once in the abdominal cavity the device allows the physician to view the ovary and then puncture and "suck up" an ovum from a mature follicle. Over the years refinements to this technique have been made and less invasive procedures are currently being used. After about 2½ days growth in a temperature-controlled environment the developing zygote, which by then has reached the 8- or 16-cell stage, is returned by the physician to the mother's uterus. If implantation is successful, growth will continue and the subsequent pregnancy will progress. In the most successful fertility clinics in the U.S., a normal term birth will occur in about 30% of in vitro fertilization attempts.

The first "test tube" baby was born in England nearly 20 years ago. Since that time, improved techniques of in vitro fertilization and advances in our knowledge of reproductive biology have made it possible for growing numbers of infertile couples to conceive and deliver healthy infants.

FIGURE 20–5 ***The Placenta: Interface Between Maternal and Fetal Circulation.*** **A,** Relationship of uterus, developing infant, and placenta. **B,** The close placement of the fetal blood supply and the maternal blood in the lacunae of the placenta permits diffusion of nutrients and other substances. It also forms a thin barrier to prevent diffusion of most harmful substances. No mixing of fetal and maternal blood occurs.

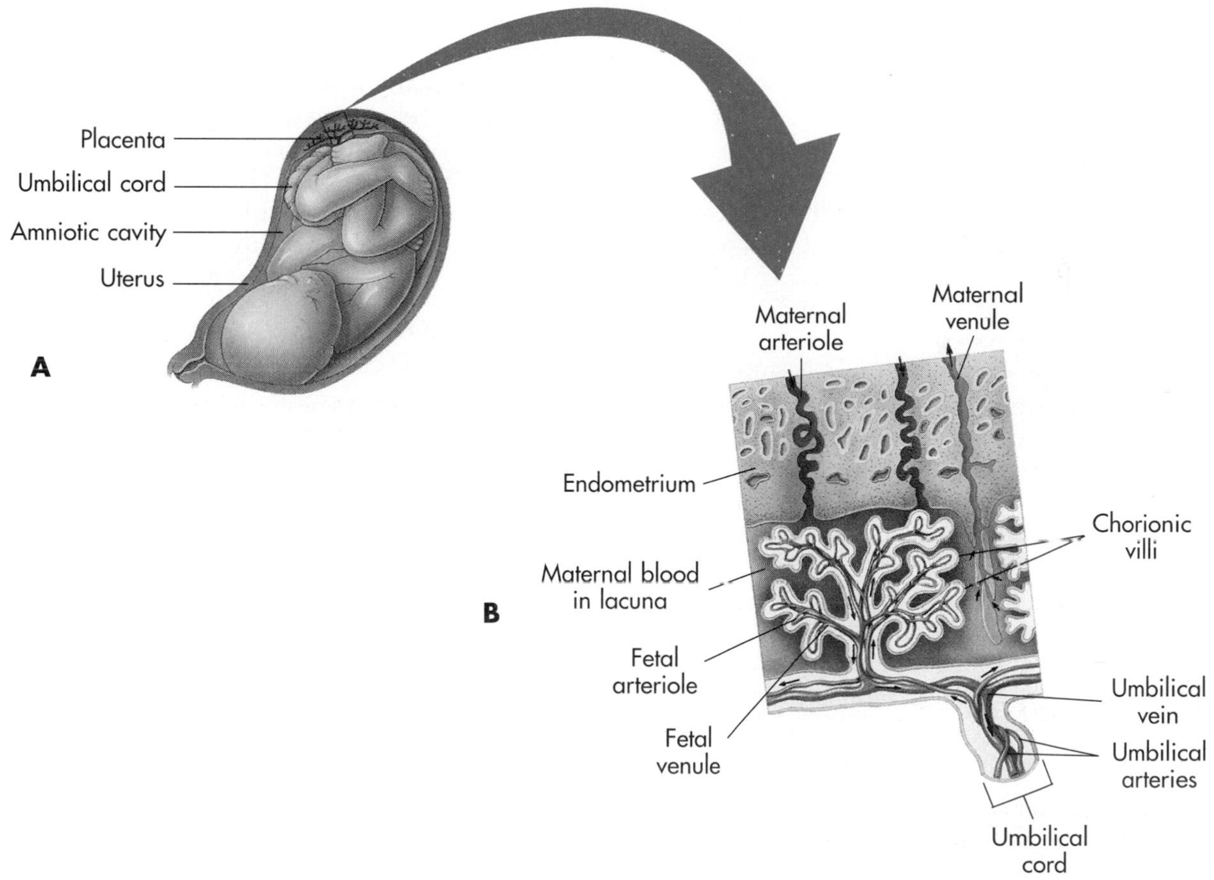

The amniotic cavity becomes a fluid-filled, shock-absorbing sac, sometimes called the *bag of waters,* in which the embryo floats during development. The **chorion** (KO-ree-on), shown in Figures 20-4 and 20-5, develops into an important fetal membrane in the **placenta** (plah-SEN-tah). The *chorionic villi* shown in Figure 20-5 connect the blood vessels of the chorion to the placenta. The placenta (Figure 20-5) anchors the developing fetus to the uterus and provides a "bridge" for the exchange of nutrients and waste products between mother and baby.

The placenta is a unique and highly specialized structure that has a temporary but very important series of functions during pregnancy. It is composed of tissues from mother and child and functions not only as a structural "anchor" and nutritive bridge, but also as an excretory, respiratory, and endocrine organ (Figure 20-5).

Placental tissue normally separates the maternal blood, which fills the lacunae of the placenta, from the fetal blood so that no intermixing occurs. The very thin layer of placental tissue that separates maternal and fetal blood also serves as an effective "barrier" that can protect the developing baby from many harmful substances that may enter the mother's bloodstream. Unfortunately, toxic substances, such as alcohol and some infectious organisms, may penetrate this protective placental barrier and injure the developing baby. The virus responsible for German measles (rubella), for example, can easily pass through the placenta and cause tragic developmental defects in the fetus.

PERIODS OF DEVELOPMENT

The length of pregnancy (about 39 weeks)—called the *gestation period*—is divided into three 3-month segments called *trimesters.* A number of terms are used to describe development during these periods known as the first, second, and third trimesters of pregnancy.

During the first trimester or 3 months of pregnancy, many terms are used. *Zygote* describes the ovum just after fertilization by a sperm cell. After about 3 days of constant cell division, the solid mass of cells, identified earlier as the *morula,* enters the uterus. Continued development transforms the morula into the hollow blastocyst, which then implants into the uterine wall.

The embryonic phase of development extends from fertilization until the end of week 8 of gestation. During this period in the first trimester, the term *embryo* is used to describe the developing individual. The fetal phase is used to indicate the period of development extending from week 9 to week 39. During this period, the term *embryo* is replaced by *fetus.*

By day 35 of gestation (Figure 20-6, *A*), the heart is beating and, although the embryo is only 8 mm (about ⅜ inch) long, the eyes and so-called limb buds, which ultimately form the arms and legs, are clearly visible. Figure 20-6, *C* shows the stage of development of the fetus at the end of the first trimester of gestation. Body size is about 7 to 8 cm (3.2 inches) long. The facial features of the fetus are apparent, the limbs are complete, and gender can be identified. By month 4 (Figure 20-6, *D,*) all organ systems are complete and in place.

FORMATION OF THE PRIMARY GERM LAYERS

Early in the first trimester of pregnancy, three layers of specialized cells develop that embryologists call the **primary germ layers** (Table 20-1). Each layer gives rise to definite structures such as the skin, nervous tissue, muscles, or digestive organs. Table 20-1 lists a number of structures derived from each primary germ layer called, respectively, **endoderm** (EN-doe-derm) or inside layer, **ectoderm** (EK-toe-derm) or outside layer, and **mesoderm** (MEZ-o-derm) or middle layer.

TABLE 20–1 Primary Germ Layer Derivatives

ENDODERM	ECTODERM	MESODERM
Lining of gastrointestinal tract	Epidermis of skin	Dermis of skin
Lining of lungs	Tooth enamel	Circulatory system
Lining of hepatic and pancreatic ducts	Lens and cornea of eye	Many glands
Kidney ducts and bladder	Outer ear	Kidneys
Anterior pituitary gland (adenohypophysis)	Nasal cavity	Gonads
Thymus gland	Facial bones	Muscle
Thyroid gland	Skeletal muscles in head	Bones (except facial)
Parathyroid gland	Brain and spinal cord	
Tonsils	Sensory neurons	
	Adrenal medulla	

FIGURE 20–6 ***Human Embryos and Fetuses.*** **A,** At 35 days. **B,** At 49 days. **C,** At the end of the first trimester. **D,** At 4 months.

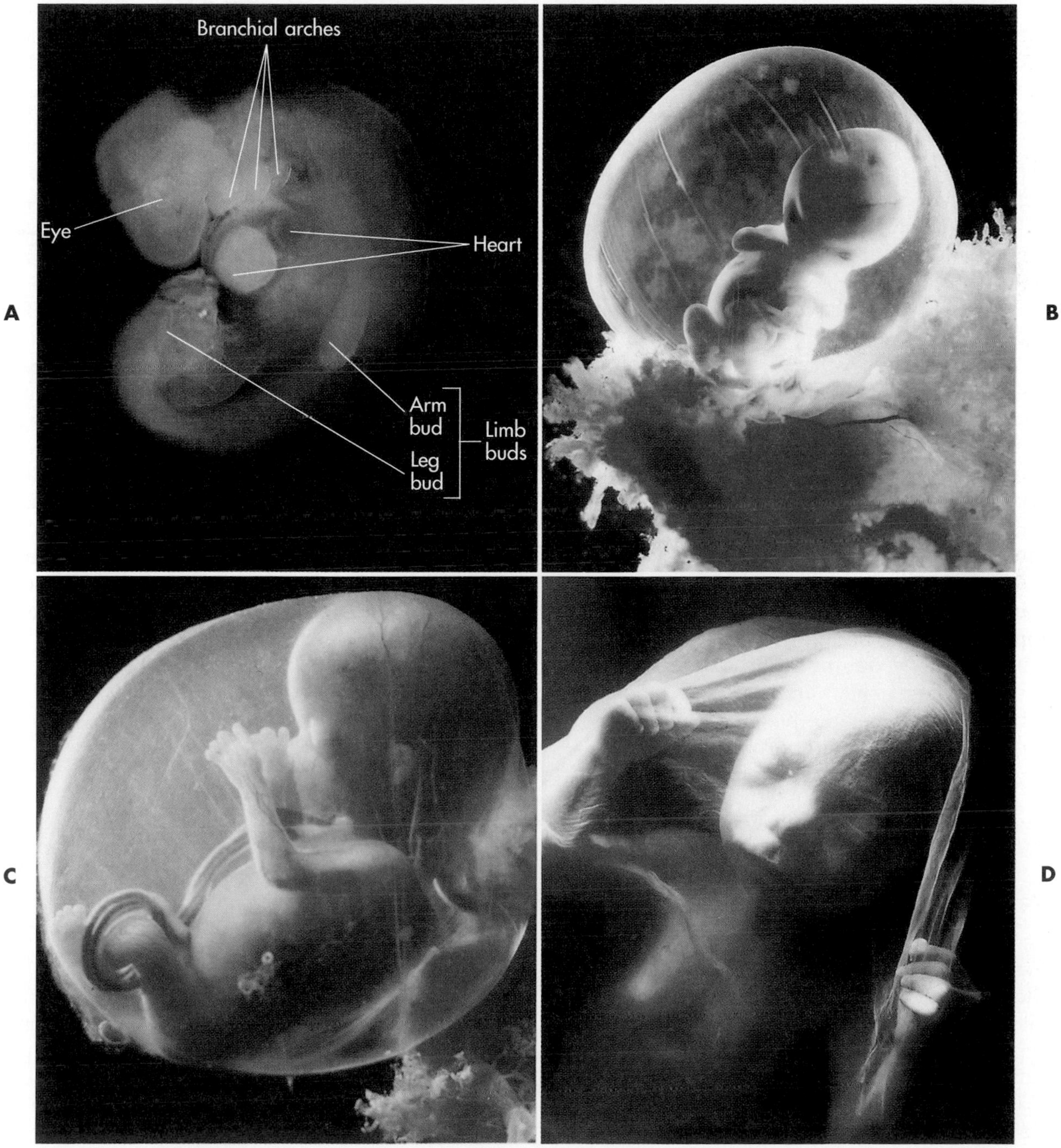

Quickening

Pregnant women usually notice fetal movement for the first time between weeks 16 and 18 of pregnancy. The term **quickening** has been used for generations to describe these first recognizable movements of the fetus. From an occasional "kick" during months 4 and 5 of pregnancy, the frequency of fetal movements steadily increases as gestation progresses. The frequency of fetal movements is an excellent indicator of the unborn baby's health.

Recent studies have shown that simply by recording the number of fetal movements each day after week 28 of pregnancy, a woman can provide her physician with extremely useful information about the health of her unborn child. Ten or more movements during a daily measurement period are considered normal.

Educating pregnant women about fetal movements and how to monitor their frequency is but one example of expanded interest in prenatal home care. Assisting pregnant women with making informed judgments about nutrition, exercise, lifestyle adjustments, and birthing options before they enter the hospital for delivery of their baby is an important and growing part of home health care services.

HISTOGENESIS AND ORGANOGENESIS

The study of how the primary germ layers develop into many different kinds of tissues is called **histogenesis** (his-toe-JEN-e-sis). The way that those tissues arrange themselves into organs is called **organogenesis** (or-ga-no-JEN-e-sis). The fascinating story of histogenesis and organogenesis in human development is long and complicated; its telling belongs to the science of embryology. But for the beginning student of anatomy, it seems sufficient to appreciate that life begins when two sex cells unite to form a single-celled zygote and that the new human body evolves by a series of processes consisting of cell differentiation, multiplication, growth, and rearrangement, all of which take place in definite, orderly sequence. Development of structure and function go hand in hand, and from 4 months of gestation, when every organ system is complete and in place, until term (about 280 days), fetal development is mainly a matter of growth. Figure 20-7, *A*, shows the normal intrauterine placement of a fetus just before birth in a full-term pregnancy.

Birth or Parturition

The process of birth or **parturition** (par-too-RISH-un) is the point of transition between the prenatal and postnatal periods of life. As pregnancy draws to a close, the uterus becomes "irritable" and, ultimately, muscular contractions begin and cause the cervix to dilate or open, thus permitting the fetus to move from the uterus through the vagina or "birth canal" to the exterior. The process normally begins with the fetus taking a head-down position against the cervix (Figure 20-7, *A*). When contractions occur, the amniotic sac or "bag of waters" ruptures, and labor begins.

STAGES OF LABOR

Labor is the process that results in the birth of a baby. It has three stages (Figure 20-7, *B* to *E*):

1. Stage one—period from onset of uterine contractions until dilation of the cervix is complete
2. Stage two—period from the time of maximal cervical dilation until the baby exits through the vagina
3. Stage three—process of expulsion of the placenta through the vagina

The time required for normal vaginal birth varies widely and may be influenced by many variables, including whether the woman has previously had a child. In most cases, stage one of labor lasts from 6 to 24 hours, and stage two lasts from a few minutes to an hour. Delivery of the placenta (stage three) normally occurs within 15 minutes after the birth of the baby.

FIGURE 20–7 ***Parturition.*** **A,** The relation of the fetus to the mother. **B,** The fetus moves into the opening of the birth canal, and the cervix begins to dilate. **C,** Dilation of the cervix is complete. **D,** The fetus is expelled from the uterus. **E,** The placenta is expelled.

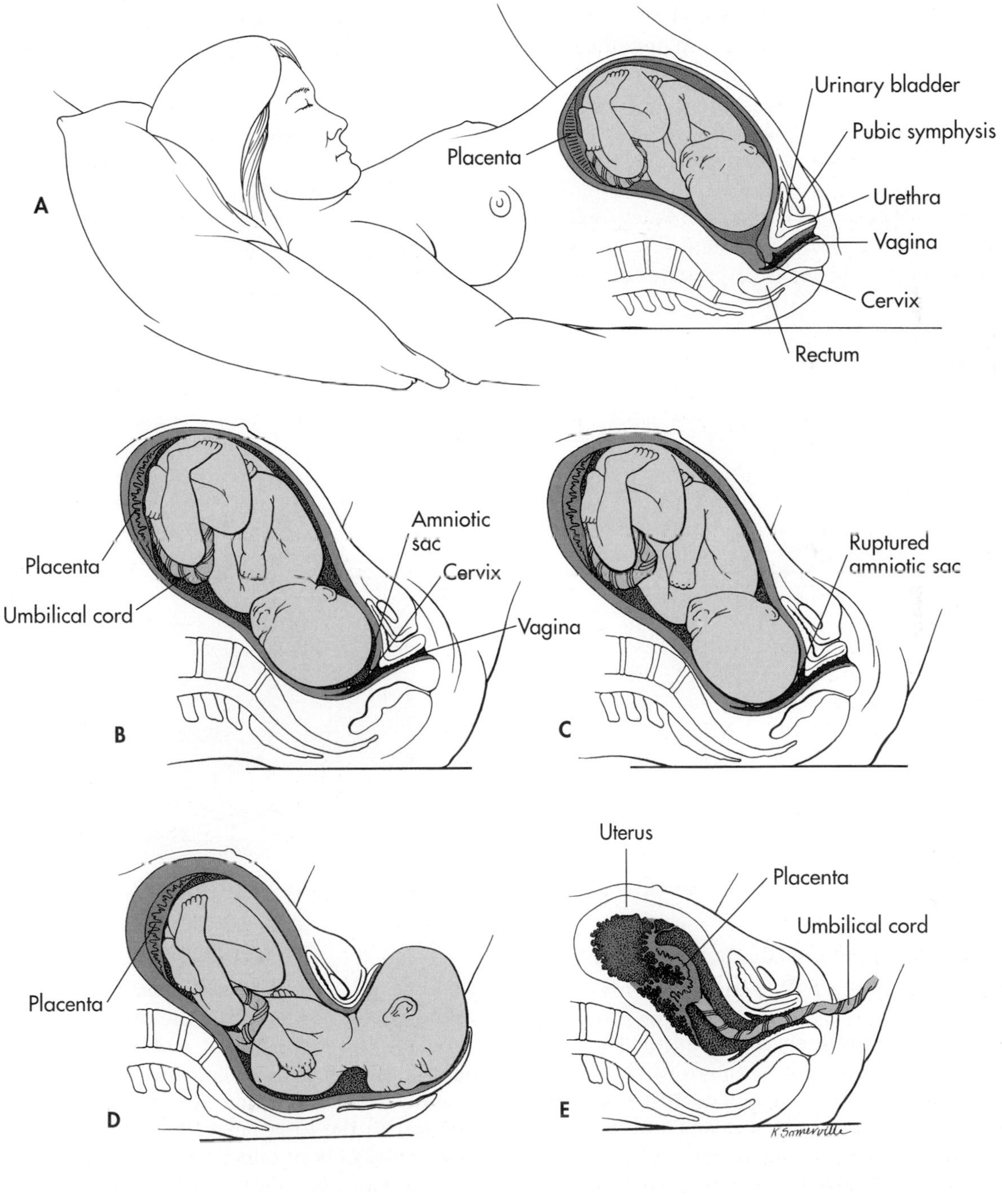

Antenatal Diagnosis and Treatment

Advances in **antenatal** (from the Latin *ante*, "before," *natus*, "birth") **medicine** now permit extensive diagnosis and treatment of disease in the fetus much like any other patient. This new dimension in medicine began with techniques by which Rh^+ babies could be given transfusions before birth.

Current procedures using images provided by ultrasound equipment (Figures *A* and *B*) allow physicians to prepare for and perform, before the birth of a baby, corrective surgical procedures such as bladder repair. These procedures also allow physicians to monitor the progress of other types of treatment on a developing fetus. Figure *A* shows placement of the ultrasound transducer on the abdominal wall. The resulting image (Figure *B*), called an *ultrasonogram*, shows a 29-week embryo. The image plane is showing the head.

A

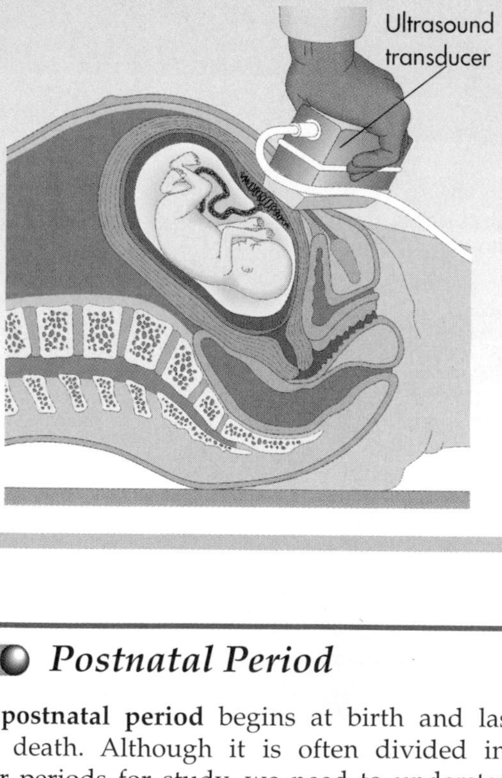

B

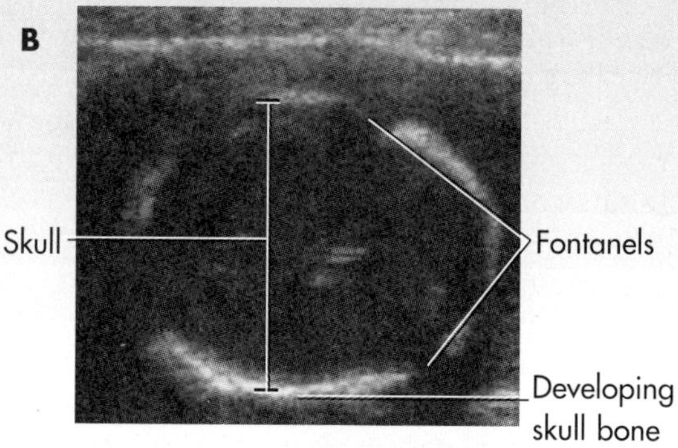

Postnatal Period

The **postnatal period** begins at birth and lasts until death. Although it is often divided into major periods for study, we need to understand and appreciate the fact that growth and development are continuous processes that occur throughout the life cycle. Gradual changes in the physical appearance of the body as a whole and in the relative proportions of the head, trunk, and limbs are quite noticeable between birth and adolescence. Note in Figure 20-8 the obvious changes in the size of bones and in the proportionate sizes between different bones and body areas. The head, for example, becomes proportionately smaller. Whereas the infant head is approximately one fourth the total height of the body, the adult head is only about one eighth the total height. The facial bones also show several changes between infancy and adulthood. In an infant the face is one eighth of the skull surface, but in an adult the face is half of the skull surface. Another change in pro-

FIGURE 20–8 ***Changes in the Proportions of Body Parts from Birth to Maturity.*** Note the dramatic differences in head size.

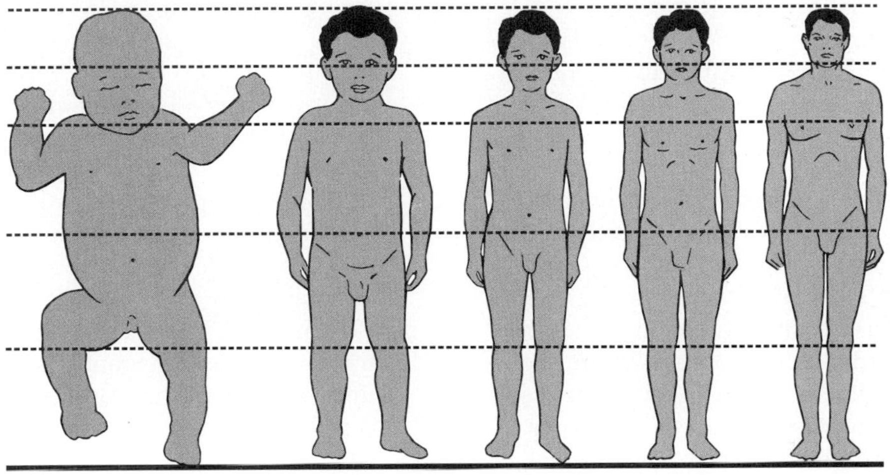

portion involves the trunk and lower extremities. The legs become proportionately longer and the trunk proportionately shorter. In addition, the thoracic and abdominal contours change, roughly speaking, from round to elliptical.

Such changes are good examples of the ever-changing and ongoing nature of growth and development. It is unfortunate that many of the changes that occur in the later years of life do not result in increased function. These degenerative changes are certainly important, however, and will be discussed later in this chapter. The following are the most common postnatal periods: (1) **infancy,** (2) **childhood,** (3) **adolescence** and **adulthood,** and (4) **older adulthood.**

FIGURE 20–9 ***The Neonate Infant.*** The umbilical cord has been cut.

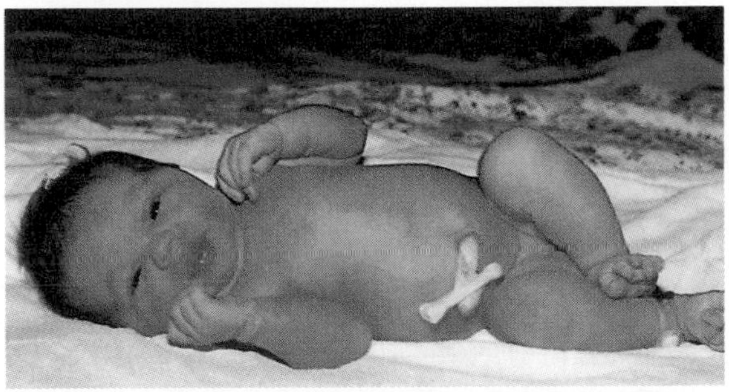

INFANCY

The period of infancy begins abruptly at birth and lasts about 18 months. The first 4 weeks of infancy are often referred to as the **neonatal** (nee-o-NAY-tal) **period** (Figure 20-9). Dramatic changes occur at a rapid rate during this short but critical period. **Neonatology** (nee-o-nay-TOL-o-jee) is the medical and nursing specialty concerned with the diagnosis and treatment of disorders of the newborn. Advances in this area have resulted in dramatically reduced infant mortality.

Many of the changes that occur in the cardiovascular and respiratory systems at birth are necessary for survival. Whereas the fetus totally depended on the mother for life support, the new-

Freezing Umbilical Cord Blood

The concept of development of blood cells from red bone marrow, a process called *hemopoiesis,* was introduced in Chapter 10. Ultimately, the presence of **"stem cells"** is required for bone marrow to produce blood cells. The fact that umbilical cord blood is rich in these stem cells has great clinical significance.

In the past, if the stem cells in the bone marrow of a child were destroyed as a result of leukemia or by chemotherapy, death would result unless a bone marrow transplant was possible. Infusion of stored umbilical cord blood obtained from the child at the time of birth is an attractive alternative. The blood is rich in stem cells, can be obtained without risk, and is much more cost-effective than a bone marrow transplant.

Removing and freezing umbilical cord blood at the time of birth may become a type of biological insurance against some types of leukemia that may affect a child later in life. Cord blood is readily available at birth and is a better source of stem cells than bone marrow. Once the umbilical cord is cut after birth, the blood that remains in the cord is simply drained into a sterile bag, frozen, and then stored in a "cryobank" in case it is needed later in life. This process, although growing in popularity, is still experimental. The Food and Drug Administration (FDA) is currently drafting guidelines for regulating commercial umbilical cord blood banks.

born infant must become totally self-supporting in terms of blood circulation and respiration immediately after birth. A baby's first breath is deep and forceful. The stimulus to breathe results primarily from the increasing amounts of carbon dioxide (CO_2) that accumulate in the blood after the umbilical cord is cut following delivery.

Many developmental changes occur between the end of the neonatal period and 18 months of age. Birth weight doubles during the first 4 months and then triples by 1 year. The baby also increases in length by 50% by the twelfth month. The "baby fat" that accumulated under the skin during the first year begins to decrease, and the plump infant becomes leaner.

Early in infancy the baby has only one spinal curvature (Figure 20-10). The lumbar curvature appears between 12 and 18 months, and the once-helpless infant becomes a toddler who can stand (Figure 20-11). One of the most striking changes to occur during infancy is the rapid development of the nervous and muscular systems. This permits the infant to follow a moving object with the eyes (2 months); lift the head and raise the chest (3 months); sit when well supported (4 months); crawl (10 months); stand alone (12 months); and run, although a bit stiffly (18 months).

FIGURE 20–10 *Normal Curvature of the Infant's Spine.*

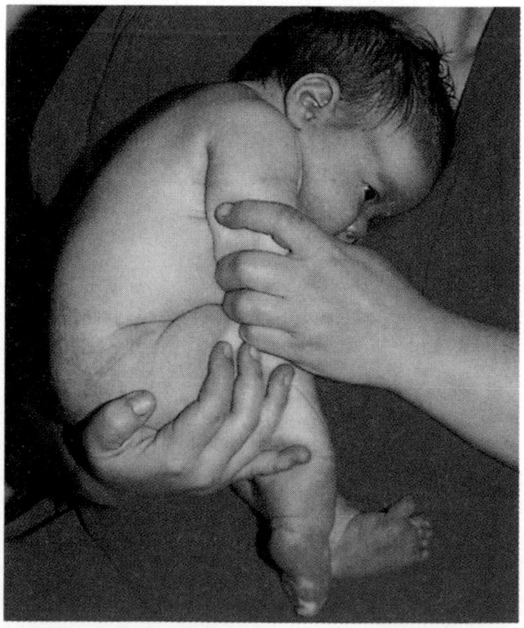

FIGURE 20–11 *Normal Lumbar Curvature of a Toddler's Spine.*

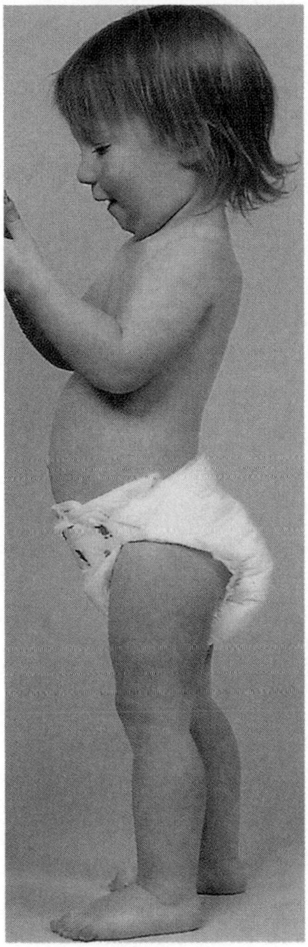

Fetal Alcohol Syndrome

Consumption of alcohol during pregnancy can have tragic effects on a developing fetus. Educational efforts to inform pregnant women about the dangers of alcohol are now receiving national attention. Even very limited consumption of alcohol during pregnancy poses significant hazards to the developing baby because alcohol can easily cross the placental barrier and enter the fetal bloodstream.

When alcohol enters the fetal blood, the potential result, called **fetal alcohol syndrome (FAS),** can cause tragic congenital abnormalities such as "small head" or **microcephaly** (my-kro-SEF-ah-lee), low birth weight, developmental disabilities such as mental retardation, and even fetal death.

CHILDHOOD

Childhood extends from the end of infancy to sexual maturity or puberty—12 to 14 years in girls and 14 to 16 years in boys. Overall, growth during early childhood continues at a rather rapid pace, but month-to-month gains become less consistent. By the age of 6 the child appears more like a preadolescent than an infant or toddler. The child becomes less chubby, the potbelly becomes flatter, and the face loses its babyish look. The nervous and muscular systems continue to develop rapidly during the middle years of childhood; by 10 years of age the child has developed numerous motor and coordination skills.

The *deciduous teeth,* which began to appear at about 6 months of age, are lost during childhood, beginning at about 6 years of age. The *permanent teeth,* with the possible exception of the third molars or wisdom teeth, have all erupted by age 14.

ADOLESCENCE AND ADULTHOOD

The average age range of **adolescence** varies but generally the teenage years (13 to 19) are used. The period is marked by rapid and intense physical growth, which ultimately results in sexual maturity. Many of the developmental changes that occur during this period are controlled by the secretion of sex hormones and are classified as **secondary sex characteristics.** Breast development is often the first sign of approaching puberty in girls, beginning about age 10. Most girls begin to menstruate at 12 to 13 years of age. In boys the first sign of puberty is often enlargement of the testicles, which begins between 10 and 13 years of age. Both sexes show a spurt in height during adolescence. In girls the spurt in height begins between the ages of 10 and 12 and is nearly complete by 14 or 15. In boys the period of rapid growth begins between 12 and 13 and is generally complete by 16.

Many developmental changes that began early in childhood are not completed until the early or middle years of **adulthood.** Examples include the maturation of bone, resulting in the full closure of the growth plates, and changes in the size and placement of other body components such as the sinuses. Many body traits do not become apparent for years after birth. Normal balding patterns, for example, are determined at the time of fertilization by heredity but do not appear until maturity As a general rule, adulthood is characterized by maintenance of existing body tissues. With the passage of years the ongoing effort of maintenance and repair of body tissues become more and more difficult. As a result, degeneration begins. It is the process of aging, and it culminates in death.

OLDER ADULTHOOD

Most body systems are in peak condition and function at a high level of efficiency during the early years of adulthood. As a person grows older, a gradual but certain decline takes place in the functioning of every major organ system in the body. The study of aging is called *gerontology.* The remainder of this chapter deals with a number of the more common degenerative changes that frequently characterize **senescence** (se-NES-ens) or older adulthood. Many of the biological changes associated with advancing age are shown in Figure 20-12. The illustration highlights the proportion of remaining function in a number of organs in older adulthood when compared with a 20-year-old person.

Effects of Aging

SKELETAL SYSTEM

In older adulthood, bones undergo changes in texture, degree of calcification, and shape. Instead of clean-cut margins, older bones develop indistinct and shaggy-appearing margins with spurs—a process called *lipping.* This type of degenerative change restricts movement because of the piling up of bone tissue around the joints. With advancing age, changes in calcification may result in reduction of bone size and in bones that are porous and subject to fracture. The lower cervical and thoracic vertebrae are the site of frequent fractures. The result is curvature of the spine and the shortened stature so typical of late adulthood. Degenerative joint diseases such as **osteoarthritis** (OS-tee-o-ar-THRYE-tis) are also common in elderly adults.

INTEGUMENTARY SYSTEM (SKIN)

With advancing age the skin becomes dry, thin, and inelastic. It "sags" on the body because of increased wrinkling and skinfolds. Pigmentation changes and the thinning or loss of hair are also common problems associated with the aging process.

URINARY SYSTEM

The number of nephron units in the kidney decreases by almost 50% between the ages of 30 and 75. Also, because less blood flows through the kidneys as an individual ages, there is a reduction in overall function and excretory capacity or the ability to produce urine. In the bladder, significant age-related problems often occur because of diminished muscle tone. Muscle atrophy (wasting) in the bladder wall results in decreased capacity and inability to empty or void completely.

RESPIRATORY SYSTEM

In older adulthood the costal cartilages that connect the ribs to the sternum become hardened or calcified. This makes it difficult for the rib cage to expand and contract as it normally does during inspiration and expiration. In time the ribs gradually become "fixed" to the sternum, and chest movements become difficult. When this occurs the rib cage remains in a more expanded position, respiratory efficiency decreases, and a condition called "barrel chest" results. With advancing years a generalized atrophy or wasting of muscle tissue takes place as the contractile muscle cells are replaced by connective tissue. This loss of muscle cells decreases the strength of the muscles associated with inspiration and expiration.

CARDIOVASCULAR SYSTEM

Degenerative heart and blood vessel disease is one of the most common and serious effects of

FIGURE 20–12 ***Some Biological Changes Associated with Maturity and Aging.*** Insets show proportion of remaining function in the organs of a person in late adulthood compared to a 20-year-old person.

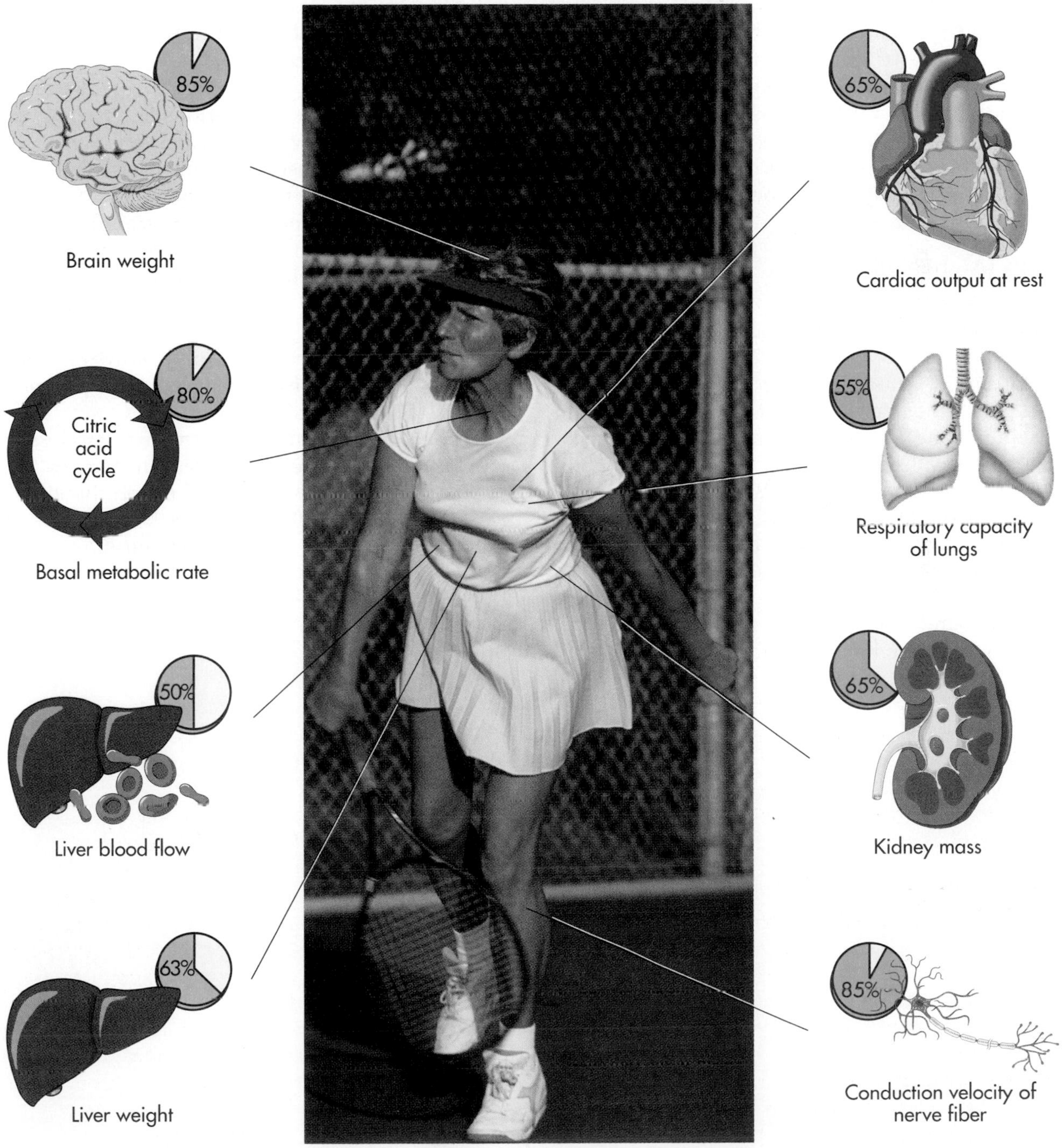

aging. Fatty deposits build up in blood vessel walls and narrow the passageway for the movement of blood, much as the buildup of scale in a water pipe decreases flow and pressure. The resulting condition, called **atherosclerosis** (ath-er-o-skle-RO-sis), often leads to eventual blockage of the coronary arteries and a "heart attack." If fatty accumulations or other substances in blood vessels calcify, actual hardening of the arteries or **arteriosclerosis** (ar-te-ree-o-skle-RO-sis) occurs. Rupture of a hardened vessel in the brain (stroke) is a frequent cause of serious disability or death in the older adult. **Hypertension** or high blood pressure is also more common.

SPECIAL SENSES

The sense organs, as a group, all show a gradual decline in performance and capacity as a person ages. Most people are farsighted by age 65 because eye lenses become hardened and lose elasticity; the lenses cannot become curved to accommodate for near vision. This hardening of the lens is called **presbyopia** (pres-bee-O-pee-ah), which means "old eye." Many individuals first notice the change at about 40 or 45 years of age, when it becomes difficult to do close-up work or read without holding printed material at arm's length. This explains the increased need, with advancing age, for bifocals or glasses that incorporate two lenses to automatically accommodate for near and distant vision. Loss of transparency of the lens or its covering capsule is another common age-related eye change. If the lens actually becomes cloudy and significantly impairs vision, it is called a **cataract** (KAT-ah-rakt) and must be removed surgically. The incidence of **glaucoma** (glaw-KO-mah), the most serious age-related eye disorder, increases with age. Glaucoma causes an increase in the pressure within the eyeball and, unless treated, often results in blindness.

In many elderly people a very significant loss of hair cells in the organ of Corti (inner ear) causes a serious decline in the ability to hear certain frequencies. In addition, the eardrum and attached ossicles become more fixed and less able to transmit mechanical sound waves. Some degree of hearing impairment is universally present in the older adult.

The sense of taste is also decreased. This loss of appetite may be caused, at least in part, by the replacement of taste buds with connective tissue cells. Only about 40% of the taste buds present at age 30 remain in an individual at age 75.

OUTLINE SUMMARY

PRENATAL PERIOD

A Prenatal period begins at conception and continues until birth (about 39 weeks)
B Science of fetal growth and development called *embryology*
C Fertilization to implantation requires about 10 days
  1 Fertilization normally occurs in outer third of oviduct (Figure 20-2)
  2 Fertilized ovum called a *zygote;* zygote is genetically complete—all that is needed for expression of hereditary traits is time and nourishment
  3 After 3 days of cell division, the zygote has developed into a solid cell mass called a *morula*
  4 Continued cell divisions of the morula produce a hollow ball of cells called a *blastocyst*
  5 Blastocyst implants in the uterine wall about 10 days after fertilization
  6 Blastocyst forms the amniotic cavity and chorion of the placenta (Figure 20-4)
  7 Placenta provides for exchange of nutrients between the mother and fetus
D Periods of development
  1 Length of pregnancy or gestation period is about 39 weeks
  2 Embryonic phase extends from fertilization to the end of week 8 of gestation
  3 Fetal phase extends from week 8 to week 39 of gestation
E Three primary germ layers appear in the developing embryo after implantation of the blastocyst (Table 20-1):
  1 Endoderm—inside layer
  2 Ectoderm—outside layer
  3 Mesoderm—middle layer
  4 All organ systems are formed and functioning by month 4 of gestation (Figure 20-6)
F Histogenesis and organogenesis
  1 Formation of new organs and tissues occurs from specific development of the primary germ layers
  2 Each primary germ layer gives rise to definite structures such as the skin and muscles
  3 Growth processes include cell differentiation, multiplication, growth, and rearrangement
  4 From 4 months of gestation until delivery, the development of the baby is mainly a matter of growth

BIRTH OR PARTURITION

A Process of birth called *parturition* (Figure 20-7)
  1 At the end of week 39 of gestation, the uterus becomes "irritable"
  2 Fetus takes head-down position against the cervix
  3 Muscular contractions begin, and labor is initiated
  4 Amniotic sac ("bag of waters") ruptures
  5 Cervix dilates
  6 Fetus moves through vagina to exterior
B Stages of labor
  1 Stage one—period from onset of uterine contractions until dilation of the cervix is complete
  2 Stage two—period from the time of maximal cervical dilation until the baby exits through the vagina
  3 Stage three—process of expulsion of the placenta through the vagina

POSTNATAL PERIOD

A Postnatal period begins at birth and lasts until death
B Divisions of postnatal period into isolated time frames can be misleading; life is a continuous process; growth and development are continuous
C Obvious changes in the physical appearance of the body in—whole and in proportion—occur between birth and maturity (Figure 20-8)
D Divisions of postnatal period
  1 Infancy
  2 Childhood
  3 Adolescence and adulthood
  4 Older adulthood
E Infancy
  1 First 4 weeks called *neonatal period* (Figure 20-9)
  2 Neonatology—medical and nursing specialty concerned with the diagnosis and treatment of disorders of the newborn
  3 Many cardiovascular changes occur at the time of birth; fetus is totally dependent on mother, whereas the newborn must immediately become totally self-supporting (respiration and circulation)
  4 Respiratory changes at birth include a deep and forceful first breath
  5 Developmental changes between the neonatal period and 18 months include:
    a Doubling of birth weight by 4 months and tripling by 1 year
    b 50% increase in body length by 12 months
    c Development of normal spinal curvature by 15 months (Figure 20-11)
    d Ability to raise head by 3 months
    e Ability to crawl by 10 months
    f Ability to stand alone by 12 months
    g Ability to run by 18 months
F Childhood
  1 Extends from end of infancy to puberty—13 years in girls and 15 in boys

2 Overall rate of growth remains rapid but decelerates
3 Continuing development of motor and coordination skills
4 Loss of deciduous or baby teeth and eruption of permanent teeth

G Adolescence and adulthood
1 Average age range of adolescence varies from 13 to 19 years
2 Period of rapid growth resulting in sexual maturity (adolescence)
3 Appearance of secondary sex characteristics regulated by secretion of sex hormones
4 Growth spurt typical of adolescence; begins in girls at about 10 and in boys at about 12
5 Growth plates fully close in adult; other structures such as the sinuses acquire adult placement
6 Adulthood characterized by maintenance of existing body tissues
7 Degeneration of body tissue begins in adulthood

H Older adulthood
1 Degenerative changes characterize older adulthood or senescence
2 Every organ system of the body undergoes degenerative changes
3 Senescence culminates in death

EFFECTS OF AGING

A Skeletal system
1 Aging causes changes in the texture, calcification, and shape of bones
2 Bone spurs develop around joints
3 Bones become porous and fracture easily
4 Degenerative joint diseases such as osteoarthritis are common

B Integumentary system (skin)
1 With age, skin "sags" and becomes:
a Thin
b Dry
c Wrinkled
2 Pigmentation problems are common
3 Frequent thinning or loss of hair occurs

C Urinary system
1 Nephron units decrease in number by 50% between ages 30 and 75
2 Blood flow to kidney and therefore ability to form urine decreases
3 Bladder problems such as inability to void completely are caused by muscle wasting in the bladder wall

D Respiratory system
1 Calcification of costal cartilages causes rib cage to remain in expanded position—barrel chest
2 Wasting of respiratory muscles decreases respiratory efficiency
3 Respiratory membrane thickens; movement of oxygen from alveoli to blood is slowed

E Cardiovascular system
1 Degenerative heart and blood vessel disease is among the most common and serious effects of aging
2 Fat deposits in blood vessels (atherosclerosis) decrease blood flow to the heart and may cause complete blockage of the coronary arteries
3 Hardening of arteries (arteriosclerosis) may result in rupture of blood vessels, especially in the brain (stroke)
4 Hypertension or high blood pressure is common in older adulthood

F Special senses
1 All sense organs show a gradual decline in performance with age
2 Eye lenses become hard and cannot accommodate for near vision; result is farsightedness in many people by age 45 (presbyopia or "old eye")
3 Loss of transparency of lens or cornea is common (cataract)
4 Glaucoma (increase in pressure in eyeball) is often the cause of blindness in older adulthood
5 Loss of hair cells in inner ear produces frequency deafness in many older people
6 Decreased transmission of sound waves caused by loss of elasticity of eardrum and fixing of the bony ear ossicles is common in older adulthood
7 Some degree of hearing impairment is universally present in the aged
8 Only about 40% of the taste buds present at age 30 remain at age 75

NEW WORDS

arteriosclerosis
atherosclerosis
blastocyst
cataract
chorion
embryology
fertilization
gestation
glaucoma
histogenesis
implantation
morula
neonate
organogenesis
parturition
presbyopia
primary germ layers
  endoderm
  ectoderm
  mesoderm
rheumatoid arthritis
senescence
zygote

CHAPTER TEST

1. The prenatal period begins at _____________ and ends at _____________.
2. The postnatal period begins at _____________ and continues until _____________.
3. The science of the development of the individual before birth is called _____________.
4. The fertilized ovum is also called a _____________.
5. The fluid-filled, shock-absorbing sac in which the embryo floats during development is called the _____________ cavity.
6. The "bridge" that permits exchange of nutrients between mother and baby before birth is called the _____________.
7. The way tissues arrange themselves into organs during development is called _____________.
8. The first 4 weeks of infancy are often referred to as the _____________ period.
9. The developmental period that extends from the end of infancy to sexual maturity is called _____________.
10. Hardening of the arteries is called _____________.
11. If the lens of the eye becomes cloudy and impairs vision, the condition is called a _____________.

Circle the T before each true statement and the F before each false statement.

T F 12. The fertilized ovum is called the *morula.*
T F 13. There are 5 primary germ layers in the developing embryo.
T F 14. In humans, all organ systems are formed and functioning by month 4 of pregnancy.
T F 15. The placenta develops in part from the fetal membrane called the *chorion.*
T F 16. Neonatology is the medical and nursing specialty concerned with the diagnosis and treatment of disorders of the newborn.
T F 17. Childhood extends from the end of infancy to sexual maturity.
T F 18. The term *senescence* refers to older adulthood.
T F 19. The kidney is unique in that it does not show degenerative changes with advancing age.
T F 20. The term *arteriosclerosis* refers to "hardening of the arteries."

REVIEW QUESTIONS

1. What biological event separates the prenatal from the postnatal period of development?
2. Define embryology, gestation, fertilization, implantation, morula, and blastocyst.
3. What is the difference between an ovum and a zygote?
4. What is the difference between an embryo and a fetus?
5. Discuss the role of the placenta in fetal development.
6. Briefly define histogenesis and organogenesis.
7. At what point in development of the fetus are all the organ systems formed and functioning?
8. When does the postnatal period begin and how long does it last?
9. List the four subdivisions of the postnatal period.
10. What is the relationship of the neonatal period to infancy? What is neonatology?
11. List five developmental changes that occur during infancy.
12. Define *senescence.*
13. Describe the degenerative changes that occur in the skeletal system as a result of aging.
14. How is the skin or integumentary system affected by aging?
15. What is the difference between atherosclerosis and arteriosclerosis?
16. Define presbyopia, glaucoma, and cataract.

CRITICAL THINKING

17. What are the primary germ layers and how are they related to development of the fetus?
18. Why is it necessary for a baby's first breath to be deep and forceful? What is the primary stimulus that causes a newborn to take its first breath?
19. Is the period of childhood the same length for both boys and girls? Explain the reason for your answer.
20. What is the average age range of adolescence? Functionally, how would the reproductive system in an individual at the end of adolescence be described?

Chemistry of Life

Appendix A

Life is chemistry. It's not quite that simple, but the more we learn about human structure and function, the more we realize that it all boils down to interactions among chemicals. The digestion of food, the formation of bone tissue, and the contraction of a muscle are all chemical processes. Thus the basic principles of anatomy and physiology are ultimately based on principles of chemistry. A whole field of science, **biochemistry,** is devoted to studying the chemical aspects of life. To truly understand the human body, it is important to understand a few basic facts about biochemistry, the chemistry of life.

Levels of Chemical Organization

Matter is anything that occupies space and has mass. Biochemists classify matter into several levels of organization for easier study. In the body, most chemicals are in the form of **molecules.** Molecules are particles of matter that are composed of one or more smaller units called **atoms.** Atoms in turn are composed of several kinds of *subatomic particles:* **protons, electrons,** and **neutrons.** (Refer to the Mini-Glossary on p. 440.)

ATOMS

Atoms are units that until recently could not be seen by scientists. New instruments, including *tunneling microscopes* and *atomic force microscopes,* produce pictures of atoms that confirm current models of how atoms are put together. At the core of each atom is a **nucleus** composed of positively charged protons and uncharged neutrons. The number of protons in the nucleus is an atom's atomic number. The number of protons and neutrons combined is the atom's **atomic mass.**

Negatively charged electrons surround the nucleus at a distance. In an electrically neutral atom, there is one electron for every proton. Electrons move about within certain limits called **orbitals.** Each orbital can hold two electrons. Orbitals are arranged into **energy levels** (shells), depending on their distance from the nucleus. The farther an orbital extends from the nucleus, the higher its energy level. The energy level closest to the nucleus has one orbital, so it can hold two electrons. The next energy level has up to four orbitals, so it can hold eight electrons. Figure 1 shows a carbon (C) atom. Notice that the first energy level (the innermost shell) contains two electrons and the outer energy level contains four electrons. The outer energy level of a carbon atom

FIGURE 1 ***A Model of the Atom.*** The nucleus—protons (+) and neutrons—is at the core. Electrons inhabit outer regions called *energy levels.* This is a carbon atom, a fact that is determined by the number of its protons. All carbon atoms (and only carbon atoms) have six protons. (One proton in the nucleus is not visible in this illustration.)

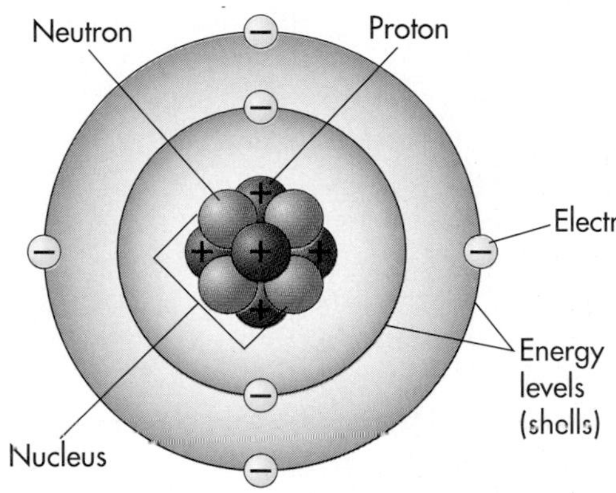

could hold up to four more electrons (for a total of eight). The number of electrons in the outer energy level of an atom determines how it behaves chemically (that is, how it may unite with other atoms). This behavior, called *chemical bonding,* will be discussed later.

ELEMENTS, MOLECULES, AND COMPOUNDS

Substances can be classified as **elements** or **compounds.** Elements are pure substances, composed of only one of over a hundred types of atoms that exist in nature. Only four kinds of atoms **(oxygen, carbon, hydrogen,** and **nitrogen)** make up about 96% of the human body. There are traces of about 20 other elements in the body. Table 1 lists some of the elements in the body. Table 1 also gives for each element its universal chemical *symbol*—the abbreviation used by chemists worldwide.

Atoms usually unite with each other to form larger chemical units called **molecules.** Some molecules are made of several atoms of the same element. *Compounds* are substances whose molecules have more than one element in them. The *formula* for a compound contains symbols for the elements in each molecule. The number of atoms of

TABLE 1 Important Elements in the Human Body

	NAME	SYMBOL	NUMBER OF ELECTRONS IN OUTER SHELL*
Major elements (over 96% of body weight)	Oxygen	O	6
	Carbon	C	4
	Hydrogen	H	1
	Nitrogen	N	5
Trace elements (examples of more than 20 trace elements found in the body)	Calcium	Ca	2
	Phosphorus	P	5
	Sodium (Latin *natrium*)	Na	1
	Potassium (Latin *kalium*)	K	1
	Chlorine	Cl	7
	Iodine	I	7

*Maximum is eight, except for hydrogen. The maximum for that element is two.

Radioactive Isotopes

Each element is unique because of the number of protons it has. In short, each element has its own *atomic number.* However, atoms of the same element can have different numbers of neutrons. Two atoms that have the same atomic number but different atomic masses are **isotopes** of the same element. An example is hydrogen. Hydrogen has three isotopes: ^{1}H (the most common isotope), ^{2}H, and ^{3}H. The figure shows that each different isotope has only one proton but different numbers of neutrons.

Some isotopes have unstable nuclei that radiate (give off) particles. Radiation particles include protons, neutrons, electrons, and altered versions of these normal subatomic particles. An isotope that emits radiation is called a **radioactive isotope.**

Radioactive isotopes of common elements are sometimes used to evaluate the function of body parts. Radioactive iodine (^{125}I) put into the body and taken up by the thyroid gland gives off radiation that can be easily measured. Thus the rate of thyroid activity can be determined. Images of internal organs can be formed by radiation scanners that plot out the location of injected or ingested radioactive isotopes. For example, radioactive technetium (^{99}Tc) is commonly used to image the liver and spleen. The radioactive isotopes ^{13}N, ^{15}O, and ^{11}C are often used to study the brain in a technique called the *PET scan.*

Radiation can damage cells. Exposure to high levels of radiation may cause cells to develop into cancer cells. Higher levels of radiation completely destroy tissues, causing *radiation sickness.* Low doses of radioactive substances are sometimes given to cancer patients to destroy cancer cells. The side effects of these treatments result from the unavoidable destruction of normal cells with the cancer cells.

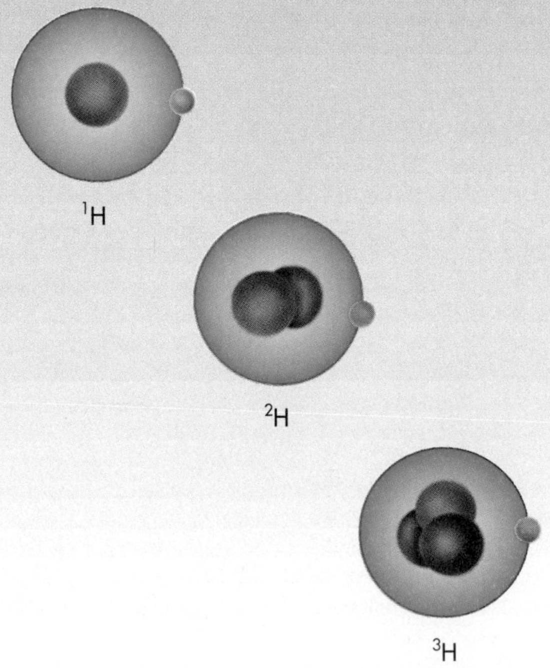

each element in the molecule is expressed as a subscript after the elemental symbol. For example, each molecule of the compound **carbon dioxide** has one carbon (C) atom and two oxygen (O) atoms; thus its molecular formula is CO_2.

Matter is composed of molecules, which are composed of atoms. Atoms are composed of protons, electrons, and neutrons. Elements are pure substances, composed of only one kind of atom. Compounds are composed of molecules having more than one kind of atom.

Chemical Bonding

Chemical bonds form to make atoms more stable. An atom is said to be chemically stable when its outer energy level is "full" (that is, when its energy shells have the maximum number of electrons they can hold). All but a handful of atoms have room for more electrons in their outermost energy level. A basic chemical principle states that atoms react with one another in ways to make their outermost energy level full. To do this, atoms can share, donate, or borrow electrons.

For example, a hydrogen atom has one electron and one proton. Its single energy shell has one electron but *can* hold two—so it's not full. If two hydrogen atoms "share" their single electrons with each other, then both will have full energy shells, making them more stable *as a molecule* than either would be as an atom. This is one example of how atoms **bond** to form molecules. Other atoms may donate or borrow electrons until the outermost energy level is full.

IONIC BONDS

One common way in which atoms make their outermost energy level full is to form **ionic bonds** with other atoms. Such a bond forms between an atom that has only one or two electrons in the outermost level (that would normally hold eight) and an atom that needs only one or two electrons to fill its outer level. The atom with one or two electrons simply "donates" its outer shell electrons to the one that needs one or two.

For example, as you can see in Table 1, the sodium (Na) atom has one electron in its outer level and the chlorine (Cl) atom has seven. Both need to have eight electrons in their outer shell. Figure 2 shows how sodium and chlorine form an ionic bond when sodium "donates" the electron in its outer shell to chlorine. Now both atoms have full outer shells (although sodium's outer shell is now one energy level lower). Because the sodium atom lost an electron, it now has one more proton that it has electrons. This makes it a positive **ion,** an electrically charged atom. Chlorine has "borrowed" an electron to become a negative ion called the *chloride* ion. Because oppositely charged particles attract one another, the sodium and chloride ions are drawn together to form a sodium chloride (NaCl) molecule—common table salt. The molecule is held together by an *ionic bond.*

Ionic molecules usually dissolve easily in water because water molecules wedge between the ions and force them apart. When this happens, we say the molecules **dissociate** (dis-SO-see-ayt) to form free ions. Molecules that form ions when dissolved in water are called **electrolytes** (el-EK-tro-lites). Chapter 17 describes mechanisms that maintain the homeostasis of electrolytes in the body. Table 2 lists some of the more important ions present in body fluids.

TABLE 2 Important Ions in Human Body Fluids

NAME	SYMBOL
Sodium	Na^+
Chloride	Cl^-
Potassium (Latin *kalium*)	K^+
Calcium	Ca^{++}
Hydrogen	H^+
Magnesium	Mg^{++}
Hydroxide	OH^-
Phosphate	$PO_4^=$
Bicarbonate	HCO_3^-

FIGURE 2 ***Ionic Bonding.*** The sodium atom donates the single electron in its outer energy level to a chlorine atom having seven electrons in its outer level. Now both have eight electrons in their outer shells. Because the electron/proton ratio changes, the sodium atom becomes a positive sodium ion. The chlorine atom becomes a negative chloride ion. The positive-negative attraction between these oppositely charged ions is called an *ionic bond.*

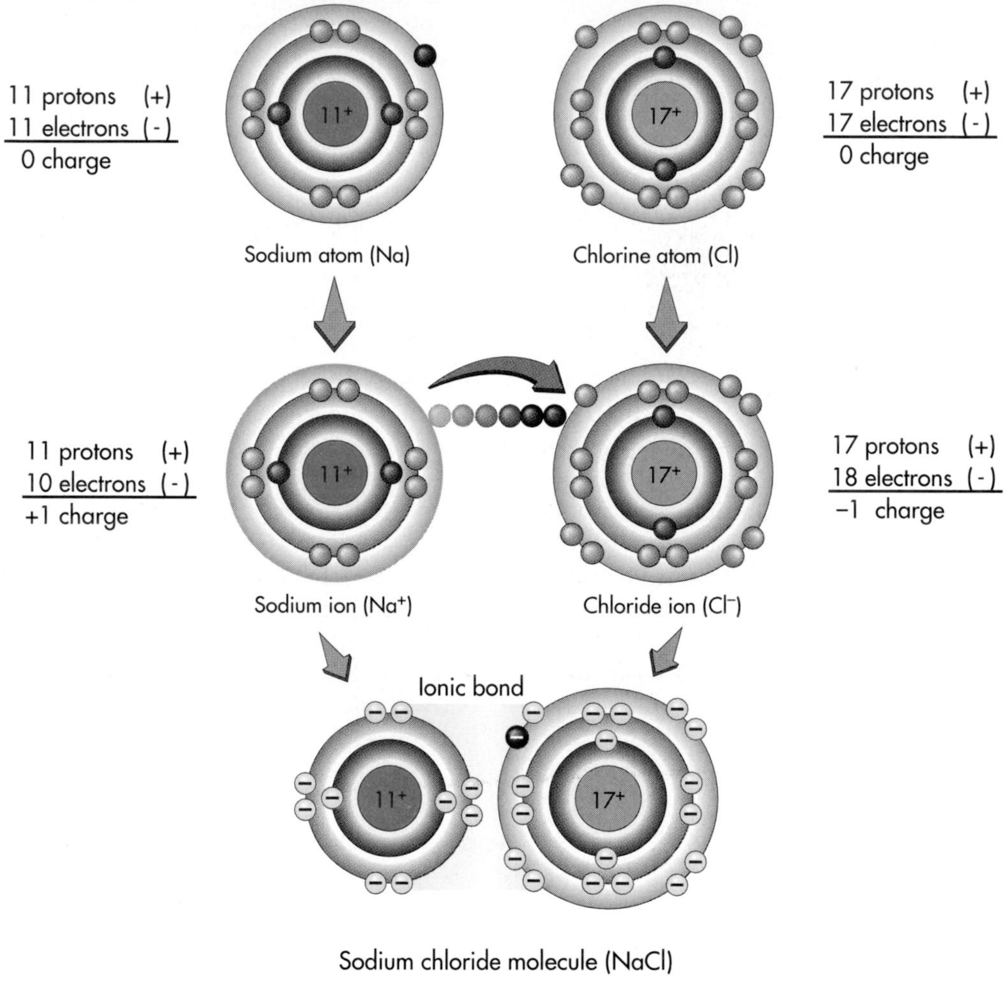

The formula of an ion always shows its charge by a superscript after the chemical symbol. Thus the sodium ion is Na^+, and the chloride ion is Cl^-. Calcium (Ca) atoms lose two electrons when they form ions, so the calcium ion formula is Ca^{++}.

COVALENT BONDS

Atoms may also fill their energy levels by sharing electrons rather than donating or receiving them. When atoms share electrons, a **covalent** (ko-VAY-lent) **bond** forms. For example, Figure 3 shows how two hydrogen atoms may move together closely so that their energy levels overlap. Each energy level contributes its one electron to the sharing relationship. This way, both outer levels have access to both electrons. Because atoms involved in a covalent bond must stay close to each other, it is not surprising that covalent bonds are not easily broken. Covalent bonds normally do not break apart in water.

FIGURE 3 ***Covalent Bonding.*** Two hydrogen atoms move together, overlapping their energy levels. Although neither gains nor loses an electron, the atoms share the electrons, forming a covalent bond.

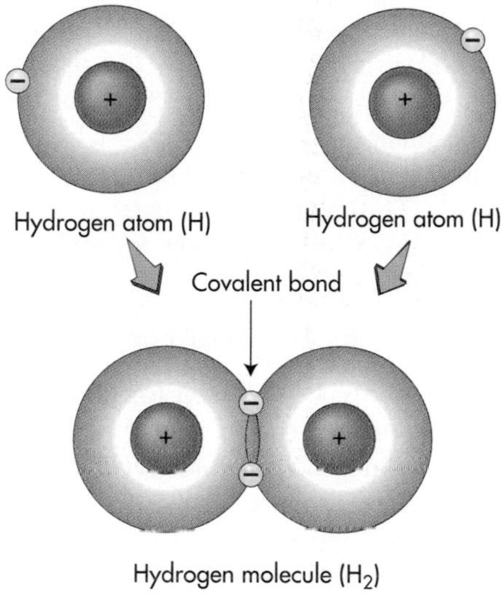

Ionic bonding occurs when one atom donates an electron to another atom and the resulting ions attract each other. In covalent bonding, atoms share electrons.

Inorganic Chemistry

In living organisms, there are two kinds of compounds: **organic** and **inorganic.** Organic compounds are composed of molecules that contain carbon-carbon (C-C) covalent bonds or carbon-hydrogen (C-H) covalent bonds—or both kinds of bonds. Few inorganic compounds have carbon atoms in them and none have C-C or C-H bonds. Organic molecules are generally larger and more complex than inorganic molecules. The human body has both kinds of compounds because both are equally important to the chemistry of life. We will discuss the chemistry of inorganic compounds first, then move on to some of the important types of organic compounds.

Metric System

Scientists, many government agencies, and increasing numbers of American industries are using or moving toward the conversion of our system of English measurements to the metric system. The metric system is a decimal system in which measurement of length is based on the *meter* (39.37 inches) and weight or mass is based on the *gram* (about 454 grams equal a pound).

A micrometer is one millionth of a meter. (*Micron* is another name for micrometer.) In the metric systems the units of length are as follows:

1 meter (m) = 39.37 inches
1 centimeter (cm) = 1/100 m
1 millimeter (mm) = 1/1,000 m
1 micrometer (μ m) or micron (μ) = 1/1,000,000 m
1 nanometer (nm) = 1/1,000,000,000 m
1 Angstrom (Å) = 1/10,000,000,000 m

Approximately equal to 1 inch:
2.5 cm
25 mm
25,000 μ m
25,000,000 nm
250,000,000 Å

WATER

One of the compounds that is most essential to life—water—is an inorganic compound. Water is the most abundant compound in the body, found in and around each cell. It is the **solvent** in which most other compounds or **solutes** are dissolved. When water is the solvent for a *mixture* (a blend of two or more kinds of molecules), the mixture is called an **aqueous solution.** An aqueous solution containing common salt (NaCl) and other molecules forms the "internal sea" of the body. Water molecules not only compose the basic internal environment of the body, but they also participate in many important *chemical reactions.* Chemical reactions are interactions among molecules in which atoms regroup into new combinations.

A common type of chemical reaction in the body is **dehydration synthesis.** In any kind of synthesis reaction, the **reactants** combine to form a larger **product.** In dehydration synthesis, reactants combine only after hydrogen (H) and oxygen (O) atoms are removed. These leftover H and O atoms come together, forming H_2O or water. As Figure 4 shows, the result is both the large product molecule and a water molecule. Just as dehydration of a cell is a loss of water from the cell and dehydration of the body is loss of fluid from the entire internal environment, dehydration synthesis is a reaction in which water is lost from the reactants.

Another common reaction in the body, **hydrolysis** (hye-DROL-i-sis), also involves water. In this reaction, water *(hydro-)* disrupts the bonds in large molecules, causing them to be broken down into smaller molecules *(lysis).* Hydrolysis is virtually the reverse of dehydration synthesis, as Figure 4 shows.

Chemical reactions always involve energy transfers. Energy is required to build the molecules. Some of that energy is stored as potential energy in the chemical bonds. The stored energy can then be released when the chemical bonds in the molecule are later broken apart. For example, a molecule called **adenosine triphosphate (ATP)** breaks apart in the muscle cells to yield the energy needed for muscle contraction (see Figure 15-2).

Chemists often use a *chemical equation* to represent a chemical reaction. In a chemical equation, the reactants are separated from the products by an arrow (→) showing the "direction" of the reaction. Reactants are separated from each other and products are separated from each other by addition signs (+). Thus the reaction *potassium and chloride combine to form potassium chloride* can be expressed as the equation:

$$K^+ + Cl^- \rightarrow KCl$$

The single arrow (→) is used for equations that occur in only one direction. For example, when hydrochloric acid (HCl) is dissolved in water, *all* of it dissociates to form H^+ and Cl^-.

$$HCl \rightarrow H^+ + Cl^-$$

The double arrow (⇆) is used for reactions that happen in "both directions" at the same time. When carbonic acid (H_2CO_3) dissolves in water, *some* of it dissociates into H^+ (hydrogen ion) and

FIGURE 4 ***Water-Based Chemistry.*** Dehydration synthesis is a reaction in which small molecules are assembled into large molecules by removing water (H and O atoms). Hydrolysis operates in the reverse direction; H and O from water is added as large molecules are broken down into small molecules.

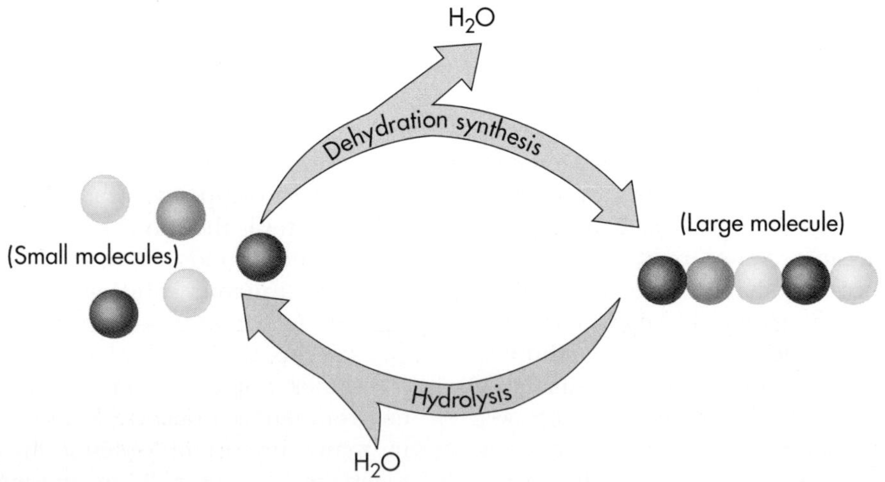

HCO_3^- (bicarbonate) but not all of it. As additional ions dissociate, previously dissociated ions bond together again forming H_2CO_3.

$$H_2CO_3 \leftrightarrows H^+ HCO_3^-$$

In short, the double arrow indicates that at any instant in time both reactants and products are present in the solution at the same time.

ACIDS, BASES, AND SALTS

Besides water, many other inorganic compounds are important in the chemistry of life. For example, **acids** and **bases** are compounds that profoundly affect chemical reactions in the body. As explained in more detail at the beginning of Chapter 18, a few water molecules dissociate to form the H^+ ion and the OH^- (hydroxide) ion:

$$\mathbf{H_2O \leftrightarrows H^+ + OH^-}$$

In pure water, the balance between these two ions is equal. However, when an acid such as hydrochloric acid (HCl) dissociates into H^+ and Cl^-, it shifts this balance in favor of excess H^+ ions. In the blood, carbon dioxide (CO_2) forms carbonic acid (H_2CO_3) when it dissolves in water. Some of the carbonic acid then dissociates to form H^+ ions and HCO_3^- (bicarbonate) ions, producing an excess of H^+ ions in the blood. Thus high CO_2 levels in the blood make the blood acidic.

Bases or **alkaline** compounds, on the other hand, shift the balance in the opposite direction. For example, sodium hydroxide (NaOH) is a base that forms OH^- ions but no H^+ ions. In short, acids are compounds that produce an excess of H^+ ions, and bases are compounds that produce an excess of OH^- ions (or a decrease in H^+).

The relative H^+ concentration is a measure of how acidic or basic a solution is. The H^+ concentration is usually expressed in units of **pH.** The formula used to calculate pH units gives a value of 7 to pure water. A higher pH value indicates a low relative concentration of H^+—a base. A lower pH value indicates a higher H^+ concentration—an acid. Figure 5 shows a scale of pH from 0 to 14. Notice that when the pH of a solution is less than 7, the scale "tips" toward the side marked "high H^+." When the pH is more than 7, the scale "tips" toward the side marked "low H^+." pH units

FIGURE 5 ***The pH Scale.*** The H^+ concentration is balanced with the OH^- concentration at pH 7. At values above 7 (low H^+), the scale tips in the basic direction. At values below 7 (high H^+), the scale tips toward the acid side.

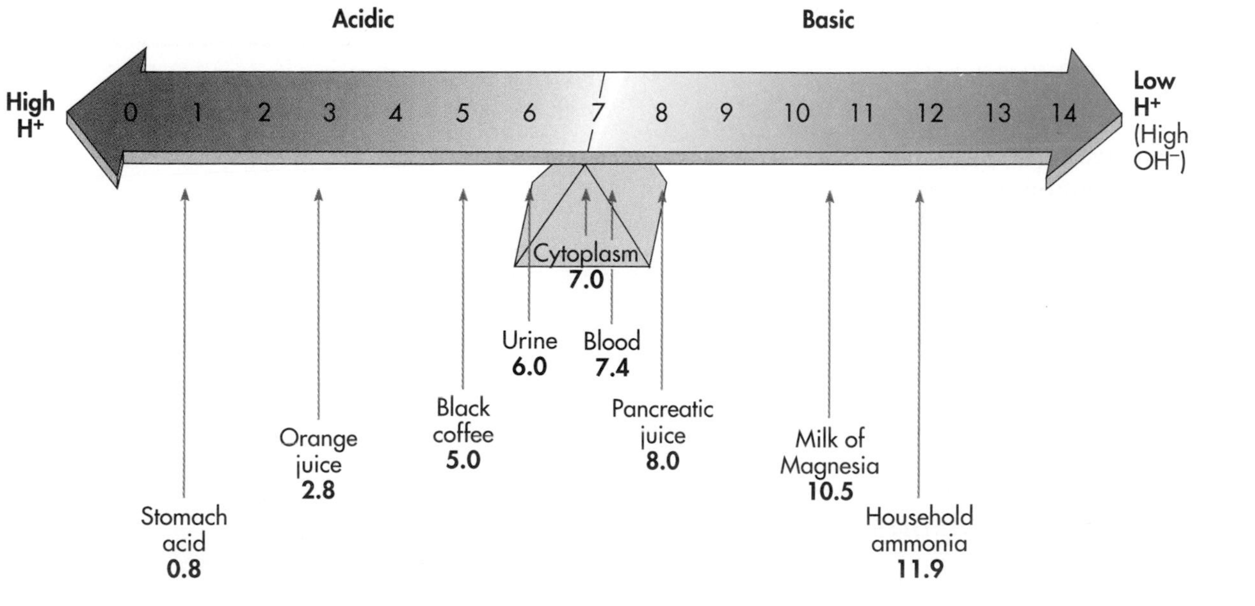

increase or decrease by factors of 10. Thus a pH 5 solution has ten times the H^+ concentration of a pH 6 solution. A pH 4 solution has a hundred times the H^+ concentration of a pH 6 solution.

A *strong acid* is an acid that completely, or almost completely, dissociates to form H^+ ions. A *weak acid*, on the other hand, dissociates very little and therefore produces few excess H^+ ions in solution.

When a strong acid and a strong base mix, excess H^+ ions may combine with the excess OH^- ions to form water. That is, they may *neutralize* each other. The remaining ions usually form neutral ionic compounds called **salts.** For example:

$$\underset{\text{acid}}{HCl} + \underset{\text{base}}{NaOH} \rightarrow H^+ + Cl^- + Na^+ + OH^- \rightarrow \underset{\text{water}}{H_2O} + \underset{\text{salt}}{NaCl}$$

The pH of body fluids affects body chemistry so greatly that normal body function can be maintained only within a narrow range of pH. The body can remove excess H^+ ions by excreting them in the urine (see Chapter 16). Another way to remove acid is by increasing the loss of CO_2 (an acid) by the respiratory system (see Chapter 13). A third way to adjust the body's pH is the use of **buffers**—chemicals in the blood that maintain pH. Buffers maintain pH balance by preventing sudden changes in the H^+ ion concentration. Buffers do this by forming a chemical system that neutralizes acids and bases as they are added to a solution. The mechanisms by which the body maintains pH homeostasis, or acid-base balance, are discussed further in Chapter 18.

Organic compounds always contain carbon (forming carbon-carbon or carbon-hydrogen bonds); few inorganic compounds even contain carbon. Biological reactions take place in aqueous solutions. In hydrolysis, chemical bonds are broken. In dehydration synthesis, bonds are formed. The pH (relative H+ concentration) of body fluids affects chemical reactions.

Organic Chemistry

Organic compounds are much more complex than inorganic compounds. In this section, we will describe the basic structure and function of each major type of organic compound found in the body: **carbohydrates, lipids** (fats), **proteins,** and **nucleic acids.** Table 3 summarizes the structure and the function of each type. Refer to this table as you read through the descriptions that follow.

CARBOHYDRATES

The name *carbohydrate* literally means "carbon (C) and water (H_2O)," signifying the types of atoms that form carbohydrate molecules. The basic unit of carbohydrate molecules is called a *monosaccharide* (mah-no-SAK-ah-ride) (Figure 6). Glucose (dextrose) is an important monosaccharide in the body; cells use it as their primary source of energy (see Chapter 15). A molecule made of two saccharide units is a double sugar or *disaccharide.* The disaccharides sucrose (table sugar) and lactose (milk sugar) are important dietary carbohydrates. After they are eaten, the body digests them to form monosaccharides that can be used as cellular fuel. Many saccharide units joined together form *polysaccharides.* Examples of polysaccharides are **glycogen** (GLY-ko-jen) and *starch.* Each glycogen molecule is a chain of glucose molecules joined together. Liver cells and muscle cells form glycogen when there is an excess of glucose in the blood, thus putting them into "storage" for later use.

FIGURE 6 ***Carbohydrates.*** Monosaccharides are single carbohydrate units joined by dehydration synthesis to form disaccharides and polysaccharides.

TABLE 3 Major Types of Organic Compounds

EXAMPLE	COMPONENTS	FUNCTIONS
Carbohydrate		
Monosaccharide (glucose, galactose, fructose)	Single monosaccharide unit	Unit as source of energy; used to build other carbohydrates
Disaccharide (sucrose, lactose, maltose)	Two monosaccharide units	Can be broken into monosaccharides
Polysaccharide (glycogen, starch)	Many monosaccharide units	Used to store monosaccharides (thus to store energy)
Lipid		
Triglyceride	One glycerol, three fatty acids	Stores energy
Phospholipid	Phosphorus-containing unit, two fatty acids	Forms cell membranes
Cholesterol	Four carbon rings at core	Transports lipids; is basis of steroid hormones
Protein		
Structural proteins (fibers)	Amino acids	Form structures of the body
Functional proteins (enzymes, hormones)	Amino acids	Facilitate chemical reactions; send signals; regulate functions
Nucleic Acid		
Deoxyribonucleic acid (DNA)	Nucleotides (contain deoxyribose)	Contains information (genetic code) for making proteins
Ribonucleic acid (RNA)	Nucleotides (contain ribose)	Serves as a copy of a portion of the genetic code

Carbohydrates have potential energy stored in their bonds. When the bonds are broken in cells, the energy is released and then trapped by the cell's chemistry to do work. Chapter 15 explains more about the process by which the body extracts energy from carbohydrates and other food molecules.

LIPIDS

Lipids are fats and oils. Fats are lipids that are solid at room temperature, such as the fat in butter and lard. Oils, such as corn oil and olive oil, are liquid at room temperature. There are several important types of lipids in the body:

1. **Triglycerides** (try-GLIS-er-ides) are lipid molecules formed by a *glycerol* unit joined to three *fatty acids* (Figure 7). Like carbohydrates, their bonds can be broken apart to yield energy (see Chapter 15). Thus triglycerides are useful in storing energy in cells for later use.

FIGURE 7 ***Triglyceride.*** Each triglyceride is composed of three fatty acid units attached to a glycerol unit.

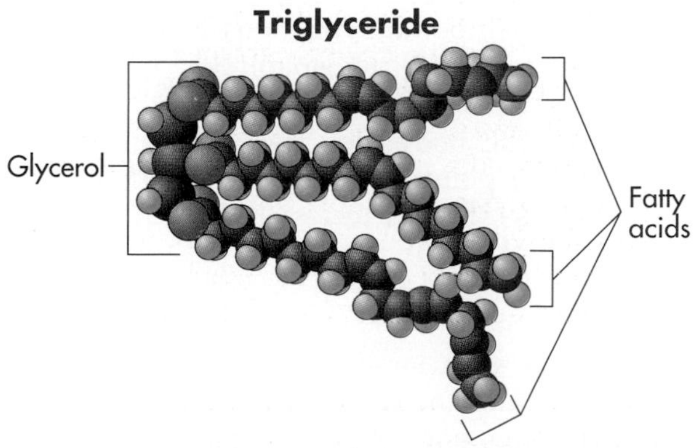

Blood Lipoproteins

A lipid such as cholesterol can travel in the blood only after it has attached to a protein molecule—forming a lipoprotein. Some of these molecules are called *high-density lipoproteins (HDLs)* because they have a high density of protein (more protein than lipid). Another type of molecule contains less protein (and more lipid), so it is called *low-density lipoprotein (LDL)*.

The cholesterol in LDLs is often called "bad" cholesterol because high blood levels of LDL are associated with **atherosclerosis,** a life-threatening blockage of arteries. LDLs carry cholesterol *to cells,* including the cells that line blood vessels. HDLs, on the other hand, carry so-called "good" cholesterol *away from cells* and toward the liver for elimination from the body. A high proportion of HDL in the blood is associated with a low risk of developing atherosclerosis. Factors such as cigarette smoking decrease HDL levels and thus contribute to risk of atherosclerosis. Factors such as exercise increase HDL levels and thus decrease the risk of atherosclerosis.

2. **Phospholipids** are similar to triglycerides but have phosphorus-containing units in them, as their name implies. The phosphorus-containing unit in each molecule forms a "head" that attracts water. Two fatty acid "tails" repel water. Figure 8, *A,* shows the head and tail of the phospholipid molecule. This structure allows them to form a stable *bilayer* in water that forms the foundation for the cell membrane. In Figure 8, *B,* the water-attracting heads face the water and the water-repelling tails face away from the water (and toward each other).
3. **Cholesterol** is a *steroid* lipid that performs several important functions in the body. It combines with phospholipids in the cell membrane to help stabilize its bilayer structure. The body also uses cholesterol as a starting point in making steroid hormones such as estrogen, testosterone, and cortisone (see Chapter 9).

PROTEINS

Proteins are very large molecules composed of basic units called **amino acids.** In addition to carbon, hydrogen, and oxygen, amino acids contain nitrogen (N). By means of a process described fully in Chapter 2, a particular sequence of amino acids is strung together and held by **peptide bonds.** Positive-negative attractions between different atoms in the long amino acid strand cause it to coil on itself and maintain its shape. The complex, three-dimensional molecule that results is a protein molecule (Figure 9).

The shape of a protein molecule determines its role in body chemistry. **Structural proteins** are shaped in ways that allow them to form essential structures of the body. Collagen, a protein with a fiber shape, holds most of the body tissues together. Keratin, another structural protein, forms a network of waterproof fibers in the outer layer of the skin. **Functional proteins** participate in chemical processes of the body. Functional proteins include some of the hormones, growth factors, cell membrane channels and receptors, and enzymes.

Enzymes are chemical catalysts. This means that they help a chemical reaction occur but are not reactants or products themselves. They participate in chemical reactions but are not changed by the reactions. Enzymes are vital to body chemistry. No reaction in the body occurs fast enough unless the specific enzymes needed for that reaction are present.

Figure 10 illustrates how shape is important to the function of enzyme molecules. Each enzyme has a shape that "fits" the specific molecules it works on much as a key fits specific locks. This explanation of enzyme action is sometimes called the **lock-and-key model.**

FIGURE 8 ***Phospholipids.*** **A,** Each phospholipid molecule has a phosphorus-containing "head" that attracts water and a lipid "tail" that repels water. **B,** Because the tails repel water, phospholipid molecules often arrange themselves so that their tails face away from water. The stable structure that results is a bilayer sheet forming a small bubble.

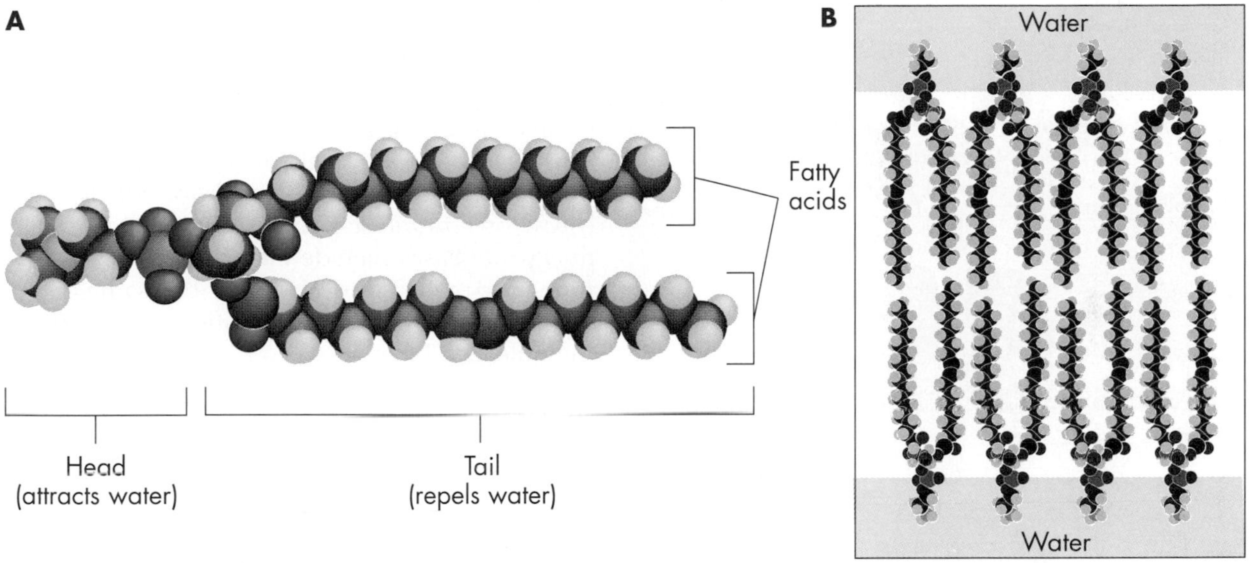

FIGURE 9 ***Protein.*** Protein molecules are large, complex molecules formed by a twisted and folded strand of amino acids. Each amino acid is connected to the next amino acid by covalent peptide bonds.

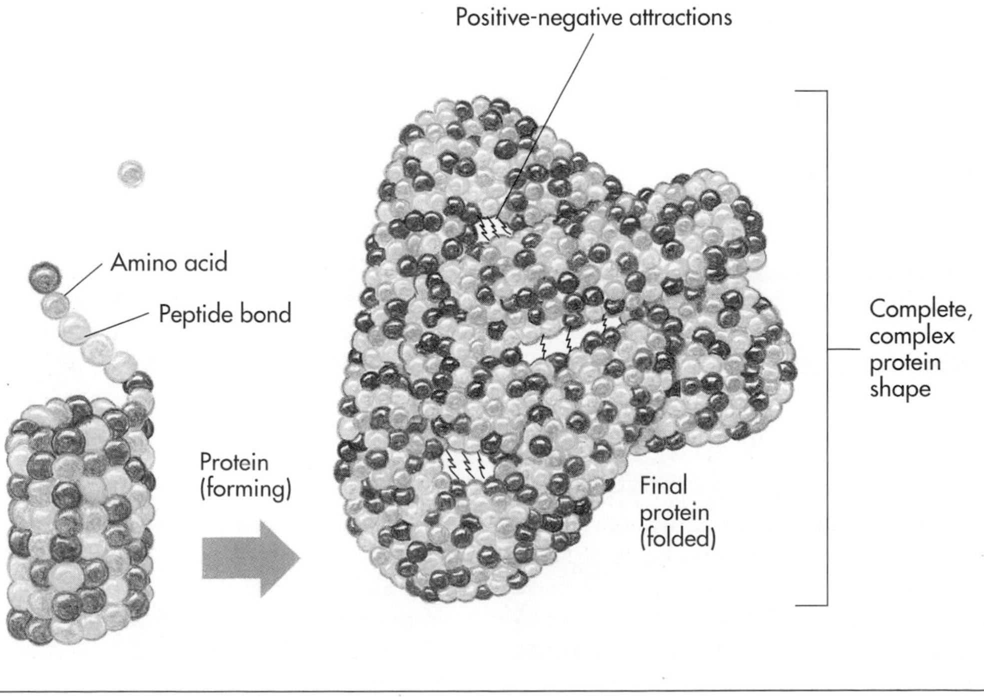

FIGURE 10 ***Enzyme Action.*** Enzymes are functional proteins whose molecular shape allows them to catalyze chemical reactions. Molecules *A* and *B* are brought together by the enzyme to form a larger molecule, *AB*.

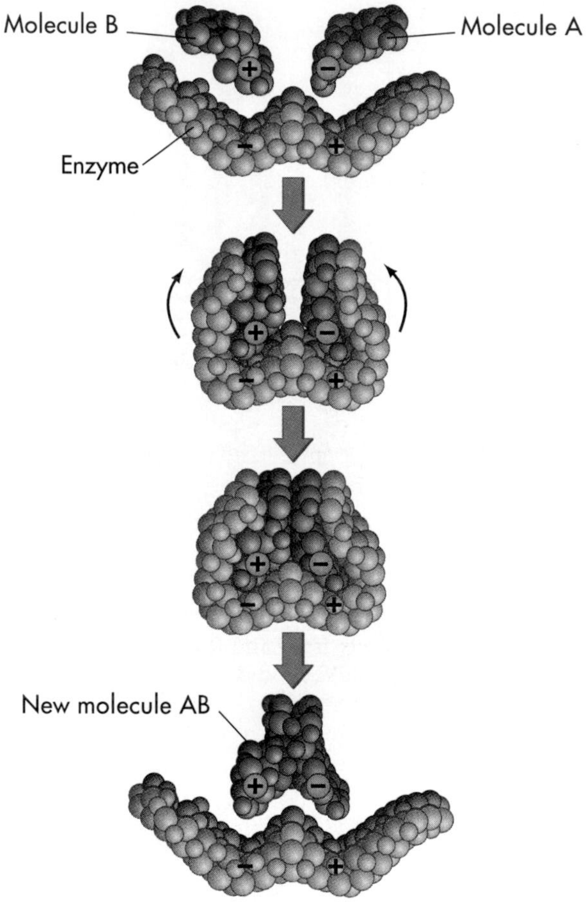

TABLE 4 Components of Nucleotides

NUCLEOTIDE	DNA	RNA
Sugar	Deoxyribose	Ribose
Phosphate	Phosphate	Phosphate
Nitrogen base	Cytosine	Cytosine
	Guanine	Guanine
	Adenine	Adenine
	Thymine	Uracil

Proteins can bond with other organic compounds and form "mixed" molecules. For example, *glycoproteins* are proteins with sugars attached. *Lipoproteins* are lipid-protein combinations.

NUCLEIC ACIDS

The two forms of nucleic acid are **deoxyribonucleic acid (DNA)** and **ribonucleic acid (RNA).** As outlined in Chapter 2, the basic building blocks of nucleic acids are called **nucleotides.** Each nucleotide consists of a *phosphate unit,* a sugar *(ribose* or *deoxyribose),* and a *nitrogen base.* DNA nucleotide bases include **adenine, thymine, guanine,** and **cytosine.** RNA uses the same set of bases, except for the substitution of **uracil** for thymine. See Table 4.

Nucleotides bind to one another to form strands or other structures. In the DNA molecule, nucleotides are arranged in a twisted, double strand called a **double helix** (Figure 11).

The sequence of different nucleotides along the DNA double helix is the "master code" for assembling proteins and other nucleic acids. *Messenger RNA (mRNA)* molecules have a sequence that forms a temporary "working copy" of the DNA code. The code in nucleic acids ultimately directs the entire symphony of living chemistry.

Carbohydrates are composed of monosaccharide units and can be broken apart to yield energy. Lipids are fat molecules composed mainly of glycerol and fatty acids and have many functions. Proteins are complex strings of amino acids. Proteins comprise body structures or regulate body functions. Nucleic acids DNA and RNA are composed of nucleotides. The sequence of nucleotides serves as a code for assembling proteins.

FIGURE 11 *DNA.* Deoxyribonucleic acid (DNA), like all nucleic acids, is composed of units called *nucleotides*. Each nucleotide has a phosphate, a sugar, and a nitrogen base. In DNA, the nucleotides are arranged in a double helix formation.

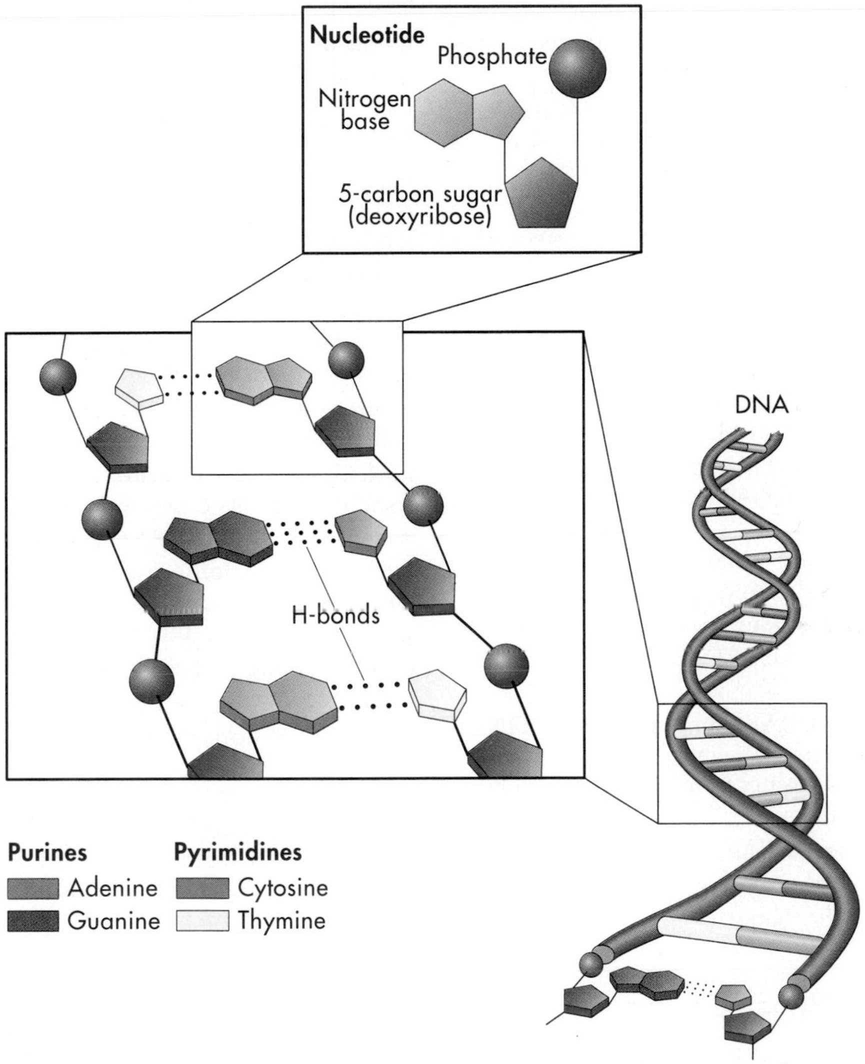

MINI-GLOSSARY

acid any substance that, when dissolved in water, contributes to an excess of H^+ ions

aqueous (AY-kwee-us) solution liquid mixture in which water is the solvent; for example, saltwater is an aqueous solution because water is the solvent

atom smallest particle of a pure substance (element) that still has the chemical properties of that substance; composed of protons, electrons, and neutrons (subatomic particles)

atomic mass combined total number of protons and neutrons in an atom

atomic number total number of protons in an atom's nucleus; atoms of each element have a characteristic atomic number

base alkaline; any substance that, when dissolved in water, contributes to an excess of OH^- ions

carbohydrate (KAR-bo-HYE-drate) organic molecule composed of one or more monosaccharides (containing C, H, and O in a 1:2:1 ratio)

compound (KOM-pound) substance whose molecules have more than one kind of element in them

covalent (ko-VAY-lent) bond chemical bond formed when atoms share electrons by overlapping their energy levels (electron shells)

dehydration (dee-hye-DRAY-shun) synthesis (SIN-the-sis) chemical reaction in which large molecules are formed by removing water from smaller molecules and joining them together

dissociation (dis-so-see-AY-shun) separation of ions as they dissolve in water

double helix (HE-lix) shape of DNA molecules; a double spiral

electrolyte (e-LEK-tro-lite) compound whose molecules dissolve in water to form ions

electron (e-LEK-tron) negatively charged particle orbiting the nucleus of an atom

element (EL-e-ment) pure substance, composed of only one type of atom

energy level limited region surrounding the nucleus of an atom at a certain distance containing electrons; also called a shell

enzyme (EN-zime) functional protein that catalyzes chemical reactions (helps them occur more rapidly)

glycogen (GLYE-ko-jen) polysaccharide consisting of a chain of glucose (monosaccharide) molecules

hydrolysis (hye-DROL-i-sis) chemical reaction in which water is added to a large molecule causing it to break apart into smaller molecules

inorganic compounds compounds whose molecules generally do not contain carbon

ionic (eye-ON-ic) bond chemical bond formed by the positive-negative attraction between two ions

lipid organic molecule usually composed of glycerol and fatty acid units; types include triglycerides, phospholipids, and cholesterol

matter any substance that occupies space and has mass

molecule (MOL-e-kyool) particle of matter composed of one or more smaller units called *atoms*

neutron (NOO-tron) electrically neutral particle within the nucleus of an atom

nucleic (noo-KLEE-ic) acid complex organic molecule composed of units called nucleotides that each include a phosphate, a five carbon sugar, and a nitrogen base

nucleus (of an atom) central core of the atom; contains protons and neutrons (hydrogen atoms have a single proton and no neutrons)

organic (or-GAN-ic) compounds compounds whose large molecules contain carbon, which forms C-C bonds and/or C-H bonds

peptide bond covalent bond linking amino acids within a protein molecule

pH unit expressing relative H^+ concentration (acidity); pH value higher than 7 is basic, pH value less than 7 is acidic, pH value equal to 7 is neutral

product any substance formed as a result of a chemical reaction

protein (PRO-teen) nitrogen-containing organic compound composed of a folded strand of amino acids

proton (PRO-ton) positively charged particle within the nucleus of an atom

reactant (ree-AK-tant) any substance entering (and being changed by) a chemical reaction

solute (SOL-yoot) substance that dissolves into another substance; for example, in saltwater the salt is the solute dissolved in water

solvent (SOL-vent) substance in which other substances are dissolved; for example, in saltwater the water is the solvent for salt

Common Medical Abbreviations, Prefixes, and Suffixes

Appendix B

ABBREVIATIONS

aa of each
ā.c̄. before meals
ad lib. as much as desired
alb. albumin
AM before noon
amt. amount
ante before
aq. water
AV. average
Ba barium
b.i.d. twice a day
b.m. bowel movement
BMR basal metabolic rate
BP blood pressure
BRP bathroom privileges
BUN blood urea nitrogen
c̄ with
CBC complete blood count
CCU coronary care unit
CHF congestive heart failure
CNS central nervous system
Co cobalt
CVA cerebrovascular accident, stroke
D & C dilation and curettage
d/c discontinue
DOA dead on arrival
Dx diagnosis
ECG electrocardiogram
EDC expected date of confinement
EEG electroencephalogram
EENT ear, eye, nose, throat
EKG electrocardiogram
ER emergency room
FUO fever of undetermined origin
GI gastrointestinal
GP general practitioner
GU genitourinary
h. hour
HCT hematocrit
Hb hemoglobin
H_2O water
h.s. at bedtime
ICU intensive care unit
KUB kidney, ureter, and bladder
MI myocardial infarction
non rep. do not repeat
NPO nothing by mouth
OR operating room
p.c. after meals
per by
PH past history
PI previous illness
PM after noon
p.r.n. as needed
q. every
q.d. every day
q.h. every hour
q.i.d. four times a day
q.n.s. quantity not sufficient

q.o.d. every other day
q.s. quantity required or sufficient
RBC red blood cell
℞ prescription
s̄ without
sp. gr. specific gravity
s̄s. one half
stat. at once, immediately
T & A tonsillectomy and adenoidectomy
T.B. tuberculosis
t.i.d. three times a day
TPR temperature, pulse, respiration
TUR transurethral resection
WBC white blood cell

PREFIXES

a- without
ab- away from
ad- to, toward
adeno- glandular
amphi- on both sides
an- without
ante- before, forward
anti- against
bi- two, double, twice
circum- around, about
contra- opposite, against
de- away from, from
di- double
dia- across, through
dis- separate from, apart
dys- difficult
e- out, away
ecto- outside
en- in
endo- in, inside
epi- on
eu- well
ex- from, out of, away from
exo- outside
extra- outside, beyond; in addition
hemi- half
hyper- over, excessive, above
hypo- under, deficient
infra- underneath, below
inter- between, among
intra- within, on the side
intro- into, within
iso- equal, like
para- beside
peri- around, beyond
post- after, behind
pre- before, in front of
pro- before, in front of
re- again
retro- backward, back
semi- half
sub- under, beneath
super- above, over
supra- above, on the upper side
syn- with, together
trans- across, beyond
ultra- excessive

SUFFIXES

-algia pain, painful
-asis condition
-blast young cell
-cele swelling
-centesis puncture for aspiration
-cide killer
-cyte cell
-ectomy cut out
-emia blood
-genesis production, development
-itis inflammation
-kinin motion, action
-logy study of
-megaly enlargement
-odynia pain
-oid resembling
-oma tumor
-osis condition
-opathy disease
-penia abnormal reduction
-pexy fixation
-phagia eating, swallowing
-phasia speaking condition
-phobia fear
-plasty plastic surgery
-plegia paralysis
-poiesis formation
-ptosis downward displacement
-rhaphy suture
-scope instrument for examination
-scopy examination
-stomy creation of an opening
-tomy incision
-uria urine

Chapter Test Answers

CHAPTER 1

1. anatomy; physiology
2. tissue
3. lateral
4. anterior; posterior
5. axial, appendicular
6. homeostasis
7. h
8. e
9. a
10. j
11. b
12. d
13. c
14. f
15. i
16. g
17. a
18. d
19. c
20. c

CHAPTER 2

1. a
2. b
3. c
4. d
5. a
6. b
7. d
8. c
9. a
10. f
11. e
12. d
13. b
14. h
15. g
16. ribosomes
17. active
18. prophase
19. epithelial
20. epithelial

CHAPTER 3

1. skin
2. bones
3. communication; integration; control; recognition
4. hormones
5. lymphatic
6. urine
7. accessory
8. alveoli
9. d
10. g
11. b
12. h
13. a
14. c
15. e
16. f

CHAPTER 4

1. epithelial; connective tissue
2. parietal; visceral
3. synovial
4. skin
5. cutaneous
6. epidermis; dermis
7. keratin
8. melanin
9. root
10. pressure
11. eccrine; apocrine
12. sebaceous
13. burns
14. d
15. g
16. e
17. a
18. c
19. b
20. f

CHAPTER 5

1. trabeculae
2. Haversian systems
3. osteoblasts; osteoclasts
4. diaphysis
5. axial; appendicular
6. sinuses
7. cervical
8. scapula; clavicle
9. radius; ulna
10. olecranon
11. carpal; phalanges
12. ileum; ischium; pubis
13. patella; tibia
14. feet
15. diarthrotic
16. F
17. T
18. F
19. F
20. T
21. F
22. T
23. T
24. F
25. T

CHAPTER 6

1. b
2. a
3. a
4. b
5. b
6. d
7. a
8. smooth or involuntary
9. tendons
10. myosin
11. sliding-filament
12. synergists
13. posture
14. oxygen debt
15. isotonic
16. plantar
17. atrophy
18. hamstrings

19. c
20. a
21. d
22. b
23. g
24. e
25. f

CHAPTER 7

1. central; peripheral
2. meninges
3. hydrocephalus
4. neurons; neuroglia
5. oligodendroglia
6. away; axon
7. synapse
8. neurotransmitters
9. dermatome
10. endorphins; enkephalins
11. hypothalamus; thalamus
12. 12; 31
13. cardiac muscle; smooth muscle; glandular epithelium
14. sympathetic; parasympathetic
15. sympathetic
16. c
17. h
18. a
19. b
20. e
21. i
22. f
23. g
24. d

CHAPTER 8

1. general
2. rods; cones
3. sclera; choroid; retina
4. iris
5. aqueous humor
6. cataracts
7. choroid
8. mechanoreceptors
9. external; middle; inner (internal)
10. malleus
11. perilymph
12. Corti
13. chemoreceptors
14. gustatory
15. g
16. a
17. i
18. c
19. b
20. h
21. d
22. f
23. e

CHAPTER 9

1. hormones
2. exocrine
3. second messenger
4. negative
5. prostaglandins
6. hypersecretion
7. thyroid stimulating
8. anterior pituitary
9. antidiuretic
10. thyroxine
11. goiter
12. glomerulosa
13. medulla
14. glucagon
15. diabetes mellitus
16. progesterone
17. testosterone
18. thymosin
19. pineal
20. estrogen
21. F
22. T
23. T
24. F
25. T
26. F
27. T
28. F
29. T
30. F
31. T
32. T
33. T
34. T
35. F

CHAPTER 10

1. b
2. b
3. d
4. a
5. c
6. d
7. a
8. b
9. serum
10. red bone marrow
11. polycythemia
12. embolus
13. antigen
14. AB
15. Rh

CHAPTER 11

1. atria; ventricles
2. myocardium
3. pericardium
4. atrioventricular
5. tricuspid
6. vena cava
7. pulmonary
8. angina pectoris
9. pacemaker
10. electrocardiogram (ECG)
11. ventricles
12. veins
13. tunica media
14. systemic
15. capillary
16. foramen ovale
17. cardiac output
18. ductus venosus
19. ductus arteriosus
20. systole
21. cardiac cycle
22. central venous pressure
23. h
24. f
25. b
26. d
27. a
28. c
29. e
30. g

CHAPTER 12

1. thoracic duct
2. lymph nodes
3. artificial
4. antibodies; complement

5. antigens
6. humoral
7. antibodies
8. lymphocytes
9. neutrophils; monocytes
10. lymphocytes
11. humoral
12. cell-mediated
13. T
14. F
15. T
16. F
17. F
18. T
19. T
20. T
21. T
22. F
23. F
24. T

CHAPTER 13

1. diffusion
2. surfactant
3. lower
4. oropharynx
5. nasopharynx
6. larynx
7. epiglottis
8. pneumothorax
9. external
10. oxyhemoglobin
11. vital capacity
12. medulla
13. alveoli
14. e
15. b
16. g
17. d
18. f
19. c
20. a

CHAPTER 14

1. mechanical; chemical
2. feces
3. accessory
4. lumen
5. mucosa
6. palates
7. crown
8. mastication
9. amylase
10. esophagus
11. chyme
12. peristalsis
13. jejunum
14. d
15. a
16. f
17. b
18. h
19. c
20. e
21. g
22. T
23. F
24. F
25. T
26. T
27. F
28. F
29. F
30. T

CHAPTER 15

1. catabolism
2. anabolism
3. metabolism
4. hepatic portal vein
5. glycolysis
6. glycogenesis
7. fats
8. vitamins
9. ATP
10. basal metabolic rate (BMR)
11. hypothalamus
12. F
13. T
14. T
15. F
16. F
17. T
18. T

CHAPTER 16

1. uremia
2. 10%
3. cortex; medulla
4. nephron
5. Bowman's capsule; glomerulus
6. proximal
7. filtration
8. osmosis
9. proximal
10. polyuria
11. pelvis
12. renal colic
13. urethra; meatus
14. incontinence
15. cystitis
16. 125
17. e
18. i
19. d
20. b
21. a
22. g
23. c
24. f
25. h

CHAPTER 17

1. intracellular
2. interstitial; plasma
3. nonelectrolytes
4. ions
5. cations; anions
6. urine
7. sodium; chloride
8. diuretic
9. edema
10. T
11. T
12. F
13. F
14. T
15. F
16. T
17. T
18. F

CHAPTER 18

1. neutral
2. alkaline; acid
3. carbonic anhydrase
4. buffers
5. carbonic
6. acidosis
7. ammonia
8. alkalosis

9. acidosis
10. homeostasis
11. f
12. b
13. j
14. d
15. a
16. h
17. c
18. e
19. g
20. i

CHAPTER 19

1. testes
2. spermatozoa
3. gonads
4. seminiferous
5. interstitial
6. prostate
7. cervix
8. progesterone
9. endometrium
10. areola
11. menarche
12. 28
13. f
14. j
15. a
16. d
17. h
18. c
19. e
20. g
21. i
22. b

CHAPTER 20

1. conception; birth
2. birth; death
3. embryology
4. zygote
5. amniotic
6. placenta
7. organogenesis
8. postnatal
9. childhood
10. arteriosclerosis
11. cataract
12. F
13. F
14. T
15. T
16. T
17. T
18. T
19. F
20. T

Glossary

abdomen (AB-doe-men) body area between the diaphragm and pelvis

abdominal cavity (ab-DOM-i-nal KAV-i-tee) the cavity containing the abdominal organs

abdominal muscles (ab-DOM-i-nal MUS-els) muscles supporting the anterior aspect of the abdomen

abdominal quadrants (ab-DOM-i-nal KWOD-rants) health professionals divide the abdomen (through the navel) into four areas to help locate specific organs

abdominal regions (ab-DOM-i-nal REE-juns) anatomists have divided the abdomen into nine regions to identify the location of organs

abdominopelvic cavity (ab-DOM-i-no-PEL-vik KAV-i-tee) term used to describe the single cavity containing the abdominal and pelvic organs

abduction (ab-DUK-shun) moving away from the midline of the body, opposite motion of adduction

absorption (ab-SORP-shun) passage of a substance through a membrane, such as skin or mucosa, into blood

accessory organ (ak-SES-o-ree OR-gan) an organ that assists other organs in accomplishing their functions

acetabulum (as-e-TAB-yoo-lum) socket in the hip bone (ox coxa or innominate bone) into which the head of the femur fits

acetylcholine (as-e-til-KO-leen) chemical neurotransmitter

acid-base balance (AS-id base BAL-ans) maintaining the concentration of hydrogen ions in body fluids

acidosis (as-i-DOE-sis) condition in which there is an excessive proportion of acid in the blood

acquired immunodeficiency syndrome (AIDS) (ah-KWIRED i-myoo-no-de-FISH-en-see SIN-drome) disease in which the HIV virus attacks the T cells, thereby compromising the body's immune system

acquired immunity (ah-KWIRED i-MYOO-ni-tee) immunity that is obtained after birth through the use of injections or exposure to a harmful agent

acromegaly (ak-ro-MEG-ah-lee) condition caused by hypersecretion of growth hormone after puberty, resulting in enlargement of facial features (for example, jaw, nose), fingers, and toes

acrosome (AK-ro-sohm) specialized structure on the sperm containing enzymes that break down the covering of the ovum to allow entry

actin (AK-tin) contractile protein found in the thin myofilaments of skeletal muscle

action potential (AK-shun po-TEN-shal) nerve impulse

active transport (AK-tiv TRANS-port) movement of a substance into and out of a living cell requiring the use of cellular energy

Addison's disease (AD-i-sons di-ZEEZ) disease of the adrenal gland resulting in low blood sugar, weight loss, and weakness

adduction (ah-DUK-shun) moving toward the midline of the body, opposite motion of abduction

adenohypophysis (ad-e-no-hye-POF-i-sis) anterior pituitary gland, which has the structure of an endocrine gland

adenoid (AD-e-noyd) literally, glandlike; adenoids, or pharyngeal tonsils, are paired lymphoid structures in the nasopharynx

adenosine diphosphate (ADP) (ah-DEN-o-sen dye-FOS-fate) molecule similar to adenosine triphosphate but containing only two phosphate groups

adenosine triphosphate (ATP) (ah-DEN-o-sen try-FOS-fate) chemical compound that provides energy for use by body cells

adipose (AD-i-pose) fat tissue

adolescence (ad-o-LES-ens) period between puberty and adulthood

adrenal cortex (ah-DREE-nal KOR-teks) outer portion of adrenal gland that secretes hormones called *corticoids*

adrenal gland (ah-DREE-nal gland) glands that rest on the top of the kidneys, made up of the cortex and medulla

adrenal medulla (ah-DREE-nal me-DUL-ah) inner portion of adrenal gland that secretes epinephrine and norepinephrine

adrenergic fibers (a-dre-NER-jik FYE-bers) axons whose terminals release norepinephrine and epinephrine

adrenocorticotropic hormone (ACTH) (ah-dree-no-kor-te-ko-TRO-pic HOR-mone) hormone that stimulates the adrenal cortex to secrete larger amounts of hormones

adulthood (ah-DULT-hood) period after adolescence

aerobic respiration (air-O-bik res-pi-RAY-shun) the stage of cellular respiration requiring oxygen

aerobic training (air-O-bik TRAIN-ing) continuous vigorous exercise requiring the body to increase its consumption of oxygen and develop the muscles' ability to sustain activity over a long period of time

afferent (AF-fer-ent) carrying or conveying toward the center (for example, an afferent neuron carries nerve impulses toward the central nervous system)

agglutinate (ah-GLOO-tin-ate) antibodies causing antigens to clump or stick together

aging process (AJ-ing PROS-es) the gradual degenerative changes that occur after young adulthood as a person ages

AIDS-related complex (ARC) (AIDS ree-LAY-ted KOM-pleks) a more mild form of AIDS that produces fever, weight loss, and swollen lymph nodes

albumin (AL-byoo-min) one of several types of proteins normally found in blood plasma, it helps thicken the blood

aldosterone (AL-doe-ste-rone) hormone that stimulates the kidney to retain sodium ions and water

alimentary canal (al-e-MEN-tar-ee kah-NAL) the digestive tract as a whole

alkalosis (al-kah-LO-sis) condition in which there is an excessive proportion of alkali in the blood, opposite of acidosis

allergy (AL-er-jee) hypersensitivity of the immune system to relatively harmless environmental antigens

all or none when stimulated, a muscle fiber will contract fully or not at all; whether a contraction occurs depends on whether the stimulus reaches the required threshold
alpha cell (AL-fah sell) pancreatic cell that secretes glucagon
alveolar duct (al-VEE-o-lar dukt) airway that branches from the smallest bronchioles; alveolar sacs arise from alveolar ducts
alveolar sac (al-VEE-o-lar sak) each alveolar duct ends in several sacs that resemble a cluster of grapes
alveolus (al-VEE-o-lus) literally, a small cavity; alveoli of lungs are microscopic saclike dilations of terminal bronchioles
amniotic cavity (am-nee-OT-ik KAV-i-tee) cavity within the blastocyst that will become a fluid-filled sac in which the embryo will float during development
amino acid (ah-MEE-no AS-id) structural units from which proteins are built
amphiarthrosis (am-fee-ar-THRO-sis) slightly movable joint such as the joint joining the two pubic bones
amylase (AM-i-lase) enzyme that digests carbohydrates
anabolic steroid (a-nah-BOL-ik STE-royd) hormones that stimulate the building of large molecules, specifically proteins in muscle and bones
anabolism (ah-NAB-o-lizm) cells making complex molecules (for example, hormones) from simpler compounds (for example, amino acids), opposite of catabolism
anal canal (AY-nal kah-NAL) terminal portion of the rectum
anaphase (AN-ah-faze) stage of mitosis; duplicate chromosomes move to poles of dividing cell
anaphylactic shock (an-ah-fi-LAK-tik shock) shock resulting from a severe allergic reaction, may be fatal
anatomical position (an-ah-TOM-i-kal po-ZISH-un) the reference position for the body, which gives meaning to directional terms
anatomy (ah-NAT-o-mee) the study of the structure of an organism and the relationships of its parts
androgen (AN-dro-jen) male sex hormone
anemia (ah-NEE-mee-ah) deficient number of red blood cells or deficient hemoglobin
anesthesia (an-es-THEE-zee-ah) loss of sensation
angina pectoris (an-JYE-nah PECK-tor-is) severe chest pain resulting when the myocardium is deprived of sufficient oxygen
angstrom (ANG-strom) unit 0.1 m (1/10,000,000,000 of a meter or about 1/250,000,000 of an inch)
anion (AN-eye-on) negatively charged particle
anorexia nervosa (an-o-REK-see-ah ner-VO-sah) a behavior involving an irrational fear of being overweight, resulting in severe weight loss due to self-starvation
antagonist muscle (an-TAG-o-nist MUS-el) those having opposing actions; for example, muscles that flex the upper arm are antagonists to muscles that extend it
antebrachial (an-tee-BRAY-kee-al) refers to the forearm
antecubital (an-tee-KYOO-bi-tal) refers to the elbow
antenatal medicine (an-tee-NAY-tal MED-i-sin) prenatal medicine
anterior (an-TEER-ee-or) front or ventral; opposite of posterior or dorsal
antibody (AN-ti-bod-ee) substance produced by the body that destroys or inactivates a specific substance (antigen) that has entered the body
antibody-mediated immunity (AN-ti-bod-ee MEE-dee-ate-ed i-MYOO-ni-tee) immunity that is produced when antibodies make antigens unable to harm the body
antidiuretic hormone (ADH) (an-ti-dye-yoo-RET-ik HOR-mone) hormone produced in the posterior pituitary gland to regulate the balance of water in the body by accelerating the reabsorption of water
antigen (AN-ti-jen) substance that, when introduced into the body, causes formation of antibodies against it
antrum (AN-trum) cavity
anuria (ah-NOO-ree-ah) absence of urine
anus (AY-nus) distal end or outlet of the rectum
aorta (ay-OR-tah) main and largest artery in the body
aortic body (ay-OR-tik BOD-ee) small cluster of chemosensitive cells that respond to carbon dioxide and oxygen levels
aortic semilunar valve (ay-OR-tic sem-i-LOO-nar valve) valve between the aorta and left ventricle that prevents blood from flowing back into the ventricle
apex (A-peks) pointed end of a conical structure
apnea (AP-nee-ah) temporary cessation of breathing
apocrine (AP-o-krin) sweat glands located in the axilla and genital regions; these glands enlarge and begin to function at puberty
appendicitis (ah-pen-di-SYE-tis) inflammation of the vermiform appendix
appendage (ah-PEN-dij) something that is attached
appendicular (a-pen-DIK-yoo-lar) refers to the upper and lower extremities of the body
appendicular skeleton (a-pen-DIK-yoo-lar SKEL-e-ton) the bones of the upper and lower extremities of the body
aqueous humor (AY-kwee-us HYOO-mor) watery fluid that fills the anterior chamber of the eye, in front of the lens
arachnoid (ah-RAK-noyd) delicate, weblike middle membrane covering the brain, the meninges
areola (ah-REE-o-lah) small space; the pigmented ring around the nipple
areolar (ah-REE-o-lar) a type of connective tissue consisting of fibers and a variety of cells embedded in a loose matrix of soft, sticky gel
arrector pili (ah-REK-tor PYE-lie) smooth muscles of the skin, which are attached to hair follicles; when contraction occurs, the hair stands up, resulting in "goose flesh"
arteriole (ar-TEER-ee-ole) small branch of an artery
artery (AR-ter-ee) vessel carrying blood away from the heart
articular cartilage (ar-TIK-yoo-lar KAR-ti-lij) cartilage covering the joint ends of bones
articulation (ar-tik-yoo-LAY-shun) joint
artificial kidney (ar-ti-FISH-al KID-nee) mechanical device that removes wastes from the blood that would normally be removed by the kidney
artificial pacemaker (ar-ti-FISH-al PAYS-may-ker) an electrical device that is implanted into the heart to treat a heart block
asexual (a-SEKS-yoo-al) one-celled plants and bacteria that do not produce specialized sex cells
assimilation (ah-sim-i-LAY-shun) when food molecules enter the cell and undergo chemical changes
association area (ah-so-shee-AY-shun AIR-ee-ah) region of the cerebral cortex of the brain that functions to put together or associate information from many parts of the brain to help make sense of or analyze the information

astrocyte (AS-tro-site) a glial cell

atherosclerosis (ath-er-o-skle-RO-sis) hardening of the arteries; lipid deposits lining the inside of the arteries

atrial natriuretic hormone (ANH) (AY-tree-al na-tree-yoo-RET-ik HOR-mone) hormone secreted by the heart cells that regulates fluid and electrolyte homeostasis

atrioventricular valves (ay-tree-o-ven-TRIK-yoo-lar valves) two valves that separate the atrial chambers from the ventricles

atrium (AY-tree-um) chamber or cavity; for example, atrium of each side of the heart

atrophy (AT-ro-fee) wasting away of tissue; decrease in size of a part; sometimes referred to as disuse atrophy

auditory tube (AW-di-toe-ree tube) tube that connects the throat with the middle ear

auricle (AW-ri-kul) part of the ear attached to the side of the head; earlike appendage of each atrium of the heart

autonomic effector (aw-toe-NOM-ik ef-FEK-tor) tissues to which autonomic neurons conduct impulses

autonomic nervous system (ANS) (aw-toe-NOM-ik NER-vus SIS-tem) division of the human nervous system that regulates involuntary actions

autonomic neuron (aw-toe-NOM-ik NOO-ron) motor neurons that make up the autonomic nervous system

AV bundle (A V BUN-dul) fibers in the heart that relay a nerve impulse from the AV node to the ventricles; also known as the bundle of His

avitaminosis (ay-vye-tah-mi-NO-sis) vitamin deficiency

axial (AK-see-al) refers to the head, neck, and torso, or trunk of the body

axial skeleton (AK-see-al SKEL-e-ton) the bones of the head, neck, and torso

axilla (AK-sil-ah) refers to the armpit

axon (AK-son) nerve cell process that transmits impulses away from the cell body

B cells (B sells) a lymphocyte; activated B cells develop into plasma cells, which secrete antibodies into the blood

Bartholin's glands (BAR-toe-lins glands) gland located on either side of the vaginal outlet that secretes mucuslike lubricating fluid; also known as greater vestibular glands

basal ganglia (BAY-sal GANG-glee-ah) see *cerebral nuclei*

basal metabolic rate (BMR) (BAY-sal met-ah-BOL-ik rate) number of calories of heat that must be produced per hour by catabolism to keep the body alive, awake, and comfortably warm

basement membrane (BASE-ment MEM-brane) the connective tissue layer of the serous membrane that holds and supports the epithelial cells

basophil (BAY-so-fil) white blood cell that stains readily with basic dyes

benign prostatic hypertrophy (be-NINE pros-TAT-ik hye-PER-tro-fee) a noncancerous enlargement of the prostate in older men

benign tumor (be-NINE TOO-mer) a relatively harmless neoplasm

beta cell (BAY-tah sell) pancreatic islet cell that secretes insulin

bicarbonate loading (bye-KAR-bo-nate LOHD-ing) ingesting large amounts of sodium bicarbonate to counteract the effects of lactic acid buildup, thereby reducing fatigue; however, there are potential dangerous side effects

biceps brachii (BYE-seps BRAY-kee-eye) the primary flexor of the forearm

biceps femoris (BYE-seps FEM-o-ris) powerful flexor of the lower leg

bicuspid (bye-KUS-pid) premolars

bicuspid valve (bye-KUS-pid valve) one of the two AV valves, it is located between the left atrium and ventricle and is sometimes called the *mitral valve*

bile (bile) substance that reduces large fat globules into smaller droplets of fat that are more easily broken down

bile duct (bile dukt) duct that drains bile into the small intestine and is formed by the union of the comman hepatic and cystic ducts

biological filtration (bye-o-LOJ-e-kal fil-TRAY-shun) process in which cells alter the contents of the filtered fluid

blackhead (BLACK-hed) when sebum accumulates, darkens, and enlarges some of the ducts of the sebaceous glands; also known as a *comedo*

bladder (BLAD-der) a sac, usually referring to the urinary bladder

blastocyst (BLAS-toe-sist) postmorula stage of developing embryo; hollow ball of cells

blister (BLIS-ter) a baglike point on the skin caused by some irritant, usually full of fluid

blood-brain barrier (blud brayn BARE-ee-er) two-ply wall formed by the wall of a capillary and the surrounding extensions of a glial cell called an *astrocyte;* it functions to prevent harmful chemicals from entering vital brain tissue

blood doping (blud DOE-ping) a practice used to improve athletic performance by removing red blood cells weeks before an event and then reinfusing them just before competition to increase the oxygen-carrying capacity of the blood

blood pressure (blud PRESH-ur) pressure of blood in the blood vessels, expressed as systolic pressure/diastolic pressure (for example, 120/80 mmHg)

blood pressure gradient (blud PRESH-ur GRAY-dee-ent) the difference between two blood pressures in the body

blood types (blud tipes) the different types of blood that are identified by certain antigens in red blood cells (A, B, AB, O, and Rh-negative or Rh-positive)

body (BOD-ee) unified and complex assembly of structurally and functionally interactive components

body composition (BOD-ee com-po-ZISH-un) assessment to identify the percentage of the body that is lean tissue and the percentage that is fat

bolus (BO-lus) a small, rounded mass of masticated food to be swallowed

bone (bone) highly specialized connective tissue whose matrix is hard and calcified

bone marrow (bone MAR-o) soft material that fills cavities of the bones; red bone marrow is vital to blood cell formation; yellow bone marrow is inactive fatty tissue

bony labyrinth (BONE-ee LAB-i-rinth) the fluid-filled complex maze of three spaces (the vestibule, semicircular canals, and cochlea) in the temporal bone

Bowman's capsule (BO-mens KAP-sul) the cup-shaped top of a nephron that surrounds the glomerulus

brachial (BRAY-kee-al) pertaining to the arm

breast (brest) anterior aspect of the chest; in females, also an accessory sex organ

bronchi (BRONG-ki) the branches of the trachea
bronchiole (BRONG-kee-ole) small branch of a bronchus
buccal (BUK-al) pertaining to the cheek
buffer (BUF-er) compound that combines with an acid or with a base to form a weaker acid or base, thereby lessening the change in hydrogen-ion concentration that would occur without the buffer
buffer pairs (BUF-er pairs) two kinds of chemical substances that prevent a sharp change in the pH of a fluid; for example, sodium bicarbonate ($NaHCO_3$) and carbonic acid (H_2CO_3)
bulbourethral gland (BUL-bo-yoo-REE-thral gland) small glands located just below the prostate gland whose mucus-like secretions lubricate the terminal portion of the urethra and contribute less than 5% of the seminal fluid volume; also known as *Cowper's glands*
bundle of His (BUN-dul of his) see AV bundle
burn (bern) an injury to tissues resulting from contact with heat, chemicals, electricity, friction, or radiant and electromagnetic energy; classified into three categories, depending on the number of tissue layers involved
bursae (BER-see) small, cushionlike sacs found between moving body parts, making movement easier
bursitis (ber-SYE-tis) inflammation of a bursa
calcaneus (kal-KAY-nee-us) heel bone; largest tarsal in the foot
calcitonin (kal-si-TOE-nin) a hormone secreted by the thyroid that decreases calcium in the blood
calorie (c) (KAL-or-ree) heat unit; the amount of heat needed to raise the temperature of 1 g of water 1° C
Calorie (C) (KAL-or-ree) heat unit; kilocalorie; the amount of heat needed to raise the temperature of 1 kilogram of water 1° C
calyx (KAY-liks) cup-shaped division of the renal pelvis
canaliculi (kan-ah-LIK-yoo-lie) an extremely narrow tubular passage or channel in compact bone
canine tooth (KAY-nine tooth) the tooth with the longest crown and the longest root, which is located lateral to the second incisor
capillary (KAP-i-lair-ee) tiny vessels that connect arterioles and venules
capillary blood pressure (KAP-i-lair-ee blud PRESH-ur) the blood pressure found in the capillary vessels
capsule (KAP-sul) found in diarthrotic joints, holds the bones of joints together while allowing movement and is made of fibrous connective tissue lined with a smooth, slippery synovial membrane
carbaminohemoglobin (kar-bam-ee-no-hee-mo-GLO-bin) the compound formed by the union of carbon dioxide with hemoglobin
carbohydrate (kar-bo-HYE-drate) organic compounds containing carbon, hydrogen, and oxygen in certain specific proportions; for example, sugars, starches, and cellulose
carbohydrate loading (kar-bo-HYE-drate LOHD-ing) the method used by athletes to increase the stores of muscle glycogen, allowing more sustained aerobic exercise
carbonic anhydrase (kar-BON-ik an-HYE-drays) the enzyme that converts carbon dioxide into carbonic acid
cardiac (KAR-dee-ak) refers to the heart
cardiac cycle (KAR-dee-ak SYE-kul) each complete heart beat, including contraction and relaxation of the atria and ventricles
cardiac muscle (KAR-dee-ak MUS-el) the specialized muscle that makes up the heart
cardiac output (KAR-dee-ak OUT-put) volume of blood pumped by one ventricle per minute
cardiac sphincter (KAR-dee-ak SFINGK-ter) a ring of muscle between the stomach and esophagus that prevents food from re-entering the esophagus when the stomach contracts
cardiac vein (KAR-dee-ak vane) any vein that carries blood from the myocardial capillary beds to the coronary sinus
cardiopulmonary resuscitation (CPR) (kar-dee-o-PUL-mo-nair-ree ree-sus-i-TAY-shun) combined external cardiac (heart) massage and artificial respiration
cardiovascular (kar-dee-o-VAS-kyoo-lar) pertaining to the heart and blood vessels
caries (KARE-eez) decay of teeth or of bone
carotid body (kah-ROT-id BOD-ee) chemoreceptor located in the carotid artery that detects changes in oxygen, carbon dioxide, and blood acid levels
carpal (KAR-pal) pertaining to the wrist
cartilage (KAR-ti-lij) a specialized, fibrous connective tissue that has the consistency of a firm plastic or gristlelike gel
catabolism (kah-TAB-o-lizm) breakdown of food compounds or cytoplasm into simpler compounds; opposite of anabolism, the other phase of metabolism
catalyst (KAT-ah-list) chemical that speeds up reactions without being changed itself
cataract (KAT-ah-rakt) opacity of the lens of the eye
catecholamines (kat-e-kol-AM-eens) norepinephrine and epinephrine
catheterization (kath-e-ter-i-ZAY-shun) passage of a flexible tube (catheter) into the bladder through the urethra for the withdrawal of urine (urinary catheterization)
cation (KAT-eye-on) positively charged particle
cavity (KAV-i-tee) hollow place or space in a tooth; dental caries
cecum (SEE-kum) blind pouch; the pouch at the proximal end of the large intestine
cell (sell) the basic biological and structural unit of the body consisting of a nucleus surrounded by cytoplasm and enclosed by a membrane
cell body (sell BOD-ee) the main part of a neuron from which the dendrites and axons extend
cell-mediated immunity (sell MEE-dee-ate-ed i-MYOO-ni-tee) resistance to disease organisms resulting from the actions of cells; chiefly sensitized T cells
cellular respiration (SELL-yoo-lar res-pi-RAY-shun) enzymes in the mitochondrial wall and matrix using oxygen to break down glucose and other nutrients to release energy needed for cellular work
centimeter (SEN-ti-mee-ter) 1/100 of a meter; approximately 2.5 cm equal 1 inch
central nervous system (CNS) (SEN-tral NER-vus SIS-tem) the brain and spinal cord
central venous pressure (SEN-tral VEE-nus PRESH-ur) venous blood pressure within the right atrium that influences the pressure in the large peripheral veins

centriole (SEN-tree-ol) one of a pair of tiny cylinders in the centrosome of a cell; believed to be involved with the spindle fibers formed during mitosis

centromere (SEN-tro-meer) a beadlike structure that attaches one chromatid to another during the early stages of mitosis

cephalic (se-FAL-ik) refers to the head

cerebellum (sair-e-BELL-um) the second largest part of the human brain that plays an essential role in the production of normal movements

cerebral cortex (se-REE-bral KOR-teks) a thin layer of gray matter made up of neuron dentrites and cell bodies that compose the surface of the cerebrum

cerebral nuclei (se-REE-bral NOOK-lee-i) islands of gray matter located in the cerebral cortex that are responsible for automatic movements and postures

cerebrospinal fluid (CSF) (se-ree-bro-SPY-nal FLOO-id) fluid that fills the subarachnoid space in the brain and spinal cord and in the cerebral ventricles

cerebrovascular accident (CVA) (se-ree-bro-VAS-kyoo-lar AK-si-dent) a hemorrhage or cessation of blood flow through cerebral blood vessels resulting in destruction of neurons; commonly called a *stroke*

cerebrum (se-REE-brum) the largest and uppermost part of the human brain that controls consciousness, memory, sensations, emotions, and voluntary movements

cerumen (se-ROO-men) ear wax

ceruminous gland (se-ROO-mi-nus gland) gland that produces a waxy substance called *cerumen* (ear wax)

cervical (SER-vi-kal) refers to the neck

cervix (SER-viks) neck; any necklike structure

chemoreceptors (kee-mo-ree-SEP-tors) receptors that respond to chemicals and are responsible for taste and smell

chest (chest) thorax

childhood (CHILD-hood) from infancy to puberty

cholecystokinin (CCK) (ko-le-sis-toe-KYE-nin) hormone secreted from the intestinal mucosa of the duodenum that stimulates the contraction of the gall bladder, resulting in bile flowing into the duodenum

chondrocyte (KON-dro-site) cartilage cell

chordae tendineae (KOR-dee ten-DIN-ee) stringlike structures that attach the AV valves to the wall of the heart

chorion (KO-ree-on) develops into an important fetal membrane in the placenta

chorionic gonadotropins (ko-ree-ON-ik go-na-doe-TRO-pins) hormones that are secreted as the uterus develops during pregnancy

chorionic villi (ko-ree-ON-ik VIL-eye) connect the blood vessels of the chorion to the placenta

choroid (KO-royd) middle layer of the eyeball that contains a dark pigment to prevent the scattering of incoming light rays

choroid plexus (KO-royd PLEK-sus) a network of brain capillaries that are involved with the production of cerebrospinal fluid

chromatids (KRO-mah-tids) a chromosome strand

cholinergic fiber (ko-lin-ER-jik FYE-ber) axons whose terminals release acetylcholine

chromatin granules (KRO-mah-tin GRAN-yools) deep-staining substance in the nucleus of cells; divides into chromosomes during mitosis

chromosome (KRO-mo-sohm) DNA molecule that has coiled to form a compact mass during mitosis or meiosis; each chromosome is composed of regions called *genes,* each of which transmits hereditary information

chyme (kime) partially digested food mixture leaving the stomach

cilia (SIL-ee-ah) hairlike projections of cells

circulatory system (SER-kyoo-lah-tor-ee SIS-tem) the system that supplies transportation for cells of the body

circumcision (ser-kum-SIZH-un) surgical removal of the foreskin or prepuce

cisterna chyli (sis-TER-nah KYE-lye) an enlarged pouch on the thoracic duct that serves as a storage area for lymph moving towards its point of entry in to the venous system

citric acid cycle (SIT-rik AS-id SYE-kul) the second series of chemical reactions in the process of glucose metabolism; it is an aerobic process

clavicle (KLAV-i-kul) collar bone, connects the upper extremity to the axial skeleton

cleavage furrow (KLEEV-ij FUR-o) appears at the end of anaphase and begins to divide the cell into two daughter cells

clitoris (KLIT-o-ris) erectile tissue located within the vestibule of the vagina

clone (klone) any of a family of many identical cells descended from a single "parent" cell

cochlea (KOKE-lee-ah) snail shell or structure of similar shape

cochlear duct (KOKE-lee-ar dukt) membranous tube within the bony cochlea

collagen (KOL-ah-jen) principle organic constituent of connective tissue

collecting tubule (ko-LEK-ting TOO-byool) a straight part of a renal tubule formed by distal tubules of several nephrons joining together

colloid (KOL-oyd) dissolved particles with diameters of 1 to 100 millimicrons (1 millimicron equals about 1/25,000,000 of an inch)

colon (KO-lon) intestine

colostomy (ko-LAH-sto-me) surgical procedure in which an artificial anus is created on the abdominal wall by cutting the colon and bringing the cut end or ends out to the surface to form an opening called a *stoma*

columnar (ko-LUM-nar) shape in which cells are higher than they are wide

combining sites (kom-BINE-ing sites) antigen-binding sites, antigen receptor regions on antibody molecule; shape of each combining site is complementary to shape of a specific antigen

compact bone (kom-PAKT bone) dense bone

compensated metabolic acidosis (KOM-pen-say-ted met-ah-BOL-ik as-i-DOE-sis) when metabolic acidosis occurs and the body is able to adjust to return the blood pH to near normal levels

complement (KOM-ple-ment) any of several inactive enzymes normally present in blood, which when activated kill foreign cells by dissolving them

complementary base pairing (kom-ple-MEN-ta-ree base PAIR-ing) bonding purines and pyridimes in DNA; adenine always binds with thymine, and cytosine always binds with guanine

complement fixation (KOM-ple-ment fik-SAY-shun) highly specialized antigen-antibody complexes are formed to destroy a foreign cell

concave (KON-kave) a rounded, somewhat depressed surface

concentric lamella (kon-SEN-trik lah-MEL-ah) ring of calcified matrix surrounding the Haversian canal

conchae (KONG-kee) shell-shaped structure; for example, bony projections into the nasal cavity

conduction (kon-DUK-shun) transfer of heat energy to the skin and then the external environment

cone (cone) receptor cell located in the retina that is stimulated by bright light

conjunctiva (kon-junk-TIE-vah) mucous membrane that lines the eyelids and covers the sclera (white portion)

connective tissue (ko-NEK-tiv TISH-yoo) most abundant and widely distributed tissue in the body; has numerous functions

connective tissue membrane (ko-NEK-tiv TISH-yoo MEM-brane) one of the two major types of body membranes; composed exclusively of various types of connective tissue

constipation (kon-sti-PAY-shun) retention of feces

contact dermatitis (KON-takt der-mah-TIE-tis) a local skin inflammation lasting a few hours or days after being exposed to an antigen

continuous ambulatory peritoneal dialysis (CAPD) (kon-TIN-yoo-us AM-byoo-lah-tor-ee pair-i-toe-NEE-al dye-AL-i-sis) an alternative form of treatment for renal failure rather than the more complex and expensive hemodialysis

contractile unit (kon-TRAK-til YOO-nit) the sarcomere, the basic functional unit of skeletal muscle

contractility (kon-TRAK-til-i-tee) the ability to contract a muscle

contraction (kon-TRAK-shun) ability of muscle cells to shorten or contract

convection (kon-VEK-shun) transfer of heat energy to air that is flowing away from the skin

convex (KON-veks) a rounded, somewhat elevated surface

coronal (ko-RO-nal) literally "like a crown"; a coronal plane divides the body or an organ into anterior and posterior regions

coronary artery (KOR-o-nair-ee AR-ter-ee) the first artery to branch off the aorta, supplies blood to the myocardium (heart muscle)

coronary bypass surgery (KOR-o-nair-ee BYE-pass SER-jer-ee) surgery to relieve severely restricted coronary blood flow; veins are taken from other parts of the body to bypass the partial blockage

coronary circulation (KOR-o-nair-ee ser-kyoo-LAY-shun) delivery of oxygen and removal of waste product from the myocardium (heart muscle)

coronary embolism (KOR-o-nair-ee EM-bo-lizm) blocking of a coronary blood vessel by a clot

coronary heart disease (KOR-o-nair-ee hart di-ZEEZ) disease (blockage or other deformity) of the vessels that supply the myocardium (heart muscle); one of the leading causes of death among adults in the United States

coronary sinus (KOR-o-nair-ree SYE-nus) area which receives deoxygenated blood from the coronary veins and empties into the right atrium

coronary thrombosis (KOR-o-nair-ree throm-BO-sis) formation of a blood clot in a coronary blood vessel

corpora cavernosa (KOR-por-ah kav-er-NO-sah) two columns of erectile tissue found in the shaft of the penis

corpus callosum (KOR-pus kal-LO-sum) where the right and left cerebral hemispheres are joined

corpus luteum (KOR-pus LOO-tee-um) a hormone-secreting glandular structure transformed after ovulation from a ruptured follicle; it secretes chiefly progesterone with some estrogen secreted as well

corpus spongiosum (KOR-pus spun-jee-O-sum) a column of erectile tissue surrounding the urethra in the penis

cortex (KOR-teks) outer part of an internal organ; for example, the outer part of the cerebrum and of the kidneys

corticoids (KOR-ti-koyds) hormones secreted by the three cell layers of the adrenal cortex

cotransport (ko-TRANS-port) active transport process in which two substances are moved together across a cell membrane; for example, sodium and glucose may be transported together across a membrane

coxal bone (KOKS-al bone) the pelvic bone or hipbone (also known as the os coxae or the innominate bone); formed by fusion of three distinct bones (ilium, ischium, and pubis) during skeletal development

cranial (KRAY-nee-al) toward the head

cranial cavity (KRAY-nee-al KAV-i-tee) space inside the skull that contains the brain

cranial nerve (KRAY-nee-al nerv) any of twelve pairs of nerves that attach to the undersurface of the brain and conduct impulses between the brain and structures in the head, neck, and thorax

craniosacral (kray-nee-o-SAY-kral) pertaining to parasympathetic nerves

cranium (KRAY-nee-um) bony vault made up of eight bones that encases the brain

crenation (kre-NAY-shun) abnormal notching in an erythrocyte due to shrinkage after suspension in a hypertonic solution

cretinism (KREE-tin-izm) dwarfism caused by hyposecretion of the thyroid gland

crista ampullaris (KRIS-tah am-pyoo-LAIR-is) a specialized receptor located within the semicircular canals that detects head movements

crown (krown) topmost part of an organ or other structure

crural (KROOR-al) refers to the leg

cryptorchidism (krip-TOR-ki-dizm) undescended testicles

cubital (KYOO-bi-tal) refers to the elbow

cuboid (KYOO-boyd) resembling a cube

cuboidal (KYOO-boyd-al) cell shape resembling a cube

Cushing's syndrome (KOOSH-ings SIN-drome) condition caused by the hypersecretion of glucocorticoids from the adrenal cortex

cuspid (KUS-pid) canine tooth, serves to pierce or tear food being eaten

cutaneous (kyoo-TANE-ee-us) pertaining to the skin

cutaneous membrane (ku-TANE-ee-us MEM-brane) primary organ of the integumentary system; the skin

cuticle (KYOO-ti-kul) skin fold covering the root of the nail

cyanosis (sye-ah-NO-sis) bluish appearance of the skin caused by deficient oxygenation of the blood

cyclic AMP (SIK-lik A M P) one of several second messengers that delivers information inside the cell and thus regulates the cell's activity

cystic duct (SIS-tik dukt) joins with the common hepatic duct to form the common bile duct

cystitis (sis-TI-tis) inflammation of the urinary bladder

cytoplasm (SYE-toe-plazm) the gellike substance of a cell exclusive of the nucleus and other organelles

deciduous (de-SID-yoo-us) temporary; shedding at a certain stage of growth; for example, deciduous teeth that are commonly referred to as *baby teeth*

deep (deep) farther away from the body's surface

deglutition (deg-loo-TISH-un) swallowing

dehydration (dee-hye-DRAY-shun) excessive loss of body water; the most common fluid imbalance; an abnormally low volume of one or more body fluids

deltoid (DEL-toyd) triangular; for example, the deltoid muscle

dendrite (DEN-drite) branching or treelike; a nerve cell process that transmits impulses toward the body

dense bone (dense bone) bone where the outer layer is hard and dense

deoxyribonucleic acid (DNA) (dee-ok-see-rye-bo-NOO-klee-ik AS-id) genetic material of the cell that carries the chemical "blueprint" of the body

depilatories (de-PIL-ah-toe-rees) hair removers

depolarization (dee-po-lar-i-ZAY-shun) the electrical activity that triggers a contraction of the heart muscle

dermal-epidermal junction (DER mal-EP-i-der-mal JUNK-shun) junction between the thin epidermal layer of the skin and the dermal layer providing support for the epidermis

dermal papillae (DER-mal pah-PIL-ee) upper region of the dermis that forms part of the dermal-epidermal junction and forms the ridges and grooves of fingerprints

dermatomes (DER-mah-tohms) skin surface areas supplied by a single spinal nerve

dermis (DER-mis) the deeper of the two major layers of the skin, composed of dense fibrous connective tissue interspersed with glands, nerve endings, and blood vessels; sometimes called the *true skin*

developmental process (de-vel-op-MEN-tal PROSS-es) changes and functions occurring during a human's early years as the body becomes more efficient and more effective

diabetes insipidus (dye-ah-BEE-teez in-SIP-i-dus) condition resulting from hyposecretion of ADH in which large volumes of urine are formed and, if left untreated, may cause serious health problems

diabetes mellitus (dye-ah-BEE-teez mell-EYE-tus) a condition resulting when the pancreatic islets secrete too little insulin, resulting in increased levels of blood glucose

dialysis (dye-AL-i-sis) separation of smaller (diffusible) particles from larger (nondiffusable) particles through a semipermeable membrane

diaphragm (DYE-ah-fram) membrane or partition that separates one thing from another; the flat muscular sheet that separates the thorax and abdomen and is a major muscle of respiration

diaphysis (dye-AF-i-sis) shaft of a long bone

diarthroses (dye-ar-THRO-sis) freely movable joint

diarrhea (dye-ah-REE-ah) defecation of liquid feces

diastole (dye-AS-toe-lee) relaxation of the heart, interposed between its contractions; opposite of systole

diastolic pressure (dye-ah-STOL-ik PRESH-ur) blood pressure in arteries during diastole (relaxation) of the heart

diencephalon (dye-en-SEF-ah-lon) "between" brain; parts of the brain between the cerebral hemispheres and the mesencephalon or midbrain

diffusion (di-FYOO-shun) spreading; for example, scattering of dissolved particles

digestion (di-JEST-chun) the breakdown of food materials either mechanically (i.e., chewing) or chemically (i.e., digestive enzymes)

digestive system (di-JEST-tiv SIS-tem) organs that work together to ensure proper digestion and absorption of nutrients

digital (DIJ-i-tal) refers to fingers and toes

discharging chambers (dis-CHARJ-ing CHAM-bers) the two lower chambers of the heart called *ventricles*

dissection (di-SEK-shun) cutting technique used to separate body parts for study

dissociate (di-SO-see-ate) when a compound breaks apart in solution

distal (DIS-tal) toward the end of a structure; opposite of proximal

distal convoluted tubule (DIS-tal KON-vo-loo-ted TOO-byool) the part of the tubule distal to the ascending limb of the loop of Henle in the kidney

disuse atrophy (DIS-yoos AT-ro-fee) when prolonged inactivity results in the muscles getting smaller in size

diuretic (dye-yoo-RET-ik) a substance that promotes or stimulates the production of urine; diuretic drugs are among the most commonly used drugs in medicine

DNA replication (DNA rep-li-KAY-shun) the unique ability of DNA molecules to make copies of themselves

dopamine (DOE-pah-meen) chemical neurotransmitter

dorsal (DOR-sal) referring to the back; opposite of ventral; in humans, the posterior is dorsal

dorsal body cavity (DOR-sal BOD-ee KAV-i-tee) includes the cranial and spinal cavities

dorsiflexion (dor-si-FLEK-shun) when the top of the foot is elevated (brought toward the front of the lower leg) with the toes pointing upward

ductless gland (DUKT-less gland) specialized gland that secretes hormones directly into the blood

ductus arteriosus (DUK-tus ar-teer-ee-O-sus) connects the aorta and the pulmonary artery, allowing most blood to bypass the fetus' developing lungs

ductus deferens (DUK-tus DEF-er-ens) a thick, smooth, muscular tube that allows sperm to exit from the epididymis and pass from the scrotal sac into the abdominal cavity; also known as the *vas deferens*

ductus venosus (DUK-tus ve-NO-sus) a continuation of the umbilical vein that shunts blood returning from the placenta past the fetus' developing liver directly into the inferior vena cava

duodenal papillae (doo-o-DEE-nal pah-PIL-ee) ducts located in the middle third of the duodenum that empty pancreatic digestive juices and bile from the liver into the small intestine; there are two ducts, the major duodenal papillae and the minor papillae

duodenum (doo-o-DEE-num) the first subdivision of the small intestine where most chemical digestion occurs

dura mater (DOO-rah MAH-ter) literally "strong or hard mother"; outermost layer of the meninges

dust cells (dust sells) macrophages that ingest particulate matter in the small air sacs of the lungs

dwarfism (DWARF-izm) condition of abnormally small stature, sometimes resulting from hyposecretion of growth hormone

dyspnea (DISP-nee-ah) difficult or labored breathing

eardrum (EAR-drum) the tympanic membrane that separates the external ear and middle ear

eccrine (EK-rin) small sweat glands distributed over the total body surface

ectoderm (EK-toe-derm) the innermost of the primary germ layers that develops early in the first trimester of pregnancy

ectopic pregnancy (ek-TOP-ik PREG-nan-see) a pregnancy in which the fertilized ovum implants some place other than in the uterus

edema (e-DEE-mah) excessive fluid in the tissues

effector (ef-FEK-tor) responding organ; for example, voluntary and involuntary muscle, the heart, and glands

efferent (EF-fer-ent) carrying from, as neurons that transmit impulses from the central nervous system to the periphery; opposite of afferent

ejaculation (ee-jak-yoo-LAY-shun) sudden discharging of semen from the body

ejaculatory duct (ee-JAK-yoo-lah-toe-ree dukt) duct formed by the joining of the ductus deferens and the duct from the seminal vesicle that allows sperm to enter the urethra

electrocardiogram (ECG) (e-lek-tro-KAR-dee-o-gram) graphic record of the heart's action potentials

electrolyte (e-LEK-tro-lite) substance that ionizes in solution, rendering the solution capable of conducting an electric current

electrolyte balance (e-LEK-tro-lite BAL-ans) homeostasis of electrolytes

electron transport system (e-LEK-tron TRANS-port SIS-tem) cellular process within mitochrondria that transfers energy from high-energy electrons from glycolysis and the citric acid cycle to ATP molecules so that the energy is available to do work in the cell

embolism (EM-bo-lizm) obstruction of a blood vessel by foreign matter carried in the bloodstream

embolus (EM-bo-lus) a blood clot or other substance (bubble of air) that is moving in the blood and may block a blood vessel

embryo (EM-bree-o) animal in early stages of intrauterine development; in humans, the first 3 months after conception

embryology (em-bree-OL-o-gee) study of the development of an individual from conception to birth

embryonic phase (em-bree-ON-ik faze) the period extending from fertilization until the end of the eighth week of gestation; during this phase the term *embryo* is used

emesis (EM-e-sis) vomiting

emptying reflex (EMP-tee-ing REE-fleks) the reflex that causes the contraction of the bladder wall and relaxation of the internal sphincter to allow urine to enter the urethra, which is followed by urination if the external sphincter is voluntarily relaxed

emulsify (e-MUL-se-fye) in digestion, when bile breaks up fats

endocarditis (en-doe-kar-DYE-tis) inflammation of the lining of the heart

endocardium (en-doe-KAR-dee-um) thin layer of very smooth tissue lining each chamber of the heart

endochondral ossification (en-doe-KON-dral os-i-fi-KAY-shun) the process in which most bones are formed from cartilage models

endocrine (EN-doe-krin) secreting into the blood or tissue fluid rather than into a duct; opposite of exocrine

endocrine glands (EN-doe-krin glands) ductless glands that are part of the endocrine system and secrete hormones into intercellular spaces

endocrine system (EN-doe-krin SIS-tem) the series of ductless glands that are found in the body

endoderm (EN-doe-derm) the outermost layer of the primary germ layers that develops early in the first trimester of pregnancy

endometrium (en-doe-MEE-tree-um) mucous membrane lining the uterus

endoneurium (en-doe-NOO-ree-um) the thin wrapping of fibrous connective tissue that surrounds each axon in a nerve

endoplasmic reticulum (ER) (en-doe-PLAS-mik re-TIK-yoo-lum) network tubules and vesicles in cytoplasm

endorphins (en-DOR-fins) chemical in central nervous system that influences pain perception; a natural painkiller

endosteum (en-DOS-tee-um) a fibrous membrane that lines the medullary cavity

endothelium (en-doe-THEE-lee-um) squamous epithelial cells that line the inner surface of the entire circulatory system and the vessels of the lymphatic system

endurance training (en-DOOR-ance TRAIN-ing) continuous vigorous exercise requiring the body to increase its consumption of oxygen and developing the muscles' ability to sustain activity over a prolonged period of time

enkephalins (en-KEF-ah-lins) peptide chemical in the central nervous system that acts as a natural painkiller

enzyme (EN-zime) biochemical catalyst allowing chemical reactions to take place

eosinophil (ee-o-SIN-o-fils) white blood cell that is readily stained by eosin

epicardium (ep-i-KAR-dee-um) the inner layer of the pericardium that covers the surface of the heart; it is also called the *visceral pericardium*

epidermis (ep-i-DER-mis) "false" skin; outermost layer of the skin

epididymis (ep-i-DID-i-mis) tightly coiled tube that lies along the top and behind the testes where sperm mature and develop the ability to swim

epiglottis (ep-i-GLOT-is) lidlike cartilage overhanging the entrance to the larynx

epinephrine (ep-i-NEF-rin) adrenaline; secretion of the adrenal medulla

epineurium (ep-i-NOO-ree-um) a tough fibrous sheath that covers the whole nerve

epiphyseal fracture (ep-i-FEEZ-ee-al FRAK-cher) when the epiphyseal plate is separated from the epiphysis or diaphysis; this type of fracture can disrupt the normal growth of the bone

epiphyseal plate (ep-i-FEEZ-ee-al plate) the cartilage plate that is between the epiphysis and the diaphysis and allows growth to occur; sometimes referred to as a *growth plate*

epiphyses (e-PIF-i-sees) ends of a long bone

episiotomy (e-piz-ee-OT-o-mee) a surgical procedure used during birth to prevent a laceration of the mother's perineum or the vagina

epithelial membrane (ep-i-THEE-lee-al MEM-brane) membrane composed of epithelial tissue with an underlying layer of specialized connective tissue

epithelial tissue (ep-i-THEE-lee-al TISH-yoo) covers the body and its parts; lines various parts of the body; forms continuous sheets that contain no blood vessels; classified according to shape and arrangement

erythroblastosis fetalis (e-rith-ro-blas-TOE-sis fee-TAL-is) a disease that may develop when an Rh-negative mother has anti-Rh antibodies and gives birth to an Rh-positive baby and the antibodies react with the Rh positive cells of the baby

erythrocytes (e-RITH-ro-sites) red blood cells

esophagus (e-SOF-ah-gus) the muscular, mucous-lined tube that connects the pharynx with the stomach; also known as the *foodpipe*

essential organs (ee-SEN-shal OR-gans) reproductive organs that must be present for reproduction to occur and are known as gonads

estrogen (ES-tro-jen) sex hormone secreted by the ovary that causes the development and maintenance of the female secondary sex characteristics and stimulates growth of the epithelial cells lining the uterus

eupnea (YOOP-nee-ah) normal respiration

eustachian tube (yoo-STAY-shun toob) tube extending from inside the ear to the throat to equalize air pressure

evaporation (ee-vap-o-RAY-shun) heat being lost from the skin by sweat being vaporized

exhalation (eks-hah-LAY-shun) moving air out of the lungs; also known as expiration

exocrine (EK-so-krin) secreting into a duct; opposite of endocrine

exocrine gland (EK-so-krin glands) glands that secrete their products into ducts that empty onto a surface or into a cavity; for example, sweat glands

expiration (eks-pi-RAY-shun) moving air out of the lungs; also known as exhalation

expiratory center (eks-PYE-rah-tor-ee SEN-ter) one of the two most important respiratory control centers, located in the medulla

expiratory muscles (eks-PYE-rah-tor-ee MUS-els) muscles that allow more forceful expiration to increase the rate and depth of ventilation; the internal intercostals and the abdominal muscles

expiratory reserve volume (ERV) (eks-PYE-rah-tor-ee re-ZERV VOL-yoom) the amount of air that can be forcibly exhaled after expiring the tidal volume (TV)

extension (ek-STEN-shun) increasing the angle between two bones at a joint

external auditory canal (eks-TER-nal AW-di-toe-ree kah-NAL) a curved tube (approximately 2.5 cm) extending from the auricle into the temporal bone, ending at the tympanic membrane

external ear (eks-TER-nal ear) the outer part of the ear that is made up of the auricle and the external auditory canal

external genitalia (eks-TER-nal jen-i-TAIL-yah) external reproductive organs

external intercostals (eks-TER-nal in-ter-KOS-tals) inspiratory muscles that enlarge the thorax, causing the lungs to expand and air to rush in

external nares (eks-TER-nal NAY-reez) nostrils

external oblique (eks-TER-nal o-BLEEK) the outermost layer of the anterolateral abdominal wall

external otitis (eks-TER-nal o-TIE-tis) a common infection of the external ear; also known as *swimmer's ear*

external respiration (eks-TER-nal res-pi-RAY-shun) the exchange of gases between air in the lungs and in the blood

extracellular fluid (ECF) (eks-trah-SELL-yoo-lar FLOO-id) the water found outside of cells located in two compartments between cells (interstitial fluid) and in the blood (plasma)

facial (FAY-shal) referring to the face

fallen arch (fallen arch) when the tendons and ligaments of the foot weaken, allowing the normally curved arch to flatten out

fallopian tubes (fal-LO-pee-an toobs) the pair of tubes that conduct the ovum from the ovary to the uterus

false ribs (fawls ribs) the eighth, ninth, and tenth pairs of ribs that are attached to the cartilage of the seventh ribs rather than the sternum

fasciculus (fah-SIK-yoo-lus) little bundle

fat (fat) one of the three basic food types; primarily a source of energy

fatigue (fah-TEEG) loss of muscle power; weakness

fat tissue (fat TISH-yoo) adipose tissue; specialized to store lipids

feces (FEE-seez) waste material discharged from the intestines

feedback control loop (FEED-bak kon-TROL loop) a highly complex and integrated communication control network, classified as negative or positive; negative feedback loops are the most important and numerous homeostatic control mechanisms

femoral (FEM-or-al) referring to the thigh

femur (FEE-mur) the thigh bone, which is the longest bone in the body

fertilization (FER-ti-li-ZAY-shun) the moment the female's ovum and the male's sperm cell unite

fetal alcohol syndrome (FAS) (FEE-tal AL-ko-hol SIN-drome) a condition that may cause congenital abnormalities in a baby that results from a woman consuming alcohol during pregnancy

fetal phase (FEE-tal faze) period extending from the eighth to the thirty-ninth week of gestation; during this phase the term *fetus* is used

fetus (FEE-tus) unborn young, especially in the later stages; in human beings, from the third month of the intrauterine period until birth

fibers (FYE-bers) threadlike structures; for example, nerve fibers

fibrin (FYE-brin) insoluble protein in clotted blood

fibrinogen (fye-BRIN-o-jen) soluble blood protein that is converted to insoluble fibrin during clotting

fibrous connective tissue (FYE-brus ko-NEK-tiv TISH-yoo) strong, nonstretchable, white collagen fibers that compose tendons

fibula (FIB-yoo-lah) the slender non-weight-bearing bone located on the lateral aspect of the leg

fight or flight syndrome (fite or flite SIN-drome) the changes produced by increased sympathetic impulses allowing the body to deal with any type of stress

filtration (fil-TRAY-shun) movement of water and solutes through a membrane by a higher hydrostatic pressure on one side

fimbriae (FIM-bree-ee) fringe

flagellum (flah-JEL-um) single projection extending from the cell surface; only example in human is the "tail" of the male sperm

flat bone (flat bone) one of the four types of bone; the frontal bone is an example of a flat bone

flat feet (flat feet) when the tendons and ligaments of the foot weaken, allowing the normally curved arch to flatten out

flexion (FLEK-shun) act of bending; decreasing the angle between two bones at the joint

floating ribs (FLOW-ting ribs) the eleventh and twelfth pairs of ribs, which are only attached to the thoracic vertebrae

fluid balance (FLOO-id BAL-ans) homeostasis of fluids; the volumes of interstitial fluid, intracellular fluid, and plasma and total volume of water remain relatively constant

fluid compartments (FLOO-id kom-PART-ments) the areas in the body where the fluid is located; for example, interstitial fluid

follicles (FOL-li-kuls) specialized structures required for hair growth

follicle-stimulating hormone (FSH) (FOL-li-kul STIM-yoo-lay-ting HOR-mone) hormone present in males and females; in males, FSH stimulates the production of sperm; in females, FSH stimulates the ovarian follicles to mature and follicle cells to secrete estrogen

fontanels (FON-tah-nels) "soft spots" on the infant's head; unossified areas in the infant skull

foramen (fo-RAY-men) small opening; for example, the vertebral foramen, which allows the spinal cord to pass through the vertebral canal

foramen ovale (fo-RAY-men o-VAL-ee) shunts blood from the right atrium directly into the left atrium, allowing most blood to bypass the baby's developing lungs

foreskin (FORE-skin) a loose-fitting retractable casing located over the glans of the penis; also know as the *prepuce*

fractal geometry (FRAK-tul jee-OM-e-tree) the study of surfaces with a seemingly infinite area, such as the lining of the small intestine

free nerve endings (free nerv END-ings) specialized receptors in the skin that respond to pain

frenulum (FREN-yoo-lum) the thin membrane that attaches the tongue to the floor of the mouth

frontal (FRON-tal) lengthwise plane running from side to side, dividing the body into anterior and posterior portions

frontal muscle (FRON-tal MUS-el) one of the muscles of facial expression; it moves the eyebrows and furrows the skin of the forehead

frontal sinusitis (FRON-tal sye-nyoo-SYE-tis) inflammation in the frontal sinus

gene (jean) one of many segments of a chromosome (DNA molecule); each gene contains the genetic code for synthesizing a protein molecule such as an enzyme or hormone

genitalia (jen-i-TAIL-yah) reproductive organs

gestation (jes-TAY-shun) the length of pregnancy, approximately 9 months in humans

gigantism (jye-GAN-tizm) a condition produced by hypersecretion of growth hormone during the early years of life; results in a child who grows to gigantic size

gland (gland) secreting structure

glandular epithelium (GLAN-dyoo-lar ep-i-THEE-lee-um) cells that are specialized for secreting activity

glans (glans) the distal end of the shaft of the penis

glaucoma (glaw-KO-mah) disorder characterized by elevated pressure in the eye

glia (GLEE-ah) supporting cells of nervous tissue; also called *neuroglia*

glioma (glee-O-mah) one of the most common types of brain tumors

globulin (GLOB-yoo-lin) a type of plasma protein that includes antibodies

glomerulus (glo-MARE-yoo-lus) compact cluster; for example, capillaries in the kidneys

glottis (GLOT-is) the space between the vocal cords

glucagon (GLOO-kah-gon) hormone secreted by alpha cells of the pancreatic islets

glucocorticoids (GCs) (gloo-ko-KOR-ti-koyds) hormones that influence food metabolism; secreted by the adrenal cortex

gluconeogenesis (gloo-ko-nee-o-JEN-e-sis) formulation of glucose or glycogen from protein or fat compounds

glucose (GLOO-kose) monosaccharide or simple sugar; the principal blood sugar

gluteal (GLOO-tee-al) of or near the buttocks

gluteus maximus (GLOO-tee-us MAX-i-mus) major extensor of the thigh and also supports the torso in an erect position

glycerol (GLIS-er-ol) product of fat digestion

glycogen (GLYE-ko-jen) polysaccharide; animal starch

glycogen loading (GLYE-ko-jen LOHD-ing) see *carbohydrate loading*

glycogenesis (glye-ko-JEN-e-sis) formation of glycogen from glucose or from other monosaccharides, fructose, or galactose

glycogenolysis (glye-ko-je-NOL-i-sis) hydrolysis of glycogen to glucose-6-phosphate or to glucose

glycolysis (glye-KOL-i-sis) the first series of chemical reactions in glucose metabolism; changes glucose to pyruvic acid in a series of anaerobic reactions

glycosuria (glye-ko-SOO-ree-ah) glucose in the urine; a sign of diabetes mellitus

goblet cells (GOB-let sells) specialized cells found in simple columnar epithelium that produce mucus

goiter (GOY-ter) enlargement of the thyroid gland

golgi apparatus (GOL-jee ap-ah-RA-tus) small sacs stacked on one another near the nucleus that makes carbohydrate compounds, combines them with protein molecules, and packages the product in a globule

golgi tendon receptors (GOL-jee TEN-don ree-SEP-tors) sensors that are responsible for proprioception

gonads (GO-nads) sex glands in which reproductive cells are formed

graafian follicle (GRAF-ee-an FOL-li-kul) a mature ovum in its sac
gradient (GRAY-dee-ent) a slope or difference between two levels; for example, blood pressure gradient: a difference between the blood pressure in two different vessels
gram (gram) the unit of measure in the metric system on which mass is based (approximately 454 grams equals one pound)
granulosa cell (gran-yoo-LO-sah sell) cell layer surrounding the oocyte
gray matter (gray MAT-er) tissue comprising cell bodies and unmyelinated axons and dendrites
greater omentum (GRATE-er o-MEN-tum) a pouchlike extension of the visceral peritoneum
growth hormone (growth HOR-mone) hormone secreted by the anterior pituitary gland that controls the rate of skeletal and visceral growth
gustatory cell (GUS-tah-tor-ee sell) cells of taste
gyrus (JYE-rus) convoluted ridge
hair follicle (hair FOL-li-kul) a small tube where hair growth occurs
hair papilla (hair pah-PIL-ah) a small, cap-shaped cluster of cells located at the base of the follicle where hair growth begins
hamstring muscles (HAM-string MUS-els) powerful flexors of the hip made up of the semimembranosus, semitendinosis, and biceps femoris muscles
Haversian canal (ha-VER-shun kah-NAL) the canal in the Haversian system that contains a blood vessel
Haversian system (hah-VER-shun SIS-tem) the circular arrangements of calcified matrix and cells that give bone its characteristic appearance
heart block (hart blok) a blockage of impulse conduction from atria to ventricles so that the heart beats at a slower rate than normal
heartburn (HART-bern) burning sensation characterized by pain and a feeling of fullness beneath the sternum caused by the esophogeal mucosa being irritated by stomach acid
Heimlich maneuver (HIME-lik mah-NOO-ver) livesaving technique used to free the trachea of objects blocking the airway
hematocrit (he-MAT-o-krit) volume percent of blood cells in whole blood
hemodialysis (hee-mo-dye-AL-i-sis) use of dialysis to separate waste products from the blood
hemoglobin (hee-mo-GLO-bin) iron-containing protein in red blood cells
hemopoiesis (hee-mo-poy-EE-sis) blood cell formation
hemopoietic tissue (hee-mo-poy-ET-ik TISH-yoo) specialized connective tissue that is responsible for the formation of blood cells and lymphatic system cells; found in red bone marrow, spleen, tonsils, and lymph nodes
heparin (HEP-ah-rin) substance obtained from the liver; inhibits blood clotting
hepatic colic flexure (he-PAT-ik KOL-ik FLEK-sher) the bend between the ascending colon and the transverse colon
hepatic ducts (he-PAT-ik dukts) drain bile out of the liver
hepatic portal circulation (he-PAT-ik POR-tal ser-kyoo-LAY-shun) the route of blood flow through the liver
hepatic portal vein (he-PAT-ik POR-tal vane) delivers blood directly from the gastrointestinal tract to the liver
herpes zoster (HER-peez ZOS-ter) "shingles," viral infection that affects the skin of a single dermatone
hiccup (HIK-up) involuntary spasmodic contraction of the diaphragm
hip (hip) the joint connecting the legs to the trunk
histogenesis (his-toe-JEN-e-sis) formation of tissues from primary germ layers of embryo
homeostasis (ho-mee-o-STAY-sis) relative uniformity of the normal body's internal environment
homeostatic mechanism (ho-mee-o-STAT-ik MEK-ah-nizm) a system that maintains a constant environment enabling body cells to function efffectively
hormone (HOR-mone) substance secreted by an endocrine gland
human immunodeficiency virus (HYOO-man i-myoo-no-de-FISH-en-see VYE-rus) the retrovirus that causes acquired immunodeficiency syndrome (AIDS)
humerus (HYOO-mer-us) the second longest bone in the body; the long bone of the arm
humoral immunity (HYOO-mor-al i-MYOO-ni-tee) antibody-mediated immunity
hybridoma (hye-brid-O-ma) fused or hybrid cells that continue to produce the same antibody as the original lymphocyte
hydrocephalus (hye-dro-SEF-ah-lus) abnormal accumulation of cerebrospinal fluid; "water on the brain"
hydrocortisone (hye-dro-KOR-ti-zone) a hormone secreted by the adrenal cortex; cortisol; compound F
hydrogen ion (HYE-dro-jen EYE-on) found in water and water solutions; produces an acidic solution; H^+
hydrostatic pressure (hye-dro-STAT-ik PRESH-ur) the force of a fluid pushing against some surface
hydroxide ion (hye-DROK-side EYE-on) found in water and water solutions; produces an alkaline solution; H^+
hymen (HYE-men) Greek for "membrane"; mucous membrane that may partially or entirely occlude the vaginal outlet
hyperacidity (hye-per-a-SID-i-tee) excessive secretion of acid; an important factor in the formation of ulcers
hypercalcemia (hye-per-kal-SEE-mee-ah) a condition in which there is harmful excesses of calcium in the blood
hyperglycemia (hye-per-glye-SEE-mee-ah) higher than normal blood glucose concentration
hyperopia (hye-per-O-pee-ah) farsightedness
hypersecretion (hye-per-se-KREE-shun) too much of a substance is being secreted
hypertension (hye-per-TEN-shun) abnormally high blood pressure
hyperthyroidism (hye-per-THYE-royd-izm) oversecretion of thyroid hormones that increases metabolic rate resulting in loss of weight, increased appetite, and nervous irritability
hypertonic (hye-per-TON-ik) a solution containing a higher level of salt (NaCl) than is found in a living red blood cell (above 0.9% NaCl)
hypertrophy (hye-PER-tro-fee) increased size of a part caused by an increase in the size of its cells
hyperventilation (hye-per-ven-ti-LAY-shun) very rapid deep respirations
hypervitaminosis (hye-per-vye-tah-mi-NO-sis) condition caused by excess amounts of vitamins; usually associated with the use of vitamin supplements

hypoglycemia (hye-po-glye-SEE-mee-ah) lower-than-normal blood glucose concentration
hyposecretion (hye-po-se-KREE-shun) too little of a substance is being secreted
hypothalamus (hye-po-THAL-ah-mus) vital neuroendocrine and autonomic control center beneath the thalamus
hypothermia (hye-po-THER-mee-ah) subnormal core body temperature below 37° C
hypothesis (hye-POTH-e-sis) a proposed explanation of an observed phenomena
hypothyroidism (hye-po-THYE-royd-izm) undersecretion of thyroid hormones; early in life results in cretinism; later in life results in myxedema
hypotonic (hye-po-TON-ik) a solution containing a lower level of salt (NaCl) than is found in a living red blood cell (below 0.9% NaCl)
hypoventilation (hye-po-ven-ti-LAY-shun) slow and shallow respirations
hysterectomy (his-te-REK-toe-mee) surgical removal of the uterus
ileocecal valve (il-ee-o-SEE-kal valv) the sphincterlike structure between the end of the small intestine and the beginning of the large intestine
ileum (IL-ee-um) the distal portion of the small intestine
iliac crest (IL-ee-ak krest) the superior edge of the illium
iliopsoas (il-ee-op-SO-as) a flexor of the thigh and an important stabilizing muscle for posture
ilium (IL-ee-um) one of the three separate bones that forms the ox coxa
immune system (i-MYOON SIS-tem) the body's defense system against disease
immunization (i-myoo-ni-ZAY-shun) deliberate artificial exposure to disease to produce acquired immunity
implantation (im-plan-TAY-shun) when a fertilized ovum implants in the uterus
inborn immunity (IN-born i-MYOO-ni-tee) immunity to disease that is inherited
incontinence (in-KON-ti-nens) when an individual voids urine involuntarily
incus (IN-kus) the anvil, the middle ear bone that is shaped like an anvil
infancy (IN-fan-see) from birth to about 18 months of age
infant respiratory distress syndrome (IN-fant RES-pi-rah-toe-ree di-STRESS SIN-drome) leading cause of death in premature babies, due to a lack of surfactant in the alveolar air sacs
inferior (in-FEER-ee-or) lower; opposite of superior
inferior vena cava (in-FEER-ee-or VEE-nah KAY-vah) one of two large veins carrying blood into the right atrium
inflammatory response (in-FLAM-ah-toe-ree re-SPONS) nonspecific immune process produced in response to injury and resulting in redness, pain, heat, and swelling and promoting movement of white blood cells to the affected area
inguinal (ING-gwi-nal) of the groin
inhalation (in-hah-LAY-shun) inspiration or breathing in; opposite of exhalation or expiration
inherited immunity (in-HAIR-i-ted i-MYOO-ni-tee) inborn immunity
inhibiting hormone (in-HIB-i-ting HOR-mone) hormone produced by the hypothalamus that slows the release of anterior pituitary hormones
insertion (in-SER-shun) attachment of a muscle to the bone that it moves when contraction occurs (as distinguished from its origin)
inspiration (in-spi-RAY-shun) inhalation, moving air into the lungs; same as inhalation, opposite of exhalation or expiration
inspiratory muscle (in-SPY-rah-tor-ee MUS-el) the muscles that increase the size of the thorax, including the diaphragm and external intercostals, and allow air to rush into the lungs
inspiratory center (in-SPY-rah-tor-ee SEN-ter) one of the two most important control centers located in the medulla; the other is the expiratory center
inspiratory reserve volume (IRV) (in-SPY-rah-tor-ee re-SERV VOL-yoom) the amount of air that can be forcibly inspired over and above a normal respiration
insulin (IN-suh-lin) hormone secreted by the pancreatic islets
integument (in-TEG-yoo-ment) refers to the skin
integumentary system (in-teg-yoo-MEN-tar-ee SIS-tem) the skin; the largest and most important organ in the body
intercalated disks (in-TER-kah-lay-ted disks) cross striations and unique dark bands that are found in cardiac muscle fibers
intercostal muscle (in-ter-KOS-tal MUS-el) the respiratory muscles located between the ribs
interferon (in-ter-FEER-on) small proteins produced by the immune system that inhibit virus multiplication
internal oblique (in-TER-nal o-BLEEK) the middle layer of the anterolateral abdominal walls
internal respiration (in-TER-nal res-pi-RAY-shun) the exchange of gases that occurs between the blood and cells of the body
interneuron (in-ter-NOO-ron) nerves that conduct impulses from sensory neurons to motor neurons
interphase (IN-ter-faze) the phase immediately before the visible stages of cell division when the DNA of each chromosome replicates itself
interstitial cell (in-ter-STISH-al sell) small specialized cells in the testes that secrete the male sex hormone, testosterone
interstitial cell-stimulating hormone (ICSH) (in-ter-STISH-al sell STIM-yoo-lay-ting HOR-mone) the previous name for luteinizing hormone in males; causes testes to develop and secrete testosterone
interstitial fluid (in-ter-STISH-al FLOO-id) fluid located in the microscopic spaces between the cells
intestine (in-TES-tin) the part of the digestive tract that is after the stomach; separated into two segments, the small and the large
intestinal gland (in-TES-ti-nal gland) thousands of glands found in the mucous membrane of the mucosa of the small intestines; secrete intestinal digestive juices
intracellular fluid (ICF) (in-tra-SELL-yoo-lar FLOO-id) a fluid located within the cells; largest fluid compartment
in vitro (in VEE-tro) refers to the glass laboratory container where a mature ovum is fertilized by a sperm
involuntary muscle (in-VOL-un-tare-ee MUS-el) smooth muscles that are not under conscious control and are found in organs such as the stomach and small intestine
involution (in-vo-LOO-shun) return of an organ to its normal size after an enlargement; also retrograde or degenerative change

ion (EYE-on) electrically charged atom or group of atoms
ion pump (EYE-on pump) a specialized cellular component that moves ions from an area of low concentration to an area of high concentration
iron deficiency anemia (EYE-ern de-FISH-en-see ah-NEE-mee-ah) when there are inadequate levels of iron in the diet so that less hemoglobin is produced; results in extreme fatigue
ischium (IS-kee-um) one of three separate bones that forms the ox coxa
isometric (eye-so-MET-rik) type of muscle contraction in which muscle does not shorten
isotonic (eye-so-TON-ik) of the same tension or pressure
jaundice (JAWN-dis) abnormal yellowing of skin, mucous membranes, and white of eyes
jejunum (je-JOO-num) the middle third of the small intestine
joints (joynts) articulation
Kaposi's sarcoma (KAH-po-sees sar-KO-mah) a type of skin cancer that can take advantage of an impaired immune system
keratin (KARE-ah-tin) protein substance found in hair, nails, outer skin cells, and horny tissues
kidney (KID-nee) organ that cleanses the blood of waste products continually produced by metabolism
kilocalorie (Kcal) (KIL-o-kal-o ree) 1000 calories
kinesthesia (kin-es-THEE-zee-ah) "muscle sense"; that is, sense of position and movement of body parts
Krause's end bulb (KROWZ end bulb) skin receptor that detects sensations of cold
Kupffer cell (KOOP-fer sell) macrophage found in spaces between liver cells
labia majora (LAY-bee-ah ma-JO-rah) "large lips" of the vulva
labia minora (LAY-bee-ah mi-NO-rah) "small lips" of the vulva
labor (LAY-bor) the process that results in the birth of the baby
lacrimal gland (LAK-ri-mal gland) the glands that produce tears, located in the upper lateral portion of the orbit
lacteal (LAK-tee-al) a lymphatic vessel located in each villus of the intestine; serves to absorb fat materials from the chyme passing through the small intestine
lactiferous duct (lak-TIF-er-us dukt) the duct that drains the grapelike cluster of milk-secreting glands in the breast
lacuna (lah-KOO-nah) space or cavity; for example, lacunae in bone contain bone cells
lambdoidal suture (LAM-doyd-al SOO-chur) the immovable joint formed by the parietal and occipital bones
lamella (lah-MEL-ah) thin layer, as of bone
lanugo (lah-NOO-go) the extremely fine and soft hair found on a newborn infant
laparoscope (LAP-ah-ro-skope) specialized optical viewing tube
laryngopharynx (lah-ring-go-FAIR-inks) the lowest part of the pharynx
larynx (LAIR-inks) the voice box located just below the pharynx; the largest piece of cartilage making up the larynx is the thyroid cartilage, commonly known as the *Adam's apple*
lateral (LAT-er-al) of or toward the side; opposite of medial
latissimus dorsi (la-TIS-i-mus DOR-si) an extensor of the upper arm
lens (lenz) the refracting mechanism of the eye that is located directly behind the pupil
leukemia (loo-KEE-mee-ah) blood cancer characterized by an increase in white blood cells
leukocyte (LOO-ko-site) white blood cells
leukocytosis (loo-ko-SYE-toe-sis) abnormally high white blood cell numbers in the blood
leukopenia (loo-ko-PEE-nee-ah) abnormally low white blood cell numbers in the blood
ligament (LIG-ah-ment) bond or band connecting two objects; in anatomy a band of white fibrous tissue connecting bones
lipase (LYE-pase) fat-digesting enzymes
lithotriptor (LITH-o-trip-tor) a specialized ultrasound generator that is used to pulverize kidney stones
liver glycogenolysis (LIV-er glye-ko-je-NOL-i-sis) chemical process by which liver glycogen is converted to glucose
longitudinal arch (lon-ji-TOO-di-nal arch) two arches, the medial and lateral, that extend lengthwise in the foot
loop of Henle (loop of HEN-lee) extension of the proximal tubule of the kidney
lumbar (LUM-bar) lower back, between the ribs and pelvis
lumbar puncture (LUM-bar PUNK-chur) when some cerebrospinal fluid is withdrawn from the subarachnoid space in the lumbar region of the spinal cord
lumen (LOO-men) the hollow space within a tube
lung (lung) organ of respiration; the right lung has three lobes and the left lung has two lobes
lunula (LOO-nyoo-lah) crescent-shaped white area under the proximal nail bed
luteinization (loo-te-ni-ZAY-shun) the formation of a golden body (corpus luteum) in the ruptured follicle
luteinizing hormone (LH) (LOO-te-nye-zing HOR-mone) acts in conjunction with follicle-stimulating hormone (FSH) to stimulate follicle and ovum maturation and release of estrogen and ovulation; known as the ovulating hormone; in males, causes testes to develop and secrete testosterone
lymph (limf) specialized fluid formed in the tissue spaces that returns excess fluid and protein molecules to the blood
lymph node (limf node) performs biological filtration of lymph on its way to the circulatory system
lymphatic capillaries (lim-FAT-ik CAP-i-lair-ees) tiny, blind-ended tubes distributed in the tissue spaces
lymphatic duct (lim-FAT-ik dukt) terminal vessel into which lymphatic vessels empty lymph; the duct then empties the lymph into the circulatory system
lymphatic system (lim-FAT-ik SIS-tem) a system that plays a critical role in the functioning of the immune system, moves fluids and large molecules from the tissue spaces and fat-related nutrients from the digestive system to the blood
lymphatic tissue (lim-FAT-ik TISH-yoo) tissue that is responsible for manufacturing lymphocytes and moncytes; found mostly in the lymph nodes, thymus, and spleen
lymphatic vessels (lim-FAT-ik VES-els) vessels that carry lymph to its eventual return to the circulatory system
lymphocytes (LIM-fo-sites) one type of white blood cell
lyse (lize) disintegration of a cell
lysosome (LYE-so-sohm) membranous organelles containing various enzymes that can dissolve most cellular compounds; hence called *digestive bags* or *suicide bags* of cells
macrophage (MAK-ro-faje) phagocytic cells in the immune system

malignant (mah-LIG-nant) cancerous growth
malleus (MAL-ee-us) hammer; the tiny middle ear bone that is shaped like a hammer
mammary gland (MAM-er-ee gland) breasts; classified as external accessory sex organs in females
mastication (mas-ti-KAY-shun) chewing
matrix (MAY-triks) the intracellular substance of a tissue; for example, the matrix of bone is calcified, whereas that of blood is liquid
mature follicle (mah-CHUR FOL-li-kul) graafian follicle
maximum oxygen consumption (Vo_{2max}) (MAX-i-mum OKS-i-jen kon-SUMP-shun) the maximum amount of oxygen taken up by the lungs, transported to the tissues and used to do work
mechanoreceptor (mek-an-o-ree-SEP-tor) receptors that are mechanical in nature; for example, equilibrium and balance sensors in the ears
medial (MEE-dee-al) of or toward the middle; opposite of lateral
mediastinum (mee-dee-as-TI-num) a subdivision in the mid-portion of the thoracic cavity
medulla (me-DUL-ah) Latin for "marrow"; hence the inner portion of an organ in contrast to the outer portion or cortex
medulla oblongata (me-DUL-ah ob-long-GAH-tah) the lowest part of the brain stem; an enlarged extension of the spinal cord; the vitals centers are located within this area
medullary cavity (MED-yoo-lair-ee KAV-i-tee) hollow area inside the diaphysis of the bone that contains yellow bone marrow
meiosis (my-O-sis) nuclear division in which the number of chromosomes are reduced to half their original number; produce gametes
Meissner's corpuscle (MIZS-ners KOR-pus-ul) a sensory receptor located in the skin close to the surface that detects light touch
melanin (MEL-ah-nin) brown skin pigment
melanocyte (me-LAN-o-site) specialized cells in the pigment layer that produce melanin
melanocyte-stimulating hormone (MSH) (me-LAN-o-site STIM-yoo-lay-ting HOR-mone) responsible for a rapid increase in the synthesis and dispersion of melanin granules in specialized skin cells
melatonin (mel-ah-TOE-nin) important hormone produced by the pineal gland that is believed to regulate the onset of puberty and the menstrual cycle; also referred to as the *third eye* because it responds to levels of light and is thought to be involved with the body's internal clock
membrane (MEM-brane) thin layer or sheet
membranous labyrinth (MEM-brah-nus LAB-i-rinth) a membranous sac that follows the shape of the bony labyrinth and is filled with endolymph
memory cell (MEM-o-ree sell) cells that remain in reserve in the lymph nodes until their ability to secrete antibodies is needed
menarche (me-NAR-kee) beginnings of the menstrual function
meninges (me-NIN-jeez) fluid-containing membranes surrounding the brain and spinal cord
menopause (MEN-o-pawz) termination of menstrual cycles
menses (MEN-seez) menstrual flow
menstrual cycle (MEN-stroo-al SYE-kul) the cyclical changes in the uterine lining
mesentery (MEZ-en-tair-ee) a large double fold of peritoneal tissue that anchors the loops of the digestive tract to the posterior wall of the abdominal cavity
mesoderm (MEZ-o-derm) the middle layer of the primary germ layers
messenger RNA (mRNA) (MES-en-jer RNA) a duplicate copy of a gene sequence on the DNA that passes from the nucleus to the cytoplasm
metabolic acidosis (met-ah-BOL-ik as-i-DOE-sis) a disturbance affecting the bicarbonate element of the bicarbonate-carbonic acid buffer pair; bicarbonate deficit
metabolic alkalosis (met-ah-BOL-ik al-kah-LO-sis) disturbance affecting the bicarbonate element of the bicarbonate-carbonic acid buffer pair; bicarbonate excess
metabolism (me-TAB-o-lizm) complex process by which food is used by a living organism
metacarpal (met-ah-KAR-pal) the part of the hand between the wrist and fingers
metaphase (MET-ah-faze) second stage of mitosis, during which the nuclear envelope and nucleolus disappear
metatarsal arch (met-ah-TAR-sal arch) the arch that extends across the ball of the foot; also called the *transverse arch*
meter (MEE-ter) a measure of length in the metric system; equal to about 39.5 inches
microcephaly (my-kro-SEF-ah-lee) a congenital abnormality in which an infant is born with a small head
microglia (my-KROG-lee-ah) one type of connective tissue found in the brain and spinal cord
micron (MY-kron) 1/1000 millimeter; 1/25,000 inch
microvilli (my-kro-VIL-eye) the brushlike border made up of epithelial cells found on each villus in the small intestine; increases the surface area for absorption of nutrients
micturition (mik-too-RISH-un) urination, voiding
midbrain (MID-brain) one of the three parts of the brain stem
middle ear (MID-ul eer) a tiny and very thin epithelium-lined cavity in the temporal bone that houses the ossicles; in the middle ear, sound waves are amplified
midsagittal (mid-SAJ-i-tal) a cut or plane that divides the body or any of its parts into two equal halves
minerals (MIN-er-als) inorganic elements or salts found naturally in the earth that are vital to the proper functioning of the body
mineralocorticoid (MC) (min-er-al-o-KOR-ti-koyd) hormone that influences mineral salt metabolism; secreted by adrenal cortex; aldosterone is the chief mineralocorticoid
mitochondria (my-toe-KON-dree-ah) threadlike structures
mitosis (my-TOE-sis) indirect cell division involving complex changes in the nucleus
mitral valve (MY-tral valv) also known as the *bicuspid valve;* located between the left atrium and ventricle
monoclonal antibody (mon-o-KLONE-al AN-ti-bod-ee) specific antibody produced from a population of identical cells
monocyte (MON-o-site) a phagocyte
mons pubis (monz PYOO-bis) skin-covered pad of fat over the symphysis pubis in the female
morula (MOR-yoo-lah) a solid mass of cells formed by the divisions of a fertilized egg

motor neuron (MO-tor NOO-ron) transmits nerve impulses from the brain and spinal cord to muscles and glandular epithelial tissues

motor unit (MO-tor YOO-nit) a single motor neuron with the muscle cells it innervates

mucocutaneous junction (myoo-ko-kyoo-TAY-nee-us JUNK-shun) the transitional area where the skin and mucous membrane meet

mucosa (myoo-KO-sah) mucous membrane

mucous membrane (MYOO-kus MEM-brane) epithelial membranes that line body surfaces opening directly to the exterior and secrete a thick, slippery material called *mucus*

mucus (MYOO-kus) thick, slippery material that is secreted by the mucous membrane and that keeps the membrane moist

multiple sclerosis (MS) (MUL-ti-pul skle-RO-sis) the most common primary disease of the central nervous system; a myelin disorder

muscle fiber (MUS-el FYE-ber) the specialized contractile cells of muscle tissue that are grouped together and arranged in a highly organized way

muscular system (MUS-kyoo-lar SIS-tem) the muscles of the body

muscularis (mus-kyoo-LAIR-is) two layers of muscle surrounding the digestive tube that produce wavelike, rhythmic contractions, called *peristalsis,* which move food material

myelin (MY-e-lin) lipoid substace found in the myelin sheath around some nerve fibers

myelinated fiber (MY-e-li-nay-ted FYE-ber) axons outside the central nervous system that are surrounded by a segmented wrapping of myelin

myeloid (MY-e-loyd) pertaining to bone marrow

myocardial infarction (my-o-KAR-dee-al in-FARK-shun) death of cardiac muscle cells resulting from inadequate blood supply as in coronary thrombosis

myocardium (my-o-KAR-dee-um) muscle of the heart

myofilaments (my-o-FIL-ah-ments) ultramicroscopic, threadlike structures found in myofibrils

myometrium (my-o-MEE-tree-um) muscle layer in the uterus

myopia (my-O-pee-ah) nearsightedness

myosin (MY-o-sin) contractile protein found in the thick filaments of skeletal muscle

myxedema (mik-se-DEE-mah) condition caused by deficiency of thyroid hormone in adults

nail body (nail BOD-ee) the visible part of the nail

nail root (nail root) the part of the nail that is hidden by the cuticle

nanometer (NAN-o-mee-ter) a measure of length in the metric system; one billionth of a meter

nares (NAY-reez) nostrils

nasal cavity (NAY-zal KAV-i-tee) the moist, warm cavities lined by mucosa located just beyond the nostrils; olfactory receptors are located in the mucosa

nasal septum (NAY-zal SEP-tum) a partition that separates the right and left nasal cavities

nasopharynx (nay-zo-FAIR-inks) the uppermost portion of the tube just behind the nasal cavities

neonatology (nee-o-nay-TOL-o-jee) diagnosis and treatment of disorders of the newborn infant

neoplasm (NEE-o-plazm) an abnormal mass of proliferating cells that may be either benign or malignant

nephritis (ne-FRY-tis) kidney disease; inflammation of the nephrons

nephron (NEF-ron) anatomical and functional unit of the kidney, consisting of the renal corpuscle and the renal tubule

nerve (nerv) collection of nerve fibers

nerve impulse (nerv IM-puls) signals that carry information along the nerves

nervous tissue (NER-vus TISH-yoo) consists of neurons and glia that provide rapid communication and control of body function

nucleic acids (noo-KLEE-ik AS-ids) the two nucleic acids are ribonucleic acid, found in the cytoplasm, and deoxyribonucleic acid, found in the nucleus

neurilemma (noo-ri-LEM-mah) nerve sheath

neurohypophysis (noo-ro-hye-POF-i-sis) posterior pituitary gland

neuromuscular junction (noo-ro-MUS-kyoo-lar JUNK-shun) the point of contact between the nerve endings and muscle fibers

neuron (NOO-ron) nerve cell, including its processes (axons and dendrites)

neurotransmitter (noo-ro-trans-MIT-ter) chemicals by which neurons communicate

neutrophil (NOO-tro-fils) white blood cell that stains readily with neutral dyes

nodes of Ranvier (nodes of rahn-vee-AY) indentations that are found between adjacent Schwann cells

norepinephrine (nor-ep-i-NEF-rin) hormone secreted by adrenal medulla; released by sympathetic nervous system

nose (noze) respiratory organ

nuclear envelope (NOO-klee-ar EN-vel-ope) membrane that surrounds the cell nucleus

nucleolus (noo-KLEE-o-lus) critical to protein formation because it "programs" the formation of ribosomes in the nucleus

nucleoplasm (NOO-klee-o-plazm) a special type of cytoplasm found in the nucleus

nucleus (NOO-klee-us) spherical structure within a cell; a group of neuron cell bodies in the brain or spinal cord

nutrition (noo-TRI-shun) food, vitamins, and minerals that are ingested and assimilated into the body

old age (old age) see *senescence*

olecranon fossa (o-LEK-rah-non FOS-ah) a large depression on the posterior surface of the humerus

olecranon process (o-LEK-rah-non PROSS-es) the large bony process of the ulna; commonly referred to as the tip of the elbow

olfaction (ol-FAK-shun) sense of smell

olfactory receptor (ol-FAK-tor-ee ree-SEP-tor) chemical receptors responsible for the sense of smell; located in the epithelial tissue in the upper part of the nasal cavity

oligodendroglia (ol-i-go-den-DROG-lee-ah) holds nerve fibers together and, more important, produces the myelin sheath around axons in the CNS

oliguria (ol-i-GOO-ree-ah) scanty amounts of urine

oocyte (O-o-site) immature stage of the female sex cell

oogenesis (o-o-JEN-e-sis) production of female gametes

oophorectomy (o-off-o-REK-toe-mee) surgical procedure to remove the ovaries

opposition (op-o-ZISH-un) moving the thumb to touch the tips of the fingers; the movement used to hold a pencil to write

optic disc (OP-tic disk) the area in the retina where the optic nerve fibers exit and there are no rods or cones; also known as a *blind spot*

oral cavity (OR-al KAV-i-tee) mouth

orbicularis oculi (or-bik-yoo-LAIR-is OK-yoo-lie) facial muscle that causes a squint

orbicularis oris (or-bik-yoo-LAIR-is O-ris) facial muscle that puckers the lips

organ (OR-gan) group of several tissue types that performs a special function

organelle (or-gah-NELL) cell organ; for example, the ribosome

organism (OR-gah-nizm) an individual living thing

organ of Corti (OR-gan of KOR-tee) the organ of hearing located in the cochlea and filled with endolymph

organogenesis (or-ga-no-JEN-e-sis) formation of organs from the primary germ layers of the embryo

origin (OR-i-jin) the attachment of a muscle to the bone that does not move when contraction occurs, as distinguished from insertion

oropharynx (o-ro-FAIR-inks) the portion of the pharynx that is located behind the mouth

osmosis (os-MO-sis) movement of a fluid through a semipermeable membrane

ossicles (OS-si-kls) little bones; found in the ears

osteoblast (OS-tee-o-blast) bone-forming cell

osteoclast (OS-tee-o-klast) bone-absorbing cell

osteocyte (OS-tee-o-site) bone cell

osteoporosis (os-tee-o-po-RO-sis) a bone disease where there is an excessive loss of calcified matrix and collagenous fibers from bone

otitis media (o-TIE-tis MEE-dee-ah) a middle ear infection

ova (O-vah) female sex cells (singular ovum)

oval window (O-val WIN-doe) a small, membrane-covered opening that separates the middle and inner ear

ovarian follicles (o-VARE-ee-an FOL-i-kuls) contain oocytes

ovaries (O-var-ees) female gonads that produce ova (sex cells)

overhydration (o-ver-hye-DRAY-shun) too large a fluid input that can put a burden on the heart

oviducts (O-vi-dukts) uterine or fallopian tubes

oxygen debt (OK-si-jen det) continued increased metabolism that occurs in a cell to remove excess lactic acid that resulted from exercise

oxyhemoglobin (ok-see-hee-mo-GLO-bin) hemoglobin combined with oxygen

oxytocin (ok-se-TOE-sin) hormone secreted by the posterior pituitary gland before and after delivering a baby; thought to initiate and maintain labor and it causes the release of breast milk into ducts for the baby to suck

pacemaker (PASE-may-ker) see *sinoatrial node*

pacinian corpuscle (pah-SIN-ee-an KOR-pus-ul) a receptor found deep in the dermis that detects pressure on the skin surface

palate (PAL-let) the roof of the mouth; made up of the hard (anterior portion of the mouth) and soft (posterior portion of the mouth) palates

palmar (PAHL-mar) palm of the hand

pancreas (PAN-kree-as) endocrine gland located in the abdominal cavity; contains pancreatic islets that secrete glucagon and insulin

pancreatic islets (pan-kree-AT-ik eye-LETS) endocrine portion of the pancreas; made up of alpha and beta cells among others

papillae (pah-PIL-ee) small, nipple-shaped elevations

paralysis (pah-RAL-i-sis) loss of the power of motion, especially voluntary motion

paranasal sinus (pair-ah-NAY-sal SYE-nus) four pairs of sinuses that have openings into the nose

parasympathetic nervous system (PNS) (par-ah-sim-pah-THE-tic NER-vus SIS-tem) part of the autonomic nervous system; ganglia are connected to the brain stem and the sacral segments of the spinal cord; controls many visceral effectors under normal conditions

parathyroid glands (pair-ah-THYE-royd glands) endocrine glands located in the neck on the posterior aspect of the thyroid gland; secrete parathyroid hormone

parathyroid hormone (PTH) (pair-ah-THYE-royd HOR-mone) hormone released by the parathryroid gland that increases the concentration of calcium in the blood

parietal (pah-RYE-i-tal) of the walls of an organ or cavity

parietal pericardium (pah-RYE-i-tal pair-i-KAR-dee-um) pericardium surrounding the heart like a loose-fitting sack to allow the heart enough room to beat

parietal portion (pah-RYE-i-tal POR-shun) serous membrane that lines the walls of a body cavity

parturition (par-too-RISH-un) act of giving birth

patella (pah-TEL-ah) small, shallow pan; the kneecap

pectoral girdle (PEK-toe-ral GIR-dul) shoulder girdle; the scapula and clavicle

pectoralis major (pek-tor-RAL-is MAY-jor) major flexor of the upper arm

pedal (PEED-al) foot

pelvic cavity (PEL-vik KAV-i-tee) the lower portion of the ventral cavity; the distal portion of the abdominopelvic cavity

pelvic girdle (PEL-vik GIR-dul) connects the legs to the trunk

pelvis (PEL-vis) basin or funnel-shaped structure

penis (PEE-nis) forms part of the male genitalia; when sexually aroused, becomes stiff to enable it to enter and deposit sperm in the vagina

pepsinogen (pep-SIN-o-jen) component of gastric juice that is converted into pepsin by hydrochloric acid

pericarditis (pair-i-kar-DYE-tis) when the pericardium becomes inflamed

pericardium (pair-i-KAR-dee-um) membrane that surrounds the heart

perilymph (PAIR-i-limf) a watery fluid that fills the bony labyrinth of the ear

perineal (pair-i-NEE-al) area between the anus and genitals; the perineum

perineum (pair-i-NEE-um) see *perineal*

periosteum (pair-i-OS-tee-um) tough, connective tissue covering the bone

peripheral (pe-RIF-er-al) pertaining to an outside surface

peripheral nervous system (PNS) (pe-RIF-er-al NER-vus SIS-tem) the nerves connecting the brain and spinal cord to other parts of the body

peristalsis (pair-i-STAL-sis) wavelike, rhythmic contractions of the stomach and intestines that move food material along the digestive tract

peritoneal space (pair-i-toe-NEE-al space) small, fluid-filled space between the visceral and parietal layers that allows the layers to slide over each other freely in the abdominopelvic cavity

peritoneum (pair-i-toe-NEE-um) large, moist, slippery sheet of serous membrane that lines the abdominopelvic cavity (parietal layer) and its organs (visceral layer)

peritonitis (pair-i-toe-NYE-tis) inflammation of the serous membranes in the abdominopelvic cavity; sometimes a serious complication of an infected appendix

permeable membrane (PER-mee-ah-bul MEM-brane) a membrane that allows passage of substances

pernicious anemia (per-NISH-us ah-NEE-mee-ah) deficiency of red blood cells due to a lack of vitamin B_{12}

peroneal muscles (per-o-NEE-al MUS-els) plantar flexors and evertors of the foot; the peroneus longus forms a support arch for the foot

perspiration (per-spi-RAY-shun) transparent, watery liquid released by glands in the skin that eliminates ammonia and uric acid and helps maintain body temperature; also known as *sweat*

phagocytes (FAG-o-sites) white blood cells that engulf microbes and digest them

phagocytosis (fag-o-sye-TOE-sis) ingestion and digestion of articles by a cell

phalanges (fah-LAN-jeez) the bones that make up the fingers and toes

pharynx (FAIR-inks) organ of the digestive and respiratory system; commonly called the *throat*

phospholipid (fos-fo-LIP-id) phosphate-containing fat molecule

photopigments (fo-toe-PIG-ments) chemicals in retinal cells that are sensitive to light

phrenic nerve (FREN-ik nerv) the nerve that stimulates the diaphragm to contract

physiology (fiz-ee-OL-o-jee) the study of body function

pia mater (PEE-ah MAH-ter) the vascular innermost covering (meninx) of the brain and spinal cord

pigment layer (PIG-ment LAY-er) the layer of the epidermis that contains the melanocytes that produce melanin to give skin its color

pineal gland (PI-nee-al gland) endocrine gland located in the third ventricle of the brain; produces melatonin

pinocytosis (pin-o-sye-TOE-sis) the active transport mechanism used to transfer fluids or dissolved substances into cells

pituitary gland (pi-TOO-i-tair-ee gland) endocrine gland located in the skull, made up of the adenohypophysis and the neurohypophysis

placenta (plah-SEN-tah) anchors the developing fetus to the uterus and provides a "bridge" for the exchange of nutrients and waste products between the mother and developing baby

plantar (PLAN-tar) pertaining to the sole of the foot

plantar flexion (PLAN-tar FLEK-shun) the bottom of the foot is directed downward; this motion allows a person to stand on his or her tip-toes

plasma (PLAZ-mah) the liquid part of the blood

plasma cells (PLAZ-mah sells) cells that secrete copious amounts of antibody into the blood

plasma membrane (PLAZ-mah MEM-brane) membrane that separates the contents of a cell from the tissue fluid; encloses the cytoplasm and forms the outer boundary of the cell

plasma protein (PLAZ-mah PRO-teen) any of several proteins normally found in the plasma; includes albumins, globulins, and fibrinogen

platelet plug (PLAYT-let plug) a temporary accumulation of platelets (thrombocytes) at the site of an injury; it precedes the formation of a blood clot

pleura (PLOOR-ah) the serous membrane in the thoracic cavity

pleural cavity (PLOOR-al KAV-i-tee) a subdivision of the thorax

pleural space (PLOOR-al space) the space between the visceral and parietal pleuras filled with just enough fluid to allow them to glide effortlessly with each breath

pleurisy (PLOOR-i-see) inflammation of the pleura

plica (PLYE-kah) multiple circular folds

pneumocystitis (noo-mo-sis-TYE-tis) a protozoan infection, most likely to invade the body when the immune system has been compromised

pneumothorax (noo-mo-THO-raks) accumulation of air in the pleural space, causing collapse of the lung

polycythemia (pol-ee-sye-THEE-mee-ah) an excessive number of red blood cells

polyuria (pol-ee-YOO-ree-ah) unusually large amounts of urine

pons (ponz) the part of the brain stem between the medulla oblongata and the midbrain

popliteal (pop-li-TEE-al) behind the knee

pore (pore) pinpoint-size openings on the skin that are outlets of small ducts from the eccrine sweat glands

posterior (pos-TEER-ee-or) located behind; opposite of anterior

posterior pituitary gland (pos-TEER-ee-or pi-TOO-i-tair-ee gland) neurohypophysis; hormones produced are ADH and oxytocin

posterior root ganglion (pos-TEER-ee-or GANG-lee-on) ganglion located near the spinal cord; where the neuron cell body of the dendrites of the sensory neuron is located

postganglionic neurons (post-gang-glee-ON-ik NOO-rons) autonomic neurons that conduct nerve impulses from a ganglion to cardiac or smooth muscle or glandular epithelial tissue

postnatal period (POST-nay-tal PEER-ee-od) the period after birth and ending at death

postsynaptic neuron (post-si-NAP-tik NOO-ron) a neuron situated distal to a synapse

posture (POS-chur) position of the body

precapillary sphincter (pree-CAP-pi-lair-ee SFINGK-ter) smooth muscle cells that guard the entrance to the capillary

preganglionic neurons (pree-gang-glee-ON-ik NOO-rons) autonomic neurons that conduct nerve impulses between the spinal cord and a ganglion

prenatal period (PREE-nay-tal PEER-i-od) the period after conception until birth
presbyopia (pres-bee-O-pee-ah) farsightedness of old age
presynaptic neuron (pree-si-NAP-tik NOO-ron) a neuron situated proximal to a synapse
primary follicles (PRYE-mare-ee FOL-i-kuls) the follicles present at puberty; covered with granulosa cells
primary germ layers (PRYE-mar-ee jerm LAY-ers) three layers of specialized cells that give rise to definite structures as the embryo develops
primary spermatocyte (PRY-mar-ee SPER-mah-toe-site) specialized cell that undergoes meiosis to ultimately form sperm
prime mover (prime MOO-ver) the muscle responsible for producing a particular movement
progesterone (pro-JES-ter-ohn) hormone produced by the corpus luteum; stimulates secretion of the uterine lining; with estrogen, helps to initiate the menstrual cycle in girls entering puberty
prolactin (pro-LAK-tin) hormone secreted by the anterior pituitary gland during pregnancy to stimulate the breast development needed for lactation
pronate (PRO-nate) to turn the palm downward
prone (prone) used to describe the body lying in a horizontal position facing downward
prophase (PRO-faze) first stage of mitosis during which chromosomes become visible
proprioceptors (pro-pree-o-SEP-tors) receptors located in the muscles, tendons, and joints; allows the body to recognize its position
prostaglandins (PGs) (pross-tah-GLAN-dins) a group of naturally occurring fatty acids that affect many body functions
prostatectomy (pross-tah-TEK-toe-mee) surgical removal of part or all of the prostate gland
prostate gland (PROSS-tate gland) lies just below the bladder; secretes a fluid that constitutes about 30% of the seminal fluid volume; helps activate sperm and helps them maintain motility
protease (PRO-tee-ase) protein-digesting enzyme
protein (PRO-teen) one of the basic nutrients needed by the body; usually involved with anabolism
protein hormone (PRO-teen HOR-mone) first messenger, provides communication between endocrine glands and target organs; triggers second messengers to affect the cell's activity
proteinuria (pro-teen-YOO-ree-ah) presence of abnormally high amounts of plasma protein in the urine; usually an indicator of kidney disease
prothrombin (pro-THROM-bin) a protein present in normal blood that is required for blood clotting
prothrombin activator (pro-THROM-bin AK-tiv-ayt-or) a protein formed by clotting factors from damaged tissue cells and platelets; it converts prothrombin into thrombin, a step essential to forming a blood clot
proximal (PROK-si-mal) next or nearest; located nearest the center of the body or the point of attachment of a structure
proximal convoluted tubule (PROK-si-mal kon-vo-LOO-ted TOOB-yool) the first segment of a renal tubule
pseudo (SOO-doe) false
pubis (PYOO-bis) joint in the midline between the two pubic bones
pulmonary artery (PUL-mo-nair-ee AR-ter-ee) artery that carries deoxygenated blood from the right ventricle to the lungs
pulmonary circulation (PUL-mo-nair-ee ser-kyoo-LAY-shun) venous blood flow from the right atrium to the lung and returning to the left atrium
pulmonary semilunar valve (PUL-mo-nair-ee sem-i-LOO-nar valv) valve located at the beginning of the pulmonary artery
pulmonary vein (PUL-mo-nair-ee vane) any vein that carries oxygenated blood from the lungs to the left atrium
pulmonary ventilation (PUL-mo-nair-ee ven-ti-LAY-shun) breathing; process that moves air in and out of the lungs
pupil (PYOO-pil) the opening in the center of the iris that regulates the amount of light entering the eye
purkinje fibers (pur-KIN-jee FYE-bers) specialized cells located in the walls of the ventricles; relay nerve impulses from the AV node to the ventricles causing them to contract
P wave (P wave) deflection on an ECG that occurs with depolarization of the atria
pyloric sphincter (pye-LOR-ik SFINGK-ter) sphincter that prevents food from leaving the stomach and entering the duodenum
pylorus (pye-LOR-us) the small narrow section of the stomach that joins the first part of the small intestine
pyramids (PEER-ah-mids) triangular-shaped divisions of the medulla of the kidney
QRS complex (QRS KOM-pleks) deflection on an ECG that occurs as a result of depolarization of the ventricles
quadriceps femoris (KWOD-re-seps fe-MOR-is) extensor of the lower leg
quickening (KWIK-en-ing) when a pregnant woman first feels recognizable movements of the fetus
radiation (ray-dee-AY-shun) flow of heat waves away from the blood
radius (RAY-dee-us) one of the two bones in the forearm; located on the thumb side of the forearm
reabsorption (ree-ab-SORP-shun) process of absorbing again that occurs in the kidneys
receiving chambers (ree-SEE-ving CHAM-bers) atria of the heart; receive blood from the superior and inferior vena cava
receptor (ree-SEP-tor) peripheral beginning of a sensory neuron's dendrite
rectum (REK-tum) distal portion of the large intestine
rectus abdominis (REK-tus ab-DOM-i-nis) muscle that runs down the middle of the abdomen; protects the abdominal viscera and flexes the spinal column
reflex (REE-fleks) involuntary action
reflex arc (REE-fleks ark) allows an impulse to travel in only one direction
reflux (REE-fluhks) back flow, as in flow of stomach contents back into esophagus
refraction (ree-FRAK-shun) bending of a ray of light as it passes from a medium of one density to one of a different density
releasing hormones (ree-LEE-sing HOR-mones) hormone produced by the hypothalamus gland that causes the anterior pituitary gland to release its hormones
renal calculi (REE-nal KAL-kyoo-lie) kidney stones

renal colic (REE-nal KOL-ik) pain caused by the passage of a kidney stone

renal corpuscle (REE-nal KOR-pus-ul) the part of the nephron located in the cortex of the kidney

renal pelvis (REE-nal PEL-vis) basinlike upper end of the ureter that is located inside the kidney

renal tubule (REE-nal TOOB-yool) one of the two principal parts of the nephron

repolarization (ree-po-lah-ri-ZAY-shun) begins just before the relaxation phase of cardiac muscle activity

reproductive system (ree-pro-DUK-tiv SIS-tem) produces hormones that permit the development of sexual characteristics and the propagation of the species

residual volume (RV) (re-ZID-yoo-al VOL-yoom) the air that remains in the lungs after the most forceful expiration

respiratory acidosis (RES-pi-rah-tor-ee as-i-DOE-sis) a respiratory disturbance that results in a carbonic acid excess

respiratory alkalosis (RES-pi-rah-tor-ee al-kah-LO-sis) a respiratory disturbance that results in a carbonic acid deficit

respiratory arrest (RES-pi-rah-tor-ee ah-REST) cessation of breathing without resumption

respiratory control centers (RES-pi-rah-tor-ee kon-TROL SEN-ters) centers located in the medulla and pons that stimulate the muscles of respiration

respiratory membrane (RES-pi-rah-tor-ee MEM-brane) the single layer of cells that makes up the wall of the alveoli

respiratory mucosa (RES-pi-rah-tor-ee myoo-KO-sah) mucus-covered membrane that lines the tubes of the respiratory tree

respiratory muscles (RES-pi-rah-tor-ee MUS-els) muscles that are responsible for the changing shape of the thoracic cavity that allows air to move in and out of the lungs

respiratory system (re-SPY-rah-tor-ee SIS-tem) the organs that allow the exchange of oxygen from the air with the carbon dioxide from the blood

respiratory tract (RES-pi-rah-tor-ee trakt) the two divisions of the respiratory system are the upper and lower respiratory tracts

reticular formation (re-TIK-yoo-lar for-MAY-shun) located in the medulla where bits of gray and white matter mix intricately

retina (RET-i-nah) innermost layer of the eyeball; contains rods and cones and continues posteriorly with the optic nerve

retroperitoneal (re-tro-pair-i-toe-NEE-al) area outside of the peritoneum

Rh-negative (R H NEG-ah-tiv) red blood cells that do not contain the antigen called *Rh factor*

RhoGAM (RO-gam) an injection of a special protein given to an Rh-negative woman who is pregnant to prevent her body from forming anti-Rh antibodies, which may harm an Rh-positive baby

Rh-positive (R H POZ-i-tiv) red blood cells that contain an antigen called *Rh factor*

ribonucleic acid (RNA) (rye-bo-noo-KLEE-ik AS-id) a nucleic acid found in the cytoplasm that is crucial to protein synthesis

ribosome (RYE-bo-sohm) organelle in the cytoplasm of cells that synthesizes proteins; also known as a protein factory

rods (rods) receptors located in the retina that are responsible for night vision

rotation (ro-TAY-shun) movement around a longitudinal axis; for example, shaking your head "no"

rugae (ROO-gee) wrinkles or folds; singular: ruga (ROO-gah)

"rule of nines" a frequently used method to determine the extent of a burn injury; the body is divided into 11 areas of 9% each to help estimate the amount of skin surface burned in an adult

sagittal (SAJ-i-tal) longitudinal; like an arrow

salivary amylase (SAL-i-vair-ee AM-i-lase) digestive enzyme found in the saliva that begins the chemical digestion of carbohydrates

saltatory conduction (SAL-tah-tor-ee kon-DUK-shun) when a nerve impulse encounters myelin and "jumps" from one node of Ranvier to the next

sarcomere (SAR-ko-meer) contractile unit of muscle; length of a myofibril between two Z bands

scapula (SKAP-yoo-lah) shoulder blade

Schwann cells (shwon sells) large nucleated cells that form myelin

sclera (SKLE-rah) white outer coat of the eyeball

scrotum (SKRO-tum) pouchlike sac that contains the testes

sebaceous gland (se-BAY-shus gland) oil-producing glands found in the skin

sebum (SEE-bum) secretion of sebaceous glands

secondary sexual characteristics (SEK-on-dair-ee SEK-shoo-al kair-ak-ter-IS-tiks) sexual characteristics that appear at the onset of puberty

second messenger (SEK-und MES-en-jer) provide communication within a hormone's target cell; for example, cyclic AMP

sella turcica (SEL-lah TER-si-kah) small depression of the sphenoid bone that contains the pituitary gland

semen (SEE-men) male reproductive fluid

semicircular canals (sem-i-SIR-kyoo-lar kah-NALS) located in the inner ear; contains a specialized receptor called *crista ampullaris* that generates a nerve impulse on movement of the head

semilunar valves (sem-i-LOO-nar valvs) valves located between the two ventricular chambers and the large arteries that carry blood away from the heart; valves found in the veins

seminal fluid (SEM-i-nal FLOO-id) semen

seminal vesicle (SEM-i-nal VES-i-kul) paired, pouchlike glands that contribute about 60% of the seminal fluid volume; rich in fructose, which is a source of energy for sperm

seminiferous tubule (se-mi-NIF-er-us TOOB-yool) long, coiled structure that forms the bulk of the testicular mass

senescence (se-NES-enz) older adulthood; aging

sensory neurons (SEN-sor-ee NOO-rons) neurons that transmit impulses to the spinal cord and brain from all parts of the body

serosa (se-RO-sah) outermost covering of the digestive tract; composed of the parietal pleura in the abdominal cavity

serotonin (sair-o-TOE-nin) a neurotransmitter that belongs to a group of compounds called *catecholamines*

serous membrane (SE-rus MEM-brane) a two-layered epithelial membrane that lines body cavities and covers the surfaces of organs

serum (SEER-um) blood plasma minus its clotting factors, still contains antibodies

shingles (SHING-guls) see *herpes zoster*
sickle cell anemia (SIK-ul sell ah-NEE-mee-ah) severe, possibly fatal, hereditary disease caused by an abnormal type of hemoglobin
sickle cell trait (SIK-ul sell trate) when only one defective gene is inherited and only a small amount of hemoglobin that is less soluble than usual is produced
sigmoid colon (SIG-moyd KO-lon) S-shaped segment of the large intestine that terminates in the rectum
sinoatrial (SA) node (sye-no-AY-tree-al node) the heart's pacemaker; where the impulse conduction of the heart normally starts; located in the wall of the right atrium near the opening of the superior vena cava
sinus (SYE-nus) a space or cavity inside some of the cranial bones
sinusitis (sye-nyoo-SYE-tis) sinus infections
skeletal muscle (SKEL-e-tal MUS-el) also known as *voluntary muscle;* muscles under willed or voluntary control
skeletal system (SKEL-e-tal SIS-tem) the bones, cartilage, and ligaments that provide the body with a rigid framework for support and protection
smooth muscle (smooth MUS-el) muscles that are not under conscious control; also known as *involuntary* or *visceral;* forms the walls of blood vessels and hollow organs
sodium-potassium pump (SO-dee-um po-TAS-ee-um pump) a system of coupled ion pumps that actively transports sodium ions out of a cell and potassium ions into the cell at the same time—found in all living cells
solute (SOL-yoot) dissolved particles in water
somatic nervous system (so-MA-tik NER-vus SIS-tem) the motor neurons that control the voluntary actions of skeletal muscles
specific immunity (spe-SI-fik i-MYOON-i-tee) the protective mechanisms that provide specific protection against certain types of bacteria or toxins
sperm (sperm) the male spermatazoon; sex cell
spermatids (SPER-mah-tids) the resulting daughter cells from the primary spermatocyte undergoing meiosis; these cells have only half the genetic material and half the chromosomes of other body cells
spermatogenesis (sper-mah-toe-JEN-e-sis) the production of sperm cells
spermatogonia (sper-mah-toe-GO-nee-ah) sperm precursor cells
spermatozoa (sper-mah-tah-ZO-ah) sperm cells (singular: spermatozoon)
sphincter (SFINGK-ter) ring-shaped muscle
spinal cavity (SPY-nal KAV-i-tee) the space inside the spinal column through which the spinal cord passes
spinal nerves (SPY-nal nervs) nerves that connect the spinal cord to peripheral structures such as the skin and skeletal muscles
spinal tracts (SPY-nal tracts) the white columns of the spinal cord that provide two-way conduction paths to and from the brain; ascending tract carries information to the brain, whereas descending tracts conduct impulses from the brain
spindle fiber (SPIN-dul FYE-ber) a network of tubules formed in the cytoplasm between the centrioles as they are moving away from each other
spirometer (spi-ROM-e-ter) an instrument used to measure the amount of air exchanged in breathing
spleen (spleen) largest lymphoid organ; filters blood, destroys worn out red blood cells, salvages iron from hemoglobin, and serves as a blood resevoir
splenectomy (splen-NEK-toe-mee) surgical removal of the spleen
splenic flexure (SPLEEN-ik FLEK-shur) where the descending colon turns downward on the left side of the abdomen
spongy bone (SPUN-jee bone) porous bone in the end of the long bone, may be filled with marrow
squamous (SKWAY-mus) scalelike
squamous suture (SKWAY-mus SOO-chur) the immovable joint between the temporal bone and the sphenoid bone
stapes (STAY-peez) tiny, stirrup-shaped bone in the middle ear
Stensen's ducts (STEN-sens dukts) the ducts of the parotid gland as they enter the mouth
sternoclavicular joint (ster-no-klah-VIK-yoo-lar joynt) the direct point of attachment between the bones of the upper extremity and the axial skeleton
sternocleidomastoid (stern-o-klye-doe-MAS-toyd) "strap" muscle located on the anterior aspect of the neck
steroid hormones (STE-royd HOR-mones) lipid-soluble hormones that pass intact through the cell membrane of the target cell and influence cell activity by acting on specific genes
stimulus (STIM-yoo-lus) agent that causes a change in the activity of a structure
stoma (STO-mah) an opening, such as the opening created in a colostomy procedure
stomach (STUM-ak) an expansion of the digestive tract between the esophagus and small intestine
stratum corneum (STRA-tum KOR-nee-um) the tough outer layer of the epidermis; cells are filled with keratin
stratum germinativum (STRA-tum JER-mi-nah-tiv-um) the innermost of the tightly packed epithelial cells of the epidermis; cells in this layer are able to reproduce themselves
strength training (strength TRAIN-ing) contracting muscles against resistance to enhance muscle hypertrophy
striated muscle (STRYE-ay-ted MUS-el) see *skeletal muscle*
stroke volume (stroke VOL-yoom) the amount of blood that is ejected from the ventricles of the heart with each beat
subcutaneous tissue (sub-kyoo-TAY-nee-us TISH-yoo) tissue below the layers of skin; made up of loose connective tissue and fat
submucosa (sub-myoo-KO-sah) connective tissue layer containing blood vessels and nerves in the wall of the digestive tract
sudoriferous gland (soo-doe-RIF-er-us gland) glands that secrete sweat; also referred as *sweat glands*
sulcus (SUL-kus) furrow or groove
superficial (soo-per-FISH-al) near the body surface
superior (soo-PEER-ee-or) higher, opposite of inferior
superior vena cava (soo-PEER-ee-or VEE-nah KAY-vah) one of two large veins returning deoxygenated blood to the right atrium
supinate (SOO-pi-nate) to turn the palm of the hand upward; opposite of pronate
supine (SOO-pine) used to describe the body lying in a horizontal position facing upward

supraclavicular (soo-prah-cla-VIK-yoo-lar) area above the clavicle

surfactant (sur-FAK-tant) a substance covering the surface of the respiratory membrane inside the alveolus, which reduces surface tension and prevents the alveoli from collapsing

suture (SOO-chur) immovable joint

sweat (swet) transparent, watery liquid released by glands in the skin that eliminates ammonia and uric acid and helps maintain body temperature; also known as *perspiration*

sympathetic nervous system (sim-pah-THE-tik NER-vus SIS-tem) part of the autonomic nervous system; ganglia are connected to the thoracic and lumbar regions of the spinal cord; functions as an emergency system

sympathetic postganglionic neurons (sim-pah-THE-tik post-gang-glee-ON-ik NOO-rons) dendrites and cell bodies are in sympathetic ganglia and axons travel to a variety of visceral effectors

sympathetic preganglionic neurons (sim-pah-THE-tik pree-gang-glee-ON-ik NOO-rons) dendrites and cell bodies are located in the gray matter of the thoracic and lumbar segments of the spinal cord; leaves the cord through an anterior root of a spinal nerve and terminates in a collateral ganglion

synapse (SIN-aps) junction between adjacent neurons

synaptic cleft (si-NAP-tik kleft) the space between a synaptic knob and the plasma membrane of a postsynaptic neuron

synaptic knob (si-NAP-tik nob) a tiny bulge at the end of a terminal branch of a presynaptic neuron's axon that contains vesicles with neurotransmitters

synarthrosis (sin-ar-THRO-sis) a joint in which fibrous connective tissue joins bones and holds them together tightly; commonly called *sutures*

synergist (SIN-er-jists) muscle that assists a prime mover

synovial fluid (si-NO-vee-al FLOO-id) the thick, colorless lubricating fluid secreted by the synovial membrane

synovial membrane (si-NO-vee-al MEM-brane) connective tissue membrane lining the spaces between bones and joints that secretes synovial fluid

system (SIS-tem) group of organs arranged so that the group can perform a more complex function than any one organ can perform alone

systemic circulation (sis-TEM-ik ser-kyoo-LAY-shun) blood flow from the left ventricle to all parts of the body and back to the right atrium

systole (SIS-toe-lee) contraction of the heart muscle

target organ cell (TAR-get OR-gan sell) organ or cell acted on by a particular hormone and responding to it

tarsals (TAR-sals) seven bones of the heel and back part of the foot; the calcaneus is the largest

taste buds (taste buds) chemical receptors that generate nerve impulses, resulting in the sense of taste

telophase (TEL-o-faze) last stage of mitosis in which the cell divides

temporal (TEM-po-ral) muscle that assists the masseter in closing the jaw

tendons (TEN-dons) bands or cords of fibrous connective tissue that attach a muscle to a bone or other structure

tendon sheath (TEN-don sheeth) tube-shaped structure lined with synovial membrane that encloses certain tendons

tenosynovitis (ten-o-sin-o-VYE-tis) inflammation of a tendon sheath

testes (TES-teez) male gonads that produce the male sex cells or sperm

testosterone (tes-TOS-te-rone) male sex hormone produced by the interstitial cells in the testes; the "masculinizing hormone"

tetanic contraction (te-TAN-ik kon-TRAK-shun) sustained contraction

tetanus (TET-ah-nus) sustained muscular contraction

thalamus (THAL-ah-mus) located just above the hypothalamus; its functions are to help produce sensations, associates sensations with emotions and plays a part in the arousal mechanism

thermoregulation (ther-mo-reg-yoo-LAY-shun) maintaining homeostasis of body temperature

thoracic duct (thor-AS-ik dukt) largest lymphatic vessel in the body

thorax (THOR-aks) chest

threshold stimulus (THRESH-hold STIM-yoo-lus) minimal level of stimulation required to cause a muscle fiber to contract

thrombin (THROM-bin) protein important in blood clotting

thrombocytes (THROM-bo-sites) also called *platelets;* play a role in blood clotting

thrombosis (throm-BO-sis) formation of a clot in a blood vessel

thrombus (THROM-bus) stationary blood clot

thymosin (THY-mo-sin) hormone produced by the thymus that is vital to the development and functioning of the body's immune system

thymus gland (THY-mus gland) endocrine gland located in the mediastinum; vital part of the body's immune system

thyroid gland (THY-royd gland) endocrine gland located in the neck that stores its hormones until needed; thyroid hormones regulate cellular metabolism

thyroid-stimulating hormone (TSH) (THY-royd STIM-yoo-lay-ting HOR-mone) a tropic hormone secreted by the anterior pituitary gland that stimulates the thyroid gland to increase its secretion of thyroid hormone

thyroxine (T_4) (thy-ROK-sin) thyroid hormone that stimulates cellular metabolism

tibia (TIB-ee-ah) shinbone

tibialis anterior (tib-ee-AL-is an-TEER-ee-or) dorsiflexor of the foot

tidal volume (TV) (TIE-dal VOL-yoom) amount of air breathed in and out with each breath

tissue (TISH-yoo) group of similar cells that perform a common function

tissue fluid (TISH-yoo FLOO-id) a dilute salt water solution that bathes every cell in the body

tissue hormone (TISH-yoo HOR-mone) prostaglandins; produced in a tissue and only diffuses a short distance to act on cells within the tissue

tissue typing (TISH-yoo TIE-ping) a procedure used to identify tissue compatability before an organ transplant

T-lymphocytes (T LIM-fo-sites) cells that are critical to the function of the immune system; produce cell-mediated immunity

tonic contraction (TON-ik kon-TRAK-shun) special type of skeletal muscle contraction used to maintain posture

tonsillectomy (ton-si-LEK-toe-mee) surgical procedure used to remove the tonsils

tonsillitis (ton-si-LIE-tis) an inflammation of the tonsils

tonsils (TON-sils) masses of lymphoid tissue; protect against bacteria; three types: palatine tonsils, located on each side of the throat; pharyngeal tonsils (adenoids), near the posterior opening of the nasal cavity; and lingual tonsils, near the base of the tongue

total metabolic rate (TMR) (TOE-tal met-ah-BOL-ik rate) total amount of energy used by the body per day

trabeculae (trah-BEK-yoo-lee) needlelike threads of spongy bone that surround a network of spaces

trachea (TRAY-kee-ah) the windpipe; the tube extending from the larynx to the bronchi

transcription (trans-KRIP-shun) when the double stranded DNA molecules unwind and form mRNA

translation (trans-LAY-shun) the synthesis of a protein by ribosomes

transverse arch (TRANS-vers arch) see *metatarsal arch*

transversus abdominis (trans-VER-sus ab-DOM-i-nis) the innermost layer of the anterolateral abdominal wall

trapezium (trah-PEE-zee-um) the carpal bone of the wrist that forms the saddle joint that allows the opposition of the thumb

trapezius (trah-PEE-zee-us) triangular muscle in the back that elevates the shoulder and extends the head backwards

triceps brachii (TRY-seps BRAY-kee-eye) extensor of the elbow

tricuspid valve (try-KUS-pid valv) the valve located between the right atrium and ventricle

trigone (TRY-gon) triangular area on the wall of the urinary bladder

triiodothyonine (T_3) (try-eye-o-doe-THY-ro-nine) thyroid hormone that stimulates cellular metabolism

tropic hormone (TRO-pik HOR-mone) hormone that stimulates another endocrine gland to grow and secrete its hormones

true ribs (troo ribs) the first seven pairs of ribs that are attached to the sternum

tumor (TOO-mer) growth of tissues in which cell proliferation is uncontrolled and progressive

tunica adventitia (TOO-ni-kah ad-ven-TISH-ah) the outermost layer found in blood vessels

tunica albuginea (TOO-ni-kah al-byoo-JIN-ee-ah) a tough, whitish membrane that surrounds each testis and enters the gland to divide it into lobules

tunica intima (TOO-ni-kah IN-tih-mah) endothelium that lines the blood vessels

tunica media (TOO-ni-kah MEE-dee-ah) the muscular middle layer found in blood vessels; the tunica media of arteries is more muscular than that of veins

T wave (T wave) deflection on an electrocardiogram that occurs with repolarization of the ventricles

twitch (twitch) a quick, jerky response to a single stimulus

tympanic (tim-PAN-ik) drumlike

ulcer (UL-ser) a necrotic open sore or lesion

ulna (UL-nah) one of the two forearm bones; located on the little finger side

ultrasonogram (ul-tra-SOHN-o-gram) a technique using sound to produce images

umbilical artery (um-BIL-i-kul AR-ter-ee) two small arteries that carry oxygen-poor blood from the developing fetus to the placenta

umbilical cord (um-BIL-i-kul cord) flexible structure connecting the fetus with the placenta, which allows the umbilical arteries and vein to pass

umbilical vein (um-BIL-i-kul vane) a large vein carrying oxygen-rich blood from the placenta to the developing fetus

urea (yoo-REE-ah) nitrogen-containing waste product

uremia (yoo-REE-mee-ah) high levels of nitrogen-containing waste products in the blood; also referred to as *uremic poisoning*

uremic poisoning (yoo-REE-mik POY-zon-ing) see *uremia*

urethra (yoo-REE-thrah) passageway for elimination of urine; in males, also acts as a genital duct that carries sperm to the exterior

urinary meatus (YOOR-i-nair-ee mee-AY-tus) external opening of the urethra

urinary system (YOOR-i-nair-ee SIS-tem) system responsible for excreting liquid waste from the body

urination (yoor-i-NAY-shun) passage of urine from the body; emptying of the bladder

urine (YOOR-in) fluid waste excreted by the kidneys

uterus (YOO-ter-us) hollow, muscular organ where a fertilized egg implants and grows

uvula (YOO-vyoo-lah) cone-shaped process hanging down from the soft palate that helps prevent food and liquid from entering the nasal cavities

vagina (vah-JYE-nah) internal tube from uterus to vulva

vas deferens (vas DEF-er-enz) see *ductus deferens*

vastus (VAS-tus) wide; of great size

vein (vane) vessel carrying blood toward the heart

ventral (VEN-tral) of or near the belly; in humans, front or anterior; opposite of dorsal or posterior

ventricles (VEN-tri-kuls) small cavities

venule (VEN-yool) small blood vessels that collect blood from the capillaries and join to form veins

vermiform appendix (VERM-i-form ah-PEN-diks) a tubular structure attached to the cecum composed of lymphatic tissue

vertebrae (VER-te-bray) bones that make up the spinal column

vertebral column (ver-TEE-bral KOL-um) the spinal column, made up of a series of separate vertebrae that form a flexible, curved rod

vestibular nerve (ves-TIB-yoo-lar nerv) a division of the vestibulocochlear nerve (the eighth cranial nerve)

vestibule (VES-ti-byool) located in the inner ear; the portion adjacent to the oval window between the semicircular canals and the cochlea

villi (VIL-eye) fingerlike folds covering the plicae of the small intestines

visceral pericardium (VIS-er-al pair-i-KAR-dee-um) the pericardium that covers the heart

visceral portion (VIS-er-al POR-shun) serous membrane that covers the surface of organs found in the body cavity

vital capacity (VC) (VYE-tal kah-PAS-i-tee) largest amount of air that can be moved in and out of the lungs in one inspiration and expiration

vitamins (VYE-tah-mins) organic molecules needed in small quantities to help enzymes operate effectively

vitreous humor (VIT-ree-us HYOO-mor) the jellylike fluid found in the eye, posterior to the lens

voiding (VOYD-ing) emptying of the bladder
volar (VO-lar) palm or sole
voluntary muscle (VOL-un-tair-ee MUS-el) see *skeletal muscle*
vulva (VUL-vah) external genitals of the female
white matter (wite MAT-er) nerves covered with white myelin
withdrawl reflex (with-DRAW-al REE-fleks) a reflex that moves a body part away from an irritating stimulus
yolk sac (yoke sak) in humans, involved with the production of blood cells in the developing embryo
zona fasciculata (ZO-nah fas-sic-yoo-LAY-tah) middle zone of the adrenal cortes that secretes glucocorticoids
zona glomerulosa (ZO-nah glo-mare-yoo-LO-sah) outer zone of the adrenal cortex that secretes mineralocorticoids
zona reticularis (ZO-nah re-tik-yoo-LAIR-is) inner zone of the adrenal cortex that secretes small amounts of sex hormones
zygomaticus (zye-go-MAT-ik-us) muscle that elevates the corners of the mouth and lips; also known as the *smiling muscle*
zygote (ZYE-gote) a fertilized ovum

Illustration/Photo Credits

Chapter 1: 1-1, 1-4, 1-8, 1-9, Rolin Graphics; 1-2, Terry Cockerham/Synapse Media Production; 1-3, 1-5, 1-6, Joan Beck; 1-7, Cynthia Alexander Turner/Terry Cockerham/Synapse Media Production/Christine Oleksyk.

Chapter 2: 2-1, 2-2, William Ober; 2-3, Lennart Nilsson; 2-4, 2-6, Tonicity box, Table 2-2, Table 2-3, Rolin Graphics; 2-5, 2-8, Joan Beck; 2-9, 2-10, 2-11, 2-12, 2-14, 2-19, 2-20, Edward Reschke; 2-13, courtesy of S. Erlandsen (from *Color Atlas of Histology,* 1992, Mosby); 2-15, 2-16, 2-18, 2-21, Phototake; 2-17, 2-22, Robert Callentine.

Chapter 3: 3-2, 3-3, 3-4, 3-5, 3-6, 3-7, 3-8, 3-9, 3-10, 3-11, 3-12, 3-13, Joan Beck.

Chapter 4: 4-1A,B, 4-2, 4-6A,B, Rolin Graphics; 4-3, Edward Reschke; 4-4, 4-7A,B, Christine Oleksyk; 4-5, David Scharf/Peter Arnold, Inc.; 4-8, Joan Beck; Home Health Care box, courtesy of Potter/Perry (from *Fundamentals of Nursing,* 1993, Mosby).

Chapter 5: 5-1, Joan Beck; 5-2, Laurie O'Keefe/John Daugherty; 5-3, Phototake; 5-5, Stephen Oh; 5-6, Network Graphics; 5-7A,B, David J. Mascaro & Associates; 5-8, 5-9, 5-10, 5-13A,B, 5-14 (Drawing), 5-15A, 5-15C, 5-16, 5-19, Ernest W. Beck; 5-11, Ron Edwards; 5-12, 5-13C, 5-14 (Photo), 5-15B, 5-15D, courtesy of B. Vidic and F.R. Suarez (from *Photographic Atlas of the Human Body,* 1984, Mosby); 5-17, Yvonne Wylie Walston; 5-18, Christine Oleksyk; 5-20, David J. Mascaro & Associates; 5-21, The Knee Joint box (Drawing), Rolin Graphics; Epiphyseal Fracture box, J.M. Booher and G.A. Thibodeau: *Athletic Injury Assessment,* St. Louis, 1985, Mosby; Palpable Bony Landmarks box, Terry Cockerham/Synapse Media Production; The Knee Joint box (Photo), Stewart Halpernin.

Chapter 6: 6-1A-C, Christine Oleksyk; 6-2, Network Graphics; 6-3A, Barbara Cousins/Rolin Graphics; 6-3B, courtesy of Dr. H.E. Huxley; 6-4, courtesy of S. Erlandsen and J. Magney (from *Color Atlas of Histology,* 1992, Mosby); 6-5A,B, 6-9A, 6-9C, 6-10A, 6-10C, Rolin Graphics; 6-6A,B, 6-7, 6-8, Intramuscular Injections box, John V. Hagen; 6-9B, 6-10B, 6-11A, 6-11C, 6-11D, Terry Cockerham/Synapse Media Production; 6-11B, Patrick Watson.

Chapter 7: 7-2A,B, 7-13, 7-16, 7-20, Rolin Graphics; 7-2C, Edward Reschke; 7-4 (Drawing), 7-7, Laurie O'Keefe/John Daugherty; 7-4 (Photo), courtesy of H.L. McCance and S. Huether (from *Pathophysiology,* 1991, Mosby); 7-5, 7-15, Barbara Cousins; 7-6A, 7-8, 7-19, Joan Beck; 7-6B, 7-15 (inset), 7-17, Herpes Zoster box (art), Network Graphics; 7-3, Barbara Cousins; 7-6 (inset), 7-14, Scott Bodell; 7-9A, 7-10A,B, William Ober; 7-9B, 7-10 (inset), 7-11 (Photo), courtesy of B. Vidic and F.R. Suarez (from *Photographic Atlas of the Human Body,* 1984, Mosby); 7-11 (Drawing), George Wassilchenko; 7-12, Christine Oleksyk; 7-18, Raychel Ciemma; Herpes Zoster box (Photo), courtesy of Thomas P. Habif (from *Clinical Dermatology,* ed. 2, 1990, Mosby).

Chapter 8: 8-1, 8-3, Christine Oleksyk; 8-2, George Wassilchenko; 8-4, Ernest W. Beck; 8-5, Table 8-1, Rolin Graphics; 8-6, 8-7A-C, Focusing on Problems box A-D, Table 8-1 (Muscle Spindles), Table 8-1 (Golgi Tendon Receptors), Network Graphics; Color Blindness box, courtesy of Ishihara (from *Tests for Colour Blindness,* Tokyo, Japan, 1973, Kanehara Shuppan Co., Ltd. provided by Washington University Department of Ophthalmology), 8-8, Joan Beck.

Chapter 9: 9-1, Joan Beck; 9-2, 9-3, Network Graphics; 9-4, 9-8, Rolin Graphics; 9-5, Barbara Cousins; 9-6, 9-9, 9-11, Ernest W. Beck; 9-10, Graphic Works; Thyroid Hormone Abnormalities box (A), Seidel, et. al. (from *Mosby's Guide to Physical Examination,* ed. 3, 1995, Mosby); Thyroid Hormone Abnormalities box (B), L.V. Bergman & Associates, Inc., Cold Springs, New York; Adrenal Hormone Abnormalities box, courtesy of Gower Medical Publishers.

Chapter 10: 10-1, Barbara Cousins; 10-2, Sickle Cell Anemia box, courtesy of G. Bevelander and J.A. Ramaley (from *Essentials of Histology,* ed. 8, Mosby); 10-3, 10-7, Rolin Graphics; 10-4A-E, courtesy of S. Erlandsen and J. Magney (from *Color Atlas of Histology,* 1992, Mosby); 10-5, courtesy of A. Arlan Hinchee; 10-6, Laurie O'Keefe/John Daugherty; 10-8, Molly Babich/John Daugherty; Table 10-1, Ernest W. Beck.

Chapter 11: 11-1, 11-7A, Ernest W. Beck; 11-2, Rusty Jones; 11-2 (inset), 11-3A,B (bottom), George J. Wassilchenko; 11-3A,B (top), Christine Oleksyk; 11-4, 11-8, 11-9, Barbara Cousins; 11-5, Joan M. Beck; 11-6, Lisa Shoemaker/Joan M. Beck; 10-10, Karen Waldo; 11-11, Rolin Graphics; 11-12, 11-15, Network Graphics; 11-13, Molly Babich; Blood Pressure Readings box, Joan M. Beck/Donna Odle.

Chapter 12: 12-1, 12-4, Joan Beck; 12-2, G. David Brown; 12-5, George Wassilchenko; 12-6, 12-11, 12-12, Rolin Graphics; 12-8, 12-9, Network Graphics; 12-10, courtesy of Emma Shelton; 12-13, courtesy of Dr. James T. Barrett.

Chapter 13: 13-1, 13-2, Heimlich Maneuver box, Joan M. Beck; 13-4, Margaret Gerrity; 13-5, George J. Wassilchenko; 13-6A, Ernest W. Beck; 13-6B, Christine Oleksyk; 13-6C, Custom Medical Stock Photos; 13-7 (Drawing), Lisa Shoemaker/Joan M. Beck; 13-7 (Photo), courtesy of S. Erlandsen and J. Magney (from *Color Atlas of Histology,* 1992, Mosby); 13-8, 13-14 (heart and lungs), Network Graphics; 13-9, 13-12, Rolin Graphics; 13-11, John Daugherty; 13-14 (inset and brain stem), William Ober.

Chapter 14: 14-1, Lisa Shoemaker; 14-2, Bill Ober; 14-3, 14-4, Table 14-2, 14-7, Rolin Graphics; 14-5, 14-6, 14-9, 14-10, 14-12, Ernest W. Beck; 14-8, G. David Brown; 14-11, courtesy of B. Vidic and F.R. Suarez (from *Photographic Atlas of the Human Body,* 1984, Mosby); 14-13, CNRI Science Photo Library/Photo Researchers; 14-14, Michael P. Schenck; Colostomy box, Network Graphics.

Chapter 15: 15-1, 15-5, Network Graphics; 15-2, 15-3, 15-4, Rolin Graphics.

Chapter 16: 16-1A, 16-3A, Christine Oleksyk; 16-1B, courtesy of Patricia Kane, University of Indiana Medical School; 16-2, David J. Mascaro; 16-3B, Dr. Andrew P. Evan, University of Indiana; 16-4, 16-8, Ernest W. Beck; 16-5, Rolin Graphics; 16-6, courtesy of Potter/Perry (*Fundamentals of Nursing,* 1993, Mosby); 16-7, courtesy of G. Bevelander and J.A. Ramaley (from *Essentials of Histology,* ed. 8, Mosby); Artificial Kidney box (Photo), Pat Watson; Artificial Kidney box (Art), Barbara Stackhouse.

Chapter 17: 17-1 (right), 17-2, Rolin Graphics; 17-3, Joan M. Beck; 17-4, Network Graphics; 17-7, Patrick Watson (from Barkauskas, et. al., *Health and Physical Assessment,* 1994, Mosby).

Chapter 18: 18-7, Laurie O'Keefe/John Daugherty.

Chapter 19: 19-1, Ronald J. Ervin; 19-2 (Photo), Lennart Nilsson; 19-2 (Art), Ernest W. Beck; 19-4A, courtesy of S. Erlandsen and J. Magney (from *Color Atlas of Histology,* 1992, Mosby); 19-4B, Barbara Cousins; 19-5A, Carolyn B. Coulam/John A. McIntyre; 19-5B, William Ober; 19-6A, Kevin A. Sommerville; 19-6B, courtesy of B. Vidic and F.R. Suarez (from *Photographic Atlas of the Human Body,* 1984, Mosby); 19-7, 19-10, George J. Wassilchenko; 19-8, 19-9, Kevin A. Sommerville/Kathy Mitchell Gray; 19-11, David J. Mascaro & Associates; 19-13, Yvonne Wylie Walston.

Chapter 20: 20-1(Art), Rolin Graphics; 20-1(Photo), 20-6, Lennart Nilsson; 20-2, Scott Bodell; 20-3, courtesy of Lucinda L. Veek, Jones Institute for Reproductive Medicine, Norfolk, Virginia; 20-4, 20-8, Ernest W. Beck; 20-5, 20-7, Kevin A. Somerville; 20-9, courtesy of Marjorie M. Pyle, for Lifecircle, Costa Mesa, California; 20-10, Ron Edwards; 20-11, Patrick Watson; Antenatal Diagnosis and Treatment box, Network Graphics.

Chemistry Appendix: A-1, A-7, A-10, A-11, Network Graphics; A-2, A-3, Precision Graphics; A-4, A-5, A-6, A-9, Rolin Graphics; S-8, J.B. Wooskey and Associates.

Index

A

A blood type, 223
AB blood type, 223
Abdomen
  arteries of, 241t
  horizontal section of, *318*
  veins of, 244t
Abdominal aorta, *318, 342*
Abdominal cavity, 5, 8t
Abdominal hysterectomy, 400
Abdominal muscles, 293
Abdominal oblique muscles, *120, 121*
Abdominal region, 10t
Abdominopelvic cavity, 5, 8t
  quadrants of, *6*
  regions of, 5, *6*
Abdominopelvic regions, 5, 6
Abducens nerve, *158*, 159t
Abduction, 127, *129*
ABO system of blood typing, 222-223
Absorption, 305
  in digestive tract, 322-323
Accessory nerve, *158*, 159t
Accessory organs
  of digestion, 48t, 54, *55*
  of reproduction, 57
Accessory sex glands
  female, 396
  male, 389-390
Acetabulum, 99
Acetazolamide (Diamox), 363
Acetylcholine, 146, 164
Acid; *see* specific acid
Acid-base balance, 370-381
Acid solution, 371
Acidification of urine
  by distal renal tubule secretion of hydrogen ions, *376*
  by tubule secretion of ammonia, *377*
Acidosis, 215, 377
  metabolic, 378
    uncompensated, 378
  respiratory, 378
Acoustic nerve, *181, 182*
Acquired immunity, 264, 265t
Acquired immunodeficiency disease, 220
Acquired immunodeficiency syndrome, 271
Acromegaly, 197
Acromion process of scapula, *89, 126*
  as palpable bony landmark, *103*
Acrosome, 388
ACTH; *see* Adrenocorticotropic hormone
Actin, 113
Action potentials, 141
Active immunity, 265
Active transport processes, 22, 25-26
Acuity, visual, 176
"Adam's apple"; *see* Thyroid cartilage
Addison's disease, 206
Adduction, 127, *129*
Adductor group of muscles, 122t, 125
Adductor longus muscle, *120*, 122t
Adductor magnus muscle, *121*
Adductor tubercle, *98*
Adenohypophysis, 196; *see also* Pituitary gland
Adenoids, 263, 284, *285*
Adenosine triphosphate, 23
  metabolism and, 330, 331
ADH; *see* Antidiuretic hormone
Adipose connective tissue, 32t, 36, 37
Adipose tissue, subcutaneous, *66*
Adolescence, 419-420
ADP; *see* Adenosine triphosphate
Adrenal cortex, *203*, 204-205
  hormones of, 193t
Adrenal glands, 51, *52*, 203-207, *342*
  location of, *192*
Adrenal hormone, abnormalities of, 206
Adrenal medulla, *203*, 205-207
  hormones of, 193t
Adrenaline, functions of, 193t
Adrenergic fibers, 164, *165*
Adrenocorticotropic hormone, 197
  functions of, 193t
  target organs for, *199*
Adulthood, 420
  older, 420
Aerobic, 329
Aerobic respiration, 21
Aerobic training, 118-119
Afferent arteriole to glomerulus, 343, *344, 345*
Afferent lymph vessels, 262
Afferent neurons, 137
Agglutination, 222, 266
Aging, effects of, 420-422
Aging processes, 12
AIDS; *see* Acquired immunodeficiency disease
Air exchanged in pulmonary ventilation, volumes of, 295-297
Air cells, ethmoidal, *283*
Airway, obstruction of, 286-287, 288
Albumins, 215, 329
Alcohol consumption during pregnancy, 419
Aldosterone, 204
  functions of, 193t
  urine volume and, 348-349
Aldosterone mechanism, 364-365
Alimentary tract, 305; *see also* Digestive tract
Alkaline solution, 371
Alkalosis, 375, 377
  metabolic, 378
  respiratory, 378
"All or none" response, 117
Allergy, 262
Alpha cells of islets of Langerhans, 207
Alveolar ducts, *280*, 287, 289
Alveolar sacs, *280*, 289
Alveoli, 54, 279, *280, 281*, 287, 289, *294*
  of breast, 396
Amenorrhea in female athletes, 401
Amino acids, 29, 322
  essential and nonessential, 333
  listing of, 333t
  synthesis of, 333
Ammonia, tubule secretion of, urine acidification by, *377*
Amniotic cavity, 409, *410*, 411
Amniotic sac, *415*
  ruptured, *415*
Amphiarthroses, 102
Ampulla, *182*, 183
Amylase, 322, *323*
  salivary, 312, 322, *323*
Anabolic steroids, abuse of, 192
Anabolism, protein, 332-333
Anaerobic, 329
Anal canal, 54, *55*, 306, 320
Anal sphincter, 320
Anaphase, *29*, 30

t indicates term found in table only; italics indicates term found in illustration only.

Anaphylactic shock, 262
Anatomical directions, 3
Anatomical neck of humerus, *96*
Anatomical position, 1, 3
Anatomy, definition of, 1
Androgens, 205
  functions of, 193t
Anemia, 218, *219*
Anesthesia, 154
Angina pectoris, 234
ANH; *see* Atrial natriuretic hormone
Animal starch; *see* Glycogen
Ankle, *9*
Antagonists, muscle, 113
Antebrachial region, *9*, 10t
Antecubital region, *9*, 10t
Antenatal diagnosis and treatment, 416
Antenatal medicine, 416
Anterior, 3, *4*
Anterior pituitary gland, 196; *see also* Pituitary gland
  hormones of, 196-198
Anterior superior iliac spine, 103
Antibody(ies)
  blood typing and, 222, 223
  of immune system, 265-267
    functions of, 265-267
  monoclonal, 267
Antibody-mediated immunity, 265
Antidiuretic hormone, 149, 198, 199
  functions of, 193t
  target organs for, *199*
  urine volume and, 348
Antigen-antibody complex, 265-266
Antigens, 265
  blood typing and, 222, 223
Antiimmunity antiallergy effect of glucocorticoids, 204
Antrum, 393
Anuria, 349
Anus, 320, *384*, *397*
Aorta, *230*, *231*, 234, 238, 241t, *242*, *245*, *247*, *319*
  abdominal, *318*, *342*
Aortic arch, *247*
Aortic arch chemoreceptors, respiration and, *298*, 299
Aortic semilunar valve, *231*, 232, *233*
Apical beat, 229
Apnea, 299
Apocrine sweat glands, 72
Appendages, 47
  of skin, 68-73
Appendicitis, 54, 320
Appendicular division of body, 8, *9*
Appendicular skeleton, 87, 94-100
Appendix, 54, *55*, *246*, *306*, *319*
  digestion and, 320
Aqueous humor, 177
Arachnoid, *154*, 155, *157*
Arches of foot, 99, *100*
Areola, 396
Areolar connective tissue, 32t, 37
Arm, *9*; *see also* Upper extremity
  bones of, *96*
  lower
    flexion and extension of, *128*
    muscles of, 128t
  superficial veins of, *244*
  upper, muscles of, 128t
Armpit, *9*
Arrector pili muscle, *66*, 69, 70
Arrest, respiratory, 299
Arterial blood, pH of, 371
Arterioles, 238, *245*
  afferent and efferent, to glomerulus, 343, *344*, *345*
  functions of, 241
Arteriosclerosis, 422
Artery(ies), 52, *53*, 238, *240*, *245*; *see also* specific artery
  functions of, 241
  major, 241t, *242*
Arthritis, 116
Articular cartilage, 82, 104
Articulations, 81; *see also* Joints
Artificial immunity, 264-265
Artificial kidney, 346, 350-351
Artificial pacemaker, 238
Ascending colon, 306t, 320
Ascending tracts, 152
Ascorbic acid, sources, functions, and symptoms of deficiency of, 334t
Assimilation of nutrients, 329
Association areas, *151*
Astrocytes, 140
Atherosclerosis, 422
Athletes
  amenorrhea in, 401
  making weight by, 362
  vitamin supplements for, 333
Atoms, 1, *2*
ATP; *see* Adenosine triphosphate
Atria, 229, *230*, *231*, *233*, *245*
Atrial natriuretic hormone, 209
  functions of, 194t
  urine volume and, 349, 362
Atrial systole, *233*, 234
Atrioventricular bundle, 237
Atrioventricular node, 237
Atrioventricular valves, 232, *233*
Atrophy
  disuse, 118
  muscle, in bladder, 420
Attracting factor of T cells, 273
Auditory area, primary, *151*
Auditory association area, *151*
Auditory canal, external, *91*, 180-181, *183*
Auditory meatus, external, *181*
Auditory ossicles, 181
Auditory tube(s), 181-182, *183*, 284, *285*
Auricle, 180, *181*
Automatic bladder, 354
Autonomic conduction paths, 162-163
Autonomic effectors, 162
Autonomic functions, 164t
Autonomic nervous system, 137, 156, 159-166
  functions of, 164t
  as whole, 164-165
Autonomic neurons, 160
Autonomic neurotransmitters, 164, *165*
Avitaminosis, 333
Axial division of body, 8, *9*
Axial skeleton, 87-94
Axillary arteries, 241t, *242*
  as pulse point, *252*
Axillary lymph nodes, *260*, 262
Axillary region, *9*, 10t
Axillary veins, *243*, 244
Axons, 137, 138, *139*
  postganglionic, parasympathetic, 164, *165*
  preganglionic
    parasympathetic, 164, *165*
    sympathetic, 164, *165*
Azidothymidine, 271
AZT; *see* Azidothymidine

B

B blood type, 223
B cells, 217t, 219, 268
  development of, 270-272
  function of, 272
B-complex vitamins, sources, functions, and symptoms of deficiency of, 334t
B-lymphocytes; *see* B cells
Bacteria, phagocytosis of, by white blood cell, *27*
Balance
  acid-base, 370-381
  of body functions, 8-12
  fluid and electrolyte, 358-369
    mechanisms that maintain, 359-367
  mechanoreceptors for, 183
Ball-and-socket joint, 104, *105*
"Barrel chest," 420
Bartholin's glands, 396
Basal ganglia, 150
Basal metabolic rate, 334
  effects of aging on, *421*
  factors determining, *335*
Base pairing, complementary, 27
Basement membrane, *33*, *281*
  of serous membranes, 63
Basic solution, 371
Basilic veins, *243*, 244
Basophils, 217t, *219*, 220
Beat, apical, 229

Bedsores, 72
Beta cells of islets of Langerhans, 207
Bicarbonate loading, 374
Biceps brachii muscle, 113, 115, *120*, 122t, 124, 128t
Biceps femoris muscle, *121*, 123t, 125
Bicuspid valve, *231*, 232, *233*, *237*
Bicuspids, 309
Bile, 316, 322
Bile duct, *316*
  hepatic, *306*
Biological filtration by lymph nodes, 261-262
Biotin, sources, functions, and symptoms of deficiency of, 334t
Birth, 414, *415*
Blackhead, 73
Bladder, *7*, 54, *56*, *321*, *342*, 352, *384*, *392*, *415*
  automatic, 354
  male, *352*
  muscle atrophy in, 420
Blastocyst, 407, *408*, *410*
"Blind spot"; *see* Optic disc
Blindness, 177
  color, 180
Blisters, 68
Blood, 214-227
  calcium in, levels of, regulation of, 202-203
  circulation of, 241; *see also* Circulation
  clotting of, platelets and, 220-222
  components of, *216*
  composition of, 215-222
  donor and recipient, results of combinations of, *222*
  flow of
    changes in, during exercise, 236
    through circulatory system, *235*, *245*
    through heart, 234
  formed elements of, 215-217
  glucose in, regulation of, 208
  pH of, 371
  supply of, to heart muscle, 234-235
  umbilical, freezing, 418
  viscosity of, blood pressure and, 251
  volume of, 215
    blood pressure and, 249
Blood-brain barrier, 140
Blood cells
  classes of, 217t
  red; *see* Red blood cells
  white, 219-220
    phagocytosis of bacteria by, *27*
Blood doping, 223
Blood plasma; *see* Plasma
Blood pressure, 248-251
  average, 251
  capillary
    blood proteins and, 367
Blood pressure—cont'd
    increase in, causing edema, 364
  factors influencing, 249-251
  fluctuations in, 251
  high, 422
  reading, 250
  understanding, 248
  venous, 251
Blood pressure gradient, 248, *249*
Blood proteins, 329
  capillary blood pressure and, 367
Blood serum, 215
Blood tissue, 32t, 38; *see also* Blood
Blood types, 222-224
Blood vessels, 238-241
  functions of, 241
  kinds of, 238
  structure of, 238, 241
Body(ies)
  changes in proportions of, from birth to maturity, 416-417
  fractal geometry of, 313
  functions of, balance of, 8-12
  membranes of
    classification of, 63-65
    integumentary system and, 62-79
  organ systems of, 46-61
  planes of, 3-5
  regions of, 8
  sections of, 3-5
  structure and function of, introduction to, 1-15
  water in, 359, *360*
Body cavities, 5-8
  organs of, *7*, 8t
Body composition, 39
Body-fat percentage, determination of, 39
Body fluids, 359
  electrolytes in, importance of, 362-367
  pH of, 371
    mechanisms that control, 371-376
Body movements, examples of, *129*
Body surface area, estimating, 74
Body temperature, 336
Body water, total volume of, homeostasis of, *363*
Body weight, proportion of, represented by water, 359, *360*
Bolus, 309
Bone(s), 32t, 37; *see also* specific bone
  arm, *96*
  carpal or wrist, 95, 97
  cranial, 90t
  development of, in newborn, *86*
  ear, 90t
  elbow joint, *96*
  facial, 90t
  finger, 95, *96*
  formation and growth of, 84-86
Bone(s)—cont'd
  hand, 95, *97*
  lipping of, 420
  long, structure of, 82
  longitudinal section of, 82
  lower extremity, 99, 100t
  metacarpal, 95, *97*
  microscopic structure of, 82-84
  remodeling of, 84
  shaft of, 82
  skull, 90t
  thigh, knee joint, and leg, *98*
  thorax, 94t, *95*
  types of, 81
  upper extremity, 94-97
  vertebral column, 92t
Bone marrow
  red, 81, 82
  yellow, 82
Bony labyrinth, 182
Bony landmarks, palpable, 103
Bowman's capsule, 343, *344*, *345*
Boxer's muscle; *see* Triceps brachii muscle
Brachial arteries, 241t, *242*
  as pulse point, *252*
  reading blood pressure at, 250
Brachial region, *9*, 10t
Brachial veins, *244*
Brachialis muscle, 113, 115, *120*
Brachiocephalic arteries, *242*
Brachiocephalic trunk, *230*
Brachiocephalic veins, *243*, 244
Brain, *7*, 51
  coverings and fluid spaces of, 154-156
  divisions of, 146-150
    functions of, 153t
  effects of aging on, *421*
  emotional, 165
  hemorrhage in, 116
  tumor in, 116, 156
Brain stem, 147, *148*
  functions of, 153t
Breast(s), *9*, 57, 396
  cancer of, 262
  lymphatic drainage of, *262*
  self-examination of, 58
Breastbone; *see* Sternum
Breathing; *see also* Respiration
  mechanics of, 290, 292-293
  types of, 299
Broca's area, *151*
Bronchi, 54, *55*, 279, *280*, 287, 289, *291*, *292*
Bronchioles, *280*, 287, 289, *291*
Buccal region, *9*, 10t
Buffer pairs, 372
Buffers, 371-375
Buffy coat, 218
Bulbourethral glands, *384*, 389-390

Bundle of His, 237
Burns, 73-75
  classification of, 75
  estimating body surface area of, 74
Bursa(e), 65, 112
  omental, *321*
Buttock, *9*

C

Cafe coronary, 288
Calcaneus, *89*, 99
  as palpable bony landmark, *103*
Calciferol, sources, functions, and symptoms of deficiency of, 334t
Calcification, bony, 84
Calcitonin, 200, 202
  functions of, 193t
Calcium
  blood levels of, regulation of, 202-203
  sources, functions, and symptoms of deficiency of, 335t
Calcium pump, 25
Calculi, renal; *see* Kidney stones
Calipers to measure body-fat percentage, 39
Calorie, 336
Calyx(calyces), renal, 341, *343*, *344*
Canal of Schlemm, *177*
Canaliculi, *83*, 84
Cancer
  breast, 262
  screening tests for, 58
Canine teeth, 309
Capillary(ies), 52, *53*, 238, 241, *245*
  functions of, 241
  lymphatic, 259, 261
  peritubular, *345*
Capillary beds, 238
Capillary blood pressure
  blood proteins and, 367
  increase in, causing edema, 364
Carbaminohemoglobin, 295
Carbohydrate loading, 332
Carbohydrates, 329
  digestion of, 322
  metabolism of, 329-332
Carbon dioxide, diffusion of, 293, *294*, 295
Carbonic acid, buffering action of, 372, *373*, 374-375
Carbonic anhydrase, 371
Cardiac center, 147
Cardiac cycle, 235
Cardiac muscle, 50, 111, *112*
Cardiac muscle tissue, 32t, 38, 39
Cardiac sphincter, 312
Cardiac veins, *230*, 235, *243*
Cardiopulmonary resuscitation, 229
Cardiovascular system, 52
  effects of aging on, 420, 422
Caries, dental, 311
Carotid arteries, *230*, 241t, *242*
  as pulse point, *252*
Carotid sinus chemoreceptors, respiration and, *298*, 299
Carpal bones, *88*, *89*, 95, 97
Carpal region, *9*, 10t
Carpal tunnel syndrome, 119
Carrier, 25
Cartilage, 32t, 37, 38, 84
  articular, 82, 104
  costal, *88*, *95*
  cricoid, *286*
  microscopic structure of, 82-84
  in newborn, *86*
  thyroid, 284, *285*, *286*
  tracheal, 286
Cartilage tissue, *84*
Catabolism
  of glucose, *330*
  of nutrients, *332*
Cataracts, 177, 422
Catecholamines, 146
Catheterization, urinary, 353
Cavity(ies)
  amniotic, 409, *410*, 411
  body, 5-8
  medullary, 82
  nasal, *55*, *185*, *280*, 283
  oral, *55*, 307-309
  pulp, 310
  in tooth, 311
CCK; *see* Cholecystokinin
Cecum, 306, *319*, 320
Celiac arteries, 241t, *242*
Cell body of neuron, 137
Cell-mediated immunity, T cells and, 273
Cell membranes, movement of substances through, 22-26
Cells, 1, *2*, 17-31
  air, ethmoidal, *283*
  alpha and beta, of islets of Langerhans, 207
  B; *see* B cells
  blood; *see* Blood cells
  composition of, 17
  daughter, *29*
  division of, 29-31
  dust, 268
  epithelial, arrangement and shape of, 31, *33*
  general characteristics of, *19*
  granulosa, 392, *393*
  gustatory, 184
  hair, sensory, of ear, *182*
  immune system, 268-273
  interstitial, of testes, 385
  Kupffer's, 268
  memory, *270*, 271, 272
Cells—cont'd
  muscle, 111
  nervous system, 137-140
  olfactory, 185
  parts of, 17-22
  photoreceptor, of eye, 178
  plasma, *270*, 271, 272
  reproduction of, heredity and, 26-31
  retinal, 178
  Schwann, 138, *139*
  size and shape of, 17
  stem, 270
  structure and function of, relationship of, 22
  target organ, 191
Cellular respiration, 21, 290
Cementum, 310
Central canal, 82
Central nervous system, 137, 146-156
Central neurons, 137
Central retinal artery, *177*
Central retinal vein, *177*
Central venous pressure, 251
Centrioles, *19*, 20t, 21, *29*
Centromere, 30
Cephalic region, *9*, 10t
Cephalic veins, *243*, 244
Cerebellum, *148*, *155*
  functions of, 149, 153t
  structure of, 149
Cerebral aqueduct, *155*, 156
Cerebral cortex, *148*, 150, *151*, *157*
  regulation of respiration by, 298
Cerebral hemisphere, *155*
Cerebral lobes, 150, *151*
Cerebral nuclei, 150
Cerebral ventricles, 155
Cerebrospinal fluid, 155-156
  flow of, 156, *157*
Cerebrovascular accident, 150
Cerebrum, *151*
  functions of, 150, 153t
  structure of, 150
Cerumen, 181
Ceruminous glands, 181
Cervical canal, *395*
Cervical curve of spine, 92, *93*
Cervical lymph nodes, *260*
Cervical nerves, *152*
Cervical region, *9*, 10t
Cervical vertebrae, *89*, 92t, *93*, *152*
Cervix, *392*, 394, *395*, *415*
Cesarean section, 394
Cheek, *9*
Chemical digestion, 322, *323*
  small intestine and, 316
Chemical level of organization, 1, *2*
Chemoreceptors, 173, 184
  respiration and, *298*, 299
Chest; *see* Thorax

Chest cavity, 5
Childhood, 419
Chlorine, sources, functions, and symptoms of deficiency of, 335t
Chlorothiazide (Diuril), 363
Choking, 286-287
Cholecystokinin, 317
Cholesterol, 17
Cholinergic fibers, 164, *165*
Chondrocytes, 37, 38, 84
Chordae tendineae, *231*, 232
Chorion, *410*, 411
  as endocrine organ, 209
Chorionic gonadotropin, functions of, 194t
Choroid, 176, *177*
Choroid plexus, 156, *157*
Chromatids, 30
Chromatin, *29*
Chromatin granules, 22
Chromosomes, 22, 27, *29*
Chyme, 312
Cilia, *19*, 20t, 21
Ciliary muscle, 176, 177
Circulation, 241-248
  blood, 241
  coronary, 234
  fetal, 247-248
    maternal and, placenta as interface between, 411-412
  hepatic portal, 245-247
  maternal and fetal, placenta as interface between, 411-412
  pulmonary, 234, *235*, 241, 244-245
  systemic, 234, *235*, 241, 244-245
Circulatory system, 48t, 52, *53*, 228-257
  blood flow through, *235*, *245*
  role of, in movement, 116
Circumcision, 391
Cisterna chyli, *260*, 261
Citric acid cycle, 329
Clavicle, *88*, *89*, 94, *95*, 97t
  area above, *9*
  in newborn, *86*
Cleavage furrow, *29*, 30
Cleft, synaptic, *145*, 146
Clitoris, *392*, 397
Clone, 271
Clotting, blood, platelets and, 220-222
Cobalt, sources, functions, and symptoms of deficiency of, 335t
Coccygeal nerve, *152*
Coccyx, *88*, *89*, 92t, *93*, *152*
Cochlea, *181*, 182
  membranous, 183
Cochlear duct, 183
Cochlear nerve, *181*, *182*, *183*
Cochlear structures, effect of sound waves on, *183*
Colic, renal, 352
Colic artery, *319*
Colic flexure; *see* Hepatic flexure; Splenic flexure
Collagen fibers of dermis, 68
Collar bone; *see* Clavicle
Collecting duct, *344*
Collecting tubule, 343, *344*, *345*
Colon, *246*, 306, *319*
Color blindness, 180
Colostomy, 324
Columnar epithelium, simple, 32t, *33*, *34*, 35
Common carotid artery, *230*, 241t, *242*
Compact bone, 82, *83*, 84
Compartments, fluid, *360*
Complement, 267
  immune system, 265
Complement-binding sites, 267
Complement fixation, 266-267, *268*
Complement proteins, 267
Complementary base pairing, 27
Composition, body, 39
Concave spinal curves, 92
Concentration gradient
  movement down, 23
  movement up, 25
Concentric lamella, 82, *83*
Conchae, 90t, *283*, 284, *285*
Conduction
  causing heat loss, 336
  saltatory, *144*, 145
Conduction paths, autonomic, 162-163
Conduction system of heart, 236-238
Condyles, *98*
Condyloid joint, 105
Condyloid process, *91*
Cones, rods and, 176, 178
Conjunctiva, 176, *177*
Connecting neurons, 137
Connective tissue, 32t, 36-38
Connective tissue membranes, *64*, 65
Consumption, oxygen, maximum, 295
Continuous ambulatory peritoneal dialysis, 351
Contraction(s)
  heart, strength of, blood pressure and, 249-250
  skeletal muscle
    movements produced by, 127-129
    types of, 117, *118*
  tonic, 115
Control center, 11
  expiratory, 297
  inspiratory, 297, *298*
  respiratory, 297, *298*
Convection causing heat loss, 336
Convex spinal curves, 92
Convoluted tubules, 343, *344*, *345*
Convolutions, cerebral, 150
Cooper, ligaments of, 396
Copper, sources, functions, and symptoms of deficiency of, 335t
Cornea, 176
Coronal plane, *4*, 5
Coronal suture, *91*, 92
Coronary, cafe, 288
Coronary arteries, *230*, 234, 241t, *242*
Coronary bypass surgery, 234
Coronary circulation, 234
Coronary embolism, 221, 234
Coronary sinus, 235
Coronary thrombosis, 221, 234
Coronary veins, 244t
Coronoid process, *96*
Corpora cavernosa, 390
Corpus callosum, *148*, 150
Corpus luteum, 208, 393, 395
Corpus spongiosum, 390
Corpuscle(s)
  Meissner's, *66*, 70-71, 174t, *175*
  Pacinian, *66*, 70-71, 174t, *175*
  renal, 341, 343, *344*, *345*
  Ruffini's, 174t, *175*
Corti, organ of, *182*, 183
Corticospinal nerve tract, *153*
Cortisol, 204
  functions of, 193t
Costal cartilage, *88*, *95*
Coverings of brain and spinal cord, 154-156
Cowper's glands; *see* Bulbourethral glands
Coxal bone, *88*, *89*, 99, 100t
CPR; *see* Cardiopulmonary resuscitation
Cranial cavity, 5, 6, 8t
Cranial nerves, 156, *158*, 159t
Cranial region, *9*, 10t
Craniosacral system, 163
Cranium, bones of, 87, 90t
Crenation, 24
Cretinism, 201
Cricoid cartilage, *286*
Crista ampullaris, 183
Crown of tooth, 310
Crural region, *9*, 10t
Cryptorchidism, 386
Cubital region, *9*, 10t
Cubital veins, *243*, 244
Cuboidal epithelium, 32t, *33*, 35-36
Cuneatus tract, *153*
Curvature
  spinal
    infant's, 418
    toddler's, 419
  of stomach, 313
Cushing's syndrome, 206
Cusp of tooth, *310*
Cuspids, 309
Cutaneous membrane, 63, 64; *see also* Skin

Cutaneous nerve, *66*
Cutaneous region, 10t
Cuticle, 71
Cyanocobalamin, sources, functions, and symptoms of deficiency of, 334t
Cyanosis, 67, 71
Cyclic adenosine monophosphate, 191-192
Cyclic AMP; *see* Cyclic adenosine monophosphate
Cystic duct of liver, *306, 316*
Cystitis, 353, 354
Cytoplasm, 17, 18-21, *408*
  organelles in, 20-21

D

Daughter cells, *29*
Decay, tooth, 311
Deciduous teeth, 309, 419
Decubitus ulcers, 72
Deep, 3, *4*
Deglutition, 322
Dehydration, 73, 367
  testing for, *367*
Deltoid muscle, *120, 121*, 122t, 124, *126*, 128t
Dendrites, 40, 137, *139*
Dense bone, 82
Dense fibrous connective tissue, 32t, 37
Dental caries, 311
Dental diseases, 311
Dentin, 310
Deoxyribonucleic acid, 22, 27
  genetic information and, *27*
  protein synthesis and, *28*
  replication of, 30
Depilatories, 71
Depolarization, 238, *239*
Dermal-epidermal junction, 68
Dermal papilla, *66*, 68
Dermatomes, 159, *160*
Dermis, 65, *66*, 67, 68
Descending colon, 306t, 320
Descending tracts, 152
Development
  growth and, 406-425
  human, early stages of, *409*
  periods of, 412
  prenatal period of, 407-414
Developmental processes, 12
Diabetes insipidus, 198
Diabetes mellitus, 208
  exercise and, 208
Dialysis, 25, 350-351
  peritoneal, continuous ambulatory, 351
Diaphragm, 5, *7*, 125, 292, *306*
Diaphysis, 82, *86*
Diarrhea, 319
Diarthroses, 102-105
Diastole, 232
Diencephalon, 147, 149
  functions of, 153t
Diffusion, 23-25
  of carbon dioxide, 293, *294*
  in exchange of gases in tissues, 295
  gas exchange in lungs and, 293, *294*
  oxygen, 293, *294*
  in respiratory system, 279
Digestion, 305, 322
  carbohydrate, 322
  chemical, 322, *323*
    small intestine and, 316
  fat, 322
  mechanical, 322
  in mouth, 307
  protein, 322
  teeth and, 309
Digestive system, 48t, 54, *55*, 304-327
  organs of, 306
Digestive tract, walls of, 305
Digital region, *9*, 10t
Directions, anatomical, 3
Disc, optic, *177*, 178
Discharging chambers of heart; *see* Ventricles
Disk(s)
  Merkel's, *175*
  intercalated, 38, *39*, 111
    conduction system of heart and, 236
Dissection, 1
Dissociation, 362
Distal, 3, *4*
Distal renal tubule secretion of hydrogen ions, urine acidification and conservation of base by, *376*
Distal tubule diuretics, 363
Disuse atrophy, 118
Diuretics, 363
Division, cell, results of, 31
DNA; *see* Deoxyribonucleic acid
Dopamine, 146
Doping, blood, 223
Dorsal, 3, *4*
Dorsal body cavity, 5, 6, 8t
Dorsal region, 10t
Dorsal root ganglion, 142
Dorsalis pedis artery as pulse point, *252*
Dorsiflexion, 127, *129*
Drainage, lymphatic, of breast, *262*
Duct(s)
  alveolar, *280*, 287, 289
  bile, hepatic, *306, 316*
  cochlear, 183
  collecting, *344*
  cystic, of liver, *306, 316*
  ejaculatory, 389, *390*
  genital, male, 57
  hepatic, *316*, 317
  lactiferous, 396
Duct(s)—cont'd
  lymphatic, 259
    area drained by, *260*
  pancreatic, *316*
  reproductive
    female, 394-396
    male, 389
  submandibular, *308*
  sweat, *66*
  thoracic, 52, *53*, 259, *260*
    area drained by, *260*
Ductless glands, 51, 191
Ductus arteriosus, *247*, 248
Ductus deferens, *384*, 389
Ductus venosus, *247*, 248
Duodenal papillae, 316
Duodenal ulcers, 314
Duodenum, *246*, 306, 314, 316, *321*
  ulcers of, 314
Dura mater, *152, 154*, 155, *157*
Dust cells, 268
Dwarfism, 197
Dyspnea, 299

E

Ear, 180-183
  bones of, 90t
  effects of aging on, 422
  external, 180-181
  infections of, 182
  inner, *181*, 182-183
  middle, 181-182
    bones of, 87
  receptors in, 176t
  swimmer's, 184
Eardrum, 181
Eccrine sweat glands, 72
ECF; *see* Extracellular fluid
ECG; *see* Electrocardiogram
Ectoderm, 412
Edema, 364
Effector(s), 143
  autonomic or visceral, 162
  in feedback loop, 11
Efferent arteriole to glomerulus, 343, *344, 345*
Efferent lymph vessels, 262
Efferent neurons, 137
Ejaculatory duct, 389, *390*
Elastic fibers of dermis, 68
Elbow, *9*, 95
  bones of, *96*
Electrocardiogram, 238, *239*
Electrocardiograph, 238
Electrolyte balance, fluid balance and, 358-369
Electrolytes, 362
  in blood plasma, 364t
  in body fluids, importance of, 362-367
  retention of, 364

Electron transfer system, 329, 330
Embolism, 221, 234
Embolus, 221
Embryo, 412, *413*
Embryology, 407
Emesis, 312, 378
Emetic drugs, 378
Emotional brain, 165
Emptying reflex, 353
Emulsification of fats, 317
Enamel of tooth, 310
Encapsulated nerve endings, 174t
Encapsulated receptors, 173, 174t
End-bulbs, Krause's, 71, 174t, *175*
Endocarditis, 232, 237
Endocardium, 232
Endochondral ossification, *85*, *86*
Endocrine glands, 51, 191
  hormones of, 193t
  location of, *192*
Endocrine system, 48t, 51, 52, 190-213
Endoderm, 412
Endolymph, *182*, 183
Endoneurium, 140, *141*
  shedding, in menstrual cycle, 395
Endoplasmic reticulum, *19*, 20-21
Endorphins, 146
Endosteum, 82
Endothelium
  of blood vessels, 238
  of lymphatic capillaries, 259
Endurance training, 118-119
Energy, measurement of, 336
Enkephalins, 146
Enzymes, 21
Eosinophils, 217t, *219*, 220
Epicardium, 232
Epicondyles, *96*, *98*
  as palpable bony landmark, *103*
Epidermis, 65, 66-68
Epididymis, *384*, 389
Epigastric region of abdominopelvic cavity, 5, *6*
Epiglottis, *200*, 284, *285*, *286*
Epinephrine, 205
  functions of, 193t
  glucose levels and, 332
Epineurium, 141
Epiphyseal fracture, 87
Epiphyseal line, *86*
Epiphyseal plate, 82, *86*
Epiphyses, 82, *86*
Episiotomy, 397
Epithelial cells, arrangement and shape of, 31, *33*
Epithelial membranes, 63-65
Epithelial tissue, 31-36
  cells of, arrangement and shape of, 31, *33*
Epithelium
  columnar, simple, 32t, *33*, *34*, 35
  cuboidal, 32t, *33*, 35-36
  olfactory, *185*
  pseudostratified, 32t, *33*, 35
  squamous
    simple, 31, 32t, *33*
      of serous membranes, 63
    stratified, 31, 32t, *33*, *34*
  transitional, stratified, 32t, *33*, 35
Equilibrium, mechanoreceptors for, 183
ERV; *see* Expiratory reserve volume
Erythroblastosis fetalis, 223, *224*
Erythrocytes; *see* Red blood cells
Esophagus, *7*, 54, *55*, *285*, 306
  digestion and, 312
Essential amino acids, 333
Estrogen(s), 208
  functions of, 194t
  production of, by ovary, 393-394
  secretion of, 198
Ethacrynic acid (Edecrin), 363
Ethmoid bone, 90t, *91*
Ethmoid sinuses, 90, 283
Ethmoidal air cells, *283*
Eupnea, 299
Eustachian tubes; *see* Auditory tubes
Evaporation causing heat loss, 336
Exchange of gases
  in lungs, 293-295
  in tissues, *294*, 295
Exercise
  blood flow changes during, 236
  diabetes mellitus and, 208
  effects of
    on immunity, 260
    on skeletal muscles, 117-119
  fluid uptake and, 317
  isometric, 117, 118
  pain suppression during, 146
  proteinuria after, 349
  skin and, 73
Exercise physiology, 12
Exocrine glands, 191
Expiration, 290, 292-293
Expiratory control center, 297
Expiratory muscles, 293
Expiratory reserve volume, 295-297
Expression, facial, muscles of, 123
Extension, 127
  of lower arm, *128*
  of lower leg, *128*
External abdominal oblique muscle, *120*, *121*
External auditory canal, *91*, 180-181, *183*
External auditory meatus, *181*
External ear, 180-181
External genitals
  female, 396-397
  male, 390-391
External nares, 283
External oblique muscle, 122t, 124, *125*
External otitis, 184
External respiration, 290
Extracellular fluid, 359
Extremity; *see* Lower extremity; Upper extremity
Eye, *9*, 176-180
  effects of aging on, 422
Eyeball, tissues of, 176

F

Face, *9*
  bones of, 87, 90t
Facial arteries, 241t, *242*
  as pulse point, *252*
Facial expression, muscles of, 123
Facial muscles, *120*
Facial nerve, *158*, 159t, *181*
Facial region, *9*, 10t
Facial veins, *243*, 244t
Fallen arches, 99
Fallopian tube; *see* Uterine tube
False ribs, 94
Farsightedness, 176, 179
Fascicles, 140, *141*
Fat
  digestion of, 322
  metabolism of, 332
Fatigue, muscle, 115
Fatty acids, 322
Fatty tissue; *see* Adipose tissue
Feces, 54
Feedback loop, 10-12
  negative, 11, 12, 194, *196*
  positive, 12, 194-195
Female accessory sex glands, 396
Female genitals, external, 396-397
Female and male skeleton, differences between, 100, *101*
Female reproductive system, 48t, 57, 391-401
  accessory organs of, 391
  essential organs of, 391
  structure of, 391, *392*
  summary of, 401
Female secondary sex characteristics, 394
Female sex glands, 208
Feminizing hormone; *see* Estrogen
Femoral arteries, 241t, *242*
  as pulse point, *252*
Femoral region, 10t
Femoral veins, *243*, 244t
Femur, *49*, *88*, *89*, *98*, 99, 100t, 115
  in newborn, *86*
Fertilization, 383, 395, *408*
  to implantation, 407-412
  in vitro, 410
Fetal alcohol syndrome, 419

Fetal circulation, 247-248
  and maternal circulation, placenta as interface between, 411-412
Fetus, 412, *413*
Fibers
  adrenergic, 164, *165*
  cholinergic, 164, *165*
  collagen or white, of dermis, 68
  elastic or yellow, of dermis, 68
  muscle, 111, 113, *114*
  myelinated, 138
  nerve, effects of aging on, *421*
  Purkinje, 237
  skeletal muscle, 38
  spindle, *29*, 30
Fibrin, 221
Fibrinogen, 215, 220-221, 329
Fibrous connective tissue, 32t, 37
Fibula, *88*, *89*, *98*, 99, 100t
  lateral malleolus of, as palpable bony landmark, *103*
  in newborn, *86*
Fight-or-flight response, 163
Filtrate, glomerular, 347
Filtration, 23t, 25
  biological, by lymph nodes, 261-262
  glomerular, 347
  urine formation and, 346-347, 348
Fimbriae of uterine tubes, 394, 407, *408*
Finger bones, 95
Fingernail, 71
Fingerprints, 68
Fingers, *9*
  opposing thumb to, 105
First-degree burn, 75
Fissures, cerebral, 150, *151*
Fitness, tissues and, 39
Fixation, complement, 266-267, *268*
Flagellum(a), *19*, 20t, 21, 22
Flat bones, 81
Flatfeet, 99
Flexion, 127
  of lower arm, *128*
  of lower leg, *128*
  plantar, *129*
Floating ribs, 94
Fluid balance, 359
  and electrolyte balance, 358-369
  mechanisms that maintain, 359-367
Fluid(s)
  body; *see* Body fluids
  cerebrospinal, 155-156
  extracellular, 359
  intake of
    and output of, sources of, 361
    regulation of, 362
  interstitial, 17, 259, 359, *360*
  intracellular, 359, *360*
  pericardial, 232
  seminal, 389
Fluid(s)—cont'd
  synovial, 65, 104
    in bursae, 112
  tissue, 17
  uptake of, exercise and, 317
Fluid compartments, 359, *360*
Fluid homeostasis, role of lymphatic system in, *260*
Fluid imbalances, 367
Fluid spaces of brain and spinal cord, 154-156
Focusing, problems with, 179
Folic acid, sources, functions, and symptoms of deficiency of, 334t
Follicle(s)
  Graafian, 392, *393*
  hair, *66*, 68, 69, 70
    infection of, *261*
  mature, 392, *393*
  ovarian, 208, 392
  primary, 392
  secondary, 393
Follicle-stimulating hormone, 197-198
  functions of, 193t
  menstrual cycle and, 400-401
  spermatogenesis and, 386
Fontanels, 92
  in newborn, *86*
Foot, *9*
  arches of, 99, *100*
  muscles of, 128t
  sole of, *9*
Footprints, 68
Foramen
  interventricular, *155*
  mental, *91*
  vertebral, 92
Foramen magnum, 147
Foramen ovale, *247*, 248
Forearm, *9*
  bones of, *96*
Forehead, *9*
Foreskin, 390-391
Fossa
  intercondylar, *98*
  olecranon, *96*
Fourth ventricle, *155*, 156, *157*
Fovea centralis, 176, *177*
Fractal geometry of body, 313
Fracture(s)
  epiphyseal, 87
  spontaneous, *86*
Free nerve endings, 71, 174t, *175*
Free ribosomes, *19*
Freezing umbilical cord blood, 418
Frenulum, 308
Frontal air sinus, *285*
Frontal bone, *88*, 90t, *91*
Frontal lobe, 150, *151*
Frontal muscle, 122t, 123, *124*
Frontal plane, *4*, 5
Frontal region, *9*, 10t
Frontal sinuses, 90, 283
Frontal sinusitis, 90, 92
FSH; *see* Follicle-stimulating hormone
Full-thickness burn, 75
Fundus
  of stomach, 313
  of uterus, 394-395
Furosemide (Lasix), 363
Furrow, cleavage, *29*, 30

G

Gallbladder, *7*, 54, *55*, *306*
  digestion and, 316-317
Gallstone, 316, 317
Gametes, 383
Ganglion, 142
  basal, 150
  posterior (dorsal) root, 142
  spinal, *154*
  sympathetic, *154*
  sympathetic chain, 163
Gas-exchange structures of lung, *281*
Gases, exchange of
  in lungs, 293-295
  respiratory system and, 279
  in tissues, *294*, 295
Gastric emptying, exercise and, 317
Gastric glands, 312
Gastric juice, 322, *323*
Gastric ulcers, 314
Gastric veins, *246*
Gastrocnemius muscle, *120*, *121*, 123t, 127, 128t
Gastroepiploic veins, *246*
Gastrointestinal tract, 54, 305; *see also* Digestive tract
Gene, 27
General sense organs, 173-175
General-adaptation syndrome, 206-207
Genetic code, 27
Genital ducts, male, 57
Genitalia
  female, 57, 396-397
  male, *56*, 57, 390-391
Genome, 27
Geometry, fractal, of body, 313
Germ layers, primary
  derivatives of, 412t
  formation of, 412
Gerontology, 420
Gestation period, 412
GH; *see* Growth hormone
Gigantism, 197
Gingiva, *310*
Gland(s); *see also* specific gland
  adrenal, 51, *52*, 203-207
    location of, *192*
  Bartholin's, 396

Gland(s)—cont'd
  bulbourethral (Cowper's), *384*, 389-390
  ceruminous, 181
  ductless, 51, 191
  endocrine, 51, 191
    hormones of, 193t
    location of, *192*
  exocrine, 191
  gastric, 312
  intestinal, 314
  lacrimal, 176
  mammary, 57
  parathyroid, 51, *52*, *200*, 202-203
    hormones of, 193t
    location of, *192*
  parotid, 311
  pineal, 51, *52*, *148*, 209
    hormones of, 194t
    location of, *192*
  pituitary; *see* Pituitary gland
  prostate; *see* Prostate gland
  salivary, 54, *55*, 191
  sebaceous, 65, *66*, 69, 72-73
  sex, 208-209
    accessory
      female, 396
      male, 389-390
  skin, 72-73
  sublingual, *308*, 311
  submandibular, 311
  sweat (sudoriferous), *66*, 72, 191
    functions of, 73
  thymus; *see* Thymus
  thyroid, 51, *52*, 200-202
    location of, *192*
  uterine, *410*
  vestibular, 396
Glans penis, *390*
Glaucoma, 177, 422
Glia, 40, 137, 138, 140
Gliding joint, 105
Glioma, 140
Globulins, 215
Glomerular filtrate, 347
Glomerular filtration, 347
Glomerulus, 343, *344*, *345*
Glossopharyngeal nerve, *158*, 159t
Glucagon, 207-208
  functions of, 194t
  glucose levels and, 332
  insulin and, 208
Glucocorticoids, 204
  antiimmunity antiallergy effect of, 204
  functions of, 193t
  gluconeogenesis and, 204
  stress responses induced by, *205*
Gluconeogenesis, glucocorticoids and, 204
Glucose, 322
  carbohydrate metabolism and, 330, 331-332
  catabolism of, *330*
  metabolism and, 329
  reabsorption of, 347
Gluteal artery, *126*
Gluteal region, *9*, 10t
Gluteal vein, *126*
Gluteus maximus muscle, *121*, 122t, 125, *126*, 128t
Gluteus medius muscle, *126*, 128t
Glycerol, 322
Glycogen, 331
Glycogen loading, 332
Glycogenesis, 331
Glycogenolysis, liver, 207-208
Glycolysis, 329
Glycosuria, 208, 347
Goiter, simple, 201
Golgi apparatus, *19*, 20t, 21, *29*
Golgi tendon receptors, 175t
Gonadotropic hormones, target organs for, *199*
Gonadotropins, 209
  chorionic, functions of, 194t
Gonads, male, 57, 383
Goose pimples, 70
Graafian follicle, 392, *393*
Gracilis muscle, *120*, 122t
Gracilis tract, *153*
Granular leukocytes, 215
  effects of exercise on, 260
Granules, chromatin, 22
Granulosa cells, 392, *393*
Gray matter, 140, *142*
Greater omentum, 321
Greater trochanter, *88*, *98*, *126*
Greater tubercle, *96*
Groin, *9*
Growth
  and development, 406-425
  hair, 69
Growth hormone, 198
  abnormalities of, 197
  functions of, 193t
  glucose levels and, 332
  insulin and, 198
  target organs for, *199*
Gustatory cells, 184
Gyri, cerebral, 150

H

Hair, 68-70
  growth of, 69
  papilla of, *66*, 69
  root of, 69
  shaft of, *66*, 69, *70*
Hair cells, sensory, of ear, *182*
Hair follicles, *66*, 68, 69, 70
  infection of, *261*
Hamstring group of muscles, *121*, 123t, 125, 128t
Hand
  anterior surface of, *9*
  bones of, 95, *97*
Hard palate, *285*, 308
Haversian systems, 37, 82
Head, *9*
  arteries of, 241t
  changes in size of, from birth to maturity, 416-417
  muscles of, 122t, 123, *124*
  sagittal section of, *285*
  veins of, 244t
Hearing, effects of aging on, 422
Heart, *7*, 229-238
  action of, 232, *233*
  anatomy of, 229-232
  apex of, 229, *230*
  blood flow through, 234
  chambers of, 229, *231*, 232
  conduction system of, 236-238
  covering sac of, 232
  effects of aging on, *421*
  hormones of, 194t
  location, size, and position of, 229
  strength of contractions of, blood pressure and, 249-250
  valves of, *231*, 232
  wall of, cross section of, *231*
"Heart attack," 234, 422
Heart block, 238
Heart failure, 251
Heart muscle, blood supply to, 234-235
Heart rate, blood pressure and, 251
Heart sounds, 232, 234
Heartbeat, blood pressure and, 249-250, 251
Heartburn, 312
Heat production, skeletal muscle and, 115
Heel bone; *see* Calcaneus
Heimlich maneuver, 287, *288*
Helicobacter pylori, ulcers and, 314
Hematocrit, 218, *219*
Hemodialysis, 350
Hemoglobin in red blood cells, 218
Hemopoiesis, 216, 418
  skeletal system and, 81
Hemopoietic tissue, 32t, 38
Hemorrhage, 249, 251
  brain, 116
Henle, loop of, 343, *344*, *345*
Heparin, 220
  to prevent excessive blood clotting, 222
Hepatic bile duct, *306*
Hepatic ducts, *316*, 317

Hepatic flexure, *306*, *319*, 320
Hepatic portal circulation, 245-247
Hepatic portal veins, *243*, 244t, 246, *247*
Hepatic veins, *243*, 244t, *246*
Heredity, cell reproduction and, 26-31
Herpes zoster, 166
Hiccup, 290
Hinge joint, 105
Hip, 99
Hip bone, *88*, *89*
Hip replacement, total, 104
His, bundle of, 237
Histogenesis, 414
HIV; *see* Human immunodeficiency virus
Homeostasis, 8, 10, 12
  body temperature, regulation of, 336, 337
  fluid, role of lymphatic system in, *260*
  respiratory system and, 279
  of total volume of body water, *363*
Hormone(s), 51, 191
  action of, mechanisms of, 191-194
  adrenal, abnormalities of, 206
  adrenocorticotropic, 197
    functions of, 193t
    target organs for, *199*
  antidiuretic, 149, 198, 199
    functions of, 193t
    target organs for, *199*
  atrial natriuretic, 209
    functions of, 194t
    urine volume and, 349, 362
  follicle-stimulating, 197-198
    functions of, 193t
    menstrual cycle and, 400-401
    spermatogenesis and, 386
  gonadotropic, target organs for, *199*
  growth; *see* Growth hormone
  hypothalamus creating, 149
  inhibiting, 199
    functions of, 193t
  interstitial cell-stimulating, 198
  lactogenic, 198
    functions of, 193t
  luteinizing, 198
    functions of, 193t
    menstrual cycle and, 400-401
  melanocyte-stimulating, 198
    functions of, 193t
    target organs for, *199*
  ovulating; *see* Luteinizing hormone
  parathyroid, 202-203
    functions of, 193t
  pituitary, 196-198, *199*
  plasma membrane and, 18
  protein, 191-192
    mechanism of action of, *192*
  releasing, 149, 199
    functions of, 193t
Hormone(s)—cont'd
  secretion of, regulation of, 194-195
  sex, 204
    functions of, 193t
  steroid, 192-194
    abuse of, 192
    mechanism of action of, *195*
  thyroid, abnormalities of, 201
  thyroid-stimulating, 197
    functions of, 193t
    target organs for, *199*
  tissue; *see* Prostaglandins
  tropic, 196-197
Human immunodeficiency virus, 271
Human sperm, *22*
Humerus, *49*, *88*, *89*, 94-95, *96*, 97t
  epicondyles of, as palpable bony landmark, *103*
  in newborn, *86*
Humoral immunity, 265
  B cells and, 272
Hybridomas, 267
Hydrocephalus, 156
Hydrochloric acid, 322
Hydrocortisone, 204
  functions of, 193t
  glucose levels and, 332
Hydrogen ions, 371
  urine acidification and conservation of base by distal renal tubule secretion of, *376*
Hydrostatic pressure, 25
Hydroxide ions, 371
Hymen, 397
Hyoid bone, 101, *200*, *285*, *286*
Hyperacidity, ulcers and, 314
Hypercalcemia, 202
Hyperglycemia, 198
Hyperopia, 179
Hypertension, 422
Hyperthyroidism, 201
Hypertonic solution, 24
Hypertrophy
  muscle, 118
  prostatic, 391
Hyperventilation, 299
Hypervitaminosis, 333
Hypochondriac regions of abdominopelvic cavity, 5, *6*
Hypogastric region of abdominopelvic cavity, 5, *6*
Hypoglossal nerve, *158*, 159t
Hypoglycemia, 198
Hypothalamus, 51, *52*, 147, *148*, 149, 198-199
  body temperature and, 336
  functions of, 153t
  hormones of, 193t
  location of, *192*
Hypothermia, 115
Hypothesis, 191
  second messenger, 191
Hypothyroidism, 201
Hypotonic solution, 24
Hypoventilation, 299
Hypoxia, 297
Hysterectomy, 400
Hysterical hyperventilation, 299

I

ICF; *see* Intracellular fluid
ICSH; *see* Interstitial cell-stimulating hormone
IF; *see* Interstitial fluid
Ileocecal valve, *306*, 318, *319*
Ileum, 306, 314, *319*
Iliac arteries, 241t, *242*, *247*, *342*
Iliac crest, 103, *126*
Iliac regions of abdominopelvic cavity, 5, *6*
Iliac spine
  anterior superior, 103
  posterior superior, *126*
Iliac veins, 244t, *243*, *342*
Iliopsoas muscle, *120*, 122t, 125, 128t
Ilium, *88*, *319*
  in newborn, *86*
Imbalance
  pH, 377-379
  fluid, 367
Immune mechanism, 219
Immune system, 263-265
  cells of, 268-273
  function of, 263
  molecules of, 265-268
Immunity
  acquired, 264, 265t
  active, 265
  antibody-mediated, 265
  artificial, 264-265
  cell-mediated, T cells and, 273
  effects of exercise on, 260
  humoral, 265
    B cells and, 272
  inborn, 264, 265t
  inherited, 264
  natural, 264-265
  nonspecific, 263-264
  passive, 265
  specific, 264-265
Immunization, 265
Immunodeficiency disease, acquired, 220
Immunodeficiency syndrome, acquired, 271
Immunodeficiency virus, human, 271
Immunosuppression, 209
Implantation, *408*, *410*
  fertilization to, 407-412
Impulses, nerve, 50, 141, 142, 143-145

In vitro fertilization, 410
Inborn immunity, 264, 265t
Incisors, 309
Incontinence, 354
Incus, 90t, *183*
Infancy, 417-418
Infant, normal spinal curvature of, 418
Infant respiratory distress syndrome, 289
Infarction, myocardial, 234, 237, 238
Infections
  ear, 182
  of hair follicle, *261*
Inferior, 3, *4*
Inferior vena cava; *see* Vena cava
Inflammatory response, 264
Inguinal canal, *125*
Inguinal lymph nodes, *260*
Inguinal regions of abdominopelvic cavity, 5, *6*, *9*, 10t
Inherited immunity, 264
Inhibiting hormones, 199
  functions of, 193t
Injection(s)
  intramuscular, 126
  subcutaneous, 68
Inner ear, *181*, 182-183
Innervation of major organs by autonomic nervous system, *161*
Insertion of muscle, 111
Inspiration, 290, 292
Inspiratory control center, 297, *298*
Inspiratory muscles, 292
Inspiratory reserve volume, 295-297
Insulin
  carbohydrate metabolism and, 331
  functions of, 194t
  glucagon and, 208
  glucose levels and, 332
  growth hormone and, 198
Insulin-dependent diabetes mellitus, 208
Integument, 63; *see also* Skin
Integumentary system, 47, 48t, *49*
  body membranes and, 62-79
  effects of aging on, 420
Interatrial septum, 232
Intercalated disks, 38, *39*, 111
  conduction system of heart and, 236
Intercondylar fossa, *98*
Intercostal muscles, 125, 292, 293
Interferon, 269
Internal oblique muscle, 122t, 124, *125*
Internal respiration, 290, 295
Internal secretions, sodium-containing, *366*
Interneuron, *142*, 137, 143
Interphase, 29-30
Interstitial cell-stimulating hormone, 198
Interstitial cells of testes, 385
Interstitial fluid, 17, 259, 359, *360*
Interventricular foramen, *155*
Interventricular septum, *231*, 232
Intestinal glands, 314
Intestinal juice, 322, *323*
Intestine, *318*
  large; *see* Colon; Large intestine
  small; *see* Small intestine
Intracellular fluid, 359, *360*
Intramuscular injections, 126
Intrapleural space, 290, *292*
Involuntary muscles, 38, 50, 111
Involuntary tissue, 40
Involution of thymus, 263
Iodine, sources, functions, and symptoms of deficiency of, 335t
Ion pumps, 25-26
Ions
  hydrogen, 371
  hydroxide, 371
  negatively charged, 364
  positively charged, 364
Ipecac, 378
Iris, 176
  muscle of, *177*
Iron, sources, functions, and symptoms of deficiency of, 335t
Iron deficiency anemia, 218
Irregular bones, 81
IRV; *see* Inspiratory reserve volume
Ischium, *88*, *89*, 99
  in newborn, *86*
Islets of Langerhans, 207-208, 318
  hormones of, 194t
Isometric contractions, 117, *118*
Isometric exercises, 117, 118
Isotonic contractions, 117, *118*
Isotonic solution, 24

J

Jaundice, 317
Jejunum, 306t, 314, *315*
Jerk reflex, 154
Joint(s), 81, 101-106; *see also* specific joint
  kinds of, 102-105
Joint capsule, 103
Jugular veins, *243*, 244
Juxtaglomerular apparatus, *345*, 346

K

Kaposi sarcoma, 271
Keratin, 67
  functions of, 73
Ketone bodies, 375
Ketosis, 375
Kidney stones, 352
  removal of, using ultrasound, 354
Kidneys, 7, 54, *56*, *247*, *318*, 341-346
  artificial, 346, 350-351
  effects of aging on, *421*
  function of, 345-346
  internal structure of, 341, *343*
Kidneys—cont'd
  location of, 341
  microscopic structure of, 341-345
Kilocalorie, 336
Knee, 106
  back of, *9*
  bones of, *98*
  torn ligaments in, *106*
Knee cap; *see* Patella
Knee-jerk reflex, 142, 143, 154
Korotkoff sounds, 250
Krause's end bulbs, 71, 174t, *175*
Kupffer's cells, 268

L

Labia majora (labium majus), *392*, 397
Labia minora (labium minus), *392*, 396, 397
Labor, stages of, 414, *415*
Lacrimal bone, 90t, *91*
Lacrimal gland, 176
Lacrimal sac, *283*, 284
Lactase, 322, *323*
Lactation, 198
Lacteals, 261
  of small intestine, 314
Lactic acid, 372, 374
  buffered by sodium bicarbonate, *374*
Lactiferous ducts, 396
Lactogenic hormone, 198
  functions of, 193t
Lacunae, 84
Lambdoidal suture, *91*, 92
Lamella, concentric, 82, *83*
Langerhans, islets of, 207-208, 318
  hormones of, 194t
Lanugo, 68
Laparoscope, 410
Large intestine, *7*, 54, *55*, 306t
  digestion and, 318-320
  divisions of, 320
Laryngopharynx, *280*, 284, *285*
Larynx, *7*, 54, *55*, *200*, 279, *280*, 284, *286*, *306*
Lateral, 3, *4*
Lateral condyle, *98*
Lateral epicondyle, *96*, *98*
  as palpable bony landmark, *103*
Lateral longitudinal arch of foot, 99, *100*
Lateral malleolus, *98*
  as palpable bony landmark, *103*
Lateral rectus muscle, *177*
Lateral ventricle, *155*, *157*
Latissimus dorsi muscle, *121*, 122t, 123, 124, *125*, 128t
Leg, *9*; *see also* Lower extremity
  bones of, *98*
  lower
    flexion and extension of, *128*
    muscles of, 128t

Lens of eye, 176, 177
Lesser trochanter, *98*
Leukemia, 220
  cord blood for, 418
Leukocytes; *see* White blood cells
Leukocytosis, 220
Leukopenia, 220
LH; *see* Luteinizing hormone
Ligaments, 104
  of Cooper, 396
Light, refraction of, by eye, 178
Lingual tonsils, 263, *285*
Lip, *308*
Lipase, 322, *323*
  pancreatic, 322, *323*
Lipping of bones, 420
Lithotriptor, 354
Liver, *7*, 54, *55*, *246*, *247*, *306*, *318*, *321*, *342*
  digestion and, 316-317
  effects of aging on, *421*
  role of, in metabolism, 329
Liver glycogenolysis, 207-208
Loading
  bicarbonate, 374
  carbohydrate or glycogen, 332
Lobes
  cerebral, 150, *151*
  of lungs, 290, *291*
Lobules, breast, 396
Logarithmic scale, *372*
Loin, *9*
Long bones, 81
  structure of, 82
Longitudinal arches of foot, 99, *100*
Loop of Henle, 343, *344*, *345*
Loop of Henle diuretics, 363
Lower extremity, *9*
  arteries of, 241t
  bones of, 99, 100t
  muscles moving, 122t-123t, 125, 127
  veins of, 244t
Lower respiratory tract, 279, *280*, 282
Lub dup sound of heart, 232, 234
Lumbar curve of spine, 92, *93*
Lumbar nerves, *152*
Lumbar puncture, 156
Lumbar region, *9*, 10t
Lumbar regions of abdominopelvic cavity, 5, *6*
Lumbar vertebrae, *89*, 92t, *93*, *152*
Lumen of digestive tract, 305
Lungs, *7*, 54, *55*, *245*, 279, *280*, 290, *291*, *292*
  effects of aging on, *421*
  exchange of gases in, 293-295
  gas-exchange structures of, *281*
  lobes of, 290, *291*
Lunula, 71
Luteinization, 198
Luteinizing hormone, 198
  functions of, 193t
  menstrual cycle and, 400-401
Lymph, 52, 259-261
  drainage of, *260*
  formation of, 259
Lymph nodes, 52, *53*, *260*, 261-262
  defense function of, 261-262
  structure of, 261
Lymph vessels, 259-261, 262
Lymphatic capillaries, 259, 261
Lymphatic drainage of breast, *262*
Lymphatic ducts, 259
  area drained by, *260*
Lymphatic system, 48t, 52, *53*, 259-263
  principal organs of, *260*
  role of, in fluid homeostasis, *260*
Lymphatic tissue, 216
Lymphatic venules, 259
Lymphatic vessels, 52, *53*
Lymphocytes, 219, 268-273
  effects of exercise on, 260
Lysis, 24
Lysosome, *19*, 20t, 21

M

Macrophage activating factor of T cells, 273
Macrophages, 268
Macula lutea, 176, *177*
Magnesium, sources, functions, and symptoms of deficiency of, 335t
Male accessory sex glands, 389-390
Male external genitals, 390-391
Male and female skeleton, differences between, 100, *101*
Male reproductive ducts, 389
Male reproductive organs, *384*
Male reproductive system, 48t, *56*, 57, 383-391
  accessory organs of, 383-384
  essential organs of, 383, 384
  structure of, 383-384
  summary of, 401
Male sex glands, 208-209
Malleolus(malleoli), *98*
  as palpable bony landmark, *103*
Malleus, 90t, 181, *183*
Malnutrition, 329
Maltase, 322, *323*
Mammary glands, 57
Mammary region, *9*, 10t
Mandible, *88*, 90t, *91*
  in newborn, *86*
Manganese, sources, functions, and symptoms of deficiency of, 335t
Marrow, bone, 81, 82
Masculinizing hormone; *see* Testosterone
Masseter muscle, 122t, 123, *124*
Master gland; *see* Pituitary gland
Mastication
  muscles of, 123
  teeth and, 309
Mastoid process, *91*
Maternal and fetal circulation, placenta as interface between, 411-412
Matter, gray and white, 140
Mature follicles, 392, *393*
Maxilla, *88*, 90t, *91*
  in newborn, *86*
Maxillary sinuses, 90, 283
Maximum oxygen consumption, 295
Meatus
  auditory, external, *181*
  urinary, 353
Mechanical digestion, 322
Mechanoreceptors, 173
  for balance and equilibrium, 183
  of ear, 180
Medial, 3, *4*
Medial condyle, *98*
Medial epicondyle, *96*
  as palpable bony landmark, *103*
Medial longitudinal arch of foot, 99, *100*
Medial malleolus of tibia as palpable bony landmark, *103*
Medial rectus muscle, *177*
Mediastinum, 5, 8t
Meditation, 165
Medulla oblongata, 147, *148*
  functions of, 153t
Medullary cavity, 82
Meiosis, 386
Meissner's corpuscle, *66*, 70-71, 174t, *175*
Melanin, 67
  functions of, 73
Melanocyte-stimulating hormone, 198
  functions of, 193t
  target organs for, *199*
Melanocytes, 67
Melatonin, 209
  functions of, 194t
Membrane(s), 63
  basement, *33*, *281*
    of serous membranes, 63
  body
    classification of, 63-65
    integumentary system and, 62-79
  cell, movement of substances through, 22-26
  connective tissue, *64*, 65
  cutaneous, 63, 64; *see also* Skin
  epithelial, 63-65
  mucous, *64*, 65
  periodontal, 310
  plasma, 17-18, *19*, 20t
    structure of, 18
  respiratory, 279, *281*, 282
  serous, 63, 64, 65

Membrane(s)—cont'd
  synovial, *64*, 65, 104
    in bursae, 112
  tympanic, 181, *183*
Membranous cochlea, 183
Membranous labyrinth, 183
Memory cells, *270*, 271, 272
Menarche, 397
Meninges, 146, 154-155
Menopause, 395
Menses, 397, 398, *399*, 400
Menstrual cycle, 395, 397-401
  changes in, control of, 400-401
Menstruation, 395
  cause of, 401
Mental foramen, *91*
Merkel endings, *175*
Merkel's disc, *175*
Mesenteric arteries, 241t, *242*, *319*
Mesenteric veins, *243*, 244t, 246, 319
Mesentery, 305, *319*, 321
Mesoderm, 412
Messenger RNA, 28
Metabolic acidosis, 378
  uncompensated, 378
Metabolic alkalosis, 378
Metabolic disturbances, 377-378
Metabolic rate, 334-336
  basal, 334
    effects of aging on, *421*
    factors determining, *335*
  total, 334
    factors determining, *335*
Metabolism, 305, 329
  carbohydrate, 329-332
  fat, 332
  nutrient, 329-333
  nutrition and, 328-339
  protein, 332-333
  role of liver in, 329
Metacarpals, *88*, *89*, 95, 97
Metaphase, *29*, 30
Metatarsal arch, 99
Metatarsals, *88*, *89*, 99, 100t
Microcephaly from fetal alcohol syndrome, 419
Microglia, 140
Microvilli of small intestine, 313, 314, *315*
Micturition, 353-354
Midbrain, 147, *148*
  functions of, 153t
Middle concha, *91*
Middle ear, 181-182
  bones of, 87
Midsagittal plane, 5
Mineralocorticoids, 204
  functions of, 193t
Minerals, 333, 335t
Mitochondrion(mitochondria), *19*, 20t, 21, *29*, *139*
Mitosis, 26-27, *29*
Mitral valve, *231*, 232, *233*, *237*
Molars, 309
Molecules, 1, *2*
  immune system, 265-268
Monoclonal antibodies, 267
Monocytes, 217t, 219
Monosynaptic synapse, *142*
Mons pubis, 396-397
Morula, 407, *408*, 412
Motor area, primary, *151*
Motor neuron, 116, 137, *142*
Motor unit, 116
Mouth, *9*, 54, *55*, 306t, 307-309
Movement(s)
  body, examples of, *129*
  produced by skeletal muscle contractions, 127-129
  role of other body systems in, 116
  of substances through cell membranes, 22-26
mRNA; *see* Messenger RNA
MS; *see* Multiple sclerosis
MSH; *see* Melanocyte-stimulating hormone
Mucocutaneous junction, 65
Mucosa
  of digestive tract, 305
  respiratory, 282
Mucous blanket of respiratory tract, 282
Mucous membranes, *64*, 65
Mucus, 65
  of respiratory mucosa, 282
Multiple sclerosis, 116, 143
Mumps, 311
Muscle(s); *see also* specific muscle
  body of, 111
  cardiac, 50, 111, *112*
  disuse atrophy of, 118
    in bladder, 420
  facial expression, 123
  fatigue of, 115
  group according to function, 128t
  head and neck, 122t, 123, *124*
  hypertrophy of, 118
  insertion of, 111
  involuntary, 38, 50, 111
  mastication, 123
  movement by, 113, 115
  moving lower extremities, 122t-123t, 125, 127
  moving upper extremities, 122t, 123-124
  origin of, 111
  skeletal; *see* Skeletal muscle
  smooth, 111, *112*
  stimulus to, 117
  striated, 111
  trunk, 122t, 124-125
Muscle(s)—cont'd
  visceral, 111
  voluntary, 38, 40, 50, 111
Muscle cells, 111
Muscle fibers, 111, 113, *114*
  skeletal, 38
Muscle spindles, 175t
Muscle tissue, 32t, 38-40, 111, *112*
Muscular system, 48t, 50, 110-135
  during infancy, 418
  role of, in movement, 116
Muscularis layer of digestive tract, 305
Myelin, 138
Myelin disorders, 143
Myelin sheath, *139*
Myelinated fibers, 138
Myeloid tissue, 216; *see also* Red bone marrow
Myocardial infarction, 234, 237, 238
Myocardium, 229
Myofilaments, thick and thin, 113, *114*
Myometrium of uterus, 394
Myopia, 179
Myosin, 113
Myxedema, 201

N

Nail bed, 71
Nail body, 71
Nails, *49*, 71
  root of, 71
Nares, external, 283
Nasal bone, *88*, 90t, *91*, *285*
Nasal cavity, *55*, *185*, *280*, 283
Nasal region, *9*, 10t
Nasal septum, 283
Nasopharynx, *280*, 284, *285*
Natriuretic hormone, atrial, 209
  urine volume and, 349, 362
Natural immunity, 264-265
Navel, *9*
Nearsightedness, 179
Neck, *9*
  arteries of, 241t
  muscles of, 122t, 123, *124*
  sagittal section of, *285*
  veins of, 244t
Negative feedback, 194, *196*
Negative feedback loops, 11, 12
Neonatal period, 417-418
Neonate, 417
Neonatology, 417
Nephrons, 341, *345*
  functions of, in urine formation, 348t
  location of, *344*
Nerve endings
  encapsulated, 174t
  free, 71, 174t, *175*
Nerve fibers, effects of aging on, *421*
Nerve impulses, 50, 141, 142, 143-145

Nerve roots, *153*, *154*
Nerve tracts, 140, *153*
Nerves, 51, 140-141, *147*; *see also* specific nerve
  cranial, 156, *158*, 159t
  cutaneous, *66*
  spinal, *152*, *154*
    structure and function of, 156, 158
Nervous system, 48t, 50-51, 136-171
  autonomic, 156, 159-166
    functions of, 164t
    as whole, 164-165
  cells of, 137-140
  central, 146-156
  divisions of, *138*
  during infancy, 418
  organs and divisions of, 137
  parasympathetic, 163
  peripheral, *147*, 156-159
  role of, in movement, 116
  somatic, 160
  sympathetic, 163
Nervous tissue, 32t, 40
Neurilemma, 138, *139*
Neuroglia, 40, 138
Neurohypophysis, 196; *see also* Pituitary gland
Neuromuscular junction, 116
Neuron pathways, 141
Neuron(s), 40, 137-138, *139*
  afferent, 137
  autonomic, 160
  central or connecting, 137
  efferent, 137
  motor, 116, 137, *142*
  postganglionic, 162
    sympathetic, 163, 164, *165*
  postsynaptic, 145, 146
  preganglionic, 160, 162
    parasympathetic, 163
  presynaptic, 145
  sensory, 137, *142*
  types of, 137
Neurotransmitters, *145*, 146
  autonomic, 164, *165*
Neutrophils, 217t, 219
Newborn
  bone development of, *86*
  spinal curves of, 92, *94*
Niacin, sources, functions, and symptoms of deficiency of, 334t
Nipple, 396
Node(s)
  atrioventricular, 237
  lymph, 52, *53*, *260*, 261-262
  of Ranvier, 138, *139*
  sinoatrial, 237
  submandibular, *260*
Nonelectrolytes, 362
Nonessential amino acids, 333
Nongranular leukocytes, 215
Non-insulin-dependent diabetes mellitus, 208
Nonspecific immunity, 263-264
Nonstriated muscle, 111
Norepinephrine, 146, 164, 205
  functions of, 193t
Normal saline, 378
Nose, *9*, 279, 283-284
  receptors in, 176t
Nuclear envelope, *19*, 21
Nucleic acids, 27
Nucleolus(nucleoli), *19*, 20t, 22
Nucleoplasm, 21-22
Nucleus, 17, *19*, 20t
  cell, 21-22, *29*
  cerebral, 150
Nutrients
  assimilation of, 329
  catabolism of, *332*
  metabolism of, 329-333
Nutrition, 329
  metabolism and, 328-339

O

O blood type, 223
Oblique muscles, 122t, 124, *125*
Obstruction, airway, 286-287, 288
Occipital arteries, 241t, *242*
Occipital bone, *89*, 90t, *91*
  in newborn, *86*
Occipital lobe, 150, *151*
Occipital region, 10t
Oculomotor nerve, 156, *158*, 159t
Older adulthood, 420
"Oldsightedness," 176
Olecranon fossa, 95, *96*
Olecranon process, 95, *96*
Olecranon region, *9*, 10t
Olfactory bulb, *185*
Olfactory cells, 185
Olfactory center, *185*
Olfactory epithelium, *185*
Olfactory nerve, *158*, 159t, *185*
Olfactory receptors, 185
Olfactory tract, *185*
Oligodendroglia, 140
Oliguria, 349
Omental bursa, *321*
Omentum, greater, 321
Oocyte, 392, *393*
Oogenesis, 393
Oophorectomy, 400
Ophthalmic region, 10t
Opposing thumb to fingers, 105
Optic disc, *177*, 178
Optic nerve, 156, *158*, 159t, *177*
Oral cavity, *55*, *283*, 307-309
Oral region, *9*, 10t
Orbicularis oculi muscle, 122t, *124*
Orbicularis oris muscle, 122t, 123, *124*
Orbit, *88*, 176
Orbital region, *9*, 10t
Organ(s), 1, *2*
  cardiovascular system, 52
  circulatory system, 48t, 52, 53
  of Corti, *182*, 183
  digestive system, 48t, 54, *55*
  digestive tract, 306t
    location of, *306*
  endocrine system, 48t, 51, 52
  innervation of, by autonomic nervous system, *161*
  integumentary system, 47, 48t, *49*
  lymphatic system, 48t, 52, *53*, *260*
  major body cavities, *7*, 8t
  muscular system, 48t, 50
  of nervous system, 137
  paired, 58
  reproductive, 48t, 54, *56*, 57
    female, 391
    male, 383-384
  respiratory system, 48t, 54, *55*
  sense, 51
    classification of, 173
    skin as, 73
  skeletal system, 47, 48t, *49*, 50
  thermoregulatory, skin as, *337*
  urinary system, 48t, 54, *56*
Organ systems of body, 46-61
Organelles, 17, 18
  in cytoplasm, 20-21
Organization
  chemical level of, 1, *2*
  structural levels of, 1, *2*
Organogenesis, 414
Origin of muscle, 111
Oropharynx, *280*, 284, *285*
Osmosis, 23t, 25
Ossicles, auditory, 181
Ossification, endochondral, *85*, *86*
Osteoarthritis, 420
Osteoblasts, 84
Osteoclasts, 84
Osteocytes, 82, *83*, 84
Osteons, 37, 82, *83*, 84
Osteoporosis, *86*
Otitis, external, 184
Otitis media, 182, 284
Ova, 57, 383
Oval window, 181, *182*, *183*
Ovarian follicles, 208, 392
Ovaries, *52*, 57, 208, 391, *393*
  functions of, 393-394
  hormones of, 194t
  location of, *192*, 392-393
  production of estrogen and progesterone by, 393-394
  structure of, 392-393
Overhydration, 367

Oviducts; *see* Uterine tubes
Ovulating hormone; *see* Luteinizing hormone
Ovulation, 398, *399*, 400
Ovum, 393, *408*
Oxygen
  diffusion of, 293, *294*
  storage of, 297
Oxygen consumption, maximum, 295
Oxygen debt, 115
Oxygen therapy, 297
Oxyhemoglobin, 218, 293
Oxytocin, 198, 199
  functions of, 193t
  target organs for, *199*

P

P wave, 238, *239*
Pacemaker, artificial, 238; *see* Sinoatrial node
Pacinian corpuscle, *66*, 70-71, 174t, *175*
Pain, suppression of, during exercise, 146
Pain receptors, 173
Palate, *285*, 308
Palatine bone, 90t
Palatine tonsils, 263, 284, *285*
Palmar region, *9*, 10t
Palpable bony landmarks, 103
Palsy, shaking; *see* Parkinson's disease
Pancreas, *7*, 51, *52*, 54, *55*, *207*, *306*, *318*, *321*
  digestion and, 317-318
  hormones of, 194t
  location of, *192*
Pancreatic duct, *316*
Pancreatic islets; *see* Islets of Langerhans
Pancreatic juice, 317, 322, *323*
Pancreatic lipase, 322, *323*
Pancreatic veins, *246*
Panhysterectomy, 400
Pantothenic acid, sources, functions, and symptoms of deficiency of, 334t
Papilla(e)
  dermal, *66*, 68
  duodenal, 316
  hair, *66*, 69
  renal, 341, *344*
  of tongue, 184
  vallate, *308*, 309
Paralysis, 116, 154
Paranasal sinuses, 90, 283
Parasympathetic nervous system, 163
Parasympathetic postganglionic axon, 164, *165*
Parasympathetic preganglionic axon, 164, *165*
Parasympathetic preganglionic neurons, 163
Parathyroid glands, 51, *52*, *200*, 202-203
  location of, *192*
Parathyroid hormones, 193t, 202-203
  functions of, 193t
Parietal bone, *89*, 90t, *91*
  in newborn, *86*
Parietal lobe, 150, *151*
Parietal peritoneum, *64*, 65, 232, *321*
Parietal pleura, 63, *64*, 290, *292*
Parietal portion of serous membrane, 63
Parkinson's disease, 150
Parotid gland, *306*, 311
Partial-thickness burn, 75
Parturition, 414, *415*
Passive immunity, 265
Passive transport processes, 22, 23-25
Patella, *88*, *98*, 99, 100t, *142*
  as palpable bony landmark, *103*
Patellar reflex, 142, 143
Patellar tendon, *142*
Pectineus muscle, *120*, 122t
Pectoral girdle, 94
Pectoralis major muscle, *120*, 122t, 123, 124, *125*, 128t
Pedal region, *9*, 10t
Pelvic bones, 99
  in newborn, *86*
Pelvic cavity, 5, 8t
Pelvic girdle, 99
Pelvic region, 10t
Pelvis
  male and female, differences between, 100, *101*
  renal, 341, *342*, *343*, *344*, 349
Penis, 54, *56*, 57, *384*, 390-391
Pepsin, 322
Pepsinogen, 322
Peptidases, 322, *323*
Pericardial fluid, 232
Pericarditis, 232
Pericardium, 232
Perilymph, 182
Perilymph space, *182*
Perineal region, 10t
Perineum, 397
Perineurium, 140, *141*
Periodontal membrane, 310
Periosteum, 82, 83, 84, 103
Peripheral nervous system, 137, *147*, 156-159
Peristalsis, 305
  stomach and, 312
Peritoneal dialysis, continuous ambulatory, 351
Peritoneal fluid, 321
Peritoneal space, *318*, 321
Peritoneum, 63, 320-322
  extensions of, 321-322
  parietal, *64*, 65
  visceral, *64*, 65
Peritubular capillaries, *345*
Permanent teeth, 309, 310, 419
Pernicious anemia, 218
Peroneal veins, *243*, 244t
Peroneus brevis muscle, *120*, *121*, 123t
Peroneus group of muscle, 127
Peroneus longus muscle, *120*, *121*, 123t, 128t
Peroneus longus muscle tendon, 127
Perspiration, 72
pH
  blood, 371
  of body fluids, 371
    mechanisms that control, 371-376
  control of
    respiratory mechanism of, 375
    urinary mechanism of, 375-376
pH imbalances, 377-379
pH range, *372*
Phagocytes, 219, 268
Phagocytosis, 26, 219, *220*
  antibodies and, 266, *269*
  of bacteria by white blood cell, *27*
Phalangeal region, *9*
Phalanges, *88*, *89*
  of lower extremity, 99, 100t
  of upper extremity, 95, 97
Pharyngeal tonsils, 263, 284, *285*
Pharynx, 54, *55*, 279, *280*, 284, 306
  digestion and, 312
Phospholipids, 17
Phosphorus, sources, functions, and symptoms of deficiency of, 335t
Photopigments, 180
Photoreceptor cells of eye, 178
Photoreceptors, 173
Phrenic nerve, 292
Physiology, 1
  exercise, 12
Pia mater, *154*, 155, *157*
Pigment, 67
Pigment containing layer of skin, *66*, 67
Pineal body, *148*
Pineal gland, 51, *52*, *148*, 209
  hormones of, 194t
  location of, *192*
Pinna, 180
Pinocytosis, 26
Pituitary gland, 51, *52*, *148*, 196-198
  hormones of, 193t, 196-198, *199*
  location of, *192*
  menstrual cycle and, 400
Pituitary stalk, 147
Pivot joint, 105
Placenta, 411-412, *415*
  as endocrine gland, 209
  fetal circulation and, 247
  hormones of, 194t
Planes, body, 3-5

Plantar flexion, 127, *129*
Plantar region, *9*, 10t
Plasma, 38, 215, 359, *360*
  electrolytes in, 364t
Plasma cells, *270*, 271, 272
Plasma membrane, 17-18, *19*, 20t
  structure of, 18
Plasma proteins, 215, 329
  decreased concentration of, causing edema, 364
Platelet plug, 220
Platelets, 217t
  blood clotting and, 220-222
  volume of, 216
Pleura, 63, *64*, 290, *292*
Pleural cavity, 5, 8t
Pleurisy, 290
Plexus, 159
  choroid, 156, *157*
Plicae of small intestine, 314, *315*
Pneumocystosis, 271
Pneumothorax, 290
Poisoning, uremic, 341
Polar bodies, 393
Polycythemia, 218, *219*
Polyuria, 349
Pons, 147, *148*, *155*
  functions of, 153t
Popliteal arteries, 241t, *242*
  as pulse point, *252*
Popliteal lymph nodes, *260*
Popliteal region, *9*, 10t
Popliteal veins, *243*, 244t
Pores, 72
Position, anatomical, 1, 3
Positive feedback, 194-195
Positive feedback loops, 12
Posterior, 3, *4*
Posterior pituitary gland, 196; *see also* Pituitary gland
  hormones of, 198
Posterior root ganglion, 142
Posterior superior iliac spine, *126*
Postganglionic axon, parasympathetic, 164, *165*
Postganglionic neurons, 162
  sympathetic, 163, 164, *165*
Postnatal period, 407, 416-420
Postsynaptic neuron, 145, 146
Posture, muscles and, 115
Potassium, sources, functions, and symptoms of deficiency of, 335t
Potassium pump, 25
Precapillary sphincter, 241
Prefrontal association area, *151*
Preganglionic axon
  parasympathetic, 164, *165*
  sympathetic, 164, *165*
Preganglionic neurons, 160, 162
  parasympathetic, 163
Pregnancy, 395
  alcohol consumption during, 419
  trimesters of, 412
  tubal, 394
Premolars, 309
Premotor area, *151*
Prenatal period, 407-414
Prepuce, 390-391, *397*
Presbyopia, 176, 422
Pressure
  blood; *see* Blood pressure
  central venous, 251
  hydrostatic, 25
Pressure receptors, 71
Pressure sores, 72
Presynaptic neuron, 145
Primary bronchi, 287
Primary follicles, 392
Primary germ layers
  derivatives of, 412t
  formation of, 412
Primary organs of digestion, 48t, 54, *55*
Primary spermatocyte, 386
Prime mover, 113
Progesterone
  functions of, 194t
  production of, by ovary, 393-394
Prolactin, 198
  functions of, 193t
  target organs for, *199*
Proliferative phase of menstrual cycle, 398, *399*, 400
Pronation, 127, *129*
Prone, 3
Prophase, *29*, 30
Proprioceptors, 173
Prostaglandin A, 195
Prostaglandin E, 195
Prostaglandin F, 195
Prostaglandins, 195-196
  groups of, 194
Prostate gland, *56*, 57, *352*, *384*, 389, *390*
  hypertrophy of, 391
Prostatectomy, 391
Prostatic urethra, *352*
Protease, 322, *323*
Protein(s)
  anabolism of, 332-333
  blood, 329
    capillary blood pressure and, 367
  complement, 267
  digestion, 322
  metabolism of, 332-333
  plasma, 215, 329
    decreased concentration of, causing edema, 364
  synthesis of, *28*
    RNA molecules and, 28
Protein hormones, 191-192
  mechanism of action of, *192*
Proteinuria after exercise, 349
Prothrombin, 220, *221*, 329
Prothrombin activator, 220, *221*
Proximal, 3, *4*
Proximal convoluted tubule, 343
Proximal tubule diuretics, 363
Pseudostratified epithelium, 32t, *33*, 35
Pterygoid process, *91*
Pubic symphysis, *415*
Pubis, *88*, 99
  in newborn, *86*
Pulmonary artery(ies), *230*, *231*, 234, *237*, *242*, *245*, *292*
Pulmonary circulation, 234, *235*, 241, 244-245
Pulmonary semilunar valve, *231*, 232, *233*
Pulmonary stretch receptors, respiration and, *298*, 299
Pulmonary trunk, *247*, *292*
Pulmonary veins, *230*, *231*, *237*, *243*, 244t, *292*
Pulmonary ventilation, 290
  volumes of air exchanged in, 295-297
Pulp cavity, 310
Pulse, 251-252
Pulse points, 251-252
Puncture, lumbar, 156
Pupil, 176, *177*
Purkinje fibers, 237
Pyloric sphincter, 313
Pylorus of stomach, 313
Pyridoxine, sources, functions, and symptoms of deficiency of, 334t

Q

QRS complex, 238, *239*
Quadrants, abdominopelvic, 6
Quadriceps femoris muscle, 125
Quadriceps group of muscles, *120*, 123t, 128t, *142*
Quickening, 414

R

Radial arteries, 241t, *242*
  as pulse point, *252*
Radial tuberosity, *96*
Radial veins, *244*
Radiation causing heat loss, 336
Radius, *88*, *89*, 95, *96*, 97
  in newborn, *86*
  styloid process of, as palpable bony landmark, *103*
Ranvier, node of, 138, *139*
Reabsorption in urine formation, 347, 348
Receiving chambers of heart; *see* Atria
Receptor(s)
  encapsulated, 173
  Golgi tendon, 175t

Receptor(s)—cont'd
of impulses, 142
influencing respiration, 299
pain, 173
sense, general, 174t, *175*
sensory, 173
in skin, 70-71
smell or olfactory, 185
stretch, *142*
pulmonary, respiration and, *298*, 299
taste, 184-185
unencapsulated, 173
Rectal artery, *319*
Rectal vein, *319*
Rectum, 54, *55*, 306, *319*, 320, *321*, *384*, *392*, *415*
Rectus abdominis muscle, *120*, 122t, 124-125
Rectus femoris muscle, *120*, 123t, 125
Rectus muscles of eye, *177*
Rectus sheath, *125*
Red blood cells
structure and function of, 217-218
volume of, 216
Red bone marrow, 81, 82, 216
Red-green color blindness, 180
Reflex(es), 143
emptying, 353
jerk, 154
knee-jerk, 142, 143, 154
patellar, 142, 143
spinal cord, 154
vomit, *379*
withdrawal, 143, 154
Reflex arcs, 141-143
Reflux, heartburn caused by, 312
Regions, body, 8
Regulation of respiration, 297-299
Releasing hormones, 149, 199
functions of, 193t
Renal arteries, 241t, *242*, *342*, *343*
Renal calculi; *see* Kidney stones
Renal calyx, *344*
Renal capsule, *343*, *344*
Renal colic, 352
Renal corpuscle, 341, 343, *344*, *345*
Renal cortex, 341, *343*
Renal medulla, 341, *343*, *344*
Renal papilla, *344*
Renal pelvis, 341, *342*, *344*, 349
Renal pyramids, 341, *343*
Renal tubule, 341, 343
Renal veins, *342*, *343*
Rennin, 322
Replacement, hip, total, 104
Replication, DNA, 30
Repolarization, 238, *239*
Reproduction, cell, 26-31
Reproductive ducts
female, 394-396
male, 389
Reproductive organs, male, *384*
Reproductive system(s), 48t, 54, *56*, 57, 382-405
analogous features of, 401t
female, 48t, 57, 391-401; *see also* Female reproductive system
male, 48t, *56*, 57, 383-391; *see also* Male reproductive system
Reserve volume
expiratory, 295-297
inspiratory, 295-297
Residual volume, 297
Respiration, 290-297
aerobic or cellular, 21
cellular, 290
external, 290
internal, 290, 295
receptors influencing, 299
regulation of, 297-299
voluntary control of, 298
Respiratory acidosis, 378
Respiratory alkalosis, 378
Respiratory arrest, 299
Respiratory center, 147
Respiratory control centers, 297, *298*
Respiratory distress syndrome, infant, 289
Respiratory disturbances, 377-378
Respiratory mechanism of pH control, 375
Respiratory membrane, 279, *281*, 282
Respiratory mucosa, 282
Respiratory muscles, *298*
Respiratory system, 48t, 54, *55*, 278-303
effects of aging on, 420
functions of, 279
role of, in movement, 116
structure of, 279
Respiratory therapist, 297
Respiratory tracts, 279, 282
lower, 279, *280*, 282
upper, 279, *280*, 282
Response, inflammatory, 264
Resuscitation, cardiopulmonary, 229
Retention
of electrolytes, 364
of sodium causing edema, 364
urinary, 353-354
Reticular formation, 147, *148*
Reticulum, endoplasmic, 20-21
rough and smooth, *19*, 20
Retina, 176, *177*
cells of, 178
Retinal artery, *177*
Retinal vein, *177*
Rh-negative blood, 223
Rh-positive blood, 223
Rh system of blood typing, 223
RhoGAM, 223
Riboflavin, sources, functions, and symptoms of deficiency of, 334t
Ribonucleic acid, 27
messenger, 28
protein synthesis and, 28-29
Ribosomes, *19*, 20
free, *19*
Ribs, *88*, *89*, 94
effects of aging on, 420
RNA; *see* Ribonucleic acid
Rods and cones, 176, 178
Root(s)
hair, 69
nail, 71
nerve, *153*, *154*
Root canal, *310*
Rotation, 127, *129*
Rough endoplasmic reticulum, *19*
Ruffini's corpuscles, 174t, *175*
Rugae, 312
"Rule of nines" for burns, 74

S

Sacral curve of spine, 92, *93*
Sacral nerves, *152*
Sacrum, *88*, *89*, 92t, *93*, *152*
in newborn, *86*
Saddle joint, 105
Sagittal plane, *4*, 5
Sagittal sinus, *243*, 244t
Saline, normal, 378
Saliva, 312
Salivary amylase, 312, 322, *323*
Salivary glands, 54, *55*, 191
digestion and, 311-312
Saltatory conduction, *144*, 145
Saphenous veins, *243*, 244t
Sarcoma, Kaposi, 271
Sarcomere, 113, *114*
Sartorius muscle, *120*, 122t, 128t
Scapula, *88*, *89*, 94, *95*, 97t
acromion process of, *126*
as palpable bony landmark, *103*
Schlemm, canal of, *177*
Schwann cells, 138, *139*
Sciatic nerve, *126*
Sclera, 176, *177*
Scrotum, *56*, 57, 384, 390-391
Sebaceous glands, 65, *66*, 69, 72-73
Sebum, 72-73
Second-degree burn, 75
Second messenger hypothesis, 191
Second messengers, 191
Secondary bronchi, 287
Secondary follicle, 393
Secondary sex characteristics
development of, 419
female, 394

Secretion(s)
distal renal tubule, of hydrogen ions, urine acidification and conservation of base by, *376*
internal, sodium-containing, *366*
tubule, of ammonia, urine acidification by, *377*
urine formation and, 348
Secretory phase of menstrual cycle, 398, *399*, 400
Sections, body, 3-5
Sella turcica, 196
Semen, 209, 389
Semicircular canals, 181, 182, 183
Semilunar valves, *231*, 232, *233*, *240*
Semimembranosus muscle, *121*, 123t, 125
Seminal fluid, 389
Seminal vesicles, *384*, 389
Seminiferous tubule, 385
Semitendinosus muscle, *121*, 123t, 125
Senescence, 420
Sensations
converting stimulus into, 173
taste, 184-185
Sense organs, 51
classification of, 173
general, 173-175
skin as, 73
special, 173, 176-185
Senses, 172-189
special, effects of aging on, 422
Sensor in feedback loop, 11
Sensory hair cells of ear, *182*
Sensory neurons, 137, *142*
Sensory receptors, 173
general, 174t, *175*
Septum
interatrial, 232
interventricular, *231*, 232
nasal, 283
Sequence of base pairs, 27
Serosa of digestive tract, 305
Serotonin, 146
Serous membranes, 63, 64, 65
Serum, blood, 215
Sex characteristics, secondary
development of, 419
female, 394
Sex glands
accessory
female, 396
male, 389-390
female, 208
male, 208-209
Sex hormones, 204
functions of, 193t
Sexes, common structural and functional characteristics between, 383
Shaft
of bone, 82
hair, *66*, 69, *70*
Shaking palsy; *see* Parkinson's disease
Shinbone; *see* Tibia
Shingles, 166
Shock, anaphylactic, 262
Short bones, 81
Shoulder, 94
Shoulder blade; *see* Scapula
Sickle cell anemia, 218
Sickle cell trait, 218
Sigmoid artery, *319*
Sigmoid colon, 306t, 320
Sigmoid vein, *319*
Simple columnar epithelium, 32t, *33*, *34*, 35
Simple cuboidal epithelium, 32t, *33*, 35-36
Simple goiter, 201
Simple squamous epithelium, 31, 32t, *33*
of serous membranes, 63
Sinoatrial node, 237
Sinus(es), 90
coronary, 235
frontal air, *285*
paranasal, 283
sagittal, *243*, 244t
sphenoidal air, *285*
Sinusitis, 283
frontal, 90, 92
Skeletal muscle, 48t, 50, 111, *112*
attachments of, *112*
contractions of
movements produced by, 127-129
types of, 117, *118*
effects of exercise on, 117-119
functions of, 113-115
general overview of, *120*, *121*
groups of, 119-127
heat production and, 115
microscopic structure of, 113, *114*
posture and, 115
structure of, 111-113, *114*
Skeletal muscle fibers, 38
Skeletal muscle tissue, 32t, 38, 39
Skeletal system, 47, 48t, *49*, 50, 80-109
effects of aging on, 420
functions of, 81
role of, in movement, 116
Skeleton
appendicular, 87, 94-100
axial, 87-94
divisions of, 87-100
male and female, differences between, 100, *101*
Skin, *49*, 63, 64, 65-75
appendages of, 68-73
body temperature and, 336, *337*
effects of aging on, 420
Skin—cont'd
exercise and, 73
functions of, 73
glands of, 72-73
layers of 65-68
microscopic view of, *66*
receptors in, 70-71
structure of, 65-68
subcutaneous layer of, 69
Skull, *9*, 87, 90-92, *148*
bones of, 87, 90t
changes in size of, from birth to maturity, 416-417
side of, *9*
Sliding filament model of skeletal muscle contraction, 113
Small intestine, *7*, 54, *55*, *246*, 306t, *321*
digestion and, 314-316
muscle layers of, *315*
section of, *307*
Smell receptors, 185
Smiling muscle; *see* Zygomaticus muscle
Smooth endoplasmic reticulum, *19*
Smooth muscle, 111, *112*
Smooth muscle tissue, 32t, 40
Sodium
internal secretions containing, *366*
reabsorption of, 347-348
retention of, causing edema, 364
sources, functions, and symptoms of deficiency of, 335t
Sodium bicarbonate
buffering action of, 372, *373*, 374-375
lactic acid buffered by, *374*
Sodium-potassium pump, 25-26
Sodium pump, 25
Soft palate, *285*, 308
"Soft spots"; *see* Fontanels
Soleus muscle, *120*, *121*, 123t, 128t
Solution
acid, 371
alkaline, 371
basic, 371
hypertonic, 24
hypotonic, 24
isotonic, 24
Somatic nervous system, 160
Somatic sensory area, primary, *151*
Somatic sensory association area, *151*
Sores, pressure, 72
Sound waves, effect of, on cochlear structures, *183*
Sounds
heart, 232, 234
Korotkoff, 250
Space
intrapleural, 290, *292*
perilymph, *182*
peritoneal, *318*, 321
subarachnoid, *157*

Special sense organs, 173, 176-185
effects of aging on, 422
Specific immunity, 264-265
Sperm(spermatozoa), *22*, 57, 208-209, 383, 388, *408*
structure of, *388*
Spermatic cord, 389
Spermatids, 386
Spermatocyte, primary, 386
Spermatogenesis, 386, *387*
Spermatogonia, 386
Sphenoid bone, 90t, *91*
Sphenoid sinuses, 90
Sphenoidal air sinus, *285*
Sphenoidal sinus, 283
Sphincter(s)
anal, 320
cardiac, 312
precapillary, 241
pyloric, 313
urethral, 353
Sphygmomanometer, 250
Spinal cavity, 5, 6, 8t
Spinal cord, *7*, 51, *147*, *148*, *153*, *154*, *155*, *157*
coverings and fluid spaces of, 154-156
functions of, 154
injury to, 116
structure of, 150-154
Spinal cord reflexes, 154
Spinal curvature
infant's, 418
toddler's, 419
Spinal ganglion, *154*
Spinal nerves, *152*, *154*
structure and function of, 156, 158
Spinal tracts, 152
Spindle fibers, *29*, 30
Spindles, muscle, 175t
Spine, 92, *93*
curves of, 92
in newborn, 92, *94*
iliac
anterior superior, 103
posterior superior, *126*
Spinocerebellar nerve tract, *153*
Spinothalamic nerve tract, *153*
Spirometer, 295
Spleen, *7*, 52, *53*, *246*, *260*, 263, *306*, *342*
Splenectomy, 263
Splenic arteries, 241t, *242*
Splenic flexure, *306*, *319*
Splenic veins, *243*, 244t, *246*, *319*
Spongy bone, 82, *83*
Spontaneous fractures, *86*
Squamous epithelium
simple, 31, 32t, *33*
of serous membranes, 63
stratified, 31, 32t, *33*, *34*
Squamous suture, *91*, 92
Stapes, 90t, 181, *183*
Starch, animal; *see* Glycogen
Stem cells, 270
Sternoclavicular joint, 94
Sternocleidomastoid muscle, *120*, *121*, 122t, 123, *124*
Sternum, *49*, *88*, 94, *95*, *292*
in newborn, *86*
Steroid hormones, 192-194
abuse of, 192
mechanism of action of, *195*
Stimulus(stimuli)
converting, into sensation, 173
muscle, 117
nervous system, 51
threshold, 117
Stoma, 324
Stomach, *7*, 54, *55*, *246*, 306, *318*, *321*
curvatures of, 313
digestion and, 312-313
divisions of, 313
emptying of, exercise and, 317
muscle layers of, 312, *313*
ulcers in, 314
Stones, kidney, 352
removal of, using ultrasound, 354
Stratified squamous epithelium, 31, 32t, *33*, *34*
Stratified transitional epithelium, 32t, *33*, 35
Stratum corneum, 66, 67, 71
functions of, 73
Stratum germinativum, 66
Strength training, 118
Stress, glucocorticoids and, 204
Stress responses induced by glucocorticoids, *205*
Stretch receptors, *142*
pulmonary, respiration and, *298*, 299
Striated muscle, 111
Stroke, 150, 422
Stroke volume, 249
Structural levels of organization, 1, *2*
Structure and function of body, introduction to, 1-15
Styloid process, *91*
of radius, *96*
as palpable bony landmark, *103*
of ulna, *96*
as palpable bony landmark, *103*
Subarachnoid space, *157*
Subclavian artery(ies), *230*, 241t, *242*
Subclavian veins, *243*, 244
Subcutaneous fatty tissue, *66*
Subcutaneous injection, 68
Subcutaneous layer of skin, 69
Subcutaneous tissue, 65-66
Sublingual gland, *306*, *308*, 311
Submandibular duct, *308*
Submandibular glands, *306*, 311
Submandibular nodes, *260*
Submucosa of digestive tract, 305
Substances, movement of, through cell membranes, 22-26
Subtotal hysterectomy, 400
Sucrase, 322, *323*
Sudoriferous glands; *see* Sweat glands
Sulci, cerebral, 150, *151*
Sunburn, 75
Superficial, 3, *4*
Superior, 3, *4*
Superior vena cava; *see* Vena cava
Supination, 127, *129*
Supine, 3
Supplements, vitamin, for athletes, 333
Suppression, urinary, 354
Supraclavicular region, *9*, 10t
Surfactant, *281*, 289
Surgery, coronary bypass, 234
Surgical neck of humerus, *96*
Sutures, 92, 102
Sweat, 72
Sweat ducts, *66*
Sweat gland, *66*, 72, 191
functions of, 73
Sweating, exercise and, 73
Swimmer's ear, 184
Sympathetic chain ganglia, 163
Sympathetic ganglion, *154*
Sympathetic nervous system, 163
Sympathetic postganglionic neurons, 163, 164, *165*
Sympathetic preganglionic axon, 164, *165*
Sympathetic trunk, *154*
Symphysis pubis, 102, *392*
Synapse, 142-143, 145-146
monosynaptic, *142*
Synaptic cleft, *145*, 146
Synaptic knob, 145-146
Synarthroses, 102
Synergists, 113
Synovial fluid, 65, 104
in bursae, 112
Synovial membranes, *64*, 65, 104
in bursae, 112
Synthesis, protein, *28*
RNA molecules and, 28
Systemic arteries, *294*
Systemic circulation, 234, *235*, 241, 244-245
Systemic veins, *294*
Systems, 1, *2*; *see also* specific system
Systole, 232, *233*, 234

T

T_3, 200
functions of, 193t
T_4, 200
functions of, 193t

T cells, 217t, 219, 262, 268, *272*
AIDS and, 271
development of, *272*, 273
functions of, 273
T-lymphocytes; *see* T cells
T wave, 238, *239*
Target organ cell, 191
Tarsal region, *9*, 10t
Tarsals, *88*, *89*, 99, 100t
Taste, sense of, effects of aging on, 422
Taste area, primary, *151*
Taste buds, 184, 309
receptors in, 176t
Taste receptors, 184-185
Taste sensations, 184-185
Teeth, 54, 309-310
decay of, 311
deciduous, 419
longitudinal section of, *310*
permanent, 419
typical, 310
Telophase, *29*, 30-31
Temperature, body, 336
Temporal artery, as pulse point, *252*
Temporal bone, 90t, *91*, *181*
Temporal lobe, 150, *151*
Temporal muscle, 122t
Temporal region, *9*, 10t
Temporalis muscle, 123, *124*
Tendon(s), 50, 111-112
patellar, *142*
Tendon receptors, Golgi, 175t
Tendon sheaths, 112
Tenosynovitis, 119
"Test tube" baby, 410
Testes, *52*, *56*, 57, 383, 384-389
functions of, 386-389
hormones of, 194t
location of, *192*
structure of, 384-385
tissue of, *385*
Testicles, self-examination of, 58
Testosterone, 209, 385
functions of, 194t
production of, by testes, 388-389
Tests, cancer screening, 58
Tetanic contractions, 117
Tetanus, 117
Thalamic center, *185*
Thalamus, *148*, 149
functions of, 149, 153t
Therapist, respiratory, 297
Therapy, oxygen, 297
Thermoreceptors, 173
Thermoregulatory organ, skin as, *337*
Thiamine, sources, functions, and symptoms of deficiency of, 334t
Thick myofilaments, 113, *114*
Thigh
bones of, *98*
muscles of, 128t
Thin myofilaments, 113, *114*
Third-degree burn, 75
Third eye; *see* Pineal gland
Third ventricle, 149, *155*, *157*
Thoracic cavity, 5, 8t
Thoracic curve of spine, 92, *93*
Thoracic duct, 52, *53*, 259, *260*
area drained by, *260*
Thoracic nerves, *152*
Thoracic region, 10t
Thoracic veins, *243*, 244t
Thoracic vertebrae, *89*, 92t, *93*, *152*
Thoracolumbar system, 163
Thorax, 94
arteries of, 241t
bones of, 94t, *95*
veins of, 244t
Three-neuron arc, 142, 143
Threshold stimulus, 117
Thrombin, 220, *221*
Thrombocytes; *see* Platelets
Thrombosis, 221, 232
Thrombus, 221
Thumbs, 105
opposing, to fingers, 105
Thymosin, 209, 263
functions of, 194t
Thymus gland, 51, 52, *53*, 209, *260*, 262-263
hormones of, 194t
location of, *192*
Thyroid cartilage, 284, *285*, *286*
Thyroid gland, 51, *52*, 200-202, *286*
location of, *192*
tissue of, *200*
Thyroid hormone, abnormalities of, 201
Thyroid-stimulating hormone, 197
functions of, 193t
target organs for, *199*
Thyroxine, 200
functions of, 193t
Tibia, *88*, *89*, *98*, 99, 100t
anterior border of, as palpable bony landmark, *103*
medial malleolus of, as palpable bony landmark, *103*
in newborn, *86*
Tibial arteries, 241t, *242*
Tibial tuberosity, *98*
Tibial veins, *243*, 244t
Tibialis anterior muscle, *120*, 123t, 127, 128t
Tidal volume, 295-297
Tissue(s), 1, 2, 31-40
adipose, subcutaneous, *66*
blood, 32t, 38; *see also* Blood
bone, 32t, 37; *see also* Bone
Tissue(s)—cont'd
cartilage, *84*
connective, 32t, 36-38
membranes of, *64*, 65
epithelial, 31-36
cells of, arrangement and shape of, 31, *33*
exchange of gases in, *294*, 295
eyeball, 176
fitness and, 39
hemopoietic, 32t, 38
involuntary, 40
lymphatic, 216
muscle, 32t, 38-40, 111
myeloid, 216; *see also* Red bone marrow
nervous, 32t, 40
subcutaneous, 65-66
thyroid gland, *200*
Tissue fluid, 17
Tissue hormones; *see* Prostaglandins
Tissue typing, 18
Tocopherol, sources, functions, and symptoms of deficiency of, 334t
Toddler, normal spinal curvature of, 419
Toe(s), *9*, 99
Toe dancer's muscle; *see* Gastrocnemius muscle
Toenails, 71
Tongue, 54, *55*, *184*, *285*, *286*, *306*, 308
Tongue-tied, 308
Tonic contraction, 115
Tonicity, 24
Tonsillectomy, 284
Tonsillitis, 284
Tonsils, 52, *53*, 263, 284
Total hip replacement, 104
Total hysterectomy, 400
Total metabolic rate, 334
factors determining, *335*
Touch, receptors for, 71
Trabeculae, 82, *83*
Trachea, *7*, 54, *55*, *200*, 279, *280*, 284-287, *306*
cartilages of, 286
obstruction of, 286-287
respiratory mucosa lining, *282*
Tract(s)
nerve, 140, *153*
olfactory, *185*
spinal, 152
Training
aerobic, 118-119
endurance, 118-119
strength, 118
Transcription, 28
Transducer, ultrasound, 416
Transitional epithelium, stratified, 32t, *33*, 35
Translation, 28-29

Transport processes
active, 22, 25-26
passive, 22, 23-25
Transverse arch of foot, 99, *100*
Transverse colon, 306t, 320, *321*
Transverse plane, *4*, 5
Transverse process, *154*
Transversus abdominis muscle, 122t, 124, *125*
Trapezium, 105
Trapezius muscle, *120*, *121*, 122t, 123, *124*, *126*
Triceps brachii muscle, 113, 115, *121*, 122t, 124, 128t
Tricuspid valve, *231*, 232, *233*, *237*
Tricuspids, 309
Trigeminal nerve, *158*, 159t
Trigone, 352
Triiodothyronine, 200
functions of, 193t
Trimesters of pregnancy, 412
Trochanter
greater, *88*, *98*, *126*
lesser, *98*
Trochlea, *96*
Trochlear nerve, *158*, 159t
Tropic hormone, 196-197
True ribs, 94
Trunk, *9*
muscles of, 122t, 124-125
Trypsin, 322
TSH; *see* Thyroid-stimulating hormone
Tubal pregnancies, 394
Tube(s)
auditory or eustachian, 181-182, *183*, 284, *285*
uterine (fallopian), 57, 394, *392*
Tubercle
adductor, *98*
greater, *96*
Tuberosity
radial, *96*
tibial, *98*
Tubule(s)
collecting, 343, *344*, *345*
convoluted, 343, *344*, *345*
renal, 341, 343
seminiferous, 385
Tubule secretion of ammonia, urine acidification by, *377*
Tumors, brain, 116, 156
Tunica adventitia, 238, *240*
Tunica albuginea, 385
Tunica intima, 238, *240*, 241
Tunica media, 238, *240*
Turkish saddle; *see* Sella turcica
TV; *see* Tidal volume
Twitch contractions, 117
Two-neuron arc, 142, 143
Tympanic membrane, 181, *183*
Type A blood, 223
Type AB blood, 223
Type B blood, 223
Type O blood, 223
Typing, tissue, 18

U

Ulcers, 314
decubitus, 72
Ulna, *88*, *89*, 95, *96*, 97
in newborn, *86*
styloid process of, as palpable bony landmark, *103*
Ulnar arteries, 241t, *242*
Ulnar veins, *244*
Ultrasonogram, 416
Ultrasound, removal of kidney stones using, 354
Ultrasound transducer, 416
Umbilical arteries, *247*, 248
Umbilical cord, 247, *415*
Umbilical cord blood, freezing, 418
Umbilical region of abdominopelvic cavity, 5, *6*, *9*, 10t
Umbilical vein, *247*, 248
Umbilicus, *125*
Uncompensated metabolic acidosis, 378
Unencapsulated receptors, 173, 174t
Universal donor blood, 223
Universal recipient blood, 223
Upper extremity(ies), *9*; *see also* Arm
arteries of, 241t
bones of, 94-97
muscles moving, 122t, 123-124
superficial veins of, *244*
veins of, 244t
Upper respiratory tract, 279, *280*, 282
Uremia, 341
Uremic poisoning, 341
Ureters, *7*, 54, *56*, *342*, *343*, *344*, 349, *352*, *384*, *392*
cross section of, *349*
Urethra, *7*, 54, *56*, 353, *384*
female, *392*, 397, *415*
male, *56*, 57, 389, *390*
prostatic, *352*
Urethral orifice, male, *390*
Urethral sphincters, 353
Urinary bladder; *see* Bladder
Urinary catheterization, 353
Urinary meatus, 353
Urinary mechanism of pH control, 375-376
Urinary system, 48t, 54, *56*, 340-357
effects of aging on, 420
Urination, 353
Urine, 54
acidification of
by distal renal tubule secretion of hydrogen ions, *376*
Urine—cont'd
by tubule secretion of ammonia, *377*
characteristics of, 346t
formation of, 346-349
functions of nephron in, 348t
retention of, 353-354
suppression of, 354
volume of, control of, 348-349
Uterine fimbriae, 407, *408*
Uterine glands, *410*
Uterine tubes, 57, *392*, 394, *395*
fertilization and, 407, *408*
parts of, 407
Uterus, 57, *392*, 394-395, *408*
Uvula, *285*, 308

V

Vagina, 57, *392*, *395*, 396, *415*
Vaginal hysterectomy, 400
Vagus nerve, 156, *158*, 159t
Vallate papillae, *308*, 309
Valve(s)
atrioventricular, 232, *233*
bicuspid, 232, *233*, *237*
heart, *231*, 232
ileocecal, *306*, 318, *319*
mitral, *231*, 232, *233*, *237*
semilunar, 232, *233*, *240*
tricuspid, 232, *233*, *237*
Vas deferens, *56*, 57, *389*
Vasomotor center, 147
Vastus intermedius muscle, 123t, 125
Vastus lateralis muscle, *120*, 123t
Vastus medialis muscle, *120*, 123t
Vastus muscles, 125
VC; *see* Vital capacity
Veins, 52, *53*, 238, *240*, 241, *245*
functions of, 241
major, *243*, 244t
Vena cava, *230*, *231*, 234, *237*, 238, *243*, 244t, *245*, *246*, *247*, *318*, *342*
Venous blood, pH of, 371
Venous blood pressure, 251
central, 251
Ventilation, pulmonary, 290
volumes of air exchanged in, 295-297
Ventral, 3, *4*
Ventral body cavity, 5, 6, 8t
Ventricles, *229*, *230*, *231*, *233*, *237*, *245*
cerebral, 155
fourth, *155*, 156, *157*
lateral, *155*, *157*
third, 149, *155*, *157*
Ventricular systole, *233*, 234
Venules, 238, *245*
functions of, 241
lymphatic, 259
Vermiform appendix; *see* Appendix

Vertebrae, 92, *93*, *292*
- cervical, *89*, *152*
- joints between, 102
- lumbar, *89*, *152*
- thoracic, *89*, *152*

Vertebral bone, *318*
Vertebral column, *88*, 92, *93*, *95*
- bones of, 92t

Vertebral foramen, 92
Vesicles, 21
- seminal, *384*, 389

Vessels
- blood, 238-241; *see also* Blood vessels
- lymphatic, 52, *53*, 259-261, 262

Vestibular glands, 396
Vestibular nerve, *181*, *182*, 183
Vestibule, *181*, 182, 183, 396, 397
Vestibulocochlear nerve, *158*, 159t
Villi of small intestine, 313, 314, *315*
Virus, human immunodeficiency, 271
Visceral effectors, 162
Visceral muscle, 111
Visceral pericardium, 232
Visceral peritoneum, *64*, 65, *321*
Visceral pleura, 63, *64*, 290, *292*
Visceral portion of serous membrane, 63
Viscosity, blood, blood pressure and, 251
Vision
- effects of aging on, 422
- problems with, 179

Visual acuity, 176
Visual association area, *151*
Visual cortex, *151*
- visual interpretation in, 180

Visual interpretation, 180
Visual pathway, 178-180
Vital capacity, 295-297
Vital centers, 147
Vitamin A, sources, functions, and symptoms of deficiency of, 334t
Vitamin B_1, sources, functions, and symptoms of deficiency of, 334t
Vitamin B_2, sources, functions, and symptoms of deficiency of, 334t
Vitamin B_3, sources, functions, and symptoms of deficiency of, 334t
Vitamin B_5, sources, functions, and symptoms of deficiency of, 334t
Vitamin B_6, sources, functions, and symptoms of deficiency of, 334t
Vitamin B_{12}, sources, functions, and symptoms of deficiency of, 334t
Vitamin C, sources, functions, and symptoms of deficiency of, 334t
Vitamin D, sources, functions, and symptoms of deficiency of, 334t
Vitamin E, sources, functions, and symptoms of deficiency of, 334t
Vitamin K
- blood clotting and, 221
- synthesis of, 318

Vitamin supplements for athletes, 333
Vitamins, 333, 334t
- B-complex, sources, functions, and symptoms of deficiency of, 334t

Vitreous humor, 177
Vocal cords, 284, *285*, *286*
Voiding, 353
Volar region, *9*, 10t
Volume
- of air exchanged in pulmonary ventilation, 295-297
- of body water, total, homeostasis of, *363*
- expiratory reserve, 295-297
- inspiratory reserve, 295-297
- residual, 297
- tidal, 295-297
- urine, control of, 348-349

Voluntary muscle(s), 38, 40, 50, 111
Vomer, 90t, *91*
Vomit reflex, *379*
Vomiting, 312, 378, *379*
Vomiting center, 378
Vulva, 57, 396

W

Water
- body, total volume of, homeostasis of, *363*
- proportion of body weight represented by, 359, *360*

Waves
- ECG, 238, *239*
- sound, effect of, on cochlear structures, *183*

Weight
- body, proportion of, represented by water, 359, *360*
- gain or loss of, metabolic rate and, 334, 336
- making, 362

Weight lifting, 118
Wernicke's area, *151*
White blood cell count, low, 220
White blood cells, 219-220
- phagocytosis of bacteria by, *27*
- volume of, 216

White fibers of dermis, 68
White matter, 140
Windpipe; *see* Trachea
Withdrawal reflex, 143, 154
Wrist, *9*
- bones of, 95, *97*

X

Xiphoid process, *88*, 94t, *95*

Y

Yellow bone marrow, 82
Yellow fibers of dermis, 68
Yolk sac, 409, *410*

Z

Z lines, 113, *114*
Zinc, sources, functions, and symptoms of deficiency of, 335t
Zona fasciculata, 204
Zona glomerulosa, 204
Zona reticularis, 204
Zygomatic bone, *88*, 90t, *91*
- as palpable bony landmark, *103*

Zygomatic region, *9*, 10t
Zygomaticus muscle, 122t, 123, *124*
Zygote, 383, 407, *408*, 412